CurrentLaw

STATUTES

1994

VOLUME ONE

AUSTRALIA
The Law Book Company
Brisbane : Sydney : Melbourne : Perth

CANADA
Carswell
Ottawa : Toronto : Calgary : Montreal : Vancouver

Agents:
Steimatzky's Agency Ltd., Tel Aviv;
N. M. Tripathi (Private) Ltd., Bombay;
Eastern Law House (Private) Ltd., Calcutta;
M.P.P. House, Bangalore;
Universal Book Traders, Delhi;
Aditya Books, Delhi;
MacMillan Shuppan KK, Tokyo;
Pakistan Law House, Karachi

Current Law

STATUTES

1994

VOLUME ONE

SWEET & MAXWELL EDITORIAL TEAM
SARAH ANDREWS
MELANIE BHAGAT
CAROLINE EADIE
ALICE EMMOTT
PHILIPPA JOHNSON
ALA KUZMICKI
SOPHIE LOWE
JON PEAKE
CERI PICKERING

W. GREEN EDITORIAL TEAM
ELANOR BOWER
CHARLOTTE HALL
PETER NICHOLSON

LONDON

SWEET & MAXWELL

EDINBURGH

W. GREEN

1995

Published by
SWEET & MAXWELL LIMITED
of South Quay Plaza, 183 Marsh Wall, London,
and W. GREEN LIMITED
of Alva Street, Edinburgh,
Typeset by MFK Typesetting Ltd., Hitchin, Herts.
and printed in Great Britain
by The Bath Press,
Bath, Avon.

ISBN This Volume only : 0 421 51910 X
As a set   : 0 421 51900 2

CONTENTS

CHRONOLOGICAL TABLE

VOLUME ONE

Annotators' names are in italic

VOLUME ONE

c.1.   Social Security Contributions Act 1994
      Professor N.J. Wikeley, Faculty of Law, University of Southampton

2.   Statutory Sick Pay Act 1994
      Professor N.J. Wikeley, Faculty of Law, University of Southampton

3.   Non-Domestic Ratings Act 1994

4.   Consolidated Fund Act 1994

5.   New Towns (Amendment) Act 1994

6.   Mental Health (Amendment) Act 1994
      Jonathan Montgomery, B.A., LL.M., Senior Lecturer in Law, University of Southampton

7.   Insolvency Act 1994
      David Milman, LL.B., Ph.D., Herbert Smith Professor of Corporate and Commercial Law, University of Manchester

8.   Transport Police (Jurisdiction) Act 1994

9.   Finance Act 1994
      Ian Ferrier, M.A., Barrister and Rupert Baldry, Barrister

10.   Race Relations (Remedies) Act 1994

11.   Road Traffic Regulation (Special Events) Act 1994
      Robert Ward, M.A., LL.B. (Cantab.), LL.M. (U.B.C.), Barrister

12.   Insolvency (No. 2) Act 1994
      Professor Phillip H. Kenny, LL.B., Dip.Crim., LL.M., Solicitor, Property Consultant, Messrs. Dickinson Dees, Newcastle upon Tyne

13.   Intelligence Services Act 1994
      Philip Kolvin and Timothy Straker, Barristers, 2–3 Gray's Inn Square, Gray's Inn, London

14.   Parliamentary Commissioner Act 1994

15. Antarctic Act 1994
    Catherine Redgwell, Senior Lecturer in Law, University of Nottingham
16. State Hospitals (Scotland) Act 1994
    Peter Nicholson, LL.B., Solicitor
17. Chiropractors Act 1994
    Jonathan Montgomery, B.A., LL.M., Senior Lecturer in Law, University of Southampton
18. Social Security (Incapacity for Work) Act 1994
    Professor N.J. Wikeley, Faculty of Law, University of Southampton
19. Local Government (Wales) Act 1994
    Paul Griffiths, The Welsh Office and Colin Crawford, Senior Lecturer, Faculty of Law, University of Birmingham

INDEX OF SHORT TITLES

STATUTES 1994

(References are to chapter numbers of 1994)

SOCIAL SECURITY (CONTRIBUTIONS) ACT 1994*

(1994 c. 1)

An Act to increase primary Class 1 contributions payable under the Social Security Contributions and Benefits Act 1992; to correct the provisions as to the appropriate national health service allocation in the case of such contributions; to clarify what reliefs are to be taken into account in assessing Class 4 contributions; and for connected purposes.

[10th February 1994]

PARLIAMENTARY DEBATES
Hansard, H.C. Vol. 234, cols. 1301, 1377; H.L. Vol. 551, cols. 9, 811, 836, 1112, 1445.

INTRODUCTION AND GENERAL NOTE
This short Act has one principal purpose: to increase the standard rate of employees' Class 1 National Insurance contributions by one per cent. to 10 per cent. (s.1). The Government has also taken the opportunity to include two subsidiary items designed to clarify existing legislation. These concern the allocation of monies from the National Insurance Fund for the National Health Service (s.2) and the liability of self-employed people with personal pensions to pay Class 4 contributions (s.3). Section 4 makes corresponding provisions for Northern Ireland.

The Bill was guillotined before Second Reading in the House of Commons (*Hansard*, H.C. Vol. 234, cols. 842–893) and allowed only six hours of debate in that House. This led to the Opposition suspending normal cross-party co-operation. The Bill was passed by both Houses without any amendments being made.

The Act received Royal Assent on February 10, 1994. However, s.1 came into effect on April 6, 1994, while the clarifying amendments in ss.2 and 3 are both retrospective in their operation (being deemed to have come into effect on October 5, 1989 and July 23, 1987 respectively).

ABBREVIATIONS
SERPS   : State Earnings Related Pension Scheme.
SSAA 1992   : The Social Security Administration Act 1992.
SSCBA 1992 : The Social Security Contributions and Benefits Act 1992.

Increase in primary Class 1 contributions

1.—(1) In section 8 of the Social Security Contributions and Benefits Act 1992 (calculation of primary Class 1 contributions), in subsection (2)(b) (by virtue of which the main primary percentage is 9 per cent.) for "9 per cent." substitute "10 per cent.".

(2) The above amendment comes into effect on 6th April 1994.

DEFINITIONS
"main primary percentage": s.122(1) of the SSCBA 1992.

GENERAL NOTE
This section increases the amount of Class 1 National Insurance contributions payable by employed earners under the SSCBA 1992. The main primary Class 1 contribution rate on earnings between the lower and upper earnings limits is increased from nine per cent. to 10 per cent. for employees who are not contracted-out of SERPS. This takes effect from April 6, 1994. The rise for those who are contracted-out is from 7.2 per cent. to 8.2 per cent. This increase, foreshadowed in the Chancellor of the Exchequer's budget statement in March 1993, is the first rise in the main contribution rate since 1983. It has been caused by the need to ensure that contri-

---

*Annotations by N.J. Wikeley, M.A. (Cantab.), Barrister, Senior Lecturer in Law, University of Birmingham.

butions meet the levels of expenditure to which the National Insurance Fund is committed. It will increase contributions to the Fund by some £1.9b. in a full year.

National health service allocation

2.—(1) In section 162(5) of the Social Security Administration Act 1992 (destination of contributions: national health service allocation), in paragraph (a) (allocation in case of primary Class 1 contributions) for the words from "the earnings" to the end substitute "so much of the earnings in respect of which those contributions were paid as exceeded the lower earnings limit but did not exceed the upper earnings limit;".

(2) After subsection (6) of that section insert—

"(6A) In the case of earners paid other than weekly, the reference in paragraph (a) of subsection (5) above to the lower or upper earnings limit shall be taken as a reference to the equivalent of that limit prescribed under section 8(3) of the Contributions and Benefits Act.".

(3) The above amendments shall be deemed to have had effect as from the commencement of the 1992 Act; and corresponding amendments to section 134 of the Social Security Act 1975 shall be deemed to have had effect as from the commencement of section 1 of the Social Security Act 1989.

DEFINITIONS

"earner": ss.3(1)(b) and 122(1) of the SSCBA 1992.
"earnings": ss.3(1)(a) and 122(1) of the SSCBA 1992.
"lower earnings limit": s.5(1)(a) of the SSCBA 1992.
"upper earnings limit": s.5(1)(b) of the SSCBA 1992.

GENERAL NOTE

From the inception of the National Insurance scheme a proportion of the contributions paid into the Fund has been allocated to the National Health Service. This section clarifies the position as regards the allocation of such funds and ensures that the law reflects what has always been understood to be the policy intention. Since earnings-related contributions were introduced in 1975, the National Health Service (NHS) allocation has been part of the percentage rate applied to earnings. In 1989 the method of calculating liability for primary Class 1 contributions was reformed, with an initial two per cent. being paid on earnings up to the lower earnings limit, and the main nine per cent. rate applied to earnings between the lower and upper earnings limits. So far as the main primary rate is concerned, 1.5 per cent. was transferred to the NHS and 7.95 per cent. to the National Insurance Fund.

It was noticed by the Department of Social Security that the existing provision governing the NHS allocation (SSAA 1992, s.162(5)) could be interpreted as meaning that no allocation was payable on variants of the main primary percentage rate. The principal group affected consists of employees contracted out of SERPS who pay the rebated main contribution rate (7.2 per cent. until April 1994; 8.2 per cent. thereafter). The policy intention was always that the allocation should be paid from the contributions of all employees with earnings above the lower earnings limit. Indeed, between October 1989 and April 1994, £4.6b. in contributions has been levied on this basis and transferred to the NHS. The purpose of this section is thus to give retrospective authority for that practice and to clarify the position for the future, as some £1b. a year is allocated from the National Insurance Fund to the NHS.

Subs. (1)

This subsection ensures that the NHS allocation is still payable where contributions have been paid on earnings between the lower and upper earnings limits at a rate which is different from the main primary percentage rate.

Subs. (2)

This subsection provides that the NHS allocation in respect of employed earners who are paid other than on a weekly basis is calculated using an equivalent lower and upper earnings limit. It is therefore consequential upon subs. (1).

Subs. (3)

This provision deems the amendments to have had effect from October 5, 1989, when s.1 of the Social Security Act 1989 came into force.

Reliefs available in calculating Class 4 contributions

3.—(1) In paragraph 3(2) of Schedule 2 to the Social Security Contributions and Benefits Act 1992 and the Social Security Contributions and Benefits (Northern Ireland) Act 1992 (computation of profits or gains for purposes of Class 4 contributions: reliefs which do not apply)—
(a) at the end of paragraph (e), omit "and"; and
(b) after paragraph (f) insert—
    "and
    (g) section 639 (personal pension contributions).".
(2) The above amendments shall be deemed to have had effect as from the commencement of those Acts; and corresponding amendments to paragraph 3(2) of Schedule 2 to the Social Security Act 1975 and the Social Security (Northern Ireland) Act 1975 shall be deemed to have had effect as from the commencement of section 31 of the Finance (No. 2) Act 1987 (deduction of personal pension contributions from relevant earnings).

GENERAL NOTE
Subsection (1) establishes that payments towards personal pensions are not allowed as a deduction by the self-employed from the profits on which their Class 4 National Insurance contributions are calculated. Subsection (2) provides that this provision shall be deemed to have had effect from July 23, 1987 (the commencement date of the Finance (No. 2) Act 1987). This effectively gives retrospective authority for the levying of some £60m. per year in Class 4 contributions since that date. These amendments do not involve any change in policy and are designed to ensure that the law reflects the principle that only genuine business expenses, and not personal expenses, are allowable. The same rule already applies to employees paying Class 1 contributions.

Corresponding provision for Northern Ireland

4. An Order in Council under paragraph 1(1)(b) of Schedule 1 to the Northern Ireland Act 1974 (legislation for Northern Ireland in the interim period) which states that it is made only for purposes corresponding to those of section 1 or 2 of this Act—
(a) shall not be subject to paragraph 1(4) and (5) of that Schedule (affirmative resolution of both Houses of Parliament), but
(b) shall be subject to annulment in pursuance of a resolution of either House of Parliament.

GENERAL NOTE
This section provides that provisions corresponding to those under ss.1 and 2 of this Act which are made under an Order in Council in Northern Ireland are subject to the negative resolution procedure. Section 3 of this Act extends to Northern Ireland by virtue of s.5(2).

Short title and extent

5.—(1) This Act may be cited as the Social Security (Contributions) Act 1994.
(2) Sections 3 and 4 and this section extend to Northern Ireland, but otherwise this Act does not extend there.

INDEX

References are to section number

STATUTORY SICK PAY ACT 1994*

(1994 c. 2)

An Act to remove the right of employers other than small employers to recover sums paid by them by way of statutory sick pay; to enable the Secretary of State to make further provision by order as to the recovery of such sums; and for connected purposes.   [10th February 1994]

PARLIAMENTARY DEBATES
 Hansard, H.C. Vol. 234, cols. 1109, 1177; Vol. 237, col. 393; H.L. Vol. 551, cols. 79, 884, 1499.

INTRODUCTION AND GENERAL NOTE

This short Act makes an important change to the law governing the recovery by employers of statutory sick pay (SSP) paid to employees. With effect from April 6, 1994, employers will no longer receive any reimbursement for SSP (s.1(1)). A significant social cost previously borne largely by the State has thus been transferred to industry. The existing rights of small employers (as defined by Regulations) to relief from the costs of SSP are preserved, albeit on a different basis. However, s.3 provides an alternative mechanism for reimbursement of SSP to all employers, regardless of size, which may come into force in April 1995, depending on the outcome of consultation by the Government with interested parties.

A consequential change to the law is that women employees aged between 60 and 65 are now entitled to SSP (s.1(2)). With this one exception, the Act has no impact on the entitlement of individuals to SSP. However, the Government also proposes to abolish the lower rate of SSP with effect from April 1995. It is estimated that this will advantage about 50,000 people in low-paid work (see cl. 7 of the Social Security (Incapacity for Work) Bill 1994).

The abolition of employers' right to reimbursement for the costs of SSP was presented by the Government as part of a package of related measures. The rate of employees' National Insurance contributions has been raised by one per cent. to 10 per cent. by the Social Security (Contributions) Act 1994 (s.1). At the same time, the Social Security (Contributions) (Re-rating and National Insurance Fund Payments) Order 1994/544 has reduced employers' contributions from 10.4 per cent. to 10.2 per cent. at the main rate and by a whole percentage point for each of the lower three rates. The effect of this reform will be to reduce annual public expenditure by an estimated gross figure of £695m. in 1994/95, rising to £720m. in 1995/96 and £750m. in 1996/97. These savings will be offset by the reduction in employers' National Insurance contributions. The Bill was guillotined before Second Reading in the House of Commons, and was subject to less than seven hours of scrutiny in the lower chamber.

Under s.5(2) the Act came into force on Royal Assent on February 10, 1994, with the exception of s.1, which came into force on April 6, 1994.

ABBREVIATIONS

    CBI   : Confederation of British Industry.
    SSAA 1992 : The Social Security Administration Act 1992.
    SSCBA 1992 : The Social Security Contributions and Benefits Act 1992.
    SSP   : statutory sick pay.
    SSPA 1991 : The Statutory Sick Pay Act 1991.

Restriction of employers' right of recovery

1.—(1) In section 158(1)(a) of the Social Security Contributions and Benefits Act 1992 (recovery by employers of amounts paid by way of statutory sick pay), sub-paragraph (ii) (recovery of 80 per cent. of payments not qualifying for small employers' relief) shall cease to have effect.

---

*Annotations by N. J. Wikeley, M.A. (Cantab.), Barrister, Senior Lecturer in Law, University of Birmingham.

(2) In consequence the following are repealed—
(a) that provision and the word "and" preceding it, and
(b) section 81(2) of the Social Security Administration Act 1992;
and in paragraph 2 of Schedule 11 to the Social Security Contributions and
Benefits Act 1992 (circumstances in which entitlement to statutory sick pay
does not arise), in sub-paragraph (a) for "over pensionable age" substitute
"over the age of 65".

DEFINITIONS
    "small employer": s.158(3) of the SSCBA 1992.

GENERAL NOTE
    This section abolishes the right of an employer to recover 80 per cent. of any SSP paid to
employees (subs. (1)). It also enables working women aged between 60 and 65 to claim SSP
(subs. (2)).

Subs. (1)
    When SSP was introduced in 1983, an employee's entitlement was limited to eight weeks of
sickness in any one tax year (increased to 26 weeks in 1986). Originally employers were reimbursed in full for the cost of SSP. The SSPA 1991 reduced this compensation to 80 per cent. and
also abolished the right of employers to an allowance to cover administrative costs and contributions paid during periods of entitlement to SSP. At the same time the right of small employers
to 100 per cent. reimbursement was preserved. A "small employer" is an employer whose gross
National Insurance liability was £16,000 or less in the 1993/94 tax year (Statutory Sick Pay (Small
Employers' Relief) Amendment Regulations 1992 (S.I. 1992 No. 797)); this threshold is to be
increased by regulations to £20,000 for the 1994/95 tax year. Small employers include almost
two-thirds of those eligible to pay SSP but cover only about 15 per cent. of the work-force.
    The arrangements for small employers' relief are maintained, but with important modifi-
cations. Under the previous arrangements small employers received 80 per cent. reimbursement
for the first six weeks, followed by 100 per cent. thereafter. Under the new system small
employers will receive no compensation whatsoever for SSP payments for the first four weeks of
an employee's absence; only after four weeks will they receive 100 per cent. relief. In practice,
however, the duration of sickness absence is typically very low. About 40 per cent. of employees
off sick are absent for fewer than four days and about 75 per cent. of sick leave cases are for less
than four weeks. It was largely because of concern expressed in the House of Lords about these
changes that the Government introduced s.3 below as an alternative mechanism for small
employers' relief.
    The principal justification advanced for placing the entire cost of SSP on employers was that
this will give employers a greater incentive to improve the health, motivation and attendance of
their employees. The Secretary of State noted that Britain has the highest rate of sick leave of
any country in the European Union with the exception of the Netherlands (*Hansard*, H.C. Vol.
234, col. 1109). The Act is also designed to reduce and simplify the administrative burden of SSP,
but the only change of any significance here, as the CBI has commented, is to relieve employers
of the burden of claiming reimbursement for the cost of SSP.

Subs. (2)
    This provision makes two changes consequential upon subs. (1). First, s.81(2) of the SSAA
1992 is repealed. That section enabled the Department of Social Security to recover under the
recoupment scheme (SSAA 1992, Pt. IV) the equivalent of 80 per cent. of any SSP paid from any
compensation payment above the small payments limit. That provision is redundant now that
the State will no longer be funding SSP for employees (other than those working for small
employers).
    The second change is that working women aged between 60 and 65 who fall sick and are
incapable for work will become eligible for SSP. At present the maximum age for entitlement to
SSP is based on pensionable age (65 for men, 60 for women). This reform is achieved by an
amendment to para. 2 of Sched. 11 to the SSCBA 1992. The reason for this change is that SSP will
become a form of pay and so subject to the E.C. Equal Treatment Directive as from April 1994,
when employers have to meet its full cost. The extension of entitlement to SSP to this group of
women workers is expected to cost employers about £10m. per year. This figure will be offset to

some extent by a reduction in employers' National Insurance contributions (see the Introduction and General Note).

Transitional and other supplementary provisions

2.—(1) The Secretary of State may by regulations make such transitional and consequential provision, and such savings, as he considers necessary or expedient for or in connection with the coming into force of the provisions of section 1 or the operation of any enactment repealed or amended by that section during any period when the repeal or amendment is not wholly in force.

(2) Section 175(2) to (4) of the Social Security Contributions and Benefits Act 1992 (general provisions as to regulations and orders) apply in relation to the power conferred by subsection (1) above as they apply in relation to a power conferred by that Act to make regulations.

(3) A statutory instrument—

(a) which contains (whether alone or with other provisions) any regulations made under subsection (1), and

(b) which is not subject to any requirement that a draft of the instrument be laid before and approved by a resolution of each House of Parliament,

shall be subject to annulment in pursuance of a resolution of either House of Parliament.

(4) The provisions of this Act apply to the Crown, and in relation to persons employed by or under the Crown, to the same extent as the provisions amended or repealed by section 1.

GENERAL NOTE

Subsections (1) and (2) merely enable the Secretary of State to make such transitional and other consequential provisions as are considered necessary or expedient in connection with the coming into force of the Act. As these are non-controversial provisions they are subject to the negative resolution procedure (subs. (3)). Subsection (4) provides that the Act applies to the Crown and to persons employed by the Crown.

The Government's intention is that, as part of the transitional arrangements, employers will be able to recover the appropriate amount of SSP paid for days of sickness up to and including April 5, 1994, even if the employer cannot actually recover that amount until after that date (*Hansard*, H.C. Vol. 234, col. 1191).

Power to make further provision as to recovery

3.—(1) In Part XI of the Social Security Contributions and Benefits Act 1992 (statutory sick pay), after section 159 insert—

> **"Power to provide for recovery by employers of sums paid by way of statutory sick pay**
>
> **159A.**—(1) The Secretary of State may by order provide for the recovery by employers, in accordance with the order, of the amount (if any) by which their payments of, or liability incurred for, statutory sick pay in any period exceeds the specified percentage of the amount of their liability for contributions payments in respect of the corresponding period.
>
> (2) An order under subsection (1) above may include provision—
>
> (a) as to the periods by reference to which the calculation referred to above is to be made,
>
> (b) for amounts which would otherwise be recoverable but which do not exceed the specified minimum for recovery not to be recoverable,
>
> (c) for the rounding up or down of any fraction of a pound which would otherwise result from a calculation made in accordance with the order, and

(d) for any deduction from contributions payments made in accordance with the order to be disregarded for such purposes as may be specified,

and may repeal sections 158 and 159 above and make any amendments of other enactments which are consequential on the repeal of those sections.

(3) In this section—

"contributions payments" means payments which a person is required by or under any enactment to make in discharge of any liability of his as an employer in respect of primary or secondary Class 1 contributions; and

"specified" means specified in or determined in accordance with an order under subsection (1).

(4) The Secretary of State may by regulations make such transitional and consequential provision, and such savings, as he considers necessary or expedient for or in connection with the coming into force of any order under subsection (1) above.".

(2) In section 176(1)(c) of the Social Security Contributions and Benefits Act 1992 (parliamentary control: orders subject to affirmative procedure), at the appropriate place insert "section 159A(1)".

(3) The Secretary of State—

(a) shall lay before each House of Parliament the draft of an order under section 159A(1) of the Social Security Contributions and Benefits Act 1992 (inserted by subsection (1) above) framed so as to come into force on or before 6th April 1995, and

(b) if the draft order is approved by a resolution of each House of Parliament, shall make the order in the form of the draft,

unless before 1st December 1994 he lays before each House of Parliament a report explaining why he does not intend to make such an order.

DEFINITIONS

"contributions payments": subs. (3).

"specified": subs. (3).

GENERAL NOTE

This section was introduced as a Government amendment at the Third Reading of the Bill in the House of Lords in response to pressure from peers at the Report stage. It represents a notable success in lobbying terms for the Federation of Small Businesses.

Under the present system, small employers are fully reimbursed for the cost of SSP paid beyond a prescribed period (formerly six weeks, now four weeks). Peers argued that this failed to provide an adequate safeguard for the employer (of whatever size) who faced a short-term problem of the sudden shortage of several key staff due to illness (*e.g.* in a flu epidemic). This section, by inserting a new s.159A into the SSCBA 1992, enables the Secretary of State to provide by order for employers to recover SSP which exceeds a specified percentage of their National Insurance contributions. The Government has indicated that such a threshold will be set so that the reimbursement costs are equivalent to those to be paid under the reformed system of small employers' relief.

It is important to note that this is an enabling provision. The Government has undertaken to consult both employers' and employees' organisations about the merits of the proposed scheme over the next year. A new scheme for reimbursement would not be introduced until April 1995. If the Government decides to proceed along these lines, a draft order bringing such a scheme into effect must be laid before each House of Parliament (subs. (3)(a)). If approved by resolution of each House, the order must then be made in the same terms as the draft (subs. (3)(b)). Such an order may repeal the existing reimbursement provisions under ss.158 and 159 of the SSCBA 1992 and make any necessary consequential amendments (subs. (1), inserting s.159A(2) of the SSCBA 1992). If the Government decides not to introduce such a scheme, the Secretary of State must lay a report before each House by December 1, 1994, explaining his reasons for not so proceeding.

Corresponding provision for Northern Ireland

4. An Order in Council under paragraph 1(1)(b) of Schedule 1 to the Northern Ireland Act 1974 (legislation for Northern Ireland in the interim period) which states that it is made only for purposes corresponding to those of sections 1 to 3 of this Act—

  (a) shall not be subject to paragraph 1(4) and (5) of that Schedule (affirmative resolution of both Houses of Parliament), but

  (b) shall be subject to annulment in pursuance of a resolution of either House of Parliament.

GENERAL NOTE

  This section provides that provisions corresponding to those under ss.1 to 3 of this Act which are made under an Order in Council in Northern Ireland are subject to the negative resolution procedure.

Citation, commencement, financial provision and extent

5.—(1) This Act may be cited as the Statutory Sick Pay Act 1994.

  (2) Section 1 comes into force on 6th April 1994; and the other provisions of this Act come into force on Royal Assent.

  (3) There shall be paid out of money provided by Parliament any expenses incurred by a Minister of the Crown in consequence of this Act.

  (4) Section 4 and this section (except subsection (3)) extend to Northern Ireland, but otherwise this Act does not extend there.

INDEX

References are to section number

NON-DOMESTIC RATING ACT 1994

(1994 c. 3)

ARRANGEMENT OF SECTIONS

An Act to make further provision with respect to non-domestic rating for the financial year beginning in 1994 and subsequent financial years; and for connected purposes. [24th February 1994]

PARLIAMENTARY DEBATES
Hansard, H.C. Vol. 235, cols. 136, 195, 365, 397; H.L. Vol. 551, cols. 327, 1089, 1512; Vol. 552, cols. 101, 181, 292, 353, 423, 517, 591, 633, 940.

INTRODUCTION
The transitional arrangements for phasing in the effects of two changes to non-domestic rating (introduction of the national non-domestic rate; compilation of new non-domestic rating lists following revaluation of non-domestic property) were amended in 1993 by non-domestic rating legislation. The 1994 Act makes further amendments to those provisions. The 1994 Act provides for (1) an alteration in the rate increases in the financial year 1994–1995 arising from the changes in non-domestic rating; (2) amendments to the powers of the Secretary of State in relation to the making of regulations providing for transitional arrangements; and (3) further requirements on the Secretary of State to make good any shortfall arising from the Act.

Limit on increase in non-domestic rates for 1994 financial year

1.—(1) The provisions of subsections (2) and (3) below have effect for setting, for the financial year beginning in 1994, the value of X in the formula in sub-paragraph (2) of paragraph 5 of Schedule 7A to the 1988 Act, being a formula relevant to the determination of the non-domestic rates for certain hereditaments.

(2) In sub-paragraph (2A) of that paragraph, for the words from "except that" to the end there shall be substituted the words "except that for the financial years beginning in 1992 and 1993 X is 100 and for the financial year beginning in 1994 X is—

(a) 110 if the hereditament falls within sub-paragraph (3) below, and

(b) 107.5 if the hereditament falls within sub-paragraph (4) below."

(3) In subsection (2) of section 2 of the 1992 Act (amendment of the Non-Domestic Rating (Transitional Period) (Amendment and Further Provision) Regulations 1990), in paragraph (a), for the words "the financial year beginning in 1992 or that beginning in 1993" there shall be substituted the words "any of the financial years beginning in 1992, 1993 and 1994".

(4) For the purpose of making similar provision in relation to certain hereditaments shown in a central non-domestic rating list, the formula in each of the following, namely—

(a) article 9 of the British Gas plc (Rateable Values) Order 1989,

(b) article 9(3) of the Electricity Supply Industry (Rateable Values) Order 1989,

(c) article 12(3) of the Railways (Rateable Values) Order 1989, and

(d) article 9(3) of the Water Undertakers (Rateable Values) Order 1989, shall have effect in relation to the financial year beginning in 1994 as if for the figure "1.2" there were substituted the figure "1.1".

(5) In this Act—
"the 1988 Act" means the Local Government Finance Act 1988;
"the 1992 Act" means the Non-Domestic Rating Act 1992;
"financial year" has the same meaning as in the 1988 Act.

Amendments of power to make special provision for 1995 onwards

2.—(1) After subsection (7) of section 58 of the 1988 Act (special provision for 1995 onwards) there shall be inserted the following subsection—
"(7A) Without prejudice to section 143(1) and (2) below, regulations under this section may include provision—
(a) imposing duties and conferring powers on valuation officers (whether as regards determinations, certificates or otherwise) in relation to the ascertainment of rateable values;
(b) as to appeals relating to things done or not done by such officers."
(2) In subsection (8) of that section for the words "relevant period" there shall be substituted the words "relevant financial year" and for the words "the period" there shall be substituted the words "the year".
(3) In subsection (9) of that section, for the words "is the same as" there shall be substituted the words "does not exceed that which".

Non-domestic rating: transitional pooling

3.—(1) Subject to subsections (2) and (3) below, the modifications of Schedule 8 to the 1988 Act (non-domestic rating: pooling) made by sections 4 and 5(1) of the 1992 Act ("the 1992 modifications") shall also have effect in relation to the financial year beginning in 1995 and subsequent financial years.
(2) In relation to the financial year beginning in 1995, the 1992 modifications shall have effect as if for paragraph (a) of paragraph 9(3A) of Schedule 8 to the 1988 Act (as set out in section 4(1) of the 1992 Act) there were substituted the following paragraph—
"(a) estimate the amount by which, if the Non-Domestic Rating Act 1994 had not been enacted, the amount calculated under sub-paragraph (3) above would have been greater than it is;".
(3) In relation to the financial year beginning in 1996 and subsequent financial years, the 1992 modifications shall have effect as if—
(a) in paragraph 9(3A) of Schedule 8 to the 1988 Act (as set out in section 4(1) of the 1992 Act), for the words "shall also" there were substituted the words "may also" and for paragraph (a) there were substituted the following paragraph—
"(a) estimate the amount by which, if regulations under section 58 above had not been made, the amount calculated under sub-paragraph (3) above would have been greater than it is;"; and
(b) in paragraph (d) of paragraph 2(1) of that Schedule (as set out in section 5(1) of the 1992 Act) for the words "the amount added" there were substituted the words "any amount added".

Financial provisions

4. There shall be paid out of money provided by Parliament any increase attributable to this Act in the sums payable out of money so provided under the 1988 Act.

Short title and extent

5.—(1) This Act may be cited as the Non-Domestic Rating Act 1994.
(2) This Act extends to England and Wales only.

INDEX

References are to section number

CONSOLIDATED FUND ACT 1994

(1994 c. 4)

An Act to apply certain sums out of the Consolidated Fund to the service of the years ending on 31st March 1993 and 1994.   [24th March 1994]

PARLIAMENTARY DEBATES
Hansard, H.C. Vol. 239, col. 1070; H.L. Vol. 550, col. 587.

INTRODUCTION
This Act authorises the Treasury to issue out of the Consolidated Fund certain sums for supply in the years ending March 31, 1993 and March 31, 1994.

Issue out of the Consolidated Fund for the year ending 31st March 1993

1. The Treasury may issue out of the Consolidated Fund of the United Kingdom and apply towards making good the supply granted to Her Majesty for the service of the year ending on 31st March 1993 the sum of £355,824,479.56.

Issue out of the Consolidated Fund for the year ending 31st March 1994

2. The Treasury may issue out of the Consolidated Fund of the United Kingdom and apply towards making good the supply granted to Her Majesty for the service of the year ending on 31st March 1994 the sum of £2,362,375,000.

Short title

3. This Act may be cited as the Consolidated Fund Act 1994.

INDEX

References are to sections

NEW TOWNS (AMENDMENT) ACT 1994

(1994 c. 5)

An Act to amend Schedule 9 to the New Towns Act 1981.

[24th March 1994]

PARLIAMENTARY DEBATES
Hansard, H.L. Vol. 550, cols. 350, 931; Vol. 551, cols. 209, 723; H.C. Vol. 239, col. 596.

INTRODUCTION
This Act makes changes to the New Towns Act 1981, Sched. 9 in relation to the Commission for the New Towns and delegation of powers, so as to include sub-committees of the Commission.

Delegation of powers

1. In Schedule 9 to the New Towns Act 1981 (which makes provision as to the Commission for the New Towns)—
  (a) in paragraph 5(2) (quorum etc. of committees)—
            (i) for "committee set up under paragraph 3 above" there shall be substituted "committee or sub-committee of the Commission", and
            (ii) after "the committee" in each place there shall be inserted "or sub-committee",
  (b) in paragraph 5(3) (validity of proceedings) for "such a committee" there shall be substituted "a committee or sub-committee of the Commission", and
  (c) there shall be added at the end—

"Delegation of powers

8. Anything authorised or required to be done by the Commission under this Act, or any other enactment—
  (a) may be done by any member of the Commission, or of its staff, who has been authorised for the purpose, whether generally or specially, by the Commission, or
  (b) may be done by any committee or sub-committee of the Commission which has been so authorised."

Short title and extent

2.—(1) This Act may be cited as the New Towns (Amendment) Act 1994.
(2) This Act extends to England and Wales only.

INDEX

References are to sections

MENTAL HEALTH (AMENDMENT) ACT 1994*

(1994 c. 6)

An Act to amend section 145(1) of the Mental Health Act 1983.

[24th March 1994]

PARLIAMENTARY DEBATES

Hansard, H.L. Vol. 550, col. 1462; Vol. 551, cols. 777, 1379, 1698; Vol. 552, col. 292; H.C. Vol. 239, col. 586.

INTRODUCTION AND GENERAL NOTE

This Act makes a minor, but important, amendment to the definition of "managers" in the Mental Health Act 1983. It remedies a drafting error in the provisions of the National Health Service and Community Care Act 1990 that amended the 1983 Act.

Under the Mental Health Act 1983 special responsibilities are laid upon the "managers" (see the *Code of Practice: Mental Health Act 1983* (1993), chaps. 22 and 24). It is the normal practice for health authorities to delegate the functions of Mental Health Act "managers" and it was intended that NHS Trusts should be able to do the same. However, the 1990 Act defined the "managers" as being the directors of the NHS Trust, not the Trust as a corporate entity. The Department of Health was advised that this precluded NHS Trust Boards from delegating their functions under the Act.

A particular problem arose from the fact that executive directors are precluded from exercising powers of discharge of detained patients (see the Mental Health Act 1983, s.23(5)). This in effect controls detention under the 1983 Act, in that declining to discharge patients is to detain them. The position was set out in a letter from the NHS Management Executive, "Mental Health Act Managers: powers of discharge under s.23" (Trust executive letter (TEL) 93/2). The discharge function is an onerous one because a panel of three of the Mental Health Act "managers" are obliged to consider whether a patient should be discharged whenever the authority for detention under s.3 is renewed (s.20(3)). This must be done after six months, 12 months and thereafter annually (s.20(1)(2)). The effect of the provisions was that non-executive directors of NHS Trusts, many of whom had little or no experience in Mental Health Act matters, were forced to deal with renewal hearings personally. They were unable to delegate this function to trained and experienced people who had previously carried it out while the hospitals were directly managed by health authorities.

A further difficulty was identified that arose from the fact that legal liability for errors would fall upon the non-executive directors personally and not upon the NHS Trust as a corporate body. The NHS Management Executive permitted NHS Trusts to accept liability on behalf of non-executive directors and to provide for this risk in one of two ways; taking out commercial insurance or funding claims under the scheme covering clinical negligence (see the "Mental Health Act: Managers' Powers of Discharge under s.23" (TEL 93/5)).

The amendment made by this Act removes the reference to directors in the definition of Mental Health Act "managers". This makes the Trust as a corporate entity, acting through its Board of Directors, the manager for the purposes of the Mental Health Act 1983. Under s.23(4) of the 1983 Act, it is possible to delegate the discharge functions to a committee or sub-committee of the Trust. NHS Trusts are empowered to set up such committees or sub-committees, membership of which need not be restricted to directors, under the NHS Trusts (Membership and Procedure) Regulations 1990 (S.I. 1990 No. 2024), reg. 15. Under s.23(5)(b) of the 1983 Act the powers of discharge cannot be exercised by people who are employees of the Trust.

In order to take advantage of the Mental Health (Amendment) Act 1994, NHS Trusts should establish a committee or sub-committee to exercise the powers of discharge. There is no need for non-executive directors to be members. However, the Trust Board remains responsible for ensuring that the requirements of the Act are complied with and many Trusts may wish to ensure that Board members are directly involved. The NHS Management Executive has indicated that it will still be possible to cover the costs of litigation in relation to functions of "managers" under s.23 of the 1983 Act through the clinical negligence scheme (see "Mental Health Act: Managers' Powers of Discharge under s.23" (TEL 94/2)).

---

* Annotations by Jonathan Montgomery, B.A., LL.M., Lecturer in Law, University of Southampton, Non-executive Director, Southampton Community Health Services NHS Trust.

COMMENCEMENT
   The Act came into force on April 14, 1994, 21 days after it received Royal Assent (s.2(3)).

EXTENT
   The Act extends to England and Wales only (see s.2(2)).

Definition of managers

1. In section 145(1) of the Mental Health Act 1983 (definitions) in the definition of "the managers", in paragraph (bb) the words "the directors of" shall be omitted.

Short title, extent and commencement

2.—(1) This Act may be cited as the Mental Health (Amendment) Act 1994.
   (2) This Act extends to England and Wales only.
   (3) This Act shall come into force twenty-one days after Royal Assent.

INDEX

References are to sections

INSOLVENCY ACT 1994*

(1994 c. 7)

An Act to amend the Insolvency Act 1986 in relation to contracts of employment adopted by administrators, administrative receivers and certain other receivers; and to make corresponding provision for Northern Ireland. [24th March 1994]

PARLIAMENTARY DEBATES

Hansard, H.C. Vol. 240, col. 23; H.L. Vol. 553, col. 622.

INTRODUCTION AND GENERAL NOTE

The Insolvency Act 1994 was rushed through Parliament in a week to remove some of the unfortunate practical consequences of the Court of Appeal ruling in *Paramount Airways (No. 3), Re* [1994] British Company Cases 172 (decided February 22, 1994). In this case the Court of Appeal, upholding the first instance ruling of Evans-Lombe J. [1993] BCC 662, held that administrators (and presumably administrative receivers) could by implication adopt the contracts of employment of employees of an insolvent company and thereby the employee entitlements would rank as a prior claim on administration enjoying priority over an administrator's claim to remuneration and expenses and also over any floating charge (see the Insolvency Act 1986, s.19(5)). These employee entitlements might include such items as payments due in lieu of notice, unpaid contributions by the employer in respect of occupational pensions and holiday pay. Where an administrator had failed to pay such sums interest thereon might also be included.

The implications of *Paramount* for administrative receivers are different but no less serious. Such employment liabilities as those described above arising through adoption would amount to a personal obligation on the part of the administrative receiver (see the Insolvency Act 1986, s.44(1)(b)), though such liabilities could be covered by his indemnity out of the company's assets (*ibid.*, s.44(1)(c)).

The aforementioned statutory provisions concede that for both administrators and administrative receivers an adoption of contracts of employment would not be presumed during the initial 14 days immediately following the appointment of the administrator or administrative receiver. The result of this combination of legal factors was that there was a strong financial incentive for insolvency practitioners to dismiss employees immediately after the 14 days had elapsed, even though that dismissal might end any hope of finding a buyer for the business.

In order to understand how this position came about one needs to investigate the origin of the statutory provisions that are at the heart of the *Paramount* case. These practical problems, it is submitted, spring from the statutory provisions themselves rather than from the perfectly sensible interpretation of the concept of the adoption of contracts of employment which found favour with the Court of Appeal. It appears that these provisions were introduced late during the passage of the Insolvency Act 1985, a short-lived statute that was almost immediately replaced by the consolidatory Insolvency Act 1986. This late legislative flurry was designed to counteract another criticised ruling of the Court of Appeal (*Nicoll* v. *Cutts* [1985] BCLC 322), where it was held that a receiver had no personal liability towards employees whose contracts of employment were continued during his stewardship. Policy-makers thought that this total denial of responsibility was unacceptable, though the provisions drafted to counteract this decision appeared to move to the other extreme without giving consideration to an acceptable compromise, which is the destination we have now arrived at via *Paramount* and the 1994 Act.

Whatever the underlying causes of the problems in this area of law there is no doubt that the *Paramount* decision came as a shock to insolvency practitioners, who for several years had been following a practice allegedly legitimised by an unreported ruling of Harman J. in *Specialised Mouldings, Re* (1987), which involved the issue of a letter to company employees stating that although their services were being retained for the moment this fact was not to be taken as an indication that the insolvency practitioner was either adopting the contract of employment or indeed assuming personal liability thereunder. The legal efficacy of this practice was expressly rejected by the Court of Appeal in *Paramount Airways (No. 3), Re (supra)*. Insolvency practitioners, alarmed by the ruling of the Court of Appeal, placed considerable pressure on the Government, playing on fears that the economic effect of the decision would be to seriously undermine the corporate rescue strategy so much in favour with government policy-makers and to produce an immediate increase in unemployment. The case was strengthened by examples

---

* Annotations by David Milman, LL.B., Ph.D., Herbert Smith Professor of Corporate and Commercial Law, University of Manchester.

such as the Leyland DAF administrative receivership where the receivers had been able to repackage the businesses of the company and sell them as going concerns saving thousands of jobs in the process. The point was made that this beneficial outcome could not have materialised had the Court of Appeal ruling preceded that receivership because the administrative receivers would have probably dismissed many of the employees after the 14-day period rather than waiting to secure a sale of the businesses.

In response to this campaign the President of the Board of Trade announced in the House of Commons on March 14, 1994 that he was going to act to neutralise the dangers posed by *Paramount Airways (No. 3), Re* (*supra*) and that any legislative action taken would be backdated to midnight that day.

It is interesting to note that the Government was forced to effect the necessary legal change through primary legislation. Increasingly, technical reforms in the field of companies' legislation are being effected through delegated legislation (authorised by many sections in the Companies Acts) and current government policy appears to be leaning towards this *modus operandi* (witness the Deregulation and Contracting Out Bill). This particular affair may well lend weight to the supporters of the use of delegated legislation in cases such as this.

The concept of a short statute designed to counteract an inconvenient decision of the courts is not a new one. Amongst the precedents for this legislation one could point to the War Damage Act 1965 (reversing *Burmah Oil Co. (Burmah Trading)* v. *Lord Advocate; Burmah Oil Co. (Burmah Concessions)* v. *Same; Burmah Oil Co. (Overseas)* v. *Same; Burmah Oil Co. (Pipe Lines)* v. *Same* [1965] A.C. 75), the Northern Ireland Act 1972 (introduced specifically to deal with *R.* (*Hume et al.*) v. *Londonderry J.J.* [1972] N.I. 91), the Wills Act (*Bravda, Re* [1968] 1 W.L.R. 479) and the Trade Disputes Act 1965 (enacted in response to *Rookes* v. *Barnard* [1964] A.C. 1129). The 1994 Act, therefore, is not a constitutional innovation, though the urgency with which it was passed meant that it came into force before the mischievous authority of the courts it was designed to combat was fully reported! The only report of the case available on March 24, 1994 when the Insolvency Act 1994 got the Royal Assent was noted in *The Times,* March 1, 1994.

The irony with this legislation is that at the end of the day it may turn out to be unnecessary because *Paramount Airways (No. 3), Re* (*supra*) may be appealed to the House of Lords.

However, regardless of subsequent developments, the exercise of Parliamentary intervention will have achieved its immediate aim in that it will have given reassurance to insolvency practitioners and removed the incentive to abandon corporate rescue. Obviously if the ruling of the Court of Appeal is upheld by the House of Lords there will still be problems for insolvency practitioners who may have adopted contracts of employment before March 15, 1994. The Government appears to have indicated that it has not ruled out further legislative intervention to rectify matters should that scenario come to pass (see the guarded comments of Lord Strathclyde, *Hansard,* H.L. Vol. 553, col. 639).

ARRANGEMENT OF THE ACT

The Act is commendably short, though drafted in such technical terms as to mean little to all but the most dedicated followers of corporate insolvency law. Basically the Act deals separately with four different types of insolvency practitioner operating within the U.K. What is interesting is that it does not seek to offer comparable reassurance to those who in English law might be termed non-administrative receivers. These would be receivers normally appointed under the Law of Property Act 1925 to enforce security over property based assets (such as hotels). Even though such receivers can incur personal liability for any contracts of employment they might adopt (see the Insolvency Act 1986, s.37(1)(a)), the Government steadfastly refused to bow to pressure from the opposition parties to bring such receivers within the protective régime inaugurated by the 1994 Act (see *Hansard,* H.C. Vol. 240, cols. 49–50 and H.L. Vol. 553, col. 642). The reasons put forward by the Government appear unconvincing — if it was necessary to introduce a statutory provision for such receivers to combat *Nicoll* v. *Cutts* (*supra*) why should not the same reasoning produce an amendment to cope with *Paramount* (*supra*)? The Government conceded that there may be a need for this legislation to be extended to non-administrative receivers but preferred to leave this issue to be considered in the wake of its forthcoming Consultative Document on corporate rescue.

Administrators: priority of liabilities under adopted contracts of employment

1.—(1) Section 19 of the Insolvency Act 1986 (vacation of office) shall be amended as provided by subsections (2) to (6) below.

(2) In subsection (3) (which provides for the next two subsections to apply where a person ceases to be administrator) for "next two" there shall be substituted "following".

(3) In subsection (5) (which provides for certain debts and liabilities incurred during administration, including those incurred under contracts of employment adopted by the administrator, to be charged on the company's property in priority to his remuneration and expenses) the words "or contracts of employment adopted" shall be omitted.

(4) After the first paragraph of that subsection there shall be inserted—

"(6) Any sums payable in respect of liabilities incurred, while he was administrator, under contracts of employment adopted by him or a predecessor of his in the carrying out of his or the predecessor's functions shall, to the extent that the liabilities are qualifying liabilities, be charged on and paid out of any such property as is mentioned in subsection (4) and enjoy the same priority as any sums to which subsection (5) applies."

(5) The second paragraph of that subsection (which provides that an administrator is not to be taken to have adopted a contract of employment by reason of any acts or omissions within 14 days after his appointment) shall become the second paragraph of the subsection inserted by subsection (4) above.

(6) At the end of the section there shall be inserted—

"(7) For the purposes of subsection (6), a liability under a contract of employment is a qualifying liability if—

(a) it is a liability to pay a sum by way of wages or salary or contribution to an occupational pension scheme, and

(b) it is in respect of services rendered wholly or partly after the adoption of the contract.

(8) There shall be disregarded for the purposes of subsection (6) so much of any qualifying liability as represents payment in respect of services rendered before the adoption of the contract.

(9) For the purposes of subsections (7) and (8)—

(a) wages or salary payable in respect of a period of holiday or absence from work through sickness or other good cause are deemed to be wages or (as the case may be) salary in respect of services rendered in that period, and

(b) a sum payable in lieu of holiday is deemed to be wages or (as the case may be) salary in respect of services rendered in the period by reference to which the holiday entitlement arose.

(10) In subsection (9)(a), the reference to wages or salary payable in respect of a period of holiday includes any sums which, if they had been paid, would have been treated for the purposes of the enactments relating to social security as earnings in respect of that period."

(7) This section shall have effect in relation to contracts of employment adopted on or after 15th March 1994.

<small>DEFINITIONS</small>
"administrator": s.8(2) of the Insolvency Act 1986.

<small>GENERAL NOTE</small>
This section counteracts some of the implications of *Paramount Airways (No. 3), Re* [1994] BCC 172 for administrators. An administrator was a new breed of insolvency practitioner who appeared in 1986, governed by the legislative framework found in Pt. II of the Insolvency Act 1986 (which also applies in Scotland). Statistically, administrators are rare entities; over the last few years approximately 100 to 200 administration orders have been granted annually, though administrators often handle the larger and more high profile cases involving corporate collapses. Administrators are primarily concerned with corporate rescue and the ruling of the Court of Appeal would seriously undermine their raison d'être.

It is worth noting that the strategy adopted by the legislature is not to deny the fact of adoption, which was the argument of the administrators in *Paramount Airways (No. 3), Re (supra)*, but instead to limit the financial consequences of adoption for insolvency practitioners. Indeed, the Minister of Corporate Affairs, Mr Neil Hamilton, appeared to confirm that his interpretation of the concept of adoption matched that of the Court of Appeal (see *Hansard*, H.C. Vol. 240, col. 40).

Subs. (1)

This subsection triggers the next five subsections and authorises changes to s.19 of the Insolvency Act 1986.

Subss. (2) to (6)

Apart from the consequential changes necessitated by the introduction of new subsections into s.19 of the Insolvency Act 1986, the key substantive change is to limit the range of liabilities arising on an adoption of contracts of employment that enjoy priority treatment currently provided for by subs. (5) of s.19 of the 1986 Act. Thus under the new subs. (6) such priority will only be afforded to "qualifying liabilities", as defined by the new subs. (7). The limitation of "qualifying liabilities" is designed to exclude such items as arrears of wages owed in respect of services provided by the employee prior to the adoption by the administrator, unpaid pension contributions due from the employing company during this earlier period and also contractual entitlements to payments in lieu of notice. These claims will not enjoy priority over the administrator's claim to remuneration nor over the floating charge, though they are at least unsecured debts of the company, and some may be preferential items or the subject of claims on the Redundancy Fund.

Subs. (7)

The changes introduced by the aforementioned provision apply to contracts of employment adopted on or after March 15, 1994. In this sense the legislation is retrospective, though it can hardly be said to take away the legitimate expectations of employees in view of the clear statement of the President of the Board of Trade on March 14, 1994. Indeed, there was some debate in Parliament as to whether the legislation should be backdated to December 30, 1986 which was the date of the coming into force of the Insolvency Act 1986 itself. Proponents of this more radical backdating (ironically largely from the opposition parties) expressed concern at the predicament of insolvency practitioners who may have unwittingly adopted contracts of employment in the past and then failed to make good sums due to employees as a result of such adoption. By treating such claims as unsecured they would inevitably fail to be met out of an insolvent company's assets, though some may have been satisfied out of the Redundancy Fund or by any purchaser of the company's businesses. Insolvency practitioners, so the argument ran, could be bankrupted by "windfall" actions brought on behalf of employees who had lost out in the last few years. The Government was not prepared to make the legislation any more retrospective than was absolutely necessary, though it has given assurances to review its position on this point if insolvency practitioners are plagued with claims from employees of companies that became insolvent some time ago (see *Hansard*, H.C. Vol. 240, col. 45).

Administrative receivers: extent of personal liability on adopted contracts of employment

2.—(1) Section 44 of the Insolvency Act 1986 (personal liability of administrative receiver for certain contracts) shall be amended as provided by subsections (2) and (3) below.

(2) In subsection (1)(b) (liability for contracts of employment adopted in carrying out his functions) after "provides) and" there shall be inserted ", to the extent of any qualifying liability,".

(3) After subsection (2) there shall be inserted—

"(2A) For the purposes of subsection (1)(b), a liability under a contract of employment is a qualifying liability if—

　(a) it is a liability to pay a sum by way of wages or salary or contribution to an occupational pension scheme,

　(b) it is incurred while the administrative receiver is in office, and

　(c) it is in respect of services rendered wholly or partly after the adoption of the contract.

(2B) Where a sum payable in respect of a liability which is a qualifying liability for the purposes of subsection (1)(b) is payable in respect of services rendered partly before and partly after the adoption of the contract, liability under subsection (1)(b) shall only extend to so much of the sum as is payable in respect of services rendered after the adoption of the contract.

(2C) For the purposes of subsections (2A) and (2B)—

(a) wages or salary payable in respect of a period of holiday or absence from work through sickness or other good cause are deemed to be wages or (as the case may be) salary in respect of services rendered in that period, and

(b) a sum payable in lieu of holiday is deemed to be wages or (as the case may be) salary in respect of services rendered in the period by reference to which the holiday entitlement arose.

(2D) In subsection (2C)(a), the reference to wages or salary payable in respect of a period of holiday includes any sums which, if they had been paid, would have been treated for the purposes of the enactments relating to social security as earnings in respect of that period."

(4) This section shall have effect in relation to contracts of employment adopted on or after 15th March 1994.

DEFINITIONS
"administrative receiver": s.29(2) of the Insolvency Act 1986.

GENERAL NOTE
Section 2 is concerned with mitigating the consequences of *Paramount Airways (No. 3), Re* [1994] BCC 172 for administrative receivers. This species of insolvency practitioner has been around for over a hundred years (under the guise of "receivers" and "managers") though it was only given the cumbersome label of "administrative receiver" in 1986. Essentially an administrative receiver is appointed out of court by a debenture holder, whose security includes a general floating charge, and his function is to realise the assets to repay the debenture holder. This process of realisation may involve the carrying on of the company's business until a suitable buyer can be found for the more attractive elements. An administrative receiver is personally liable, under s.44(1)(b) of the Insolvency Act 1986, for contracts of employment he adopts and the wide view of adoption taken by the Court of Appeal in *Paramount* created as many potential problems for this type of insolvency practitioner as for administrators. Indeed, bearing in mind the statistical scarcity of administrators and the relative ubiquity of administrative receivership (there are several thousand cases recorded each year, though the numbers do fluctuate), the practical problems here were greatly magnified. In spite of the legal differences on adoption of contracts of employment the solution adopted by the legislature for the administrative receivership scenario is exactly the same as for a case of administration; there may be adoption but exposure to liability is limited.

Subs. (1)
This indicates that the change in the law is to be effected through amendments to s.44 of the Insolvency Act 1986.

Subss. (2) and (3)
The amendments to s.44 of the Insolvency Act 1986 are designed to limit the personal liability of administrative receivers on adopted contracts of employment to "qualifying liabilities". These are defined in the same terms as for s.1 above. Note the possibility of apportionment where the supply of services straddles the adoption by the administrative receiver.

Subs. (4)
See the note to s.1(7) above.

Receivers (Scotland): extent of personal liability on, and agency in relation to, adopted contracts of employment

3.—(1) Section 57 of the Insolvency Act 1986 (agency and personal liability of receiver for certain contracts) shall be amended as provided by subsections (2) to (4) below.

(2) After subsection (1) there shall be inserted—

"(1A) Without prejudice to subsection (1), a receiver is deemed to be the agent of the company in relation to any contract of employment adopted by him in the carrying out of his functions."

(3) In subsection (2) (liability for certain contracts entered into or adopted in carrying out receiver's functions), after "provides, and" there shall be inserted ", to the extent of any qualifying liability,".

(4) After subsection (2) there shall be inserted—

"(2A) For the purposes of subsection (2), a liability under a contract of employment is a qualifying liability if—

    (a) it is a liability to pay a sum by way of wages or salary or contribution to an occupational pension scheme,

    (b) it is incurred while the receiver is in office, and

    (c) it is in respect of services rendered wholly or partly after the adoption of the contract.

(2B) Where a sum payable in respect of a liability which is a qualifying liability for the purposes of subsection (2) is payable in respect of services rendered partly before and partly after the adoption of the contract, liability under that subsection shall only extend to so much of the sum as is payable in respect of services rendered after the adoption of the contract.

(2C) For the purposes of subsections (2A) and (2B)—

    (a) wages or salary payable in respect of a period of holiday or absence from work through sickness or other good cause are deemed to be wages or (as the case may be) salary in respect of services rendered in that period, and

    (b) a sum payable in lieu of holiday is deemed to be wages or (as the case may be) salary in respect of services rendered in the period by reference to which the holiday entitlement arose.

(2D) In subsection (2C)(a), the reference to wages or salary payable in respect of a period of holiday includes any sums which, if they had been paid, would have been treated for the purposes of the enactments relating to social security as earnings in respect of that period."

(5) This section shall have effect in relation to contracts of employment adopted on or after 15th March 1994.

<small>DEFINITIONS</small>
"receiver": s.70 of the Insolvency Act 1986.

<small>GENERAL NOTE</small>
"Administrative receivership" is not a term used in Scottish corporate insolvency law. The Scots having only accepted the concept of receivership in 1972 have not yet adopted the more cumbersome label that has been attached to what is essentially the same institution in England and Wales. The Scottish law of receivership is based therefore upon a discrete set of provisions in the Insolvency Act 1986, namely ss.50–71. Consequently the Insolvency Act 1994 is required to make special amendments to cater for the *Paramount* problem in Scotland.

Subs. (1)
This indicates that the solution to the *Paramount* problem is being engineered through amendments to s.57 of the Insolvency Act 1986.

Subss. (2) to (4)
The effect of these changes is to limit personal liability of Scottish receivers for contracts of employment adopted by them. The qualifying liability criterion is used again. See the note to s.2 above.

Subs. (5)
See the note to s.1(7) above.

Corresponding provision for Northern Ireland

4. Schedule 1 to this Act (which makes provision for Northern Ireland corresponding to that made by sections 1 and 2 above) shall have effect.

<small>DEFINITIONS</small>
"administrator": art. 21(2) of the Insolvency (Northern Ireland) Order 1989 (S.I. 1989 No. 2405 (N.I. 19)).
"administrative receiver": art. 5 of the Insolvency (Northern Ireland) Order 1989 (S.I. 1989 No. 2405 (N.I. 19)).

The major reforms of corporate insolvency law introduced into English law in 1985/6 did not surface in Northern Ireland until 1991 when the Insolvency (Northern Ireland) Order 1989 (S.I. 1989 No. 2405 (N.I. 19)) was brought into force. It is therefore necessary to incorporate special amending provisions into that Order. Details of these amendments are outlined in Sched. 1; in essence they duplicate ss.1 and 2 dealing with contracts of employment adopted by administrators and administrative receivers in Northern Ireland by making the appropriate amendments to arts. 31 and 54 of the 1989 Order.

Short title, repeals and extent

5.—(1) This Act may be cited as the Insolvency Act 1994.

(2) The enactments mentioned in Schedule 2 to this Act are hereby repealed to the extent specified in the third column of that Schedule.

(3) The extent of any amendment or repeal of an enactment made by this Act is the same as that of the enactment amended or repealed.

GENERAL NOTE

Subs. (1)
This Act started off as the Insolvency (No. 2) Bill because there was already an Insolvency Bill 1994 progressing through Parliament when the significance of the *Paramount* affair became apparent. The second Bill was the first to receive the Royal Assent hence its short title.

Subs. (2)
Schedule 2 deals with repeals, though in substance this legislation is concerned with amendment by substitution.

Subs. (3)
This is a convenient shorthand formula used to explain the territorial extent of the 1994 Act. It is a pity that an opportunity was not taken to clarify the position as to whether these provisions apply to administrations and administrative receiverships of foreign companies—compare here the conflicting signs coming from *Dallhold Estates (U.K.) Pty.* [1992] BCC 394 with *International Bulk Commodities, Re* [1992] 3 W.L.R. 238.

SCHEDULES

Section 4   SCHEDULE 1

CORRESPONDING PROVISION FOR NORTHERN IRELAND

1.—(1) Article 31 of the Insolvency (Northern Ireland) Order 1989 (vacation of office) shall be amended as follows.

(2) In paragraph (3) (which provides for paragraphs (4) and (5) to apply where a person ceases to be administrator) for "paragraphs (4) and (5)" there shall be substituted "the following paragraphs".

(3) In paragraph (5) (which provides for certain debts and liabilities incurred during administration, including those incurred under contracts of employment adopted by the administrator, to be charged on the company's property in priority to his remuneration and expenses) the words "or contracts of employment adopted" and the words from "and for the purpose" to the end shall be omitted.

(4) At the end there shall be inserted—

"(6) Any sums payable in respect of liabilities incurred, while he was administrator, under contracts of employment adopted by him or a predecessor of his in the carrying out of his or the predecessor's functions shall, to the extent that the liabilities are qualifying liabilities, be charged on and paid out of any such property as is mentioned in paragraph (4) and enjoy the same priority as any sums to which paragraph (5) applies; and for the purpose of this paragraph the administrator is not to be taken to have adopted a contract of employment by reason of anything done or omitted to be done within 14 days from his appointment.

(7) For the purposes of paragraph (6), a liability under a contract of employment is a qualifying liability if—

(a) it is a liability to pay a sum by way of wages or salary or contribution to an occupational pension scheme, and

(b) it is in respect of services rendered wholly or partly after the adoption of the contract.

(8) There shall be disregarded for the purposes of paragraph (6) so much of any qualifying liability as represents payment in respect of services rendered before the adoption of the contract.

(9) For the purposes of paragraphs (7) and (8)—

(a) wages or salary payable in respect of a period of holiday or absence from work through sickness or other good cause are deemed to be wages or (as the case may be) salary in respect of services rendered in that period, and

(b) a sum payable in lieu of holiday is deemed to be wages or (as the case may be) salary in respect of services rendered in the period by reference to which the holiday entitlement arose.

(10) In paragraph (9)(a), the reference to wages or salary payable in respect of a period of holiday includes any sums which, if they had been paid, would have been treated for the purposes of the statutory provisions relating to social security as earnings in respect of that period."

2.—(1) Article 54 of the Insolvency (Northern Ireland) Order 1989 (personal liability of administrative receiver for certain contracts) shall be amended as follows.

(2) In paragraph (1)(b) (liability for contracts of employment adopted in carrying out his functions) after "provides" and" there shall be inserted ", to the extent of any qualifying liability,".

(3) After paragraph (2) there shall be inserted—

"(2A) For the purposes of paragraph (1)(b), a liability under a contract of employment is a qualifying liability if—

(a) it is a liability to pay a sum by way of wages or salary or contribution to an occupational pension scheme,

(b) it is incurred while the administrative receiver is in office, and

(c) it is in respect of services rendered wholly or partly after the adoption of the contract.

(2B) Where a sum payable in respect of a liability which is a qualifying liability for the purposes of paragraph (1)(b) is payable in respect of services rendered partly before and partly after the adoption of the contract, liability under paragraph (1)(b) shall only extend to so much of the sum as is payable in respect of services rendered after the adoption of the contract.

(2C) For the purposes of paragraphs (2A) and (2B)—

(a) wages or salary payable in respect of a period of holiday or absence from work through sickness or other good cause are deemed to be wages or (as the case may be) salary in respect of services rendered in that period, and

(b) a sum payable in lieu of holiday is deemed to be wages or (as the case may be) salary in respect of services rendered in the period by reference to which the holiday entitlement arose.

(2D) In paragraph (2C)(a), the reference to wages or salary payable in respect of a period of holiday includes any sums which, if they had been paid, would have been treated for the purposes of the statutory provisions relating to social security as earnings in respect of that period."

3. The preceding provisions shall have effect in relation to contracts of employment adopted on or after 15th March 1994.

GENERAL NOTE

See the note to s.4 above.

Section 5   SCHEDULE 2

REPEALS

Chapter	Short title	Extent of repeal
1986 c.45.	The Insolvency Act 1986.	In section 19(5), the words "or contracts of employment adopted".
S.I. 1989/2405 (N.I. 19).	The Insolvency (Northern Ireland) Order 1989.	In Article 31(5), the words "or contracts of employment adopted" and the words from "and for the purpose" to the end.

GENERAL NOTE

See the commentary on s.5(2) above.

INDEX

References are to sections

TRANSPORT POLICE (JURISDICTION) ACT 1994

(1994 c. 8)

An Act to make further provision with respect to the jurisdiction of transport police. [24th March 1994]

PARLIAMENTARY DEBATES
Hansard, H.C. Vol. 240, col. 52; H.L. Vol. 553, cols. 622, 809, 826.

INTRODUCTION

This Act amends the British Transport Commission Act 1949, s.53 and repeals the Railways Act 1993, s.132(5) to extend the jurisdiction of the British Transport Police. It enables them to act as constables in England and Wales in, on and in the vicinity of premises of any subsidiary of the British Railways Board, and anywhere in England and Wales in matters connected with or affecting any of the Board's subsidiaries or a police services user or their undertakings. The Act also makes transitional provision to ensure that British Transport Police constables appointed before the amendments come into force have the same jurisdiction as those appointed afterwards.

Amendment of the British Transport Commission Act 1949

1.—(1) Section 53 of the British Transport Commission Act 1949 (which makes provision in relation to transport police, including provision with respect to jurisdiction) shall, in its application to England and Wales, be amended in accordance with subsections (2) to (4) below.

(2) In subsection (1) (which, subject to subsection (2), makes provision for the appointment and jurisdiction of transport police constables and which was amended by the Railways Act 1993) for the words "subsection (2)" there shall be substituted the words "subsections (1A) and (2)".

(3) For the proviso to subsection (1) (which restricts the jurisdiction of transport police constables) there shall be substituted the following subsection—

"(1A) Except to the extent that any other enactment confers more extensive powers on a constable appointed under subsection (1) of this section, any constable so appointed shall, for the duration of his appointment, only act as a constable—

    (a) in, on and in the vicinity of any policed premises; and

    (b) elsewhere, in relation to matters connected with or affecting—

        (i) the British Railways Board,

        (ii) a subsidiary of that Board, or

        (iii) a police services user,

    or the undertaking of any person falling within subparagraph (i), (ii) or (iii) of this paragraph;

and, if and to the extent that he is acting as a constable in pursuance of a transport police services agreement, he shall (without prejudice to the foregoing limitations) only so act in accordance with the terms of that agreement."

(4) For subsection (3) (definitions) there shall be substituted—

"(3) In this section—

"police services user" means any person who is a party to a transport police services agreement, other than the British Railways Board or a subsidiary of that Board;

"policed premises" means—

    (a) any land, building or other structure, or any rolling stock, which is owned or used by, leased or hired to, or under the management of, the British Railways Board or a subsidiary of that Board; or

    (b) any land, building or other structure, or any rolling stock—

(i) which is owned or used by, leased or hired to, or under the management of, a police services user; and

(ii) in respect of which the services of constables appointed under subsection (1) of this section are made available to that police services user under or by virtue of a transport police services agreement;

"rolling stock" has the meaning given in section 83 of the Railways Act 1993;

"transport police services agreement" means an agreement made (whether before or after the passing of this Act) between—

(a) the British Railways Board, acting under or by virtue of any other enactment, and

(b) any other person,

for making the services of constables appointed under subsection (1) of this section available to that other person;

"subsidiary" has the meaning given in section 736 of the Companies Act 1985."

(5) Without prejudice to section 17(2) of the Interpretation Act 1978, any person who, immediately before the coming into force of this Act, is or is deemed to have been appointed to act as a constable throughout England and Wales under section 53 of the British Transport Commission Act 1949 shall, as from the coming into force of this Act, be deemed to have been appointed so to act under that section as amended by this Act.

Short title, commencement, repeals and extent

2.—(1) This Act may be cited as the Transport Police (Jurisdiction) Act 1994.

(2) This Act shall come into force on 1st April 1994.

(3) Section 132(5) of the Railways Act 1993 (which sets out the jurisdiction of the transport police in relation to certain agreements) shall cease to have effect.

(4) The enactments mentioned in the Schedule to this Act are hereby repealed to the extent specified in the third column of that Schedule.

(5) Section 1 of this Act extends to England and Wales only.

(6) This Act does not extend to Northern Ireland.

SCHEDULE

ENACTMENTS REPEALED

Chapter	Short title	Extent of repeal
1978 c.xxi.	The British Railways Act 1978.	Section 25(4).
1993 c.43.	The Railways Act 1993.	Section 132(5). In Schedule 10, paragraph 1(3).

INDEX

References are to sections

FINANCE ACT 1994*

(1994 c. 9)

ARRANGEMENT OF SECTIONS

PART I

CUSTOMS AND EXCISE

CHAPTER I

GENERAL

Rates of duty

CHAPTER II

APPEALS AND PENALTIES

VAT and duties tribunals

Civil penalties

Assessments to excise duty or to penalties

Customs and excise reviews and appeals

Supplemental provisions

CHAPTER III

CUSTOMS: ENFORCEMENT POWERS

*Annotations by Ian Ferrier, M.A., Barrister and Rupert Baldry, Barrister.

146. Minor corrections.

An Act to grant certain duties, to alter other duties, and to amend the law relating to the National Debt and the Public Revenue, and to make further provision in connection with Finance.   [3rd May 1994]

PARLIAMENTARY DEBATES
Hansard, H.C. Vol. 236, cols. 166, 633, 764, 819; Vol. 239, col. 884; Vol. 241, cols. 745, 891; H.L. Vol. 554, col. 927.

INTRODUCTION AND GENERAL NOTE

This Act was the first to result from the new system whereby the Budget is presented in the Autumn, along with the Chancellor's Autumn Statement on proposed government spending, instead of the traditional date in the Spring. During the transitional period there were two Budgets in 1993, on March 16, presented by Mr Norman Lamont, and on November 30, presented by Mr Kenneth Clarke.

During the intervening period, a slow economic recovery continued. With a public sector deficit still close to £50 billion, Mr Clarke had to look for further sources of revenue, which he attempted to do without impeding recovery or creating controversy such as that caused by Mr Lamont's imposition of VAT on domestic fuel and power. As well as introducing two new taxes, Mr Clarke raised further revenue by continuing to erode the value of various reliefs, including mortgage interest relief.

Surprise was expressed that the Finance Act 1994, following just nine months after the Finance Act 1993 (c. 34), was even longer than its predecessor. This reflects to some extent a regrettable, but possibly inevitable, trend towards greater complexity in fiscal legislation, but can also be attributed to a number of special measures, some of a rather technical character, among which the following may be noted:

(1) a new system of appeals on customs and excise duties is introduced, together with associated powers for the Customs and Excise (ss.7–27 and Scheds. 4 and 5);

(2) Air Passenger Duty is introduced, generally at £10 on international journeys and £5 on domestic journeys (ss.28–44 and Sched. 6);

(3) Insurance Premium Tax is introduced, charged at 2.5 per cent. on most insurance except life policies (ss.48–74 and Sched. 7);

(4) an Enterprise Investment Scheme is introduced, to replace the Business Expansion Scheme, which expired at the end of 1993 (s.137 and Sched. 15);

(5) companies are offered an alternative system for the taxation of dividends from their foreign income (s.138 and Sched. 16);

(6) following on the code for taxation of companies' exchange gains and losses in the FA 1993 (c. 34), further provisions are introduced for taxing interest rate and currency contracts (ss.147–177 and Sched. 18);

(7) the administration of income tax is extensively changed by a move towards self-assessment and the abolition of the preceding year basis of assessment for individuals and partnerships (ss.178–218 and Scheds. 19–20);

(8) detailed provisions are necessary to deal with fiscal aspects of the privatisation of British Rail under the Railways Act 1993 (c. 43) (s.252 and Sched. 24).

ABBREVIATIONS

ACT	:	Advance Corporation Tax
APD	:	air passenger duty
BES	:	Business Expansion Scheme
CAA 1990 (c. 1)	:	Capital Allowance Act 1990
CATS	:	Central Area Transmission System
CEMA 1979 (c. 2)	:	Customs and Excise Management Act 1979
DFP	:	Distributable Foreign Profit
EIS	:	Enterprise Investment Scheme
FID	:	Foreign income dividend
FII	:	Franked Investment Income
ICTA 1988 (c. 1)	:	Income and Corporation Taxes Act 1988
IPT	:	insurance premium tax
MIRAS	:	Mortgage interest relief at source
NIC	:	National Insurance Contributions
TCGA 1992 (c. 12)	:	Taxation of Chargeable Gains Act 1992
TMA 1970 (c. 9)	:	Taxes Management Act 1970
VATA 1983 (c. 55)	:	Value Added Tax Act 1983
VEP	:	Vehicle Excise Duty

PART I

CUSTOMS AND EXCISE

CHAPTER I

GENERAL

Rates of Duty

Wine, made-wine and cider

1.—(1) For the Table of rates of duty in Schedule 1 to the Alcoholic Liquor Duties Act 1979 (wine and made-wine) there shall be substituted the Table in Schedule 1 to this Act.

(2) In section 62(1) of that Act (cider) for "£22.39" there shall be substituted "£22.82".

(3) This section shall be deemed to have come into force on 1st January 1994.

GENERAL NOTE

The duty on cider is increased by 1.9 per cent. For the duty on wine see the General Note to Sched. 1. The duty on beer and spirits remains unchanged.

In a change of practice, the new rates do not come into force until one month after the date of the Budget, *i.e.* after the Christmas holiday period.

Tobacco products

2.—(1) For the Table in Schedule 1 to the Tobacco Products Duty Act 1979 there shall be substituted—

"TABLE

1. Cigarettes	An amount equal to 20 per cent. of the retail price plus £52.33 per thousand cigarettes.
2. Cigars	£77.58 per kilogram.
3. Hand-rolling tobacco	£81.86 per kilogram.
4. Other smoking tobacco and chewing tobacco	£34.26 per kilogram."

(2) This section shall be deemed to have come into force at 6 o'clock in the evening of 30th November 1993.

GENERAL NOTE

The specific duty on all tobacco products is increased by 7.3 per cent. The *ad valorem* duty additionally charged on cigarettes remains at 20 per cent.

The Chancellor has announced his intention of increasing tobacco duties on average by at least 3 per cent. a year in real terms, in order to discourage smoking.

Hydrocarbon oil

3.—(1) In section 6(1) of the Hydrocarbon Oil Duties Act 1979 for "£0.3058" (duty on light oil) and "£0.2514" (duty on heavy oil) there shall be substituted "£0.3314" and "£0.2770" respectively.

(2) In section 11(1) of that Act (rebate on heavy oil) for "£0.0105" (fuel oil) and "£0.0149" (gas oil) there shall be substituted "£0.0116" and "£0.0164" respectively.

(3) In section 14(1) of that Act (rebate on light oil for use as furnace fuel) for "£0.0105" there shall be substituted "£0.0116".

(4) This section shall be deemed to have come into force at 6 o'clock in the evening of 30th November 1993.

GENERAL NOTE

The duty on light oil (effectively, leaded petrol) is increased by 8.5 per cent. and the duty on heavy oil (effectively, diesel road fuel) is increased by 10 per cent. The rebate on unleaded petrol is left unchanged, so producing a 10 per cent. increase in duty. Other rebates are adjusted to produce a 10 per cent. increase in duty.

The Chancellor has announced his intention to increase road fuel duties on average by at least 5 per cent. in real terms in future Budgets, in order to restrain carbon dioxide emissions.

Bus fuel duty rebate, introduced by the FA 1965 (c. 25), s.92 and payable at 100 per cent. since the FA 1974 (c. 30), s.54, is to be restricted for the first time by being held at pre-Budget levels, resulting in an increase of 29 per cent. in bus operators' fuel costs.

Vehicles excise duty

4.—(1) The Vehicles (Excise) Act 1971 shall be amended as follows.

(2) In section 2(1)(b) (six month licences), for "£35" there shall be substituted "£50".

(3) In Schedule 1 (annual rates of duty on motorcycles), in Part I, paragraph 4(a) (special provision about old motorcycles in Northern Ireland) shall be omitted.

(4) In Schedule 2 (annual rates of duty on hackney carriages)—

(a) in Part I, paragraph 3 (special provision about vehicles used partly for private purposes) and paragraph 5 (special provision for Northern Ireland) shall be omitted; and

(b) in the second column of the first entry in the Table set out in Part II (hackney carriages with seating capacity under nine), for "125" there shall be substituted "130".

(5) In Schedule 4 (annual rates of duty on goods vehicles), in the Table set out in paragraph 4(1) (articulated vehicles), there shall be inserted at the end—

38,000	44,000	—	—	—	2,730	2,730	1,240

(6) In Schedule 4, in paragraph 6 (farmers' goods vehicles and showmen's goods vehicles), sub-paragraph (6)(a), (c) and (d) (exceptional cases where rate is not determined according to sub-paragraphs (3) to (5)) shall be omitted.

(7) In Schedule 5 (annual rates of duty on vehicles not falling within Schedules 1 to 4A), in the second column of paragraph 2 in the Table set out in Part II (vehicles other than those constructed before 1947), for "125.00" there shall be substituted "130.00".

(8) This section shall apply in relation to licences taken out after 30th November 1993.

GENERAL NOTE

Sundry changes are made to the vehicle excise duty (VED) régime.

Subs. (2)

The threshold below which six-monthly licensing is not available is increased from £35 to £50.

Subs. (3)

The concessionary rate for motorcycles in Northern Ireland will now apply to those registered before 1933, as in Great Britain, rather than 1935.

Subs. (4)

The provision under which hackney carriages used partly for private purposes are licensed in the class for cars and small vans is abolished. The rate of VED is increased from £125 to £130.

Subs. (5)

Rates of duty are specified for articulated lorries between 38,000 kg and 44,000 kg used in combined transport (*i.e.* journeys to and from a railhead carrying a swap body or container).

Subs. (6)

Rates of VED for certain farmers' and showmens' vehicles are omitted. They will instead be licensed under other provisions at 60 per cent. and 25 per cent. of the main lorry VED rates respectively.

Subs. (7)

VED for cars and small vans constructed after 1947 is increased from £125 to £130.

Other provisions

Vehicles excise duty: miscellaneous provisions

5. Schedule 2 to this Act (which contains miscellaneous provisions relating to vehicles excise duty) shall have effect.

GENERAL NOTE

Schedule 2 introduces amendments preparatory to the consolidation of the VED legislation; see further the General Note to Sched. 2.

Gaming machine licence duty

6. Schedule 3 to this Act (which makes amendments to the Betting and Gaming Duties Act 1981 about gaming machine licence duty) shall have effect.

GENERAL NOTE

Schedule 3 amends the Betting and Gaming Duties Act 1981 (c. 63) with respect to administrative arrangements for the issue of gaming machine licences; see further the General Note to Sched. 3.

CHAPTER II

APPEALS AND PENALTIES

VAT and duties tribunals

GENERAL NOTE
The European Community Customs Code, Art. 243, requires Member States to provide appeal procedures for customs and excise duties. Until now, appeal in the U.K. has only been available in a limited and unsatisfactory way. A general system of appeal is now provided to the VAT tribunal, which is renamed the VAT and duties tribunal. The opportunity is taken to bring the system of penalties for customs and excise duties into line with those for VAT and to provide (in Chap. III) further enforcement powers in relation to customs duties.

VAT and duties tribunals

7.—(1) As from the coming into force of this section the tribunals for which provision is made by Schedule 8 to the Value Added Tax Act 1983 (value added tax tribunals)—
  (a) shall be known as the VAT and duties tribunals; and
  (b) shall (in addition to their jurisdiction in relation to matters relating to value added tax) have the jurisdiction in relation to matters relating to customs and excise which is conferred by this Chapter.
(2) Accordingly—
  (a) the President of Value Added Tax Tribunals and any Vice-President of Value Added Tax Tribunals shall be known after the coming into force of this section as, respectively, the President of the VAT and Duties Tribunals and a Vice-President of the VAT and Duties Tribunals; and
  (b) references in the Value Added Tax Act 1983 or in any other enact-ment, or in any subordinate legislation, to a value added tax tribunal, to the President of Value Added Tax Tribunals or to a Vice-President of Value Added Tax Tribunals, and any cognate expressions, shall be construed in accordance with subsection (1) and paragraph (a) above.
(3) In the following provisions of this Chapter references to an appeal tri-bunal are references to a VAT and duties tribunal.
(4) Sections 25 and 29 of the Finance Act 1985 (settling of appeals by agreement and enforcement of decisions of tribunal) shall have effect as if—
  (a) the references to section 40 of the Value Added Tax Act 1983 included references to this Chapter; and
  (b) references to value added tax included references to any relevant duty.
(5) Without prejudice to the generality of the power conferred by para-graph 9 of Schedule 8 to the Value Added Tax Act 1983 (rules of procedure for tribunals), rules under that paragraph may provide for costs awarded against an appellant on an appeal by virtue of this Chapter to be recoverable, and for any directly applicable Community legislation relating to any rel-evant duty or any enactment so relating to apply, as if the amount awarded were an amount of duty which the appellant is required to pay.
(6) In Part I of Schedule 1 to the Tribunals and Inquiries Act 1992 (tri-bunals under direct supervision of Council on Tribunals), for the entry begin-ning "Value added tax" there shall be substituted the following entry—

"VAT and duties   44. VAT and duties tribunals for
                                   England and Wales and for North-
                                   ern Ireland, constituted in accord-
                                   ance with Schedule 8 to the Value
                                   Added Tax Act 1983 (c. 55)."

(7) In Part II of Schedule 1 to that Act of 1992 (tribunals under supervision of Scottish Committee of the Council), for the entry beginning "Value added tax" there shall be substituted the following entry—

"VAT and duties   63. VAT and duties tribunals for Scotland constituted in accordance with Schedule 8 to the Value Added Tax Act 1983 (c. 55)."

GENERAL NOTE

The VAT tribunals, which have existed since the introduction of VAT in 1973, are renamed the VAT and duties tribunals, with consequential changes to other legislation.

Subs. (5)

This permits rules of procedure to be made to allow costs awarded against an appellant to be recovered as if it were duty.

Civil penalties

Penalty for evasion of excise duty

8.—(1) Subject to the following provisions of this section, in any case where—

(a) any person engages in any conduct for the purpose of evading any duty of excise, and

(b) his conduct involves dishonesty (whether or not such as to give rise to any criminal liability),

that person shall be liable to a penalty of an amount equal to the amount of duty evaded or, as the case may be, sought to be evaded.

(2) References in this section to a person's evading a duty of excise shall include references to his obtaining or securing, without his being entitled to it—

(a) any repayment, rebate or drawback of duty;

(b) any relief or exemption from or any allowance against duty; or

(c) any deferral or other postponement of his liability to pay any duty or of the discharge by payment of any such liability,

and shall also include references to his evading the cancellation of any entitlement to, or the withdrawal of, any such repayment, rebate, drawback, relief, exemption or allowance.

(3) In relation to any such evasion of duty as is mentioned in subsection (2) above, the reference in subsection (1) above to the amount of duty evaded or sought to be evaded shall be construed as a reference to the amount of the repayment, rebate, drawback, relief, exemption or allowance or, as the case may be, the amount of the payment which, or the liability to make which, is deferred or otherwise postponed.

(4) Where a person is liable to a penalty under this section—

(a) the Commissioners or, on appeal, an appeal tribunal may reduce the penalty to such amount (including nil) as they think proper; and

(b) an appeal tribunal, on an appeal relating to a penalty reduced by the Commissioners under this subsection, may cancel the whole or any part of the reduction made by the Commissioners.

(5) Neither of the following matters shall be a matter which the Commissioners or any appeal tribunal shall be entitled to take into account in exercising their powers under subsection (4) above, that is to say—

(a) the insufficiency of the funds available to any person for paying any duty of excise or for paying the amount of the penalty;

(b) the fact that there has, in the case in question or in that case taken with any other cases, been no or no significant loss of duty.

(6) Statements made or documents produced by or on behalf of a person shall not be inadmissible in—

   (a) any criminal proceedings against that person in respect of any offence in connection with or in relation to any duty of excise, or

   (b) any proceedings against that person for the recovery of any sum due from him in connection with or in relation to any duty of excise,

by reason only that any of the matters specified in subsection (7) below has been drawn to his attention and that he was, or may have been, induced by that matter having been brought to his attention to make the statements or produce the documents.

   (7) The matters mentioned in subsection (6) above are—

   (a) that the Commissioners have power, in relation to any duty of excise, to assess an amount due by way of a civil penalty, instead of instituting criminal proceedings;

   (b) that it is the Commissioners' practice, without being able to give an undertaking as to whether they will make such an assessment in any case, to be influenced in determining whether to make such an assessment by the fact (where it is the case) that a person has made a full confession of any dishonest conduct to which he has been a party and has given full facilities for an investigation;

   (c) that the Commissioners or, on appeal, an appeal tribunal have power to reduce a penalty under this section, as provided in subsection (4) above; and

   (d) that, in determining the extent of such a reduction in the case of any person, the Commissioners or tribunal will have regard to the extent of the co-operation which he has given to the Commissioners in their investigation.

   (8) Where, by reason of conduct falling within subsection (1) above, a person is convicted of an offence, that conduct shall not also give rise to liability to a penalty under this section.

GENERAL NOTE

The system of civil penalties for infractions of the VAT code, introduced as a result of the recommendations of the Keith Committee, is now extended to excise duty. This section deals with dishonest evasion. The penalty can amount to 100 per cent., *i.e.* the total of the duty evaded, but this may be mitigated by the Customs and Excise or, on appeal, by the tribunal. Insufficiency of funds or the amount of net duty loss do not provide grounds for mitigation.

Where a person makes statements or produces documents in response to assurances from the Customs and Excise that full co-operation may result in civil rather than criminal proceedings, these statements or documents may nonetheless be admissible in subsequent criminal proceedings. However, a criminal conviction will rule out subsequent civil proceedings.

Penalties for contraventions of statutory requirements

   9.—(1) This section applies, subject to section 10 below, to any conduct in relation to which any enactment (including an enactment contained in this Act or in any Act passed after this Act) provides for the conduct to attract a penalty under this section.

   (2) Any person to whose conduct this section applies shall be liable—

   (a) in the case of conduct in relation to which provision is made by subsection (4) below or any other enactment for the penalty attracted to be calculated by reference to an amount of, or an amount payable on account of, any duty of excise, to a penalty of whichever is the greater of 5 per cent. of that amount and £250; and

   (b) in any other case, to a penalty of £250.

   (3) Subject to section 13(3) and (4) below, in the case of any conduct to which this section applies which is conduct in relation to which provision is made by subsection (4) or (5) below or any other enactment for that conduct to attract daily penalties, the person whose conduct it is—

   (a) shall be liable, in addition to an initial penalty under subsection (2) above, to a penalty of £20 for every day, after the first, on which the conduct continues, but

(b) shall not, in respect of the continuation of that conduct, be liable to further penalties under subsection (2) above.

(4) Where any conduct to which this section applies consists in a failure, in contravention of any subordinate legislation, to pay any amount of any duty of excise or an amount payable on account of any such duty, then, in so far as that would not otherwise be the case—

(a) the penalty attracted to that contravention shall be calculated by reference to the amount unpaid; and

(b) the contravention shall also attract daily penalties.

(5) Where—

(a) a contravention of any provision made by or under any enactment consists in or involves a failure, before such time as may be specified in or determined in accordance with that provision, to send a return to the Commissioners showing the amount which any person is or may become required to pay by way of, or on account of, any duty of excise, and

(b) that contravention attracts a penalty under this section,

that contravention shall also attract daily penalties.

(6) Where, by reason of any conduct to which this section applies, a person is convicted of an offence, that conduct shall not also give rise to liability to a penalty under this section.

(7) If it appears to the Treasury that there has been a change in the value of money since the passing of this Act or, as the case may be, the last occasion when the power conferred by this subsection was exercised, they may by order substitute for any sum for the time being specified in subsection (2) or (3) above such other sum as appears to them to be justified by the change.

(8) The power to make an order under subsection (7) above—

(a) shall be exercisable by statutory instrument subject to annulment in pursuance of a resolution of the House of Commons; but

(b) shall not be exercisable so as to vary the penalty for any conduct occurring before the coming into force of the order.

(9) Schedule 4 to this Act (which provides for the conduct to which this section applies, repeals the summary offences superseded by this section and makes related provision with respect to forfeiture) shall have effect.

GENERAL NOTE

This section extends the civil penalty system to a large number of contraventions of excise law listed in Sched. 4 and these contraventions cease to be summary offences under the criminal law. There are three types of penalty:

(i) "geared penalties": these are 5 per cent. of any amount due.

(ii) "fixed penalties": where a geared penalty is less than £250, a fixed penalty of that amount will apply.

(iii) "daily penalties": a daily penalty of £20 may also be exigible in cases provided for under subss. (4) and (5).

These penalties may be varied by the Treasury by Statutory Instrument, subject to the negative resolution procedure in the House of Commons.

A criminal conviction precludes a civil penalty in respect of the same matter.

Exceptions to liability under section 9

10.—(1) Subject to subsection (2) below and to any express provision to the contrary made in relation to any conduct to which section 9 above applies, such conduct shall not give rise to any liability to a penalty under that section if the person whose conduct it is satisfies the Commissioners or, on appeal, an appeal tribunal that there is a reasonable excuse for the conduct.

(2) Where it appears to the Commissioners or, on appeal, an appeal tribunal that there is no reasonable excuse for a continuation of conduct for which there was at first a reasonable excuse, liability for a penalty under section 9 above shall be determined as if the conduct began at the time when there ceased to be a reasonable excuse for its continuation.

(3) For the purposes of this section—
 (a) an insufficiency of funds available for paying any duty or penalty due shall not be a reasonable excuse; and
 (b) where reliance is placed by any person on another to perform any task, then neither the fact of that reliance nor the fact that any conduct to which section 9 above applies was attributable to the conduct of that other person shall be a reasonable excuse.

GENERAL NOTE
 As with the parallel provisions for VAT, mitigation is not allowed for penalties under s.9, but they may be remitted altogether if a reasonable excuse is shown. Shortage of funds or reliance on another person are not in themselves reasonable excuses. There have been many appeals to tribunals in relation to reasonable excuses under the VAT legislation. For the approach which the courts have taken, see *Customs and Excise Commissioners* v. *Salevon; Same* v. *Harris* [1989] STC 907 and *Customs and Excise Commissioners* v. *Steptoe* [1992] STC 757, C.A.

Breaches of walking possession agreements

11.—(1) This section applies where—
 (a) by virtue of section 117 of the Management Act or section 28 of the Betting and Gaming Duties Act 1981, a person ("the person levying the distress") is empowered or authorised to distrain any property of another person ("the person in default"); and
 (b) the person levying the distress and the person in default have entered into a walking possession agreement.
 (2) In this section a "walking possession agreement" means an agreement under which, in consideration of the property distrained upon being allowed to remain in the custody of the person in default and of the delaying of its sale, the person in default—
 (a) acknowledges that the property specified in the agreement is under distraint and held in walking possession; and
 (b) undertakes that, except with the consent of the Commissioners and subject to such conditions as they may impose, he will not remove or allow the removal of any of the specified property from the premises named in the agreement.
 (3) Subject to subsection (4) below, if the person in default is in breach of the undertaking contained in a walking possession agreement, he shall be liable to a penalty equal to one-half of the unpaid duty or penalty which gives rise to the distraint.
 (4) The person in default shall not be liable to a penalty under subsection (3) above if he satisfies the Commissioners or, on appeal, an appeal tribunal that there is a reasonable excuse for the breach in question.
 (5) This section does not extend to Scotland.

GENERAL NOTE
 A walking possession agreement occurs when the Customs and Excise seize goods in settlement of a duty or penalty, but leave them in the charge of the debtor, to allow him to continue his business, in return for an undertaking not to remove them from the premises. Breach of a walking possession agreement will attract a civil penalty of 50 per cent. of the debt.

Assessments to excise duty or to penalties

Assessments to excise duty

12.—(1) Subject to subsection (4) below, where it appears to the Commissioners—

(a) that any person is a person from whom any amount has become due in respect of any duty of excise; and

(b) that there has been a default falling within subsection (2) below,

the Commissioners may assess the amount of duty due from that person to the best of their judgment and notify that amount to that person or his representative.

(2) The defaults falling within this subsection are—

(a) any failure by any person to make, keep, preserve or produce as required or directed by or under any enactment any returns, accounts, books, records or other documents;

(b) any omission from or inaccuracy in any returns, accounts, books, records or other documents which any person is required or directed by or under any enactment to make, keep, preserve or produce;

(c) any failure by any person to take or permit to be taken any step which he is required under Schedule 1 or 3 to the Betting and Gaming Duties Act 1981 to take or to permit to be taken;

(d) any unreasonable delay in performing any obligation the failure to perform which would be a default falling within this subsection.

(3) Where an amount has been assessed as due from any person and notified in accordance with this section, it shall, subject to any appeal under section 16 below, be deemed to be an amount of the duty in question due from that person and may be recovered accordingly, unless, or except to the extent that, the assessment has subsequently been withdrawn or reduced.

(4) An assessment of the amount of any duty of excise due from any person shall not be made under this section at any time after whichever is the earlier of the following times, that is to say—

(a) subject to subsection (5) below, the end of the period of six years beginning with the time when his liability to the duty arose; and

(b) the end of the period of one year beginning with the day on which evidence of facts, sufficient in the opinion of the Commissioners to justify the making of the assessment, comes to their knowledge;

but this subsection shall be without prejudice, where further evidence comes to the knowledge of the Commissioners at any time after the making of an assessment under this section, to the making of a further assessment within the period applicable by virtue of this subsection in relation to that further assessment.

(5) Subsection (4) above shall have effect as if the reference in paragraph (a) to six years were a reference to twenty years in the case of any assessment to any amount of duty the assessment or payment of any of which has been postponed or otherwise affected by—

(a) conduct in respect of which any person (whether or not the person assessed)—

(i) has become liable to a penalty under section 8 above, or

(ii) has been convicted of an offence of fraud or dishonesty; or

(b) any conduct in respect of which proceedings for an offence of fraud or dishonesty would have been commenced or continued against any person (whether or not the person assessed), but for their having been compounded under section 152(a) of the Management Act.

(6) The reference in subsection (4) above to the time when a person's liability to a duty of excise arose are references—

(a) in the case of a duty of excise on goods, to the excise duty point; and

(b) in any other case, to the time when the duty was charged.

(7) In this section references to an offence of fraud or dishonesty include references to an offence under any of the following provisions, that is to say—

(a) sections 100(3), 136(1), 159(6), 167(1), 168(1), 170(1) and (2) and 170B(1) of the Management Act,

(b) section 24(6) of the Betting and Gaming Duties Act 1981 and paragraph 13(3) of Schedule 1, paragraph 7(3) of Schedule 2 and paragraph 16(1) of Schedule 3 to that Act,
(c) section 31(1) and (3) of the Finance Act 1993, and
(d) section 41(1) and (3) below,
and also include references to attempting or conspiring to commit an offence
of fraud or dishonesty and to inciting the commission of such an offence.

(8) In this section "representative", in relation to a person appearing to the
Commissioners to be a person from whom any amount has become due in
respect of any duty of excise, means his personal representative or trustee in
bankruptcy, any receiver or liquidator appointed in relation to that person or
any of his property or any other person acting in a representative capacity in
relation to that person.

GENERAL NOTE
The section permits the Customs and Excise to assess excise duty underpaid, not paid or
overclaimed, subject to time-limits. This replaces an existing power to estimate excise duty due;
failure to pay an estimate on demand is a criminal offence.

Subs. (1)
The power to assess arises where a person has been in default.

Subs. (2)
This lists the defaults giving rise to the power to assess.

Subs. (3)
An assessment may be recovered as duty payable, subject to the appeal procedure.

Subss. (4) and (5)
A normal time-limit of six years applies to the raising of assessments, increased to 20 years in
cases of fraud or dishonesty. Further assessments may be made where new facts come to light.
The offences of fraud or dishonesty involved are further detailed in subs. (7).

Subs. (6)
Time-limits run from the duty point (for goods) and the date when duty was charged (for
excise-dutiable activities). For excise duty point, see the Finance (No. 2) Act 1992 (c. 48), s.1 and
regulations made thereunder.

Subs. (8)
Assessments may be notified to a person's "representative", defined in wide terms.

Assessments to penalties

13.—(1) Where any person is liable to a penalty under this Chapter, the
Commissioners may assess the amount due by way of penalty and notify that
person, or his representative, accordingly.

(2) An assessment under this section may be combined with an assessment
under section 12 above, but any notification for the purposes of any such
combined assessment shall separately identify any amount assessed by way
of a penalty.

(3) In the case of any amount due from any person by way of a penalty
under section 9 above for conduct consisting in a contravention which
attracts daily penalties—
(a) a notification of an assessment under this section shall specify a date,
   being a date no later than the date of the notification, to which the
   penalty as assessed is to be calculated; and
(b) if the contravention continues after that date, a further assessment, or
   (subject to this subsection) further assessments, may be made under
   this section in respect of any continuation of the contravention after
   that date.
(4) If—

(a) a person is assessed to a penalty in accordance with paragraph (a) of subsection (3) above, and

(b) the contravention to which that penalty relates is remedied within such period after the date specified for the purposes of that subsection in the notification of assessment as may for the purposes of this subsection be notified to that person by the Commissioners,

that contravention shall be treated for the purposes of this Chapter as having been remedied, and accordingly the conduct shall be deemed to have ceased, immediately before that date.

(5) If an amount has been assessed as due from any person and notified in accordance with this section, then unless, or except to the extent that, the assessment has subsequently been withdrawn or reduced, that amount shall, subject to any appeal under section 16 below, be recoverable as if it were an amount due from that person as an amount of the appropriate duty.

(6) In subsection (5) above "the appropriate duty" means—

(a) the duty of excise (if any) by reference to an amount of which the penalty in question is calculated; or

(b) where there is no such duty, the duty of excise the provisions relating to which are contravened by the conduct giving rise to the penalty or, if those provisions relate to more than one duty, such of the duties as appear to the Commissioners and are certified by them to be relevant in the case in question.

(7) In this section "representative", in relation to a person liable to a penalty under this Chapter, means his personal representative or trustee in bankruptcy, any receiver or liquidator appointed in relation to that person or any of his property or any other person acting in a representative capacity in relation to that person.

GENERAL NOTE

This section provides for penalties to be assessed and for penalty amounts to be recoverable as duty.

Subs. (2)

A penalty assessment may be combined with an assessment under s.12, but the amounts must be separately identified.

Subs. (3)

The assessment must specify the date to which the penalty has been calculated, in the case of daily penalties. Further assessments may be raised if the contravention continues.

Subs. (4)

The Customs and Excise may allow time for a contravention to be remedied.

Subss. (5) and (6)

Amounts assessed as penalties are recoverable as the appropriate duty, defined as the duty in relation to which the penalty is calculated. Where more than one duty is involved, or none, the Customs and Excise may nominate the duty which seems most relevant to them.

Customs and excise reviews and appeals

Requirement for review of a decision

14.—(1) This section applies to the following decisions, not being decisions under this section or section 15 below, that is to say—

(a) any decision by the Commissioners, in relation to any customs duty or to any agricultural levy of the European Community, as to—
    (i) whether or not, and at what time, anything is charged in any case with any such duty or levy;
    (ii) the rate at which any such duty or levy is charged in any case, or the amount charged;
    (iii) the person liable in any case to pay any amount charged, or the amount of his liability; or
    (iv) whether or not any person is entitled in any case to relief or to any repayment, remission or drawback of any such duty or levy, or the amount of the relief, repayment, remission or drawback to which any person is entitled;
(b) so much of any decision by the Commissioners that a person is liable to any duty of excise, or as to the amount of his liability, as is contained in any assessment under section 12 above;
(c) so much of any decision by the Commissioners that a person is liable to any penalty under any of the provisions of this Chapter, or as to the amount of his liability, as is contained in any assessment under section 13 above; and
(d) any decision by the Commissioners or any officer which is of a description specified in Schedule 5 to this Act.
(2) Any person who is—
(a) a person whose liability to pay any relevant duty or penalty is determined by, results from or is or will be affected by any decision to which this section applies,
(b) a person in relation to whom, or on whose application, such a decision has been made, or
(c) a person on or to whom the conditions, limitations, restrictions, prohibitions or other requirements to which such a decision relates are or are to be imposed or applied,
may by notice in writing to the Commissioners require them to review that decision.
(3) The Commissioners shall not be required under this section to review any decision unless the notice requiring the review is given before the end of the period of forty-five days beginning with the day on which written notification of the decision, or of the assessment containing the decision, was first given to the person requiring the review.
(4) For the purposes of subsection (3) above it shall be the duty of the Commissioners to give written notification of any decision to which this section applies to any person who—
(a) requests such a notification;
(b) has not previously been given written notification of that decision; and
(c) if given such a notification, will be entitled to require a review of the decision under this section.
(5) A person shall be entitled to give a notice under this section requiring a decision to be reviewed for a second or subsequent time only if—
(a) the grounds on which he requires the further review are that the Commissioners did not, on any previous review, have the opportunity to consider certain facts or other matters; and
(b) he does not, on the further review, require the Commissioners to consider any facts or matters which were considered on a previous review except in so far as they are relevant to any issue to which the facts or matters not previously considered relate.
(6) If it appears to the Commissioners that there is any description of decisions falling to be made for the purposes of any provision of—
(a) the Community Customs Code,
(b) any Community legislation made for the purpose of implementing that Code, or

(c) any enactment or subordinate legislation so made,
which are not decisions to which this section otherwise applies, the Commissioners may by regulations provide for this section to apply to decisions of that description as it applies to the decisions mentioned in subsection (1) above.

(7) The power to make regulations under subsection (6) above shall be exercisable by statutory instrument subject to annulment in pursuance of a resolution of either House of Parliament and shall include power—

(a) to provide, in relation to any description of decisions to which this section is applied by any such regulations, that section 16(4) below shall have effect as if those decisions were of a description specified in Schedule 5 to this Act; and

(b) to make such other incidental, supplemental, consequential and transitional provision as the Commissioners think fit.

GENERAL NOTE
Before appealing to a tribunal against a customs or excise decision, the taxpayer is required to ask the Customs and Excise to review the decision.

Subs. (1)
This lists the decisions to which the section applies. They include decisions about: amounts of customs duty or agricultural levy, including whether they are chargeable and if so when, the chargeable rate, the person liable and the amount of liability; whether a person is entitled to duty or levy relief or repayment, and if so the amount and; liability under assessments under ss.12 and 13. Further reviewable decisions are listed under Sched. 5.

Subss. (2)–(5)
A review may be initiated by a request in writing within 45 days of the written notification of the decision, which must be given on request. A further review can only be required where there are new facts or matters to be considered.

Subss. (6) and (7)
The Customs and Excise may add to the categories of reviewable decisions by Statutory Instrument, subject to annulment by either House of Parliament.

Review procedure

15.—(1) Where the Commissioners are required in accordance with this Chapter to review any decision, it shall be their duty to do so and they may, on that review, either—

(a) confirm the decision; or

(b) withdraw or vary the decision and take such further steps (if any) in consequence of the withdrawal or variation as they may consider appropriate.

(2) Where—

(a) it is the duty of the Commissioners in pursuance of a requirement by any person under section 14 above to review any decision; and

(b) they do not, within the period of forty-five days beginning with the day on which the review was required, give notice to that person of their determination on the review,

they shall be assumed for the purposes of this Chapter to have confirmed the decision.

(3) The Commissioners shall not by virtue of any requirement under this Chapter to review a decision have any power, apart from their power in pursuance of section 8(4) above, to mitigate the amount of any penalty imposed under this Chapter.

In reviewing a decision, the Customs and Excise may confirm it, withdraw it or vary it and take such further steps as may be appropriate. If they do not notify their determination of the review within 45 days, they are deemed to have confirmed it. No power of mitigation exists, except in the case of a penalty under s.8.

Appeals to a tribunal

16.—(1) Subject to the following provisions of this section, an appeal shall lie to an appeal tribunal with respect to any of the following decisions, that is to say—
(a) any decision by the Commissioners on a review under section 15 above (including a deemed confirmation under subsection (2) of that section); and
(b) any decision by the Commissioners on such review of a decision to which section 14 above applies as the Commissioners have agreed to undertake in consequence of a request made after the end of the period mentioned in section 14(3) above.

(2) An appeal under this section shall not be entertained unless the appellant is the person who required the review in question.

(3) An appeal which relates to, or to any decision on a review of, any decision falling within any of paragraphs (a) to (c) of section 14(1) above shall not be entertained if any amount is outstanding from the appellant in respect of any liability of the appellant to pay any relevant duty to the Commissioners (including an amount of any such duty which would be so outstanding if the appeal had already been decided in favour of the Commissioners) unless—
(a) the Commissioners have, on the application of the appellant, issued a certificate stating either—
(i) that such security as appears to them to be adequate has been given to them for the payment of that amount; or
(ii) that, on the grounds of the hardship that would otherwise be suffered by the appellant, they either do not require the giving of security for the payment of that amount or have accepted such lesser security as they consider appropriate;
(b) the tribunal to which the appeal is made decide that the Commissioners should not have refused to issue a certificate under paragraph (a) above and are satisfied that such security (if any) as it would have been reasonable for the Commissioners to accept in the circumstances has been given to the Commissioners.

(4) In relation to any decision as to an ancillary matter, or any decision on the review of such a decision, the powers of an appeal tribunal on an appeal under this section shall be confined to a power, where the tribunal are satisfied that the Commissioners or other person making that decision could not reasonably have arrived at it, to do one or more of the following, that is to say—
(a) to direct that the decision, so far as it remains in force, is to cease to have effect from such time as the tribunal may direct;
(b) to require the Commissioners to conduct, in accordance with the directions of the tribunal, a further review of the original decision; and
(c) in the case of a decision which has already been acted on or taken effect and cannot be remedied by a further review, to declare the decision to have been unreasonable and to give directions to the Commissioners as to the steps to be taken for securing that repetitions of the unreasonableness do not occur when comparable circumstances arise in future.

(5) In relation to other decisions, the powers of an appeal tribunal on an appeal under this section shall also include power to quash or vary any

decision and power to substitute their own decision for any decision quashed on appeal.

(6) On an appeal under this section the burden of proof as to—

(a) the matters mentioned in subsection (1)(a) and (b) of section 8 above,

(b) the question whether any person has acted knowingly in using any substance or liquor in contravention of section 114(2) of the Management Act, and

(c) the question whether any person had such knowledge or reasonable cause for belief as is required for liability to a penalty to arise under section 22(1) or 23(1) of the Hydrocarbon Oil Duties Act 1979 (use of fuel substitute or road fuel gas on which duty not paid),

shall lie upon the Commissioners; but it shall otherwise be for the appellant to show that the grounds on which any such appeal is brought have been established.

(7) An appeal tribunal shall not, by virtue of anything contained in this section, have any power, apart from their power in pursuance of section 8(4) above, to mitigate the amount of any penalty imposed under this Chapter.

(8) References in this section to a decision as to an ancillary matter are references to any decision of a description specified in Schedule 5 to this Act which is not comprised in a decision falling within section 14(1)(a) to (c) above.

GENERAL NOTE

This deals with the heart of the new provisions, the right to appeal the result of a review by the Customs and Excise to a VAT and duties tribunal. Appeals under s.14(1)(a)–(c) may not be entertained, where any duty is outstanding, unless the Customs and Excise have issued a certificate stating that adequate security is given or that hardship would be caused. The tribunal may review the decision of the Customs and Excise on this point.

Subs. (4)

In relation to the ancillary matters dealt with in Sched. 5, the tribunal's powers are restricted to setting aside the decision, requiring the Customs and Excise to review it again, and where the decision cannot be remedied, requiring the Customs and Excise to take such steps as are necessary to ensure that an unreasonable decision does not recur in future.

Subs. (5)

In relation to the matters dealt with under s.14(1)(a)–(c), the tribunal may additionally quash or vary a decision and substitute its own.

Subs. (6)

The burden of proof lies on the Customs and Excise in the following cases:

(i) dishonest evasion under s.8.

(ii) the use of prohibited substances under the Customs and Excise Management Act 1979 (c. 2), s.114(2);

(iii) the use of petrol substitutes or road fuel gas on which duty has not been paid (Hydrocarbon Oil Duties Act 1979 (c. 5), ss.22(1) and 23(1)).

In all other cases the burden of proof lies on the taxpayer.

Subs. (7)

Mitigation is only available to the tribunal in cases of penalties for dishonest evasion of duty.

Supplemental provisions

Interpretation

17.—(1) Subject to the following provisions of this section, expressions used in this Chapter and in the Management Act have the same meanings in this Chapter as in that Act.

(2) In this Chapter—

"appeal tribunal" shall be construed in accordance with section 7(3) above;

"conduct" includes any act, omission or statement;

"contravention" includes a failure to comply, and cognate expressions shall be construed accordingly;

"the Community Customs Code" means the Regulation of the Council of the European Communities dated 12th October 1992 (EEC) No. 2913/92 for establishing the Community Customs Code;

"the Management Act" means the Customs and Excise Management Act 1979;

"relevant duty" means any Community customs duty or agricultural levy of the European Community or any duty of excise; and

"subordinate legislation" has the same meaning as in the Interpretation Act 1978.

(3) For the purposes of this Chapter a contravention consisting in a failure to do something at or before a particular time shall be taken to continue after that time until the thing is done, and references in this Chapter to the remedying of such a contravention shall be construed accordingly.

(4) References in this Chapter to a duty of excise do not include references to vehicles excise duty.

GENERAL NOTE

This contains general interpretation provisions and excludes vehicle excise duty from the scope of the appeal system.

Consequential modifications of enactments

18.—(1) Subject to subsection (2) below, references in the Management Act to a penalty shall not include references to a penalty under this Chapter.

(2) Section 117 of the Management Act (execution and distress against revenue traders) shall have effect—

  (a) as if any amount assessed as due from any person by way of a penalty under this Chapter, not being an amount in relation to which subsection (4) below applies, were an amount of excise duty payable by that person; and

  (b) with the substitution, in subsection (7A)—

      (i) for "estimated under section 116A above" of "assessed under section 12 of the Finance Act 1994"; and

      (ii) for the word "estimated", in the second and third places where it occurs, of "assessed".

(3) Section 127 of the Management Act (determination of disputes as to duties on imported goods) shall cease to have effect; and for subsection (5) of section 40 of the Value Added Tax Act 1983 (which provides for there to be no appeal with respect to any matter falling to be determined in accordance with section 127 of the Management Act) there shall be substituted the following subsection—

    "(5) No appeal shall lie under this section with respect to the subject-matter of any decision which by virtue of section 24 above is a decision to which section 14 of the Finance Act 1994 (decisions subject to review) applies unless the decision—

      (a) relates exclusively to one or both of the following matters, namely whether or not section 16(3) above applies in relation to the importation of the goods in question and (if it does not) the rate of tax charged on those goods; and

      (b) is not one in respect of which notice has been given to the Commissioners under section 14 of that Act requiring them to review it."

(4) Sections 28 and 29 of the Betting and Gaming Duties Act 1981 (distress and poinding) shall apply, as they apply in relation to any amount recover-

able by way of general betting duty, in relation to any amount assessed as due from any person by way of a penalty incurred under this Chapter with respect to conduct connected with a duty or licence under that Act.

(5) In section 29A(1)(d) of that Act of 1981 (certificate to be evidence of certain matters), for the words "or estimate made in pursuance of this Act" there shall be substituted "made in pursuance of this Act or in any assessment made under section 12 of the Finance Act 1994".

(6) In section 35(1)(c) of the Finance Act 1993 (certificate to be evidence of certain matters), for the words "in an estimate made under section 116A of the Customs and Excise Management Act 1979" there shall be substituted "in any assessment made under section 12 of the Finance Act 1994".

(7) In section 827 of the Taxes Act 1988 (VAT penalties etc.), after subsection (1) there shall be inserted the following subsection—

"(1A) Where a person is liable to make a payment by way of a penalty under any of sections 8 to 11 of the Finance Act 1994 (penalties relating to excise), that payment shall not be allowed as a deduction in computing any income, profits or losses for any tax purposes."

(8) Subsections (1), (2) and (4) above shall be without prejudice to section 13(5) above; and subsection (7) above shall have effect in relation to any chargeable period ending after the coming into force of the provision which provides for the imposition of the penalty in question.

GENERAL NOTE
This contains consequential amendments to other statutes relating to excise duties and VAT.

Subs. (7)
A civil penalty under ss.8 and 11 is not deductible for income tax or corporation tax purposes.

Commencement of Chapter

19.—(1) Subject to section 18(8) above, this Chapter shall come into force on such day as the Commissioners may by order made by statutory instrument appoint, and different days may be appointed under this subsection for different provisions and for different purposes.

(2) An order under this section may make such transitional provision and savings as appear to the Commissioners to be appropriate in connection with the bringing into force by such an order of any provision of this Chapter.

(3) Nothing in any provision of this Chapter shall, in respect of conduct occurring before the coming into force of that provision, impose or affect any liability to any civil or criminal penalty or any liability of goods to forfeiture.

GENERAL NOTE
The new provisions will be brought into effect by Statutory Instrument.

CHAPTER III

CUSTOMS: ENFORCEMENT POWERS

GENERAL NOTE
The purpose of this Chapter is to extend to customs duty the control techniques already used by the Customs and Excise for VAT and excise duty. These are based on the audit by Customs and Excise officers of the commercial records kept by businesses. The new provisions supersede existing powers in the CEMA 1979 (c. 2), except so far as these relate to restricted goods and goods liable to an export refund under Common Agricultural Policy arrangements.

The corresponding powers for excise duties may be found in the CEMA 1979 (c. 2), ss.118A–G (added by the FA 1991 (c. 31), Sched. 5) and for VAT in the VATA 1983 (c. 55), Sched. 7.

Interpretation, etc.

20.—(1) This Chapter applies to any person carrying on a trade or business which consists of or includes any of the following activities—

 (a) importing or exporting any goods of a class or description subject to a duty of customs (whether or not in fact chargeable with that duty);

 (b) producing, manufacturing or applying a process to them;

 (c) buying, selling or dealing in them;

 (d) handling or storing them;

 (e) financing or facilitating any activity mentioned in paragraphs (a) to (d) above.

 (2) In subsection (1) above "duty of customs" includes any agricultural levy of the European Community.

 (3) In this Chapter—

 (a) "customs goods" means any goods mentioned in paragraph (a) of subsection (1) above; and

 (b) any reference to the business of a person to whom this Chapter applies is a reference to the trade or business carried on by him as mentioned in that subsection.

 (4) This Chapter shall have effect and be construed as if it were contained in the Customs and Excise Management Act 1979.

 (5) In consequence of the provision made by sections 21 to 27 below, any power under—

 (a) section 75A, 75B or 75C of the Customs and Excise Management Act 1979 to require a person importing or exporting goods to keep or preserve records, or

 (b) section 77A, 77B or 77C of that Act to require a person to furnish information or produce documents relating to imported or exported goods,

shall cease to be exercisable in relation to a person to the extent that the goods in question are customs goods.

GENERAL NOTE

 This section applies the powers within the Chapter to any person whose trade or business involves an activity relating to goods subject to any customs duty or agricultural levy of the E.C.

Requirements about keeping records

 21.—(1) The Commissioners may by regulations require any person to whom this Chapter applies—

 (a) to keep such records as may be prescribed in the regulations; and

 (b) to preserve those records—

   (i) for such period not exceeding four years as may be prescribed in the regulations, or

   (ii) for such lesser period as the Commissioners may require.

 (2) The Commissioners may also require any person mentioned in subsection (3) below—

 (a) to keep such records as they may specify; and

 (b) to preserve those records for such period not exceeding four years as they may require.

 (3) The person referred to is any person who—

 (a) is not carrying on a trade or business which consists of or includes the importation or exportation of customs goods, but

 (b) is concerned in some other capacity in such importation or exportation.

 (4) A duty imposed under subsection (1)(b) or (2)(b) above to preserve records may be discharged by the preservation of the information contained in them by such means as the Commissioners may approve.

 (5) On giving approval under subsection (4) above, the Commissioners may impose such reasonable requirements as appear to them necessary for securing that the information will be as readily available to them as if the records themselves had been preserved.

 (6) Regulations under this section may—

(a) make different provision for different cases; and
(b) be framed by reference to such records as may be specified in any notice published by the Commissioners in pursuance of the regulations and not withdrawn by a further notice.

(7) Any person who fails to comply with a requirement imposed by virtue of this section shall be liable on summary conviction to a penalty not exceeding level 3 on the standard scale.

GENERAL NOTE
The Customs and Excise may make regulations requiring any person referred to in s.20 to keep records of their business activity and to preserve such records for up to four years. The parallel provisions for excise duties and VAT may be found in the CEMA 1979 (c. 2), ss.118A, 118G and the VATA 1983 (c. 55), Sched. 7, para. 7.

Records and rules of evidence

22.—(1) Where any information is preserved by approved means as mentioned in section 21(4) above, a copy of any document in which it is contained shall, subject to subsection (2) below, be admissible in evidence in any proceedings, whether civil or criminal, to the same extent as the records themselves.

(2) A statement contained in a document produced by a computer shall not by virtue of subsection (1) above be admissible in evidence—
(a) in civil proceedings in England and Wales, except in accordance with sections 5 and 6 of the Civil Evidence Act 1968;
(b) in criminal proceedings in England and Wales, except in accordance with sections 69 and 70 of the Police and Criminal Evidence Act 1984 and Part II of the Criminal Justice Act 1988;
(c) in civil proceedings in Scotland, except in accordance with sections 5 and 6 of the Civil Evidence (Scotland) Act 1988;
(d) in criminal proceedings in Scotland, except in accordance with Schedule 3 to the Prisoners and Criminal Proceedings (Scotland) Act 1993;
(e) in civil proceedings in Northern Ireland, except in accordance with sections 2 and 3 of the Civil Evidence Act (Northern Ireland) 1971; and
(f) in criminal proceedings in Northern Ireland, except in accordance with Article 68 of the Police and Criminal Evidence (Northern Ireland) Order 1989 and Part II of the Criminal Justice (Evidence, Etc.) (Northern Ireland) Order 1988.

GENERAL NOTE
Copies of documents are made admissible as evidence to the same extent as the records themselves. This is also the case for documents generated by a computer in accordance with the legislation specified in subs. (2).

Furnishing of information and production of documents

23.—(1) Every person to whom this Chapter applies shall furnish the Commissioners, within such time and in such form as they may reasonably require, with such information relating to his business as they may reasonably specify.

(2) Every person to whom this Chapter applies shall, if required to do so by an officer, produce or cause to be produced for inspection by the officer—
(a) at that person's principal place of business or at such other place as the officer may reasonably require, and
(b) at such time as the officer may reasonably require,
any documents which relate to his business.

(3) Where it appears to an officer that any documents which relate to a business of a person to whom this Chapter applies are in the possession of another person, the officer may require that other person, at such time and

place as the officer may reasonably require, to produce those documents or cause them to be produced.

(4) For the purposes of this section, the documents which relate to a business of a person to whom this Chapter applies shall be taken to include—

(a) any profit and loss account and balance sheet, and

(b) any documents required to be kept by virtue of section 21(1) above.

(5) Every person mentioned in section 21(3) above shall furnish the Commissioners, within such time and in such form as they may reasonably require, with such information relating to the importation or exportation of customs goods in which he is concerned as they may reasonably specify.

(6) Every person mentioned in section 21(3) above shall, if required to do so by an officer, produce or cause to be produced for inspection by the officer at such time and place as the officer may reasonably require, any documents which relate to the importation or exportation of customs goods in which he is concerned.

(7) An officer may take copies of, or make extracts from, any document produced under this section.

(8) If it appears to an officer to be necessary to do so, he may, at a reasonable time and for a reasonable period, remove any document produced under this section.

(9) Where a document is removed under subsection (8) above—

(a) if the person from whom the document is removed so requests, he shall be given a record of what was removed;

(b) if the document is reasonably required for the proper conduct of any business, the person by whom the document was produced or caused to be produced shall be provided as soon as practicable with a copy of the document free of charge;

(c) if the document is lost or damaged, the Commissioners shall be liable to compensate the owner of it for any expenses reasonably incurred by him in replacing or repairing it.

(10) If a person claims a lien on any document produced by him under subsection (3) or (6) above—

(a) the production of the document shall be without prejudice to the lien; and

(b) the removal of the document under subsection (8) above shall not be regarded as breaking the lien.

(11) Any person who fails to comply with a requirement imposed under this section shall be liable on summary conviction to a penalty not exceeding level 3 on the standard scale.

GENERAL NOTE

A trader involved with customs goods is required to furnish information or produce documents about his business to the Customs and Excise. The requirement extends to the production of documents by others in whose possession they may be. The documents, which include profit and loss accounts and balance sheets, may be copied or removed, subject to the provision of a record or a copy of a document so removed.

Power of entry

24. Where an officer has reasonable cause to believe that—

(a) any premises are used in connection with a business of a person to whom this Chapter applies, and

(b) any customs goods are on those premises,

he may at any reasonable time enter and inspect those premises and inspect any goods found on them.

GENERAL NOTE

Powers of entry and inspection are given to Customs and Excise officers in relation to premises used in connection with customs goods.

Order for production of documents

25.—(1) Where, on an application by an officer, a justice is satisfied that there are reasonable grounds for believing—
  (a) that an offence in connection with a duty of customs is being, has been or is about to be committed, and
  (b) that any information or documents which may be required as evidence for the purpose of any proceedings in respect of such an offence is in the possession of any person,
he may make an order under this section.

(2) An order under this section is an order that the person who appears to the justice to be in possession of the information or documents to which the application relates shall—
  (a) furnish an officer with the information or produce the document,
  (b) permit an officer to take copies of or make extracts of any document produced, and
  (c) permit an officer to remove any document which he reasonably considers necessary,
not later than the end of the period of seven days beginning with the date of the order or the end of such longer period as the order may specify.

(3) In this section "justice" means a justice of the peace or, in relation to Scotland, a justice within the meaning of section 462 of the Criminal Procedure (Scotland) Act 1975.

GENERAL NOTE
A magistrate, upon application, may order the production of documents or information potentially required as evidence in connection with a customs duty offence.

Procedure when documents are removed

26.—(1) An officer who removes any document in the exercise of a power conferred under section 25 above shall, if so requested by a person showing himself—
  (a) to be the occupier of premises from which it was removed, or
  (b) to have had custody or control of it immediately before the removal,
provide that person with a record of what he removed.

(2) The officer shall provide the record within a reasonable time from the making of the request for it.

(3) Subject to subsection (7) below, if a request for permission to be granted access to any document which—
  (a) has been removed by an officer, and
  (b) is retained by the Commissioners for the purposes of investigating an offence,
is made to the officer in charge of the investigation by a person who had custody or control of the document immediately before it was so removed or by someone acting on behalf of such a person, the officer shall allow the person who made the request access to it under the supervision of an officer.

(4) Subject to subsection (7) below, if a request for a photograph or copy of any such document is made to the officer in charge of the investigation by a person who had custody or control of the document immediately before it was so removed, or by someone acting on behalf of such a person, the officer shall—
  (a) allow the person who made the request access to it under the supervision of an officer for the purpose of photographing it or copying it, or
  (b) photograph or copy it, or cause it to be photographed or copied.

(5) Where any document is photographed or copied under subsection (4)(b) above, the photograph or copy shall be supplied to the person who made the request.

(6) The photograph or copy shall be supplied within a reasonable time from the making of the request.

(7) There is no duty under this section to grant access to, or to supply a photograph or copy of, any document if the officer in charge of the investigation for the purposes of which it was removed has reasonable grounds for believing that to do so would prejudice—

(a) that investigation;

(b) the investigation of an offence other than the offence for the purposes of the investigation of which the document was removed; or

(c) any criminal proceedings which may be brought as a result of—
  (i) the investigation of which he is in charge; or
  (ii) any such investigation as is mentioned in paragraph (b) above.

(8) Any reference in this section to the officer in charge of the investigation is a reference to the person whose name and address are endorsed on the order concerned as being the officer in charge of it.

GENERAL NOTE

A Customs and Excise officer removing documents in the exercise of an order under s.25, is required to provide access to, or copies of the documents, unless this would prejudice an investigation or criminal proceedings.

Failure of officer to comply with requirements under section 26

27.—(1) Where, on an application made as mentioned in subsection (2) below, the appropriate judicial authority is satisfied that a person has failed to comply with a requirement imposed by section 26 above, the authority may order that person to comply with the requirement within such time and in such manner as may be specified in the order.

(2) An application under subsection (1) above shall be made—

(a) in the case of a failure to comply with any of the requirements imposed by subsections (1) and (2) of section 26 above, by the occupier of the premises from which the document in question was removed or by the person who had custody or control of it immediately before it was so removed, and

(b) in any other case, by the person who has such custody or control.

(3) In this section "the appropriate judicial authority" means—

(a) in England and Wales, a magistrates' court;

(b) in Scotland, the sheriff; and

(c) in Northern Ireland, a court of summary jurisdiction, as defined in Article 2(2)(a) of the Magistrates' Courts (Northern Ireland) Order 1981.

(4) Any application for an order under this section—

(a) in England and Wales, shall be made by way of complaint; or

(b) in Northern Ireland, shall be made by way of civil proceedings upon complaint.

(5) Sections 21 and 42(2) of the Interpretation Act (Northern Ireland) 1954 (rules and orders regulating procedure of courts etc. and assignment of business to particular courts) shall apply as if any reference in those provisions to any enactment included a reference to this section.

GENERAL NOTE

Where a Customs and Excise officer fails to comply with the requirements of s.26, he may be ordered to do so by the appropriate judicial authority.

CHAPTER IV

AIR PASSENGER DUTY

The duty

GENERAL NOTE
  Faced with a £50 billion deficit, the Chancellor had to find additional sources of revenue. Given the Government's reluctance to increase rates of direct tax and the limitations on its freedom of action regarding VAT imposed by the E.C. Sixth Directive, it was essential to extend the tax base. A duty on all air passengers from U.K. airports offered a convenient method of doing this. Air travel has benefited from a zero rate of VAT and virtually duty-free fuel. The new duty will raise more than a third of a billion pounds per annum.

Air passenger duty

28.—(1) A duty to be known as air passenger duty shall be charged in accordance with this Chapter on the carriage on a chargeable aircraft of any chargeable passenger.

(2) Subject to the provisions of this Chapter about accounting and payment, the duty in respect of any carriage on an aircraft of a chargeable passenger—

  (a) becomes due when the aircraft first takes off on the passenger's flight, and

  (b) shall be paid by the operator of the aircraft.

(3) Subject to section 29 below, every aircraft designed or adapted to carry persons in addition to the flight crew is a chargeable aircraft for the purposes of this Chapter.

(4) Subject to sections 31 and 32 below, every passenger on an aircraft is a chargeable passenger for the purposes of this Chapter if his flight begins at an airport in the United Kingdom.

(5) In this Chapter, "flight", in relation to any person, means his carriage on an aircraft; and for the purposes of this Chapter, a person's flight is to be treated as beginning when he first boards the aircraft and ending when he finally disembarks from the aircraft.

GENERAL NOTE
  This section introduces air passenger duty (APD) on the carriage on a chargeable aircraft of any chargeable passenger. The operator of the aircraft is liable for the duty. Every passenger-carrying aircraft is a chargeable aircraft (subject to s.29) and every passenger on a flight beginning in the U.K. is a chargeable passenger (subject to ss.31 and 32). A flight begins with embarkation and ends with final disembarkation.

Chargeable aircraft

29.—(1) Where—

  (a) the authorised take-off weight in respect of an aircraft is less than ten tonnes, or

  (b) an aircraft is not authorised to seat twenty or more persons (excluding members of the flight crew and cabin attendants),

the aircraft is not a chargeable aircraft for the purposes of this Chapter.

(2) In this section "take-off weight", in relation to an aircraft, means the total weight of the aircraft and its contents when taking off; and for the purposes of this section the authorised take-off weight of an aircraft is less than ten tonnes if—

  (a) there is a certificate of airworthiness in force in respect of the aircraft showing that the maximum authorised take-off weight (assuming the most favourable circumstances for take-off) is less than ten tonnes, or

  (b) the Commissioners are satisfied that the aircraft is not designed or adapted to take off when its take-off weight is ten tonnes or more (assuming the most favourable circumstances for take-off) or the aircraft belongs to a class or description of aircraft in respect of which the Commissioners are so satisfied.

(3) For the purposes of this section an aircraft is not authorised as mentioned in subsection (1)(b) above it—

(a) there is a certificate of airworthiness in force in respect of the aircraft showing that the maximum number of persons who may be seated on the aircraft (excluding members of the flight crew and cabin attendants) is less than twenty, or

(b) the Commissioners are satisfied that the aircraft is not designed or adapted to seat twenty or more persons (excluding members of the flight crew and cabin attendants) or the aircraft belongs to a class or description of aircraft in respect of which the Commissioners are so satisfied.

(4) In this section "certificate of airworthiness" has the same meaning as in the Air Navigation Order.

GENERAL NOTE

A *de minimis* provision excludes aircraft with an authorised take-off weight of less than 10 tonnes or authorised seating of less than 20 passengers.

The rate of duty

30.—(1) Air passenger duty shall be charged on the carriage of each chargeable passenger at the rate appropriate for the place where the passenger's journey ends.

(2) If that place is—

(a) in the United Kingdom or another member State or in any territory for whose external relations the United Kingdom or any other member State is responsible, and

(b) in the area specified in subsection (3) below,

the rate is £5.

(3) The area referred to in subsection (2) above is the area bounded by the meridians of longitude 32°W and 32°E and the parallels of latitude 26°N and 81°N.

(4) In any other case, the rate of £10.

(5) Subject to subsection (6) below, the journey of a passenger whose agreement for carriage is evidenced by a ticket ends for the purposes of this section at his final place of destination.

(6) Where in the case of such a passenger—

(a) his journey includes two or more flights, and

(b) any of those flights is not followed by a connected flight,

his journey ends for those purposes where the first flight not followed by a connected flight ends.

(7) The journey of any passenger whose agreement for carriage is not evidenced by a ticket ends for those purposes where his flight ends.

(8) For the purposes of this Chapter, successive flights are connected if (and only if) they are treated under an order as connected.

GENERAL NOTE

The rate of APD is set at £5 for flights within the E.C. and £10 for other flights. A geographical limitation excludes the French overseas departments and the Faroe islands from the E.C. rate. Journeys by connected flights, to be defined by statutory order, are treated as ending at the final place of destination to where the passenger has a ticket.

Passengers: exceptions

31.—(1) Where in the case of a passenger whose agreement for carriage is evidenced by a return ticket—

(a) he is a chargeable passenger in relation to a flight on his outward journey, and

(b) his final place of destination in relation to that journey is in the United Kingdom,

he is not a chargeable passenger in relation to a flight on his return journey.

(2) Subsection (1) above does not apply if—

(a) either his outward journey or his return journey includes two or more flights, and

(b) in relation to any of those flights (other than the first) on the journey in question, he would (apart from that subsection) be a chargeable passenger.

(3) A passenger whose agreement for carriage is evidenced by a ticket is not a chargeable passenger in relation to a flight which is the second or a subsequent flight on his journey if—

(a) the prescribed particulars of the flight are shown on the ticket, and

(b) that flight and the previous flight are connected.

(4) A child who—

(a) has not attained the age of two years, and

(b) is not allocated a separate seat before he first boards the aircraft,

is not a chargeable passenger.

(5) A passenger not carried for reward is not a chargeable passenger if he is carried—

(a) in pursuance of any requirement imposed under any enactment, or

(b) for the purpose only of inspecting matters relating to the aircraft or the flight crew.

(6) Regulations may provide for subsection (1) above to have effect as if the reference in paragraph (a) to a person who is a chargeable passenger in relation to a flight on his outward journey included a person whose outward journey began at an airport in the Isle of Man.

GENERAL NOTE
    Where a passenger has a return ticket within the U.K., he is not charged to APD on the return leg of his journey. This does not apply where either journey includes two or more flights, subject to the relief for connected flights. Children aged under two who are not allocated separate seats and non-paying passengers carrying out inspection or monitoring duties (*e.g.* on behalf of the Civil Aviation Authority) are not chargeable. Provision is made to prevent double taxation if the Isle of Man introduces APD.

Change of circumstances after ticket issued etc.

    32.—(1) This section applies in the case of a person whose agreement for carriage is evidenced by a ticket.

(2) Where—

(a) at the time the ticket is issued or, if it is altered, at the time it is last altered, he would not (assuming there is no change of circumstances) be a chargeable passenger in relation to any flight in the course of his journey, and

(b) by reason only of a change of circumstances not attributable to any act or default of his, he arrives at or departs from an airport in the course of that journey on a flight the prescribed particulars of which were not shown on his ticket at that time,

he shall not by reason of the change of circumstances be treated as a chargeable passenger in relation to that flight.

(3) Where—

(a) at the time the ticket is issued or, if it is altered, at the time it is last altered, he would (assuming there is no change of circumstances) be a chargeable passenger in relation to one or more flights ("the proposed chargeable flights") in the course of his journey,

(b) by reason only of a change of circumstances not attributable to any act or default of his, he arrives at or departs from an airport in the course of that journey on a flight the prescribed particulars of which were not shown on his ticket at that time, and

(c) but for this subsection he would by reason of the change be a chargeable passenger in relation to a number of flights exceeding the number of the proposed chargeable flights,

he shall not by reason of the change of circumstances be treated as a chargeable passenger in relation to that flight.

GENERAL NOTE
This section is designed to deal with cases of *force majeure*, where, due to circumstances beyond a passenger's control, the flight plans set out in the passenger's ticket are changed. In such cases the passenger will not be charged to duty or additional duty, as applicable.

Persons liable for the duty

Registration of aircraft operators

33.—(1) The Commissioners shall under this section keep a register of aircraft operators.

(2) The operator of a chargeable aircraft becomes liable to be registered under this section if the aircraft is used for the carriage of any chargeable passengers.

(3) A person who has become liable to be registered under this section ceases to be so liable if the Commissioners are satisfied at any time—

(a) that he no longer operates any chargeable aircraft, or

(b) that no chargeable aircraft which he operates will be used for the carriage of chargeable passengers.

(4) A person who is not registered and has not given notice under this subsection shall, if he becomes liable to be registered at any time, give written notice of that fact to the Commissioners not later than the end of the prescribed period beginning with that time.

(5) Notice under subsection (4) above shall be in such form, be given in such manner and contain such information as the Commissioners may direct.

(6) If a person who is required to give notice under subsection (4) above fails to do so, his failure shall attract a penalty under section 9 above which, if any amount of duty is then due from him and unpaid, shall be calculated by reference to that amount.

(7) Regulations may make provision as to the information to be included in, and the correction of, the register kept under this section.

(8) In particular, the regulations may provide—

(a) for the inclusion in the register of persons who have not given notice under this section but appear to the Commissioners to be liable to be registered.

(b) for persons who are liable to be registered—
    (i) not to be included in, or
    (ii) to be removed from,
the register in prescribed circumstances,

(c) for the removal from the register of persons who have ceased to be so liable, and

(d) for the time from which an entry in the register is to be effective (which may be earlier than the time when the entry is first made in the register).

GENERAL NOTE
Under s.28(2), the operator of the aircraft is liable for APD. Aircraft operators are required to register with the Customs and Excise under conditions to be prescribed by Statutory Order. Failure to comply will attract a penalty under s.9.

Fiscal representatives

34.—(1) An aircraft operator who—
(a) is or is liable to be registered, and
(b) does not meet the requirements of subsection (3) below,
is required to have a fiscal representative.

(2) In this Chapter "fiscal representative", in relation to an aircraft operator, means a person who meets those requirements and stands appointed by the operator for the purposes of this section.

(3) A person meets the requirements of this subsection if—
(a) he has any business establishment or other fixed establishment in the United Kingdom, or
(b) if he is an individual, he has his usual place of residence in the United Kingdom.

(4) Where any person is appointed under this section to be the fiscal representative of any aircraft operator (in this section referred to as his "principal"), then, subject to subsection (5) below, the fiscal representative—
(a) shall be entitled to act on his principal's behalf for any of the purposes of the enactments relating to duty,
(b) shall, subject to such provisions as may be made by regulations, secure (where appropriate by acting on his principal's behalf) his principal's compliance with and discharge of the obligations and liabilities to which his principal is subject by virtue of those enactments, and
(c) shall be personally liable in respect of any failure of his principal to comply with or discharge any such obligation or liability as if the obligations and liabilities imposed on his principal were imposed jointly and severally on the fiscal representative and his principal.

(5) A fiscal representative shall not be liable by virtue of subsection (4) above himself to be registered under section 33 above, but regulations may—
(a) require the names of fiscal representatives to be shown in such manner as may be prescribed against the names of their principals in the register kept under that section, and
(b) make it the duty of a fiscal representative, for the purposes of registration, to notify the Commissioners, within such period as may be prescribed, that his appointment has taken effect or has ceased to have effect.

<small>GENERAL NOTE</small>
Aircraft operators who are liable to be registered, but do not have any business or other fixed establishment in the U.K., are required to appoint a "fiscal representative" to account for duty on their behalf. The fiscal representative will be jointly and severally liable for APD.

Fiscal representatives: supplementary

35.—(1) Regulations may make provision about—
(a) the manner in which a person is to be appointed as a fiscal representative, and
(b) the circumstances in which a person is to be treated as having ceased to be a fiscal representative.

(2) If any aircraft operator who is required to have a fiscal representative fails to appoint such a representative before the prescribed time, his failure shall attract a penalty under section 9 above.

(3) Any failure of a fiscal representative to give any notice which he is required to give by regulations under section 34(5)(b) above shall attract a penalty under section 9 above.

<small>GENERAL NOTE</small>
The rules governing fiscal representatives are to be made by Statutory Instrument.

Security for payment of duty

36.—(1) The Commissioners may require—
(a) any operator of an aircraft who is or is liable to be registered, or
(b) any fiscal representative,
to provide such security, or further security, as they may think appropriate
for the payment of any duty which is or may become due from the operator.

(2) Any failure by a person to provide any security which he is required by
the Commissioners to provide under subsection (1) above shall attract a penalty under section 9 above.

(3) For the purposes of this section, a person shall not be treated as having
been required to provide security under subsection (1) above unless the
Commissioners have either—
(a) served notice of the requirement on him, or
(b) taken all such other steps as appear to them to be reasonable for bringing the requirement to his attention.

GENERAL NOTE
    The Customs and Excise may require an aircraft operator, or his fiscal representative, to
provide appropriate security for the payment of APD.

Handling agents

37.—(1) Where any amount of duty becomes payable at any time by the
operator of an aircraft and, within the period of ninety days beginning with
that time, that amount, or any other amount which becomes payable by him
within the period, is not paid, the Commissioners may give notice under this
section to any handling agent of his.

(2) If any operator of an aircraft who is required to have a fiscal representative fails to appoint such a representative before the prescribed time, the
Commissioners may give notice under this section to any handling agent of
his.

(3) In this Chapter "handling agent", in relation to the operator of an aircraft ("the principal"), means any person (other than an individual) who,
under an agreement with the principal, makes arrangements for—
(a) the allocation of seats to passengers on aircraft operated by the principal, or
(b) the supervision of the boarding of such aircraft by passengers.

(4) A notice under this section—
(a) may be given on the ground referred to in subsection (1) above only if
the Commissioners consider it necessary to do so for the protection of
the revenue, and
(b) may at any time be withdrawn by the Commissioners.

(5) A notice under this section shall become effective on the date stated in
it or, if later, the time when the notice is received by the handling agent and
shall continue to be effective until withdrawn.

(6) If, where a notice given to a handling agent under this section is
effective—
(a) the allocation of seats to passengers on aircraft operated by his principal, or the supervision of the boarding of such aircraft by passengers, is
carried out in pursuance of arrangements made by him under any
agreement with his principal, and
(b) any duty payable in respect of those passengers is not paid,
the handling agent shall be liable jointly and severally with his principal for
the payment of the duty.

GENERAL NOTE

Where APD remains unpaid for 90 days, or a fiscal representative is not appointed within the period prescribed by regulations, the Customs and Excise may notify a handling agent that he will be jointly and severally liable with his principal for any future APD unpaid.

"Handling agent" is defined as a person other than an individual who makes arrangements for the allocation of seats or the supervision of boarding.

Accounting for and payment of duty

38.—(1) Regulations shall require aircraft operators who are registered or liable to be registered—

    (a) to keep accounts for the purposes of duty in such form and manner as may be prescribed, and

    (b) to make returns in respect of duty—

        (i) by reference to such periods as may be prescribed or as may be allowed by the Commissioners, in relation to a particular operator, in accordance with regulations, and

        (ii) at such time and in such manner as may be prescribed or specified.

(2) Any person from whom any duty is due shall pay the duty at such time and in such manner as may be prescribed or specified.

(3) In this section "specified" means specified in a notice published, and not withdrawn, by the Commissioners.

(4) Any failure by any person to comply with regulations under this section shall, unless he is complying with the corresponding provisions of such a notice, attract a penalty under section 9 above and, in the case of any failure to keep accounts, daily penalties.

GENERAL NOTE

The rules governing the keeping of accounts and the making of returns for APD will be prescribed by Statutory Instrument.

Schemes for simplifying operation of reliefs etc.

39.—(1) If in the opinion of the Commissioners it is expedient to do so in the light of difficulties encountered or expected to be encountered by any registered operator in obtaining and recording information about passengers and their journeys, they may in accordance with the provisions of this section prepare a scheme for the registered operator.

(2) Any scheme so prepared shall specify the period for which it is to have effect.

(3) A scheme prepared for a registered operator shall relate only to passengers—

    (a) who are carried on chargeable aircraft operated by that operator,

    (b) whose flights begin in the United Kingdom, and

    (c) who are not passengers of a description mentioned in section 31(4) or (5) above;

and in this section any reference to the relevant passengers of a registered operator is a reference to passengers who fall within this subsection in relation to him.

(4) A scheme for a registered operator shall provide, in relation to passengers who are relevant passengers of his in the period specified in the scheme, for methods of calculating—

    (a) how many of those relevant passengers may be treated as passengers who are not chargeable passengers, and

    (b) how many of them may be treated as passengers on the carriage of whom duty shall be charged at the rate mentioned in section 30(2) above.

(5) A calculation provided for by the scheme may be provided by reference to such factors as appear to the Commissioners to be expedient in the circumstances, including in particular information—

(a) derived from surveys of passengers carried on chargeable aircraft operated by the operator for whom the scheme is prepared, or

(b) relating to airports and routes used by that operator,

whether obtained before or during the specified period.

(6) No scheme prepared in accordance with this section shall be of any effect unless the registered operator for whom it is prepared elects in writing to be bound by it for the specified period.

(7) If the registered operator makes such an election the scheme shall have effect for the specified period and subsection (8) below shall apply.

(8) This Chapter shall have effect for the specified period as if, except in accordance with provision made to the contrary by the scheme (by virtue of subsection (4) above)—

(a) each of the passengers who are relevant passengers of the registered operator were chargeable passengers, and

(b) duty were charged on the carriage of each of them at the rate mentioned in section 30(4) above.

(9) Regulations may make further provision with respect to schemes under this section, including in particular provision amending this section.

GENERAL NOTE

This section, introduced during the committee stage, enables the Customs and Excise to agree schemes with aircraft operators for calculating duty by reference to surveys of numbers of passengers carried or by reference to airports and routes used. The scheme will determine how many passengers are to be treated as not chargeable and how many are to be charged at the £5 and £10 rate.

The section may be supplemented or amended by Statutory Instrument.

Administration and enforcement

Administration and enforcement

40.—(1) Air passenger duty shall be a duty of excise and, accordingly, shall be under the care and management of the Commissioners.

(2) Schedule 6 to this Act (administration and enforcement) shall have effect.

GENERAL NOTE

APD is made a duty of excise and so is placed under the care and management of the Customs and Excise (*cf.* the CEMA 1979 (c. 2), s.6(2)).

The provisions regarding administration and enforcement are set out in Sched. 6. See further the General Note to Sched. 6.

Offences

41.—(1) A person who is knowingly concerned—

(a) in the fraudulent evasion (by him or another person) of duty, or

(b) in taking steps with a view to such fraudulent evasion,

is guilty of an offence.

(2) A person guilty of an offence under subsection (1) above is liable—

(a) on summary conviction, to a penalty of—

(i) the statutory maximum, or

(ii) if greater, treble the amount of the duty evaded or sought to be evaded, or to imprisonment for a term not exceeding six months, or to both, or

  (b) on conviction on indictment, to a penalty of any amount or to imprisonment for a term not exceeding seven years, or to both.

(3) A person who in connection with duty—

  (a) makes a statement that he knows to be false in a material particular or recklessly makes a statement that is false in a material particular, or

  (b) with intent to deceive, produces or makes use of a book, account, return or other document that is false in a material particular,

is guilty of an offence.

(4) A person guilty of an offence under subsection (3) above is liable—

  (a) on summary conviction, to a penalty of the statutory maximum or to imprisonment for a term not exceeding six months, or to both, or

  (b) on conviction on indictment, to a penalty of any amount or to imprisonment for a term not exceeding two years, or to both.

GENERAL NOTE

Fraudulent evasion of APD is a criminal offence carrying a penalty of up to three times the amount of duty evaded plus six-months' imprisonment on summary conviction, an unlimited penalty and seven-years' imprisonment on conviction on indictment.

The making of false statements or the production of false documents in connection with APD carries a penalty of the statutory maximum plus six-months' imprisonment on summary conviction, an unlimited penalty and two-years' imprisonment on conviction on indictment.

Supplementary

Regulations and orders

42.—(1) In this Chapter "regulations" means regulations made by the Commissioners and "order" means an order made by the Treasury.

(2) Regulations and orders may make different provision for different cases or circumstances and make incidental, supplemental, saving or transitional provision.

(3) Any power to make regulations or an order is exercisable by statutory instrument.

(4) No order which appears to the Treasury to extend the circumstances in which passengers are to be treated as chargeable passengers shall be made unless a draft of the order has been laid before and approved by the House of Commons.

(5) Any other order, and any regulations, shall be subject to annulment in pursuance of a resolution of the House of Commons.

GENERAL NOTE

Regulations and orders relating to APD are to be made by Statutory Instrument, subject to the negative resolution procedure in the House of Commons, save for orders which appear to the Treasury to extend the scope of the duty, which are subject to the affirmative resolution procedure.

Interpretation

43.—(1) In this Chapter—

  "accounting period" means any period prescribed or allowed for the purposes of section 38 above,

  "agreement for carriage", in relation to the carriage of any person, means the agreement or arrangement under which he is carried, whether the carriage is by a single carrier or successive carriers,

"Air Navigation Order" has the same meaning as in the Civil Aviation Act 1982,

"airport" means any aerodrome (within the meaning of that Act),

"carriage" means carriage wholly or partly by air, and "carried" is to be read accordingly,

"connected", in relation to any flights, has the meaning given by section 30(8) above,

"document" includes information recorded in any form,

"duty" means air passenger duty,

"fiscal representative" has the meaning given by section 34(2) above,

"flight" has the meaning given by section 28(5) above,

"operator", in relation to any aircraft, means the person having the management of the aircraft for the time being,

"passenger", in relation to any aircraft, means—

(a) where the operator is an air transport undertaking (within the meaning of the Air Navigation Order), any person carried on the aircraft other than—

(i) a member of the flight crew,

(ii) a cabin attendant, or

(iii) a person who is not carried for reward, who is an employee of any aircraft operator and who satisfies such other requirements as may be prescribed, and

(b) in any other case, any person carried on the aircraft for reward,

"prescribed" means prescribed by regulations,

"reward", in relation to the carriage of any person, includes any form of consideration received or to be received wholly or partly in connection with the carriage, irrespective of the person by whom or to whom the consideration has been or is to be given, and

"ticket" means a document or documents evidencing an agreement (wherever made) for the carriage of any person.

(2) Subject to subsection (3) below, in this Chapter, in relation to a passenger whose agreement for carriage is evidenced by a ticket—

"journey" means the journey from his original place of departure to his final place of destination, and

"original place of departure" and "final place of destination" mean the original place of departure and the final place of destination indicated on his ticket.

(3) For the purposes of this Chapter, where the agreement for carriage of a passenger by air is evidenced by a ticket, the ticket is a return ticket if (and only if) it covers his return by air to the airport from which he originally departed; and, in such a case, there is both an outward and a return journey and the return journey is the journey from the final place of destination on the outward journey to that airport.

(4) Subject to the preceding provisions of this section, expressions used in this Chapter and in the Customs and Excise Management Act 1979 have the same meaning as in that Act.

GENERAL NOTE

This section contains definitions for the purposes of APD. Where not otherwise stated, definitions in the CEMA 1979 (c. 2) apply.

Commencement

44.—(1) This Chapter applies to any carriage of a passenger on an aircraft which begins after 31st October 1994.

(2) For the purpose of determining whether or not a person is a chargeable passenger in relation to any carriage on an aircraft beginning after that date, the provisions of section 31 above and any order made by virtue of that sec-

tion shall be treated as having applied to any such carriage of that person which began on or before that date as they would apply to any such carriage of that person beginning after that date.

GENERAL NOTE

Air passenger duty commences as from November 1, 1994.

PART II

VALUE ADDED TAX

Misdeclaration etc.

45.—(1) Section 14 of the Finance Act 1985 (misdeclaration or neglect resulting in understatement or overclaim) shall be amended as follows.

(2) In subsection (4), for the words from "aggregate of" to the end there is substituted "amount of the understatement of liability or, as the case may be, overstatement of entitlement referred to, in relation to that period, in subsection (1) above".

(3) In subsection (5A), for "subsections (4B) and (5) above" there is substituted "this section".

(4) This section shall have effect in relation to any prescribed accounting period beginning on or after such day as the Treasury may by order made by statutory instrument appoint.

GENERAL NOTE

In *Customs and Excise Commissioners* v. *P. & O. Steam Navigation Co.* [1994] STC 259, the Court of Appeal set aside a penalty of £100,000 which had been imposed on the company for an error of £300,000 in one month's return which was corrected by a compensating error in the following month. While accepting the principle of the *P. & O.* decision, the amendment to the FA 1985 (c. 54), s.14 seeks to confine it to cases where the compensating error explicitly corrects the original error.

Repayment supplement

46.—(1) Section 20 of the Finance Act 1985 (repayment supplement) shall be amended as follows.

(2) In subsection (1) (supplement of 5 per cent. or £30, whichever is greater) for "£30" there shall be substituted "£50".

(3) In subsection (2)(a) (return or claim must be received not later than one month after last day on which it is required) the words "one month after" shall be omitted.

(4) This section shall apply where the requisite return or claim is received after the expiry of the period of one month beginning with the day after that on which this Act is passed.

GENERAL NOTE

The provisions in the FA 1985 (c. 54), s.20 (as substituted by the FA 1988 (c. 39), s.20) regarding the repayment supplement which the Customs and Excise are required to pay in the event of undue delay in the payment of VAT claims are amended in two respects. First, the minimum amount payable is increased from £30 to £50. Secondly, claims will not qualify for repayment supplement unless they are submitted by the due date. Previously one month's tolerance was allowed.

Set-off of credits

47.—(1) Section 21 of the Finance Act 1988 (set-off of credits) shall become subsection (1) of that section and the following subsections shall be inserted in that section after subsection (1), that is to say—

"(2) Subsection (1) above shall not apply in the case of any such amount as is mentioned in paragraph (a) of that subsection where that amount became due to the person in question—

(a) at a time when that person's estate was vested in any other person as that person's trustee in bankruptcy;

(b) at a time when that person's estate was vested in any other person as that person's interim trustee or permanent trustee;

(c) at a time, other than a time before the appointment of a liquidator, when that person was being wound up, either voluntarily or by the court;

(d) at a time when an administration order was in force in relation to that person;

(e) at a time when there was an administrative receiver of that person;

(f) at a time when—

(i) a voluntary arrangement approved in accordance with Part I or VIII of the Insolvency Act 1986, or Part II or Chapter II of Part VIII of the Insolvency (Northern Ireland) Order 1989, or

(ii) a deed of arrangement registered in accordance with the Deeds of Arrangement Act 1914 or Chapter I of Part VIII of that Order of 1989,

was in force in relation to that person; or

(g) at a time when that person's estate was vested in any other person as that person's trustee under a trust deed.

(3) In subsection (2) above—

(a) "administration order" means an administration order under Part II of the Insolvency Act 1986 or an administration order within the meaning of Article 5(1) of the Insolvency (Northern Ireland) Order 1989;

(b) "administrative receiver" means an administrative receiver within the meaning of section 251 of that Act of 1986 or Article 5(1) of that Order of 1989; and

(c) "interim trustee", "permanent trustee" and "trust deed" have the same meanings as in the Bankruptcy (Scotland) Act 1985."

(2) This section shall have effect in relation to amounts becoming due on or after such day as the Commissioners of Customs and Excise may by order made by statutory instrument appoint.

GENERAL NOTE

By extra-statutory concession, the provisions of the FA 1988 (c. 39), s.21 regarding set-off of credits is not applied in cases of firms subject to bankruptcy, liquidation or trading under a voluntary arrangement. The amendment puts the concession in statutory form and extends it to firms trading in receivership and under an administration order.

PART III

INSURANCE PREMIUM TAX

The basic provisions

GENERAL NOTE

Under the E.C. Sixth Directive the provision of insurance is exempt from VAT, but it is permissible to levy a separate tax on insurance premiums, and this is now introduced as insurance premium tax (IPT). It will be levied at 2.5 per cent. on the general insurance of risks in the U.K. Exceptions from its scope include reinsurance, the insurance of ships, aircraft and international transit goods, export credits and long-term insurance, including life assurance and assurance for endowment mortgages. The expected yield of IPT is more than £750 million per annum.

Insurance premium tax

48.—(1) A tax, to be known as insurance premium tax, shall be charged in accordance with this Part.

(2) The tax shall be under the care and management of the Commissioners of Customs and Excise.

GENERAL NOTE
This section introduces insurance premium tax (IPT). As an indirect tax, its administration is entrusted to the Customs and Excise.

Charge to tax

49. Tax shall be charged on the receipt of a premium by an insurer if the premium is received—
(a) under a taxable insurance contract, and
(b) on or after 1st October 1994.

GENERAL NOTE
This is the charging section for IPT. It is introduced as from October 1, 1994.

Chargeable amount

50.—(1) Tax shall be charged by reference to the chargeable amount.
(2) For the purposes of this Part, the chargeable amount is such amount as, with the addition of the tax chargeable, is equal to the amount of the premium.
(3) Subsection (2) above shall have effect subject to section 69 below.

GENERAL NOTE
The chargeable amount is the proportion of the premium which, when added to the tax charged on it, gives the total premium, *i.e.* premiums received will be deemed to include tax. This is subject to s.69, which provides for the chargeable amount to be reduced when a contract of insurance provides cover for both exempt and non-exempt matters.

Rate of tax

51. Tax shall be charged at the rate of 2·5 per cent.

GENERAL NOTE
The rate of IPT is set at 2.5 per cent.

Liability to pay tax

52.—(1) Tax shall be payable by the person who is the insurer in relation to the contract under which the premium is received.
(2) Subsection (1) above shall have effect subject to any regulations made under section 65 below.

GENERAL NOTE
Primary liability to pay is laid on the insurer, although the insured may be liable in certain cases under regulations made in pursuance of s.65.
There is no definition of "insurer" in the legislation, since the term is well understood in other contexts.

Administration

Registration of insurers

53.—(1) A person who—
(a) receives, as insurer, premiums in the course of a taxable business, and
(b) is not registered,
is liable to be registered.
(2) A person who—
(a) at any time forms the intention of receiving, as insurer, premiums in the course of a taxable business, and
(b) is not already receiving, as insurer, premiums in the course of another taxable business,

shall notify the Commissioners of those facts.

(3) A person who at any time—

(a) ceases to have the intention of receiving, as insurer, premiums in the course of a taxable business, and

(b) has no intention of receiving, as insurer, premiums in the course of another taxable business,

shall notify the Commissioners of those facts.

(4) Where a person is liable to be registered by virtue of subsection (1) above the Commissioners shall register him with effect from the time when be begins to receive premiums in the course of the business concerned; and it is immaterial whether or not he notifies the Commissioners under subsection (2) above.

(5) Where a person—

(a) notifies the Commissioners under subsection (3) above,

(b) satisfies them of the facts there mentioned, and

(c) satisfies them that no tax is unpaid in respect of premiums received in the course of any taxable business concerned,

the Commissioners shall cancel his registration with effect from the earliest practicable time after he ceases to receive, as insurer, premiums in the course of any taxable business.

(6) For the purposes of this section regulations may make provision—

(a) as to the time within which a notification is to be made;

(b) as to the circumstances in which premiums are to be taken to be received in the course of a taxable business;

(c) as to the form and manner in which any notification is to be made and as to the information to be contained in or provided with it;

(d) requiring a person who has made a notification to notify the Commissioners if any information contained in or provided in connection with it is or becomes inaccurate;

(e) as to the correction of entries in the register.

(7) References in this section to receiving premiums are to receiving premiums on or after 1st October 1994.

GENERAL NOTE

This section provides for the registration and deregistration of insurers receiving premiums on taxable policies. Persons covering risks in the U.K. are liable to register whether or not they have a place of business here.

Subss. (2) and (3)

These impose the basic requirements to register and deregister.

Subs. (4)

An insurer is liable to be registered even if he has not gone through the registration procedure.

Subs. (5)

Deregistration will be effected when the Customs and Excise are satisfied that the notification is correct and no tax remains outstanding.

Subs. (6)

Procedural aspects of registration and notification will be covered by regulations.

Accounting for tax and time for payment

54. Regulations may provide that a registrable person shall—

(a) account for tax by reference to such periods (accounting periods) as may be determined by or under the regulations;

  (b) make, in relation to accounting periods, returns in such form as may be prescribed and at such times as may be so determined;

  (c) pay tax at such times and in such manner as may be so determined.

GENERAL NOTE

    The method and timing of payment of IPT will also be covered by regulations. The Government have decided that returns and payments shall be made quarterly.

Credit

  55.—(1) Regulations may provide that where an insurer has paid tax and all or part of the premium is repaid, the insurer shall be entitled to credit of such an amount as is found in accordance with prescribed rules.

  (2) Regulations may provide that where—

  (a) by virtue of regulations made under section 68 below tax is charged in relation to a premium which is shown in the accounts of an insurer as due to him,

  (b) that tax is paid, and

  (c) it is shown to the satisfaction of the Commissioners that the premium, or part of it, will never actually be received by or on behalf of the insurer,

the insurer shall be entitled to credit of such an amount as is found in accordance with prescribed rules.

  (3) Regulations may make provision as to the manner in which an insurer is to benefit from credit, and in particular may make provision—

  (a) that an insurer shall be entitled to credit by reference to accounting periods;

  (b) than an insurer shall be entitled to deduct an amount equal to his total credit for an accounting period from the total amount of tax due from him for the period;

  (c) that if no tax is due from an insurer for an accounting period but he is entitled to credit for the period, the amount of the credit shall be paid to him by the Commissioners;

  (d) that if the amount of credit to which an insurer is entitled for an accounting period exceeds the amount of tax due from him for the period, an amount equal to the excess shall be paid to him by the Commissioners;

  (e) for the whole or part of any credit to be held over to be credited for a subsequent accounting period;

  (f) as to the manner in which a person who has ceased to be registrable is to benefit from credit.

  (4) Regulations under subsection (3)(c) or (d) above may provide that where at the end of an accounting period an amount is due to an insurer who has failed to submit returns for an earlier period as required by this Part, the Commissioners may withhold payment of the amount until he has complied with that requirement.

  (5) Regulations under subsection (3)(e) above may provide for credit to be held over either on the insurer's application or in accordance with general or special directions given by the Commissioners from time to time.

  (6) Regulations may provide that—

  (a) no deduction or payment shall be made in respect of credit except on a claim made in such manner and at such time as may be determined by or under regulations;

  (b) payment in respect of credit shall be made subject to such conditions (if any) as the Commissioners think fit to impose, including conditions as to repayment in specified circumstances;

  (c) deduction in respect of credit shall be made subject to such conditions (if any) as the Commissioners think fit to impose, including conditions as to the payment to the Commissioners, in specified circumstances, of an amount representing the whole or part of the amount deducted.

(7) Regulations may require a claim by an insurer to be made in a return required by provision made under section 54 above.

(8) Regulations may provide that where—

(a) all or any of the tax payable in respect of a premium has not been paid, and

(b) the circumstances are such that a person would be entitled to credit if the tax had been paid,

prescribed adjustments shall be made as regards any amount of tax due from any person.

GENERAL NOTE

This section provides for regulations to be made to permit the credit of tax to insurers where premiums are repaid, to specify the conditions of such credit, and establish the operation of the credit mechanism.

Subs. (2)

This deals with credits where the insurer has opted to be taxed on the written premium basis (see s.68).

Subs. (3)

The credit system will operate generally like the VAT system for off-setting input tax against output tax, with refunds to the taxpayer where appropriate.

Subs. (4)

Where a credit is due to an insurer who has failed to submit returns for an earlier period, the Customs and Excise may withhold payment until the insurer has made the returns.

Subs. (5)

Credits may also be held over on the insurer's application or in accordance with general or special directions of the Customs and Excise.

Subs. (6)

Deduction or payment in respect of a credit may be subject to a claim or such conditions as the Customs and Excise may impose, including conditions relating to payment or repayment of the credit.

Subss. (7) and (8)

A claim may be required to be made in a s.54 return. Where tax in respect of a premium has not been paid, but a credit would be exigible if it had been, appropriate adjustment may be made in respect of the tax due.

Power to assess

56.—(1) In a case where—

(a) a person has failed to make any returns required to be made under this Part,

(b) a person has failed to keep any documents necessary to verify returns required to be made under this Part,

(c) a person has failed to afford the facilities necessary to verify returns required to be made under this Part, or

(d) it appears to the Commissioners that returns required to be made by a person under this Part are incomplete or incorrect,

the Commissioners may assess the amount of tax due from the person concerned to the best of their judgment and notify it to him.

(2) Where a person has for an accounting period been paid an amount to which he purports to be entitled under regulations made under section 55 above, then, to the extent that the amount ought not to have been paid or would not have been paid had the facts been known or been as they later turn out to be, the Commissioners may assess the amount as being tax due from him for that period and notify it to him accordingly.

(3) Where a person is assessed under subsections (1) and (2) above in respect of the same accounting period the assessments may be combined and notified to him as one assessment.

(4) Where the person failing to make a return, or making a return which appears to the Commissioners to be incomplete or incorrect, was required to make the return as a personal representative, trustee in bankruptcy, trustee in sequestration, receiver, liquidator or person otherwise acting in a representative capacity in relation to another person, subsection (1) above shall apply as if the reference to tax due from him included a reference to tax due from that other person.

(5) An assessment under subsection (1) or (2) above of an amount of tax due for an accounting period shall not be made after the later of the following—

    (a) two years after the end of the accounting period;

    (b) one year after evidence of facts, sufficient in the Commissioners' opinion to justify the making of the assessment, comes to their knowledge;

but where further such evidence comes to their knowledge after the making of an assessment under subsection (1) or (2) above another assessment may be made under the subsection concerned in addition to any earlier assessment.

(6) In a case where—

    (a) as a result of a person's failure to make a return for an accounting period the Commissioners have made an assessment under subsection (1) above for that period,

    (b) the tax assessed has been paid but no proper return has been made for the period to which the assessment related, and

    (c) as a result of a failure to make a return for a later accounting period, being a failure by the person referred to in paragraph (a) above or a person acting in a representative capacity in relation to him, as mentioned in subsection (4) above, the Commissioners find it necessary to make another assessment under subsection (1) above,

then, if the Commissioners think fit, having regard to the failure referred to in paragraph (a) above, they may specify in the assessment referred to in paragraph (c) above an amount of tax greater than that which they would otherwise have considered to be appropriate.

(7) Where an amount has been assessed and notified to any person under subsection (1) or (2) above it shall be deemed to be an amount of tax due from him and may be recovered accordingly unless, or except to the extent that, the assessment has subsequently been withdrawn or reduced.

(8) For the purposes of this section notification to—

    (a) a personal representative, trustee in bankruptcy, trustee in sequestration, receiver or liquidator, or

    (b) a person otherwise acting in a representative capacity in relation to another person,

shall be treated as notification to the person in relation to whom the person mentioned in paragraph (a) above, or the first person mentioned in paragraph (b) above, acts.

General Note

The Customs and Excise is empowered to make assessments of IPT, which are then recoverable as if they were IPT. The general provisions relating to assessments are as follows:

Subs. (1)

Assessments may be raised on a best of judgment basis in cases of failure to make returns or to keep documents or afford facilities necessary to verify returns, or where it appears to the Customs and Excise that returns are incomplete or incorrect.

Subs. (2)
Assessments may also be raised where a credit has been incorrectly paid.

Subs. (3)
Assessments under subss. (1) and (2) in respect of the same accounting period may be combined.

Subs. (4)
Subsection (1) applies to persons acting in a representative capacity.

Subs. (5)
The normal time-limit for assessment is two years after the accounting period in question, or one year after the relevant facts come to the knowledge of the Customs and Excise. The limit may be extended if further facts come to light.

Subs. (6)
Where a subs. (1) assessment has been paid, but no proper return has been made for that period, then a further assessment for a later period for which no return has been made may be increased to an amount larger than the Customs and Excise would otherwise have considered appropriate.

Subs. (7)
An assessment duly notified is deemed to be tax due.

Subs. (8)
Notification to a subs. (4) representative is treated as notification to the person concerned.

Tax representatives

Tax representatives

57.—(1) Where at any time (a relevant time) a person who is an insurer—
(a) is registered, or liable to be registered, under section 53 above, and
(b) does not have any business establishment or other fixed establishment in the United Kingdom,
this section shall have effect with a view to securing that another person is the insurer's tax representative at that time.

(2) If, at the time the insurer first falls within subsection (1) above, the insurer has a representative fulfilling the requirements of section 10 of the Insurance Companies Act 1982—
(a) the Commissioners shall be taken to approve that person at that time as the insurer's tax representative, and
(b) that person shall be the insurer's tax representative at any relevant time falling after the time mentioned in paragraph (a) above and before the Commissioners' approval is withdrawn.

(3) If, at the time the insurer first falls within subsection (1) above, the insurer does not have a representative fulfilling the requirements of section 10 of the Insurance Companies Act 1982, the insurer shall take action as mentioned in subsection (4) below.

(4) The insurer takes action as mentioned in this subsection if—
(a) he requests the Commissioners to approve a particular person as his tax representative, and
(b) the request is made with a view to securing that a person approved by the Commissioners becomes the insurer's tax representative within the relevant period.

(5) If the Commissioners approve a person as the insurer's tax representative in a case where action has been taken as mentioned in subsection (4) above, that person shall be the insurer's tax representative at any relevant time falling after the Commissioners' approval is given and before their approval is withdrawn.

(6) Subsection (7) below applies where the Commissioners believe that the revenue would not be sufficiently protected if—

(a) a person were to become the insurer's tax representative by virtue of subsection (2) above, or

(b) a person who by virtue of any of the provisions of this section is the insurer's tax representative were to continue to be so.

(7) If the Commissioners require the insurer to take action as mentioned in subsection (4) above the insurer shall comply with that requirement.

(8) In a case where—

(a) a person is the insurer's tax representative,

(b) the insurer withdraws his agreement that that person should act as his tax representative, or that person withdraws his agreement to act as the insurer's tax representative, or the insurer and that person agree that that person should no longer be the insurer's tax representative, and

(c) that person notifies the Commissioners accordingly,

the Commissioners shall be taken to have withdrawn their approval of that person at the time they inform the insurer that they have received the notification, and that person shall cease at that time to be the insurer's tax representative.

(9) Where subsection (8) above applies the insurer shall take action as mentioned in subsection (4) above.

(10) If at any time after the insurer first falls within subsection (1) above—

(a) the insurer (otherwise than in pursuance of a duty under subsection (3), (7) or (9) above) requests the Commissioners to approve a particular person as his tax representative, and

(b) the Commissioners approve that person,

that person shall be the insurer's tax representative at any relevant time falling after the Commissioners' approval is given and before their approval is withdrawn.

(11) The Commissioners may at any time direct that a person who is an agent of the insurer and is specified in the direction shall be the insurer's tax representative; and—

(a) the direction shall be taken to signify the Commissioners' approval of that person as the insurer's tax representative;

(b) that person shall be the insurer's tax representative at any relevant time falling after the Commissioners' direction is made and before their approval is withdrawn;

(c) the direction shall not prejudice any duty of the insurer under subsection (3), (7) or (9) above;

(d) subsection (8) above shall not apply in the case of the person specified in the direction.

(12) Where the Commissioners approve a person under this section as the insurer's tax representative—

(a) at the time the approval is given they shall be taken to withdraw their approval of any person who was the insurer's tax representative immediately before the approval was given, and

(b) that person shall cease at that time to be the insurer's tax representative.

(13) The fact that a person ceases to be an insurer's tax representative shall not prevent his subsequent approval under this section.

(14) The Commissioners may not withdraw their approval of a person as a tax representative except by virtue of subsection (8) or (12) above.

(15) Regulations may make provision as to the time at which—

(a) the Commissioners' approval is to be treated as given in a case where action has been taken as mentioned in subsection (4) above or a request has been made as mentioned in subsection (10) above;

(b) the Commissioners are to be taken to inform the insurer under subsection (8) above;

(c) a direction of the Commissioners is to be treated as made under sub-
    section (11) above.

(16) The relevant period for the purposes of subsection (4) above is—

(a) where subsection (4) above applies by virtue of subsection (3) above,
    the period of 30 days beginning with the day on which the insurer first
    falls within subsection (1) above;

(b) where subsection (4) above applies by virtue of subsection (7) above,
    the period of 30 days beginning with the day on which the requirement
    mentioned in subsection (7) above is made;

(c) where subsection (4) above applies by virtue of subsection (9) above,
    the period of 30 days beginning with the day on which the person men-
    tioned in subsection (8) above ceases to be the insurer's tax
    representative;

but if in any case the Commissioners allow a longer period than that found
under paragraphs (a) to (c) above, the relevant period is that longer period.

GENERAL NOTE

This section, which was extensively amended in Committee to strengthen its requirements,
requires an insurer with no establishment in the U.K. to appoint a tax representative and lays
down the conditions associated with such an appointment.

Subs. (1)

The purpose of the section is to ensure that a non-resident insurer has a tax representative in
the U.K.

Subs. (2)

A general representative fulfilling the requirements of the Insurance Companies Act 1982 (c.
50), s.10 is taken to be the tax representative.

Subss. (3)–(5)

These require a non-resident insurer without a general representative to ask the Customs and
Excise to approve someone as his tax representative.

Subss. (6) and (7)

Where the Customs and Excise are not satisfied with a general or other tax representative,
they may require the insurer to nominate someone else.

Subss. (8) and (9)

Where the insurer or the tax representative wish to end the arrangement, it terminates
on notification to the Customs and Excise. The insurer must then nominate another tax
representative.

Subs. (10)

A tax representative may be appointed other than under the mandatory provisions of subss.
(3), (5) and (7).

Subs. (11)

The Customs and Excise may direct that an insurer's agent shall be his tax representative. In
such a case the option to terminate the arrangement under subs. (8) does not apply.

Subs. (12)

Approval of a new tax representative implies withdrawal of approval of the previous
representative.

Subs. (13)
A previous tax representative may be subsequently reappointed.

Subs. (14)
The Customs and Excise may not withdraw approval of a tax representative except under subss. (8) and (12) (presumably without prejudice to their power to require a new one to be appointed under subss. (6) and (7)).

Subs. (15)
Regulations will provide times at which the Customs and Excise will be deemed to have taken action under subss. (4)(8)(10) and (11).

Subs. (16)
Where an insurer has to take action under sub. (4), he must do so within 30 days of the relevant time, unless the Customs and Excise allow him longer.

Rights and duties of tax representatives

58.—(1) Where a person is an insurer's tax representative at any time, the tax representative—
    (a) shall be entitled to act on the insurer's behalf for the purposes of legislation relating to insurance premium tax,
    (b) shall secure (where appropriate by acting on the insurer's behalf) the insurer's compliance with and discharge of the obligations and liabilities to which the insurer is subject by virtue of legislation relating to insurance premium tax (including obligations and liabilities arising before the person became the insurer's tax representative), and
    (c) shall be personally liable in respect of any failure to secure the insurer's compliance with or discharge of any such obligation or liability, and in respect of anything done for purposes connected with acting on the insurer's behalf,
as if the obligations and liabilities imposed on the insurer were imposed jointly and severally on the tax representative and the insurer.
    (2) A tax representative shall not be liable by virtue of subsection (1) above himself to be registered under this Part, but regulations may—
    (a) require the registration of the names of tax representatives against the names of the insurers in any register kept under this Part;
    (b) make provision for the deletion of the names of persons who cease to be tax representatives.
    (3) A tax representative shall not by virtue of subsection (1) above be guilty of any offence except in so far as—
    (a) the tax representative has consented to, or connived in, the commission of the offence by the insurer,
    (b) the commission of the offence by the insurer is attributable to any neglect on the part of the tax representative, or
    (c) the offence consists in a contravention by the tax representative of an obligation which, by virtue of that subsection, is imposed both on the tax representative and on the insurer.
    (4) Subsection (1)(b) above shall have effect subject to such provisions as may be made by regulations.

GENERAL NOTE

Subs. (1)
Tax representatives are responsible for the insurer's compliance with the legislation and are jointly and severally liable with the insurer for non-compliance.

Regulations may require the recording of the tax representative's name against the insurer's and its deletion where applicable in any register that is kept.

Subs. (3)
This restricts a tax representative's liability for offences to cases where he colluded in the commission of an offence, or where the offence was caused by his neglect, or where he is in any event jointly and severally liable.

Subs. (4)
Regulations may further amplify a tax representative's compliance duties.

Review and appeal

Review of Commissioners' decisions

59.—(1) This section applies to any decision of the Commissioners with respect to any of the following matters—
    (a) the registration or cancellation of registration of any person under this Part;
    (b) whether tax is chargeable in respect of a premium or how much tax is chargeable;
    (c) whether a person is entitled to credit by virtue of regulations under section 55 above or how much credit a person is entitled to or the manner in which he is to benefit from credit;
    (d) an assessment under section 56 above or the amount of such an assessment;
    (e) any refusal of an application under section 63 below;
    (f) whether a notice may be served on a person by virtue of regulations made under section 65 below;
    (g) an assessment under regulations made under section 65 below or the amount of such an assessment;
    (h) whether a scheme established by regulations under section 68 below applies to an insurer as regards an accounting period;
    (i) the requirement of any security under paragraph 24 of Schedule 7 to this Act or its amount;
    (j) any liability to a penalty under paragraphs 12 to 19 of Schedule 7 to this Act;
    (k) the amount of any penalty or interest specified in an assessment under paragraph 25 of Schedule 7 to this Act;
    (l) a claim for the repayment of an amount under paragraph 8 of Schedule 7 to this Act;
    (m) any liability of the Commissioners to pay interest under paragraph 22 of Schedule 7 to this Act or the amount of the interest payable.
    (2) Any person who is or will be affected by any decision to which this section applies may by notice in writing to the Commissioners require them to review the decision.
    (3) The Commissioners shall not be required under this section to review any decision unless the notice requiring the review is given before the end of the period of 45 days beginning with the day on which written notification of the decision, or of the assessment containing the decision, was first given to the person requiring the review.
    (4) For the purposes of subsection (3) above it shall be the duty of the Commissioners to give written notification of any decision to which this section applies to any person who—

(a) requests such a notification,

(b) has not previously been given written notification of that decision, and

(c) if given such a notification, will be entitled to require a review of the decision under this section.

(5) A person shall be entitled to give a notice under this section requiring a decision to be reviewed for a second or subsequent time only if—

(a) the grounds on which he requires the further review are that the Commissioners did not, on any previous review, have the opportunity to consider certain facts or other matters, and

(b) he does not, on the further review, require the Commissioners to consider any facts or matters which were considered on a previous review except in so far as they are relevant to any issue not previously considered.

(6) Where the Commissioners are required in accordance with this section to review any decision, it shall be their duty to do so; and on the review they may withdraw, vary or confirm the decision.

(7) In a case where—

(a) it is the duty under this section of the Commissioners to review any decision, and

(b) they do not, within the period of 45 days beginning with the day on which the review was required, give notice to the person requiring it of their determination on the review,

they shall be assumed for the purposes of this Part to have confirmed the decision.

(8) The Commissioners shall not by virtue of any requirement under this section to review a decision have any power, apart from their power in pursuance of paragraph 13 of Schedule 7 to this Act, to mitigate the amount of any penalty imposed under this Part.

GENERAL NOTE

Before appealing to a tribunal against a decision in relation to IPT, the taxpayer is required to ask the Customs and Excise to review the decision. The procedure follows that laid down for appeals in relation to Customs and Excise decisions (ss.14 and 15).

In relation to any of the decisions listed in subs. (1), the taxpayer or any person affected may require the Customs and Excise to review the decision by written notice given within 45 days (subss. (2), (3)).

To facilitate appeals, the Customs and Excise are required where necessary to give written notification of any relevant decision (subs. (4)). A second review may be demanded when new facts or new issues emerge (subs. (5)). On the review, the Customs and Excise may withdraw, confirm or vary the decision (subs. (6)). If they have not responded within 45 days, they are deemed to have confirmed the decision (subs. (7)). On a review, the mitigation powers of the Customs and Excise are confined to the civil penalties for fraudulent evasion of IPT under Sched. 7, para. 13 (subs. (8)).

Appeals

60.—(1) Subject to the following provisions of this section, an appeal shall lie to an appeal tribunal with respect to any of the following decisions—

(a) any decision by the Commissioners on a review under section 59 above (including a deemed confirmation under subsection (7) of that section);

(b) any decision by the Commissioners on such review of a decision referred to in section 59(1) above as the Commissioners have agreed to undertake in consequence of a request made after the end of the period mentioned in section 59(3) above.

(2) Without prejudice to paragraph 3 of Schedule 7 to this Act, nothing in subsection (1) above shall be taken to confer on a tribunal any power to vary an amount assessed by way of penalty or interest except in so far as it is necessary to reduce it to the amount which is appropriate under paragraphs 12 to 21 of that Schedule.

(3) Where an appeal is made under this section by a person who is required to make returns by virtue of regulations under section 54 above, the appeal shall not be entertained unless the appellant—
  (a) has made all the returns which he is required to make by virtue of those regulations, and
  (b) has paid the amounts shown in those returns as payable by him;
but the restriction in paragraph (b) above shall not apply in the case of an appeal against a decision with respect to the matter mentioned in section 59(1)(i) above.

(4) Where the appeal is against a decision with respect to any of the matters mentioned in paragraphs (b) and (d) of section 59(1) above it shall not be entertained unless—
  (a) the amount which the Commissioners have determined to be payable as tax has been paid or deposited with them, or
  (b) on being satisfied that the appellant would otherwise suffer hardship the Commissioners agree or the tribunal decides that it should be entertained notwithstanding that that amount has not been so paid or deposited.

(5) Where on an appeal against a decision with respect to any of the matters mentioned in section 59(1)(d) above—
  (a) it is found that the amount specified in the assessment is less than it ought to have been, and
  (b) the tribunal gives a direction specifying the correct amount,
the assessment shall have effect as an assessment of the amount specified in the direction and that amount shall be deemed to have been notified to the appellant.

(6) Where on an appeal under this section it is found that the whole or part of any amount paid or deposited in pursuance of subsection (4) above is not due, so much of that amount as is found not to be due shall be repaid with interest at such rate as the tribunal may determine.

(7) Where on an appeal under this section it is found that the whole or part of any amount due to the appellant by virtue of regulations under section 55(3)(c) or (d) or (f) above has not been paid, so much of that amount as is found not to have been paid shall be paid with interest at such rate as the tribunal may determine.

(8) Where an appeal under this section has been entertained notwithstanding that an amount determined by the Commissioners to be payable as tax has not been paid or deposited and it is found on the appeal that that amount is due the tribunal may, if it thinks fit, direct that that amount shall be paid with interest at such rate as may be specified in the direction.

(9) On an appeal against an assessment to a penalty under paragraph 12 of Schedule 7 to this Act, the burden of proof as to the matters specified in paragraphs (a) and (b) of sub-paragraph (1) of paragraph 12 shall lie upon the Commissioners.

(10) Sections 25 and 29 of the Finance Act 1985 (settling of appeals by agreement and enforcement of certain decisions of tribunal) shall have effect as if—
  (a) the references to section 40 of the Value Added Tax Act 1983 included references to this section, and
  (b) the references to value added tax included references to insurance premium tax.

GENERAL NOTE

Subs. (1)
  An appeal may be made to the VAT and duties tribunal against a s.59 decision.

Subs. (2)
  The tribunal's power of mitigation may only be exercised in relation to penalties or interest under Sched. 7, paras. 12–21.

Subs. (3)
　An appeal will not be entertained unless the taxpayer has made his returns and paid the IPT due, except where security has been required.

Subs. (4)
　Except on grounds of hardship, an appeal relating to liability to IPT or an assessment to IPT will not be entertained unless the relevant tax has been paid.

Subs. (5)
　Where the tribunal decides to increase an assessment, this will take effect as an increased assessment.

Subs. (6)
　Tax paid under subs. (4) which is found not to be due will be repaid with interest at a rate to be determined by the tribunal.

Subs. (7)
　Credits due under s.55 but unpaid will also carry interest.

Subs. (8)
　Where unpaid tax is found to be due, the tribunal has a discretion to award interest.

Subs. (9)
　Where dishonest evasion of tax is alleged by the Customs and Excise with a view to the imposition of a civil penalty, the burden of proof lies on them.

Subs. (10)
　The provisions of the VAT legislation regarding the settling of appeals by agreement and the enforcement of tribunal decisions apply to IPT.

Review and appeal: commencement

　61. Sections 59 and 60 above shall come into force on such day as may be appointed by order.

General Note
　The review and appeal procedure will come into force on a date to be appointed by the Customs and Excise.

Miscellaneous

Partnership, bankruptcy, transfer of business, etc.

　62.—(1) Regulations may make provision for determining by what persons anything required by this Part to be done by an insurer is to be done where the business concerned is carried on in partnership or by another unincorporated body.
　(2) The registration under this Part of an unincorporated body other than a partnership may be in the name of the body concerned; and in determining whether premiums are received by such a body no account shall be taken of any change in its members.
　(3) Regulations may make provision for determining by what person anything required by this Part to be done by an insurer is to be done in a case

where insurance business is carried on by persons who are underwriting members of Lloyd's and are members of a syndicate of such underwriting members.

(4) Regulations may—

(a) make provision for the registration for the purposes of this Part of a syndicate of underwriting members of Lloyd's;

(b) provide that for purposes prescribed by the regulations no account shall be taken of any change in the members of such a syndicate;

and regulations under paragraph (a) above may modify section 53 above.

(5) As regards any case where a person carries on a business of an insurer who has died or become bankrupt or incapacitated or been sequestrated, or of an insurer which is in liquidation or receivership or in relation to which an administration order is in force, regulations may—

(a) require the person to inform the Commissioners of the fact that he is carrying on the business and of the event that has led to his carrying it on;

(b) make provision allowing the person to be treated for a limited time as if he were the insurer;

(c) make provision for securing continuity in the application of this Part where a person is so treated.

(6) Regulations may make provision for securing continuity in the application of this Part in cases where a business carried on by a person is transferred to another person as a going concern.

(7) Regulations under subsection (6) above may in particular provide—

(a) for liabilities and duties under this Part of the transferor to become, to such extent as may be provided by the regulations, liabilities and duties of the transferee;

(b) for any right of either of them to repayment or credit in respect of tax to be satisfied by making a repayment or allowing a credit to the other;

but the regulations may provide that no such provision as is mentioned in paragraph (a) or (b) of this subsection shall have effect in relation to any transferor and transferee unless an application in that behalf has been made by them under the regulations.

GENERAL NOTE

Subs. (1)

Regulations will be made to determine liability for compliance where the insurer is a partnership or other unincorporated body.

Subss. (2)–(4)

These subsections were inserted at Committee Stage to clarify the position of Lloyd's.

The Government's purpose is that underwriting syndicates should be treated in the same way as ordinary insurance companies, except for their accounting arrangements. Each syndicate that does business in the U.K. is expected to register, although the Lloyd's premium signing office will generally account for IPT on behalf of the syndicate. The ultimate liability for tax will remain with those who are members of the syndicate when the particular liability concerned arises.

Subs. (5)

Regulations will cover administrative requirements for a person carrying on the business of an insurer who has died, become bankrupt or incapacitated, or is in liquidation or receivership.

Subss. (6) and (7)

Regulations will also cover the situation where an insurance business is transferred as a going concern. Such regulations will cater for the transfer of liabilities and duties, and right to credit and repayments, from the transferor to the transferee, where a joint application has been made to the Customs and Excise in that behalf.

Groups of companies

63.—(1) Where under the following provisions of this section any bodies corporate are treated as members of a group, for the purposes of this Part—

(a) any taxable business carried on by a member of the group shall be treated as carried on by the representative member,

(b) the representative member shall be taken to be the insurer in relation to any taxable insurance contract as regards which a member of the group is the actual insurer,

(c) any receipt by a member of the group of a premium under a taxable insurance contract shall be taken to be a receipt by the representative member, and

(d) all members of the group shall be jointly and severally liable for any tax due from the representative member.

(2) Two or more bodies corporate are eligible to be treated as members of a group if each of them falls within subsection (3) below and—

(a) one of them controls each of the others,

(b) one person (whether a body corporate or an individual) controls all of them, or

(c) two or more individuals carrying on a business in partnership control all of them.

(3) A body falls within this subsection if it is resident in the United Kingdom or it has an established place of business in the United Kingdom.

(4) Where an application to that effect is made to the Commissioners with respect to two or more bodies corporate eligible to be treated as members of a group, then—

(a) from the beginning of an accounting period they shall be so treated, and

(b) one of them shall be the representative member,

unless the Commissioners refuse the application; and the Commissioners shall not refuse the application unless it appears to them necessary to do so for the protection of the revenue.

(5) Where any bodies corporate are treated as members of a group and an application to that effect is made to the Commissioners, then, from the beginning of an accounting period—

(a) a further body eligible to be so treated shall be included among the bodies so treated,

(b) a body corporate shall be excluded from the bodies so treated,

(c) another member of the group shall be substituted as the representative member, or

(d) the bodies corporate shall no longer be treated as members of a group,

unless the application is to the effect mentioned in paragraph (a) or (c) above and the Commissioners refuse the application.

(6) The Commissioners may refuse an application under subsection (5)(a) or (c) above only if it appears to them necessary to do so for the protection of the revenue.

(7) Where a body corporate is treated as a member of a group as being controlled by any person and it appears to the Commissioners that it has ceased to be so controlled, they shall, by notice given to that person, terminate that treatment from such date as may be specified in the notice.

(8) An application under this section with respect to any bodies corporate must be made by one of those bodies or by the person controlling them and must be made not less than 90 days before the date from which it is to take effect, or at such later time as the Commissioners may allow.

(9) For the purposes of this section a body corporate shall be taken to control another body corporate if it is empowered by statute to control that

body's activities or if it is that body's holding company within the meaning of section 736 of the Companies Act 1985; and an individual or individuals shall be taken to control a body corporate if he or they, were he or they a company, would be that body's holding company within the meaning of that section.

GENERAL NOTE
This section was inserted at Committee Stage in response to requests from the insurance industry. It will simplify the registration and accounting procedures for insurers structured as several different companies by allowing them to be treated as a single entity for the purposes of making returns and accounting for tax. The section is based on similar provisions for other taxes (see, for example, the VATA 1983 (c. 55), s.29).

Subs. (1)
Where companies are treated as a group, the representative member acts for the group in relation to IPT, although they all remain jointly and severally liable.

Subss. (2) and (3)
Companies may apply for group treatment if they are all resident or have an established place of business in the U.K. and one controls the others or one person or a partnership controls all of them.

Subs. (4)
An application for group treatment may not be refused by the Customs and Excise except for the protection of the revenue.

Subss. (5) and (6)
Further applications may be made by adding or deleting members, changing the representative member or ending group treatment. Applications for adding members or changing the representative member may be refused by the Customs and Excise for the protection of the revenue.

Subs. (7)
Where it appears to the Customs and Excise that a group member has ceased to be under the control of a person, they will terminate its group treatment by notice to that person.

Subs. (8)
Applications with respect to group treatment must be made 90 days before the effective date, unless the Customs and Excise so allow.

Subs. (9)
Control is to be construed in line with the Companies Act 1985 (c. 6), s.736.

Information, powers, penalties, etc.

64. Schedule 7 to this Act (which contains provisions relating to information, powers, penalties and other matters) shall have effect.

GENERAL NOTE
This section introduces Sched. 7, which contains sundry administrative and penalty provisions. See further the General Note to Sched. 7.

Liability of insured in certain cases

65.—(1) Regulations may make provision under this section with regard to any case where at any time—
   (a) an insurer does not have any business establishment or other fixed establishment in the United Kingdom, and
   (b) no person is the insurer's tax representative by virtue of section 57 above.
   (2) Regulations may make provision allowing notice to be served in accordance with the regulations on—
   (a) the person who is insured under a taxable insurance contract, if there is one insured person, or

(b) one or more of the persons who are insured under a taxable insurance contract, if there are two or more insured persons;

and a notice so served is referred to in this section as a liability notice.

(3) Regulations may provide that if a liability notice has been served in accordance with the regulations—

(a) the Commissioners may assess to the best of their judgment the amount of any tax due in respect of premiums received by the insurer under the contract concerned after the material date and before the date of the assessment, and

(b) that amount shall be deemed to be the amount of tax so due.

(4) The material date is—

(a) where there is one person on whom a liability notice has been served in respect of the contract, the date when the notice was served or such later date as may be specified in the notice;

(b) where there are two or more persons on whom liability notices have been served in respect of the contract, the date when the last of the notices was served or such later date as may be specified in the notices.

(5) Regulations may provide that where—

(a) an assessment is made in respect of a contract under provision included in the regulations by virtue of subsection (3) above, and

(b) the assessment is notified to the person, or each of the persons, on whom a liability notice in respect of the contract has been served,

the persons mentioned in subsection (6) below shall be jointly and severally liable to pay the tax assessed, and that tax shall be recoverable accordingly.

(6) The persons are—

(a) the person or persons mentioned in subsection (5)(b) above, and

(b) the insurer.

(7) Where regulations make provision under subsection (5) above they must also provide that any provision made under that subsection shall not apply if, or to the extent that, the assessment has subsequently been withdrawn or reduced.

(8) Regulations may make provision as to the time within which, and the manner in which, tax which has been assessed is to be paid.

(9) Where any amount is recovered from an insured person by virtue of regulations made under this section, the insurer shall be liable to pay to the insured person an amount equal to the amount recovered; and regulations may make provision requiring an insurer to pay interest where this subsection applies.

(10) Regulations may make provision for adjustments to be made of a person's liability in any case where—

(a) an assessment is made under section 56 above in relation to the insurer, and

(b) an assessment made by virtue of regulations under this section relates to premiums received (or assumed for the purposes of the assessment to be received) within a period which corresponds to any extent with the accounting period to which the assessment under section 56 relates.

(11) Regulations may make provision as regards a case where—

(a) an assessment made in respect of a contract by virtue of regulations under this section relates to premiums received (or assumed for the purposes of the assessment to be received) within a given period, and

(b) an amount of tax is paid by the insurer in respect of an accounting period which corresponds to any extent with that period;

and the regulations may include provision for determining whether, or how much of, any of the tax paid as mentioned in paragraph (b) above is attributable to premiums received under the contract in the period mentioned in paragraph (a) above.

(12) Regulations may—

(a) make provision requiring the Commissioners, in prescribed circumstances, to furnish prescribed information to an insured person;

(b) make provision requiring any person on whom a liability notice has been served to keep records, to furnish information, or to produce documents for inspection or cause documents to be produced for inspection;

(c) make such provision as the Commissioners think is reasonable for the purpose of facilitating the recovery of tax from the persons having joint and several liability (rather than from the insurer alone);

(d) modify the effect of any provision of this Part.

(13) Regulations may provide for an insured person to be liable to pay tax assessed by virtue of the regulations notwithstanding that he has already paid an amount representing tax as part of a premium.

GENERAL NOTE

This section is designed to provide protection for the revenue in cases where an offshore insurer has no U.K. tax representative.

The substantive provisions are to be made by regulations. These will allow the Customs and Excise to serve liability notices and assessments on the customers of such offshore insurers. Where the customer has to pay, he will be entitled to recover the amount from the insurer with interest. Assessments may be adjusted where the insurer has also been assessed, or has paid the tax. However, the customer may be liable for IPT even if he has already paid it as part of his premium.

The Customs and Excise are given wide ancillary powers, including power to modify the effect of any provision of Pt. III (though only in relation to the situation where an offshore insurer has no U.K. tax representative).

Directions as to amounts of premiums

66.—(1) This section applies where—

(a) anything is received by way of premium under a taxable insurance contract, and

(b) the amount of the premium is less than it would be if it were received under the contract in open market conditions.

(2) The Commissioners may direct that the amount of the premium shall be taken for the purposes of this Part to be such amount as it would be if it were received under the contract in open market conditions.

(3) A direction under subsection (2) above shall be given by notice in writing to the insurer, and no direction may be given more than three years after the time of the receipt.

(4) Where the Commissioners make a direction under subsection (2) above in the case of a contract they may also direct that if—

(a) anything is received by way of premium under the contract after the giving of the notice or after such later date as may be specified in the notice, and

(b) the amount of the premium is less than it would be if it were received under the contract in open market conditions,

the amount of the premium shall be taken for the purposes of this Part to be such amount as it would be if it were received under the contract in open market conditions.

(5) For the purposes of this section a premium is received in open market conditions if it is received—

(a) by an insurer standing in no such relationship with the insured person as would affect the premium, and

(b) in circumstances where there is no other contract or arrangement affecting the parties.

(6) For the purposes of this section it is immaterial whether what is received by way of premium is money or something other than money or both.

Where a premium is less than its amount would be in open market conditions, the Customs and Excise may direct that tax should be accounted for on the open market value of the insurance cover to which the premium relates. A direction may not be given more than three years after the receipt of the premium.

Open market conditions exist where there is no such relationship between the insurer and insured as would affect the premium and there is no other contract or arrangement affecting the parties.

Deemed date of receipt of certain premiums

67.—(1) In a case where—
(a) a premium under a contract of insurance is received by the insurer after 30th November 1993 and before 1st October 1994, and
(b) the period of cover for the risk begins on or after 1st October 1994,
for the purposes of this Part the premium shall be taken to be received on 1st October 1994.

(2) Subsection (3) below applies where—
(a) a premium under a contract of insurance is received by the insurer after 30th November 1993 and before 1st October 1994,
(b) the period of cover for the risk begins before 1st October 1994 and ends after 30th September 1995, and
(c) the premium, or any part of it, is attributable to such of the period of cover as falls after 30th September 1995.

(3) For the purposes of this Part—
(a) so much of the premium as is attributable to such of the period of cover as falls after 30th September 1995 shall be taken to be received on 1st October 1994;
(b) so much as is so attributable shall be taken to be a separate premium.

(4) If a contract relates to more than one risk subsection (1) above shall have effect as if the reference in paragraph (b) to the risk were to any given risk.

(5) If a contract relates to more than one risk, subsections (2) and (3) above shall apply as follows—
(a) so much of the premium as is attributable to any given risk shall be deemed for the purposes of those subsections to be a separate premium relating to that risk;
(b) those subsections shall then apply separately in the case of each given risk and the separate premium relating to it;
and any further attribution required by those subsections shall be made accordingly.

(6) Subsections (1) and (4) above do not apply in relation to a contract if the contract belongs to a class of contract as regards which the normal practice is for a premium to be received by or on behalf of the insurer before the date when cover begins.

(7) Subsections (2), (3) and (5) above do not apply in relation to a contract if the contract belongs to a class of contract as regards which the normal practice is for cover to be provided for a period exceeding 12 months.

(8) Any attribution under this section shall be made on such basis as is just and reasonable.

This is an anti-avoidance measure, to prevent insurers forestalling the tax by accepting premiums between November 30, 1993 (Budget day) and October 1, 1994 (when IPT is introduced) in relation to cover after that date. Such premiums will be deemed to be received on October 1, 1994. This will not apply where it is normal practice in the insurance industry for premiums to be received before cover begins.

Where a premium is received between November 30, 1993 and October 1, 1994 and the cover begins before October 1, 1994 and ends after September 30, 1995, the part relating to the period after September 30, 1995 will be treated as a separate premium received on October 1, 1994. This will not apply in cases where it is normal practice for cover to be provided for a period exceeding 12 months.

Special accounting schemes

68.—(1) Regulations may make provision establishing a scheme in accordance with the following provisions of this section; and in this section "a relevant accounting period", in relation to an insurer, means an accounting period as regards which the scheme applies to the insurer.

(2) Regulations may provide that if an insurer notifies the Commissioners that the scheme should apply to him as regards accounting periods beginning on or after a date specified in the notification and prescribed conditions are fulfilled, then, subject to any provision made under subsection (9) below, the scheme shall apply to the insurer as regards accounting periods beginning on or after that date.

(3) Regulations may provide that where—

(a) an entry is made in the accounts of an insurer showing a premium under a taxable insurance contract as due to him, and

(b) the entry is made as at a particular date which falls within a relevant accounting period,

then (whether or not that date is one on which the premium is actually received by the insurer or on which the premium would otherwise be treated for the purposes of this Part as received by him) the premium shall for the purposes of this Part be taken to be received by the insurer on that date or, in prescribed circumstances, to be received by him on a different date determined in accordance with the regulations.

(4) Where regulations make provision under subsection (3) above they may also provide that, for the purposes of this Part, the amount of the premium shall be taken to be the amount which the entry in the accounts treats as its amount.

(5) Regulations may provide that provision made under subsections (3) and (4) above shall apply even if the premium, or part of it, is never actually received by the insurer or on his behalf; and the regulations may include provision that, where the premium is never actually received because the contract under which it would have been received is never entered into or is terminated, the premium is nonetheless to be taken for the purposes of this Part to be received under a taxable insurance contract.

(6) Regulations may provide that any provision made under subsection (4) above shall be subject to any directions made under section 66 above.

(7) Regulations may provide that where a premium is treated as received on a particular date by virtue of provision made under subsection (3) above and there is another date on which the premium—

(a) is actually received by the insurer, or

(b) would, apart from the regulations, be treated for the purposes of this Part as received by him,

the premium shall be taken for the purposes of this Part not to be received by him on that other date.

(8) Regulations may provide that provision made under subsection (7) above shall apply only to the extent that there is no excess of the actual amount of the premium over the amount which, by virtue of regulations under this section or of a direction under section 66 above, is to be taken for the purposes of this Part to be its amount; and the regulations may include provision that where there is such an excess, the excess amount shall be taken for the purposes of this Part to be a separate premium and to be received by the insurer on a date determined in accordance with the regulations.

(9) Regulations may provide that if a notification has been given in accordance with provision made under subsection (2) above and subsequently—

(a) the insurer gives notice to the Commissioners that the scheme should not apply to him as regards accounting periods beginning on or after a date specified in the notice, or

(b) the Commissioners give notice to the insurer that the scheme is not to apply to him as regards accounting periods beginning on or after a date specified in the notice,

then, if prescribed conditions are fulfilled, the scheme shall not apply to the insurer as regards an accounting period beginning on or after the date specified in the notice mentioned in paragraph (a) or (b) above unless the circumstances are such as may be prescribed.

(10) Regulations may include provision—

(a) enabling an insurer to whom the scheme applies as regards an accounting period to account for tax due in respect of that period on the assumption that the scheme will apply to him as regards subsequent accounting periods;

(b) designed to secure that, where the scheme ceases to apply to an insurer, any tax which by virtue of provision made under paragraph (a) above has not been accounted for is accounted for and paid.

(11) Regulations may provide that where—

(a) an entry in the accounts of an insurer shows a premium as due to him,

(b) the entry is made as at a date falling before 1st October 1994,

(c) tax in respect of the receipt of the premium would, apart from the regulations, be charged by reference to a date (whether or not the date on which the premium is actually received by the insurer) falling on or after 1st October 1994,

(d) the date by reference to which tax would be charged falls within a relevant accounting period, and

(e) prescribed conditions are fulfilled,

the premium, or such part of it as may be found in accordance with prescribed rules, shall be taken for the purposes of this Part to have been received by the insurer before 1st October 1994.

(12) Without prejudice to subsection (13) below, regulations may include provision modifying any provision made under this section so as to secure the effective operation of the provision in a case where a premium consists wholly or partly of anything other than money.

(13) Regulations may modify the effect of any provision of this Part.

(14) The reference in subsection (3)(a) above to a premium under a taxable insurance contract includes a reference to anything that, although not actually received by or on behalf of the insurer, would be such a premium if it were so received.

GENERAL NOTE

This section was introduced at Committee Stage in response to a request by the insurance industry. Under s.49, IPT is charged on a cash basis, *i.e.* when premiums are received, but most insurance companies operate on a premium written basis, under which the premium may be written into the company's accounts at a different time. The purpose of the section is to allow them to account for IPT on that basis.

The implementation of the section is to be carried out by regulations. The framework of the regulations is that an insurer may opt to account for IPT on the premium written basis, and that this will be effective until either he or the Customs and Excise terminate the arrangement.

It is anticipated that insurance companies will be given the option either of accounting for tax only on contracts entered into after October 1, 1994 but not to claim IPT offset on credits relating to premiums written before October 1, 1994 for which tax has not been accounted; or to account for tax on a strict written premium basis. This would mean accounting for tax on some contracts before October 1, 1994 but would allow an IPT offset on credits, even where those relate to premiums on which IPT was not paid.

Reduced chargeable amount

69.—(1) Where a contract provides cover for one or more exempt matters and also provides cover for one or more non-exempt matters, for the purposes of this Part the chargeable amount is such amount as, with the addition of the tax chargeable, is equal to the difference between—

(a) the amount of the premium, and

(b) such part of the premium as is attributable to the exempt matter or matters.

(2) In applying subsection (1) above, any amount that is included in the premium as being referable to tax (whether or not the amount corresponds to the actual amount of tax payable in respect of the premium) shall be taken to be wholly attributable to the non-exempt matter or matters; and, subject to that, any attribution under subsection (1) above shall be made on such basis as is just and reasonable.

(3) For the purposes of this section an exempt matter is any matter such that, if it were the only matter for which the contract provided cover, the contract would not be a taxable insurance contract.

(4) For the purposes of this section a non-exempt matter is a matter which is not an exempt matter.

(5) If the contract relates to a lifeboat and lifeboat equipment, the lifeboat and the equipment shall be taken together in applying this section.

(6) If a matter for which the contract provides cover is loss of or damage to goods in foreign or international transit, the matter is not an exempt matter for the purposes of this section unless the insured enters into the contract in the course of a business carried on by him.

GENERAL NOTE

Where a premium covers taxable and non-taxable insurance, an apportionment will be made on a just and reasonable basis.

Lifeboat equipment is taken together with the lifeboat in applying the section (see s.70(2)(f)).

Insurance covering loss or damage for goods in foreign or international transit (see s.70(2)(k)) is not exempt unless entered into by the insured in the course of business.

Supplementary

Interpretation: taxable insurance contracts

70.—(1) Subject to the following provisions of this section, any contract of insurance is a taxable insurance contract.

(2) A contract is not a taxable insurance contract if it fulfils one or more of the following conditions—

(a) the contract is a contract of reinsurance;

(b) the contract is one whose effecting and carrying out constitutes business of one or more of the classes specified in Schedule 1 to the Insurance Companies Act 1982 (long term business) and constitutes only such business;

(c) the contract relates only to a motor vehicle where the conditions mentioned in subsection (3) below are satisfied;

(d) the contract relates only to a commercial ship and is a contract whose effecting and carrying out constitutes business of one or more of the relevant classes and constitutes only such business;

(e) the contract relates only to a lifeboat and is a contract whose effecting and carrying out constitutes business of one or more of the relevant classes and constitutes only such business;

(f) the contract relates only to a lifeboat and lifeboat equipment and is such that, if it related only to a lifeboat, it would fall within paragraph (e) above;

(g) the contract relates only to a commercial aircraft and is a contract whose effecting and carrying out constitutes business of one or more of the relevant classes and constitutes only such business;

(h) the contract relates to one risk which is situated outside the United Kingdom;

(i) the contract relates to two or more risks each of which is situated outside the United Kingdom;

(j) the contract relates only to loss of or damage to goods in foreign or international railway rolling stock;

(k) the contract relates only to loss of or damage to goods in foreign or international transit and the insured enters into the contract in the course of a business carried on by him;

(l) the contract relates only to credit granted in relation to relevant supplies falling within section 1(1) of the Export and Investment Guarantees Act 1991.

(3) The conditions referred to in subsection (2)(c) above are that—

(a) the vehicle is used, or intended for use, by a handicapped person in receipt of a disability living allowance by virtue of entitlement to the mobility component or of a mobility supplement,

(b) the insured lets such vehicles on hire to such persons in the course of a business consisting predominantly of the provision of motor vehicles to such persons, and

(c) the insured does not in the course of the business let such vehicles on hire to such persons on terms other than qualifying terms.

(4) For the purposes of subsection (3)(c) above a vehicle is let on qualifying terms to a person (the lessee) if the consideration for the letting consists wholly or partly of sums paid to the insured by—

(a) the Department of Social Security,

(b) the Department of Health and Social Services for Northern Ireland, or

(c) the Ministry of Defence,

on behalf of the lessee in respect of the disability living allowance or mobility supplement to which the lessee is entitled.

(5) For the purposes of subsection (2)(d) and (e) above the relevant classes are classes 1, 6 and 12 of the classes specified in Part I of Schedule 2 to the Insurance Companies Act 1982 (ships, accident, third-party etc.).

(6) For the purposes of subsection (2)(g) above the relevant classes are classes 1, 5 and 11 of the classes specified in Part I of Schedule 2 to the Insurance Companies Act 1982 (aircraft, accident, third-party etc.).

(7) In deciding whether a contract relates to lifeboat equipment the nature of the risks concerned is immaterial, and they may (for example) be risks of dying or sustaining injury or of loss or damage.

(8) For the purposes of subsection (2)(l) above relevant supplies are—

(a) any supply of goods where the supply is to be made outside the United Kingdom or where the goods are to be exported from the United Kingdom;

(b) any supply of services where the services are to be performed outside the United Kingdom.

(9) Regulations may make provision for determining for the purposes of subsection (8) above—

(a) the place where a supply of goods is to be regarded as made;

(b) the place where services are to be regarded as performed.

(10) For the purposes of this section—

(a) "handicapped" means chronically sick or disabled;

(b) "disability living allowance" means a disability living allowance within the meaning of section 71 of the Social Security Contributions and Benefits Act 1992 or section 71 of the Social Security Contributions and Benefits (Northern Ireland) Act 1992;

(c) "mobility supplement" means a mobility supplement within the meaning of article 26A of the Naval, Military and Air Forces etc. (Disablement and Death) Service Pensions Order 1983, article 25A of the Personal Injuries (Civilians) Scheme 1983, article 3 of the Motor Vehicles (Exemption from Vehicles Excise Duty) Order 1985 or article 3 of the Motor Vehicles (Exemption from Vehicles Excise Duty) (Northern Ireland) Order 1985.

(11) This section has effect subject to section 71 below.

(12) This section and section 71 below have effect for the purposes of this Part.

GENERAL NOTE
This important section establishes the scope of IPT through the definition of a taxable insurance contract and those circumstances in which an insurance contract is not taxable and so exempt from the tax.

Contracts in relation to the following matters are not taxable:

(i) reinsurance;

(ii) long-term insurance as defined in the Insurance Companies Act 1982 (c. 50), Sched. 1. This includes most life assurance;

(iii) the insurance of adapted vehicles on lease to disabled drivers through the charity *Motability*. This exemption was added at Report Stage through a back-bench initiative;

(iv) certain insurance of commercial air and sea transport and international railway rolling-stock. The relevant types of business are defined in the Insurance Companies Act 1982 (c. 50), Sched. 2, Pt. I, paras. 1, 5 and 11 and paras. 1, 6 and 12 for air and sea transport respectively;

(v) insurance of lifeboats and their equipment;

(vi) insurance of commercial goods in international transit and export credit;

(vii) insurance of risks situated outside the U.K.

Taxable insurance contracts: power to change definition

71.—(1) Provision may be made by order that—

(a) a contract of insurance that would otherwise not be a taxable insurance contract shall be a taxable insurance contract if it falls within a particular description;

(b) a contract of insurance that would otherwise be a taxable insurance contract shall not be a taxable insurance contract if it falls within a particular description.

(2) A description referred to in subsection (1) above may be by reference to the nature of the insured or by reference to such other factors as the Treasury think fit.

(3) Provision under this section may be made in such way as the Treasury think fit, and in particular may be made by amending this Part.

(4) An order under this section may amend or modify the effect of section 69 above in such way as the Treasury think fit.

GENERAL NOTE
The Treasury is given the power to amend s.70 by Statutory Instrument, subject to approval by affirmative order of the House of Commons within 28 days.

Interpretation: premium

72.—(1) In relation to a taxable insurance contract, a premium is any payment received under the contract by the insurer, and in particular includes any payment wholly or partly referable to—

(a) any risk,

(b) costs of administration,
(c) commission,
(d) any facility for paying in instalments or making deferred payment
      (whether or not payment for the facility is called interest), or
(e) tax.

(2) A premium may consist wholly or partly of anything other than money, and references to payment in subsection (1) above shall be construed accordingly.

(3) Where a premium is to any extent received in a form other than money, its amount shall be taken to be—

(a) an amount equal to the value of whatever is received in a form other
      than money, or
(b) if money is also received, the aggregate of the amount found under
      paragraph (a) above and the amount received in the form of money.

(4) The value to be taken for the purposes of subsection (3) above is open market value at the time of the receipt by the insurer.

(5) The open market value of anything at any time shall be taken to be an amount equal to such consideration in money as would be payable on a sale of it at that time to a person standing in no such relationship with any person as would affect that consideration.

(6) Where (apart from this subsection) anything received under a contract by the insurer would be taken to be an instalment of a premium, it shall be taken to be a separate premium.

(7) Where anything is received by any person on behalf of the insurer—

(a) it shall be treated as received by the insurer when it is received by the
      other person, and
(b) the later receipt of the whole or any part of it by the insurer shall be
      disregarded.

(8) In a case where—

(a) a payment under a taxable insurance contract is made to a person (the
      intermediary) by or on behalf of the insured, and
(b) the whole or part of the payment is referable to commission to which
      the intermediary is entitled,

in determining for the purposes of subsection (7) above whether, or how much of, the payment is received by the intermediary on behalf of the insurer any of the payment that is referable to that commission shall be regarded as received by the intermediary on behalf of the insurer notwithstanding the intermediary's entitlement.

(9) References in subsection (8) above to a payment include references to a payment in a form other than money.

(10) This section has effect for the purposes of this Part.

GENERAL NOTE
   The section provides a comprehensive definition of premium. A major change from the original proposal in that commission is included in the premium. Premiums paid other than in money are to be valued on an open market basis between independent parties. Instalments are to be treated as separate premiums. Payments received by an intermediary, including commission to which the intermediary is entitled, are to be treated as received by the insurer.

Interpretation: other provisions

   73.—(1) Unless the context otherwise requires—
       "accounting period" shall be construed in accordance with section 54
           above;
       "appeal tribunal" means a VAT and duties tribunal;
       "authorised person" means any person acting under the authority of the
           Commissioners;

"the Commissioners" means the Commissioners of Customs and
Excise;

"conduct" includes any act, omission or statement;

"insurer" means a person or body of persons (whether incorporated or
not) carrying on insurance business;

"legislation relating to insurance premium tax" means this Part (as
defined by subsection (9) below), any other enactment (whenever
passed) relating to insurance premium tax, and any subordinate
legislation made under any such enactment;

"prescribed" means prescribed by an order or regulations under this
Part;

"tax" means insurance premium tax;

"tax representative" shall be construed in accordance with section 57
above;

"taxable business" means a business which consists of or includes the
provision of insurance under taxable insurance contracts;

"taxable insurance contract" shall be construed in accordance with section 70 above.

(2) A risk is situated in the United Kingdom if, by virtue of section 96A(3)
of the Insurance Companies Act 1982, it is situated in the United Kingdom
for the purposes of that Act.

(3) A registrable person is a person who—

(a) is registered under section 53 above, or

(b) is liable to be registered under that section.

(4) A commercial ship is a ship which is—

(a) of a gross tonnage of 15 tons or more, and

(b) not designed or adapted for use for recreation or pleasure.

(5) A commercial aircraft is an aircraft which is—

(a) of a weight of 8,000 kilogrammes or more, and

(b) not designed or adapted for use for recreation or pleasure.

(6) A lifeboat is a vessel used or to be used solely for rescue or assistance at
sea; and lifeboat equipment is anything used or to be used solely in connection with a lifeboat.

(7) Foreign or international railway rolling stock is railway rolling stock
used principally for journeys taking place wholly or partly outside the United
Kingdom.

(8) Goods in foreign or international transit are goods in transit where
their carriage—

(a) begins and ends outside the United Kingdom,

(b) begins outside but ends in the United Kingdom, or

(c) ends outside but begins in the United Kingdom.

(9) A reference to this Part includes a reference to any order or regulations
made under it and a reference to a provision of this Part includes a reference
to any order or regulations made under the provision, unless otherwise
required by the context or any order or regulations.

(10) This section has effect for the purposes of this Part.

GENERAL NOTE

Subs. (1)
This provides the formal definition of terms used in Pt. III.

Subs. (2)
The definition in the Insurance Companies Act 1982 (c. 50), s.96A(3) is derived from E.C.
general insurance directives.

Subss. (4) and (5)
Commercial ships or aircraft are over 15 tons or 8,000 kg respectively and are not for recreation or pleasure.

Subs. (7)

International railway stock is stock used principally for journeys wholly or partly outside the U.K., *e.g. Eurostar.*

Subs. (8)

Goods are in international transit where the carriage at least commences or ends outside the U.K.

Orders and regulations

74.—(1) The power to make an order under section 61 above shall be exercisable by the Commissioners, and the power to make an order under any other provision of this Part shall be exercisable by the Treasury.

(2) Any power to make regulations under this Part shall be exercisable by the Commissioners.

(3) Any power to make an order or regulations under this Part shall be exercisable by statutory instrument.

(4) An order under section 71 above shall be laid before the House of Commons; and unless it is approved by that House before the expiration of a period of 28 days beginning with the date on which it was made it shall cease to have effect on the expiration of that period, but without prejudice to anything previously done under the order or to the making of a new order.

(5) In reckoning any such period as is mentioned in subsection (4) above no account shall be taken of any time during which Parliament is dissolved or prorogued or during which the House of Commons is adjourned for more than four days.

(6) A statutory instrument containing an order or regulations under this Part (other than an order under section 71 above) shall be subject to annulment in pursuance of a resolution of the House of Commons.

(7) Any power to make an order or regulations under this Part—

(a) may be exercised as regards prescribed cases or descriptions of case;

(b) may be exercised differently in relation to different cases or descriptions of case.

(8) An order or regulations under this Part may include such supplementary, incidental, consequential or transitional provisions as appear to the Treasury or the Commissioners (as the case may be) to be necessary or expedient.

(9) No specific provision of this Part about an order or regulations shall prejudice the generality of subsections (7) and (8) above.

GENERAL NOTE

This section is of some importance since much of the machinery of IPT is to be effected by orders and regulations.

Both orders and regulations are made by Statutory Instrument, orders by the Treasury and regulations by the Customs and Excise. Exceptionally, the order bringing into effect the review and appeal procedure under ss.59 and 60 will be made by the Customs and Excise.

Statutory Instruments will be subject to the negative resolution procedure in the House of Commons, except for an order under s.71 changing the scope of IPT, which will be subject to the passage of an affirmative resolution within 28 days.

PART IV

INCOME TAX, CORPORATION TAX AND CAPITAL GAINS TAX

CHAPTER I

GENERAL

Income tax: charge, rates and reliefs

Charge and rates of income tax for 1994–95

75.—(1) Income tax shall be charged for the year 1994–95, and for that year—
   (a) the lower rate shall be 20 per cent.,
   (b) the basic rate shall be 25 per cent., and
   (c) the higher rate shall be 40 per cent.
   (2) For the year 1994–95 section 1(2) of the Taxes Act 1988 shall apply as if—
   (a) the amount specified in paragraph (aa) were £3,000 (the lower rate limit), and
   (b) the amount specified in paragraph (b) were £23,700 (the basic rate limit);
and accordingly section 1(4) of that Act (indexation) shall not apply for the year 1994–95.

GENERAL NOTE
  For 1994–1995 the lower rate of tax of 20 per cent. applies to the first £3,000 of income. The basic rate remains at 25 per cent. and the higher rate is 40 per cent. on income over £23,700.

Personal allowance

76. Section 257 of the Taxes Act 1988 (personal allowance) shall apply for the year 1994–95 as if the amounts specified in it were the same as the amounts specified in it as it applies for the year 1993–94, and accordingly section 257C(1) of that Act (indexation) so far as relating to section 257 shall not apply for the year 1994–95.

GENERAL NOTE
  For 1994–1995 the ordinary personal allowances and personal age allowances remain as for 1993 and 1994, *i.e.* £3,445 for individuals aged under 65; £4,200 for those aged between 65 and 74 and £4,370 for those aged 75 and over. The income limit above which the personal age allowances are abated (see the ICTA 1988 (c. 1), s.257(5)) is unchanged at £14,200, as for 1993–1994.

Rate of relief to married couples etc.

77.—(1) The provisions of section 256 of the Taxes Act 1988 (general provision as to personal reliefs) shall become subsection (1) of that section and after that subsection there shall be inserted the following subsections—
   "(2) Where under any provision of this Chapter the relief to which a person is entitled for any year of assessment consists in an income tax reduction calculated by reference to a specified amount, the effect of that relief shall be that the amount of that person's liability for that year to income tax on his total income shall be the amount to which he would have been liable apart from that provision less whichever is the smaller of—
   (a) the amount equal to 20 per cent. of the specified amount; and
   (b) the amount which reduces his liability to nil.
   (3) In determining for the purposes of subsection (2) above the amount of income tax to which a person would be liable apart from any provision providing for an income tax reduction, no account shall be taken—
   (a) where that provision is section 259 or 261A, of any income tax reduction under any of the other provisions of this Chapter;

(b) where that provision is section 262(1), of any income tax reduction under any of the other provisions of this Chapter except section 259 or 261A; or

(c) whatever that provision—

    (i) of any relief by way of a reduction of liability to tax which is given in accordance with any arrangements having effect by virtue of section 788 or by way of a credit under section 790(1); or

    (ii) of any tax at the basic rate on so much of that person's income as is income the income tax on which he is entitled to charge against any other person or to deduct, retain or satisfy out of any payment;

but paragraph (a) above, so far as it relates to any income tax reduction under section 261A, is without prejudice to the provisions of subsection (2) of that section."

(2) In section 257A of that Act (married couple's allowance)—

(a) in subsection (1), for the words from "to a deduction" onwards there shall be substituted "for that year to an income tax reduction calculated by reference to £1,720";

(b) in subsection (2), for the words from "to a deduction" to "the deduction" there shall be substituted "for that year to an income tax reduction calculated by reference to £2,665 (instead of to the reduction"; and

(c) in subsection (3), for the words from "to a deduction" to "the deduction" there shall be substituted "for that year to an income tax reduction calculated by reference to £2,705 (instead of to the reduction".

(3) In section 259(2) of that Act (additional personal allowance), for "to a deduction from his total income of" there shall be substituted "for that year to an income tax reduction calculated by reference to".

(4) In section 261A(1) of that Act (additional personal allowance for a year in which spouses separate), for "to a deduction from his total income of" there shall be substituted "for that year to an income tax reduction calculated by reference to".

(5) In subsection (1) of section 262 of that Act (widow's bereavement allowance)—

(a) in paragraph (a), for "to a deduction from her total income of" there shall be substituted "to an income tax reduction calculated by reference to"; and

(b) in paragraph (b), for "to a deduction of" there shall be substituted "to an income tax reduction calculated by reference to".

(6) The Taxes Act 1988 and the Taxes Management Act 1970 shall have effect with the amendments specified in Schedule 8 to this Act (which supplements the provisions of this section).

(7) This section and Schedule 8 to this Act shall have effect for the year 1994–95 and, subject to the following provisions of this section, for subsequent years of assessment.

(8) For the year 1995–96 and subsequent years of assessment section 256(2)(a) of the Taxes Act 1988 shall have effect with the substitution of "15 per cent" for the words "20 per cent."

(9) For the year 1995–96, section 257A of the Taxes Act 1988 shall have effect—

(a) as if the same amount (namely £1,720) were specified in subsection (1) as is specified in that subsection as it applies for the year 1994–95;

(b) as if the amount specified in subsection (2) were "£2,995"; and

(c) as if the amount specified in subsection (3) were "£3,035".

(10) Section 257C(1) of the Taxes Act 1988 (indexation), so far as relating to section 257A (1) to (3) of that Act, shall not apply for the year 1994–95 or

for the year 1995–96 but shall not be prevented by anything in this section from applying for the year 1996–97 or any subsequent year of assessment.

GENERAL NOTE
The ordinary married couple's allowance, the single parent's allowance and the widow's bereavement allowance are frozen at £1,720 for 1994–1995 and 1995–1996. The married couple's age allowance (one spouse aged between 65 and 74) is increased to £2,665 for 1994–1995 and to £2,995 for 1995–1996. The higher married couple's age allowance (one spouse aged 75 and over) is increased to £2,705 for 1994–1995 and to £3,305 for 1995–1996.
From 1994–1995 onwards, the allowances are to be given by reduction from the claimant's income tax liability instead of by deduction from total income. The reduction is restricted to (a) 20 per cent. (15 per cent. for 1995–1996 onwards) of the amount of the allowance or (b) the amount which reduces the income tax liability to nil, if lower.

Amount by reference to which MCA is reduced

78. Section 257A(5) of the Taxes Act 1988 (reduction of married couple's allowance if claimant's total income exceeds a certain amount) shall apply for the year 1994–95 as if the amount specified in it were the same as the amount specified in it as it applies for the year 1993–94, and accordingly section 257C(1) of that Act (indexation) so far as relating to section 257A(5) shall not apply for the year 1994–95.

GENERAL NOTE
The income limit for married couple's age allowance is frozen at £14,200 for 1994–1995 as for 1993–1994.

Relief for maintenance payments

79.—(1) Sections 347A and 347B of the Taxes Act 1988 and section 38 of the Finance Act 1988 (which contain provision with respect to the deductions from income allowed on account of maintenance payments) shall have effect in relation to payments becoming due on or after 6th April 1994 with the following modifications.

(2) Section 347A (which restricts the making of deductions) shall apply to any payment made—

(a) in pursuance of any obligation which falls within paragraphs (a) to (c) of subsection (4) of section 36 of the Finance Act 1988 (existing obligations) and is an obligation under an order made by a court, a written or oral agreement or a deed executed for giving effect to an agreement, and

(b) for the benefit, maintenance or education of a person (whether or not the person to whom the payment is made) who attained the age of 21 on or before the day on which the payment became due but after 5th April 1994,

as if that obligation were not an existing obligation within the definition contained in that subsection.

(3) In subsection (2) of section 347B (relief for qualifying maintenance payments)—

(a) the words "Notwithstanding section 347A(1)(a) but" shall be omitted; and

(b) for the words from "in computing" to "to deduct" there shall be substituted "for a year of assessment to an income tax reduction calculated by reference to".

(4) In subsection (3) of section 347B (restriction of relief to amount of married couple's allowance), for the words from the beginning to "exceed"

there shall be substituted "The amount by reference to which any income tax reduction is to be calculated under this section shall be limited to".

(5) In subsection (5) of section 347B (other payments attracting relief), for "otherwise than under this section" there shall be substituted "by virtue of section 36(3) of the Finance Act 1988 but otherwise than in accordance with section 38(2)(a) of that Act".

(6) After subsection (5) of section 347B there shall be inserted the following subsections—

"(5A) Where any person is entitled under this section for any year of assessment to an income tax reduction calculated by reference to the amount determined in accordance with subsections (2) to (5) above ('the relevant amount'), the amount of that person's liability for that year to income tax on his total income shall be the amount to which he would have been liable apart from this section less whichever is the smaller of—

(a) the amount equal to the appropriate percentage of the relevant amount; and

(b) the amount which reduces his liability to nil;

and in this subsection 'the appropriate percentage' means 20 per cent. for the year 1994–95 and 15 per cent. for the year 1995–96 and subsequent years of assessment.

(5B) In determining for the purposes of subsection (5A) above the amount of income tax to which a person would be liable apart from any income tax reduction under this section, no account shall be taken of—

(a) any income tax reduction under Chapter I of Part VII;

(b) any relief by way of a reduction of liability to tax which is given in accordance with any arrangements having effect by virtue of section 788 or by way of a credit under section 790(1); or

(c) any tax at the basic rate on so much of that person's income as is income the income tax on which he is entitled to charge against any other person or to deduct, retain or satisfy out of any payment."

(7) In subsection (3) of section 38 (amount of relief in transitional cases for persons making payments), for the words from the word "aggregate", in the first place where it occurs, to "exceed" there shall be substituted "amount (if any) by which the relevant aggregate exceeds the amount specified in section 257A(1) of the Taxes Act 1988 for the year; and in this subsection and subsection (3A) below 'the relevant aggregate' means whichever is the smaller of the following, that is to say, the aggregate amount of the payments made by him which fall due in that year and to which this section applies and".

(8) After subsection (3) of section 38 there shall be inserted the following subsection—

"(3A) Sections 347A and 347B of the Taxes Act 1988 (except, in the case of section 347A, so far as it restricts the extent to which any payment is to be treated as forming part of the income of the person to whom it is made or any other person) shall have effect as if so much of the relevant aggregate for any year of assessment as does not exceed the amount specified for that year in section 257A(1) of that Act were a qualifying maintenance payment made otherwise than in pursuance of an existing obligation."

GENERAL NOTE

Relief for maintenance payments made under obligations which arose after March 14, 1988 is restricted to 20 per cent. for 1994–1995 and 15 per cent. for 1995–1996 on the first £1,720 of payments.

From 1994–1995 onwards, the relief will be given by income tax reduction in line with the relief for the married couple's allowance. Relief for the first £1,720 of maintenance payments made under obligations which existed as at March 14, 1988 will be given as above. The excess over £1,720 and up to the lesser of the aggregate payments due in the tax year and the amount in respect of which the payer was entitled to relief for 1988–1989, continues to qualify as a deduction from total income.

The ICTA 1988 (c. 1), s.347A is amended so that relief is no longer available for maintenance payments paid to children once they reach the age of 21 after April 5, 1994; conversely the payments are not treated as the recipient's income. This applies whether the payments are made directly to the person for whose benefit they are made or whether they are made to a third party.

Limit on relief for interest

80. For each of the years 1994–95 and 1995–96 the qualifying maximum defined in section 367(5) of the Taxes Act 1988 (limit on relief for interest on certain loans) shall be £30,000.

GENERAL NOTE

The maximum loan on which mortgage interest relief is available is unchanged at £30,000 for 1994–1995 and 1995–1996.

Mortgage interest relief etc.

81.—(1) For subsection (1) of section 353 of the Taxes Act 1988 (general provision for relief for interest payments) there shall be substituted the following subsection—

"(1) Where a person pays interest in any year of assessment, that person, if he makes a claim to the relief, shall for that year of assessment be entitled (subject to sections 354 to 368) to relief in accordance with this section in respect of so much (if any) of the amount of that interest as is eligible for relief under this section by virtue of sections 354 to 365."

(2) After that subsection there shall be inserted the following subsections—

"(1A) Where a person is entitled for any year of assessment to relief under this section in respect of any amount of interest which—

(a) is eligible for that relief by virtue of section 354 or 365, and

(b) so far as eligible by virtue of section 354, is so eligible in a case which falls, or is treated as falling, within section 355(1)(a), 356 or 358,

that relief shall consist in an income tax reduction for that year calculated by reference to that amount.

(1B) Where a person is entitled for any year of assessment to relief under this section in respect of any amount of interest which—

(a) is eligible for that relief otherwise than by virtue of section 354 or 365, or

(b) is eligible for that relief by virtue of section 354 in a case falling within section 355(1)(b),

that relief shall consist (subject to sections 237(5)(b) and 355(4)) in a deduction or set-off of that amount from or against that person's income for that year.

(1C) Without prejudice to subsection (1E) below, where the whole or any part of an amount of interest is eligible for relief under this section by virtue of section 354 in a case which (apart from this subsection) would fall, or be treated as falling, within both section 355(1)(a) or 356 and section 355(1)(b), then that case shall be treated for the purposes of this section and the following provisions of this Act—

(a) except in relation to payments to which an election made for the purposes of this subsection by the person entitled to the relief applies, as falling within section 355(1)(b) and not within section 355(1)(a) or 356; and

(b) in relation to payments to which such an election does apply, as falling within section 355(1)(a) or, as the case may be, 356, and not within section 355(1)(b).

(1D) An election for the purposes of subsection (1C)—

    (a) shall be made, and may be withdrawn, by the giving of written notice to an officer of the Board;

    (b) shall apply to every payment of interest which—

        (i) is made after the time specified in the notice of that election as the time as from which it takes effect; and

        (ii) is not made after a time specified in a notice of the withdrawal of that election as the time as from which that election is withdrawn;

    (c) shall not be made so as to take effect as from any time except the beginning of a year of assessment or a time as from which the conditions for the case to fall, or be treated as falling, within both section 355(1)(a) or 356 and section 355(1)(b) have begun to be satisfied in relation to payments of interest on the loan in question;

    (d) shall not be withdrawn except as from the beginning of a year of assessment; and

    (e) shall not be made so as to take effect, and shall not be withdrawn, as from any time before the beginning of the year of assessment immediately before that in which the notice of the election or, as the case may be, of the withdrawal is given to an officer of the Board.

(1E) Where any person is entitled for any year of assessment to relief under this section in respect of any amount of interest as is eligible for that relief partly as mentioned in subsection (1A) above and partly as mentioned in subsection (1B) above, that amount of interest shall be apportioned between the cases to which each of those subsections applies without regard to what parts of the total amount borrowed remain outstanding but according to the following factors, that is to say—

    (a) the proportions of the total amount borrowed which were applied for different purposes; and

    (b) in the case of so much of any amount of interest which is, or in pursuance of an apportionment under paragraph (a) above is treated as, eligible for relief by virtue of section 354, the different uses to which the land or other property in question is put from time to time;

and subsection (1A) or (1B) above shall apply accordingly in relation to the interest apportioned to the case to which that subsection applies.

(1F) Where any person is entitled under this section for any year of assessment to an income tax reduction calculated by reference to an amount of interest, the amount of that person's liability for that year to income tax on his total income shall be the amount to which he would have been liable apart from this section less whichever is the smaller of—

    (a) the amount equal to the applicable percentage of that amount of interest; and

    (b) the amount which reduces his liability to nil.

(1G) In subsection (1F) above 'the applicable percentage'—

    (a) in relation to so much of any interest as is eligible for relief under this section by virtue of section 354, means 20 per cent.; and

    (b) in relation to so much of any interest as is eligible for relief under this section by virtue of section 365, means the percentage which is the basic rate for the year of assessment in question;

but, in relation to any payment of interest which (whenever falling due) is made in the year 1995–96 or any subsequent year of assessment, paragraph (a) above shall have effect with the substitution of '15 per cent.' for '20 per cent.'

(1H) In determining for the purposes of subsection (1F) above the amount of income tax to which a person would be liable apart from any income tax reduction under this section, no account shall be taken of—

(a) any income tax reduction under Chapter I of Part VII or section 347B;

(b) any relief by way of a reduction of liability to tax which is given in accordance with any arrangements having effect by virtue of section 788 or by way of a credit under section 790(1); or

(c) any tax at the basic rate on so much of that person's income as is income the income tax on which he is entitled to charge against any other person or to deduct, retain or satisfy out of any payment."

(3) In subsection (1) of section 369 of that Act (deduction at source of mortgage interest relief), for the words from "income tax" onwards there shall be substituted "the applicable percentage thereof." and after that subsection there shall be inserted the following subsection—

"(1A) In subsection (1) above 'the applicable percentage'—

(a) in relation to so much of any payment of relevant loan interest as is not a payment in relation to which paragraph (b) below has effect, means 20 per cent.; and

(b) in relation to so much of any payment as—

(i) has become due before 6th April 1994; or

(ii) being a payment becoming due on or after 6th April 1994, would, apart from section 353(2), be eligible for relief under section 353 by virtue of section 365,

means the percentage which is the basic rate for the year of assessment in which the payment has become or becomes due;

but, in relation to any payment of interest which becomes due in the year 1995–96 or any subsequent year of assessment, paragraph (a) above shall have effect with the substitution of '15 per cent.' for '20 per cent.' "

(4) For subsections (3) to (5B) of section 369 of that Act (provisions balancing deduction of relevant loan interest from income against charge to tax) there shall be substituted the following subsection—

"(3) The following payments, that is to say—

(a) payments of relevant loan interest to which this section applies, and

(b) payments which would be such payments but for section 373(5),

shall not be allowable as deductions for any purpose of the Income Tax Acts except in so far as they fall to be treated as such payments by virtue only of section 375(2) and would be allowable apart from this subsection."

(5) Schedule 9 to this Act (which for the purposes of or in connection with the provisions of this section makes further modifications of certain enactments in relation to tax relief on interest payments) shall have effect.

(6) The preceding provisions of this section and that Schedule—

(a) shall have effect in relation to payments of interest made on or after 6th April 1994 (whenever falling due); and

(b) shall also have effect, so far as they relate to relevant loan interest, in relation to any payments of interest becoming due on or after 6th April 1994 which have been made at any time before that date but on or after 30th November 1993.

(7) Any provision made before the passing of this Act by reference to the basic rate of income tax and contained in any instrument or agreement under or in accordance with which payments of relevant loan interest have been or are to be made shall be taken, in relation to any such payment as is mentioned in subsection (6)(a) or (b) above, to have been made, instead, by reference to a rate which, in the case of that payment, is the applicable percentage for the purposes of subsection (1) of section 369 of the Taxes Act 1988.

(8) Section 377 of the Taxes Act 1988 (variation of terms of repayment of certain loans) shall have effect—
  (a) as if the references in subsections (3), (4) and (7) of that section to a change in the basic rate of income tax included references to the amendments having effect by virtue of this section and to any change in the applicable percentage for the time being specified in section 369(1A) of that Act; and
  (b) in relation to any notice under section 377(2)(a) of that Act the effective date of which is on or after 6th April 1994, as if the reference to tax at the basic rate for the year of assessment in which that date falls, were a reference to tax at a rate equal to the percentage which is the applicable percentage for the purposes of section 369(1) of that Act in relation to payments becoming due in that year of assessment.

(9) In this section "relevant loan interest" has the same meaning as in Part IX of the Taxes Act 1988.

GENERAL NOTE
The ICTA 1988 (c. 1), s.353(1) is amended so that relief is available (subject to the ICTA 1988 (c. 1), ss.354–368) for any interest paid after April 5, 1994, without the previous complicated restrictions in that subsection. This will benefit non-U.K. resident borrowers since their interest payments need not have a U.K. source to be eligible for relief.

The rate of relief for mortgage interest (including those within MIRAS) is reduced to 20 per cent. for 1994–1995 and 15 per cent. from 1995–1996 onwards. Relief for mortgage interest due before April 6, 1994 and for interest on loans to buy life annuities remains unchanged at 25 per cent.

From 1994–1995 onwards, where relief is not given by deduction at source under MIRAS, relief will be given by income tax reduction (in line with the relief for the married couple's allowance) and is limited to the amount of income tax to which the individual would otherwise be liable. In determining the taxpayer's income tax liability, interest relief is calculated before other reliefs due to the taxpayer.

Relief for interest on other eligible loans (including interest on property that is let) continues to be given by deduction from taxable income. If the property is partly main residence and partly let, the relief is given by deduction from taxable income, unless the borrower elects, in writing, for the relief to be given by way of income tax reduction. If the loan was used for more than one purpose or there is a change of use in the property, the interest is to be apportioned between the parts qualifying for relief by income tax reduction and by deduction from taxable income respectively.

Relief for blind persons

82.—(1) In section 265(1) of the Taxes Act 1988 (blind person's allowance) for "£1,080" there shall be substituted "£1,200".

(2) This section shall apply for the year 1994–95 and subsequent years of assessment.

GENERAL NOTE
The blind person's allowance is increased to £1,200 for 1994–1995 and subsequent years.

Medical insurance

83. Schedule 10 to this Act (which contains provisions about medical insurance) shall have effect.

Relief for vocational training

84.—(1) In subsection (1) of section 32 of the Finance Act 1991 (relief for vocational training), after paragraph (c) there shall be inserted the following paragraphs—
  "(ca) the individual has attained school-leaving age and, if under the age of nineteen, is not a person who is being provided with full-time education at a school,
  (cb) the individual undertakes the course neither wholly nor mainly for recreational purposes or as a leisure activity,".

(2) In subsection (10) of that section, the words after paragraph (b) (which exclude from the qualifying courses those programmes of activity capable of counting towards a qualification at the highest defined level) shall be omitted.

(3) After subsection (10) of that section there shall be inserted the following subsection—

"(11) In this section—

'school' means any institution at which full-time education is provided to persons at least some of whom are under school-leaving age; and

'school-leaving age' means the age of sixteen."

(4) This section has effect in relation to payments made on or after 1st January 1994.

GENERAL NOTE

From January 1, 1994 tax relief for vocational training is extended to all levels of the National Vocational Qualifications. As from that date, relief is no longer available for (a) children aged up to 18 in full-time education at a school, and (b) training undertaken wholly or mainly for recreational purposes or as a leisure activity.

Corporation tax charge and rate

Charge and rate of corporation tax for 1994

85. Corporation tax shall be charged for the financial year 1994 at the rate of 33 per cent.

GENERAL NOTE

The rate of corporation tax for the 1994 financial year is 33 per cent.

Small companies

86.—(1) For the financial year 1994—

(a) the small companies' rate shall be 25 per cent., and

(b) the fraction mentioned in section 13(2) of the Taxes Act 1988 (marginal relief for small companies) shall be one fiftieth.

(2) In section 13(3) of that Act (limits of marginal relief) in paragraphs (a) and (b)—

(a) for "£250,000" there shall be substituted "£300,000", and

(b) for "£1,250,000" there shall be substituted "£1,500,000".

(3) Subsection (2) above shall have effect for the financial year 1994 and subsequent financial years; and where by virtue of that subsection section 13 of the Taxes Act 1988 has effect with different relevant maximum amounts in relation to different parts of a company's accounting period, then for the purposes of that section those parts shall be treated as if they were separate accounting periods and the profits and basic profits of the company for that period shall be apportioned between those parts.

GENERAL NOTE

The small companies rate remains at 25 per cent. The profit limit for the small companies rate is increased to £300,000. Marginal relief applies up to £1,500,000. The marginal relief fraction is unchanged at one-fiftieth giving a marginal rate of 35 per cent. on profits between £300,000 and £1,500,000. The new limits apply for the 1994 financial year onwards.

Benefits in kind

Car fuel

87.—(1) In section 158 of the Taxes Act 1988 (car fuel) for the Tables in subsection (2) (tables of cash equivalents) there shall be substituted—

"TABLE A

Cylinder capacity of car in cubic centimetres	Cash equivalent
1,400 or less	£640
More than 1,400 but not more than 2,000	£810
More than 2,000	£1,200

TABLE AB

Cylinder capacity of car in cubic centimetres	Cash equivalent
2,000 or less	£580
More than 2,000	£750

TABLE B

Description of car	Cash equivalent
Any car	£1,200"

(2) This section shall have effect for the year 1994–95 and subsequent years of assessment.

GENERAL NOTE
    The scale charges for fuel provided for private motoring in a company car, has been increased, for 1994–1995 and subsequent tax years. The FA 1993 (c. 34), Sched. 3, para. (6) which prospectively set the charges for 1994–1995 is made redundant.

Beneficial loan arrangements

88.—(1) In section 160(1) of the Taxes Act 1988 (charge to tax of benefit of loan obtained by reason of employment) for the words following paragraph (b) there shall be substituted—
    "an amount equal to whatever is the cash equivalent of the benefit of the loan for that year shall, subject to the provisions of this Chapter, be treated as emoluments of the employment, and accordingly chargeable to tax under Schedule E; and where that amount is so treated, the employee is to be treated as having paid interest on the loan in that year of the same amount.
    (1A) Interest treated as paid by virtue of subsection (1) above—
    (a) shall be treated as paid for all the purposes of the Tax Acts (other than this Chapter, including Schedule 7), but shall not be treated for any purpose as income of the person making the loan or be treated as relevant loan interest to which section 369 applies, and
    (b) shall be treated as accruing during, and paid by the employee at the end of, the year or, if different, the period in the year during which he is employed in employment to which this Chapter applies and the loan is outstanding.
    (1B) All the loan between the same lender and borrower which—
    (a) are outstanding at any time, as to any amount, in any year,
    (b) are not qualifying loans, and
    (c) are made in the same currency,
are, if a cash equivalent for them falls to be ascertained, to be treated for the purposes of subsections (1) and (1A) above and Part II of Schedule 7 as a single loan.

(1C) In this section and section 161 "qualifying loan" means any loan made to any person where, assuming interest is being paid on the loan (whether or not it is in fact being paid), the whole or any part of the interest—

(a) is eligible for relief under section 353 or would be so eligible but for subsection (2) of that section or section 357(1)(b), or

(b) is deductible in computing the amount of the profits or gains to be charged under Case I or II of Schedule D in respect of a trade, profession or vocation carried on by him."

(2) At the end of section 160(5) of that Act (interpretation, including "official rate of interest") there shall be added—

"and, without prejudice to the generality of section 178 of the Finance Act 1989, regulations under that section may make different provision in relation to a loan outstanding for the whole or part of a year if—

(i) it was made in the currency of a country or territory outside the United Kingdom,

(ii) the benefit of the loan is obtained by reason of the employment of a person who normally lives in that country or territory, and

(iii) that person has lived in that country or territory at some time in the period of six years ending with that year".

(3) For section 161(1) of that Act (exemption for loans the cash equivalent of which does not exceed £300) there shall be substituted—

"(1) The cash equivalent of the benefit of any such loan as is referred to in section 160(1) is not to be treated as emoluments of the employment if—

(a) at no time in the year does the amount outstanding on the loan (or, if two or more such loans as are referred to in section 160(1) are outstanding in the year, the aggregate of the amounts outstanding on them) exceed £5000, or

(b) where paragraph (a) above does not apply, the loan is not a qualifying loan and at no time in the year does the amount outstanding on the loan (or, if two or more such loans as are referred to in section 160(1) and are not qualifying loans are outstanding in the year, the aggregate of the amounts outstanding on them) exceed £5000.

(1A) Section 160(1) does not in any year apply to a loan made at any time in that or an earlier year by a person in the ordinary course of a business carried on by him which includes the lending of money if—

(a) comparable loans were available, at the time the loan in question was made, to all those who might be expected to avail themselves of the services which he provides in the course of that business,

(b) of the total number of the loan in question and comparable loans made by him at or about the time the loan in question was made, a substantial proportion were made to members of the public at large with whom he was dealing at arm's length, and

(c) the loan in question, and comparable loans in general made by him at or about that time to members of the public at large with whom he was dealing at arm's length, are held on the same terms and, if those terms differ from the terms applicable immediately after the loan was first made, they were imposed in the ordinary course of his business.

(1B) For the purposes of subsection (1A) above, a loan is comparable to the loan in question if it is made for the same or similar purposes, and on the same terms and conditions, as that loan."

(4) In Schedule 7 to that Act (beneficial loan arrangements)—

(a) in paragraph 1(5) for "Sub-paragraph (2) above does" there shall be substituted "Sub-paragraphs (2) and (4) above do" and the words "his employer, being" shall cease to have effect, and

(b) Parts III to V shall cease to have effect.

(5) In determining for the purposes of section 161(1A) and (1B) of that Act (inserted by this section) whether any loans made by any person before 1st June 1994 are made or held on the same terms or conditions, there shall be left out of account any amounts, by way of fees, commission or other incidental expenses, incurred for the purpose of obtaining any of those loans by the persons to whom they are made.

(6) This section shall have effect for the year 1994–95 and subsequent years of assessment.

GENERAL NOTE

An employee in receipt of a reduced rate or interest free loan is to be taxed under Sched. E on the cash equivalent of the benefit (the "official rate" of interest applied to the loan). Such an employee is deemed to have paid interest equal to the amount charged and may claim relief on beneficial "qualifying loans". Relief, however, is restricted to 20 per cent. (15 per cent. from 1995–1996 onwards) as with other home loans. The deemed interest is treated as accruing during and paid at the end of, the year of assessment (if the loan ceases, or the employment is terminated, during the year, the accrual period and deemed payment date change accordingly).

When calculating the cash equivalent, all non-qualifying loans in the same currency from the same lender that are outstanding in the tax year are to be treated as a single loan. The previous exemption from tax where the cash equivalent on beneficial loans did not exceed £300 is replaced with an exemption for loans totalling up to £5,000.

Loans provided to employees on the same terms as loans regularly provided to the general public by the employer in the course of his business are exempt from the Sched. E charge. The Treasury may set different "official rates" of interest for foreign currency loans to employees who live or have lived abroad. The provisions above have effect for the year 1994–1995 and subsequent years.

Vouchers and credit-tokens

89.—(1) Section 141 of the Taxes Act 1988 (non-cash vouchers) shall be amended as follows.

(2) In subsection (1)—

(a) in paragraph (a), for the words from "the expense incurred" to "exchanged;" there shall be substituted "the expense incurred ("the chargeable expense")—

    (i) by the person at whose cost the voucher and the money, goods or services for which it is capable of being exchanged are provided,

    (ii) in or in connection with that provision;" and

(b) the words following paragraph (b) shall be omitted.

(3) In subsection (6B), in paragraph (a) for the words "the person providing the non-cash voucher" there shall be substituted "the person at whose cost the voucher and the entertainment are provided".

(4) Section 142 of the Taxes Act 1988 (credit-tokens) shall be amended as follows.

(5) In subsection (1)(a), for the words from "expense incurred" to "obtained;" there shall be substituted "the expense incurred—

    (i) by the person at whose cost the money, goods or services are provided,

    (ii) in or in connection with that provision;".

(6) In subsection (3) for the words "providing the credit-token as mentioned in subsection (1)(a) above" there shall be substituted "mentioned in subsection (1)(a)(i) above".

(7) In subsection (3B), in paragraph (a) for the words "providing the credit-token" there shall be substituted "mentioned in subsection (1)(a)(i) above".

(8) Section 143 of the Taxes Act 1988 (cash vouchers) shall be amended as follows.

(9) In subsection (1) for the words from "(and in particular section 203)" to "paid by his employer" there shall be substituted "—
    (a) he shall be treated as having received".

(10) In subsection (3) for the words "in providing the voucher by the person who provides it" there shall be substituted "by the person at whose cost the voucher is provided".

(11) In subsection (4)—
    (a) in paragraph (a) for the words "in providing the voucher by the person who provides it" there shall be substituted "by the person at whose cost the voucher, stamp or similar document is provided"; and
    (b) in the words following paragraph (b) for the words from "the expense incurred" to the end there shall be substituted "the expense incurred by the person mentioned in paragraph (a) above shall be treated as reduced by the difference or part of the difference mentioned in paragraph (b) above."

(12) Section 144 of the Taxes Act 1988 (supplementary provisions relating to sections 141 to 143) shall be amended as follows.

(13) In subsection (1)—
    (a) for the words "or credit-tokens" there shall be substituted ", credit-tokens or cash vouchers"; and
    (b) for the words "141 or 142" there shall be substituted "141, 142 or 143".

(14) In subsection (3)—
    (a) for the words "141 or 142" there shall be substituted "141, 142 and 143"; and
    (b) for the words "by him of non-cash" there shall be substituted "of".

GENERAL NOTE

Non-cash vouchers
An employee who receives a non-cash voucher by reason of his employment is to be taxed on the amount incurred by the person at whose cost the voucher and the money, goods or services are provided in or in connection with their provision. This provision is effective from May 3, 1994.

The exemption from tax in the ICTA 1988 (c. 1), s.141(6B) is amended to ensure that the person at whose cost the voucher and entertainment are provided must not be the employer or a person connected with the employer and that neither the employer nor a connected person have directly or indirectly provided the entertainment.

Credit tokens
Parallel changes are made to the rules governing the provision of credit tokens.

Cash vouchers
The definition of cash voucher is amended so that it refers to the expense incurred by the person at whose cost the voucher is provided. The provision of a cash voucher is treated as a receipt of an emolument by the employee and subject to PAYE under s.130 below.

Chargeable gains

Annual exempt amount for 1994–95

90. For the year 1994–95 section 3 of the Taxation of Chargeable Gains Act 1992 (annual exempt amount) shall have effect as if the amount specified in subsection (2) were £5,800, and accordingly subsection (3) of that section (indexation) shall not apply for that year.

GENERAL NOTE
The annual exempt amount for capital gains tax remains unchanged at £5,800.

Relief on re-investment

91.—(1) Schedule 11 to this Act (which extends the relief on re-investment for individuals and trustees provided by Chapter IA of Part V of the Taxation of Chargeable Gains Act 1992) shall have effect.

(2) That Schedule shall have effect in relation to disposals made on or after 30th November 1993.

(3) In section 164H(1) of that Act—

(a) for "is greater than" there shall be substituted "exceeds", and

(b) at the end there shall be added "or half the value of the company's assets as a whole (whichever is the greater); and section 294(3) and (4) of the Taxes Act (meaning of value of company's assets as a whole) applies for the purposes of his subsection as it applies for the purposes of section 294 of that Act".

(4) Subsection (3) above shall apply to determine whether a company is a qualifying company on or after 30th November 1993.

GENERAL NOTE

Schedule 11 (extension of roll-over relief on reinvestment) is introduced. For the purposes of entrepreneur relief, a company is not a qualifying company if the value of its interests in land exceeds the greater of half its chargeable assets or half its total assets.

Relief on retirement

92.—(1) In paragraph 13(1) of Schedule 6 to the Taxation of Chargeable Gains Act 1992 (amount available for relief on retirement)—

(a) in paragraph (a) (gains not exceeding appropriate percentage of £150,000) for "£150,000" there shall be substituted "£250,000", and

(b) in paragraph (b) (half gains not exceeding that percentage of £150,000 to £600,000) for "£150,000" and "£600,000" there shall be substituted respectively "£250,000" and "£1 million".

(2) This section shall have effect in relation to disposals made on or after 30th November 1993.

GENERAL NOTE

For disposals made after November 29, 1993, the limits for full retirement relief and half retirement relief are increased to £250,000 and £1 million respectively.

Indexation losses

93.—(1) In section 53 of the Taxation of Chargeable Gains Act 1992 (indexation allowance), in subsection (1), for the words following "contrary" to the end of paragraph (c) there shall be substituted "if on the disposal of an asset there is an unindexed gain, an allowance ("the indexation allowance") shall be allowed against the unindexed gain—

(a) so as to give the gain for the purposes of this Act, or

(b) if the indexation allowance equals or exceeds the unindexed gain, so as to extinguish it (in which case the disposal shall be one on which, after taking account of the indexation allowance, neither a gain nor a loss accrues)".

(2) In subsection (2) of that section—

(a) for "subsection (1) above" there shall be substituted "this Chapter",

(b) for paragraph (a) there shall be substituted—

"(a) "unindexed gain" means the amount of the gain on the disposal computed in accordance with this Part", and

(c) in paragraph (b), for "gain or loss" there shall be substituted "gain".

(3) After that subsection there shall be inserted—

"(2A) Notwithstanding anything in section 16 of this Act, this section shall not apply to a disposal on which a loss accrues."

(4) In section 55 of that Act (assets acquired on a no gain/no loss disposal), after subsection (6) there shall be inserted—

"(7) The rules in subsection (8) below apply (after the application of section 53 but before the application of section 35(3) or (4)) to give the gain or loss for the purposes of this Act where—

(a) subsection (6) above applies to the disposal (the "disposal in question") of an asset by any person (the "transferor"), and

(b) but for paragraph (b) of that subsection, the consideration the transferor would be treated as having given for the asset would include an amount or amounts of indexation allowance brought into account by virtue of section 56(2) on any disposal made before 30th November 1993.

(8) The rules are as follows—

(a) where (apart from this subsection) there would be a loss, an amount equal to the rolled-up indexation shall be added to it so as to increase it,

(b) where (apart from this subsection) the unindexed gain or loss would be nil, there shall be a loss of an amount equal to the rolled-up indexation, and

(c) where (apart from this subsection)—

(i) there would be an unindexed gain, and

(ii) the gain or loss would be nil but the amount of the indexation allowance used to extinguish the gain would be less than the rolled-up indexation,

the difference shall constitute a loss.

(9) In this section the "rolled-up indexation" means, subject to subsections (10) and (11) below, the amount or, as the case may be, the aggregate of the amounts referred to in subsection (7)(b) above; and subsections (10) and (11) below shall, as well as applying on the disposal in question, be treated as having applied on any previous part disposal by the transferor.

(10) Where, for the purposes of any disposal of the asset by the transferor, any amount falling within any, or any combination of, paragraphs (a) to (c) of section 38(1) is required by any enactment to be excluded, reduced or written down, the amount or aggregate referred to in subsection (9) above (or so much of it as remains after the application of this subsection and subsection (11) below on a previous part disposal) shall be reduced in proportion to any reduction made in the amount falling within the paragraph, or the combination of paragraphs, in question.

(11) Where the transferor makes a part disposal of the asset at any time, then, for the purposes of that and any subsequent disposal, the amount or aggregate referred to in subsection (9) above (or so much of it as remains after the application of this subsection and subsection (10) above on a previous part disposal by him or after the application of subsection (10) above on the part disposal) shall be apportioned between the property disposed of and the property which remains in the same proportions as the sums falling within section 38(1)(a) and (b)."

(5) In section 56 of that Act (amount of consideration on no gain/no loss disposals)—

(a) in subsection (2) for the words preceding paragraph (a) there shall be substituted "On a no gain/no loss disposal by any person ("the transferor")", and

(b) after that subsection there shall be added—

"(3) Where apart from this subsection—

(a) a loss would accrue on the disposal of an asset, and

(b) the sums allowable as a deduction in computing that loss would include an amount attributable to the application of the assumption in subsection (2) above on any no gain/no loss disposal made on or after 30th November 1993,

those sums shall be determined as if that subsection had not applied on any such disposal made on or after that date and the loss shall be reduced accordingly or, if those sums are then equal to or less than the consideration for the disposal, the disposal shall be one on which neither a gain nor a loss accrues.

(4) For the purposes of this section a no gain/no loss disposal is one which, by virtue of any enactment other than section 35(4), 53(1) or this section, is treated as a disposal on which neither a gain nor a loss accrues to the person making the disposal."

(6) In section 110 of that Act (indexation allowance for share pools), after subsection (6) there shall be inserted—

"(6A) Where a disposal to a person acquiring or adding to a new holding is treated by virtue of any enactment as one on which neither a gain nor a loss accrues to the person making the disposal—

(a) section 56(2) shall not apply to the disposal (and, accordingly, the amount of the consideration shall not be calculated on the assumption that a gain of an amount equal to the indexation allowance accrues to the person making the disposal), but

(b) an amount equal to the indexation allowance on the disposal shall be added to the indexed pool of expenditure for the holding acquired or, as the case may be, held by the person to whom the disposal is made (and, where it is added to the indexed pool of expenditure for a holding so held, it shall be added after any increase required by subsection (8)(a) below)."

(7) Sections 103 (collective investment schemes, etc.), 111 (building society etc. shares), 182 to 184 (groups and associated companies) and 200 (oil industry assets) of that Act (all of which relate to indexation allowance) shall cease to have effect.

(8) In Schedule 7A to that Act (restriction on set-off of pre-entry losses), in paragraph 2—

(a) in sub-paragraph (2), for the definitions of "B" and "C" there shall be substituted—

"B is the amount of the item of relevant allowable expenditure for which an amount falls to be determined under this paragraph;

C is the total amount of all the relevant allowable expenditure",

(b) in sub-paragraph (4), "except in relation to the calculation of any indexed rise" shall cease to have effect,

(c) after sub-paragraph (8) there shall be inserted—

"(8A) Where by virtue of section 55(8) the allowable loss accruing on the disposal of a pre-entry asset, or any part of the loss, is attributable to an amount ("the rolled-up amount") of rolled-up indexation (as defined in section 55(9) to (11)), then, for the purposes of this paragraph—

(a) the total amount of all the relevant allowable expenditure shall be treated as increased by the rolled-up amount, and

(b) the amount of each item of relevant allowable expenditure shall be treated as increased by so much (if any) of the rolled-up amount as is attributable to that item.

(8B) Where—

(a) section 56(3) applies on the disposal of a pre-entry asset on which an allowable loss accrues, and

(b) in accordance with that subsection, the total amount of all the relevant allowable expenditure is reduced by any amount ("the global reduction"), the amount of each item of relevant allowable expenditure shall be treated for the purposes of this paragraph as reduced by so much (if any) of the global reduction as is attributable to that item", and

(d) in sub-paragraph (9), the definition of "indexed rise" shall cease to have effect.

(9) In paragraph 4 of that Schedule—

(a) in sub-paragraph (12) the words from "together" to the end, and

(b) sub-paragraph (13),

shall cease to have effect.

(10) In paragraph 5 of that Schedule, after sub-paragraph (2) there shall be inserted—

"(2A) In determining for the purposes of sub-paragraph (2)(a) above the amount of any loss which would have accrued if the asset had been disposed of at the relevant time at its market value at that time—

(a) it shall be assumed that the amendments of this Act made by section 93(1) to (5) of the Finance Act 1994 (indexation losses) had effect in relation to that disposal and, accordingly,

(b) references in those amendments and in subsection (11) of that section to November 30, 1993 shall be read as references to the day on which the relevant time falls."

(11) This section shall have effect in relation to disposals made on or after 30th November 1993 and Schedule 12 to this Act (which gives transitional relief) shall have effect for the years 1993–94 and 1994–95.

GENERAL NOTE

Restriction of indexation allowance

For disposals made after November 29, 1993, indexation allowance may only reduce or extinguish chargeable gains and may not create or increase a capital loss.

Assets acquired on a no gain/no loss disposal

In relation to assets acquired after March 31, 1982 by way of a no gain/no loss transaction, the acquirer's base cost includes any indexation allowance assumed to be given on the transaction.

If the asset is disposed of after November 29, 1993 other than by way of a no gain/no loss disposal, at a loss, that loss may be increased by the rolled up indexation. If neither a gain nor a loss accrues on the disposal, a loss equal to the rolled up indexation is treated as accruing if a gain accrues on the disposal which is less than the indexation allowance, the gain is converted into a loss if the rolled up indexation loss exceeds the gain.

If the asset is disposed of after November 29, 1993 in a no gain/no loss disposal and the disposal would otherwise result in a loss, the indexation allowance assumed to be given on the previous no gain/no loss transaction is deducted from the loss. If disregarding the indexation allowance would convert the loss into a gain, the disposal is treated as one in which neither a gain nor loss accrues.

Set-off of pre-entry losses

94.—(1) Schedule 7A to the Taxation of Chargeable Gains Act 1992 (set off pre-entry losses) shall be amended as follows.

(2) In sub-paragraph (3)(a) of paragraph 2 (calculation of pre-entry proportion of loss), for "assumption applying by virtue of sub-paragraphs (4) and (5)" there shall be substituted "assumptions applying by virtue of sub-paragraphs (4) to (6B)", and for sub-paragraph (7) of that paragraph there shall be substituted the following sub-paragraphs—

"(6A) Notwithstanding anything in section 56(2), where in the case of the disposal of any pre-entry asset—

(a) any company has at any time between the relevant time and the time of the disposal acquired that asset or the equivalent asset, and

(b) the acquisition was either an acquisition in pursuance of a disposal on which there is treated by virtue of section 171 as having been neither a gain nor a loss accruing or an acquisition by virtue of which an asset is treated as the equivalent asset,

the items of relevant allowable expenditure and the times when those items shall be treated as having been incurred shall be determined for the purposes of this paragraph on the assumptions specified in sub-paragraph (6B) below.

(6B) Those assumptions are that—

(a) the company by reference to which the asset in question is a pre-entry asset, and

(b) the company mentioned in sub-paragraph (6A) above and every other company which has made an acquisition which, in relation to the disposal of that asset, falls within that sub-paragraph,

were the same person and, accordingly, that the pre-entry asset had been acquired by the company disposing of it at the time when it or the equivalent asset would have been treated for the purposes of this paragraph as acquired by the company mentioned in paragraph (a) above.

(7) In sub-paragraphs (5) to (6B) above the references to the equivalent asset, in relation to another asset acquired or disposed of by any company, are references to any asset which falls in relation to that company to be treated (whether by virtue of paragraph 1(8) above or otherwise) as the same as the other asset or which would fall to be so treated after applying, as respects other assets, the assumptions for which those sub-paragraphs provide."

(3) In paragraph 9(2)(c) (cases where a group is relevant if a company was a member of it in the accounting period in which it joined another relevant group), after "paragraph (a)" there shall be inserted "or (b)".

(4) This section shall apply in relation to the making in respect of any loss of any deduction from a chargeable gain where either the gain or the loss is one accruing on or after 11th March 1994.

GENERAL NOTE

The TCGA 1992 (c. 12), Sched. 7A is amended to block two loopholes.

Where a pre-entry asset is transferred to other group members prior to its disposal outside the group, the time apportionment rules in para. 2 previously treated the asset as having been acquired, albeit at a cost equal to base cost, when it was transferred inter-group, effectively allowing the pre-entry loss restrictions in that paragraph to be side-stepped. Schedule 7, para. 2 is amended to block this loophole so that all companies acquiring the asset inter-group and the company having the pre-entry asset when it joined the group, are treated as if they were the same person.

Schedule 7A, para. 9 is amended to stop schemes whereby a company having unrealised losses is acquired by a group to shelter a prospective gain and is then sold to another group and the loss realised. The amendment ensures the loss may not set-off against the gain.

The provisions apply to chargeable gains or capital losses realised after March 10, 1994.

Commodity and financial futures

95.—(1) In section 143 of the Taxation of Chargeable Gains Act 1992 (commodity and financial futures and qualifying options), subsection (4) shall cease to have effect and for subsection (6) there shall be substituted the following subsections—

"(6) In any case where, in the course of dealing in commodity or financial futures, a person has entered into a futures contract and—

(a) he has not closed out the contract (as mentioned in subsection (5) above), and

(b) he becomes entitled to receive or liable to make a payment, whether under the contract or otherwise, in full or partial settlement of any obligations under the contract, then, for the purposes of this Act, he shall be treated as having disposed of an asset (namely, that entitlement or liability) and the payment received or made by him shall be treated as consideration for the disposal or, as the case may be, as incidental costs to him of making the disposal.

(7) Section 46 shall not apply to obligations under—

(a) a commodity or financial futures contract which is entered into by a person in the course of dealing in such futures on a recognised futures exchange; or

(b) a commodity or financial futures contract to which an authorised person or listed institution is a party.

(8) In this section—

'authorised person' has the same meaning as in the Financial Services Act 1986, and

'listed institution' has the same meaning as in section 43 of that Act."

(2) This section shall apply in relation to contracts entered into on or after 30th November 1993.

GENERAL NOTE

The settlement of unclosed commodity and financial futures for cash is treated as the disposal of an asset and the payment received or made is treated as the disposal proceeds, or the costs of the disposal. The capital gains tax wasting provisions do not apply to commodity and financial futures dealt in on a recognised futures exchange or to which an authorised person or listed institution is a party.

Cash-settled options

96.—(1) After section 144 of the Taxation of Chargeable Gains Act 1992 (options and forfeited deposits) there shall be inserted the following section—

"Cash-settled options

144A.—(1) In any case where—

(a) an option is exercised; and

(b) the nature of the option (or its exercise) is such that the grantor of the option is liable to make, and the person exercising it is entitled to receive, a payment in full settlement of all obligations under the option,

subsections (2) and (3) below shall apply in place of subsections (2) and (3) of section 144.

(2) As regards the grantor of the option—

(a) he shall be treated as having disposed of an asset (namely, his liability to make the payment) and the payment made by him shall be treated as incidental costs to him of making the disposal; and

(b) the grant of the option and the disposal shall be treated as a single transaction and the consideration for the option shall be treated as the consideration for the disposal.

(3) As regards the person exercising the option—

(a) he shall be treated as having disposed of an asset (namely, his entitlement to receive the payment) and the payment received by him shall be treated as the consideration for the disposal;

(b) the acquisition of the option (whether directly from the grantor or not) and the disposal shall be treated as a single transaction and the cost of acquiring the option shall be treated as expenditure allowable as a deduction under section 38(1)(a) from the consideration for the disposal; and

(c) for the purpose of computing the indexation allowance (if any) on the disposal, the cost of the option shall be treated (notwithstanding paragraph (b) above) as incurred when the option was acquired.

(4) In any case where subsections (2) and (3) above would apply as mentioned in subsection (1) above if the reference in that subsection to full settlement included a reference to partial settlement, those subsections and subsections (2) and (3) of section 144 shall both apply but with the following modifications—

(a) for any reference to the grant or acquisition of the option there shall be substituted a reference to the grant or acquisition of so much of the option as relates to the making and receipt of the payment or, as the case may be, the sale or purchase by the grantor; and

(b) for any reference to the consideration for, or the cost of or of acquiring, the option there shall be substituted a reference to the appropriate proportion of that consideration or cost.

(5) In this section 'appropriate proportion' means such proportion as may be just and reasonable in all the circumstances."

(2) This section shall apply in relation to options granted on or after 30th November 1993.

GENERAL NOTE

Section 144A is inserted into the TCGA 1992 (c. 12). The exercise of a call option which results in a cash payment is treated as the disposal of an asset and the payment made falls to be taken into account as the disposal proceed in relation to the grantor of the option. The same rules apply to cash payments paid in partial settlement, with appropriate apportionment.

Settlements with foreign element: information

97.—(1) The Taxation of Chargeable Gains Act 1992 shall be amended as mentioned in subsections (2) to (4) below.

(2) In Chapter II of Part III (settlements) the following section shall be inserted after section 98—

"Settlements with foreign element: information

98A. Schedule 5A to this Act (which contains general provisions about information relating to settlements with a foreign element) shall have effect."

(3) The following Schedule shall be inserted after Schedule 5—

"SCHEDULE 5A

SETTLEMENTS WITH FOREIGN ELEMENT: INFORMATION

1. In this Schedule "the commencement day" means the day on which the Finance Act 1994 was passed.

2.—(1) This paragraph applies if—

(a) a settlement was created before 19th March 1991,

(b) on or after the commencement day a person transfers property to the trustees otherwise than under a transaction entered into at arm's length and otherwise than in pursuance of a liability incurred by any person before that day,

(c) the trustees are not resident or ordinarily resident in the United Kingdom at the time the property is transferred, and

(d) the transferor knows, or has reason to believe, that the trustees are not so resident or ordinarily resident.

(2) Before the expiry of the period of twelve months beginning with the relevant day, the transferor shall deliver to the Board a return which—

(a) identifies the settlement, and

(b) specifies the property transferred, the day on which the transfer was made, and the consideration (if any) for the transfer.

(3) For the purposes of sub-paragraph (2) above the relevant day is the day on which the transfer is made.

3.—(1) This paragraph applies if a settlement is created on or after the commencement day, and at the time it is created—

(a) the trustees are not resident or ordinarily resident in the United Kingdom, or

(b) the trustees are resident or ordinarily resident in the United Kingdom but fall to be regarded for the purposes of any double taxation relief arrangements as resident in a territory outside the United Kingdom.

(2) Any person who—

(a) is a settlor in relation to the settlement at the time it is created, and

(b) at that time fulfils the condition mentioned in sub-paragraph (3) below,

shall, before the expiry of the period of three months beginning with the relevant day, deliver to the Board a return specifying the particulars mentioned in sub-paragraphs (4) below.

(3) The condition is that the person concerned is domiciled in the United Kingdom and is either resident or ordinarily resident in the United Kingdom.

(4) The particulars are—

(a) the day on which the settlement was created;

(b) the name and address of the person delivering the return;

(c) the names and addresses of the persons who are the trustees immediately before the delivery of the return.

(5) For the purposes of sub-paragraph (2) above the relevant day is the day on which the settlement is created.

4.—(1) This paragraph applies if a settlement is created on or after 19th March 1991, and at the time it is created—

(a) the trustees are not resident or ordinarily resident in the United Kingdom, or

(b) the trustees are resident or ordinarily resident in the United Kingdom but fall to be regarded for the purposes of any double taxation relief arrangements as resident in a territory outside the United Kingdom.

(2) Any person who—

(a) is a settlor in relation to the settlement at the time it is created,

(b) at that time does not fulfil the condition mentioned in sub-paragraph (3) below, and

(c) first fulfils that condition at a time falling on or after the commencement day,

shall, before the expiry of the period of twelve months beginning with the relevant day, deliver to the Board a return specifying the particulars mentioned in sub-paragraph (4) below.

(3) The condition is that the person concerned is domiciled in the United Kingdom and is either resident or ordinarily resident in the United Kingdom.

(4) The particulars are—

(a) the day on which the settlement was created;

(b) the name and address of the person delivering the return;

(c) the names and addresses of the persons who are the trustees immediately before the delivery of the return.

(5) For the purposes of sub-paragraph (2) above the relevant day is the day on which the person first fulfils the condition as mentioned in paragraph (c) of that sub-paragraph.

5.—(1) This paragraph applies if—

(a) the trustees of a settlement become at any time (the relevant time) on or after the commencement day neither resident nor ordinarily resident in the United Kingdom, or

(b) the trustees of a settlement, while continuing to be resident and ordinarily resident in the United Kingdom, become at any time (the relevant time) on or after the commencement day trustees who fall to be regarded for the purposes of any double taxation relief arrangements as resident in a territory outside the United Kingdom.

(2) Any person who was a trustee of the settlement immediately before the relevant time shall, before the expiry of the period of twelve months beginning with the relevant day, deliver to the Board a return specifying—

(a) the day on which the settlement was created,

(b) the name and address of each person who is a settlor in relation to the settlement immediately before the delivery of the return, and

(c) the names and addresses of the persons who are the trustees immediately before the delivery of the return.

(3) For the purposes of sub-paragraph (2) above the relevant day is the day when the relevant time falls.

6.—(1) Nothing in paragraph 2, 3, 4 or 5 above shall require information to be contained in the return concerned to the extent that—

(a) before the expiry of the period concerned the information has been provided to the Board by any person in pursuance of the paragraph concerned or of any other provision, or

(b) after the expiry of the period concerned the information falls to be provided to the Board by any person in pursuance of any provision other than the paragraph concerned.

(2) Nothing in paragraph 2, 3, 4 or 5 above shall require a return to be delivered if—

(a) before the expiry of the period concerned all the information concerned has been provided to the Board by any person in pursuance of the paragraph concerned or of any other provision, or

(b) after the expiry of the period concerned all the information concerned falls to be provided to the Board by any person in pursuance of any provision other than the paragraph concerned."

(4) In Schedule 5, paragraphs 11 to 14 (information) shall be omitted.

(5) Subsection (4) above shall have effect where the relevant day falls on or after the day on which this Act is passed.

(6) In the Table in section 98 of the Taxes Management Act 1970 (penalties) at the end of the second column there shall be inserted—

"Paragraphs 2 to 6 of Schedule 5A to the 1992 Act."

GENERAL NOTE

Section 98A and Sched. 5A (settlements with foreign element: information) are inserted into the TCGA 1992 (c. 12). Schedule 5A for the most part re-enacts the TCGA 1992 (c. 12), Sched. 5, paras. 11–14 (the provisions which hitherto gave the Revenue extensive information powers in respect of non-resident trusts) which are now deleted. As part of Sched. 5, which was introduced by s.86 of the TCGA 1992 (c. 12), paras. 11–14 only applied to foreign settlements in which the settlor at some time in the year of assessment had an interest. Schedule 5A however, applies, effective from Royal Assent, to all foreign settlements whether the settlor has an interest or not.

Profit-related pay

The distributable pool

98.—(1) Schedule 8 to the Taxes Act 1988 (profit-related pay schemes: conditions for registration) shall be amended as follows.

(2) After paragraph 13 (determination of distributable pool by method A) there shall be inserted—

"13A.—(1) Where a scheme includes provision by virtue of paragraph 13(4) or (5) above the scheme must be so framed that in arriving at the profits for the base year or for the previous profit period any profit-related pay and any secondary Class I contributions in respect of it are accorded the same accountancy treatment as is accorded to any profit-related pay and any secondary Class I contributions in respect of it in arriving at the profits in the profit period.

(2) In sub-paragraph (1) above—

(a) "profit-related pay" means profit-related pay under whatever scheme;

(b) "secondary Class I contributions" means secondary Class I contributions under Part I of the Social Security Act 1975 or Part I of the Social Security (Northern Ireland) Act 1975 or Part I of the Social Security Contributions and Benefits Act 1992 or Part I of the Social Security Contributions and Benefits (Northern Ireland) Act 1992.

(3) Sub-paragraph (1) above shall apply notwithstanding anything in paragraph 19 below.

(4) Where a scheme includes provision by virtue of paragraph 13(4) above the scheme must also include provision that if the pay for the profit period is less than the pay for the base year or for the previous profit period (as the case may be) the percentage to be applied for the purposes of the provision included by virtue of paragraph 13(4) above shall be the increased percentage (instead of any other percentage).

(5) The increased percentage must be one arrived at by—

(a) taking the percentage that would be applied for the purposes of the provision included by virtue of paragraph 13(4) above apart from the provision included by virtue of sub-paragraph (4) above, and

(b) adding the percentage found by expressing the difference in pay as a percentage of the profits for the base year or for the previous profit period (as the case may be).

(6) For the purposes of this paragraph—

(a) the pay for the profit period or for previous profit period or for the base year is the pay paid to employees in respect of employment in the period or year concerned in the employment unit concerned;

(b) the difference in pay is the difference between the pay for the profit period and the pay for the previous profit period or for the base year (as the case may be);

and any profit-related pay shall be ignored in applying paragraph (a) above."

(3) After paragraph 14 (determination of distributable pool by method B) there shall be inserted—

"14A.—(1) Where a scheme includes provision to give effect to paragraph 14(3) above or provision by virtue of paragraph 14(4) above the scheme must be so framed that in arriving at the profits in the preceding period of 12 months any profit-related pay and any secondary Class I contributions in respect of it are accorded the same accountancy treatment as is accorded to any profit-related pay and any secondary Class I contributions in respect of it in arriving at the profits in the profit period.

(2) Where a scheme includes provision by virtue of paragraph 14(5) above the scheme must be so framed that in arriving at the profits in the relevant period of 12 months any profit-related pay and any secondary Class I contributions in respect of it are accorded the same accountancy treatment as is accorded to any profit-related pay and any secondary Class I contributions in respect of it in arriving at the profits in the profit period; and for this purpose the relevant period of 12 months is the period of 12 months immediately preceding the first or only profit period to which the scheme relates.

(3) In sub-paragraphs (1) and (2) above—
(a) "profit-related pay" means profit-related pay under whatever scheme;
(b) "secondary Class I contributions" means secondary Class I contributions under Part I of the Social Security Contributions and Benefits Act 1992 or Part I of the Social Security Contributions and Benefits (Northern Ireland) Act 1992.

(4) Sub-paragraphs (1) and (2) above shall apply notwithstanding anything in paragraph 19 below.

(5) Where a scheme includes provision by virtue of paragraph 14(4) above the scheme must also include provision that if the pay for the profit period is less than the pay for the preceding period of 12 months the percentage to be applied for the purposes of the provision included by virtue of paragraph 14(4) above shall be the increased percentage (instead of any other percentage).

(6) The increased percentage must be one arrived at by—
(a) taking the percentage that would be applied for the purposes of the provision included by virtue of paragraph 14(4) above apart from the provision included by virtue of sub-paragraph (5) above, and
(b) adding the percentage found by expressing the difference in pay as a percentage of the profits in the preceding period of 12 months.

(7) For the purposes of this paragraph—
(a) the pay for the profit period or for the preceding period of 12 months is the pay paid to employees in respect of employment in the period concerned in the employment unit concerned;
(b) the difference in pay is the difference between the pay for the profit period and the pay for the preceding period of 12 months; and any profit-related pay shall be ignored in applying paragraph (a) above."

(4) This section shall have effect in relation to any scheme not registered before 1st December 1993.

GENERAL NOTE

The new paras. 13A and 14A are inserted into Sched. 8 to the ICTA 1988 (c. 1) to tighten the rules for calculating the upper limit on profits which must be brought into account when calculating profit related pay (PRP) for a particular period.

Paragraph 13A provides that where a method A PRP scheme includes either an upper percentage limit or a lower profits limit, the scheme must ensure that in calculating profits for both the current profit period and the previous profit period (or base year), PRP and National Insurance Contributions on PRP are treated in the same way for accountancy purposes. For this purpose, PRP includes PRP payable under any scheme, not just the particular scheme. Further if a method A scheme for an employment unit includes an upper percentage limit, the scheme must contain a provision ensuring that if the pay given to employees in the unit in the current profit period is less than the pay given to employees in the same unit for the previous profit period or base year, the increased percentage is to apply instead. The increased percentage is the basic percentage that would have applied under the scheme in the absence of the new rules plus the percentage which represents the difference in pay as between the current profit period and the previous profit period or base year expressed as a percentage of the profits for that earlier period.

Paragraph 14A applies similar rules to a method B PRP scheme.

The new provisions apply to schemes registered after November 29, 1993.

Parts of undertakings

99.—(1) Schedule 8 to the Taxes Act 1988 shall also be amended by inserting the following paragraphs after paragraph 22 (which, with paragraph 21, applies to schemes relating to parts of undertakings)—

"23.—(1) In a case where—

(a) paragraph 21 above applies to a scheme, and

(b) method A (specified in paragraph 13 above) is employed for the purposes of the scheme,

the scheme must contain provisions which comply with this paragraph and which apply as regards each profit period to which the scheme relates.

(2) The scheme must ensure that no payments are made under it by reference to a given profit period if the percentage mentioned in paragraph 13(1) above exceeds the permitted percentage.

(3) The scheme must ensure that the permitted percentage is a percentage found by—

(a) taking the pay paid to employees in respect of employment in the relevant year in the employment unit to which the other scheme mentioned in paragraph 22(1)(a) above relates or (if there are two or more other schemes) the aggregate of the pay paid to employees in respect of employment in the relevant year in the employment units to which the other schemes relate;

(b) taking the profit-related pay paid to employees in respect of employment in the relevant year in the employment unit to which the other scheme mentioned in paragraph 22(1)(a) above relates or (if there are two or more other schemes) the aggregate of the profit-related pay paid to employees in respect of employment in the relevant year in the employment units to which the other schemes relate;

(c) taking the pay paid to employees in respect of employment in the relevant year in the employment unit to which the scheme mentioned in paragraph 21 above relates;

(d) taking the fraction whose denominator is equal to the number of whole pounds found under paragraph (a) above and whose numerator is equal to the number of whole pounds found under paragraph (b) above;

(e) multiplying the amount found under paragraph (c) above by the fraction found under paragraph (d) above;

(f) taking the profits for the relevant year of the undertaking mentioned in paragraph 21 above;

(g) expressing the amount found under paragraph (e) above as a percentage of the amount found under paragraph (f) above;

(h) taking the percentage found under paragraph (g) above as the permitted percentage.

(4) The scheme must ensure that the relevant year is a period of 12 months identified in the scheme and ending at a time within the period of two years immediately preceding the given profit period.

24.—(1) In a case where—

(a) paragraph 21 above applies to a scheme, and

(b) method B (specified in paragraph 14 above) is employed for the purposes of the scheme, the scheme must contain provisions which comply with this paragraph and which apply as regards each profit period to which the scheme relates.

(2) The scheme must ensure that no payments are made under it by reference to the first or only profit period to which the scheme relates if the notional pool mentioned in paragraph 14(1)(a) above exceeds the permitted limit.

(3) The scheme must also ensure that no payments are made under it by reference to a given profit period other than the first if the distributable pool for the previous profit period (mentioned in paragraph 14(1) (b) above) exceeds the permitted limit.

(4) The scheme must ensure that the permitted limit is a limit found by—

(a) taking the pay paid to employees in respect of employment in the relevant year in the employment unit to which the other scheme mentioned in paragraph 22(1)(a) above relates or (if there are two or more other schemes) the aggregate of the pay paid to employees in respect of employment in the relevant year in the employment units to which the other schemes relate;

(b) taking the profit-related pay paid to employees in respect of employment in the relevant year in the employment unit to which the other scheme mentioned in paragraph 22(1)(a) above relates or (if there are two or more other schemes) the aggregate of the profit-related pay paid to employees in respect of employment in the relevant year in the employment units to which the other schemes relate;

(c) taking the pay paid to employees in respect of employment in the relevant year in the employment unit to which the scheme mentioned in paragraph 21 above relates;

(d) taking the fraction whose denominator is equal to the number of whole pounds found under paragraph (a) above and whose numerator is equal to the number of whole pounds found under paragraph (b) above;

(e) multiplying the amount found under paragraph (c) above by the fraction found under paragraph (d) above;

(f) taking the amount found under paragraph (e) above as the permitted limit.

(5) The scheme must ensure that the relevant year is—

(a) a period of 12 months identified in the scheme and ending at a time within the period of two years immediately preceding the first or only profit period to which the scheme relates (in the case of provisions contained in the scheme by virtue of sub-paragraph (2) above);

(b) a period of 12 months identified in the scheme and ending at a time within the period of two years immediately preceding the given profit period (in the case of provisions contained in the scheme by virtue of sub-paragraph (3) above)."

(2) This section shall have effect in relation to any scheme not registered before 1st December 1993.

GENERAL NOTE

Paragraphs 23 and 24 are inserted into Sched. 8 to the ICTA 1988 (c. 1) to ensure that PRP payable to employees in a special scheme is not disproportionately greater than the PRP paid under other schemes to employees in the same business.

For special schemes registered after November 30, 1993, the scheme must ensure that its fixed percentage (if it is a method A scheme) or notional/distributable pool (if it is a method B scheme) does not exceed a limit calculated by reference to the ratio of total pay to PRP in the other scheme[s] registered for the business in question. The ratio is to be calculated by reference to the figures for pay and PRP paid for a specified earlier period.

Profit sharing schemes

Relevant age for purpose of appropriate percentage

100.—(1) Schedule 10 to the Taxes Act 1988 (profit sharing schemes) shall be amended as follows.

(2) In paragraph 3 (the appropriate percentage for purposes of tax charge) the words from "In this paragraph" to the end of the paragraph shall be omitted.

(3) The following paragraph shall be inserted after paragraph 3—

"3A.—(1) In paragraph 3 above the reference to the relevant age shall be construed as follows.

(2) Where the scheme is approved before 25th July 1991 and the event occurs before 30th November 1993, the relevant age is pensionable age.

(3) Where—

(a) the scheme is approved before 25th July 1991,

(b) the event occurs on or after 30th November 1993,

(c) the scheme defines the period of retention by reference to the age of 60 for both men and women, and

(d) the reference to that age is incorporated in the definition by virtue of an alteration approved by the Board under paragraph 4 of Schedule 9 before the event occurs,

the relevant age is 60.

(4) Where—

(a) the scheme is approved before 25th July 1991,

(b) the event occurs on or after 30th November 1993, and

(c) sub-paragraph (3) above does not apply,

the relevant age is pensionable age.

(5) Where the scheme is approved on or after 25th July 1991, the relevant age is the specified age."

GENERAL NOTE

The relevant age (by reference to which the appropriate percentage of 50 per cent. is applied) in relation to profit sharing schemes approved before July 25, 1991, is amended.

The relevant age for such schemes is 60 for both men and women if the event giving rise to the charge occurs after November 29, 1993 and the scheme has previously been altered to define the age of retention by reference to the age of 60 for both men and women. If the event giving rise to the charge occurs before November 30, 1993 or the event occurs after November 30, 1993 and the scheme has not been altered as provided above, the relevant age is 65 for men and 60 for women.

Acceptance of qualifying corporate bonds for shares

101.—(1) Schedule 10 to the Taxes Act 1988 (profit sharing schemes) shall be amended as mentioned in subsections (2) to (4) below.

(2) In paragraph 1 (limitations on contractual obligations of participants) in sub-paragraph (1) the following paragraph shall be inserted after paragraph (c)—

"(cc) directing the trustees to accept an offer of a qualifying corporate bond, whether alone or with cash or other assets or both, for his shares if the offer forms part of a general offer which is made as mentioned in paragraph (c) above; or".

(3) In paragraph 1 the following sub-paragraph shall be inserted after sub-paragraph (3)—

"(4) In sub-paragraph (1)(cc) above "qualifying corporate bond" shall be construed in accordance with section 117 of the 1992 Act."

(4) The following paragraph shall be inserted after paragraph 5 (company reconstructions)—

"5A.—(1) Paragraph 5(2) to (6) above apply where there occurs in relation to any of a participant's shares ("the original holding") a relevant transaction which would result in a new holding being equated with the original holding for the purposes of capital gains tax, were it not for the fact that what would be the new holding consists of or includes a qualifying corporate bond; and "relevant transaction" here means a transaction mentioned in Chapter II of Part IV of the 1992 Act.

(2) In paragraph 5(2) to (6) above as applied by this paragraph—

(a) references to a company reconstruction are to the transaction referred to in sub-paragraph (1) above;

(b) references to the new holding are to what would be the new holding were it not for the fact mentioned in sub-paragraph (1) above;

(c) references to the original holding shall be construed in accordance with sub-paragraph (1) above (and not paragraph 5(1));

(d) references to shares, in the context of the new holding, include securities and rights of any description which form part of the new holding.

(3) In sub-paragraph (1) above "qualifying corporate bond" shall be construed in accordance with section 117 of the 1992 Act."

(5) In paragraph 32(1) of Schedule 9 to the Taxes Act 1988 (requirements applicable to profit sharing schemes) for "or (c)" there shall be substituted ", (c) or (cc)".

(6) In paragraph 33(a) of Schedule 9 to the Taxes Act 1988 (which provides that the trust instrument must contain certain provision by reference to new shares within the meaning of paragraph 5 of Schedule 10) the reference to paragraph 5 of Schedule 10 shall be construed as including a reference to that paragraph as applied by paragraph 5A.

(7) Subsections (2) and (3) above shall have effect where a direction is made on or after the day on which this Act is passed.

(8) Subsection (4) above shall have effect where what would be the new holding comes into being on or after the day on which this Act is passed; but this is subject to subsection (13) below.

(9) Subsection (5) above shall have effect in relation to any scheme not approved before the day on which this Act is passed.

(10) In a case where—

(a) a scheme is approved before the day on which this Act is passed, and

(b) on or after that day the trust instrument is altered in such a way that paragraph 32(1) of Schedule 9 to the Taxes Act 1988 would be fulfilled if subsection (5) above applied in relation to the scheme,

subsection (5) above shall apply in relation to the scheme with effect from the time the alteration is made.

(11) Subsection (6) above shall have effect in relation to any scheme not approved before the day on which this Act is passed.

(12) In a case where—

(a) a scheme is approved before the day on which this Act is passed, and

(b) on or after that day the trust instrument is altered in such a way that paragraph 33(a) of Schedule 9 to the Taxes Act 1988 would be fulfilled if subsection (6) above applied in relation to the scheme,

subsection (6) above shall apply in relation to the scheme with effect from the time the alteration is made.

(13) In a case where—

(a) a scheme is approved before the day on which this Act is passed,

(b) subsection (4) above would apply in relation to the scheme by virtue of subsection (8) above and apart from this subsection, and

(c) the trust instrument is not altered as mentioned in subsection (12)(b) above before what would be the new holding comes into being,

subsection (4) above shall not apply in relation to the scheme.

(14) Subsection (6) above shall not imply a contrary intention for the purposes of section 20(2) of the Interpretation Act 1978 in its application to other references to paragraph 5 of Schedule 10 to the Taxes Act 1988.

This enables trustees of an approved profit-sharing scheme, as from Royal Assent, to retain in the scheme trust qualifying corporate bonds which they receive from the company whose shares they hold is reconstructed or taken over. The bonds may in due course be distributed tax-free to scheme participants.

Employee share ownership trusts

Employee share ownership trusts

102. Schedule 13 to this Act (which contains provisions about employee share ownership trusts) shall have effect.

Retirement benefits schemes

The administrator

103.—(1) The following section shall be inserted after section 611 of the Taxes Act 1988—

"Definition of the administrator
611AA.—(1) In this Chapter references to the administrator, in relation to a retirement benefits scheme, are to the person who is, or the persons who are, for the time being the administrator of the scheme by virtue of the following provisions of this section.
(2) Subject to subsection (7) below, where—
(a) the scheme is a trust scheme, and
(b) at any time the trustee, or any of the trustees, is or are resident in the United Kingdom,
the administrator of the scheme at that time shall be the trustee or trustees of the scheme.
(3) Subject to subsection (7) below, where—
(a) the scheme is a non-trust scheme, and
(b) at any time the scheme sponsor, or any of the scheme sponsors, is or are resident in the United Kingdom,
the administrator of the scheme at that time shall be the scheme sponsor or scheme sponsors.
(4) At any time when the trustee of a trust scheme is not resident in the United Kingdom or (if there is more than one trustee) none of the trustees is so resident, the trustee or trustees shall ensure that there is a person, or there are persons—
(a) resident in the United Kingdom, and
(b) appointed by the trustee or trustees to be responsible for the discharge of all duties relating to the scheme which are imposed on the administrator under this Chapter.
(5) At any time when the scheme sponsor of a non-trust scheme is not resident in the United Kingdom or (if there is more than one scheme sponsor) none of the scheme sponsors is so resident, the scheme sponsor or scheme sponsors shall ensure that there is a person, or there are persons—
(a) resident in the United Kingdom, and
(b) appointed by the scheme sponsor or scheme sponsors to be responsible for the discharge of all duties relating to the scheme which are imposed on the administrator under this Chapter.

(6) Without prejudice to subsections (4) and (5) above—

  (a) the trustee or trustees of a trust scheme, or

  (b) the scheme sponsor or scheme sponsors of a non-trust scheme,

may at any time appoint a person who is, or persons who are, resident in the United Kingdom to be responsible for the discharge of all duties relating to the scheme which are imposed on the administrator under this Chapter.

(7) Where at any time there is or are a person or persons—

  (a) for the time being appointed under subsection (4), (5) or (6) above as regards a scheme, and

  (b) resident in the United Kingdom,

the administrator of the scheme at that time shall be that person or those persons (and no other person).

(8) Any appointment under subsection (4), (5) or (6) above—

  (a) must be in writing, and

  (b) if made after the time when the scheme is established, shall constitute an alteration of the scheme for the purposes of section 591B(2).

(9) In this section—

  (a) references to a trust scheme are to a retirement benefits scheme established under a trust or trusts;

  (b) references to the trustee or trustees, in relation to a trust scheme and to a particular time, are to the person who is the trustee, or the persons who are the trustees, of the scheme at that time;

  (c) references to a non-trust scheme are to a retirement benefits scheme not established under a trust or trusts, and

  (d) references to the scheme sponsor or scheme sponsors, in relation to a retirement benefits scheme and to a particular time, are references to any person who established the scheme and is in existence at that time or, if more than one, all such persons."

(2) In consequence of subsection (1) above, in section 612(1) of the Taxes Act 1988 (interpretation of Chapter I of Part XIV) the definition of "administrator" shall cease to have effect.

(3) This section—

  (a) so far as it relates to section 591B(1) of the Taxes Act 1988, shall apply in relation to notices given on or after the day on which this Act is passed;

  (b) so far as it relates to section 593(3) of that Act, shall apply in relation to contributions paid on or after that day;

  (c) so far as it relates to section 596A(3) of that Act, shall apply in relation to benefits received on or after that day;

  (d) so far as it relates to sections 598(2) and (4), 599(3) and 599A(2) of that Act, shall apply in relation to payments made on or after that day;

  (e) so far as it relates to section 602(1) and (2) of that Act and regulations made under section 602, shall apply in relation to amounts becoming recoverable on or after that day;

  (f) so far as it relates to section 604(1) of that Act, shall apply in relation to applications made on or after that day;

  (g) so far as it relates to section 605(1) and (4) of that Act, shall apply in relation to notices given on or after that day.

GENERAL NOTE

A new s.611AA is inserted into the ICTA 1988 (c. 1). The trustees of a retirement benefit scheme (or the scheme sponsors, in the case of a scheme not set up under trust) are treated as the administrators responsible for the tax affairs of a tax-approved retirement benefit scheme provided at least one of the trustees or scheme sponsors is U.K. resident. The trustees and sponsors may (must if they are all non-U.K. resident) appoint (which must be in writing) a U.K. resident to fulfil that role.

The provisions have effect from May 3, 1994 (Royal Assent).

Default of administrator etc.

104.—(1) The following section shall be substituted for section 606 of the Taxes Act 1988—

"**Default of administrator etc.**
606.—(1) This section applies in relation to a retirement benefits scheme if at any time—
  (a) there is no administrator of the scheme, or
  (b) the person who is, or all of the persons who are, the administrator of the scheme cannot be traced, or
  (c) the person who is, or all of the persons who are, the administrator of the scheme is or are in default for the purposes of this section.
(2) If the scheme is a trust scheme, then—
  (a) if subsection (1)(b) or (c) above applies and at the time in question the condition mentioned in subsection (3) below is fulfilled, the trustee or trustees shall at that time be responsible for the discharge of all duties imposed on the administrator under this Chapter (whenever arising) and liable for any tax due from the administrator in the administrator's capacity as such (whenever falling due);
  (b) if subsection (1)(a) above applies, or subsection (1)(b) or (c) above applies and at the time in question the condition mentioned in subsection (3) below is not fulfilled, the employer shall at that time be so responsible and liable;
and paragraph (b) above shall apply to a person in his capacity as the employer even if he is also the administrator, or a trustee, of the scheme.
(3) The condition is that there is at least one trustee of the scheme who—
  (a) can be traced,
  (b) is resident in the United Kingdom, and
  (c) is not in default for the purposes of this section.
(4) If the scheme is a non-trust scheme, then—
  (a) if subsection (1)(b) or (c) above applies and at the time in question the condition mentioned in subsection (5) below is fulfilled, the scheme sponsor or scheme sponsors shall at that time be responsible for the discharge of all duties imposed on the administrator under this Chapter (whenever arising) and liable for any tax due from the administrator in the administrator's capacity as such (whenever falling due);
  (b) if subsection (1)(a) above applies, or subsection (1)(b) or (c) above applies and at the time in question the condition mentioned in subsection (5) below is not fulfilled, the employer shall at that time be so responsible and liable;
and paragraph (b) above shall apply to a person in his capacity as the employer even if he is also the administrator of the scheme, or a scheme sponsor.
(5) The condition is that there is at least one scheme sponsor who—
  (a) can be traced,
  (b) is resident in the United Kingdom, and
  (c) is not in default for the purposes of this section.
(6) Where at any time—
  (a) paragraph (b) or (c) of subsection (1) above applies in relation to a scheme, and
  (b) a person is by virtue of this section responsible for the discharge of any duties, or liable for any tax, in relation to the scheme,
then at that time the person or persons mentioned in paragraph (b) or (as the case may be) paragraph (c) of subsection (1) above shall not, by

reason only of being the administrator of the scheme, be responsible for the discharge of those duties or liable for that tax.

(7) Where the scheme is a trust scheme and the employer is not a contributor to the scheme, subsection (2) above shall have effect as if—

   (a) for "the employer", in the first place where those words occur, there were substituted "the scheme sponsor or scheme sponsors", and

   (b) for "the employer", in the second place where those words occur, there were substituted "scheme sponsor".

(8) Where the scheme is a non-trust scheme and the employer is not a contributor to the scheme, subsection (4) above shall have effect as if paragraph (b) and the words after that paragraph were omitted.

(9) No liability incurred under this Chapter—

   (a) by the administrator of a scheme, or

   (b) by a person by virtue of this section,

shall be affected by the termination of a scheme or by its ceasing to be an approved scheme or to be an exempt approved scheme.

(10) Where by virtue of this section a person becomes responsible for the discharge of any duties, or liable for any tax, the Board shall, as soon as is reasonably practicable, notify him of that fact; but any failure to give such notification shall not affect that person's being responsible or liable by virtue of this section.

(11) A person is in default for the purposes of this section if—

   (a) he has failed to discharge any duty imposed on him under this Chapter, or

   (b) he has failed to pay any tax due from him by virtue of this Chapter,

and (in either case) the Board consider the failure to be of a serious nature.

(12) References in this section to a trust scheme, a non-trust scheme, trustees and scheme sponsors shall be construed in accordance with section 611AA.

(13) References in this section to the employer include, where the employer is resident outside the United Kingdom, references to any branch or agent of the employer in the United Kingdom, and in this subsection "branch or agent" has the meaning given by section 118(1) of the Management Act.

(14) This section does not apply for the purposes of sections 602 and 603 and Schedule 22."

(2) In consequence of subsection (1) above, in section 607(3)(b)(iii) of the Taxes Act 1988 for the words "section 606(1) and (3)" there shall be substituted "section 606(2)(b), (4)(b), (7), (8) and (13)".

(3) This section shall apply where the time in question falls on or after the day on which this Act is passed.

GENERAL NOTE

The ICTA 1988 (c. 1), s.606 is rewritten. If there is no scheme administrator or he cannot be traced or he defaults on his duties, responsibility passes to the scheme trustees or sponsors (provided at least one of the scheme trustees or sponsors is U.K. resident) and as a last resort, to the employer, except in the case of default by the administrator of free-standing additional voluntary contribution schemes, where the final responsibility will rest with the scheme sponsors.

Information

105.—(1) The Taxes Act 1988 shall be amended in accordance with subsections (2) and (3) below.

(2) In section 605 (information) at the beginning there shall be inserted the following subsections—

"(1A) The Board may by regulations make any of the following provisions—

(a) provision requiring prescribed persons to furnish to the Board at prescribed times information relating to any of the matters mentioned in subsection (1B) below;

(b) provision enabling the Board to serve a notice requiring prescribed persons to furnish to the Board, within a prescribed time, particulars relating to any of those matters;

(c) provision enabling the Board to serve a notice requiring prescribed persons to produce to the Board, within a prescribed time, documents relating to any of those matters;

(d) provision enabling the Board to serve a notice requiring prescribed persons to make available for inspection on behalf of the Board books, documents and other records, being books, documents and records which relate to any of those matters;

(e) provision requiring prescribed persons to preserve for a prescribed time books, documents and other records, being books, documents and records which relate to any of those matters.

(1B) The matters referred to in subsection (1A) above are—

(a) an approved scheme;

(b) a relevant statutory scheme;

(c) an annuity contract by means of which benefits provided under an approved scheme or a relevant statutory scheme have been secured;

(d) a retirement benefits scheme which is not an approved scheme but in relation to which an application for approval for the purposes of this Chapter has been made.

(1C) A person who fails to comply with regulations made under subsection (1A)(e) above shall be liable to a penalty not exceeding £3,000.

(1D) Regulations under subsection (1A) above may make different provision for different descriptions of case.

(1E) In subsection (1A) above "prescribed" means prescribed by regulations made under that subsection."

(3) Subsections (1) and (2) of section 605 shall cease to have effect.

(4) In section 98 of the Taxes Management Act 1970 (penalties for failure to provide information etc.)—

(a) in the first column of the Table after the entry "regulations under section 602;" there shall be inserted the entry "regulations under section 605(1A)(b) to (d);";

(b) in the first column of the Table for the entry "section 605(1), (2), (3)(b) and (4);" there shall be substituted the entry "section 605(3)(b) and (4);";

(c) in the second column of the Table after the entry "regulations under section 602;" there shall be inserted the entry "regulations under section 605(1A)(a);".

(5) Subsections (3) and (4)(b) above shall come into force on such day as the Treasury may by order appoint.

GENERAL NOTE

Regulations may be made: to specify what information must be produced about the tax affairs of approved occupational pension schemes; to allow notices calling for information or documents to be served; to authorise the inspection of records and other documents and to specify how long information and other scheme records should be retained.

Penalties of up to £3,000 may be imposed for failure to provide information or particulars or to deliver documents.

False statements etc.

106.—(1) The following section shall be inserted after section 605 of the Taxes Act 1988—

"False statements etc.
    605A.—(1) A person who fraudulently or negligently makes a false statement or false representation on making an application for the approval for the purposes of this Chapter of—
    (a) a retirement benefits scheme, or
    (b) an alteration in such a scheme,
shall be liable to a penalty not exceeding £3,000.
    (2) In a case where—
    (a) a person fraudulently or negligently makes a false statement or false representation, and
    (b) in consequence that person, or any other person, obtains relief from or repayment of tax under this Chapter,
the person mentioned in paragraph (a) above shall be liable to a penalty not exceeding £3,000."
    (2) This section shall apply in relation to things done or omitted after the day on which this Act is passed.

GENERAL NOTE
    A new s.605A is inserted into the ICTA 1988 (c. 1). Penalties of up to £3,000 may be imposed if a false statement (a) is made in order to obtain tax approval of, or obtain an alteration of, a retirement benefit scheme; or (b) results in relief or repayment of tax being obtained.

Discretionary approval

107.—(1) Section 591 of the Taxes Act 1988 (discretionary approval of retirement benefits schemes) shall be amended as follows.
    (2) In subsection (2)(g) (annuity contracts)—
    (a) after "relevant benefits" there shall be inserted "falling within subsection (2A) below";
    (b) the words "approved by the Board and" shall be omitted.
    (3) The following subsection shall be inserted after subsection (2)—
    "(2A) Relevant benefits fall within this subsection if they correspond with benefits that could be provided by an approved scheme, and for this purpose—
    (a) a hypothetical scheme (rather than any particular scheme) is to be taken, and
    (b) benefits provided by a scheme directly (rather than by means of an annuity contract) are to be taken."
    (4) This section shall apply in relation to a scheme not approved by virtue of section 591 of the Taxes Act 1988 before 1st July 1994.

GENERAL NOTE
    The ICTA 1988 (c. 1), s.591 is amended. Revenue approval for approved deferred annuity contracts is no longer required; instead, benefits payable under such contracts must be of a type and amount that an approved scheme could provide.

Taxation of benefits of non-approved schemes

108.—(1) Section 596A of the Taxes Act 1988 (taxation of benefits under non-approved schemes) shall be amended as follows.

(2) In subsection (4), at the beginning there shall be inserted "Subject to subsection (9) below".

(3) For subsection (6) there shall be substituted—

"(6) Tax shall not be charged under this section in the case of—

    (a) any pension or annuity which is chargeable to tax under Schedule E by virtue of section 19(1); or

    (b) any pension or other benefit chargeable to tax under section 58."

(4) In subsection (7)—

    (a) for the words "by virtue of section 19(1)1", in the first place where they occur, there shall be substituted "as mentioned in subsection (6)(a) above";

    (b) in paragraph (a), for the words "subsection (6) above" there shall be substituted "subsection (6)(a) above"; and

    (c) in paragraph (b) for the words "section 19(1)1" there shall be substituted "section 19(1)".

(5) For subsections (8) and (9) there shall be substituted—

"(8) Subject to subsection (9) below, tax shall not be charged under this section (or section 19(1) or 148) in the case of a lump sum where—

    (a) the employer has paid any sum or sums with a view to the provision of any relevant benefits under a retirement benefits scheme;

    (b) an employee has been assessed to tax in respect of the sum or sums by virtue of section 595(1); and

    (c) the lump sum is provided under the scheme to the employee, any person falling within section 595(5) in relation to the employee or any other individual designated by the employee.

(9) Where any of the income or gains accruing to the scheme under which the lump sum is provided is not brought into charge to tax, tax shall be charged under this section on the amount of the lump sum received less any deduction applicable under subsection (10) or (11) below.

(10) Subject to subsection (11) below, the deduction applicable is the aggregate of—

    (a) any sum or sums in respect of which the employee has been assessed as mentioned in subsection (8)(b) above, and

    (b) any sum or sums paid by the employee,

which in either case were paid by way of contribution to the provision of the lump sum.

(11) Where—

    (a) the lump sum is provided under the scheme on the disposal of a part of any asset or the surrender of any part of or share in any rights in any asset, and

    (b) the employee, any person falling within section 595(5) in relation to the employee or any person connected with the employee has any right to receive or any expectation of receiving a further lump sum (or further lump sums) under the scheme on a further disposal of any part of the asset or a further surrender of any part of or share in any rights in the asset,

the deduction applicable shall be determined in accordance with the formula in subsection (12) below.

(12) The formula is—

$$D = S \times \frac{A}{B}$$

(13) For the purposes of the formula in subsection (12) above—

    D is the deduction applicable;

       S is the aggregate amount of any sum or sums of a description mentioned in paragraphs (a) and (b) of subsection (10) above;

       A is the amount of the lump sum received in relation to which the deduction applicable falls to be determined;

       B is the market value of the asset in relation to which the disposal or surrender occurred, on the assumption that the valuation is made immediately before the disposal or surrender.

     (14) An individual may not claim that a deduction is applicable in relation to a lump sum more than once.

     (15) For the purposes of subsections (8) and (9) above, it shall be assumed unless the contrary is shown—

       (a) that no sums have been paid, and the employee has not been assessed in respect of any sums paid, with a view to the provision of relevant benefits;

       (b) that the income or gains accruing to a scheme under which the benefit is provided are not brought into charge to tax; and

       (c) that no deduction is applicable under subsection (10) or (11) above.

     (16) Section 839 shall apply for the purposes of subsection (11) above.

     (17) In subsection (13) above "market value" shall be construed in accordance with section 272 of the 1992 Act."

   (6) The amendments of section 596A made by this section shall have effect in relation to retirement benefit schemes—

     (a)   entered into on or after 1st December 1993, or

     (b)   entered into before that day if the scheme is varied on or after that day with a view to the provision of the benefit.

   (7) Subject to subsection (8) below, in the Taxes Act 1988—

     (a)   in section 188(1), paragraph (c), and

     (b)   in section 189, paragraph (b),

(exemption from tax where recipient of benefit or lump sum chargeable to tax in respect of sums paid or treated as paid with a view to the provision of the benefit or lump sum) shall cease to have effect in relation to any benefit provided or lump sum paid on or after 1st December 1993.

   (8) The repeals made by subsection (7) above shall not have effect in relation to any benefit provided or lump sum paid on or after 1st December 1993 in pursuance of a scheme or arrangement entered into before that day unless the scheme or arrangement is varied on or after that day with a view to the provision of the benefit or lump sum.

GENERAL NOTE

   A lump sum received from a funded, unapproved retirement benefit scheme (FURBS) which has not been subject to U.K. tax, is chargeable to tax on the difference between the amount received and the total contributions paid in. If the lump sum is paid by means of the disposal of part of an asset, or the surrender of part of or share in any rights in any asset and the employee (or anyone connected with him) is entitled to receive or to expect a further lump sum or sums in the future, only a proportion of the contributions are allowable.

   The provisions apply to retirement benefit schemes made or varied after November 29, 1993.

Annuities

Annuities derived from personal pension schemes

   109.—(1) In Chapter IV of Part XIV of the Taxes Act 1988 (personal pension schemes) the following shall be inserted after section 648—

"Annuities: charge to tax

Annuities: charge under Schedule E

648A.—(1) Subject to subsection (2) below, where funds held for the purposes of an approved personal pension scheme are used to acquire an annuity—

    (a) the annuity shall be charged to tax under Schedule E and section 203 shall apply accordingly;

    (b) the annuity shall not be charged to tax under Case III of Schedule D.

(2) As respects any approved personal pension scheme the Board may direct that, until such date as the Board may specify, annuities acquired with funds held for the purposes of the scheme shall be charged to tax as annual payments under Case III of Schedule D, and tax shall be deductible under sections 348 and 349 accordingly."

(2) This section shall apply in relation to payments which are made under annuities on or after 6th April 1995.

<small>GENERAL NOTE</small>

The new s.648A is inserted into the ICTA 1988 (c. 1). Annuities paid by approved personal pension schemes fall within PAYE as from April 6, 1995.

Annuities derived from retirement benefits schemes

110.—(1) In section 597 of the Taxes Act 1988 (pensions paid under retirement benefits schemes generally charged under Schedule E) the following subsection shall be inserted after subsection (2)—

"(3) Without prejudice to subsection (1) above, where funds held for the purposes of any scheme which is approved or is being considered for approval under this Chapter are used to acquire an annuity—

    (a) the annuity shall be charged to tax under Schedule E and section 203 shall apply accordingly;

    (b) the annuity shall not be charged to tax under Case III of Schedule D."

(2) This section shall apply in relation to payments which are made under annuities on or after the day on which this Act is passed.

<small>GENERAL NOTE</small>

Where trustees of a retirement benefit scheme use trust funds to purchase an annuity for a scheme member instead of paying a pension out of those funds, the annuity remains taxable under PAYE.

The provisions apply to payments made on or after Royal Assent.

Authorised unit trusts

Rate of corporation tax

111.—(1) In section 468E of the Taxes Act 1988 (authorised unit trusts: corporation tax), for subsection (2) (deemed rate of corporation tax) there shall be substituted—

"(2) The rate of corporation tax—

    (a) for the financial year 1993, shall be deemed to be 22.5 per cent.; and

(b) subject to subsection (3) below and section 468EE, for any other financial year shall be deemed to be the rate at which income tax at the basic rate is charged for the year of assessment which begins on 6th April in the financial year concerned."

(2) After that section there shall be inserted—

"Corporation tax: cases where lower rate applies
468EE.—(1) Where this subsection applies, the rate of corporation tax for the financial year shall be deemed to be the rate at which income tax at the lower rate is charged for the year of assessment which begins on 6th April in that financial year.

(2) Subsection (1) above only applies—

(a) for the financial year 1994 and subsequent financial years; and

(b) where, on a claim made within the period of twelve months from the end of accounting period which or part of which falls in the financial year concerned, it is shown to the satisfaction of the inspector that throughout that accounting period the condition in subsection (3) below is fulfilled by the investments subject to the trusts of the authorised unit trust.

(3) The condition in this subsection is fulfilled by the investments if the market value of such of those investments as are qualifying investments does not exceed 60 per cent. of the market value of all those investments.

(4) For the purposes of subsection (3) above "qualifying investments" means any of the following investments—

(a) any money placed at interest;

(b) any security—

(i) including any loan stock or similar security whether of the Government of the United Kingdom or of any other government or of any public or local authority in the United Kingdom or elsewhere, or of any company, and whether secured or unsecured, but

(ii) excluding shares in a company;

(c) any shares in a building society; and

(d) an entitlement to a share in the investments subject to the trusts of another authorised unit trust, unless, throughout the relevant period, the condition in subsection (5) below is fulfilled by the investments subject to the trusts of that other authorised unit trust.

(5) The condition in this subsection is fulfilled by the investments if the market value of such of the investments as fall within paragraphs (a) to (c) of subsection (4) above does not exceed 60 per cent. of the market value of all those investments.

(6) In subsection (4)(d) above "the relevant period" means the accounting period in relation to which by virtue of subsection (2)(b) above the question whether the entitlement is a "qualifying investment" falls to be determined.

(7) For the purpose of this section "investment" does not include cash awaiting investment.

(8) The Treasury may by order amend this section so as to extend or restrict the meaning of qualifying investments for the purposes of subsection (3) above.

(9) An order under subsection (8) above may contain such transitional provision as the Treasury think necessary or expedient."

GENERAL NOTE

For the financial year 1994 the deemed corporation tax rate applicable to authorised unit trusts is 25 per cent. This is reduced to 20 per cent. if, on a claim made within 12 months after the end of the unit trust's accounting period, it is shown that throughout the accounting period, less than 60 per cent. (either directly or indirectly via an investment in another unit trust) of the value of the unit trust's investments were "qualifying investments" (broadly, debt instruments and deposits and building society shares).

The Treasury may by regulations extend or reduce the categories of qualifying investments and such regulations may contain transitional provisions as are deemed necessary or expedient.

Distributions of authorised unit trusts

112. Schedule 14 to this Act (distributions of authorised unit trusts) shall have effect.

Umbrella schemes

113.—(1) In section 468 of the Taxes Act 1988 (authorised unit trusts), in subsection (6) (definitions) at the beginning there shall be inserted "Subject to subsections (7) to (9) below".

(2) After that subsection there shall be added—

"(7) Each of the parts of an umbrella scheme shall be regarded for the purposes of this Chapter as an authorised unit trust and the scheme as a whole shall not be so regarded.

(8) In this section, "umbrella scheme" means a unit trust scheme—

(a) which provides arrangements for separate pooling of the contributions of the participants and the profits or income out of which payments are to be made to them;

(b) under which the participants are entitled to exchange rights in one pool for rights in another; and

(c) in the case of which an order under section 78 of the Financial Services Act 1986 is in force;

and any reference to a part of an umbrella scheme is a reference to such of the arrangements as relate to a separate pool.

(9) In relation to a part of an umbrella scheme, any reference—

(a) to investments subject to the trusts of an authorised unit trust, shall have effect as a reference to such of the investments as under the arrangements form part of the separate pool to which the part of the umbrella scheme relates; and

(b) to a unit holder, shall have effect as a reference to a person for the time being having rights in that separate pool."

(3) In section 469 of the Taxes Act 1988 (other unit trusts)—

(a) in subsection (1)(a) (application of section) for the words "that is not an authorised unit trust" there shall be substituted "that is neither an authorised unit trust nor an umbrella scheme"; and

(b) after subsection (6) there shall be inserted—

"(6A) In this section "umbrella scheme" has the same meaning as in section 468."

(4) Subject to what follows, the amendments made by subsections (1) to (3) above shall have effect on and after 1st April 1994 in relation to unit trust schemes and their participants.

(5) Nothing in those amendments shall have effect before the relevant date in relation to a unit trust scheme which immediately before 1st April 1994 falls within the definition of an umbrella scheme contained in those amendments.

(6) In this section "the relevant date", means, in relation to a unit trust scheme, the day after the end of the last distribution period of the scheme which commences before 1st April 1994.

(7) On and after the relevant date, the amendments made by subsections (1) to (3) above shall have effect in relation to a scheme—

(a) to which subsection (5) above applies, and

(b) which immediately before the relevant date falls within the definition of an umbrella scheme contained in those amendments, subject to subsections (8) to (10) below.

(8) The amendments made by subsections (1) to (3) above shall not prevent the trustees of the scheme on and after the relevant date—

(a) making a claim under section 239(3) of the Taxes Act 1988 (carry back of surplus advance corporation tax) in respect of accounting periods of the scheme ending before the relevant date; or

(b) continuing anything which immediately before that date was in the process of being done for the purposes of tax in relation to such accounting periods.

(9) Where immediately before the relevant date the trustees of the scheme are entitled to carry forward an excess under—

(a) section 75(3) of the Taxes Act 1988 (carry forward of management expenses and sums treated as management expenses), or

(b) section 241 of that Act (carry forward of franked investment income), then, on the relevant date, that right shall be translated into a right in each successor company to carry forward a proportionate part of that excess.

(10) Where immediately before the relevant date the trustees of the scheme have an amount of surplus advance corporation tax which—

(a) has not been dealt with under subsection (3) of section 239 of the Taxes Act 1988, and

(b) is due to be treated under subsection (4) of that section as if it were advance corporation tax paid by them in their next accounting period, then, on and after the relevant date, a proportionate part of that amount shall be treated as paid under subsection (4) of that section by each successor company in its first accounting period.

(11) In subsections (9) and (10) above "successor company" means, in relation to a scheme, each part of the scheme which on the relevant date becomes an authorised unit trust.

GENERAL NOTE

This section ensures, by amendment of the ICTA 1988 (c. 1), s.468, that where an authorised unit trust is divided into sub-funds, the sub-funds are treated as if they were separate authorised unit trusts for corporation tax purposes. A proportionate part of surplus ACT, surplus franked investment income and surplus management expenses of the umbrella scheme may be carried forward to each of the separate successor unit trusts. Provision is made for surplus ACT generated after April 1, 1994 to be carried back.

The provisions apply from April 1, 1994.

Exchange gains and losses

Assets and liabilities

114.—(1) In section 154 of the Finance Act 1993 (definitions connected with assets) the following subsections shall be inserted after subsection (5)—

"(5A) The question whether a company becomes unconditionally entitled at a particular time to an asset falling within section 153(1)(a) above shall be determined without reference to the fact that there is or is not a later time when, or before which, the whole or any part of the debt is required to be paid.

(5B) Where an asset falling within section 153(1)(a) above consists of a right to interest—

(a) a company becomes unconditionally entitled to the asset at the time when or (as the case may be) before which the interest is required to be paid to the company, and

(b) subsection (5A) above shall not apply."

(2) In that section the following subsections shall be inserted after subsection (13)—

"(13A) In a case where—
(a) a company would (apart from this subsection) become entitled to an asset at a particular time (the earlier time) by virtue of subsections (1) to (11) above,
(b) the asset falls within section 153(1)(a) above and the debt concerned is a debt on a security, or the asset is a share,
(c) the time at which the company, in drawing up its accounts, regards itself as becoming entitled to the asset is a time (the later time) later than the earlier time, and
(d) the accounts are drawn up in accordance with normal accountancy practice,
the company shall be taken to become entitled to the asset at the later time and not at the earlier time.
(13B) In a case where—
(a) a company would (apart from this subsection) cease to be entitled to an asset at a particular time (the earlier time) by virtue of subsections (1) to (11) above,
(b) the asset falls within section 153(1)(a) above and the debt concerned is a debt on a security, or the asset is a share,
(c) the time at which the company, in drawing up its accounts, regards itself as ceasing to be entitled to the asset is a time (the later time) later than the earlier time, and
(d) the accounts are drawn up in accordance with normal accountancy practice,
the company shall be taken to cease to be entitled to the asset at the later time and not at the earlier time."
(3) In section 155 of that Act (definitions connected with liabilities) the following subsections shall be inserted after subsection (4)—
"(4A) The question whether a company becomes unconditionally subject at a particular time to a liability falling within section 153(2)(a) above shall be determined without reference to the fact that there is or is not a later time when, or before which, the whole or any part of the debt is required to be paid.
(4B) Where a liability falling within section 153(2)(a) above consists of a duty to pay interest—
(a) a company becomes unconditionally subject to the liability at the time when or (as the case may be) before which the company is required to pay the interest, and
(b) subsection (4A) above shall not apply."

GENERAL NOTE
Amendments are made to the FA 1993 (c. 34), ss.154 and 155. A company is treated as becoming unconditionally (a) entitled to a qualifying asset, or (b) subject to a liability on a qualifying asset, from when the obligation to pay arises. Where the debt represents interest the latter rule does not apply; instead the company is treated as becoming unconditionally entitled to the interest, or subject to a liability to pay the interest, when (or before) it is due.
Where a company, in accordance with normal accountancy practice, accounts for the acquisition or disposal of shares or securities in its accounts at a later date than the contract date, that later date may be used in computing exchange gains or losses.

Currency contracts: net payments

115.—(1) In section 126 of the Finance Act 1993 (accrual on currency contracts) the following subsection shall be inserted after subsection (1)—
"(1A) In deciding whether a contract falls within subsection (1) above it is immaterial that the rights and duties there mentioned may be exercised and discharged by a payment made to or, as the case may require, by the qualifying company of an amount (in whatever currency) designed to represent any difference in value at the specified time between the two payments referred to in that subsection."

(2) In section 146 of that Act (early termination of currency contract) the following subsection shall be inserted after subsection (1)—
> "(1A) This section also applies where—
>> (a) a qualifying company ceases to be entitled to rights and subject to duties under a currency contract, and
>> (b) it so ceases by virtue of the making of a payment to or by the company of an amount (in whatever currency) designed to represent any difference in value at the specified time between the two payments referred to in section 126(1) above."

(3) In section 164(2) of that Act (definition of currency contract for purposes of the Chapter) after "(1)" there shall be inserted "and (1A)".

GENERAL NOTE

Subs. (1)
The definition of currency contracts in the FA 1993 (c. 34), s.126 is amended to include contracts which provide for net payments rather than the actual exchange of the currencies.

Subs. (2)
The FA 1993 (c. 34), s.146 is amended to ensure that it applies where a currency contract is terminated by a net payment.

Currency contracts: matching

116.—(1) Schedule 15 to the Finance Act 1993 (alternative calculation) shall be amended as follows.

(2) The following shall be inserted after paragraph 4—

"Currency contracts: matching

4A.—(1) Regulations may provide that where—
(a) as regards a contract an initial exchange gain or initial exchange loss accrues to a company for an accrual period under section 126 (5) of this Act or would so accrue apart from regulations under this Schedule,
(b) the relevant duty is eligible to be matched on any day in the accrual period with an asset held by the company, and such other conditions as may be prescribed are fulfilled, and
(c) an election is made in accordance with the regulations to match the duty with the asset on any such day and the election has effect by virtue of the regulations,
the amount of the gain or loss shall be found in accordance with the alternative method of calculation.

(2) Regulations may also provide that as regards any day in respect of which an election has effect the accrued amount shall be ascertained in accordance with prescribed rules.

(3) The reference in sub-paragraph (1) above to the relevant duty is to the duty to which, under the contract, the company becomes subject as regards the second currency (within the meaning given by section 126 of this Act).

(4) Where regulations are made under this paragraph, sub-paragraphs (3) to (12) of paragraph 4 above shall apply as they apply where regulations are made under that paragraph; but in the application of those sub-paragraphs by virtue of this sub-paragraph—

(a) the references to a liability in sub-paragraphs (3), (4), (9) and (11) shall be construed as references to a duty,

(b) the references to liabilities in sub-paragraphs (3) and (4) shall be construed as references to duties, and

(c) the reference in sub-paragraph (11)(a) to sub-paragraph (1) of paragraph 4 shall be construed as a reference to sub-paragraph (1) above."

(3) The following paragraph shall be inserted after paragraph 5—

"5A.—(1) This paragraph applies where regulations under both paragraph 2 and paragraph 4A above apply—

(a) as regards the same contract, and

(b) for the same accrual period.

(2) Regulations may provide that, as regards any day falling within the period and identified in accordance with prescribed rules, and accrued amount shall be ascertained in accordance with rules prescribed under this paragraph (rather than provisions made under either of those paragraphs)."

(4) In paragraph 6—

(a) for "paragraphs 2 to 5 above" there shall be substituted "the relevant paragraphs";

(b) at the end there shall be inserted "; and the relevant paragraphs are paragraphs 2, 3, 4 and 5 above."

(5) In paragraph 7 for "5" there shall be substituted "5A".

GENERAL NOTE

Paragraphs 4A and 5A are inserted into Sched. 15 to the FA 1993 (c. 34) to enable regulations to be made permitting a company to match non-monetary assets (instead of borrowings) with a currency contract.

Capital allowances

Expenditure on machinery or plant

117.—(1) At the end of section 83 of the Capital Allowances Act 1990 (interpretation of Part II, which relates to machinery and plant) there shall be added—

"(7) Schedule AA1 (which excludes certain expenditure from the expression 'expenditure on the provision of machinery or plant') shall have effect."

and before Schedule A1 to that Act there shall be inserted—

"SCHEDULE AA1

EXCLUSIONS FROM EXPENDITURE ON MACHINERY OR PLANT

Buildings

1.—(1) For the purposes of this Act expenditure on the provision of machinery or plant does not include any expenditure on the provision of a building.

(2) For the purposes of this Schedule 'building' includes an asset in the building—

(a) which is incorporated into the building, or

(b) which, by reason of being moveable or otherwise, is not so incorporated, but is of a kind normally incorporated into buildings;

and in particular includes any asset in or in connection with the building included in any of the items in column 1 or column 2 of the following Table ('Table 1').

(3) Sub-paragraph (1) above does not affect the question whether expenditure on the provision of—

(a) any asset falling within column 2 of Table 1,
(b) any cold store,
(c) any caravan provided mainly for holiday lettings,
(d) any building provided for testing aircraft engines run within the building, or
(e) any moveable building intended to be moved in the course of the trade,

is for the purposes of this Act expenditure on the provision of machinery or plant.

(4) Table 1 is to be read subject to the notes following it.

TABLE 1

(1) *Assets included in the expression* *'building'*	(2) *Assets so included, but expenditure on which* *is unaffected by the Schedule*
A. Walls, floors, ceilings, doors, gates, shutters, windows and stairs.	1. Electrical, cold water, gas and sewerage systems— (a) provided mainly to meet the particular requirements of the trade, or (b) provided mainly to serve particular machinery or plant used for the purposes of the trade.
	2. Space or water heating systems; powered systems of ventilation, air cooling or air purification; and any ceiling or floor comprised in such systems.
B. Mains services, and systems, of water, electricity and gas.	3. Manufacturing or processing equipment; storage equipment, including cold rooms; display equipment; and counters, checkouts and similar equipment.
	4. Cookers, washing machines, dishwashers, refrigerators and similar equipment; washbasins, sinks, baths, showers, sanitary ware and similar equipment; and furniture and furnishings.
C. Waste disposal systems.	5. Lifts, hoists, escalators and moving walkways.
	6. Sound insulation provided mainly to meet the particular requirements of the trade.
D. Sewerage and drainage systems.	7. Computer, telecommunication and surveillance systems (including their wiring or other links).
	8. Refrigeration or cooling equipment.
E. Shafts or other structures in which lifts, hoists, escalators and moving walkways are installed.	9. Sprinkler equipment and other equipment for extinguishing or containing fire; fire alarm systems.
	10. Burglar alarm systems.
	11. Any machinery (including devices for providing motive power) not within any other item in this column.
F. Fire safety systems.	12. Strong rooms in bank or building society premises; safes.

(1) *Assets included in the expression 'building'*	(2) *Assets so included, but expenditure on which is unaffected by the Schedule*
	13. Partition walls, where moveable and intended to be moved in the course of the trade.
	14. Decorative assets provided for the enjoyment of the public in the hotel, restaurant or similar trades.
	15. Advertising hoardings; and signs, displays and similar assets.
	16. Swimming pools (including diving boards, slides and structures on which such boards or slides are mounted).

Notes:
1. An asset does not fall within column 2 if its principal purpose is to insulate or enclose the interior of the building or provide an interior wall, a floor or a ceiling which (in each case) is intended to remain permanently in place.
2. 'Electrical systems' include lighting systems.

Structures, assets and works

2.—(1) for the purposes of this Act expenditure on the provision of machinery or plant does not include any expenditure on—
  (a) the provision of structures or other assets to which this paragraph applies, or
  (b) any works involving the alteration of land.
(2) This paragraph applies to any structure or other asset which falls within column 1 of the following Table ('Table 2').
(3) Sub-paragraph (1) above does not affect the question whether—
  (a) any expenditure falling within column 2 of Table 2, or
  (b) any expenditure on the provision of any asset of a description within any of the items in column 2 of Table 1,
is for the purposes of this Act expenditure of the provision of machinery or plant.
(4) Table 2 is to be read subject to the notes following it.

TABLE 2

(1) *Structures and assets*	(2) *Expenditure which is unaffected by the Schedule*
A. Any tunnel, bridge, viaduct, aqueduct, embankment or cutting.	1. Expenditure on the alteration of land for the purpose only of installing machinery or plant.
B. Any way or hard standing, such as a pavement, road, railway or tramway, a park for vehicles or containers, or an airstrip or runway.	2. Expenditure on the provision of dry docks. 3. Expenditure on the provision of any jetty or similar structure provided mainly to carry machinery or plant.
C. Any inland navigation, including a canal or basin or a navigable river.	4. Expenditure on the provision of pipelines, or underground ducts or tunnels with a primary purpose of carrying utility conduits. 5. Expenditure on the provision of towers provided to support floodlights.

(1) *Structures and assets*	*(2)* *Expenditure which is unaffected by* *the Schedule*
D. Any dam, reservoir or barrage (including any sluices, gates, generators and other equipment associated with it).	6. Expenditure on the provision of any reservoir incorporated into a water treatment works or on the provision of any service reservoir of treated water for supply within any housing estate or other particular locality.
E. Any dock.	7. Expenditure on the provision of silos provided for temporary storage or on the provision of storage tanks.
	8. Expenditure on the provision of slurry pits or silage clamps.
F. Any dike, sea wall, weir or drainage ditch.	9. Expenditure on the provision of fish tanks or fish ponds.
G. Any structure not within any other item in this column.	10. Expenditure on the provision of rails, sleepers and ballast for a railway or tramway.
	11. Expenditure on the provision of structures and other assets for providing the setting for any ride at an amusement park or exhibition.
	12. Expenditure on the provision of fixed zoo cages.

Notes:

1. 'Dock' includes—

(a) any harbour, wharf, pier, marina or jetty, and

(b) any other structure in or at which vessels may be kept or merchandise or passengers may be shipped or unshipped.

2. An industrial structure, that is, anything (other than a building) which is or is to be an industrial building or structure as defined in section 18, is not within item G in column 1; and that section, as it applies for the purposes of this note, shall have effect as if—

(a) in subsection (1)(b), after 'electricity' there were inserted 'gas',

(b) after that paragraph there were inserted—

'(ba) for the purposes of a trade which consists in the provision of telecommunication, television or radio services; or', and

(c) in subsection (9), after the definition of 'foreign plantation', there were inserted—

' "gas undertaking" means an undertaking for the extraction, production, processing or distribution of gas'.

Land

3.—(1) For the purposes of this Act expenditure on the provision of machinery or plant does not include expenditure on the acquisition of any interest in land.

(2) This paragraph does not apply for the purposes of Part II to any asset which is so installed or otherwise fixed in or to any description of land as to become, in law, part of that land.

General exemptions

4. Paragraphs 1(1) and 2(1) above do not apply to any expenditure to which section 67, 67A, 68, 69, 70 or 71 applies.

Interpretation

5.—(1) In this Schedule—
(a) 'structure' means a fixed structure of any kind, other than a building, and
(b) references to the provision of any building, structure or other asset include references to its construction or acquisition.

(2) Nothing in this Schedule affects the question whether expenditure on the provision of any glasshouse which is constructed so that the required environment (that is, air, heat, light, irrigation and temperature) for growing plants is provided automatically by means of devices which are an integral part of its structure is, for the purposes of this Act, expenditure on the provision of machinery or plant.

(3) The definition of 'land' in Schedule 1 to the Interpretation Act 1978, in its application for the purposes of this Schedule, shall have effect with the omission of the words 'buildings and other structures'; and, subject to that, 'interest in land' in paragraph 3 above has the same meaning as in Chapter VI of Part II."

(2) This section shall have effect in relation to expenditure incurred on or after 30th November 1993 unless—
(a) it is incurred before 6th April 1996 in pursuance of a contract entered into before 30th November 1993, or
(b) it is incurred before 6th April 1996 in pursuance of a contract entered into, for the purpose of securing that the obligations under a contract entered into before 30th November 1993 are complied with, on or after 30th November 1993.

GENERAL NOTE

At present there is no general statutory definition of plant for capital allowance purposes. This has led to a profusion of case law where it has been unclear whether a particular asset qualified as plant. New Sched. AA1 is inserted into the CAA 1990 (c. 1) which provides new rules which are designed to make the boundaries clearer by providing that land, buildings and structures cannot qualify as plant. Expenditure on building and structures which specific decisions of the court have shown to be plant are unaffected by these new rules.

The first columns of Tables 1 and 2 specifically list those items of expenditure which fall within the definition of building and structure.

The second columns of Tables 1 and 2 list those items of expenditure which are unaffected by the new rules, the existing case law will apply to them although this does not necessarily mean that they will qualify as plant.

Expenditure on the acquisition of any interest in land does not qualify as plant except in so far as it relates to a machinery or plant fixture. The new rules do not apply to expenditure on: thermal insulation; computer software; films; tapes and disks; fire safety; safety on sports grounds or personal security.

Schedule AA1 has effect in relation to expenditure incurred after November 29, 1993 unless it is incurred before April 5, 1996 in pursuance of contractual obligations entered into before November 30, 1993.

Expenditure on machinery or plant: notification

118.—(1) A first year allowance shall not be made under—
(a) section 22 of the Capital Allowances Act 1990 (first-year allowances in respect of expenditure on machinery or plant), or
(b) section 41 of the Finance Act 1971 (provision corresponding to section 22 applicable to earlier chargeable periods),
for any chargeable period (whenever ending) unless the relevant condition is fulfilled with respect to that period.
(2) For the purposes of—

(a) section 25(1) of the 1990 Act (meaning of qualifying expenditure for the purposes of writing-down allowances for expenditure on machinery or plant), and

(b) section 44(4) of the 1971 Act (provision corresponding to section 25(1) applicable to earlier chargeable periods),

no expenditure may form part of a person's qualifying expenditure for any chargeable period (whenever ending) unless the relevant condition is fulfilled with respect to that period.

(3) The relevant condition is fulfilled with respect to a chargeable period ending on or after 30th November 1993 if notice of the expenditure is given to the inspector, in such form as the Board may require, not later than two years after the end of that period.

(4) The relevant condition is fulfilled with respect to a chargeable period ending before 30th November 1993 if—

(a) the expenditure was included in a computation which—

(i) was required to be made for any tax purpose,

(ii) was given before that date to an inspector, and

(iii) was not contained in a document prepared primarily for a purpose which was not a tax purpose; or

(b) notice of the expenditure is given to the inspector, in such form as the Board may require, not later than three years after the end of that period; or

(c) if the chargeable period ends on or after 1st December 1990, notice of the expenditure is so given before the passing of this Act.

(5) If in a particular case it appears to the Board appropriate to do so, having regard to all the circumstances of the case (including in particular any unforeseeable circumstances which have delayed the giving of any notice or computation), they may extend the period within which for the purposes of subsection (3) or (4) above any notice or computation is to be given to the inspector.

(6) For the purposes of the provisions mentioned in subsection (2) above expenditure which has not formed part of a person's qualifying expenditure for a previous chargeable period may not form part of his qualifying expenditure for a subsequent chargeable period unless the machinery or plant on which the expenditure was incurred belongs to that person at some time in that subsequent period or its basis period.

(7) No relief shall be given under section 33 or 42 of the Taxes Management Act 1970 in respect of a claim of error or mistake to the extent that the error or mistake consists of or arises from a failure to fulfil the relevant condition in relation to a chargeable period.

(8) In this section "the 1990 Act" means the Capital Allowances Act 1990 and "the 1971 Act" means the Finance Act 1971; and expressions used in subsections (1) to (6) above have the same meaning as in the 1990 Act or (as the case may be) the 1971 Act.

(9) Any such adjustment as is appropriate in consequence of this section may be made (whether by way of discharge or repayment of tax, the making of an assessment or otherwise).

GENERAL NOTE

Capital allowances in respect of expenditure on machinery or plant may only be made if the expenditure is notified to the inspector within two years (three years for chargeable periods ending before November 30, 1993) of the end of the period to which the claim relates, in a form approved by the Board.

The Board have discretionary powers to extend these time-limits. For chargeable periods ending before November 30, 1993 inclusion of the expenditure in a tax computation submitted before that date constitutes notice for these purposes. Where expenditure is not notified within the relevant time-limits, writing down allowances may be claimed for a subsequent period, provided the asset in question belongs to the claimant in that subsequent period or basis period and notification for that later period is given on time.

Transactions between connected persons

119.—(1) Section 158(2) of the Capital Allowances Act 1990 (election exercisable in the case of transactions between connected persons, etc.) shall be assumed always to have had effect subject to the amendments made by section 117(2) and (3) of the Finance Act 1993 (transactions between connected persons: qualifying hotels, commercial buildings and scientific research expenditure).

(2) Paragraph 4(2) of Schedule 7 to the Capital Allowances Act 1968 (provision corresponding to section 158(2)) shall be assumed always to have had effect subject to amendments corresponding to those made to section 158(2) of the 1990 Act by section 117(2) and (3) of the Finance Act 1993.

GENERAL NOTE
This enables a person to elect to treat a sale, taking place before March 16, 1993, of qualifying hotels, commercial buildings in enterprise zones and assets representing scientific research expenditure, to a connected person, as taking place at their tax written down value.

Balancing charge on realisation of capital value

120.—(1) The Capital Allowances Act 1990 shall be amended as follows:
(2) In section 4 (balancing adjustments)—
(a) in subsection (1) (events giving rise to an adjustment), after "or" at the end of paragraph (d) there is inserted—
"(dd) any capital value is realised (within the meaning of section 4A), or",
and for "subsection (2)" there is substituted "subsections (2) and (9A)", and
(b) after subsection (9) there is inserted—
"(9A) No balancing allowance shall be made by reason of any event falling within subsection (1)(dd) above; and (subject to that) in relation to such an event—
(a) this Part and (so far as relating to it) Part VIII shall have effect as if references to sale, insurance, salvage or compensation moneys were references to the capital value realised, and
(b) subsections (5) to (7) and (9) above shall have effect as if immediately after the event the capital expenditure were reduced by the amount of the capital value realised".
(3) After that section there is inserted—

"Realisation of capital value

4A.—(1) Where any capital expenditure has been incurred on the construction of a building or structure and, while the building or structure is an industrial building or structure or after it has ceased to be one—
(a) an amount of capital value is paid which is attributable to an interest in land (the 'subordinate interest') to which the relevant interest in the building or structure is or will be subject, and
(b) the payment is made not more than seven years after the agreement relating to the capital expenditure was entered into or (if the agreement was conditional) the time when the agreement became unconditional,
capital value of that amount is realised for the purposes of this Part on making the payment.

(2) For the purposes of this section, capital value is attributable to the subordinate interest if—

(a) it is paid in consideration of the grant of the subordinate interest,

(b) it is paid in lieu of any rent payable by the person entitled to the subordinate interest or paid in consideration of the assignment of such rent, or

(c) it is paid in consideration of the surrender of the subordinate interest or the variation or waiver of any of the terms on which it was granted.

(3) For the purposes of this section, 'capital value'—

(a) means any capital sum and includes what would have been a capital sum if it had taken the form of a money payment, and 'payment' and 'paid' shall be interpreted accordingly, but

(b) does not include so much of any sum as corresponds to any amount of rent or profits falling to be computed by reference to that sum under section 34 of the principal Act (premium, etc. treated as rent or Schedule D profits).

(4) Where—

(a) no premium is given in consideration of the grant of the subordinate interest or any premium given is less than the amount which would have been given by way of premium if the transaction had been at arm's length, and

(b) no commercial rent is payable in respect of the subordinate interest,

subsection (2) above shall have effect as if the amount referred to in paragraph (a) above (and not any premium actually given) were paid on and in consideration of the grant of the interest.

(5) Where—

(a) any rent payable in respect of the subordinate interest is assigned, the subordinate interest is surrendered or any of the terms on which the subordinate interest was granted are varied or waived, but

(b) no value is given in consideration of the event concerned, or any value given in consideration of the event concerned is less than the amount that would have been given if the transaction had been at arm's length,

subsection (2) above shall have effect as if that amount (and not any value actually given) were paid on and in consideration of the event concerned.

(6) Where any value given in lieu of any rent payable by the person entitled to the subordinate interest is less than the amount that would have been given if the transaction had been at arm's length, subsection (2) above shall have effect as if that amount (and not any value actually given) had been paid.

(7) This section shall apply with the omission of subsection (1)(b) above in any case where—

(a) arrangements under which the person entitled to the relevant interest acquired it include provision in respect of the subsequent sale of the relevant interest, the subsequent grant out of the relevant interest of an interest in land or any other event on which capital value attributable to the subordinate interest would be, or be treated as, paid, and

(b) either the provision concerned requires such a sale, grant or other event to occur or such a sale, grant or other event is substantially more likely to occur than if the provision had not been made;

and the reference to arrangements in paragraph (a) above includes any arrangements made in connection with the acquisition of the relevant interest.

(8) This section does not apply to the grant of any interest in land to which an election under section 11 applies.

(9) In this section 'interest in land' means—

(a) a leasehold estate in the land (whether in the nature of a head-lease, sub-lease or under-lease),

(b) an easement or servitude, and

(c) a licence to occupy land;

and references to granting an interest in land include agreeing to grant any interest falling within paragraphs (a) to (c) above.

(10) In this section 'commercial rent' means such rent as may reasonably be expected to have been required in respect of the subordinate interest (having regard to any premium given in consideration of the grant of the interest) if the transaction had been at arm's length.

(11) For the purposes of this section, where—

(a) an agreement is made to pay in respect of any event an amount of capital value which would be attributable to the subordinate interest, and

(b) the agreement is made or (if the agreement is conditional) becomes unconditional before the expiry of the period of seven years referred to in subsection (1)(b) above, but the event occurs, or any payment in consideration of the event is made, afterwards,

the event or payment shall be treated as occurring or made before the expiry of the period.

(12) For the purposes of this section, an agreement relates to any capital expenditure referred to in subsection (1) above if—

(a) it is the agreement under which the expenditure was incurred, or

(b) where the expenditure is deemed for the purposes of sections 1 to 8 to have been incurred by a person who acquired the relevant interest, it is the agreement under which he acquired the relevant interest.

(13) In the application of this section to Scotland—

(a) references to assignment shall be read as references to assignation, and

(b) references to a leasehold estate in land shall be read as references to a lease of land."

(4) In section 5 (restriction of balancing allowance where interest has been sold subject to subordinate interest), after subsection (2) there is inserted—

"(2A) Where the net proceeds to the relevant person of the sale fall to be increased or determined under subsection (2) above, those proceeds as so increased or determined shall be taken to be reduced by the amount of any capital value realised before the sale".

(5) In section 6 (buildings, etc. in enterprise zones), in subsection (4), after "4(1)" there is inserted "4A(1)".

(6) In section 8 (writing off expenditure)—

(a) after subsection (12A) there is inserted—

"(12B) Where any event occurs to which section 4(1)(dd) applies, there shall be treated as written off as at the time of the event an amount equal to the capital value realised", and

(b) in subsection (13), for "(12A)" there is substituted "(12B)".

(7) Subject to subsection (8) below, this section applies—

(a) where capital expenditure has been incurred under a relevant contract, or

(b) where capital expenditure is deemed for the purposes of sections 1 to 8 to have been incurred by a person who under a relevant contract acquires the relevant interest;

and "relevant contract" means a contract entered into on or after 13th January 1994 or a conditional contract entered into before that date which becomes unconditional after 25th February 1994.

(8) This section applies to capital expenditure on the construction of a building or structure only if the expenditure, or, in the case of expenditure

falling within subsection (7)(b) above, the actual expenditure on the construction of the building or structure to which the expenditure so falling relates, is incurred, or is incurred under a contract entered into, at a time when the site of the building or structure is wholly or mainly in an enterprise zone, being a time not more than 10 years after the site was first included in the zone.

GENERAL NOTE

The new s.4A is inserted into the CAA 1990 (c. 1) and other amendments are made to s.4 of that Act.

Where a capital value is realised: (a) on the occasion of the grant of a subordinate interest out of the relevant interest in a building or structure situated in an enterprise zone or (b) on the surrender of the subordinate interest or the variation or waiver of any of the terms on which it was granted or (c) in lieu of rent payable by the person entitled to the subordinate interest or in consideration for the assignment of such rent, it is treated as a balancing event giving rise to a balancing adjustment. If the adjustment results in a balancing allowance, it is ignored.

Where the capital value realised on a transaction falling within (a) to (c) is less than the capital value realisable if the transaction was at arm's length, the arm's length value is substituted.

The provisions do not apply where the capital value is realised more than seven years after the agreement relating to the capital expenditure was entered into or the time when that agreement became unconditional but do apply if the event falling within (a) to (c) above occurs or the capital value is paid after the seven-year period but the agreement in question is made or becomes unconditional within the seven-year period. The seven-year limit does not apply if the relevant interest was acquired under arrangements which included provision relating to the subsequent sale of the relevant interest, the subsequent grant of the subordinate interest or any other event on which capital value attributable to the subordinate interest would be or would be treated as, paid.

"Capital value" includes money and the value of any other form of consideration but excludes premiums treated as rent.

The provisions apply only if the expenditure on construction was incurred under a contract: (i) which is entered into after January 12, 1994, or (ii) a contract which is entered into before that date which becomes unconditional after February 25, 1994.

Used buildings etc. in enterprise zones

121.—(1) Where—
- (a) the relevant interest in a building or structure is sold on a date falling after the expiry of the period of two years beginning with the date on which the building or structure was first used, and
- (b) that period ends, and the date on which the relevant interest is sold falls, within the period beginning with 13th January 1994 and ending with 31st August 1994,

paragraphs (c) and (d) of section 10B(1) of the Capital Allowances Act 1990 (purchaser of building etc. in enterprise zone within two years of first use eligible for allowances) shall have effect as if the period there referred to were the period beginning with the date on which the building or structure was first used and ending with 31st August 1994.

(2) Expressions used in this section and in Part I of the Capital Allowances Act 1990 have the same meaning as in that Part.

GENERAL NOTE

If an enterprise zone building is sold within two years after being brought into use and provided its first use occurred after December 15, 1991, the purchaser is entitled to enterprise zone allowances. This section amends the CAA 1990 (c. 1), s.10B to extend the two-year time-limit to August 31, 1994 if the two-year period ends, and the date on which the relevant interest is sold falls within the period between January 13, 1994 and August 31, 1994.

Securities

Sale and repurchase of securities; deemed manufactured payments

122. After section 737 of the Taxes Act 1988 there shall be inserted the following sections—

"Sale and repurchase of securities: deemed manufactured payments

737A.—(1) This section applies where on or after the appointed day a person (the transferor) agrees to sell any securities, and under the same or any related agreement the transferor or another person connected with him—

(a) is required to buy back the securities, or

(b) acquires an option, which he subsequently exercises, to buy back the securities;

but this section does not apply unless the conditions set out in subsection (2) below are fulfilled.

(2) The conditions are that—

(a) as a result of the transaction, a dividend which becomes payable in respect of the securities is receivable otherwise than by the transferor,

(b) the dividend is not, by virtue of any other provision of the Tax Acts, treated as income of the transferor,

(c) there is no requirement under any agreement mentioned in subsection (1) above for a person to pay to the transferor on or before the relevant date an amount representative of the dividend, and

(d) it is reasonable to assume that, in arriving at the repurchase price of the securities, account was taken of the fact that the dividend is receivable otherwise than by the transferor.

(3) For the purposes of subsection (2) above the relevant date is the date when the repurchase price of the securities becomes due.

(4) Where it is a person connected with the transferor who is required to buy back the securities, or who acquires the option to buy them back, references in the following provisions of this section to the transferor shall be construed as references to the connected person.

(5) Where this section applies, section 737 and Schedule 23A and dividend manufacturing regulations shall apply as if—

(a) the relevant person were required, under the arrangements for the transfer of the securities, to pay to the transferor an amount representative of the dividend mentioned in subsection (2)(a) above,

(b) a payment were made by that person to the transferor in discharge of that requirement, and

(c) the payment were made on the date when the repurchase price of the securities becomes due.

(6) In subsection (5) above "the relevant person" means—

(a) where subsection (1)(a) above applies, the person from whom the transferor is required to buy back the securities;

(b) where subsection (1)(b) above applies, the person from whom the transferor has the right to buy back the securities;

and in that subsection "dividend manufacturing regulations" means regulations under Schedule 23A (whenever made).

Interpretation of section 737A

737B.—(1) In section 737A and this section "securities" means United Kingdom equities, United Kingdom securities or overseas securities; and—

(a) where the securities mentioned in section 737A(1) are United Kingdom securities, references in section 737A to a dividend shall be construed as references to a periodical payment of interest;

(b) where the securities mentioned in section 737A(1) are overseas securities, references in section 737A to a dividend shall be construed as references to an overseas dividend.

(2) In this section "United Kingdom equities", "United Kingdom securities", "overseas securities" and "overseas dividend" have the meanings given by paragraph 1(1) of Schedule 23A.

(3) For the purposes of section 737A agreements are related if each is entered into in pursuance of the same arrangement (regardless of the date on which either agreement is entered into).

(4) In section 737A "the repurchase price of the securities" means—
  (a) where subsection (1)(a) of that section applies, the amount which, under any agreement mentioned in section 737A(1), the transferor or connected person is required to pay for the securities bought back, or
  (b) where subsection (1)(b) of that section applies, the amount which under any such agreement the transferor or connected person is required, if he exercises the option, to pay for the securities bought back.

(5) In section 737A and subsection (4) above references to buying back securities include references to buying similar securities.

(6) For the purposes of subsection (5) above securities are similar if they entitle their holders to the same rights against the same persons as to capital and interest and the same remedies for the enforcement of those rights, notwithstanding any difference in the total nominal amounts of the respective securities or in the form in which they are held or the manner in which they can be transferred; and "interest" here includes dividends.

(7) For the purposes of section 737A and subsection (4) above—
  (a) a person who is connected with the transferor and is required to buy securities sold by the transferor shall be treated as being required to buy the securities back notwithstanding that it was not he who sold them, and
  (b) a person who is connected with the transferor and acquires an option to buy securities sold by the transferor shall be treated as acquiring an option to buy the securities back notwithstanding that it was not he who sold them.

(8) Section 839 shall apply for the purposes of section 737A and this section.

(9) In section 737A "the appointed day" means such day as the Treasury may by order appoint, and different days may be appointed in relation to—
  (a) United Kingdom equities,
  (b) United Kingdom securities, and
  (c) overseas securities.

Deemed manufactured payments: further provisions
737C.—(1) This section applies where section 737A applies.

(2) Subsection (3) below applies where—
  (a) the dividend mentioned in section 737A(2)(a) is a dividend on United Kingdom equities, and
  (b) by virtue of section 737A(5), section 737 and paragraph 2 of Schedule 23A apply, or paragraph 2 of Schedule 23A applies, in relation to the payment which is treated under section 737A(5) as having been made;
and in subsection (3) below "the deemed manufactured dividend" means that payment.

(3) Where this subsection applies—
  (a) the amount of the deemed manufactured dividend shall be taken to be an amount equal to the amount of the dividend mentioned in section 737A(2)(a);

(b) the repurchase price of the securities shall be treated, for the purposes of the Tax Acts other than section 737A and of the 1992 Act, as increased by an amount equal to the gross amount of the deemed manufactured dividend.

(4) In subsection (3) above the reference to the gross amount of the deemed manufactured dividend is to the aggregate of—

(a) the amount of the deemed manufactured dividend, and

(b) the amount of the tax credit that would have been issued in respect of the deemed manufactured dividend had the deemed manufactured dividend in fact been a dividend on the United Kingdom equities.

(5) Subsection (6) below applies where—

(a) the dividend mentioned in section 737A(2)(a) is a periodical payment of interest on United Kingdom securities, and

(b) by virtue of section 737A(5), section 737 applies in relation to the payment which is treated under section 737A(5) as having been made;

and in subsection (6) below "the deemed manufactured interest" means the payment referred to in paragraph (b) above.

(6) Where this subsection applies, the amount of the deemed manufactured interest shall be taken to be an amount equal to the gross amount of the periodical payment referred to in subsection (5)(a) above reduced by an amount equal to income tax thereon at the basic rate for the year of assessment in which that periodical payment is made.

(7) Subsection (8) below applies where—

(a) the dividend mentioned in section 737A(2)(a) is a periodical payment of interest on United Kingdom securities, and

(b) by virtue of section 737A(5), paragraph 3 of Schedule 23A applies in relation to the payment which is treated under section 737A(5) as having been made (whether or not section 737 also applies in relation to that payment);

and in subsection (8) below "the deemed manufactured interest" means the payment referred to in paragraph (b) above.

(8) Where this subsection applies—

(a) the gross amount of the deemed manufactured interest shall be taken to be the amount found under paragraph 3(4) of Schedule 23A;

(b) any deduction which, by virtue of paragraph 3 of Schedule 23A, is required to be made out of the gross amount of the deemed manufactured interest shall be deemed to have been made.

(9) Where subsections (6) and (8) above apply, or where subsection (8) above applies, the repurchase price of the securities shall be treated, for the purposes of the Tax Acts other than section 737A and of the 1992 Act, as increased by the gross amount of the deemed manufactured interest.

(10) Subsection (11) below applies where—

(a) the dividend mentioned in section 737A(2)(a) is an overseas dividend, and

(b) by virtue of section 737A(5), paragraph 4 of Schedule 23A applies in relation to the payment which is treated under section 737A(5) as having been made;

and in subsection (11) below "the deemed manufactured overseas dividend" means that payment.

(11) Where this subsection applies—

(a) the gross amount of the deemed manufactured overseas dividend shall be taken to be the amount found under paragraph 4(5)(b) and (c) of Schedule 23A;

(b) any deduction which, by virtue of paragraph 4 of Schedule 23A, is required to be made out of the gross amount of the deemed manufactured overseas dividend shall be deemed to have been made;

(c) the repurchase price of the securities shall be treated, for the purposes of the Tax Acts other than section 737A and of the 1992 Act, as increased by the gross amount of the deemed manufactured overseas dividend.

(12) In this section—

(a) "United Kingdom equities", "United Kingdom securities" and "overseas dividend" have the meanings given by paragraph 1(1) of Schedule 23A;

(b) "the repurchase price of the securities" shall be construed in accordance with section 737B(4)."

GENERAL NOTE

The new ss.737A, 737B and 737C are inserted into the ICTA 1988 (c. 1).

Section 737A of the ICTA 1988

This section sets out the circumstances where there is deemed to be a payment of a manufactured dividend and the tax consequences.

Where:

(a) on or after the appointed day, a person ("the transferor") agrees to sell securities and under the same or related agreement he (or a connected person); (i) has to repurchase the securities, or (ii) acquires an option, which he subsequently exercises, to repurchase the securities; and

(b) a dividend is received in respect of the securities other than by the transferor; and

(c) the dividend is not treated for tax purposes as the transferor's income and no manufactured payment is to be made to the transferor to compensate him for not receiving the dividend; and

(d) it can reasonably be assumed that the repurchase price has been reduced to compensate the transferor for not receiving the dividend,

the manufactured dividend provisions of the ICTA 1988 (c. 1), s.737 and Sched. 23A are to apply as if the person from whom the transferor repurchases the securities (whether under the agreement or the option) had actually made a manufactured payment to the transferor on the date when the repurchase price becomes due.

If the connected person repurchases the securities, he is deemed to have received the manufactured payment.

Section 737B of the ICTA 1988

This defines various terms used in s.737A above. The appointed day is to be fixed by Treasury Order and different dates may be appointed for U.K. equities, U.K. securities and overseas securities.

Section 737C of the ICTA 1988

The amount of the deemed manufactured payment for the purposes of s.737A above, is:

(a) where the manufactured payment is a dividend on U.K. equities, the amount received by the manufacturer;

(b) where the manufactured payment is a payment of interest on U.K. securities and the payment falls within the ICTA 1988 (c. 1), Sched. 23A, para. 3, the gross interest received by the manufacturer less any deduction required to be made from the actual payment under that paragraph, otherwise it is the gross interest received by the manufacturer less income tax at the basic rate for the year in which the actual interest was received;

(c) where the manufactured payment is an overseas dividend, the aggregate of the net dividend after deduction of overseas tax, the overseas tax so deducted and any overseas tax credit in respect of the dividend.

The repurchase price of the securities is treated as increased by the gross amount of the (i) deemed manufactured dividend, or (ii) deemed manufactured interest payment, or (iii) deemed manufactured overseas dividend, as appropriate.

Manufactured payments

123.—(1) In section 715 of the Taxes Act 1988 (exceptions from provisions about deemed sums and reliefs under the accrued income scheme) in subsection (6) (exceptions in certain cases where section 737 has effect) after "section 737" there shall be inserted "or paragraph 3 or 4 of Schedule 23A".

(2) In Schedule 23A to the Taxes Act 1988 (manufactured dividends and interest) paragraph 5 (dividends and interest passing through the market) shall be amended as mentioned in subsections (3) to (5) below.

(3) In sub-paragraph (2) (dividend which manufactured payment represents not to be treated as income of the payment manufacturer) the word "and" at the end of paragraph (b) shall be omitted and at the end of paragraph (c) there shall be inserted "and

    (d) relief shall not be given under any provision of the Tax Acts to the payment manufacturer in respect of the manufactured payment."

(4) In sub-paragraph (4) (dividend which subsequent manufactured payment represents not to be treated as income of the subsequent manufacturer) the word "and" at the end of paragraph (b) shall be omitted and at the end of paragraph (c) there shall be inserted "and

    (d) relief shall not be given under any provision of the Tax Acts to the payment manufacturer or any subsequent manufacturer in respect of the manufactured payment or any subsequent manufactured payment."

(5) After sub-paragraph (6) there shall be inserted—

"(7) In this paragraph "relief" means relief by way of—

    (a) deduction in computing profits or gains; or

    (b) deduction or set off against income or total profits."

(6) Subsection (1) above shall apply where any of the contracts mentioned in section 715(6) of the Taxes Act 1988 is made on or after 30th November 1993.

(7) Subsections (2) to (5) above shall apply in relation to payments made on or after 30th November 1993.

GENERAL NOTE

Subss. (1) and (6)

The exemption from the accrued income scheme legislation in the ICTA 1988 (c. 1), s.715(6) is extended to cover manufactured payments within the ICTA 1988 (c. 1), Sched. 23A, paras. 3 and 4. The amendments apply to relevant contracts entered into after November 29, 1993.

Subss. (2)–(5)

Where a payment manufacturer receives an actual dividend or interest payment and passes it on to another person, the dividend or interest payment is treated as income of the recipient and not of the payment manufacturer. Further the payment manufacturer cannot claim tax relief in respect of the manufactured payment.

The amendments apply to payments after November 29, 1993.

Overseas dividend manufacturers: limitation of double taxation relief

124. The following sub-paragraph shall be inserted after sub-paragraph (7) of paragraph 4 of Schedule 23A to the Taxes Act 1988—

"(7A) Dividend manufacturing regulations may provide that where a person who is an overseas dividend manufacturer is entitled to relief under Part XVIII (or would be apart from provision made under this sub-paragraph) and the circumstances are such as may be prescribed—

    (a) his entitlement shall be extinguished, or

(b) if the regulations so provide, the amount of the relief shall be reduced to such extent as may be found in accordance with prescribed rules."

GENERAL NOTE
Regulations may be made denying or restricting double taxation relief to an overseas dividend manufacturer as specified in the regulations.

PAYE

GENERAL NOTE
Sections 125–133 extend the scope of PAYE to prevent employers paying their employees in unusual ways (such as gold bars or coffee beans). Such arrangements provide a cash-flow benefit to the employees as the tax due (but for the new provisions) would otherwise have been collected after the end of the tax year.

Payment by intermediary

125. After section 203A of the Taxes Act 1988 there shall be inserted—

"PAYE: payment by intermediary
203B.—(1) Subject to subsection (2) below, where any payment of, or on account of, assessable income of an employee is made by an intermediary of the employer, the employer shall be treated, for the purposes of PAYE regulations, as making a payment of that income of an amount equal to the amount determined in accordance with subsection (3) below.
(2) Subsection (1) above does not apply if the intermediary (whether or not he is a person to whom section 203 and PAYE regulations apply) deducts income tax from the payment he makes and accounts for it in accordance with PAYE regulations.
(3) The amount referred to is—
(a) if the amount of the payment made by the intermediary is an amount to which the recipient is entitled after deduction of any income tax, the aggregate of the amount of that payment and the amount of any income tax due; and
(b) in any other case, the amount of the payment made by the intermediary.
(4) For the purposes of this section, a payment of, or on account of, assessable income of an employee is made by an intermediary of the employer if it is made—
(a) by a person acting on behalf of the employer and at the expense of the employer or a person connected with him; or
(b) by trustees holding property for any persons who include or class of persons which includes the employee.
(5) Section 839 applies for the purposes of subsection (4) above."

GENERAL NOTE
The new s.203B is inserted into the ICTA 1988 (c. 1). A payment of, or on account of, assessable income by an intermediary of an employer, to an employee, is treated as made by the employer for the purposes of the PAYE regulations, unless the intermediary (whether or not the PAYE regulations apply to him) operates PAYE on the payment and accounts for the income tax. Liability is on the grossed up amount where the employee receives a net sum free of tax. A payment is made by the intermediary if it is made by a person acting on behalf of the employer

and at the expense of the employer or a connected person or made by trustees holding property for a class of persons which includes the employee.

Employees working for persons other than their employers, etc.

GENERAL NOTE
    The new s.203C–203E are inserted into the ICTA 1988 (c. 1). They replace the Income Tax (Employment) Regulations 1993 (S.I. 1993 No. 744), reg. 4 which is revoked with effect from the date of Royal Assent (see s.133 below).

126.—(1) After section 203B of the Taxes Act 1988 (which is inserted by section 125 above) there shall be inserted—

"PAYE: employee of non-UK employer
    203C.—(1) This subsection applies where—
    (a) an employee during any period works for a person ("the relevant person") who is not his employer;
    (b) any payment of, or on account of, assessable income of the employee in respect of work done in that period is made by a person who is the employer or an intermediary of the employer;
    (c) PAYE regulations do not apply to the person making the payment or, if he makes the payment as an intermediary of the employer, the employer; and
    (d) income tax is not deducted or accounted for in accordance with the regulations by the person making the payment or, if he makes the payment as an intermediary of the employer, the employer.
    (2) Where subsection (1) above applies, the relevant person shall be treated, for the purposes of PAYE regulations, as making a payment of the assessable income of the employee of an amount equal to the amount determined in accordance with subsection (3) below.
    3) The amount referred to is—
    (a) if the amount of the payment actually made is an amount to which the recipient is entitled after deduction of any income tax, the aggregate of the amount of that payment and the amount of any income tax due; and
    (b) in any other case, the amount of the payment actually made.
    (4) In this section and sections 203D and 203E "work", in relation to an employee, means the performance of any duties of the office or employment of the employee and any reference to his working shall be construed accordingly.
    (5) Subsections (4) and (5) of section 203B apply for the purposes of this section as they apply for the purposes of that section.

PAYE: employee non-resident, etc.
    203D.—(1) This section applies in relation to an employee in a year of assessment only if—
    (a) he is not resident or, if resident, not ordinarily resident in the United Kingdom; and
    (b) he works or will work in the United Kingdom and also works or is likely to work outside the United Kingdom.
    (2) Where in relation to any year of assessment it appears to an officer of the Board that—
    (a) some of the income of an employee to whom this section applies is assessable to income tax under Case II of Schedule E, but
    (b) an as yet unascertainable proportion of the income may prove not to be assessable,

the officer may, on an application made by the appropriate person, give a direction for determining a proportion of any payment made in that year of, or on account of, income of the employee which shall be treated for the purposes of PAYE regulations as a payment of assessable income of the employee.

(3) In this section "the appropriate person" means—

(a) the person designated by the employer for the purposes of this section; or

(b) if no person is so designated, the employer.

(4) An application for a direction under subsection (2) above shall provide such information as is available and is relevant to the giving of the direction.

(5) A direction under subsection (2) above—

(a) shall specify the employee to whom and the year of assessment to which it relates;

(b) shall be given by notice to the appropriate person; and

(c) may be withdrawn by notice to the appropriate person from a date specified in the notice.

(6) The date so specified may not be earlier than thirty days from the date on which the notice of the withdrawal is given.

(7) Where—

(a) a direction under subsection (2) above has effect in relation to an employee to whom this section applies, and

(b) a payment of, or on account of, the income of the employee is made in the year of assessment to which the direction relates,

the proportion of the payment determined in accordance with the direction shall be treated for the purposes of PAYE regulations as a payment of assessable income of the employee.

(8) Where in any year of assessment—

(a) no direction under subsection (2) above has effect in relation to an employee to whom this section applies, and

(b) any payment is made of, or on account of, the income of the employee,

the entire payment shall be treated for the purposes of PAYE regulations as a payment of assessable income of the employee.

(9) Subsections (7) and (8) above are without prejudice to—

(a) any assessment in respect of the income of the employee in question; and

(b) any right to repayment of income tax overpaid and any obligation to pay income tax underpaid.

PAYE: mobile UK workforce

203E.—(1) This subsection applies where it appears to the Board that—

(a) a person ("the relevant person") has entered into or is likely to enter into an agreement that employees of another person ("the contractor") shall in any period work for, but not as employees of, the relevant person;

(b) payments of, or on account of, assessable income of the employees in respect of work done in that period are likely to be made by or on behalf of the contractor; and

(c) PAYE regulations would apply on the making of such payments but it is likely that income tax will not be deducted or accounted for in accordance with the regulations.

(2) Where subsection (1) above applies, the Board may give a direction that, if—

(a) any employees of the contractor work in any period for, but not as employees of, the relevant person, and

   (b) any payment is made by the relevant person in respect of work done by the employees in that period,
income tax shall be deducted in accordance with the provisions of this section by the relevant person on making that payment.

   (3) A direction under subsection (2) above—

   (a) shall specify the relevant person and the contractor to whom it relates;

   (b) shall be given by notice to the relevant person; and

   (c) may at any time be withdrawn by notice to the relevant person.

   (4) The Board shall take such steps as are reasonably practicable to ensure that the contractor is supplied with a copy of any notice given under subsection (3) above which relates to him.

   (5) Where—

   (a) a direction under subsection (2) above has effect, and

   (b) any employees of the contractor specified in the direction work for, but not as employees of. the relevant person so specified,
income tax shall, subject to and in accordance with PAYE regulations, be deducted by the relevant person on making any payment in respect of that work as if so much of the payment as is attributable to work done by each employee were a payment of assessable income of that employee."

GENERAL NOTE

Section 203C

   Where an employee works for a person (the relevant person) in the U.K., and is paid by his employer (or an intermediary of the employer) to whom the PAYE regulations do not apply (for example because they lack the required U.K. tax presence), the relevant person is liable to operate PAYE on the payments made to the employee (grossed up where the payment represents an amount which the employee is entitled to after deduction of any income tax).

Section 203D

   Where a non-resident employee works partly in the U.K. and partly abroad, so that a part of his emoluments are taxable under Sched. E, Case II, the employer must operate PAYE on the total emoluments unless the Revenue (upon application by the employer or a person designated by him) gives a direction as to the amount on which PAYE is to operate.

Section 203E

   This applies where employees of X ("the contractor") work for Y ("the relevant person") and Y pays X for the employees' services. The Board may direct that Y apply PAYE on payments made for the work done by the employees if it appears likely that X will fail to apply PAYE on payments made to the employees.

Tradeable assets

   127. After section 203E of the Taxes Act 1988 (which is inserted by section 126 above) there shall be inserted—

"PAYE: tradeable assets

   203F.—(1) Where any assessable income of an employee is provided in the form of a tradeable asset, the employer shall be treated, for the purposes of PAYE regulations, as making a payment of that income of an amount equal to the amount specified in subsection (3) below.

   (2) For the purposes of subsection (1) above "tradeable asset" means—

   (a) any asset capable of being sold or otherwise realised on a recognised investment exchange (within the meaning of the Financial Services Act 1986) or the London Bullion Market;

   (b) any asset capable of being sold or otherwise realised on any market for the time being specified in PAYE regulations; and

   (c) any other asset for which, at the time when the asset is provided, trading arrangements exist.

(3) The amount referred to is—

(a) in the case of an asset falling within subsection (2)(a) or (b) above, the amount for which it is capable of being sold or the amount for which it can be realised on the exchange or market in question; and

(b) in the case of an asset for which trading arrangements exist at the time when the asset is provided, the amount which is obtained under those arrangements.

(4) For the purposes of subsection (2) above, "asset" does not include—

(a) any payment actually made of, or on account of, assessable income;

(b) any non-cash voucher, credit-token or cash voucher (as defined in sections 141 to 143); or

(c) any description of property for the time being excluded from the scope of this section by PAYE regulations.

(5) Subject to subsection (4) above, for the purposes of subsection (2) above "asset" includes any property and in particular any right or interest falling within any paragraph in Part I of Schedule 1 to the Financial Services Act 1986."

GENERAL NOTE

The new s.203F is inserted into the ICTA 1988 (c. 1). If an employee receives Sched. E income in the form of a tradeable asset, the employer is treated for PAYE purposes as making a payment of income.

"Tradeable asset" means an asset which is realisable on a recognised investment exchange, the London Bullion Market, a market specified in PAYE regulations or for which trading arrangements exist at the time the asset is provided.

The amount to which PAYE applies is the amount the asset can be realised for on the specified market in question or the amount which can be obtained for it under the trading arrangements in question.

"Asset" includes any property as well as a right or interest within the FA 1986 (c. 41), Pt. I, but excludes actual payments, non-cash vouchers, credit tokens or cash vouchers. As to the meaning of trading arrangements, see the ICTA 1988 (c. 1), s.203H (s.129 below).

Non-cash vouchers

128. After section 203F of the Taxes Act 1988 (which is inserted by section 127 above) there shall be inserted—

"PAYE: non-cash vouchers

203G.—(1) Where a non-cash voucher to which this section applies is received by an employee, the employer shall be treated, for the purposes of PAYE regulations, as making a payment of assessable income of the employee of an amount equal to the amount ascertained in accordance with section 141(1)(a).

(2) This section applies to a non-cash voucher to which section 141(1) applies if—

(a) either of the two conditions set out below is fulfilled with respect to the voucher; and

(b) the voucher is not of a description for the time being excluded from the scope of this section by PAYE regulations.

(3) The first condition is fulfilled with respect to a voucher if it is capable of being exchanged for goods—

(a) which, at the time when the voucher is provided, are capable of being sold or otherwise realised on an exchange or market falling within section 203F(2)(a) or (b); or

(b) for which, at the time when the voucher is provided, trading arrangements exist.

(4) The second condition is fulfilled with respect to a voucher if, at the time when the voucher is provided, the voucher itself—
  (a) is capable of being sold or otherwise realised on an exchange or market falling within section 203F(2)(a) or (b); or
  (b) is a voucher for which trading arrangements exist."

GENERAL NOTE
The new s.203G is inserted into the ICTA 1988 (c. 1). Where an employee receives a non-cash voucher, which is not excluded from the scope of this section by PAYE regulations, the employer is treated for PAYE purposes as making a payment of assessable income, equal to an amount determined by the ICTA 1988 (c. 1), s.141(1)(a).

A non-cash voucher is one which either is a tradeable asset (as to which see s.203F above) or which can be exchanged for goods which are themselves tradeable assets.

Credit-tokens

129. After section 203G of the Taxes Act 1988 (which is inserted by section 128 above) there shall be inserted—

"PAYE: credit-tokens
203H.—(1) Subject to subsection (3) below, on each occasion on which an employee uses a credit-token provided to him by reason of his employment to obtain—
  (a) money, or
  (b) goods falling within subsection (2) below,
the employer shall be treated, for the purposes of PAYE regulations, as making a payment of assessable income of the employee of an amount equal to the amount ascertained in accordance with section 142(1)(a).

(2) Goods fall within this subsection if, at the time when they are obtained, they are goods—
  (a) which are capable of being sold or otherwise realised on an exchange or market falling within section 203F(2)(a) or (b); or
  (b) for which trading arrangements exist.

(3) PAYE regulations may make provision for excluding from the scope of this section any description of use of a credit-token.

(4) In this section "credit-token" has the same meaning as in section 142."

GENERAL NOTE
The new s.203H is inserted into the ICTA 1988 (c. 1). Whenever an employee uses a credit token provided by reason of his employment to obtain money or tradeable assets (as to which see s.203F above), the employer is treated for PAYE purposes as making a payment of assessable income, equal to the amount determined by the ICTA 1988 (c. 1), s.142(1)(a). PAYE regulations may exclude from the scope of this section, certain uses of credit tokens.

Cash vouchers

130. After section 203H of the Taxes Act 1988 (which is inserted by section 129 above) there shall be inserted—

"PAYE: cash vouchers
203I.—(1) Subject to subsection (2) below, where a cash voucher to which section 143(1) applies is received by an employee, the employer shall be treated, for the purposes of PAYE regulations, as making a payment of assessable income of the employee of an amount equal to the amount ascertained in accordance with section 143(1)(a).

(2) PAYE regulations may make provision for excluding from the scope of this section the provision of cash vouchers in such description of circumstances as may be specified in the regulations."

GENERAL NOTE
   The new s.203I is inserted into the ICTA 1988 (c. 1). Where a cash voucher is received by an employee, the employer is treated for PAYE purposes as making a payment of assessable income, equal to an amount determined by s.143(1)(a). PAYE regulations may exclude vouchers from the scope of this section.

Supplementary

131. After section 203I of the Taxes Act 1988 (which is inserted by section 130 above) there shall be inserted—

"S.203B to s.203I: accounting for tax

203J.—(1) Where an employer makes a notional payment of assessable income of an employee, the obligation to deduct income tax shall have effect as an obligation on the employer to deduct income tax at such time as may be prescribed by PAYE regulations from any payment or payments he actually makes of, or on account of, such income of that employee.

(2) For the purposes of this section—
(a) a notional payment is a payment treated as made by virtue of any of sections 203B, 203C and 203F to 203I, other than a payment whose amount is determined in accordance with section 203B(3)(a) or 203C(3)(a); and
(b) any reference to an employer includes a reference to a person who is treated as making a payment by virtue of section 203C(2).

(3) Where, by reason of an insufficiency of payments actually made, the employer is unable to deduct the amount (or the full amount) of the income tax as required by virtue of subsection (1) above, the obligation to deduct income tax shall have effect as an obligation on the employer to account to the Board at such time as may be prescribed by PAYE regulations for an amount of income tax equal to the amount of income tax he is required, but is unable, to deduct.

(4) PAYE regulations may make provision—
(a) with respect to the time when any notional payment (or description of notional payment) is made;
(b) applying (with or without modifications) any specified provisions of the regulations for the time being in force in relation to deductions from actual payments to amounts accounted for in respect of any notional payments;
(c) with respect to the collection and recovery of amounts accounted for in respect of notional payments.

(5) Any amount which an employer deducts or for which he accounts as mentioned in subsections (1) and (3) above shall be treated as an amount paid by the employee in question in respect of his liability to income tax for such year of assessment as may be specified in PAYE regulations.

"Trading arrangements"

203K.—(1) "Trading arrangements" in sections 203F to 203H shall be construed in accordance with this section.

(2) Trading arrangements—
(a) for an asset, are arrangements for the purpose of enabling the person to whom the asset is provided to obtain an amount similar to the expense incurred in the provision of the asset;
(b) for goods for which a non-cash voucher is capable of being exchanged, are arrangements for the purpose of enabling the per-

son to whom the voucher is provided to obtain an amount similar
to the expense incurred in the provision of the goods;
(c) for a non-cash voucher, are arrangements for the purpose of
enabling the person to whom the voucher is provided to obtain an
amount similar to the expense incurred as mentioned in section
141(1)(a);
(d) for goods obtained by the use of a credit-token, are arrangements
for the purpose of enabling the person to whom the credit-token
is provided to obtain an amount similar to the expense incurred in
the provision of the goods.
(3) For the purposes of subsection (2) above—
(a) any reference to enabling a person to obtain an amount
includes—
(i) a reference to enabling a class or description of persons
which includes that person to obtain the amount; and
(ii) a reference to enabling an amount to be obtained by any
means, including in particular by using an asset or goods as security for a loan or an advance; and
(b) an amount is similar to an expense incurred if it is greater than,
equal to or not substantially less than that expense.
(4) PAYE regulations may exclude any description of arrangements
from being trading arrangements for the purposes of sections 203F to
203H.
203L.—(1) In sections 203B to 203J "employee" means a person holding an office or employment under or with any other person, and (subject to section 203J(2)(b)) any reference to the employer is a reference
to that other person.
(2) In section 203B to 203J "assessable" means assessable to income
tax under Schedule E.
(3) In sections 203B to 203K and this section "PAYE regulations"
means regulations under section 203.
(4) PAYE regulations made by virtue of any of sections 203B to 203K
may—
(a) make different provision for different classes of case;
(b) contain such incidental, consequential and supplementary provision as appears to the Board to be expedient."

GENERAL NOTE
The new ss.203J–203L are inserted into the ICTA 1988 (c. 1).

Section 203J
An employer who makes a notional payment to an employee must deduct tax from any actual
payments made to the employee. He must account to the Revenue for any tax he is unable to
deduct from actual payments because of an insufficiency of such payments. Tax deducted by the
employer or accounted for to the Revenue is treated as tax paid by the employee in respect of his
tax liability for such year of assessment as is prescribed in PAYE regulations.
Employer includes a relevant person. Notional payment is any payment within ss.203B, 203C
and 203F–203I.
PAYE regulations may be made, or modified, to cover notional payments.

Section 203K
Trading arrangements are defined for the purposes of ss.203F–203H and constitute arrangements which enable an employee who is provided with assets, non-cash vouchers, goods or credit
tokens, to obtain an amount similar to the expense incurred in providing the assets, goods, etc.
An employee is enabled to obtain an amount if he belongs to the class of persons who can
obtain the amount or if he can use the asset or goods as security for a loan or advance.
An amount is similar to an expense incurred if it is greater than, equal to or not substantially
less than the expense.

Payments etc. received free of tax

132. After section 144 of the Taxes Act 1988 there shall be inserted—

"Payments etc. received free of tax
144A.—(1) In any case where—
(a) an employer is treated, by virtue of any of sections 203B to 203I, as having made a payment of income of an employee which is assessable to income tax under Schedule E,
(b) the employer is required, by virtue of section 203J(3), to account for an amount of income tax ("the due amount") in respect of that payment, and
(c) the employee does not, before the end of the period of thirty days from the date on which the employer is treated as making that payment, make good the due amount to the employer,
the due amount shall be treated as income of the employee which arises on the date mentioned in paragraph (c) above and is assessable to income tax under Schedule E.
(2) In this section any reference to an employer includes a reference to a person who is treated as making a payment by virtue of section 203C(2)."

GENERAL NOTE
The new s.144A is inserted into the ICTA 1988 (c. 1). Under the ICTA 1988 (c. 1), s.203J(3) (see s.131 above) an employer who makes a notional payment to an employee must account to the Revenue for any income tax he is unable to deduct from actual payments made to the employee. If the employee, within 30 days of the date on which the deemed payment is made, fails to reimburse the employer the tax, he is treated as having received Sched. E income equal to that amount on the date on which the payment was made.

PAYE regulations: past cases

133.—(1) Regulation 4 of the 1993 Regulations (intermediate employers) is hereby revoked; but in relation to any time before its revocation it shall be deemed to have been validly made.
(2) Regulation 3 of the 1973 Regulation (intermediate employers) shall, in relation to any time before its revocation, be deemed to have been validly made.
(3) Where, at any time before the passing of this Act—
(a) a payment has been made of, or on account of, any income of an employee not resident or, if resident, not ordinarily resident in the United Kingdom,
(b) at the time when the payment was made it appeared that some of the income would be assessable to income tax under Case II of Schedule E, but that some of the income might prove not to be assessable to income tax under that Schedule, and
(c) the payment or any proportion of it was treated for the purposes of the 1993 Regulations or the 1973 Regulations as a payment to which the regulations applied,
then the treatment of that payment or that proportion of the payment as being a payment to which the regulations applied shall be deemed to have been lawful.
(4) In this section—
(a) "employee" means a person holding an office or employment under or with any other person;
(b) "the 1993 Regulations" means the Income Tax (Employments) Regulations 1993; and

(c) "the 1973 Regulations" means the Income Tax (Employments) Regulations 1973.

GENERAL NOTE
Regulation 4 of the Income Tax (Employment) Regulations 1993 (S.I. 1993 No. 744) is revoked with effect from Royal Assent, but is deemed together with revoked reg. 3 of the corresponding 1973 Regulations to have been validly made. The treatment of payments made in accordance with these regulations before they were revoked is deemed to have been lawful.

Miscellaneous provisions about companies

Controlled foreign companies

134.—(1) In Schedule 25 to the Taxes Act 1988, Part I (acceptable distribution policy) shall be amended as follows.

(2) In paragraph 2 (acceptable distribution policies for both trading and non-trading companies)—

(a) in sub-paragraph (1)—

(i) for "sub-paragraph (2)" there is substituted "paragraph 2A",

(ii) in paragraph (a), "or for some other period which, in whole or in part, falls within that accounting period" is omitted,

(iii) in paragraph (b), for "the period for which it is paid" there is substituted "that period",

(iv) in paragraph (d) for "proportion" there is substituted "amount" and for "represents at least" there is substituted "is not less than", and

(v) the words following paragraph (d) are omitted,

(b) sub-paragraph (2) is omitted, and

(c) for sub-paragraph (3) there is substituted—

"(3) For the purposes of this paragraph and paragraph 2A below, a dividend which is not paid for the period or periods the profits of which are, in relation to the dividend, the relevant profits for the purposes of section 799 shall be treated (subject to sub-paragraph (3A) below) as so paid.

(3A) For the purposes of this paragraph and paragraph 2A below—

(a) where a dividend is paid for a period which is not an accounting period but falls wholly within an accounting period, it shall be treated as paid for that accounting period, and

(b) where a dividend ("the actual dividend") is paid for a period which falls within two or more accounting periods—

(i) it shall be treated as if it were a number of separate dividends each of which is paid for so much of the period as falls wholly within an accounting period, and

(ii) the necessary apportionment of the amount of the actual dividend shall be made to determine the amount of the separate dividends."

(3) After that paragraph there is inserted—

"2A.—(1) Paragraph 2 above shall have effect in accordance with this paragraph to determine whether a controlled foreign company which is not a trading company pursues an acceptable distribution policy in respect of a particular accounting period ("the relevant accounting period").

(2) Subject to sub-paragraph (4) below, where the distribution condition is satisfied in relation to the relevant accounting period, then, in addition to any dividend which falls within paragraph 2(1)(a) above apart from this paragraph—

(a) any dividend which is paid for the accounting period ("the preceding period") which immediately precedes the relevant
accounting period and is not an excluded period shall be treated
as falling within that paragraph, and

(b) if the distribution condition is satisfied in relation to the preceding period, any dividend which is paid for the accounting period
which immediately precedes the preceding period and is not an
excluded period shall be treated as falling within that paragraph,

and so on; and in this sub-paragraph "dividend" means a dividend not
paid out of specified profits.

(3) For the purposes of this paragraph, the distribution condition is
satisfied in relation to any accounting period if—

(a) a dividend or dividends are paid for the period to persons resident
in the United Kingdom,

(b) the amount or, as the case may be, aggregate amount of any dividends falling within paragraph (a) above is not less than—
(i) the relevant profits for that period, or
(ii) where paragraph 2(4) or (5) above applies (with the
modifications of paragraph 2 made by sub-paragraph (5)
below), the appropriate portion of those profits, and

(c) any dividends falling within that paragraph are paid not later than
the time by which any dividend paid for the relevant accounting
period is required by paragraph 2(1)(b) above to be paid;

or if there are no relevant profits for the period.

(4) Where, by reason only of the fact that a company pursued an
acceptable distribution policy in respect of any accounting period ("the
earlier period") earlier than the relevant accounting period, no direction could be given in respect of the earlier period under section 747(1),
sub-paragraph (2) above shall apply to any dividend required to be
taken into account for the purpose of showing that the company pursued
an acceptable distribution policy in respect of the earlier period only to
the extent (if any) to which that dividend was not required to be taken
into account for that purpose.

(5) The modifications of paragraph 2 above referred to in sub-
paragraph (3)(b) above are that—

(a) the references in sub-paragraphs (4) and (5) to the accounting
period in question are to be read as references to the accounting
period for which the dividend or dividends are paid,

(b) the references in those sub-paragraphs to sub-paragraph (1)(d)
are to be read as references to sub-paragraph (3)(b) above,
and

(c) the reference in the definition of "X" in sub-paragraph (6) to
available profits is to be read as a reference to relevant profits.

(6) Paragraph 2(1)(d) above shall have effect as if for "50 per cent. of
the company's available profits" there were substituted "90 per cent. of
the company's net chargeable profits".

(7) In paragraph 2(6) above, the definition of "X" shall have effect as
if the reference to available profits were a reference to net chargeable
profits.

(8) For the purposes of this paragraph—

(a) a period is an excluded period if it is an accounting period in
respect of which a direction is given under section 747(1),
and

(b) relevant profits for any accounting period are the profits which
would be the relevant profits of that period for the purposes of
section 799 if a dividend were actually paid for that period."

(4) In paragraph 3 of that Schedule (available profits)—
(a) after sub-paragraph (4) there is inserted—

"(4A) Subject to sub-paragraph (5) below, for the purposes of this Part of this Schedule, the net chargeable profits of a controlled foreign company for any accounting period are—
(a) its chargeable profits for that period, less
(b) the amount (if any) which, if a direction were given under section 747(1) in respect of the period, would be the company's unrestricted creditable tax for that period;
and for the purposes of this sub-paragraph "unrestricted creditable tax" in relation to a company's accounting period means the amount which would be its creditable tax for that period if the reference in section 751(6)(a) to Part XVIII did not include section 797", and
(b) in sub-paragraph (5), after "available profits" there is inserted "or, where the company is not a trading company, the chargeable profits".

(5) This section shall apply to determine whether a controlled foreign company pursues an acceptable distribution policy in respect of accounting periods ending on or after 30th November 1993.

GENERAL NOTE
Paragraphs 2 and 3 of Sched. 25 to the ICTA 1988 (c. 1) are amended; new para. 2A is inserted into that Schedule.
A dividend is treated as paid for the accounting period out of whose profits it is paid. If it is paid out of the profits of a period which spans more than one accounting period it is treated (apportioned as necessary) as separate dividends paid for each of those periods.

Para. 2A
For accounting periods ending after November 29, 1993 the distribution standard for a non-trading controlled foreign company is 90 per cent. of the company's "net chargeable profits" (previously "available profits"). When considering the 90 per cent. distribution standard for any period, distributions of earlier periods to the extent that they exceeded the required distribution standard for those periods, may be taken into account so long as there is an unbroken chain of earlier periods with excess distributions.

Prevention of avoidance of corporation tax

135.—(1) In the Taxes Act 1988, immediately before section 768 there shall be inserted—

"Change in company ownership corporation tax
767A.—(1) Where it appears to the Board that—
(a) there has been a change in the ownership of a company ("the tax-payer company"),
(b) any corporation tax assessed on the tax-payer company for an accounting period beginning before the change remains unpaid at any time after the relevant date, and
(c) any of the three conditions mentioned below is fulfilled,
any person mentioned in subsection (2) below may be assessed by the Board and charged (in the name of the tax-payer company) to an amount of corporation tax in accordance with this section.
(2) The persons are—
(a) any person who at any time during the relevant period before the change in the ownership of the tax-payer company had control of it;
(b) any company of which the person mentioned in paragraph (a) above has at any time had control within the period of three years before that change.
(3) In subsection (2) above, "the relevant period" means—
(a) the period of three years before the change in the ownership of the tax-payer company; or

(b) if during the period of three years before that change ("the later change") there was a change in the ownership of the tax-payer company ("the earlier change"), the period elapsing between the earlier change and the later change.

(4) The first condition is that—

(a) at any time during the period of three years before the change in the ownership of the tax-payer company the activities of a trade or business of that company cease or the scale of those activities become small or negligible; and

(b) there is no significant revival of those activities before that change occurs.

(5) The second condition is that at any time after the change in the ownership of the tax-payer company, but under arrangements made before that change, the activities of a trade or business of that company cease or the scale of those activities become small or negligible.

(6) The third condition is that—

(a) at any time during the period of six years beginning three years before the change in the ownership of the tax-payer company there is a major change in the nature or conduct of a trade or business of that company;

(b) there is a transfer or there are transfers of assets of the tax-payer company to a person mentioned in subsection (7) below or to any person under arrangements which enable any of those assets or any assets representing those assets to be transferred to a person mentioned in subsection (7) below;

(c) that transfer occurs or those transfers occur during the period of three years before the change in the ownership of the tax-payer company or after that change but under arrangements made before that change; and

(d) the major change mentioned in paragraph (a) above is attributable to that transfer or those transfers.

(7) The persons are—

(a) any person mentioned in subsection (2)(a) above; and

(b) any person connected with him.

(8) The amount of tax charged in an assessment made under this section must not exceed the amount of the tax which, at the time of that assessment, remains unpaid by the tax-payer company.

(9) For the purposes of this section the relevant date is the date six months from the date on which the corporation tax is assessed as mentioned in subsection (1)(b) above.

(10) Any assessment made under this section shall not be out of time if made within three years from the date on which the liability of the tax-payer company to corporation tax for the accounting period mentioned in subsection (1)(b) above is finally determined.

Change of company ownership: supplementary

767B.—(1) In relation to corporation tax assessed under section 767A—

(a) section 86 of the Management Act (interest on overdue tax), in so far as it has effect in relation to accounting periods ending on or before 30th September 1993, and

(b) section 87A of that Act (corresponding provision for corporation tax due for accounting periods ending after that date),

shall have effect as if the references in section 86 of the reckonable date and in section 87A to the date when the tax becomes due and payable were, respectively, references to the date which is the reckonable date in relation to the tax-payer company and the date when the tax became due and payable by the tax-payer company.

(2) A payment in pursuance of an assessment under section 767A shall not be allowed as a deduction in computing any income, profits or losses for any tax purposes; but any person making such a payment shall be entitled to recover an amount equal to the payment from the tax-payer company.

(3) In subsection (2) above the reference to a payment in pursuance of an assessment includes a reference to a payment of interest under section 86 or 87A of the Management Act (as they have effect by virtue of subsection (1) above).

(4) For the purposes of section 767A, "control", in relation to a company, shall be construed in accordance with section 416 as modified by subsections (5) and (6) below.

(5) In subsection (2)(a) for "the greater part of" there shall be substituted "50 per cent. of".

(6) For subsection (3) there shall be substituted—

"(3) Where two or more persons together satisfy any of the conditions in subsection (2) above and do so by reason of having acted together to put themselves in a position where they will in fact satisfy the condition in question, each of those persons shall be treated as having control of the company."

(7) In section 767A(6) "a major change in the nature or conduct of a trade or business" includes any change mentioned in any of paragraphs (a) to (d) of section 245(4); and also includes a change falling within any of those paragraphs which is achieved gradually as the result of a series of transfers.

(8) In section 767A(6) "transfer", in relation to an asset, includes any disposal, letting or hiring of it, and any grant or transfer of any right, interest or licence in or over it, or the giving of any business facilities with respect to it.

(9) Section 839 shall apply for the purposes of section 767A(7).

(10) Subsection (9) of section 768 shall apply for the purposes of section 767A as it applies for the purposes of section 768."

(2) Section 769 (rules for ascertaining change of ownership of company) shall be amended as follows.

(3) In subsections (1), (2) and (5) for the words "section 768", in each place where they occur, there shall be substituted "sections 767A, 768".

(4) After subsection (2) there shall be inserted—

"(2A) Where—

(a) persons, whether company members or not, possess extraordinary rights or powers under the articles of association or under any other document regulating the company, and

(b) because of that fact ownership of the ordinary share capital may not be an appropriate test of whether there has been a change in the ownership of the company,

then, in considering whether there has been a change in the ownership of the company for the purposes of section 767A, holdings of all kinds of share capital, including preference shares, or of any particular category of share capital, or voting power or any other kind of special power may be taken into account instead of ordinary share capital."

(5) After subsection (8) there shall be inserted—

"(9) Subsection (8) above shall not apply in relation to section 767A."

(6) The amendments made by this section shall have effect in relation to any change in ownership occurring on or after 30th November 1993 other than a change occurring in pursuance of a contract entered into before that day.

GENERAL NOTE
The new ss.767A and 767B are inserted into the ICTA 1988 (c. 1).

Section 767A of the ICTA 1988
Where a company's ownership changes and its corporation tax for any accounting period beginning before the change remains unpaid six months after it has been assessed on the company, then if any of the following conditions are met the tax may be assessed on any person who had control of the company during the relevant period or any company which was controlled by such persons during the three years before the change. The conditions are:
  (a) that in the three years before the ownership change, the company's activities ceased or became small or negligible with no revival of those activities; or
  (b) at any time after the ownership change but under arrangements made before the change, the company's activities ceased or became small or negligible; or
  (c) that there is a major change, within the six years beginning three years before the change, in the nature or conduct of the company's trade or business which is attributable to the transfer (occurring within three years either side of the ownership change, under arrangements made before the change) of assets, directly or indirectly, to a person who had control of the company before the ownership change or any person connected with him or any other company which he controlled.
The relevant period is either three years before the ownership change or the period between the change and a previous ownership change if less than three years. An assessment must be made within three years from the date of the determination of the company's corporation tax liability for the accounting period.

Section 767B of the ICTA 1988
Interest is chargeable on tax assessed under s.767A. Neither the tax nor the interest is deductible for corporation tax purposes but the person paying the tax may recover it from the company concerned. The definition of control in the ICTA 1988 (c. 1), s.416 is applied here except that 50 per cent. control suffices. The meaning of major change and transfer are extended.

Parts of trades: computations in different currencies

136.—(1) The following section shall be inserted after section 94 of the Finance Act 1993 (computations in different currencies for different parts of trades)—

"Parts of trades: petroleum extraction companies
94A.—(1) If a trade carried on by a petroleum extraction company is a ring fence trade—
  (a) subsection (1) of section 94 above shall not apply as regards the trade, but
  (b) regulations may make provision under that section as regards a case where in an accounting period the company carries on the trade and the condition mentioned in subsection (2) below is fulfilled.
(2) The condition is that—
  (a) part of the trade consists of activities which relate to oil and are carried on under the authority of a petroleum licence in the United Kingdom or a designated area, and
  (b) part of the trade consists of activities which relate to gas and are carried on under the authority of a petroleum licence in the United Kingdom or a designated area.
(3) For the purposes of this section—
  (a) a petroleum licence is a licence granted under the Petroleum (Production) Act 1934 or the Petroleum (Production) Act (Northern Ireland) 1964;
  (b) a petroleum extraction company is a company which carries on activities under the authority of such a licence;
  (c) a designated area is an area designated by Order in Council under section 1(7) of the Continental Shelf Act 1964.
(4) For the purposes of this section "ring fence trade" means activities which—

(a) fall within any of paragraphs (a) to (c) of subsection (1) of section 492 of the Taxes Act 1988 (oil extraction etc.), and
(b) constitute a separate trade (whether by virtue of that subsection or otherwise).
(5) For the purposes of this section—
(a) "oil" means such substance as falls within the meaning of oil contained in section 502(1) of the Taxes Act 1988 and is not gas;
(b) "gas" means such substance as falls within the meaning of oil contained in section 502(1) of the Taxes Act 1988 and is gas of which the largest component by volume, measured at a temperature of 15 degrees centigrade and a pressure of one atmosphere, is methane or ethane or a combination of those gases."
(2) In section 95(6) of the Finance Act 1993 (commencement of provisions about currency to be used for computations) for "94" there shall be substituted "94A".

GENERAL NOTE
The new s.94A is inserted into the FA 1993 (c. 34). Where a petroleum extraction company carries on a ring-fence trade which consists partly of oil extraction activities and partly of gas extraction activities, regulations under s.94 may provide for different currencies to be used in computing for corporation tax purposes the basic profits or losses (before capital allowances) of different parts of the trade.

Miscellaneous

Enterprise investment scheme

137.—(1) Schedule 15 to this Act shall have effect to revive Chapter III of Part VII of the Taxes Act 1988 (relief for investment in corporate trades) in relation to shares issued on or after 1st January 1994.
(2) That Chapter shall have effect in relation to such shares with the amendments made by that Schedule; and, in relation to such shares, that Chapter as so amended shall apply for the year 1993–94 and subsequent years of assessment.
(3) The Taxation of Chargeable Gains Act 1992 shall have effect with the amendments made by that Schedule.

Foreign income dividends

138. Schedule 16 to this Act (which contains provisions about foreign income dividends) shall have effect.

Taxation of incapacity benefit

139.—(1) For the year 1995–96 and subsequent years of assessment incapacity benefit, except—
(a) benefit payable for an initial period of incapacity, and
(b) so much of any benefit as is attributable in any case to an increase in respect of a child,
shall be treated as income for the purposes of the Income Tax Acts and charged to income tax under Schedule E.
(2) Subsection (1) above shall not apply to incapacity benefit to which a person is entitled for any day of incapacity for work falling in a period of incapacity for work which is treated for the purposes of that benefit as having

begun before 13th April 1995 if the part of that period which is treated as having fallen before that date includes a day for which that person was entitled to invalidity benefit.

(3) Incapacity benefit shall for the purposes of this section be a benefit in relation to which section 41 of the Finance Act 1989 (year of assessment in which benefit to be charged) applies.

(4) Enactments relating to the payment of incapacity benefit shall have effect subject to such provision as may be contained for the purposes of this section in regulations under section 203 of the Taxes Act 1988 (PAYE regulations).

(5) In this section—

"incapacity benefit" means any benefit which by virtue of provisions contained in the Social Security (Incapacity for Work) Act 1994 or any corresponding provisions made for Northern Ireland is to be known as incapacity benefit;

"initial period of incapacity", in relation to incapacity benefit, means any period for which that benefit is payable as short-term incapacity benefit at the rate which (apart from any increase or addition) is the lower of the rates applicable to short-term incapacity benefit; and

"invalidity benefit" means invalidity benefit under Part II of the Social Security Contributions and Benefits Act 1992 or under Part II of the Social Security Contributions and Benefits (Northern Ireland) Act 1992.

GENERAL NOTE

Incapacity benefits (other than benefits paid during the first 26 weeks of incapacity or benefits paid in respect of children) are to be chargeable to tax under Sched. E from 1995–1996 onwards. Incapacity benefit paid to a person, who was entitled to invalidity benefit immediately before April 13, 1995, for a period of incapacity that commenced before that date, are exempt from tax. Benefits will be charged in the tax year in which they accrue regardless of when payment is made. Tax may be deducted from incapacity benefits under PAYE.

Restriction on deduction from income

140.—(1) Section 808 of the Taxes Act 1988 (restriction on deduction of interest or dividends from trading income) shall be amended as follows—

(a) for "a banking business, an insurance business or a business consisting wholly or partly in dealing in securities" there shall be substituted "a business";

(b) for "or dividend" there shall be substituted ", dividend or royalties";

(c) the words "In this section 'securities' includes stocks and shares" shall be omitted.

(2) This section shall apply where it is sought to exclude receipts from income or profits of an accounting period beginning on or after 30th November 1993.

GENERAL NOTE

Previously, non-resident persons carrying on a banking or insurance business or dealing in securities business in the U.K., were under the ICTA 1988 (c. 1), s.808 denied relief for losses to the extent that the losses arose as a result of excluding from trading income, interest or dividend income which are tax exempt under a double tax treaty. This section extends the provisions in s.808 so as to include royalties which are exempt from U.K. tax under a double tax treaty and applies that section to all businesses in the U.K., whatever their nature.

The amendments apply to accounting periods beginning after November 29, 1993.

Expenditure involving crime

141.—(1) Section 577A of the Taxes Act 1988 (certain expenditure involving crime not to be deducted and not to be included in expenses of management) shall be amended as follows.

(2) After subsection (1) there shall be inserted—

"(1A) In computing profits or gains chargeable to tax under Schedule A or Schedule D, no deduction shall be made for any expenditure incurred in making a payment induced by a demand constituting—
  (a) the commission in England or Wales of the offence of blackmail under section 21 of the Theft Act 1968,
  (b) the commission in Northern Ireland of the offence of blackmail under section 20 of the Theft Act (Northern Ireland) 1969, or
  (c) the commission in Scotland of the offence of extortion."

(3) In subsection (2) for "Such expenditure" there shall be substituted "Any expenditure mentioned in subsection (1) or (1A) above".

(4) This section shall apply in relation to expenditure incurred on or after 30th November 1993.

GENERAL NOTE
Expenditure incurred after November 29, 1993 in making a payment as a result of blackmail (in England, Wales or Northern Ireland) or extortion (in Scotland) is not deductible for Sched. A or Sched. D purposes nor allowable as management expenses.

Mortgage interest payable under deduction of tax: qualifying lenders

142.—(1) In section 376 of the Taxes Act 1988 (qualifying lenders)—
  (a) in subsection (4)(p), for "prescribed under subsection (5) below" there shall be substituted "for the time being registered under section 376A below" and for "Treasury" there shall be substituted "Board"; and
  (b) subsection (5) shall be omitted.

(2) The following section shall be inserted in the Taxes Act 1988 after section 376—

"The register of qualifying lenders

376A.—(1) The Board shall maintain, and publish in such manner as they consider appropriate, a register for the purposes of section 376(4).

(2) If the Board are satisfied that an applicant for registration is entitled to be registered, they may register the applicant generally or in relation to any description of loan specified in the register, with effect from such date as may be so specified; and a body which is so registered shall become a qualifying lender in accordance with the terms of its registration.

(3) The registration of any body may be varied by the Board—
  (a) where it is general, by providing for it to be in relation to a specified description of loan, or
  (b) where it is in relation to a specified description of loan, by removing or varying the reference to that description of loan,
and where they do so, they shall give the body written notice of the variation and of the date from which it is to have effect.

(4) If it appears to the Board at any time that a body which is registered under this section would not be entitled to be registered if it applied for registration at that time, the Board may by written notice given to the body cancel its registration with effect from such date as may be specified in the notice.

(5) The date specified in a notice under subsection (3) or (4) above shall not be earlier than the end of the period of 30 days beginning with the date on which the notice is served.

(6) Any body which is aggrieved by the failure of the Board to register it under this section, or by the variation or cancellation of its registration, may, by notice given to the Board before the end of the period of

30 days beginning with the date on which the body is notified of the Board's decision, require the matter to be determined by the Special Commissioners; and the Special Commissioners shall thereupon hear and determine the matter in like manner as an appeal."

(3) Any body which is, immediately before the date on which this Act is passed, a prescribed body for the purposes of section 376 of the Taxes Act 1988 (by virtue of an order made under subsection (5) of that section) shall be entitled to be entered in the register maintained under section 376A of that Act as a qualifying lender except that if it was, immediately before that date, a qualifying lender only in relation to such description of loan as was specified in the order, it shall be entitled to be entered in the register as a qualifying lender only in relation to that description of loan.

(4) Until such time as the Board enter any such body in the register, that body shall be deemed to have been registered in accordance with its entitlement.

GENERAL NOTE

The Treasury procedure of admitting lenders to the MIRAS scheme by prescribing them as qualifying lenders by order made by Statutory Instrument, is replaced with a simpler registration procedure to be administered by the Revenue. In future lenders will be entered on a register maintained by the Revenue.

Premiums referred to pension business

143.—(1) The Taxes Act 1988 shall be amended as follows.

(2) In section 431(4) (insurance companies: premiums to be referred to pension business) in paragraph (d) (annuity contracts)—
   (a) the words "approved by the Board and" shall be omitted;
   (b) after "as defined by section 612(1)" there shall be inserted "and falling within section 431AA".

(3) In section 431(4) in paragraph (e) (annuity contracts entered into in substitution)—
   (a) the words "approved by the Board" shall be omitted;
   (b) after "paragraph (d) above" there shall be inserted "and by means of which relevant benefits as defined by section 612(1) and falling within section 431AA (but no other benefits) are secured".

(4) The following section shall be inserted after section 431—

"Relevant benefits for purposes of section 431(4)(d) and (e)

431AA.—(1) Subsection (2) below applies where—
   (a) section 431(4)(d)(i) applies, or
   (b) section 431(4)(e) applies and the contract within section 431(4)(d) was entered into for the purposes of a scheme falling within section 431(4)(d)(i).

(2) In such a case, relevant benefits fall within this section if they correspond with benefits that could be provided by a scheme approved under Chapter I of Part XIV, and for this purpose—
   (a) a hypothetical scheme (rather than any particular scheme) is to be taken, and
   (b) benefits provided by a scheme directly (rather than by means of an annuity contract) are to be taken.

(3) Subsection (4) below applies where—
   (a) subsection 431(4)(d)(ii) applies, or
   (b) section 431(4)(e) applies and the contract within section 431(4)(d) was entered into for the purposes of a scheme falling within section 431(4)(d)(ii).

(4) In such a case, relevant benefits fall within this section if they correspond with benefits that could be provided by a scheme which is a relevant statutory scheme for the purposes of Chapter I of Part XIV, and for this purpose—
- (a) a hypothetical scheme (rather than any particular scheme) is to be taken, and
- (b) benefits provided by a scheme directly (rather than by means of an annuity contract) are to be taken.

(5) Subsection (6) below applies where—
- (a) section 431(4)(d)(iii) applies, or
- (b) section 431(4)(e) applies and the contract within section 431(4)(d) was entered into for the purposes of a fund falling within section 431(4)(d)(iii).

(6) In such a case, relevant benefits fall within this section if they correspond with benefits that could be provided by a fund to which section 608 applies, and for this purpose—
- (a) a hypothetical fund (rather than any particular fund) is to be taken, and
- (b) benefits provided by a fund directly (rather than by means of an annuity contract) are to be taken."

(5) This section shall apply in relation to an annuity contract entered into on or after 1st July 1994; and in the case of an annuity contract entered into in substitution for another it is immaterial when that other was entered into.

GENERAL NOTE
  The ICTA 1988 (c. 1), s.431 is amended to remove the requirement of obtaining prior Revenue approval for annuities purchased by an approved pension scheme. Instead new s.431AA defines the benefits which may be secured by annuity contracts.
  The provisions apply to annuity contracts entered into on or after July 1, 1994.

Debts released in voluntary arrangement: relief from tax

144.—(1) In the Taxes Act 1988, in section 74 (general rules as to deductions not allowable), for paragraph (j) (debts not allowable except in certain circumstances) there shall be substituted—
  "(j) any debts except—
      (i) a bad debt proved to be such;
      (ii) a debt or part of a debt released by the creditor wholly and exclusively for the purposes of his trade, profession or vocation as part of a relevant arrangement or compromise; and
      (iii) a doubtful debt to the extent estimated to be bad, meaning, in the case of the bankruptcy or insolvency of the debtor, the debt except to the extent that any amount may reasonably be expected to be received on the debt;".

(2) The provisions of that section shall become subsection (1) of that section and after that subsection there shall be inserted—
  "(2) In paragraph (j) of subsection (1) above "relevant arrangement or compromise" means—
- (a) a voluntary arrangement which has taken effect under or by virtue of the Insolvency Act 1986 or the Insolvency (Northern Ireland) Order 1989; or
- (b) a compromise or arrangement which has taken effect under section 425 of the Companies Act 1985 or Article 418 of the Companies (Northern Ireland) Order 1986."

(3) In the Taxes Act 1988—
- (a) in section 94 (debts deducted and subsequently released) after the word "released" where it first occurs, and
- (b) in section 103(4)(b) (debts deducted before, but released after, discontinuance of trade, etc.) after the word "released",

there shall be inserted "otherwise than as part of a relevant arrangement or compromise".

(4) The provisions of section 94 of the Taxes Act 1988 shall become subsection (1) of that section and after that subsection there shall be inserted—

"(2) In subsection (1) above 'relevant arrangement or compromise' has the same meaning as in section 74."

(5) After section 103(4) of the Taxes Act 1988 there shall be inserted—

"(4A) In subsection (4)(b) above 'relevant arrangement or compromise' has the same meaning as in section 74."

(6) Subsection (1) above shall have effect, for the purposes of determining (in computing the amount of profits or gains to be charged under Case I or Case II of Schedule D) whether any sum should be deducted in respect of any debt, in relation to debts—

(a) proved to be bad,

(b) released as part of—

(i) a voluntary arrangement which has taken effect under or by virtue of the Insolvency Act 1986 or the Insolvency (Northern Ireland) Order 1989, or,

(ii) a compromise or arrangement which has taken effect under section 425 of the Companies Act 1985 or Article 418 of the Companies (Northern Ireland) Order 1986, and

(c) estimated to be bad,

if the proof, release or estimation occurs on or after 30th November 1993.

(7) Subsection (3) above shall have effect in relation to the release on or after 30th November 1993 of the whole or any part of any debt.

GENERAL NOTE

Section 74(j) is amended to ensure trade debts released as part of a voluntary arrangement, under the Insolvency Act 1986 (c. 45) or the equivalent Northern Ireland legislation or a compromise or arrangement under the Companies Act 1985 (c. 6), s.425 or the Companies (Northern Ireland) Order 1986, art. 418, are allowable as a trading deduction. Sections 94 and 103(4)(b) are amended to ensure that debts released as part of a voluntary arrangement or arrangement or compromise under the companies legislation are not treated as receipts or post-cessation receipts respectively of the debtor's trade.

The amendments apply to debts released after November 29, 1993.

Relief for business donations

145.—(1) In sections 79(11) and 79A(7) of the Taxes Act 1988 (contributions to local enterprise agencies, training and enterprise councils and local enterprise companies made before 1st April 1995 to be deductible as expenses), for "1995" (in both places) there shall be substituted "2000".

(2) Section 79A of that Act shall be amended as follows.

(3) In subsection (1), after "training and enterprise council" there shall be inserted "business link organisation" and in subsection (3) after "council" there shall be inserted "organisation".

(4) In subsection (5), before paragraph (a) there shall be inserted—

"(aa) "business link organisation" means any person authorised by or on behalf of the Secretary of State to use a service mark (within the meaning of the Trade Marks (Amendment) Act 1984) designated by the Secretary of State for the purposes of this paragraph".

(5) In subsection (7), after "1st April 1990" there shall be inserted "or, in the case of a contribution to a business link organisation, 30th November 1993".

GENERAL NOTE

The period of relief (for contributions to local enterprise agencies, training and enterprise councils and local enterprise companies) in ss.79(11) and 79A(7) of the ICTA 1988 (c. 1) has been extended by five years to April 1, 2000. In addition, relief is available for contributions made between November 30, 1993 and March 31, 2000 to Business Link Organisations.

Minor corrections

146. Schedule 17 to this Act (which corrects various mistakes made in or introduced into the Taxes Act 1988) shall have effect.

CHAPTER II

INTEREST RATE AND CURRENCY CONTRACTS

GENERAL NOTE

Sections 147 to 177 and Sched. 18 introduce provisions for the taxation of financial instruments used by companies for managing interest rate and currency risks. The provisions are the result of three consultative documents on the matter: (a) *Tax treatment of swap fees* (issued on March 14, 1989); (b) *Financial instruments: The tax treatment of financial instruments for managing interest rate risk* (issued on August 29, 1991); and (c) *Financial instruments: Draft clauses on the tax treatment of financial instruments for managing interest rate and currency risks* (issued by the Revenue on August 20, 1993), as well as extensive discussion between the Revenue and representative bodies on those documents. The provisions take effect for accounting periods commencing on or after a day to be appointed by the Treasury.

Qualifying contracts

Qualifying contracts

147.—(1) For the purposes of this Chapter—
  (a) an interest rate contract or option, or
  (b) a currency contract or option,
is a qualifying contract as regards a qualifying company if the company becomes entitled to rights or subject to duties under the contract or option on or after its commencement day.

(2) Where both immediately before and at the beginning of its commencement day—
  (a) a company to which this paragraph applies is entitled to rights or subject to duties under an interest rate contract or option, or
  (b) a qualifying company is entitled to rights or subject to duties under a currency contract or option,
for the purposes of this Chapter the company shall be treated as becoming entitled or subject to them at the beginning of that day.

(3) A qualifying company is a company to which paragraph (a) of subsection (2) above applies if its commencement day falls outside the period of 12 months beginning with the appointed day.

(4) For the purposes of this Chapter—
  (a) a company's commencement day is the first day of its first accounting period to begin after the day preceding the appointed day; and
  (b) the appointed day is such day as the Treasury may by order appoint.

GENERAL NOTE

A qualifying contract is an interest rate contract or option, or a currency contract or option entered into, or acquired, by a qualifying company on or after its commencement date. Existing currency contracts or options held by a qualifying company on its commencement day are treated as acquired on that day, as are interest rate contracts or options provided the company's commencement day is more than 12 months after the appointed day.

Instruments falling outside the definition of qualifying contract, *e.g.* commodity-linked and equity-linked swaps are excluded.

Contracts which may become qualifying contracts

148.—(1) A qualifying company is a company to which this section applies if its commencement day falls within the period of 12 months beginning with the appointed day.

(2) Subject to subsection (3) below, all quasi-qualifying contracts which, at the end of the period of six years beginning with its commencement day, are held by a company to which this section applies shall be treated for the purposes of this Chapter as if the company became entitled to rights or subject to duties under them on the first day of its first accounting period beginning after the end of the period of six years.

(3) Subject to subsection (5) below, if a company to which this section applies so elects, all quasi-qualifying contracts held by the company on its commencement day shall be treated for the purposes of this Chapter as if the company became entitled to rights or subject to duties under them on that day.

(4) An election by a company under subsection (3) above shall be irrevocable and shall be made by notice served on the inspector before the end of the period of three months beginning with its commencement day.

(5) A company may not make an election under subsection (3) above at a time when it is a member but not the principal company of a group unless the company did not become a member of the group until after the relevant day.

(6) An election under subsection (3) above by a company which is the principal company of a group shall have effect also as an election by any other company to which this section applies and which on the relevant day is a member of the group.

(7) Subsection (6) above shall apply in relation to a company notwithstanding that the company ceases to be a member of the group at any time after the relevant day except where—

(a) the company is an outgoing company in relation to the group, and
(b) the election relating to the group is made after the company ceases to be a member of the group.

(8) In this section—

"outgoing company", in relation to a group of companies, means a company which ceases to be a member of the group before the end of the period during which an election under subsection (3) above could be made in relation to it and at a time when no such election has been made;

"quasi-qualifying contract", in relation to a qualifying company, means an interest rate contract or option which would be a qualifying contract if the company became entitled to rights or subject to duties under it on or after the company's commencement day;

"the relevant day" means the principal company's commencement day.

(9) Section 170 of the Taxation of Chargeable Gains Act 1992 (groups of companies) shall have effect for the purposes of this section as for those of sections 171 to 181 of that Act.

GENERAL NOTE

Interest rate contracts and options held by a company on its commencement day, which falls within 12 months of the appointed day, may be treated as qualifying contracts. An election is necessary and must be made within three months of the company's commencement day. If no election is made, any contracts or options still held six years after the commencement date are subject to the financial instrument provisions (*i.e.* ss.147–177 of this Act). The election is to be made by the principal company of the group, where the qualifying company is a member of a group, unless the latter company joins the group after the principal company's commencement date. Companies leaving a group continue to be subject to this rule unless the outgoing company ceases to be a member of the group before the principal company makes the election.

Interest rate and currency contracts and options

Interest rate contracts and options

149.—(1) A contract is an interest rate contract for the purposes of this Chapter if—

(a) the condition mentioned below is fulfilled, and

(b) the only transfers of money or money's worth for which the contract provides are payments falling within subsection (2), (3) or (4) or section 151 below.

(2) The condition is that under the contract, whether unconditionally or subject to conditions being fulfilled, a qualifying company becomes entitled to a right to receive, or becomes subject to a duty to make, at a time specified in the contract a variable rate payment.

(3) An interest rate contract may include provision under which, as the consideration or part of the consideration for a payment falling within subsection (2) above, the qualifying company becomes subject to a duty to make, or (as the case may be) becomes entitled to a right to receive, at a time specified in the contract a fixed or fixed rate payment.

(4) In so far as the rights and duties mentioned in subsections (2) and (3) above relate to two payments—
(a) which fall to be made at the same time, and
(b) of which one falls to be made to and the other by the qualifying company,
it is immaterial for the purposes of this section that those rights and duties may be exercised and discharged by a payment made to or, as the case may require, by the company of an amount equal to the difference between the amounts of those payments.

(5) Each of the following, namely—
(a) an option to enter into an interest rate contract, and
(b) an option to enter into such an option,
is an interest rate option for the purposes of this Chapter if the only transfers of money or money's worth for which it provides are payments falling within section 151 below.

(6) In this section—
"fixed payment" means a payment of a fixed amount specified in the contract;
"fixed rate payment" means a payment the amount of which falls to be determined (wholly or mainly) by applying to a notional principal amount specified in the contract, for a period so specified, a rate the value of which at all times is the same as that of a fixed rate of interest so specified;
"variable rate payment" means a payment the amount of which falls to be determined (wholly or mainly) by applying to a notional principal amount specified in the contract, for a period so specified, a rate the value of which at any time is the same as that of a variable rate of interest so specified.

GENERAL NOTE
An interest rate contract must entitle a qualifying company to pay or receive a variable rate payment (whether conditional or unconditional), a fixed payment or a fixed rate payment, at a contractually specified time. Such receipts and payments may be netted provided they all fall due at the same time. Payments specified in s.151 below may also be made under the contract.
An interest rate option is an option to enter into an interest rate contract or option provided the only payments under the option are those specified in s.151.

Currency contracts and options

150.—(1) A contract is a currency contract for the purposes of this Chapter if—
(a) the condition mentioned below is fulfilled, and
(b) the only transfers of money or money's worth for which the contract provides are payments falling within subsection (2), (3), (4) or (9) or section 151 below.

(2) The condition is that under the contract a qualifying company—

(a) becomes entitled to a right and subject to a duty to receive payment at a specified time of a specified amount of one currency (the first currency), and

(b) becomes entitled to a right and subject to a duty to pay in exchange and at the same time a specified amount of another currency (the second currency).

(3) A currency contract may include provision under which the qualifying company—

(a) becomes entitled to a right to receive at a time specified in the contract a payment the amount of which falls to be determined (wholly or mainly) by applying a specified rate of interest to a specified amount of the first currency, and

(b) becomes subject to a duty to make at a time so specified a payment the amount of which falls to be determined (wholly or mainly) by applying a specified rate of interest to a specified amount of the second currency.

(4) A currency contract may also include provision under which the qualifying company—

(a) becomes entitled to a right and subject to a duty to receive payment at a specified time of a specified amount of the second currency, and

(b) becomes entitled to a right and subject to a duty to pay in exchange and at the same time a specified amount of the first currency.

(5) In subsections (3) and (4) above—

(a) any reference to a time is a reference to a time earlier than that specified in the contract for the purposes of subsection (2) above, and

(b) any reference to a specified rate of interest is a reference to a rate the value of which at any time is the same as that of the specified rate of interest.

(6) Each of the following, namely—

(a) an option to enter into a currency contract, and

(b) an option to enter into such an option,

is a currency option for the purposes of this Chapter if the only transfers of money or money's worth for which it provides are payments falling within section 151 below.

(7) An option the exercise of which at any time would result in a qualifying company—

(a) becoming entitled to a right and subject to a duty to receive payment at that time of a specified amount of one currency, and

(b) becoming entitled to a right and subject to a duty to pay in exchange and at that time a specified amount of another currency,

is a currency option for the purposes of this Chapter if the only transfers of money or money's worth for which it provides are payments falling within this subsection and section 151 below.

(8) Where, in the case of a contract which is subject to a condition precedent, the fulfilment of the condition at any time would result in a qualifying company becoming entitled and subject as mentioned in paragraphs (a) and (b) of subsection (7) above, that subsection and the following provisions of this Chapter shall have effect as if—

(a) the contract before the fulfilment of the condition were such an option as is mentioned in that subsection,

(b) the fulfilment of the condition were the exercise of the option, and

(c) the contract after the fulfilment of the condition were the contract resulting from the exercise of the option.

(9) It is immaterial for the purposes of this section that the rights and duties mentioned in subsection (2), (4) or (7) above may be exercised and discharged by a payment made to or, as the case may require, by the qualifying company of an amount (in whatever currency) which, at the specified time or

the time when the option is exercised, is equivalent in value to the difference between—
   (a) the local currency equivalent at that time of one of the payments there mentioned, and
   (b) the local currency equivalent at that time of the other of those payments.
(10) Subsection (9) above shall be read as applying equally to such of the rights and duties mentioned in subsection (3) above as fall to be exercised and discharged at the same time, and for that purpose shall have effect with such modifications as may be requisite.

GENERAL NOTE
   A currency contract must entitle a qualifying company to exchange an amount of currency ("the first currency") for an amount of another currency ("the second currency"), at a specified time (see subs. (2)). It may also provide for: (i) payments, determined by applying specified rates of interest to specified amounts of the first and second currencies, to be made or received at a specified time, before the exchange date in subs. (2); (ii) an exchange, at a specified time, before the exchange date in subs. (2) of specified amounts of the first currency and second currency and (iii) payments falling within s.151 below (see subss. (3)(4) and (5)).
   A currency option is (a) an option to enter into a currency contract or option; or (b) an option to buy or sell specified amounts of currency at or within a specified time, provided in either case the only transfers of value under the option are those falling within s.151 below (see subss. (6) and (7)).
   A currency contract may provide for the initial (see subs. (4)) or final exchange of currencies (see subs. (2)) to be netted and settled in a local currency equivalent. A currency option may provide for the exchange of currencies on exercise to be netted and settled in a local currency equivalent (see subs. (9)).

Provisions which may be included

151.—(1) An interest rate contract or option, or a currency contract or option, may include provision under which the qualifying company—
   (a) becomes entitled to a right to receive a payment in consideration of its entering into the contract or option, or
   (b) becomes subject to a duty to make a payment in consideration of another person's entering into the contract or option.
(2) An interest rate contract or option, or a currency contract or option, may also include provision for all or any of the following—
   (a) a payment of a reasonable fee for arranging the contract or option;
   (b) a payment of reasonable costs incurred in respect of the contract or option;
   (c) a payment for securing, or made in consequence of, the variation or termination of the contract or option; and
   (d) a payment by way of compensation for, or made in consequence of, a failure to comply with the contract or option.

GENERAL NOTE
   The following payments may be made under interest rate contracts or options or currency contracts without jeopardising their status as a qualifying contract:
   (a) payments made or received for entering into the contract or option;
   (b) reasonable fees for arranging the contract or option;
   (c) reasonable fees incurred in respect of the contract or option;
   (d) payments for varying or terminating the contract or option;
   (e) compensation payments arising from a failure to comply with the contract or option.

Provisions which may be disregarded

152.—(1) Where—
   (a) but for the inclusion in a contract or option of provisions for one or

more transfers of money or money's worth, the contract or option would be a qualifying contract; and

(b) as regards the qualifying company and the relevant time, the present value of the transfer, or the aggregate of the present values of the transfers, is small when compared with the aggregate of the present values of all relevant payments,

the contract or option shall be treated for the purposes of section 149 or, as the case may be, section 150 above as if those provisions were not included in it.

(2) For the purposes of subsection (1) above—

(a) any present value of a relevant payment which is a negative value shall be treated as if it were the equivalent positive value; and

(b) any relevant payment the amount of which represents the difference between two other amounts shall be treated as if it were a payment of an amount equal to the aggregate of those amounts.

(3) In this section—

"relevant payments" means—

(a) in relation to a contract, qualifying payments under the contract;

(b) in relation to an option, qualifying payments under the option and payments which, if it were exercised, would be qualifying payments under the contract arising by virtue of its exercise;

"the relevant time" means the time when the contract or option was entered into or, if later, the time when the provisions were included in the contract or option.

GENERAL NOTE

A contract which provides for non-qualifying payments is still a qualifying contract if, at the relevant time, the aggregate of the present value of such payments is small compared with the aggregate of the present value of all qualifying payments which may be made under the contract.

For options, qualifying payments includes such payments which would arise if the option were exercised. Where qualifying payments are netted, the payment is treated as if it were a payment of their aggregate. The "present value" of a relevant payment with a negative value is treated as a positive value.

Other basic definitions

Qualifying payments

153.—(1) Subject to subsections (2) to (5) below, in this Chapter "qualifying payment" means—

(a) in relation to a qualifying contract which is an interest rate contract, a payment falling within section 149(2), (3) or (4) above;

(b) in relation to a qualifying contract which is a currency contract, a payment falling within subsection (3) or (9) of section 150 above;

(c) in relation to a qualifying contract which is a currency option, a payment falling within subsection (9) of that section; and

(d) in relation to any qualifying contract, a payment falling within section 151 above.

(2) In this Chapter "qualifying payment" includes, in relation to a qualifying contract—

(a) a payment which, if it were a payment under the contract, would be a payment falling within section 151 above; and

(b) a payment for securing the acquisition or disposal of the contract.

(3) Where a qualifying company closes out a qualifying contract which is an interest rate or currency contract by entering into another contract with obligations which are reciprocal to those of the qualifying contract—

(a) any payment received by the company in consideration of its entering into the reciprocal contract, or paid by the company in consideration of another person's entering into that contract, is for the purposes of this Chapter a qualifying payment in relation to the qualifying contract; and

(b) all other payments under the reciprocal contract, and all subsequent payments under the qualifying contract, shall be ignored for all purposes of the Tax Acts.

(4) Subsection (5) below applies where, in the case of a qualifying contract which is a currency contract, there is a difference between—

(a) the local currency equivalent, at the time immediately after the qualifying company becomes entitled to rights and subject to duties under the contract, of the amount of the first currency (the first currency equivalent), and

(b) the local currency equivalent, at that time, of the amount of the second currency (the second currency equivalent).

(5) The amount of the difference shall be treated for the purposes of this Chapter—

(a) where the first currency equivalent exceeds the second currency equivalent, as a qualifying payment received by the qualifying company at the time specified in the contract for the purposes of section 150(2) above, and

(b) where the first currency equivalent is less than the second currency equivalent, as a qualifying payment made by the qualifying company at that time.

GENERAL NOTE
Qualifying payments means:
(a) variable rate, fixed and fixed rate and netted payments under an interest rate contract falling within s.149(2)(3) and (4); and
(b) interest related payments under a currency contract within s.150(3) and payments under a currency contract or option which are netted and settled in the local currency equivalent under s.150(9); and
(c) payments within s.151.

Any payment which if made under the contract would fall within s.151 as well as payments for securing the acquisition or disposal of the contract are also qualifying payments as are payments made or received for entering into a reciprocal contract to close out an interest rate or currency contract and any payments made under the original and reciprocal contract are to be ignored for the purposes of the Taxes Acts. The difference between the local currency equivalents of the first and second currencies when the company acquired the contract is a qualifying payment made or received at the exchange date specified in s.150(2), above.

Qualifying companies

154.—(1) Subject to subsections (2) and (3) below, any company is a qualifying company for the purposes of this Chapter.

(2) Where a unit trust scheme is an authorised unit trust as respects an accounting period the trustees (who are deemed to be a company for certain purposes by section 468(1) of the Taxes Act 1988) are not, as regards that period, a qualifying company for the purposes of this Chapter.

(3) A company which is approved for the purposes of section 842 of the Taxes Act 1988 (investment trusts) for an accounting period is not, as regards that period, a qualifying company for the purposes of this Chapter so far as it relates to currency contracts and options.

(4) In this section—

"authorised unit trust" has the same meaning as in section 468 of the Taxes Act 1988;

"unit trust scheme" has the same meaning as in section 469 of that Act.

GENERAL NOTE
All companies are qualifying companies with the exception of authorised unit trusts and approved investment trusts (but only in relation to currency contracts and options).

Accrual of profits and losses

Accrual of profits and losses

155.—(1) Where, as regards a qualifying contract held by a qualifying company and an accounting period, amount A exceeds amount B, a profit on the contract of an amount equal to the excess accrues to the company for the period.

(2) Where, as regards a qualifying contract held by a qualifying company and an accounting period, amount B exceeds amount A, a loss on the contract of an amount equal to the excess accrues to the company for the period.

(3) Subsections (4) and (5) below have effect for the purposes of this section, sections 158 and 161 to 167 below and paragraph 2 of Schedule 18 to this Act; and any reference in any of those sections or that paragraph to amount A or amount B is a reference to that amount after the making of any adjustments under such of those sections as precede that section or paragraph.

(4) Where as regards a qualifying contract a qualifying company's profit or loss for an accounting period falls to be computed on a mark to market basis incorporating a particular method of valuation—

(a) amount A is the aggregate of—

(i) the amount or aggregate amount of the qualifying payment or payments becoming due and payable to the company in the period, and

(ii) any increase for the period, or the part of the period for which the contract is held by the company, in the value of the contract as determined by that method, and

(b) amount B is the aggregate of—

(i) the amount or aggregate amount of the qualifying payment or payments becoming due and payable by the company in the period, and

(ii) any reduction for the period, or the part of the period for which the contract is held by the company, in the value of the contract as so determined.

(5) Where as regards a qualifying contract a qualifying company's profit or loss for an accounting period falls to be computed on a particular accruals basis—

(a) amount A is so much of the qualifying payment or payments received or falling to be received by the company as is allocated to the period on that basis, and

(b) amount B is so much of the qualifying payment or payments made or falling to be made by the company as is so allocated.

(6) Where a qualifying contract is such a contract by reason of being treated, by virtue of section 152 above, as if any provisions for one or more transfers of money or money's worth were not included in it—

(a) so much of any qualifying payment as relates to the transfer or transfers shall be ignored for the purposes of subsections (4) and (5) above, and

(b) so much of any such increase or reduction as is mentioned in paragraph (a) or (b) of subsection (4) above as so relates shall be ignored for the purposes of that subsection.

(7) Subject to subsection (8) below, where a qualifying contract—

(a) becomes held by a qualifying company at any time in an accounting period, or

(b) ceases to be so held at any such time,

it shall be assumed for the purposes of subsection (4) above that its value is nil immediately after it becomes so held or, as the case may be, immediately before it ceases to be so held.

(8) Subsection (7)(b) above does not apply where a qualifying contract is discharged by the making of payments none of which is a qualifying payment for the purposes of this Chapter.

GENERAL NOTE

A profit arises on a qualifying contract in an accounting period if amount A exceeds amount B and a loss arises if amount B exceeds amount A, and the difference between the two is the profit or loss.

Where the mark to market basis of accounting is adopted:

Amount A is the aggregate of qualifying payments due and payable to the company in the period and any increase in the value of the contract in the same period, or part of the period for which the contract is held by the company; and

Amount B is the aggregate of qualifying payments due and payable by the company in the period and any decrease in the value of the contract in the same period or part of the period for which the contract is held by the company.

Where an accruals basis is adopted:

Amount A is the aggregate of qualifying payments received or receivable by the company as is allocated to the period; and

Amount B is the aggregate of qualifying payments paid or payable by the company as is allocated to the period.

The definition of amounts A and B also applies to ss.158, 161 and 167 and para. (2) of Sched. 18 with any necessary adjustments required by those sections or paragraph. Any payments or transfers of value disregarded under s.152 are to be excluded from the calculation of amounts A and B. Where the mark to market basis of accounting is used, the value of a qualifying contract immediately after its acquisition, or before its disposal, is nil unless the contract, when it ceases to be held, is discharged by payments which are not qualifying payments.

Basis of accounting: general

156.—(1) Where, for the purposes of a qualifying company's accounts, profits and losses for an accounting period on a qualifying contract held by the company are computed on—

(a) a mark to market basis of accounting which satisfies the requirements of this section, or

(b) an accruals basis of accounting which satisfies those requirements,

profits and losses for the period on the contract shall be computed on that basis for the purposes of this Chapter.

(2) Where subsection (1) above does not apply in the case of a qualifying contract held by a qualifying company and an accounting period, profits and losses for the period on the contract shall be computed for the purposes of this Chapter on a mark to market or accruals basis of accounting which—

(a) satisfies the requirements of this section, and

(b) is specified in an agreement between the company and the inspector or, in default of such an agreement, in a notice served on the company by the inspector.

(3) A mark to market basis of accounting satisfies the requirements of this section as regards a qualifying contract if—

(a) computing the profits or losses on the contract on that basis is in accordance with normal accountancy practice;

(b) all relevant payments under the contract are allocated to the accounting periods in which they become due and payable; and

(c) the method of valuation adopted is such as to secure the contract is brought into account at a fair value.

(4) An accruals basis of accounting satisfies the requirements of this section as regards a qualifying contract if—

(a) computing the profits or losses on the contract on that basis is in accordance with normal accountancy practice;

(b) all relevant payments under the contract are allocated to the accounting periods to which they relate, without regard to the accounting periods in which they are made or received, or become due and payable; and

    (c) where such payments relate to two or more such periods, they are apportioned between those periods on a just and reasonable basis.

    (5) In determining whether, as regards a qualifying contract, a relevant payment is dealt with as mentioned in subsection (4) above—

    (a) regard shall be had to the accounting period or periods to which any reciprocal payment or payments are allocated, and to the basis on which any such payment or payments are apportioned between two or more such periods, but

    (b) no regard shall be had to the accounting period or periods to which any other payment or payments are allocated, or to the basis on which any such payment or payments are so apportioned.

    (6) References in this section to a qualifying company's accounts shall be construed as follows—

    (a) in the case of a company formed and registered under the Companies Act 1985, as references to its accounts drawn up in accordance with the requirements of that Act;

    (b) in the case of a company formed and registered under the Companies (Northern Ireland) Order 1986, as references to its accounts drawn up in accordance with the requirements of that Order;

    (c) in any other case, as references to the accounts which it is required to keep under the law of its home State or, if it is not so required to keep accounts, such of its accounts as most closely correspond to the accounts mentioned in paragraph (a) above;

and for the purposes of paragraph (c) above the home State of a company is the country or territory under whose law the company is incorporated.

    (7) In this section—

    "fair value", in relation to a qualifying contract, means the amount which, if the qualifying company disposed of the contract to a knowledgeable and willing party dealing at arm's length, it would be able to obtain or, as the case may be, would have to pay;

    "reciprocal payment", in relation to a relevant payment, means another such payment which is the consideration or part of the consideration for that payment;

    "relevant payment" means a qualifying payment made or received, or falling to be made or received, by the company.

    (8) In the above definition of "reciprocal payment", the second reference to a relevant payment includes a reference to any payment which—

    (a) is subject to a condition precedent, and

    (b) would be a relevant payment if the condition were fulfilled.

GENERAL NOTE

Tax profits or losses on qualifying contracts may be computed following the accounting treatment of qualifying contracts provided the qualifying company accounts for qualifying contracts on an acceptable mark to market basis or an acceptable accruals basis of accounting.

A mark to market basis of accounting is acceptable if: (a) profits or losses on qualifying contracts are computed in accordance with normal accountancy practice; (b) qualifying payments are allocated to the periods in which they become due and payable; and (c) all qualifying contracts are included in the accounts at fair value.

An accrual basis of accounting is acceptable if: (a) profits or losses on qualifying contracts are computed in accordance with normal accountancy practice; (b) qualifying payments are allocated to the period to which they relate regardless of when they become due and payable or are made or received; and (c) payments relating to two or more periods are allocated on a just and reasonable basis.

If the company adopts a different basis of accounting, the tax profits or losses on qualifying contracts are to be computed using either a mark to market basis or an accruals basis as agreed between the company and the inspector, or in the absence of agreement as specified by the inspector in a notice.

Basis of accounting for linked currency options

157.—(1) As regards a qualifying contract which is a linked currency option, a qualifying company's profit or loss for an accounting period shall be computed on a mark to market basis of accounting.

(2) Accordingly if, as regards such an option, a qualifying company's profit or loss for an accounting period would, apart from subsection (1) above, fall to be computed on an accruals basis of accounting, that profit or loss shall be computed for the purposes of this Chapter on a mark to market basis of accounting which—

    (a) satisfies the requirements of section 156 above, or would satisfy those requirements if paragraph (a) of subsection (3) of that section were omitted, and

    (b) is specified in an agreement between the company and the inspector or, in default of such an agreement, in a notice served on the company by the inspector.

(3) A currency option is a linked currency option for the purposes of this section if each of the conditions mentioned below is fulfilled.

(4) The first condition is that—

    (a) in the case of an option exercisable by the qualifying company against the other party, another currency option is exercisable by that party against the company; or

    (b) in the case of an option exercisable by the other party against the qualifying company, another currency option is exercisable by the company against that party.

(5) For the purposes of subsection (4) above, another currency option which is exercisable by or against an associated company of the qualifying company, or by or against an associated company of the other party to the currency option in question, shall be treated as exercisable by or against the qualifying company or that party.

(6) The second condition is that the terms of the two options are such that—

    (a) they must be exercised (if at all) at the same, or substantially the same, time, and

    (b) the rights and duties under the contract which would arise if the one option were exercised are the same, or substantially the same, as those under the contract which would arise if the other option were exercised.

(7) Where the currency option in question is such an option by virtue of section 150(8) above, subsections (4) and (5) above shall be construed as if—

    (a) any reference to an option being exercisable by any person were a reference to a contract subject to a condition precedent the fulfilment of which would result in a transfer of value to that person, and

    (b) any reference to an option being exercisable against any person were a reference to a contract subject to a condition precedent the fulfilment of which would result in a transfer of value by that person.

(8) For the purposes of subsection (7) above there is a transfer of value to or by any person if, immediately after the fulfilment of the condition, the value of that person's net assets is more or, as the case may be, less than it would have been but for the fulfilment of the condition.

(9) Any reference in subsection (8) above to the value of a person's net assets being more or less than it would have been but for the fulfilment of the condition includes a reference to the value of that person's net liabilities being less or, as the case may be, more than it would have been but for the fulfilment of the condition.

(10) In this section "associated company" shall be construed in accordance with section 416 of the Taxes Act 1988 and any reference to a currency option is a reference to one which is a qualifying contract.

GENERAL NOTE

Tax profits or losses on linked currency options are to be computed on a mark to market basis of accounting which satisfies s.156 (except that it is not necessary that profits or losses be computed in accordance with normal accountancy practice). The basis must be agreed with the inspector, or in the absence of agreement as specified by the inspector in a notice. A linked currency is one where there is another currency option between the same parties (including associated companies of these parties) and both options must be exercised (if at all) at substantially the same time and the rights and duties that would arise under the contracts if the options were exercised are substantially the same.

Contracts subject to a condition precedent (see s.150(8)) the fulfilment of which would result in a transfer of value, are to be treated as linked currency options.

Adjustments for changes in basis of accounting

158.—(1) Subsections (2) to (5) below apply where, as regards a qualifying contract and an accounting period, a qualifying company's profit or loss is computed on a basis of accounting (the new basis) other than that adopted for the immediately preceding accounting period.

(2) There shall be added to amount A an amount equal to any amount, or the aggregate of any amounts—

(a) which have not been included in amount A for a preceding accounting period, and

(b) which would have been so included if the new basis had been adopted for that period.

(3) There shall be deducted from amount A or, as the case may require, added to amount B an amount equal to any amount, or the aggregate of any amounts—

(a) which have been included in amount A for a preceding accounting period, and

(b) which would not have been so included if the new basis had been adopted for that period.

(4) There shall be added to amount B an amount equal to any amount, or the aggregate of any amounts—

(a) which have not been included in amount B for a preceding accounting period, and

(b) which would have been so included if the new basis had been adopted for that period.

(5) There shall be deducted from amount B or, as the case may require, added to amount A an amount equal to any amount, or the aggregate of any amounts—

(a) which have been included in amount B for a preceding accounting period, and

(b) which would not have been so included if the new basis had been adopted for that period.

(6) Subject to subsection (7) below, subsections (2) to (5) above also apply where a contract or option becomes a qualifying contract by virtue of section 147(2) or 148(2) or (3) above at the beginning of the first day of an accounting period of a qualifying company.

(7) Where subsections (2) to (5) above apply by virtue of subsection (6) above, they shall have effect as if—

(a) any reference to the new basis were a reference to the basis of accounting on which, as regards the qualifying contract, the company's profit or loss for the accounting period is calculated,

(b) any reference to being or not being included in amount A for a preceding accounting period were a reference to being or not being taken into account as receipts or increases in value in computing the company's profits or losses for such a period, and

(c) any reference to being or not being included in amount B for a preceding accounting period were a reference to being or not being taken into account as deductions or reductions in value in computing the company's profits or losses for such a period.

GENERAL NOTE

Where a qualifying company changes the basis of accounting for computing profits and losses on qualifying contracts, then in the period in which the change takes place:
- (a) amounts A and B are to be increased by amounts which were not taken into account in an earlier period but which would have been under the new basis;
- (b) amounts A and B are to be decreased (or amounts B and A increased respectively) by amounts which have already been taken into account in an earlier period but which would not have been under the new basis.

A similar adjustment is made where existing contracts or options become qualifying contracts on a qualifying company's commencement day or six years after its commencement day.

Treatment of profits and losses

Trading profits and losses

159.—(1) Subsections (2) and (3) below apply where—
- (a) as regards a qualifying contract a profit or loss accrues to a qualifying company for an accounting period, and
- (b) the qualifying contract was at any time in the period held by the company for the purposes of a trade or part of a trade carried on by it.

(2) If throughout the accounting period the qualifying contract was held by the company solely for the purposes of the trade or part, the whole of the profit or loss shall be treated for the purposes of the Tax Acts as a profit or loss of the trade or part for the period.

(3) In any other case the profit or loss shall be apportioned on a just and reasonable basis and so much as is attributable to the trade or part shall be treated for the purposes of the Tax Acts as a profit or loss of the trade or part for the period.

(4) The preceding provisions of this section apply notwithstanding anything in section 74 of the Taxes Act 1988 (general rules as to deductions not allowable).

GENERAL NOTE

Profits or losses on qualifying contracts held solely for the purposes of the trade are treated as income or expenses of the trade and the ICTA 1988 (c. 1), s.74 is disapplied. If the contract is held partly for the purposes of the trade, the profits or losses are apportioned accordingly on a just and reasonable basis to determine the part attributable to the trade.

As to the treatment of non-trading profits or losses, see s.160 below.

Non-trading profits and losses

160.—(1) In a case where—
- (a) as regards a qualifying contract a profit or loss accrues to a qualifying company for an accounting period, and
- (b) the whole or part of the profit or loss does not fall to be treated for the purposes of the Tax Acts as a profit or loss of a trade or part of a trade for the period,

the whole or part (as the case may be) shall be treated for the purposes of this section as a non-trading profit or loss of the company for the period.

(2) Subsections (5), (6) and (9) of section 129 and sections 130 to 133 of the Finance Act 1993 (non-trading exchange gains and losses) shall have effect as if—
- (a) any reference to an amount which a company is treated as receiving in an accounting period by virtue of section 129 included a reference to an amount equal to any non-trading profit of the company for the period, and
- (b) any reference to a loss which a company is treated as incurring in an accounting period by virtue of that section included a reference to an amount equal to any non-trading loss of the company for the period;

and (unless the contrary intention appears) any reference in the following provisions of this Chapter to any of those provisions of that Act is a reference to that provision so far as it has effect in relation to such non-trading profits or losses.

(3) For the purposes of subsection (2) above, any reference in the provisions there mentioned which falls to be construed as a reference to a qualifying company for the purposes of Chapter II of Part II of the Finance Act 1993 (exchange gains and losses) shall be construed as including a reference to a qualifying company for the purposes of this Chapter.

(4) Case VI of Schedule D shall for the purposes of corporation tax extend to companies not resident in the United Kingdom, so far as those companies are chargeable to tax on profits which, in the case of companies resident in the United Kingdom, fall within that Case by virtue of section 130 of the Finance Act 1993.

GENERAL NOTE
Non-trading profits or losses (*i.e.* profits or losses or qualifying contracts not treated as trading profits or losses under s.159 above) are treated as non-trading exchange gains or losses for the purposes of the FA 1993 (c. 34), s.129(5)(6) and (9) and ss.130–133.

Special cases

Termination etc. of qualifying contracts

161.—(1) This section applies where at any time (the relevant time) in an accounting period of a qualifying company—
  (a) a qualifying contract held by the company is terminated,
  (b) such a contract is disposed of by the company, or
  (c) a contract held by the company is so varied as to cease to be such a contract.

(2) If, as regards the contract and the period, amounts A and B fall to be determined under section 155(5) above—
  (a) there shall be deducted from amount A or, as the case may require, added to amount B so much of any qualifying payment as has not become due and payable to the company before the relevant time but has been included in amount A for the period or any previous accounting period, and
  (b) there shall be deducted from amount B or, as the case may require, added to amount A so much of any qualifying payment as has not become due and payable by the company before the relevant time but has been included in amount B for the period or any previous accounting period.

GENERAL NOTE
Where, in any period, a qualifying contract which has been accounted for on an accruals basis (under s.155(5) above) is terminated, disposed of or varied so as to cease to be a qualifying contract, amounts A and B are to be adjusted to ensure that payments due but not paid or received before the date of disposal, termination, etc., but which have previously been taken into account, are left out of account.

Exchange gains and losses on currency contracts

162. Where, as regards a currency contract held by a qualifying company and an accounting period, amounts A and B fall to be determined under section 155(4) above—
  (a) the amount of any exchange gain which as regards the contract accrues to the company for the period shall be deducted from amount A or, as the case may require, added to amount B; and
  (b) the amount of any exchange loss which as regards the contract accrues to the company for the period shall be deducted from amount B or, as the case may require, added to amount A.

GENERAL NOTE

Where amounts A and B are calculated on a mark to market basis, any exchange gain accruing on a currency contract in any period is to be deducted from amount A (or added to amount B) and vice versa in the case of exchange losses accruing in any period.

Irrecoverable payments

163.—(1) Subsections (2) and (3) below apply in any case where—

(a) a qualifying company is entitled to a right to receive a qualifying payment, and

(b) the inspector is satisfied, on a claim made within two years after the end of an accounting period of the company, that the whole or any part of the payment outstanding immediately before the end of that period could at that time reasonably have been regarded as having become irrecoverable in that period.

(2) If, as regards the contract and the period, amounts A and B fall to be determined under section 155(4) above, an amount equal to so much of the payment as—

(a) is considered to have become irrecoverable in the period, and

(b) became due and payable in the period or any previous accounting period,

shall be deducted from amount A, or as the case may require, added to amount B.

(3) If, as regards the contract and the period, amounts A and B fall to be determined under section 155(5) above, an amount equal to so much of the payment as—

(a) is considered to have become irrecoverable in the period, and

(b) was allocated to the period or any previous accounting period,

shall be deducted from amount A, or as the case may require, added to amount B.

(4) In any case where—

(a) as regards a qualifying contract and an accounting period of a qualifying company, an amount has been deducted or added as mentioned in subsection (2) or (3) above, and

(b) the whole or any part of so much of the qualifying payment as was considered irrecoverable is recovered in a later accounting period of the company,

an amount equal to so much of the payment as is so recovered shall, as regards the qualifying contract and the later accounting period, be deducted from amount B, or as the case may require, added to amount A.

GENERAL NOTE

Relief is available where a qualifying payment (or a part thereof) due to a company, is shown to be irrecoverable immediately before the end of an accounting period. The irrecoverable amount is to be deducted from amount A (or added to amount B as appropriate) for the accounting period concerned. The claim for relief must be made within two years of that accounting period. If the amount is subsequently recovered, amount B is to be decreased (or amount A increased) in the period in which the recovery occurs.

Released payments

164.—(1) Subsections (2) and (3) below apply in any case where—

(a) a qualifying company is subject to a duty to make a qualifying payment, and

(b) at any time in any accounting period of the company, the whole or any part of the payment then outstanding is released by the person to whom the duty is owed.

(2) If, as regards the contract and the period, amounts A and B fall to be determined under section 155(4) above, an amount equal to so much of the payment as—

(a) is released in the period, and

(b) became due and payable, in the period or any previous accounting period,

shall be deducted from amount B, or as the case may require, added to amount A.

(3) If, as regards the contract and the period, amounts A and B fall to be determined under section 155(5) above, an amount equal to so much of the payment as—

(a) is released in the period, and

(b) was allocated to the period or any previous accounting period,

shall be deducted from amount B, or as the case may require, added to amount A.

GENERAL NOTE

Where a qualifying company is released (wholly or partly) from the obligation to make a qualifying payment, an adjustment is to be made to amount B (or amount A as appropriate) to disallow a deduction for the payment (or part thereof) which will never be made.

Anti-avoidance and related provisions

Transfers of value by qualifying companies

165.—(1) Subsection (2) below applies where, as a result of—

(a) a qualifying company entering into a relevant transaction on or after its commencement day, or

(b) the expiry on or after a qualifying company's commencement day of an option held by the company which, until its expiry, was a qualifying contract,

there is a transfer of value by the qualifying company to an associated company or an associated third party.

(2) For the accounting period of the qualifying company in which the transaction was entered into or the option expired, there shall be deducted from amount B or, as the case may require, added to amount A an amount equal to the value transferred by that company.

(3) For the purposes of subsection (1) above there is a transfer of value by the qualifying company to an associated company or an associated third party if, immediately after the transaction or expiry—

(a) the value of the qualifying company's net assets is less, and

(b) the value of the associated company's or associated third party's net assets is more,

than it would have been but for the transaction or expiry; and the amount by which the value mentioned in paragraph (a) above is less is the value transferred by the qualifying company for the purposes of subsection (2) above.

(4) Any reference in subsection (3) above to the value of a person's net assets being less or more than it would have been but for the transaction or expiry includes a reference to the value of that person's net liabilities being more or, as the case may be, less than it would have been but for the transaction or expiry.

(5) In applying subsection (3) above, no account shall be taken of any such payment as is mentioned in section 151(2)(a) or (b) above.

(6) A third party, that is to say, a person who is not an associated company, is an associated third party for the purposes of this section at the time when the relevant transaction is entered or the option expires if, at that time, each of the two conditions mentioned below is fulfilled.

(7) The first condition is that relevant transaction is entered into or the option is allowed to expire in pursuance of arrangements made with the third party.

(8) The second condition is that, in pursuance of those arrangements, a transfer of value has been or will be made to an associated company (directly

or indirectly) by the third party or by a company which was at the time when the arrangements were made an associated company of that party.

(9) Where it appears to the inspector that there is a transfer of value by the qualifying company to a third party, he may be notice in writing require the company, within such time (which shall not be less than 30 days) as may be specified in the notice, to furnish to the inspector such information—

(a) as is in its possession or power, and

(b) as the inspector reasonably requires for the purpose of determining whether the third party is an associated third party for the purposes of this section.

(10) Subsection (3) above shall (with the necessary modifications) apply for the purposes of subsections (7) to (9) above as it applies for the purposes of subsection (1) above.

(11) In this section—

"associated company" shall be construed in accordance with section 416 of the Taxes Act 1988;

"relevant transaction" means a transaction as a result of which—

(a) a qualifying company becomes party to a qualifying contract, or

(b) the terms of a qualifying contract to which a qualifying company is party are varied;

and any reference to an associated company is, unless the contrary intention appears, a reference to an associated company of the qualifying company.

GENERAL NOTE

If a qualifying company, on or after its commencement day, transfers value to an associated company or an associated third party, by (a) entering into or varying the terms of a qualifying contract or (b) by abandoning an interest rate or currency option which was a qualifying contract prior to its expiry, amount B is to be reduced (or amount A increased as appropriate) by the value transferred, in the period in which the transaction takes place.

There is a transfer of value if (i) the qualifying company's net assets have decreased (or its net liabilities increased) and (ii) the other party's net assets are increased (or net liabilities decreased), as a result of the transaction. Payments made for arranging, or reasonable fees incurred in respect of, the contract or option are ignored. The amount transferred is the reduction referred to in (i) above.

An associated third party is a party which has entered into arrangements to receive a transfer of value from a qualifying company and to make a transfer of value to an associate of the qualifying company. The inspector may, by service of notice on the qualifying company, call for information to determine if a third party is an associated third party for the purposes of these rules.

Transfers of value to associated companies

166.—(1) Subsection (2) below applies where subsection (2) of section 165 above applies and either—

(a) the transfer of value by the qualifying company is to an associated company which it itself a qualifying company; or

(b) the transfer of value by the qualifying company is to an associated third party, and the transfer of value mentioned in subsection (8) of that section—

(i) is to an associated company which is itself a qualifying company, and

(ii) results from that company entering into a relevant transaction.

(2) For the corresponding accounting period or periods of the associated company, there shall be deducted from amount A or, as the case may require, added to amount B an amount equal to the value transferred to the associated company.

(3) Subsection (3) of section 165 above shall (with the necessary modifications) apply for the purposes of subsection (2) above as it applies for the purposes of subsection (2) of that section.

(4) In subsection (2) above "corresponding accounting period or periods", in relation to the associated company, means the accounting period or periods of that company comprising or together comprising the accounting period of the qualifying company in which the transaction was entered into or the option expired, and any necessary apportionment shall be made between corresponding accounting periods if more than one.

(5) In this section any expressions which are also used in section 165 above shall be construed in accordance with the provisions of that section.

GENERAL NOTE

This ensures that where a transfer of value within s.165 above is made by a qualifying company, an adjustment corresponding to that arising under s.165(2) is made to amounts A or B of the transferee-associated company in the corresponding accounting period. Apportionment is necessary where the accounting periods of the qualifying company and the associated company do not directly correspond.

Transactions not at arm's length

167.—(1) A transaction entered into on or after a qualifying company's commencement day is a relevant transaction for the purposes of this section if as a result of the transaction—
  (a) the qualifying company becomes party to a qualifying contract, or
  (b) the terms of a qualifying contract to which the qualifying company is party are varied.
  (2) Subsections (3) to (5) below apply where—
  (a) if the parties to a relevant transaction had been dealing at arm's length, the transaction—
      (i) would not have been entered into at all, or
      (ii) would have been entered into on different terms, and
  (b) the Board direct that those subsections shall apply,
but subject, in a case falling within paragraph (a)(ii) above, to the modifications made by subsection (7) below.
  (3) For each relevant accounting period for the whole of which the other party is a qualifying company, the following deductions shall be made—
  (a) from amount B, a deduction of such amount as may be necessary to reduce amount B to nil, and
  (b) from amount A, a deduction of such amount as may be necessary to reduce amount A to nil.
  (4) For each relevant accounting period for any part of which the other party is not a qualifying company, the following deductions shall be made—
  (a) from amount B, a deduction of such amount as may be necessary to reduce amount B to nil, and
  (b) from amount A, a deduction of the same amount or (where that amount exceeds amount A) a deduction of so much of that amount as may be necessary to reduce amount A to nil.
  (5) For each relevant accounting period (except the first) for any part of which the other party is not a qualifying company, there shall also be deducted from amount A or, as the case may require, added to amount B such amount as may be necessary to secure that amount C does not exceed amount D where—
  (a) amount C is any amount by which the aggregate of adjusted amounts A exceeds the aggregate of adjusted amounts B, and
  (b) amount D is any amount by which the aggregate of unadjusted amounts A exceeds the aggregate of unadjusted amounts B.
  (6) In subsection (5) above—
    "adjusted" means adjusted under subsections (4) and (5) above and "unadjusted" shall be construed accordingly;

"the aggregate of adjusted amounts A", in relation to a relevant
accounting period, means the aggregate of—
    (a) adjusted amount A for that period, and
    (b) adjusted amount A for each preceding relevant accounting
    period,
and similar expressions shall be construed accordingly.

(7) In a case falling within subsection (2)(a)(ii) above—
(a) subsections (3) to (5) above shall have effect as if any reference to
amount A or amount B were a reference to the relevant proportion of
that amount; and
(b) the definitions in subsection (6) above of "the aggregate of adjusted
amounts A" and similar expressions shall have effect as if any reference to adjusted amount A were a reference to the adjusted relevant
proportion of amount A;
and in this subsection "the relevant proportion" means such proportion as
may be just and reasonable having regard to the differences between the
terms mentioned in subsection (2)(a)(ii) above and the terms on which the
relevant transaction was actually entered into.

(8) In applying subsections (2) and (7) above—
(a) no account shall be taken of any transfer of value in respect of which
an adjustment is made under section 165 or 166 above, but
(b) subject to that, all factors shall be taken into account.

(9) The factors which may be so taken into account include—
(a) in a case where the qualifying contract is an interest rate contract or
option, any notional principal amounts and rates of interest that would
have been involved;
(b) in a case where the qualifying contract is a currency contract or option,
any currencies and amounts that would have been involved; and
(c) in either case, any transactions which are related to the relevant
transaction.

(10) In this section "relevant accounting period", in relation to a relevant
transaction, means—
(a) the accounting period of the qualifying company in which the transaction was entered into, and
(b) each subsequent accounting period of that company for the whole or
part of which it is party to the contract.

GENERAL NOTE
This section applies to transactions entered into on or after a qualifying company's commencement date which result in a qualifying contract being entered into or its terms varied, and
the transaction would, if the parties had been at arm's length, not have been entered into at all or
would have been entered into on different terms and the Board directs that the provisions
should apply (see subss. (1) and (2)).
If the contract would not have been entered into if the parties were acting at arm's length, and
the counterparty is a qualifying company, in each relevant accounting period adjustments are to
be made to amounts A and B to reduce them to nil, effectively disregarding the contract (see
subs. (3)).
Where the counterparty is not a qualifying company, for each relevant accounting period,
amount B is to be reduced to nil and amount A is to be reduced by the amount of the loss, or
reduced to nil if the loss exceeds the gain. In subsequent relevant accounting periods further
adjustments are made to ensure that on a cumulative basis the net gain is taxed, and the net loss
disallowed (see subss. (4) and (5)).
Where the transaction would have been entered into on different terms if the parties were
acting at arm's length, similar adjustments are to be made but only to the relevant proportion.
The relevant proportion is such proportion as may be determined to be just and reasonable
having regard to the terms on which the transaction would have been entered into on an arm's
length basis (see subs. (7)). In determining whether or not a transaction is at arm's length, all
factors, other than adjustments for transfers of value under ss.165 and 166, are to be taken into
account (see subs. (8)).

"Relevant accounting period" is the period in which the transaction was entered into and each subsequent accounting period over the life of the contract (see subs. (10)).

Qualifying contracts with non-residents

168.—(1) Subject to subsections (3) to (5) below, subsections (4) and (5) of section 167 above ("the relevant subsections") also apply where, as a result of any transaction entered into on or after a qualifying company's commencement day—

    (a) the qualifying company and a non-resident, that is, a person who is not resident in the United Kingdom, both become party to a qualifying contract;

    (b) the qualifying company becomes party to a qualifying contract to which a non-resident is party; or

    (c) a non-resident becomes party to a qualifying contract to which the qualifying company is party.

(2) For the purposes of the relevant subsections as so applied, the definition of "relevant accounting period" in subsection (10) of that section shall have effect as if—

    (a) any reference to a relevant transaction were a reference to the transaction mentioned in subsection (1) above; and

    (b) in paragraph (b), for the words "it is" there were substituted the words "both it and the non-resident are".

(3) The relevant subsections shall not apply where the qualifying company is a bank, building society or financial trader and—

    (a) it holds the qualifying contract solely for the purposes of a trade or part of a trade carried on by it in the United Kingdom, and

    (b) it is party to the contract otherwise than as a agent or nominee of another person.

(4) The relevant subsections shall not apply where—

    (a) the non-resident holds the qualifying contract solely for the purposes of a trade or part of a trade carried on by him in the United Kingdom through a branch or agency, and

    (b) he is party to the contract otherwise than as agent or nominee of another person.

(5) The relevant subsections shall not apply where arrangements made with the government of the territory in which the non-resident is resident—

    (a) have effect by virtue of section 788 of the Taxes Act 1988, and

    (b) make provision, whether for relief or otherwise, in relation to interest (as defined in the arrangements).

(6) Where the non-resident is party to the contract as agent or nominee of another person, subsection (5) above shall have effect as if the reference to the territory in which the non-resident is resident were a reference to the territory in which that other person is resident.

General Note

A qualifying contract between a qualifying company and a non-resident person is (regardless of its terms) treated as one which would not have been entered into at all by parties dealing at arm's length so that the provisions in s.167(4) and (5) above apply. Where the qualifying company or the non-resident person becomes a party to the contract, the provisions apply during the period when both are parties to the contract.

The provisions do not apply (a) where the qualifying company is a bank, building society or financial trader which is not acting as an agent or nominee for another person and which holds the contract solely for the purposes of its U.K. trade (or part of the trade); or (b) where the non-resident, who is not acting as an agent or nominee for another person, holds the contract solely for the purposes of a trade (or part of a trade) carried on in the U.K. through a branch or agency; or (c) if a double taxation agreement containing an interest article exists between the U.K. and the territory of the counterparty.

Miscellaneous

Insurance and mutual trading companies

169.—(1) Subject to the provisions of Schedule 18 to this Act and subsection (2) below, this Chapter shall apply in relation to insurance companies and mutual trading companies as it applies in relation to other qualifying companies.

(2) The Treasury may by regulations provide that this Chapter shall have effect in relation to currency contracts held by insurance companies with such modifications as may be specified in the regulations.

(3) Regulations under subsection (2) above may make different provision as respects contracts held for different purposes or in different circumstances.

GENERAL NOTE

The provisions (*i.e.* ss.146–177 of this Act) are, subject to Sched. 18 below, applied to insurance and mutual trading companies. The Treasury may by regulations modify the application of those sections to currency contracts held by insurance companies.

Investment trusts

170.—(1) For the purpose of determining whether a qualifying company may be approved for the purposes of section 842 of the Taxes Act 1988 (investment trusts) for any accounting period, any non-trading profits which the company is treated for the purposes of section 160 above as having for that period shall be treated as income derived from shares or securities.

(2) In this section "shares" has the same meaning as in section 842 of the Taxes Act 1988.

GENERAL NOTE

Non-trading profits on interest rate contracts and options held by investment trusts are treated as income derived from shares or securities.

Charities

171.—(1) Section 505 of the Taxes Act 1988 (charities: general) shall have effect, in relation to any qualifying company established for charitable purposes only, as if the reference in subsection (1)(c)(ii) to any yearly interest or other annual payment included a reference to any annual profits or gains which the company is treated as receiving in any accounting period by virtue of section 130 of the Finance Act 1993 (non-trading exchange gains: charge to tax).

(2) As regards a qualifying company so established, no part of the relievable amount for any accounting period may be set off against any income which, if it had been applied for charitable purposes only, would have been exempt by virtue of section 505 of the Taxes Act 1988.

(3) In subsection (2) above "the relievable amount" has the same meaning as in section 131 of the Finance Act 1993 (relief for non-trading exchange losses).

GENERAL NOTE

Non-trading profits on qualifying contracts held by qualifying companies which are charities are exempt from tax under Sched. D and non-trading losses may not be relieved against income which, had it been applied for charitable purposes, would have been exempt from tax under the ICTA 1988 (c. 1), s.505.

Partnerships involving qualifying companies

172.—(1) Subject to the provisions of this section, this Chapter shall have effect as if qualifying partnerships were qualifying companies.

(2) A partnership is a qualifying partnership for the purposes of this section if one or more of the partners are qualifying companies.

(3) Subsections (4) to (6) below apply where—
(a) one or more of the members of a qualifying partnership are not qualifying companies, and
(b) as regards one or more qualifying contracts, one or more profits or losses accrue to the partnership for an accounting period.
(4) Two computations of the profits and losses for the period shall be made under subsection (1) of section 114 of the Taxes Act 1988 (partnerships involving companies: special rules for computing profits and losses)—
(a) one (the first computation) on the basis that the partnership is a qualifying partnership, and
(b) the other (the second computation) on the basis that the partnership is not such a partnership.
(5) The first computation shall be used for the purpose of determining, under subsection (2) of that section, the share or shares of such of the partners as are qualifying companies.
(6) The second computation shall be used for the purpose of determining, under that subsection, the share or shares of such of the partners as are not qualifying companies.

GENERAL NOTE
This applies the financial instrument provisions (*i.e.* ss.146–177 of this Act) to "qualifying partnerships", *i.e.* a partnership having one or more partners who are qualifying companies. If profits or losses accrue on qualifying contracts, held by a qualifying partnership where not all the partners are qualifying companies, two computations are to be done, one on the basis that the partnership is a qualifying company and the other on the basis that it is not. This determines the respective entitlements of those partners who are qualifying companies and those which are not.

Supplemental

Prevention of double charging etc.

173.—(1) Subsection (2) below applies to any amount—
(a) which under or by virtue of this Chapter is chargeable to corporation tax as profits of a qualifying company, or
(b) which falls to be taken into account as a receipt in computing for the purposes of this Chapter the profits or losses of such a company.
(2) An amount to which this subsection applies—
(a) shall not otherwise than under or by virtue of this Chapter be chargeable to corporation tax as profits of the company,
(b) shall not be taken into account as a receipt in computing for other purposes of the Tax Acts the profits or losses of the company, and
(c) for the purposes of the Taxation of Chargeable Gains Act 1992, shall be excluded from the consideration for a disposal of assets taken into account in the computation of the gain.
(3) Subsection (4) below applies to any amount—
(a) which is allowable as a deduction in computing for the purposes of this Chapter the profits or losses of a qualifying company, or
(b) which under or by virtue of this Chapter is allowable as a deduction in computing any other income or profits or gains or losses of such a company for the purposes of the Tax Acts, or
(c) which, although not so allowable as a deduction in computing any losses, would be so allowable but for an insufficiency of income or profits or gains;
and that subsection applies to any such amount irrespective of whether effect is or would be given to the deduction in computing the amount of tax chargeable or by discharge or repayment of tax or in any other way.

(4) An amount to which this subsection applies—
  (a) shall not be allowable as a deduction in computing for other purposes of the Tax Acts the profits or losses of the company,
  (b) shall not otherwise than under or by virtue of this Chapter be allowable as a deduction in computing any other income or profits or gains or losses of the company for the purposes of the Tax Acts,
  (c) shall not be treated as a charge on income for the purposes of corporation tax, and
  (d) shall be excluded from the sums allowable under section 38 of the Taxation of Chargeable Gains Act 1992 as a deduction in the computation of the gain.
(5) In this section—
  (a) references to the purposes of this Chapter include references to the purposes of subsections (5), (6) and (9) of section 129 and sections 130 to 133 of the Finance Act 1993 (non-trading exchange gains and losses), and
  (b) references to other purposes of the Tax Acts are references to the purposes of those Acts other than those of this Chapter.

GENERAL NOTE
Amounts which, under the financial instrument provisions (*i.e.* ss.146–177 of this Act), are taken into account as profits or receipts, or are allowable as deductions, may not be taxed or correspondingly allowed under other existing legislation even if relief under the financial instrument provisions cannot be obtained due to insufficient income, profits or gains.

Prevention of deduction of tax

174. Notwithstanding anything in section 349 of the Taxes Act 1988 or any other provision of the Tax Acts, a qualifying company shall not be required, on making a qualifying payment, to deduct out of it any sum representing an amount of income tax on it.

GENERAL NOTE
A qualifying company, on making a qualifying payment, need not deduct withholding tax.

Transitional provisions

175.—(1) In a case where—
  (a) at any time, a currency contract held by a qualifying company becomes a qualifying contract by virtue of section 147(2) above, and
  (b) at that time, it is held for the purposes of a trade or part of a trade carried on by the company,
subsection (4) of section 153 above shall have effect in relation to the contract and the company as if section 147(2) above applied for the purposes of this Chapter except those of that subsection.
  (2) In a case where—
  (a) at any time in an accounting period of a qualifying company, a currency contract held by the company becomes a qualifying contract by virtue of section 147(2) above, and
  (b) at all times in the period when the contract is so held, it is held otherwise than for the purposes of a trade or part of a trade carried on by the company,
section 158 above shall have effect in relation to the contract and the period as if subsections (2) and (4) were omitted.

GENERAL NOTE
This sets out transitional rules for existing currency contracts which become qualifying contracts on a company's commencement day under s.147(2) above. If such a contract is held for the purposes of the trade, any forward premium or discount is to be computed from the date the company became party to the contract and not from its commencement date. If the contract is held for non-trade purposes, only the forward premium or discount accruing after a company

commencement date is to be taken into account as a profit or loss. Any adjustments which fall to be made under s.158 above, are to be ignored. Thus any differences between the old basis of computing profits and losses and the basis adopted under the financial instrument provisions are not immediately charged on the company's commencement day.

Minor and consequential amendments

176.—(1) In section 434A(1) of the Taxes Act 1988 (limitations on loss relief and group relief), for the words from "under" to "Part X" there shall be substituted the following paragraphs—
"(a) under Chapter II (loss relief) or Chapter IV (group relief) of Part X, or
(b) under Chapter II of Part II of the Finance Act 1993 so far as it has effect in relation to losses treated as non-trading losses for the purposes of section 160 of the Finance Act 1994,".
(2) In Schedule 27 to that Act (distributing funds) in paragraph 5 (United Kingdom equivalent profits) the following sub-paragraph shall be substituted for sub-paragraph (2A)—
"(2A) In applying sub-paragraph (1) above the effect of the following shall be ignored, namely—
(a) sections 125 to 133 of the Finance Act 1993 (exchange gains and losses), and
(b) sections 159 and 160 of, and paragraph 1 of Schedule 18 to, the Finance Act 1994 (treatment of profits and losses on interest rate and currency contracts)."

GENERAL NOTE
Non-trading losses on qualifying contracts held by an insurance company carrying on a life assurance business may not be relieved against the policy-shareholder's share of the profits (as defined by the FA 1989 (c. 26), s.88) (see subs. (1)). The provisions in the FA 1993 (c. 34), ss.125–133 and the FA 1994 (c. 9), ss.159 and 160 and Sched. 18, para. (1) are to be ignored when calculating the U.K. equivalent profits of offshore distribution funds (see subs. (2)).

Interpretation of Chapter II

177.—(1) In this Chapter—
"appointed day" has the meaning given by section 147(4) above;
"bank" means any of the following—
(a) the Bank of England;
(b) any institution authorised under the Banking Act 1987; and
(c) a European authorised institution which has lawfully established a branch in the United Kingdom for the purpose of accepting deposits;
"commencement day" has the meaning given by section 147(4) above;
"currency contract" and "currency option" shall be construed in accordance with section 150 above;
"deposit" has the same meaning as in the Banking Act 1987;
"European authorised institution" has the same meaning as in the Banking Coordination (Second Council Directive) Regulations 1992;
"financial trader" means any of the following—
(a) an authorised person under Chapter III of Part I of the Financial Services Act 1986;
(b) an exempted person under section 43 of that Act;
(c) a European authorised institution which has lawfully established a branch in the United Kingdom for the purpose of carrying on investment business; and
(d) any person not falling within paragraphs (a) to (c) above who is approved by the Board for the purposes of this paragraph;

"inspector" includes any officer of the Board;

"insurance company" means a company to which Part II of the Insurance Companies Act 1982 applies;

"interest rate contract" and "interest rate option" shall be construed in accordance with section 149 above;

"investment business" has the same meaning as in the Financial Services Act 1986;

"mutual trading company" means a company carrying on any business of mutual trading or mutual insurance or other mutual business;

"qualifying company" has the meaning given by section 154 above;

"qualifying contract" has the meaning given by section 147(1) above;

"qualifying payment" shall be construed in accordance with section 153 above.

(2) For the purposes of this Chapter—

(a) a company becomes entitled to rights or subject to duties under an interest rate contract or option, or a currency contract or option, when it becomes party to the contract or option; and

(b) a company holds such a contract or option at a particular time if it is then entitled to rights or subject to duties under it;

and it is immaterial for the purposes of paragraph (b) above when the rights or duties fall to be exercised or performed.

(3) Any provision of this Chapter other than section 167 above which requires any amount (the relevant amount) to be deducted from amount A or, as the case may require, added to amount B shall be construed as requiring the following deductions or additions to be made—

(a) where amount A is not less than the relevant amount, a deduction from amount A of an amount equal to the relevant amount;

(b) where amount A is less than the relevant amount but is more than nil—

(i) a deduction from amount A of an amount equal to so much of the relevant amount as may be necessary to reduce amount A to nil, and

(ii) an addition to amount B of an amount equal to the remainder of the relevant amount;

(c) where amount A is nil, an addition to amount B of an amount equal to the relevant amount.

(4) Subsection (3) above shall be read as applying equally to any such provision which requires any amount to be deducted from amount B or, as the case may be, added to amount A, and for that purpose shall have effect with such modifications as may be requisite.

(5) In this Chapter expressions which are not defined or otherwise explained but are used in Chapter II of Part II of the Finance Act 1993 (exchange gains and losses) have the same meanings as in that Chapter.

(6) The Treasury may by order amend any of sections 149 to 153 above; and any such order may—

(a) make corresponding amendments to section 126 of the Finance Act 1993;

(b) make consequential amendments to such of the provisions of this Chapter or Chapter II of Part II of that Act as relate to currency contracts; and

(c) contain such other consequential provisions, and such supplementary, incidental or transitional provisions, as appear to the Treasury to be necessary or expedient.

GENERAL NOTE

Various terms in ss.147 to 177 and Sched. 18 are defined. Definitions contained in the foreign exchange legislation in the FA 1993 (c. 34) are applied as necessary. The Treasury may make regulations with such supplementary, incidental, consequential or transitional provisions as appear necessary or expedient, and may amend ss.147 to 153 and make corresponding and consequential amendments to the FA 1993 (c. 34), ss.125 to 170 and the FA 1994 (c. 9), ss.147 to 177.

CHAPTER III

MANAGEMENT: SELF-ASSESSMENT

GENERAL NOTE

This Chapter, and Chap. IV, implement two aspects of the continuing changes in the administration of the tax system. The first important change, the introduction of the "Pay and File" system for corporation tax, was brought into operation from the end of 1993. Chapter III extends the changes to tax returns for self-employed individuals and partnerships taxed under Sched. D. Chapter IV abolishes the preceding year basis which has applied for most Sched. D assessments since the introduction of income tax at the end of the eighteenth century. Further provisions will be introduced next year dealing with the obligations of an employer with respect to an employee taxed under Sched. E.

The format of Chap. III is to amend the basic statute, the Taxes Management Act 1970 (c. 9) (TMA). The more important amendments are in ss.178–199, and other amendments are in Sched. 19.

Income tax and capital gains tax

Personal and trustee's returns

178.—(1) For subsection (1) of section 8 of the Management Act (personal return) there shall be substituted the following subsections—

"(1) For the purpose of establishing the amounts in which a person is chargeable to income tax and capital gains tax for a year of assessment, he may be required by a notice given to him by an officer of the Board—

(a) to make and deliver to the officer, on or before the day mentioned in subsection (1A) below, a return containing such information as may reasonably be required in pursuance of the notice, and

(b) to deliver with the return such accounts, statements and documents, relating to information contained in the return, as may reasonably be so required.

(1A) The day referred to in subsection (1) above is—

(a) the 31st January next following the year of assessment, or

(b) where the notice under this section is given after the October next following the year, the last day of the period of three months beginning with the day on which the notice is given.

(1B) In the case of a person who carries on a trade, profession, or business in partnership with one or more other persons, a return under this section shall include each amount which, in any relevant statement, is stated to be equal to his share of any income, loss or charge for the period in respect of which the statement is made.

(1C) In subsection (1B) above "relevant statement" means a statement which, as respects the partnership, falls to be made under section 12AB of this Act for a period which includes, or includes any part of, the year of assessment or its basis period."

(2) For subsection (1) of section 8A of the Management Act (trustee's return) there shall be substituted the following subsections—

"(1) For the purpose of establishing the amounts in which a trustee of a settlement, and the settlors and beneficiaries, are chargeable to income tax and capital gains tax for a year of assessment, an officer of the Board may by a notice given to the trustee require the trustee—

(a) to make and deliver to the officer, on or before the day mentioned in subsection (1A) below, a return containing such information as may reasonably be required in pursuance of the notice, and

(b) to deliver with the return such accounts, statements and documents, relating to information contained in the return, as may reasonably be so required;

and a notice may be given to any one trustee or separate notices may be given to each trustee or to such trustees as the officer thinks fit.

(1A) The day referred to in subsection (1) above is—

(a) 31st January next following the year of assessment, or

(b) where the notice under this section is given after the 31st October next following the year, the last day of the period of three months beginning with the day on which the notice is given."

GENERAL NOTE

The new s.8 of the TMA 1970 (c. 9) sets the date for the submission of tax returns as January 31 following the year of assessment (which ends on April 5). Where a notice to submit a return is given after October 31, a three-month deadline applies.

The new s.8A of the TMA 1970 (c. 9) applies similar provisions to trustees.

Returns to include self-assessment

179. For section 9 of the Management Act there shall be substituted the following section—

"Returns to include self-assessment

9.—(1) Subject to subsection (2) below, every return under section 8 or 8A of this Act shall include an assessment (a self-assessment) of the amounts in which, on the basis of the information contained in the return, the person making the return is chargeable to income tax and capital gains tax for the year of assessment.

(2) A person shall not be required to comply with subsection (1) above if he makes and deliver his return for a year of assessment—

(a) on or before the 30th September next following the year, or

(b) where the notice under section 8 or 8A of this Act is given after the 31st July next following the year, within the period of two months beginning with the day on which the notice is given.

(3) Where, in making and delivering a return, a person does not comply with subsection (1) above, an officer of the Board shall if subsection (2) above applies, and may in any other case—

(a) make the assessment on his behalf on the basis of the information contained in the return, and

(b) send him a copy of the assessment so made;

and references in the following provisions of this Act to a person's self-assessment include references to an assessment made on a person's behalf under this subsection.

(4) Subject to subsection (5) below—

(a) at any time before the end of the period of nine months beginning with the day on which a person's return is delivered, an officer of the Board may by notice to that person so amend that person's self-assessment as to correct any obvious errors or mistakes in the return (whether errors of principle, arithmetical mistakes or otherwise); and

(b) at any time before the end of the period of twelve months beginning with the filing date, a person may by notice to an officer of the Board so amend his self-assessment as to give effect to any amendments to his return which he has notified to such an officer.

(5) No amendment of a self-assessment may be made under subsection (4) above at any time during the period—

(a) beginning with the day on which an officer of the Board gives notice of his intention to enquire into the return, and

(b) ending with the day on which the officer's enquiries into the return are completed.

(6) In this section and section 9A of this Act 'the filing date' means the day mentioned in section 8(1A) or, as the case may be, section 8A(1A) of this Act."

GENERAL NOTE

The new s.9 of the TMA 1970 (c. 9) introduces the principle of self-assessment. The taxpayer, instead of merely supplying the information on which an inspector (or other Revenue official) will make an assessment, can personally complete the calculation of his liability. If he does not wish to do so, the inspector will make the calculation, but the return must be submitted by September 30, or within two months where a notice to submit a return has been served after July 31.

The inspector may notify the taxpayer within nine months of corrections to the self-assessment where there are obvious errors and mistakes. Likewise, the taxpayer may amend his self-assessment within 12 months of January 31 or the later deadline in s.178 ("the filing date"). These provisions do not apply if the inspector is conducting an enquiry into the return.

Power to enquire into returns

180. After section 9 of the Management Act there shall be inserted the following section—

"Power to enquire into returns

9A.—(1) An officer of the Board may enquire into—

(a) the return on the basis of which a person's self-assessment was made under section 9 of this Act, or

(b) any amendment of that return on the basis of which that assessment has been amended by that person,

if, before the end of the period mentioned in subsection (2) below, he gives notice in writing to that person of his intention to do so.

(2) The period referred to in subsection (1) above is—

(a) in the case of a return delivered or amendment made on or before the filing date, the period of twelve months beginning with that date;

(b) in the case of a return delivered or amendment made after that date, the period ending with the quarter day next following the first anniversary of the day on which the return or amendment was delivered or made;

and the quarter days for the purposes of this subsection are 31st January, 30th April, 31st July and 31st October.

(3) A return or amendment which has been enquired into under subsection (1) above shall not be the subject of a further notice under that subsection."

GENERAL NOTE

The new s.9A of the TMA 1970 (c. 9) empowers the inspector (or other qualified Revenue official) to launch an enquiry within 12 months of the filing date (as defined in s.178) or, in the case of a return or amendment made at some other time, by the quarter date (January 31, April 30, July 31 and October 31) following the anniversary of the return or amendment.

A code of practice will be published for the conduct of enquiries. A second enquiry may not be launched.

Corporation tax

Return of profits

181.—(1) In subsection (1) of section 11 of the Management Act (return of profits), after the words "as may", in both places where they occur, there shall be inserted the word "reasonably".

(2) In subsection (1A) of that section, after the words "a company may", in both places where they occur, there shall be inserted the word "reasonably".

(3) After subsection (2) of that section there shall be inserted the following subsections—

"(2A) In the case of a company which carries on a trade, profession or business in partnership with one or more other persons, a return under this section shall include each amount which, in any relevant statement, is stated to be equal to its share of any income, loss or charge for the period in respect of which the statement is made.

(2B) In subsection (2A) above 'relevant statement' means a statement which, as respects the partnership, falls to be made under section 12AB of this Act for a period which includes, or includes any part of, the period in respect of which the return is required."

GENERAL NOTE

Subss. (1) and (2)
Following discussion in Committee, this extends to corporation tax a requirement of reasonableness in relation to information required by the inspector in connection with a return.

Subs. (3)
The new subsections (2A) and (2B) of s.11 of the TMA 1970 (c. 9) require a company which is trading in partnership to include in its return its total income from the partnership, computed in accordance with s.12AB (see s.185, *infra*).

Return of profits to include self-assessment

182. After section 11 of the Management Act there shall be inserted the following section—

"Return of profits to include self-assessment

11AA.—(1) Every return under section 11 of this Act for an accounting period shall include an assessment (a self-assessment) of the amount in which, on the basis of the information contained in the return, the company is chargeable to corporation tax for that period.

(2) Subject to subsection (3) below—

(a) at any time before the end of the period of nine months beginning with the day on which a company's return is delivered, an officer of the Board may by notice to the company so amend the company's self-assessment as to correct any obvious errors or mistakes in the return (whether errors of principle, arithmetical mistakes or otherwise); and

(b) at any time before the end of the period of twelve months beginning with the filing date, a company may by notice to an officer of the Board so amend its self-assessment as to give effect to any amendments to its return which it has notified to such an officer.

(3) No amendment of a self-assessment may be made under subsection (2) above at any time during the period—

(a) beginning with the day on which an officer of the Board gives notice of his intention to enquire into the return, and

(b) ending with the day on which the officer's enquiries into the return are completed.

(4) In this section and section 11AB of this Act 'the filing date' means the day mentioned in section 11(4) of this Act."

GENERAL NOTE
The new s.11AA of the TMA 1970 (c. 9) extends the principle of self-assessment to corporation tax. The self-assessment is not optional, as in the case of income tax, and must be submitted with the return.

Otherwise, the provisions of s.179 apply.

Power to enquire into return of profits

183. After section 11AA of the Management Act there shall be inserted the following section—

"Power to enquire into return of profits

11AB.—(1) An officer of the Board may enquire into—

(a) the return on the basis of which a company's self-assessment was made under section 11AA of this Act, or

(b) any amendment of that return on the basis of which that assessment was amended under subsection (2)(b) of that section,

if, before the end of the period mentioned in subsection (2) below, he gives notice in writing to the company of his intention to do so.

(2) The period referred to in subsection (1) above is—

(a) in the case of a return delivered or amendment made on or before the filing date, the period of twelve months beginning with that date;

(b) in the case of a return delivered or amendment made after that date, the period ending with the quarter day next following the first anniversary of the day on which the return or amendment was delivered or made;

and the quarter days for the purposes of this subsection are 31st January, 30th April, 31st July and 31st October.

(3) A return or amendment which has been enquired into under subsection (1) above shall not be the subject of a further notice under that subsection."

<small>GENERAL NOTE</small>
The new s.11AB of the TMA 1970 (c. 9) allows the inspector to launch an enquiry into a corporation tax return under the same conditions as those set out for income tax in s.180.

Partnerships

Partnership return

184. After section 12 of the Management Act there shall be inserted the following section—

"Partnerships

Partnership return

12AA.—(1) Where a trade, profession or business is carried on by two or more persons in partnership, for the purpose of facilitating—

(a) the assessment to income tax for a year of assessment, and

(b) the assessment to corporation tax for any period,

of each partner who is liable to be so assessed, an officer of the Board may act under subsection (2) or (3) below (or both).

(2) An officer of the Board may by a notice given to the partners require such person as is identified in accordance with rules given with the notice—

(a) to make and deliver to the officer in respect of such period as may be specified in the notice, on or before such day as may be so specified, a return containing such information as may reasonably be required in pursuance of the notice, and

(b) to deliver with the return such accounts and statements as may reasonably be so required.

(3) An officer of the Board may by notice given to any partner require the partner—

(a) to make and deliver to the officer in respect of such period as may be specified in the notice, on or before such day as may be so specified, a return containing such information as may reasonably be required in pursuance of the notice, and

(b) to deliver with the return such accounts and statements as may reasonably be so required;

and a notice may be given to any one partner or separate notices may be given to each partner or to such partners as the officer thinks fit.

(4) In the case of a partnership which includes one or more individuals, the day specified in a notice under subsection (2) or (3) above shall not be earlier than—

(a) the 31st January next following the year of assessment concerned, or

(b) where the notice under this section is given after the 31st October next following the year, the last day of the period of three months beginning with the day on which the notice is given.

(5) In the case of a partnership which includes one or more companies, the day specified in a notice under subsection (2) or (3) above shall not be earlier than—

(a) the first anniversary of the end of the relevant period, or

(b) where the notice under this section is given more than nine months after the end of the relevant period, the last day of the period of three months beginning with the day on which the notice is given;

and the relevant period for the purposes of this subsection and subsection (6) below is the period in respect of which the return is required.

(6) Every return under this section shall include—

(a) a declaration of the name, residence and tax reference of each of the persons who have been partners—

(i) for the whole of the relevant period, or

(ii) for any part of that period,

and, in the case of a person falling within sub-paragraph (ii) above, of the part concerned; and

(b) a declaration by the person making the return to the effect that it is to the best of his knowledge correct and complete.

(7) Every return under this section shall also include, if the notice under subsection (2) or (3) above so requires—

(a) with respect to any disposal of partnership property during a period to which any part of the return relates, the like particulars as if the partnership were liable to tax on any chargeable gain accruing on the disposal, and

(b) with respect to any acquisition of partnership property, the particulars required under section 12(2) of this Act.

(8) A notice under this section may require different information, accounts and statements for different periods or in relation to different descriptions of source of income.

(9) Notices under this section may require different information, accounts and statements in relation to different descriptions of partnership.

(10) In this section 'residence', in relation to a company, means its registered officer."

GENERAL NOTE

The new s.12AA of the TMA 1970 (c. 9), which prospectively replaces the existing s.9 of the TMA 1970 (c. 9) as from 1996–97, brings the provisions for partnership returns in line with the new system.

As regards a partnership which has individual and corporate members, the due date for submission of returns will be determined by the later date on which it is due. The return from the partnership is due on the later of the two dates that apply to the individual and to the corporate member.

Otherwise, the provisions of the existing s.9 of the TMA 1970 (c. 9) generally apply.

Partnership return to include partnership statement

185. After section 12AA of the Management Act there shall be inserted the following section—

"Partnership return to include partnership statement

12AB.—(1) Every return under section 12AA of this Act shall include a statement (a partnership statement) of the following amounts, namely—

(a) in the case of each period of account ending within the period in respect of which the return is made—

(i) the amount of income or loss from each source which, on the basis of the information contained in the return, has accrued to or has been sustained by the partnership for that period, and

(ii) the amount of each charge which, on that basis, was a charge on the income of the partnership for that period; and

(b) in the case of each such period and each of the partners, the amount which, on that basis, is equal to his share of that income, loss or charge.

(2) Subject to subsection (3) below—

(a) at any time before the end of the period of nine months beginning with the day on which a person's return is delivered, an officer of the Board may by notice to that person so amend that person's partnership statement as to correct any obvious errors or mistakes in the return (whether errors of principle, arithmetical mistakes or otherwise); and

(b) at any time before the end of the period of twelve months beginning with the filing date, a person may by notice to an officer of the board so amend his partnership statement as to give effect to any amendments to his return which he has notified to such an officer.

(3) No amendment of a partnership statement may be made under subsection (2) above at any time during the period—

(a) beginning with the day on which an officer of the Board gives notice of his intention to enquire into the return, and

(b) ending with the day on which the officer's enquiries into the return are completed.

(4) Where a partnership statement is amended under subsection (2) above, the officer shall by notice to the partners so amend their self-assessments under section 9 or 11AA of this Act as to give effect to the amendments of the partnership statement.

(5) In this section—

'filing date' means the day specified in the notice under subsection (2) or, as the case may be, subsection (3) of section 12AA of this Act;

'period of account', in relation to a partnership, means any period for which accounts are drawn up."

GENERAL NOTE

The new s.12AB of the TMA 1970 (c. 9) creates a new requirement for partnership returns to include a statement of the total income, losses and charges of the partnership, together with an allocation of these amounts between the partners. The statement is subject to similar provisions for amendment by the taxpayer or the Revenue as those relating to an individual self-assessment (see s.179, introducing the new s.9(4) and (5) of the TMA 1970 (c. 9)), but is not itself a self-assessment because the partnership as an entity will not be subject to tax under self-assessment.

Power to enquire into partnership return

186. After section 12AB of the Management Act there shall be inserted the following section—

"Power to enquire into partnership return

12AC.—(1) An officer of the Board may enquire into—
  (a) the return on the basis of which a person's partnership statement was made under section 12AB of this Act, or
  (b) any amendment of that return on the basis of which that statement has been amended by that person,
if, before the end of the period mentioned in subsection (2) below, he gives notice in writing of his intention to do so to that person or any successor of that person.
(2) The period referred to in subsection (1) above is—
  (a) in the case of a return delivered or amendment made on or before the filing date, the period of twelve months beginning with that date;
  (b) in the case of a return delivered or amendment made after that date, the period ending with the quarter day next following the first anniversary of the day on which the return or amendment was delivered or made;
and the quarter days for the purposes of this subsection are 31st January, 31st April, 31st July and 31st October.
(3) The giving of notice under subsection (1) above at any time shall be deemed to include the giving of notice under section 9A(1) or, as the case may be, section 11AB(1) of this Act to each partner who—
  (a) at that time, has made a return under section 9 of 11 of this Act, or
  (b) at any subsequent time, makes such a return.
(4) A return or amendment which has been enquired into under subsection (1) above shall not be the subject of a further notice under that subsection.
(5) In this section 'the filing date' means the day specified in the notice under subsection (2) or, as the case may be, subsection (3) of section 12AA of this Act.
(6) In this Act 'successor', in relation to a person who—
  (a) has made and delivered a return under section 12AA of this Act, but
  (b) is no longer a partner or is otherwise no longer available,
means such other partner who may at any time be nominated for the purposes of this subsection by the majority of the partners at that time, and 'predecessor' and 'successor', in relation to a person so nominated, shall be construed accordingly."

GENERAL NOTE
   A power to enquire into partnership returns is conferred similar to that for individual and company returns (see ss.180, 183, *supra*). An assurance was given at Committee Stage that the Revenue would seek to ensure that all members of a partnership which has ended are aware of the liability that it is pursuing from former members of the partnership.

Enquiries: procedure

Power to call for documents

187. Immediately before section 20 of the Management Act there shall be inserted the following section—

"Power to call for documents for purposes of certain enquiries

19A.—(1) This section applies where an officer of the Board gives notice under section 9A(1), 11AB(1) or 12AC(1) of this Act to any person (the taxpayer) of his intention to enquire into—
  (a) the return on the basis of which the taxpayer's self-assessment or partnership statement was made, or
  (b) any amendment of that return on the basis of which that assessment or statement has been amended by the taxpayer.

(2) For the purpose of enquiring into the return or amendment, the officer may at the same or any subsequent time by notice in writing require the taxpayer, within such time (which shall not be less than 30 days) as may be specified in the notice—
  (a) to produce to the officer such documents as are in the taxpayer's possession or power and as the officer may reasonably require for the purpose of determining whether and, if so, the extent to which the return is incorrect or incomplete or the amendment is incorrect, and
  (b) to furnish the officer with such accounts or particulars as he may reasonably require for that purpose.

(3) To comply with a notice under subsection (2) above, copies of documents may be produced instead of originals; but—
  (a) the copies must be photographic or otherwise by way of facsimile; and
  (b) if so required by a notice in writing given by the officer, in the case of any document specified in the notice, the original must be produced for inspection by him within such time (which shall not be less than 30 days) as may be specified in the notice.

(4) The officer may take copies of, or make extracts from, any document produced to him under subsection (2) or (3) above.

(5) A notice under subsection (2) above does not oblige the taxpayer to produce documents or furnish accounts or particulars relating to the conduct of any pending appeal by him.

(6) An appeal may be brought against any requirement imposed by a notice under subsection (2) above to produce any document or to furnish any accounts or particulars.

(7) An appeal under subsection (6) above must be brought within the period of 30 days beginning with the date on which the notice under subsection (2) above is given.

(8) Subject to subsection (9) below, the provisions of this Act relating to appeals shall have effect in relation to an appeal under subsection (6) above as they have effect in relation to an appeal against an assessment to tax.

(9) On an appeal under subsection (6) above section 50(6) to (8) of this Act shall not apply but the Commissioners may—
  (a) if it appears to them that production of the document or the furnishing of the accounts or particulars was reasonably required by the officer of the Board for the purpose mentioned in subsection (2) above, confirm the notice under that subsection so far as relating to the requirement; or
  (b) if it does not so appear to them, set aside that notice so far as so relating.

(10) Where, on an appeal under subsection (6) above, the Commissioners confirm the notice under subsection (2) above so far as relating to any requirement, the notice shall have effect in relation to that requirement as if it had specified 30 days beginning with the determination of the appeal.

(11) Neither the taxpayer nor the officer of the Board shall be entitled to require a case to be stated under section 56 of this Act following the determination of an appeal under subsection (6) above.

(12) Where this section applies by virtue of a notice given under section 12AC(1) of this Act, any reference in this section to the taxpayer includes a reference to any predecessor or successor of his."

GENERAL NOTE

The new s.19A of the TMA 1970 (c. 9) gives the Revenue power to require the production of documents or furnishing of accounts from a taxpayer, but not from a third party, when an enquiry is launched. The restrictions on the more general powers under the TMA 1970 (c. 9), ss.20 and 20A contained in s.20B do not apply, but the taxpayer is given the right to appeal to commissioners. The decision of the commissioners on the reasonableness of the Revenue's requirement is not subject to appeal by way of case stated.

Copies of documents may be produced, but must be photographic or by way of facsimile, since evidence provided in photocopy form is relatively easy to tamper with. The inspector may ask to see the original.

Maximum, or where applicable, minimum time-limits of 30 days apply for the purposes of the section.

Amendment of self-assessment

188. Immediately before section 29 of the Management Act there shall be inserted the following section—

"Amendment of self-assessment where enquiries made.

28A.—(1) This section applies where an officer of the Board gives notice under section 9A(1) or 11AB(1) of this Act to any person (the taxpayer) of his intention to enquire into—
  (a) the return on the basis of which the taxpayer's self-assessment was made, or
  (b) any amendment of that return on the basis of which an amendment (the taxpayer's amendment) of that assessment has been made by the taxpayer.

(2) If, at any time before the officer's enquiries are completed, the officer is of opinion that—
  (a) the tax contained in the taxpayer's self-assessment is insufficient and, in a case falling within subsection (1)(b) above, the deficiency is attributable (wholly or partly) to the taxpayer's amendment, and
  (b) unless the assessment is immediately so amended as to make good the deficiency or, as the case may be, so much of the deficiency as is so attributable, there is likely to be a loss of tax to the Crown,

he may by notice to the taxpayer amend the assessment accordingly.

(3) At any time in the period of 30 days beginning with the day on which the officer's enquiries are completed, the taxpayer may so amend his self-assessment—
  (a) as to make good any deficiency or eliminate any excess which, on the basis of the conclusions stated in the officer's notice under subsection (5) below, is a deficiency or excess which could be made good or eliminated under subsection (4) below; or
  (b) in a case falling within subsection (1)(a) above where the return was made before the end of the period of twelve months begin-

ning with the filing date, as to give effect to any amendments to the return which he has notified to the officer.

(4) If, at any time in the period of 30 days beginning immediately after the period mentioned in subsection (3) above, the officer is of opinion that—

(a) the tax contained in the taxpayer's self-assessment is insufficient or excessive, and

(b) in a case falling within subsection (1)(b) above, the deficiency or excess is attributable (wholly or partly) to the taxpayer's amendment,

he may by notice to the taxpayer so amend the assessment as to make good or eliminate the deficiency or excess or, where paragraph (b) above applies, so much of the deficiency or excess as is so attributable.

(5) Subject to subsection (6) below, the officer's enquiries shall be treated as completed at such time as he by notice—

(a) informs the taxpayer that he has completed his enquiries, and

(b) states his conclusions as to the amount of tax which should be contained in the taxpayer's self-assessment.

(6) At any time before a notice is given under subsection (5) above the taxpayer may apply to the Commissioners for a direction that the officer shall give such a notice within such period as may be specified in the direction; and the Commissioners shall give such a direction unless they are satisfied that the officer has reasonable grounds for not giving such a notice.

(7) Proceedings under subsection (6) above shall be heard and determined in the same way as an appeal.

(8) In this section 'filing date' means the day mentioned in section 8(1A), section 8A(1A) or, as the case may be, section 11(4) of this Act."

GENERAL NOTE

The new s.28A of the TMA 1970 (c. 9) enables amendments to be made to a person's self-assessment once the inspector has commenced enquiries into the return on which it is based and sets the procedure for bringing those enquiries to a conclusion.

Subs. (2)

The inspector can amend an assessment immediately during the enquiry if he feels there is likely to be a loss of tax otherwise.

Subs. (3)

The taxpayer can amend his self-assessment to give effect to any amendments he wishes to make within 30 days of the completion of the inspector's enquiries. Where the return was delivered within 12 months after the filing date, these may cover any aspect, otherwise they are restricted to matters which the inspector has concluded require amendment.

Subs. (4)

After the taxpayer has had his opportunity to amend his self-assessment under subs. (3), the inspector may, within 30 days, amend it within the same parameters.

Subs. (5)

The inspector's enquiry is completed when he gives notice to the taxpayer that he has done so and advises his conclusions as to how much tax is due.

Subss. (6) and (7)

The taxpayer can apply to commissioners to direct the inspector to complete his enquiry within a specified period. Such an application is treated as an appeal.

Amendment of partnership statement

189. After section 28A of the Management Act there shall be inserted the following section—

"Amendment of partnership statement where enquiries made

28B.—(1) This section applies where an officer of the Board gives notice under section 12AC(1) of this Act to any person (the taxpayer) of his intention to enquire into—

(a) the return on the basis of which the taxpayer's partnership statement was made, or

(b) any amendment of that return on the basis of which an amendment (the taxpayer's amendment) of that statement has been made by the taxpayer.

(2) At any time in the period of 30 days beginning with the day on which the officer's enquiries are completed, the taxpayer may so amend his partnership statement—

(a) as to make good any deficiency or eliminate any excess which, on the basis of the conclusions stated in the officer's notice under subsection (5) below, is a deficiency or excess which could be made good or eliminated under subsection (3) below; or

(b) in a case falling within subsection (1)(a) above where the return made before the end of the period of twelve months beginning with the filing date, as to give effect to any amendments to the return which he has notified to the officer.

(3) If, at any time in the period of 30 days beginning immediately after the period mentioned in subsection (2) above, the officer is of opinion that—

(a) any amount contained in the taxpayer's partnership statement is insufficient or excessive, and

(b) in a case falling within subsection (1)(b) above, the deficiency or excess is attributable (wholly or partly) to the taxpayer's amendment,

he may by notice to the taxpayer so amend the statement as to make good or eliminate the deficiency or excess or, where paragraph (b) above applies, so much of the deficiency or excess as is so attributable.

(4) Where a partnership statement is amended under this section, the officer shall by notice to each of the partners so amend his self-assessment under section 9 or 11AA of this Act as to give effect to the amendments of the partnership statement.

(5) Subject to subsection (6) below, the officer's enquiries shall be treated as completed at such time as he by notice—

(a) informs the taxpayer that he has completed his enquiries, and

(b) states his conclusions as to the amounts which should be contained in the taxpayer's partnership statement.

(6) Subsections (6) and (7) of section 28A of this Act apply for the purposes of subsection (5) above as they apply for the purposes of subsection (5) of that section.

(7) In this section 'filing date' means the day specified in the notice under subsection (2) or, as the case may be, subsection (3) of section 12AA of this Act.

(8) Any reference in this section to the taxpayer includes a reference to any predecessor or successor of his."

GENERAL NOTE

The new s.28B of the TMA 1970 (c. 9) follows through for partnerships, *mutatis mutandis*, the provisions of s.28A for other taxpayers inserted by s.188, *supra.*

Determinations and assessments to protect revenue

Determination of tax where no return delivered

190. After section 28B of the Management Act there shall be inserted the following section—

"Determination of tax where no return delivered

28C.—(1) Where—
   (a) a notice has been given to any person under section 8, 8A or 11 of this Act (the relevant section), and
   (b) the required return is not delivered on or before the filing date,
an officer of the Board may make a determination of the amounts in which, to the best of his information and belief, the person who should have made the return is chargeable to income tax and capital gains tax for the year of assessment or (as the case may be) is chargeable to corporation tax for the accounting period.

(2) Notice of any determination under this section shall be served on the person in respect of whom it is made and shall state the date on which it is issued.

(3) Until such time (if any) as it is superseded by a self-assessment made under section 9 or 11AA of this Act (whether by the taxpayer or an officer of the Board) on the basis of information contained in a return under the relevant section, a determination under this section shall have effect for the purposes of Parts VA, VI, IX and XI of this Act as if it were such a self-assessment.

(4) Where—
   (a) an officer of the Board has commenced any proceedings for the recovery of any tax charged by a determination under this section; and
   (b) before those proceedings are concluded, the determination is superseded by such a self-assessment as is mentioned in subsection (3) above,
those proceedings may be continued as if they were proceedings for the recovery of so much of the tax charged by the self-assessment as is due and payable and has not been paid.

(5) No determination under this section, and no self-assessment superseding such a determination, shall be made otherwise than—
   (a) before the end of the period of five years beginning with the filing date; or
   (b) in the case of such a self-assessment, before the end of the period of twelve months beginning with the date of the determination.

(6) In this section 'the filing date' means the day mentioned in section 8(1A), section 8A(1A) or, as the case may be, section 11(4) of this Act."

GENERAL NOTE
Where a return has been issued to a taxpayer and is overdue, the inspector can issue to the taxpayer an estimated determination of the tax due. The determination can be superseded by a self-assessment, but until it is, it is treated as a self-assessment for the purposes of collection, interest and proceedings for recovery.

There is a time-limit of five years for a determination, with a further 12 months for the taxpayer to supersede it by a self-assessment.

Assessment where loss of tax discovered

191.—(1) For section 29 of the Management Act there shall be substituted the following section—

"Assessment where loss of tax discovered

29.—(1) If an officer of the Board or the Board discover, as regards any person (the taxpayer) and a chargeable period—

(a) that any profits which ought to have been assessed to tax have not been assessed, or

(b) that an assessment to tax is or has become insufficient, or

(c) that any relief which has been given is or has become excessive,

the officer or, as the case may be, the Board may, subject to subsections (2) and (3) below, make an assessment in the amount, or the further amount, which ought in his or their opinion to be charged in order to make good to the Crown the loss of tax.

(2) Where—

(a) the taxpayer has made and delivered a return under section 8, 8A or 11 of this Act in respect of the relevant chargeable period, and

(b) the situation mentioned in subsection (1) above is attributable to an error or mistake in the return as to the basis on which his liability ought to have been computed,

the taxpayer shall not be assessed under that subsection in respect of the chargeable period there mentioned if the return was in fact made on the basis or in accordance with the practice generally prevailing at the time when it was made.

(3) Where the taxpayer has made and delivered a return under section 8, 8A or 11 of this Act in respect of the relevant chargeable period, he shall not be assessed under subsection (1) above—

(a) in respect of the chargeable period mentioned in that subsection; and

(b) in the case of a return under section 8 or 8A, in the same capacity as that in which he made and delivered the return,

unless one of the two conditions mentioned below is fulfilled.

(4) The first condition is that the situation mentioned in subsection (1) above is attributable to fraudulent or negligent conduct on the part of the taxpayer or a person acting on his behalf.

(5) The second condition is that at the time when an officer of the Board—

(a) ceased to be entitled to give notice of his intention to enquire into the taxpayer's return under section 8, 8A or 11 of this Act in respect of the relevant chargeable period; or

(b) informed the taxpayer that he had completed his enquiries into that return,

the officer could not have been reasonably expected, on the basis of the information made available to him before that time, to be aware of the situation mentioned in subsection (1) above.

(6) For the purposes of subsection (5) above, information is made available to an officer of the Board if—

(a) it is contained in the taxpayer's return under section 8, 8A or 11 of this Act in respect of the relevant chargeable period (the return), or in any accounts, statements or documents accompanying the return;

(b) it is contained in any claim made as regards the relevant chargeable period by the taxpayer acting in the same capacity as that in which he made the return, or in any accounts, statements or documents accompanying any such claim;

(c) it is contained in any documents, accounts or particulars which, for the purposes of any enquiries into the return or any such claim by an officer of the Board, are produced or furnished by the taxpayer to the officer, whether in pursuance of a notice under section 19A of this Act or otherwise; or

　　(d) it is information the existence of which, and the relevance of which as regards the situation mentioned in subsection (1) above—

　　　　(i) could reasonably be expected to be inferred by an officer of the Board from information falling within paragraphs (a) to (c) above; or

　　　　(ii) are notified in writing by the taxpayer to an officer of the Board.

　(7) In subsection (6) above—

　　(a) any reference to the taxpayer's return under section 8, 8A or 11 of this Act in respect of the relevant chargeable period includes—

　　　　(i) a reference to any return of his under that section for either of the two immediately preceding chargeable periods; and

　　　　(ii) where the return is under section 8 and the taxpayer carries on a trade, profession or business in partnership, a reference to any return with respect to the partnership under section 12AA of this Act for the relevant chargeable period or either of those periods; and

　　(b) any reference in paragraphs (b) to (d) to the taxpayer includes a reference to a person acting on his behalf.

　(8) An objection to the making of an assessment under this section on the ground that neither of the two conditions mentioned above is fulfilled shall not be made otherwise than on an appeal against the assessment.

　(9) Any reference in this section to the relevant chargeable period is a reference to—

　　(a) in the case of the situation mentioned in paragraph (a) or (b) of subsection (1) above, the chargeable period mentioned in that subsection; and

　　(b) in the case of the situation mentioned in paragraph (c) of that subsection, the chargeable period in respect of which the claim was made.

　(10) In this section 'profits'—

　　(a) in relation to income tax, means income,

　　(b) in relation to capital gains tax, means chargeable gains, and

　　(c) in relation to corporation tax, means profits as computed for the purposes of that tax."

　(2) This section, so far as it relates to partnerships whose trades, professions or businesses are set up and commenced before 6th April 1994, has effect as respects the year 1997–98 and subsequent years of assessment.

GENERAL NOTE

　The substituted s.29 of the TMA 1970 (c. 9) continues the protection given to the Revenue by the previous s.29 by allowing the raising of further assessments when a discovery is made. The ambit of "discovery" is fairly wide (see *Cenlon Finance Co.* v. *Ellwood* [1962] A.C. 782), but some protection is afforded to taxpayers within the section.

Subs. (2)

　A discovery assessment may not be made where an erroneous return was nevertheless based on the practice prevailing at the time.

Subss. (3)–(5):

　Further, a discovery assessment may not be made unless one of two conditions is satisfied:

　(i) fraudulent or negligent conduct is involved;

　(ii) the inspector could not reasonably have been expected to be aware of the position on the basis of information made available to him.

Subs. (6)

Information is "made available" where it is in the taxpayer's return or accompanying documents, or in a claim or accompanying documents, or in documents produced during an enquiry, or could reasonably be expected to be inferred by the inspector or is notified to him by the taxpayer. In the last case, the relevance of the information must also be reasonably inferrable.

Subs. (7)

Information "made available" for the purposes of a return includes information in the returns for the two previous years.

Subs. (8)

An appeal is necessary to overturn an assessment where the taxpayer alleges that neither of the conditions in subss. (3)–(5) is satisfied.

For most purposes the new provisions come into effect from 1996–1997 (see s.199), but for partnerships formed before April 6, 1994, not until 1997–1998.

Payment of tax

Payments on account of income tax

192. After Part V of the Management Act there shall be inserted the following section—

"PART VA

PAYMENT OF TAX

Payments on account of income tax

59A.—(1) This section applies to any person (the taxpayer) as regards a year of assessment if as regards the immediately preceding year—
  (a) he has been assessed to income tax under section 9 of this Act in any amount, and
  (b) that amount (the assessed amount) exceeds the amount of any income tax which has been deducted at source, and
  (c) the amount of the excess (the relevant amount) is not less than such amount as may be prescribed by regulations made by the Board, and
  (d) the proportion which the relevant amount bears to the assessed amount is not less than such proportion as may be so prescribed.
  (2) Subject to subsection (3) below, the taxpayer shall make two payments on account of his liability to income tax for the year of assessment—
  (a) the first on or before the 31st January in that year, and
  (b) the second on or before the following 31st July;
and, subject to subsection (4) below, each of those payments on account shall be of an amount equal to 50 per cent. of the relevant amount.
  (3) If, at any time before the 31st January next following the year of assessment, the taxpayer makes a claim under this subsection stating—
  (a) his belief that he will not be assessed to income tax for that year, or that the amounts in which he will be so assessed will not exceed the amount of income tax deducted at source, and
  (b) his grounds for that belief,
each of the payments on account shall not be, and shall be deemed never to have been, required to be made.
  (4) If, at any time before the 31st January next following the year of assessment, the taxpayer makes a claim under this subsection stating—
  (a) his belief that the amount in which he will be assessed to income tax for that year will exceed the amount of income tax deducted at source by a stated amount which is less than the relevant amount, and

(b) his grounds for that belief,
the amount of each of the payments on account required to be made shall be, and shall be deemed always to have been, equal to 50 per cent. of the stated amount.

(5) Where the taxpayer makes a claim under subsection (3) or (4) above, there shall be made all such adjustments, whether by the repayment of amounts paid on account or otherwise, as may be required to give effect to the provisions of that subsection.

(6) Where the taxpayer fraudulently or negligently makes any incorrect statement in connection with a claim under subsection (3) or (4) above, he shall be liable to a penalty not exceeding the difference between—

    (a) the amount which would have been payable on account if he had made a correct statement, and

    (b) the amount of the payment on account (if any) made by him.

(7) The provisions of the Income Tax Acts as to the recovery of income tax shall apply to an amount falling to be paid on account of tax in the same manner as they apply to an amount of tax.

(8) In this section any reference to income tax deducted at source is a reference to—

    (a) income tax deducted or treated as deducted from any income or treated as paid on any income, or

    (b) any amount which, in respect of the year of assessment, is to be deducted at source under section 203 of the principal Act in a subsequent year, or is a tax credit to which section 231 of that Act applies."

GENERAL NOTE

The new s.59A of the TMA 1970 (c. 9) provides rules for payments on account of income tax during and shortly after the end of the year of assessment.

Subs. (1)

Interim payments apply to an assessment under s.9 of the TMA 1970 (c. 9) (see s.179, *supra*) where the amount assessed for the preceding year exceeds the amount of income tax deducted at source by at least a specified amount or a proportion to be prescribed by regulations.

Subs. (2)

Interim payments will be made on January 31 and July 31. This is one month later than at present (although the preceding year basis now applies).

Subs. (3)

Interim payments are not required if the taxpayer claims that he will not be assessed to income tax for that year, or that the assessment will not exceed tax deducted at source, and states his reasons for the claim.

Subs. (4)

The amount of interim payments is reduced proportionately where the taxpayer claims, with reasons, that his income tax for that year of assessment will be less than for the preceding year by a stated amount.

Subs. (5)

Claims under subss. (3) or (4) will give rise to all necessary adjustments.

Subs. (6)

A fraudulent or negligent claim under subss. (3) or (4) will give rise to a penalty up to the amount of the tax underpaid.

Subss. (7) and (8)

The normal tax recovery machinery applies to interim payments. Tax deducted at source includes PAYE for a subsequent year (see the Income and Corporation Taxes Act 1988 (c. 1), s.203) or an advance corporation tax (ACT) credit on a dividend (*ibid.*, s.231).

Payment of income tax and capital gains tax

193. After section 59A of the Management Act there shall be inserted the following section—

"Payment of income tax and capital gains tax

59B.—(1) Subject to subsection (2) below, the difference between—

(a) the amount of income tax and capital gains tax contained in a person's self-assessment under section 9 of this Act for any year of assessment, and

(b) the aggregate of any payments on account made by him in respect of that year (whether under section 59A of this Act or otherwise) and any income tax which in respect of that year has been deducted at source,

shall be payable by him or (as the case may be) repayable to him as mentioned in subsection (3) or (4) below.

(2) The following, namely—

(a) any amount which, in the year of assessment, is deducted at source under section 203 of the principal Act in respect of a previous year, and

(b) any amount which, in respect of the year of assessment, is to be deducted at source under that section in a subsequent year, or is a tax credit to which section 231 of that Act applies,

shall be respectively deducted from and added to the aggregate mentioned in subsection (1)(b) above.

(3) In a case where the person—

(a) gave the notice required by section 7 of this Act within six months from the end of the year of assessment, but

(b) was not given notice under section 8 or 8A of this Act until after the 31st October next following that year,

the difference shall be payable or repayable at the end of the period of three months beginning with the day on which the notice under section 8 or 8A was given.

(4) In any other case, the difference shall be payable or repayable on or before the 31st January next following the year of assessment.

(5) Where a person's self-assessment under section 9 of this Act is amended under section 9(4), section 28A(2), (3) or (4) or section 30B(2) of this Act, any amount of tax which is payable or repayable by virtue of the amendment shall, subject to section 55(6) and (9) of this Act, be payable or (as the case may be) repayable—

(a) in a case where notice of the amendment is given after, or less than 30 days before, the day given by subsection (3) or (4) above, on or before the day following the end of the period of 30 days beginning with the day on which notice is given; and

(b) in any other case, on or before the day given by subsection (3) or (4) above.

(6) Any amount of income tax or capital gains tax which is payable by virtue of an assessment made under section 29 of this Act shall be payable on the day following the end of the period of 30 days beginning with the day on which the notice of assessment is given.

(7) In this section any reference to income tax deducted at source is a reference to income tax deducted or treated as deducted from any income or treated as paid on any income."

GENERAL NOTE

The new s.59B of the TMA 1970 (c. 9) introduces rules for the final balancing payment of income tax and capital gains tax liability for year of assessment, normally by January 31 following the year of assessment.

Subs. (1)

The difference between the self-assessment and interim payments plus tax deducted at source is payable, or repayable, as the case may be.

Subs. (2)

PAYE deductions in respect of a previous year, and PAYE deductions in respect of a subsequent year, and dividend tax credits, are to be respectively deducted from and added to the interim payments.

Subss. (3) and (4)

Where a return has been issued after October 31 (but not as the result of a failure to notify chargeability under s.7) the date for the balancing payment is three months from the issue of the return. In every other case it is January 31 following the year of assessment.

Subs. (5)

Additional tax on an amended assessment, if not postponed, is payable within 30 days of the amendment, if later than the date in subss. (3) and (4).

Subs. (6)

An assessment under the substituted s.29 (see s.191, *supra*) is likewise payable within 30 days.

Surcharges on unpaid income tax and capital gains tax

194. After section 59B of the Management Act there shall be inserted the following section—

"Surcharges on unpaid income tax and capital gains tax

59C.—(1) This section applies in relation to any income tax or capital gains tax which has become payable by a person (the taxpayer) in accordance with section 55 or 59B of this Act.

(2) Where any of the tax remains unpaid on the day following the expiry of 28 days from the due date, the taxpayer shall be liable to a surcharge equal to 5 per cent. of the unpaid tax.

(3) Where any of the tax remains unpaid on the day following the expiry of 6 months from the due date, the taxpayer shall be liable to a further surcharge equal to 5 per cent. of the unpaid tax.

(4) Where the taxpayer has incurred a penalty under section 7, 93(5) or 95 of this Act, no part of the tax by reference to which that penalty was determined shall be regarded as unpaid for the purposes of subsection (2) or (3) above.

(5) An officer of the Board may impose a surcharge under subsection (2) or (3) above; and notice of the imposition of such a surcharge—

(a) shall be served on the taxpayer, and

(b) shall state the day on which it is issued and the time within which an appeal against the imposition of the surcharge may be brought.

(6) A surcharge imposed under subsection (2) or (3) above shall carry interest at the rate applicable under section 178 of the Finance Act 1989 from the end of the period of 30 days beginning with the day on which the surcharge is imposed until payment.

(7) An appeal may be brought against the imposition of a surcharge under subsection (2) or (3) above within the period of 30 days beginning with the date on which the surcharge is imposed.

(8) Subject to subsection (9) below, the provisions of this Act relating to appeals shall have effect in relation to an appeal under subsection (7) above as they have effect in relation to an appeal against an assessment to tax.

(9) On an appeal under subsection (7) above section 50(6) to (8) of this Act shall not apply but the Commissioners may—

(a) if it appears to them that, throughout the period of default, the taxpayer had a reasonable excuse for not paying the tax, set aside the imposition of the surcharge; or

(b) if it does not so appear to them, confirm the imposition of the surcharge.

(10) Inability to pay the tax shall not be regarded as a reasonable excuse for the purposes of subsection (9) above.

(11) The Board may in their discretion—

(a) mitigate any surcharge under subsection (2) or (3) above, or

(b) stay or compound any proceedings for the recovery of any such surcharge,

and may also, after judgment, further mitigate or entirely remit the surcharge.

(12) In this section—

'the due date', in relation to any tax, means the date on which the tax becomes due and payable;

'the period of default', in relation to any tax which remained unpaid after the due date, means the period beginning with that date and ending with the day before that on which the tax was paid."

GENERAL NOTE

The new s.59C of the TMA 1970 (c. 9) introduces a surcharge for unpaid income tax and capital gains tax, due under s.55 or s.59B.

Subs. (2)

A surcharge of five per cent. applies 28 days after the due date.

Subs. (3)

A further surcharge of five per cent. applies six months after the due date.

Subs. (4)

A double charge of surcharge and penalties under ss.7, 93(5) or 95 of the TMA 1970 (c. 9) is prevented.

Subs. (5)

A surcharge is imposed by notice. During the Committee Stage, the Government gave an assurance that a surcharge would not be imposed where tax was paid late as a result of a bona fide mistake on a self-assessment which was later corrected.

Subs. (6)

Interest runs on unpaid surcharges after 30 days.

Subss. (7)–(9)

An appeal against a surcharge may be brought within 30 days. The commissioners have no power to mitigate, but may set aside the surcharge if the taxpayer has a reasonable excuse.

Subs. (10)

Inability to pay is not in itself a reasonable excuse. For cases in which the courts have looked into circumstances surrounding inability to pay as providing a reasonable excuse in the context of VAT see *Customs and Excise Commissioners* v. *Salevon; Same* v. *Harris* [1989] STC 907 and *Customs and Excise Commissioners* v. *Steptoe* [1992] STC 757, C.A.

Subs. (11)

The Revenue may mitigate or entirely remit a surcharge.

Payment of corporation tax

195. After section 59C of the Management Act there shall be inserted the following section—

"Payment of corporation tax

59D.—(1) Corporation tax for an accounting period shall be due and payable on the day following the expiry of nine months from the end of that period.

(2) If, with respect to any accounting period—

(a) a company has paid an amount of corporation tax; and

(b) at any time before an assessment to corporation tax for the period becomes final, the company has grounds for believing that, by reason of a change in the circumstances of the case since the tax was paid, the amount paid exceeds the company's probable liability for corporation tax,

the company may, by notice given to an officer of the Board on or after the date which, under section 826 of the principal Act, is the material date in relation to that tax, make a claim for the repayment to the company of the amount of that excess.

(3) A notice under subsection (2) above shall state the amount which the company considers should be repaid and the grounds referred to in paragraph (b) of that subsection.

(4) If, apart from this subsection, a claim would fall to be made under subsection (2) above at a time when—

(a) the company has appealed against, or against an amendment of, such an assessment as is referred to in paragraph (b) of that subsection, but

(b) that appeal has not been finally determined,

that subsection shall have effect as if, for the words from 'make a claim' to 'excess', there were substituted the words 'apply to the Commissioners to whom the appeal stands referred for a determination of the amount which should be repaid to the company pending a determination of the company's liability for the accounting period in question'.

(5) An application under subsections (2) and (4) above shall be determined in the same way as an appeal.

(6) Where on an appeal against, or against an amendment of, an assessment to corporation tax a company makes an application under section 55(3) or (4) of this Act, that application may be combined with an application under subsections (2) and (4) above (relating to tax which was paid prior to the assessment)."

GENERAL NOTE

The new s.59D of the TMA 1970 (c. 9) moves the rules for payment of corporation tax from the ICTA 1988 (c. 1), s.10 to the TMA 1970 (c. 9). These rules are: that corporation tax is due nine months after the end of an accounting period; that the company may subsequently claim repayment of excess tax paid; that the claim may be taken to commissioners if an appeal is still open and that an application to postpone tax under s.55 may be heard at the same time as an application under this section.

Miscellaneous and supplemental

Management: other amendments

196. Schedule 19 to this Act (which makes other amendments relating to the management of tax) shall have effect.

GENERAL NOTE

This section introduces Sched. 19 which makes further amendments relating to the management of tax to effect the introduction of self-assessment. See further the General Note to Sched. 19.

Construction of certain references

197.—(1) In the Tax Acts and the Gains Tax Acts, any reference (however expressed) to a person being assessed to tax, or being charged to tax by an assessment, shall be construed as including a reference to his being so assessed, or being so charged—

(a) by a self-assessment under section 9 or 11AA of the Management Act, or

(b) by a determination under section 28C of that Act (which, until super-seded by such a self-assessment, has effect as if it were one).

(2) In this section "the Gains Tax Acts" means the Taxation of Chargeable Gains Act 1992 and all other enactments relating to capital gains tax.

GENERAL NOTE

References in the Tax Acts (see the ICTA 1988 (c. 1), s.831(2)) and the Gains Tax Acts (the Taxation of Chargeable Gains Act 1992 (c. 12) and all other enactments relating to capital gains tax) to someone being assessed to tax or charged to tax by an assessment are extended to include his being assessed or charged by a self-assessment under the TMA 1970 (c. 9), ss.9 or 11AA or by a determination under s.28C (see ss.179, 182 and 190, *supra*).

Transitional provisions

198.—(1) Section 59A of the Management Act shall have effect as regards the year 1996–97 as if—
(a) the reference in subsection (1)(a) to a person being assessed to income tax under section 9 of that Act were a reference to his being assessed to income tax under section 29 of that Act;
(b) the reference in subsection (1)(b) to the assessed amount were a reference to the difference between that amount and the amount of any income tax charged at a rate other than the basic rate on any income—
   (i) from which tax has been deducted otherwise than under section 203 of the Taxes Act 1988,
   (ii) from or on which income tax is treated as having been deducted or paid, or
   (iii) which is chargeable under Schedule F;
(c) subsection (2) required—
   (i) the first payment on account to be of an amount equal to the aggregate of the relevant proportion of the relevant amount and 50 per cent. of the difference between the relevant amount and that proportion of that amount, and
   (ii) the second payment on account to be of an amount equal to 50 per cent. of that difference; and
(d) subsection (4) provided that, in the circumstances there mentioned—
   (i) the amount of the first payment on account required to be made should be, and should be deemed always to have been, equal to the aggregate of the relevant proportion of the stated amount and 50 per cent. of the difference between the stated amount and that proportion of that amount, and
   (ii) the amount of second payment on account required to be made should be, and should be deemed always to have been, equal to 50 per cent. of that difference.

(2) In subsection (1) above "relevant proportion" means the proportion which the amount of tax charged under Schedule A or any of Cases III to VI of Schedule D for the year 1995–96 bears to the assessed amount.

(3) In the case of a partnership whose trade, profession or business is set up and commenced before 6th April 1994, section 59B of the Management Act shall have effect, as respects each partner and the year 1996–97, as if his share of any income tax to which the partnership is assessed for that year were income tax which in respect of that year had been deducted at source.

GENERAL NOTE

This section introduces provisions regarding payment in 1996–1997, the year of transition from the preceding year basis to the current year basis.

Subs. (1)

Various transitional amendments are made to the new s.59A (see s.192, *supra*). Reference to s.29 (as it stands at present) is substituted for the reference to s.9. Any income tax charged at a rate other than the basic rate on income from which tax has been deducted is excluded from the assessed amount. The first payment on account for that year will be equal to all of the relevant proportion of the tax due for the preceding year together with half of the balance. The element of the first interim payment relating to the relevant proportion cannot be reduced under s.59A(4).

Subs. (2)
The "relevant proportion" in subs. (1) is defined as the proportion of the tax assessed for 1995–1996 relating to tax charged under Sched. A or Sched. D, Cases III–VI.

Subs. (3)
For a partnership commencing before April 6, 1994, the definition of tax deducted at source for the purposes of determining the balancing payment due under s.59B (see s.193, *supra*) is extended to include the share of a partner in the tax assessed on the partnership.

Interpretation and commencement of Chapter III

199.—(1) In this Chapter "the Management Act" means the Taxes Management Act 1970.
(2) Unless the contrary intention appears, this Chapter—
(a) so far as it relates to income tax and capital gains tax, has effect as respects the year 1996–97 and subsequent years of assessment, and
(b) so far as it relates to corporation tax, has effect as respects accounting periods ending on or after the appointed day.
(3) For the purposes of this Chapter the appointed day is such day, not earlier than 1st April 1996, as the Treasury may by order appoint.

GENERAL NOTE
The new system will apply from 1996–1997 for income tax and capital gains tax and from an appointed day (not before April 1, 1996) for corporation tax.

CHAPTER IV

CHANGES FOR FACILITATING SELF-ASSESSMENT

GENERAL NOTE
Sections 200–218 below provide the rules for computation of income assessable under Sched. D on a current year basis and apply from 1994–1995 onwards in relation to new businesses set up after, or a new source of income arising after, April 5, 1994 and in all other cases from 1996–1997 onwards.

Assessment under Cases I and II of Schedule D

Assessment on current year basis

200. For section 60 of the Taxes Act 1988 there shall be substituted the following section—

"Assessment on current year basis

60.—(1) Subject to subsection (2) below and section 63A, income tax shall be charged under Cases I and II of Schedule D on the full amount of the profits or gains of the year of assessment.
(2) Where, in the case of a trade, profession or vocation, a basis period for the year of assessment is given by subsection (3) below or sections 61 to 63, the profits or gains of that period shall be taken to be the profits or gains of the year.
(3) Subject to sections 61 to 63, the basis period for a year of assessment is as follows—
(a) if the year is the first year of assessment in which there is an accounting date which falls not less than 12 months after the com-

mencement date, the period of 12 months ending with that
accounting date; and

(b) if there is a basis period for the immediately preceding year and
that basis period is not given by section 61, the period of 12
months beginning immediately after the end of that basis period.

(4) In the case of a person who, if he had not died, would under the
provisions of this section and sections 61 to 63A have become chargeable to income tax for any year, the tax which would have been so
chargeable—

(a) shall be assessed and charged on his personal representatives,
and

(b) shall be a debt due from and payable out of his estate.

(5) In this section and sections 61 to 63—

'accounting date', in relation to a year of assessment, means a
date in the year to which accounts are made up or, where
there are two or more such dates, the latest of those dates;

'the commencement date' and 'the commencement year' mean
respectively the date on which and the year of assessment
in which the trade, profession or vocation is set up and
commenced."

GENERAL NOTE

A new current year basis of assessment for Sched. D, Cases I and II is introduced by the
substitution of new s.60 in the ICTA 1988 (c. 1).

Income tax is to be charged on the full amount of the profits of the year of assessment (see
s.60(1)). If, however, the basis period of assessment is set by the ICTA 1988 (c. 1), s.60(3) or ss.61
to 63, the profits of that period are assessable instead (see s.60(2)). For the first year of assessment in which there is an accounting date which falls at least 12 months after the date of commencement, the basis period is the 12 months to the accounting date (see s.60(3)(a)). This sets
the basis period for subsequent years for the purposes of subs. (3)(b). The basis period for the
next year of assessment is the 12 months following the basis period for the year which preceded it
(where there was such a period). This rule does not apply where the basis period for the preceding year is given by new s.61 of the ICTA 1988 (c. 1) (see s.201 below and s.60(3)(b)).

If a taxpayer dies, his personal representatives are chargeable in his stead and the tax is payable out of the estate (see s.60(4)).

Basis of assessment at commencement

201. For section 61 of the Taxes Act 1988 there shall be substituted the
following section—

"Basis of assessment at commencement

61.—(1) Notwithstanding anything in section 60, where the year of
assessment is the commencement year, the computation of the profits or
gains chargeable to income tax under Case I or II of Schedule D shall be
made on the profits or gains arising in the year.

(2) Subject to section 63, where the year of assessment is the year next
following the commencement year and—

(a) there is an accounting date in the year and the period beginning
with the commencement date and ending with the accounting
date is a period of less than 12 months; or

(b) the basis period for the year would, apart from this subsection, be
given by section 62(2) and the period beginning with the commencement date and ending with the new date in the year is a
period of less than 12 months,

the basis period for the year is the period of 12 months beginning with
the commencement date.

(3) In this section 'the new date' has the same meaning as in section 62."

GENERAL NOTE

The basis period for the year of commencement is from commencement to the following April 5. The ICTA 1988, s.60(3)(a) and (b) (see s.200 above) will then apply to determine the basis period for the second and subsequent years of assessments.

Where: (a) the first year's accounts are for a period of less than 12 months and the accounting date falls in the second year of assessment; or (b) no accounts are drawn up to a date in the second year of assessment, then the basis period for the second year of assessment is the 12 months beginning with the commencement date.

Change of basis period

202. For section 62 of the Taxes Act 1988 there shall be substituted the following section—

"Change of basis period

62.—(1) Subsection (2) below applies where, in the case of a trade, profession or vocation—
- (a) an accounting change, that is, a change from one accounting date ('the old date') to another ('the new date'), is made or treated as made in a year of assessment; and
- (b) either section 62A applies or the year of assessment is the year next following or next but one following the commencement year.

(2) The basis period for the year of assessment is as follows—
- (a) if the year is the year next following the commencement year or the relevant period is a period of less than 12 months, the period of 12 months ending with the new date in the year; and
- (b) if the relevant period is a period of more than 12 months, that period;

and in this subsection 'the relevant period' means the period beginning immediately after the end of the basis period for the preceding year and ending with the new date in the year.

(3) Where subsection (2) above does not apply as respects an accounting change made or treated as made in a year of assessment ('the first year'), this section and section 62A shall have effect in relation to the next following year ('the second year') as if the change had not been made or treated as made.

(4) As a consequence of subsection (3) above—
- (a) an accounting change shall be treated as made in the second year if the date or, as the case may be, the latest date in that year to which accounts are made up is a date other than the date of the end of the basis period for the first year; and
- (b) no such change shall be treated as made in the second year if that date is the date of the end of that period.

(5) For the purposes of this section an accounting change is made in the first year of assessment in which accounts are not made up to the old date, or accounts are made up to the new date, or both."

GENERAL NOTE

The ICTA 1988 (c. 1), s.62 is revised. It determines basis periods where a business changes its accounting date. The Inland Revenue practice as set out in leaflet IR 26, will cease to apply.

Where there is a change of accounting date and either (a) the change takes place in the second or third year of assessment or (b) the conditions in the ICTA 1988 (c. 1), s.62A (see s.203 below) are satisfied, then there will be a new basis period. The basis period will be the 12 months to the new accounting date if the relevant period is less than 12 months or the year concerned is the second year of assessment, otherwise the basis period is the relevant period itself. Any overlap profits for overlap periods are dealt with under the new ICTA 1988 (c. 1), s.63A (see s.205

below). The change of accounting date is treated as taking place in the year in which accounts are made up to the new date, or if there is a year in which no accounting date falls, that year. Where neither (a) nor (b) above are satisfied, the basis period continues to be the 12 months ending on the old accounting date (by apportioning the profits shown in the accounts), until the taxpayer satisfies those conditions (the basis period will then be determined by the above provisions) or reverts to the original accounting date.

"Relevant period" is the period from the end of the basis period for the previous year of assessment to the new accounting date. The taxpayer is given the opportunity to satisfy conditions (a) or (b) above by treating the year of change as deferred to the following year.

Conditions for such a change

203. After section 62 of the Taxes Act 1988 there shall be inserted the following section—

"Conditions for such a change

62A.—(1) This section applies in relation to an accounting change if the following are fulfilled, namely—

(a) the first and second conditions mentioned below, and

(b) either the third or the fourth condition so mentioned.

(2) The first condition is that the first accounting period ending with the new date does not exceed 18 months.

(3) The second condition is that notice of the accounting change is given to an officer of the Board on or before the 31st January next following the year of assessment.

(4) The third condition is that no accounting change as respects which section 62(2) has applied has been made or treated as made in any of the five years immediately preceding the year of assessment.

(5) The fourth condition is that—

(a) the notice required by the second condition sets out the reasons for which the change is made; and

(b) either the officer is satisfied that the change is made for bona fide commercial reasons or he does not, within 60 days of receiving the notice, give notice to the person carrying on the trade, profession or vocation that he is not so satisfied.

(6) An appeal may be brought against the giving of a notice under subsection (5)(b) above within the period of 30 days beginning with the date on which the notice is given.

(7) Subject to subsection (8) below, the provisions of the Management Act relating to appeals shall have effect in relation to an appeal under subsection (6) above as they have effect in relation to an appeal against an assessment to tax.

(8) On an appeal under subsection (6) above section 50(6) to (8) of the Management Act shall not apply but the Commissioners may—

(a) if they are satisfied that the change is made for bona fide commercial reasons, set the notice under subsection (5)(b) above aside; or

(b) if they are not so satisfied, confirm that notice.

(9) Obtaining a tax advantage shall not be regarded as a bona fide commercial reason for the purposes of subsections (5) and (8) above.

(10) In this section—

(a) 'accounting period' means a period for which accounts are made up, and

(b) expressions which are also used in section 62 have the same meanings as in that section."

General Note

This sets out the conditions which must be met if a change in accounting date (other than a change taking place in the second or third year of assessment) is to result in a change of the basis period.

The conditions are: the accounting period ending with the new accounting date are not to exceed 18 months; the Revenue must be notified of the accounting change by January 31 in the year following the year of assessment in which the change is deemed to take place by virtue of new s.62(5) (see s.202 above); and either there must have been no change of accounting date (which had effect for tax purposes) for that business within the five years preceding the year of assessment (other than a change taking place in the second or third year of assessment) or there has been a change of accounting date within that five-year period but it was made for bona fide commercial reasons.

Obtaining a tax advantage is not to be regarded as a bona fide commercial reason. Tax advantage is not defined and is to be given its ordinary meaning. The Revenue view is that it includes cashflow advantage as well as a net reduction in tax liabilities. Provision is made for the taxpayer to appeal against the Revenue rejection of a change of accounting date on bona fide commercial grounds.

Basis of assessment on discontinuance

204. For section 63 of the Taxes Act 1988 there shall be substituted the following section—

"Basis of assessment on discontinuance

63. Where a trade, profession or vocation is permanently discontinued in a year of assessment other than the commencement year, the basis period for the year shall be the period beginning—
   (a) where the year is the year next following the commencement year, immediately after the end of the commencement year, and
   (b) in any other case, immediately after the end of the basis period for the preceding year of assessment,
and (in either case) ending with the date on which the trade, profession or vocation is permanently discontinued."

GENERAL NOTE
The basis period for the year of cessation runs from the end of the basis period for the preceding year to the date of discontinuance. Where the cessation takes place in the second year of assessment, the basis period is from April 6 to the date of discontinuance.

Overlap profits and overlap losses

205. After section 63 of the Taxes Act 1988 there shall be inserted the following section—

"Overlap profits and overlap losses

63A.—(1) Where, in the case of any trade, profession or vocation, the basis period for a year of assessment is given by section 62(2)(b), a deduction shall be made in computing the profits or gains of that year of an amount equal to that given by the formula in subsection (2) below.
   (2) The formula referred to in subsection (1) above is—

$$A \times \frac{B - C}{D}$$

where—
   A = the aggregate of any overlap profits less the aggregate of any amounts previously deducted under subsection (1) above;

   B = the number of days in the basis period;

   C = the number of days in the year of assessment;

   D = the aggregate of the overlap periods of any overlap profits less the aggregate number of days given by the variable "B – C" in any previous applications of this subsection.

   (3) Where, in the case of any trade, profession or vocation, the basis period for a year of assessment is given by section 63, a deduction shall

be made in computing the profits or gains of that year of an amount equal to—
  (a) the aggregate of any overlap profits, less
  (b) the aggregate of any amounts deducted under subsection (1) above.
  (4) Where, in the case of any trade, profession or vocation, an amount of a loss would, apart from this subsection, fall to be included in the computations for two successive years of assessment, that amount shall not be included in the computation for the second of those years.
  (5) In this section—
    'overlap profit' means an amount of profits or gains which, by virtue of sections 60 to 62, is included in the computations for two successive years of assessment; and
    'overlap period', in relation to an overlap profit, means the number of days in the period in which the overlap profit arose."

GENERAL NOTE
  Relief is available for "overlap profits", i.e. profits which under the ICTA 1988 (c. 1), ss.60–62 (see ss.200–202 above) are included in two successive years of assessment.
  Where a change of accounting date results in the basis period for a year of assessment exceeding 12 months, the profits of the long basis period are to be reduced by an amount ascertained as follows:

$$\frac{A \times B - C}{D}$$

A = the total overlap profit not previously deducted as overlap relief;
B = the number of days in the long basis period;
C = the number of days in the year of assessment (366 in a leap year);
D = the number of days in the overlap period to which A relates.

  Any overlap profits not so relieved are deducted from profits assessed for the year of cessation. If a loss-making period is included in two successive years of assessment, the loss is treated as nil in the second year.

Assessment under Cases III to VI of Schedule D

Basis of assessment under Case III

  206. For section 64 of the Taxes Act 1988 there shall be substituted the following section—

  "Case III assessments

    64. Income tax under Case III of Schedule D shall be computed on the full amount of the income arising within the year of assessment, and shall be paid on the actual amount of that income, without any deduction."

GENERAL NOTE
  The ICTA 1988 (c. 1), s.64 is replaced from April 6, 1994 for new sources of income and from April 6, 1997 for sources of income existing at April 6, 1994 but which continue beyond April 6, 1998. Schedule D, Case III income is to be assessed on a strictly fiscal year basis.

Basis of assessment under Cases IV and V

  207.—(1) In subsection (1) of section 65 of that Act (Case IV and V assessments: general), the words "and sections 66 and 67" and the words "the year preceding" shall cease to have effect.
  (2) In subsection (3) of that section—
  (a) after the words "Cases I and II of Schedule D" there shall be inserted the words "(including sections 60 to 63A and 113)"; and
  (b) the words from "Nothing in this subsection" to the end shall cease to have effect.

(3) In subsection (5) of that section, the words "subject to sections 66 and 67" and the words "the year preceding", in each place where they occur, shall cease to have effect.

(4) Sections 66 and 67 of that Act (special rules for fresh income and special rules where source of income disposed of or yield ceases) shall cease to have effect.

(5) In subsection (1) of section 68 of that Act (special rules where property etc. situated in Republic of Ireland), for the words "sections 65 or 66" there shall be substituted the words "section 65".

(6) In its application to trades, professions or vocations set up and commenced before 6th April 1994, subsection (2) above has effect as respects the year 1997–98 and subsequent years of assessment.

GENERAL NOTE

The ICTA 1988 (c. 1), s.65 is amended from April 6, 1994 for new sources of income and from April 6, 1997 for sources of income existing at April 6, 1994 but which continue beyond April 6, 1998.

Schedule D, Cases IV and V income is to be assessed on a strictly fiscal year basis on the amount arising, or if appropriate remitted to the U.K., in the year of assessment. The new Sched. D, Case I (see s.200 above) current year basis of assessment will apply to income from foreign trades, professions and vocations (from April 6, 1997 if they were trading as at April 6, 1994, otherwise from April 6, 1994) although the income remains assessable under Cases IV and V. Property in the Republic of Ireland remains assessable on an arising basis, whether remitted to the U.K. or not.

Basis of assessment under Case VI

208. For section 69 of the Taxes Act 1988 there shall be substituted the following section—

"Case VI assessments

69. Income tax under Case VI of Schedule D shall be computed on the full amount of the profits or gains arising in the year of assessment."

GENERAL NOTE

The ICTA 1988 (c. 1), s.69 is substituted from April 6, 1994 for new sources of income and from April 6, 1997 for sources of income existing at April 6, 1994 but which continue beyond April 6, 1998.

Schedule D, Case VI income is to be assessed on a strict actual year basis without any option for any averaging method.

Loss relief

Loss relief: general

209.—(1) For subsection (1) and (2) of section 380 of the Taxes Act 1988 (set-off against general income) there shall be substituted the following subsections—

"(1) Where in any year of assessment any person sustains a loss in any trade, profession, vocation or employment carried on by him either solely or in partnership, he may, by notice given within twelve months from the 31st January next following that year, make a claim for relief from income tax on—

(a) so much of his income for that year as is equal to the amount of the loss or, where it is less than that amount, the whole of that income; or

(b) so much of his income for the last preceding year as is equal to that amount or, where it is less than that amount, the whole of that income;

but relief shall not be given for the loss or the same part of the loss both under paragraph (a) and under paragraph (b) above.

(2) Any relief claimed under paragraph (a) of subsection (1) above in respect of any income shall be given in priority to any relief claimed in respect of that income under paragraph (b) of that subsection."

(2) In subsection (2) of section 381 of that Act (further relief for individuals for losses in early years of trade), for the words "an amount of the claimant's income equal to the amount of the loss" there shall be substituted the words "so much of the claimant's income as is equal to the amount of the loss or, where it is less than that amount, the whole of that income".

(3) For subsections (3) and (4) of section 382 of that Act (provisions supplementary to sections 380 and 381) there shall be substituted the following subsections—

"(3) Subject to subsection (4) below, for the purposes of sections 380 and 381, the amount of a loss sustained in a trade, profession or vocation shall be computed in like manner and in respect of the same period as the profits or gains arising or accruing from the trade, profession or vocation are computed under the provisions of the Income Tax Acts applicable to Case I or II of Schedule D.

(4) An amount of a loss which, apart from this subsection, would fall to be included in the computations for two successive years of assessment shall not be included in the computation for the second of those years."

(4) For subsection (1) of section 385 of that Act (carry-forward against subsequent profits) there shall be substituted the following subsection—

"(1) Where a person has, in any trade, profession or vocation carried on by him either alone or in partnership, sustained a loss (to be computed as mentioned in subsections (3) and (4) of section 382) in respect of which relief has not been wholly given either under section 380 or any provision of the Income Tax Acts—

   (a) he may make a claim requiring that any part of the loss for which relief has not been so given shall be set off for the purposes of income tax against the income of the trade, profession or vocation for subsequent years of assessment; and

   (b) where he makes such a claim, the income from the trade, profession or vocation in any subsequent year of assessment shall be treated as reduced by that part of the loss, or by so much of that part as cannot, on that claim, be relieved against such income of an earlier year of assessment."

(5) Subsections (3) and (8) of that section shall cease to have effect.

(6) In subsection (1) of section 388 of that Act (carry-back of terminal losses) for the words "the three years of assessment last preceding that in which the discontinuance occurs" there shall be substituted the words "the year of assessment in which the discontinuance occurs and the three years last preceding it".

(7) In their application to trades, professions or vocations set up and commenced before 6th April 1994, subsections (3) to (5) above have effect as respects the year 1997–98 and subsequent years of assessment.

GENERAL NOTE

Several changes are made to the loss relief provisions in the ICTA 1988 (c. 1), ss.380–389, effective from April 6, 1997 for pre-April 6, 1994 businesses and from April 6, 1994 for new businesses.

Section 380 of the ICTA 1988 (c. 1) is amended to ensure loss relief is given against total income of either the year of the loss or the preceding year (the taxpayer decides which year takes priority).

The relief for either year is restricted to the lesser of the claimant's total income or the amount of the loss. A claim is necessary which must be made within 12 months of January 31 following the year in which the loss arises. Relief for a current year loss takes precedence over relief for a loss sustained in the following year but which is carried back. Section 381 of the ICTA 1988 (c. 1) is amended to ensure that loss relief is available up to the lesser of the claimant's total income or the amount of the loss.

Subs. (3)

Section 382 of the ICTA 1988 (c. 1) is amended to ensure (a) that relief is to be given by reference to a loss of an accounts year not that of a fiscal year and (b) a loss which is included in a computation for two successive years of assessment is to be included in the computation of the first year only.

Subs. (4)

Section 385 of the ICTA 1988 (c. 1) is amended to ensure that on a claim being made, losses will be carried forward and relieved automatically against first available profits. It will no longer be necessary to make a separate claim for each profitable year in which relief is sought. The claim must be made within five years of January 31 following the year in which the loss arises.

Subs. (6)

Section 388 of the ICTA 1988 (c. 1) is amended to ensure terminal loss relief is available in the year of assessment in which cessation takes place and the three preceding years. Previously, if there was a loss in the final 12 months of trading but a profit assessable in the final tax year, terminal loss relief could not be given against that profit.

Subs. (7)

Subsections (3) to (5) above apply from 1997–1998 to businesses in existence at April 6, 1994.

Relief for losses on unquoted shares

210.—(1) For subsections (1) and (2) of section 574 of the Taxes Act 1988 (relief for individuals for losses on unquoted shares) there shall be substituted the following subsections—

"(1) Where an individual who has subscribed for shares in a qualifying trading company incurs an allowable loss (for capital gains tax purposes) on the disposal of the shares in any year of assessment, he may, by notice given within twelve months from the 31st January next following that year, make a claim for relief from income tax on—

(a) so much of his income for that year as is equal to the amount of the loss or, where it is less than that amount, the whole of that income; or

(b) so much of his income for the last preceding year as is equal to that amount or, where it is less than that amount, the whole of that income;

but relief shall not be given for the loss or the same part of the loss both under paragraph (a) and under paragraph (b) above.

Where such relief is given in respect of the loss or any part of it, no deduction shall be made in respect of the loss or (as the case may be) that part under the 1992 Act.

(2) Any relief claimed under paragraph (a) of subsection (1) above in respect of any income shall be given in priority to any relief claimed in respect of that income under paragraph (b) of that subsection; and any relief claimed under either paragraph in respect of any income shall be given in priority to any relief claimed in respect of that income under section 380 or 381."

(2) This section has effect as respects the year 1994–95 and subsequent years of assessment.

GENERAL NOTE

The ICTA 1988 (c. 1), s.574(1) and (2) are amended from 1994–1995. A capital gains tax loss arising on the disposal of shares in qualifying companies may be relieved against income of (a) the year of the loss or (b) the preceding year. A claim is necessary which must be made within 12 months of January 31 following the year in which the loss arises.

Relief for the same loss may not be given twice nor is capital gains tax relief available where income tax relief is allowed. A current year loss set-off takes precedence over relief for a loss sustained in the following year which is carried back. Relief under the new provisions takes priority over relief for trading losses under the ICTA 1988 (c. 1), ss.380 or 381.

Capital allowances

Income tax allowances and charges in taxing a trade etc.

211.—(1) For section 140 of the Capital Allowances Act 1990 there shall be substituted the following section—

"Income tax allowances and charges in taxing a trade etc.

140.—(1) In computing for the purposes of income tax a person's income for any period of account there shall be made all such deductions and additions as are required to give effect to the provisions of Parts I to VI and this Part which relate to allowances and charges in respect of capital expenditure; and subsection (2) below and section 141 have effect as respects allowances and charges which fall to be made under those provisions as they apply for the purposes of income tax.

(2) Allowances and charges which fall to be made for any period of account in taxing a trade under the provisions of Parts I to VI and this Part as they apply for the purposes of income tax shall be given effect by treating the amount of any allowance as a trading expense of the trade in that period, and by treating the amount on which any such charge is to be made as a trading receipt of the trade in that period.

(3) Any claim made by a person for an allowance falling to be made to him in taxing his trade shall be made in his return of income for income tax purposes, and section 42 of the Taxes Management Act 1970 shall not apply to any such claim.

(4) This section shall apply in relation to professions, vocations, employments and offices as it applies in relation to trades.

(5) Deductions allowable in taxing a trade under the provisions of Part VII as they apply for the purposes of income tax shall be given effect in accordance with subsections (1) and (2) above.

(6) In the application of subsection (2) above to allowances and charges which fall to be made under the provisions of Part I, references to a trade shall be treated as including references to an undertaking treated by virtue of section 21(5A) as carried on by way of trade."

(2) Subject to section 214(7) below, this section and sections 212 to 214 below, in their application to trades, professions or vocations set up and commenced before 6th April 1994 or employments or offices entered into before that date, have effect as respects the year 1997–98 and subsequent years of assessment.

GENERAL NOTE
The CAA 1990 (c. 1), s.140 is substituted from April 6, 1997 for pre-April 6, 1994 businesses and from April 6, 1994 for new businesses.

Capital allowances which are given in taxing the trade are to be treated as trading receipts and balancing charges as trading expenses of the taxpayer's period of account. A claim for capital allowances is to be made by inclusion in the claimant's tax return. Scientific research allowances continue to be given as expenses of the trade.

These provisions also apply to professions, vocations, employments and offices.

Chargeable periods for income tax purposes

212.—(1) For section 160 of the Capital Allowances Act 1990 there shall be substituted the following section—

"Meaning of 'period of account'

160.—(1) In this Act as it applies for income tax purposes, 'period of account' has the meaning given by the following provisions of this section.

(2) In the case of a person to or on whom an allowance or charge falls to be made in taxing his trade, profession or vocation, 'period of account' means, subject to subsections (3) and (4) below, any period for which accounts are made up for the purposes of the trade, profession or vocation.

(3) For the purposes of subsection (2) above—

(a) where two periods of account overlap, the period common to both shall be deemed to fall in the first period of account only; and

(b) where there is an interval between two periods of account, the interval shall be deemed to be part of the first period of account.

(4) For the purposes of subsection (2) above, where a period of account ('the original period') would, apart from this subsection, be a period of more than 18 months, that period shall be deemed to be divided into as many separate periods of account—

(a) the first beginning with the commencement date of the original period; and

(b) each subsequent one beginning with an anniversary of that date, as may be necessary to secure that none of those periods of account is a period of more than 12 months.

(5) In the case of any other person to or on whom an allowance or charge falls to be made under Parts I to VI or this Part, 'period of account' means any year of assessment.

(6) Any reference in this section to the overlapping of two periods shall be construed as including a reference to the coincidence of two periods or to the inclusion of one period in another, and references to the period common to both of two periods shall be construed accordingly."

(2) In subsection (2) of section 161 of that Act (other interpretative provisions), for the definitions of "chargeable period" and related expressions there shall be substituted the following definitions—

" 'chargeable period' means an accounting period of a company or a period of account, and a reference to a 'chargeable period related to' the incurring of expenditure, or a sale or other event, is a reference to the chargeable period in which the expenditure is incurred, or the sale or other event takes place;".

GENERAL NOTE

The CAA 1990 (c. 1), s.160 is substituted from April 6, 1997 for pre-April 6, 1994 businesses and from April 6, 1994 for new businesses.

"Period of account" in relation to a trade, profession or vocation is any period for which accounts are made up; in every other case it means the year of assessment. Where two periods of account overlap or there is an interval between them, the overlap period or the interval is treated as falling within the first period of account. Where accounts are made up for a period exceeding 18 months, the period is divided into separate 12-month periods of accounts and any remaining period of account.

Capital allowances given by discharge or repayment of tax, under the CAA 1990 (c. 1), s.141, are to be given for years of assessment.

The definition of chargeable period in the CAA 1990 (c. 1), s.161(2) is substituted.

Other amendments of Capital Allowances Act 1990

213.—(1) In the Capital Allowances Act 1990 the following words, in each place where they occur, shall cease to have effect, namely—

"or its basis period";

"or of which the basis periods end on or before that date";

"or, as the case may be, in its basis period";

"or in the basis period for which";

"or, as the case may be, its basis period"; and

"or the basis periods for which".

(2) In subsection (2) of section 3 of that Act (writing down allowances for industrial buildings and structures), after the word "less" there shall be inserted the words "or more" and after the word "reduced" there shall be inserted the words "or increased".

(3) In section 8 of that Act (writing off of expenditure on industrial buildings and structures)—

(a) in subsection (5), in paragraph (a), the words from "or" to the end shall cease to have effect; and

(b) in subsection (13), for paragraph (d) there shall be substituted the following paragraph—

"(d) the periods of account of that other person in respect of that trade had, in the case of each year of assessment, ended immediately before the beginning of the next following year of assessment."

(4) In subsection (2)(a) of section 24 of that Act (writing-down allowances and balancing adjustments), for sub-paragraph (ii) there shall be substituted the following sub-paragraph—

"(ii) a proportionately reduced or, as the case may require, increased percentage of the excess if the period is a period of less or more than a year, or the trade has been carried on for part only of the period;".

(5) In subsection (3) of section 34 of that Act (writing-down allowances etc. for expensive motor cars), for paragraphs (a) and (b) there shall be substituted the following paragraphs—

"(a) except in a case falling within paragraph (b) below, £3,000 or, if the period is a period of less or more than a year, that amount proportionately reduced or, as the case may require, increased,

(b) if, by virtue of section 153, the person carrying on the trade is regarded as having incurred a part only of the expenditure actually incurred on the provision of the motor car, a proportionate part of £3,000 or, if the period is a period of less or more than a year, that part proportionately reduced or, as the case may require, increased."

(6) In subsection (1)(b) of section 35 of that Act (contributions to expenditure on expensive motor cars), for the words "or, if the chargeable period is part only of a year, that amount proportionately reduced" there shall be substituted the words "or, if the chargeable period is a period of less or more than a year, that amount proportionately reduced or, as the case may require, increased".

(7) In subsection (2) of section 85 of that Act (writing down allowances), after the word "less" there shall be inserted the words "or more" and after the word "reduced" there shall be inserted the words "or increased".

(8) For subsection (6) of section 98 of that Act (mineral extraction: writing down and balancing allowances), there shall be substituted the following subsection—

"(6) If a chargeable period is a period of less or more than a year or if the trade has been carried on for part only of it, the percentage appropriate under subsection (5) above shall be correspondingly reduced or, as the case may require, increased."

(9) In subsection (1) of section 134 of that Act (allowances for expenditure on dredging), the words from "but where a writing-down allowance" to the end shall cease to have effect.

(10) For subsections (5) to (7) of section 137 of that Act (allowances for capital expenditure on scientific research) there shall be substituted the following subsection—

"(5) The relevant chargeable period shall be the chargeable period in which the expenditure was incurred or, if it was incurred before the setting up and commencement of the trade, the chargeable period beginning with that setting up and commencement."

(11) In subsection (5) of section 161 of that Act (other interpretative provisions), for the words from "or in charging" to the end there shall be substituted the words "or income tax."

GENERAL NOTE

This section makes a number of amendments to the CAA 1990 (c. 1), which are consequential upon the changes introduced by ss.211 and 212 above. References to basis periods in the CAA 1990 (c. 1) are deleted. Since a period of account, for capital allowances purposes, may now exceed 12 months (but not 18 months–see s.212 above) or may be less than 12 months, various amendments are made to ensure writing down allowances are proportionately increased or reduced by reference to the length of the period in respect of which the allowance is made.

The amendments apply to new businesses from April 6, 1994 and from 1997–1998 for businesses existing at April 6, 1994.

Amendments of other enactments

214.—(1) In the Taxes Act 1988, the following provisions shall cease to have effect, namely—
  (a) in section 96 (farming and market gardening: relief for fluctuating profits), in subsection (7), paragraph (b);
  (b) section 383 (extension of right to set-off to capital allowances);
  (c) in section 384 (restrictions on right of set-off), in subsection (1), the words "(including any amount in respect of capital allowances which, by virtue of section 383, is to be treated as a loss)", and in subsection (2), the words "or an allowance in respect of expenditure incurred", paragraph (b) and the word "or" immediately preceding that paragraph;
  (d) in section 388 (carry-back of terminal losses), in subsection (6), paragraphs (b) and (d) and the word "and" immediately preceding paragraph (d), and in subsection (7), the words from the beginning to "an earlier year: and"; and
  (e) in section 389 (supplementary provisions relating to carry-back of terminal losses), subsections (5) to (7).
(2) In subsection (6) of section 384 of that Act—
  (a) for the words "There shall be disregarded for the purposes of section 383 any allowances" there shall be substituted the words "There shall be disregarded for the purposes of sections 380 and 381 so much of any loss as derives from any allowances"; and
  (b) for the words "the year of the loss (as defined in section 383)" there shall be substituted the words "the year of assessment in which the loss was sustained".
(3) In subsection (1) of section 397 of that Act (restriction of relief in case of farming and market gardening)—
  (a) after the word "loss", in the second place where it occurs, there shall be inserted the words ", computed without regard to capital allowances,"; and
  (b) the words from "and where" to the end shall cease to have effect.
(4) In subsection (4)(a) of section 520 of that Act (allowances for expenditure on purchase of patent rights), for sub-paragraph (ii) there shall be substituted the following sub-paragraph—
  "(ii) a proportionately reduced or, as the case may require, increased percentage of the excess if the period is a period of less or more than a year, or the trade has been carried on for part only of the period;".
(5) In the following provisions of that Act, namely—
  (a) section 521 (provisions supplementary to section 520);
  (b) section 528 (manner of making allowances and charges); and
  (c) section 530 (disposal of know-how),

the words "or its basis period", in each place where they occur, shall cease to have effect.

(6) In subsection (2)(a) of section 530 of that Act (disposal of know-how), for sub-paragraph (ii) there shall be substituted the following sub-paragraph—

"(ii) a proportionately reduced or, as the case may require, increased percentage of the excess if the period is a period of less or more than a year, or the trade has been carried on for part only of the period;".

(7) Subsection (1)(a) above—

(a) except in its application to a trade set up and commenced on or after 6th April 1994, has effect where the first of the two years of assessment to which the claim relates is the year 1996–97 or any subsequent year, and

(b) in its application to a trade so set up and commenced, has effect where the first of those two years of assessment is the year 1995–96 or any subsequent year.

GENERAL NOTE

This section makes a number of amendments to the ICTA 1988 (c. 1), which are consequential upon the changes introduced by ss.211 and 212 above.

The amendments apply to new businesses from April 6, 1994 and from 1997–1998 for businesses existing at April 6, 1994.

Subs. (7)

The existing capital allowance provisions will apply to existing farming businesses up to 1996 and 1997, *i.e.* 1995–96 and 1996–97 profits will be averaged before deducting capital allowance but 1996–97 and 1997–98 profits and subsequent pairs of years will be averaged after deducting capital allowance.

Miscellaneous and supplemental

Treatment of partnerships

215.—(1) For section 111 of the Taxes Act 1988 there shall be substituted the following section—

"Treatment of partnerships

111.—(1) Where a trade or profession is carried on by two or more persons in partnership, the partnership shall not, unless the contrary intention appears, be treated for the purposes of the Tax Acts as an entity which is separate and distinct from those persons.

(2) So long as a trade or profession ('the actual trade or profession') is carried on by persons in partnership, and each of those persons is chargeable to income tax, the profits or gains or losses arising from the trade or profession shall be computed for the purposes of income tax in like manner as if the partnership were an individual.

(3) A person's share in the profits or gains or losses of the partnership which for any period are computed in accordance with subsection (2) above shall be determined according to the interests of the partners during that period; and income tax shall be chargeable or, as the case may require, loss relief may be claimed as if—

(a) that share derived from a trade or profession ('the deemed trade or profession') carried on by the person alone;

(b) the deemed trade or profession was set up and commenced by him at the time when he became a partner or, where the actual trade or profession was previously carried on by him alone, the time when the actual trade was set up and commenced; and

(c) the deemed trade or profession is permanently discontinued by him at the time when he ceases to be a partner or, where the actual trade or profession is subsequently carried on by him alone, the time when the actual trade or profession is permanently discontinued.

(4) Where—

(a) subsections (2) and (3) above apply in relation to the profits or gains or losses of a trade or profession carried on by persons in partnership, and

(b) other income accrues to those persons by virtue of their being partners,

that other income shall be chargeable to tax by reference to the same periods as if it were profits or gains arising from the trade or profession.

(5) Subsections (1) to (3) above apply, with the necessary modifications, in relation to a business as they apply in relation to a trade."

(2) In section 114 of that Act (special rules for computing profits or losses), after the word "trade"—

(a) in subsection (1), in each place where it occurs;

(b) in subsection (2); and

(c) in subsection (3), in the first place where it occurs,

there shall be inserted the words "profession or business".

(3) The following provisions of that Act shall cease to have effect, namely—

(a) in section 114, in subsection (3), the words from "except that" to the end, and subsection (4);

(b) in section 115 (provisions supplementary to section 114), subsections (1) to (3) and (6); and

(c) in section 277 (personal reliefs: partnerships), in subsection (1), the words "Subject to subsection (2) below", paragraph (c) and the word "and" immediately preceding that paragraph, and subsection (2).

(4) This section and section 216 below—

(a) except in their application to partnerships mentioned in subsection (5) below, have effect as respects the year 1997–98 and subsequent years of assessment, and

(b) in its application to partnerships so mentioned, have effect as respects the year 1994–95 and subsequent years of assessment.

(5) The partnerships referred to in subsection (4) above are partnerships—

(a) whose trades, professions or businesses are set up and commenced on or after 6th April 1994; and

(b) which are not partnership firms to which section 112(3) of the Taxes Act 1988 (partnerships controlled abroad) applies.

GENERAL NOTE

Fundamental changes are made to the taxation of partnerships. Partners will no longer be assessed jointly in the partnership's name. Instead each partner will be charged individually in connection with his share of the partnership profits and losses (according to his interest in the partnership in the basis period) and have his own overlap period and overlap relief on joining and leaving the partnership as well as his own individual adjustment on a change of the partnership accounting date. Other income accruing to a partner from the partnership is to be assessed by reference to the partnership basis period even if it is chargeable under a different Schedule or Case and would normally be assessed on a strictly fiscal year basis.

Where all the partners are individual, the partnership profits are to be computed as if the partnership were an individual. Where some of the partners are companies, two computations will be required: one along corporation tax lines and one along income tax lines to determine the profit shares of the corporate partners and individual partners respectively.

The new rules apply from April 6, 1997 onwards to partnerships in existence at April 6, 1994 and in every other case from April 6, 1994 onwards. Where, after April 5, 1994, there is a change in partners without a valid continuation election under the ICTA 1988 (c. 1), s.113(2), the new rules apply immediately to the new firm.

Effect of change in ownership of trade, profession or vocation

216.—(1) For subsection (2) of section 113 of the Taxes Act 1988 (effect of change in ownership of trade, profession or vocation) there shall be substituted the following subsection—

"(2) Where—

(a) there is such a change as is mentioned in subsection (1) above, and

(b) a person engaged in carrying on the trade, profession or vocation immediately before the change continues to be so engaged immediately after it,

subsection (1) above shall not apply to treat the trade, profession or vocation as discontinued or a new one as set up and commenced."

(2) Subsections (3) to (5) of that section and, in subsection (6) of that section, the words from "and where" to the end shall cease to have effect.

(3) The following provisions of that Act shall cease to have effect, namely—

(a) in section 96 (farming and market gardening: relief for fluctuating profits), in subsection (6) the words from "except that" to the end;

(b) in section 380 (set-off against general income), subsection (3);

(c) in section 381 (further relief in early years of trade), subsection (6);

(d) in section 384 (restrictions on right of set-off), subsection (5);

(e) in section 385 (carry-forward against subsequent profits), subsections (2) and (5);

(f) in section 386 (carry-forward where business transferred to a company), subsection (4); and

(g) in section 389 (supplementary provisions relating to carry-back of terminal losses), subsection (3).

(4) For subsection (4) of section 389 of that Act, there shall be substituted the following subsection—

"(4) For the purposes of this section and section 388 a trade, profession or vocation shall be treated as discontinued, and a new one as set up and commenced, when it is so treated for the purposes of section 111 or 113."

(5) Subsection (3)(a) above—

(a) except in its application to a trade set up and commenced on or after 6th April 1994, has effect where the first of the two years of assessment to which the claim relates is the year 1996–97 or any subsequent year, and

(b) in its application to a trade so set up and commenced, has effect where the first of those two years of assessment is the year 1995–96 or any subsequent year.

GENERAL NOTE

Subs. (1)

Where at least one person continues to be a partner before and after a change in the membership of the partnership, the trade, profession, etc., is treated as continuing. There is no need to make a continuation election. The opening year and cessation provisions will apply to those partners joining or leaving the partnership.

Subs. (2)

The ICTA 1988 (c. 1), s.389(4) is amended to enable a partner to claim terminal loss relief on leaving the partnership (see subs. (4)).

Subs. (5)

For continuing farming partnerships, claims under the ICTA 1988 (c. 1), s.96 for 1995–96 and 1996–97 are to be made at the partnership level, and for 1996–97 and 1997–98 and subsequent pairs of years, claims are to be made at the individual level. For farming partnerships which commence after April 5, 1994 all claims are to be made at the individual level.

Double taxation relief in respect of overlap profits

217.—(1) In subsection (1) of section 804 of the Taxes Act 1988 (relief against income tax in respect of income arising in years of commencement), for the words "any income arising in the years of commencement" there shall be substituted the words "any income which is an overlap profit".

(2) For subsection (5) of that section there shall be substituted the following subsections—

"(5) Subsections (5A) and (5B) below apply where—

(a) credit against income tax for any year of assessment is allowed by virtue of subsection (1) above in respect of any income which is an overlap profit ('the original income'), and

(b) the original income or any part of it contributes to an amount which, by virtue of section 63A(1) or (3), is deducted in computing the profits or gains of a subsequent year of assessment ('the subsequent year').

(5A) The following shall be set off one against the other, namely—

(a) the difference between—

(i) the amount of the credit which, under this Part (including this section), has been allowed against income tax in respect of so much of the original income as contributes as mentioned in subsection (5) above, and

(ii) the amount of the credit which, apart from this section, would have been so allowed; and

(b) the amount of credit which, on the assumption that no amount were deducted by virtue of section 63A(1) or (3), would be allowable under this Part against income tax in respect of income arising in the subsequent year from the same source as the original income.

(5B) The person chargeable in respect of the income (if any) arising in the subsequent year from the same source as the original income shall—

(a) if the amount given by paragraph (a) of subsection (5A) above exceeds that given by paragraph (b) of that subsection, be treated as having received in that year a payment chargeable under Case VI of Schedule D of an amount such that income tax on it at the basic rate is equal to the excess; and

(b) if the amount given by paragraph (b) of subsection (5A) above exceeds that given by paragraph (a) of that subsection, be allowed for that year under this Part an amount of credit equal to the excess.

(5C) For the purposes of subsections (5) to (5B) above, it shall be assumed that, where an amount is deducted by virtue of section 63A(1), each of the overlap profits included in the aggregate of such profits contributes to that amount in the proportion which that overlap profit bears to that aggregate."

(3) In subsection (8) of that section—

(a) immediately before the definition of "overseas tax" there shall be inserted the following definition—

" 'overlap profit' means an amount of profits or gains which, by virtue of sections 60 to 62, is included in the computations for two successive years of assessment;"; and

(b) the definitions of "non-basis period" and "years of commencement" and the words "references to the enactments relating to cessation are references to sections 63, 67 and 113" shall cease to have effect.

GENERAL NOTE

The ICTA 1988 (c. 1), s.804 is amended to ensure that under simplified assessing, double tax relief will be available against overlap profits. There may be a clawback of relief if overlap relief becomes available under the new s.63A of the ICTA 1988 (c. 1) (see s.205 above).

The amount clawed back is chargeable under Sched. D, Case VI at the basic rate such that the tax due equals the excess credit.

Commencement, transitional provisions and savings

218.—(1) Unless the contrary intention appears, this Chapter—

(a) except in its application to a trade set up and commenced on or after 6th April 1994 or income from a source arising to a person on or after that date, has effect as respects the year 1996–97 and subsequent years of assessment, and

(b) in its application to a trade so set up and commenced or income from a source so arising, has effect as respects the year 1994–95 and subsequent years of assessment.

(2) Any reference in subsection (1) above to a trade includes a reference to a profession, vocation, employment or office.

(3) Where the first underwriting year of the underwriting business of a member of Lloyd's is the year 1994, subsection (1) above shall have effect in relation to that business as if it had been set up and commenced on 6th April 1994.

(4) Where, as respects income from any source, income tax is to be charged under Case IV or V of Schedule D by reference to the amounts of income received in the United Kingdom, the source shall be treated for the purposes of subsection (1) above as arising on the date on which the first amount of income is so received.

(5) This Chapter shall have effect subject to the transitional provisions and savings contained in Schedule 20 to this Act.

GENERAL NOTE

The provisions in ss.200 to 218 apply from 1994–1995 onwards in relation to new businesses commenced, or a new source of income arising, after April 5, 1994 and in all other cases from 1997–1998 onwards. 1996 and 1997 are the transitional years and the transitional provisions are contained in Sched. 20 below. Income assessed under Sched. D, Cases IV or V on a remittance basis, is regarded as first arising to a taxpayer on the date of the first remittance.

CHAPTER V

LLOYD'S UNDERWRITERS: CORPORATIONS ETC.

Main provisions

GENERAL NOTE

The FA 1993 (c. 34) ss.171–184 and Scheds. 19 and 20 introduced a new system for taxing members of Lloyd's. The requirement for further legislation has arisen primarily from the decision by Lloyd's to admit corporate members from January 1, 1994. The rules for corporate members conform with the "pay and file" system which has applied generally to companies since October 1993.

Changes are also made to the basis of assessing individual members to conform with the rules for self-assessment and taxation of income on a current year basis in ss.178–218, *supra.*

Taxation of profits

219.—(1) Corporation tax for any accounting period on the profits arising from a corporate member's underwriting business shall be computed on the profits of that accounting period.

(2) As respects the profits arising to a corporate member for any accounting period directly from its membership of one or more syndicates, or from assets forming part of a premiums trust fund—

(a) the aggregate of those profits shall be computed for tax purposes under Case I of Schedule D; and

(b) accordingly, no part of those profits shall be computed for those purposes under any other Schedule or any other Case of Schedule D.

(3) The profits arising to a corporate member for any accounting period—
(a) from assets forming part of an ancillary trust fund; or
(b) from assets employed by it in, or in connection with, its underwriting business,

shall be computed for tax purposes under Case I of Schedule D if, and to the extent that, they do not fall to be computed for those purposes under any other Schedule or any other Case of Schedule D.

(4) Where the profits arising for any accounting period from the assets of a corporate member's premiums trust fund include dividends or other distributions of a company resident in the United Kingdom, subsection (2) above shall apply in relation to those distributions (and any associated tax credits) notwithstanding anything in section 11(2)(a) or 208 of the Taxes Act 1988.

(5) In section 20(2) of the Taxes Act 1988 (Schedule F), after the words "section 171 of the Finance Act 1993" there shall be inserted the words "or section 219 of the Finance Act 1994".

GENERAL NOTE
This section provides that the profits of a corporate member's underwriting business are to be chargeable to corporation tax as trading profits within the rules of Sched. D, Case I. The tax for a company's accounting period is to be chargeable on the profits of that accounting period. The profits from an ancillary trust fund (see s.223, *infra*) or other assets used by it in connection with its underwriting business are computed under Sched. D, Case I if they are not already computed otherwise.

Dividends from U.K. resident companies are included in the Sched. D, Case I income. Such dividends are accordingly excluded from Sched. F.

Accounting period in which certain profits or losses arise

220.—(1) For the purposes of section 219 above and all other purposes of the Corporation Tax Acts, the profits or losses arising to a corporate member in any accounting period directly from its membership of one or more syndicates, or from assets forming part of a premiums trust fund, shall be taken to be—
(a) if two underwriting years each fall partly within that period, the aggregate of the apportioned parts of those profits or losses in those years; and
(b) if a single underwriting year falls wholly or partly within that period, those profits or losses or (as the case may be) the apportioned part of those profits or losses in that year.

(2) Subject to the provisions of this Chapter, for the purposes of subsection (1) above and all other purposes of the Corporation Tax Acts—
(a) the profits or losses arising to a corporate member in any underwriting year directly from its membership of one or more syndicates shall be taken to be those of any previous year or years which are declared in that year; and
(b) the profits or losses arising to a corporate member in any underwriting year from assets forming part of a premiums trust fund shall be taken to be those allocated under the rules or practice of Lloyd's to any previous year or years the profits or losses of which are declared in that year.

(3) In this section "apportioned part", in relation to the profits or losses of an underwriting year, means a part apportioned under section 72 of the Taxes Act 1988.

GENERAL NOTE
This section sets out the accounting period in which profits and losses arising directly to a corporate member from syndicate membership or from assets forming part of a premiums trust

fund are to be treated as arising. They are to be determined by reference to the profits declared in an underwriting year, *e.g.* the profits of a corporate member who joins Lloyd's in 1994 would be declared in June 1997, according to Lloyd's current practice, and the tax liability will crystallise in January 1998. Any apportionments required will be on a time basis.

Assessment and collection of tax

221.—(1) Subject to subsection (2) below, Schedule 19 (Lloyd's underwriters: assessment and collection of tax) to the Finance Act 1993 ("the 1993 Act") shall apply in relation to corporate members as it applies in relation to other members.

(2) In its application to a corporate member, paragraph 13 of that Schedule shall have effect as if—
  (a) in sub-paragraph (3)(b), the reference to the members' agent of each member were a reference to each corporate member itself;
  (b) after sub-paragraph (3A) there were inserted the following sub-paragraph—
     "(3B) The provisions of this paragraph relating to the payment of tax credits have effect notwithstanding anything in section 231(2) of the Taxes Act 1988.";
  (c) in sub-paragraph (4), the reference to section 824 of the Taxes Act 1988 were a reference to section 826 of that Act (interest on tax overpaid); and
  (d) in sub-paragraph (4A), the reference to the members' agent of a member were a reference to a corporate member itself, the reference to section 171 of the 1993 Act were a reference to section 219 of this Act and each reference to the Income Tax Acts were a reference to the Corporation Tax Acts.

GENERAL NOTE
  The provisions of the FA 1993 (c. 34), Sched. 19 that presently apply for assessing and collecting tax on individual members of Lloyd's are extended to corporate members with the necessary amendments to accommodate companies.

Trust funds

Premiums trust funds

222.—(1) For the purposes of the Corporation Tax Acts—
  (a) a corporate member shall be treated as absolutely entitled as against the trustees to the assets forming part of a premiums trust fund belonging to it; and
  (b) where a deposit required by a regulatory authority in a country or territory outside the United Kingdom is paid out of such a fund, the money so paid shall be treated as still forming part of that fund.

(2) Where an asset forms part of a corporate member's premiums trust fund at the beginning of any underwriting year, for the purposes of the Corporation Tax Acts—
  (a) the trustees of the fund shall be treated as acquiring it on that day, and
  (b) they shall be treated as paying in respect of the acquisition an amount equal to the value of the asset at the time of the acquisition.

(3) Where an asset forms part of a corporate member's premiums trust fund at the end of any underwriting year, for the purposes of the Corporation Tax Acts—
  (a) the trustees of the fund shall be treated as disposing of it on that day, and
  (b) they shall be treated as obtaining in respect of the disposal an amount equal to the value of the asset at the time of the disposal.

(4) Subsection (5) below applies where the following state of affairs exists at the beginning of any underwriting year or the end of any such year—

(a) securities have been transferred by the trustees of a corporate member's premiums trust fund in pursuance of an arrangement mentioned in section 129(1), (2) or (2A) of the Taxes Act 1988,

(b) the transfer was made to enable another person to fulfil a contract or to make a transfer,

(c) securities have not been transferred in return, and

(d) section 129(3) of that Act applies to the transfer made by the trustees.

(5) The securities transferred by the trustees shall be treated for the purposes of subsections (2) and (3) above as if they formed part of the corporate member's premiums trust fund at the beginning or (as the case may be) the end of the underwriting year concerned.

(6) Subsections (2) to (5) above do not apply to FOTRA securities forming part of a corporate member's premiums trust fund at the beginning or end of any underwriting year if it is a non-resident United Kingdom trader in the year.

(7) In subsection (6) above—

"FOTRA securities" has the same meaning as in section 715 of the Taxes Act 1988 (exceptions from accrued income scheme);

"non-resident United Kingdom Trader" shall be construed in accordance with subsection (5) of that section.

GENERAL NOTE

This section ensures that a corporate member, and not the trustees, is to be treated as the owner of the assets in its premiums trust fund for corporation tax purposes. It also provides for the assets to be treated as acquired at their value at the beginning of each underwriting year and disposed of for their value at the end of the year. Assets from such a fund used to satisfy regulatory requirements in another country are treated as still being part of the fund.

The other provisions of the section follow those applicable to individuals in the FA 1993 (c. 34), s.174.

Ancillary trust funds

223. A corporate member shall be treated for the purposes of the Corporation Tax Acts as absolutely entitled as against the trustees to the assets forming part of an ancillary trust fund belonging to it.

GENERAL NOTE

As with individual members (see the FA 1993 (c. 34), s.176(1)) corporate members of Lloyd's are treated as the owners of the assets in their ancillary trust funds for corporation tax purposes.

Other special cases

Reinsurance to close

224.—(1) Subject to subsection (2) below, section 177 of the 1993 Act (reinsurance to close) shall apply for the purposes of this Chapter as it applies for the purposes of Chapter III of Part II of that Act (Lloyd's underwriters: individuals).

(2) That section as so applied shall have effect as if—

(a) the member by whom the premium is payable were required to be a corporate member;

(b) the member to whom the premium is payable might, but need not, be such a member; and

(c) any reference to the purposes of income tax were a reference to the purposes of corporation tax.

GENERAL NOTE

The reinsurance to close provisions of the FA 1993 (c. 34), s.177 apply to corporate members as for individual members.

Stop-loss and quota share insurance

225.—(1) In computing for the purposes of corporation tax the profits of a corporate member's underwriting business, each of the following shall be deductible as an expense, namely—

(a) any premium payable by it under a stop-loss insurance, and any repayment of insurance money paid to it under such an insurance; and

(b) any amount payable by it under a quota share contract, irrespective of the purpose for which the contract was entered into.

(2) Subject to subsection (3) below, the following provisions apply where any insurance money is payable to a corporate member under a stop-loss insurance in respect of a loss in its underwriting business—

(a) if the underwriting year in which the loss is declared falls within two or more accounting periods, the apportioned part of the insurance money shall be treated as a trading receipt in computing the profits arising from the business for each of those periods; and

(b) if the underwriting year in which the loss is declared falls within a single accounting period, the insurance money shall be treated as a trading receipt in computing the profits arising from the business for that period.

(3) Where, as respects the payment of any such insurance money as is mentioned in subsection (2) above—

(a) the inspector is not notified of the payment at least 30 days before the time after which any assessment or further assessment of profits for any of the accounting periods or (as the case may be) the accounting period is precluded by section 34 of the Management Act (ordinary time limit), and

(b) the inspector is not entitled, after that time, to make any such assessment or further assessment by virtue of section 36 (fraudulent or negligent conduct) of that Act,

that subsection shall have effect in relation to the apportioned part of that insurance money or (as the case may be) that insurance money as if, instead of that accounting period, it referred to the accounting period in which the payment is made.

(4) In this section—

"apportioned part", in relation to any insurance money, means a part apportioned under section 72 of the Taxes Act 1988;

"quota share contract" means any contract between a corporate member and another person which—

(a) is made in accordance with the rules or practice of Lloyd's; and

(b) provides for that other person to take over any rights and liabilities of the member under any of the syndicates of which it is a member.

GENERAL NOTE

In computing the profits of a corporate member's underwriting business, amounts payable to secure protection against losses (stop-loss insurance) or to transfer its liabilities to someone else (quota share contracts) are deductible. The amounts payable are to be matched, in most instances, with the losses that gave rise to the claim. The provisions generally follow those applicable to individual members in the FA 1993 (c. 34), s.178.

Miscellaneous

Provisions which are not to apply

226.—(1) Sections 92 to 95 of the 1993 Act (corporation tax: currency to be used) shall not apply for the purposes of computing for the purposes of corporation tax the profits or losses of a corporate member's underwriting business.

(2) No asset forming part of or liability attaching to a premiums trust fund of a corporate member shall be a qualifying asset or liability for the purposes of Chapter II of Part II of the 1993 Act (exchange gains and losses); and no contract forming part of such a fund shall be a currency contract for those purposes.

(3) No contract or option forming part of a premiums trust fund of a corporate member shall be a qualifying contract for the purposes of Chapter II of this Part of this Act (interest rate and currency contracts and options).

GENERAL NOTE

The section sets out certain provisions which apply generally to the taxation of companies but are not to apply to corporate members of Lloyd's. These provisions are concerned with foreign currency (the FA 1993 (c. 34), ss.92–95), exchange gains and losses (the FA 1993 (c. 34), Pt. II, Chap. II) and interest rate and currency contracts (the FA 1994 (c. 9), Pt. IV, Chap. II, *supra*).

Cessation: final underwriting year

227.—(1) This section applies where a corporate member ceases to carry on its underwriting business, whether by reason of being wound up or otherwise.

(2) Subject to the provisions of any regulations made by the Board—

(a) the member's final underwriting year shall be that in which its deposit at Lloyd's is paid over to it or its liquidator, and

(b) the member's underwriting business shall be treated as continuing until the end of that year.

GENERAL NOTE

The final underwriting year of a corporate member of Lloyd's is that in which its deposit is paid over to it or its liquidator (*cf.* the FA 1993 (c. 34), s.179 for individual members) subject to regulations by the Revenue.

Lloyd's underwriters: individuals

228.—(1) Chapter III of Part II of the 1993 Act (Lloyd's underwriters: individuals) shall have effect subject to the amendments specified in Schedule 21 to this Act.

(2) The following provisions shall cease to have effect, namely—

(a) section 627 of the Taxes Act 1988 (elections by Lloyd's underwriters with respect to retirement annuities);

(b) in section 641 of that Act, subsection (2) (elections by Lloyd's underwriters with respect to carry-back of contributions); and

(c) in section 183 of the 1993 Act, subsection (3) (amendments of sections 627(5) and 641(2) of the Taxes Act 1988).

(3) Subject to any provision to the contrary, the provisions of Schedule 21 to this Act have effect for the year 1994–95 and subsequent years of assessment.

(4) Subsection (2) above has effect for the year 1997–98 and subsequent years of assessment.

GENERAL NOTE

This section introduces Sched. 21, which introduces changes to the scheme for the taxation of individual members of Lloyd's as set out in the FA 1993 (c. 34). See further the General Note to Sched. 21.

It also removes provisions that allowed individual members of Lloyd's to make modified elections relating to the year in which retirement annuity payments and contributions to personal pension schemes were treated as having been paid.

Supplemental

Regulations

229. The Board may by regulations provide—

(a) for the assessment and collection of tax charged in accordance with section 219 above (so far as not provided for by Schedule 19 to the 1993 Act as applied by section 221 above);

(b) for making, in the event of any changes in the rules or practice of Lloyd's, such amendments of this Chapter as appear to the Board to be expedient having regard to those changes;

(c) for modifying the application of this Chapter in cases where a syndicate continues after the end of its closing year or a corporate member becomes insolvent or otherwise ceases to carry on its underwriting business;

(d) for giving credit for foreign tax.

GENERAL NOTE
The regulation-making power conferred by this section corresponds with that already available under the FA 1993 (c. 34), s.182.

Interpretation and commencement

230.—(1) In this Chapter, unless the context otherwise requires—

"the 1993 Act" means the Finance Act 1993;

"ancillary trust fund", in relation to a corporate member, does not include a premiums trust fund but, subject to that, means any trust fund required or authorised by the rules of Lloyd's, or required by a members' agent or regulating trustee of the corporate member;

"closing year"—

(a) in relation to an underwriting year, means the underwriting year next but one following that year; and

(b) in relation to a syndicate, means the closing year of the underwriting year for which it was formed;

"corporate member" means a body corporate which is a member of Lloyd's and is or has been an underwriting member;

"inspector" includes any officer of the Board;

"the Management Act" means the Taxes Management Act 1970;

"managing agent", in relation to a syndicate and an underwriting year, means—

(a) the person registered as a managing agent at Lloyd's who was acting as such an agent for the syndicate at the end of that year, or

(b) such other person as may be determined in accordance with regulations made by the Board;

"member" means a member of Lloyd's who is or has been an underwriting member;

"members' agent", in relation to a corporate member, means a person registered as a members' agent at Lloyd's who has been appointed by the corporate member to act as its members' agent in respect of all or any part of its underwriting business;

"premiums trust fund" means such a trust fund as is referred to in section 83 of the Insurance Companies Act 1982;

"prescribed" means prescribed by regulations made by the Board;

"profits" includes gains;

"regulating trustee", in relation to a corporate member, means a person designated as such by the terms of any trust deed by which a premiums trust fund of the corporate member is constituted;

"stop-loss insurance" means any insurance taken out by a corporate member against losses in its underwriting business;

"syndicate" means a syndicate of underwriting members of Lloyd's formed for an underwriting year;

"underwriting business", in relation to a corporate member, means its underwriting business as a member of Lloyd's;

"underwriting year" means the calendar year.

(2) For the purposes of this Chapter, unless the contrary intention appears—

(a) the profits or losses of a corporate member's underwriting business include profits or losses arising to it—

    (i) from assets forming part of a premiums trust fund or an ancillary trust fund; or

    (ii) from assets employed by it in, or in connection with, its underwriting business; and

(b) any charge made on a corporate member by the managing agent of a syndicate of which it is a member, and any expense incurred on its behalf by the managing agent of such a syndicate, shall be treated as expenses arising directly from its membership of that syndicate.

(3) Subject to any provision to the contrary, the provisions of this Chapter have effect for accounting periods ending on or after January 1, 1994 or, as the case may require, for the underwriting year 1994 and subsequent underwriting years.

GENERAL NOTE

The interpretation provisions correspond with those in the FA 1993 (c. 34), s.184, with necessary adaptations for the introduction of corporate members.

The new legislation will generally take effect for accounting periods ending on or after January 1, 1994, or for the underwriting year 1994 and subsequent underwriting years.

PART V

OIL TAXATION

CHAPTER I

ELECTION BY REFERENCE TO PIPE-LINE USAGE

Election by reference to pipe-line with excess capacity

231.—(1) The provisions of this Chapter apply where, on or before 1st January 1996, a participator in a taxable field makes, in accordance with Part I of Schedule 22 to this Act, an election with respect to that field by reference to a pipe-line—

(a) which is a qualifying asset;

(b) which is used or intended to be used for transporting oil in circumstances which give rise or are expected to give rise to tariff receipts;

(c) which, at the date of the election, is at least 25 kilometres in length; and

(d) for which the initial usage fraction does not exceed one-half.

(2) A participator may not make an election—

(a) unless the field to which the election applies is (or, as the case may be, is intended to be) the chargeable field in relation to the tariff receipts referred to in subsection (1)(b) above; or

(b) if the first chargeable period of that field ended on or before 30th June 1982; or

(c) if the participator's net profit period with respect to that field ended on or before 30th June 1993;

and for the purposes of paragraph (c) above no account shall be taken of the operation of section 113 of the Finance Act 1981 (loss following net profit period).

(3) If there is more than one pipe-line by reference to which the electing participator could, apart from this subsection, make an election (with respect to the same field) he may make an election only by reference to that pipe-line which is the longer or longest.

(4) In this Chapter, in relation to a pipe-line or an election made by reference to a pipe-line, "the initial usage fraction" means the fraction of which—

(a) the numerator is the daily contracted and production throughput of oil in relation to the pipe-line on 16th March 1993; and

(b) the denominator is the design capacity of the pipe-line, expressed on a daily basis.

(5) Subject to subsection (6) below, where an election is in operation it shall apply to all those assets which, by reference to the field to which the election applies, are at the date of the election or subsequently become—

(a) qualifying assets in relation to the electing participator; and

(b) assets to which are or are expected to be referable any tariff receipts of the electing participator attributable to that field.

(6) If the electing participator specifies in his election that the election is to be limited to oil which is, or is expected to be, transported by the pipe-line by reference to which the election is made, the election shall apply only to such of the assets referred to in subsection (5) above as, in whole or in part, are or subsequently become used in connection with that oil.

(7) For the purposes of this Chapter, unless it is just and reasonable to determine some other quantity of oil, the daily contracted and production throughput of oil in relation to a pipe-line on 16th March 1993 is the aggregate of—

(a) the maximum daily capacity specified in contracts then in force for the use of the pipe-line (whether at that date or in the future) for transporting oil won from any taxable field (including the field to which the election applies); and

(b) the maximum expected daily throughput, otherwise than pursuant to such contracts, of oil transported by the pipe-line and won from the field to which the election applies or any other taxable field, being the throughput ascertained by reference to what was at that date the most recent development plan applicable to the field to which the election applies or, as the case may be, the other taxable field.

(8) For the purposes of this Chapter, unless it is just and reasonable to determine some other capacity, the design capacity of a pipe-line is that which is specified for the pipe-line as a whole in what was, on 16th March 1993, the most recent development plan applicable to the field to which the election applies or, as the case may be, the pipe-line itself.

GENERAL NOTE

This section, together with ss.232–234 and Sched. 22, was introduced at Committee Stage following a Budget day announcement that a new petroleum revenue tax (PRT) option for companies with interests in North Sea oil or gas fields that had not yet recovered their costs and had pipelines largely intended to transport production from other fields. Participators in the recently commissioned Central Area Transmission System (CATS) pipeline had a particular transitional problem, because it was designed with substantial spare capacity and is an asset of fields with relatively low profitability. New pipelines will pay only corporation tax, while CATS participators will have no prospect of early effective PRT relief on their expenditure, but will face a full PRT charge on their tariff receipts. The cost to the Exchequer of the new option depends on various factors but might be around £20 million per annum from the year 2000.

An election for the optional treatment may be made in respect of a pipeline at least 25 km in length and with at least 50 per cent. unused capacity and must be made by January 1, 1996. The procedure for an election is contained in Sched. 22, Pt. I.

Restriction on electing participator's allowable expenditure on elected assets

232.—(1) This section has effect in relation to expenditure which is incurred on an asset to which an election applies; and in this section "allowable or allowed", in relation to any expenditure, means allowable or allowed under any of the expenditure relief provisions.

(2) Subject to the following provisions of this section, in the case of expenditure incurred before the date of the election, the amount which, apart from

this section, would be allowable or allowed in the case of the electing partici-pator shall be reduced by multiplying it by the initial usage fraction.

(3) Subject to subsection (5) below, in the case of expenditure incurred on or after the date of the election, the amount which, apart from this section, would be allowable or allowed in the case of the electing participator shall be reduced to nil.

(4) Where, after 30th November 1993 and before the date of the election, expenditure was incurred on an asset to which the election applies and—

(a) apart from this section, that expenditure would have qualified for sup-plement by virtue of paragraph (c) or paragraph (d) of subsection (5) of section 3 of the principal Act, and

(b) the effect of the expenditure is to increase the maximum capacity of the pipe-line by reference to which the election was made above its design capacity or to increase the capacity of any asset used or to be used for the initial treatment or initial storage of oil transported by the pipe-line above its development plan capacity,

that expenditure shall be treated for the purposes of the application of sub-sections (2) and (3) above as if it had been incurred after the date of the election.

(5) Where, at the date of the election, an asset to which the election applies is for the time being leased or hired under a contract which was entered into before 16th March 1993, any expenditure—

(a) which is incurred on or after the date of the election on the leasing or hiring of the asset under the contract, and

(b) which is not of a description falling within paragraphs (a) and (b) of subsection (4) above,

shall be treated for the purposes of the application of subsections (2) and (3) above as if it had been incurred before the date of the election.

(6) For the purposes of subsection (4)(b) above, the development plan capacity of any asset used or to be used for the initial treatment or initial storage of oil transported by a pipe-line is—

(a) the maximum capacity of that asset as specified in what, on 16th March 1993, was the most recent development plan applicable to the field to which the election applies or, as the case may be, to the asset itself; or

(b) if no such maximum capacity was so specified in relation to an asset, its actual maximum capacity on that date or, if there was no such capacity on that date, nil.

(7) Where a claim under Schedule 5 or Schedule 6 to the principal Act relates to the allowance of any expenditure to which subsection (2) above applies, the amount claimed shall take account of the operation of that sub-section; and where subsection (3) above applies to any expenditure, no such claim shall be made with respect to it.

(8) Where a claim has been made under Schedule 5 or Schedule 6 to the principal Act with respect to any expenditure and, subsequently, an election is made which has the effect of altering the amount of expenditure which is allowable or allowed,—

(a) a notice of variation such as is mentioned in paragraph 9 of Schedule 5 to the principal Act may be served after the end of the period referred to in sub-paragraph (1) of that paragraph if it is served before the expiry of the period of three years beginning on the date of the elec-tion; and

(b) if the effect of such a notice is that the net profit period with respect to the field to which the election applies is changed, the change shall not (by virtue of section 231(2) above) affect the validity of the election.

(9) Nothing in this section affects the determination of the question whether an asset is a qualifying asset for the purposes of the 1983 Act and, accordingly, for that purpose, the preceding provisions of this section shall be disregarded in determining whether any expenditure is allowable or allowed.

GENERAL NOTE
    Expenditure on the elected assets before the date of the election will be allowable only to the extent of the usage of the pipeline at that time. Expenditure thereafter will get no PRT relief. However, incremental expenditure incurred between Budget day and the date of election will get no PRT relief, while leasing costs will continue to get relief after the election to the extent of the usage, provided the asset concerned was in place by March 16, 1993.

Tax relief for certain receipts of an electing participator

    233.—(1) If any sum—
    (a) is received or receivable by the electing participator on or after the date of an election, and
    (b) is so received or receivable from a participator in a non-taxable field in respect of the use, in connection with that non-taxable field, of an asset to which the election applies or the provision of services or other business facilities of whatever kind in connection with that use, and
    (c) would, apart from this section, constitute a tariff receipt attributable to the field to which the election applies,
that sum shall not be regarded as a tariff receipt for the purposes of the Oil Taxation Acts.
    (2) If any sum—
    (a) is received or receivable by the electing participator on or after the date of an election, and
    (b) is so received or receivable in respect of the disposal of an asset to which the election applies or of an interest in such an asset, and
    (c) constitutes a disposal receipt of the electing participator attributable to the field to which the election applies,
that sum shall, for the purposes of the Oil Taxation Acts, be taken to be reduced in accordance with subsection (4) below.
    (3) Any reference in subsection (1) or subsection (2) above to a sum received or receivable includes a reference to an amount which (apart from this section) would be treated as a tariff receipt or disposal receipt by virtue of paragraph 5 of Schedule 2 to the 1983 Act (acquisition and disposal of qualifying assets otherwise than at arm's length).
    (4) Unless it is just and reasonable to make a different reduction, the reduction referred to in subsection (2) above shall be determined by reference to that applicable under subsection (2) or subsection (3) of section 232 above to the expenditure incurred on the asset concerned so that if, for the purposes of determining under those subsections the amount of that expenditure which was allowed or allowable,—
    (a) the whole or any part of that expenditure was reduced by multiplying it by the initial usage fraction, or
    (b) the whole or any part of that expenditure was reduced to nil,
a similar reduction shall apply to the whole or, as the case may require, to each correspondingly proportionate part of any sum falling within subsection (2) above.
    (5) In this section "the Oil Taxation Acts" means Parts I and III of the principal Act, the 1983 Act and any other enactment relating to petroleum revenue tax.

GENERAL NOTE
    Tariffs receipts from non-taxable fields after an election is made and accepted are free from PRT from the date of receipt of the election. Disposals of elected assets at arm's length will be subject to a restricted PRT charge, usually by reference to the extent of usage.

Interpretation of Chapter and supplementary provisions

    234.—(1) In this Chapter "the 1983 Act" means the Oil Taxation Act 1983 and expressions used in this Chapter have the same meaning as in that Act.
    (2) In this Chapter—

(a) "election" means an election under section 231 above and "electing participator" means a participator who makes or has made an election;

(b) "the expenditure relief provisions" means sections 3 and 4 of the principal Act and section 3 of the 1983 Act; and

(c) "the initial usage fraction" shall be construed in accordance with section 231(4) above.

(3) In this Chapter—

(a) any reference to the assets to which an election applies is a reference to the pipe-line by reference to which the election is made together with the assets determined in accordance with subsections (5) and (6) of section 231 above;

(b) any reference to the net profit period is a reference to the chargeable period which is the net profit period for the purposes of section 111 of the Finance Act 1981 (restriction of expenditure supplement); and

(c) any reference to a development plan is a reference to a consent for, or programme of, development granted, served or approved by the Secretary of State.

(4) Any reference in this Chapter to expenditure incurred on an asset is a reference to expenditure (whether or not of a capital nature) which—

(a) is incurred in acquiring, bringing into existence or enhancing the value of the asset, or

(b) is incurred (for any of the purposes mentioned in section 3(1) of the principal Act) by reference to the use of the asset in connection with a taxable field,

other than expenditure which, in the hands of the recipient, constitutes a tariff receipt.

(5) For the purposes of this Chapter—

(a) an election is "in operation" if it has been accepted by the Board; and

(b) the date of an election which is in operation is the date on which the election was received by the Board.

(6) The provisions of Part II of Schedule 22 to this Act shall have effect for supplementing the preceding provisions of this Chapter.

(7) The Board may make all such amendments of assessments or determinations or of decisions on claims as may be necessary in consequence of the provisions of this Chapter.

GENERAL NOTE

This is the general interpretation provision for ss.231–233. It also introduces supplementary provisions in Sched. 22, Pt. II.

CHAPTER II

MISCELLANEOUS

Valuation of oil

235.—(1) With respect to chargeable periods ending after 31st December 1993, subsection (5A) of section 2 of the Oil Taxation Act 1975 (special rules for valuation of oil consisting of gas which is disposed of in a sale at arm's length on terms including transportation costs etc.) shall be amended as follows—

(a) for the words "oil consisting of gas" there shall be substituted "oil";

(b) for the word "gas", in each place where it subsequently occurs, there shall be substituted "oil";

(c) for the words "for delivery at a place" there shall be substituted "or another country for delivery at another place in or"; and

(d) in paragraph (ii) after the words "United Kingdom", in the second place where they occur, there shall be inserted "or, in the case of oil first landed in another country, at the place in that or any other country".

(2) In Schedule 3 to that Act, in each of paragraphs 2(3) and 2A(3) for "(2)(e)" there shall be substituted "(2)(f)".

(3) In Schedule 10 to the Finance Act 1987 (nomination scheme for disposals and appropriations of oil), in paragraph 4 (timing of nominations)—
  (a) in sub-paragraph (1) for the words "sub-paragraph (2)" there shall be substituted "sub-paragraphs (2) and (2A)"; and
  (b) after sub-paragraph (2) there shall be inserted—
    "(2A) Where the proposed transaction has a transaction base date later than 31st December 1993, sub-paragraph (1) above has effect with the substitution for the reference to the second business day of a reference to the first business day."

(4) In paragraph 11 of that Schedule (a participator's aggregate nominated proceeds for a month), in sub-paragraph (2) for the words "sub-paragraph (2A)" there shall be substituted "sub-paragraphs (2A) and (2B)" and after sub-paragraph (2A) there shall be inserted the following sub-paragraph—
    "(2B) In the case of a nominated transaction which is a disposal to which subsection (5A) of section 2 of the principal Act applies, for the amount which, apart from this sub-paragraph, would be the nominated price for the purposes of sub-paragraph (2) above there shall be substituted the amount which, under that subsection, is deemed to be the price received or receivable for the oil in question."

GENERAL NOTE
This section makes two changes to the rules governing the amounts chargeable to PRT from the sale of oil.

First, it provides that where North Sea crude is sold at arm's length on terms which include delivery to a buyer at a place which is not the nearest reasonable place of delivery, the amount chargeable to PRT shall be the price at which the oil would have been sold if it had been delivered at that place. This ensures coincidence for PRT in such cases between the point of valuation and the point to which costs are allowed.

Second, it reduces by one day the time participators have in which to nominate sales of their own production for the purpose of establishing the taxable value of that production under the PRT nomination scheme for disposals and appropriations of oil.

Both changes apply from January 1, 1994.

Valuation of certain light gases

236.—(1) Subject to subsection (2) below, the principal Act shall have effect subject to the amendments in Schedule 23 to this Act, being—
  (a) amendments altering the rules for determining the market value of certain light gases for the purposes of petroleum revenue tax; and
  (b) amendments consequential upon, or incidental to, those amendments.

(2) The amendments in Schedule 23 to this Act do not have effect in relation to any light gases if, before 1st January 1994, an election was made under section 134 of the Finance Act 1982 (alternative valuation of certain ethane) or section 109 of the Finance Act 1986 (alternative valuation of certain light gases) and the election applies to those gases.

(3) No election may be made after 31st December 1993 under section 134 of the Finance Act 1982 or section 109 of the Finance Act 1986; and, accordingly—
  (a) in subsection (2) of the said section 134, after the word "section" there shall be inserted "must be made before 1st January 1994 and"; and
  (b) in subsection (1) of the said section 109, after the word "section" there shall be inserted "before 1st January 1994".

(4) In section 12 of the principal Act (interpretation), in subsection (1) after the definition of "licensee" there shall be inserted—
    " "light gases", except in relation to an election under section 134 of the Finance Act 1982 or section 109 of the Finance Act 1986, means oil

consisting of gas of which the largest component by volume over any chargeable period, measured at a temperature of 15 degrees centigrade and a pressure of one atmosphere, is methane or ethane or a combination of those gases".

GENERAL NOTE

This section, together with Sched. 23, amends the PRT rules for determining the market value of gas disposed of otherwise than at arm's length. The new rules do not apply to gas in respect of which an election was made under the old rules (the FA 1982 (c. 39), s.134 and the FA 1986 (c. 41), s.109) but the old rules cease to apply from January 1, 1994.

A definition of "light gases" for the purpose of the new rules is inserted into the Oil Taxation Act 1975 (c. 22).

Abortive exploration expenditure

237.—(1) In section 5 of the principal Act (allowance of abortive exploration expenditure incurred before 16th March 1983), after subsection (2) there shall be inserted the following subsection—

"(2A) For the purpose only of determining under paragraph (c) of subsection (1) above whether expenditure is or is likely to become allowable for any oil field, it shall be assumed that any oil field which, apart from this subsection, would be a non-taxable field is or, as the case may be, will be a taxable field and, accordingly, that section 185(4)(e) of the Finance Act 1993 (no expenditure allowable for non-taxable fields) does not apply."

(2) Subsection (1) above shall be deemed to have come into force at the same time as Part III of the Finance Act 1993 (27th July 1993).

(3) The Board may make all such amendments of assessments or determinations or of decisions on claims as may be necessary in consequence of the preceding provisions of this section.

GENERAL NOTE

This section confirms that the circumstances in which the former allowance for abortive exploration expenditure incurred before March 16, 1983 is available against current PRT liabilities are unchanged as the result of the prospective abolition of PRT in the FA 1993 (c. 34).

Disposals of assets producing tariff receipts

238.—(1) With respect to disposals made after 30th November 1993, paragraph 5 of Schedule 2 to the Oil Taxation Act 1983 (acquisition and disposal of qualifying assets otherwise than at arm's length: limit on tariff and disposal receipts) shall be amended in accordance with subsections (2) and (3) below; and in this subsection "disposal" has the same meaning as in that paragraph.

(2) In sub-paragraph (1) of paragraph 5, at the end of paragraph (c), and in place of the amendment made by section 190(5)(b) of the Finance Act 1993, there shall be inserted "and

(d) the use of the asset will be wholly by that person in connection with a taxable field in which he is a participator (and accordingly, and in particular, there will be no use giving rise to tariff receipts)";

and for the words "those receipts", where they next occur, there shall be substituted "the receipts referred to in paragraphs (b) and (c) above".

(3) In sub-paragraph (3) of paragraph 5, for paragraph (b) there shall be substituted the following paragraph—

"(b) the disposal does not fall within sub-paragraph (1) above, and".

(4) The Board may make all such amendments of assessments or determinations or of decisions on claims as may be necessary in consequence of the preceding provisions of this section.

GENERAL NOTE

PRT is charged where the disposal of an operational asset is to an affiliate at market value rather than any actual proceeds paid. This rule is extended to include all assets generating tariff receipts, *e.g.* pipelines.

PART VI

STAMP DUTY

Execution of deeds

239.—(1) In section 122 of the Stamp Act 1891 (definitions)—

(a) after subsection (1) there shall be inserted—

"(1A) For the purposes of this Act a deed (or, in Scotland, a deed for which delivery is required) shall be treated as executed when it is delivered or, if it is delivered subject to conditions, when the conditions are fulfilled", and

(b) at the end of the definition of "executed" and "execution" in subsection (1) there shall be added "(but subject to subsection (1A) of this section)".

(2) In section 27 of the Stamp Duties Management Act 1891 (definitions), in the definition of "executed" and "execution", for the words following "execution" there shall be substituted "have the same meaning as in the Stamp Act 1891".

(3) This section shall apply to any instrument except one which, on or before 7th December 1993, has been executed for the purposes of the Stamp Act 1891 as that Act has effect before amendment by this section.

GENERAL NOTE

Some doubt had been expressed about the meaning of "execution" for stamp duty in Scotland. The stamp duty on a document is generally fixed by reference to its date of execution. The section provides that where a document is a deed which requires delivery in order to be effective, it will not be regarded as executed until it has been delivered as well as signed.

This is not regarded as changing the law in England, Wales and Northern Ireland.

Time for presenting agreements for leases

240.—(1) If there are presented for stamping at the same time in pursuance of the Stamp Act 1891—

(a) an agreement for a lease or tack, and

(b) the lease or tack which gives effect to the agreement,

and the duty (if any) chargeable on the agreement is paid, the agreement shall be treated for the purposes of section 15 of that Act (penalty upon stamping instruments after execution) as if it had been first executed when the lease or tack which gives effect to the agreement was first executed.

(2) No lease or tack shall be treated as duly stamped unless—

(a) it contains a certificate that there is no agreement to which it gives effect, or

(b) it is stamped with a stamp denoting—

(i) that there is an agreement to which it gives effect which is not chargeable with duty, or

(ii) the duty paid on the agreement to which it gives effect.

(3) For the purposes of this section a lease or tack gives effect to an agreement if the lease or tack is granted subsequent to the agreement and either is in conformity with the agreement or relates to substantially the same property and term as the agreement.

(4) Subsection (1) above shall apply to agreements executed on or after 6th May 1994; and subsection (2) above shall apply to any lease or tack executed on or after that day.

GENERAL NOTE

The Revenue had received legal advice that agreements for leases, as well as leases themselves, need to be stamped. The section provides that where an agreement for lease and the lease to which it relates are presented for stamping at the same time and any duty on the agreement is paid, for penalty purposes the agreement is treated as if executed at the same time as the lease. A lease itself must contain a certificate that there is no relative agreement or must bear a stamp denoting the duty paid (if any) on the agreement to which it gives effect. There is no question of a double charge on the agreement and the lease itself.

Exchange, partition, etc.

241.—(1) Where—

(a) the consideration for the transfer or vesting of any estate or interest in land or the grant of any lease or tack consists of or includes any property, and

(b) for the purposes of stamp duty chargeable under or by reference to the heading "Conveyance or Transfer on sale" in Schedule 1 to the Stamp Act 1981 no amount or value is, apart from this section, attributed to that property on that transfer, vesting or grant,

then, for those purposes, the consideration or, as the case may be, the consideration so far as relating to that property shall be taken to be the market value of the property immediately before the instrument in question is executed and accordingly the instrument shall be charged with ad valorem duty under that heading.

(2) For the purposes of this section the market value of property at any time is the price which that property might reasonably be expected to fetch on a sale at that time in the open market.

(3) Stamp duty shall not be chargeable under the heading "Exchange or Excambion" in Schedule 1 to the Stamp Act 1891, and section 73 of that Act (exchange and partition or division) shall cease to apply to the exchange of property; and, accordingly, in that section the words from first "upon" to "heritable property, or" and the words "exchange or" shall cease to have effect.

(4) In that section, as amended by subsection (3) above, for "real or heritable property" there shall be substituted "estate or interest in land".

(5) In Schedule 1 to that Act, in paragraph (3) of the heading "Lease or Tack" (consideration consisting of money, stock or security charged as on a conveyance on sale), for "or security" there shall be substituted "security or other property".

(6) This section shall apply to instruments executed after 7th December 1993, not being instruments executed in pursuance of a contract made before 30th November 1993.

GENERAL NOTE

This section is an anti-avoidance provision. Some transactions which were in substance sales, or grants of leases, of land were documented as exchanges in order to reduce or avoid stamp duty.

In future, exchanges of land or buildings will be treated as transfers for chargeable consideration with duty payable on both transfers. The open market value of one interest in land or buildings received in exchange for another will be regarded as its purchase price for stamp duty purposes. On a sale of land or buildings it will not matter for stamp duty what type of assets are received in payment.

Where consideration not ascertainable from conveyance or lease

242.—(1) Where, for the purposes of stamp duty chargeable under or by reference to the heading "Conveyance or Transfer on sale" in Schedule 1 to the Stamp Act 1891, the consideration, or any part of the consideration, for—

(a) the transfer or vesting of any estate or interest in land, or

(b) the grant of any lease or tack,

cannot, apart from this subsection, be ascertained at the time the instrument in question is executed, the consideration for the transfer, vesting or grant shall for those purposes be taken to be the market value immediately before the instrument is executed of the estate or interest transferred or vested or, as the case may be, the lease or tack granted.

(2) Where, for the purposes of stamp duty chargeable under paragraph (3) of the heading "Lease or Tack" in Schedule 1 to that Act, the rent, or any part

of the rent, payable under any lease or tack cannot, apart from this subsection, be ascertained at the time it is executed, the rent shall for those purposes be taken to be the market rent at that time.

(3) For the purposes of this section—

(a) the cases where consideration or rent cannot be ascertained at any time do not include cases where the consideration or rent could be ascertained on the assumption that any future event mentioned in the instrument in question were or were not to occur, and

(b) the market rent of a lease or tack at any time is the rent which the lease or tack might reasonably be expected to fetch at that time in the open market,

and in this section "market value" has the same meaning as in section 241 above.

(4) This section shall apply to instruments executed after 7th December 1993.

GENERAL NOTE

If the price payable for an interest in land cannot be ascertained at the time the transfer document is executed (and could not be ascertained by reference to a possible future event specified in the document) stamp duty will be payable on the open market value of the property (or on the market premium and/or the market rent in the case of a new lease).

Previously, duty in such cases was charged at a fixed rate of 50p on a sale and £2 on a lease.

Agreements to surrender leases

243.—(1) Where, in pursuance of any agreement, any lease is surrendered (or, in Scotland, renounced) at any time otherwise than by deed, the agreement shall be treated for the purposes of any duty chargeable under the Stamp Act 1891 as if it were a deed executed at that time effecting the surrender (or, as the case may be, renunciation).

(2) This section shall apply to any agreement made after 7th December 1993.

GENERAL NOTE

This section is directed against an avoidance device under which a valuable lease is created out of a freehold interest and is then surrendered to a third party without a deed of surrender in order to save duty on the sale to the third party of the freehold.

The section provides that where, following an agreement, a lease is surrendered otherwise than by deed, for stamp duty purposes the agreement will be treated as a deed effecting the surrender.

Production of documents on transfer of land in Northern Ireland

244.—(1) Subject to section 245 below, on the occasion of—

(a) any transfer on sale of any freehold interest in land in Northern Ireland, or

(b) the grant, or any transfer on sale, of any lease of such land,

the transferee, lessee or proposed lessee shall produce to the Commissioners the instrument by means of which the transfer is effected or the lease granted or agreed to be granted, as the case may be.

(2) Any transferee, lessee or proposed lessee required to produce any instrument under subsection (1) above shall produce with it a document (signed by him or by some person on his behalf and showing his address) giving such particulars as may be prescribed.

(3) Any person who, within thirty days—

(a) after the execution of an instrument which he is required under subsection (1) above to produce, or

(b) in the case of such an instrument executed at a place outside Northern Ireland, after it is first received in Northern Ireland,

fails to comply with that subsection or subsection (2) above shall be liable on summary conviction to a fine not exceeding level 1 on the standard scale.

(4) Where any agreement for any lease of land in Northern Ireland is produced to the Commissioners together with a document (signed as mentioned in subsection (2) above) giving such particulars as may be prescribed—

(a) it shall not be necessary to produce to them the instrument granting the lease, or any further such document as is referred to in that subsection, unless that instrument is inconsistent with the agreement, but

(b) the Commissioners shall, if any such instrument is produced to them and application is made for that purpose, denote on the instrument that it has been produced to them.

(5) Notwithstanding anything in section 12 of the Stamp Act 1891, no instrument required by this section to be produced to the Commissioners shall be deemed, for the purposes of section 14 of that Act, to be duly stamped unless it is stamped with a stamp denoting that the instrument has been so produced.

GENERAL NOTE

This section, together with s.245, supersedes the present rules under which documents for land transfers and leases in Northern Ireland are required to be produced to the Stamp Office. In future, a Particulars Delivered form, summarising details of the transaction to be prescribed by regulation, will have to be produced to the Stamp Office along with the conveyancing document.

Production of documents: supplementary

245.—(1) Section 244 above shall not apply to any instrument (an "exempt instrument") falling within any prescribed class; but regulations may, in respect of exempt instruments or such descriptions of exempt instruments as may be prescribed, require such a document as is mentioned in subsection (2) of that section to be furnished in accordance with the regulations to the Commissioner of Valuation for Northern Ireland.

(2) The Information contained in any document produced to the Commissioners under section 244(2) above shall be available for use by the Commissioner of Valuation for Northern Ireland.

(3) Any person who fails to comply with any requirement imposed by virtue of subsection (1) above shall be liable on summary conviction to a fine not exceeding level 3 on the standard scale.

(4) Section 244 above shall also not apply to any instrument which relates solely to—

(a) incorporeal hereditaments or to a grave or right of burial, or

(b) land subject to land purchase annuities which are registered in the Land Registry in Northern Ireland.

(5) In this section and section 244 above—

"lease"—

(a) includes an underlease or other tenancy and an agreement for a lease, underlease or tenancy, but

(b) does not include a mortgage, charge or lien on any property for securing money or money's worth,

and "lessee" and "grant" shall be construed accordingly,

"prescribed" means prescribed by regulations, and

"regulations" means regulations made by the Commissioners under this section.

(6) The power to make regulations under this section shall be exercisable by statutory instrument which shall be subject to annulment in pursuance of a resolution of the House of Commons.

(7) Regulations under this section may make different provision for different cases.

(8) This section and section 244 above shall come into force on such day as the Treasury may by order made by statutory instrument appoint.

GENERAL NOTE
Documents recording transactions below the stamp duty threshold will be enabled to bypass the Stamp Office and go direct to the appropriate registrar.
Similar arrangements to ss.244 and 245 already exist for England, Wales and Scotland.

PART VII

INHERITANCE TAX

Rate bands: no indexation in 1994

246. The Table substituted by section 72(1) of the Finance (No. 2) Act 1992 shall apply to chargeable transfers made in the year beginning 6th April 1994, and accordingly section 8(1) of the Inheritance Tax Act 1984 (indexation of rate bands) shall not apply to such transfers.

GENERAL NOTE
The threshold for inheritance tax remains at £150,000.

Business and agricultural relief

247.—(1) In section 113B of the Inheritance Tax Act 1984 (replacement business property)—
  (a) in subsections (2)(a) and (5)(b), for "twelve months" substitute, in each case, "the allowed period"; and
  (b) in subsection (8), at the end add "and "allowed period" means the period of three years or such longer period as the Board may allow".
  (2) In section 124B of the Act of 1984 replacement agricultural property)—
  (a) in subsections (2)(a) and (5)(b), for "twelve months" substitute, in each case, "the allowed period"; and
  (b) in subsection (8), at the end add "and "allowed period" means the period of three years or such longer period as the Board may allow".
  (3) This section applies in relation to transfers of value made, and other events occurring, on or after 30th November 1993.

GENERAL NOTE
The period within which a donee, who receives and then sells property eligible for business or agricultural property relief, must acquire a replacement property to avoid losing the relief is extended from 12 months to three years, or such longer period as the Revenue may allow.

Corporate Lloyd's underwriters

248.—(1) No property forming part of a premiums trust fund or ancillary trust fund of a corporate member shall be relevant property for the purposes of Chapter III of Part III of the Inheritance Tax Act 1984 (settlements without interests in possession).
  (2) In this section "ancillary trust fund", "corporate member" and "premiums trust fund" have the same meanings as in Chapter V of Part IV of this Act (Lloyd's underwriters: corporations etc.).

GENERAL NOTE
This section is an adjunct to the provisions in ss.219 and 230, *supra*, relating to the taxation of corporate members of Lloyd's. It ensures that the assets forming part of a corporate member's

premiums trust fund or ancillary trust fund are excluded from the definition of relevant property for the purposes of inheritance tax provisions relating to settlements without interests in possession.

PART VIII

MISCELLANEOUS AND GENERAL

Companies treated as non-resident

Certain companies treated as non-resident

249.—(1) A company which—
(a) would (apart from this section) be regarded as resident in the United Kingdom for the purposes of the Taxes Acts, and
(b) is regarded for the purposes of any double taxation relief arrangements as resident in a territory outside the United Kingdom and not resident in the United Kingdom,
shall be treated for the purposes of the Taxes Acts as resident outside the United Kingdom and not resident in the Untied Kingdom.

(2) For the purpose of deciding whether the company is regarded as mentioned in subsection (1)(b) above it shall be assumed that—
(a) the company has made a claim for relief under the arrangements, and
(b) in consequence of the claim it falls to be decided whether the company is to be regarded as mentioned in subsection (1)(b) above.

(3) This section shall apply whether the company would otherwise be regarded as resident in the United Kingdom for the purposes of the Taxes Acts by virtue of section 66(1) of the Finance Act 1988 (company incorporated in UK to be regarded as resident there) or by virtue of some other rule of law.

(4) In this section—
(a) "double taxation relief arrangements" means arrangements having effect by virtue of section 788 of the Taxes Act 1988;
(b) "the Taxes Acts" has the same meaning as in the Taxes Management Act 1970.

(5) This section shall be deemed to have come into force on 30th November 1993.

GENERAL NOTE
    This section amends the rules on company residence for certain dual-resident companies, *i.e.* companies which are regarded as resident for tax purposes by both the U.K. and another country. It provides that where a dual-resident company is regarded as not resident in the U.K. for the purposes of the double taxation agreement between the two countries, it will be treated as not resident for all U.K. tax purposes from November 30, 1993.

Companies treated as non-resident: supplementary

250.—(1) Sections 130(1) to (6) and 131(1) to (5) of the Finance Act 1988 (securing payment of outstanding tax) shall not apply where the company concerned ceases to be resident in the United Kingdom on 30th November 1993 solely by virtue of the coming into force of section 249 above.

(2) References in section 179 of the Taxation of Chargeable Gains Act 1992 to a company ceasing to be a member of a group of companies do not apply to cases where a company ceases to be a member of a group by virtue of that company, or another company, ceasing to be resident in the United Kingdom on 30th November 1993 solely by virtue of the coming into force of section 249 above.

(3) Subsection (4) below applies where—
(a) a company ceases to be resident in the United Kingdom on 30th November 1993 solely by virtue of the coming into force of section 249 above, and

(b) by virtue of section 185(2) of the Taxation of Chargeable Gains Act 1992 it is deemed to have disposed of assets immediately before the time it so ceases.

(4) In such a case—

(a) if the company makes an actual disposal of the assets on or before the day when (apart from this subsection) corporation tax is due and payable in respect of the deemed disposal, the tax shall be due and payable on that day;

(b) in any other case the tax shall be due and payable on the day the company makes an actual disposal of the assets or on 30th November 1999 (whichever falls first).

(5) Where subsection (4) above applies, for the purposes of section 87A of the Taxes Management Act 1970 (interest on overdue corporation tax) the tax shall be treated as becoming due and payable on the relevant day in accordance with section 10 of the Taxes Act 1988; and the relevant day is the day on which the tax is due and payable by virtue of subsection (4) above.

(6) If the company makes an actual disposal of part of the assets subsections (4) and (5) above shall be applied separately as regards the different parts and the tax shall be apportioned (and carry interest) accordingly.

GENERAL NOTE
Certain provisions which would otherwise apply when a dual-resident company ceased to be resident in the U.K. as a result of s.249 are relaxed. The requirement to notify the Revenue and to discharge outstanding tax liabilities is removed. The capital gains liability where a company ceases to be a member of a group as a result of the change will not arise. The capital gains charge on the deemed disposal of assets is deferred until the asset is actually disposed of, but not beyond November 30, 1999.

Companies treated as non-resident: repeals

251.—(1) For the purposes of this section—

(a) the relevant date is 30th November 1993;

(b) the 1992 Act is the Taxation of Chargeable Gains Act 1992.

(2) In section 468F of the Taxes Act 1988 the following shall be omitted—

(a) in subsection (1)(c) the words "and not a dual resident";

(b) in subsection (8) the definition of "dual resident";

and this subsection shall have effect where the date of payment is the relevant date or later.

(3) In sections 742(8) and 745(4) of the Taxes Act 1988 the words ", or regarded for the purposes of any double taxation arrangements having effect by virtue of section 788 as resident in a territory outside the United Kingdom," shall be omitted; and—

(a) subject to paragraph (b) below, the omissions shall apply in relation to transfers of assets and associated operations on or after the relevant date;

(b) in so far as the omission in subsection (4) of section 745 relates to subsections (3)(b) and (5) of that section, it shall be deemed to have come into force on the relevant date.

(4) Sections 749(4A) and 751(2)(bb) of the Taxes Act 1988 shall be omitted; and this subsection shall be deemed to have come into force on the relevant date.

(5) Section 139(3) of the 1992 Act shall be omitted; and this subsection shall have effect in relation to acquisitions on or after the relevant date.

(6) Section 160 of the 1992 Act shall be omitted; and this subsection shall have effect where the disposal of the old assets (or of the interest in them) is made on or after the relevant date or the acquisition of the new assets is made (or the acquisition of the interest in them is made or the unconditional contract for their acquisition is entered into) on or after the relevant date.

(7) The following provisions shall be omitted—

(a) in section 166(2) of the 1992 Act the words "or a company" and the words "or company";

(b) in section 171(2) of that Act, paragraph (e) and the word "or" immediately preceding it;

(c) section 172(3)(a) of that Act;

and this subsection shall have effect in relation to disposals on or after the relevant date.

(8) In section 175(2) of the 1992 Act the words from "or a company which" to the end of paragraph (b) shall be omitted; and this subsection shall have effect where the disposal of the old assets (or of the interest in them) or the acquisition of the new assets (or of the interest in them) is made on or after the relevant date.

(9) Section 186 of the 1992 Act shall be omitted together with the following in section 187—

(a) in subsection (1)(a) the words "or 186";

(b) in subsection (6) the words "or, as the case may be, section 186(2)," and the words "or, as the case may be, section 186(1)";

and this subsection shall have effect where the company concerned becomes on or after the relevant date a company which falls to be regarded as mentioned in section 186(1).

(10) Section 188 of the 1992 Act shall be omitted; and this subsection shall be deemed to have come into force on the relevant date.

(11) In section 211(3) of the 1992 Act the words "(and would not be a gain on which, under any double taxation relief arrangements, it would not be liable to tax)" shall be omitted; and this subsection shall have effect where the transfer is made on or after the relevant date.

(12) Section 61(3) of the Finance Act 1993 shall be omitted; and this subsection shall be deemed to have come into force on the relevant date.

GENERAL NOTE

This section repeals the special rules to prevent avoidance of tax by companies which are regarded as resident for U.K. tax purposes but as not resident for the purposes of a double taxation agreement. These rules are no longer needed since the companies would be treated as non-resident for all tax purposes under s.249.

The rules related to the following matters: (i) authorised unit trusts (subs. (2)); (ii) transfer of assets abroad (subs. (3)); (iii) controlled foreign companies (subs. (4)); (iv) reconstruction or amalgamation involving transfer of business (subs. (5)); (v) roll-over relief (subs. (6)); (vi) gifts to non-residents (subs. (7)(a)); (vii) transfers within groups (subs. (7)(b) and (c) and (8)); (viii) deemed disposal of assets on ceasing to be liable to U.K. taxation (subs. (9)); (ix) deemed disposal of certain assets (subs. (10)); (x) transfers of long-term insurance business (subs. (11)); (xi) interest, etc., on debts between associated companies (subs. (12)).

Privatisations

Railways

252.—(1) Schedule 24 to this Act (which makes provision in connection with transfers and other disposals under or by virtue of the Railways Act 1993) shall have effect.

(2) Paragraphs 4(1) and 17 of that Schedule, and this section so far as relating to those provisions, shall be taken to have come into force on 5th November 1993 (the date on which the Railways Act 1993 was passed).

(3) Subject to subsection (2) above, this section and that Schedule shall be taken to have come into force on 11th January 1994.

GENERAL NOTE

This section introduces Sched. 24, which deals with the tax treatment of the reorganisation of British Rail under the provisions of the Railways Act 1993 (c. 43). The main effect of the provisions is to prevent taxable profits or allowable losses arising as a consequence of the reorganisation and to enable certain successor companies to inherit British Rail's tax position in relation to the activities and assets transferred. The transfers are to be effected by way of "relevant transfers" provided for in statutory restructuring schemes (see the Railways Act 1993 (c. 43), Pt. II). The schedule also includes provisions to maintain the present tax treatment of travel benefits for employees of British Rail before January 11, 1994, who earn less than £8,500 a year.

Northern Ireland Airports Limited

253. Schedule 25 to this Act (which makes provision in connection with the transfer of the undertaking of Northern Ireland Airports Limited) shall have effect.

GENERAL NOTE
   This section introduces Sched. 25, which is designed to facilitate the privatisation of Northern Ireland Airports Limited.

Management

Practice and procedure in connection with appeals

254.—(1) Section 56B of the Taxes Management Act 1970 (regulations about practice and procedure in connection with appeals) shall be amended as follows.
   (2) In subsection (2)(b) (documents to be made available for inspection by Commissioners or by officers of the Board) for "the Commissioners or by officers of the Board" there shall be substituted "specified persons".
   (3) The following subsection shall be inserted after subsection (2)—
      "(2A) In subsection (2)(b) above "specified persons" means such of the following as may be specified in the regulations—
      (a) the Commissioners;
      (b) any party to the appeal;
      (c) officers of the Board."

GENERAL NOTE
   The regulations which the Lord Chancellor is to make under the TMA 1970 (c. 9), s.56B may provide for the Commissioners to require the provision of information and production of documents by the Revenue as well as by the taxpayer. It is intended to extend the right initially to the Special Commissioners and to the General Commissioners later, after the assessment procedure is simplified.

Calling for documents of taxpayers and others

255.—(1) Section 20 of the Taxes Management Act 1970 (power to call for documents) shall be amended as follows.
   (2) The following subsections shall be inserted after subsection (7A)—
      "(7AB) A Commissioner who has given his consent under subsection (7) above shall neither take part in, nor be present at, any proceedings on, or related to, any appeal brought—
      (a) in the case of a notice under subsection (1) above, by the person to whom the notice applies, or
      (b) in the case of a notice under subsection (3) above, by the taxpayer concerned,
      if the Commissioner has reason to believe that any of the required information is likely to be adduced in evidence in those proceedings.
      (7AC) In subsection (7AB) above "required information" means any document or particulars which were the subject of the proposed notice with respect to which the Commissioner gave his consent."
   (3) The following subsections shall be inserted after subsection (8D)—
      "(8E) An inspector who gives a notice under subsection (1) or (3) above shall also give to—
      (a) the person to whom the notice applies (in the case of a notice under subsection (1) above), or

(b) the taxpayer concerned (in the case of a notice under subsection (3) above),

a written summary of his reasons for applying for consent to the giving of the notice.

(8F) Subsection (8E) above does not apply, in the case of a notice under subsection (3) above, if by virtue of section 20B(1B) a copy of that notice need not be given to the taxpayer.

(8G) Subsection (8E) above does not require the disclosure of any information—

(a) which would, or might, identify any person who has provided the inspector with any information which he took into account in deciding whether to apply for consent; or

(b) if the Commissioner giving the required consent has given a direction that that information is not to be subject to the obligation imposed by that subsection.

(8H) A General or Special Commissioner shall not give a direction under subsection (8G) above unless he is satisfied that the inspector has reasonable grounds for believing that disclosure of the information in question would prejudice the assessment or collection of tax."

GENERAL NOTE

This section amends the TMA 1970 (c. 9), s.20, which covers the Revenue's general power to obtain information from taxpayers and third parties. It provides new safeguards for taxpayers who are subject to information notices.

The new subss. (7AB) and (7AC) debar a Commissioner who has consented to the issue of a s.20 notice from participating in further proceedings where the required information is likely to be adduced.

The new subss. (8E)–(8H) require an inspector issuing a s.20 notice to provide the taxpayer with a written summary of his reasons for the application for consent, unless the Commissioner has agreed that the taxpayer need not be notified of the issue of a notice to a third party, because there are reasonable grounds for suspecting fraud. The requirement does not apply where the disclosure might identify an informer or where the Commissioner so directs. However, the Commissioner may only give such a direction where he is satisfied that the inspector has reasonable grounds for believing that disclosure of the information in question would prejudice the assessment or collection of tax. The words "or assist in the evasion or avoidance of tax" at the end of new subs. (8H) were withdrawn by the Government at Report Stage after widespread concern was expressed in the Committee at their breadth.

Further proposed amendments to s.20A, contained in cl. 241 of the Finance Bill, which would have considerably widened the Revenue's power to call for the papers of a tax accountant, were withdrawn by the Government for further consultation.

Assigned matters

Minor corrections

256.—(1) The provisions mentioned in subsection (2) below (which enable revenue traders and taxable persons to be required to keep records) shall be amended in accordance with subsections (3) and (4) below (which correct minor errors in those provisions so far as they relate to the admissibility in evidence of the recorded information).

(2) The provisions are—

(a) in the Customs and Excise Management Act 1979, section 118A; and

(b) in Schedule 7 to the Value Added Tax Act 1983, paragraph 7.

(3) In subsection (6) and sub-paragraph (5) of those provisions—

(a) in paragraph (c) for the words "sections 13 and 14 of the Law Reform (Miscellaneous Provisions) (Scotland) Act 1968" there shall be substituted "sections 5 and 6 of the Civil Evidence (Scotland) Act 1988"; and

(b) in paragraph (d), for the words "except in accordance with the said sections 13 and 14" to the end there shall be substituted "except in accordance with Schedule 3 to the Prisoners and Criminal Proceedings (Scotland) Act 1993".

(4) Subsection (7) and sub-paragraph (6) of those provisions shall be omitted.

GENERAL NOTE
   This section, inserted at Report Stage, corrects errors not only in the Finance Bill as originally drafted but in the legislation as it stood. References to the obsolete Law Reform (Miscellaneous Provisions) (Scotland) Act 1968 (c. 70) are replaced by references to the Civil Evidence (Scotland) Act 1988 (c. 32) and the Prisoners and Criminal Proceedings (Scotland) Act 1993 (c. 9). The matters covered relate to the admissibility of documents as evidence.

General

Interpretation and construction

257.—(1) In this Act "the Taxes Act 1988" means the Income and Corporation Taxes Act 1988.

(2) Part V of this Act shall be construed as one with Part I of the Oil Taxation Act 1975, and in Part V of that Act is referred to as "the principal Act".

(3) Part VI of this Act shall be construed as one with the Stamp Act 1891.

Repeals

258. The enactments specified in Schedule 26 to this Act (which include provisions which are already spent) are hereby repealed to the extent specified in the third column of that Schedule, but subject to any provision of that Schedule.

Short title

259. This Act may be cited as the Finance Act 1994.

SCHEDULES

Section 1   SCHEDULE 1

TABLE OF RATES OF DUTY ON WINE AND MADE-WINE

PART I

WINE OR MADE-WINE OF A STRENGTH NOT EXCEEDING 22 PER CENT.

Description of wine or made-wine	Rates of duty per hectolitre
	£
Wine or made-wine of a strength not exceeding 2 per cent.	13.48
Wine or made-wine of a strength exceeding 2 per cent. but not exceeding 3 per cent.	22.46
Wine or made-wine of a strength exceeding 3 per cent. but not exceeding 4 per cent.	31.45
Wine or made-wine of a strength exceeding 4 per cent. but not exceeding 5 per cent.	40.44
Wine or made-wine of a strength exceeding 5 per cent. but not exceeding 5.5 per cent.	49.42
Wine or made-wine of a strength exceeding 5.5 per cent. but not exceeding 15 per cent. and not being sparkling	134.77
Sparkling wine or sparkling made-wine of a strength exceeding 5.5 per cent. but not exceeding 15 per cent.	222.55
Wine or made-wine of a strength exceeding 15 per cent. but not exceeding 22 per cent.	207.33

Part II

Wine or made-wine of a strength exceeding 22 per cent.

Description of wine or made-wine	Rates of duty per litre of alcohol in the wine or made-wine
	£
Wine or made-wine of a strength exceeding 22 per cent.	19.81

General Note

The rate of duty on wine and made-wine is increased by 1.9 per cent. for strengths up to 15 per cent. For strengths between 15 and 22 per cent. the rate is reduced by 5.9 per cent.

The duty on strengths over 22 per cent. remains unchanged.

Section 5   SCHEDULE 2

Vehicles Excise Duty: Miscellaneous Provisions

1.—(1) Section 1 of the Vehicles (Excise) Act 1971 (charge of duty) shall be amended as follows.

(2) In subsection (3) (charge in respect of keeping a vehicle on a road), for the words "be deemed" onwards there shall be substituted "be chargeable—

(a) where one or more vehicle licences have previously been issued under this Act for the use of the vehicle, by reference to the rate currently applicable to a vehicle of the same description as that of the vehicle on the occasion of the issue of that licence (or the last of those licences), and

(b) otherwise, by reference to whichever of the rates specified in Schedule 5 to this Act is applicable to a vehicle constructed at the same time as the vehicle."

(3) Subsection (4) (which provides that section 1 does not make lawful the keeping of a vehicle which is unlawful apart from that section) shall be omitted.

2. In section 3(3) of that Act (collection of duty), the words "the restoration of any forfeiture and" shall be omitted.

3. In section 4(1)(b) of that Act (exemption for fire brigade vehicles), for "local authority" there shall be substituted "fire authority".

4. In section 6(3) of that Act (recovery of duty by Secretary of State where VAT becomes chargeable on vehicle supplied for export), for the words from "there shall be recoverable" to the end of paragraph (b) there shall be substituted "duty shall be payable—

(a) by the person by whom the vehicle was acquired from its manufacturer in respect of the whole period since the registration of the vehicle; or

(b) by any other person who is for the time being the keeper of the vehicle in respect of the period since the vehicle was first kept by that other person,".

5. In section 7(2) of that Act (exemption for vehicles of disabled persons)—

(a) after "physical" there shall be inserted "or mental", and

(b) in paragraph (c), after "subsection" there shall be inserted "or by reason of the continued operation of the provisions mentioned in section 12(1) of the Finance (No. 2) Act 1992".

6. In section 12(6) of that Act (regulations providing for issue of new licences), for "may be lost or destroyed" there shall be substituted "are or may be lost, stolen, destroyed or damaged".

7. In section 16(4) of that Act (trade licences), the words following paragraph (b) shall be omitted.

8.—(1) Section 18 of that Act (alteration of vehicle or of its use) shall be amended as follows.

(2) Subsections (8) and (9) (power to exempt farmers' goods vehicles from liability to pay duty at higher rate) shall be omitted.

(3) In subsection (10) (Northern Ireland), for the words from "as if" to "substituted" there shall be substituted "as if after subsection (7) there were inserted".

9. Section 21 of that Act (hackney carriage signs) shall be omitted.

10. In section 22 of that Act (failure to fix mark etc.), in the version of paragraph (b) of the proviso to subsection (1) which is set out in subsection (4), for "no opportunity" there shall be substituted "no reasonable opportunity".

11.—(1) Section 23 of that Act as set out in paragraph 20 of Part I of Schedule 7 to that Act (registration regulations) shall be amended as follows.

(2) In subsection (1)—

(a) in paragraph (b) (particulars of register), for "the prescribed fee" there shall be substituted "a fee of such amount as appears to the Secretary of State reasonable in the circumstances of the case", and

(b) in paragraph (e) (registration documents), for "may be lost or destroyed" there shall be substituted "are or may be lost, stolen, destroyed or damaged".

(3) In subsection (2)(c) (replacement plates), for the words "such plates" onwards there shall be substituted "trade plates which are or may be lost, stolen, destroyed or damaged".

(4) The following subsection shall be inserted after subsection (4)—

"(5) Regulations under subsection (3) above which require a person to furnish information relating to vehicles exempted from duty by reason of the continued operation of the provisions mentioned in section 12(1) of the Finance (No. 2) Act 1992 may require him to furnish in addition such evidence of the facts giving rise to the exemption as is prescribed by the regulations."

12. In section 25(1) of that Act (review of Secretary of State's decisions relating to motor traders etc.)—

(a) in paragraph (c), for "motor trader or vehicle tester within the meaning of section 16 of this Act" there shall be substituted "person entitled to make one", and

(b) for "dealer, trader, tester or other person" there shall be substituted "person".

13.—(1) Section 26A of that Act (dishonoured cheques) shall be amended as follows.

(2) In subsection (2)(b)(iv), for the words "a new" onwards there shall be substituted "there first had effect a new licence for the vehicle specified in the application for the licence or (in the case of a trade licence) a new trade licence to be used for the same description of vehicles."

(3) In subsection (3), for the words "period, was" onwards there shall be substituted "period—

(a) in the case of a vehicle licence, was applicable to a vehicle of the description specified in the application, and

(b) in the case of a trade licence, was applicable to a vehicle falling within paragraph 2 of Part II of Schedule 5 to this Act or, if the licence was to be used only for vehicles to which Schedule 1 to this Act applies, to a vehicle falling within paragraph 3 of Part II of that Schedule."

(4) In subsection (4), after "section in the case of" there shall be inserted "a vehicle licence for".

14. In section 28(1) of that Act (legal proceedings in England and Wales and Northern Ireland), for ", 18(4) or 26(1) or (2) there shall be substituted "or 18(4)".

15. In section 33 of that Act (burden of proof), after "16(7)" there shall be inserted ", 18(4)".

16. Section 36 of that Act (fractions of a new penny) shall be omitted.

17.—(1) Section 37 of that Act (regulations) shall be amended as follows.

(2) In subsection (1) (matters which may be dealt with in regulations)—

(a) in paragraph (a), after "provision for different" there shall be inserted "cases or", and

(b) in paragraph (c), after "incidental" there shall be inserted ", consequential".

(3) In subsection (2) (fees), for "23(c)" there shall be substituted "23(2)(c)".

18.—(1) No order shall be made under section 39(2) of that Act (transitional modifications in Part I of Schedule 7 to that Act to cease to have effect on a day appointed by order) in relation to any of the provisions of that Part of that Schedule which are specified in sub-paragraph (2) below.

(2) The provisions of Part I of Schedule 7 which are referred to in sub-paragraph (1) above are paragraphs 1 to 9, 11, 13, 16, 17, 17A, 20 and 24 and, so far as it relates to section 26(1) of that Act, paragraph 23.

19.—(1) Schedule 4 to that Act (annual rates of duty on goods vehicles) shall be amended as follows.

(2) In paragraph 1(1) (basic rate of duty), for "paragraphs 5 and" there shall be substituted "paragraph" and the following paragraph shall be inserted after paragraph (a)—

"(aa) which has a plated gross weight or plated train weight exceeding 7,500 kilograms but has such a weight only by virtue of paragraph 9(2A)(c) below and is not a vehicle of a prescribed class; or".

(3) Paragraph 5 (special types) shall be omitted.

(4) In paragraph 11 (exempted vehicles), the following sub-paragraph shall be inserted after sub-paragraph (c)—

"(cc) a haulage vehicle within the meaning of that Schedule;".

(5) In paragraphs 14, 14A and 14B (no extra charge to duty where tractor unit used with semi-trailer with fewer axles than envisaged by licence), for "the tractor unit shall, when so used, be taken to be licensed in accordance with the requirements of this Act" there shall be substituted "duty at a higher rate shall not become chargeable under section 18 of this Act".

(6) In paragraph 15(1), in the definition of "goods vehicle", the words "(including a tricycle as defined in Schedule 1 to this Act and weighing more than 425 kilograms unladen)" shall be omitted.

20.—(1) Part I of Schedule 7 to that Act (transitional modifications) shall be amended as follows.

(2) Paragraphs 1(c), 3(b), 18, 19, 21 and 22 and, so far as it relates to section 26(2) of that Act, paragraph 23 shall be omitted.

(3) In paragraph 12, for "(4) and (5)" there shall be substituted "(4) to (5)" and the following subsections shall be substituted for the subsections set out in that paragraph—

"(4) A trade licence may be taken out—

(a) for one calendar year;

(b) for a period of six months beginning with the first day of January or of July; or

(c) where subsection (4A) below applies, for a period of seven, eight, nine, ten or eleven months beginning with the first day of any month other than January or July.

(4A) This subsection applies where the person taking out the licence—

(a) is not a motor trader or vehicle tester (having satisfied the Secretary of State as mentioned in subsection (1A) above); or

(b) does not hold any existing trade licence.

(5) The rate of duty applicable to a trade licence—

(a) if the licence is taken out for a calendar year, shall be—

(i) the annual rate currently applicable to a vehicle falling within paragraph 3 of Part II of Schedule 1 to this Act if the licence is to be used only for vehicles to which that Schedule 1 applies; and

(ii) otherwise, the annual rate currently applicable to a vehicle falling within paragraph 2 of Part II of Schedule 5 to this Act;

(b) if the licence is taken out for a period of six months, shall be fifty-five per cent. of the rate applicable to the corresponding trade licence taken out for a calendar year; and

(c) if the licence is taken out for a period of seven, eight, nine, ten or eleven months, shall be the aggregate of—

(i) fifty-five per cent. of the rate applicable to the corresponding trade licence taken out for a calendar year, and

(ii) one-sixth of the amount arrived at under sub-paragraph (i) above in respect of each month in the period in excess of six.

(5A) In determining a rate of duty under subsection (5)(b) or (c) any fraction of five pence—

(a) if it exceeds two and a half pence, shall be treated as five pence; and

(c) otherwise, shall be disregarded."

21.—(1) Section 11 of the Finance Act 1976 (information about goods vehicles and trailers) shall be amended as follows.

(2) In subsection (2), the following paragraph shall be substituted for paragraph (b) (details of plated weights etc.)—

"(b) the vehicle's plated gross weight or plated train weight, or (in Northern Ireland) relevant maximum weight or relevant maximum train weight, within the meaning of Schedule 4 to the said Act of 1971;".

(3) In paragraph (c) of that subsection (details of laden weight)—

(a) for "such plated weights" there shall be substituted "such weight", and

(b) the words "or, if it falls" onwards shall be omitted.

(4) In subsection (3) (trailers), for the words from the beginning to "Act)" there shall be substituted "In section 23(3) of the said Act of 1971 as set out in paragraph 20 of Part I of Schedule 7 to that Act".

22. In section 12(2)(a) of that Act (inspection of vehicles to which a registration mark is requested to be assigned), the words "either" and ", or elsewhere" shall be omitted.

23. In section 8(4) of the Finance Act 1978 (offences in relation to exempt licences), after "above" there shall be inserted "or any of the provisions mentioned in section 12(1) of the Finance (No. 2) Act 1992".

24. In Article 34 of the Road Traffic (Northern Ireland) Order 1981 (obligatory vehicle test certificates), the following paragraph shall be substituted for paragraph (3)—

"(3) For the purposes of paragraph (2)(b) there shall be disregarded—

(a) the use of a vehicle before it is sold or supplied by retail; and
(b) the use of a vehicle to which a motor dealer has assigned a mark under section 20 of the Vehicles (Excise) Act 1971 before it is registered by the Secretary of State under section 19(1)(b) of that Act."

25. In section 47 of the Road Traffic Act 1988 (obligatory test certificates), the following subsection shall be substituted for subsection (4)—
    "(4) For the purposes of subsection (2)(b) above there shall be disregarded—
    (a) the use of a vehicle before it is sold or supplied by retail, and
    (b) the use of a vehicle to which a motor dealer has assigned a mark under section 20 of the Vehicles (Excise) Act 1971 before it is registered by the Secretary of State under section 19(1)(b) of that Act."

26.—(1) Section 11 of the Finance Act 1989 (power to make provision for retention of registration marks) shall be amended as follows.
    (2) In subsection (2), the following paragraphs shall be inserted after paragraph (i)—
    "(ia) for allowing a person to be nominated when an application for the grant of a right of retention is made or to be nominated at a later time;
    (ib) for allowing a different person to be nominated in place of a person already nominated;
    (ic) for the manner in which a nomination is to be made and for the payment of a specified fee where a nomination is made in specified circumstances;".
    (3) The following subsection shall be inserted after subsection (3)—
    "(3ZA) An extension or nomination shall be exempt from a fee payable by virtue of subsection (2)(f) or (ic) above if the Secretary of State considers it appropriate in the circumstances of the case."

27.—(1) Section 12 of that Act (provision for sale of registration marks) shall be amended as follows.
    (2) In subsection (3), the following paragraphs shall be inserted after paragraph (i)—
    "(ia) for allowing a person to be nominated when a relevant right is acquired or to be nominated at a later time;
    (ib) for allowing a different person to be nominated in place of a person already nominated;
    (ic) for the manner in which a nomination is to be made and for the payment of a specified fee where a nomination is made in specified circumstances;".
    (3) The following subsection shall be inserted after subsection (5)—
    "(5A) An extension or nomination shall be exempt from a fee payable by virtue of subsection (3)(f) or (ic) above if the Secretary of State considers it appropriate in the circumstances of the case."

28. Section 128 of the Finance Act 1990 (power to provide for repayment of fees and charges) shall apply to any power by virtue of this Schedule to make provision under section 11 or 12 of the Finance Act 1989 for the payment of any fee as it applies to powers conferred before the Finance Act 1990 was passed.

29. Paragraphs 20(2), 24 and 25 shall come into force on 1st June 1994.

GENERAL NOTE

The amendments made by this Schedule fall into two categories: (1) pre-consolidation amendments including the repeal of obsolete provisions; (2) other amendments which correct absurdities or anomalies in the legislation, *e.g.* some provisions apply for no discernible reason to vehicle licences but not to trade licences.

None of the amendments make any substantial change to the law.

Section 6   SCHEDULE 3

AMENDMENTS ABOUT GAMING MACHINE LICENCE DUTY

Licences for periods beginning on or after 1st May 1994

1.—(1) The Betting and Gaming Duties Act 1981 shall be amended as follows.
(2) For section 21(3) (period of gaming machine licences) there is substituted—

"(3) A gaming machine licence may be granted for a period of a month, or of any number of months not exceeding twelve, beginning on any day of any month".

(3) Section 22(5) (rates of duty) is omitted.

(4) For section 23 (amount of duty) there is substituted—

"Amount of duty

23.—(1) The amount of duty payable on a gaming machine licence shall be—

  (a) the appropriate amount for the machine which it authorises, or

  (b) if it authorises two or more machines, the aggregate of the appropriate amounts for each of those machines.

(2) The appropriate amount for each machine shall be determined in accordance with the following Table by reference to—

  (a) the period for which the licence is granted, and

  (b) whether the machine falls within column 2 or column 3 of the Table,

and references in this Part to a rate of gaming machine licence duty are references to the rate in column 2 or the rate in column 3.

TABLE

(1) Period (in months) for which licence granted	(2) Small prize or five-penny machines	(3) Other machines
	£	£
1	50	125
2	90	230
3	130	335
4	170	435
5	210	540
6	245	630
7	290	735
8	330	840
9	365	930
10	405	1,035
11	425	1,090
12	450	1,150"

(5) In section 24 (restrictions on number of licences)—

  (a) subsection (2),

  (b) in subsections (3) and (4), "such", and

  (c) in subsection (6)(a), the words from "or" at the end of sub-paragraph (i) to "greater", are omitted.

(6) In section 26 (supplementary provisions), in subsection (4)—

  (a) "section 22(5) or" is omitted, and

  (b) for "those provisions" there is substituted "that provision".

(7) In Part II of Schedule 4 (supplementary provisions) for paragraphs 6 and 7 (applications and duration of licences) there is substituted—

"6. An application for a gaming machine licence shall be made to the Commissioners in such form and manner as they may require.

7. The period for which a gaming machine licence is granted shall begin with the day on which application for the licence is received by the Commissioners or, if a later day is specified for that purpose in the application, with that day; and the licence shall expire at the end of that period."

(8) Paragraphs 9 to 11A of that Schedule (amendment, etc.) shall not apply at any time before 1st May 1994 to any licence in relation to which this paragraph has effect.

(9) This paragraph shall have effect in relation to gaming machine licences granted for any period beginning on or after 1st May 1994.

Special licences

2. No special licence (as defined in section 21(2) of the Betting and Gaming Duties Act 1981) may be granted for any period beginning on or after 1st May 1994.

3.—(1) Accordingly, that Act shall be amended as follows.

(2) In section 21, for the words following "force" in subsection (1) to the end of subsection (2) there is substituted—

"a licence granted under this Part of this Act with respect to the premises.

(2) Such a licence shall be known as a gaming machine licence".

(3) Section 21A (special licences) is omitted.

(4) In section 24—

(a) in subsection (3), the words from, "but" to the end are omitted, and

(b) in subsection (4), the words "or there are special licences in force with respect to those machines" are omitted.

(5) In paragraph 8 of Schedule 4 (transfer of licences), in sub-paragraph (1), for paragraphs (a) and (b) there is substituted "transfer a gaming machine licence in respect of any premises to a successor in title to the interest in those premises of the person to whom the licence was granted".

(6) Paragraph 11(2) of that Schedule is omitted.

(7) In paragraph 12 of that Schedule (display of licence), for "an ordinary licence" there is substituted "a gaming machine licence".

(8) In paragraph 13(1) of that Schedule (labelling etc. of machines), for paragraphs (a) and (b) there is substituted "gaming machines provided on any premises in respect of which a gaming machine licence is in force".

(9) In paragraph 18 of that Schedule (forfeiture), for paragraphs (a) and (b) there is substituted "those machines which are authorised by the gaming machine licence or licences produced to him".

(10) Paragraph 4(2) below shall cease to have effect.

(11) This paragraph shall come into force on 1st May 1995.

GENERAL NOTE

Various changes are made to the Betting and Gaming Duties Act 1981 (c. 63) so far as it relates to the issue of gaming machine licences.

Para. (1)

To assist the tourist trade in seasonal resorts, gaming machine licences may be granted for a period of a month, or of any number of months up to 12, beginning on any day of any month. This replaces the existing system of quarterly, biannual or annual licences.

A new rate structure is introduced covering small prize or five-penny machines (these comprise machines where the value of prizes from a single game cannot exceed £6 and five-penny machines where prizes can exceed £6) and other machines, where the stake exceeds 5p. Small prize five-penny machines are not liable to duty.

The application procedure is simplified.

Paras. (2) and (3)

As a corollary, the facility for issuing special licences, granted in respect of machines rather than premises, is abolished. This was originally introduced by the F.A. 1984 (c. 43), Sched. 3.

Seasonal licences

4.—(1) In Part I of Schedule 4 to that Act (exemptions), for paragraph 4 (and the cross-heading preceding it) there shall be substituted—

"*Seasonal licences*

4.—(1) If at any time during March of any year there has previously been granted a seasonal licence for that year authorising the provision of any number of small-prize machines on any premises and that licence has not been surrendered, it shall be treated for the purposes of this Act as authorising the provision at that time of that number of small-prize machines on the premises.

(2) Where a seasonal licence is granted for any year authorising the provision of any number of small-prize machines on any premises, and the licence is not surrendered, it shall be treated for the purposes of this Act as authorising during October of that year the provision of that number of small-prize machines on the premises.

(3) Subject to sub-paragraph (4) below, in this Schedule "seasonal licence", in relation to any year, means a gaming machine licence expressed to authorise only the provision of small-prize machines on any premises for the period of six months beginning with 1st April in that year.

(4) A licence in respect of any premises is not a seasonal licence in relation to any year if any gaming machine licence has been granted in respect of those premises for any period which includes the whole or any part of the preceding winter period.

(5) If in relation to any year—

(a) a seasonal licence is granted in respect of any premises, and

(b) another gaming machine licence is granted (whether before or after the grant of the seasonal licence or after the surrender of the seasonal licence) in respect of those premises for any period which includes the whole or any part of the following winter period (and does not include the whole or any part of the preceding winter period),

there shall (unless an amount has already become payable under this sub-paragraph in respect of the seasonal licence) be payable on the seasonal licence on the relevant date an additional amount of duty.

(6) The additional amount is the difference between the duty payable (apart from this paragraph) on that licence at the time it was granted and the amount that would have been so payable if the licence had been granted for a period of eight months or, in a case where the seasonal licence has been surrendered before the beginning of September, seven months.

(7) In sub-paragraph (5) above, the "relevant date" means—

(a) the date on which the seasonal licence is granted, or

(b) the date on which the other licence is granted,

whichever is the later.

(8) In this paragraph "winter period" means November to February."

(2) The references in paragraph 4(4) and (5)(b) of that Schedule (as inserted by this paragraph) to a licence in respect of any premises include a reference to any special licence in respect of any machine on those premises.

(3) Sections 21(3) and 23 of that Act (as inserted by this Schedule) shall have effect for the purposes of paragraph 4(6) of that Schedule (as so inserted) in relation to gaming machine licences granted for the period of six months beginning with 1st April 1994.

(4) This paragraph shall have effect in relation to gaming machine licences granted for any period beginning on or after 1st April 1994.

Amendment and surrender of licences

5.—(1) Part II of Schedule 4 to that Act shall be amended as follows.

(2) Paragraphs 9 and 10 (amendment of licences) are omitted.

(3) In paragraph 11 (surrender of licence), for sub-paragraph (1) there is substituted—

"(1) The holder of a gaming machine licence may surrender it to the proper officer at any time.

(1A) On the surrender of the licence the holder shall be entitled to repayment of duty of the following amount.

(1B) That amount is the difference between—

(a) the amount of duty actually paid on the licence, and

(b) the amount (if less) that would have been paid if the period for which the licence was granted had been reduced by the number of complete months in that period which have not expired,

and for the purposes of this paragraph a seasonal licence is to be treated as granted for the period of eight months beginning with 1st March".

(4) Paragraph 11A (reduction of duty in certain cases) is omitted.

(5) Sub-paragraph (3) above shall not apply to special licences; and sections 21(3) and 23 of that Act (as inserted by this Schedule) shall have effect for the purposes of paragraph 11(1B)(b) of that Schedule (as so inserted) in relation to gaming machine licences granted for any period beginning before 1st May 1994.

(6) This paragraph shall come into force on 1st May 1994.

GENERAL NOTE

Para. (4)

Seasonal licences will continue to be issued for the period April 1–September 30 (with an extension, where applicable, to March and October) and will cover only small prize machines.

Anti-avoidance provisions ensure that a seasonal licence cannot be obtained in respect of a machine which has been licensed during the preceding winter period, *i.e.* November to February.

Para. (5)
With the new flexibility on the issue of licences, the provisions for amendment of licences are redundant and are accordingly abolished. Where licences are surrendered, a refund will be made based on the original cost minus the cost for the period of use in complete months.

Section 9   SCHEDULE 4

PENALTIES FOR STATUTORY CONTRAVENTIONS

PART I

CONTRAVENTIONS UNDER THE MANAGEMENT ACT

1. The Management Act shall be amended in accordance with the following provisions of this Part of this Schedule.
2.—(1) In subsection (6) of section 92 (offence of making alteration in or addition to approved warehouse), for the words from "he shall be liable" onwards there shall be substituted "the making of the alteration or addition shall attract a penalty under section 9 of the Finance Act 1994 (civil penalties)."
(2) For subsection (8) of that section (offence of contravening condition or direction given in connection with the approval of a waterhouse) there shall be substituted the following subsection—

"(8) Where any person contravenes or fails to comply with any condition imposed or direction given by the Commissioners under this section, his contravention or failure to comply shall attract a penalty under section 9 of the Finance Act 1994 (civil penalties)."
3. In section 93(6) (offence of failing to comply with any warehousing regulations or with any condition, restriction or requirement imposed under any warehousing regulations), for the words from "he shall be liable" onwards there shall be substituted "his failure to comply shall attract a penalty under section 9 of the Finance Act 1994 (civil penalties)."
4. In section 100J (offence and forfeiture in the case of a contravention of REDS regulations), for the words from "he shall be liable" onwards there shall be substituted "his contravention or failure to comply shall attract a penalty under section 9 of the Finance Act 1994 (civil penalties), and any goods in respect of which any person contravenes any provision of any such regulations, or fails to comply with any such condition or restriction, shall be liable to forfeiture."
5. In section 101(4) (offence of failing to produce licence after being requested to do so)—
(a) for "a reasonable time" there shall be substituted "one month"; and
(b) for the words from "he shall be liable" onwards there shall be substituted "his failure shall attract a penalty under section 9 of the Finance Act 1994 (civil penalties)."
6.—(1) In subsection (2) of section 107 (offence of failing to display notice or comply with directions as to the form and manner of a notice), for the words from "he shall be liable" onwards there shall be substituted "his contravention or failure to comply shall attract a penalty under section 9 of the Finance Act 1994 (civil penalties)."
(2) In subsection (3) of that section (offence of affixing misleading notice), for the words from "he shall be liable" onwards there shall be substituted "his doing so shall attract a penalty under section 9 of the Finance Act 1994 (civil penalties)."
7. In section 108(4) (offence of contravening directions in relation to premises etc. entered under the revenue trade provisions), for the words from "he shall be liable" onwards there shall be substituted "his contravention or failure to comply shall attract a penalty under section 9 of the Finance Act 1994 (civil penalties)."
8.—(1) In subsection (1) of section 111 (using premises or article without having entered them), for the words from "he shall be liable" to the words "and any", in the first place where they occur, there shall be substituted "his use of the premises or article shall attract a penalty under section 9 of the Finance Act 1994 (civil penalties), and any".
(2) Subsection (2) of that section (fraudulent use of entered premises or article) shall cease to have effect.
9. In section 114(2) (offence of using prohibited substance or liquor), for the words from "he shall be liable" onwards there shall be substituted "his use of that substance or liquor in that manner shall attract a penalty under section 9 of the Finance Act 1994 (civil penalties); but section 10 of that Act (exception for cases of reasonable excuse) shall not apply in relation to conduct attracting a penalty by virtue of this subsection."

10.—(1) In subsection (4) of section 115 (offence of tampering etc. with specimen)—

(a) for "any person other than an officer" there shall be substituted "the revenue trader"; and

(b) for the words from "he shall be liable" onwards there shall be substituted "his doing so shall attract a penalty under section 9 of the Finance Act 1994 (civil penalties)."

(2) After that subsection there shall be inserted the following subsection—

"(5) For the purposes of subsection (4) above and without prejudice to section 10(1) of the Finance Act 1994 (exception for cases of reasonable excuse), conduct by an employee of the revenue trader or by any other person entitled to act on the trader's behalf in connection with his trade shall be deemed to be conduct by that trader except in so far as he took all reasonable steps to prevent it."

11. In section 116(3) (offence of failing to pay duty on demand), for the words from "the trader shall" onwards there shall be substituted "the trader's failure to pay the duty on demand shall attract a penalty under section 9 of the Finance Act 1994 (civil penalties) which shall be calculated by reference to the amount of the duty demanded and shall also attract daily penalties."

12. In section 118G (offences in connection with record keeping etc. by revenue traders), for the words from "he shall be liable" onwards there shall be substituted "his failure to comply shall attract a penalty under section 9 of the Finance Act 1994 (civil penalties) and, in the case of any failure to keep records, shall also attract daily penalties.

13.—(1) In subsection (1) of section 170A (offence of handling goods subject to unpaid duty)—

(a) in paragraph (b), for the words from "the duty" to "its payment" there shall be substituted "a payment of duty on the goods is outstanding and"; and

(b) for the words after that paragraph there shall be substituted—

"the conduct of that person falling within paragraph (a) above shall attract a penalty under section 9 of the Finance Act 1994 (civil penalties) which shall be calculated by reference to the amount of the unpaid duty."

(2) In subsection (2) of that subsection (defences), for the words before paragraph (a) there shall be substituted—

"(2) Section 10 of the Finance Act 1994 (exception to civil penalty in cases of reasonable excuse) shall not apply in relation to conduct attracting a penalty by virtue of subsection (1) above; but such conduct shall not give rise to any liability to a penalty under section 9 of that Act if the person whose conduct it is satisfies the Commissioners or, on appeal, a VAT and duties tribunal, that he—".

PART II

CONTRAVENTIONS UNDER THE ALCOHOLIC LIQUOR DUTIES ACT 1979

14. The Alcoholic Liquor Duties Act 1979 shall be amended in accordance with the following provisions of this Part of this Schedule.

15. In section 8(2) (offence of contravening condition of remission of duty on spirits used for medical or scientific purposes), for the words from "then" onwards there shall be substituted "his contravention or failure to comply shall attract a penalty under section 9 of the Finance Act 1994 (civil penalties)."

16. In section 10(2) (offence of contravening condition of remission of duty on spirits used in art or manufacture), for the words from "then" onwards there shall be substituted "his contravention or failure to comply shall attract a penalty under section 9 of the Finance Act 1994 (civil penalties)."

17.—(1) In subsection (3) of section 13 (offence and forfeiture in the case of a contravention of regulations etc. applying to the manufacture of spirits)—

(a) for the words from "he shall" to "continues" there shall be substituted "his contravention or failure to comply shall attract a penalty under section 9 of the Finance Act 1994 (civil penalties)"; and

(b) for the words from "in respect of which" onwards there shall be substituted "in respect of which any person contravenes any such regulation, or fails to comply with any such regulation, condition, restriction or requirement, shall be liable to forfeiture."

(2) Subsection (4) of that section (power to vary penalty under subsection (3)) shall cease to have effect.

(3) In subsection (5) of that section (offence and forfeiture in the case of a contravention of any condition imposed with respect to any process of manufacture involving spirits), for the

words from "he shall be liable" onwards there shall be substituted "his contravention or failure to comply shall attract a penalty under section 9 of the Finance Act 1994 (civil penalties), and any spirits in respect of which any person contravenes or fails to comply with any such condition shall be liable to forfeiture."

18.—(1) In subsection (4) of section 15 (offence of failing to provide accommodation for officer in charge of a distiller's warehouse), for the words from "he shall" to "but nothing" there shall be substituted "his failure shall attract a penalty under section 9 of the Finance Act 1994 (civil penalties); but nothing".

(2) For subsection (5) of that section there shall be substituted the following subsection—

"(5) Where, after the approval of a distiller's warehouse, the distiller by whom it is provided makes, without the previous consent of the Commissioners, an alteration in or addition to that warehouse, the making of the alteration or addition shall attract a penalty under section 9 of the Finance Act 1994 (civil penalties)."

(3) In subsection (7) of that section (offence and forfeiture in the case of a contravention of regulations relating to a distiller's warehouse), for the words from "he shall" onwards there shall be substituted "his contravention or failure to comply shall attract a penalty under section 9 of the Finance Act 1994 (civil penalties), and any spirits in respect of which any person contravenes any such regulation, or fails to comply with any such regulation or condition, shall be liable to forfeiture."

(4) Subsection (8) of that section (power to vary penalty under subsection (7)) shall cease to have effect.

19.—(1) In subsection (2) of section 16 (offence and forfeiture in the case of a contravention of regulations relating to racking at a distillery), for the words from "he shall be liable" onwards there shall be substituted "his contravention or failure to comply shall attract a penalty under section 9 of the Finance Act 1994 (civil penalties), and any spirits in respect of which any person contravenes or fails to comply with any such regulation shall be liable to forfeiture."

(2) In subsection (3) of that section (forfeiture and offence in the case of an excess of stock), for the words from "the distiller shall be liable" onwards there shall be substituted "there shall be deemed to have been conduct by the distiller attracting a penalty under section 9 of the Finance Act 1994 (civil penalties)."

20. In section 18(6) (rectifying or compounding spirits in contravention of an excise licence), for the words from "he shall be liable" onwards there shall be substituted "his doing so shall attract a penalty under section 9 of the Finance Act 1994 (civil penalties)."

21.—(1) In subsection (2) of section 19 (offence and forfeiture in the case of contraventions of obligations imposed by or under regulations relating to the rectifying etc. of spirits), for the words from "he shall" onwards there shall be substituted "his contravention or failure to comply shall attract a penalty under section 9 of the Finance Act 1994 (civil penalties), and any spirits and any other article in respect of which any person contravenes any such regulation, or fails to comply with any such regulation, condition, requirement or restriction, shall be liable to forfeiture."

(2) Subsection (3) of that section (power to vary penalty under subsection (2)) shall cease to have effect.

22. In each of subsections (1) and (2) of section 20 (forfeiture and offences in the case of an excess or deficiency of stock), for the words from "the rectifier shall be liable" onwards there shall be substituted "there shall be deemed to have been conduct by the rectifier attracting a penalty under section 9 of the Finance Act 1994 (civil penalties)."

23.—(1) In subsection (3) of section 21 (offences in the case of certain contravention of restrictions relating to rectifiers), for the words from "he shall be liable" onwards there shall be substituted "the contravention of that subsection shall attract a penalty under section 9 of the Finance Act 1994 (civil penalties) or, as the case may be, there shall be deemed to have been conduct by the rectifier attracting such a penalty."

(2) For subsection (4) of that section (disqualification from holding a licence) there shall be substituted the following subsection—

"(4) Where—

(a) a rectifier becomes liable and is assessed to a penalty by virtue of subsection (3) above, and

(b) the assessment is not more than three years after the making of a previous assessment to a previous penalty to which he became liable by virtue of that subsection,

then his licence shall become void and he shall be disqualified from holding a licence as a rectifier for a period of three years from the date on which the assessment to the penalty mentioned in paragraph (a) above is made."

(3) Where a person has been convicted of an offence under subsection (3) of that section within the period of three years before the coming into force of sub-paragraph (2) above—

(a) that sub-paragraph shall be without prejudice to the continuation to the end of the appropriate three year period of any disqualification under subsection (4) of that section which is in force when that sub-paragraph comes into force; and

(b) subsection (4) of that section, as amended by that sub-paragraph, shall have effect as if the conviction were an assessment to a penalty to which that person was liable by virtue of subsection (3) of that section.

24. In section 22(9) (offence and forfeiture in the case of a contravention of regulations relating to drawback on compounds), for the words from "then" onwards there shall be substituted "his contravention or failure to comply shall attract a penalty under section 9 of the Finance Act 1994 (civil penalties), and any article in respect of which any person contravenes or fails to comply with any such regulation shall be liable to forfeiture."

25. In section 24(4) (offence of contravening provisions restricting the carrying on of other trades by a distiller or rectifier), for the words from "he shall be liable" onwards there shall be substituted "his contravention or failure to comply shall attract a penalty under section 9 of the Finance Act 1994 (civil penalties)."

26.—(1) In subsection (1) of section 33 (offence and forfeiture in the case of the use of spirits relieved from spirits duty), in the words after paragraph (c), for the words from "he shall" to "greater" there shall be substituted "his doing so shall, unless he has complied with the requirements specified in subsection (2) below, attract a penalty under section 9 of the Finance Act 1994 (civil penalties)".

(2) In subsection (5) of that section (contravention of enforcement regulations), for the words from "he shall be liable" onwards there shall be substituted "his contravention or failure to comply shall attract a penalty under section 9 of the Finance Act 1994 (civil penalties)."

27. For subsection (2) of section 34 (offence of contravening prohibition on grogging) there shall be substituted the following subsection—

"(2) A contravention of this section shall attract a penalty under section 9 of the Finance Act 1994 (civil penalties)."

28. In section 35(3) (contravention of regulations as to returns etc. relating to importation, manufacture, sale or use of alcohols), for the words from "he shall be liable" onwards there shall be substituted "his contravention or failure to comply shall attract a penalty under section 9 of the Finance Act 1994 (civil penalties)."

29. In section 41A(8) (offence and forfeiture in the case of a contravention of a condition of registration), for the words from "he shall be liable" onwards there shall be substituted "his contravention or failure to comply shall attract a penalty under section 9 of the Finance Act 1994 (civil penalties), and any beer in respect of which any person contravenes or fails to comply with any such conditions shall be liable to forfeiture."

30. In section 44(2) (offence of contravening condition imposed in connection with remission of duty on beer used for the purposes of research or experiment), for the words from "then" onwards there shall be substituted "his contravention or failure to comply shall attract a penalty under section 9 of the Finance Act 1994 (civil penalties)."

31. In section 46(2) (offence of contravening regulations relating to the remission of duty on spoilt beer), for the words from "he shall be liable" onwards there shall be submitted "his contravention or failure to comply shall attract a penalty under section 9 of the Finance Act 1994 (civil penalties)."

32.—(1) In subsection (4) of section 47 (offence of failing to apply for registration as a brewer), for the words from "he shall be liable" to "scale;" there shall be substituted "his failure shall attract a penalty under section 9 of the Finance Act 1994 (civil penalties)".

(2) In subsection (5) of that section (offence and forfeiture in the case of the production of beer by an unregistered person), for the words from "he shall be liable" onwards there shall be substituted "his doing so shall attract a penalty under section 9 of the Finance Act 1994 (civil penalties) which shall be calculated by reference to the amount of duty charged on the beer produced, and the beer produced and any worts found on those premises shall be liable to forfeiture."

33. For subsection (3) of section 49 (offence and forfeiture in the case of a contravention of beer regulations) there shall be substituted the following subsection—

"(3) Where any person contravenes or fails to comply with any regulation made under this section, his contravention or failure to comply shall attract a penalty under section 9 of the Finance Act 1994 (civil penalties), and any article or substance in respect of which any person contravenes or fails to comply with any such regulation shall be liable to forfeiture."

34. In section 54(5) (offence of producing wine on unlicensed premises), for the words from "he shall" to "and the wine" there shall be substituted "his doing so shall attract a penalty under section 9 of the Finance Act 1994 (civil penalties) which shall be calculated by reference to the amount of duty charged on the wine produced, and the wine".

35. In section 55(6) (offence of producing made-wine on unlicensed premises), for the words from "he shall" to "and the made-wine" there shall be substituted "his doing so shall attract a penalty under section 9 of the Finance Act 1994 (civil penalties) which shall be calculated by reference to the amount of duty charged on the made-wine produced, and the made-wine".

36. In section 55A(3) (offence of contravening regulations relating to wine or made-wine of a certain strength)—
(a) for "Any person who" there shall be substituted "Where any person"; and
(b) for the words from "shall be liable" to "scale" there shall be substituted "his contravention or failure to comply shall attract a penalty under section 9 of the Finance Act 1994 (civil penalties)".

37. In section 56(2) (offence and forfeiture in the case of a contravention of regulations relating to wine and made-wine), for the words from "he shall be liable" onwards there shall be substituted "his contravention or failure to comply shall attract a penalty under section 9 of the Finance Act 1994 (civil penalties), and any article in respect of which any person contravenes or fails to comply with any such regulation shall be liable to forfeiture."

38. For subsection (2) of section 59 (offence of rendering wine or made-wine sparkling) there shall be substituted the following subsection—
"(2) Where any person contravenes subsection (1) above or is concerned in such a contravention, his contravention or, as the case may be, his being so concerned shall attract a penalty under section 9 of the Finance Act 1994 (civil penalties)."

39. In section 61(2) (offence of contravening regulations relating to the remission of duty on spoilt wine or made-wine), for the words from "he shall be liable" onwards there shall be substituted "his contravention or failure to comply shall attract a penalty under section 9 of the Finance Act 1994 (civil penalties)."

40.—(1) In subsection (4) of section 62 (offence of producing cider on unlicensed premises), for the words from "he shall" to "and the cider" there shall be substituted "his doing so shall attract a penalty under section 9 of the Finance Act 1994 (civil penalties) which shall be calculated by reference to the amount of duty charged on the cider made, and the cider".
(2) In subsection (6) of that section (offence and forfeiture in the case of a contravention of regulations made for the purposes of managing the duty on cider), for the words from "he shall be liable" onwards there shall be substituted "his contravention or failure to comply shall attract a penalty under section 9 of the Finance Act 1994 (civil penalties), and any article in respect of which any person contravenes or fails to comply with any such regulation shall be liable to forfeiture."

41. In section 64(2) (offence of contravening regulations relating to the remission of duty on spoilt cider), for the words from "he shall be liable" onwards there shall be substituted "his contravention or failure to comply shall attract a penalty under section 9 of the Finance Act 1994 (civil penalties)."

42. In section 67(2) (offence and forfeiture in the case of any contravention of regulations regulating the keeping of dutiable liquors by wholesalers and retailers), for the words from "he shall be liable" onwards there shall be substituted "his contravention or failure to comply shall attract a penalty under section 9 of the Finance Act 1994 (civil penalties), and any liquor, container or utensil in respect of which any person contravenes or fails to comply with any such regulation shall be liable to forfeiture."

43.—(1) In subsection (3) of section 69 (offences relating to the carrying on of businesses by wholesalers and retailers), for the words from "he shall be liable" onwards there shall be substituted "his contravention or failure to comply shall attract a penalty under section 9 of the Finance Act 1994 (civil penalties)."
(2) In subsection (4) of that section (offence relating to the sending out or selling of spirits by a retailer), for the words from "he shall be liable" onwards there shall be substituted "his contravention or failure to comply shall attract a penalty under section 9 of the Finance Act 1994 (civil penalties)."

44.—(1) In subsection (1) of section 71 (penalty of misdescribing liquor as spirits) for the words from "that person shall" to "liquor or that" there shall be substituted "his doing so shall attract a penalty under section 9 of the Finance Act 1994 (civil penalties) unless the duty chargeable on spirits has been paid in respect of no less than 97.5 per cent. of the liquor or".
(2) In subsection (3) of that section, for "guilty of an offence under this section" there shall be substituted "liable to a penalty under section 9 of the Finance Act 1994 (civil penalties)".
(3) For subsection (4) of that section there shall be substituted the following subsection—
"(4) Any liquor or other article by means of or in relation to which there is a contravention of subsection (1) above shall be liable to forfeiture."

45. In section 75(5) (offence of unlicensed methylation of spirits)—
(a) for "Any person who" there shall be substituted "Where any person"; and

(b) for the words from "shall be liable" onwards there shall be substituted "his doing so shall attract a penalty under section 9 of the Finance Act 1994 (civil penalties)."

46.—(1) In subsection (3) of section 77 (offence of contravening regulations relating to methylated spirits or any condition, restriction or requirement imposed under any such regulations), for the words from "he shall be liable" onwards there shall be substituted "his contravention or failure to comply shall attract a penalty under section 9 of the Finance Act 1994 (civil penalties)."

(2) In subsection (4) of that section (offence of unlicensed dealing in methylated spirits), for the words from "he shall be liable" onwards there shall be substituted "his doing so shall attract a penalty under section 9 of the Finance Act 1994 (civil penalties)."

(3) In subsection (5) of that section (forfeiture), for "an offence under subsection (3) or (4) above is committed" there shall be substituted "there is such a contravention or failure to comply as is mentioned in subsection (3) above or any such dealing as is mentioned in subsection (4) above".

47. In section 78(4) (offence and forfeiture in the case of a person having unlicensed methylated spirits in his possession), for the words from "he shall be liable" to "and the" there shall be substituted "his having them in his possession shall attract a penalty under section 9 of the Finance Act 1994 (civil penalties), and the".

48. In section 82(2) (offence and forfeiture in the case of a contravention of regulations relating to stills), for the words from "he shall be liable" onwards there shall be substituted "his contravention or failure to comply shall attract a penalty under section 9 of the Finance Act 1994 (civil penalties), and any still or part thereof in respect of which any person contravenes or fails to comply with any such regulation shall be liable to forfeiture."

Part III

Contraventions under the Hydrocarbon Oil Duties Act 1979

49. The Hydrocarbon Oil Duties Act 1979 shall be amended in accordance with the following provisions of this Part of this Schedule.

50.—(1) In subsection (3) of section 10 (offences in connection with use etc. of oil that has been relieved of duty for a purpose which does not qualify for relief)—
(a) for "A person who" there shall be substituted "Where any person"; and
(b) for the words from "shall be liable" to "greater" there shall be substituted "his use or acquisition of the oil or, as the case may be, his becoming so liable shall attract a penalty under section 9 of the Finance Act 1994 (civil penalties)".

(2) In subsection (4) of that section (offence of supplying for a use that does not qualify for relief)—
(a) for "A person who" there shall be substituted "Where any person";
(b) for the words from "shall be liable" to "greater, if" there shall be substituted "and"; and
(c) at the end there shall be inserted "his supplying the oil shall attract a penalty under section 9 of the Finance Act 1994 (civil penalties)".

51.—(1) In subsection (1) of section 13 (offences in connection with use etc. of heavy oil)—
(a) for "A person who" there shall be substituted "Where any person"; and
(b) for the words from "shall be liable" to "greater" there shall be substituted "his use of the oil or, as the case may be, his becoming so liable shall attract a penalty under section 9 of the Finance Act 1994 (civil penalties)".

(2) In subsection (2) of that section (offence of supplying heavy oil for a use in contravention of section 12(2))—
(a) for "A person who" there shall be substituted "Where any person";
(b) for the words from "shall be liable" to "greater, where" there shall be substituted "and"; and
(c) at the end there shall be inserted "his supplying the oil shall attract a penalty under section 9 of the Finance Act 1994 (civil penalties)."

52.—(1) In subsection (4) of section 14 (offences in connection with use etc. of oil in the case of which rebate has been allowed)—
(a) for "A person who" there shall be substituted "Where any person"; and
(b) for the words from "shall be liable" to "greater" there shall be substituted "his use or acquisition of the oil or, as the case may be, his becoming so liable shall attract a penalty under section 9 of the Finance Act 1994 (civil penalties)".

(2) In subsection (5) of that section (offence of supplying for a use for which no rebate is allowed)—

(a) for "A person who" there shall be substituted "Where any person";

(b) for the words from "shall be liable" to "greater, if" there shall be substituted "and"; and

(c) at the end there shall be inserted "his supplying the oil shall attract a penalty under section 9 of the Finance Act 1994 (civil penalties)."

53. In section 18(5) (offence in certain circumstances of using or relanding oil), for the words from "he shall be liable" onwards there shall be substituted "his use or relanding of the oil or any part of it shall attract a penalty under section 9 of the Finance Act 1994 (civil penalties), and, in the case of any contravention falling within paragraph (b) of this subsection, the oil relanded shall be liable to forfeiture."

54. In section 20AA(4) (offence and forfeiture in the case of a contravention of the regulations relating to reliefs), for paragraph (a) there shall be substituted the following paragraph—

"(a) his contravention or failure to comply shall attract a penalty under section 9 of the Finance Act 1994 (civil penalties); and".

55. In section 21(3) (offence and forfeiture in the case of a contravention of regulations relating to administration or enforcement)—

(a) for "A person who" there shall be substituted "Where any person"; and

(b) for the words from "shall be liable on" onwards there shall be substituted "his contravention or failure to comply shall attract a penalty under section 9 of the Finance Act 1994 (civil penalties), and any goods in respect of which any person contravenes or fails to comply with any such regulation shall be liable to forfeiture."

56.—(1) In subsection (1) of section 22 (offence and forfeiture in the case of the use of fuel substitute for a chargeable purpose without duty have been paid)—

(a) for "A person who" there shall be substituted "Where any person"; and

(b) for the words from "shall be liable on" onwards there shall be substituted "his putting the liquid to that use shall attract a penalty under section 9 of the Finance Act 1994 (civil penalties), and any goods in respect of which any person contravenes this subsection shall be liable to forfeiture."

(2) After that subsection there shall be inserted the following subsection—

"(1A) Section 10 of the Finance Act 1994 (exception for cases of reasonable excuse) shall not apply in relation to conduct attracting a penalty by virtue of subsection (1) above."

57.—(1) In subsection (1) of section 23 (offence and forfeiture in the case of the use etc. of road fuel gas without duty having been paid)—

(a) for "A person who" there shall be substituted "Where any person"; and

(b) for the words from "shall be liable on" onwards there shall be substituted "his use of the road fuel gas or, as the case may be, his taking it as fuel into that vehicle shall attract a penalty under section 9 of the Finance Act 1994 (civil penalties), and any goods in respect of which a person contravenes this subsection shall be liable to forfeiture."

(2) After that subsection there shall be inserted the following subsection—

"(1A) Section 10 of the Finance Act 1994 (exception for cases of reasonable excuse) shall not apply in relation to conduct attracting a penalty by virtue of subsection (1) above."

58. In section 24(4) (offence and forfeiture in the case of a contravention of regulations relating to incidental matters)—

(a) for "A person who" there shall be substituted "Where any person"; and

(b) for the words from "shall be liable on" onwards there shall be substituted "his contravention or failure to comply shall attract a penalty under section 9 of the Finance Act 1994 (civil penalties), and any goods in respect of which any person contravenes or fails to comply with any such regulation shall be liable to forfeiture."

PART IV

CONTRAVENTIONS UNDER THE TOBACCO PRODUCTS DUTY ACT 1979

59. In section 7(2) of the Tobacco Products Duty Act 1979 (offence and forfeiture in the case of a contravention of regulations for the management of the duty etc.), for the words from "he shall be liable" onwards there shall be substituted "his failure to comply shall attract a penalty under section 9 of the Finance Act 1994 (civil penalties), and any article in respect of which any person fails to comply with any such regulation, or which is found on premises in respect of which any person has failed to comply with any such regulation, shall be liable to forfeiture."

PART V

CONTRAVENTIONS UNDER THE BETTING AND GAMING DUTIES ACT 1981

60. The Betting and Gaming Duties Act 1981 shall be amended in accordance with the following provisions of this Part of this Schedule.

61. In section 24(5) (offence where gaming machine provided without there being a licence in force)—

(a) for "any person who at the time when it is so provided" there shall be substituted "the provision of the machine shall attract a penalty under section 9 of the Finance Act 1994 (civil penalties) and, for the purposes of the application of that section to the conduct attracting the penalty, the provision of the machine shall be treated as the conduct of each of the persons who, at the time when the gaming machine is provided"; and

(b) the words after paragraph (f) shall be omitted.

62.—(1) In paragraph 13 of Schedule 1 (enforcement), for sub-paragraphs (1) and (2) there shall be substituted—

"(1) Where any person—

(a) fails to pay any general betting duty or pool betting duty payable by him, or

(b) contravenes or fails to comply with any of the provisions of, or of any regulations made under, any of paragraphs 2, 4 and 6 to 10 above,

his failure to pay, contravention or failure to comply shall attract a penalty under section 9 of the Finance Act 1994 (civil penalties) which, in the case of a failure to pay, shall be calculated by reference to the amount of duty payable.

(2) Any such failure to pay as is mentioned in sub-paragraph (1)(a) above shall also attract daily penalties.

(2A) Any person who obstructs any officer in the exercise of his functions in relation to general betting duty or pool betting duty shall be guilty of an offence and liable on summary conviction to a penalty of level 4 on the standard scale."

(2) In paragraph 14(3) of that Schedule (offence of failing to produce permit within period reasonably required)—

(a) the word "reasonably" shall be omitted; and

(b) for the words from "he shall be guilty" onwards there shall be substituted "his failure shall attract a penalty under section 9 of the Finance Act 1994 (civil penalties)."

(3) In paragraph 15 of that Schedule (forfeiture and cancellation of licence on second or subsequent conviction),—

(a) in sub-paragraph (1), for "paragraph 13(1) or (3) above" there shall be substituted "paragraph 13(3) above" and the words from "(not being" to "9 above)" shall be omitted; and

(b) in paragraph (a) of that sub-paragraph, for the words from "the conviction" to "other person)" there shall be substituted "there has been at least one previous occasion on which that or another person has been either—

(i) convicted of an offence under paragraph 13(3) above; or

(ii) assessed to a penalty to which he was liable under section 8 of the Finance Act 1994 (penalty for evasion),

in respect of conduct taking place".

63.—(1) In paragraph 7 of Schedule 2 (enforcement), for sub-paragraphs (1) and (2) there shall be substituted—

"(1) Where any person contravenes or fails to comply with any of the provisions of, or of any regulations made under, paragraph 3 above, his contravention or failure to comply shall attract a penalty under section 9 of the Finance Act 1994 (civil penalties).

(1A) Any person who obstructs any officer in the exercise of his functions in relation to the duty on gaming licences shall be guilty of an offence and liable on summary conviction to a penalty of level 5 on the standard scale."

(2) In sub-paragraph (5) of that paragraph, for "sub-paragraphs (1)(b) and" there shall be substituted "sub-paragraph".

64.—(1) In sub-paragraph (3) of paragraph 16 of Schedule 3 (offence of contravening provision made by or under that Schedule)—

(a) for "Any person who" there shall be substituted "Where any person"; and

(b) for the words after paragraph (b) there shall be substituted—

"his contravention or failure to comply shall attract a penalty under section 9 of the Finance Act 1994 (civil penalties)."

(2) Sub-paragraph (4) of that paragraph (continuing offences) shall cease to have effect.

65.—(1) In sub-paragraph (1) of paragraph 16 of Schedule 4 (offence of contravening provision made by or under that Schedule), for the words from "he shall be guilty" onwards there shall be substituted "his contravention, failure to comply or refusal shall attract a penalty under section 9 of the Finance Act 1994 (civil penalties)."

(2) Sub-paragraph (2) of that paragraph (continuing offences) shall cease to have effect.

PART VI

PART VI

CONTRAVENTIONS RELATING TO LOTTERY DUTY

66. Chapter II of Part I of the Finance Act 1993 shall be amended in accordance with the following provisions of this Part of this Schedule.

67. In section 27(4) (offence of failing to pay duty)—

(a) for "A person who" there shall be substituted "Where a person"; and

(b) for the words from "is guilty" onwards there shall be substituted "his failure so to make the payment shall attract a penalty under section 9 of the Finance Act 1994 (civil penalties) which shall be calculated by reference to the amount which has not been paid and shall also attract daily penalties."

68. In each of sections 28(3) and 29(8) (offences of contravening regulations made for the purposes of lottery duty)—

(a) for "A person who" there shall be substituted "Where a person"; and

(b) for the words from "is guilty" onwards there shall be substituted "his contravention or failure to comply shall attract a penalty under section 9 of the Finance Act 1994 (civil penalties)."

GENERAL NOTE

This Schedule lists the procedural offences under excise law which cease to be liable for summary prosecution and are instead liable to civil penalties under s.9.

Part I, paras. (1)–(13), deals with contraventions under the Customs and Excise Management Act 1979 (c. 2).

Part II, paras. (14)–(48), covers the Alcoholic Liquor Duties Act 1979 (c. 4).

Part III, paras. (49)–(58), covers the Hydrocarbon Oil Duties Act 1979 (c. 5).

Part IV, para. (59), covers the Tobacco Products Duty Act 1979 (c. 7).

Part V, paras. (60)–(65), covers the Betting and Gaming Duties Act 1981 (c. 63).

Part VI, paras. (66)–(68), covers the lottery duty introduced by the FA 1993 (c. 34), ss.24–41.

In appropriate cases, forfeiture of goods will continue to apply in addition to the civil penalty.

Section 14   SCHEDULE 5

DECISIONS SUBJECT TO REVIEW AND APPEAL

The Community Customs Code etc.

1. The following decisions, so far as they are made for the purposes of the Community Customs Code and are decisions the authority for which is not contained in provisions outside that Code and any directly applicable Community legislation made for the purpose of implementing that Code, that is to say—

(a) any decision in relation to any goods as to whether or not the entry, unloading or transhipment of the goods, or their release by or to any person or for any purpose, is to be allowed or otherwise permitted;

(b) any decision as to whether or not permission for the examination of, or the taking of samples from, any goods presented to the Commissioners is to be granted;

(c) any decision as to the route to be used for the movement of any goods;

(d) any other decision as to whether or not the requirements of any procedure for goods which are to be or have been presented to the Commissioners, or any other formalities in relation to any such goods, have been satisfied or complied with or are to be waived, or as to the measures to be taken, including any requirements to be imposed, in consequence of the inability or other failure of any person to comply with the required procedure;

(e) any decision in relation to any place or area as to whether or not it is to be, or to continue to be, designated or approved for any purpose;

(f) any decision, in any particular case, as to whether or not the carrying out of any processing or other operations or the use of any procedure is to be, or to continue to be, authorised or approved;

(g) any decision in relation to—

(i) the establishment or operation of any warehouse or other facility, or

(ii) the construction of any building,

as to whether or not its establishment, operation or construction or the person by whom it is to be established, operated or constructed, is to be, or to continue to be, authorised or approved for any purpose;

(h) any decision consisting in the imposition of a requirement to supply information or assistance, or to furnish any document or other evidence, to the Commissioners or any officer or of a requirement to be present or represented when anything is done in relation to any goods;

(i) any decision to take or retain samples of any goods or as to the examination or analysis to which any goods or samples are to be subjected;

(j) any decision as to whether or not any person is to bear any of the expenses of the supply of any information by or on behalf of the Commissioners or as to the amount of any such expenses to be borne by any person;

(k) any decision as to whether or not any amount due in respect of any customs duty or any agricultural levy of the European Community is to bear interest or as to the rate at which or period for which any such amount is to bear interest;

(l) any decision, in relation to a decision mentioned in any of the preceding sub-paragraphs, as to the conditions subject to which the decision so mentioned is made or, as the case may be, the matters to which that decision relates have effect;

(m) any decision as to whether or not any person is to be required to give any security for the fulfilment, in whole or in part, of—

    (i) any obligation to pay any customs duty or any agricultural levy of the European Community; or

    (ii) any obligation to comply with a condition of any permission, designation, approval, authorisation or requirement mentioned in any of the preceding sub-paragraphs or with any provision for the purposes of which any decision falling within any of those sub-paragraphs is made,

or as to the form or amount of, or the conditions of, any such security;

(n) any decision as to the time at which or the period within which any obligation to pay any customs duty or agricultural levy of the European Community or to do any other thing required by virtue of the Community Customs Code is to be complied with;

(o) any decision as to whether or not a decision falling within this paragraph is to be varied or revoked, including a decision as to whether or not the time at which any such decision is to take effect is to be deferred.

The Management Act

2.—(1) The following decisions under or for the purposes of the Management Act, that is to say—

(a) any decision for the purposes of section 20, 22 or 25 as to whether or not an approval of a place as an approved wharf, as an examination station or as a transit shed is to be given or withdrawn or as to the conditions subject to which any such approval is given;

(b) any decision as to whether or not any permission for any of the purposes of section 21 (control of movement of aircraft) is to be given or withdrawn or as to the conditions subject to which any such permission is given;

(c) any decision as to whether or not approval of a pipe-line for the purposes of section 24 (control of movement of goods by pipe-line) is to be given or withdrawn or as to the conditions subject to which any such approval is given;

(d) any decision as to whether or not expenses incurred by the Commissioners are to be borne by any person by virtue of section 29(3) (expenses of detention etc. of ships, aircraft and vehicles) or as to the amount of the expenses to be so borne;

(e) any decision consisting in the giving of a direction under section 30(1) (control of uncleared goods);

(f) any decision by virtue of subsection (2A) of section 31 (control of movement of goods) as to whether or not the requirements of any regulations under subsection (1) of that section are to be relaxed, as to whether or not substituted requirements are to be imposed or as to the terms of any such substituted requirements;

(g) any decision consisting in the imposition of a requirement by virtue of subsection (3) of section 33 (requirements as to record keeping) on a person in control of an aerodrome who is not licensed under any enactment relating to air navigation or as to what is or is not to be approved (whether or not in relation to such a requirement) for the purposes of paragraph (a) of that subsection;

(h) any decision as to whether or not permission is to be given to any person for the purposes of section 39 (entry of surplus stores);

(i) any decision for the purposes of section 40 that any goods are to be deposited in a Queen's warehouse;

(j) any decision for the purposes of section 47 as to whether or not goods are allowed to be removed for transit or trans-shipment or as to the conditions subject to which they are removed;

(k) any decision as to the conditions subject to which any permission is given for the purposes of section 48 (temporary importation);

(l) any decision for the purposes of section 63 (entry outwards) as to whether or not entry outwards is to be made of any ship or goods or as to the conditions subject to which any such entry outwards is to be made;

(m) any decision consisting in the imposition of a requirement under section 77, 79 or 80 to produce or furnish any document or other evidence or information;

(n) any decision for the purposes of section 92 (approval of warehouses)—

    (i) as to whether or not any approval is to be given to any place as a warehouse or any consent is to be given to any alteration in or addition to any warehouse;

    (ii) as to the conditions subject to which any approval or consent is given for the purposes of that section; or

    (iii) for the withdrawal of any such approval or consent;

(o) any decision as to whether or not any amount is payable to the Commissioners in pursuance of section 99 (provision as to deposit in Queen's warehouse) or as to the amount to be so paid by any person;

(p) any decision for the purposes of section 100G (registered excise dealers and shippers) as to whether or not, and in which respects, any person is to be, or to continue to be, approved and registered or as to the conditions subject to which any person is approved and registered;

(q) any decision as to the conditions subject to which any drawback is allowed or payable under section 132 or 134;

(r) any decision under section 152(b) as to whether or not anything forfeited or seized under the customs and excise Acts is to be restored to any person or as to the conditions subject to which any such thing is so restored;

(s) any decision under section 157 as to whether or not any person is to be required to give any security for the observance of any condition, as to the form or amount of, or the conditions of, any such security or as to the cancellation of any bond;

(t) any decision consisting in the giving or imposition of a direction or requirement for the purposes of section 158 (power to require the provision of facilities) or any decision as to whether or not an approval is to be given for the purposes of any such direction.

(2) Any decision which is made under or for the purposes of any regulations under any of sections 3, 31 or 93 of the Management Act (application to pipe-lines, control of movement of goods and warehousing regulations) and is—

(a) a decision in relation to any goods as to whether or not they may be moved, deposited, kept, secured, treated in any manner, removed or made available to any person or as to the conditions subject to which they are moved, deposited, kept, secured, treated in any manner, removed or made available to any person ;

(b) a decision as to whether or not any person or place is to be, or to continue to be, authorised or approved in any respect for any purpose or as to the conditions subject to which any person or place is so authorised or approved; or

(c) a decision as to whether or not any person is to be required to give any security for the fulfilment of any obligation or as to the form or amount of, or the conditions of, any such security.

(3) Any decision which is made under or for the purposes of any regulations under section 35(4), 42 or 66 of the Management Act (report inwards, procedure in relation to goods on arrival etc. or in relation to goods for exportation) and is—

(a) a decision as to whether or not any permission is to be given for the purpose of dispensing with any of the requirements of any such regulations;

(b) a decision consisting in the imposition or variation of any requirement in exercise of any power conferred by any such regulations; or

(c) a decision as to whether or not any approval, authority or permission is to be given or granted for the purpose of determining the manner in which any requirement imposed by or under any such regulations is to be performed.

(4) Any decision which is made under or for the purposes of any regulations under section 127A of the Management Act (deferment of duty) and is—

(a) a decision as to whether or not any person or place is to be, or to continue to be, approved for any purpose connected with the deferment of duty or as to the conditions subject to which any person or place is so approved;

(b) a decision as to the amount of duty that may be deferred in any case; or

(c) a decision as to whether or not any person is to be required to give any security for the fulfilment of any obligation or as to the form or amount of, or the conditions of, any such security.

The Alcoholic Liquor Duties Act 1979

3.—(1) The following decisions under or for the purposes of the Alcoholic Liquor Duties Act 1979, that is to say—

(a) any decision for the purposes of section 6 (power to exempt angostura bitters) as to whether or not to give a direction that any bitters are to be treated as not being spirits or as to the conditions subject to which any such direction is given;

(b) any decision for the purposes of section 7 (exemption of spirits used for medical purposes) as to whether or not to recognise any article as used for medical purposes;

(c) any decision for the purposes of section 8 (remission of duty on spirits used for medical purposes etc.)—

(i) as to the use to which any article is or is to be put or as to the purposes for which it is or is to be used; or

(ii) as to the conditions subject to which the receipt and delivery of any spirits is permitted as mentioned in that section;

(d) any decision for the purposes of section 9 or 10 (remission of duty on spirits for methylation or for use in art or manufacture) as to whether or not permission or authorisation for any person to receive, or for the delivery of, any spirits without payment of duty is to be granted or withdrawn or as to the conditions subject to which any such permission or authorisation is granted;

(e) any decision as to whether or not any goods are to be directed under section 11 (goods not for human consumption) to be treated as not containing spirits or as to the conditions subject to which any goods are directed to be so treated;

(f) any decision for the purposes of section 12 (licences to manufacture spirits) as to whether or not a licence under that section is to be granted or as to the suspension or revocation of such a licence or as to the conditions subject to which such a licence is granted;

(g) any decision for the purposes of section 15 (distillers' warehouses)—

(i) as to whether or not any approval is to be given to any place as a warehouse or any consent is to be given to any alteration in or addition to any warehouse;

(ii) as to the conditions subject to which any approval or consent is given for the purposes of that section; or

(iii) for the withdrawal of any such approval or consent;

(h) any decision for the purposes of section 18 (licences for rectifiers and compounders)—

(i) as to whether or not any person is to be granted a licence as a rectifier or compounder or permission to compound spirits without a licence;

(ii) as to the conditions subject to which any such licence or permission is granted; or

(iii) as to the revocation or withdrawal of any such licence or permission;

(i) any decision for the purposes of section 32 (transfer of spirits in a distiller's warehouse) as to whether or not any person is to be required to give any security for the payment of any duty or as to the form or amount of, or the conditions of, any such security;

(j) any decision as to whether or not drawback is to be allowed in any case under section 42 (drawback on exportation etc.) or as to the conditions subject to which drawback is so allowed;

(k) any decision as to whether or not any duty is to be remitted or repaid under section 44 (remission or repayment of duty on beer used for the purposes of research or experiment) or as to the conditions subject to which any duty is so remitted or repaid;

(l) any decision for the purposes of section 49A as to whether or not any drawback is to be set against an amount chargeable in respect of excise duty on beer or as to the conditions subject to which any drawback is set against any such amount;

(m) any decision as to whether or not any permission for the purposes of section 57 or 58 (mixing of made-wine or wine with spirits) is to be given or withdrawn or as to the conditions subject to which any such permission is given;

(n) any decision as to whether or not any permission for the purposes of subsection (1) or (2) of section 69 (restrictions applying to wholesalers and retailers of spirits) is to be given or withdrawn or as to the conditions subject to which any such permission is given;

(o) any decision as to whether or not an authorisation or licence for the purposes of section 75 (methylated spirits and denatured alcohol) is to be granted to any person or as to the revocation or suspension of any such authorisation or licence.

(2) Any decision which is made under or for the purposes of any regulations under section 13 or 77 of the Alcoholic Liquor Duties Act 1979 (regulation of the manufacture of spirits, methylated spirits and denatured alcohol) and is a decision as to whether or not any premises, plant or process is to be, or to continue to be, approved for any purpose or as to the conditions subject to which any premises, plant or process is so approved.

(3) Any decision which is made under or for the purposes of section 55, or any regulations under section 56, of the Alcoholic Liquor Duties Act 1979 (regulation of the making of wine and made-wine) and is a decision as to whether or not a licence under that section is to be granted or cancelled.

The Hydrocarbon Oil Duties Act 1979

4.—(1) The following decisions under or for the purposes of the Hydrocarbon Oil Duties Act 1979—

    (a) any decision under section 9 (delivery of oil for home use etc.) as to whether or not permission is to be given for the delivery of anything without payment of duty or as to the conditions subject to which any such permission is given;

    (b) any decision as to whether or not a consent is to be given for the purposes of section 10(1) (consent to certain uses of oil delivered for home use) or as to the conditions subject to which any such consent is given;

    (c) any decision as to whether or not a consent is to be given for the purposes of section 14(2) (consent to certain uses of rebated oil) or as to the conditions subject to which any such consent is given;

    (d) any decision consisting in a determination for the purposes of section 17(3) (determination of use of oil etc. for different purposes);

    (e) any decision as to the conditions subject to which any payment is to be made to any person in accordance with section 20(3) (payments in respect of contaminated or mixed substances).

(2) Any decision which is made under or for the purposes of any regulations made or having effect as if made under section 21 or 24 of the Hydrocarbon Oil Duties Act 1979 and is—

    (a) a decision as to whether or not any person is to be required to give any security for any duty which is or may become due, or as to the form or amount of, or the conditions of, any such security; or

    (b) a decision as to whether or not any person is to be, or to continue to be, approved for the purposes of section 9(1) or (4), 14(1) or 19A(1) of that Act or as to the conditions subject to which any person is so approved.

GENERAL NOTE

    This Schedule lists decisions, on what are described in s.16(4) as "ancillary matters", which the Customs and Excise may be required to review, with possible appeal to a tribunal thereafter. These are detailed as follows in the Schedule.

Para. (1)

    Decisions relating to the Community Customs Code. It was the requirement to have an appeal procedure in relation to the Code which prompted this legislation.

Para. (2)

    Decisions relating to a number of matters under the Customs and Excise Management Act 1979 (c. 2). Decisions in relation to seizure and forfeiture of goods will continue to be dealt with by magistrates' courts, subject to possible appeal to the European Court.

Para. (3)

    Decisions relating to a number of matters under the Alcoholic Liquor Duties Act 1979 (c. 4).

Para. (4)

    Decisions relating to a number of matters under the Hydrocarbon Oil Duties Act 1979 (c. 5).

The Tobacco Products Duty Act 1979

5. Any decision which is made under or for the purposes of any regulations made under section 2 or 7 of the Tobacco Products Duty Act 1979 and is—

    (a) a decision as to whether or not any duty is remitted or repaid or as to the conditions subject to which it is remitted or repaid; or

    (b) a decision as to whether or not any premises are to be, or to continue to be, registered for any purpose or as to the conditions subject to which any premises are so registered.

The Betting and Gaming Duties Act 1981

6.—(1) The following decisions under or for the purposes of the Betting and Gaming Duties Act 1981, that is to say—

(a) any decision as to whether or not a permit under paragraph 5 of Schedule 1 (permit for carrying on pool betting business) is to be granted to any person or as to the revocation of such a permit;

(b) any decision under paragraph 10(2) of Schedule 3 (registration of bingo promoters) as to the conditions subject to which any person is to be, or to continue to be, registered as a bingo-promoter.

(2) Any decision which is made under or for the purposes of—

(a) any regulations under paragraph 2 of Schedule 1 to the Betting and Gaming Duties Act 1981 (regulations in relation to general betting duty), or

(b) paragraph 10(2) of Schedule 3 to that Act,

and is a decision as to whether or not any person is to be required to give any security for any duty which is or may become due, or as to the form or amount of, or the conditions of, any such security.

The Finance Act 1993

7. Any decision as to whether or not any person is to be or to continue to be registered under section 29 of the Finance Act 1993 (registration for the purposes of lottery duty) and any decision which is made under or for the purposes of any regulations under that section and is a decision as to whether or not any person is to be required to give any security for the payment of any lottery duty that may become due, or as to the form or amount of, or the conditions of, any such security.

Chapter III of Part I of this Act

8.—(1) Any decision made under or for the purposes of any regulations under section 21 of this Act or for the purposes of subsection (2) of that section which is—

(a) a decision consisting in the imposition or variation of any requirement as to the records which are to be kept by any person;

(b) a decision as to the manner in which any record or information is to be preserved or is to be made available to the Commissioners; or

(c) a decision as to the period for which any record or information is to be preserved.

(2) Any decision for the purposes of section 23 of this Act which is—

(a) a decision consisting in the imposition or variation of any requirement as to the information or documents which are to be furnished or produced by any person, including any decision as to the time or place at which, period within which or form in which anything is to be furnished or produced in pursuance of that section; or

(b) a decision as to the removal of any document produced under that section or as to the period for which such a document may be removed.

Chapter IV of Part I of this Act

9. The following decisions under or for the purposes of Chapter IV of Part I of this Act, that is to say—

(a) any decision under regulations made by virtue of section 33 to register, or not to register, any person as an aircraft operator in the register kept under that section or to remove a person so registered from the register;

(b) any decision under such regulations to show, or not to show, the name of any person as a fiscal representative in that register or to remove a name from the register;

(c) any decision under section 36 to require a person to provide security, including any decision as to the form or amount of the security; and

(d) any decision to give a person a notice under section 37.

Interpretation of Schedule

10.—(1) In this Schedule references to any decision as to the conditions subject to which any other decision (whether or not specified in this Schedule) is made include references to—

(a) any decision as to whether the other decision should be made subject to or to the imposition of any conditions, limitations, restrictions, prohibitions or other requirements, either from the time when the other decision takes effect or in exercise of any power to impose them subsequently;

(b) any decision as to the terms of any conditions, limitations, restrictions, prohibitions or other requirements imposed or applied in relation to that other decision;

(c) any decision as to the period for which any licence, approval, permission or other authorisation to which the other decision relates is to have effect or as to any variation of that period; and

(d) any decision as to whether any conditions, limitations, restrictions, prohibitions or other requirements so imposed or applied are to be revoked, suspended or cancelled or as to whether or in what respect their terms are at any time to be varied;

but those references do not include references to any decision as to the enforcement of any condition, restriction or prohibition in criminal proceedings, by the seizure or forfeiture of goods or, for purposes connected with any duty of excise, by any other means.

(2) References in this Schedule to decisions as to the exercise of any power to require security for the fulfilment of any obligation, the observance of any conditions or the payment of any duty shall be without prejudice to any reference to decisions as to the excise of any general power in the case in question to impose conditions in connection with the making of any other decision and shall include references to the exercise of any power to require further security for the fulfilment of that obligation, the observance of those conditions or, as the case may be, the payment of that duty.

GENERAL NOTE

Para. (5)
Decisions under the Tobacco Products Duty Act 1979 (c. 7), ss.2 and 7, relating to payment or repayment of duty or to the registration of premises, or the conditions under which premises are registered.

Para. (6)
Decisions relating to a number of matters under the Betting and Gaming Duties Act 1981 (c. 63).

Para. (7)
Decisions relating to registration for lottery duty and any requirement to give security for the payment of the duty or the conditions of such security under the FA 1993 (c. 34), s.29 or regulations made thereunder.

Para. (8)
Decisions under the FA 1994 (c. 9), ss.21(2) and 23 relating to the keeping of records and the furnishing of information or the production and removal of documents.

Para. (9)
Decisions relating to air passenger duty under the FA 1994 (c. 9), ss.33, 36 and 37.

Para. (10)
Conditions attached to decisions are also reviewable as are decisions to require further security or to require security in the exercise of a general as distinct from a specific power.

Section 40   SCHEDULE 6

AIR PASSENGER DUTY: ADMINISTRATION AND ENFORCEMENT

Application of excise enactments

1.—(1) The Customs and Excise Management Act 1979 shall have effect for the purposes of Chapter IV of Part I of this Act in relation to—

(a) any person who is or is liable to be registered,

(b) any fiscal representative, and

(c) any handling agent where a notice given to him under section 37 of this Act is effective,

as it has effect in relation to revenue traders, but with the modifications mentioned in sub-paragraph (2), and paragraphs 3 and 4, below.

(2) That Act shall have effect, in relation to any person to whom sub-paragraph (1) above applies, as if—

(a) the reference in section 112(1) (power of entry) to vehicles included aircraft,

   (b) section 116 (payment of duty) were omitted,

   (c) in section 117 (execution and distress)—

        (i) the references to goods liable to any excise duty included tickets, and

        (ii) the references to the trade in respect of which duty is imposed were to the trade or business by virtue of which sub-paragraph (1) above applies to him, and

   (d) any power under section 118B(1)(b) to require any person who is or is liable to be registered to produce or cause to be produced any such documents as are referred to in that subsection included power to require his fiscal representative to produce them.

2. Section 118B of that Act shall have effect for the purposes of Chapter IV of Part I of this Act in relation to any person who, in the course of a trade or business carried on by him, issues or arranges for the issue of tickets as if—

   (a) he were a revenue trader, and

   (b) the references to services supplied by or to him in the course or furtherance of a business were to services supplied by or to him in the course of issuing or arranging for the issue of tickets.

3.—(1) A notice may require any person to whom paragraph 1 above applies to furnish, at specified times and in the specified form, any such information to the Commissioners as he could be required by the Commissioners to furnish under subsection (1) of section 118B; and any such requirement shall have effect as a requirement under that subsection.

(2) A notice may require any person to whom paragraph 1 or 2 above applies to produce or cause to be produced for inspection by an officer, at specified places and times, any such documents as he could be required by the officer to produce under that subsection; and any such requirement shall have effect as a requirement under that subsection.

(3) In this paragraph—

"notice" means a notice published, and not withdrawn, by the Commissioners, and "specified" means specified in such a notice.

4. In relation to any person to whom paragraph 1 or 2 above applies—

   (a) that Act shall have effect as if "document" had the same meaning as in Chapter IV of Part I of this Act, and

   (b) that Act and this Schedule shall have effect as if any reference to the production of any document, in the case of information recorded otherwise than in legible form, were to producing a copy of the information in legible form.

Information

5.—(1) Any person having the management of an airport shall, if required to do so by the Commissioners—

   (a) give notice to the Commissioners, within such time and in such form as they may reasonably require, stating whether or not he holds or has at any time held any information relating to the matters mentioned in sub-paragraph (3) below and, if he does or has done, stating the general nature of the information, and

   (b) furnish to the Commissioners, within such time and in such form as they may reasonably require, such information relating to such matters as they may reasonably specify.

(2) Any such person shall, if required to do so by an officer, produce any documents relating to those matters, or cause them to be produced, for inspection by that officer.

(3) The matters referred to in sub-paragraphs (1) and (2) above are—

   (a) whether or not any aircraft is a chargeable aircraft,

   (b) who is the operator of any aircraft,

   (c) whether or not any person is a handling agent of the operator of any aircraft, and

   (d) whether or not any duty is payable on the carriage of any person and, if so, the amount of duty.

(4) Documents produced under sub-paragraph (2) above shall be produced, at such time as the officer may reasonably require, at the principal place of business of the person required to produce them or cause them to be produced or at such other place as the officer may reasonably require.

(5) An officer may take copies of, or make extracts from, any document produced under this paragraph.

(6) If it appears to an officer to be necessary to do so, he may, at a reasonable time and for a reasonable period, remove any document produced under this paragraph.

(7) Where an officer removes a document under sub-paragraph (6) above, then—

   (a) if the person from whom it is removed so requests, the officer shall give him a receipt for the document,

(b) if the document is reasonably required for the proper conduct of any business, the officer shall, as soon as practicable, provide a copy of the document, free of charge, to the person by whom it was produced or caused to be produced, and

(c) if the document is lost or damaged, the Commissioners shall be liable to compensate the owner for any expenses reasonably incurred by him in replacing or repairing it.

(8) Any reference in this paragraph to the production of a document, in the case of information recorded otherwise than in legible form, is to producing a copy of the information in legible form.

(9) Any failure by a person having the management of an airport to comply with a requirement imposed under this paragraph shall attract a penalty under section 9 of this Act.

Application of Chapter II

6. An appeal which relates to duty shall not be entertained under section 16 of this Act at any time if any return which the appellant is required by regulations made by virtue of section 38 of this Act to make has not at that time been made.

GENERAL NOTE

This Schedule contains the general administrative provisions relating Air Passenger Duty (APD) introduced by ss.28–44. APD is an excise duty and accordingly the general approach to the collection of excise duties applies.

Para. (1)

The provisions of the CEMA 1979 (c. 2) relating to revenue traders are applied to aircraft operators, their fiscal representatives and their handling agents (see s.37) with the modifications listed in subpara. (2).

Para. (2)

The duty of revenue traders in the CEMA 1979 (c. 2), s.118(B) to provide information and produce documents is extended to travel agencies.

Para. (3)

The Customs and Excise are given power to specify by notice the precise requirements for compliance under paras. (1) and (2).

Para. (4)

The definition of "document" in s.42, which includes information recorded in any form, is applied for the purposes of paras. (1) and (2). It must be provided in legible form.

Para. (5)

This paragraph, added at Committee Stage, is an important part of the control effort. It enables the Customs and Excise to require the production of information provided to airports by airlines. The information relates to the circumstances giving rise to liability to air passenger duty (APD). An airport operator failing to comply is subject to penalty under s.9.

Para. (6)

The right of appeal to a VAT and duties tribunal under s.16 does not apply unless all requisite returns have been made.

Interest payable to Commissioners

7.—(1) Where an assessment of duty due from any person ("the person assessed") is made under section 12 of this Act and any of the conditions in sub-paragraph (2) below is fulfilled, the whole of the amount assessed shall, subject to paragraph 8 below, carry interest at the specified rate from the reckonable date until payment.

(2) The conditions are—

(a) that the assessment relates to an accounting period in respect of which either a return has previously been made or an earlier assessment has already been notified to the person assessed, or

(b) that the assessment relates to an accounting period which exceeds one month and begins on the date on which the person assessed was, or became liable to be, registered.

(3) In a case where—

(a) the circumstances are such that an assessment of duty due from any person could have been made and, if it had been made, the conditions in sub-paragraph (2) above would have been fulfilled, but

(b) before such an assessment was made the duty was paid (so that no such assessment was necessary),

the whole of the amount paid shall carry interest at the specified rate from the reckonable date until the date on which it was paid.

(4) In this paragraph and paragraph 8 below the "reckonable date" means the latest date on which a return is required to be made under Chapter IV of Part I of this Act for the accounting period to which the amount assessed or paid relates; and interest under this paragraph shall run from the reckonable date even if that date is a non-business day, within the meaning of section 92 of the Bills of Exchange Act 1882.

(5) Interest under this paragraph shall be paid without any deduction of income tax.

8.—(1) Where on an appeal by any person ("the appellant") to a tribunal under section 16 of this Act against an assessment of duty—

(a) it is found that the whole or any part of the duty was due from him, and

(b) the amount due, or any part of that amount, has not been paid and no cash security has been given for it,

that amount or, as the case may be, that part of it shall carry interest at such rate as the tribunal may determine from the reckonable date until payment.

(2) In sub-paragraph (1) above, "cash security" means such adequate security as enables the Commissioners to place the amount in question on deposit.

(3) Interest under this paragraph shall be paid without any deduction of income tax.

Interest payable by the Commissioners

9.—(1) Where, due to an error on the part of the Commissioners, a person has paid by way of duty an amount which was not due and which the Commissioners are in consequence liable to repay to him, they shall (subject to the following provisions of this paragraph and paragraph 10) pay interest to him on that amount at the specified rate for the applicable period (if and to the extent that they would not be liable to do so apart from this paragraph).

(2) For the purposes of this paragraph the applicable period is the period—

(a) beginning with the date on which the payment is received by the Commissioners, and

(b) ending with the date on which they authorise payment of the amount on which the interest is payable;

but in determining that period for those purposes there shall be left out of account any period referable to the raising and answering of any reasonable enquiry relating to any matter giving rise to, or otherwise connected with, the person's entitlement to interest under this paragraph.

(3) In determining for the purposes of sub-paragraph (2) above whether any period is referable to the raising and answering of such an enquiry as is there mentioned, there shall be taken to be so referable any period which begins with the date on which the Commissioners first consider it necessary to make such an enquiry and ends with the date on which the Commissioners—

(a) satisfy themselves that they have received a complete answer to the enquiry, or

(b) determine not to make the enquiry or (if they have made it) not to pursue it further;

but excluding so much of that period as may be prescribed.

(4) For the purposes of sub-paragraph (3) above it is immaterial—

(a) whether any enquiry is in fact made, or

(b) whether any enquiry is or might have been made of the person referred to in sub-paragraph (1) above or of an authorised person or of some other person.

(5) The Commissioners shall only be liable to pay interest under this paragraph on a claim made in writing for that purpose.

(6) No claim shall be made under this paragraph after the expiry of six years from the date on which the claimant discovered the error or could with reasonable diligence have discovered it.

(7) Any reference in this paragraph to receiving a payment from the Commissioners includes a reference to the discharge, by way of set-off, of their liability to make it.

10.—(1) Where a person ("the appellant") who appeals to a tribunal under section 16 of this Act against an assessment of duty has paid, or given cash security for, the whole or any part of the duty, sub-paragraph (2) below shall apply if the tribunal find that the whole or any part of the amount paid or secured is not due.

(2) The Commissioners shall pay interest to the appellant, at such rate as the tribunal may determine, on—

(a) so much of the duty paid as is found not to be due or,

(b) so much of the cash security as relates to duty found not to be due,

for the period beginning with the payment of duty or, as the case may be, giving of the cash security and ending with its repayment.

(3) In this paragraph "cash security" means such adequate security as enables the Commissioners to place the amount in question on deposit.

Interest: specified rate

11.—(1) In paragraphs 7 and 9 above, "the specified rate" means such rate as may be specified in an order.
(2) An order specifying rates of interest—
(a) may specify different rates for different purposes,
(b) shall apply to interest for periods beginning on or after the date when the order is expressed to come into force, whether or not interest runs from before that date.

Evidence by certificate

12.—(1) A certificate of the Commissioners—
(a) that a person was or was not, on any date specified in the certificate, registered or liable to be registered under section 33 of this Act,
(b) that the name of any person was or was not, on any date so specified, shown as the fiscal representative of any person in the register kept under that section,
(c) that any aircraft was or was not, on any date so specified, a chargeable aircraft,
(d) that any return required to be made under regulations made by virtue of section 38 of this Act had not, on any date so specified, been made, or
(e) that any duty shown as due in such a return, or in an assessment under section 12 of this Act, had not, on any date so specified, been paid,
shall be sufficient evidence of that fact until the contrary is proved.
(2) A photograph of any document furnished to the Commissioners for the purposes of Chapter IV of Part I of this Act and certified by them to be such a photograph shall be admissible in any proceedings, whether civil or criminal, to the same extent as the document itself.
(3) Any document purporting to be a certificate under sub-paragraph (1) or (2) above shall be taken to be such a certificate until the contrary is proved.

Preferential debt

13.—(1) In Schedule 6 to the Insolvency Act 1986 (categories of preferential debts) in Category 2 (debts due to Customs and Excise) after paragraph 5B there shall be inserted—
"5C. Any amount which is due by way of air passenger duty from the debtor at the relevant date and which became due within the period of six months next before that date."
(2) In Schedule 3 to the Bankruptcy (Scotland) Act 1985 (list of preferred debts) at the end of paragraph 2 (debts due to Customs and Excise) there shall be added—
"(6) Any amount which is due by way of air passenger duty from the debtor at the relevant date and which became due within the period of six months next before that date."
(3) In Schedule 4 to the Insolvency (Northern Ireland) Order 1989 (categories of preferential debts) in Category 2 (debts due to Customs and Excise) after paragraph 5B there shall be inserted—
"5C. Any amount which is due by way of air passenger duty from the debtor at the relevant date and which became due within the period of six months next before that date."

GENERAL NOTE

Para. (7)
Interest is payable to the Customs and Excise in the event of late payment of APD. It runs generally from the date on which a return is required to be made until the date of payment.

Para. (8)
Likewise, interest is payable on duty found to be due by the tribunal where it has not been paid or secured by a cash deposit.

Para. (9)
Interest is also payable by the Customs and Excise on a refund of APD, where the payment was made due to official error. Periods relating to the raising and answering of enquiries are excluded (*cf.* the VATA 1983 (c. 55), s.38A).
Interest will only be payable on a claim being made within six years.

Para. (10)
Likewise, interest is payable on APD paid or secured by a cash deposit which is found by the tribunal to be not due.

Para. (11)
Tribunals may set the rate of interest in the case of appeals. In other cases it is set by Treasury order.

Para. (12)
The Customs and Excise may provide evidence about registration, returns, fiscal representatives and chargeable aircraft by means of a certificate.

Para. (13)
APD, for a six-month period, is added to the categories of preferential debt under the Insolvency Act 1986 (c. 45), Sched. 6 and the corresponding Scottish and Northern Irish legislation.

Section 64	SCHEDULE 7

INSURANCE PREMIUM TAX

PART I

INFORMATION

Records

1.—(1) Regulations may require registrable persons to keep records.

(2) Regulations under sub-paragraph (1) above may be framed by reference to such records as may be specified in any notice published by the Commissioners in pursuance of the regulations and not withdrawn by a further notice.

(3) Regulations may require any records kept in pursuance of the regulations to be preserved for such period not exceeding six years as may be specified in the regulations.

(4) Any duty under regulations to preserve records may be discharged by the preservation of the information contained in them by such means as the Commissioners may approve; and where that information is so preserved a copy of any document forming part of the records shall (subject to the following provisions of this paragraph) be admissible in evidence in any proceedings, whether civil or criminal, to the same extent as the records themselves.

(5) The Commissioners may, as a condition of approving under sub-paragraph (4) above any means of preserving information contained in any records, impose such reasonable requirements as appear to them necessary for securing that the information will be as readily available to them as if the records themselves had been preserved.

(6) A statement contained in a document produced by a computer shall not by virtue of sub-paragraph (4) above be admissible in evidence—

(a) in civil proceedings in England and Wales, except in accordance with sections 5 and 6 of the Civil Evidence Act 1968;

(b) in criminal proceedings in England and Wales, except in accordance with sections 69 and 70 of the Police and Criminal Evidence Act 1984 and Part II of the Criminal Justice Act 1988;

(c) in civil proceedings in Scotland, except in accordance with sections 5 and 6 of the Civil Evidence (Scotland) Act 1988;

(d) in criminal proceedings in Scotland, except in accordance with Schedule 3 to the Prisoners and Criminal Proceedings (Scotland) Act 1993;

(e) in civil proceedings in Northern Ireland, except in accordance with sections 2 and 3 of the Civil Evidence Act (Northern Ireland) 1971;

(f) in criminal proceedings in Northern Ireland, except in accordance with Article 68 of the Police and Criminal Evidence (Northern Ireland) Order 1989 and Part II of the Criminal Justice (Evidence, Etc.) (Northern Ireland) Order 1988.

Other provisions

2.—(1) Every person who is concerned (in whatever capacity) in a taxable business shall furnish to the Commissioners such information relating to taxable insurance contracts entered into in the course of the business as the Commissioners may reasonably require.

(2) Every person who makes arrangements for other persons to enter into any taxable insurance contract shall furnish to the Commissioners such information relating to that contract as the Commissioners may reasonably require.

(3) Every person who—

(a) is concerned in a business that is not a taxable business, and
(b) has been involved in the entry into any taxable insurance contract providing cover for any matter associated with the business,
shall furnish to the Commissioners such information relating to that contract as the Commissioners may reasonably require.

(4) The information mentioned in sub-paragraph (1), (2) or (3) above shall be furnished within such time and in such form as the Commissioners may reasonably require.

3.—(1) Every person who is concerned (in whatever capacity) in a taxable business shall upon demand made by an authorised person produce or cause to be produced for inspection by that person any documents relating to taxable insurance contracts entered into in the course of the business.

(2) Every person who makes arrangements for other persons to enter into any taxable insurance contract shall upon demand made by an authorised person produce or cause to be produced for inspection by that person any documents relating to that contract.

(3) Every person who—
(a) is concerned in a business that is not a taxable business, and
(b) has been involved in the entry into any taxable insurance contract providing cover for any matter associated with the business,
shall upon demand made by an authorised person produce or cause to be produced for inspection by that person any documents relating to that contract.

(4) Where, by virtue of any of sub-paragraphs (1) to (3) above, an authorised person has power to require the production of any documents from any person, he shall have the like power to require production of the documents concerned from any other person who appears to the authorised person to be in possession of them; but where any such other person claims a lien on any document produced by him, the production shall be without prejudice to the lien.

(5) The documents mentioned in sub-paragraphs (1) to (4) above shall be produced—
(a) at the principal place of business of the person on whom the demand is made or at such other place as the authorised person may reasonably require, and
(b) at such time as the authorised person may reasonably require.

(6) An authorised person may take copies of, or make extracts from, any document produced under any of sub-paragraphs (1) to (4) above.

(7) If it appears to him to be necessary to do so, an authorised person may, at a reasonable time and for a reasonable period, remove any document produced under any of sub-paragraphs (1) to (4) above and shall, on request, provide a receipt for any document so removed; and where a lien is claimed on a document produced under sub-paragraph (4) above the removal of the document under this sub-paragraph shall not be regarded as breaking the lien.

(8) Where a document removed by an authorised person under sub-paragraph (7) above is reasonably required for the proper conduct of a business he shall, as soon as practicable, provide a copy of the document, free of charge, to the person by whom it was produced or caused to be produced.

(9) Where any documents removed under the powers conferred by this paragraph are lost or damaged the Commissioners shall be liable to compensate their owner for any expenses reasonably incurred by him in replacing or repairing the documents.

GENERAL NOTE
This Schedule contains the rather extensive provisions considered necessary for the enforcement of insurance premium tax.

Para. (1)
The Customs and Excise have power to require registrable persons (see s.73(3)) to keep such records as they may specify by regulation or notice in pursuance of the regulations for a period of up to six years. They may approve arrangements for alternative modes of preserving records. Computer printouts will be admissible in court in accordance with the relevant statutes.

Para. (2)
The requirement to provide information within a reasonable time extends to insurers, brokers and insurance policy holders.

Para. (3)
The same people, and anyone else in possession of documents, may be required to produce them on demand to a Customs and Excise official at such place and time as he may be reasonable. The official may copy the documents or remove them for a reasonable period. Where they are removed, a copy must be provided where required and compensation paid if they are lost or damaged.

PART II

POWERS

Entry, arrest, etc.

4.—(1) For the purpose of exercising any powers under this Part of this Act an authorised person may at any reasonable time enter premises used in connection with the carrying on of a business.

(2) In a case where—

(a) a justice of the peace is satisfied on information on oath that there is reasonable ground for suspecting that a fraud offence which appears to be of a serious nature is being, has been or is about to be committed on any premises or that evidence of the commission of such an offence is to be found there, or

(b) in Scotland a justice, within the meaning of section 462 of the Criminal Procedure (Scotland) Act 1975, is satisfied by evidence on oath as mentioned in paragraph (a) above,

he may issue a warrant in writing authorising any authorised person to enter those premises, if necessary by force, at any time within one month from the time of the issue of the warrant and search them.

(3) A person who enters the premises under the authority of the warrant may—

(a) take with him such other persons as appear to him to be necessary;

(b) seize and remove any documents or other things whatsoever found on the premises which he has reasonable cause to believe may be required as evidence for the purposes of proceedings in respect of a fraud offence which appears to him to be of a serious nature;

(c) search or cause to be searched any person found on the premises whom he has reasonable cause to believe to be in possession of any such documents or other things;

but no woman or girl shall be searched except by a woman.

(4) The powers conferred by a warrant under this paragraph shall not be exercisable—

(a) by more than such number of authorised persons as may be specified in the warrant,

(b) outside such times of day as may be so specified, or

(c) if the warrant so provides, otherwise than in the presence of a constable in uniform.

(5) An authorised person seeking to exercise the powers conferred by a warrant under this paragraph or, if there is more than one such authorised person, that one of them who is in charge of the search shall provide a copy of the warrant endorsed with his name as follows—

(a) if the occupier of the premises concerned is present at the time the search is to begin, the copy shall be supplied to the occupier;

(b) if at that time the occupier is not present but a person who appears to the authorised person to be in charge of the premises is present, the copy shall be supplied to that person;

(c) if neither paragraph (a) nor paragraph (b) above applies, the copy shall be left in a prominent place on the premises.

(6) Where an authorised person has reasonable grounds for suspecting that a fraud offence has been committed he may arrest anyone whom he has reasonable grounds for suspecting to be guilty of the offence.

(7) In this paragraph "a fraud offence" means an offence under any provision of paragraph 9(1) to (5) below.

Removal of documents etc.

5.—(1) An authorised person who removes anything in the exercise of a power conferred by or under paragraph 4 above shall, if so requested by a person showing himself—

(a) to be the occupier of premises from which it was removed, or

(b) to have had custody or control of it immediately before the removal,

provide that person with a record of what he removed.

(2) The authorised person shall provide the record within a reasonable time from the making of the request for it.

(3) Subject to sub-paragraph (7) below, if a request for permission to be allowed access to anything which—

(a) has been removed by an authorised person, and

(b) is retained by the Commissioners for the purposes of investigating an offence,

is made to the officer in overall charge of the investigation by a person who had custody or control of the thing immediately before it was so removed or by someone acting on behalf of such a person, the officer shall allow the person who made the request access to it under the supervision of an authorised person.

(4) Subject to sub-paragraph (7) below, if a request for a photograph or copy of any such thing is made to the officer in overall charge of the investigation by a person who had custody or

control of the thing immediately before it was so removed, or by someone acting on behalf of such a person, the officer shall—
   (a) allow the person who made the request access to it under the supervision of an authorised person for the purpose of photographing it or copying it, or
   (b) photograph or copy it, or cause it to be photographed or copied.
(5) Subject to sub-paragraph (7) below, where anything is photographed or copied under sub-paragraph (4)(b) above the officer shall supply the photograph or copy, or cause it to be supplied, to the person who made the request.
(6) The photograph or copy shall be supplied within a reasonable time from the making of the request.
(7) There is no duty under this paragraph to allow access to, or to supply a photograph or copy of, anything if the officer in overall charge of the investigation for the purposes of which it was removed has reasonable grounds for believing that to do so would prejudice—
   (a) that investigation,
   (b) the investigation of an offence other than the offence for the purposes of the investigation of which the thing was removed, or
   (c) any criminal proceedings which may be brought as a result of the investigation of which he is in charge or any such investigation as is mentioned in paragraph (b) above.
(8) Any reference in this paragraph to the officer in overall charge of the investigation is a reference to the person whose name and address are endorsed on the warrant concerned as being the officer so in charge.
6.—(1) Where, on an application made as mentioned in sub-paragraph (2) below, the appropriate judicial authority is satisfied that a person has failed to comply with a requirement imposed by paragraph 5 above, the authority may order that person to comply with the requirement within such time and in such manner as may be specified in the order.
(2) An application under sub-paragraph (1) above shall be made—
   (a) in the case of a failure to comply with any of the requirements imposed by sub-paragraphs (1) and (2) of paragraph 5 above, by the occupier of the premises from which the thing in question was removed or by the person who had custody or control of it immediately before it was so removed, and
   (b) in any other case, by the person who had such custody or control.
(3) In this paragraph "the appropriate judicial authority" means—
   (a) in England and Wales, a magistrates' court;
   (b) in Scotland, the sheriff;
   (c) in Northern Ireland, a court of summary jurisdiction, as defined in Article 2(2)(a) of the Magistrates' Court (Northern Ireland) Order 1981.
(4) In England and Wales and Northern Ireland, an application for an order under this paragraph shall be made by way of complaint; and sections 21 and 42(2) of the Interpretation Act (Northern Ireland) 1954 shall apply as if any reference in those provisions to any enactment included a reference to this paragraph.

GENERAL NOTE

Para. (4)
The Customs and Excise may enter premises by force, if authorised by a warrant issued by a justice of the peace. A warrant authorises seizure of documents and confers powers of search of individuals. The warrant may specify the number of officials conducting the raid, the times at which it may be carried out, and may require the presence of a police officer. A copy of the warrant must be supplied to the occupier or the person in charge or left on the premises. An official may arrest anyone on reasonable suspicion of an offence under para. (9).

Para. (5)
Where documents are seized in a para. (4) raid, the official concerned is obliged to provide a record of them. The official in charge of the investigation is obliged to grant access to documents and to provide facilities for photographing or copying them, unless it would prejudice the investigation. The name and address of the official in charge will be endorsed on the warrant.

Para. (6)
Where the Customs and Excise fail to meet the requirements of para. (5), they may be ordered to do so on complaint to a magistrates' court, or by similar procedures in Scotland and Northern Ireland.

PART III

RECOVERY

Recovery of tax etc.

7.—(1) Tax due from any person shall be recoverable as a debt due to the Crown.

(2) In the Insolvency Act 1986, in section 386(1) (preferential debts) the words "insurance premium tax," shall be inserted after "VAT," and in Schedule 6 (categories of preferential debts) the following paragraph shall be inserted after paragraph 3—

"3A. Any insurance premium tax which is referable to the period of 6 months next before the relevant date (which period is referred to below as "the 6-month period").

For the purposes of this paragraph—
- (a) where the whole of the accounting period to which any insurance premium tax is attributable falls within the 6-month period, the whole amount of that tax is referable to that period; and
- (b) in any other case the amount of any insurance premium tax which is referable to the 6-month period is the proportion of the tax which is equal to such proportion (if any) of the accounting period in question as falls within the 6-month period;

and references here to accounting periods shall be construed in accordance with Part III of the Finance Act 1994."

(3) In the Bankruptcy (Scotland) Act 1985, Schedule 3 (preferred debts) shall be amended as mentioned in sub-paragraphs (4) and (5) below.

(4) In paragraph 2 the following sub-paragraph shall be inserted after sub-paragraph (1)—

"(1A) Any insurance premium tax which is referable to the period of six months next before the relevant date."

(5) The following shall be inserted after paragraph 8—

"*Periods to which insurance premium tax referable*

8A.—(1) For the purpose of paragraph 2(1A) of Part I of this Schedule—
- (a) where the whole of the accounting period to which any insurance premium tax is attributable falls within the period of six months next before the relevant date ("the relevant period"), the whole amount of that tax shall be referable to the relevant period; and
- (b) in any other case the amount of any insurance premium tax which shall be referable to the relevant period shall be the proportion of the tax which is equal to such proportion (if any) of the accounting period in question as falls within the relevant period.

(2) In sub-paragraph (1) above "accounting period" shall be construed in accordance with Part III of the Finance Act 1994."

(6) In the Insolvency (Northern Ireland) Order 1989, in Article 346(1) (preferential debts) the words "insurance premium tax" shall be inserted after "VAT" and in Schedule 4 (categories of preferential debts) the following paragraph shall be inserted after paragraph 3—

"3A. Any insurance premium tax which is referable to the period of 6 months next before the relevant date (which period is referred to below as "the 6-month period").

For the purposes of this paragraph—
- (a) where the whole of the accounting period to which any insurance premium tax is attributable falls within the 6-month period, the whole amount of that tax is referable to that period; and
- (b) in any other case the amount of any insurance premium tax which is referable to the 6-month period is the proportion of the tax which is equal to such proportion (if any) of the accounting period in question as falls within the 6-month period;

and references here to accounting periods shall be construed in accordance with Part III of the Finance Act 1994."

(7) Regulations may make provision in respect of England and Wales and Northern Ireland—
- (a) for authorising distress to be levied on the goods and chattels of any person refusing or neglecting to pay any tax due from him or any amount recoverable as if it were tax due from him;
- (b) for the disposal of any goods or chattels on which distress is levied in pursuance of the regulations;
- (c) for the imposition and recovery of costs, charges, expenses and fees in connection with anything done under the regulations.

(8) Regulations may make provision in respect of Scotland—

(a) for obtaining a summary warrant for the poinding, sale and disposal of proceeds of sale, in accordance with Schedule 5 to the Debtors (Scotland) Act 1987, of the moveable property of any person refusing or neglecting to pay any tax due from him or any amount recoverable as if it were tax due from him;

(b) for the imposition and recovery of expenses, charges and fees in connection with anything done under the regulations.

Recovery of overpaid tax

8.—(1) Where a person has paid an amount to the Commissioners by way of tax which was not tax due to them, they shall be liable to repay the amount to him.

(2) The Commissioners shall only be liable to repay an amount under this paragraph on a claim being made for the purpose.

(3) It shall be a defence, in relation to a claim under this paragraph, that repayment of an amount would unjustly enrich the claimant.

(4) No amount may be claimed under this paragraph after the expiry of six years from the date on which it was paid, except where sub-paragraph (5) below applies.

(5) Where an amount has been paid to the Commissioners by reason of a mistake, a claim for the repayment of the amount under this paragraph may be made at any time before the expiry of six years from the date on which the claimant discovered the mistake or could with reasonable diligence have discovered it.

(6) A claim under this paragraph shall be made in such form and manner and shall be supported by such documentary evidence as may be prescribed by regulations.

(7) Except as provided by this paragraph, the Commissioners shall not be liable to repay an amount paid to them by way of tax by virtue of the fact that it was not tax due to them.

GENERAL NOTE

Para. (7)
Insurance premium tax is recoverable as a debt due to the Crown, and is added to the categories of preferential debt under the insolvency and bankruptcy legislation in England, Wales, Scotland and Northern Ireland. Regulations may provide for distress (in England, Wales and Northern Ireland) or poinding (in Scotland) in relation to unpaid IPT.

Para. (8)
The Customs and Excise are obliged to refund any IPT overpaid on a claim being made within six years of the payment or the discovery that it was mistakenly paid, but not if it would unjustly enrich the claimant.

PART IV

PENALTIES

Criminal offences

9.—(1) A person is guilty of an offence if—
(a) being a registrable person, he is knowingly concerned in, or in the taking of steps with a view to, the fraudulent evasion of tax by him or another registrable, or
(b) not being a registrable person, he is knowingly concerned in, or in the taking of steps with a view to, the fraudulent evasion of tax by a registrable person.

(2) Any reference in sub-paragraph (1) above to the evasion of tax includes a reference to the obtaining of a payment under regulations under section 55(3)(c) or (d) or (f) of this Act.

(3) A person is guilty of an offence if with the requisite intent—
(a) he produces, furnishes or sends, or causes to be produced, furnished or sent, for the purposes of this Part of this Act any document which is false in a material particular, or
(b) he otherwise makes use for those purposes of such a document;
and the requisite intent is intent to deceive or to secure that a machine will respond to the document as if it were a true document.

(4) A person is guilty of an offence if in furnishing any information for the purposes of this Part of this Act he makes a statement which he knows to be false in a material particular or recklessly makes a statement which is false in a material particular.

(5) A person is guilty of an offence by virtue of this sub-paragraph if his conduct during any specified period must have involved the commission by him of one or more offences under the preceding provisions of this paragraph; and the preceding provisions of this sub-paragraph apply whether or not the particulars of that offence or those offences are known.

(6) A person is guilty of an offence if—

(a) he enters into a taxable insurance contract, or

(b) he makes arrangements for other persons to enter into a taxable insurance contract,

with reason to believe that tax in respect of the contract will be evaded.

(7) A person is guilty of an offence if he enters into taxable insurance contracts without giving security (or further security) he has been required to give under paragraph 24 below.

Criminal penalties

10.—(1) A person guilty of an offence under paragraph 9(1) above shall be liable—

(a) on summary conviction, to a penalty of the statutory maximum or of three times the amount of the tax, whichever is the greater, or to imprisonment for a term not exceeding six months or to both;

(b) on conviction on indictment, to a penalty of any amount or to imprisonment for a term not exceeding seven years or to both.

(2) The reference in sub-paragraph (1) above to the amount of the tax shall be construed, in relation to tax itself or a payment falling within paragraph 9(2) above, as a reference to the aggregate of—

(a) the amount (if any) falsely claimed by way of credit, and

(b) the amount (if any) by which the gross amount of tax was falsely understated.

(3) A person guilty of an offence under paragraph 9(3) or (4) above shall be liable—

(a) on summary conviction, to a penalty of the statutory maximum or, where sub-paragraph (4) below applies, to the alternative penalty there specified if it is greater, or to imprisonment for a term not exceeding six months or to both;

(b) on conviction on indictment, to a penalty of any amount or to imprisonment for a term not exceeding seven years or to both.

(4) In a case where—

(a) the document referred to in paragraph 9(3) above is a return required under this Part of this Act, or

(b) the information referred to in paragraph 9(4) above is contained in or otherwise relevant to such a return,

the alternative penalty is a penalty equal to three times the aggregate of the amount (if any) falsely claimed by way of credit and the amount (if any) by which the gross amount of tax was understated.

(5) A person guilty of an offence under paragraph 9(5) above shall be liable—

(a) on summary conviction, to a penalty of the statutory maximum or (if greater) three times the amount of any tax that was or was intended to be evaded by his conduct, or to imprisonment for a term not exceeding six months or to both;

(b) on conviction on indictment, to a penalty of any amount or to imprisonment for a term not exceeding seven years or to both;

and paragraph 9(2) and sub-paragraph (2) above shall apply for the purposes of this sub-paragraph as they apply respectively for the purposes of paragraph 9(1) and sub-paragraph (1) above.

(6) A person guilty of an offence under paragraph 9(6) above shall be liable on summary conviction to a penalty of level 5 on the standard scale or three times the amount of the tax, whichever is the greater.

(7) A person guilty of an offence under paragraph 9(7) above shall be liable on summary conviction to a penalty of level 5 on the standard scale.

(8) In this paragraph—

(a) "credit" means credit for which provision is made by regulations under section 55 of this Act;

(b) "the gross amount of tax" means the total amount of tax due before taking into account any deduction for which provision is made by regulations under section 55(3) of this Act.

Criminal proceedings etc.

11. Sections 145 to 155 of the Customs and Excise Management Act 1979 (proceedings for offences, mitigation of penalties and certain other matters) shall apply in relation to offences under paragraph 9 above and penalties imposed under paragraph 10 above as they apply in relation to offences and penalties under the customs and excise Acts as defined in that Act.

Civil penalties

12.—(1) In a case where—

(a) for the purpose of evading tax, a registrable person does any act or omits to take any action, and

(b) his conduct involves dishonesty (whether or not it is such as to give rise to criminal liability),

he shall be liable to a penalty equal to the amount of tax evaded, or (as the case may be) sought to be evaded, by his conduct; but this is subject to sub-paragraph (7) below.

(2) The reference in sub-paragraph (1)(a) above to evading tax includes a reference to obtaining a payment under regulations under section 55(3)(c) or (d) or (f) of this Act in circumstances where the person concerned is not entitled to the sum.

(3) The reference in sub-paragraph (1) above to the amount of tax evaded or sought to be evaded is a reference to the aggregate of—

(a) the amount (if any) falsely claimed by way of credit, and

(b) the amount (if any) by which the gross amount of tax was falsely understated.

(4) In this paragraph—

(a) "credit" means credit for which provision is made by regulations under section 55 of this Act;

(b) "the gross amount of tax" means the total amount of tax due before taking into account any deduction for which provision is made by regulations under section 55(3) of this Act.

(5) Statements made or documents produced by or on behalf of a person shall not be inadmissible in any such proceedings as are mentioned in sub-paragraph (6) below by reason only that it has been drawn to his attention—

(a) that, in relation to tax, the Commissioners may assess an amount due by way of a civil penalty instead of instituting criminal proceedings and, though no undertaking can be given as to whether the Commissioners will make such an assessment in the case of any person, it is their practice to be influenced by the fact that a person has made a full confession of any dishonest conduct to which he has been a party and has given full facilities for investigation, and

(b) that the Commissioners or, on appeal, an appeal tribunal have power under paragraph 13 below to reduce a penalty under this paragraph,

and that he was or may have been induced thereby to make the statements or produce the documents.

(6) The proceedings referred to in sub-paragraph (5) above are—

(a) any criminal proceedings against the person concerned in respect of any offence in connection with or in relation to tax, and

(b) any proceedings against him for the recovery of any sum due from him in connection with or in relation to tax.

(7) Where, by reason of conduct falling within sub-paragraph (1) above, a person is convicted of an offence (whether under this Part of this Act or otherwise) that conduct shall not also give rise to liability to a penalty under this paragraph.

13.—(1) Where a person is liable to a penalty under paragraph 12 above the Commissioners or, on appeal, an appeal tribunal may reduce the penalty to such amount (including nil) as they think proper.

(2) In the case of a penalty reduced by the Commissioners under sub-paragraph (1) above an appeal tribunal, on an appeal relating to the penalty, may cancel the whole or any part of the reduction made by the Commissioners.

(3) None of the matters specified in sub-paragraph (4) below shall be matters which the Commissioners or any appeal tribunal shall be entitled to take into account in exercising their powers under this paragraph.

(4) Those matters are—

(a) the insufficiency of the funds available to any person for paying any tax due or for paying the amount of the penalty;

(b) the fact that there has, in the case in question or in that case taken with any other cases, been no or no significant loss of tax.

14.—(1) A person who fails to comply with section 53(2) of this Act shall be liable to a penalty equal to 5 per cent. of the relevant tax or, if it is greater or the circumstances are such that there is no relevant tax, to a penalty of £250; but this is subject to sub-paragraphs (3) and (4) below.

(2) In sub-paragraph (1) above "relevant tax" means the tax (if any) for which the person concerned is liable for the period which—

(a) begins on the date with effect from which he is, in accordance with section 53 of this Act, required to be registered, and

(b) ends on the date on which the Commissioners received notification of his liability to be registered.

(3) Conduct falling within sub-paragraph (1) above shall not give rise to liability to a penalty under this paragraph if the person concerned satisfies the Commissioners or, on appeal, an appeal tribunal that there is a reasonable excuse for his conduct.

(4) Where, by reason of conduct falling within sub-paragraph (1) above—

(a) a person is convicted of an offence (whether under this Part of this Act or otherwise), or

(b) a person is assessed to a penalty under paragraph 12 above,

that conduct shall not also give rise to liability to a penalty under this paragraph.

(5) If it appears to the Treasury that there has been a change in the value of money since the passing of this Act or, as the case may be, the last occasion when the power conferred by this sub-paragraph was exercised, they may by order substitute for the sum for the time being specified in sub-paragraph (1) above such other sum as appears to them to be justified by the change.

(6) An order under sub-paragraph (5) above shall not apply in relation to a failure which ended on or before the date on which the order comes into force.

15.—(1) This paragraph applies if a person fails to comply with—

(a) a requirement imposed by regulations made under section 54 of this Act to pay the tax due in respect of any period within the time required by the regulations, or

(b) a requirement imposed by regulations made under that section to furnish a return in respect of any period within the time required by the regulations;

and sub-paragraphs (2) and (3) below shall have effect subject to sub-paragraphs (5) and (6) below and paragraph 25(7) below.

(2) The person shall be liable to a penalty equal to 5 per cent. of the tax due or, if it is greater, to a penalty of £250.

(3) The person—

(a) shall be liable, in addition to an initial penalty under sub-paragraph (2) above, to a penalty of £20 for every relevant day when he fails to pay the tax or furnish the return, but

(b) shall not in respect of the continuation of the failure be liable to further penalties under sub-paragraph (2) above;

and a relevant day is any day falling after the time within which the tax is required to be paid or the return is required to be furnished.

(4) For the purposes of sub-paragraph (2) above the tax due—

(a) shall, if the person concerned has furnished a return, be taken to be the tax shown in the return as that for which he is accountable in respect of the period in question, and

(b) shall, in any other case, be taken to be such tax as has been assessed for that period and notified to him under section 56(1) of this Act.

(5) A failure falling within sub-paragraph (1) or (3) above shall not give rise to liability to a penalty under this paragraph if the person concerned satisfies the Commissioners or, on appeal, an appeal tribunal that there is a reasonable excuse for the failure.

(6) Where, by reason of a failure falling within sub-paragraph (1) or (3) above—

(a) a person is convicted of an offence (whether under this Part of this Act or otherwise), or

(b) a person is assessed to a penalty under paragraph 12 above,

that failure shall not also give rise to liability to a penalty under this paragraph.

(7) If it appears to the Treasury that there has been a change in the value of money since the passing of this Act or, as the case may be, the last occasion when the power conferred by this sub-paragraph was exercised, they may by order substitute for the sums for the time specified in sub-paragraphs (2) and (3) above such other sums as appear to them to be justified by the change.

(8) An order under sub-paragraph (7) above shall not apply to a failure which began before the date on which the order comes into force.

16.—(1) This paragraph applies where—

(a) by virtue of regulations made under section 65 of this Act a liability notice (within the meaning of that section) is served on an insured person,

(b) by virtue of such regulations that person is liable to pay an amount of tax which has been assessed in accordance with the regulations, and

(c) that tax is not paid within the time required by the regulations;

and sub-paragraphs (2) and (3) below shall have effect subject to sub-paragraphs (4) and (5) below and paragraph 25(7) below.

(2) The person shall be liable to a penalty equal to 5 per cent. of the tax assessed as mentioned in sub-paragraph (1) above or, if it is greater, to a penalty of £250.

(3) The person—

(a) shall be liable, in addition to an initial penalty under sub-paragraph (2) above, to a penalty of £20 for every relevant day when the tax is unpaid, but

(b) shall not in respect of the continuation of the non-payment of the tax be liable to further penalties under sub-paragraph (2) above;

and a relevant day is any day falling after the time within which the tax is required to be paid.

(4) A person shall not be liable to a penalty by virtue of this paragraph if he satisfies the Commissioners or, on appeal, an appeal tribunal that he took all reasonable steps to ensure that the tax mentioned in sub-paragraph (1)(b) above was paid within the time required by the regulations.

(5) Where, by reason of a failure to pay tax, a person is convicted of an offence (whether under this Part of this Act or otherwise), that failure shall not also give rise to liability to a penalty under this paragraph.

(6) If it appears to the Treasury that there has been a change in the value of money since the passing of this Act or, as the case may be, the last occasion when the power conferred by this sub-paragraph was exercised, they may by order substitute for the sums for the time being specified in sub-paragraphs (2) and (3) above such other sums as appear to them to be justified by the change.

(7) An order under sub-paragraph (6) above shall not apply in relation to any failure to pay tax that was required to be paid before the date on which the order comes into force.

17.—(1) If a person fails to comply with—
(a) section 53(3) of this Act,
(b) any provision of paragraph 2 or 3 above, or
(c) a requirement imposed by any regulations made under this Part of this Act, other than a requirement falling within sub-paragraph (2) below,

he shall be liable to a penalty of £250; but this is subject to sub-paragraphs (3) and (4) below.

(2) A requirement falls within this sub-paragraph if it is—
(a) a requirement imposed by regulations made under section 54 of this Act to pay the tax due in respect of any period within the time required by the regulations,
(b) a requirement imposed by regulations made under that section to furnish a return in respect of any period within the time required by the regulations,
(c) a requirement imposed by regulations made under section 65 of this Act to pay tax within the time required by the regulations, or
(d) a requirement specified for the purposes of this sub-paragraph by regulations.

(3) A failure falling within sub-paragraph (1) above shall not give rise to liability to a penalty under this paragraph if the person concerned satisfies the Commissioners or, on appeal, an appeal tribunal that there is a reasonable excuse for the failure.

(4) Where by reason of a failure falling within sub-paragraph (1) above—
(a) a person is convicted of an offence (whether under this Part of this Act or otherwise), or
(b) a person is assessed to a penalty under paragraph 12 above,

that failure shall not also give rise to liability to a penalty under this paragraph.

(5) If it appears to the Treasury that there has been a change in the value of money since the passing of this Act or, as the case may be, the last occasion when the power conferred by this sub-paragraph was exercised, they may by order substitute for the sum for the time being specified in sub-paragraph (1) above such other sum as appears to them to be justified by the change.

(6) An order under sub-paragraph (5) above shall not apply in relation to a failure which began before the date on which the order comes into force.

18.—(1) A person who—
(a) by virtue of subsection (3), (7) or (9) of section 57 of this Act becomes subject to a duty to take action as mentioned in subsection (4) of that section, and
(b) fails to take action as so mentioned,

shall be liable to a penalty of £10,000; but this is subject to sub-paragraph (2) below.

(2) A failure falling within sub-paragraph (1) above shall not give rise to liability to a penalty under this paragraph if the person concerned satisfies the Commissioners or, on appeal, an appeal tribunal that there is a reasonable excuse for the failure.

(3) If it appears to the Treasury that there has been a change in the value of money since the passing of this Act or, as the case may be, the last occasion when the power conferred by this sub-paragraph was exercised, they may by order substitute for the sum for the time being specified in sub-paragraph (1) above such other sum as appears to them to be justified by the change.

(4) An order under sub-paragraph (3) above shall not apply in relation to a case where the duty mentioned in sub-paragraph (1) above was imposed before the date on which the order comes into force.

19.—(1) This paragraph applies where—
(a) in accordance with regulations under paragraph 7(7) above a distress is authorised to be levied on the goods and chattels of a person (a person in default) who has refused or neglected to pay any tax due from him or any amount recoverable as if it were tax due from him, and

(b) the person levying the distress and the person in default have entered into a walking possession agreement.

(2) For the purposes of this paragraph a walking possession agreement is an agreement under which, in consideration of the property distrained upon being allowed to remain in the custody of the person in default and of the delaying of its sale, the person in default—

(a) acknowledges that the property specified in the agreement is under distraint and held in walking possession, and

(b) undertakes that, except with the consent of the Commissioners and subject to such conditions as they may impose, he will not remove or allow the removal of any of the specified property from the premises named in the agreement.

(3) Subject to sub-paragraph (4) below, if the person in default is in breach of the undertaking contained in a walking possession agreement, he shall be liable to a penalty equal to half of the tax or other amount referred to in sub-paragraph (1)(a) above.

(4) The person in default shall not be liable to a penalty under sub-paragraph (3) above if he satisfies the Commissioners or, on appeal, an appeal tribunal that there is a reasonable excuse for the breach in question.

(5) This paragraph does not extend to Scotland.

20. For the purposes of paragraphs 14(3), 15(5), 17(3), 18(2) and 19(4) above—

(a) an insufficiency of funds available for paying any amount is not a reasonable excuse, and

(b) where reliance is placed on any other person to perform any task, neither the fact of that reliance nor any conduct of the person relied upon is a reasonable excuse.

General Note

Para. (9)

The following are made criminal offences:

    (i) fraudulent evasion of IPT;

  (ii) the production of false documents;

 (iii) the deliberate or reckless making of false statements;

 (iv) conduct which must have involved the commission of offences under (i)–(iii) above;

  (v) taking out insurance or making arrangements for it believing that IPT will be evaded;

 (vi) writing insurance without giving security required under para. (24).

Para. (10)

The above offences attract the following penalties:

    (i) on summary conviction, the statutory maximum or three times the tax, whichever is greater plus six months; on indictment an unlimited penalty plus seven years;

 (ii), (iii) and (iv) similar penalties, related to the amount of tax involved;

  (v) level 5 on the standard scale or three times the amount of the tax, if greater;

 (vi) level 5 on the standard scale.

Para. (11)

The general provisions in the CEMA 1979 (c. 2), ss.145–155 relating to legal proceedings apply to IPT.

Para. (12)

As has been the case for some time with VAT, and now with excise duty (see ss.8–11), a system of civil penalties is provided for IPT. At Committee Stage, the Government gave assurances that penalties would not be applied in cases of genuine misunderstanding or unfamiliarity with the requirements in the first year of the operation of IPT. Insurers would not be penalised for a first default in the first year, unless it was thought that deliberate evasion or manipulation was involved.

This paragraph imposes a penalty equal to the amount of IPT dishonestly evaded. Discussions regarding full disclosure with a view to a civil penalty will not preclude the use of statements and documents in subsequent criminal proceedings, but a criminal conviction precludes a civil penalty.

Para. (13)

A penalty under para. (12) may be varied by the Customs and Excise or the tribunal. Insufficiency of funds or the fact that there has been no significant loss of tax are not matters which may be taken into account.

Para. (14)

Failure to register for IPT attracts a penalty of 5 per cent. of the tax due for the period of non-registration, subject to a minimum penalty of £250. The reasonable excuse defence applies.

A criminal conviction or a para. (12) penalty excludes a para. (14) penalty. The fixed penalty may be revalorised by Treasury order.

Para. (15)
Failure to submit returns or pay tax due attracts similar penalties to para. (14) plus £20 per day for the period of non-compliance. The other provisions of para. (14) also apply.

Para. (16)
Similar provisions to para. (15) apply in the case of an insured who has an assessment served on him.

Para. (17)
Failure to deregister, to provide information or produce documents when required, or to comply with other regulatory requirements, attracts a penalty of £250. The other provisions of para. (14) also apply.

Para. (18)
Offshore insurers who fail to appoint a tax representative are liable to a penalty of £10,000. Again, the reasonable excuse defence applies and the penalty may be revalorised by Treasury order.

Para. (19)
Breach of a walking possession agreement entered into when distress is levied under para. (7) attracts a penalty of half the tax in question. The reasonable excuse defence applies.

Para. (20)
As with the parallel VAT provisions, insufficiency of funds or reliance on another person do not form a reasonable excuse for an insurer who is penalised. In *Customs and Excise Commissioners* v. *Steptoe* [1992] STC 757, the Court of Appeal held that while insufficiency of funds was not of itself a reasonable excuse, the underlying cause of the insufficiency, *e.g.* the dilatoriness in paying by a main or sole customer, might provide such an excuse.

PART V

INTEREST

Interest on tax etc.

21.—(1) Where an assessment is made under any provision of section 56 of this Act, the whole of the amount assessed shall carry interest at the prescribed rate from the reckonable date until payment; but this is subject to sub-paragraph (2) and paragraph 25(7) below.
(2) Sub-paragraph (1) above shall not apply in relation to an assessment under section 56(1) of this Act unless at least one of the following conditions is fulfilled, namely—
(a) that the assessment relates to an accounting period in respect of which either a return has previously been made, or an earlier assessment has already been notified to the person concerned;
(b) that the assessment relates to an accounting period which exceeds three months and begins on the date with effect from which the person was, or was required to be, registered under this Part of this Act.
(3) In a case where—
(a) the circumstances are such that a relevant assessment could have been made, but
(b) before such an assessment was made the tax due or other amount concerned was paid (so that no such assessment was necessary),
the whole of the amount paid shall carry interest at the prescribed rate from the reckonable date until the date on which it was paid; and for the purposes of this sub-paragraph a relevant assessment is an assessment in relation to which sub-paragraph (1) above would have applied if the assessment had been made.
(4) The references in sub-paragraphs (1) and (3) above to the reckonable date shall be construed as follows—
(a) where the amount assessed or paid is such an amount as is referred to in subsection (2) of section 56 of this Act, the reckonable date is the seventh day after the day on which a written instruction was issued by the Commissioners directing the making of the payment of the amount which ought not to have been paid to the person concerned;
(b) in all other cases the reckonable date is the latest date on which (in accordance with regulations under this Part of this Act) a return is required to be made for the accounting period to which the amount assessed or paid relates;

and interest under this paragraph shall run from the reckonable date even if that date is a non-business day, within the meaning of section 92 of the Bills of Exchange Act 1882.

(5) In this paragraph "the prescribed rate" means such rate as may be prescribed by order; and such an order—

(a) may prescribe different rates for different purposes;

(b) shall apply to interest for periods beginning on or after the date when the order is expressed to come into force, whether or not interest runs from before that date.

(6) Interest under this paragraph shall be paid without any deduction of income tax.

Interest payable by Commissioners

22.—(1) Where, due to an error on the part of the Commissioners, a person—

(a) has paid to them by way of tax an amount which was not tax due and which they are in consequence liable to repay to him,

(b) has failed to claim payment of an amount to the payment of which he was entitled in pursuance of provision made under section 55(3)(c), (d) or (f) of this Act, or

(c) has suffered delay in receiving payment of an amount due to him from them in connection with tax,

then, if and to the extent that they would not be liable to do so apart from this paragraph, they shall (subject to the following provisions of this paragraph) pay interest to him on that amount for the applicable period.

(2) Interest under this paragraph shall be payable at such rate as may from time to time be prescribed by order, and—

(a) any such order may prescribe different rates for different purposes;

(b) any such order shall apply to interest for periods beginning on or after the date on which the order is expressed to come into force, whether or not interest runs from before that date.

(3) The applicable period, in a case falling within sub-paragraph (1)(a) above, is the period—

(a) beginning with the date on which the payment is received by the Commissioners, and

(b) ending with the date on which they authorise payment of the amount on which the interest is payable.

(4) The applicable period, in a case falling within sub-paragraph (1)(b) or (c) above, is the period—

(a) beginning with the date on which, apart from the error, the Commissioners might reasonably have been expected to authorise payment of the amount on which the interest is payable, and

(b) ending with the date on which they in fact authorise payment of that amount.

(5) In determining the applicable period for the purposes of this paragraph, there shall be left out of account any period referable to the raising and answering of any reasonable enquiry relating to any matter giving rise to, or otherwise connected with, the person's entitlement to interest under this paragraph.

(6) In determining for the purposes of sub-paragraph (5) above whether any period is referable to the raising and answering of such an enquiry as is there mentioned, there shall be taken to be so referable any period which begins with the date on which the Commissioners first consider it necessary to make such an enquiry and ends with the date on which the Commissioners—

(a) satisfy themselves that they have received a complete answer to the enquiry, or

(b) determine not to make the enquiry or (if they have made it) not to pursue it further;

but excluding so much of that period as may be prescribed by regulations.

(7) For the purposes of sub-paragraph (6) above it is immaterial—

(a) whether any enquiry is in fact made;

(b) whether any enquiry is or might have been made of the person referred to in sub-paragraph (1) above or of an authorised person or of some other person.

(8) The Commissioners shall only be liable to pay interest under this paragraph on a claim made in writing for that purpose.

(9) No claim shall be made under this paragraph after the expiry of six years from the date on which the claimant discovered the error or could with reasonable diligence have discovered it.

(10) Any reference in this paragraph to receiving a payment from the Commissioners includes a reference to the discharge, by way of set-off, of their liability to make it.

23.—(1) In a case where—

(a) any interest is payable by the Commissioners to a person on a sum due to him under this Part of this Act, and

(b) he is a person to whom regulations under section 55 of this Act apply, the interest shall be treated as an amount to which he is entitled by way of credit in pursuance of the regulations.

(2) Sub-paragraph (1) above shall be disregarded for the purpose of determining a person's entitlement to interest or the amount of interest to which he is entitled.

GENERAL NOTE

Para. (21)
Assessments under s.56 carry interest, where there has either been a previous return or earlier assessment, or relates to a period exceeding three months from the date when the insurer became liable to be registered. Interest also runs in circumstances where an assessment could have been made. Interest runs either from seven days after the Customs and Excise have ordered repayment of an excessive credit or the date when a return should have been made. Interest rates will be set by Treasury order.

Para. (22)
The Customs and Excise are liable to pay interest where as a result of their error a taxpayer has been overcharged or undercredited or has suffered delay in receiving a repayment. The period for which interest runs excludes time referrable to the raising and answering of reasonable enquiries, although part of that may be excluded by regulation. Interest, the rate of which will be set by Treasury order, is payable only on a claim being made within a six-year limitation period.

Para. (23)
Interest due will be included, where applicable, in the s.55 credit procedure.

PART VI

MISCELLANEOUS

Security for tax

24. Where it appears to the Commissioners requisite to do so for the protection of the revenue they may require a registrable person, as a condition of his entering into taxable insurance contracts, to give security (or further security) of such amount and in such manner as they may determine for the payment of any tax which is or may become due from him.

Assessments to penalties etc.

25.—(1) Where a person is liable—
(a) to a penalty under any of paragraphs 12 to 19 above, or
(b) for interest under paragraph 21 above,
the Commissioners may, subject to sub-paragraph (2) below, assess the amount due by way of penalty or interest (as the case may be) and notify it to him accordingly; and the fact that any conduct giving rise to a penalty under any of paragraphs 12 to 19 above may have ceased before an assessment is made under this paragraph shall not affect the power of the Commissioners to make such an assessment.

(2) In the case of the penalties and interest referred to in the following paragraphs of this sub-paragraph, the assessment under this paragraph shall be of an amount due in respect of the accounting period which in the paragraph concerned is referred to as the relevant period—
(a) in the case of a penalty under paragraph 12 above relating to the evasion of tax, the relevant period is the accounting period for which the tax evaded was due;
(b) in the case of a penalty under paragraph 12 above relating to the obtaining of a payment under regulations under section 55(3)(c) or (d) or (f) of this Act, the relevant period is the accounting period in respect of which the payment was obtained;
(c) in the case of interest under paragraph 21 above, the relevant period is the accounting period in respect of which the tax (or amount assessed as tax was due.

(3) In a case where the amount of any penalty or interest falls to be calculated by reference to tax which was not paid at the time it should have been and that tax cannot be readily attributed to any one or more accounting periods, it shall be treated for the purposes of this Part of this Act as tax due for such period or periods as the Commissioners may determine to the best of their judgment and notify to the person liable for the tax and penalty or interest.

(4) Where a person is assessed under this paragraph to an amount due by way of any penalty or interest falling within sub-paragraph (2) above and is also assessed under subsection (1) or (2) of

section 56 of this Act for the accounting period which is the relevant period under sub-paragraph (2) above, the assessments may be combined and notified to him as one assessment, but the amount of the penalty or interest shall be separately identified in the notice.

(5) Sub-paragraph (6) below applies in the case of—

(a) an amount due by way of penalty under paragraph 15 or 16 above;

(b) an amount due by way of interest under paragraph 21 above.

(6) Where this sub-paragraph applies in the case of an amount—

(a) a notice of assessment under this paragraph shall specify a date, being not later than the date of the notice, to which the aggregate amount of the penalty or, as the case may be, the amount of interest which is assessed is calculated, and

(b) if the penalty or interest continues to accrue after that date, a further assessment or further assessments may be made under this paragraph in respect of amounts which so accrue.

(7) If, within such period as may be notified by the Commissioners to the person liable to the penalty under paragraph 15 or 16 above or for the interest under paragraph 21 above—

(a) a failure falling within paragraph 15(3) above is remedied,

(b) the tax referred to in paragraph 16(1) above is paid, or

(c) the amount referred to in paragraph 21(1) above is paid,

it shall be treated for the purposes of paragraph 15, 16 or 21 above (as the case may be) as remedied or paid on the date specified as mentioned in sub-paragraph (6)(a) above.

(8) Where an amount has been assessed and notified to any person under this paragraph it shall be recoverable as if it were tax due from him unless, or except to the extent that, the assessment has subsequently been withdrawn or reduced.

(9) Subsection (8) of section 56 of this Act shall apply for the purposes of this paragraph as it applies for the purposes of that section.

Assessments: time limits

26.—(1) Subject to the following provisions of this paragraph, an assessment under—

(a) any provision of section 56 of this Act, or

(b) paragraph 25 above,

shall not be made more than six years after the end of the accounting period concerned or, in the case of an assessment under paragraph 25 above of an amount due by way of a penalty which is not a penalty referred to in sub-paragraph (2) of that paragraph, six years after the event giving rise to the penalty.

(2) An assessment under paragraph 25 above of—

(a) an amount due by way of any penalty referred to in sub-paragraph (2) of that paragraph, or

(b) an amount due by way of interest,

may be made at any time before the expiry of the period of two years beginning with the time when the amount of tax due for the accounting period concerned has been finally determined.

(3) In relation to an assessment under paragraph 25 above, any reference in sub-paragraph (1) or (2) above to the accounting period concerned is a reference to that period which, in the case of the penalty or interest concerned, is the relevant period referred to in sub-paragraph (2) of that paragraph.

(4) If tax has been lost—

(a) as a result of conduct falling within paragraph 12(1) above or for which a person has been convicted of fraud, or

(b) in circumstances giving rise to liability to a penalty under paragraph 14 above,

an assessment may be made as if, in sub-paragraph (1) above, each reference to six years were a reference to twenty years.

Supplementary assessments

27. If, otherwise than in circumstances falling within subsection (5)(b) of section 56 of this Act, it appears to the Commissioners that the amount which ought to have been assessed in an assessment under any provision of that section or under paragraph 25 above exceeds the amount which was so assessed, then—

(a) under the like provision as that assessment was made, and

(b) on or before the last day on which that assessment could have been made, the Commissioners may make a supplementary assessment of the amount of the excess and shall notify the person concerned accordingly.

Disclosure of information

28.—(1) Notwithstanding any obligation not to disclose information that would otherwise apply, the Commissioners may disclose information—

(a) to the Secretary of State, or

(b) to an authorised officer of the Secretary of State,

for the purpose of assisting the Secretary of State in the performance of his duties.

(2) Notwithstanding any such obligation as is mentioned in sub-paragraph (1) above—

(a) the Secretary of State, or

(b) an authorised officer of the Secretary of State,

may disclose information to the Commissioners or to an authorised officer of the Commissioners for the purpose of assisting the Commissioners in the performance of duties in relation to tax.

(3) Information that has been disclosed to a person by virtue of this paragraph shall not be disclosed by him except—

(a) to another person to whom (instead of him) disclosure could by virtue of this paragraph have been made, or

(b) for the purpose of any proceedings connected with the operation of any provision of, or made under, any enactment in relation to insurance or to tax.

(4) References in the preceding provisions of this paragraph to an authorised officer of the Secretary of State are to any person who has been designated by the Secretary of State as a person to and by whom information may be disclosed under this paragraph.

(5) The Secretary of State shall notify the Commissioners in writing of the name of any person designated under sub-paragraph (4) above.

Evidence by certificate

29.—(1) A certificate of the Commissioners—

(a) that a person was or was not at any time registered under section 53 of this Act,

(b) that any return required by regulations under section 54 of this Act has not been made or had not been made at any time, or

(c) that any tax shown as due in a return made in pursuance of regulations made under section 54 of this Act, or in an assessment made under section 56 of this Act, has not been paid,

shall be sufficient evidence of that fact until the contrary is proved.

(2) Any document purporting to be a certificate under sub-paragraph (1) above shall be taken to be such a certificate until the contrary is proved.

Service of notices etc.

30. Any notice, notification or requirement to be served on, given to or made of any person for the purposes of this Part of this Act may be served, given or made by sending it by post in a letter addressed to that person or his tax representative at the last or usual residence or place of business of that person or representative.

No deduction of penalties or interest

31. In section 827 of the Taxes Act 1988 (no deduction for penalties etc.) the following subsection shall be inserted after subsection (1A)—

"(1B) Where a person is liable to make a payment by way of—

(a) penalty under any of paragraphs 12 to 19 of Schedule 7 to the Finance Act 1994 (insurance premium tax), or

(b) interest under paragraph 21 of that Schedule,

the payment shall not be allowed as a deduction in computing any income, profits or losses for any tax purposes."

Destination of receipts

32. All money and securities for money collected or received for or on account of the tax shall—

(a) if collected or received in Great Britain, be placed to the general account of the Commissioners kept at the Bank of England under section 17 of the Customs and Excise Management Act 1979;

(b) if collected or received in Northern Ireland, be paid into the Consolidated Fund of the United Kingdom in such manner as the Treasury may direct.

Provisional collection of tax

33. In section 1(1) of the Provisional Collection of Taxes Act 1968 after "value added tax," there shall be inserted "insurance premium tax,".

34.—(1) In a case where—
(a) by virtue of a resolution having effect under the Provisional Collection of Taxes Act 1968 has been paid at a rate specified in the resolution, and
(b) by virtue of section 1(6) or (7) or 5(3) of that Act any of that tax is repayable in consequence of the restoration in relation to the premium concerned of a lower rate,
the amount repayable shall be the difference between the tax paid by reference to the actual chargeable amount at the rate specified in the resolution and the tax that would have been payable by reference to the actual chargeable amount at the lower rate.

(2) In sub-paragraph (1) above the "actual chargeable amount" means the chargeable amount by reference to which tax was paid.

(3) In a case where—
(a) by virtue of a resolution having effect under the Provisional Collection of Taxes Act 1968 tax is chargeable at a rate specified in the resolution, but
(b) before the tax is paid it ceases to be chargeable at that rate in consequence of the restoration in relation to the premium concerned of a lower rate,
the tax chargeable at the lower rate shall be charged by reference to the same chargeable amount as that by reference to which tax would have been chargeable at the rate specified in the resolution.

Adjustment of contracts

35.—(1) Where, after the making of a contract of insurance and before a given premium is received by the insurer under the contract, there is a change in the tax chargeable on the receipt of the premium, then, unless the contract otherwise provided, there shall be added to or deducted from the amount payable as the premium an amount equal to the difference between—
(a) the tax chargeable had the change not been made, and
(b) the tax in fact chargeable.

(2) References in sub-paragraph (1) above to a change in the tax chargeable include references to a change to or from no tax being chargeable.

(3) Where this paragraph applies, the amount of the premium shall not be treated as altered for the purposes of calculating tax.

GENERAL NOTE

Para. (24)
The Customs and Excise may require security for the payment of any IPT.

Para. (25)
Penalties under paras. (12)–(19) or interest under para. (21) may be assessed on the taxpayer. Where penalties or interest cannot readily be attributed to particular accounting periods, the Customs and Excise are to allocate them to the best of their judgment. An assessment under this paragraph may be combined with a s.56 assessment for the same period, with the penalty or interest separately identified. A para. (15) or (16) penalty or para. (21) interest assessment will notify the date to which the penalty or interest has been calculated. Further assessments may be made in the event of continued default. A default remedied within a period notified by the Customs and Excise will be treated as made by the date to which the penalty or interest was calculated.

Para. (26)
A normal time-limit of six years applies to assessments, but in cases of dishonest conduct (para. (12)) or of failure to register (para. (14)) the time-limit is increased to 20 years.

Para. (27)
Supplementary assessments may be made in appropriate circumstances.

Para. (28)
Mutual disclosure of information may take place between the Customs and Excise and other government departments for the purpose of assisting either party in their duties. Further disclos-

ure may not be made except for the purpose of proceedings in connection with legislation relating to insurance or tax.

Para. (29)
A Customs and Excise certificate shall be taken as evidence of matters under ss.53, 54 and 56 until the contrary is proved.

Para. (30)
Notices may be served by post to the residence or place of business of the person concerned.

Para. (31)
IPT interest and penalties, like those in relation to VAT and excise duties, are not deductible for income or corporation tax purposes.

Para. (32)
Normal procedures apply to the banking of IPT receipts (see, *e.g.* the VATA 1983 (c. 55), Sched. 7, para. 1(2)).

Para. (33)
Budget resolutions have the same temporary effect for IPT as for other taxes until the Finance Act 1994 is passed.

Para. (34)
This covers the situation where a Budget resolution increases the rate of IPT but the related section of the Finance Act 1994 fails to become law. Tax overpaid will be repayable and tax not yet paid will be chargeable at the lower rate.

Para. (35)
Insurance contracts may be adjusted to take account of the introduction of IPT or any future change in rate.

Section 77   SCHEDULE 8

SUPPLEMENTAL PROVISIONS RELATING TO PERSONAL RELIEFS

The Taxes Act 1988

1. In section 257A(6) of the Taxes Act 1988 (relief confined to one deduction), for "deduction" there shall be substituted "income tax reduction".
2.—(1) In subsections (1) and (2) of section 257BA of that Act (elections as to transfer of relief under section 257A)—
   (a) for the words "to deduct from her total income", in each place where they occur, there shall be substituted "to an income tax reduction calculated by reference to"; and
   (b) for the words "that he is entitled to deduct under section 257A", in each place where they occur, there shall be substituted "by reference to which the calculation of the income tax reduction to which he is entitled under section 257A is to be made".
   (2) In subsection (3) of that section—
   (a) for "to deduct from his total income" there shall be substituted "to an income tax reduction calculated by reference to";
   (b) for "the amount, if any, that he is already entitled to deduct" there shall be substituted "any income tax reduction to which he is already entitled"; and
   (c) for "that she is entitled to deduct by virtue of that election" there shall be substituted "by reference to which the calculation of the income tax reduction to which she is entitled by virtue of that election is to be made".
   (3) Any election made for the purposes of section 257BA of the Taxes Act 1988 which—
   (a) has been made before the coming into force of this paragraph, and
   (b) apart from this paragraph, would have effect in accordance with that section for the year 1994–95 or any subsequent year,
shall so have effect as if it were an election for the purposes of that section as amended by this paragraph.
   3.—(1) In subsection (1) of section 257BB of that Act (transfer of relief where it is not all used), for paragraph (b) and the words after that paragraph there shall be substituted—
      "(b) the amount of the reduction to which he is entitled is determined in accordance with section 256(2)(b) or, by virtue of his having no income tax liability to which that reduction is applicable, is nil,

his wife shall be entitled (in addition to any reduction to which she is entitled by virtue of an election under section 257BA) to an income tax reduction calculated by reference to an amount equal to the unused part of the amount by reference to which her husband's income tax reduction fell to be calculated in pursuance of section 257A and any election under section 257BA."

(2) In subsection (3) of that section, for paragraph (b) and the words after that paragraph there shall be substituted—

"(b) the amount of the reduction to which she is entitled is determined in accordance with section 256(2)(b) or, by virtue of her having no income tax liability to which that reduction is applicable, is nil,

her husband shall be entitled (in addition to any other reduction to which he is entitled by virtue of section 257A) to an income tax reduction calculated by reference to an amount equal to the unused part of the amount by reference to which his wife's income tax reduction fell to be calculated in pursuance of that election."

(3) After that subsection there shall be inserted the following subsection—

"(3A) In this section references, in relation to such an amount as is mentioned in subsection (1)(b) or (3)(b), to the unused part of an amount by reference to which any income tax reduction fell to be calculated are references to so much of it (including, where the amount so mentioned is nil, all of it) as has no practical effect on the determination of the amount so mentioned."

(4) Subsection (6) of that section (calculation of amount left after deductions of a person's total income) shall cease to have effect.

4.—(1) Where the year in question for the purposes of subsection (5) of section 257D of the Taxes Act 1988 (transitional relief in the case of a husband with excess allowances) is the year 1994–95, deductions by virtue of any of sections 257A to 262 of that Act shall be disregarded in determining the deductions which a wife is taken for the purposes of paragraph (c) of that subsection to have been entitled to make from her total income for the year immediately preceding the year in question.

(2) In section 257D(5)(d) of that Act, the words "section 257A and" shall be omitted.

5. In section 257F(c) of that Act, after "257A" there shall be inserted "or, as the case may be, an income tax reduction under that section".

6.—(1) In subsection (1)(b) of section 259 of that Act (additional personal allowance not available to a person entitled to the married couple's allowance), for "to a deduction from his total income" there shall be substituted "to an income tax reduction".

(2) In subsection (3) of that section (entitlement confined to only one deduction), for "deduction" there shall be substituted "income tax reduction".

(3) In subsection (4A) of that section—

(a) for the words "a deduction", in the first and third places where they occur, there shall be substituted "an income tax reduction"; and

(b) for the words "a deduction", in the second place where they occur, there shall be substituted "a reduction".

7.—(1) In subsection (1)(b) of section 260 of that Act (apportionment of relief under section 259), for the words from "the deduction" to "equal" there shall be substituted "the income tax reduction to which each of them is entitled under that section shall be calculated, subject to subsection (2) below, by reference".

(2) In subsection (2) of that section, for the words from "the deduction" to "equal" there shall be substituted "the income tax reduction to which he is entitled for that year under section 259 shall be calculated by reference".

8.—(1) In subsection (2) of section 261A of that Act (additional personal allowance for a year in which spouses separate), for the words from "that he is entitled to deduct" onwards there shall be substituted "by reference to which the income tax reduction to which he is entitled under subsection (1) above is calculated shall be treated as reduced by the amount by reference to which the income tax reduction in which that relief consists is, or but for section 256(2)(b) would be, calculated (or to nil where the latter amount is equal to or exceeds the amount which is to be treated as reduced)."

(2) In subsection (4) of that section, for "deduction" there shall be substituted "income tax reduction".

(3) In subsection (5) of that section—

(a) in paragraph (a), for "relief to which those persons are entitled shall not exceed" there shall be substituted "income tax reductions to which those persons are entitled shall not exceed an amount equal to an income tax reduction calculated (in accordance with section 256(2)(a)) by reference to"; and

(b) in paragraph (c), for the words from "the deduction" to "equal" there shall be substituted "the income tax reduction to which each of them is entitled under section 259 or this section shall be calculated by reference".

9.—(1) In subsection (2) of section 262 of that Act (widow's bereavement allowance)—

(a) for the words "a deduction from her total income", where they occur in paragraphs (a) and (b), there shall be substituted "an income tax reduction"; and

(b) for the words after paragraph (b) there shall be substituted—

"the income tax reduction mentioned in paragraph (b) above shall instead be made (without a claim being made and in accordance with section 257A) in relation to her late husband's liability to tax for that year as if there had been no such election."

(2) For subsections (3) and (4) of that section (cases where allowance transferred back to deceased would be unused) there shall be substituted the following subsections—

"(3) If the amount of an income tax reduction falling to be made by virtue of subsection (2) above in relation to the liability of a widow's late husband—

(a) is less by virtue of section 256(2)(b) than the income tax reduction which, but for subsection (2) above, would have been made in her case by virtue of the election mentioned in that subsection, or

(b) by virtue of his having no income tax liability to which that reduction is applicable, is nil,

the widow shall be entitled (in addition to any reduction to which she is entitled by virtue of subsection (1) above and without making a further claim) to an income tax reduction calculated by reference to an amount equal to the unused part of the amount by reference to which the income tax reduction transferred to the late husband in pursuance of subsection (2) above would have fallen to be calculated.

(3A) In subsection (3) above the references, in relation to an amount to which paragraph (a) or (b) of that subsection applies, to the unused part of an amount by reference to which any income tax reduction would have fallen to be calculated are references to so much of it (including, where paragraph (b) of that subsection applies, all of it) as has no practical effect on the determination of the amount to which that paragraph applies."

10. In section 265(3)(b) of that Act (blind person's allowance), the words from "section 257A" to "or under" shall be omitted.

11. In section 276 of that Act (effect of relief on charges on income), after subsection (1) there shall be inserted the following subsection—

"(1A) In subsection (1) above the references to relief under this Chapter do not include references to relief consisting in such an income tax reduction as is mentioned in section 256(2)."

12. In section 796(1) of that Act (limits on credit for foreign tax), after the words "foreign tax", in the second place where they occur, there shall be inserted "but allowing for the making of any other income tax reduction under the Income Tax Acts".

The Taxes Management Act 1970 (c. 9)

13. In section 37A of the Taxes Management Act 1970 (effect of assessment where allowances transferred)—

(a) after the word "person's", in the first place where it occurs, there shall be inserted "liability to income tax or";

(b) for the words from "any deduction made" to "spouse" there shall be substituted "any income tax reduction or deduction from total income made in the case of that person's spouse"; and

(c) for the words from "and where" onwards there shall be substituted "and the entitlement in that case of the first-mentioned person for the year in question to any income tax reduction or deduction from total income shall be treated as correspondingly reduced."

GENERAL NOTE

Paras. (1)–(11)
Numerous amendments are made to Pt. VII, Chap. 1 of the ICTA 1988 (c. 1) to reflect the fact that from 1994–1995 the married couple's allowance, single parent's allowance and widow's bereavement allowance are now given by income tax reduction instead of by deduction from taxable income (see s.77).

Para. (12)
Relief for foreign tax is to be given after taking into account any income tax reductions given in respect of the married couple's allowance and other personal allowances.

MORTGAGE INTEREST RELIEF ETC.

The Taxes Act 1988

1. For paragraph (o) of section 74 of the Taxes Act 1988 (deduction of relevant loan interest in computing profits and gains) there shall be substituted the following paragraph—
"(o) any interest in so far as the payment of that interest is or would be, otherwise than by virtue of section 375(2), either—
    (i) a payment of interest to which section 369 applies, or
    (ii) a payment of interest to which that section would apply but for section 373(5);".

2. In section 237(5)(b) of the Taxes Act 1988 (no deduction for interest from or against income consisting of bonus issues etc.), for "under section 353" there shall be substituted "in accordance with section 353(1B)".

3. Subsections (4) and (5) of section 353 of the Taxes Act 1988 (restriction of relief to basic rate tax) shall cease to have effect.

4. In section 355(4) of the Taxes Act 1988 (relief where eligibility is by virtue only of section 355(1)(b))—
  (a) for the words from "where" to "but" there shall be substituted "falling within subsection (1)(b) above shall be given only against income from the letting of any land, caravan or house-boat (whether or not the land, caravan or house-boat in question), but"; and
  (b) for the words "the first-mentioned land, caravan or house-boat" there shall be substituted "the land, caravan or house-boat in question".

5. In section 356(1) of the Taxes Act 1988 (job-related accommodation), for "Section 355(1)" there shall be substituted "Section 355(1)(a)".

6. In section 356A(3) of the Taxes Act 1988 ("the sharer's limit") after "is", in the second place where it occurs, there shall be inserted "or but for section 353(1C)(a) would be".

7.—(1) In sections 356D(1) and 357(1) of the Taxes Act 1988, for "eligible for relief under section 353 by virtue of section 355(1)(a) or 356(1)" there shall, in each case, be substituted ", in a case falling or treated as falling within section 355(1)(a), 356 or 358, eligible for relief under section 353 by virtue of section 354".

(2) In sections 357A(7) and 357B(1)(c) and (6) of that Act, for "by virtue of section 355(1)(a) or 356(1)" there shall, in each case, be substituted "and is such that the conditions for the case to fall, or be treated as falling, within section 355(1)(a), 356 or 358 are satisfied".

(3) In section 357C(1)(e) of that Act, for "by virtue of section 355(1)(a) or 356(1)" there shall be substituted "and would have been such that the conditions for the case to fall, or be treated as falling, within section 355(1)(a), 356 or 358 were satisfied".

(4) In section 357C(2) of that Act, for "by virtue of section 355(1)(a) or 356(1)" there shall be substituted "and was such that the conditions for the case to fall, or be treated as falling, within section 355(1)(a), 356 or 358 were satisfied".

8. In section 358 of the Taxes Act 1988 (relief where borrower deceased), after subsection (4) there shall be inserted the following subsection—
    "(4A) References in this Act to a case falling within this section shall not include references to a case falling within section 355(1)(b) where the interest paid by the personal representatives or trustees is eligible for relief under section 353 apart from the assumptions for which subsection (3) above provides."

9. In section 368(1) of the Taxes Act 1988 (interest in respect of which relief given not allowable as deduction for any other purpose), for "for any other purpose of the Income Tax Acts" there shall be substituted "for any purpose of the Income Tax Acts except so far as it is so allowable in accordance with subsection (1B) of that section."

10.—(1) In subsection (2) of section 370 of the Taxes Act 1988 (conditions for interest to be treated as relevant loan interest)—
  (a) after "section 353(2)" there shall be inserted "and any other provision applying to interest falling to be treated as relevant loan interest"; and
  (b) for "from section 74(o) and, where applicable," there shall be substituted "(where applicable) from".

(2) After subsection (6) of that section there shall be inserted the following subsection—
    "(6A) In disregarding section 353(2) for the purposes of subsection (2)(c) above, section 353(1C) and (1D) shall apply for determining whether or not the condition in section 355(1) or 356(1) is fulfilled as (but for section 353(2)) they would apply for the purpose of determining whether or not the case falls, or is treated as falling, within section 355(1)(a) or 356."

11. In section 375(3) of the Taxes Act 1988 (liability of borrower for excess where deduction should not have been made), for the words from "entitles" to "been allowed" there shall be

substituted "shall be taken as regards the borrower as entitling him to any deduction or to retain any amount deducted and, accordingly, where any amount that has been deducted exceeds the amount which ought to have been deducted".

The Finance Act 1993 (c. 34)

12. Subsection (7) of section 57 of the Finance Act 1993 (transitional provision for bridging loans made before 6th April 1991) shall cease to have effect.

General Note

Paras. (1)–(11)
Numerous amendments are made to various provisions in the ICTA 1988 (c. 1), mainly consequential upon the revision of the ICTA 1988 (c. 1), s.353 by s.81 above. The amendments apply to (a) interest payments (whenever due) made after April 5, 1994 (including those made under MIRAS) and (b) interest payments due after April 5, 1994 but paid between November 30, 1993 and that date.

Para. (12)
Transitional relief at the higher rate for bridging loans is no longer available after April 6, 1994.

Section 83   SCHEDULE 10

Medical insurance

Introductory

1. In this Schedule "the 1989 Act" means the Finance Act 1989.

Reduction of relief

2.—(1) Section 54 of the 1989 Act (relief on premiums for medical insurance) shall be amended as follows.
(2) In subsection (3) (relief by deduction from income) for the words from "it shall be deducted" to the end of the subsection there shall be substituted "the individual shall be entitled to relief under this subsection in respect of the payment; and (except where subsections (4) to (6) below apply) relief under this subsection shall be given—
(a) in accordance with subsections (3A) to (3C) below, and
(b) only on a claim made for the purpose."
(3) The following subsections shall be inserted after subsection (3)—
"(3A) Where an individual is entitled to relief under subsection (3) above in respect of one or more payments made in a given year of assessment, the amount of his liability for that year of assessment to income tax on his total income shall be the amount to which he would be liable apart from this section less whichever is the smaller of—
(a) the amount found under subsection (3B) below, and
(b) the amount which reduces his liability to nil.
(3B) The amount referred to in subsection (3A)(a) above is an amount found by—
(a) taking the amount of the payment referred to in subsection (3A) above or (as the case may be) the aggregate amount of the payments there referred to, and
(b) finding an amount equal to tax on the amount taken under paragraph (a) above at the basic rate for the year of assessment concerned.
(3C) In determining for the purposes of subsection (3A) above the amount of income tax to which a person would be liable apart from this section, no account shall be taken of—
(a) any income tax reduction under Chapter I of Part VII of the Taxes Act 1988 or under section 347B of that Act;
(b) any income tax reduction under section 353(1A) of the Taxes Act 1988;
(c) any relief by way of a reduction of liability to tax which is given in accordance with any arrangements having effect by virtue of section 788 of the Taxes Act 1988 or by way of a credit under section 790(1) of that Act;
(d) any tax at the basic rate on so much of that person's income as is income the income tax on which he is entitled to charge against any other person or to deduct, retain or satisfy out of any payment."
(4) This paragraph shall apply in relation to payments made on or after 6th April 1994.

3.—(1) In sections 257D(8) and 265(3) of the Taxes Act 1988 (total income after deductions) paragraph (d) (deduction on account of payments to which section 54(5) of the 1989 Act applies to be disregarded) shall be omitted.

(2) This paragraph shall apply in relation to payments made on or after 6th April 1994.

Surviving spouse

4.—(1) In section 54 of the 1989 Act the following subsection shall be inserted after subsection (2)—

"(2A) In a case where—

(a) a payment is made in respect of a premium under a contract at a time when the contract meets the requirement in subsection (2) above by virtue of paragraph (c) of that subsection, and

(b) a payment is made under the same contract at a time after one of the individuals has died and when the contract does not (apart from this subsection) meet the requirement in subsection (2) above by virtue only of the fact that the surviving spouse is not aged 60 or over at the time,

for the purposes of subsection (2) above in its application to the contract the surviving spouse shall be deemed to be aged 60 or over at the time mentioned in paragraph (b) above."

(2) This paragraph shall apply where the first or only payment to be made in respect of a premium under the contract after the death occurs is made on or after 6th April 1994.

Small benefits and abolition of certification

5.—(1) Section 55 of the 1989 Act (eligible contracts) shall be amended as follows.

(2) In subsection (2) (conditions for contract's being eligible) the following paragraphs shall be inserted after paragraph (b)—

"(ba) at the relevant time the contract satisfies the conditions set out in subsection (2A) below,

(bb) the contract is not one in the case of which subsection (2D) below applies,".

(3) Also in subsection (2)—

(a) after paragraph (c) there shall be inserted "and", and

(b) paragraph (e) and the word "and" immediately preceding it shall be omitted.

(4) The following subsections shall be inserted after subsection (2)—

"(2A) The conditions referred to in subsection (2)(ba) above are that—

(a) the contract either provides indemnity in respect of all or any of the costs of all or any of the treatments, medical services and other matters for the time being specified in regulations made by the Treasury, or in addition to providing indemnity of that description provides cash benefits falling within rules for the time being so specified,

(b) the contract does not confer any right other than such a right as is mentioned in paragraph (a) above or is for the time being specified in regulations made by the Treasury,

(c) the premium under the contract is reasonable, and

(d) the contract satisfies such other requirements as are for the time being specified in regulations made by the Treasury.

(2B) In a case where—

(a) at the relevant time the contract confers a material right, or more than one such right, but

(b) the total cost to the insurer of providing benefits in pursuance of the material right or (as the case may be) in pursuance of all the material rights would not exceed the prescribed sum,

the contract shall not thereby be regarded as failing to satisfy at the relevant time the condition set out in subsection (2A)(b) above.

(2C) For the purposes of subsection (2B) above a material right is a right which—

(a) is not a right such as is mentioned in subsection (2A)(a) above or such as is for the time being specified in regulations made under subsection (2A)(b) above, and

(b) is not a right to a cash benefit.

(2D) This subsection applies in the case of a contract (the main contract) if—

(a) at least one other contract is entered into which is a contract (a collateral contract) under which a benefit is provided in consideration of the insured's entering into the main contract, and

(b) the cost to the insurer of fulfilling his obligations under the collateral contract (or, if there is more than one collateral contract, of fulfilling his obligations under all of them) exceeds the prescribed sum."

(5) Subsections (3) to (6) shall be omitted.

(6) In subsection (9) (approved benefit) for "mentioned in section 56(3)(a) below" there shall be substituted the following paragraphs—

"(a) mentioned in subsection (2A)(a) above, or

(b) for the time being specified in regulations made under subsection (2A)(b) above."

(7) The following subsections shall be inserted after subsection (9)—

"(10) For the purposes of this section a benefit is also an approved benefit if it is not a cash benefit and—

(a) it is a single benefit provided otherwise than as mentioned in subsection (9) above and the cost to the insurer of providing it does not exceed the prescribed sum, or

(b) it is one of a number of benefits provided otherwise than as mentioned in subsection (9) above and the total cost to the insurer of providing the benefits does not exceed the prescribed sum.

(11) In this section the reference to a premium, in relation to a contract of insurance, is to any amount payable under the contract to the insurer.

(12) For the purposes of this section the prescribed sum is £30.

(13) The Treasury may by order substitute for the sum for the time being specified in subsection (12) above such sum as may be specified in the order; and any such substitution shall have effect in relation to cases where the relevant time falls on or after such date as is specified in the order."

(8) This paragraph shall apply where the time which is the relevant time for the purposes of section 55 falls on or after 1st July 1994.

6. The Board shall not certify a contract under section 56 of the 1989 Act in such a way that the certification is expressed to take effect on or after 1st July 1994.

GENERAL NOTE

This Schedule amends the rules which grant tax relief on medical insurance premiums to U.K. resident individuals aged 60 and over.

Para. (2)

Relief for qualifying medical insurance premiums is limited to 25 per cent. Relief continues to be given by deduction at source from premium payments. If this is not possible, then on the making of a claim, relief will be given by income tax reduction. From 1994–95 onwards relief will not be given by a deduction from taxable income. The reduction is limited to the taxpayer's income tax liability assuming relief would not be available. The changes apply to payments made after April 5, 1994.

Para. (4)

A surviving spouse aged under 60 may continue to receive tax relief on a joint medical insurance policy, following the death of a co-spouse aged over 60, provided the surviving spouse's age is the only failure to satisfy the requirements in the FA 1989 (c. 26), s.54(2). The changes apply to payments made after April 5, 1994.

Para. (5)

From July 1, 1994, medical insurance contracts need not be certified by the Revenue in order for their premiums to qualify for tax relief. The conditions that had to be met in order for certification to be granted are re-enacted as conditions that must be met if premium payments under the contract are to be eligible for tax relief. Non-cash benefits of up to £30 (this amount may be amended by Treasury order) may be provided without disqualifying the contract. New s.55(2D) of the FA 1989 (c. 26) ensures this limit is not avoided by the use of linked collateral contracts. This paragraph has effect as from July 1, 1994.

Section 91   SCHEDULE 11

EXTENSION OF ROLL-OVER RELIEF ON RE-INVESTMENT

1. Chapter IA of Part V of the Taxation of Chargeable Gains Act 1992 shall be amended as follows.

Disposals on which relief available

2. In section 164A—

(a) in subsection (1)(a), for the words following "('the re-investor')" there is substituted "on any disposal by him of any asset ('the asset disposed of'); and",

(b) in subsection (2), "Subject to section 164C" is omitted and for "initial holding" (in three places) there is substituted "asset disposed of",

(c) subsections (3) to (7) are omitted,

(d) in subsection (9), for "initial holding" there is substituted "asset disposed of", and

(e) for subsection (12) there is substituted—

"(12) Without prejudice to section 52(4), where consideration is given for the acquisition of any assets some of which are shares to the acquisition of which a claim under this section relates and some of which are not, the consideration shall be apportioned in such manner as is just and reasonable".

3. For section 164B there is substituted—

"Roll-over relief on re-investment by trustees

164B.—(1) Subject to the following provisions of this section, section 164A shall apply, as it applies in such a case as is mentioned in subsection (1) of that section, where there is—

(a) a disposal by the trustees of a settlement of any asset comprised in any settled property to which this section applies, and

(b) such an acquisition by those trustees of eligible shares in a qualifying company as would for the purposes of that section be an acquisition of a qualifying investment at a time in the qualifying period.

(2) This section applies—

(a) to any settled property in which the interests of the beneficiaries are not interests in possession, if all the beneficiaries are individuals, and

(b) to any settled property in which the interests of the beneficiaries are interests in possession, if any of the beneficiaries are individuals,

and references in this section to individuals include any charity.

(3) If, at the time of the disposal of the asset mentioned in subsection (1)(a) above, the settled property comprising that asset is property to which this section applies by virtue of subsection (2)(b) above but not all the beneficiaries are individuals, then—

(a) only the relevant proportion of the gain which would accrue to the trustees on the disposal shall be taken into account for the purposes of section 164A(2)(a)(i), and

(b) no reduction under section 164A(2) shall be made in respect of the whole or any part of the balance of the gain.

(4) Section 164A shall not apply by virtue of this section in a case where, at the time of the disposal of the asset mentioned in subsection (1)(a) above, the settled property which comprises that asset is property to which this section applies by virtue of subsection (2)(a) above unless, immediately after the acquisition of shares mentioned in subsection (1)(b) above, the settled property comprising the shares is also property to which this section applies by virtue of subsection (2)(a) above.

(5) Section 164A shall not apply by virtue of this section in a case where, at the time of the disposal of the asset mentioned in subsection (1)(a) above, the settled property which comprises that asset is property to which this section applies by virtue of subsection (2)(b) above unless, immediately after the acquisition of shares mentioned in subsection (1)(b) above—

(a) the settled property comprising the shares is also property to which this section applies by virtue of subsection (2)(b) above, and

(b) if not all the beneficiaries are individuals, the relevant proportion is not less than the proportion which was the relevant proportion at the time of the disposal of the asset mentioned in subsection (1)(a) above.

(6) If, at any time, in the case of settled property to which this section applies by virtue of subsection (2)(b) above, both individuals and others have interests in possession, the relevant proportion at that time is the proportion which the amount specified in paragraph (a) below bears to the amount specified in paragraph (b) below, that is—

(a) the total amount of the income of the settled property, being income the interests in which are held by beneficiaries who are individuals, and

(b) the total amount of all the income of the settled property.

(7) Where, in the case of any settled property in which any beneficiary holds an interest in possession, one or more beneficiaries ("the relevant beneficiaries") hold interests not in possession, this section shall apply as if—

(a) the interests of the relevant beneficiaries were a single interest in possession, and

(b) that interest were held, where all the relevant beneficiaries are individuals, by an individual and, in any other case, by a person who is not an individual.

(8) In this section references to interests in possession do not include interests for a fixed term."

4. Sections 164C to 164E are omitted.

5. In section 164H(1), "within the meaning of section 164C" is omitted.

6. In section 164L(10), for the words following "trustees or" there is substituted "any individual or charity by virtue of whose interest, at the time of the acquisition, section 164B applies to the settled property".

GENERAL NOTE
    This Schedule extends the availability of reinvestment relief for gains realised by individuals and most trustees, after November 29, 1993, which are reinvested in qualifying investments. Briefly, all gains are now eligible for reinvestment relief.

Para. (2)
    Reinvestment relief is now available on the disposal of any chargeable asset.

Para. (3)
    The TCGA 1992 (c.12), s.164B is rewritten. The trustees of *any* settlement may now claim reinvestment relief, provided the beneficiaries are all individuals both when the asset is disposed of and when the qualifying investment is acquired. Where not all of the beneficiaries of an interest in possession trust are individuals, a proportion of the gain corresponding to the proportion of the trust fund held for the benefit of the individuals qualifies for relief. Where a part of the trust fund is held partly on interest in possession trusts and partly on discretionary trusts, the latter is deemed to be an interest in possession settlement held by individuals provided all the discretionary beneficiaries are individuals. Interests for a fixed term do not count as interests in possession. References to individuals include references to charities.

Paras. (4)–(6)
    Amendments are made to reflect the extension of relief to all disposals by individuals and most trustees, and to delete redundant provisions.

Acquisitions on which relief available

7. For section 164A(8) there is substituted—
    "(8) For the purposes of this section, a person who acquires any eligible shares in a qualifying company shall be regarded as acquiring a qualifying investment unless, where the asset disposed of consisted of shares in or other securities of any company ('the initial holding'), the qualifying company—
    (a) is the company in which the initial holding subsisted, or
    (b) is a company that was, at the time of the disposal of the initial holding, or is, at the time of the acquisition of the qualifying investment, a member of the same group of companies as the company in which the initial holding subsisted."

Retirement relief

8. Section 164A(11) is omitted and after section 164B there is inserted—

"Interaction with retirement relief
    164BA.—(1) The provisions of section 164A for making any reduction shall apply before any provisions for calculating the amount of, or giving effect to, any relief under section 163 or 164; and references in that section and this to a chargeable gain (except the second reference in subsection (4)(a) below) shall be construed accordingly.
    (2) Subsection (3) below applies where—
    (a) any claim for relief is made under section 164A in respect of any chargeable gain, and
    (b) apart from this Chapter, the whole or any part of that gain would be relieved under section 163 or 164.
    (3) For the purpose of giving relief under section 163 or 164, any reduction under section 164A shall be treated as having been made first against the unrelieved part of the chargeable gain; and only the amount (if any) which is equal to the unrelieved part of the chargeable gain after that reduction shall be treated as exceeding the amount available for relief.
    (4) For the purposes of this section—
    (a) the unrelieved part of a chargeable gain is so much of that gain as, apart from this Chapter, would constitute a chargeable gain after the application of the appropriate paragraph of Schedule 6,
    (b) 'amount available for relief' has the same meaning as in the appropriate paragraph of that Schedule, and
    (c) the 'appropriate paragraph' means, as the case may be, paragraph 6, 7(1)(b) or 8(1)(b)."

Clawback

9.—(1) In section 164F—

(a) for subsection (1) there is substituted—

"(1) This section shall apply where a person has acquired any eligible shares in a qualifying company ('the acquired holding') for a consideration which is treated as reduced, under section 164A or this section, by any amount ('the held-over gain')",

(b) in subsection (3), for the words from "either" to the end of paragraph (b) there is substituted "charged on any disposal or under this section",

(c) for subsection (4) there is substituted—

"(4) For the purposes of this section the whole or a part of any held-over gain on the acquisition of the acquired holding shall be treated—

(a) in accordance with subsection (4A) below as charged on any disposal in relation to which the whole or any part of the held-over gain falls to be taken into account in determining the chargeable gain or allowable loss accruing on the disposal, and

(b) as charged under this section so far as it falls to be disregarded in accordance with subsection (11) below.

(4A) In the case of any such disposal as is mentioned in subsection (4)(a) above, the amount of the held-over gain charged on that disposal—

(a) shall, except in the case of a part disposal, be the amount taken into account as so mentioned, and

(b) in the case of a part disposal, shall be calculated by multiplying the following, that is to say—

(i) so much of the amount of the held-over gain as has not already been charged on a previous disposal, and

(ii) the fraction used in accordance with section 42(2) for determining, subject to any deductions in pursuance of this Chapter, the amount allowable as a deduction in the computation of the gain accruing on the disposal in question",

(d) in subsection (5)—

(i) in paragraph (a) "or 164D" is omitted, and

(ii) in paragraph (c), for the words from "section 164D(4)" to the end there is substituted "subsections (4) and (4A) above",

(e) in subsection (10), "(within the meaning of section 164D)" is omitted, and

(f) after that subsection there is inserted—

"(10A) Where (apart from this subsection) a chargeable gain of any amount would by virtue of subsection (2) above accrue to the person who acquired the acquired holding but, within the period mentioned in subsection (10B) below, that person acquires a qualifying investment (within the meaning of section 164A), that person shall, on making a claim as respects the qualifying investment, be treated—

(a) as if the amount of the gain were reduced by whichever is the smallest of the following—

(i) the actual amount or value of the consideration for the acquisition of the qualifying investment,

(ii) in the case of a qualifying investment acquired otherwise than by a transaction at arm's length, the market value of that investment at the time of its acquisition,

(iii) the amount specified for the purposes of this subsection in the claim, and

(b) as if the amount or value of the consideration for the acquisition of the qualifying investment were reduced by the amount of the reduction made under paragraph (a) above;

but paragraph (b) above shall not affect the treatment for the purposes of this Act of the other party to the transaction involving the qualifying investment.

(10B) The period referred to in subsection (10A) above is the period (not including any period before the acquisition of the acquired holding) which begins 12 months before and ends three years after the time when the chargeable gain accrues or would but for that subsection accrue, together with any such further period after the disposal as the Board may by notice allow."

(2) Section 164F as amended by sub-paragraph (1) above shall have effect as follows—

(a) the reference in subsection (1) to consideration treated as reduced under section 164A includes consideration treated as reduced under section 164D,

(b) the reference in subsection (3) to a gain having been charged on any disposal includes any gain having been carried forward from any disposal of shares, and

(c) the amounts referred to in subsection (4A)(a) and (b)(i) shall be treated as reduced by any amounts carried forward from any disposal of shares.

(3) References in sub-paragraph (2) above to an amount being carried forward from a disposal of shares are references to the reduction by that amount, in accordance with section 164D(3)(a), of the amount of the consideration for the disposal of those shares.

Anti-avoidance

10. In section 164L—
(a) after subsection (10) there is inserted—
"(10A) For the purposes of this Chapter, where—
(a) a person has acquired any eligible shares in a qualifying company ('the acquired holding') for a consideration which is treated as reduced under this Chapter by any amount ('the held-over gain'), and
(b) after that acquisition, he acquires eligible shares in a relevant company,
he shall not be regarded in relation to his acquisition of those shares in the relevant company as acquiring a qualifying investment for the purposes of section 164A.
(10B) For the purposes of subsection (10A) above a company is a relevant company if—
(a) where that person has disposed of any of the acquired holding, it is the company in which the acquired holding has subsisted or a company which was a member of the same group of companies as that company at any time since the acquisition of the acquired holding,
(b) it is a company in relation to the disposal of any shares in which there has been a claim under this Chapter such that, without that or an equivalent claim, there would have been no held-over gain in relation to the acquired holding, or
(c) it is a company which, at the time of the disposal or acquisition to which the claim relates, was a member of the same group of companies as a company falling within paragraph (b) above", and
(b) in subsection (11), for the definition of "chargeable business assets" there is substituted—
" 'chargeable business asset', in relation to any company, means a chargeable asset (including goodwill but not including shares or securities or other assets held as investments) which is, or is an interest in, an asset used for the purposes of a trade, profession, vocation, office or employment carried on by—
(a) the individual acquiring the shares,
(b) any personal company of that individual,
(c) a member of a trading group of which the holding company is a personal company of that individual, or
(d) a partnership of which that individual is a member".

Miscellaneous

11. In section 164N, after subsection (1) there is inserted—
"(1A) Every asset of a company is for the purposes of this Chapter a chargeable asset of that company at any time, except one on the disposal of which by the company at that time no gain accruing to the company would be a chargeable gain".

GENERAL NOTE

Para. (7)
The TCGA 1992 (c. 12), s.164A(8) is amended. The qualifying investment may now be any number of ordinary shares in the qualifying company. The investment does not qualify if the asset disposed of consisted of shares in the qualifying company, or a company in the same group of companies.

Para. (8)
The new s.164BA is inserted into the TCGA 1992 (c. 12). Reinvestment relief is given before retirement relief and is set first against the part of the gain (assuming there is no reinvestment relief) not eligible for retirement relief.

Para. (9)
Consequential amendments are made to s.164F. Subparagraphs (1)(a) and (c) of para. (9) re-enact repealed s.164(1)(4) and (5). New subparas. (10A) and (10B) (inserted by subparagraph (f)) allow gains clawed back under the clawback provisions to be reinvested in a further qualifying investment within the period commencing from 12 months before and ending three years after the event giving rise to the clawback occurs. Any gains rolled over into replacement shares under the repealed s.164D remain subject to the clawback provisions.

Para. (10)

Relief cannot be claimed for shares in a qualifying company if the claimant has disposed of shares in that company or in a company in the same group, whether or not relief has been claimed in respect of those shares.

Para. (11)

Subsection (5) of the repealed s.164C is re-enacted by s.164N.

Section 93   SCHEDULE 12

INDEXATION LOSSES: TRANSITIONAL RELIEF

Introductory

1. This Schedule applies in relation to chargeable gains and allowable losses accruing to—
(a) an individual, or
(b) the trustees of a settlement made before 30th November 1993;
(referred to in this Schedule as "the taxpayer").

2.—(1) This paragraph applies for the purposes of this Schedule, and the determinations required by this paragraph to be made shall be made without regard to paragraphs 4 to 7 below.

(2) If an allowable loss accrues on a disposal made on or after 30th November 1993 and, under the old indexation rules, a greater allowable loss would have accrued, there is an indexation loss in respect of the disposal equal to the amount by which the allowable loss which would have accrued under the old indexation rules exceeds the allowable loss accruing on the disposal.

(3) If a disposal made on or after 30th November 1993 is one on which neither a gain nor a loss accrues and, under the old indexation rules, an allowable loss would have accrued, there is an indexation loss in respect of the disposal equal to the amount of the allowable loss that would have accrued under the old indexation rules.

(4) If the total amount of chargeable gains accruing to the taxpayer in any year of assessment for which this Schedule has effect exceeds the allowable losses accruing in that year, there is a relevant gain for that year equal to the amount of the excess.

3.—(1) The cases in which the appropriation of an asset by the taxpayer is treated under section 161(1) of the 1992 Act (appropriations to and from stock) as a disposal of the asset include cases in which, if he had sold the asset for its market value, an allowable loss would have accrued to him under the old indexation rules.

(2) Where, but for an election under subsection (3) of section 161 of the 1992 Act—
(a) an asset appropriated by the taxpayer would have been treated as disposed of as mentioned in subsection (1) of that section, and
(b) paragraph 2(2) or (3) above would have applied on the disposal,
paragraphs 1 and 2 above and 6 and 7 below shall apply, as if the asset had been so treated, to determine for the purposes of subsection (3) of that section any increase to be made in the amount of any allowable loss; and the appropriation of the asset is referred to below as a "relevant appropriation".

(3) Sections 574 to 576 of the Taxes Act (relief for individual on disposal of shares in qualifying trading company) shall apply if an individual who has subscribed for shares as mentioned in section 574(1) disposes of them in circumstances where paragraph 2(3) above applies as they apply in other cases.

(4) Where a person makes a claim for relief under subsection (1) of section 574 in the case of a disposal in respect of which there is an indexation loss (referred to below as a "section 574 disposal")—
(a) paragraphs 6 and 7 below shall apply to determine any increase to be made, for the purposes of that subsection, in the amount of the allowable loss, and
(b) paragraphs 4 and 5 below shall apply to so much only of the indexation loss as is not relieved under that section.

(5) References in this paragraph and paragraphs 6 and 7 below to an increase in any loss include, in circumstances where paragraph 2(3) above applies, a reference to the creation of the loss.

Capital gains tax

4.—(1) Where in the case of any taxpayer—
(a) there is a relevant gain for the year 1993–94,
(b) the relevant gain exceeds the exempt amount for that year, and
(c) there are indexation losses in respect of any disposals made in that year,

then, for the purposes of the 1992 Act, the amount by which the total amount of chargeable gains accruing to the taxpayer in that year exceeds the allowable losses accruing in the year shall be reduced by the amount mentioned in sub-paragraph (2) below, and shall be so reduced before the deduction of any allowable losses carried forward from any previous year or carried back under section 62 from any subsequent year.

(2) The amount referred to in sub-paragraph (1) above is so much of the total of indexation losses in respect of disposals made in that year as does not exceed—

(a) £10,000, or

(b) the amount by which the relevant gain exceeds the exempt amount for the year,

whichever is the smaller.

5.—(1) Where in the case of any taxpayer—

(a) there is a relevant gain for the year 1994–95,

(b) the relevant gain exceeds the exempt amount for that year, and

(c) there are indexation losses in respect of any disposals made in that year or unused indexation losses for the previous year,

then, for the purposes of the 1992 Act, the amount by which the total amount of chargeable gains accruing to the taxpayer in the year 1994–95 exceeds the allowable losses accruing in that year shall be reduced by the amount mentioned in sub-paragraph (2) below, and shall be so reduced before the deduction of any allowable losses carried forward from any previous year or carried back under section 62 from any subsequent year.

(2) The amount referred to in sub-paragraph (1) above is so much of the total of indexation losses in respect of disposals made in the year 1994–95, plus any unused indexation losses for the previous year, as does not exceed—

(a) £10,000 less the aggregate of—

(i) the amount of any reduction made under paragraph 4(1) above for the previous year, and

(ii) any increase made under paragraph 6(2) below for the previous year, or

(b) the amount by which the relevant gain exceeds the exempt amount for the year 1994–95,

whichever is the smaller.

(3) For the purposes of this paragraph, if the total amount of indexation losses in respect of disposals made by the taxpayer in the year 1993–94 exceeds the aggregate of—

(a) the amount of any reduction made under paragraph 4(1) above for that year, and

(b) any increase made under paragraph 6(2) below for that year,

there are unused indexation losses for that year of an amount equal to the excess.

Income tax

6.—(1) This paragraph applies where, at any time in the period beginning with 30th November 1993 and ending with 5th April 1994, the taxpayer makes any relevant appropriation or any section 574 disposal; and for the purposes of this paragraph there shall be determined—

(a) the amount of any reduction for the year 1993–94 which (disregarding relevant appropriations and section 574 disposals) would be made under paragraph 4(1) above, and

(b) the amounts of any indexation losses in respect of relevant appropriations or section 574 disposals made in that period.

(2) If the aggregate of the amounts referred to in sub-paragraph (1)(a) and (b) above does not exceed £10,000, the amount of any allowable loss referable to such an appropriation or disposal shall be increased by any indexation loss in respect of it.

(3) In any other case, notwithstanding anything in paragraphs 4 and 5 above—

(a) the aggregate of—

(i) the amount of any reduction for the year 1993–94 to be made under paragraph 4(1) above, and

(ii) the amount of any indexation losses in respect of relevant appropriations or section 574 disposals made in the period referred to in sub-paragraph (1) above,

shall be equal to £10,000 and shall be allocated as the taxpayer may determine between that reduction and increases in allowable losses referable to such appropriations or disposals, and

(b) no reduction shall be made under paragraph 5 above or 7 below for the year 1994–95.

7.—(1) This paragraph applies where, at any time in the year 1994–95, the taxpayer makes any relevant appropriation or any section 574 disposal; and for the purposes of this paragraph there shall be determined—

(a) the amount of any reduction for that year which (disregarding relevant appropriations and section 574 disposals) would be made under paragraph 5(1) above, and

(b) the amounts of any indexation losses in respect of relevant appropriations or section 574 disposals made in that year.

(2) If the aggregate of the amounts referred to in sub-paragraph (1)(a) and (b) above does not exceed the limit for 1994–95, that is—

(a) £10,000, less

(b) the aggregate of the amount of any reduction made under paragraph 4(1) above for the year 1993–94 and of any increases made under paragraph 6(2) above for that year,

the amount of any allowable loss referable to such an appropriation or disposal shall be increased by any indexation loss in respect of it.

(3) In any other case, notwithstanding anything in paragraph 5 above, the aggregate of the amount of any reduction for the year 1994–95 to be made under paragraph 5(1) above and of the amount of any indexation losses in respect of relevant appropriations or section 574 disposals made in that year—

(a) shall be equal to the limit for 1994–95, and

(b) shall be allocated as the taxpayer may determine between that reduction and increases in allowable losses referable to such appropriations or disposals.

Supplementary

8.—(1) In this Schedule—

"the 1992 Act" means the Taxation of Chargeable Gains Act 1992, and

"the old indexation rules" means the 1992 Act as it would have effect if—

(a) the amendments made by subsections (1) to (5) of section 93 of this Act, and

(b) the repeal of section 103 (collective investment schemes, etc.) and section 111 (building societies) of the 1992 Act by subsection (7) of section 93 of this Act,

had not come into force.

(2) Other expressions not defined in this Schedule but used both in it and in the 1992 Act have the same meaning as in that Act.

(3) References in this Schedule to the reduction of any amount include its reduction to nil.

GENERAL NOTE

This Schedule provides transitional relief for indexation losses accruing between November 30, 1993 and April 5, 1995.

Para. (1)

The relief is only available to individuals and to trustees of settlements created prior to November 30, 1993.

Para. (2)

An indexation loss means the allowable loss or greater allowable loss that would have accrued on disposals between November 30, 1993 and April 5, 1995, under the old indexation rules.

Para. (4)

Up to £10,000 of indexation losses accruing between November 30, 1993 and April 5, 1994 may be used to reduce chargeable gains accruing in 1993–1994 (after deducting the £5,800 annual exemption but before relief for capital losses are brought forward).

Para. (5)

If the £10,000 limit is not exhausted in 1993 and 1994, then the unused balance may be used to reduce chargeable gains accruing in 1994 and 1995 (computed as in para. (4) above). Any indexation losses still not used by April 5, 1995 are lost forever.

Paras. (3)(6) and (7)

Where an asset is appropriated to trading stock between November 30, 1993 and April 5, 1995 and an election made under the TCGA 1992 (c. 12), s.161(3), the increase in the Case I acquisition cost may include any indexation loss.

If an election is made under the ICTA 1988 (c. 1), s.574 for losses on unquoted shares in trading companies to be set off against income, the amount allowed may include any indexation losses on the shares. However indexation losses on appropriations to trading stock and s.574 disposals together with indexation losses on other disposals may not exceed the £10,000 limit for 1993–94 and 1994–95 in paras. (4) and (5) above. The £10,000 is allocated as the taxpayer chooses.

Section 102   SCHEDULE 13

<small>EMPLOYEE SHARE OWNERSHIP TRUSTS</small>

Introduction

1. The Finance Act 1989 shall be amended as provided in this Schedule.

Trustees

2. In Schedule 5, in paragraph 3 (trustees) the following sub-paragraph shall be inserted after sub-paragraph (4)—
"(5) This paragraph applies in relation to trusts established on or before the day on which the Finance Act 1994 was passed."
3. In Schedule 5, the following paragraphs shall be inserted after paragraph 3—
"3A. Where a trust is established after the day on which the Finance Act 1994 was passed, the trust deed must make provision as mentioned in one of paragraphs (a) to (c) below—
(a) provision for the establishment of a body of trustees and complying with paragraph 3(2) to (4) above;
(b) provision for the establishment of a body of trustees and complying with paragraph 3B(2) to (9) below;
(c) provision that at any time while the trust subsists there must be a single trustee.
3B.—(1) The following are the provisions that must be complied with under paragraph 3A(b) above.
(2) The trust deed must—
(a) appoint the initial trustees;
(b) contain rules for the retirement and removal of trustees;
(c) contain rules for the appointment of replacement and additional trustees.
(3) The trust deed must be so framed that at any time while the trust subsists the conditions set out in sub-paragraph (4) below are fulfilled as regards the persons who are then trustees; and in that sub-paragraph "the relevant time" means that time.
(4) The conditions are that—
(a) the number of trustees is not less than three;
(b) all the trustees are resident in the United Kingdom;
(c) the trustees include at least one person who is a professional trustee and at least two persons who are non-professional trustees;
(d) at least half of the non-professional trustees were, before being appointed as trustees, selected in accordance with sub-paragraph (7) or (8) below;
(e) all the trustees so selected are persons who are employees of companies which fall within the founding company's group at the relevant time, and who do not have and have never had a material interest in any such company.
(5) For the purposes of this paragraph a trustee is a professional trustee at a particular time if—
(a) the trustee is then a trust corporation, a solicitor, or a member of such other professional body as the Board may at that time allow for the purposes of this sub-paragraph,
(b) the trustee is not then an employee or director of any company then falling within the founding company's group, and
(c) the trustee meets the requirements of sub-paragraph (6) below;
and for the purposes of this paragraph a trustee is a non-professional trustee at a particular time if the trustee is not then a professional trustee for those purposes.
(6) A trustee meets the requirements of this sub-paragraph if—
(a) he was appointed as an initial trustee and, before being appointed as trustee, was selected by (and only by) the persons who later became the non-professional initial trustees, or
(b) he was appointed as a replacement or additional trustee and, before being appointed as trustee, was selected by (and only by) the persons who were the non-professional trustees at the time of the selection.

(7) Trustees are selected in accordance with the sub-paragraph if the process of selection is one under which—

(a) all the persons who are employees of the companies which fall within the founding company's group at the time of the selection, and who do not have and have never had a material interest in any such company, are (so far as is reasonably practicable) given the opportunity to stand for selection,

(b) all the employees of the companies falling within the founding company's group at the time of the selection are (so far as is reasonably practicable) given the opportunity to vote, and

(c) persons gaining more votes are preferred to those gaining less.

(8) Trustees are selected in accordance with this sub-paragraph if they are selected by persons elected to represent the employees of the companies falling within the founding company's group at the time of the selection.

(9) For the purposes of this paragraph a company falls within the founding company's group at a particular time if—

(a) it is at that time resident in the United Kingdom, and

(b) it is the founding company or it is at that time controlled by the founding company.

3C.—(1) This paragraph applies where the trust deed provides that at any time while the trust subsists there must be a single trustee.

(2) The trust deed must—

(a) be so framed that at any time while the trust subsists the trustee is a company which at that time is resident in the United Kingdom and controlled by the founding company;

(b) appoint the initial trustee;

(c) contain rules for the removal of any trustee and for the appointment of a replacement trustee.

(3) The trust deed must be so framed that at any time while the trust subsists the company which is then the trustee is a company so constituted that the conditions set out in sub-paragraph (4) below are then fulfilled as regards the persons who are then directors of the company; and in that sub-paragraph "the relevant time" is that time and "the trust company" is that company.

(4) The conditions are that—

(a) the number of directors is not less than three;

(b) all the directors are resident in the United Kingdom;

(c) the directors include at least one person who is a professional director and at least two persons who are non-professional directors;

(d) at least half of the non-professional directors were, before being appointed as directors, selected in accordance with sub-paragraph (7) or (8) below;

(e) all the directors so selected are persons who are employees of companies which fall within the founding company's group at the relevant time, and who do not have and have never had a material interest in any such company.

(5) For the purposes of this paragraph a director is a professional director at a particular time if—

(a) the director is then a solicitor or a member of such other professional body as the Board may at that time allow for the purposes of this sub-paragraph,

(b) the director is not then an employee of any company then falling within the founding company's group,

(c) the director is not then a director of any such company (other than the trust company), and

(d) the director meets the requirements of sub-paragraph (6) below;

and for the purposes of this paragraph a director is a non-professional director at a particular time if the director is not then a professional director for those purposes.

(6) A director meets the requirements of this sub-paragraph if—

(a) he was appointed as an initial director and, before being appointed as director, was selected by (and only by) the persons who later became the non-professional initial directors, or

(b) he was appointed as a replacement or additional director and, before being appointed as director, was selected by (and only by) the persons who were the non-professional directors at the time of the selection.

(7) Directors are selected in accordance with this sub-paragraph if the process of selection is one under which—

(a) all the persons who are employees of the companies which fall within the founding company's group at the time of the selection, and who do not have and have never had a material interest in any such company, are (so far as is reasonably practicable) given the opportunity to stand for selection,

(b) all the employees of the companies falling within the founding company's group at the time of the selection are (so far as is reasonably practicable) given the opportunity to vote, and

(c) persons gaining more votes are preferred to those gaining less.

(8) Directors are selected in accordance with this sub-paragraph if they are selected by persons elected to represent the employees of the companies falling within the founding company's group at the time of the selection.

(9) For the purposes of this paragraph a company falls within the founding company's group at a particular time if—

(a) it is at that time resident in the United Kingdom, and

(b) it is the founding company or it is at that time controlled by the founding company."

4. In Schedule 5, the following shall be inserted at the end of paragraph 12 (position after trust's establishment)—

"This paragraph applies in relation to trusts established on or before the day on which the Finance Act 1994 was passed."

5. In Schedule 5, the following paragraph shall be inserted after paragraph 12—

"12A.—(1) Subject to sub-paragraphs (2) and (3) below, a trust which was at the time it was established a qualifying employee share ownership trust shall continue to be one.

(2) If the trust deed makes provision under paragraph 3A(a) above, the trust shall not be a qualifying employee share ownership trust at any time when the requirements mentioned in paragraph 3(3)(a) to (f) above are not satisfied.

(3) If the trust deed makes provision under paragraph 3A(b) above, the trust shall not be a qualifying employee share ownership trust at any time when the conditions mentioned in paragraph 3B(4)(a) to (e) above are not satisfied.

(4) If the trust deed makes provision under paragraph 3A(c) above, the trust shall not be a qualifying employee share ownership trust at any time when—

(a) there is not a single trustee,

(b) the trustee is not a company which is resident in the United Kingdom and controlled by the founding company, or

(c) the conditions mentioned in paragraph 3C(4)(a) to (e) above are not satisfied as regards the directors of the trustee.

(5) This paragraph applies in relation to trusts established after the day on which the Finance Act 1994 was passed."

Securities

6.—(1) Section 69 (chargeable events) shall be amended as follows.

(2) In subsection (1)(c) (retention of securities at expiry of seven years from acquisition) for "period of seven years" there shall be substituted "qualifying period".

(3) After subsection (4) there shall be inserted—

"(4A) For the purposes of subsection (1)(c) above the qualifying period is—

(a) seven years, in the case of trusts established on or before the day on which the Finance Act 1994 was passed;

(b) twenty years, in the case of other trusts;

and for this purpose a trust is established when the deed under which it is established is executed."

7.—(1) Paragraph 9 of Schedule 5 (transfer of securities) shall be amended as follows.

(2) In sub-paragraph (1)(b) for "period of seven years" there shall be substituted "qualifying period".

(3) After sub-paragraph (2) there shall be inserted—

"(2A) For the purposes of sub-paragraph (1) above the qualifying period is—

(a) seven years, in the case of trusts established on or before the day on which the Finance Act 1994 was passed;

(b) twenty years, in the case of other trusts."

Interpretation

8. In Schedule 5, the following paragraph shall be inserted after paragraph 16—

"17. For the purposes of this Schedule a trust is established when the deed under which it is established is executed."

GENERAL NOTE

This Schedule relaxes the statutory requirements which must be satisfied by an Employee Share Ownership Trust (ESOT) if it is to qualify for certain tax reliefs. Such trusts established before May 3, 1994 may take advantage of the changes by executing new trust deeds.

Para. (2)
ESOTs established on or before May 3, 1994 must have a body of trustees which conforms with the FA 1989 (c. 26), Sched. 5, para. (3).

Para. (3)
ESOTs established after May 3, 1994 have a choice of three possible trust structures:
(a) the previous statutory structure (see the FA 1989 (c. 26), Sched. 5, para. (3));
(b) a paritarian trust structure;
(c) a single corporate trustee.
The paritarian trust structure must have at least three U.K. resident trustees with:—
(i) at least one professional trustee (trust corporation, solicitor or member of another professional body approved by the Revenue). (The professional trustee may not be an employee or director of any company within the founding company's group and must be selected by the other non-professional trustees); and
(ii) at least two non-professional trustees of which half must be employees of companies within the founding company's group, who do not have and have never had a material interest (*i.e.* 5 per cent. of the ordinary share capital) in any such company and who have either been selected (i) by a process under which all the employees within the founding company's group are (so far as reasonably practicable) given the opportunity to stand for election or to vote for those standing; or (ii) by persons elected to represent those employees.
A corporate trustee must be a U.K. resident company controlled by the founding company, with a board of directors composed in the same way as the trustees of the paritarian trust—the legislation is virtually identical to that applicable to paritarian trusts with the substitution of "directors" for "trustees".

Para. (6)
For ESOTs established after May 3, 1994, the maximum period for the retention of securities by trustees is increased from seven to 20 years.

Para. (8)
A trust is established when its deed is executed.

Section 112   SCHEDULE 14

DISTRIBUTIONS OF AUTHORISED UNIT TRUSTS

GENERAL NOTE
This Schedule introduces changes to the taxation of distributions by authorised unit trusts.

1. Chapter III of Part XII of the Taxes Act 1988 shall be amended in accordance with paragraphs 2 to 5 of this Schedule.

The new sections

2. The following sections shall be inserted immediately before section 469—

"*Distributions of authorised unit trusts: general*

Interpretation
468H.—(1) This section has effect for the interpretation of sections 468I to 468R.
(2) The making of a distribution by an authorised unit trust to a unit holder includes investing an amount on behalf of the unit holder in respect of his accumulation units.
(3) In relation to an authorised unit trust—
(a) "distribution period" means a period by reference to which the total amount available for distribution to unit holders is ascertained; and
(b) "distribution accounts" means accounts showing how that total amount is computed.
(4) The distribution date for a distribution period of an authorised unit trust is—
(a) the date specified by or in accordance with the terms of the trust for any distribution for that distribution period; or
(b) if no date is so specified, the last day of that distribution period.
(5) In this Chapter references to foreign income dividends shall be construed in accordance with Chapter VA of Part VI.
(6) Sections 468I to 468R do not apply to an authorised unit trust which is also an approved personal pension scheme (within the meaning of Chapter IV of Part XIV).

Section 468H of the ICTA 1988
This defines terms used in ss.468H to 468R. Sections 468H to 468R do not apply to authorised unit trusts which are approved personal pension schemes.

Distribution accounts
468I.—(1) The total amount shown in the distribution accounts as available for distribution to unit holders shall be shown as available for distribution in one of the ways set out below.

(2) It may be shown as available for distribution as dividends which are not foreign income dividends.

(3) It may be shown as available for distribution as foreign income dividends.

(4) It may be shown as available for distribution as yearly interest.

(5) It may be divided into—

(a) a part shown as available for distribution as dividends which are not foreign income dividends; and

(b) a part shown as available for distribution as foreign income dividends.

(6) Amounts deriving from income under Schedule A may not be included in any amount shown in the distribution accounts as available for distribution as yearly interest.

(7) Where distribution accounts show an amount as available for distribution to unit holders in the way set out in subsection (5) above there shall not be any discrimination between unit holders having accumulation units and other unit holders (or between unit holders on other grounds).

GENERAL NOTE

Section 468I of the ICTA 1988
Amounts available for distribution may be treated as franked payments, as foreign income dividends (FIDs), as yearly interest or as part dividends and part FIDs. Sched. A income may not be treated as yearly interest.

Dividend and foreign income distributions

Dividend distributions
468J.—(1) Subsection (2) below applies where the total amount or a part of the total amount shown in the distribution accounts as available for distribution to unit holders is shown as available for distribution as dividends which are not foreign income dividends.

(2) The Tax Acts shall have effect as if the total amount or, as the case may be, the part were dividends on shares paid on the distribution date by the company referred to in section 468(1) to the unit holders in proportion to their rights.

(3) The trustees of an authorised unit trust may not make an election under section 246A in respect of dividends paid by virtue of this section.

(4) In the following provisions of this Chapter "a dividend distribution" means a dividend treated as paid by virtue of subsection (2) above.

GENERAL NOTE

Section 468J of the ICTA 1988
Dividend distributions are treated as if they were franked payments paid out to unit holders in proportion to their rights, on the distribution date.

Foreign income distributions
468K.—(1) Subsection (2) below applies where the total amount or a part of the total amount shown in the distribution accounts as available for distribution to unit holders is shown as available for distribution as foreign income dividends.

(2) The Tax Acts shall have effect (subject to what follows) as if the total amount or, as the case may be, the part were foreign income dividends on shares paid on the distribution date by the company referred to in section 468(1) to the unit holders in proportion to their rights.

(3) In relation to the paying of foreign income dividends by authorised unit trusts Chapter VA of Part VI shall have effect as if the following provisions were omitted—

(a) sections 246A and 246B (provisions with respect to election to pay foreign income dividends);

(b) sections 246K to 256M (special provisions for subsidiaries); and

(c) sections 246S to 246W (international headquarters companies).

(4) In the following provisions of this Chapter "a foreign income distribution" means a foreign income dividend treated as paid by virtue of subsection (2) above.

GENERAL NOTE

Section 468K of the ICTA 1988

Foreign income distributions are treated as if they were FIDs paid out to unit holders in proportion to their rights on the distribution date. A simplified version of the FID Scheme contained in Sched. 15 below is to apply to unit trusts.

Interest distributions

Interest distributions

468L.—(1) Subsection (2) below applies where the total amount shown in the distribution accounts as available for distribution to unit holders is shown as available for distribution as yearly interest.

(2) The Tax Acts shall have effect (subject to what follows) as if the total amount were payments of yearly interest made on the distribution date by the company referred to in section 468(1) to the unit holders in proportion to their rights.

(3) In the following provisions of this Chapter "an interest distribution" means a payment of yearly interest treated as made by virtue of subsection (2) above.

(4) The obligation under section 349(2) to deduct a sum in its application to an interest distribution is subject to sections 468M and 468N (and, in its application to an interest distribution to a unit holder in respect of his accumulation units, is an obligation to deduct a sum out of the amount being invested on the unit holder's behalf).

(5) Interest distributions shall not be a charge on income for the purposes of section 338(1) but any interest distributions for a distribution period which are interest distributions with respect to which the obligation under section 349(2) (if and to the extent that it applies) is complied with shall be allowed as a deduction against the profits of the authorised unit trust for the accounting period in which the last day of that distribution period falls.

(6) The deduction mentioned in subsection (5) above may be made—

(a) in computing the total profits for the accounting period, after the deduction of any expenses deductible in computing profits apart from section 75 and either before or after the deduction under that section of sums disbursed as expenses of management; or

(b) against total profits as reduced by any other relief from tax or against total profits not so reduced.

(7) Where in any accounting period the amount deductible by virtue of subsection (5) above exceeds the amount from which the deduction is made—

(a) the excess may be carried forward to the succeeding accounting period; and

(b) the amount so carried forward shall be treated as if it were deductible in that succeeding accounting period by virtue of subsection (5) above.

GENERAL NOTE

Section 468L of the ICTA 1988

Interest distributions are treated as if they were payments of yearly interest made to unit holders in proportion to their rights, on the distribution date. Interest distributions do not constitute charges on income but are deductible in computing profits of the unit trust for the accounting period in which the last day of the distribution period falls. Any unrelieved amounts may be carried forward and relieved in succeeding accounting periods. Unless exempt under ss.468M and 468N, interest distributions are subject to deduction of income tax at source, even if the yearly interest is reinvested in the unit trust instead of being paid to the unit holder.

Deduction of tax (simple case)

468M.—(1) Subsection (2) below applies where—

(a) an interest distribution is made for a distribution period to a unit holder; and

(b) the gross income entered in the distribution accounts for the purpose of computing the total amount available for distribution to unit holders derives from eligible income entirely.

(2) Where this subsection applies, the obligation to deduct under section 349(2) shall not apply to the interest distribution to the unit holder is the residence condition is on the distribution date fulfilled with respect to him.

(3) Section 468O makes provision with respect to the circumstances in which the residence condition is fulfilled with respect to a unit holder.

(4) Subject to subsection (5) below, in this Chapter "eligible income" means—

(a) any interest on a security which falls within paragraph 5(5)(d) of Schedule 19AA;

(b) any interest on a security which is a quoted Eurobond for the purposes of section 124;

(c) any dividends falling within section 17(1)3;

(d) any proceeds or other realisation falling within section 17(1)4;

(e) any amount taxable by virtue of section 123;

(f) any other amount, if it is not subject to income tax by deduction.

(5) "Eligible income" does not include—

(a) franked investment income;

(b) income under Schedule A;

(c) any foreign income dividend;

(d) any amount afforded relief from taxation imposed under the laws of a territory outside the United Kingdom under arrangements having effect by virtue of section 788 in relation to that territory.

Deduction of tax (mixed funds)

468N.—(1) Subsection (2) below applies where—

(a) an interest distribution is made for a distribution period to a unit holder; and

(b) the gross income entered in the distribution accounts for the purposes of computing the total amount available for distribution to unit holders does not derive from eligible income entirely.

(2) Where this subsection applies, the obligation to deduct under section 349(2) shall not apply to the relevant amount of the interest distribution to the unit holder if the residence condition is on the distribution date fulfilled with respect to him.

(3) Section 468O makes provision with respect to the circumstances in which the residence condition is fulfilled with respect to a unit holder.

(4) This is how to calculate the relevant amount of the interest distribution—

$$R = A \times \frac{B}{C}$$

Where—

R = the relevant amount;

A = the amount of the interest distribution before deduction of tax to the unit holder in question;

B = such amount of the gross income as derives from eligible income;

C = the amount of the gross income.

(5) In subsection (4) above the references to the gross income are references to the gross income entered as mentioned in subsection (1)(b) above.

GENERAL NOTE

Sections 468M and 468N of the ICTA 1988

Interest distributions may be paid gross to non-resident unit holders, including personal representatives of deceased unit holders, if they are wholly derived from eligible income (broadly speaking income which would not be subject to deduction of tax if received directly by a non-resident investor). Where only part of the interest distribution is derived from eligible income, a proportion of the interest distribution, corresponding to the proportion which the gross eligible income bears to the total gross income, may be paid gross to non-U.K. resident unitholders.

Residence condition

468O.—(1) For the purposes of sections 468M and 468N, the residence condition is fulfilled with respect to a unit holder if—

(a) there is a valid declaration made by him that he is not ordinarily resident in the United Kingdom; or

(b) he holds the rights as a personal representative of a unit holder and—
      (i) before his death the deceased made a declaration valid at the time of his death that he was not ordinarily resident in the United Kingdom; or
      (ii) the personal representative has made a declaration that the deceased, immediately before his death, was not ordinarily resident in the United Kingdom.
(2) For the purposes of sections 468M and 468N, the residence condition is also fulfilled with respect to a unit holder if the unit holder is a company and there is a valid declaration made by the company that it is not resident in the United Kingdom.
(3) The Board may by regulations make such provision as appears to them to be necessary or expedient modifying the application of this section and section 468P in relation to interest distributions made to or received under a trust.
(4) Regulations under subsection (3) above may—
(a) make different provision for different cases; and
(b) contain such supplementary, incidental, consequential or transitional provision as appears to the Board to be appropriate.

GENERAL NOTE

Section 468O of the ICTA 1988
A non-resident unitholder (including companies, individuals or personal representatives of deceased unitholders) must make a valid declaration of non-residence in writing.

Residence declarations
468P.—(1) A declaration made for the purposes of section 468O must—
(a) be in such form as may be required or authorised by the Board;
(b) be made in writing to the trustees of the authorised unit trust in question; and
(c) contain any details or undertakings required by subsections (2) to (4) below.
(2) A declaration made as mentioned in section 468O(1)(a) or (b)(i) must contain—
(a) the name and principal residential address of the person making it; and
(b) an undertaking that he will notify the trustees if he becomes ordinarily resident in the United Kingdom.
(3) A declaration made as mentioned in section 468O(1)(b)(ii) must contain the name of the deceased and his principal residential address immediately before his death.
(4) A declaration made as mentioned in section 468O(2) must contain—
(a) the name of the company making it and the address of its registered or principal office; and
(b) an undertaking that the company will notify the trustees if it becomes resident in the United Kingdom.
(5) For the purposes of determining whether an interest distribution should be made with or without any deduction, the trustees may not treat a declaration as valid if—
(a) they receive a notification in compliance with an undertaking under subsection (2) or (4) above that the person in question has become ordinarily resident or, as the case may be, resident in the United Kingdom; or
(b) they come into possession of information by some other means which indicates that the person in question is or may be ordinarily resident or, as the case may be, resident in the United Kingdom;
but, subject to that, they are entitled to treat the declaration as valid.
(6) The trustees shall, on being required to do so by a notice given by an officer of the Board, make available for inspection by such an officer any declarations made to them under this section or any specified declaration or description of declarations.
(7) Where a notice has been given to the trustees under subsection (6) above, the declarations shall be made available within such time as may be specified in the notice and the person carrying out the inspection may take copies of or extracts from them.
(8) The Board may by regulations make provision for giving effect to this section, including in particular provision requiring trustees and managers of authorised unit trusts to supply information and make available books, documents and other records for inspection on behalf of the Board.
(9) Regulations under subsection (8) above may—
(a) make different provision for different cases; and
(b) contain such supplementary, incidental, consequential or transitional provision as appears to the Board to be appropriate.

GENERAL NOTE

Section 468P of the ICTA 1988
  This contains the requirements for a valid residence declaration.

Distributions to corporate unit holder

Dividend distribution to corporate unit holder
  468Q.—(1) Subsection (2) below applies where—
  (a) a dividend distribution for a distribution period is made to a unit holder by the trustees of an authorised unit trust; and
  (b) on the distribution date for that distribution period the unit holder is within the charge to corporation tax.
  (2) For the purpose of computing corporation tax chargeable in the case of the unit holder the unfranked part of the dividend distribution shall be deemed—
  (a) to be an annual payment and not a dividend distribution, a foreign income distribution or an interest distribution; and
  (b) to have been received by the unit holder after deduction of income tax at the lower rate for the year of assessment in which the distribution date falls, from a corresponding gross amount.
  (3) This is how to calculate the unfranked part of the dividend distribution—

$$U = \left((A + B) \times \frac{C}{D} \right) - B$$

Where—
  U = the unfranked part of the dividend distribution to the unit holder;
  A = the amount of the dividend distribution;
  B = the amount of any foreign income distribution for the distribution period for which that dividend distribution is made to the unit holder;
  C = such amount of the gross income as does not derive from franked investment income;
  D = the amount of the gross income.

  (4) If the calculation in accordance with subsection (3) above produces a value of U that is less than O, it shall be assumed for the purposes of this section that no part of the dividend distribution is unfranked.
  (5) Where the unit holder is on the distribution date the manager of the scheme, subsection (2) above shall not apply in so far as the rights in respect of which the dividend distribution is made are held by him in the ordinary course of his business as manager of the scheme.
  (6) For the purposes of this section the references to the gross income are references to the gross income entered in the distribution accounts for the purpose of computing the total amount available for distribution to unit holders for the distribution period in question.

Foreign income distribution to corporate unit holder
  468R.—(1) Subsection (2) below applies where—
  (a) a foreign income distribution for a distribution period is made to a unit holder by the trustees of an authorised unit trust; and
  (b) on the distribution date for that distribution period the unit holder is within the charge to corporation tax.
  (2) The provisions of subsections (2) to (6) of section 468Q shall have effect, with the necessary modifications, in relation to the foreign income distribution as they have effect in relation to a dividend distribution, and in particular as if for the provisions of subsection (3) of that section there were substituted the provisions of subsection (3) below.
  (3) This is how to calculate the unfranked part of the foreign income distribution—

$$U = \left((A + B) \times \frac{E}{D} \right) - A$$

Where—
  U = the unfranked part of the foreign income distribution to the unit holder in question;
  A = the amount of any dividend distribution for the distribution period for which that foreign income distribution is made to the unit holder;

B = the amount of that foreign income distribution;
E = such amount of the gross income as does not derive from foreign income dividends;
D = the amount of the gross income."

Other amendments

3.—(1) Section 468 (authorised unit trusts) shall be amended as follows.

(2) At the end of subsection (1) there shall be inserted "but paragraph (b) above is without prejudice to the making of distributions which are interest distributions (within the meaning of section 468L) to unit holders".

(3) Subsection (2) (notional dividends of authorised unit trusts) shall be omitted.

(4) In subsection (3) for the words "subsections (1) and (2) above" there shall be substituted "subsection (1) above".

(5) In subsection (6) the definition of "distribution period" shall be omitted.

4. Sections 468F and 468G shall cease to have effect.

5. In section 469 (other unit trusts), in subsection (6) (meaning of "distribution period") for the words "has the same meaning as in section 468, but" there shall be substituted "means a period beginning on or after 1st April 1987 over which income from the investments subject to the trusts is aggregated for the purposes of ascertaining the amount available for distribution to unit holders, but".

6. In section 834(3) of the Taxes Act 1988 (date on which dividends treated as paid) for the words from "except in so far as" to the end there shall be substituted "except in so far as Chapter III of Part XII makes other provision for dividends treated as paid by virtue of that Chapter".

Commencement

7.—(1) Subject to sub-paragraph (2) below, this Schedule shall have effect in relation to distribution periods beginning on or after 1st April 1994.

(2) Nothing in the amendments made by this Schedule shall be taken to permit—
(a) the total amount shown in the distribution accounts for a distribution period of an authorised unit trust, or
(b) a part of that total amount,
to be shown as available for distribution as foreign income dividends unless the distribution date for that distribution period is 1st July 1994 or a subsequent date.

GENERAL NOTE

Sections 468Q and 468R of the ICTA 1988
The unfranked part of a dividend distribution or a foreign income distribution made to a corporate unitholder is treated as unfranked investment income from which lower rate income tax (for the year of assessment in which the distribution date falls) has been deducted. The formula for ascertaining the unfranked part of the dividend distribution is:

$$\left(\frac{\text{dividend}}{\text{distribution}} + \frac{\text{foreign income}}{\text{distribution}} \times \frac{\text{total non-FII income}}{\text{total income}} \right) - \frac{\text{foreign income}}{\text{distributions}}$$

The same formula applies for ascertaining the unfranked part of a foreign income distribution but total non-FID is to be substituted in place of total non-FII income.

Para. (7)
This Schedule applies to distribution periods commencing after March 31, 1994.

Section 137   SCHEDULE 15

ENTERPRISE INVESTMENT SCHEME

GENERAL NOTE
This Schedule contains the provisions for the Enterprise Investment Scheme (EIS) which replaced the previous Business Expansion Scheme (BES) with effect from January 1, 1994. The new scheme is introduced by extensive amendments to the BES provisions.

| *Para. (2)*
Section 289 is replaced with three new sections; ss.289, 289A and 289B.

Amendments of the Taxes Act 1988

1. Chapter III of Part VII of the Taxes Act 1988 shall be amended as follows:
2. For section 289 (the relief) and the heading preceding it there is substituted—

"ENTERPRISE INVESTMENT SCHEME

Eligibility for relief
  289.—(1) For the purposes of this Chapter, an individual is eligible for relief, subject to the following provisions of this Chapter, if—
  (a) eligible shares in a qualifying company for which he has subscribed are issued to him and, under section 291, he qualifies for relief in respect of those shares,
  (b) the shares are issued in order to raise money for the purpose of a qualifying business activity, and
  (c) the money raised by the issue is employed not later than the time mentioned in sub-section (3) below wholly for the purpose of that activity.
  (2) In this Chapter 'qualifying business activity', in relation to a company, means—
  (a) the company or any subsidiary—
        (i) carrying on a qualifying trade which, on the date the shares are issued, it is carrying on, or
        (ii) preparing to carry on a qualifying trade which, on that date, it intends to carry on wholly or mainly in the United Kingdom and which it begins to carry on within two years after that date,
      but only if, at any time in the relevant period when the qualifying trade is carried on, it is carried on wholly or mainly in the United Kingdom,
  (b) the company or any subsidiary carrying on research and development—
        (i) which, on the date the shares are issued, it is carrying on or which it begins to carry on immediately afterwards, and
        (ii) from which it is intended that a qualifying trade which the company or any subsidiary will carry on wholly or mainly in the United Kingdom will be derived,
      but only if, at any time in the relevant period when the research and development or the qualifying trade derived from it is carried on, it is carried on wholly or mainly in the United Kingdom, or
  (c) the company or any subsidiary carrying on oil exploration—
        (i) which, on the date the shares are issued, it is carrying on or begins to carry on immediately afterwards, and
        (ii) from which it is intended that a qualifying trade which the company or any subsidiary will carry on wholly or mainly in the United Kingdom will be derived,
      but only if, at any time in the relevant period when the oil exploration or the qualifying trade derived from it is carried on, it is carried on wholly or mainly in the United Kingdom.
  (3) The time referred to in subsection (1)(c) above is—
  (a) the end of the period of twelve months beginning with the issue of the eligible shares, or
  (b) in the case of money raised only for the purpose referred to in subsection (2)(a) above, the end of that period or, if later, the end of the period of twelve months beginning when the company or subsidiary concerned begins to carry on the qualifying trade,
and for the purposes of this Chapter, the condition in subsection (1)(c) above does not fail to be satisfied by reason only of the fact that an amount of money which is not significant is employed for another purpose.
  (4) Subsection (2)(c) above shall not apply unless—
  (a) throughout the period of three years beginning with the date on which the shares were issued, the company or any subsidiary holds an exploration licence which was granted to it, or to another subsidiary,
  (b) the exploration is carried out solely within the area to which the licence applies, and
  (c) on the date on which the shares were issued, neither the company nor any subsidiary held an appraisal licence or a development licence relating to that area or any part of that area.
  (5) Where, at any time after the issue of the shares but before the end of the period mentioned in subsection (4)(a) above, the company or any subsidiary comes to hold an

appraisal licence or development licence which relates to the area, or any part of the area, to which the exploration licence relates, the exploration licence and that other licence shall be treated for the purposes of subsection (4)(a) above as a single exploration licence.

(6) An individual is not eligible for relief in respect of any shares unless the shares are subscribed, and issued, for bona fide commercial purposes and not as part of a scheme or arrangement the main purpose or one of the main purposes of which is the avoidance of tax.

(7) In this Chapter 'eligible shares' means new ordinary shares which, throughout the period of five years beginning with the date on which they are issued, carry no present or future preferential right to dividends or to a company's assets on its winding up and no present or future preferential right to be redeemed.

(8) Section 312(1A)(b) applies to determine the relevant period for the purposes of this section.

GENERAL NOTE

Section 289
Relief is available to a "qualifying individual" who subscribes for eligible shares issued by a "qualifying company" in order to finance a "qualifying business activity", carried on or to be carried on by the company or its subsidiary. The activity must be carried on wholly or mainly in the U.K. during the three years from the share issue date or if later, from the date the trade commences.

"Qualifying business activity" is a qualifying trade; or research and development or oil exploration from which a qualifying trade will be derived. Activities preparatory to carrying on a qualifying trade also qualify if the trade is commenced within two years after the share issue date. The money raised must be employed wholly for that activity within 12 months (a) from the share issue date, or (b) from the date the trade commences if the company was not trading at the share issue date. Eligible shares are ordinary shares which, during the first five years from their issue, carry no preferential rights to be redeemed, to dividends or to assets on a winding up. Relief is not available unless the shares are issued for bona fide commercial purposes and not as part of a scheme the main purpose or one of the main purpose of which is the avoidance of tax.

Form of relief
289A.—(1) Where an individual eligible for relief in respect of any amount subscribed for eligible shares makes a claim, then, subject to the following provisions of this Chapter, the amount of his liability for the year of assessment in which the shares were issued ('the current year') to income tax on his total income shall be the following amount.

(2) That amount is the amount to which he would be so liable apart from this section less whichever is the smaller of—
(a) an amount equal to tax at the lower rate for the current year on the amount or, as the case may be, the aggregate of the amounts subscribed for eligible shares issued in that year in respect of which he is eligible for relief, and
(b) the amount which reduces his liability to nil.

(3) Subject to subsection (4) below, if in the case of any issue of relevant shares, that is, shares—
(a) which are issued before 6th October in the current year, and
(b) in respect of the amount subscribed for which the individual is eligible for relief,
the individual so requests in his claim, subsection (1) above shall apply as if, in respect of such part of that issue as may be specified in his claim, the shares had been issued in the preceding year of assessment; and his liability to income tax for both years of assessment shall be determined accordingly.

(4) Not more than half of the relevant shares comprised in any issue may be treated by virtue of subsection (3) above as issued in the previous year; and the number of relevant shares (comprised in any issues) so treated as issued in a particular year shall not be such that the total amount subscribed for them exceeds £15,000.

(5) In determining for the purposes of subsection (2) above the amount of income tax to which a person would be liable apart from this section, no account shall be taken of—
(a) any income tax reduction under Chapter I of Part VII of this Act or under section 347B,
(b) any income tax reduction under section 353(1A),
(c) any income tax reduction under section 54(3A) of the Finance Act 1989,
(d) any relief by way of reduction of liability to tax which is give in accordance with any arrangements having effect by virtue of section 788 or by way of a credit under section 790(1), or

(e) any tax at the basic rate on so much of that person's income as is income the income tax on which he is entitled to charge against any other person or to deduct, retain or satisfy out of any payment.

(6) A claim for relief shall not be allowed unless subsection (7) below is complied with but, where it is complied with, the relief may be given at any time when it appears that the conditions for the relief may be satisfied.

(7) This subsection is complied with if—

(a) in the case of shares issued for the purpose of a qualifying business activity falling within paragraph (a) of section 289(2), the company or subsidiary concerned has carried on the trade for four months,

(b) in the case of shares issued for the purpose of a qualifying business activity falling within paragraph (b) of that subsection or within both paragraph (a) and paragraph (b) of that subsection, the company or subsidiary concerned has carried on the research and development for four months, and

(c) in the case of shares issued for the purpose of a qualifying business activity falling within paragraph (c) of that subsection, the company or subsidiary concerned has carried on the exploration for four months.

(8) Where—

(a) the company or subsidiary concerned, by reason of its being wound up, or dissolved without winding up, carries on a trade for a period shorter than four months, and

(b) it is shown that the winding up or dissolution was for bona fide commercial reasons and not as part of a scheme or arrangement the main purpose or one of the main purposes of which was the avoidance of tax,

subsection (7)(a) above shall have effect as if it referred to that shorter period.

(9) Where effect is given to a claim for relief by repayment of tax, section 824 shall have effect in relation to the repayment as if the time from which the twelve months mentioned in subsections (1)(a) and (3)(a) of that section are to be calculated were the end of the year of assessment in which the shares are issued or, if subsection (7) above is first complied with in a later year, the end of that later year.

GENERAL NOTE

Section 289A of the ICTA 1988
EIS relief is given by income tax reduction for the tax year in which the shares were issued. The reduction is restricted to (a) lower rate income tax on the amount subscribed, or (b) the amount which reduces the taxpayer's tax liability to nil, if lower. A claim for relief is not allowable until the qualifying business activity concerned has been carried on for four months; once this condition appears to be satisfied relief may be given at any time. A shorter period than four months may be allowed where the company is wound-up or dissolved for bona fide commercial reasons. The taxpayer may claim that up to half of the eligible shares issued before October 6 in a tax year should be treated as if they had been issued in the preceding year, up to £15,000 may be carried back in this way. Where EIS relief results in a repayment of tax, no repayment supplement is payable for the first 12 months after the end of the tax year (a) in which the shares were issued, or (b) if later, in which the company completes four months carrying on the qualifying activity.

Attribution of relief to shares
289B.—(1) References in this Chapter, in relation to any individual, to the relief attributable to any shares or issue of shares shall be read, subject to the provisions of this Chapter providing for the reduction or withdrawal of relief, as references to any reduction made in the individual's liability to income tax which is attributed to those shares or that issue in accordance with this section.

(2) Where an individual's liability to income tax is reduced in any year of assessment ('the current year') under section 289A, then—

(a) where the reduction is given by reason of an issue of shares made (or treated as made) in the current year, the amount of the reduction shall be attributed to that issue, and

(b) where the reduction is given by reason of two or more issues of shares made (or treated as made) in the current year, the reduction—

(i) shall be apportioned between those issues in the same proportions as the amount subscribed by the individual for each issue, and

(ii) shall be attributed to those issues accordingly.

(3) Where under this section an amount of any reduction of income tax is attributed to an issue of shares ('the original issue') in a company to an individual—

   (a) a proportionate part of that amount shall be attributed to each share comprised in the original issue, and

   (b) if any bonus shares in that company which are eligible shares are issued to him at any subsequent time—

      (i) a proportionate part of the total amount attributed immediately before that time to shares comprised in the original issue shall be attributed to each of the shares in the holding comprising those shares and the bonus shares, and

      (ii) this Chapter shall apply as if the original holding had comprised all those shares.

(4) Subject to subsection (5) below, in this Chapter references to an issue of shares in any company to an individual are to any shares in the company issued to him on the same day.

(5) Where section 289A(1) applies in the case of any issue of shares as if part of the issue had been issued in a previous year, this section and the following provisions of this Chapter (except section 290(1)) shall have effect as if that part and the remainder were separate issues of shares (and that part had been issued on a day in the previous year).

(6) Where, at a time when any relief is attributable to, or to any part of, any issue of shares, the relief falls to be withdrawn or reduced under this Chapter—

   (a) where it falls to be withdrawn, the relief attributable to each of the shares in question shall be reduced to nil, and

   (b) where it falls to be reduced by any amount, the relief attributable to each of the shares in question shall be reduced by a proportionate part of that amount."

3.—(1) In section 290 (minimum and maximum subscriptions), for subsection (2) there is substituted—

   "(2) An individual shall not be eligible for relief in any year of assessment in respect of any amount subscribed for eligible shares exceeding £100,000 (whether the shares are issued in that or a subsequent year)."

(2) Sub-paragraph (1) above shall have effect for the year 1994–95 and subsequent years of assessment.

(3) An individual shall not be eligible for relief in respect of the year 1993–94 in respect of any amount subscribed for eligible shares (whether the shares are issued in that or a subsequent year) which, when aggregated with the amounts (if any) on which relief is claimed under the old scheme in respect of that year, exceeds £40,000.

(4) In this paragraph the "old scheme" means Chapter III of Part VII of the Taxes Act 1988 as it had effect before the amendments made by this Schedule.

4.—(1) In section 290A (restriction of relief)—

   (a) for subsection (1) there is substituted—

     "(1) Where—

     (a) a company raises any amount through the issue of eligible shares, and

     (b) the aggregate of that amount and of all other amounts (if any) so raised within the period mentioned in subsection (2) below exceeds £1 million,

    the relief shall not be given in respect of the excess",

   (b) in subsection (4), for "£750,000" there is substituted "£1 million",

   (c) subsection (10) and the definition of "prospectus" in subsection (11) are omitted, and

   (d) after subsection (11) there is added—

     "(12) Section 312(1A)(b) applies to determine the relevant period for the purposes of this section."

(2) References in that section to amounts raised through the issue of eligible shares include amounts raised through the issue before 1st January 1994 of shares which were eligible shares under the old scheme; and the "old scheme" has the same meaning as in paragraph 3 above.

5. For section 291 (individuals qualifying for relief) there is substituted—

GENERAL NOTE

Section 289B of the ICTA 1988

EIS relief is attributed to each issue of EIS shares in proportion to the amounts subscribed. The relief attributed to each issue is then apportioned equally between each share including any bonus shares added to the holding. Shares issued on the same day are treated as a single issue. Where an EIS investor makes a claim for part of the relief in respect of a single issue of shares in the preceding tax year, the issue is split and part is treated as issued on the actual share date and the remainder as issued in the previous year. Where EIS relief in respect of an issue of shares is reduced, a proportional amount of relief attributable to each share is withdrawn.

Para. (3)
  The maximum total subscriptions eligible for EIS relief is £100,000. For 1993 and 1994 BES and EIS subscriptions are aggregated and the maximum limit is the BES limit, of £40,000.

Para. (4)
  The ICTA 1988 (c. 1), s.290A is amended. The maximum amount that can be raised by a company under EIS is increased to £1 million, effective from January 1, 1994. The period to which the £1 million limit applies is the same as for BES but amounts raised through BES issues are to be taken into account if they fall within the period. The limit of £5 million for qualifying shipping trades is unchanged. The anti-avoidance rules in subs. (4), which prevent a qualifying business activity being divided among a number of companies, is similarly amended to increase the limit to £1 million.

Para. (5)
  The ICTA 1988 (c. 1), s.291 is replaced by ss.291, 291A and 291B which determine whether an individual qualifies for EIS relief.

"Individuals qualifying for relief
  291.—(1) An individual qualifies for relief in respect of eligible shares in a company (referred to in this section and sections 291A and 291B as the 'issuing company') if—
    (a) he subscribes for the shares on his own behalf, and
    (b) subject to section 291A(4), he is not at any time in the relevant period connected with the company.
  (2) For the purposes of this section and sections 291A and 291B, an individual is connected with the issuing company if he, or an associate of his, is—
    (a) an employee of, or of a partner of, the issuing company or any subsidiary,
    (b) a partner of the issuing company or any subsidiary, or
    (c) subject to section 291A, a director of, or of a company which is a partner of, the issuing company or any subsidiary,
  or if he, or an associate of his, is so connected by virtue of section 291B.
  (3) In subsection (2) above 'subsidiary', in relation to the issuing company, means a 51 per cent. subsidiary of the issuing company—
    (a) whether it becomes such a subsidiary before, during or after the year of assessment in respect of which the individual concerned claims relief, and
    (b) whether or not it is such a subsidiary while he or his associate is such an employee, partner or director.
  (4) For the purposes of subsections (2) and (3) above and section 291A, in the case of a person who is both a director and an employee of a company—
    (a) references (however expressed) to him in his capacity as a director of the company include him in his capacity as an employee of the company, but
    (b) (apart from that) he is not to be treated as an employee of the company.
  (5) Section 312(1A)(a) applies to determine the relevant period for the purposes of this section and sections 291A and 291B.

GENERAL NOTE

Section 291 of the ICTA 1988
  Relief is available if (a) the investor subscribes for eligible shares on his own behalf, and (b) neither he nor an associate is an employee, partner or director of the issuing company, or any 51 per cent. subsidiary, throughout the relevant period (as defined in the ICTA 1988 (c. 1), s.312(1A)(a)). Directors are not treated as employees. An EIS investor need not be U.K. resident.

Connected persons: directors
  291A.—(1) An individual is not connected with the issuing company by reason only that he, or an associate of his, is a director of that or another company unless he or his associate (or a partnership of which he or his associate is a member)—
    (a) receives a payment from the issuing company or a related person during the relevant period, or
    (b) is entitled to receive such a payment in respect of that period or any part of it.
  (2) In this section—
    (a) 'related person', in relation to the issuing company, means—
        (i) any company of which the individual or his associate is a director and which is a subsidiary or a partner of the issuing company or of a subsidiary, and

     (ii) any person connected with the issuing company or with a company falling within subparagraph (i) above, and

(b) any reference to a payment to an individual includes a payment made to him indirectly or to his order or for his benefit.

(3) For the purposes of subsection (1) above there shall be disregarded—

(a) any payment or reimbursement of travelling or other expenses wholly, exclusively and necessarily incurred by him or his associate in the performance of his duties as a director,

(b) any interest which represents no more than a reasonable commercial return on money lent to the issuing company or a related person,

(c) any dividend or other distribution which does not exceed a normal return on the investment,

(d) any payment for the supply of goods which does not exceed their market value,

(e) any payment of rent for any property occupied by the issuing company or a related person which does not exceed a reasonable and commercial rent for the property, and

(f) any reasonable and necessary remuneration which—

     (i) is paid for services rendered to the issuing company or related person in the course of a trade or profession (not being secretarial or managerial services of a kind provided by the person to whom they are rendered), and

     (ii) is taken into account in computing the profits or gains of the trade or profession under Case I or II of Schedule D or would be so taken into account if it fell in a period on the basis of which those profits or gains are assessed under that Schedule.

(4) An individual ('the subscriber') who subscribes for eligible shares ('the relevant shares') may qualify for the relief notwithstanding his connection with the company at any time in the relevant period if—

(a) he is so connected by reason only of his, or his associate's, being a director of, or of a company which is a partner of, the issuing company or a subsidiary in receipt of, or entitled to receive, remuneration as such, and

(b) the following conditions are satisfied;

and in this subsection and subsection (5) below 'remuneration' includes any benefit or facility.

(5) The conditions are that—

(a) in relation to the director (whether he is the subscriber or his associate), his remuneration, or the remuneration to which he is entitled, (leaving out of account any reasonable and necessary remuneration falling within subsection (3)(f) above) consists only of remuneration which is reasonable remuneration for services rendered to the company of which he is a director in his capacity as such,

(b) the subscriber was issued with eligible shares (whether the relevant shares or a previous issue of eligible shares) at a time when he had never been—

     (i) connected with the issuing company, or

     (ii) an employee of any person who previously carried on the trade carried on by the issuing company, and

(c) where the issue of the relevant shares did not satisfy paragraph (b) above, they were not issued after the end of the period of five years beginning with the date of the latest issue of eligible shares which satisfied that paragraph,

and in paragraph (b) above 'trade' includes any business, profession or vocation, and the reference to a trade previously carried on includes part of such a trade.

(6) In this section 'subsidiary', in relation to the issuing company, means a 51 per cent. subsidiary of the issuing company.

GENERAL NOTE

Section 291A of the ICTA 1988

An EIS investor is not connected with the issuing company if he or his associate are unremunerated directors (*i.e.* a director who neither receives, nor is entitled to receive, a payment from the company or a related person) throughout the relevant period. For this purpose certain payments to the directors are disregarded including rent for property occupied by the company. An EIS investor or an associate who is a paid director of the company or a related person may claim EIS relief for eligible shares issued before he or she became a paid director if (a) the remuneration is reasonable, and (b) prior to the share issue date he had never been connected with the company nor had he been employed by a predecessor in its trade. Provided the director does not become otherwise connected with the company, he may also qualify for relief in respect of eligible shares which are issued within five years from the latest of those earlier issues which were issued when the director was not connected with the company in any way.

Connected persons: persons interested in capital etc. of company

291B.—(1) An individual is connected with the issuing company if he directly or indirectly possesses or is entitled to acquire more than 30 per cent. of—

(a) the issued ordinary share capital of the company or any subsidiary,

(b) the loan capital and issued share capital of the company or any subsidiary, or

(c) the voting power in the company or any subsidiary.

(2) An individual is connected with the issuing company if he directly or indirectly possesses or is entitled to acquire such rights as would, in the event of the winding up of the company or any subsidiary or in any other circumstances, entitle him to receive more than 30 per cent. of the assets of the company or subsidiary (the 'company in question') which would then be available for distribution to equity holders of the company in question.

(3) For the purposes of subsection (2) above—

(a) the persons who are equity holders of the company in question, and

(b) the percentage of the assets of the company in question to which the individual would be entitled,

shall be determined in accordance with paragraphs 1 and 3 of Schedule 18, taking references in paragraph 3 to the first company as references to an equity holder and references to a winding up as including references to any other circumstances in which assets of the company in question are available for distribution to its equity holders.

(4) An individual is connected with a company if he has control of it or of any subsidiary.

(5) Where an individual subscribes for shares in a company with which (apart from this subsection) he is not connected, he shall nevertheless be treated as connected with it if he subscribes for the shares as part of any arrangement which provides for another person to subscribe for shares in another company with which (assuming it to be an issuing company) that or any other individual who is a party to the arrangement is connected.

(6) In this section 'subsidiary', in relation to the issuing company, means a 51 per cent. subsidiary of the issuing company—

(a) whether it becomes such a subsidiary before, during or after the year of assessment in respect of which the individual concerned claims relief, and

(b) whether or not it is such a subsidiary while he has, or is entitled to acquire, such capital, voting power, rights or control as are mentioned in this section.

(7) For the purposes of this section the loan capital of a company shall be treated as including any debt incurred by the company—

(a) for any money borrowed or capital assets acquired by the company,

(b) for any right to receive income created in favour of the company, or

(c) for consideration the value of which to the company was (at the time when the debt was incurred) substantially less than the amount of the debt (including any premium on it).

(8) For the purposes of this section an individual shall be treated as entitled to acquire anything which he is entitled to acquire at a future date or will at a future date be entitled to acquire, and there shall be attributed to any person any rights or powers of any other person who is an associate of his.

(9) In determining for the purposes of this section whether an individual is connected with a company, no debt incurred by the company or any subsidiary by overdrawing an account with a person carrying on a business of banking shall be treated as loan capital of the company or subsidiary if the debt arose in the ordinary course of that business.

(10) Section 840 applies for the purposes of this section."

6. In section 292 (parallel trades)—

(a) in subsection (1), for the words preceding paragraph (a) there is substituted "An individual is not eligible for relief in respect of any shares in a company if, at the date mentioned in subsection (2) below", and

(b) in subsection (4)(a) for "any of its subsidiaries" there is substituted "any company which is a 51 per cent. subsidiary of that company on the date referred to in subsection (2) above".

7. In section 293 (qualifying companies)—

(a) for subsections (1) to (3) there is substituted—

"(1) Subject to section 294, a company is a qualifying company (whether it is resident in the United Kingdom or elsewhere) if it complies with the requirements of this section.

(2) The company must, throughout the relevant period, be an unquoted company and be—

(a) a company which exists wholly for the purpose of carrying on one or more qualifying trades or which so exists apart from purposes capable of having no significant effect (other than in relation to incidental matters) on the extent of the company's activities, or

(b) a company whose business consists wholly of—

(i) the holding of shares or securities of, or the making of loans to, one or more qualifying subsidiaries of the company, or

(ii) both the holding of such shares or securities, or the making of such loans, and the carrying on of one or more qualifying trades.

(3) In this section 'qualifying subsidiary', in relation to a company, means a subsidiary of a kind which that company may hold by virtue of section 308",

(b) subsection (4) is omitted,

(c) in subsection (7), at the end there is inserted "or would not be fully paid up if any undertaking to pay cash to the company at a future date were disregarded",

(d) for subsection (8) there is substituted—

"(8) Subject to section 308, the company must not—

(a) at any time in the relevant period control (or together with any person connected with it control) another company or be under the control of another company (or another company and any other person connected with that other company), or

(b) at any such time be a 51 per cent. subsidiary of another company or itself have a 51 per cent. subsidiary.

and no arrangements must be in existence at any time in that period by virtue of which the company could fall within paragraph (a) or (b) above.

(8A) Section 312(1A)(b) applies to determine the relevant period for the purposes of this section and sections 294, 295 and 296", and

(e) subsections (9) to (11) are omitted.

8. In section 294 (companies with interests in land), in subsection (1), for the words preceding paragraph (a) there is substituted "Subject to section 296, a company is not a qualifying company in relation to any shares if at any time during the relevant period".

9. In section 296 (provisions supplementary to section 294), subsection (6) is omitted.

10. In section 297 (qualifying trades)—

(a) in subsection (1), "(6) and" is omitted,

(b) in subsection (2)—

(i) in paragraph (a), for "commodities, shares, securities, land or futures" there is substituted "land, in commodities or futures or in shares, securities or other financial instruments",

(ii) in paragraph (g), after "another person" there is inserted "(other than a company of which the company providing the services or facilities is the subsidiary)", and

(iii) paragraphs (h) and (j) are omitted,

(c) in subsection (5), for the words preceding paragraph (a) there is substituted "A trade shall not be treated as failing to comply with this section by reason only that it consists to a substantial extent of receiving royalties or licence fees if", and

(d) in subsection (9), for "289(1)(d)" there is substituted "289(2)(c)".

11. In section 298 (supplementary provisions)—

(a) for subsection (4) there is substituted—

"(4) The Treasury may by order amend section 297 and this section in such manner as they consider expedient",

(b) in subsection (5), the definition of "property development" is omitted,

(c) at the end of that subsection there is inserted—

"and section 312(1A)(b) shall apply to determine the relevant period for the purposes of that section", and

(d) subsections (6) to (8) are omitted.

12. For section 299 (disposal of shares) there is substituted—

"Disposal of shares

299.—(1) Where an individual makes any disposal of eligible share before the end of the relevant period, then—

(a) if the disposal is made otherwise than by way of a bargain made at arm's length, any relief attributable to those shares shall be withdrawn, and

(b) in the case of any disposal made by way of a bargain made at arm's length—

(i) if, apart from this subsection, the relief attributable to those shares is greater than the amount mentioned in subsection (2) below, it shall be reduced by that amount, and

    (ii) if sub-paragraph (i) above does not apply, any relief attributable to those shares shall be withdrawn.

    (2) The amount referred to in subsection (1) above is an amount equal to tax at the lower rate for the year of assessment for which the relief was given on the amount or value of the consideration which the individual receives for the shares.

    (3) Where, in relation to any issue of shares held by any person, the disposal referred to in subsection (1) above is a disposal of part of the shares, that subsection shall apply to the relief that was attributable to that part.

    (4) Where an individual's liability to income tax has been reduced in any year of assessment under section 289A in respect of any issue of shares and the amount of the reduction ('A') is less than the amount ('B') which is equal to tax at the lower rate for that year on the amount subscribed for the issue, subsection (2) above shall have effect as if the amount or value referred to in that subsection were reduced by multiplying it by the fraction—

$$\frac{A}{B}$$

    (5) Where an option, the exercise of which would bind the grantor to purchase any shares, is granted to an individual during the relevant period, any relief attributable to the shares to which the option relates shall be withdrawn.

    (6) Where any relief is attributable to shares of any class in a company which have been issued to an individual at different times, any disposal by him of shares of that class shall be treated for the purposes of this section as relating to those issued earlier rather than to those issued later.

    (7) Where relief is attributable to any shares which have by virtue of any such allotment as is mentioned in section 126(2)(a) of the 1992 Act (not being an allotment for payment) fallen to be treated under section 127 of that Act as the same asset as a new holding, a disposal of the whole or part of the new holding shall be treated for the purposes of this section as a disposal of the whole or a corresponding part of those shares.

    (8) For the purposes of this section—

    (a) shares in a company shall not be treated as being of the same class unless they would be so treated if dealt with on the Stock Exchange,

    (b) references to a disposal of shares include references to the grant of an option the exercise of which would bind the grantor to sell the shares, and

    (c) section 312(1A)(a) applies to determine the relevant period."

GENERAL NOTE

Section 291B of the ICTA 1988
    The new s.291B revives the old BES rules, that an individual is connected with the issuing company if he directly or indirectly possesses or is entitled (together with his associates) to acquire more than 30 per cent. of (a) the issued share capital or issued share and loan capital, or (b) the voting power, or (c) assets on a winding-up of the company or any 51 per cent. subsidiary. Loan capital includes money borrowed and assets acquired by the company but a bank overdraft is excluded. The rights of an associate are attributed to an investor.

Paras. (6)(8)(9) and (11)
    Minor amendments are made to the ICTA 1988 (c. 1), ss.292, 294, 296 and 298, respectively, to accommodate the new rules for EIS.

Para. (7)
    The ICTA 1988 (c. 1), s.293 is amended. A qualifying company is no longer required to be U.K. resident and incorporated. The company must exist wholly (previously "wholly or substantially wholly") for the purposes of carrying one or more qualifying trades or be a holding company or financing company of such a company. All shares must be fully paid and not subject to undertakings to make future payments to the company. Other minor amendments are made to the section to accommodate the new rules for EIS.

Para. (10)
    The ICTA 1988 (c. 1), s.297 is amended to add dealings in financial instruments to the list of forbidden activities. Property development and farming are removed from the list.

Para. (12)
    The ICTA 1988 (c. 1), s.299 is substituted. EIS relief is wholly withdrawn if shares are disposed of within the relevant period in a non-arm's length disposal. An arm's length disposal reduces

EIS relief originally given, by an amount equal to the lower tax rate (for the tax year in which the relief was given) applied to the consideration received (X). If the original relief (A) was less than lower rate tax on the amount subscribed for the shares (B), the reduction in relief, *i.e.* X is further reduced by the fraction A/B (s.299(4)). On a part disposal of the shares, the original relief attributable to that part is to be taken into account. The grant of a call option over eligible shares within the five-year period disbars relief. Shares are deemed to be disposed of on a first in first out basis and bonus shares are treated as part of a shareholding.

13. In section 299A (loan linked investments)—
(a) in subsection (1), for the words preceding paragraph (a) there is substituted "An individual is not eligible for relief in respect of any shares in a company if", and
(b) after subsection (2) there is inserted—
"(3) Section 312(1A)(a) applies to determine the relevant period for the purposes of this section."
14. In section 300 (value received from company)—
(a) for subsection (1) there is substituted—
"(1) Subsection (1A) below applies where an individual who subscribes for eligible shares in a company—
(a) has, before the issue of the shares but within the relevant period, received any value from the company, or
(b) after their issue but before the end of the relevant period, receives any such value.
(1A) Where any relief is attributable to those shares, then (unless the amount of the relief has already been reduced on account of the value received)—
(a) if it is greater than the amount mentioned in subsection (1B) below, it shall be reduced by that amount, and
(b) if paragraph (a) above does not apply, the relief shall be withdrawn.
(1B) The amount referred to in subsection (1A) above is an amount equal to tax at the lower rate for the year of assessment for which the relief was given on the amount of the value received; and section 299(4) above applies for the purposes of this subsection as it applies for the purposes of subsection (2) of that section.
(1C) References in subsection (1) above to the receipt of value from a company include references to the receipt of value from a 51 per cent. subsidiary of that company, whether it becomes such a subsidiary before or after the individual concerned receives any value from it; and other references to the company in this section and section 301 shall be read accordingly.
(1D) Notwithstanding anything in subsection (2) below, for the purposes of this section an individual is not to be treated as receiving value from a company by reason only of the payment to him, or any associate of his, of any remuneration for services rendered to the company as a director if the remuneration is reasonable remuneration.
(1E) Section 291(4) applies for the purposes of subsection (1D) above as it applies for the purposes of section 291A, and the reference in subsection (1D) above to the payment of remuneration includes the provision of any benefit or facility", and
(b) in subsection (2)—
(i) in paragraph (c), for "291(3)(a) or (e)" there is substituted "291A(3)(a) or (f)", and
(ii) in paragraph (h), for "section 291(3)(a), (b), (c), (d) or (e)" there is substituted "any of the paragraphs of section 291A(3)".
15. In section 301 (provisions supplementary to section 300)—
(a) subsections (1) and (2) are omitted,
(b) after subsection (6) there is inserted—
"(6A) Section 312(1A)(a) applies to determine the relevant period for the purposes of section 300", and
(c) subsection (7) is omitted.
16. In section 302 (replacement capital)—
(a) for subsection (1) there is substituted—
"(1) Any relief attributable to any shares in a company held by an individual shall be withdrawn if—
(a) at any time in the relevant period, the company or any subsidiary—
(i) begins to carry on as its trade or as part of its trade a trade which was previously carried on at any time in that period otherwise than by the company or any subsidiary, or
(ii) acquires the whole, or a greater part, of the assets used for the purposes of a trade previously so carried on, and

(b) subsection (2) below applies in relation to that individual",
(b) in subsection (3), for the words preceding paragraph (a) there is substituted "Any relief attributable to any shares in a company held by an individual shall be withdrawn if",
(c) after subsection (4) there is inserted—

"(4A) In determining whether any relief attributable to any shares in a company (the 'issuing company') held by a person who—
    (a) is a director of, or of a company which is a partner of, the issuing company or any subsidiary, and
    (b) is in receipt of, or entitled to receive, remuneration as such a director falling within section 291A(5)(a),

is to be withdrawn, the second reference in paragraph (b) of each of subsections (2) and (3) above and, so far as relating to those paragraphs, in subsection (1)(a)(i) above to any time in the relevant period shall be read as a reference to any time before the end of the relevant period.

(4B) Section 291(4) applies for the purposes of subsection (4A) above as it applies for the purposes of section 291A, and in subsection (4A) above 'remuneration' includes any benefit or facility", and
(d) in subsection (5)—
    (i) for the definition of "subsidiary" there is substituted—
        " 'subsidiary' means a company which would be a subsidiary if the relevant period for the purposes of section 308 were the period referred to in section 312(1A)(a)" and
    (ii) at the end of that subsection there is inserted—
        "and section 312(1A)(a) applies to determine the relevant period for the purposes of this section".

17. In section 303 (value received by persons other than claimants)—
(a) for subsection (1) there is substituted—

"(1) Where any relief is attributable to any shares in a company held by an individual, subsection (1A) below shall apply if at any time in the relevant period the company or any subsidiary repays, redeems or repurchases any of its share capital which belongs to any member other than—
    (a) that individual, or
    (b) another individual the relief attributable to whose shares in the company is thereby withdrawn or reduced by virtue of section 299 or 300(2)(a),

or makes any payment to any such member for giving up his right to any of the share capital of the company or subsidiary on its cancellation or extinguishment.

(1A) The relief—
    (a) if it is greater than the amount mentioned in subsection (1B) below, shall be reduced by that amount, and
    (b) if paragraph (a) above does not apply, shall be withdrawn.

(1B) The amount referred to in subsection (1A) above is an amount equal to tax at the lower rate for the year of assessment for which the relief was given on the amount receivable by the member or, if greater, the nominal value of the share capital in question; and section 299(4) above applies for the purposes of this subsection as it applies for the purposes of subsection (2) of that section",
(b) in subsection (3), for "291(4)" there is substituted "291B(1)" and for "291" there is substituted "291B",
(c) after subsection (6) there is inserted—

"(6A) The reference in subsection (3) above to the receipt of value from a company includes the receipt of value from a subsidiary, and the reference to the company in subsection (6) above shall be read accordingly",
(d) subsection (8) is omitted,
(e) after subsection (9) there is inserted—

"(9A) References in this section to a subsidiary of a company are references to a 51 per cent. subsidiary of the company, whether it becomes such a subsidiary before or after the redemption, repayment, repurchase or payment in question or, as the case may be, the receipt of value in question.

(9B) Section 312(1A)(a) applies to determine the relevant period for the purposes of this section", and
(f) subsection (10) and (11) are omitted.
18. For section 304 (husband and wife) there is substituted—

"Husband and wife

304.—(1) Section 299(1) shall not apply to a disposal of shares to which an amount of relief is attributable made by a married man to his wife or a married woman to her husband at a time when they are living together.

(2) Where such shares issued to one of them ('the transferor') are transferred to the other ('the transferee') by a transaction *inter vivos* to which that section does not apply, this Chapter shall have effect, in relation to any subsequent disposal or other event, as if—

(a) the transferee were the person who had subscribed for the shares,

(b) the transferee's liability to income tax had been reduced under section 289A in respect of those shares for the same year of assessment as that for which the transferor's liability was so reduced and, accordingly, that amount of relief had continued to be attributable to the shares notwithstanding the transfer.

(3) Any assessment for reducing or withdrawing the relief by reason of any such disposal or other event shall be made on the transferee".

GENERAL NOTE

Para. (14)

If an EIS investor receives any value from the issuing company (or any 51 per cent. subsidiary) during the relevant period, the relief originally given is to be reduced by an amount equal to the lower tax rate (for the tax year in which the relief was given) applied to the value received. Section 299(4) is applied if the original relief given is less than the lower rate tax on the amount subscribed for the shares. Reasonable remuneration received for services rendered as a director are ignored.

Paras. (13)(15) and (16)

Minor amendments are made to the ICTA 1988 (c. 1), ss.299A, 301 and 302 respectively to accommodate the new EIS rules.

Para. (17)

The ICTA 1988 (c. 1), s.303 is amended to reflect the fact that EIS relief is given by income tax reduction. Where s.303(1) applies the EIS relief originally given is to be reduced by an amount equal to the lower tax rate (for the tax year in which the relief was given) applied to the amount receivable or the nominal value of the shares redeemed, if greater. Section 299(4) is applied if the original relief given is less than lower rate tax on the amount subscribed for the shares. Other minor amendments are made to s.303 to accommodate the new EIS rules.

Para. (18)

Section 304 is substituted. Disposals between spouses are ignored for the purpose of s.299 (see para. (12) above); instead the transferee spouse is treated as having subscribed for the shares and as having received any EIS relief previously given to the transferor.

19. For section 305 (re-organisation of share capital) there is substituted—

"Reorganisation of share capital

305.—(1) Subsection (2) below applies where—

(a) there is by virtue of any allotment in the relevant period, being such an allotment for payment as is mentioned in section 126(2)(a) of the 1992 Act, a reorganisation affecting ordinary shares,

(b) immediately before the reorganisation an amount of relief ('X') is attributable to the shares, and

(c) both—

(i) the amount subscribed for the shares ('Z'), and

(ii) the market value of the shares immediately before the reorganisation,

exceed the market value of the shares immediately after the reorganisation.

(2) Where this subsection applies, the relief attributable to the shares shall be reduced by the following amount—

$$\frac{X \times Y}{Z}$$

where 'Y' is whichever is the smaller of the amounts by which Z, and the market value of the shares immediately before the reorganisation, exceed the market value of the shares immediately after the reorganisation.

(3) Subsection (2) above also applies where—

(a) an individual, who at any time in the relevant period has received, or become entitled to receive, in respect of any ordinary shares in a company, a provisional allotment of shares in or debentures of the company, disposes of his rights, and

(b) that subsection would have applied if he had not disposed of the rights but the allotment had been made to him by virtue of those rights.

(4) Section 312(1A)(a) applies to determine the relevant period for the purposes of this section".

GENERAL NOTE

Para. (19)

Section 305 is substituted. If, within the relevant period, new shares are allotted for consideration, under a company reconstruction, in respect of a holding of EIS shares, the EIS relief originally given (X) to an investor is to be reduced if the market value of the old shares after the reorganisation is less than (a) the amount subscribed for the EIS shares (Z), and (b) the market value of those shares before the reorganisation. The relief is reduced by the fraction:

$$\frac{X \times Y}{Z}$$

where Y is the lesser of the two shortfalls. The same reduction also applies, if the investor disposes of his entitlement under a rights issue, instead of taking up the shares.

20. After section 305 there is inserted—

"Relief for loss on disposal of shares

305A.—(1) Section 574 shall apply on the disposal by an individual of shares to which relief is attributable as it applies to a disposal by him of shares in a qualifying trading company for which he has subscribed ('qualifying trading company' and 'subscribed' having for this purpose the same meaning as in that section).

(2) For the purposes of that section (as applied by this) sections 575(1) and (3) and 576(2) and (3) shall apply".

21. In section 306 (claims)—

(a) in subsection (1)—

(i) in paragraph (a), for "289(8)(a), (b) or (c)" there is substituted "289A(7)(a), (b) or (c)", and

(ii) for paragraph (b) there is substituted—

"(b) not later than twelve months after an inspector authorises the issue of a certificate for the purposes of subsection (2) below",

(b) after subsection (3) there is inserted—

"(3A) A company may not furnish an inspector with a statement in respect of any shares issued in any year of assessment—

(a) later than two years after the end of that year of assessment, or

(b) if the period of four months referred to in subsection (1)(a) above ended after the end of that year, later than two years after the end of that period,

but section 289B(5) shall not apply for the purposes of this subsection",

(c) in subsection (8), for "entitled to" there is substituted "eligible for",

(d) in subsection (10), the second sentence is omitted, and

(e) after that subsection there is inserted—

"(11) Section 312(1A)(b) applies to determine the relevant period for the purposes of this section".

22. In section 307 (withdrawal of relief)—

(a) in subsection (1), the words from "but" to the end are omitted,

(b) for subsection (2) there is substituted—

"(1A) Relief may not be withdrawn, in relation to shares issued by a company on any date, on the ground that the company is not a qualifying company or that the requirements of section 289(1)(b) or (c) are not met unless—

(a) the company has given notice under section 310, or

(b) an inspector has given notice to the company stating that, by reason of that ground, the whole or any part of the relief given to individuals to whom the shares were issued on that date was not, in his opinion, due.

(1B) The giving of notice by an inspector under subsection (1A) above shall be taken, for the purposes of the provisions of the Management Act relating to appeals against decisions on claims, to be a decision refusing a claim made by the company.

(2) Subject to subsections (3) to (7) below, no assessment for withdrawing relief may be made, and no notice may be given under subsection (1A) above, more than six years after the end of the year of assessment—

(a) in which the time mentioned in section 289(3) falls, or

(b) in which the event by reason of which the claimant ceases to be eligible for relief occurs,

whichever is the later",

(c) in subsection (6)—

(i) in paragraph (a), for "289(11)" there is substituted "289(6)",

(ii) after that paragraph there is inserted—

"(aa) in the case of relief withdrawn by virtue of section 289(1)(c), the date on which the relief was granted", and

(iii) after paragraph (c) there is inserted—

"(cca) in the case of relief withdrawn by virtue of section 299(5), the date on which the option was granted",

(d) after subsection (8) there is inserted—

"(8A) References in this section to the withdrawal of relief include its reduction", and

(e) subsection (9) is omitted.

23. In section 308 (application to subsidiaries)—

(a) after subsection (5) there is inserted—

"(5A) Section 312(1A)(b) applies to determine the relevant period for the purposes of this section", and

(b) subsection (6) is omitted.

24. Section 309 (further provisions as to subsidiaries) is omitted.

25. In section 310 (information)—

(a) in subsection (1), for "304(2) to (6)" there is substituted "304",

(b) in subsection (2), for "289(11)" there is substituted "289(1)(c) or (6)"

(c) in subsection (5), for "289(11), 291(10)" there is substituted "289(6), 291B(5)",

(d) in subsection (6), for "289(11)" (in both places) there is substituted "289(6)" and for "291(10)" there is substituted "291B(5)", and

(e) subsections (10) and (11) are omitted.

26. In section 311 (nominees, etc.)—

(a) in subsection (2), for the words preceding "this Chapter" there is substituted "Where eligible shares are held on a bare trust for two or more beneficiaries", and

(b) in subsection (2B), for the words preceding paragraph (a) there is substituted—

"In any case where this subsection applies, sections 289A and 298B shall have effect as if".

27. In section 312 (interpretation)—

(a) in subsection (1)—

(i) in the definition of "control", for "291(7), 308(2) and 309(6)(a)" there is substituted "291B(4) and 308(2)",

(ii) after the definition of "director" there is inserted—

" 'eligible for relief' has the meaning given by section 289(1),

'eligible shares' has the meaning given by section 289(7)",

(iii) the definition of "fixed rate preference share capital" is omitted,

(iv) the definition of "the relevant period" is omitted,

(v) for the definition of "the relief" and "relief" there is substituted—

" 'relief' means relief under this Chapter,

'subsidiary', in relation to any company (except in the expression '51 per cent. subsidiary' or where otherwise defined), means a subsidiary of that company of a kind which that company may hold under section 308,

'51 per cent. subsidiary', in relation to any company, means (except in the case of references to a company which is a 51 per cent. subsidiary on a particular date or at a particular time) a company which is a 51 per cent. subsidiary of that company at any time in the relevant period (applying subsection (1A)(a) below)", and

(vi) for the definition of "unquoted company" there is substituted—

" 'unquoted company' means a company none of whose shares, stocks, debentures or other securities are marketed to the general public",

(b) after that subsection there is inserted—

"(1A) In any provision of this Chapter 'relevant period', in relation to relief in respect of any eligible shares issued by a company, means whichever of the following periods is applied for the purposes of that provision (disregarding section 289B(5))—

    (a) the period beginning with the incorporation of the company (or, if the company was incorporated more than two years before the date on which the shares were issued, beginning two years before that date) and ending five years after the issue of the shares, and

    (b) the period beginning with the date on which the shares were issued and ending either—

        (i) three years after that date, or

        (ii) in a case falling within section 289(2)(a) where the company or subsidiary concerned had not begun to carry on the trade in question on that date, three years after the date on which it begins to carry on that trade.

(1B) For the purposes of the definition of 'unquoted company' in subsection (1) above, shares, stocks, debentures or other securities are marketed to the general public if they are—

    (a) listed on a recognised stock exchange,

    (b) listed on a designated exchange in a country outside the United Kingdom, or

    (c) dealt in on the Unlisted Securities Market or dealt in outside the United Kingdom by such means as may be designated.

(1C) In subsection (1B) above "designated" means designated by an order made by the Board for the purposes of that subsection; and an order made for the purposes of paragraph (b) of that subsection may designate an exchange by name, or by reference to any class or description of exchanges, including a class or description framed by reference to any authority or approval given in a country outside the United Kingdom.

(1D) Section 828(1) does not apply to an order made for the purposes of subsection (1B) above.

(1E) Where a company is an unquoted company at the time when any shares are issued, it shall not be treated for the purposes of this Chapter as ceasing to be an unquoted company in relation to those shares at any subsequent time by reason only that any shares, stocks, debentures or other securities of the company are at that time listed on an exchange, or dealt in by any means, designated by such an order if the order was made after the shares were issued",

(c) in subsection (2), for "section 291" there is substituted "sections 291 to 291B",

(d) for subsections (4) and (5) there is substituted—

    "(4) In this Chapter—

    (a) references in any provision to the reduction of any relief attributable to any shares include a reference—

        (i) to the reduction of the relief to nil, and

        (ii) where no relief has yet been given, to the reduction of the amount which apart from that provision would be the relief, and

    (b) references to the withdrawal of any relief, in respect of any shares, are to the withdrawal of the relief attributable to those shares or, in a case where no relief has yet been given, to ceasing to be eligible for relief in respect of those shares.

(5) For the purposes of this Chapter, the market value at any time of any asset shall be taken to be the price which it might reasonably be expected to fetch on a sale at that time in the open market free from any interest or right which exists by way of security in or over it", and

(e) in subsection (7), for "289(1)(d)" there is substituted "289(2)(c)".

GENERAL NOTE

Para. (20)

An allowable loss accruing on the disposal of EIS shares may be relieved against income under the ICTA 1988 (c. 1), s.574.

Para. (21)

The ICTA 1988 (c. 1), s.306 is amended. A claim for EIS relief must be made within the period commencing after the initial four months of qualifying business activity expires and ending 12 months after the inspector authorises the issue of the EIS certificate. A s.306(3) statement must be submitted within two years from the end of the tax year in which (a) the shares were issued, or (b) the four months referred to above ends, if later. Other amendments are made to s.306 to accommodate the new EIS rules.

Para. (22)
The ICTA 1988 (c. 1), s.307 is amended. EIS relief may only be withdrawn after the inspector has given notice to the company that relief is not due or the company has itself given notice, under the ICTA 1988 (c. 7), s.310. A company may appeal against a notice given by the inspector. No notice and no assessment to withdraw relief may be issued six years after the end of the tax year in which (a) the time allowed for using moneys subscribed for eligible shares expired, or (b) the event occasioning the withdrawal of relief occurs, if later. Other amendments are made to s.307 to accommodate the new EIS rules.

Paras. (23)–(27)
Sections 308–312 are amended. A new definition of relevant period is introduced (para. (27)).

Amendments of the Taxation of Chargeable Gains Act 1992

28. The Taxation of Chargeable Gains Act 1992 shall be amended as follows:
29. In section 150 (business expansion schemes), at the end of subsection (1) there is inserted "and references in this section to Chapter III of Part VII of the Taxes Act or any provision of that Chapter are to that Chapter or provision as it applies in relation to shares issued before 1st January 1994".
30. After that section there is inserted—

"Enterprise investment scheme
150A.—(1) For the purpose of determining the gain or loss on any disposal of eligible shares by an individual where—
(a) an amount of relief is attributable to the shares, and
(b) apart from this subsection there would be a loss,
the consideration given by him for the shares shall be treated as reduced by the amount of the relief.
(2) Subject to subsection (3) below, if on any disposal of eligible shares by an individual after the end of the period referred to in section 312(1A)(a) of the Taxes Act where an amount of relief is attributable to the shares, there would (apart from this subsection) be a gain, the gain shall not be a chargeable gain.
(3) Where—
(a) an individual's liability to income tax has been reduced (or treated by virtue of section 304 of the Taxes Act (husband and wife) as reduced) for any year of assessment under section 289A of that Act in respect of any issue of shares, and
(b) the amount of the reduction ('A') is less than the amount ('B') which is equal to tax at the lower rate for that year on the amount subscribed for the issue,
then, if there is a disposal of the shares on which there is a gain, subsection (2) above shall apply only to so much of the gain as is found by multiplying it by the fraction—

$$\frac{A}{B}$$

(4) Any question as to—
(a) which of any shares issued to a person at different times a disposal relates, being shares to which relief is attributable, or
(b) whether a disposal relates to shares to which relief is attributable or to other shares, shall for the purposes of capital gains tax be determined as for the purposes of section 299 of the Taxes Act; and Chapter I of this Part shall have effect subject to the foregoing provisions of this subsection.
(5) Sections 104, 105 and 107 shall not apply to shares to which relief is attributable.
(6) Where—
(a) an individual holds shares which form part of the ordinary share capital of a company, and
(b) relief is attributable to some of the shares but not others,
then, if there is within the meaning of section 126 a reorganisation affecting those shares, section 127 shall apply (subject to the following provisions of this section) separately to the shares to which relief is attributable and to the other shares (so that shares of each kind are treated as a separate holding of original shares and identified with a separate new holding).

(7) Where—

(a) an individual holds shares ('the existing holding') which form part of the ordinary share capital of a company,

(b) there is, by virtue of any such allotment for payment as is mentioned in section 126(2)(a), a reorganisation affecting the existing holding, and

(c) immediately following the reorganisation, relief is attributable to the existing holding or the allotted shares,

sections 127 to 130 shall not apply in relation to the existing holding.

(8) Sections 135 and 136 shall not apply in respect of shares to which relief is attributable.

(9) Where the relief attributable to any shares is reduced by virtue of section 305(2) of the Taxes Act—

(a) the sums allowable as deductions from the consideration in the computation, for the purposes of capital gains tax, of the gain or loss accruing to an individual on the disposal of any of the allotted shares or debentures shall be taken to include the amount of the reduction apportioned between the allotted shares or (as the case may be) debentures in such a way as appears to the inspector, or on appeal to the Commissioners concerned, to be just and reasonable, and

(b) the sums so allowable on the disposal (in circumstances in which the preceding provisions of this section do not apply) of any of the shares referred to in section 305(1)(a) shall be taken to be reduced by the amount mentioned in paragraph (a) above, similarly apportioned between those shares.

(10) There shall be made all such adjustments of capital gains tax, whether by way of assessment or by way of discharge or repayment of tax, as may be required in consequence of the relief being given or withdrawn.

(11) Chapter III of Part VII of the Taxes Act (enterprise investment scheme) applies for the purposes of this section to determine whether relief is attributable to any shares and, if so, the amount of relief so attributable; and 'eligible shares' has the same meaning as in that Chapter.

(12) References in this section to Chapter III of Part VII of the Taxes Act or any provision of that Chapter are to that Chapter or provision as it applies in relation to shares issued on or after 1st January 1994".

31. At the end of section 164M of that Act (exclusion of double relief) there is inserted "but the reference in this section to that Chapter is to that Chapter as it applies in relation to shares issued before 1st January 1994".

32.—(1) After that section there is inserted—

"Exclusion of double relief

164MA. If a person makes a claim for relief under Chapter III of Part VII of the Taxes Act (enterprise investment scheme) in respect of any shares, those shares shall not be, or be treated as ever having been, eligible shares".

(2) This paragraph has effect in relation to shares issued on or after 1st January 1994.

33. In section 164N(1), in the definition of "eligible shares", for "and 164M" there is substituted "164M and 164MA".

34. In section 231(1)(d), "(business expansion scheme)" is omitted.

GENERAL NOTE

Para. (29)

This ensures that the TCGA 1992 (c. 12), s.150 applies only to shares which qualified for BES or business start-up scheme relief.

Para. (30)

The new TCGA 1992 (c. 12), s.150A is introduced. Losses arising on the disposal of eligible shares are allowable but their acquisition cost is to be reduced by any EIS relief. The loss may be relieved against income under the ICTA 1988 (c. 1), s.574. Where eligible shares are disposed of more than five years after their issue any gains accruing are wholly exempt, provided EIS relief was given at the lower rate of income tax on the amount subscribed. If the relief was restricted to the investor's income tax liability for the year, a corresponding proportion of the gain is exempt. The share-pooling rules in the TCGA 1992 (c. 12) do not apply to EIS shares. If, under s.305 (para. (19) above) EIS relief is reduced, the acquisition costs are increased by the reduction.

Paras. (31)–(34)

Reinvestment relief is not available for reinvestments in shares for which BES or EIS relief is claimed; nor can such shares constitute replacement assets for roll-over relief on the disposal of EIS shares into an employee share ownership trust.

SCHEDULE 16

FOREIGN INCOME DIVIDENDS

PART I

THE NEW CHAPTER

1. In Part VI of the Taxes Act 1988 (company distributions, tax credits etc.) the following Chapter shall be inserted after Chapter V—

"CHAPTER VA

FOREIGN INCOME DIVIDENDS

GENERAL NOTE
   This Schedule introduces the Foreign Income Dividend (FID) Scheme. Multinational companies with substantial non-U.K. income face the potential problem that due to relief for foreign taxes paid they may have no U.K. corporation tax to set against ACT payable on dividends. The FID scheme is aimed at enabling such companies to reclaim at least some of that ACT.

Election by company paying dividend

Election by company paying dividend
   246A.—(1) Where a company pays a dividend, the dividend shall be treated as a foreign income dividend for the purposes of this Chapter if the company elects for it to be so treated in accordance with this section and section 246B.
   (2) An election may not be made under this section as regards a dividend unless the dividend is paid, or to be paid, in cash.
   (3) An election may not be made under this section as regards a dividend which is paid, or to be paid, to a person by virtue of his holding a share in respect of which there are arrangements for the holder to choose whether, or in what form, dividends are to be paid; and the arrangements may be for the holder to choose to be paid a dividend by a company other than the one which issued the share.
   (4) Where at a given time—
   (a) a company pays one dividend in respect of two or more shares of the same class, and
   (b) payment is on the same terms as respects all the shares involved,
an election may not be made under this section as regards any of the dividends unless an election is made as regards each of the dividends.
   (5) Where at a given time—
   (a) a company pays two or more dividends in respect of each of two or more shares of the same class, and
   (b) payment is on the same terms as respects all the shares involved,
an election may not be made under this section as regards any one of the dividends in respect of a given share unless an election is also made as regards the corresponding dividend in respect of each of the other shares involved.
   (6) Subject to subsection (7) below, a company which has more than one class of share capital may not make an election under this section as regards any dividend.
   (7) In a case where—
   (a) a company has more than one class of share capital,
   (b) at a given time the company pays a dividend in respect of each share of each such class, and
   (c) all of those dividends are paid on the same terms,
the company may elect that each of those dividends is to be treated as a foreign income dividend.
   (8) For the purposes of subsection (7) above a dividend is paid on the same terms as another dividend if the relevant proportion in the case of each dividend is the same; and the relevant proportion, in relation to a dividend, is the proportion which the amount of the dividend bears to the nominal value of the share in respect of which the dividend is paid.
   (9) For the purposes of subsections (6) and (7) above fixed-rate preference shares shall not be treated as constituting a class of share capital; and "fixed-rate preference shares" shall be construed in accordance with section 95(5).
   (10) Where an election is made under this section as regards a dividend in respect of which an election is in force under section 247(1)—

(a) the election under this section shall have effect as if it were also a notice to the collector under section 247(3) stating that the paying company does not wish the election
under section 247(1) to have effect in relation to the dividend as regards which the
election under this section is made;

(b) if the election under this section is revoked, the revocation shall have effect as if it
were also a revocation of the notice deemed by paragraph (a) above;

(c) the notice deemed by paragraph (a) above may not be revoked otherwise than as
mentioned in paragraph (b) above;

(d) if the notice deemed by paragraph (a) above is revoked it shall be treated as never
having been made.

GENERAL NOTE
Sections 246A–246Y are inserted into the ICTA 1988 (c. 1).

Section 246A of the ICTA 1988
A company may elect to treat a cash dividend as a FID. An election cannot be made if the
shareholder can choose whether, or in what form a dividend is to be paid, or for it to be paid by a
company that did not issue the shares. Nor may an election be made unless it is in respect of all
corresponding dividends paid on the same class of shares involved. An election may be made in
respect of dividends paid on different classes of share capital (ignoring fixed rate preference
shares) provided that the dividends were paid at the same time and on the same terms in respect
of each share of each class.

Procedure for making election
246B.—(1) An election under section 246A—
(a) must be made by a notice to the inspector;
(b) must be made not later than the time the dividend is paid;
(c) may be revoked by a further notice to the inspector before that time (without prejudice to the making of another election as regards the same dividend);
(d) cannot be revoked after the dividend is paid.
(2) A notice under subsection (1)(a) above must—
(a) identify the dividend in respect of which the election is made, and
(b) be in such form as the Board may require.
(3) Where section 246A(4), (5) or (7) applies—
(a) the same notice must be used to elect as regards all the dividends concerned, and
(b) the notice may identify the dividends concerned, or any of them, by means of a general description.

Recipient of foreign income dividend

No tax credit for recipient
246C. Section 231(1) shall not apply where the distribution there mentioned is a foreign
income dividend.

Individuals etc.
246D.—(1) Where a company pays a foreign income dividend in a case in which an individual is beneficially entitled to the dividend, that individual shall be treated as having
received on the date of the payment income of an amount which, if reduced by an amount
equal to income tax on that income at the lower rate for the year of assessment in which the
date of the payment fell, would be equal to the amount of the dividend.
(2) Where subsection (1) above applies—
(a) no assessment shall be made on the individual in respect of income tax at the lower
rate on that income but he shall be treated as having paid tax at the lower rate on it or,
if his total income is reduced by any deductions, on so much of it as is part of his total
income as so reduced;
(b) no repayment shall be made of income tax treated by virtue of paragraph (a) above as
having been paid;
(c) to the extent that it would not otherwise be so treated, that income shall be treated as
income to which (without prejudice to paragraph (a) above) section 207A shall be
taken to apply as it applies to income chargeable under Schedule F;
(d) that income shall be treated for the purposes of sections 348 and 349(1) as not
brought into charge to income tax.
(3) Where a company pays a foreign income dividend to the personal representatives of a
deceased person as such during the administration period, the amount of income which, if

the case had been one in which an individual was beneficially entitled to the dividend, that individual would be treated under subsection (1) above as having received shall be deemed for the purposes of Part XVI to be part of the aggregate income of the estate of the deceased; and the preceding provisions of this subsection shall be construed as if they were contained in Part XVI.

(4) Where a company pays a foreign income dividend to trustees and the dividend is income to which section 686 applies—

  (a) there shall be ascertained the amount of income which, if the case had been one in which an individual was beneficially entitled to the dividend, that individual would be treated under subsection (1) above as having received;

  (b) income of that amount shall be treated as having arisen to the trustees on the date of the payment and as if it had been chargeable to income tax at the lower rate.

  (c) paragraphs (a) to (d) of subsection (2) above shall, with the substitution of "income" for "total income" and with all other necessary modifications, apply to that income as they apply to income which an individual is treated as having received under subsection (1) above.

(5) Subsections (1) and (1A) of section 233 shall not apply where the distribution mentioned in either of those subsections is a foreign income dividend.

GENERAL NOTE

Section 246B of the ICTA 1988
An election must be made to the inspector by the time the dividend is paid, in a form approved by the Board and must identify the dividend in respect of which the election is made.

Section 246C of the ICTA 1988
The recipient of a FID is not entitled to a tax credit.

Section 246D of the ICTA 1988
Individuals beneficially entitled to FIDs are treated as receiving income equal to the FID grossed up at the lower rate and which has borne lower rate tax, which is not repayable. A FID may not be used to cover charges. FIDs are taxable either at the lower rate or the higher rate and if applicable will be treated as the highest part of a taxpayer's income. The treatment for the individual recipient matches that of stock dividends. The rules are applied to personal representatives and trustees of a discretionary trust with suitable modifications.

Companies: payments and receipts

Foreign income dividend not franked payment
246E. A foreign income dividend shall not constitute a distribution for the purposes of the definition of "franked payment" in section 238(1).

Calculation of ACT where company receives foreign income dividend
246F.—(1) Where in any accounting period a company receives foreign income dividends, the company shall not be liable to pay advance corporation tax in respect of foreign income dividends paid by it in that period unless the amount of the foreign income dividends paid by it in that period exceeds the amount of the foreign income dividends received by it in that period.

(2) If in an accounting period there is such an excess, advance corporation tax shall be payable on an amount equal to the excess.

(3) If the amount of foreign income dividends received by a company in an accounting period exceeds the amount of the foreign income dividends paid by it in that period the excess shall be carried forward to the next accounting period and treated for the purposes of this section (including any further application of this subsection) as foreign income dividends received by the company in that period.

(4) This section shall have effect subject to section 246T and paragraph 2(6) of Schedule 23A.

(5) Without prejudice to section 238(5), Schedule 13 shall apply for the purpose of regulating the manner in which effect is to be given to this section.

Information relating to foreign income dividends
246G.—(1) Where section 234A applies by virtue of the fact that a foreign income dividend is paid by a company, references in that section to an appropriate statement shall be construed as references to a written statement—

(a) in such form as the Board may require,

(b) showing the amount of the dividend paid,

(c) showing the date of the payment, and

(d) stating that the dividend carries no entitlement to a tax credit;

and in such a case section 234A(7) shall not apply.

(2) In a case where—

(a) a requirement is imposed on a company under section 234A(2) or (3) in relation to a foreign income dividend paid by it, and

(b) the company fails to comply with the requirement,

no election may be made by the company under section 246J or 246K as regards the dividend or any part of it.

Power of inspector to require information

246H.—(1) This section applies where a return made by a company for a return period in accordance with Schedule 13 shows that the company has paid foreign income dividends in the period.

(2) The inspector may by notice require the company to furnish him within such time (not being less than 30 days) as may be specified in the notice with such further information relating to the dividends as he may reasonably require for the purposes of any enactment relating to foreign income dividends.

(3) Without prejudice to the generality of subsection (2) above, the notice may require information as to the persons to whom dividends are paid.

GENERAL NOTE

Section 246E of the ICTA 1988
A FID is not a franked payment.

Section 246F of the ICTA 1988
ACT is payable on the excess of FIDs paid over FIDs received in any period. Any excess of FIDs received over FIDs paid in a period may be carried forward to the next period and is treated as FIDs received in that period. The ICTA 1988 (c. 1), Sched. 13 is applied to FIDs.

Section 246G of the ICTA 1988
A recipient of a FID is entitled to a statement in an approved form, showing the amount and date of payment and stating that the FID carries no tax credit. Where the ICTA 1988 (c. 1), s.234A(2)(3) applies to a FID and the company fail to comply, no election may be made under ss.246J or 246K to match the dividend or (part thereof) with distributable foreign profit (DFP).

Section 246H of the ICTA 1988
A company which has paid FIDs may be required to supply further information, including information about the recipients, relating to those FIDs.

Foreign source profit and distributable foreign profit

Foreign source profit and distributable foreign profit

246I.—(1) Where for an accounting period of a company there is any income, or any chargeable gain, in respect of which double taxation relief is afforded, then so much of that income or gain as forms part of the company's chargeable profits for the period is a foreign source profit of the company for the period.

(2) Subsection (3) below applies where in the accounting period concerned there is any deduction to be made for charges on income, expenses of management or other amounts which can be deducted from or set against or treated as reducing profits of more than one description.

(3) In finding for the purposes of this section whether, or how much of, any income or gain forms part of the company's chargeable profits for the period the company may allocate the deduction in such amounts and to such of its profits for the period as it thinks fit.

(4) Where a company has a foreign source profit for an accounting period, such part of it as exceeds the relevant amount of tax is for the purposes of this Chapter a distributable foreign profit of the company for the period.

(5) Where the amount of foreign tax payable in respect of the foreign source profit exceeds the amount of corporation tax payable, before double taxation relief is afforded, in respect of that profit, the relevant amount of tax is the amount of foreign tax payable in respect of that profit.

(6) Where subsection (5) above does not apply, the relevant amount of tax is an amount equal to the aggregate of—

(a) the amount of foreign tax payable in respect of the foreign source profit, and

(b) the amount of corporation tax payable in respect of that profit after double taxation relief is afforded.

(7) In this section "double taxation relief" means—

(a) relief under double taxation arrangements which takes the form of a credit allowed against corporation tax, or

(b) unilateral relief under section 790(1) which takes that form;

and "double taxation arrangements" here means arrangements having effect by virtue of section 788.

(8) References in this section to a company's chargeable profits for an accounting period are to the amount of its profits for that period on which corporation tax falls finally to be borne; and section 238(4) shall apply for the purposes of this subsection.

" (9) For the purposes of this section foreign tax is any tax, imposed by the laws of a territory outside the United Kingdom, for which double taxation relief is afforded.

(10) Section 788(5) shall apply for the purposes of this section.

GENERAL NOTE

Section 246I of the ICTA 1988
A company's foreign source profit for any period is its income or gains which are chargeable to corporation tax and in respect of which double tax relief (whether treaty or unilateral relief) is afforded. A company's DFP is the excess of foreign source profits after deducting foreign tax and any remaining corporation tax liability on that profit after double tax relief.

Matching of dividend with distributable foreign profit

Matching of dividend with distributable foreign profit
246J.—(1) Where a company pays a foreign income dividend in an accounting period it may elect that the dividend (or part of it) shall be matched with (or with part of) a distributable foreign profit of the company; and subsections (2) to (6) below shall have effect with regard to matching.

(2) Different parts of a dividend may be matched with different distributable foreign profits or parts; and different dividends, or parts of different dividends, may be matched with different parts of the same distributable foreign profit.

(3) A foreign income dividend (or part of one) may be matched with a distributable foreign profit (or part of one) only if the amount of the distributable foreign profit or part is equal to the amount of the dividend or part.

(4) Subject to subsection (5) below, where a company pays a foreign income dividend in a given accounting period the dividend (or part of it) may only be matched with (or with part of) a distributable foreign profit of the company for that period or for the accounting period immediately preceding it, but without the need to exhaust distributable foreign profits for one of those periods before taking those for the other period.

(5) Where a company pays a foreign income dividend in a given accounting period the dividend (or part of it) may be matched with (or with part of) a distributable foreign profit of the company for any subsequent accounting period, but only if there is no amount of unmatched distributable foreign profit of the company for the given period and no such amount for the accounting period immediately preceding the given period.

(6) Where a distributable foreign profit (or part of one) has been matched with a foreign income dividend (or part of one) it cannot be matched with another foreign income dividend or part.

GENERAL NOTE

Section 246J of the ICTA 1988
A company may elect to match all or part of a paid FID with all or part of its DFP of the same or the immediately preceding period. Unmatched FIDs may be carried forward and matched in subsequent periods. Where DFP have been matched with FIDs they may not be matched with other FIDs.

Matching subsidiaries
246K.—(1) This section applies where a company (the subsidiary) is a 51 per cent. subsidiary of another company (the parent); but this is subject to section 246L.

(2) In a case where—

(a) an accounting period of the subsidiary coincides with, or with part of, an accounting period of the parent, and

(b) the subsidiary has a distributable foreign profit for its accounting period,

the whole of the profit is for the purposes of this section an eligible profit for the parent's accounting period.

(3) In a case where—

(a) part of an accounting period of the subsidiary coincides with, or with part of, an accounting period of the parent, and

(b) the subsidiary has a distributable foreign profit for its accounting period,

then, to the extent of the appropriate fraction, the profit is for the purposes of this section an eligible profit for the parent's accounting period.

(4) The appropriate fraction is one—

(a) whose numerator is equal to the number of the days in the subsidiary's accounting period that coincide with days in the parent's accounting period, and

(b) whose denominator is equal to the number of the days in the subsidiary's accounting period.

(5) Where the parent pays a foreign income dividend in an accounting period it may elect that the dividend (or part of it) shall be matched with (or with part of) an eligible profit; and subsections (6) to (11) below shall have effect with regard to matching.

(6) No election as to matching may be made unless the subsidiary gives its written consent in such form as the Board may require.

(7) Different parts of a dividend may be matched with different eligible profits or parts; and different dividends, or parts of different dividends, may be matched with different parts of the same eligible profit.

(8) A foreign income dividend (or part of one) may be matched with an eligible profit (or part of one) only if the amount of the eligible profit or part is equal to the amount of the dividend or part.

(9) Subject to subsection (10) below, where the parent pays a foreign income dividend in a given accounting period the dividend (or part of it) may only be matched with (or with part of) an eligible profit for that period or for the accounting period immediately preceding it, but without the need to exhaust eligible profits for one of those periods before taking those for the other period.

(10) Where the parent pays a foreign income dividend in a given accounting period the dividend (or part of it) may be matched with (or with part of) an eligible profit for any subsequent accounting period, but only if there is no amount of unmatched eligible profit derived from the same subsidiary for the given period and no such amount for the accounting period immediately preceding the given period.

(11) Where an eligible profit (or part of one) has been matched with a foreign income dividend (or part of one) it cannot be matched with another foreign income dividend or part.

(12) References in this section to a company apply only to bodies corporate; and in determining for the purposes of this section whether one company is a 51 per cent. subsidiary of another company, that other company shall be treated as not being the owner—

(a) of any share capital which it owns directly in a body corporate if a profit on the sale of the shares would be treated as a trading receipt of its trade, or

(b) of any share capital which it owns indirectly, and which is owned directly by a body corporate for which a profit on the sale of the shares would be a trading receipt.

GENERAL NOTE

Section 246K of the ICTA 1988

A parent may elect to match all or part of a paid FID with all or part of its 51 per cent. subsidiary's DFP of the same or immediately preceding accounting period. Any unmatched FIDs may be carried forward and matched with the subsidiary's DFP of a subsequent period. Apportionment is necessary where only a part of the subsidiary's accounting period coincides with, or with part of, the parent's accounting period, to ascertain the DFP available for matching. The subsidiary must give its written consent to the election.

Requirement as to subsidiaries

246L.—(1) Section 246K(5) does not apply unless the subsidiary is a 51 per cent. subsidiary of the parent throughout the relevant period (determined under subsection (3) or (4) below).

(2) In this section "the payment period" means the accounting period of the parent in which it pays the dividend as regards which an election under section 246K is proposed.

(3) If the proposed election involves only eligible profits deriving from an accounting period of the subsidiary coinciding with the payment period, the relevant period is the payment period.

(4) In any other case the relevant period is one that—

(a) begins with the beginning of the payment period or (if earlier) the beginning of the first or only relevant accounting period of the subsidiary, and

(b) ends with the end of the payment period or (if later) the end of the last or only relevant accounting period of the subsidiary.

(5) For the purposes of subsection (4) above a relevant accounting period of the subsidiary is an accounting period of the subsidiary for which there is a distributable foreign profit which—

(a) is (as to the whole or part) an eligible profit, and

(b) would, under the proposed election, be to any extent matched with the dividend as regards which the election is proposed.

(6) Section 246K(12) shall apply in determining for the purposes of this section whether the subsidiary is a 51 per cent. subsidiary of the parent at any given time.

GENERAL NOTE

Section 246L of the ICTA 1988
Only 51 per cent. subsidiaries of the parent throughout the relevant period are eligible. In applying the 51 per cent. test, shares held as stock are excluded.

Matching: further provisions
246M.—(1) Where a parent elects under section 246K as regards an eligible profit for an accounting period, the following rules shall have effect for the purposes of this Chapter—

(a) to the extent provided for in the election, the eligible profit shall be treated as a separate distributable foreign profit of the parent for the parent's accounting period and as matched;

(b) the distributable foreign profit mentioned in section 246K(2)(b) or (3)(b) shall be treated as reduced accordingly or (depending on the circumstances) as extinguished;

(c) the foreign source profit of which the distributable foreign profit mentioned in section 246K(2)(b) or (3)(b) forms a part shall be treated as correspondingly divided between the parent and the subsidiary or (depending on the circumstances) as a foreign source profit of the parent alone for its accounting period.

(2) Where an election is made under section 246J or 246K with regard to anything which is or represents a distributable foreign profit of a subsidiary (or part of such a profit) no further election can be made with regard to it under the other section.

GENERAL NOTE

Section 246M of the ICTA 1988
A s.246K election reduces or extinguishes the subsidiary's eligible profit and its foreign source profit is correspondingly divided between the parent and subsidiary accordingly. The subsidiary's eligible profit is treated as the parent's DFP and matched accordingly.

Repayment or set-off of advance corporation tax

ACT to be repaid or set off against corporation tax liability
246N.—(1) This section and section 246Q apply where—

(a) a company pays a foreign income dividend in an accounting period (the relevant period), and

(b) the company does not treat itself as an international headquarters company at any time in the period by virtue of section 246S(9).

(2) In a case where—

(a) the company pays an amount of advance corporation tax in respect of qualifying distributions actually made by it in the relevant period,

(b) the amount, or part of it, is available to be dealt with under this section, and

(c) there is as regards the company an amount of notional foreign source advance corporation tax for the relevant period,

an amount of the advance corporation tax paid shall be repaid to the company, or set off, or partly repaid and partly set off, in accordance with this section and section 246Q.

(3) In the following provisions of this section "the relevant advance corporation tax" means the advance corporation tax paid as mentioned in subsection (2)(a) above.

(4) The amount of the relevant advance corporation tax to be repaid or (as the case may be) set off, or partly repaid and partly set off, is whichever of the following is smaller—

(a) so much of the relevant advance corporation tax as is available to be dealt with under this section;

(b) so much of the relevant advance corporation tax as is equal to the amount which is, as regards the company, the amount of notional foreign source advance corporation tax for the relevant period (found under section 246P).

(5) So much of the relevant advance corporation tax as remains after deducting the aggregate of the deductible amounts is available to be dealt with under this section; and each of the following is a deductible amount—

(a) an amount equal to so much (if any) of the relevant advance corporation tax as has been repaid;

(b) an amount equal to so much (if any) of the relevant advance corporation tax as has been set off against the company's corporation tax liability for the relevant period under section 239(1) or, if there is—

(i) any amount of advance corporation tax from a preceding accounting period,

(ii) any amount of surrendered advance corporation tax, or

(iii) any amount of advance corporation tax from a succeeding accounting period,

as would have been so set off if there had been no amounts as mentioned in subparagraphs (i) to (iii) above;

(c) an amount equal to so much (if any) of the relevant advance corporation tax as has been dealt with under section 239(3);

(d) an amount equal to so much (if any) of the relevant advance corporation tax as is advance corporation tax the benefit of which has been surrendered by the company under section 240;

(e) an amount equal to so much (if any) of the relevant advance corporation tax as has been set off against the company's corporation tax liability for the relevant period by virtue of the previous application of this section and section 246Q.

(6) For the purposes of subsection (5)(b) above—

(a) advance corporation tax from a preceding accounting period is advance corporation tax which by virtue of section 239(4) is treated for the purposes of section 239 as paid by the company in respect of distributions made by it in the relevant period;

(b) surrendered advance corporation tax is advance corporation tax which by virtue of section 240 is so treated;

(c) advance corporation tax from a succeeding accounting period is advance corporation tax which by virtue of section 239(3) is so treated;

and in applying subsection (5)(b) above in a case where there is any amount as mentioned in subsection (5)(b)(i) to (iii), it shall be assumed that the company would not have surrendered the benefit of any of the relevant advance corporation tax under section 240.

(7) No amount shall be repaid or set off under this section and section 246Q unless the company makes a claim for the purpose.

| GENERAL NOTE

Section 246N of the ICTA 1988

A company (other than an international headquarters company) which pays a FID in an accounting period may claim that the lesser of: (a) surplus ACT (calculated in accordance with subs. (5)) paid in respect of qualifying distributions made in that period; and (b) notional foreign source ACT (defined in s.246P below) for that period, be wholly or partly repaid or set off (in accordance with s.246Q below).

Notional foreign source advance corporation tax

246P.—(1) As regards the company mentioned in section 246N(1), the amount of notional foreign source advance corporation tax for the relevant period is the amount of advance corporation tax which—

(a) the company would have paid in respect of distributions made by it in the relevant period, and

(b) would not have been set off against the company's corporation tax liability for the relevant period under section 239(1), on the assumptions mentioned in subsection (2) below.

(2) The assumptions are that—

(a) the qualifying foreign income dividends were the only distributions made by the company in the relevant period,

(b) no distributions were received (or treated for the purposes of section 246F as received) by the company in the relevant period,

(c) no amounts of advance corporation tax were by virtue of section 239(3) or (4) or section 240 treated for the purposes of section 239 as having been paid in respect of distributions made by the company in the relevant period,

(d) the benefit of the advance corporation tax paid in respect of distributions made by the company in the relevant period was not surrendered under section 240;

(e) the company's profits for the relevant period on which corporation tax fell finally to be borne consisted of the matched foreign source profits and no other profits, and

(f) the amount of corporation tax charged in respect of a matched foreign source profit actually arising in an accounting period other than the relevant period was found by reference to—

(i) the rate of foreign tax, within the meaning given by section 246I(9), actually chargeable in respect of the profit (having regard to the time when it arose), and

(ii) the rate of corporation tax that would have applied had the profit arisen in the relevant period.

(3) A foreign income dividend is a qualifying foreign income dividend if—

(a) it is a matched foreign income dividend paid by the company in the relevant period, and

(b) the company has elected for it to be a qualifying foreign income dividend.

(4) A foreign income dividend the whole of which is, at the material time, matched with the whole or part of a distributable foreign profit of the company is a matched foreign income dividend.

(5) Where there is a foreign income dividend only part of which is at the material time matched as mentioned in subsection (4) above, the part of the dividend which at that time is so matched shall be treated for the purposes of this section as a separate dividend and, accordingly, as a matched foreign income dividend.

(6) The company may elect that matched foreign income dividends paid by it in the relevant period are qualifying foreign income dividends only if the amount found under paragraph (a) of subsection (7) below exceeds the amount found under paragraph (b) of that subsection; and where there is such an excess the election may only be made as regards matched foreign income dividends whose total amount is the same as or less than the amount of the excess.

(7) The amounts referred to in subsection (6) above are—

(a) the total amount of foreign income dividends paid by the company in the relevant period (other than excluded dividends);

(b) the total amount of foreign income dividends received (or treated for the purposes of section 246F as received) by the company in the relevant period;

and for the purposes of this subsection an excluded dividend is a foreign income dividend which by virtue of section 246G(2) is not capable of being matched.

(8) A matched foreign source profit is a foreign source profit of which a matched distributable foreign profit forms part; and for the purposes of this subsection "a matched distributable foreign profit" means a distributable foreign profit of the company the whole or part of which is, at the material time, matched with a qualifying foreign income dividend, or with part of such a dividend, or with different such dividends or parts.

(9) Where the matched foreign source profit is a foreign source profit of which a partly matched distributable foreign profit forms part, for the purposes of any calculation required by subsections (1) and (2) above the amount of the matched foreign source profit shall be taken to be reduced by an amount which bears to the full amount of the matched foreign source profit the same proportion as the unmatched part of the distributable foreign profit bears to the amount of the distributable foreign profit.

(10) For the purposes of subsection (9) above—

(a) "a partly matched distributable foreign profit" means a distributable foreign profit of the company part of which is not, at the material time, matched as mentioned in subsection (8) above, and

(b) "the unmatched part of the distributable foreign profit" shall be construed accordingly.

(11) For the purposes of this section—

(a) "the relevant period" shall be construed in accordance with section 246N(1);

(b) "the material time" means the time at which the claim mentioned in section 246N(7) is made.

(12) References in this section to matching shall be construed in accordance with sections 246J to 246M.

(13) Section 238(4) shall apply for the purposes of this section.

GENERAL NOTE

Section 246P of the ICTA 1988
This defines "notional foreign source ACT" for the purposes of s.246N above as being the amount of ACT that would have been surplus in a period, assuming that ACT was paid solely in relation to FIDs paid in that period which the company matches with DFP.

Repayment or set-off: supplementary
246Q.—(1) Subsections (2) and (3) below shall have effect to determine whether the amount which is the smaller of the amounts found under section 246N(4) is to be repaid, set off, or partly repaid and partly set off.

(2) If at the time when it falls to be determined whether the amount mentioned in subsection (1) above is to be repaid or set off—

(a) advance corporation tax paid (or treated for the purposes of section 239 as paid) by the company in respect of distributions made by it in the relevant period has so far as possible been set against its liability to corporation tax for the period under section 239(1), but

(b) the company's liability to corporation tax for the period is to any extent undischarged,

the amount mentioned in subsection (1) above shall so far as possible be set off against the company's liability to corporation tax for the relevant period (and an amount of that liability equal to the amount so set off shall accordingly be discharged); and any excess of the amount mentioned in subsection (1) above over the amount so set off shall be repaid.

(3) Where paragraph (a) of subsection (2) above applies but paragraph (b) of that subsection does not, the whole of the amount mentioned in subsection (1) above shall be repaid.

(4) No amount shall be repayable under section 246N and this section until the expiry of nine months from the end of the relevant period.

(5) An amount of advance corporation tax which has been dealt with under section 246N and this section—

(a) shall not be set off under section 239(1) against the company's liability to corporation tax for any accounting period;

(b) shall not be available for the purposes of a claim under section 240.

(6) A return made by the company for the relevant period under section 11 of the Management Act, or an amendment of such a return, shall be treated as a claim for the purposes of section 246N and this section if the return or (as the case may be) the amendment contains such particulars as the inspector may require.

(7) A claim for those purposes which is not made by means of a return under section 11 of the Management Act, or by means of an amendment of such a return, shall be supported by such particulars as the inspector may require.

(8) In a case where—

(a) a claim is made under section 246N and this section, and

(b) by virtue of the claim, an amount of advance corporation tax is repaid or set off which has already been set off by virtue of section 239(4) against the company's corporation tax liability for an accounting period falling after the accounting period to which the claim relates,

the set-off by virtue of section 239(4) of that amount shall be treated for the purposes of section 252 as if it ought not to have been made.

(9) In determining for the purposes of subsection (8) above whether an amount repaid or set off by virtue of a claim under section 246N and this section is an amount which has already been set off against the company's corporation tax liability for an accounting period, amounts of advance corporation tax repaid or set off by virtue of that claim shall be treated as having been set off against that liability only after any other amounts of advance corporation tax that were capable of being set off against that liability have been taken into account.

(10) Where section 252 applies by virtue of this section the reference in subsection (5) of that section to the Management Act shall be treated as not including a reference to section 34 of that Act.

(11) In this section "the relevant period" shall be construed in accordance with section 246N(1).

GENERAL NOTE

Section 246Q of the ICTA 1988
This lays down the machinery for providing ACT relief calculated under s.246N above. Surplus ACT which becomes repayable for an accounting period must first be set against any outstanding corporation tax liability for the period and only the balance is repayable. ACT repayments may only be made nine months after the end of the period. A claim for ACT relief may be made in the company's corporation tax return for the relevant period or in any other form and must in either case, contain the particulars required by the inspector.

Supplementary claims
246R.—(1) This section applies where—
(a) a claim is made under sections 246N and 246Q, and
(b) at any time after the claim is made the company makes an election under section 246J(5) or 246K(10) matching profits with dividends paid in the accounting period to which the claim relates.

(2) The company may as regards that accounting period make a further claim under sections 246N and 246Q (a supplementary claim) so as to take account of the election.

(3) Subsections (5) and (6) below shall apply in determining for the purposes of the supplementary claim the amount of notional foreign source advance corporation tax for the accounting period to which that claim relates.

(4) In subsections (5) and (6) below a "previously counted dividend" means a foreign income dividend (or part of one) which was included in an election made by the company under section 246P for the purposes of an earlier claim as regards the accounting period (and which, accordingly, was treated as a qualifying foreign income dividend for those purposes).

(5) In applying section 246P for the purposes of the supplementary claim, a previously counted dividend shall be treated as not being a qualifying foreign income dividend notwithstanding the election mentioned in subsection (4) above; and the company may not include the previously counted dividend in any further election made under section 246P for the purposes of the supplementary claim.

(6) In relation to an election which the company proposes to make under section 246P for the purposes of the supplementary claim, section 246P(6) shall have effect as if for the reference to matched foreign income dividends whose total amount is the same as or less than the amount of the excess there mentioned there were substituted a reference to matched foreign income dividends whose total amount, when added to the total amount of the previously counted dividends, give an amount which is equal to or less than the amount of that excess.

(7) A company may make more than one supplementary claim as regards any accounting period.

GENERAL NOTE

Section 246R of the ICTA 1988
A company which has claimed ACT relief in respect of a FID for an accounting period may make supplementary claims when it matches DFP with FIDs paid in the same period.

International headquarters companies

International headquarters companies
246S.—(1) For the purposes of this Chapter a company is an international headquarters company in an accounting period if—
(a) at least one of the first three conditions (set out in subsections (2) to (5) below) is fulfilled, and
(b) the fourth condition (set out in subsection (7) below) is fulfilled;
but the fourth condition need not be fulfilled if the second condition is fulfilled.

(2) The first condition is that—
(a) the company is wholly owned by another company throughout the accounting period, and

(b) that other company is a foreign held company in the accounting period.

(3) The second condition is that—

(a) the company is wholly owned by another company throughout the accounting period,

(b) that other company is not resident in the United Kingdom at any time in the accounting period,

(c) throughout the accounting period, and the period of 12 months immediately preceding it, the shares in that other company are quoted in the official list of a recognised stock exchange other than a stock exchange in the United Kingdom,

(d) at a time falling within the accounting period or the period of 12 months immediately preceding it, shares in that other company have been the subject of dealings on a recognised stock exchange other than a stock exchange in the United Kingdom, and

(e) throughout the accounting period, and the period of 12 months immediately preceding it, the shares in that other company are not quoted in the official list of a recognised stock exchange in the United Kingdom;

but this is subject to subsection (8) below.

(4) For the purposes of subsection (3)(e) above, shares that (apart from this subsection) would be regarded as quoted in the official list of a recognised stock exchange shall be regarded as not being so quoted if the issuer of the shares is not subject, in relation to them, to the full requirements applicable by virtue of listing rules to the listing of shares on that exchange; and in this subsection "listing rules" shall be construed in accordance with section 142(6) of the Financial Services Act 1986.

(5) The third condition is that—

(a) at each given time in the accounting period each shareholder of the company owns at least 5 per cent. of the company's share capital, and

(b) the test mentioned in subsection (6) below is satisfied.

(6) The test is that at each given time in the accounting period at least 80 per cent. of the company's share capital is owned by—

(a) persons who are not companies and who are not resident in the United Kingdom at any time in the accounting period,

(b) companies which are foreign held companies in the accounting period, or

(c) persons falling within paragraph (a) above and companies falling within paragraph (b) above.

(7) The fourth condition is that at each given time in the accounting period not more than 20 per cent. of the company's ordinary share capital is ultimately owned by persons who are not companies and are resident in the United Kingdom; and where any shares are not directly owned by a person who is not a company their ultimate ownership shall be found by tracing ownership through any corporate holders to persons who are not companies on such basis as is reasonable.

(8) Notwithstanding subsection (3) above, the second condition shall also be treated as fulfilled in relation to a company (the company concerned) and an accounting period if—

(a) the company concerned is throughout the accounting period wholly owned by another company, and that other company is throughout the period wholly owned by a company which satisfies the conditions set out in subsection (3)(b) to (e) above,

(b) there are two or more companies (intermediary companies) which throughout the accounting period beneficially own between them all the share capital of the company concerned, and there is another company which throughout the period wholly owns all the intermediary companies and which satisfies the conditions set out in subsection (3)(b) to (e) above, or

(c) there are two or more companies (relevant companies) which throughout the accounting period beneficially own between them all the share capital of the company concerned, and one of the relevant companies is a company which throughout the period wholly owns all the other relevant companies and which satisfies the conditions set out in subsection (3)(b) to (e) above;

and in determining for the purposes of this subsection whether a particular company satisfies the conditions set out in subsection (3)(b) to (e) above, references in subsection (3)(b) to (e) to "that other company" shall be construed as references to that particular company.

(9) Where a company pays a foreign income dividend, for the purposes of this Chapter it may treat itself as an international headquarters company if—

(a) in the company's opinion it is likely to be an international headquarters company in the accounting period in which the dividend is paid, and

(b) in a case where the dividend is paid in the company's second accounting period or a subsequent accounting period, it is an international headquarters company in the immediately preceding accounting period;

and for the purposes of paragraph (a) above the company's opinion held at the time the dividend is paid is to be taken.

(10) For the purposes of this section a company is a foreign held company in an accounting period if—

(a) at each given time in the accounting period at least 80 per cent. of the company's share capital is owned by persons who are not resident in the United Kingdom at any time in the accounting period, or

(b) throughout the accounting period the company is wholly owned by another company and at each given time in the accounting period at least 80 per cent. of that other company's share capital is owned by persons who are not resident in the United Kingdom at any time in the accounting period.

(11) For the purposes of this section a company wholly owns another company if the first company is the beneficial owner of all the share capital of the second company.

(12) For the purposes of this section the question whether a person owns a particular percentage of a company's share capital at a particular time shall be determined by—

(a) assuming that a general meeting of the company is held at that time;

(b) taking the number of votes carried by the company's share capital and capable of being cast at such a meeting;

(c) taking the number of those votes capable of being so cast by the person concerned by virtue of the company's share capital beneficially owned by him;

(d) expressing the number found under paragraph (c) above as a percentage of the number found under paragraph (b) above;

(e) taking the percentage found under paragraph (d) above as the percentage of the company's share capital owned by that person at that time.

(13) Subsection (12) above shall not apply for the purposes of subsection (7) above; and in subsection (7) references to ownership shall be construed as references to beneficial ownership.

GENERAL NOTE

Section 246S of the ICTA 1988

This defines an international headquarters company (IHC). A company is an IHC in any period if it satisfies conditions (b) or conditions (a) or (c) and (d), namely:—

(a) the company is wholly owned by a foreign-held company throughout that period;

(b) the company is wholly owned, throughout that period, by a non-U.K. resident company whose shares, throughout that period and the previous 12 months, are traded and quoted on an overseas recognised stock exchange;

(c) the company is one in which non-residents own 80 per cent. of its shares and each own at least five per cent. of the shares;

(d) the company is one in which, at any time in that period, U.K. resident persons (other than companies) own less than 20 per cent. of the shares. Ultimate ownership may be traced on a reasonable basis through corporate owners to persons who are not companies.

A company is a foreign-held company if throughout the accounting period: (i) non-residents own 80 per cent. of its shares at any time in that period; or (ii) it is wholly owned by a company with such non-resident shareholders. A company may treat itself as an IHC in an accounting period in which it paid a FID if it expects to be an IHC in that period and it was an IHC in the preceding period.

Liability to pay ACT displaced

246T.—(1) This section applies where—

(a) a company pays a foreign income dividend in an accounting period, and

(b) at the time it pays the dividend the company treats itself as an international headquarters company by virtue of section 246S(9).

(2) The company shall not be liable to pay advance corporation tax in respect of the dividend.

(3) This section shall have effect subject to section 246V.

GENERAL NOTE

Section 246T of the ICTA 1988

A company which treats itself as an IHC may pay a FID without paying ACT.

Settlement of liability by IHC as to ACT

246U.—(1) This section applies where—

(a) at any time when it pays a dividend in an accounting period a company treats itself as an international headquarters company by virtue of section 246S(9), and

(b) the company is an international headquarters company in the accounting period.

(2) If amount A exceeds amount B, the company shall be liable to pay an amount equal to the excess as if the amount were advance corporation tax payable in respect of a distribution made by the company in the last return period falling within the accounting period; and "return period" here has the same meaning as in Schedule 13.

(3) If amount B exceeds amount A, an amount equal to the excess shall be paid to the company in accordance with this section; and the payment shall be treated as if it were a repayment of advance corporation tax which—

(a) was paid by the company in respect of distributions made by it in the accounting period, and

(b) falls to be repaid under sections 246N and 246Q.

(4) Amount A is the total amount of the advance corporation tax which by virtue of section 246T and paragraph 3A of Schedule 13 the company is not liable to pay, and has not paid, in respect of dividends paid by it in the accounting period.

(5) Amount B is the amount (if any) of the advance corporation tax which would be required to be repaid, or set off, or partly repaid and partly set off, under sections 246N and 246Q if the company—

(a) had not treated itself as an international headquarters company at any time in the accounting period, and

(b) had, at the expiry of nine months from the end of the accounting period, made a claim as regards the accounting period in accordance with sections 246N and 246Q.

(6) Where an amount of advance corporation tax actually paid by the company in respect of qualifying distributions made by it in the accounting period has been dealt with under section 239(3), or the benefit of such an amount has been surrendered under section 240, in applying section 246N(5)(c) and (d) by virtue of subsection (5) above it shall be assumed that an equivalent amount of advance corporation tax would have been so dealt with or (as the case may be) that the benefit of an equivalent amount of advance corporation tax would have been so surrendered.

(7) No amount shall be paid under subsection (3) above unless the company makes a claim for payment; and—

(a) a return made by the company for the accounting period under section 11 of the Management Act, or

(b) an amendment of such a return,

shall be treated as a claim for payment if the return or (as the case may be) the amendment contains such particulars as the inspector may require.

(8) A claim which is not made by means of a return under section 11 of the Management Act, or by means of an amendment of such a return, shall be supported by such particulars as the inspector may require.

(9) No amount shall be payable under subsection (3) above until the expiry of nine months from the end of the accounting period.

GENERAL NOTE

Section 246U of the ICTA 1988

An IHC which has paid a FID in any period and treats itself as an IHC is liable to pay the excess of amount A over amount B as if it were ACT, nine months after the end of the accounting period, and to claim the excess of amount B over amount A as if it were ACT paid by it, which is repayable under ss.246N and 246Q. Amount A is the ACT which is not payable under s.246T above because the company is an IHC, amount B is the ACT which would be repaid or set off (in whole or in part), assuming the company had not treated itself as an IHC and made a claim under ss.246N and 246Q.

Settlement of liability by non-IHC as to ACT

246V.—(1) This section applies where—

(a) at any time when it pays a dividend in an accounting period a company treats itself as an international headquarters company by virtue of section 246S(9), and

(b) the company is not an international headquarters company in the accounting period.
(2) Section 246T shall not apply, and shall be treated as never having applied, as regards the dividend.
(3) Sections 246N and 246Q shall apply as if the company had not treated itself as an international headquarters company at any time in the period by virtue of section 246S(9).

GENERAL NOTE

Section 246V of the ICTA 1988
An assessment may be made to recover any ACT due where a company pays a FID and treats itself as an IHC and it subsequently fails to qualify as an IHC. ACT relief under ss.246N and 246Q is nevertheless available.

Payments and repayments where further matching takes place
246W.—(1) Subsection (2) below applies where—
(a) a company pays an amount under section 246U(2) as regards an accounting period,
(b) the company makes an election under section 246J(5) or 246K(10) matching profits with dividends paid in that accounting period, and
(c) had the election been made before the relevant time, the company would not have been required to pay some or all of the amount mentioned in paragraph (a) above.
(2) The company shall be entitled to repayment of so much of the amount mentioned in subsection (1)(a) above as it would not have been required to pay if the election had been made before the relevant time.
(3) Subsection (4) below applies where—
(a) a company either pays an amount under section 246U(2) as regards an accounting period or is paid an amount under section 246U(3) as regards the period,
(b) the company makes an election under section 246J(5) or 246K(10) matching profits with dividends paid in that accounting period, and
(c) had the election been made before the relevant time, the company would have been entitled under section 246U(3) to be paid an amount which was not in fact paid to it.
(4) The company shall be entitled to payment of the amount mentioned in subsection (3)(c) above.
(5) Any repayment under subsection (2) above shall (without prejudice to section 246U(2)) be treated as if it were a repayment of advance corporation tax which—
(a) was paid by the company in respect of a distribution made by it in the last return period falling within the accounting period mentioned in subsection (1) above, and
(b) falls to be repaid under sections 246N and 246Q.
(6) In relation to a repayment under subsection (2) above which by virtue of subsection (5) above is treated as a repayment of advance corporation tax, the material date for the purposes of section 826 shall be the date when advance corporation tax in respect of distributions made by the company in the return period mentioned in subsection (5) above became (or, as the case may be, would have become) due and payable; and accordingly subsection (2A) of section 826 shall not apply in relation to the repayment.
(7) Any payment under subsection (4) above shall be treated as if it were a repayment of advance corporation tax which—
(a) was paid by the company in respect of distributions made by it in the accounting period mentioned in subsection (3) above, and
(b) falls to be repaid under sections 246N and 246Q.
(8) Subsections (7) and (8) of section 246U shall apply in relation to payments and repayments under this section as they apply in relation to payments under section 246U(3).
(9) For the purposes of this section—
(a) "the relevant time" means the expiry of nine months from the end of the accounting period mentioned in subsection (1) or (3) above;
(b) "return period" has the same meaning as in Schedule 13.

GENERAL NOTE

Section 246W of the ICTA 1988
A company which has paid ACT under s.246U(2) above in respect of a FID (because amount A exceeds amount B) may elect to match the FID with DFP of that period. It is then entitled to a

repayment of the ACT, together with interest. A similar procedure entitles a company to claim ACT under s.246U(3) (because amount B exceeds amount A) although it had not made the election within the relevant time.

Adjustments

Adjustments where profits or foreign tax altered
    246X.—(1) This section applies where a company is paid or repaid an amount under any provision of this Chapter, or sets off under any such provision an amount against a liability of the company to corporation tax, and either—
    (a) there is any alteration of the profits of a company for an accounting period which renders the payment or repayment, or the amount set off, excessive or insufficient, or
    (b) there is any alteration of an amount of tax payable under the laws of a territory outside the United Kingdom which renders the payment or repayment, or the amount set off, excessive or insufficient.
    (2) Where there is any such alteration as is mentioned in subsection (1) above the company may revise any election made under section 246J or 246K or 246P in such manner as is just and reasonable having regard to the alteration.
    (3) Where there is any such alteration as is mentioned in subsection (1) above, then such adjustments shall be made of any calculation required by this Chapter as are just and reasonable having regard to the alteration and to any revision made under subsection (2) above; and payments or repayments shall be made accordingly.

GENERAL NOTE

Section 246X of the ICTA 1988
    Elections previously made under ss.246J, 246K or 246P may be revised to reflect adjustments to the company's profits or its foreign tax liabilities.

Application of this Chapter

Application of this Chapter
    246Y. This Chapter shall have effect in relation to—
    (a) any dividend paid on or after 1st July 1994;
    (b) any foreign source profit consisting of income for, or a chargeable gain for, an accounting period beginning on or after 1st July 1993."

GENERAL NOTE

Section 246Y of the ICTA 1988
    The FID regime applies to dividends paid after June 30, 1994 and to foreign source profits of accounting periods beginning after June 30, 1993.

PART II

LIABILITY FOR AND COLLECTION OF ADVANCE CORPORATION TAX

    2. In section 14 of the Taxes Act 1988 (advance corporation tax and qualifying distributions) in subsection (3) for the words "section 241" there shall be substituted "sections 241 and 246F".
    3.—(1) Schedule 13 to the Taxes Act 1988 (collection of advance corporation tax) shall be amended as follows.
    (2) In paragraph 1 (duty to make returns) for sub-paragraph (1) there shall be substituted—
    "(1) A company shall for each of its accounting periods make, in accordance with this Schedule, returns to the collector of—
    (a) the franked payments made and franked investment income received by it in that period,
    (b) the foreign income dividends paid and foreign income dividends received by it in that period, and
    (c) the advance corporation tax (if any) payable by it in respect of the franked payments made and foreign income dividends paid by it in that period;
    and references in this Schedule to foreign income dividends shall be construed in accordance with Chapter VA of this Part."
    (3) In paragraph 1, for sub-paragraph (4) there shall be substituted—
    "(4) Subject to paragraphs 4(2), 4A(2) and 7(3) below, no return need be made under this Schedule by a company for any period in which it has—

    (a) made no franked payments, and

    (b) paid no foreign income dividends."

(4) In paragraph 2 (contents of return) for sub-paragraph (1) there shall be substituted—

  "(1) Subject to paragraphs 7(2), 3A(2) and 9A(2) below, the return made by a company for any return period shall show—

    (a) the amount of the franked payments, if any, made by it in that period,

    (b) the amount of franked investment income, if any, received by it in that period,

    (c) if any advance corporation tax is payable in respect of the franked payments, the amount thereof,

    (d) the amount of the foreign income dividends, if any, paid by it in that period,

    (e) the amount of the foreign income dividends, if any, received by it in that period, and

    (f) if any advance corporation tax is payable in respect of the foreign income dividends paid, the amount thereof."

(5) In paragraph 2, after sub-paragraph (4) there shall be inserted—

  "(5) For the purposes of paragraph (e) of sub-paragraph (1) above the amount of foreign income dividends received by a company in a return period shall be treated as including the excess, if any, of—

    (a) any amount carried forward under section 246F(3) to the accounting period for which the return is made, and

    (b) any amount of foreign income dividends received by the company in that accounting period but before the beginning of the return period,

over the amount of any foreign income dividends paid by the company in that accounting period but before the beginning of the return period.

  (6) For the purposes of paragraph (f) of sub-paragraph (1) above advance corporation tax shall be payable in respect of foreign income dividends paid in a return period if—

    (a) the amount shown under paragraph (d) of that sub-paragraph exceeds the amount shown under paragraph (e) of that sub-paragraph, or

    (b) no amount is shown under paragraph (e) of that sub-paragraph;

and the amount of that tax shall be calculated at the rate of advance corporation tax in force for the financial year in which the return period ends on an amount equal to that excess or, if no amount is shown under sub-paragraph (1)(e) above, to the amount shown under sub-paragraph (1)(d) above."

(6) In paragraph 3 (payment of tax)—

(a) in sub-paragraph (1) after the words "franked payments" there shall be inserted "and foreign income dividends", and

(b) in sub-paragraph (3) after the words "franked payment" there shall be inserted "or foreign income dividend".

(7) After paragraph 3 there shall be inserted—

               "International headquarters companies

  3A.—(1) This paragraph and paragraph 3B below apply where—

    (a) a company pays a foreign income dividend in a return period, and

    (b) at the time it pays the dividend the company treats itself as an international headquarters company by virtue of section 246S(9).

  (2) The return made by the company for the return period—

    (a) shall state that the company has so treated itself;

    (b) shall show the basis on which it has so treated itself;

    (c) shall not include the amount of the dividend in the amount shown under paragraph 2(1)(d) above;

    (d) shall state separately that the dividend was paid and show its amount.

  (3) The dividend shall be treated for the purposes of section 246F(1) and (2), paragraph 2(5) above and paragraph 4A below as if it had not been paid.

  3B.—(1) Without prejudice to paragraph 3 above, if at any time before the end of the accounting period in which the return period mentioned in paragraph 3A(1) above falls the inspector is not satisfied that there was a reasonable basis for the company treating itself as mentioned in paragraph 3A(1) he may make an assessment on the company to the best of his judgment; and any advance corporation tax due under an assessment made by virtue of this sub-paragraph shall be treated for the purposes of interest on unpaid tax as having been payable at the time when it would have been payable if the company had not so treated itself.

  (2) Where an assessment which takes account of the dividend mentioned in paragraph 3A(1) above is made under sub-paragraph (1) above, then, subject to any appeal—

(a) the company shall be deemed for the purposes of Chapter VA of this Part not to have treated itself as an international headquarters company by virtue of section 246S(9) at the time it paid the dividend;

(b) paragraph 3A(3) above shall not apply to the dividend.

(3) In a case where—

(a) the company is not an international headquarters company in the accounting period in which the return period mentioned in paragraph 3A(1) above falls, and

(b) as regards any relevant return period amount X exceeds amount Y,

after the end of the accounting period the inspector may make an assessment on the company for an amount of advance corporation tax equal to the excess; and a relevant return period is a return period falling within the accounting period in question.

(4) For the purposes of sub-paragraph (3) above—

(a) amount X is the amount of advance corporation tax which, if the company had not treated itself as an international headquarters company at any time in the accounting period and had made a return for the relevant return period under paragraph 2 above accordingly, would have been payable by the company in respect of the relevant return period under paragraph 2(6) above;

(b) amount Y is the aggregate of the amounts mentioned in sub-paragraph (5) below.

(5) The amounts referred to in sub-paragraph (4)(b) above are—

(a) the amount (if any) of advance corporation tax which was in fact payable by the company under paragraph 2(6) above in respect of the relevant return period,

(b) any amount of advance corporation tax to which the company has been assessed under sub-paragraph (1) above in respect of that period, and

(c) any amount of advance corporation tax to which the company has been assessed under paragraph 3 above in respect of that period and which is attributable to foreign income dividends.

(6) Any advance corporation tax due under an assessment made by virtue of sub-paragraph (3) above shall be treated for the purposes of interest on unpaid tax as having been payable at the time when it would have been payable if the company had not treated itself as an international headquarters company at any time in the accounting period."

(8) In paragraph 4 (receipt of franked investment income after payment of advance corporation tax) in sub-paragraph (2) after the words "any franked payments" there shall be inserted ", or paid any foreign income dividends,".

(9) After paragraph 4 there shall be inserted—

"Receipt of foreign income dividends after payment of advance corporation tax

4A.—(1) This paragraph shall have effect where—

(a) a return has been made of foreign income dividends paid in any return period falling within an accounting period and advance corporation tax has been paid in respect of those dividends, and

(b) the company receives foreign income dividends after the end of the return period but before the end of the accounting period.

(2) The company shall make a return under paragraph 1 above for the return period in which the foreign income dividends are received whether or not it has made any franked payments, or paid any foreign income dividends, in that period, and, subject to sub-paragraphs (3) to (5) below, shall be entitled to repayment of any advance corporation tax paid (and not repaid) in respect of foreign income dividends paid in the accounting period in question.

(3) If no foreign income dividends were paid by the company in the return period for which a return is made by virtue of sub-paragraph (2) above (the relevant return period), the amount of the repayment shall not exceed the amount which would have been payable under paragraph 2 above as regards the relevant return period if the company—

(a) had paid in the period foreign income dividends of an amount equal to the foreign income dividends actually received by it in the period and had paid in the period no other foreign income dividends or franked payments, and

(b) had received in the period no foreign income dividends or franked investment income.

(4) If at least one foreign income dividend was paid by the company in the relevant return period and the amount of the foreign income dividends received by it in the period exceeds the amount of the foreign income dividends paid by it in the period, the amount of the repayment shall not exceed the amount which would have been payable under paragraph 2 above as regards the relevant return period if the company—

(a) had paid in the period foreign income dividends of an amount equal to the foreign income dividends actually received by it in the period and had paid in the period no other foreign income dividends or franked payments, and

(b) had received in the period foreign income dividends of an amount equal to the foreign income dividends actually paid by it in the period and had received in the period no other foreign income dividends or franked investment income.

(5) If at least one foreign income dividend was paid by the company in the relevant return period and the amount of the foreign income dividends paid by it in the period exceeds the amount of the foreign income dividends received by it in the period, the company shall not be entitled to a repayment under this paragraph as regards the relevant return period."

(10) After paragraph 6 there shall be inserted—

"*Claims for set-off in respect of foreign income dividends received by a company*

6A.—(1) Where under paragraph 2 or 4A above foreign income dividends received by a company fall to be taken into account in determining—

(a) whether advance corporation tax is payable or repayable, or

(b) the amount of such tax which is payable or repayable,

the inclusion of the foreign income dividends in the appropriate return shall be treated as a claim by the company to have them so taken into account, and any such claim shall be supported by such evidence as the inspector may reasonably require.

(2) Paragraph 6 above shall apply in relation to a claim under this paragraph as it applies in relation to a claim under paragraph 5 above."

(11) In paragraph 7 (qualifying distributions which are not payments and payments of uncertain nature) in sub-paragraph (3) for the words from "and if" to "that period" there shall be substituted "and if in that period no franked payment (apart from that distribution or payment) is made and no foreign income dividend is paid".

(12) After paragraph 9 there shall be inserted—

"*Manufactured foreign income dividends*

9A.—(1) This paragraph applies in any case where, by virtue of paragraph 2(2) and (6) of Schedule 23A, a company is treated as having paid a foreign income dividend.

(2) No amount shall be shown under paragraph 2(1)(d) above in respect of the dividend which is treated as having been paid, but the company's return for the return period in which the dividend is treated as having been paid shall state separately that it was treated as paid and shall show its amount."

(13) This paragraph shall have effect in relation to any return period ending after 30th June 1994.

GENERAL NOTE

Part II

Para. (2)
The ICTA 1988 (c. 1), s.14 is amended to include s.246F.

Para. (3)
The ICTA 1988 (c. 1), Sched. 13, which details the machinery for the collection of ACT, is amended. The return to be made by a company for each accounting period must now include FIDs paid and received and the ACT (if any) payable thereon. Provisions dealing with IHCs are introduced. The provisions in para. (3) apply to return periods ending after June 30, 1994.

PART III

INSURANCE COMPANIES ETC.

4. In section 431(2) of the Taxes Act 1988 (interpretative provisions relating to insurance companies) the following shall be inserted after the definition of "closing liabilities"—

" "foreign income dividends" shall be construed in accordance with Chapter VA of Part VI;".

5.—(1) Section 434 of the Taxes Act 1988 (franked investment income etc.) shall be amended as follows.

(2) In subsection (1) after "income of" there shall be inserted ", or foreign income dividends arising to,".

(3) In subsection (2) after "income of" there shall be inserted ", and foreign income dividends arising to,".

(4) The following subsections shall be inserted after subsection (3A)—

"(3B) The policy holders' share of foreign income dividends received in respect of investments held in connection with a company's life assurance business shall be left out of account in determining, under subsection (7) of section 13, the foreign income dividends forming part of the company's profits for the purposes of that section.

(3C) The policy holders' share of any income or chargeable gain arising in respect of investments held in connection with a company's life assurance business shall be left out of account in ascertaining any foreign source profit of the company of the purposes of Chapter VA of Part VI.

(3D) The policy holders' share of foreign income dividends received in respect of investments held in connection with a company's life assurance business shall be left out of account in ascertaining, for the purposes of sections 246F(1) and (3) and Schedule 13, the amount of the foreign income dividends received by the company."

(5) In subsection (6A) the word "and" at the end of paragraph (a) shall be omitted and after that paragraph there shall be inserted—

"(aa) "the policy holders' share" of any foreign income dividends is so much of the income they represent as is not the shareholders' share within the meaning of that section,

(ab) "the policy holders' share" of any income (other than franked investment income) is so much of that income as is not the shareholders' share within the meaning of that section,

(ac) "the policy holders' share" of any chargeable gain is so much of that gain as is equal to the amount that, if the gain were income, would not be the shareholders' share within the meaning of that section, and".

6.—(1) Section 438 of the Taxes Act 1988 (pension business: exemption from tax) shall be amended as follows.

(2) The following subsection shall be inserted after subsection (3)—

"(3AA) Subject to subsection (6B) below, the exclusion by section 208 from the charge to corporation tax of foreign income dividends shall not prevent such dividends being taken into account as part of the profits in computing under section 436 income from pension business."

(3) In subsection (6) the words from "being" to "that profit," shall be omitted.

(4) The following subsections shall be inserted after subsection (6A)—

"(6B) If for any accounting period there is, apart from this subsection, a profit arising to an insurance company from pension business and computed under section 436, and the company so elects as respects all or any part of the relevant foreign income dividends arising to it in that period, subsection (3AA) above shall not apply to the foreign income dividends to which the election relates.

(6C) In subsection (6B) above "relevant foreign income dividends" means the shareholders' share of foreign income dividends within subsection (1) above; and for this purpose "the shareholders' share" of any foreign income dividends is so much of the income they represent as is the shareholders' share within the meaning of section 89 of the Finance Act 1989.

(6D) If in the same accounting period both relevant franked investment income and relevant foreign income dividends arise to the company—

(a) only one election may be made under subsections (6) and (6B) above;

(b) the election may be made as regards both relevant franked investment income and relevant foreign income dividends (subject to paragraph (c) below);

(c) the election may not be made as regards relevant foreign income dividends unless the election is made as regards all the company's relevant franked investment income arising in the period.

(6E) Where an election is made under one or both of subsections (6) and (6B) above, the elected amount must not exceed the amount of the profit which (apart from the election) arises to the company for accounting period from pension business and is computed under section 436; and the elected amount is—

(a) the amount of franked investment income to which the election relates (where the election is made under subsection (6) alone);

(b) the amount of the foreign income dividends to which the election relates (where the election is made under subsection (6B) alone);

(c) the aggregate amount of the franked investment income and the foreign income dividends to which the election relates (where the election is made under subsections (6) and (6B))."

(5) In subsection (7) for "subsection (6) above" there shall be substituted "this section".

7. In section 458 of the Taxes Act 1988 (capital redemption business) in subsection (2)(a) after "income of" there shall be inserted ", and foreign income dividends arising to,".

8.—(1) Section 802 of the Taxes Act 1988 (UK insurance companies trading overseas) shall be amended as follows.

(2) In subsection (2)(a) after "franked investment income" there shall be inserted ", foreign income dividends".

(3) The following subsection shall be inserted after subsection (3)—

"(4) In this section "foreign income dividends" shall be construed in accordance with Chapter VA of Part VI."

9.—(1) Section 89 of the Finance Act 1989 (policy holders' share of profits) shall be amended as follows.

(2) In subsection (2) after paragraph (b) there shall be inserted ", and

(c) the shareholders' share of any foreign income dividends arising to the company in the period in respect of investments held in connection with the business."

(3) The following subsection shall be inserted after subsection (2)—

"(2A) For the purposes of subsection (2) above—

(a) "foreign income dividends" shall be construed in accordance with Chapter VA of Part VI;

(b) the shareholders' share of any foreign income dividends is so much of the income they represent as is the shareholders' share."

PART IV

OTHER PROVISIONS

Penalties

10. In the first column of the Table in section 98 of the Taxes Management Act 1970 (penalties for failure to furnish particulars etc.) the following entry shall be inserted after the entry relating to section 234 of the principal Act—

"section 246H;".

Small companies' relief

11.—(1) Section 13 of the Taxes Act 1988 (small companies' relief) shall be amended as follows.

(2) In subsection (7) (definition of profits for purposes of small companies' relief) after "companies within the group" there shall be inserted "and with the addition of foreign income dividends arising to the company".

(3) The following subsection shall be inserted after subsection (8)—

"(8A) In this section "foreign income dividends" shall be construed in accordance with Chapter VA of Part VI."

Expenses of management

12.—(1) Section 75 of the Taxes Act 1988 (expenses of management: investment companies) shall be amended as follows.

(2) In subsection (2) after "franked investment income," there shall be inserted "foreign income dividends,".

(3) The following subsection shall be inserted after subsection (5)—

"(6) In this section "foreign income dividends" shall be construed in accordance with Chapter VA of Part VI."

Group income

13. In section 247 of the Taxes Act 1988 (dividends etc. paid by one member of a group to another) the following subsection shall be inserted after subsection (5)—

"(5A) Subsections (1) to (3) above shall not apply to foreign income dividends; and "foreign income dividends" shall be construed in accordance with Chapter VA of Part VI."

GENERAL NOTE

Part III

Paras. (4)–(9)
The legislation dealing with the taxation of insurance companies is amended to accommodate the FID regime.

Para. (10)
Penalties may be imposed for failure to supply information requested in a s.246H notice.

Part IV

Para. (11)
FIDs are to be included in a company's profits when determining whether small companies' relief is available for any period.

Para. (12)
FIDs may not be deducted from management expenses.

Para. (13)
A group income election may not be made in respect of FIDs.

Mutual business etc.

14.—(1) Section 490 of the Taxes Act 1988 (companies carrying on a mutual business or not carrying on a business) shall be amended as follows.
(2) In subsection (1) after "(including group income)" there shall be inserted "or out of foreign income dividends".
(3) In subsection (4) after "franked investment income" there shall be inserted "or foreign income dividends".
(4) The following subsection shall be inserted after subsection (4)—
"(5) In this section "foreign income dividends" shall be construed in accordance with Chapter VA of Part VI."

GENERAL NOTE

Para. (14)
FIDs received by a company carrying on a mutual business are treated in the same way as FII.

Discretionary trusts

15. In section 687 of the Taxes Act 1988 (payments under discretionary trusts) in subsection (3) the following paragraph shall be inserted after paragraph (aa)—
"(aaa) the amount of tax at a rate equal to the difference between the lower rate and the rate applicable to trusts on any sum treated, under section 246D(4), as income of the trustees;";
and in paragraph (a) of that subsection after "(aa)" there shall be inserted ", (aaa)".

GENERAL NOTE

Para. (15)
FIDs received by trustees of a discretionary trust are chargeable to 15 per cent. tax (the difference between the lower rate of income tax and the 35 per cent. special rate applicable to such trusts).

Personal representatives

16. In section 701 of the Taxes Act 1988 (interpretation of Part XVI) in subsection (8) (meaning of aggregate income) before "249(5)," there shall be inserted "246D(3),".

GENERAL NOTE

Para. (16)
FIDs received by personal representatives are to be included in the aggregate income of the estate.

Purchase and sale of securities

17.—(1) Section 731 of the Taxes Act 1988 (application and interpretation of provisions relating to purchase and sale of securities) shall be amended as follows.
(2) In subsection (9), in the definition of "interest" the words from "and in applying" to the end of paragraph (b) shall be omitted.
(3) The following subsections shall be inserted after subsection (9)—
"(9A) In applying references in the relevant provisions to interest in relation to a qualifying distribution other than a foreign income dividend—
(a) "gross interest" means the qualifying distribution together with the tax credit to which the recipient of the distribution is entitled in respect of it, and
(b) "net interest" means the qualifying distribution exclusive of any such tax credit.
(9B) In applying references in the relevant provisions to interest in relation to a foreign income dividend paid in circumstances where section 246D(1), (3) or (4) applies—
(a) "gross interest" means the amount of the income arrived at under section 246D(1) by reference to the dividend, and
(b) "net interest" means the dividend.
(9C) Where a foreign income dividend is paid in circumstances other than those where section 246D(1), (3) or (4) applies—
(a) in applying section 735(2) in relation to the dividend the words "the gross amount corresponding with" shall be disregarded, and
(b) in applying references in the relevant provisions (including section 735(2)) to interest in relation to the dividend "net interest" means the dividend.
(9D) In this section "foreign income dividend" shall be construed in accordance with Chapter VA of Part VI."

GENERAL NOTE

Para. (17)
A FID is to be grossed up for the purposes of the ICTA 1988 (c. 1), s.731.

Manufactured dividends

18.—(1) Section 737 of the Taxes Act 1988 (manufactured dividends: treatment of tax deducted) shall be amended as follows.
(2) In subsection (3) (cases where section 737(1) does not apply) at the end of paragraph (b) there shall be inserted "or", and after that paragraph there shall be inserted the following paragraph—
"(c) the manufactured dividend is representative of a foreign income dividend."
(3) In subsection (6) after the definition of "dividend manufacturing regulations" there shall be inserted the following definition—
" "foreign income dividend" shall be construed in accordance with Chapter VA of Part VI;".
19. In Schedule 23A to the Taxes Act 1988, in paragraph 2 (manufactured dividends on United Kingdom equities) the following sub-paragraphs shall be inserted after sub-paragraph (5)—
"(6) In a case where—
(a) the dividend of which the manufactured dividend is representative is a foreign income dividend, and
(b) the dividend manufacturer is a company resident in the United Kingdom,
the manufactured dividend shall, in addition to being treated as mentioned in sub-paragraph (2) above, be treated for all purposes of the Tax Acts as if it were a foreign income dividend; but in such a case the dividend manufacturer shall not by virtue of sub-paragraph (2) above be liable to pay advance corporation tax in respect of the manufactured dividend.
(7) In a case where—
(a) the dividend of which the manufactured dividend is representative is a foreign income dividend, and
(b) the dividend manufacturer is not a company resident in the United Kingdom (so that, were the dividend of which the manufactured dividend is representative not a foreign income dividend, section 737 would apply in relation to the dividend manufacturer),

in relation to the recipient and all persons claiming title through or under him the manufactured dividend shall, in addition to being treated as mentioned in sub-paragraph (3)(a) above, be treated as if it were a foreign income dividend.

(8) In this paragraph "foreign income dividend" shall be construed in accordance with Chapter VA of Part VI."

GENERAL NOTE

Paras. (18)–(19)
A manufactured dividend representing a FID which is paid by a U.K. resident dividend manufacturer is treated as a FID and the manufacturer is not liable to pay ACT thereon. The recipient of such a dividend paid by a non-U.K. resident manufacturer is treated as if he had received a FID.

Interest on tax overpaid

20.—(1) Section 826 of the Taxes Act 1988 shall be amended as follows.

(2) In subsection (1) the following paragraph shall be inserted after paragraph (a)—
"(aa) a repayment falls to be made under section 246N and 246Q of advance corporation tax paid by a company in respect of distributions made by it in such an accounting period; or".

(3) The following subsection shall be inserted after subsection (2)—
"(2A) In relation to advance corporation tax paid by a company in respect of distributions made by it in an accounting period, the material date for the purposes of this section is the date on which corporation tax for that accounting period became (or, as the case may be, would have become) due and payable in accordance with section 10."

GENERAL NOTE

Para. (20)
Interest on a repayment of ACT made under s.246N or s.246Q runs from nine months after the end of the accounting period concerned.

Section 146   SCHEDULE 17

MINOR CORRECTIONS

1. Section 43(1) of the Taxes Act 1988 shall have effect, and be deemed always to have had effect, as if the words "or IV" were omitted.

2.—(1) Subsection (1) of section 271 of that Act shall have effect, and be deemed always to have had effect, as if—
(a) the words "or contract", wherever they occur, were omitted;
(b) in paragraph (b), the words "or the contract was made after that date" were omitted; and
(c) in paragraph (c), the words "or, as the case may be, the body with which the contract was made" were omitted.

(2) Subsection (2) of that section shall have effect, and be deemed always to have had effect, as if paragraph (b) and the word "or" immediately preceding it were omitted.

3. Subsection (6) of section 356D of that Act shall have effect, and be deemed always to have had effect, as if for the words from "in relation" onwards there were substituted "so that, in determining what (if any) part of the amount on which qualifying interest is payable is the part exceeding the limit, interest on a later loan shall be eligible for relief only to the extent that the whole amount of the limit has not been used in relation to any earlier loan or loans."

4. Section 431(5) of that Act shall have effect, and be deemed always to have effect, as if for "Subsection (4)(c)" there were substituted "Subsection (4)(f)".

5. Section 561(2)(c) of that Act shall have effect, and be deemed always to have had effect, as if for "subsection (4)" there were substituted "subsection (6)".

6. Section 576(5) of that Act (in its application as amended by the Taxation of Chargeable Gains Act 1992) shall have effect, and be deemed always to have had effect, as if after "128(2)" there were inserted "of the 1992 Act".

7. Section 768(6) of that Act (in its application as amended by the Capital Allowances Act 1990) shall have effect, and be deemed always to have had effect, as if for "section 161(5)" there were substituted "section 161(6)".

8. Sections 842(4) and 843(2) of that Act (in their application as amended by the Taxation of Chargeable Gains Act 1992) shall have effect, and be deemed always to have had effect, as if, in each case, for "the 1990 Act" there were substituted "the 1992 Act".

9. Paragraph 8(b) of Schedule 11 to that Act (in its application as amended by the Capital Allowances Act 1990) shall have effect, and be deemed always to have had effect, as if the words "Chapter II of Part I of the 1968 Act or" were omitted.

GENERAL NOTE

Various provisions in the ICTA 1988 (c. 1) are amended to correct errors that arose during the consolidation of various enactments into the Taxes Acts 1988 or when that Act was subsequently amended by other Acts.

Section 169   SCHEDULE 18

INTEREST RATE AND CURRENCY CONTRACTS: INSURANCE AND MUTUAL TRADING COMPANIES

Life assurance business; I minus E

1.—(1) Subject to sub-paragraph (2) below, sub-paragraph (3) below applies where—
  (a) a qualifying contract was at any time in an accounting period of an insurance company held by the company for the purposes of any life assurance business carried on by it, and
  (b) the I minus E basis is applied for the period in respect of that business.
(2) Where the qualifying contract was held partly for the purposes of the life assurance business and partly for other purposes—
  (a) the profit or loss on the contract for the period shall be apportioned on a just and reasonable basis, and
  (b) any reference in sub-paragraph (3) below to that profit or loss shall be construed as a reference to so much of it as is referable to the life assurance business.
(3) Notwithstanding anything in section 159 of this Act—
  (a) no part of the profit or loss on the contract for the period shall be treated for the purposes of the Tax Acts as a profit or loss of a trade or part of a trade, and
  (b) accordingly, the whole of that profit or loss shall be treated for the purposes of this paragraph as a non-trading profit or loss;
and any reference in the following provisions of this paragraph to a non-trading profit or loss is a reference to a profit or loss which is treated as a non-trading one by virtue of paragraph (b) above.
(4) Section 432A of the Taxes Act 1988 (insurance companies: apportionment of income and gains) shall have effect as if—
  (a) any reference to income arising from assets of an insurance company's long term business fund or overseas life assurance fund included a reference to any non-trading profit or loss of an insurance company; and
  (b) any reference to income arising from or attributable to assets linked solely to a particular category of business included a reference to any non-trading profit or loss which derives from a qualifying contract which is so linked.
(5) Section 438 of the Taxes Act 1988 (pension business: exemption from tax) shall have effect as if the reference in subsection (1) to income from investments and deposits of so much of an insurance company's life assurance fund and separate annuity fund, if any, as is referable to pension business included a reference to so much of any non-trading profit of such a company as is so referable.
(6) So much of any non-trading loss of an insurance company as is referable to pension business or overseas life assurance business shall not be allowable as a deduction in computing for the purposes of this Chapter the profits or losses of the company; and subsection (5)(a) of section 173 of this Act applies for the purposes of this sub-paragraph as it applies for the purposes of that section.
(7) Where, as regards as insurance company and an accounting period, one or more non-trading profits or losses of the company for the period are referable to basic life assurance and general annuity business, subsections (5), (6) and (9) of section 129 and sections 130 and 131 of the Finance Act 1993 (non-trading exchange gains and losses) shall apply for the purposes of this paragraph as if—
  (a) any reference to any amount or amounts a company is treated as receiving in the period by virtue of section 129 were a reference to the amount or amounts of any non-trading profit or profits which are referable to that class of business,

(b) any reference to the amount or amounts of any loss or losses a company is treated as incurring in the period by virtue of that section were a reference to the amount or amounts of any non-trading loss or losses which are so referable, and

(c) for subsections (3) to (14) of section 131 there were substituted the following subsection—
"(3) The relievable amount shall be set off for the purposes of corporation tax against income of the accounting period which is referable to basic life assurance and general annuity business; and that income shall be treated as reduced accordingly."

Life assurance business: Case I of Schedule D

2.—(1) Subject to sub-paragraph (2) below, sub-paragraphs (3) and (4) below apply where—

(a) a qualifying contract was at any time in an accounting period of an insurance company held by the company for the purposes of any life assurance business carried on by it, and

(b) the profits of the company in respect of that business are, for the purposes of the Tax Acts, computed in accordance with the provisions of the Taxes Act 1988 applicable to Case I of Schedule D.

(2) Where the qualifying contract was held partly for the purposes of the life assurance business and partly for other purposes—

(a) amounts A and B for the period shall be apportioned on a just and reasonable basis, and

(b) any reference in sub-paragraph (3) or (4) below to either of those amounts shall be construed as a reference to so much of it as is referable to the life assurance business.

(3) Notwithstanding anything in sections 159 and 160 of this Act, amount A for the period shall not—

(a) under or by virtue of this Chapter be chargeable to corporation tax as profits of the company, or

(b) be taken into account as a receipt in computing for the purposes of this Chapter the profits or losses of the company.

(4) Notwithstanding anything in those sections, amount B for the period shall not—

(a) be allowable as a deduction in computing for the purposes of this Chapter the profits or losses of the company, or

(b) under or by virtue of this Chapter be allowable as a deduction in computing any other income or profits or gains or losses of the company for the purposes of the Tax Acts.

(5) Subsection (5)(a) of section 173 of this Act applies for the purposes of this paragraph as it applies for the purposes of that section.

Non-life mutual business

3.—(1) Subject to sub-paragraph (2) below, sub-paragraph (3) below applies where a qualifying contract was at any time in an accounting period of a mutual trading company held by the company for the purposes of any non-life mutual business carried on by it.

(2) Where the qualifying contract was held partly for the purposes of the non-life mutual business and partly for other purposes—

(a) the profit or loss on the contract for the period shall be apportioned on a just and reasonable basis, and

(b) any reference in sub-paragraph (3) below to that profit or loss shall be construed as a reference to so much of it as is referable to the non-life mutual business.

(3) Notwithstanding anything in section 159 of this Act—

(a) no part of the profit or loss on the contract for the period shall be treated for the purposes of the Tax Acts as a profit or loss of a trade or part of a trade, and

(b) accordingly, the whole of that profit or loss shall be treated for the purposes of section 160 of this Act as a non-trading profit or loss.

Interpretation

4. In this Schedule—

"the I minus E basis" means the basis commonly so called (under which a company carrying on life assurance business is charged to tax on that business otherwise than under Case I of Schedule D);

"life assurance business" includes annuity business;

"non-life mutual business" means any mutual trading, or any mutual insurance or other mutual business, which (in either case) is not life assurance business.

GENERAL NOTE

Para. (1)
Profits or losses on qualifying contracts held for the purposes of a life assurance business to which the I minus E basis applies are treated as non-trading profits or losses (apportioned if necessary if the contract is held partly for such business and partly for other purposes) and charged or allowed under Sched. D, Case VI. Non-trading profits on qualifying contracts which are referrable to pension business are exempt from tax. Non-trading losses referrable to pension business or overseas life assurance business are not deductible in computing the profits or losses of the company.

The Finance Act 1993 (c. 34), s.129(5)(6) and (9) and ss.130–131 are to apply to non-trading profits or losses which are referrable to the basic life assurance and general annuity business. Non-trading losses referrable to the basic life assurance and general annuity business, must be set off against income of that business for the period for which it is so referrable.

Para. (2)
Profits or losses arising on qualifying contracts held for the purposes of a life assurance business whose profits are computed on a Case I basis are to be chargeable under the FA 1989 (c. 26), s.83(1)–(3) and the ICTA 1988 (c. 1), ss.432A–432E (apportioned if necessary where the contract is held partly for such business and partly for other purposes) instead of the financial instrument provisions in the FA 1994 (c. 9).

Para. (3)
Profits or losses arising on qualifying contracts held for the purposes of a non-life mutual business are treated as non-trading profits or losses (apportioned if necessary if the contract is held partly for such business and partly for other purposes) and charged or allowed under Sched. D, Case VI.

Section 196   SCHEDULE 19

MANAGEMENT: OTHER AMENDMENTS

PART I

AMENDMENT OF MANAGEMENT ACT

Notice of liability to income tax and capital gains tax

GENERAL NOTE
This Schedule makes amendments, to the TMA 1970 (c. 9) in paras. (1) to (36), to the ICTA 1988 (c. 1) in paras. (37)–(43) and to sundry other statutes in paras. (43)–(46). These are supplemental to other amendments made to the TMA 1970 (c. 9) by ss.178–195 to facilitate the introduction of self-assessment.

1.—(1) For section 7 of the Management Act there shall be substituted the following section—

"Notice of liability to income tax and capital gains tax
7.—(1) Every person who—
(a) is chargeable to income tax or capital gains tax for any year of assessment, and
(b) has not received a notice under section 8 of this Act requiring a return for that year of his total income and chargeable gains,

shall, subject to subsection (3) below, within six months from the end of that year, give notice to an officer of the Board that he is so chargeable.

(2) In the case of a person who is chargeable as mentioned in subsection (1) above as a trustee of a settlement, that subsection shall have effect as if the reference to a notice under section 8 of this Act were a reference to a notice under section 8A of this Act.

(3) A person shall not be required to give notice under subsection (1) above in respect of a year of assessment if for that year his total income consists of income from sources falling within subsections (4) to (7) below and he has no chargeable gains.

(4) A source of income falls within this subsection in relation to a year of assessment if—

(a) all payments of, or on account of, income from it during that year, and

(b) all income from it for that year which does not consist of payments,

have or has been taken into account in the making of deductions or repayments of tax under section 203 of the principal Act.

(5) A source of income falls within this subsection in relation to any person and any year of assessment if all income from it for that year has been or will be taken into account—

(a) in determining that person's liability to tax, or

(b) in the making of deductions or repayments of tax under section 203 of the principal Act.

(6) A source of income falls within this subsection in relation to any person and any year of assessment if all income from it for that year is—

(a) income from which income tax has been deducted;

(b) income from or on which tax is treated as having been deducted or paid; or

(c) income chargeable under Schedule F,

and that person is not for that year liable to tax at a rate other than the basic rate or the lower rate.

(7) A source of income falls within this subsection in relation to any person and any year of assessment if all income from it for that year is income from which he could not become liable to tax under a self-assessment made under section 9 of this Act in respect of that year.

(8) If any person, for any year of assessment, fails to comply with subsection (1) above, he shall be liable to a penalty not exceeding the amount of the tax—

(a) in which he is assessed under section 9 or 29 of this Act in respect of that year, and

(b) which is not paid on or before 31st January next following that year."

(2) This paragraph has effect as respects the year 1995–96 and subsequent years of assessment.

GENERAL NOTE

The new s.7 of the TMA 1970 (c. 9) reduces from 12 months to six the period within which taxpayers must notify their liability to income tax or capital gains tax following the end of a year of assessment if they have not received a s.8 notice. Penalties will be determined in relation to tax due but unpaid by January 31 following that year of assessment. The new section comes into force for the year 1995–1996.

European Economic Interest Groupings

2. In subsection (2) of section 12A of the Management Act (European Economic Interest Groupings), for the words "making assessments to income tax, corporation tax and capital gains tax on members of a grouping" there shall be substituted the words "securing that members of a grouping are assessed to income tax and capital gains tax or (as the case may be) corporation tax".

GENERAL NOTE

The amendment to s.12A of the TMA 1970 (c. 9) allows an inspector (or other Revenue official) to serve notices on European Economic Interest Groupings for the purpose of securing that assessments are made rather than simply making assessments.

Records for purposes of returns

3. After section 12A of the Management Act there shall be inserted the following section—

"Records

Records to be kept for purposes of returns

12B.—(1) Any person who may be required by a notice under section 8, 8A, 11 or 121AA of this Act (or under any of those sections as extended by section 12 of this Act) to make and deliver a return for a year of assessment or other period shall—

(a) keep all such records as may be requisite for the purpose of enabling him to make and deliver a correct and complete return for the year or period; and

(b) preserve those records until the end of whichever of the following is the later, namely—

(i) the day mentioned in subsection (2) below; and

(ii) where a return delivered by him is enquired into by an officer of the Board, the day on which, by virtue of section 28A(5) or 28B(5) of this Act, the officer's enquiries are treated as completed.

(2) The day referred to in subsection (1) above is—

(a) in the case of a person carrying on a trade, profession or business alone or in partnership or a company, the fifth anniversary of 31st January next following the year of assessment or (as the case may be) the sixth anniversary of the end of the period;

(b) in any other case, the first anniversary of 31st January next following the year of assessment or, where a return is delivered by the person concerned after that date, the quarter day next following the first anniversary of the day on which the return is delivered;

and the quarter days for the purposes of this subsection are 31st January, 30th April, 31st July and 31st October.

(3) In the case of a person carrying on a trade, profession or business alone or in partnership—

(a) the records required to be kept and preserved under subsection (1) above shall include records of the following, namely—

(i) all amounts received and expended in the course of the trade, profession or business and the matters in respect of which the receipts and expenditure take place, and

(ii) in the case of a trade involving dealing in goods, all sales and purchases of goods made in the course of the trade; and

(b) the duty under that subsection shall include a duty to preserve until the day mentioned in subsection (2) above all supporting documents relating to such items as are mentioned in paragraph (a)(i) or (ii) above.

(4) The duty under subsection (1) above to preserve records may be discharged by the preservation of the information contained in them; and where information is so preserved a copy of any document forming part of the records shall be admissible in evidence in any proceedings before the Commissioners to the same extent as the records themselves.

(5) Any person who fails to comply with subsection (1) above in relation to a year of assessment or accounting period shall be liable to a penalty not exceeding £3,000.

(6) For the purposes of this section—

(a) a person engaged in the letting of property shall be treated as carrying on a trade; and

(b) 'supporting documents' includes accounts, books, deeds, contracts, vouchers and receipts."

GENERAL NOTE

The new s.12B of the TMA 1970 (c. 9) requires taxpayers to keep records to enable them to make complete and correct returns. Trading records are to be kept for six years and other records for one year. The records required include details of all amounts received and expended and, where applicable, details of sales and purchases of goods, together with "all supporting documents". Records may be retained in a different medium from the original documentation. Failure to comply attracts a penalty of up to £3,000.

At Committee Stage, the Government gave an assurance that guidance would be issued so that the taxpayer can be clear about what records to keep to discharge the new duty.

Recovery of overpayment of tax etc.

4.—(1) After subsection (1A) of section 30 of the Management Act (recovery of overpayment of tax etc.) there shall be inserted the following subsection—

"(1B) Subsections (2) to (8) of section 29 of this Act shall apply in relation to an assessment under subsection (1) above as they apply in relation to an assessment under subsection (1) of that section; and subsection (4) of that section as so applied shall have effect as if the reference to the loss of tax were a reference to the repayment of the amount of tax which ought not to have been repaid."

(2) For subsection (5) of that section there shall be substituted the following subsection—

"(5) An assessment under this section shall not be out of time under section 34 of this Act if it is made before the end of whichever of the following ends the later, namely—

(a) the chargeable period following that in which the amount assessed was repaid or paid as the case may be, or

(b) where a return delivered by the person concerned, or an amendment of such a return, is enquired into by an officer of the Board, the period ending with the day on which, by virtue of section 28A(5) of this Act, the officer's enquiries are treated as completed."

GENERAL NOTE

The amendments to s.30 of the TMA 1970 (c. 9) apply the restrictions in s.29(2)–(8) (see the General Note to s.191, *supra*) to the making of an assessment to recover tax over-repaid and extends the period in which such assessments can be raised to the conclusion of an inquiry into a return or an amendment to it.

Assessing procedure

5.—(1) After section 30 of the Management Act there shall be inserted the following section—

"**Assessing procedure**
30A.—(1) Except as otherwise provided, all assessments to tax which are not self-assessments shall be made by an officer of the Board.
(2) All income tax which falls to be charged by an assessment which is not a self-assessment may, notwithstanding that it was chargeable under more than one Schedule, be included in one assessment.
(3) Notice of any such assessment shall be served on the person assessed and shall state the date on which it is issued and the time within which any appeal against the assessment may be made.
(4) After the notice of any such assessment has been served on the person assessed, the assessment shall not be altered except in accordance with the express provisions of the Taxes Acts.
(5) Assessments to tax which under any provision in the Taxes Acts are to be made by the Board shall be made in accordance with this section."
(2) This paragraph, so far as it relates to partnerships whose trades, professions or businesses are set up and commenced before 6th April 1994, has effect as respects the year 1997–98 and subsequent years of assessment.

GENERAL NOTE
The new s.30A of the TMA 1970 (c. 9) provides a procedure based on the existing powers for assessment under the present s.29 to enable the Revenue to raise assessments in future where a self-assessment has not been made. The paragraph does not apply until 1997–1998 for partnerships which commenced before April 6, 1994.

Amendment of partnership statement where loss of tax discovered

6. After section 30A of the Management Act there shall be inserted the following section—

"**Amendment of partnership statement where loss of tax discovered**
30B.—(1) Where an officer of the Board or the Board discover, as regards a partnership statement made by any person (the representative partner) in respect of any period—
(a) that any profits which ought to have been included in the statement have not been so included, or
(b) that an amount of profits so included is or has become insufficient, or
(c) that any relief claimed by the representative partner is or has become excessive,
the officer or, as the case may be, the Board may, subject to subsections (3) and (4) below, by notice to that partner so amend the statement as to make good the omission or deficiency or eliminate the excess.
(2) Where a partnership statement is amended under subsection (1) above, the officer shall by notice to each of the relevant partners so amend their self-assessments under section 9 or 11AA of this Act as to give effect to the amendments of the partnership statement.
(3) Where the situation mentioned in subsection (1) above is attributable to an error or mistake as to the basis on which the partnership statement ought to have been made, no amendment shall be made under that subsection if that statement was in fact made on the basis or in accordance with the practice generally prevailing at the time when it was made.
(4) No amendment shall be made under subsection (1) above unless one of the two conditions mentioned below is fulfilled.
(5) The first condition is that the situation mentioned in subsection (1) above is attributable to fraudulent or negligent conduct on the part of—

(a) the representative partner or a person acting on his behalf, or

(b) a relevant partner or a person acting on behalf of such a partner.

(6) The second condition is that at the time when an officer of the Board—

(a) ceased to be entitled to give notice of his intention to enquire into the representative partner's return under section 12AA of this Act; or

(b) informed that partner that he had completed his enquiries into that return,

the officer could not have been reasonably expected, on the basis of the information made available to him before that time, to be aware of the situation mentioned in subsection (1) above.

(7) Subsections (6) and (7) of section 29 of this Act apply for the purposes of subsection (6) above as they apply for the purposes of subsection (5) of that section; and those subsections as so applied shall have effect as if—

(a) any reference to the taxpayer were a reference to the representative partner;

(b) any reference to the taxpayer's return under section 8, 8A or 11 were a reference to the representative partner's return under section 12AA of this Act; and

(c) sub-paragraph (ii) of paragraph (a) of subsection (7) were omitted.

(8) An objection to the making of an amendment under subsection (1) above on the ground that neither of the two conditions mentioned above is fulfilled shall not be made otherwise than on an appeal against the amendment.

(9) In this section—

'profits' has the same meaning as in section 29 of this Act;

'relevant partner' means a person who was a partner at any time during the period in respect of which the partnership statement was made.

(10) Any reference in this section to the representative partner includes, unless the context otherwise requires, a reference to any successor of his."

GENERAL NOTE

The new s.30B of the TMA 1970 (c. 9) deals with amendments to partnership statements (as to which see the General Note to s.185, *supra*) mainly where a loss of tax or grant of excessive relief has been discovered. The general conditions of the new s.29 apply, *mutatis mutandis* (see the General Note to s.191, *supra*). The commencement provision of para. (5) applies.

Right of appeal

7. For subsections (1) to (3) of section 31 of the Management Act (right of appeal) there shall be substituted the following subsections—

"(1) Subject to subsection (1A) below, an appeal may be brought against—

(a) an amendment under section 28A(2) or (4) of this Act of a self-assessment, or

(b) an amendment under section 28B(3) or 30B(1) of this Act of a partnership statement, or

(c) an assessment to tax which is not a self-assessment,

by a notice of appeal in writing given within 30 days after the date on which the notice of amendment or assessment was issued.

(1A) An appeal against an amendment under subsection (2) of section 28A of this Act of a self-assessment shall not be heard and determined before the officer who made the amendment gives notice under subsection (5) of that section that he has completed his enquiries.

(2) The notice of appeal shall be given to the officer of the Board by whom the notice of amendment or assessment was given.

(3) The appeal shall be to the Special Commissioners if—

(a) the appeal involves any question of the application of any of sections 660 to 685 and 695 to 702 of the principal Act, or

(b) in the case of an appeal against an assessment, the assessment was made by the Board."

GENERAL NOTE

The amendments to s.31 of the TMA 1970 (c. 9) extend the appeal provisions to amendments made by the inspector after carrying out enquiries into a return or partnership statement and discovery amendments to a partnership statement under s.30B and delete references to specific assessments which are henceforth mentioned generically in subs. (1).

Error or mistake

8.—(1) In subsection (1) of section 33 of the Management Act (error or mistake)—

(a) after the words "an assessment" there shall be inserted the words "(whether under section 9 or 11AA of this Act or otherwise)"; and

(b) for the words from "six years" to "made" there shall be substituted the words—

"(a) in the case of an assessment to income tax or capital gains tax, five years after 31st January next following the year of assessment to which the return relates; and

(b) in the case of an assessment to corporation tax, six years after the end of the accounting period to which the return relates,".

(2) The proviso to subsection (2) of that section shall cease to have effect and after that subsection there shall be inserted the following subsection—

"(2A) No relief shall be given under this section in respect of—

(a) an error or mistake as to the basis on which the liability of the claimant ought to have been computed where the return was in fact made on the basis or in accordance with the practice generally prevailing at the time when it was made; or

(b) an error or mistake in a claim which is included in the return."

GENERAL NOTE

The amendments to s.33 of the TMA 1970 (c. 9) extend the relief for error or mistake to self-assessments and tie the period within which claims may be made to the due date for filing returns.

9. After section 33 of the Management Act there shall be inserted the following section—

"Error or mistake in partnership statement

33A.—(1) This section applies where, in the case of a trade, profession or business carried on by two or more persons in partnership, those persons allege that the tax charged by self-assessments of theirs under section 9 or 11AA of this Act was excessive by reason of some error or mistake in a partnership statement.

(2) One of those persons (the representative partner) may, not later than five years after the filing date, by notice in writing make a claim to the Board for relief.

(3) On receiving the claim the Board shall inquire into the matter and shall, subject to subsection (5) below, so amend the partnership statement so as to give such relief in respect of the error or mistake as is reasonable or just.

(4) Where a partnership statement is amended under subsection (3) above, the Board shall by notice to each of the relevant partners so amend their self-assessments under section 9 or 11AA of this Act as to give effect to the amendment of the partnership statement.

(5) No relief shall be given under this section in respect of an error or mistake as to the basis on which the liability of the partners ought to have been computed where the partnership statement was in fact made on the basis or in accordance with the practice generally prevailing at the time when it was made.

(6) In determining the claim the Board—

(a) shall have regard to all the relevant circumstances of the case, and

(b) in particular shall consider whether the granting of relief would result in the exclusion from charge to tax of any part of the profits of any of the partners;

and for the purposes of this subsection the Board may take into consideration the liability of the partners and their self-assessments in respect of chargeable periods other than that to which the claim relates.

(7) If any appeal is brought from the decision of the Board on the claim, the Special Commissioners shall hear and determine the appeal in accordance with the principles to be followed by the Board in determining claims under this section.

(8) Neither the representative partner nor the Board shall be entitled to require a case to be stated under section 56 of this Act otherwise than on a point of law arising in connection with the computation of profits.

(9) In this section—

'filing date' has the same meaning as in section 12AC of this Act;

'profits' has the same meaning as in section 33 of this Act;

'relevant partner' means a person who was a partner at any time during the period in respect of which the partnership statement was made.

(10) Any reference in this section to the representative partner includes, unless the context otherwise requires, a reference to any successor of his."

GENERAL NOTE

The new s.33A of the TMA 1970 (c. 9) enables claims for error or mistake relief to be made in respect of partnership statements (see s.185). The general principles of s.33 apply.

Time limits for assessments

10. In subsection (1) of section 34 of the Management Act (ordinary time limit of six years), for the words from "six years" to the end there shall be substituted the words—
"(a) in the case of an assessment to income tax or capital gains tax, five years after 31st January next following the year of assessment to which it relates; and
(b) in the case of an assessment to corporation tax, six years after the end of the accounting period to which it relates."

11.—(1) In subsection (1) of section 36 of the Management Act (fraudulent or negligent conduct), for the words from "twenty years" to the end there shall be substituted the words—
"(a) in the case of an assessment to income tax or capital gains tax, twenty years after 31st January next following the year of assessment to which it relates; and
(b) in the case of an assessment to corporation tax, twenty-one years after the end of the accounting period to which it relates."
(2) For subsection (2) of that section there shall be substituted the following subsection—
"(2) Where the person in default carried on a trade, profession or business with one or more other persons at any time in the period for which the assessment is made, an assessment in respect of the profits or gains of the trade, profession or business for the purpose mentioned in subsection (1) above may be made not only on the person in default but also on his partner or any of his partners."

12. In subsections (1) and (2) of section 40 of the Management Act (assessments on personal representatives), for the words "the third year next following the year of assessment" there shall be substituted the words "the period of three years beginning with 31st January next following the year of assessment".

GENERAL NOTE

Paras. (10)–(12)
The amendment to s.34 of the TMA 1970 (c. 9) changes the ordinary time-limit for making assessments from six years to five years from the filing date or six years from the end of the accounting period for a company. Similar adjustments are made to the 20 year time-limit in s.36 for assessments in cases of fraud or negligence and the three-year time-limit for assessments on personal representatives.

Claims etc.

13. For section 42 of the Management Act there shall be substituted the following section—

"Procedure for making claims etc.
42.—(1) Where any provision of the Taxes Acts provides for relief to be given, or any other thing to be done, on the making of a claim, this section shall, unless otherwise provided, have effect in relation to the claim.
(2) Subject to subsection (3) below, where notice has been given under section 8, 8A, 11 or 12AA of this Act, a claim shall not at any time be made otherwise than by being included in a return under that section if it could, at that or any subsequent time, be made by being so included.
(3) Subsection (2) above shall not apply in relation to any claim which falls to be taken into account in the making of deductions or repayments of tax under section 203 of the principal Act.
(4) A claim made by a company for payment of a tax credit shall be made by being included in a return under section 11 of this Act.
(5) The references in subsections (2) and (4) above to a claim being included in a return include references to a claim being so included by virtue of an amendment of the return; and the reference in subsection (4) above to a claim for payment includes a reference to a claim resulting in payment.
(6) In the case of a trade, profession or business carried on by persons in partnership, a claim under any of the provisions mentioned in subsection (7) below shall be made—
(a) where subsection (2) above applies, by being included in a return under section 12AA of this Act, and
(b) in any other case, by such one of those persons as may be nominated by them for the purpose.
(7) The provisions are—
(a) sections 84, 91B, 101(2), 120(2), 401, 471, 472, 484, 504, 531, 534, 535, 537A, 538, 570, 571(4), 579(4), 723(3), 732(4), 810 of, and paragraphs 2, 6 and 11 of Schedule 5 to, the principal Act;

(b) section 43(5) of the Finance Act 1989;
(c) sections 1, 11, 17, 22, 23, 24, 25, 30, 31, 33, 37, 48, 49, 53, 55, 68(5), 68(9), 77, 78, 124A, 129(2), 140(3), 141 and 158 of the Capital Allowances Act 1990; and
(d) sections 41 and 42 of the Finance (No. 2) Act 1992.

(8) A claim may be made on behalf of an incapacitated person by his trustee, guardian, tutor or curator; and a person who under Part VIII of this Act has been charged with tax on the profits of another person may make any such claim for relief by discharge or repayment of that tax.

(9) Where a claim has been made (whether by being included in a return under section 8, 8A, 11 or 12AA of this Act or otherwise) and the claimant subsequently discovers that an error or mistake has been made in the claim, the claimant may make a supplementary claim within the time allowed for making the original claim.

(10) This section shall apply in relation to any elections and notices as it applies in relation to claims.

(11) Schedule 1A to this Act shall apply as respects any claim, election or notice which—
(a) is made otherwise than by being included in a return under section 8, 8A, 11 or 12AA of this Act, and
(b) does not fall to be taken into account in the making of deductions or repayments of tax under section 203 of the principal Act.

(12) Schedule 2 to this Act shall have effect as respects the Commissioners to whom an appeal lies under Schedule 1A to this Act.

(13) In this section 'profits'—
(a) in relation to income tax, means income,
(b) in relation to capital gains tax, means chargeable gains, and
(c) in relation to corporation tax, means profits as computed for the purposes of that tax."

14. In subsection (1) of section 43 of the Management Act (time limit for making claims), for the words from "within six years" to the end there shall be substituted the words—
"(a) in the case of a claim with respect to income tax or capital gains tax, within five years from 31st January next following the year of assessment to which it relates; and
(b) in the case of a claim with respect to corporation tax, within six years from the end of the accounting period to which it relates."

15.—(1) In subsection (1) of section 43A of the Management Act (further assessments: claims etc.), for the words "section 29(3) of this Act" there shall be substituted the words "section 29 of this Act".

(2) This paragraph, so far as it relates to partnerships whose trades, professions or businesses are set up and commenced before 6th April 1994, has effect as respects the year 1997–98 and subsequent years of assessment.

GENERAL NOTE

Paras. (13)–(15)
The new s.42 of the TMA 1970 (c. 9) amends the procedure for making claims (to which are added the giving of elections and notices). An important innovation is that claims should be made in returns if that is possible and, if so, may not be made otherwise. A new Sched. 1A (see para. 35, *infra*) deals with claims made otherwise than in a return.
The amendments to ss.43 and 43A are consequential.

Determination of Commissioners

16. In subsection (2) of section 46 of the Management Act (determination of Commissioners), after the words "Save as otherwise provided in the Taxes Acts" there shall be inserted the words "and in particular save as provided by section 29 of this Act".

GENERAL NOTE
The amendment to s.46 of the TMA 1970 (c. 9) expressly draws attention to the provisions contained in the new s.29 (see s.191, *supra*).

Procedure on appeal

17.—(1) For subsections (6) and (7) of section 50 of the Management Act (procedure on appeal) there shall be substituted the following subsections—
"(6) If, on an appeal, it appears to the majority of the Commissioners present at the hearing, by examination of the appellant on oath or affirmation, or by other lawful evidence—

(a) that, by reason of an amendment under section 28A(2) or (4) of this Act, the appellant is overcharged by a self-assessment;

(b) that, by reason of an amendment under section 28B(3) or 30B(1) of this Act, any amounts contained in a partnership statement are excessive; or

(c) that the appellant is overcharged by an assessment other than a self-assessment, the assessment or amounts shall be reduced accordingly, but otherwise the assessment or statement shall stand good.

(7) If, on an appeal, it appears to the Commissioners—

(a) that the appellant is undercharged to tax by a self-assessment which has been amended under section 28A(2) or (4) of this Act;

(b) that any amounts contained in a partnership statement which has been amended under section 28B(3) or 30B(1) of this Act are insufficient; or

(c) that the appellant is undercharged by an assessment other than a self-assessment, the assessment or amounts shall be increased accordingly."

(2) In subsection (8) of that section, after the words "an assessment" there shall be inserted the words "(other than a self-assessment)".

(3) After that subsection there shall be inserted the following subsection—

"(9) Where any amounts contained in a partnership statement are reduced under subsection (6) above or increased under subsection (7) above, an officer of the Board shall by notice to the partners so amend their self-assessment under section 9 or 11AA of this Act as to give effect to the reductions or increases of those amounts."

GENERAL NOTE

The amendments to s.50 of the TMA 1970 (c. 9) introduce provisions relating to appeals to the Commissioners against notices of an amendment to a self-assessment by the Revenue.

Postponement of tax pending appeal

18.—(1) For subsection (1) of section 55 of the Management Act there shall be substituted the following subsection—

"(1) This section applies to an appeal to the Commissioners against—

(a) an amendment made under section 28A(2) or (4) of this Act of a self-assessment,

(b) an assessment to tax made under section 29 of this Act,

(c) an assessment to income tax made under Schedule 16 to the principal Act (income tax on company payments) other than an assessment charging tax the time for the payment of which is given by paragraph 4(1) or 9 of that Schedule, or

(d) a notice under subsection (1) or (3) of section 753 of that Act where, before the appeal is determined, the appellant is assessed to tax under section 747(4)(a) of that Act by reference to an amount of chargeable profits specified in that notice."

(2) In the following provisions of that section, for the word "assessment", in each place where it occurs, there shall be substituted the words "amendment or assessment".

GENERAL NOTE

The amendments to s.55 of the TMA 1970 (c. 9) apply the postponement application rules to an amendment to a self-assessment by the Revenue following an enquiry and remove redundant references to tax charged under different schedules.

Collection and recovery

19.—(1) In subsection (1) of section 65 of the Management Act (magistrates' courts), for paragraphs (a) and (b) and the words "the tax" immediately following those paragraphs there shall be substituted the words "the amount of—

(a) any payment on account for the time being due and payable under section 59A of this Act, or

(b) any income tax and capital gains tax for the time being due and payable under any assessment (whether under section 9 of this Act or otherwise), does not exceed £2,000, the payment of tax".

(2) In subsection (3) of that section, for the words "any tax charged under Schedule E" there shall be substituted the following paragraphs—

"(a) any such payment as is mentioned in subsection (1)(a) above, or

(b) any income tax for the time being due and payable under any assessment under section 9 of this Act,".

20. In section 69 of the Management Act (collection of interest on tax)—

(a) for the words "Interest charged under Part IX of this Act" there shall be substituted the words "A penalty imposed under Part II, VA or X of this Act, a surcharge imposed under Part VA of this Act and interest charged under Part IX of this Act"; and

(b) for the words "if it is interest on tax" there shall be substituted the words "if it is a penalty or surcharge imposed in respect of, or if it is interest on, tax".

21.—(1) In subsection (2) of section 70 of the Management Act (evidence), for the words "that interest is payable" to "another collector" there shall be substituted the words—

"(a) that a penalty under Part II, VA or X of this Act, that a surcharge is payable under Part VA of this Act or that interest is payable under Part IX of this Act, and

(b) that payment of the penalty, surcharge or interest has not been made to him or, to the best of his knowledge and belief, to any other collector or to any person acting on his behalf or on behalf of another collector,".

(2) Subsection (3) of that section shall cease to have effect.

22.—(1) After section 70 of the Management Act there shall be inserted the following section—

"Payments by cheque

70A.—(1) For the purposes of this Act and the provisions mentioned in subsection (2) below, where—

(a) any payment to an officer of the Board or the Board is made by cheque, and

(b) the cheque is paid on its first presentation to the banker on whom it is drawn,

the payment shall be treated as made on the day on which the cheque was received by the officer or the Board.

(2) The provisions are—

(a) sections 824 to 826 of the principal Act (repayment supplements and interest on tax overpaid); and

(b) section 283 of the 1992 Act (repayment supplements)."

(2) This paragraph has effect as respects cheques received on or after 6th April 1996.

GENERAL NOTE

Para. (19)

The amount of tax which may be sued for in the magistrates' courts is increased from £1,000 to £2,000. The one year time-limit is applied generally, not as previously to Sched. E only.

Para. (20)

Section 69 of the TMA 1970 (c. 9), which treats interest as if it were tax for collection and recovery proceedings, is amended to include penalties and surcharge.

Para. (21)

The amendments to s.70 of the TMA 1970 (c. 9) extend the information that can be covered in a collector's certificate of non-payment to include surcharge and penalties as well as interest.

Para. (22)

The new s.70A of the TMA 1970 (c. 9) provides that a payment by cheque is treated as being made when the cheque is received.

Interest on overdue tax or tax recovered

23.—(1) For section 86 of the Management Act there shall be substituted the following section—

"Interest on overdue income tax and capital gains tax

86.—(1) The following, namely—

(a) any amount on account of income tax which on any date becomes due and payable in accordance with section 59A of this Act, and

(b) any income tax or capital gains tax which on any date becomes due and payable in accordance with section 59B(3) or (4) of this Act,

shall carry interest at the rate applicable under section 178 of the Finance Act 1989 from that date until payment.

(2) Any income tax or capital gains tax which becomes due and payable in accordance with section 55 or section 59B(5) or (6) of this Act shall carry interest at the rate applicable under section 178 of the Finance Act 1989 from the relevant date until payment; and in this subsection 'the relevant date' means the date mentioned in section 59B(3) or (4) of this Act.

(3) Subsections (1) and (2) above apply even if the date there mentioned is a non-business day within the meaning of section 93 of the Bills of Exchange Act 1882.

(4) Where as regards a year of assessment—

(a) any person makes a claim under subsection (3) or (4) of section 59A of this Act in respect of both of the amounts (the section 59A amounts) payable by him in accordance with that section, and

(b) an amount (the section 59B amount) becomes payable by him in accordance with section 59B of this Act, or would become so payable but for one or more payments on account made otherwise than under section 59A of this Act,

interest shall be payable under this section as if each of the section 59A amounts had been equal to the aggregate of that amount and 50 per cent. of the section 59B amount, or the amount given by section 59A(2) of this Act, whichever is the less.

(5) Where subsection (4) above applies as regards a year of assessment, so much (if any) of 50 per cent. of the section 59B amount as does not affect the amount of interest payable on either of the section 59A amounts shall be added to 50 per cent. of the section 59B amount for the purpose of determining the amount of interest payable on the other of those amounts.

(6) Where as regards a year of assessment—

(a) any person makes a claim under subsection (3) or (4) of section 59A of this Act in respect of one of the amounts (the section 59A amount) payable by him in accordance with that section, and

(b) an amount (the section 59B amount) becomes payable by him in accordance with section 59B of this Act, or would become so payable but for one or more payments on account made otherwise than under section 59A of this Act,

interest shall be payable under this section as if the section 59A amount had been equal to the aggregate of that amount and the section 59B amount, or the amount given by section 59A(2) of this Act, whichever is the less.

(7) Where as regards a year of assessment—

(a) two amounts (the section 59A amounts) become payable by any person in accordance with section 59A of this Act, and

(b) an amount (the section 59B amount) subsequently becomes repayable to him in accordance with section 59B of this Act,

so much of any interest payable under this section on either of the section 59A amounts as is not attributable to the amount (if any) by which that amount exceeds 50 per cent. of the section 59B amount shall be remitted.

(8) Where subsection (7) above applies, so much (if any) of 50 per cent. of the section 59B amount as does not affect the amount of interest remittable as respects either of the 59A amounts shall be added to 50 per cent. of the section 59B amount for the purpose of determining the amount of interest remittable as respects the other of those amounts.

(9) Where as regards a year of assessment—

(a) a single amount (the section 59A amount) becomes payable by any person in accordance with section 59A of this Act, and

(b) an amount (the section 59B amount) subsequently becomes repayable to him in accordance with section 59B of this Act,

so much of any interest payable under this section on the section 59A amount as is not attributable to the amount (if any) by which that amount exceeds the section 59B amount shall be remitted.

(10) In determining for the purposes of subsections (4) to (9) above the amount which is payable by or repayable to any person in accordance with section 59B of this Act, no account shall be taken of any amount which is payable by him by way of capital gains tax."

(2) This paragraph, so far as it relates to partnerships whose trades, professions or businesses are set up and commenced before 6th April 1994, has effect as respects the year 1997–98 and subsequent years of assessment.

24. In subsection (1) of section 87A of the Management Act (interest on overdue corporation tax etc.) for the words "section 10 of the principal Act" there shall be substituted the words "section 59D of this Act".

GENERAL NOTE

Para. (23)
   The substituted s.86 of the TMA 1970 (c. 9) amends the rules for charging interest on overdue income tax and capital gains tax. Interest will run on interim and balancing payments from the due date until payment. Where tax is postponed under s.55 on an amendment to a self-assessment or an assessment under s.29, interest will normally run from January 31 following the year of assessment. Where a claim to reduce both interim payments is made which is found to be excessive and a balancing payment becomes payable or would have become payable but for being paid previously, interest will run on the amount of interim payment which should have been paid. This is capped at either 50 per cent. of the previous year's liability or the sum of the reduced amount of the interim payment plus 50 per cent. of the balancing payment, whichever is lower.
   Where the two interim payments are unequal amounts and adding 50 per cent. of the balancing payment to one brings it above the cap, the excess of the balancing payment is transferred to the other interim payment. Where a claim to reduce an interim payment is made which is found to be excessive, giving rise to an actual or potential balancing payment, interest runs on the interim payment which should have been made. Where both interim payments have been reduced and there is a balancing repayment due, interest paid on amounts in excess of the interim payments that should have been made will be remitted. The interest position is adjusted where the interim payments are of unequal amounts. Where a claim is made to reduce only one interim payment and there is a repayment due at the balancing payment date interest paid on an amount in excess of the interim payment that should have been made will be remitted.
   Capital gains tax is excluded from the calculation of interest due on unpaid interim payments.

Para. (24)
   The amendment to s.87A of the TMA 1970 (c. 9) follows from the change in reference to the due date for payment of corporation tax from s.10 of the ICTA 1988 (c. 1) to s.59D of the TMA 1970 (c. 9) (see s.195, *supra*).

Penalties

25. For section 93 of the Management Act there shall be substituted the following section—

"Failure to make return for income tax and capital gains tax
   93.—(1) This section applies where—
   (a) any person (the taxpayer) has been required by a notice served under or for the purposes of section 8 or 8A of this Act (or either of those sections as extended by section 12 of this Act) to deliver any return, and
   (b) he fails to comply with the notice.
   (2) The taxpayer shall be liable to a penalty which shall be £100.
   (3) If, on an application made to them by an officer of the Board, the General or Special Commissioners so direct, the taxpayer shall be liable to a further penalty or penalties not exceeding £60 for each day on which the failure continues after the day on which he is notified of the direction (but excluding any day for which a penalty under this subsection has already been imposed).
   (4) If—
   (a) the failure by the taxpayer to comply with the notice continues after the end of the period of six months beginning with the filing date, and
   (b) no application is made under subsection (3) above before the end of that period,
   the taxpayer shall be liable to a further penalty which shall be £100.
   (5) Without prejudice to any penalties under subsections (2) to (4) above, if—
   (a) the failure by the taxpayer to comply with the notice continues after the anniversary of the filing date, and
   (b) there would have been a liability to tax shown in the return,
   the taxpayer shall be liable to a penalty of an amount not exceeding the liability to tax which would have been so shown.
   (6) No penalty shall be imposed under subsection (3) above in respect of a failure at any time after the failure has been remedied.
   (7) If the taxpayer proves that the liability to tax shown in the return would not have exceeded a particular amount, the penalty under subsection (2) above, together with any penalty under subsection (4) above, shall not exceed that amount.
   (8) On an appeal against the determination under section 100 of this Act of a penalty under subsection (2) or (4) above, neither section 50(6) to (8) nor section 100B(2) of this Act shall apply but the Commissioners may—

(a) if it appears to them that, throughout the period of default, the taxpayer had a reasonable excuse for not delivering the return, set the determination aside; or

(b) if it does not so appear to them, confirm the determination.

(9) References in this section to a liability to tax which would have been shown in the return are references to an amount which, if a proper return had been delivered on the filing date, would have been payable by the taxpayer under section 59B of this Act for the year of assessment.

(10) In this section—

'the filing date' meas the day mentioned in section 8(1A) or, as the case may be, section 8A(1A) of this Act;

'the period of default', in relation to any failure to deliver a return, means the period beginning with the filing date and ending with the day before that on which the return was delivered."

26. After section 93 of the Management Act there shall be inserted the following section—

"Failure to make partnership return

93A.—(1) This section applies where, in the case of a trade, profession or business carried on by two or more persons in partnership—

(a) a partner (the representative partner) has been required by a notice served under or for the purposes of section 12AA(2) or (3) of this Act to deliver any return, and

(b) he fails to comply with the notice.

(2) Each relevant partner shall be liable to a penalty which shall be £100.

(3) If, on an application made to them by an officer of the Board, the General or Special Commissioners so direct, each relevant partner shall be liable, for each day on which the failure continues after the day on which the representative partner is notified of the direction (but excluding any day for which a penalty under this subsection has already been imposed), to a further penalty or penalties not exceeding £60.

(4) If—

(a) the failure by the representative partner to comply with the notice continues after the end of the period of six months beginning with the filing date, and

(b) no application is made under subsection (3) above before the end of that period, each relevant partner shall be liable to a further penalty which shall be £100.

(5) No penalty shall be imposed under subsection (3) above in respect of a failure at any time after the failure has been remedied.

(6) Where, in respect of the same failure to comply, penalties under subsection (2), (3) or (4) above are determined under section 100 of this Act as regards two or more relevant partners—

(a) no appeal against the determination of any of those penalties shall be brought otherwise than by the representative partner;

(b) any appeal by that partner shall be a composite appeal against the determination of each of those penalties; and

(c) section 100B(3) of this Act shall apply as if that partner were the person liable to each of those penalties.

(7) On an appeal against a determination under section 100 of this Act of a penalty under subsection (2) or (4) above, neither section 50(6) to (8) nor section 100B(2) of this Act shall apply but the Commissioners may—

(a) if it appears to them that, throughout the period of default, the representative partner had a reasonable excuse for not delivering the return, set the determination aside; or

(b) if it does not so appear to them, confirm the determination.

(8) In this section—

'the filing date' means the day specified in the notice under section 12AA(2) or (3) of this Act;

'the period of default', in relation to any failure to deliver a return, means the period beginning with the filing date and ending with the day before that on which the return was delivered;

'relevant partner' means a person who was a partner at any time during the period in respect of which the return was required."

GENERAL NOTE

Para. (25)

The substituted s.93 of the TMA 1970 (c. 9) provides fixed, daily and tax-geared penalties for failures to make returns under ss.8 and 8A (see s.178, *supra*).

There is a penalty of £100 for failure to deliver a return on time, followed by a further penalty of £60 per day where the Revenue applies to the Commissioners for a direction to this effect. A further penalty of £100 arises six months after the due date. After a year, an additional penalty not exceeding the amount of tax due becomes exigible.

The £60 per day penalty ceases after the return has been delivered. The fixed penalties of £100 are restricted in total to the amount of tax due. The Commissioners may set aside the fixed penalties if the taxpayer shows a reasonable excuse.

Para. (26)
The new s.93A of the TMA 1970 (c. 9) provides fixed and daily penalties for failure to make a partnership return. The fixed penalty of £100 and the daily penalty of £60 apply under the same conditions as in s.93 (see para. 25, *supra*) to each partner. Appeals against penalties may only be brought by the representative partner, *i.e.* the partner required to deliver a return by a notice under s.12AA.

27.—(1) In subsection (1) of section 95 of the Management Act (incorrect return or accounts for income tax or capital gains tax), for the words "section 8 or 8A or 9 of this Act (or any of those sections" there shall be substituted the words "section 8 or 8A of this Act (or either of those sections".

(2) In subsection (3) of that section, the words from "and the references" to the end shall cease to have effect.

28. After section 95 of the Management Act there shall be inserted the following section—

"Incorrect partnership return or accounts
95A.—(1) This section applies where, in the case of a trade, profession or business carried on by two or more persons in partnership—
    (a) a partner (the representative partner)—
        (i) delivers an incorrect return of a kind mentioned in section 12AA of this Act, or
        (ii) makes any incorrect statement or declaration in connection with such a return, or
        (iii) submits to an officer of the Board any incorrect accounts in connection with such a return, and
    (b) either he does so fraudulently or negligently, or his doing so is attributable to fraudulent or negligent conduct on the part of a relevant partner.
(2) Each relevant partner shall be liable to a penalty not exceeding the difference between—
    (a) the amount of income tax or corporation tax payable by him for the relevant period (including any amount of income tax deducted at source and not repayable), and
    (b) the amount which would have been the amount so payable if the return, statement, declaration or accounts made or submitted by the representative partner had been correct;
and in determining each such penalty, regard shall be had only to the fraud or negligence, or the fraudulent or negligent conduct, mentioned in subsection (1)(b) above.
(3) Where, in respect of the same return, statement, declaration or accounts, penalties under subsection (2) above are determined under section 100 of this Act as regards two or more relevant partners—
    (a) no appeal against the determination of any of those penalties shall be brought otherwise than by the representative partner;
    (b) any appeal by that partner shall be a composite appeal against the determination of each of those penalties; and
    (c) section 100B(3) of this Act shall apply as if that partner were the person liable to each of those penalties.
(4) In this section—
    'relevant partner' means a person who was a partner at any time during the relevant period;
    'relevant period' means the period in respect of which the return was made."
29. After section 97 of the Management Act there shall be inserted the following section—

"Failure to produce documents under section 19A
97AA.—(1) Where a person fails to comply with a notice or requirement under section 19A(2) or (3) of this Act, he shall be liable, subject to subsection (4) below—
    (a) to a penalty which shall be £50, and
    (b) if the failure continues after a penalty is imposed under paragraph (a) above, to a further penalty or penalties not exceeding the relevant amount for each day on which

the failure continues after the day on which the penalty under that paragraph was imposed (but excluding any day for which a penalty under this paragraph has already been imposed).

(2) In subsection (1)(b) above 'the relevant amount' means—

(a) in the case of a determination of a penalty by an officer of the Board under section 100 of this Act, £30;

(b) in the case of a determination of a penalty by the Commissioners under section 100C of this Act, £150.

(3) An officer of the Board authorised by the Board for the purposes of section 100C of this Act may commence proceedings under that section for any penalty under subsection (1)(b) above, notwithstanding that it is not a penalty to which subsection (1) of section 100 of this Act does not apply by virtue of subsection (2) of that section.

(4) No penalty shall be imposed under subsection (1) above in respect of a failure within that subsection at any time after the failure has been remedied."

30.—(1) For subsection (2) of section 98B of the Management Act (European Economic Interest Groupings) there shall be substituted the following subsections—

"(2) Subsections (2A) to (4) below apply where a grouping or member of a grouping required by a notice given under section 12A of this Act to deliver a return or other document fails to comply with the notice.

(2A) The grouping or member shall be liable to a penalty not exceeding £300 multiplied by the number of members of the grouping at the time of the failure to comply.

(2B) If, on an application made to them by an officer of the Board, the General or Special Commissioners so direct, the grouping or member shall be liable, for each day on which the failure continues after the day on which the grouping or member is notified of the direction (but excluding any day for which a penalty under this subsection has already been imposed), to a further penalty or penalties not exceeding £60 multiplied by the number of members of the grouping at the end of that day."

(2) In subsection (3) of that section, for the words "subsection (2)" there shall be substituted the words "subsection (2A) or (2B)".

(3) In subsection (4) of that section, for the words "subsection (2)" there shall be substituted the words "subsections (2A) and (2B)".

31.—(1) In subsection (1) of section 100B of the Management Act (appeals against penalty determinations), after the words "subject to" there shall be inserted the words "sections 93, 93A and 95A of this Act".

(2) At the beginning of subsection (2) of that section there shall be inserted the words "Subject to sections 93(8) and 93A(7) of this Act".

32. In subsection (2) of section 103 of the Management Act (time limit for penalties), for the words "the end of the chargeable period" there shall be substituted the words "the 31st January next following the chargeable period".

33. After section 103 of the Management Act there shall be inserted the following section—

"Interest on penalties

103A. A penalty under any of the provisions of Part II or VA or this Part of this Act shall carry interest at the rate applicable under section 178 of the Finance Act 1989 from the date on which it becomes due and payable until payment."

GENERAL NOTE

Para. (27)

The amendments to s.95 of the TMA 1970 (c. 9) remove the reference to partnership returns, which are now catered for by the new s.95A.

Para. (28)

The new s.95A of the TMA 1970 (c. 9) provides a penalty where the representative partner delivers an incorrect partnership return, makes an incorrect statement or declaration or submits incorrect accounts either through his own fraud or negligence or that of one of his partners. Each partner is liable to a penalty up to the amount of his tax underdeclared, but only in respect of his own fraud or negligence. Appeals may only be brought by the representative partner.

Para. (29)

The new s.97AA of the TMA 1970 (c. 9) specifies penalties for failure to provide information required under the new s.19A (see s.187, *supra*). The penalty is set at £50 followed by a daily amount of up to £30, if determined by the inspector, or up to £150 if determined by the commissioners on application by the inspector.

Para. (30)
The amendments to s.98B of the TMA 1970 (c. 9) ensure that penalties charged on a European Economic Interest Grouping are multiplied by the number of members of the grouping.

Para. (31)
The amendments to s.100B of the TMA 1970 (c. 9) are consequential.

Para. (32)
The amendment to s.103 of the TMA 1970 (c. 9) ties the time-limit for penalties on personal representatives in relation to a deceased to the filing date rather than the end of a chargeable period.

Para. (33)
The new s.103A of the TMA 1970 (c. 9) ensures that interest can be charged on penalties as well as on tax and surcharge.

Interpretation

34.—(1) In subsection (1) of section 118 of the Management Act (interpretation), after the definition of "return" there shall be inserted the following definitions—
" 'successor', in relation to a person who has made and delivered a return under section 12AA of this Act, and 'predecessor' and 'successor', in relation to the successor of such a person, shall be construed in accordance with section 12AC(6) of this Act;".
(2) Subsection (3) of that section (effect of assessments in partnership name) shall cease to have effect.
(3) Sub-paragraph (2) above, so far as it relates to partnership whose trades, professions or businesses are set up and commenced before 6th April 1994, has effect as respects the year 1997–98 and subsequent years of assessment.

Claims etc. not included in returns

35. After Schedule 1 to the Management Act there shall be inserted the following Schedule—

"SCHEDULE 1A

CLAIMS ETC. NOT INCLUDED IN RETURNS

Preliminary

1. In this Schedule—
'claim' means a claim, election or notice as respects which this Schedule applies;
'partnership claim' means a claim made in accordance with section 42(6)(b) of this Act;
'profits' has the same meaning as in section 42 of this Act;
'relevant partner', in relation to a partnership claim, means any person who was a partner at any time during the period in respect of which the claim is made;
'successor', in relation to a person who—
(a) has made a partnership claim, but
(b) is no longer a partner or is otherwise no longer available,
means such other partner who may at any time be nominated for the purposes of this paragraph by the majority of the partners at that time, and 'predecessor' and 'successor', in relation to a person so nominated, shall be construed accordingly.

Making of claims

2.—(1) Subject to any provision in the Taxes Acts for a claim to be made to the Board, every claim shall be made to an officer of the Board.
(2) No claim requiring the repayment of tax shall be made unless the claimant has documentary proof that the tax has been paid by deduction or otherwise.
(3) A claim shall be made in such form as the Board may determine.
(4) The form of claim shall provide for a declaration to the effect that all the particulars given in the form are correctly stated to the best of the information and belief of the person making the claim.
(5) The form of claim may require—

(a) a statement of the amount of tax which will be required to be discharged or repaid in order to give effect to the claim;

(b) a return of profits to be made in support of the claim; and

(c) any such particulars of assets acquired as may be required in a return by virtue of section 12 of this Act.

(6) In the case of a claim made by or on behalf of a person who is not resident, or who claims to be not resident or not ordinarily resident or not domiciled, in the United Kingdom, an officer of the Board or the Board may require a statement or declaration in support of the claim to be made by affidavit.

Amendments of claims

3.—(1) Subject to sub-paragraph (2) below—

(a) at any time before the end of the period of nine months beginning with the day on which a claim is made, an officer of the Board may by notice to the claimant so amend the claim as to correct any obvious errors or mistakes in the return (whether errors of principle, arithmetical mistakes or otherwise); and

(b) at any time before the end of the period of twelve months beginning with the day on which the claim is made, the claimant may amend his claim by notice to an officer of the Board.

(2) No amendment of a claim may be made under sub-paragraph (1) above at any time during the period—

(a) beginning with the day on which an officer of the Board gives notice of his intention to enquire into the claim, and

(b) ending with the day on which the officer's enquiries into the claim are completed.

Giving effect to claims and amendments

4.—(1) An officer of the Board or the Board shall, as soon as practicable after a claim other than a partnership claim is made, or such a claim is amended under paragraph 3 above, give effect to the claim or amendment by discharge or repayment of tax.

(2) An officer of the Board or the Board shall, as soon as practicable after a partnership claim is made, or such a claim is amended under paragraph 3 above, give effect to the claim or amendment, as respects each of the relevant partners, by discharge or repayment of tax.

Power to enquire into claims

5.—(1) An officer of the Board may enquire into—

(a) a claim made by any person, or

(b) any amendment made by any person of a claim made by him,

if, before the end of the period mentioned in sub-paragraph (2) below, he gives notice in writing of his intention to do so to that person or, in the case of a partnership claim, any successor of that person.

(2) The period referred to in sub-paragraph (1) above is the period ending with the quarter day next following the first anniversary of the day on which the claim or amendment was made; and the quarter days for the purposes of this subsection are 31st January, 30th April, 31st July and 31st October.

(3) A claim or amendment which has been enquired into under sub-paragraph (1) above shall not be the subject of a further notice under that sub-paragraph.

Power to call for documents for purposes of enquiries

6.—(1) This paragraph applies where an officer of the Board gives notice under paragraph 5 above to any person (the claimant) of his intention to enquire into—

(a) a claim made by the claimant, or

(b) any amendment made by the claimant of such a claim.

(2) For the purpose of enquiring into the claim or amendment, the officer may at the same or any subsequent time by notice in writing require the claimant, within such time (which shall not be less than 30 days) as may be specified in the notice—

(a) to produce to the officer such documents as are in the claimant's possession or power and as the officer may reasonably require for the purpose of determining whether and, if so, the extent to which the claim or amendment is incorrect, and

(b) to furnish the officer with such accounts or particulars as he may reasonably require for that purpose.

(3) Subsections (3) to (11) of section 19A of this Act apply for the purposes of this paragraph as they apply for the purposes of that section; and those subsections as so applied shall have effect as if any reference to subsection (2) of that section were a reference to sub-paragraph (2) above.

(4) Where this paragraph applies in relation to a partnership claim, any reference in this paragraph to the claimant includes a reference to any predecessor or successor of his.

Amendments of claims where enquiries made

7.—(1) This paragraph applies where an officer of the Board gives notice under paragraph 5(1) above to any person (the claimant) of his intention to enquire into—

(a) a claim made by the claimant, or

(b) any amendment made by the claimant of such a claim.

(2) At any time in the period of 30 days beginning with the day on which the officer's enquiries are completed, the claimant may so amend his claim—

(a) as to eliminate or make good any excess or deficiency which, on the basis of the conclusions stated in the officer's notice under sub-paragraph (4) below, is an excess or deficiency which could be made good or eliminated under sub-paragraph (3) below; or

(b) as to give effect to any amendments to the claim which he has notified to the officer.

(3) If, at any time in the period of 30 days beginning immediately after the period mentioned in sub-paragraph (2) above, the officer is of opinion that—

(a) the claimant's claim is excessive or insufficient, and

(b) in a case falling within sub-paragraph (1)(b) above, the excess or deficiency is attributable (wholly or partly) to the claimant's amendment,

the officer may by notice to the claimant so amend the claim as to eliminate or make good the excess or deficiency or, where paragraph (b) above applies, so much of the excess or deficiency as is so attributable.

(4) Subject to sub-paragraph (5) below, the officer's enquiries shall be treated as completed at such time as he by notice—

(a) informs the claimant that he has completed his enquiries, and

(b) states his conclusions as to the amount which should be the amount of the claimant's claim.

(5) Subsections (6) and (7) of section 28A of this Act apply for the purposes of sub-paragraph (4) above as they apply for the purposes of subsection (5) of that section.

(6) Where this paragraph applies in relation to a partnership claim, any reference in this paragraph to the claimant includes a reference to any predecessor or successor of his.

Giving effect to such amendments

8.—(1) An officer of the Board or the Board shall, within 30 days of a claim other than a partnership claim being amended under paragraph 7(2) or (3) above, give effect to the amendment by making such adjustment as may be necessary, whether—

(a) by way of assessment on the claimant, or

(b) by discharge of tax or, on proof to the satisfaction of the officer or the Board that any tax has been paid by the claimant by deduction or otherwise, by repayment of tax.

(2) An officer of the Board or the Board shall, within 30 days of a partnership claim being amended under paragraph 7(2) or (3) above, give effect to the amendment, as respects each of the relevant partners, by making such adjustment as may be necessary, whether—

(a) by way of assessment on the partner, or

(b) by discharge of tax or, on proof to the satisfaction of the officer or the Board that any tax has been paid by the partner by deduction or otherwise, by repayment of tax.

(3) An assessment made under sub-paragraph (1) or (2) above shall not be out of time if it is made within the time mentioned in that sub-paragraph.

Appeals against such amendments

9.—(1) An appeal may be brought against an amendment made under paragraph 7(3) above by giving written notice to the officer within 30 days of the amendment being made.

(2) Where, in the case of such an appeal, the issues arising include—

(a) any question arising under section 278 of the principal Act (personal relief for non-residents);

(b) any question of residence, ordinary residence or domicile; or

(c) the question whether a fund is one to which section 615(3) of that Act applies (pension funds for service abroad), the time for bringing the appeal shall be three months from the making of the amendment under paragraph 7(3) above.

(3) On an appeal under this paragraph, the Commissioners may vary the amendment appealed against whether or not the variation is to the advantage of the appellant.

(4) Where an amendment made under paragraph 7(3) above is varied, whether by the Commissioners or by the order of any court, paragraph 8 above shall (with the necessary modifications) apply in relation to the variation as it applied in relation to the amendment."

GENERAL NOTE

Para. (34)
The amendments to s.118 of the TMA 1970 (c. 9) remove the provision deeming a partnership assessment to be made on the partners for Scottish law purposes and defines the successor of a person who has delivered a partnership return in accordance with s.12AC(5) (see s.186, *supra*).

Para. (35)
The new Sched. 1A to the TMA 1970 (c. 9) concerns claims which are not included in returns. The Revenue can determine the form of a claim and amend it for obvious error within nine months. The claimant may amend it within 12 months, provided an enquiry is not in progress. Claims are to be given effect to as soon as practicable. The Revenue are given similar powers to enquire into claims as they have in relation to returns and also to require the production of documents in this connection. After an inquiry the taxpayer may amend his claim within 30 days, and the Revenue may further amend it within another 30 days. The provisions of s.28A(6), (7) (see s.188, *supra*) apply. The Revenue must give effect to an amended claim within 30 days, even if this is outside normal time-limits. Appeals may be brought against a Revenue amendment of a claim within 30 days, or three months if it concerns certain issues of residence or domicile.

36.—(1) In paragraph 1 of Schedule 2 to the Management Act (jurisdiction in appeals on claims)—
  (a) in sub-paragraph (1), for the words "the decision of an inspector on a claim" there shall be substituted the words "an amendment of a claim"; and
  (b) in sub-paragraphs (1A) and (1B), for the words "the inspector or other officer of the Board" there shall be substituted the words "the officer of the Board".

(2) In paragraph 2 of that Schedule, for the words "from a decision of an inspector on a claim", in both places where they occur, there shall be substituted the words "against an amendment of a claim".

(3) For paragraph 3 of that Schedule there shall be substituted the following paragraph—

"Supplemental

3. Any reference in this Schedule to an amendment of a claim is a reference to such an amendment made under paragraph 6(3) of Schedule 1A to this Act."

GENERAL NOTE
This makes consequential amendments to Sched. 2 to the TMA 1970 (c. 9).

PART II

AMENDMENTS OF TAXES ACT 1988

Time limits for claims under section 96

37.—(1) In subsection (8) of section 96 of the Taxes Act 1988 (farming and market gardening: relief for fluctuating profits)—
  (a) for the words "two years after the end of" there shall be substituted the words "twelve months from 31st January next following"; and
  (b) for the words "before the end of" there shall be substituted the words "before 31st January next following".

(2) This paragraph has effect where the first of the two years of assessment to which the claim relates is the year 1996–97 or any subsequent year.

Interest on Schedule E tax

38. In subsection (2)(dd) of section 203 of the Taxes Act 1988 (PAYE), the words from "(being not less" to "due)" shall cease to have effect.

Time limits for claims under sections 534 and 537A

39. In subsection (5) of section 534 of the Taxes Act 1988 (relief for copyright payments etc.), for the words from "and such a claim" to the end there shall be substituted the words "and such a claim may be made at any time not later than seven years from 31st January next following the year of assessment in which the work's first publication occurs."

40. In subsection (5) of section 537A of the Taxes Act 1988 (relief for payments in respect of designs), for the words from "and such a claim" to "eight years after" there shall be substituted the words "and such a claim may be made at any time not later than seven years from 31st January next following the year of assessment in which".

GENERAL NOTE

Para. (37)
The amendment to s.96 of the ICTA 1988 (c. 1) ties the time-limit for claims to the filing date rather than the end of the year of assessment.

Para. (38)
The removal of the words in brackets from s.203 of the ICTA 1988 (c. 1) permits the removal of the one year period in the PAYE regulations before repayment supplement starts to run on PAYE over-deducted.

Paras. (39) and (40)
The amendments to ss.534 and 537A of the ICTA 1988 (c. 1) tie the time-limit for claims to the filing dates rather than the end of the year of assessment.

Repayment supplements: income tax

41.—(1) For subsection (1) of section 824 of the Taxes Act 1988 (repayment supplements: individuals and others) there shall be substituted the following subsection—
    "(1) Subject to the following provisions of this section, a repayment made by the Board on an officer of the Board of any of the following, namely—
        (a) an amount paid on account of income tax under section 59A of the Management Act;
        (b) any income tax paid by or on behalf of an individual for a year of assessment;
        (c) a surcharge imposed under section 59C of that Act; and
        (d) a penalty incurred by an individual under any of the provisions of that Act,
    shall be increased under this section by an amount (a 'repayment supplement') equal to interest on the amount repaid at the rate applicable under section 178 of the Finance Act 1989 for the period (if any) between the relevant time and the date on which the order for the repayment is issued."
(2) For subsection (3) of that section there shall be substituted the following subsection—
    "(3) For the purposes of subsection (1) above—
        (a) if the repayment is of an amount paid on account of income tax, the relevant time is either the date on which the amount became due and payable in accordance with section 59A of the Management Act or, if later, the date on which the amount was paid;
        (b) if the repayment is of income tax, the relevant time is either 31st January next following the year of assessment for which the tax was charged or, if later, the date on which the tax was paid; and
        (c) if the repayment is of a penalty or surcharge, the relevant time is either the date following the expiry of 30 days from the date on which the penalty or surcharge was incurred or imposed or, if later, the date on which the penalty or surcharge was paid."
(3) The following shall cease to have effect, namely—
(a) subsection (5) of that section;
(b) in subsection (9) of that section the words "a partnership" and the words "(within the meaning of section 111 of the Finance Act 1989)"; and
(c) subsection (10) of that section.
(4) This paragraph, so far as it relates to partnerships whose trades, professions or businesses are set up and commenced before 6th April 1994, has effect as respects the year 1997–98 and subsequent years of assessment.

GENERAL NOTE
The amendments to s.824 of the ICTA 1988 (c. 1) change the repayment supplement rules to remove the time-lag and achieve payment/repayment symmetry. Interest on overpayments to the Revenue will run from the date of payment rather than from up to 12 months later.

Interest on tax overpaid

42. In subsection (2) of section 826 of the Taxes Act 1988 (interest on tax overpaid), for the words "section 10" there shall be substituted the words "action 59D of the Management Act (payment of corporation tax)".

Time limits for elections under Schedule 5

43.—(1) In sub-paragraph (3) of paragraph 2 of Schedule 5 to the Taxes Act 1988 (farming: election for the herd basis), for the words from "not later" to the end there shall be substituted the following paragraphs—

"(a) in the case of an election by a person chargeable to income tax, not later than twelve months from 31st January next following the qualifying year of assessment;

(b) in the case of an election on behalf of persons in partnership, not later than twelve months from 31st January next following the year of assessment in which the qualifying period of account ends; and

(c) in the case of an election by a person chargeable to corporation tax, not later than two years from the end of the qualifying accounting period."

(2) In sub-paragraph (4) of that paragraph, for paragraphs (a) and (b) there shall be substituted the following paragraphs—

"(a) in a case falling within sub-paragraph (3)(a) above, for the qualifying year of assessment and all subsequent years;

(b) in a case falling within sub-paragraph (3)(b) above, for the qualifying period of account and all subsequent periods of account; and

(c) in a case falling within sub-paragraph (3)(c) above, for the qualifying accounting period and all subsequent accounting periods."

(3) After that sub-paragraph there shall be inserted the following sub-paragraphs—

"(5) Where, in a case falling within sub-paragraph (3)(a) above, the commencement year immediately precedes the qualifying year of assessment, sub-paragraph (4)(a) above shall have effect as if the reference to the qualifying year of assessment were a reference to the commencement year.

(6) In this paragraph—

'commencement year', in relation to a person chargeable to income tax, means the year of assessment in which his trade is set up and commenced;

'period of account', in relation to persons in partnership, means any period for which accounts are drawn up;

'qualifying accounting period', in relation to a person chargeable to corporation tax, means the first accounting period during the whole or part of which it kept a production herd of the class in question;

'qualifying period of account', in relation to persons in partnership, means the first period of account during the whole or part of which those persons kept such a herd;

'qualifying year of assessment', in relation to a person chargeable to income tax, means the first year of assessment after the commencement year for which the amount of profits or gains or losses in respect of his farming is computed for tax purposes by reference to the facts of a period during the whole or part of which he kept such a herd."

(4) In paragraph 6 of that Schedule, for sub-paragraphs (2) to (4) there shall be substituted the following sub-paragraphs—

"(2) An election for the herd basis made by virtue of sub-paragraph (1) above shall only be valid if made—

(a) in the case of an election by a person chargeable to income tax, not later than twelve months from January 31 next following the qualifying year of assessment;

(b) in the case of an election on behalf of persons in partnership, not later than twelve months from January 31 next following the year of assessment in which the qualifying period of account ends; and

(c) in the case of an election by a person chargeable to corporation tax, not later than two years from the end of the qualifying accounting period."

(3) An election for the herd basis made by virtue of sub-paragraph (1) above shall, notwithstanding paragraph 2(4) above, have effect—

(a) in a case falling within sub-paragraph (2)(a) above, for the qualifying year of assessment and all subsequent years;

(b) in a case falling within sub-paragraph (2)(b) above, for the qualifying period of account and all subsequent periods of account; and

(c) in a case falling within sub-paragraph (2)(c) above, for the qualifying accounting period and all subsequent accounting periods."
(4) In this paragraph—
'period of account', in relation to persons in partnership, means any period for which accounts are drawn up;
'qualifying accounting period', in relation to a person chargeable to corporation tax, means the first accounting period in which the compensation is relevant;
'qualifying period of account', in relation to persons in partnership, means the first period of account in which the compensation is relevant;
'qualifying year of assessment', in relation to a person chargeable to income tax, means the first year of assessment for which the amount of profits or gains or losses in respect of his farming falls to be computed for tax purposes by reference to the facts of a period in which the compensation is relevant."

GENERAL NOTE

Para. (42)
The amendment to s.826 of the ICTA 1988 (c. 1) is consequent on the moving of the rules for payment of corporation tax from s.10 of the ICTA 1988 (c. 1) (which is repealed) to the new s.59D of the TMA 1970 (c. 9) (see s.195, *supra*).

Para. (43)
The amendments to Sched. 5 to the ICTA 1988 (c. 1), which deal with elections for the herd basis for farm animals, tie the time-limits within which elections can be made to the filing date rather than the end of the year of assessment.

PART III

AMENDMENTS OF OTHER ENACTMENTS

Setting of rates of interest

44. In subsection (2)(f) of section 178 of the Finance Act 1989 (setting of rates of interest), for the words "sections 86, 86A, 87, 87A, and 88" there shall be substituted the words "sections 59C, 86, 86A, 87, 87A, 88 and 103A".

Class 4 contributions

45. In subsection (1) of section 16 of the Social Security Contributions and Benefits Act 1992 (application of Income Tax Acts to class 4 contributions), for paragraph (b) there shall be substituted the following paragraph—
"(b) the provisions of Part VA (payment of tax) and Part X (penalties) of the Taxes Management Act 1970,".

Repayment supplements: capital gains tax

46.—(1) In subsection (1) of section 283 of the Taxation of Chargeable Gains Act 1992 (repayment supplements)—
(a) for the words from "for which" to "that year of assessment" there shall be substituted the words "a repayment of that tax is made by the Board or an officer of the Board", and
(b) for the words "the end of the tax month in which" there shall be substituted the words "the date on which".
(2) For subsection (2) of that section there shall be substituted the following subsection—
"(2) For the purposes of subsection (1) above, the relevant time is either 31st January next following the year of assessment for which the tax was payable or, if later, the date on which the tax was paid."
(3) In subsection (4) of that section, for the words from "partnership" to "section 701(9) of that Act)" there shall be substituted the words "trust or".
(4) Subsection (5) of that section shall cease to have effect.

GENERAL NOTE

Para. (44)
The amendment to the FA 1989 (c. 26), s.178, which deals with the setting of interest rates by a formula under statutory instrument, extends its scope to cover interest on the new charges which have been introduced.

Para. (45)

The amendment to the Social Security Contributions and Benefits Act 1992 (c. 4) makes it clear that a surcharge can be imposed on late payment of Class 4 National Insurance contributions as well as on late payment of income tax, with which they are collected.

Para. (46)

The amendments to s.283 of the TCGA 1992 (c. 12), which provides for the payment of a repayment supplement on repayments of capital gains tax, bring it into line with the new repayment supplement rules for income tax. The requirement for U.K. residence is also removed for repayment supplement to individuals or trusts.

Section 218   SCHEDULE 20

CHANGES FOR FACILITATING SELF-ASSESSMENT: TRANSITIONAL PROVISIONS AND SAVINGS

Assessment under Cases I and II of Schedule D

1.—(1) Subject to paragraph 3(2) below, this paragraph applies in the case of a trade, profession or vocation set up and commenced before 6th April 1994 and continuing after 5th April 1997.

(2) The basis period for the year 1996–97 shall be as follows—

(a) where an accounting date falls within the year, the period of twelve months ending with that accounting date; and

(b) in any other case, the period of twelve months ending with 5th April 1997.

(3) Where the basis period for the year 1996–97 is given by paragraph (b) of sub-paragraph (2) above, section 62 of the Taxes Act 1988 shall have effect in relation to the accounting change by virtue of which that paragraph applies as if that change were made in the first year of assessment in which accounts are made up to the new date.

(4) In this paragraph "accounting date" and "the new date" have the same meanings as in section 62 of the Taxes Act 1988.

2.—(1) Subject to paragraph 3(2) and (4) below, this paragraph applies in the case of a trade, profession or vocation set up and commenced before 6th April 1994 and continuing after 5th April 1997.

(2) Subject to sub-paragraph (3) below, sections 60 to 63A of the Taxes Act 1988 shall have effect in relation to the year 1996–97 as if they required income tax under Case I or II of Schedule D to be charged on the appropriate percentage of the aggregate of—

(a) the full amount of the profits or gains of the basis for that year, and

(b) the full amount of the profits or gains of the relevant period.

(3) Where, in the case of the year 1995–96, the period on the profits or gains of which income tax is chargeable under Case I or II of Schedule D is that year, sub-paragraph (2) above shall have effect as if for the words from "the appropriate percentage" to the end there were substituted the words "the full amount of the profits or gains of that year".

(4) Section 63A of the Taxes Act 1988 shall have effect as if the amount of profits or gains of the basis period for the year 1997–98 which arise before 6th April 1997 were an overlap profit for the purposes of that section.

(5) In this paragraph—

"the appropriate percentage" means the following expressed as a percentage, that is, 365 divided by the number of days in the basis period for the year 1996–97 and the relevant period taken together;

"the relevant period" means the period which—

(a) begins immediately after the end of the period on the profits or gains of which tax is chargeable for the year 1995–96, and

(b) ends immediately before the beginning of the basis period for the year 1996–97.

3.—(1) In the case of a trade, profession or vocation set up and commenced before 6th April 1994 and ceasing before 6th April 1997, sections 60 to 63 of the Taxes Act 1988 shall have effect as if sections 200 to 205 of this Act had not been enacted.

(2) If, in the case of a trade, profession or vocation set up and commenced before 6th April 1994 and ceasing on or after 6th April 1997 but before 6th April 1998, an officer of the Board so directs—

(a) paragraphs 1 and 2 above shall not apply, and

(b) sections 60 to 63 of the Taxes Act 1988 shall have effect as if sections 200 to 205 of this Act had not been enacted.

(3) Sub-paragraph (4) below applies where, in the case of a trade, profession or vocation set up and commenced before 6th April 1994 and ceasing on or after 6th April 1998 but before 6th April 1999, the profits or gains arising in the year 1996–97 exceed—

(a) the amount on which income tax has been charged for that year; or

(b) the amount on which income tax would have been charged for that year if no deduction or set-off under section 385 of the Taxes Act 1988 had been allowed.

(4) Notwithstanding anything in sections 60 to 63A of the Taxes Act 1988, if an officer of the Board so directs, income tax for the year 1996–97 shall be charged instead, but subject to any deduction or set-off under section 385 of that Act, on the amount of the profits or gains arising in that year.

(5) All such adjustments shall be made, whether by way of an assessment to tax or a reduction or discharge of such an assessment or otherwise, as may be necessary to give effect to a direction under sub-paragraph (2) or (4) above.

Assessment under Case III of Schedule D

4.—(1) Subject to sub-paragraph (3) below, this paragraph applies in the case of income which—

(a) is from a source arising before 6th April 1994 and continuing after 5th April 1998, and

(b) is chargeable to tax under Case III of Schedule D.

(2) Section 64 of the Taxes Act 1988 shall have effect in relation to the year 1996–97 as if it required income tax under Case III of Schedule D to be computed on 50 per cent. of the aggregate of—

(a) the full amount of the income arising within that year; and

(b) the full amount of the income arising within the year 1995–96.

(3) This paragraph does not apply if section 66(1)(c) of that Act applied in relation to the year 1995–96.

5. In the case of income which—

(a) is from a source arising before 6th April 1994 and ceasing before 6th April 1998, and

(b) is chargeable to tax under Case III of Schedule D,

sections 64, 66–67 of the Taxes Act 1988 shall have effect as if section 206 of this Act had not been enacted.

GENERAL NOTE

Para. (1)

The basis period for 1996–1997, for businesses in existence at April 5, 1994 and which continue after April 5, 1997, is the 12 months to the date in 1996–1997 to which the accounts are drawn up or, if there is no such date, the tax year 1996–1997.

Para. (2)

The assessment for 1996–1997, for businesses falling within para. 1 above, will be based on the "appropriate percentage" of the total of: (i) the profits (calculated under the new ICTA 1988 (c. 1), ss.60–63A) for the basis period (determined under para. 1 above) and (ii) the profits of the relevant period. If the profits for 1995–1996 were assessed on an actual basis, the assessment for 1996–1997 will be based on the profits of the tax year (apportioning accounts profits as appropriate).

Para. (3)

If a business in existence at April 5, 1994 ceases before April 6, 1997, the old rules in the ICTA 1988 (c. 1), s.63(1) will determine the assessment for 1996–1997. Adjustments may also be made to 1994–1995 and 1995–1996. If the cessation occurs in 1997–1998, the tax for 1996–1997 is calculated applying the transitional rules in para. 2 above initially, but the Revenue may apply the old rules in the ICTA 1988 (c. 1), ss.60–63 if this results in higher assessable profits for 1995–1996 and 1996–1997. If the cessation occurs in 1998–1999, the Revenue may assess the profits for 1996–1997 on an actual basis instead of under the rules in para. 2 above, if this results in higher assessable profits for 1996–1997.

Paras. (4)–(5)

If the Sched. D, Case III income source first arose before April 6, 1994 and continues beyond April 5, 1998, the year 1996–1997 is to be assessed on half the aggregate of the full amount of the income arising in 1995–1996 and 1996–1997. If 1995–1996 was assessed on an actual basis, 1996–1997 is also assessed on an actual basis. If the source ceases before April 6, 1998, the old rules in the ICTA 1988 (c. 1), ss.60–63 apply throughout. The Revenue may assess the penultimate year on an actual basis if this yields higher chargeable income.

Assessment under Cases IV and V of Schedule D

6.—(1) This paragraph applies in the case of income which—
  (a) is from a source arising before 6th April 1994 and continuing after 5th April 1998, and
  (b) is chargeable to tax under Case IV or V of Schedule D.
  (2) Subject to sub-paragraph (3) below, section 65 of the Taxes Act 1988 shall have effect in relation to the year 1996–97 as if—
  (a) subsection (1) required income tax chargeable under Case IV or V of Schedule D to be computed on 50 per cent. of the aggregate of—
      (i) the full amount of the income arising within that year; and
      (ii) the full amount of the income arising within the year 1995–96,
  subject (in either case) to the deductions and allowances there mentioned in the case of income not received in the United Kingdom;
  (b) paragraph (a) of subsection (5) required income tax chargeable under Case IV of Schedule D to be computed on 50 per cent. of the aggregate of—
      (i) the full amount, so far as it can be computed, of the sums received in the United Kingdom in that year; and
      (ii) the full amount, so far as it can be computed, of the sums received in the United Kingdom in the year 1995–96,
  without (in either case) any deduction or abatement; and
  (c) paragraph (b) of that subsection required income tax chargeable under Case V of Schedule D to be computed on 50 per cent. of the aggregate of—
      (i) the full amount of the actual sums received in the United Kingdom in that year; and
      (ii) the full amount of the actual sums received in the United Kingdom in the year 1995–96,
  without (in either case) any deduction or abatement other than as there mentioned.
  (3) Sub-paragraph (2) above does not apply if section 66(1)(c) of that Act applied in relation to the year 1995–96.
  (4) Section 63A of the Taxes Act 1988 (as applied by section 65(3) of that Act) shall have effect as if the amount of profits or gains of the basis period for the year 1997–98 which arise before 6th April 1997 were an overlap profit for the purposes of that section.
  7. In the case of income which—
  (a) is from a source arising before 6th April 1994 and ceasing before 6th April 1998, and
  (b) is chargeable to tax under Case IV or V of Schedule D,
sections 65 to 68 of that Act shall have effect as if section 207 of this Act and its associated repeals had not been enacted.

Loss relief

8. Sections 380(1) and 574(1) of the Taxes Act 1988 (as substituted by sections 209(1) and 210(1) of this Act) shall have effect as respects the years 1994–95 and 1995–96 as if for the words "twelve months from 31st January next following" there were substituted the words "two years after".

Capital allowances

9.—(1) This paragraph applies in the case of a trade, profession or vocation set up and commenced before 6th April 1994 and continuing after 5th April 1997.
  (2) Section 140 of the Capital Allowances Act 1990 shall have effect as if the allowances which fall to be made in taxing the trade, profession or vocation for the first period of account ending after 5th April 1997 under the provisions of that Act as they apply for the purposes of income tax included any allowance or part of any allowance—

(a) which falls to be made in taxing the trade, profession or vocation for the year 1996–97, or is carried forward to that year from a previous year of assessment, and

(b) to which full effect cannot be given in the year 1996–97.

GENERAL NOTE

Paras. (6)–(7)
These paragraphs contain the transitional provisions for Sched. D, Cases IV and V income, where the source first arose before April 6, 1994 and continues beyond April 5, 1998. The rules follow closely those applicable to Case III income (see paras. 4–5 above), with adjustments for the remittance basis for non-U.K. domiciled residents.

Para. (8)
This ensures that the time-limit for loss relief claims for losses sustained in 1994–1995 and 1995–1996 remains two years from the end of the tax year.

Para. (9)
Unrelieved capital allowances for 1996–1997 or earlier years, which are carried forward under the CAA 1990 (c. 1), s.140(4), are treated as newly due for the first period of account ending after April 5, 1997. This ensures that they may be carried forward as losses of the trade, if still unrelieved in 1997–1998.

Double taxation relief

10.—(1) Subject to paragraph 12(2) below, this paragraph applies in the case of—

(a) a trade, profession or vocation set up and commenced before 6th April 1994 and continuing after 5th April 1998; or

(b) income from a source arising before the former date and continuing after the latter date.

(2) Subject to sub-paragraph (3) below, the amount of foreign tax to be taken into account in determining whether and, if so what credit is allowable under Part XVIII of the Taxes Act 1988 against income tax which, in respect of income from any source, is chargeable under Case I or II of Schedule D for the year 1996–97 shall be the appropriate percentage of the aggregate of—

(a) the amount of foreign tax paid on income from that source arising in the basis period for that year, and

(b) the amount of foreign tax paid on income from that source arising in the relevant period.

(3) Where the period on the profits or gains of which income tax is chargeable under Case I or II of Schedule D for the year 1995–96 is that year, sub-paragraph (2) above shall have effect as if for the words from "the appropriate percentage" to the end there were substituted the words "the amount of foreign tax paid on income arising in that year".

(4) Where—

(a) the amount of the profits or gains on which income tax is chargeable under Case I or II of Schedule D for the year 1996–97 is given by paragraph 2(2) above, and

(b) that amount includes income from any source in respect of which credit is allowable under Part XVIII of the Taxes Act 1988,

the amount of income from that source to be taken into account in determining what credit is so allowable shall be the appropriate percentage of the aggregate of the full amount of the income of the basis period for that year and the full amount of the income of the relevant period.

(5) The amount of foreign tax to be taken into account in determining whether and, if so, what credit is allowable under Part XVIII of the Taxes Act 1988 against income tax which, in respect of income from any source, is chargeable for the year 1996–97 under Case IV or V of Schedule D shall be 50 per cent. of the aggregate of—

(a) the amount of foreign tax paid on income from that source arising, or (as the case may require) received in the United Kingdom, in that year; and

(b) the amount of foreign tax paid on income from that source arising, or (as the case may require) received in the United Kingdom, in the year 1995–96.

(6) In this paragraph—

"the appropriate percentage" and "the relevant period" have the same meanings as in paragraph 2 above;

"double taxation arrangements" means arrangements having effect by virtue of section 788 of the Taxes Act 1988;

"foreign tax" means tax chargeable under the law of a territory outside the United Kingdom for which credit may be allowed under double taxation arrangements or section 790(1) of that Act.

11.—(1) Subject to paragraph 12(2) below, this paragraph applies in the case of—

(a) a trade, profession or vocation set up and commenced before 6th April 1994 and continuing after 5th April 1998; or

(b) income from a source arising before the former date and continuing after the latter date.

(2) Sub-paragraph (3) below applies where—

(a) credit against income tax for the year 1995–96 or any earlier year of assessment is or has been allowed by virtue of subsection (1) of section 804 of the Taxes Act 1988 in respect of any income ("the original income"), and

(b) the source of that income ceases in a subsequent year of assessment ("the subsequent year").

(3) The following shall be set off one against the other, namely—

(a) the amount of the credit which, under Part XVIII of the Taxes Act 1988 (including section 804), has been allowed against income tax in respect of the original income, and

(b) the aggregate of—

    (i) the amount of the credit which, apart from that section, would have been so allowed, and

    (ii) the difference between the amount of the credit which, on the assumptions mentioned in sub-paragraph (4) below, would have been allowed under Part XVIII of that Act for the year 1996–97 and the amount of credit which has been so allowed;

and if the amount given by paragraph (a) exceeds that given by paragraph (b) above, the person chargeable in respect of income (if any) arising in the subsequent year from the same source as the original income shall be treated as having received in that year a payment chargeable under Case VI of Schedule D of an amount such that income tax on it at the basic rate is equal to the excess.

(4) The assumptions are—

(a) that the words "the appropriate percentage of" were omitted from paragraph 2(2) above;

(b) that the words "50 per cent. of" were omitted from paragraphs (a), (b) and (c) of paragraph 6(2) above; and

(c) that paragraph 10 above had not been enacted.

(5) Where the period on the income of which income tax is chargeable for the year 1996–97 is that year, sub-paragraph (3) above shall have effect as if for paragraph (b) there were substituted the following paragraph—

"(b) the amount of the credit which, apart from that section, would have been so allowed;".

(6) Any reference in sub-paragraph (2) or (3) above to section 804 or Part XVIII of the Taxes Act 1988 includes a reference to the corresponding provisions of any earlier enactments.

(7) Any payment which a person is treated by virtue of sub-paragraph (3) above as having received shall not on that account constitute income of his for any of the purposes of the Income Tax Acts other than that sub-paragraph and in particular no part of it shall constitute profits or gains brought into charge to income tax for the purposes of section 348 of the Taxes Act 1988.

12.—(1) In the case of—

(a) a trade, profession or vocation set up and commenced before 6th April 1994 and ceasing before 6th April 1998, being a trade, profession or vocation in respect of which a direction has been given under paragraph 3(2) above, or

(b) income from a source arising before the former date and ceasing before the latter date, being income to which paragraph 7 above applies,

section 804 of the Taxes Act 1988 shall have effect as if section 217 of this Act and its associated repeals had not been enacted.

(2) In the case of a trade, profession or vocation set up and commenced before 6th April 1994 and ceasing on or after 6th April 1998 but before 6th April 1999, being a trade, profession or vocation in respect of which a direction has been given under paragraph 3(4) above—

(a) paragraphs 10 and 11 above shall not apply, and

(b) section 804 of the Taxes Act 1988 shall have effect as if section 217 of this Act and its associated repeals had not been enacted.

13. Paragraphs 2(2) and 6(2) above shall have effect as if any reference to the full amount of any profits or gains, or the full amount of any income, were a reference to that amount after any reduction which is treated as made by section 811 of the Taxes Act (deduction for foreign tax where no credit allowable).

Supplemental

14.—(1) In this Schedule—

(a) any reference to a source of income arising before any date ("the earlier date") and continuing after or ceasing before some other date ("the later date") is a reference to a source of income arising to any person before the earlier date and continuing to be possessed by that person after, or (as the case may be) ceasing to be possessed by that person before, the later date; and

(b) any reference to a source of income includes a reference to a part of such a source.

(2) Where, as respects income from any source, income tax is to be charged under Case IV or V of Schedule D by reference to the amounts of income received in the United Kingdom, the source shall be treated for the purposes of this Schedule as arising on the date on which the first amount of income is so received.

GENERAL NOTE

Para. (10)

The foreign tax credit for 1996–1997 for Case I profits, which first arose before April 6, 1994 and continued beyond April 6, 1998 is limited to half the aggregate of the foreign tax paid on income arising in 1995–1996 and 1996–1997. If the profits for 1995–1996 were assessed on a current year basis, the foreign tax credit for 1996–1997 is the amount of foreign tax paid in respect of 1996–1997 income. The foreign tax credit for 1996–1997 for Sched. D, Cases IV and V income where the source first arose before April 6, 1994 and continues beyond April 6, 1998, is half the aggregate of the foreign tax paid on income arising or remitted in 1995–1996 and 1996–1997.

Para. (11)

This ensures that excess foreign tax credit, which has been allowed more than once under the opening provisions under the old rules, may be clawed back on a cessation.

Para. (12)

Where a source for which double tax credit is given ceases before April 6, 1998 or in 1998–1999 and the Revenue has directed under para. 3(2) or (4) above that the actual basis should apply, the old rules for calculating the excess foreign tax credit apply for 1996–1997.

Para. (13)

Where the foreign tax is allowed as an expense instead of as a credit, the transitional calculations are made on the net amount.

Section 228   SCHEDULE 21

LLOYD'S UNDERWRITERS: INDIVIDUALS

Year of assessment in which profits or losses arise

1.—(1) After subsection (2) of section 171 of the 1993 Act (taxation of profits and allowance of losses) there shall be inserted the following subsection—

"(2A) Where the profits arising for any year of assessment from the assets of a member's premiums trust fund include dividends which are foreign income dividends for the purposes of Chapter VA of the Taxes Act 1988, subsection (2) above shall apply in relation to the actual amount of those dividends notwithstanding anything in section 246D of that Act."

(2) Subsection (3) of that section shall cease to have effect.

(3) In this paragraph—

(a) sub-paragraph (1) has effect for the year 1992–93 and subsequent years of assessment; and

(b) sub-paragraph (2) has effect for the year 1996–97 and subsequent years of assessment.

2.—(1) In subsection (1) of section 172 of the 1993 Act (year of assessment in which profits or losses arise), for paragraphs (a) and (b) there shall be substituted the following paragraphs—

"(a) in the case of profits or losses arising directly from his membership of one or more syndicates, those of any previous year or years which are declared in the corresponding underwriting year;

(b) in the case of profits or losses arising from assets forming part of a premiums trust fund, those allocated under the rules or practice of Lloyd's to any previous year or years the profits or losses of which are declared in the corresponding underwriting year; and".

(2) Sub-paragraph (1) above does not have effect for the years 1994–95, 1995–96 and 1996–97, but in relation to those years that section shall have effect as if paragraphs (a) and (b) of subsection (1) were omitted.

Premiums trust funds

3. For subsection (1) of section 174 of the 1993 Act (premiums trust funds) there shall be substituted the following subsection—

"(1) For the purposes of the Income Tax Acts and the Gains Tax Acts—

(a) a member shall be treated as absolutely entitled as against the trustees to the assets forming part of a premiums trust fund of his; and

(b) where a deposit required by a regulatory authority in a country or territory outside the United Kingdom is paid out of such a fund, the money so paid shall be treated as still forming part of that fund."

Reinsurance to close

4.—(1) After subsection (4) of section 177 of the 1993 Act (reinsurance to close) there shall be inserted the following subsection—

"(5) This section also applies in any case where the member to whom the premium is payable is a corporate member within the meaning of Chapter V of Part IV of the Finance Act 1994."

(2) This paragraph has effect for the underwriting year 1993 and subsequent underwriting years.

Stop-loss and quota share insurance

5.—(1) In subsection (2) of section 178 of the 1993 Act (stop-loss and quota share insurance)—

(a) for the word "him" there shall be substituted the words "a member"; and

(b) for the word "arose" there shall be substituted the words "was declared".

(2) This paragraph has effect as respects insurance money and other amounts payable in respect of losses declared in the underwriting year 1997 or subsequent underwriting years.

Cessation etc.

6.—(1) In section 179 of the 1993 Act (cessation: final year of assessment), subsection (3) and, in subsection (2), the words "to subsection (3) below and" shall cease to have effect.

(2) After that section there shall be inserted the following section—

"**Death of member**

179A.—(1) This section applies where a member ceases to carry on his underwriting business by reason of death.

(2) For the purposes of assessing the profits of the member's underwriting business, the member shall be treated as having died at the end of the year of assessment which corresponds to the underwriting year immediately preceding that in which he actually died.

(3) For the purposes of the Income Tax Acts—

(a) the carrying on of the member's underwriting business by his personal representatives shall not be treated as a change in the persons engaged in the carrying on of that business; and

(b) subject to the provisions of any regulations made by the Board, the business shall be treated as continuing until the member's deposit at Lloyd's is paid over to his personal representatives."

(3) This paragraph has effect in any case where the member dies after the end of the year 1993–94.

Regulations

7.—(1) In section 182 of the 1993 Act (regulations), subsections (2) to (4) shall cease to have effect.

(2) This paragraph has effect for the year 1997–98 and subsequent years of assessment.

Interpretation

8.—(1) In subsection (1) of section 184 of the 1993 Act (interpretation and commencement)—

(a) in the definition of "ancillary trust fund", the words "or the managing agent of a syndicate of which he is a member" shall cease to have effect; and

(b) in the definition of "member", for the words "a member of Lloyd's who" there shall be substituted the words "an individual who is a member of Lloyd's and".

(2) In subsection (2)(c) of that section, for the word "agent", in both places where it occurs, there shall be substituted the words "managing agent".

GENERAL NOTE
   This Schedule makes changes to the tax regime for individual underwriters at Lloyd's consequent to the move to a distribution year basis and the acceptance of corporate members. It also clarifies some aspects of the legislation in the FA 1993 (c. 34).

Para. (1)
   Where foreign income dividends are included in the profits from a member's premium trust fund assets, only the actual amount of the dividend is brought into charge. The paragraph also removes, from 1996–1997 onwards, a provision that allowed members to claim relief for Lloyd's losses against other income of the year of assessment before the loss arose.

Para. (2)
   This paragraph changes the definition of when profits arise to members and sets out the dates from which the changes are to take effect. The profits or losses of a year of assessment arising directly from syndicate membership or from assets forming part of a premiums trust fund are to be determined by reference to the profits declared in the underwriting year that ends in the year of assessment. Thus, the results of the underwriting year 1994, which will not be declared until June 1997, instead of being taxed at the tax rates prevailing in 1994, will be taxed at the rates prevailing in 1997.

Para. (3)
   Assets in a member's premiums trust fund used to satisfy regulatory requirements in other countries are to be treated as still being part of the fund.

Para. (4)
   The reinsurance to close provisions of the FA 1993 (c. 34), s.177 are amended to allow their application where the premium is payable to a corporate member.

Para. (5)
   Minor changes are made to the FA 1993 (c. 34), s.178 to reflect corporate membership of Lloyd's and the change to the distribution year basis.

Para. (6)
   The new s.179A of the FA 1993 (c. 34) amends the provisions concerning the death of a member after April 5, 1994:
   (i) for the purpose of assessing profits, the date of death is the end of the year of assessment that corresponds to the underwriting year immediately preceding the underwriting year in which the member dies;
   (ii) the business is treated as continuing until his deposit is paid over to his personal representatives;
   (iii) after his death, the business is treated as being continued without change in the persons engaged in it.
   The second provision is subject to regulations by the Revenue.

Para. (7)
   Regulation-making powers which are otiose with the move to a distribution year basis are removed.

Para. (8)
   A fund required by a managing agent is removed from the definition of ancillary trust fund.

Assessment and collection of tax

9.—(1) In Schedule 19 to the 1993 Act (assessment and collection of tax), in sub-paragraph (1) of paragraph 2 (returns by managing agent), for the words "after the end of the closing year for a year of assessment" there shall be substituted the words "after the beginning of a year of assessment".
   (2) In sub-paragraph (2) of that paragraph, for the words "the 1st September next following the end of the closing year for the year of assessment" there shall be substituted the words "1st September in the year of assessment".
   (3) This paragraph has effect for the year 1997–98 and subsequent years of assessment.

10. Part II of that Schedule (payments on account of tax) shall cease to have effect.

11.—(1) After sub-paragraph (3) of paragraph 13 of that Schedule (repayment of tax deducted etc. from investment income) there shall be inserted the following sub-paragraph—

"(3A) For the purposes of this paragraph a member who is not resident in the United Kingdom shall be treated as entitled to all such tax credits in respect of qualifying distributions as he would be entitled to if he were so resident."

(2) After sub-paragraph (4) of that paragraph there shall be inserted the following sub-paragraph—

"(4A) Where any payment of a tax credit is made under sub-paragraph (1)(b) above—

(a) each apportioned part of the tax credit which is paid to the members' agent of a member under sub-paragraph (3)(b) above shall be treated, for the purposes of section 171 of this Act and all other purposes of the Income Tax Acts, as part of the profits arising to the member from assets forming part of a premiums trust fund; but

(b) subject to that, the tax credit shall be ignored for all purposes of the Income Tax Acts."

(3) This paragraph has effect as respects the underwriting year 1992 and subsequent underwriting years.

Special reserve funds

12.—(1) In Schedule 20 to the 1993 Act (special reserve funds), in paragraph 1(1) (preliminary), after the definition of "overall premium limit" there shall be inserted the following definition—

" 'payment', unless the contrary intention appears, means a payment in money;".

(2) In paragraph 7(2) of that Schedule (payments out of fund on cessation), for the words "money's worth" there shall be substituted the words "in assets forming part of the fund".

(3) This paragraph has effect for the year 1992–93 and subsequent years of assessment.

13.—(1) For paragraph 8 of that Schedule (entitlement of member for tax purposes) there shall be substituted the following paragraph—

"8.—(1) Subject to sub-paragraph (2) below, a member shall be treated for the purposes of the Income Tax Acts and the Gains Tax Acts as absolutely entitled as against the trustees to the assets forming part of his special reserve fund.

(2) Where an asset is disposed of by a member to the trustees of his special reserve fund, nothing in sub-paragraph (1) above shall affect the operation of the Gains Tax Acts in relation to that disposal."

(2) This paragraph has effect for the year 1994–95 and subsequent years of assessment.

14.—(1) In sub-paragraphs (1) to (4) of paragraph 10 of that Schedule (tax consequences of payments into and out of fund), for the word "corresponding", in each place where it occurs, there shall be substituted the word "relevant".

(2) After sub-paragraph (4) of that paragraph there shall be inserted the following sub-paragraph—

"(5) In this paragraph 'the relevant underwriting year', in relation to a year of assessment, means the underwriting year next but two before its corresponding underwriting year."

(3) Sub-paragraphs (1) and (2) above do not have effect for the years 1994–95, 1995–96 and 1996–97, but in relation to those years that Schedule shall have effect as if paragraph 10 were omitted.

15.—(1) In sub-paragraph (2) of paragraph 11 of that Schedule (tax consequences of cessation), for the words "the final year of assessment" there shall be substituted the words "the relevant year of assessment" and for the words "the relevant year" there shall be substituted the words "the relevant underwriting year".

(2) In sub-paragraphs (3) and (4) of that paragraph, for the words "the relevant year" there shall be substituted the words "the penultimate underwriting year".

(3) For sub-paragraph (5) of that paragraph there shall be substituted the following sub-paragraph—

"(5) In this paragraph, subject to the provisions of any regulations made by the Board—

'the penultimate underwriting year' means the underwriting year immediately preceding that in which the member's deposit at Lloyd's is paid over to him or his personal representatives or assigns;

'the relevant underwriting year' means—

(a) in the case of a member who dies before his deposit at Lloyd's is paid over to him or his assigns, the underwriting year immediately preceding that corresponding to the relevant year of assessment; and

(b) in any other case, the underwriting year immediately preceding that in which his deposit at Lloyd's is paid over to him or his assigns;

'the relevant year of assessment' means—

(a) in the case of a member who dies before his deposit at Lloyd's is paid over to him or his assigns, the year of assessment at the end of which he is treated, by virtue of section 179A(2) of this Act, as having died; and

(b) in any other case, his final year of assessment."

16.—(1) In sub-paragraph (1) of paragraph 13 of that Schedule (winding up of old-style funds), the words from "and a transfer" to the end shall cease to have effect.

(2) After sub-paragraph (5) of that paragraph there shall be inserted the following sub-paragraph—

"(6) A transfer or payment under this paragraph of an amount of capital shall be in money or in assets forming part of the fund or both, as the member may direct."

(3) This paragraph has effect for the year 1992–93 and subsequent years of assessment.

GENERAL NOTE

Para. (9)
The definition of the dates by which managing agents are required to make returns of syndicate profits and losses is changed from 1997–1998 onwards.

Para. (10)
The system of payments on account of tax by the member's agent ceases to operate.

Para. (11)
The first amendment to the FA 1993 (c. 34), Sched. 19, para. 13 ensures that non-resident members are entitled to tax credits. The second ensures that the appropriate proportion of tax credits paid to a member's agent is included as part of the profit arising to the member from assets forming part of a premiums trust fund, but is ignored for all other purposes of the Income Tax Acts.

Para. (12)
Payment out of a special reserve fund generally means payment in money, except on cessation, when it may be payment in kind.

Para. (13)
Where a member disposes of assets in his special reserve fund to the trustees, the normal capital gains tax rules will operate.

Para. (14)
The provisions in the FA 1993 (c. 34), Sched. 20, para. 10 dealing with the tax consequences of payments into and out of a member's special reserve fund are amended to take account of the move to a distribution year basis.

Para. (15)
The provisions in the FA 1993 (c. 34), Sched. 20, para. 11 which deal with the tax consequences for special reserve funds on cessation are similarly amended.

Para. (16)
This contains a minor drafting clarification regarding the winding up of old-style funds.

Sections 231 and 234   SCHEDULE 22

SUPPLEMENTARY PROVISIONS AS TO ELECTIONS BY REFERENCE TO PIPE-LINE USAGE

PART I

PROCEDURE FOR AND IN CONNECTION WITH AN ELECTION

The election

1.—(1) An election shall be made by serving it on the Board, shall be in such form as may be prescribed by the Board and shall contain such information as the Board may reasonably require with respect to—

(a) the oil field to which the election is to apply, the pipe-line by reference to which the election is being made and whether the election is to be limited in accordance with subsection (6) of section 231 of this Act;

(b) all other assets which, if the election were to be accepted, would at the date of the election be assets to which the election applies;

(c) the electing participator's interest in those assets;

(d) the sums to which, if the election is accepted, it is reasonable to expect that section 233 of this Act will apply and the sources, quantities and descriptions of oil which will give rise to those sums;

(e) any other oil field (whether taxable or non-taxable) in connection with which any of the assets referred to in paragraph (b) above is or is expected to be used or in respect of which services or other business facilities in connection with that use are or are expected to be provided; and

(f) the initial usage fraction and the amounts which make up the numerator and the denominator of that fraction.

(2) The reference in sub-paragraph (1)(e) above to an oil field includes a reference to any area which the electing participator expects might be determined as an oil field under Schedule 1 to the principal Act.

(3) An election shall include a declaration that it is correct and complete to the best of the knowledge and belief of the electing participator.

(4) An election shall be irrevocable.

Conditions for acceptance of an election

2.—(1) The Board shall reject an election if they are not satisfied—

(a) that the conditions relating to the pipe-line in paragraphs (a) to (d) of subsection (1) or in subsection (3) of section 231 of this Act are fulfilled; or

(b) that the conditions relating to the oil field or the participator in subsection (2) of that section are fulfilled; or

(c) that, if the election were to be accepted, the assets to which the election would apply (having regard to any limitation under subsection (6) of that section) have the capacity and characteristics, and are otherwise suitable, to handle the quantities and descriptions of oil specified in accordance with paragraph 1(1)(d) above.

(2) Subject to sub-paragraph (3) below, the Board shall also reject an election if it appears to them—

(a) that any of the information required to be contained in the election by virtue of paragraph 1(1) above is incorrect; or

(b) that, after receiving notice in writing from the Board, the electing participator has failed to furnish to the Board on or before the specified date any information which the Board have reasonably required either with respect to the matters specified in paragraph 1(1) above or for the purpose of satisfying themselves as to the matters referred to in sub-paragraph (1) above.

(3) Before rejecting an election under sub-paragraph (2)(a) above the Board may, if they think fit, by notice in writing give the electing participator an opportunity to correct any error in the information and, if he does so, the information shall then be treated as having been provided in the correct form.

(4) In sub-paragraph (2)(b) above "the specified date" means such date as may be specified in the notice concerned, being a date not earlier than one month after the date on which the notice was given.

(5) A notice under sub-paragraph (2)(b) above shall be given within the period of three months beginning on the date on which the election was received by the Board.

Notice of acceptance or rejection

3.—(1) Notice of the acceptance or rejection of an election shall be served on the electing participator before the expiry of the period of three months beginning on whichever of the following dates is the later or latest—

(a) the date on which the election was received by the Board;

(b) if a notice was given under paragraph 2(2)(b) above relating to the election, the date or, as the case may be, the last date which is the specified date, as defined in paragraph 2(4) above, in relation to such a notice;

(c) if a notice was given under paragraph 2(3) above relating to the election, the date on which that notice was given.

(2) If no such notice of acceptance or rejection is so served, the Board shall be deemed to have accepted the election and to have served notice of their acceptance on the last day of the period referred to in sub-paragraph (1) above.

Appeals

4.—(1) Where the Board serve notice on an electing participator under paragraph 3 above rejecting an election, he may appeal to the Special Commissioners against the notice.

(2) An appeal under sub-paragraph (1) above shall be made by notice of appeal served on the Board within thirty days beginning on the date of the notice in respect of which the appeal is brought.

(3) Where, at any time after the service of notice of appeal under this paragraph and before the determination of the appeal by the Commissioners, the Board and the appellant agree that the notice in respect of which the appeal is brought should stand or that the election to which it related should be accepted with or without modification, the same consequences shall ensue as if the Commissioners had determined the appeal to that effect.

(4) On the hearing of an appeal under this paragraph, the Commissioners shall either dismiss the appeal or allow it; and if the Commissioners allow the appeal, they shall direct either—

  (a) that the election shall be accepted; or
  (b) that the election shall have effect subject to such modifications as may be specified in the direction and shall be accepted in its modified form.

(5) Sub-paragraphs (2), (8) and (11) of paragraph 14 of Schedule 2 to the principal Act shall apply in relation to an appeal against a notice under paragraph 3 above rejecting an election as they apply in relation to an appeal against an assessment or determination made under the principal Act.

(6) Any reference in this Chapter to an election accepted by the Board shall be construed as including a reference to an election accepted in pursuance of an appeal under this paragraph.

Information to the responsible person

5.—(1) Within thirty days of the relevant date, the electing participator shall furnish to the responsible person for the field to which the election applies (or would apply if the election were accepted) a copy of—

  (a) any election made by him; and
  (b) any notice under paragraph 3 above accepting or rejecting the election.

(2) For the purposes of sub-paragraph (1) above, the relevant date is—

  (a) in the case of an election made by the electing participator, the date on which it was served on the Board; and
  (b) in the case of a notice under paragraph 3 above, the date on which the electing participator received it.

(3) In a case where paragraph 9 below applies (or would apply if an election were accepted) sub-paragraphs (1) and (2) above shall require the electing participator additionally to furnish copies of the same documents to the responsible person for any non-chargeable field mentioned in sub-paragraph (3) of that paragraph.

(4) In a case where paragraph 11 below applies (or would apply if an election were accepted) sub-paragraphs (1) and (2) above shall require the electing participator additionally to furnish copies of the same documents to the old participator referred to in that paragraph.

Penalties for incorrect information

6. Where a participator fraudulently or negligently furnishes any incorrect information or makes any incorrect declaration in or in connection with an election he shall be liable to a penalty not exceeding—

  (a) in the case of negligence, £50,000, and
  (b) in the case of fraud, £100,000.

Re-opening election decisions on grounds of incorrect information

7.—(1) Without prejudice to paragraph 6 above, this paragraph applies if, at any time after notice of the acceptance of an election has been served by the Board, it appears to the Board that, as a result of an error in the information furnished to the Board, the election should not have been accepted.

(2) If, in a case where this paragraph applies, either—

(a) the error was attributable, in whole or in part, to the fraudulent or negligent conduct of the electing participator or a person acting on his behalf, or

(b) on the error coming to the notice of the electing participator, or a person acting on his behalf, the error was not remedied without unreasonable delay,

the Board may serve on the electing participator and on the responsible person for the field to which the election applies a notice rescinding the acceptance and stating what appears to the Board to be the correct position.

(3) When a notice under sub-paragraph (2) above becomes effective, the election shall be treated as having been rejected in accordance with paragraph 3 above.

(4) If, in a case where this paragraph applies,—

(a) neither of the conditions in sub-paragraph (2) above is fulfilled, and

(b) the Board are of the opinion that, if the correct information had been furnished, the election could have been accepted,

the election shall be treated as having been made and accepted subject to such modifications (being modifications to correct the effect of the error) as the Board may direct, by notice served on the electing participator and on the responsible person for the field to which the election applies.

(5) A notice served under sub-paragraph (2) or sub-paragraph (4) above shall become effective either—

(a) on the expiry of the period during which notice of appeal against the notice may be served on the Board under paragraph 8 below without such notice of appeal being served; or

(b) where such notice of appeal is served, when the notice can no longer be varied or quashed by the Special Commissioners or by the order of any court.

Appeals against re-opening notices

8.—(1) This paragraph applies where the Board serve notice under sub-paragraph (2) or sub-paragraph (4) of paragraph 7 above; and in the following provisions of this paragraph such a notice is referred to as a "re-opening notice".

(2) The electing participator may, by notice of appeal served on the Board within thirty days beginning on the date of the re-opening notice, appeal to the Special Commissioners against the re-opening notice.

(3) A notice of appeal under sub-paragraph (2) above shall sate the grounds on which the appeal is brought.

(4) An appeal under this paragraph may at any time be abandoned by notice served on the Board by the electing participator.

(5) A re-opening notice may be withdrawn at any time before it becomes effective.

(6) In any case where—

(a) the electing participator serves notice of appeal against a re-opening notice served under sub-paragraph (4) of paragraph 7 above, and

(b) before the appeal is determined by the Special Commissioners, the Board and the electing participator agree as to the modifications necessary to correct the effect of the error concerned,

the re-opening notice shall take effect subject to such modifications as may be necessary to give effect to that agreement; and thereupon the appeal shall be treated as having been abandoned.

(7) Subject to sub-paragraph (8) below, on an appeal against a re-opening notice the Special Commissioners may vary the notice, quash the notice or dismiss the appeal; and the notice may be varied whether or not the variation is to the advantage of the electing participator.

(8) The provisions relating to the variation of a re-opening notice referred to in sub-paragraph (7) above shall not apply in respect of any such notice served under sub-paragraph (2) of paragraph 7 above.

GENERAL NOTE

This Schedule contains, in Pt. I, the procedure in relation to an election under s.231. It also contains, in Pt. II, supplementary provisions in relation to ss.231–233.

Part I

This lays down the procedure for an election. It must be in the form prescribed by the Revenue and will be irrevocable. The Revenue may reject the election if they are not satisfied that it fulfils the conditions or it is incorrect or incomplete. Notice of acceptance or rejection must be given, normally within three months. The electing participator has a right of appeal to the Special Commissioners within 30 days.

Where an election is accepted (directly or on appeal) the electing participator will then notify the "responsible person" for the field (see the Oil Taxation Act 1975 (c. 22), Sched. 2, para. 4) so that the responsible person can subsequently claim reduced expenditure relief in respect of that participator.

Negligence in connection with an election attracts a penalty of £50,000 and fraud a penalty of £100,000.

An election based on incorrect information may be revoked, subject to appeal.

PART II

SUPPLEMENTARY PROVISIONS

Assets used in connection with more than one taxable field

9.—(1) The provisions of this paragraph apply where—
(a) an election is in operation; and
(b) any of the assets to which the election applies is used or expected to be used in connection with two or more taxable fields.

(2) Any reference in this paragraph to allowable expenditure has the same meaning as in Part II of Schedule 1 to the 1983 Act and is a reference to expenditure incurred on an asset to which the election applies.

(3) Sub-paragraph (4) below applies if, by virtue of paragraph 5 of Schedule 1 to the 1983 Act (which, in a case falling within this paragraph, provides for the apportionment of allowable expenditure between two or more fields), any part of the allowable expenditure is apportioned to a taxable field (a "non-chargeable field") other than the field to which the election applies.

(4) Where this sub-paragraph applies, then, so far as concerns the electing participator (as a participator in a non-chargeable field), section 232 of this Act shall apply in relation to that part of the allowable expenditure which is apportioned to the non-chargeable field as it applies in relation to the part apportioned to the field to which the election applies.

Transfer of interests

10.—(1) If, while an election is in operation, the electing participator (or a person who is treated as an electing participator by virtue of this paragraph) transfers the whole or part of his interest in the field to which the election applies, then, so far as concerns that interest or part, the new participator shall thereafter be treated as the electing participator for the purposes of this Chapter, other than paragraph 11 below, and, in particular,—
(a) any restriction on the amount of expenditure allowed or allowable by virtue of section 232 of this Act shall continue to apply to any expenditure relief transferred to the new participator under paragraph 6 of Schedule 17 to the Finance Act 1980; and
(b) any relief from tax under section 233 of this Act shall apply in relation to the new participator as it applied in relation to the old participator.

(2) If, in a case where paragraph 9 above applies, the electing participator, as a participator in the non-chargeable field (within the meaning of that paragraph) transfers the whole or part of his interest in that field, sub-paragraph (1) above (except paragraph (b)) shall apply in relation to that transfer as if—
(a) any reference to the field to which the election applies were a reference to the non-chargeable field; and
(b) any reference to the electing participator were a reference to him in his capacity as a participator in the non-chargeable field.

(3) In sub-paragraph (1) above the expressions "the old participator" and "the new participator" have the same meaning as in Schedule 17 to the Finance Act 1980.

11.—(1) This paragraph applies in any case where—
(a) the electing participator acquired the whole or any part of his interest in the field to which the election applies as a result of a transfer to which Part I of Schedule 17 to the Finance Act 1980 applies (so that the electing participator is the new participator); and
(b) some or all of the relief in respect of any expenditure incurred (before the transfer) on any asset to which the election applies did not fall to be transferred to the electing participator (whether by virtue of paragraph 6 or paragraph 7 of that Schedule).

(2) With regard to so much of the expenditure referred to in sub-paragraph (1)(b) above as falls to be taken into account under paragraph (b)(i) or paragraph (c)(i) of subsection (9) of section 2 of the principal Act in computing, for any chargeable period ending before the transfer period, the assessable profit or allowable loss accruing to the old participator or any predecessor of his, section 232 of this Act shall apply in the case of the old participator or, as the case may be, his predecessor as it is expressed to apply in the case of the electing participator.

(3) If, as a result of the operation of sub-paragraph (2) above, there is a reduction in the amount which would otherwise be the accumulated capital expenditure of the old participator at

the end of the last chargeable period before the transfer period, paragraph 8 of Schedule 17 to the Finance Act 1980 shall be taken to have transferred a correspondingly reduced amount to the electing participator.

(4) In this paragraph—

(a) the expressions "the old participator", "the new participator" and "the transfer period" have the same meaning as in Schedule 17 to the Finance Act 1980; and

(b) any reference to a predecessor of the old participator is a reference to a person who (before the transfer referred to in sub-paragraph (1)(a) above) transferred the whole or part of his interest in the field to which the election applies either to the old participator or to another person who is a predecessor in title of the old participator in respect of that interest or part.

Transfer of elected assets

12.—(1) This paragraph applies if there is a disposal of an asset which, immediately before the disposal or at an earlier time, was an asset to which an election applies; and in this paragraph—

(a) "the asset transferred" means the asset so disposed of;

(b) "the vendor" means the electing participator or other person by whom the asset is disposed of.

(2) Where a person has incurred expenditure on the acquisition of a transferred asset, he shall be treated for the purposes of the expenditure relief provisions as having incurred that expenditure only to the extent that it does not exceed the amount which, having regard to section 232 of this Act or the previous operation of this paragraph, was (in the case of the vendor) allowable under those provisions immediately before the disposal in respect of his expenditure on the asset.

(3) Any expenditure incurred on the asset after the disposal shall be left out of account for the purposes of the expenditure relief provisions.

Restriction of relief for expenditure incurred after 30th November 1993 and before the date of an election

13.—(1) This paragraph applies if, after 30th November 1993 and before the date of an election, expenditure was incurred by the electing participator under a contract—

(a) for the acquisition from any other person of, or of an interest in, an asset to which the election applies; or

(b) for the provision by any other person of services or other business facilities of whatever kind in connection with the use of an asset to which the election applies.

(2) If, in a case where this paragraph applies, the other person referred to in paragraph (a) or paragraph (b) of sub-paragraph (1) above ("the contractor") has performed his obligations by entering into one or more further contracts, the contractor shall be treated for the purposes of subsection (2) of section 191 of the Finance Act 1993 (time when expenditure is incurred) as having performed his obligations under the contract only to the extent that, at that time, the asset or interest in question has been acquired by or, as the case may be, the services or other business facilities have been provided to, the electing participator.

GENERAL NOTE

Part II

An apportionment will be made where assets are used in connection with more than one taxable field. Elections will continue to be valid in cases of transfers of interests or of elected assets. Expenditure on assets between Budget day and the date of an election is restricted to what had been contracted for by Budget day.

Section 236   SCHEDULE 23

AMENDMENTS OF THE PRINCIPAL ACT RELATING TO VALUATION OF LIGHT GASES

1.—(1) In section 2 (assessable profits and allowable losses), in subsection (5) (amounts to be included in calculation of gross profit or loss) in each of paragraphs (b) and (c), after the word "oil", in the first place where it occurs, there shall be inserted "(not being light gases)" and after paragraph (c) there shall be inserted—

"(ca) the market value, ascertained in accordance with paragraph 3A of Schedule 3 to this Act, of so much of any light gases so won and disposed of by him otherwise than in sales at arm's length as was delivered by him in the period; and (cb) the market value, ascertained in accordance with paragraph 3A of Schedule 3 to this Act, of so much of any light gases so won as was relevantly appropriated by him in the period without being disposed of; and".

(2) In subsection (9) of that section (amounts to be taken into account in determining amount of debit or credit in respect of expenditure), in paragraph (a)—

    (a) in sub-paragraph (i) the words "or, as the case may be" shall be omitted;

    (b) in that sub-paragraph after the words "delivery was made" there shall be inserted the words "or (in the case of light gases) its market value as determined in accordance with paragraph 3A of Schedule 3 to this Act, as the case may require"; and

    (c) at the end of sub-paragraph (ii) there shall be inserted the words "or (in the case of light gases) the market value as determined in accordance with paragraph 3A of Schedule 3 to this Act".

2. In Schedule 2 (management and collection of PRT), in paragraph 2(2) (returns by participators), in paragraph (a)(iii) after the words "delivery was made" and in paragraph (b)(ii) after the word "made" there shall be inserted the words "or (in the case of light gases) the market value as determined in accordance with paragraph 3A of Schedule 3 to this Act".

3.—(1) In Schedule 3 (miscellaneous provisions relating to PRT), in paragraph 2 (definition of market value of oil)—

    (a) at the beginning of sub-paragraph (1) there shall be inserted the words "Except in the case of light gases"; and

    (b) at the end of that sub-paragraph there shall be added the words "and, accordingly, references in the following provisions of this paragraph to oil do not apply to light gases".

(2) In paragraph 2A of that Schedule (definition of market value of oil consisting of or including gas), after sub-paragraph (1) there shall be inserted the following sub-paragraph—

    "(1A) Sub-paragraphs (2) and (3) below also apply where the market value of any light gases falls to be ascertained under paragraph 3A below."

(3) In sub-paragraph (2) of paragraph 2A, after the words "paragraph 2 above", in each place where they occur, there shall be inserted "or, as the case may require, sub-paragraph (2)(b) of paragraph 3A below".

(4) In sub-paragraph (3) of paragraph 2A, after the words "paragraph 2", in the first place where they occur, there shall be inserted "or, as the case may require, in accordance with paragraph 3A below".

(5) Sub-paragraph (4) of paragraph 2A shall be omitted.

4. After paragraph 3 of Schedule 3 (aggregate market value of oil) there shall be inserted—

"Definition of market value of light gases

3A.—(1) The market value of any light gases for the purposes of this Part of this Act is the price at which, having regard to all the circumstances relevant to the disposal or appropriation in question, light gases of that kind might reasonably have been expected to be sold under a contract of sale satisfying the conditions specified in sub-paragraph (2) below.

(2) The conditions referred to in sub-paragraph (1) above are that—

    (a) the contract is for the sale of the gases at arm's length to a willing buyer;

    (b) the contract requires the gases to have been subjected to appropriate initial treatment before delivery; and

    (c) the contract requires the gases to be delivered—

        (i) in the case of gases extracted in the United Kingdom, at the place of extraction; or

        (ii) in the case of gases extracted from strata in the sea bed and subsoil of the territorial sea of the United Kingdom or of a designated area, at the place in the United Kingdom or another country at which the seller could reasonably be expected to deliver the gases or, if there is more than one such place, the one nearest to the place of extraction.

(3) If the circumstances referred to in sub-paragraph (1) above are such that the price referred to in that sub-paragraph might reasonably be expected to include—

    (a) any such payments as are referred to in subsection (2) of section 114 of the Finance Act 1984 (treatment of certain payments relating to gas sales), or

    (b) any capacity payments, as defined in subsection (5) of that section,

section 114 of the Finance Act 1984 shall apply accordingly in relation to the notional contract specified in sub-paragraph (1) above as it applies in relation to an actual contract.

(4) This paragraph has effect subject to sub-paragraphs (2) and (3) of paragraph 2A above."

GENERAL NOTE

This Schedule contains the new rules for valuing light gases (ethane and methane). The market value of light gases is to be used in calculating a field participator's petroleum revenue tax (PRT) assessable profits and losses. This replaces the existing rules, under which participators elect for a long-term pricing formula.

The new Oil Taxation Act 1975 (c. 22), Sched. 3, para. 3A provides for market value to be the price at which gas would have been sold under a notional contract meeting certain basic arm's length conditions and taking account of all circumstances relevant to the particular disposal. If any special pricing mechanisms would have applied if the gas being valued had been sold at arm's length then the special tax rules which apply in such cases are to apply to that gas.

Section 252   SCHEDULE 24

PROVISIONS RELATING TO THE RAILWAYS ACT 1993

Interpretation

1.—(1) In this Schedule—

"the Allowances Act" means the Capital Allowances Act 1990;

"the Board" means the British Railways Board;

"fixture" has the same meaning as it has in Chapter VI of Part II of the Allowances Act;

"franchise company" has the meaning given by section 85(8) of the Railways Act 1993;

"the Franchising Director" means the Director of Passenger Rail Franchising;

"the Gains Act" means the Taxation of Chargeable Gains Act 1992;

"predecessor", in relation to any relevant transfer, means the body from which the property, rights or liabilities in question are transferred by virtue of the restructuring scheme in question;

"property", "rights" and "liabilities" have the same meaning as they have in Part II of the Railways Act 1993;

"publicly owned railway company" has the same meaning as it has in the Railways Act 1993;

"relevant transfer" means a transfer of any property, rights or liabilities by virtue of a restructuring scheme;

"restructuring scheme" means a section 85 transfer scheme made by, or pursuant to a direction of, the Secretary of State, if and to the extent that the transfer scheme provides for the transfer of property, rights or liabilities from—

         (a) the Board,

         (b) a wholly owned subsidiary of the Board,

         (c) a publicly owned railway company, or

         (d) a company which is wholly owned by the Franchising Director,

to any other body falling within paragraphs (a) to (d) above;

"section 85 transfer scheme" means a scheme made under or by virtue of section 85 of the Railways Act 1993;

"subsidiary" has the meaning given by section 736 of the Companies Act 1985;

"successor company" has the same meaning as it has in Part II of the Railways Act 1993;

"transfer date" shall be construed in accordance with section 85(6) of the Railways Act 1993;

"transfer scheme" means a scheme made under or by virtue of section 85 or 86 of the Railways Act 1993;

"transferee", in relation to a relevant transfer, means the body to which the property, rights or liabilities in question are transferred by virtue of the restructuring scheme in question;

"wholly owned subsidiary" has the meaning given by section 736 of the Companies Act 1985.

(2) Section 151(2) and (3) for the Railways Act 1993 (companies wholly owned by the Crown or the Franchising Director) shall have effect for the purposes of this Schedule as it has effect for the purposes of that Act.

(3) Any reference in this Schedule to "assignment" shall be construed in Scotland as a reference to "assignation".

(4) This Schedule—

(a) so far as it relates to income tax, shall be construed as one with the Income Tax Acts,

(b) so far as it relates to corporation tax, shall be construed as one with the Corporation Tax Acts, and

(c) so far as it relates to capital allowances, shall be construed as one with the Capital Allowances Acts.

Chargeable gains: transfer to be without gain or loss

2.—(1) For the purposes of the Gains Act, where there is a relevant transfer, the disposal of property, rights and liabilities which is constituted by that transfer shall, subject to the following provisions of this Schedule, be taken, in relation to the transferee as well as the predecessor, to be for a consideration such that no gain or loss accrues to the predecessor.

(2) Section 35(3)(d) of the Gains Act (list of provisions for transfers without gain or loss for purposes of provisions applying to assets held on 31st March 1982) shall have effect with the omission of the word "and" at the end of sub-paragraph (vii) and with the insertion, after sub-paragraph (viii), of the following sub-paragraph—

"(ix) paragraphs 2(1), 7(2), 11(3) and (4) and 25(2) of Schedule 24 to the Finance Act 1994;".

(3) Section 171(1) of the Gains Act (which makes provision in relation to the disposal of assets from one member of a group of companies to another member of the group) shall not apply where the disposal in question is a relevant transfer.

Chargeable gains: receipt of compensation or insurance policies

3.—(1) Subsection (4) of section 23 of the Gains Act (adjustments where compensation or insurance money used for purchase of replacement asset) shall have effect in accordance with sub-paragraph (3) below in any case where—

(a) there is a relevant transfer such that—

(i) any capital sum received by the predecessor by way of compensation for the loss or destruction of any asset, or under a policy of insurance of the risk of the loss or destruction of any asset, becomes available to the transferee; or

(ii) any right of the predecessor to receive such a sum is transferred to the transferee, and the transferee receives that sum; and

(b) the transferee acquires an asset in circumstances where—

(i) had there been no such relevant transfer, and

(ii) had the predecessor acquired the asset by the application of that sum,

the predecessor would be treated for the purposes of that subsection as having so acquired the asset in replacement for the asset lost or destroyed.

(2) Subsection (5) of that section (adjustments where a part of any compensation or insurance money is used for the purchase of a replacement asset) shall have effect in accordance with sub-paragraph (3) below in any case where—

(a) there is a relevant transfer such that—

(i) any capital sum received by the predecessor by way of compensation for the loss or destruction of any asset, or under a policy of insurance of the risk of the loss or destruction of any asset, becomes available to the transferee; or

(ii) any right of the predecessor to receive such a sum is transferred to the transferee, and the transferee receives that sum; and

(b) the transferee acquires an asset in circumstances where—

(i) had there been no such relevant transfer, and

(ii) had the predecessor acquired the asset by the application of all of that sum except for a part which was less than the amount of the gain (whether all chargeable gain or not) accruing on the disposal of the asset lost or destroyed,

the predecessor would be treated for the purposes of that subsection as having so acquired the asset in replacement for the asset in replacement for the asset lost or destroyed.

(3) In a case falling within sub-paragraph (1) or (2) above, subsection (4) or, as the case may be, subsection (5) of section 23 of the Gains Act shall have effect as if the transferee and the predecessor were the same person, except that—

(a) in a case falling within sub-paragraph (1)(a)(i) or (2)(a)(i) above—

(i) any claim under the subsection in question must be made by the predecessor and the transferee; and

(ii) any adjustment to be made in consequence of paragraph (a) of that subsection shall be made for the purposes only of the taxation of the predecessor; and

(b) in a case falling within sub-paragraph (1)(a)(ii) or (2)(a)(ii) above—

(i) any claim under the subsection in question must be made by the transferee; and

(ii) any adjustment to be made in consequence of paragraph (a) of that subsection shall be made for the purposes only of the taxation of the transferee.

Chargeable gains: section 30 of the Gains Act

4.—(1) Nothing in Part II or III of the Railways Act 1993, and no instrument or agreement made, or other thing done, under or by virtue of either of those Parts, shall be regarded as a scheme or arrangement for the purposes of section 30 of the Gains Act (value-shifting).

(2) In any case where—

(a) an asset which is the subject of a relevant transfer or qualifying disposal has previously been the subject of a scheme or arrangements falling within subsection (1) of that section,

(b) in consequence, subsection (5) of that section (consideration on disposal to be treated as increased for certain purposes) would, apart from sub-paragraph (3) below, have had effect in relation to the consideration for the relevant transfer or qualifying disposal, and

(c) the consideration for the relevant transfer or qualifying disposal falls to be determined under paragraph 2 above or paragraph 7(2), 11(3) or 25(2) below,

sub-paragraph (3) below shall apply.

(3) Where this sub-paragraph applies—

(a) the said subsection (5) shall not have effect in relation to the consideration for the relevant transfer or qualifying disposal; but

(b) on the first subsequent disposal of the asset which is neither a relevant transfer or qualifying disposal nor a group disposal—

(i) that subsection shall have effect in relation to the consideration for that disposal (whether or not it would otherwise have done so); and

(ii) the increase that falls to be made under that subsection shall be so calculated as to include any increase which would, but for paragraph (a) above, have fallen to be made in relation to the relevant transfer or qualifying disposal.

(4) In this paragraph—

"group disposal" means a disposal which falls to be treated by virtue of section 171(1) of the Gains Act as made for a consideration such that no gain or loss accrues to the person making the disposal;

"qualifying disposal" means—

(a) a disposal to which paragraph 7(2) below applies; or

(b) a disposal falling within paragraph 11(3) or 25(2) below.

Chargeable gains: section 41 of the Gains Act

5. Subsection (1) of section 174 of the Gains Act (which applies section 41 of that Act to cases where assets have been acquired without gain or loss) shall have effect, without prejudice to paragraph 2 above or paragraph 7(2), 11(3) or (4) or 25(2) below, where there has been—

(a) a relevant transfer,

(b) a disposal to which paragraph 7(2) below applies, or

(c) a disposal falling within paragraph 11(3) or (4) or 25(2) below,

as if the asset to which the transfer or disposal relates had thereby been transferred and acquired in relevant circumstances, within the meaning of that subsection.

Chargeable gains: roll-over relief

6.—(1) Subject to the following provisions of this paragraph, where any asset, or any interest in an asset, is the subject of a relevant transfer, sections 152 to 160 of the Gains Act (roll-over relief on replacement of business assets) shall have effect as if—

(a) the asset or interest had been acquired by the transferee—

(i) at the time at which, and for the consideration for which, the predecessor acquired it; and

(ii) for the purpose of the asset's use in a trade carried on by the transferee (and not wholly or partly for the purpose of realising a gain from the disposal of the asset or interest), but only to the extent that the predecessor's acquisition was for the purpose of the asset's use in a trade carried on by him (and not wholly or partly for the purpose of realising a gain from the disposal of the asset or interest);

(b) throughout the period during which the asset or interest was owned by the predecessor, it had been owned by the transferee; and

(c) to the extent that the predecessor—

(i) used the asset, or

(ii) in the case of an asset falling within head A of Class 1 in section 155 of that Act, used and occupied the asset,

during that period for the purposes of a trade carried on by him, the transferee had used or, as the case may be, used and occupied the asset for the purposes of a trade carried on by him.

(2) In any case where—
(a) a held-over gain would, but for the provisions of section 154 of the Gains Act (depreciating assets), have been carried forward to a depreciating asset, and
(b) that asset is the subject of a relevant transfer,
that section shall have effect as if the gain had accrued to, and the claim for it to be held over had been made by, the transferee and as if the predecessor's acquisition of the depreciating asset had been the transferee's acquisition of that asset.

(3) Where an asset, or an interest in an asset, is the subject of a relevant transfer, the predecessor shall not be entitled at any time after the coming into force of the relevant transfer to make any claim under section 152 or 153 of the Gains Act in respect of his acquisition of the asset or interest.

(4) Where an asset, or an interest in an asset, is the subject of a relevant transfer, the transferee shall not, by virtue of any provision of this Schedule, be treated for the purposes of sections 152 to 154 of the Gains Act as having applied the whole or any part of the consideration for any disposal—
(a) in acquiring the asset or interest by virtue of the relevant transfer; or
(b) in acquiring the asset or interest as postulated in sub-paragraph (1)(a) above, if the predecessor has made a claim under section 152 or 153 of that Act in respect of his acquisition of the asset or interest.

(5) Without prejudice to paragraph 1(4)(b) above, expressions used in sub-paragraph (2) above and in section 154 of the Gains Act have the same meaning in that sub-paragraph as they have in that section.

Chargeable gains: agreements and instruments by virtue of section 91(1)(c) of the Railways Act 1993

7.—(1) Sub-paragraph (2) below applies to any disposal effected pursuant to an obligation imposed by a section 85 transfer scheme by virtue of section 91(1)(c) of the Railways Act 1993 (obligations to enter into agreements or execute instruments) if the person making the disposal is—
(a) the Board,
(b) a wholly owned subsidiary of the Board,
(c) a publicly owned railway company, or
(d) a company which is wholly owned by the Franchising Director,
and the person to whom the disposal is made is either a person falling within paragraphs (a) to (d) above or the Franchising Director.

(2) A disposal to which this sub-paragraph applies shall be taken for the purposes of corporation tax on chargeable gains, in relation to the person to whom the disposal is made as well as the person making the disposal, to be effected for a consideration such that no gain or loss accrues to the person making the disposal.

(3) Section 171(1) of the Gains Act (transfers within a group) shall not apply where the disposal in question is one to which sub-paragraph (2) above applies.

(4) Section 17 of that Act (disposals and acquisitions treated as made at market value) shall not have effect in relation to a disposal or the corresponding acquisition if—
(a) the disposal is effected pursuant to an obligation imposed by a section 85 transfer scheme by virtue of section 91(1)(c) of the Railways Act 1993,
(b) the person making the disposal is either a person falling within paragraphs (a) to (d) of sub-paragraph (1) above or the Franchising Director, and
(c) the person making the corresponding acquisition is neither a person falling within those paragraphs nor the Franchising Director,
unless the person making the disposal is connected with the person to whom the disposal is made.

(5) In this paragraph, "the corresponding acquisition", in the case of any disposal, means the acquisition made by the person to whom the disposal is made.

Chargeable gains: group transactions

8.—(1) For the purposes of section 179 of the Gains Act (company ceasing to be a member of a group), where any company ("the degrouped company") ceases, by virtue of a qualifying transaction, to be a member of a group of companies, the degrouped company shall not, by virtue of that qualifying transaction, be treated under that section as having sold, and immediately reacquired, any asset acquired from a company which was at the time of acquisition a member of that group.

(2) Where sub-paragraph (1) above applies in relation to any asset, section 179 of the Gains Act shall have effect on the first subsequent occasion on which the degrouped company ceases to

be a member of a group of companies (the "subsequent group"), otherwise than by virtue of a qualifying transaction, as if both the degrouped company and the company from which the asset was acquired had been members of the subsequent group at the time of acquisition.

(3) Where, disregarding any preparatory transactions, a company would be regarded for the purposes of section 179 of the Gains Act (and, accordingly, of this paragraph) as ceasing to be, or becoming, a member of a group of companies by virtue of a qualifying transaction, it shall be regarded for those purposes as so doing by virtue of the qualifying transaction and not by virtue of any preparatory transactions.

(4) In this paragraph—

　　"preparatory transaction" means anything done under or by virtue of Part II of the Railways Act 1993 for the purpose of initiating, advancing or facilitating the qualifying transaction in question;

　　"qualifying transaction" means—

　　　　(a) a relevant transfer;

　　　　(b) any other transfer or disposal under or by virtue of section 85, 88(6) or (7) or 89 of the Railways Act 1993.

(5) Expressions used in this paragraph and in section 179 of the Gains Act have the same meaning in this paragraph as they have in that section.

Chargeable gains: disposal of debts

9.—(1) Where by virtue of any relevant transfer—

(a) any debt owed to the predecessor is transferred to the transferee, and

(b) the predecessor would, apart from this sub-paragraph, be the original creditor in relation to that debt for the purposes of section 251 of the Gains Act (disposal of debts),

that Act shall have effect as if the transferee and not the predecessor were the original creditor for those purposes.

(2) Where, by virtue of any relevant transfer, any obligations of the predecessor under a guarantee of the repayment of a loan are transferred to the transferee, the transferee shall be treated for the purposes of section 253(4) of the Gains Act (relief for guarantors) as a person who gave the guarantee.

(3) In any case where—

(a) by virtue of any relevant transfer, a debt owed to the predecessor is transferred to the transferee,

(b) that debt is either—

　　　　(i) a right to the repayment of any amount outstanding as principal on a loan which is a qualifying loan for the purposes of either of sections 253 and 254 of the Gains Act (relief for irrecoverable debts owed by traders and payments under guarantees), or

　　　　(ii) a right to recover any amount paid under a guarantee of the payment of such a loan or of a loan which would be such a loan but for section 253(1)(c) of that Act (exclusion of debts not on security), and

(c) no allowable loss in respect of the amount mentioned in paragraph (b)(i) or (ii) above has been claimed by the predecessor under either of sections 253 and 254 of that Act before the coming into force of the relevant transfer,

those sections shall have effect with the modifications set out in sub-paragraph (4) below.

(4) Those modifications are—

(a) that the loan or, as the case may be, the guarantee shall be treated as if it had been made or given by the transferee, and

(b) that any payment made under the guarantee by the predecessor shall be treated as if it had been made by the transferee,

and those sections shall accordingly have effect as if there had been no assignment of the right to recover the principal of the loan or of any right to recover an amount paid under the guarantee.

(5) In any case where—

(a) a debt falling within sub-paragraph (3)(b) above is transferred by virtue of a relevant transfer, and

(b) before the coming into force of the relevant transfer, the predecessor has claimed a loss in respect of the amount mentioned in sub-paragraph (3)(b)(i) or (ii) above under section 253 or 254 of the Gains Act,

the relevant transfer shall not be treated as an assignment of the debt for the purposes of those sections and sub-paragraph (2) above shall not have effect in relation to the transferee, so far as relating to the amount mentioned in paragraph (b) above.

(6) In any case where—

(a) any right to the recovery of an amount falling within subsection (3) of section 253 of the Gains Act (relief in respect of certain irrecoverable loans) is transferred by virtue of a relevant transfer,

(b) an allowable loss determined by reference to that amount has been treated under that subsection as accruing to the predecessor, and

(c) the whole or any part of that amount is at any time recovered by the transferee or by a company in the same group of companies as the transferee,

that Act shall have effect as if a chargeable gain equal to so much of the allowable loss as corresponds to the amount recovered had accrued to the transferee or, as the case may be, to the company in the same group as the transferee.

(7) In any case where—

(a) any right to the recovery of an amount falling within subsection (4) of section 253 of the Gains Act is transferred by virtue of a relevant transfer,

(b) an allowable loss determined by reference to that amount has been treated under that subsection as accruing to the predecessor, and

(c) the whole or any part of the amount mentioned in subsection (4)(a), or the whole or any part of the amount of the payment mentioned in subsection (4)(b), of that section is at any time recovered by the transferee or by a company in the same group of companies as the transferee,

that Act shall have effect as if a chargeable gain equal to so much of the allowable loss as corresponds to the amount recovered had accrued to the transferee or, as the case may be, to the company in the same group as the transferee.

(8) In any case where—

(a) any right to recovery of the relevant outstanding amount, as defined in subsection (11) of section 254 of the Gains Act, is transferred by virtue of a relevant transfer,

(b) an allowable loss determined by reference to that amount has been treated under subsection (2) of that section (relief for debts on qualifying corporate bonds) as accruing to the predecessor, and

(c) the whole or any part of that amount is at any time recovered by the transferee or by a company in the same group of companies as the transferee,

that Act shall have effect as if a chargeable gain equal to so much of the allowable loss as corresponds to the amount recovered and accrued to the transferee or, as the case may be, to the company in the same group as the transferee.

(9) In any case where sub-paragraph (6), (7) or (8) above applies in relation to an allowable loss, subsections (7) and (8) of section 253 of the Gains Act and subsection (10) of section 254 of that Act (which deem a chargeable gain to arise where an amount treated as an allowable loss is recovered by another company in the same group) shall not apply in relation to that allowable loss.

(10) Expressions used in this paragraph and in section 253 or 254 of the Gains Act have the same meaning in this paragraph as they have in that section.

Chargeable gains: assets held before 6th April 1965

10. Schedule 2 to the Gains Act (assets held on 6th April 1965) shall have effect in relation to any assets which vest in the transferee by virtue of a relevant transfer as if—

(a) the predecessor and the transferee were the same person; and

(b) those assets, to the extent that they were in fact acquired or provided by the predecessor, were acquired or, as the case may be, provided by the transferee.

Chargeable gains: miscellaneous disposals and acquisitions

11.—(1) In this paragraph, "relevant disposal" means—

(a) a disposal by virtue of a section 85 transfer scheme, other than a restructuring scheme, to the extent that the scheme provides for the transfer of property, rights and liabilities of—

    (i) the Board,

    (ii) a wholly owned subsidiary of the Board,

    (iii) a publicly owned railway company, or

    (iv) a company which is wholly owned by the Franchising Director,

to a franchise company or to the Franchising Director;

(b) a disposal pursuant to a direction under section 88(6) or (7) or 89 of the Railways Act 1993;

(c) a disposal by or pursuant to an agreement or instrument made or executed, transaction effected or direction given under or by virtue of paragraph 2, 3 or 14(2) of Schedule 8 to that Act, in a case where the transfer scheme in question is a section 85 transfer scheme, other than a restructuring scheme; or

(d) a disposal pursuant to a requirement imposed under paragraph 7(2)(b) of that Schedule, in a case where the transfer to which that Schedule applies is a transfer by virtue of a section 85 transfer scheme.

(2) Subject to sub-paragraph (3) below, section 17 of the Gains Act (disposals and acquisitions treated as made at market value) shall not have effect—

(a) in relation to a relevant disposal or the corresponding acquisition,

(b) in relation to an acquisition by a franchise company, in a case where the corresponding disposal is a disposal by the Franchising Director by virtue of a section 85 transfer scheme, or

(c) in relation to a disposal of a historical record or artefact in accordance with directions under section 125 of the Railways Act 1993 (railway heritage),

unless, in a case falling within paragraph (a) or (b) above, the person making the disposal is connected with the person making the acquisition.

(3) Where there is a relevant disposal of an asset of—

(a) the Board,

(b) a subsidiary of the Board,

(c) a publicly owned railway company, or

(d) a company wholly owned by the Franchising Director,

to the Franchising Director or a company wholly owned by the Crown, the disposal shall be taken for the purposes of the Gains Act, in relation to the person making the disposal and, if the disposal is made to a company wholly owned by the Crown, the person to whom the disposal is made, to be for a consideration such that no gain or loss accrues on the disposal.

(4) Where there is a disposal of a historical record or artefact in accordance with directions under section 125 of the Railways Act 1993 and the disposal is either—

(a) for a consideration not exceeding the sums which are allowable as a deduction under section 38 of the Gains Act (consideration for, and incidental costs of, original acquisition etc), or

(b) for no consideration,

the disposal shall be taken for the purposes of the Gains Act, in relation to the person to whom the disposal is made as well as the person making the disposal, to be for a consideration such that no gain or loss accrues on the disposal.

(5) In this paragraph—

"the corresponding acquisition", in the case of any disposal, means the acquisition made by the person to whom the disposal is made;

"the corresponding disposal" in the case of any acquisition, means the disposal to the person by whom the acquisition is made.

GENERAL NOTE

The Schedule adapts the tax law to make provision for the restructuring and privatisation of British Rail under the Railways Act 1993 (c. 43). Unlike previous privatisations, this does not involve the disposal of the entire business as a going concern to the public by way of a share offer, but the dismantling of British Rail itself. The bulk of British Rail's assets will be taken over by *Railtrack*, which will own the track, signalling and stations and by three regional companies that will own the rolling-stock. Passenger services will be gradually transferred to private sector management by franchising arrangements and freight and parcel services will be sold outright.

The purpose of the Schedule is to ensure that this complicated process does not entail tax consequences which would hinder an orderly implementation of the Railways Act 1993. The general principles are that transfers of assets in the course of restructuring should not entail a possible charge to capital gains tax and that successor companies in the private sector should not have the benefit of British Rail's tax losses but should step into British Rail's shoes so far as capital allowances are concerned.

Para. (1)

This contains general interpretation provisions.

Paras. (2)–(11)

These contain the provisions relating to chargeable gains and losses. A no gain/no loss situation applies in relation to transfers of assets (para. (2)). Relief under the TCGA 1992 (c. 12), s.23 is preserved in specified circumstances (para. (3)). The anti-avoidance provisions of the

TCGA 1992 (c. 12), s.30 are disapplied in certain circumstances (para. (4)). The provisions of TCGA 1992 (c. 12), ss.41 and 174 restricting losses where capital allowances have been given is applied to assets transferred on a no gain/no loss basis (para. (5)). The right to roll-over relief under TCGA 1992 (c. 12), ss.152–160 is preserved in certain circumstances after a relevant transfer (para. (6)). Where transactions are entered into pursuant to an obligation imposed under the Railways Act 1993 (c. 43), s.91(1)(c), no chargeable gain or loss arises in respect of a transfer between certain specified public sector bodies, but where transfers are made to other bodies for a consideration, that is taken into account for computing gains and losses (para. (7)). The TCGA 1992 (c. 12), s.179 is disapplied when a company ceases to be a member of a group as the result of a "qualifying transaction" (*i.e.* a transfer under the Railways Act 1993 (c. 43), ss.85, 88(6) or (7), or 89), but applies when the company next leaves a group (para. (8)). Relief under the TCGA 1992 (c. 12), ss.253 and 254 is preserved in the case of a relevant transfer (para. (9)). The successor under a relevant transfer retains the exemption for gains accruing before April 6, 1965 (para. (10)). Gains and losses on other transfers between specified public sector bodies are deferred (para. (11)).

Transfers of trading stock

12.—(1) This paragraph applies in any case where—
(a) by virtue of a relevant transfer, any trading stock belonging to a trade carried on by the predecessor ("the predecessor's trade") vests in the transferee, and
(b) the trading stock is acquired by the transferee as trading stock for the purposes of a trade which he carries on or which he begins to carry on after the relevant transfer ("the transferee's trade").

(2) Where this paragraph applies, the trading stock in question shall, for the purposes (whether in relation to the predecessor or the transferee) of computing for the purposes of the Corporation Tax Acts the profits or gains of the predecessor's trade and the transferee trade,—
(a) be taken to have been both disposed of by the predecessor and acquired by the transferee in the course of those trades and (subject to that) at the time when the transfer comes into force; and
(b) be valued in each case as if that disposal and acquisition had been for a consideration which in relation to the predecessor would have resulted in neither a profit nor a loss being brought into account in respect of the disposal in the accounting period of the predecessor which is current at that time.

(3) In this paragraph "trading stock" has the same meaning as in section 100 of the Taxes Act 1988.

Transfer of rights to receipts

13. Where, by virtue of any relevant transfer, there is transferred any right of the predecessor to receive any amount which is for the purposes of corporation tax—
(a) an amount brought into account as a trading receipt of the precedessor for any accounting period ending before the time when the transfer comes into force, or
(b) an amount falling to be so brought into account if it is assumed, where it is not the case, that the accounting period of the predecessor current on the day before the transfer comes into force ends immediately before that time,
the transfer shall not require any modification of the way in which that amount has been and is to be treated in relation to the predecessor for those purposes or entitle any amount due or paid in respect of that right to be treated as a trading receipt of the transferee for any accounting period.

Transfer of liabilities

14.—(1) If the whole or any part of the amount of a liability transferred by virtue of a relevant transfer falls, for the purposes of corporation tax,—
(a) to be brought into account as deductible in computing the predecessor's profits, or any description of the predecessor's profits, for any accounting period ending before the time when the transfer comes into force, or
(b) to be so brought into account if it is assumed, where it is not the case, that the accounting period of the predecessor current on the day before the transfer comes into force ends immediately before that time,
then the transfer shall not require any modification of the way in which that amount or, as the case may be, that part of that amount has been or is to be treated in relation to the predecessor for those purposes or entitle any amount due or paid in respect of that liability or, as the case may be, the corresponding part of that liability to be deductible in computing the transferee's profits, or any description of the transferee's profits, for any accounting period.

(2) If and to the extent that the amount of any liability which, in consequence of any relevant transfer, falls to be discharged by the transferee is an amount which would (but for that and any other transfer) have fallen to be deductible in computing the predecessor's profits, or any description of the predecessor's profits, for any accounting period beginning with the coming into force of the transfer or at any subsequent time, that amount shall, to that extent,—

    (a) not be so deductible; but

    (b) subject to sub-paragraph (3) below, be deductible in computing the transferee's profits to the same extent as if the transferee had become subject to the obligation in pursuance of which the liability arises or has arisen at the same time and for the same consideration, and otherwise on the same terms and in the circumstances, as the predecessor;

and for the purposes of this sub-paragraph it shall be assumed, where it is not the case, that the accounting period of the predecessor current on the day before the transfer comes into force ends immediately before the coming into force of that transfer.

(3) For the purposes of corporation tax, where any relevant transfer has the effect that any liability falls to any extent to be discharged by the transferee instead of by the predecessor, the amounts deductible in computing the transferee's profits, or any description of the transferee's profits, for any accounting period shall not include any amount in respect of so much of that liability as falls to be so discharged unless it is an amount which (but for that and any other transfer) would have fallen to be deductible in computing the predecessor's profits, or any description of the predecessor's profits, for any accounting period beginning or ending after the coming into force of that transfer.

(4) The preceding provisions of this paragraph shall apply in relation to the deduction of charges on income against the total profits of the predecessor or transferee for any period as they apply in relation to the deduction of any amount in the computation for that period of the profits of the predecessor or, as the case may be, of the transferee.

(5) For the purposes of Chapter II of Part VI of the Taxes Act 1988 (definition of distributions), where in the case of any relevant transfer any consideration given or treated as given in respect of a security relating to—

    (a) any liability, or

    (b) the use of the principal to which any liability, being a liability to interest or an equivalent liability, relates,

would fall (apart from this sub-paragraph) to be regarded for those purposes as new consideration received by the predecessor, that consideration shall be treated instead, to the extent that it relates to so much of the liability as falls in consequence of the transfer to be discharged by the transferee, as if it were new consideration received by the transferee.

Trading losses

15.—(1) Subject to the following provisions of this paragraph, where as a result of a relevant transfer, the predecessor falls to be regarded for the purposes of section 343 of the Taxes Act 1988 (company reconstruction without change of ownership) as ceasing to carry on a trade and the transferee falls to be regarded for the purposes of that section as beginning to carry on that trade—

    (a) the transferee shall not, by virtue of those matters, be entitled to any relief under section 393(1) (trading losses) of that Act to which it would, apart from this paragraph, have been entitled by virtue of section 343(3) of that Act; and

    (b) after the coming into force of the relevant transfer, the loss in question shall continue to be regarded for the purposes of the Corporation Tax Acts as a loss incurred in the trade for the time being carried on by the predecessor to the same extent as it would have been so regarded apart from the relevant transfer (and shall be eligible for relief accordingly).

(2) The following provisions of this paragraph apply in any case where—

    (a) a restructuring scheme makes express provision for the transfer from the predecessor to the transferee of the right to obtain tax relief in respect of such an amount of the predecessor's unrelieved trading losses or unrelieved transferred losses as may be specified in, or determined in accordance with, the scheme; and

    (b) after the relevant date the transferee carries on, or begins to carry on, any trade (whether or not the trade, or a part of the trade, carried on by the predecessor);

and any reference in this paragraph to a transferred loss is a reference to the amount mentioned in paragraph (a) above.

(3) The transferee shall be entitled to relief under section 393(1) of the Taxes Act 1988 for the transferred loss, as for a loss sustained by the transferee in carrying on its trade, but the trans-

ferred loss may only be set off against trading income of the transferee which arises in an accounting period throughout which the transferee is a public sector railway company.

(4) Where the transferee ceases to be a public sector railway company, it shall be assumed for the purposes of giving relief by virtue of sub-paragraph (3) above that—

(a) on the occasion of the cessation (unless a true accounting period of the transferee ends then) an accounting period of the transferee ends and a new one begins, the new accounting period to end with the end of the true accounting period; and

(b) the amount of the trading income for the accounting period of the transferee against which the relief may be allowed is apportioned to the component accounting periods;

and any apportionment under this sub-paragraph shall be on a time basis according to the respective lengths of the component accounting periods except that, if it appears that that method would work unreasonably or unjustly, such other method shall be used as appears just and reasonable.

(5) Relief by virtue of sub-paragraph (3) above in respect of a transferred loss shall be given against the trading income of any accounting period of the transferee before relief is given against that income in respect of losses incurred by the transferee after the relevant date.

(6) As from the relevant date—

(a) the amount of the predecessor's unrelieved transferred losses (if any) shall be regarded for the purposes of this paragraph as reduced by an amount equal to the transferred loss; and

(b) if the transferred loss exceeds the amount of the predecessor's unrelieved transferred losses before the reduction under paragraph (a) above, or if there are no such losses, the predecessor's unrelieved trading losses shall be regarded for the purposes of the Corporation Tax Acts as reduced by the amount of that excess or, as the case may be, by an amount equal to the transferred loss.

(7) Without prejudice to the generality of sub-paragraphs (1) and (3) above, if the conditions in subsection (1) of section 343 of the Taxes Act 1988 become satisfied at any time on or after the relevant date in relation to any trade (or, where subsection (8) of that section applies, any part of a trade which falls to be treated for the purposes of that section as a separate trade), the company which is the successor, within the meaning of that section, shall not become entitled to relief by virtue of subsection (3) of that section in respect of any amount for which the company which is the predecessor, within the meaning of that section, would have been entitled to relief by virtue of sub-paragraph (3) above had it continued to carry on the trade (or the part of the trade which falls to be treated as a separate trade).

(8) Subject to sub-paragraph (9) below, the provisions of a restructuring scheme providing for the determination of the amount which is to be that of any transferred loss may include provision—

(a) for such a determination to be made by the Secretary of State in such manner as may be described in the scheme;

(b) for any amount determined to be calculated by reference to such factors, or to the opinion of such person, as may be so described; and

(c) for a determination under those provisions to be capable of being modified, on one or more occasions, in such manner and in such circumstances as may be so described.

(9) The consent of the Treasury shall be required for the making or modification of a determination of any such amount as is mentioned in sub-paragraph (8) above; and the consent of the transferee shall also be required for any such modification after the coming into force of the relevant transfer.

(10) Where there is a determination, or a modification of a determination, for any purposes of this paragraph, all necessary adjustments shall be made by making assessments or by repayment or discharge of tax, and shall be so made notwithstanding any limitation on the time within which assessments may be made.

(11) For the purposes of this paragraph, a transferee is at any time a "public sector railway company" if, and only if, it is at that time—

(a) the Board;

(b) a wholly owned subsidiary of the Board;

(c) a publicly owned railway company; or

(d) a company wholly owned by the Crown.

(12) In this paragraph—

"the relevant date" means the date on which the transfer mentioned in sub-paragraph (2)(a) above takes effect;

"trading income" has the same meaning as it has in section 393 of the Taxes Act 1988;

"unrelieved trading losses" means any losses—

(a) which were incurred by the predecessor in carrying on a trade in accounting periods ending before the relevant date, or

(b) for which the predecessor has, by virtue of section 343(3) of the Taxes Act 1988, become entitled to relief under section 393(1) of that Act,

and which would, apart from the restructuring scheme mentioned in sub-paragraph (2)(a) above, have fallen to be set off under the said section 393(1) against trading income of the predecessor arising in the accounting period in which the relevant date falls;

"unrelieved transferred losses" means so much of a transferred loss as would, apart from the restructuring scheme mentioned in sub-paragraph (2)(a) above, have fallen to be set off under section 393(1) of the Taxes Act 1988, as it applies by virtue of sub-paragraph (3) above, against trading income of the predecessor arising in the accounting period in which the relevant date falls.

(13) It shall be assumed for the purposes of the definition of "unrelieved trading losses" and "unrelieved transferred losses" in sub-paragraph (12) above (if it is not in fact the case) that the trading income mentioned in those definitions is at least equal to the aggregate amount of the losses in question of each of those descriptions.

No reduction in allowable losses on extinguishment of certain liabilities

16. Where any of the liabilities of a successor company are extinguished by virtue of section 106(1) of the Railways Act 1993, section 400 of the Taxes Act 1988 (reduction of allowable losses on write-off of government investment) shall not have effect in relation to any amount of government investment in a body corporate which, apart from this paragraph, would thereby fall to be regarded as written-off for the purposes of that section.

Group relief

17.—(1) The existence of the powers of the Secretary of State of the Franchising Director under Part II of the Railways Act 1993 shall not be regarded as constituting arrangements falling within subsection (1) or (2) of section 410 of the Taxes Act 1988 (arrangements for the transfer of a company to another group or consortium).

(2) Nothing in Part II of the Railways Act 1993, and no direction given by the Secretary of State under or by virtue of any provision of that Part, shall be regarded as constituting option arrangements for the purposes of paragraph 5B of Schedule 18 to the Taxes Act 1988.

(3) Arrangements relating to the transfer, pursuant to any provision of Part II of the Railways Act 1993, of shares of a subsidiary of the Board to—

(a) the Secretary of State,
(b) the Franchising Director,
(c) a publicly owned railway company,
(d) a company which is wholly owned by the Crown, or
(e) a person acting on behalf of a person falling within any of paragraphs (a) to (d) above,

shall not, so far as so relating, be regarded as constituting arrangements falling within subsection (1)(b)(i) or (ii) of section 410 of the Taxes Act 1988.

(4) Arrangements relating to the transfer, by virtue of a section 85 transfer scheme, of the whole or any part of a trade carried on by the Board or a wholly owned subsidiary of the Board to—

(a) a publicly owned railway company, or
(b) a company wholly owned by the Franchising Director,

shall not, so far as so relating, be regarded as constituting arrangements falling within section 410(1)(b)(iii) of the Taxes Act 1988.

(5) Arrangements relating to the transfer, pursuant to any provision of Part II of the Railways Act 1993, of shares of a subsidiary of the Board, or shares of a company owned by a consortium, to—

(a) the Secretary of State,
(b) the Franchising Director,
(c) a publicly owned railway company,
(d) a company which is wholly owned by the Crown, or
(e) a person acting on behalf of a person falling within any of paragraphs (a) to (d) above,

shall not, so far as so relating, be regarded as constituting arrangements falling within section 410(2)(b)(ii) of the Taxes Act 1988.

(6) None of sub-paragraphs (3) to (5) above shall have effect in relation to any arrangements if—

(a) notwithstanding the provisions of those sub-paragraphs, the arrangements to any extent fall within section 410(1) or (2) of the Taxes Act 1988; or
(b) the arrangements form part of a series of subsisting arrangements which to any extent—

(i) relate to the transfer of any shares or assets of, or the whole or any part of the trade carried on by, a company to which the first-mentioned arrangements relate, and

(ii) notwithstanding the provisions of sub-paragraphs (3) to (5) above, fall within section 410(1) or (2) of the Taxes Act 1988.

(7) Section 413(6)(a) of the Taxes Act 1988 (company owned by a consortium) shall have effect for the purposes of sub-paragraph (5) above as it has effect for the purposes of Chapter IV of Part X of that Act.

(8) In this paragraph—

"arrangements" has the same meaning as in section 410 of the Taxes Act 1988;

"shares" includes stock.

Securities issued under section 98 or 106 of the Railways Act 1993

18.—(1) Subject to sub-paragraph (2) below, any shares issued by a relevant company in pursuance of section 98 or 106 of the Railways Act 1993 (initial share holding in, and extinguishing of certain liabilities of, successor companies) shall be treated for the purposes of the Corporation Tax Acts as if they had been issued wholly in consideration of a subscription paid to that company (and attributable equally between those shares) of an amount equal—

(a) in the case of shares issued under section 98 of that Act, to the value, as at the transfer date, of the property, rights and liabilities vested in that company in accordance with the transfer scheme mentioned in subsection (1) of that section, or

(b) in the case of shares issued under section 106 of that Act, to the amount of the liabilities extinguished by the order under subsection (1) of that section,

reduced, in either case, by the principal sum payable under any debentures issued by the company in pursuance of the section in question.

(2) Where two or more classes of share are issued by a relevant company in pursuance of section 98 or, as the case may be, section 106 of the Railways Act 1993—

(a) the issued shares of each of those classes shall be valued, as at the day on which, in consequence of section 98(4) or, as the case may be, section 106(5) of that Act, no more shares can be directed to be issued by the company under the section in question;

(b) the amount of the consideration mentioned in sub-paragraph (1) above shall be apportioned between those classes of share in proportion to the aggregate value of the issued shares of each of those classes, as determined pursuant to paragraph (a) above; and

(c) the portion attributed to any class of share pursuant to paragraph (b) above shall be divided by the number of issued shares of that class, the resulting amount being referred to in the following provisions of this sub-paragraph as the "appropriate price" for a share of that class;

and each of the issued shares of any of those classes shall be treated for the purposes of the Corporation Tax Acts as if it had been issued wholly in consideration of a subscription paid to the relevant company of an amount equal to the appropriate price for a share of that class.

(3) Any debenture issued by a relevant company in pursuance of section 98 or 106 of the Railways Act 1993 shall be treated for the purposes of the Corporation Tax Acts as if it had been issued—

(a) wholly in consideration of a loan made to that company of an amount equal to the principal sum payable under the debenture; and

(b) wholly and exclusively for the purposes of the trade or business carried on by that company.

(4) If any debenture issued as mentioned in sub-paragraph (3) above includes provisions for the payment of a sum expressed as interest in respect of a period which falls wholly or partly before the issue of the debenture, any payment made in pursuance of that provision in respect of that period shall be treated for the purposes of the Corporation Tax Acts as if the debenture had been issued at the commencement of that period and, accordingly, as interest on the principal sum payable under the debenture.

(5) The value required to be determined for the purposes of sub-paragraph (1)(a) or (2)(a) above is market value, as defined in section 272 of the Gains Act.

(6) In this paragraph—

"company" means a body corporate;

"relevant company" means a company which is—

(a) a successor company; or

(b) in the application of this paragraph in relation to shares or debentures issued pursuant to section 106 of the Railways Act 1993, the company, or one of the companies, wholly owning (within the meaning of that section) the successor company whose liabilities are extinguished by the order under subsection (1) of that section.

Leased assets

19.—(1) For the purposes of section 781 of the Taxes Act 1988 (assets leased to traders and others), where the interest of the lessor or the lessee under a lease, or any other interest in an asset, vests in any person by virtue of a relevant transfer—

(a) the transfer shall (notwithstanding anything in section 783(4) of that Act) be treated as made without any capital sum having been obtained in respect of that interest by the predecessor or the transferee; and

(b) in a case where the interest is an interest under a lease, payments made by the predecessor under the lease before the coming into force of the transfer shall be treated as if they had been made under that lease by the transferee.

(2) No charge shall arise under section 781(1) of the Taxes Act 1988 by virtue of section 783(2) of that Act in a case where the capital sum mentioned in section 781(1)(b)(i) or (ii) of that Act is the consideration obtained (or treated by section 783(4) of that Act as obtained) by the Board on a disposal pursuant to a direction under Part II of the Railways Act 1993 of securities of a subsidiary of the Board.

(3) The grant of a lease of an asset—

(a) by a person to an associate of his, pursuant to an obligation imposed by a restructuring scheme by virtue of section 91(1)(c) of the Railways Act 1993,

(b) by a person to an associate of his, pursuant to paragraph 2 of Schedule 8 to that Act in connection with a restructuring scheme, or

(c) by the Board, any of the Board's wholly owned subsidiaries, a publicly owned railway company or a company wholly owned by the Franchising Director to an associate of the grantor, pursuant to a direction under that Act,

shall be treated for the purposes of section 781 of the Taxes Act 1988 (notwithstanding anything in section 783(4) of that Act) as made without any capital sum having been obtained by the grantor.

(4) No charge shall arise under section 781(1) of the Taxes Act 1988 in a case where the capital sum mentioned in section 781(1)(b)(i) or (ii) of that Act is the consideration obtained (or treated by section 783(4) of that Act as obtained) on a disposal of, or of an interest in, rolling stock by—

(a) the Board,

(b) a wholly owned subsidiary of the Board,

(c) a publicly owned railway company,

(d) a company wholly owned by the Franchising Director, or

(e) a body which, at the time when it acquired the rolling stock, fell within paragraph (b), (c) or (d) above,

in any case where before, at or after the time when the disposal is made the lessee's interest in a lease of the rolling stock has belonged to an associate of the person making the disposal.

(5) Section 782 of the Taxes Act 1988 (leased assets: special cases) shall not apply to payments made by—

(a) the Board,

(b) a wholly owned subsidiary of the Board,

(c) a publicly owned railway company,

(d) a company wholly owned by the Franchising Director,

(e) a successor company, or

(f) a franchise company,

under a lease of an asset which at any time before the creation of the lease was used by a body falling within paragraphs (a) to (d) above for the purposes of a trade carried on by that body and which was, when so used, owned by that body.

(6) Section 781 of the Taxes Act 1988 shall not, by virtue of sub-paragraph (5) above, apply to any payments to which, by virtue of section 782 of that Act, it would not have applied apart from that sub-paragraph.

(7) In this paragraph—

"asset" has the meaning given by section 785 of the Taxes Act 1988;

"associate" shall be construed in accordance with section 783(10) of that Act;

"capital sum" has the meaning given by section 785 of that Act;

"lease" has the meaning given by section 785 of that Act;

"rolling stock" has the meaning given by section 83(1) of the Railways Act 1993;

"securities" has the meaning given by section 142 of the Financial Services Act 1986.

GENERAL NOTE

Paras. (12)–(19)

These contain provisions relating to income tax and corporation tax. Trading stock moves under a relevant transfer on a fiscally neutral basis (para. (12)) as do rights to receipts (para. (13)) and transfers of liabilities (para. (14)). Trading losses remain available to a public sector successor, but not to a private sector successor (para. (15)). Where debt is written off under the Railways Act 1993 (c. 43), s.106, s.400 of the ICTA 1988 (c. 1) is disapplied, so that the write-off does not affect tax losses (para. (16)). The right to group relief is preserved despite the powers vested in the Secretary of State or the Franchising Director under Railways Act 1993 (c. 43), Pt. II (para. (17)). Securities issued under Railways Act 1993 (c. 43), ss.98 or 106 for no consideration are deemed to have been issued for consideration (para. (18)). The anti-avoidance provisions of the ICTA 1988 (c. 1), ss.781 and 782 relating to leased assets are disapplied in circumstances where they would come into play only because of transactions brought about by provisions in the Railways Act 1993 (c. 43) (para. (19)).

Continuity in relation to capital allowances etc. where trade transferred

20.—(1) Subject to the following provisions of this Schedule, where, apart from this paragraph—

(a) the predecessor would be treated for the purposes of the Corporation Tax Acts as having ceased, by virtue of the coming into force of a relevant transfer, to carry on any trade, and

(b) the transferee would be treated as having begun, on the coming into force of that transfer, to carry it on,

then the trade shall not be treated as permanently discontinued, nor a new trade as set up, for the purposes of the allowances and charges provided for by the Capital Allowances Acts, but sub-paragraphs (2) to (4) below shall apply.

(2) Subject to sub-paragraphs (3) and (4) below, in a case falling within sub-paragraph (1) above—

(a) there shall be made to or on the transferee in accordance with the Capital Allowances Acts all such allowances and charges as would, if the predecessor had continued to carry on the trade, have fallen to be made to or on the predecessor; and

(b) the amount of any such allowance or charge shall be computed as if—

(i) the transferee had been carrying on the trade since the predecessor began to do so; and

(ii) everything done to or by the predecessor had been done to or by the transferee (but so that the relevant transfer itself, so far as it relates to any assets in use for the purpose of the trade, shall not be treated as giving rise to any such allowance or charge).

(3) For the purposes of the Corporation Tax Acts, only such amounts (if any) as may be specified in or determined in accordance with the restructuring scheme providing for a relevant transfer shall be allocated to the transferee in respect of expenditure by reference to which capital allowances may be made by virtue of sub-paragraph (2) above in relation to anything to which the transfer relates.

(4) Sub-paragraph (2) above shall affect the amounts falling to be taken into account in relation to the predecessor as expenditure by reference to which capital allowances may be made only so far as necessary to give effect to a reduction of any such amount by a sum equal to so much of that amount as is allocated to the transferee as mentioned in sub-paragraph (3) above.

(5) Subject to sub-paragraph (6) below, the provisions of a restructuring scheme providing for the determination of any amount which for the purposes of sub-paragraph (3) above is to be allocated, in the case of any relevant transfer, to the transferee may include provision—

(a) for such a determination to be made by the Secretary of State in such manner as may be described in the scheme;

(b) for any amount determined to be calculated by reference to such factors or to the opinion of such person as may be so described; and

(c) for a determination under those provisions to be capable of being modified, on one or more occasions, in such manner and in such circumstances as may be so described.

(6) The consent of the Treasury shall be required for the making or modification of a determination of any such amount as is mentioned in sub-paragraph (5) above; and the consent of the transferee shall also be required for any such modification after the coming into force of the relevant transfer.

(7) This sub-paragraph applies in any case where assets which are the subject of a relevant transfer became vested in the predecessor by virtue of a transfer made by a company; and in any such case—

    (a) if the predecessor held a direct or indirect interest in the company at the time of the transfer by the company, that interest shall be treated for the purposes of sub-paragraph (2)(b)(ii) above as if it had instead been held by the transferee;

    (b) if the company held a direct or indirect interest in the predecessor at the time of the transfer by the company, the interest which the company held in the predecessor shall be treated for the purposes of sub-paragraph (2)(b)(ii) above as if it had instead been the corresponding interest in the transferee; and

    (c) if there was a person who, at the time of the transfer by the company, held—

        (i) a direct or indirect interest in the predecessor, and

        (ii) a direct or indirect interest in the company,

the interest which that person held at that time in the predecessor shall be treated for the purposes of sub-paragraph (2)(b)(ii) above as if it had instead been the corresponding interest in the transferee.

(8) Neither section 343 of the Taxes Act 1988 (company reconstructions without change of ownership) nor section 77 of the Allowances Act (successions to trades: connected persons) shall have effect in a case falling within sub-paragraph (1) above.

(9) In determining whether sub-paragraph (1) above has effect in relation to a relevant transfer in a case where—

    (a) the predecessor continues to carry on any trade or part of a trade after the coming into force of the transfer, or

    (b) the transferee was carrying on any trade before the coming into force of the transfer,

the trade or part of a trade which is continued or, as the case may be, was being carried on shall for the purposes of that sub-paragraph be treated in relation to any trade or part of a trade which is transferred by virtue of the transfer as a separate trade and shall accordingly be disregarded.

(10) Where there is a determination, or a modification of a determination, for any purposes of this paragraph, all necessary adjustments shall be made by making assessments or by repayment or discharge of tax, and shall be so made notwithstanding any limitation on the time within which assessments may be made.

Capital allowances in certain cases where paragraph 20 does not apply

21.—(1) The Capital Allowances Acts shall have effect in accordance with this paragraph in relation to any property if—

    (a) it is property to which a relevant transfer relates; and

    (b) paragraph 20 above does not apply in relation to its transfer to the transferee;

and in this paragraph "the relevant scheme", in relation to property to which a relevant transfer relates, means the restructuring scheme that provides for that transfer.

(2) In any case where—

    (a) subsection (6) of section 21 of the Allowances Act (transfer of industrial building or structures to be deemed to be sale at market price) applies on the relevant transfer in relation to the property, and

    (b) the relevant scheme contains provision for the sale of that property which is deemed to occur by virtue of that subsection to be deemed for the purposes of the Capital Allowances Acts to be at a price specified in or determined in accordance with the scheme,

that deemed sale shall be treated as a sale at the price so specified or determined (instead of at the price determined by virtue of that subsection or any other provision of those Acts), sections 157 and 158 of the Allowances Act shall not apply and that provision of the scheme shall have an equivalent effect in relation to the expenditure which the transferee is to be treated as having incurred in making the corresponding purchase.

(3) Where the property is plant or machinery which would, for the purposes of the Capital Allowances Acts, be treated on the coming into force of the relevant transfer as disposed of by the predecessor to the transferee and the relevant scheme contains provision for the disposal value of that property to be deemed for the purposes of those Acts to be of such amount as may be specified in or determined in accordance with the scheme—

    (a) that provision shall have effect, instead of section 26(1) or 59 of the Allowances Act, for determining an amount as the disposal value of the property or, as the case may be, as the price at which any fixture is to be treated as sold;

    (b) the transferee shall be deemed to have incurred expenditure of that amount on the provision of that property; and

(c) in the case of a fixture, the expenditure which falls to be treated as incurred by the trans-feree shall be deemed for the purposes of section 54 of that Act to be incurred by the giving of a consideration consisting in a capital sum of that amount.

(4) Sub-paragraphs (5) and (6) of paragraph 20 above shall apply in relation to any determination of any amount in accordance with any provision made by a restructuring scheme for the purposes of this paragraph as they apply for the purposes of a determination such as is mentioned in those sub-paragraphs.

(5) Where there is a determination, or a modification of a determination, for any purposes of this paragraph, all necessary adjustments shall be made by making assessments or by repayment or discharge of tax, and shall be so made notwithstanding any limitation on the time within which assessments may be made.

Capital allowances: actual consideration to be the disposal value in certain other cases

22.—(1) In this paragraph, "relevant disposal" means—
(a) a disposal by virtue of a section 85 transfer scheme, other than a restructuring scheme, to the extent that the scheme provides for the transfer of property, rights and liabilities of—
    (i) the Board,
    (ii) a wholly owned subsidiary of the Board,
    (iii) a publicly owned railway company, or
    (iv) a company which is wholly owned by the Franchising Director,
to a franchise company or to the Franchising Director;
(b) a disposal pursuant to a direction under section 89 of the Railways Act 1993;
(c) a disposal in accordance with directions under section 125 of that Act;
(d) a disposal by or pursuant to an agreement or instrument made or executed, transaction effected or direction given under or by virtue of paragraph 2, 3 or 14(2) of Schedule 8 to that Act, in a case where the transfer scheme in question is a section 85 transfer scheme, other than a restructuring scheme; or
(e) a disposal pursuant to a requirement imposed under paragraph 7(2)(b) of that Schedule, in a case where the transfer to which that Schedule applies is a transfer by virtue of a section 85 transfer scheme.

(2) A relevant disposal of the relevant interest in—
(a) an industrial building or structure, or
(b) a qualifying hotel or a commercial building or structure,
shall be treated for the purposes of Part I of the Allowances Act, and the other provisions of that Act which are relevant to that Part, as a sale of that relevant interest; and sections 157 and 158 of that Act (sales between connected persons or without change of control) shall not have effect in relation to that sale.

(3) Where there is a relevant disposal of machinery or plant, the amount which, in consequence of that disposal, is to be brought into account as the disposal value of that machinery or plant for the purposes of section 24 of the Allowances Act (balancing adjustments) shall, subject to section 26(2) and (3) of that Act (disposal value of machinery or plant not to exceed capital expenditure incurred on its provision) be taken—
(a) if consideration is given in respect of the relevant disposal, to be an amount equal to the amount or value of that consideration, or
(b) if no such consideration is given, to be nil,
notwithstanding any other provision of the Capital Allowances Acts.

(4) Where, in consequence of a relevant disposal, a fixture is treated by section 57(2) of the Allowances Act as ceasing to belong to a person at any time, the amount which, in consequence of that disposal, is to be brought into account as the disposal value of the fixture for the purposes of section 24 of that Act shall, subject to section 26(2) and (3) of that Act, be taken—
(a) if consideration is given in respect of the relevant disposal, to be an amount equal to that portion of the amount or value of that consideration which falls (or, if the person to whom the relevant disposal is made were entitled to an allowance, would fall) to be treated for the purposes of Part II of that Act as expenditure incurred by that person on the provision of the fixture, or
(b) if no such consideration is given, to be nil,
notwithstanding any other provision of the Capital Alliances Acts.

Sale and lease-back: limitation on tax reliefs

23.—(1) Section 779 of the Taxes Act 1988 (sale and lease back) shall not apply by virtue of subsection (1) or (2) of that section in any case where the liability of the transferor, or of the person associated with the transferor, is—

(a) a liability under an access agreement, within the meaning of Part I of the Railways Act 1993;

(b) a liability under an agreement or instrument made or executed—

(i) pursuant to an obligation imposed by a restructuring scheme by virtue of section 91(1)(c) of that Act; or

(ii) pursuant to paragraph 2 of Schedule 8 to that Act;

(c) a liability under an exempt lease; or

(d) a liability to pay exempt rent or to make other exempt payments.

(2) A lease is "exempt" for the purposes of sub-paragraph (1)(c) above if—

(a) the transfer mentioned in subsection (1) of section 779 of the Taxes Act 1988 is—

(i) a transfer by virtue of a restructuring scheme;

(ii) a transfer pursuant to an obligation imposed by a restructuring scheme by virtue of section 91(1)(c) of the Railways Act 1993; or

(iii) a transfer pursuant to paragraph 2 of Schedule 8 to that Act; and

(b) the lease is granted after that transfer and otherwise than pursuant to—

(i) an obligation imposed by a restructuring scheme by virtue of section 91(1)(c) of the Railways Act 1993; or

(ii) paragraph 2 of Schedule 8 to that Act.

(3) Rent or other payments are "exempt" for the purposes of paragraph (d) of sub-paragraph (1) above if—

(a) the rent or other payments would, apart from that paragraph, be rent or other payments to which section 779 of the Taxes Act 1988 applies by virtue of subsection (1) or (2) of that section;

(b) the transfer mentioned in subsection (1) or, as the case may be, subsection (2)(a) of that section is—

(i) a transfer by virtue of a restructuring scheme;

(ii) a transfer pursuant to an obligation imposed by a restructuring scheme by virtue of section 91(1)(c) of the Railways Act 1993; or

(iii) a transfer pursuant to paragraph 2 of Schedule 8 to that Act; and

(c) the transaction or series of transactions mentioned in subsection (1)(b) or, as the case may be, subsection (2)(b) of the said section 779 is effected after that transfer.

(4) In this paragraph "transferor", "lease" and "rent" have the same meaning as they have in section 779 of the Taxes Act 1988 and "associated" shall be construed in accordance with subsection (11) of that section.

Sales of land with right to reconveyance

24. No charge to tax shall arise by virtue of section 36 of the Taxes Act 1988 (charge on sale of land with right to reconveyance) where the sale in question is constituted by a disposition to a franchise company—

(a) by virtue of a transfer scheme;

(b) pursuant to an obligation imposed by a transfer scheme by virtue of section 91(1)(c) of the Railways Act 1993; or

(c) pursuant to paragraph 2 of Schedule 8 to that Act.

Modifications of restructuring scheme

25.—(1) Subject to sub-paragraph (2) below, where the effect of a restructuring scheme is modified in pursuance of an agreement or direction under paragraph 2 or 3 of Schedule 8 to the Railways Act 1993, the Corporation Tax Acts and this Schedule shall have effect as if—

(a) the scheme originally made had been the scheme as modified; and

(b) anything done by or in relation to the preceding holder had, so far as relating to the property, rights or liabilities affected by the modification, been done by or in relation to the subsequent holder.

(2) A disposal of an asset—

(a) which is effected in pursuance of an agreement or direction under paragraph 2 of Schedule 8 to the Railways Act 1993, and

(b) which is either the grant of a lease of land or the creation of other liabilities and rights over land,

shall be taken for the purposes of corporation tax on chargeable gains, in relation to the person to whom the disposal is made as well as the person making the disposal, to be effected for a consideration such that no gain or loss accrues to the person making the disposal.

(3) Section 171(1) of the Gains Act (transfers within a group) shall not apply where the disposal in question falls within sub-paragraph (2) above.

(4) Any reference in sub-paragraph (1) or (2) above to an agreement or direction under paragraph 2 or 3 of Schedule 8 to the Railways Act 1993 includes a reference to such an agreement or direction as varied in accordance with a direction given by the Secretary of State under paragraph 14(2) of that Schedule.

(5) For the purposes of sub-paragraph (1)(b) above—

"the preceding holder" means the person who without the modification in question—

(a) became, by virtue of the restructuring scheme in question, entitled or subject to the property, rights or liabilities affected by the modification, or

(b) remained, notwithstanding the restructuring scheme in question, entitled or subject to the property, rights or liabilities affected by the modification,

as the case may be;

"the subsequent holder" means the person who, in consequence of the modification in question, becomes, or resumes being, entitled or subject to the property, rights or liabilities affected by the modification.

Income tax exemption for certain interest

26. Where liability for a loan made to the Board is vested in a successor company by virtue of a section 85 transfer scheme, the vesting shall not affect any direction given, or having effect as if given, by the Treasury under section 581 of the Taxes Act 1988 (income tax exemption for interest on foreign currency securities) in respect of the loan.

Employee benefits: transport vouchers

27.—(1) This paragraph applies to any person (an "eligible person")—

(a) who on January 11, 1994 was in the employment of—

(i) the Board,

(ii) a wholly owned subsidiary of the Board, or

(iii) any other subsidiary of the Board which, at that date, was a passenger transport undertaking; and

(b) who at that date was provided, or was eligible to be provided, by reason of that employment, with a transport voucher falling within subsection (6) of section 141 of the Taxes Act 1988 (exclusion of subsection (1) of that section in relation to certain transport vouchers);

but this sub-paragraph is subject to sub-paragraph (2) below.

(2) This paragraph shall not apply, or shall cease to apply, to a person if, on or after 11th January 1994, any of the following conditions became or becomes satisfied in his case, that is to say—

(a) he ceases, otherwise than—

(i) by virtue of anything done under or by virtue of, or pursuant to, the Railways Act 1993, or

(ii) by virtue of any other enactment or statutory instrument, in consequence of anything so done,

to be in the employment of a person falling within sub-paragraph (i) or, as the case may be, sub-paragraph (ii) or (iii) of sub-paragraph (1)(a) above;

(b) he is not in the employment of any person engaged in the railway industry; or

(c) the continuity of the period of his employment is broken.

(3) Subsection (6) of section 141 of the Taxes Act 1988 shall, if and so long as the conditions in sub-paragraph (4) below are satisfied, have effect in relation to a transport voucher provided for an eligible person, notwithstanding—

(a) that the employer of the eligible person does not fall to be regarded as a passenger transport undertaking;

(b) that the arrangements under which the transport voucher is provided were not in operation on 25th March 1982; or

(c) that the passenger transport services which may be obtained by means of the transport voucher are provided, in whole or in part, otherwise than as mentioned in paragraphs (a) to (d) of that subsection;

but this sub-paragraph is subject to sub-paragraph (2) above.

(4) The conditions mentioned in sub-paragraph (3) above are—

(a) that the eligible person is in the employment of an employer engaged in the railway industry;

(b) that the transport voucher is provided by reason of the eligible person's being in the employment of such an employer;

(c) that the transport voucher is intended to enable the eligible person or a relation of his to obtain passenger transport services; and

(d) that the current transport voucher benefits in the case of the eligible person are not significantly better than the former transport voucher benefits for comparable employees.

(5) The Secretary of State may, with the consent of the Treasury, by order prescribe for any
purposes of this paragraph circumstances—

    (a) in which a person who ceases, or ceased, as mentioned in sub-paragraph (2)(a) above to
be in the employment there mentioned shall be treated—

        (i) as if he had not ceased to be in that employment, or

        (ii) as if he had not so ceased to be in that employment;

    (b) in which a person shall be treated for a period during which he is not or was not in the
employment of any person engaged in the railway industry as if he were or had been in the
employment of such a person;

    (c) in which a break in the continuity of a person's period of employment shall be disre-
garded; or

    (d) in which a transport voucher shall be treated as if it were, or had been, provided for a
person by reason of his being in the employment of an employer engaged in the railway
industry.

(6) The employers who are to be regarded for the purposes of this paragraph as "engaged in
the railway industry" are those who carry on activities of a class or description specified for the
purposes of this sub-paragraph in an order made by the Secretary of State with the consent of the
Treasury; and the Secretary of State may so specify any class or description of activity which, in
his opinion, falls within, or is related to or connected with, the railway industry.

(7) Any power to make an order under this paragraph shall be exercisable by statutory instrument; and a statutory instrument containing such an order shall be subject to annulment pursuant to a resolution of the House of Commons.

(8) In determining for the purposes of sub-paragraph (4)(d) above whether the current transport voucher benefits in the case of an eligible person are not significantly better than the former
transport voucher benefits for comparable employees, regard shall be had, in particular, to—

    (a) the passenger transport services which may be, or (as the case may be) might have been,
obtained by means of transport vouchers under the arrangements in question,

    (b) whether, and (if so) the extent to which, free or concessionary travel is or (as the case may
be) was available under those arrangements,

    (c) the rate of any discount to the standard fare which is or (as the case may be) was available
in the case of concessionary travel under those arrangements, and

    (d) any limitations on the availability or use of transport vouchers under the arrangements in
question.

(9) Apart from paragraph 18, so much of Schedule 13 to the Employment Protection (Consolidation) Act 1978 as has effect for the purpose of ascertaining whether any period of employment is continuous shall apply for the purposes of this paragraph as it applies for the purposes of
that Act, except that, in the case of an employee—

    (a) who is employed for less than 16 hours, but for at least one hour, in any week, or

    (b) whose relations with the employer are governed during the whole or part of a week by a
contract of employment which normally involves employment for less than 16 hours, but
for at least one hour, weekly,

that Schedule shall so apply in relation to that employee and that week with the modifications in
sub-paragraph (10) below.

(10) Those modifications are that the said Schedule 13 shall have effect—

    (a) as if paragraph 3 provided for any week—

        (i) during the whole or part of which the employee's relations with the employer are
governed otherwise than by a contract of employment which requires him to be
employed for a minimum number of hours weekly, and

        (ii) in which the employee is employed for one hour or more,

    to count in computing a period of employment;

    (b) as if paragraph 4 provided for any week during the whole or part of which the employee's
relations with the employer are governed by a contract of employment which normally
involves employment for at least one hour, but for less than 16 hours, weekly to count in
computing a period of employment; and

    (c) as if paragraphs 5 to 7 and, in paragraphs 9, 10 and 15, the references to paragraph 5, were
omitted.

(11) Expressions used in sub-paragraph (9) or (10) above and in Schedule 13 to the Employment Protection (Consolidation) Act 1978 have the same meaning in that sub-paragraph as they
have in that Schedule.

(12) In this paragraph—

"the current transport voucher benefits", in the case of an eligible person, means the totality of the benefits which, by reason of his employment by an employer engaged in the railway industry, are available in the year in question—

(a) to the eligible person, and

(b) to relations of his,

by way of transport voucher under the arrangements under which the transport voucher in question is provided;

"the former transport voucher benefits for comparable employees", in the case of an eligible person, means the totality of the benefits which would, by reason of the employment by the Board of a person of similar status to the eligible person ("the comparable person"), have been available in the year 1993–94—

(a) to the comparable person, and

(b) to relations of his,

by way of transport voucher under arrangements in operation on 25th March 1982.

(13) Subject to paragraph 1(1) and sub-paragraphs (11) and (12) above, expressions used in this paragraph and in section 141 of the Taxes Act 1988 have the same meaning in this paragraph as they have in that section.

(14) This paragraph has effect—

(a) in relation to transport vouchers received by an employee on or after 11th January 1994; and

(b) in relation to expense incurred on or after that date in, or in connection with, the provision of—

(i) any transport voucher, or

(ii) the money, goods or services for which it is capable of being exchanged,

irrespective of when the transport voucher falls to be regarded as received by the employee in question.

GENERAL NOTE

Paras. (20)–(22)

These deal with capital allowances. Balancing charges or allowances will not arise on assets which are subject to a restructuring scheme where a trade is transferred; alternatively, the transferee will be able to claim the same allowances as the transferor could have claimed (para. (20)). Similar treatment is accorded in the case of other relevant transfers (para. (21)). In the case of other relevant disposals, including those to the private sector, balancing charges and allowances are computed in accordance with the actual consideration given rather than market value (para. (22)).

Para. (23)

This disapplies the anti-avoidance provisions in the ICTA 1992 (c. 1), s.779 regarding sale and lease-back transactions, in the context of certain transactions under the Railways Act 1993.

Para. (24)

The charge under the ICTA 1988 (c. 1), s.36 on sale of land with a right to reconveyance is disapplied where the sale is to a franchise company within the terms of the Railways Act 1993 (c. 43).

Para. (25)

A modified restructuring scheme is treated as far as possible in the same way as the original scheme for tax purposes.

Para. (26)

Income tax exemption for interest on foreign currency securities under the ICTA 1988 (c. 1), s.581 is unaffected by a transfer scheme under Railways Act 1993 (c. 43), s.85.

Para. (27)

The exemption from tax on travel concessions to employees in the public transport industry earning less than £8,500 a year is maintained where British Rail personnel leave by reason of the Railways Act 1993 and continue to work in the industry and receive similar concessions.

Finance Act 1994

SCHEDULE 25

NORTHERN IRELAND AIRPORTS LIMITED

Interpretation

1.—(1) In this Schedule—
   "the final accounting period" means the last complete accounting period of NIAL ending
      before the transfer date;
   "the Holding Company" means the Northern Ireland Transport Holding Company estab-
      lished under section 47 of the Transport Act (Northern Ireland) 1967;
   "NIAL" means the subsidiary of the Holding Company incorporated under the name of
      Northern Ireland Airports Limited;
   "the Order" means the Airports (Northern Ireland) Order 1994 and any reference to an
      Article is to an Article of the Order;
   "the successor company" means the company nominated under Article 51(1) as the suc-
      cessor company for the purposes of the Order;
   "the transfer date" means the day appointed under Article 54(2);
   "the transferred trade" means the trade carried on by NIAL and transferred under Article
      54(2) to the successor company.
(2) This Schedule, so far as it relates to corporation tax on chargeable gains, shall be construed
as one with the Taxation of Chargeable Gains Act 1992.

Transfers from NIAL to successor company: general

2.—(1) The following shall apply for the purposes of the Corporation Tax Acts—
(a) the transferred trade shall be treated as having been, at the time when it began to be
    carried on by NIAL and at all times since that time, a separate trade carried on by the
    successor company;
(b) the trade carried on by the successor company on and after the transfer date shall be
    treated as the same trade as that which, by virtue of paragraph (a) above, it is treated as
    having carried on before that date;
(c) all property, rights and liabilities of NIAL which are transferred under Article 54(2) to the
    successor company shall be treated as having been, at the time when they became vested
    in NIAL and at all times since that time, property, rights and liabilities of the successor
    company; and
(d) anything done by NIAL in relation to any property, rights and liabilities which are trans-
    ferred under Article 54(2) to the successor company shall be deemed to have been done
    by the successor company.
(2) This paragraph shall have effect in relation to accounting periods beginning after the final
accounting period.

Roll-over relief

3.—(1) This paragraph applies where NIAL has, before the transfer date, disposed of (or of its
interest in) any assets used, throughout the period of ownership, wholly or partly for the purposes of the transferred trade.
(2) Sections 152 to 156 of the Taxation of Chargeable Gains Act 1992 (roll-over relief on
replacement of business assets) shall have effect in relation to that disposal as if NIAL and the
successor company were the same person.

Transfers from Holding Company to successor company

4.—(1) This paragraph applies where under Article 54(2) an asset of the Holding Company is
transferred to the successor company.
(2) The disposal of the asset by the Holding Company shall be taken for the purposes of
corporation tax on chargeable gains to be effected for a consideration of such amount as would
secure that on the disposal neither a gain nor a loss would accrue to the Holding company.

(3) In section 35(3)(d) of the Taxation of Chargeable Gains Act 1992 after sub-paragraph (ix) there shall be inserted—
    "(x) paragraph 4(2) of Schedule 25 to the Finance Act 1994."

Leasehold interests in industrial buildings or structures

5.—(1) This paragraph applies where—
(a) NIAL is entitled, under a lease granted by the Holding Company, to a leasehold interest in a building or structure,
(b) by virtue of Article 52(2)(b) that interest is deemed to have been surrendered by NIAL,
(c) under Article 52(3) the Holding Company and NIAL enter into a lease under which NIAL is entitled to a leasehold interest ("the new interest") in the property, and
(d) under Article 54(2) that interest is transferred to the successor company.
(2) For the purposes of the 1990 Act—
(a) the surrender shall be deemed to be for such an amount (by way of sale, insurance, salvage or compensation moneys) as would secure that no balancing allowance or balancing charge would be made to or on NIAL by reason of the surrender ("the surrender value");
(b) the successor company shall be treated for the purposes of the 1990 Act—
      (i) as if the new interest were the relevant interest in relation to the capital expenditure incurred on the construction of the property; and
      (ii) as if the amount of the residue of that expenditure immediately after the transfer of the new interest were equal to the surrender value.
(3) In this paragraph—
    "the 1990 Act" means the Capital Allowances Act 1990;
    "balancing allowance" and "balancing charge" have the same meanings as in section 4 of the 1990 Act;
    "the property" means the building or structure referred to in sub-paragraph (1); and
    "relevant interest" has the same meaning as in section 20 of the 1990 Act.

Securities of successor company

6.—(1) Any share issued by the successor company under Article 57 shall be treated for the purposes of the Corporation Tax Acts as if it had been issued wholly in consideration of a subscription paid to the company of an amount equal to the nominal value of the share.
(2) Any debenture issued by the successor company under Article 57 shall be treated for the purposes of the Corporation Tax Acts as if it had been issued—
(a) wholly in consideration of a loan made to the company of an amount equal to the principal sum payable under the debenture, and
(b) wholly and exclusively for the purposes of the trade carried on by the company.
(3) If any such debenture includes provision for the payment of a sum expressed as interest in respect of a period which falls wholly or partly before the issue of the debenture, any payment made in pursuance of that provision in respect of that period shall be treated for the purposes of the Corporation Tax Acts as if the debenture had been issued at the commencement of that period and, accordingly, as interest on the principal sum payable under the debenture.

GENERAL NOTE
    The Schedule deals with the tax treatment of the pre-privatisation reorganisation of *Northern Ireland Airports Limited* (NIAL) under the provisions of the Airports (Northern Ireland) Order 1994 and the transfer scheme under the Order. The main effect is to prevent capital gains or losses arising on the reorganisation and to enable a successor company to inherit NIAL's tax position in relation to the activities transferred. It also deals with the tax consequences of secondary transfers under the Order between NIAL, Northern Ireland Transport Holding Company and the Department of the Environment (Northern Ireland).

       SCHEDULE 26

REPEALS

PART I

VEHICLES EXCISE DUTY

(1) RATES

Chapter	Short title	Extent of repeal
1971 c. 10	The Vehicles (Excise) Act 1971.	In Schedule 1, in Part I, paragraph 4(a). In Schedule 2, in Part I, paragraphs 3 and 5. In Schedule 4, paragraph 6(6)(a), (c) and (d).
1985 c. 54.	The Finance Act 1985.	Section 4(4).
1991 c. 31.	The Finance Act 1991.	In Schedule 3, in Part I, paragraph 21.
1993 c. 34.	The Finance Act 1993.	Section 17(3)(a) and (7)(b). Section 20(3).

These repeals have effect in relation to licences taken out after 30th November 1993.

(2) TRANSITIONAL MODIFICATIONS

Chapter	Short title	Extent of repeal
1971 c. 10.	The Vehicles (Excise) Act 1971.	In section 2A(1), the words "(other than licences for one calendar year)". In Schedule 7, in Part I, paragraphs 1(c), 3(b), 18, 19, 21, and 22 and, so far as it relates to section 26(2), paragraph 23.

These repeals come into force on 1st June 1994.

(3) OTHER PROVISIONS

Chapter	Short title	Extent of repeal
1971 c. 10.	The Vehicles (Excise) Act 1971.	Section 1(4). In section 3(3), the words "the restoration of any forfeiture and". Section 4(3)(a). In section 16(4), the words following paragraph (b). In section 18, subsections (8) and (9) and, in subsection (10), paragraph (b) and the word "and" immediately preceding it. Section 21. In section 22, in subsection (1), the words "or sign to be exhibited", "or 21" and "or exhibited" and, in subsection (2), the words "or sign exhibited" and "or sign". In section 23, as set out in paragraph 20 of Part I of Schedule 7, in subsection (1)(f), the words "or the signs" and "or signs". In section 25, in subsection (1), in paragraph (a), the words "temporary licences or" and, in paragraph (b), the words from the beginning to "allocated to the dealer in pursuance of this Act or" and, in subsec-

Chapter	Short title	Extent of repeal
		tion (2), the words "requirement or" (in both places). In section 26, in subsection (1), the words "or sign to be exhibited" and "or 21" and, in subsection (2)(a), the words "temporary licences or". In section 28(1), "11(2),". In section 29(4), "11(2),". In section 35(2), the words "and forfeitures" (in both places). Section 36. In section 37— in subsection (3), as set out in paragraph 22 of Part I of Schedule 7, "2(5), 11(3), 14,", in subsection (3A), as so set out, "14," and "14 or", and in subsection (4), "11(3), 14, 15(1), 17(1),". In Schedule 4, paragraph 5 and, in paragraph 15(1), in the definition of "goods vehicle", the words "(including a tricycle as defined in Schedule 1 to this Act and weighing more than 425 kilograms unladen)".
1976 c. 40	The Finance Act 1976.	In section 11, in subsection (2)(c), the words "or, if it falls" onwards and subsection (5). In section 12(2)(a), the words "either" and ", or elsewhere".
1983 c. 28.	The Finance Act 1983.	In Schedule 3, in Part II, paragraph 9.
1986 c. 41.	The Finance Act 1986.	In Schedule 2, in Part I, in paragraph 4, in sub-paragraph (5), in paragraph (a), the words ", including those words where they appear in the subsection as set out in paragraph 12 of Part I of Schedule 7," and paragraph (c) and sub-paragraph (7)(b).
1987 c. 16.	The Finance Act 1987.	In Schedule 1, in Part III, paragraphs 16(2) and 18(2) and (3).
1988 c. 53.	The Road Traffic Offenders Act 1988.	In Schedule 5, the entry relating to the Vehicles (Excise) Act 1971.
1988 c. 54.	The Road Traffic (Consequential Provisions) Act 1988.	In Schedule 3, paragraph 15.
1990 c. 29.	The Finance Act 1990.	In Schedule 2, in Part II, paragraph 6(1) to (3).
1991 c. 31.	The Finance Act 1991.	In Schedule 3, Part II.
1993 c.34.	The Finance Act 1993.	In section 19(2), the words "including that subsection as set out in paragraph 12 of Part I of Schedule 7".

PART II

GAMING MACHINE LICENCE DUTY

Chapter	Short title	Extent of repeal
1981 c. 63.	The Betting and Gaming Duties Act 1981.	Section 21A. Section 22(5). In section 24, subsection (2), in subsections (3) and (4) the word "such", in subsection

Chapter	Short title	Extent of repeal
		(3) the words from "but" to the end, in subsection (4) the words "or there are special licences in force with respect to those machines" and in subsection (6)(a) the words from "or" at the end of sub-paragraph (i) to "greater". In section 26, in subsection (4) the words "section 22(5) or".
1982 c. 39.	The Finance Act 1982.	In Schedule 4, paragraphs 9, 10 and 11A. In Schedule 3, paragraphs 9, 11 and 15.
1984 c. 43.	The Finance Act 1984.	In Schedule 3, paragraphs 3 to 5, 6(b) to (d) and (f), 7(3) to (7) and (9) to (11).
1985 c. 54.	The Finance Act 1985.	In Schedule 5, paragraphs 2, 3(1) and 9(1).
1987 c. 16.	The Finance Act 1987.	Section 4. Section 5(1), (4) and (5).
1993 c. 34.	The Finance Act 1993.	Section 15. In section 16, subsections (4)(b) and (5).

These repeals have effect in accordance with Schedule 3 to this Act.

PART III

EXCISE DUTIES: ENFORCEMENT AND APPEALS

Chapter	Short title	Extent of repeal
1979 c. 2	The Customs and Excise Management Act 1979.	Section 111(2). In section 113(4), the words from "and the trader" onwards. Section 116A. Section 127.
1979 c. 4.	The Alcoholic Liquor Duties Act 1979.	Section 13(4). Section 15(8). Section 19(3).
1979 c. 7.	The Tobacco Products Duty Act 1979.	Section 8(3).
1981 c. 35.	The Finance Act 1981.	In schedule 8— (a) in paragraph 2(d), paragraph (ii) and the word "and" immediately preceding it; (b) paragraph 7; (c) in paragraph 12, in sub-paragraph (b), the words from "and after" onwards and sub-paragraph (c); (d) in paragraph 14, the words from "and after" in sub-paragraph (c) to the end of sub-paragraph (d); and (e) in paragraph 15, sub-paragraph (c) and the word "and" immediately preceding it.
1981 c. 63.	The Betting and Gaming Duties Act 1981.	In section 24(5), the words after paragraph (f). In Schedule 1— (a) paragraph 11; (b) in paragraph 14(3), the word "reasonably", and (c) in paragraph 15(1), the words from "(not being" to "9 above)". In Schedule 2, paragraph 5 and, in paragraph 7(6), the words "(1) or".

Chapter	Short title	Extent of repeal
1985 c. 54. 1989 c. 26. 1992 c. 48.	The Finance Act 1985. The Finance Act 1989. The Finance (No. 2) Act 1992.	In Schedule 3, paragraphs 14 and 16(4). In Schedule 4, paragraph 16(2). In Schedule 5, paragraph 9(2). Section 15. In Schedule 2, paragraph 2(6).

Section 19 of this Act applies to these repeals as it applies to Chapter II of Part I of this Act.

PART IV

VALUE ADDED TAX

Chapter	Short title	Extent of repeal
1985 c. 54.	The Finance Act 1985.	In section 20(2)(a) the words "one month after".

This repeal has effect in accordance with section 46 of this Act.

PART V

INCOME TAX, CORPORATION TAX AND CAPITAL GAINS TAX

(1) RELIEFS

Chapter	Short title	Extent of repeal
1988 c. 1.	The Income and Corporation Taxes Act 1988.	Section 257BB(6). In section 257D(5)(d), the words "section 257A and". In section 265(3)(b), the words from "section 257A" to "or under". In section 347B(2), the words "Notwithstanding section 347A(1)(a) but".
1988 c. 39. 1992 c. 48.	The Finance Act 1988. The Finance (No. 2) Act 1992.	In Schedule 3, paragraph 33. In Schedule 5, paragraph 8(2).

The repeals in section 347B of the Income and Corporation Taxes Act 1988 and in the Finance Act 1988 have effect in relation to payments becoming due on or after 6th April 1994 and the other repeals have effect in accordance with section 77(7) of this Act.

(2) INTEREST RELIEF

Chapter	Short title	Extent of repeal
1988 c. 1.	The Income and Corporation Taxes Act 1988.	Section 257D(8)(a). Section 265(3)(a). Section 353(4) and (5).
1991 c. 31. 1992 c. 12.	The Finance Act 1991. The Taxation of Chargeable Gains Act 1992.	Section 27(1) to (5) and (7). In section 6(1), the words "353(4), 369(3A)", the words "certain interest etc. and" and paragraph (a).
1992 c. 48.	The Finance (No. 2) Act 1992.	In section 19, in subsection (3), the words "353(5), 369(3B)" and subsection (5).
1993 c. 34.	The Finance Act 1993.	Section 57(7). In Schedule 6, in paragraph 1, the words "353(5), 369(3B)".

These repeals have effect in accordance with section 81(6) of this Act.

(3) MEDICAL INSURANCE

Chapter	Short title	Extent of repeal
1988 c. 1.	The Income and Corporation Taxes Act 1988.	In section 257D(8), paragraph (d).
1989 c. 26.	The Finance Act 1989.	In section 55, in subsection (2) paragraph (e) and the word "and" immediately preceding it, and subsections (3) to (6).

1. The repeals in the Income and Corporation Taxes Act 1988 have effect in accordance with paragraph 3 of Schedule 10 to this Act.
2. The repeals in the Finance Act 1989 have effect in accordance with paragraph 5 of that Schedule.

(4) VOCATIONAL TRAINING

Chapter	Short title	Extent of repeal
1991 c. 31.	The Finance Act 1991.	In section 32(10), the words after paragraph (b).

This repeal comes into force in accordance with section 84(4) of this Act.

(5) BENEFICIAL LOANS

Chapter	Short title	Extent of repeal
1988 c. 1.	The Income and Corporation Taxes Act 1988.	In section 160(4), the words from "and Part III" to the end. Section 167(2A). Section 191B(14). In Schedule 7, in paragraph 1(5) the words "his employer being" and Parts III to V.
1991 c. 31.	The Finance Act 1991.	Section 31. In Schedule 6, paragraphs 2 and 5.

These repeals have effect in accordance with section 88(5) of this Act.

(6) VOUCHERS

Chapter	Short title	Extent of repeal
1988 c. 1.	The Income and Corporation Taxes Act 1988.	In section 141(1), the words following paragraph (b).

(7) RELIEF ON RE-INVESTMENT

Chapter	Short title	Extent of repeal
1992 c. 12.	The Taxation of Chargeable Gains Act 1992.	In section 164A, in subsection (2) the words "Subject to section 164C", and subsections (3) to (7) and (11).

Chapter	Short title	Extent of repeal
		Sections 164C to 164E. In section 164F, in subsection (5)(a) the words "or 164D" and in subsection (10) the words "(within the meaning of section 164D)". In section 164H(1), the words "within the meaning of section 164C".

These repeals have effect in accordance with section 91(2) of this Act.

(8) INDEXATION ALLOWANCE

Chapter	Short title	Extent of repeal
1992 c. 12.	The Taxation of Chargeable Gains Act 1992.	In section 56(1)(a), the words "or loss". Section 103. Section 111. Sections 182 to 184. Section 200. In Schedule 7A, in paragraph 2(4) the words "except in relation to the calculation of any indexed rise", in paragraph 2(9) the definition of "indexed rise", in paragraph 4(12) the words from "together" to the end and paragraph 4(13).
1993 c. 34.	The Finance Act 1993.	In Schedule 17, paragraph 8.

These repeals have effect in acordance with section 93(11) of this Act.

(9) COMMODITY AND FINANCIAL FUTURES

Chapter	Short title	Extent of repeal
1992 c. 12.	The Taxation of Chargeable Gains Act 1992.	Section 143(4).

This repeal has effect in accordance with section 95(2) of this Act.

(10) SETTLEMENTS WITH FOREIGN ELEMENT: INFORMATION

Chapter	Short title	Extent of repeal
1970 c. 9.	The Taxes Management Act 1970.	In the Table in section 98, in the second column the entry relating to paragraphs 11 to 14 of Schedule 5 to the Taxation of Chargeable Gains Act 1992.
1992 c. 12.	The Taxation of Chargeable Gains Act 1992.	In Schedule 5, paragraphs 11 to 14.

These repeals have effect in accordance with section 97 of this Act.

(11) Profit sharing schemes

Chapter	Short title	Extent of repeal
1988 c. 1.	The Income and Corporation Taxes Act 1988.	In Schedule 10, in paragraph 3 the words from "In this paragraph" to the end of the paragraph.

(12) Retirement benefits schemes

Chapter	Short title	Extent of repeal
1988 c. 1.	The Income and Corporation Taxes Act 1988.	In section 188(1), paragraph (c). In section 189, paragraph (b). In section 591(2)(g) the words "approved by the Board and". Section 605(1) and (2). In section 612(1), the definition of "administrator".

1. The repeals in section 188 and 189 have effect in accordance with section 108 of this Act.
2. The repeal in section 591 has effect in accordance with section 107 of this Act.
3. The repeal of section 605(1) and (2) has effect in accordance with section 105 of this Act.
4. The repeal in section 612(1) has effect in accordance with section 103 of this Act.

(13) Authorised unit trusts

Chapter	Short title	Extent of repeal
1988 c. 1.	The Income and Corporation Taxes Act 1988.	In section 468, subsection (2), and in subsection (6) the definition of "distribution period". Sections 468F and 468G.
1993 c. 34.	The Finance Act 1993.	In Schedule 6, paragraphs 4, 5 and 25(2).

These repeals have effect in accordance with section 111 of and Schedule 14 to this Act.

(14) Manufactured payments

Chapter	Short title	Extent of repeal
1988 c. 1.	The Income and Corporation Taxes Act 1988.	In paragraph 5 of Schedule 23A, in sub-paragraphs (2) and (4) the word "and" at the end of paragraph (b).

These repeals have effect in accordance with section 123 of this Act.

(15) Controlled Foreign Companies

Chapter	Short title	Extent of repeal
1988 c. 1.	The Income and Corporation Taxes Act 1988.	In paragraph 2 of Schedule 25, in sub-paragraph (1), in paragraph (a) the words "or for some other period which, in whole or in part, falls within that accounting period" and the words following paragraph (d), and sub-paragraph (2).

These repeals have effect in accordance with section 134(5) of this Act.

(16) REPEALS CONNECTED WITH FOREIGN INCOME DIVIDENDS

Chapter	Short title	Extent of repeal
1988 c. 1.	The Income and Corporation Taxes Act 1988.	In section 434(6A) the words "and" at the end of paragraph (a). In section 438(6) the words from "being" to "that profit,". In section 731(9), in the definition of "interest" the words from "and in applying" to the end of paragraph (b).

(17) ENTERPRISE INVESTMENT SCHEME

Chapter	Short title	Extent of repeal
1988 c. 1.	The Income and Corporation Taxes Act 1988.	In section 257D(8)(b), the words "or under section 289". In section 265(3)(b), the words "or under section 289". In section 290A, subsection (10) and, in subsection (11), the definition of "prospectus". In section 293, subsection (4) and subsections (9) to (11). Section 296(6). In section 297, in subsection (1) the words "(6) and" and in subsection (2) paragraphs (h) and (j). In section 298, in subsection (5) the definition of "property development" and subsections (6) to (8). Section 301(1), (2) and (7). Section 303(8), (10) and (11). In section 306(10), the second sentence. In section 307, in subsection (1) the words from "but" to the end and subsection (9). Section 308(6). Section 309. Section 310(10) and (11). In section 312, in subsection (1) the definitions of "fixed-rate preference share capital" and "the relevant period".
1988 c. 39.	The Finance Act 1988.	Section 50. Schedule 4.
1990 c. 29.	The Finance Act 1990.	Section 73.
1992 c. 12.	The Taxation of Chargeable Gains Act 1992.	In section 231(1)(d) the words "(business expansion scheme)".
1992 c. 48.	The Finance (No. 2) Act 1992.	Sections 38 to 40.

These repeals have effect in relation to shares issued on or after 1st January 1994.

(18) DEDUCTION FROM INCOME

Chapter	Short title	Extent of repeal
1988 c. 1.	The Income and Corporation Taxes Act 1988.	In section 808 the words "In this section "securities" includes stocks and shares."

This repeal has effect in accordance with section 140 of this Act.

(19) QUALIFYING LENDERS

Chapter	Short title	Extent of repeal
1988 c. 1.	The Income and Corporation Taxes Act 1988.	Section 376(5). In section 379, the words "except in section 376(4) and (5)". In section 828(4), "376(5)".

(20) PREMIUMS REFERRED TO PENSION BUSINESS

Chapter	Short title	Extent of repeal
1988 c. 1.	The Income and Corporation Taxes Act 1988.	In section 431(4), in paragraph (d) the words "approved by the Board and" and in paragraph (e) the words "approved by the Board".

These repeals have effect in accordance with section 143 of this Act.

(21) BUSINESS DONATIONS

Chapter	Short title	Extent of repeal
1990 c. 29.	The Finance Act 1990.	Section 75.

(22) MINOR CORRECTIONS

Chapter	Short title	Extent of repeal
1965 c. 25.	The Finance Act 1965.	Section 87. Schedule 21.
1966 c. 18.	The Finance Act 1966.	In Schedule 5, paragraph 19. In Schedule 6, paragraph 23.
1970 c. 9.	The Taxes Management Act 1970.	In Schedule 4, paragraph 6.
1970 c. 10.	The Income and Corporation Taxes Act 1970.	In Schedule 15, in Part I of the Table in paragraph 11, the entry relating to the Finance Act 1966.
1988 c. 1.	The Income and Corporation Taxes Act 1988.	In section 43(1), the words "or IV". In section 271— 　(a) in subsection (1)— 　　　(i) the words "or contract", wherever they occur, 　　　(ii) in paragraph (b), the words "or the contract was made after that date", and 　　　(iii) in paragraph (c), the words "or, as the case may be, the body with which the contract was made", and 　(b) in subsection (2), paragraph (b) and the word "or" immediately preceding it. Section 614(1). In Schedule 11, in paragraph 8(b), the words "Chapter II of Part I of the 1968 Act or".

The repeals in sections 43 and 271 of, and Schedule 11 to, the Income and Corporation Taxes Act 1988 have effect in accordance with Schedule 17 to this Act.

(23) MANAGEMENT: SELF-ASSESSMENT ETC.

Chapter	Short title	Extent of repeal
1970 c. 9.	The Taxes Management Act 1970.	In section 11(1), the words "inspector or other". Section 11A. In section 12, subsections (1) and (4). In section 33(2), the proviso. In section 95(3), the words from "and the references" to the end. Section 118(3).
1975 c. 45.	The Finance (No. 2) Act 1975.	Section 67(1).
1988 c. 1.	The Income and Corporation Taxes Act 1988.	Section 5. Section 10. In section 203(2)(dd), the words from "(being not less" to "due)". Section 478. In section 824, subsection (5), in subsection (9), the words "a partnership" and the words "(within the meaning of section 111 of the Finance Act 1989)", and subsection (10).
1992 c. 12.	The Taxation of Chargeable Gains Act 1992.	Section 283(5).

1. The repeal of section 118(3) of the Taxes Management Act 1970 has effect in accordance with section 199(2) of, and paragraph 34(3) of Schedule 19 to, this Act.
2. The repeal of section 5 of the Income and Corporation Taxes Act 1988—
   (a)　except so far as it relates to partnerships whose trades, professions or businesses are set up and commenced before 6th April 1994, has effect in accordance with section 199(2) of this Act; and
   (b)　so far as it so relates, has effect as respects the year 1997–98 and subsequent years of assessment.
3. The repeals in section 824 of the Income and Corporation Taxes Act 1988 has effect in accordance with section 199(2) of, and paragraph 41(4) of Schedule 19 to, this Act.
4. The other repeals have effect in accordance with section 199(2) of this Act.

(24) CHANGES FOR FACILITATING SELF-ASSESSMENT

Chapter	Short title	Extent of repeal
1988 c. 1.	The Income and Corporation Taxes Act 1988.	In section 65, in subsection (1), the words "and sections 66 and 67" and the words "the year preceding", in subsection (3), the words from "Nothing in this subsection" to the end, and in subsection (5), the words "subject to sections 66 and 67" and the words "the year preceding", in each place where they occur. Sections 66 and 67. In section 96, in subsection (5), paragraph (b), in subsection (6), the words from "except that" to the end, and in subsection (7), paragraph (b). In section 113, in subsection (1), the words "and of section 114(3)(b)", subsections (3) to (5) and, in subsection (6), the words from "and where" to the end. In section 114, in subsection (3), the words from "except that" to the end, and subsection (4).

Chapter	Short title	Extent of repeal
		In section 115, subsections (1) to (3) and (6). In section 277, in subsection (1), the words "Subject to subsection (2) below", paragraph (c) and the word "and" immediately preceding that paragraph, and subsection (2). Section 380(3). Section 381(6). Section 383. In section 384, in subsection (1), the words "(including any amount in respect of capital allowances which, by virtue of section 383, is to be treated as a loss)", in subsection (2), the words "or an allowance in respect of expenditure incurred", paragraph (b) and the word "or" immediately preceding that paragraph, and subsection (5). In section 385, subsections (2), (3), (5) and (8). Section 386(4). In section 388, in subsection (6), paragraphs (b) and (d) and the words "and" immediately preceding paragraph (d), and in subsection (7), the words from the beginning to "an earlier year; and". In section 389, subsections (3) and (5) to (7). In section 397(1), the words from "and where" to the end. In section 521, in subsections (1) and (2), the words "or its basis period". In section 528(1), the words "or its basis period". In section 530, in subsections (4) and (5), the words "or its basis period". In section 804(8), the definitions of "non-basis period" and "years of commencement" and the words "references to the enactments relating to cessation are references to sections 63, 67 and 113".
1990 c. 1.	The Capital Allowances Act 1990.	In section 3, in subsections (1) and (2B) to (4), the words "or its basis period", in each place where they occur. In section 4(10), the words "or of which the basis periods end on or before that date". In section 7, in subsections (2) and (3), the words "or its basis period". In section 8, in subsection (3), the words "or its basis period", and in subsection (5), in paragraph (a), the words from "or" to the end. In section 9(3), the words "or its basis period". In section 19(3), the words "or its basis period", in each place where they occur. In section 21(8), the words "or its basis period". In section 23(2), the words "or its basis period".

Chapter	Short title	Extent of repeal
		In section 24, in subsections (6), (6A) and (7), the words "or its basis period", in each place where they occur.
		In section 25, in subsections (1) and (7), the words "or its basis period".
		In section 33(3), the words "or, as the case may be, in its basis period".
		In section 37, in subsections (2) and (9), the words "or its basis period", in subsection (5), the words "or, as the case may be, in its basis period" and, in subsection (6), the words "or in the basis period for which".
		In section 42(4), the words "or in the basis period for which".
		In section 46(1), the words "or in the basis period for which".
		In section 47(1), the words "or in the basis period for which".
		In section 48, in subsections (3), (4) and (5), the words "or its basis period".
		In section 49(2), the words "or its basis period".
		In section 61(5), the words "or its basis period".
		In section 62A(6), the words "or its basis period".
		In section 67(6), the words "or its basis period".
		In section 73(3), the words "or its basis period".
		In section 79, in subsections (3) and (5), the words "or its basis period", in each place where they occur.
		In section 85, in subsections (1), (3) and (4), the words "or its basis period", in each place where they occur.
		In section 87(6), the words "or of which the basis periods end on or before that date".
		In section 93(3), the words "or its basis period".
		In section 99, in subsections (1) and (4), the words "or its basis period".
		In section 101, in subsections (2) and (6) to (8), the words "or its basis period".
		In section 121(4), the words "or its basis period" and the words "or, as the case may be, its basis period".
		In section 124(3), the words "or its basis period".
		In section 126(2), the words "or its basis period", in each place where they occur.
		In section 128(1), the words "or its basis period".
		In section 129(3), the words "or the basis periods for which".
		In section 134(1), the words from "but where a writing-down allowance" to the end.
		In section 138(7), the words "or its basis period".

Chapter	Short title	Extent of repeal
		In section 148(7), the words "or its basis period".
		In section 159, in subsections (4) and (6), the words "or its basis period".
		In section 159A(4), the words "or its basis period".
1991 c. 31.	The Finance Act 1991.	In section 72(8), the words "383(6), (7) and (8)".
1994 c. 9.	The Finance Act 1994.	In section 118(6), the words "or its basis period".

1. The repeal in section 65(3) of the Income and Corporation Taxes Act 1988 has effect in accordance with sections 207(6) and 218(1)(b) of this Act.
2. The repeal in section 96(6) of the Income and Corporation Taxes Act 1988 has effect in accordance with section 216(5) of this Act.
3. The repeal in section 96(7) of the Income and Corporation Taxes Act 1988 has effect in accordance with section 214(7) of this Act.
4. The following repeals, namely—
   (a) the repeals in sections 113, 114, 115, 277, 380, 381 and 386 of the Income and Corporation Taxes Act 1988;
   (b) the repeal of subsection (5) of section 384 of that Act;
   (c) the repeal of subsections (2) and (5) of section 385 of that Act; and
   (d) the repeal of subsection (3) of section 389 of that Act,
have effect in accordance with section 215(4) of this Act.
5. The following repeals, namely—
   (a) the repeals in sections 384(1) and (2), 388, 397, 521, 528 and 530 of the Income and Corporation Taxes Act 1988;
   (b) the repeal of section 383 of that Act;
   (c) the repeal of subsections (5) to (7) of section 389 of that Act;
   (d) the repeals in the Capital Allowances Act 1990;
   (e) the repeal in section 72 of the Finance Act 1991; and
   (f) the repeal in section 118 of the Finance Act 1994,
have effect in accordance with sections 211(2) and 218(1)(b) of this Act.
6. The repeals of subsections (3) and (8) of section 385 of the Income and Corporation Taxes Act 1988 have effect in accordance with section 209(7) of this Act.
7. The other repeals have effect in accordance with section 218(1) of this Act.

(25) LLOYD'S UNDERWRITERS

Chapter	Short title	Extent of repeal
1988 c. 1.	The Income and Corporation Taxes Act 1988.	Section 627.
		Section 641(2).
1993 c. 34.	The Finance Act 1993.	Section 171(3).
		In section 179, in subsection (2), the words "to subsection (3) below and", and subsection (3).
		In section 182, subsections (2) to (4).
		Section 183(3).
		In section 184(1), the words "or the managing agent of a syndicate of which he is a member".
		In Schedule 19, Part II.
		In Schedule 20, in paragraph 13(1), the words from "and a transfer" to the end.

1. The repeals in the Income and Corporation Taxes Act 1988 and in section 183 of the Finance Act 1993 have effect in accordance with section 228(4) of this Act.
2. The repeal in section 171 of the Finance Act 1993 has effect in accordance with paragraph 1(3)(b) of Schedule 21 to this Act.

3. The repeals in section 179 of the Finance Act 1993 have effect in accordance with paragraph 6(3) of that Schedule.
4. The repeals in section 182 of the Finance Act 1993 have effect in accordance with paragraph 7(2) of that Schedule.
5. The repeal in paragraph 13(1) of Schedule 20 to the Finance Act 1993 has effect in accordance with paragraph 16(3) of that Schedule.
6. The other repeals have effect in accordance with section 228(3) of this Act.

PART VI

OIL TAXATION

Chapter	Short title	Extent of repeal
1975 c. 22.	The Oil Taxation Act 1975.	In section 2(9)(a)(i), the words "or, as the case may be". In Schedule 3, in paragraph 2A, sub-paragraph (4).
1993 c. 34.	The Finance Act 1993.	Section 190(5)(b).

1. The repeals in the Oil Taxation Act 1975 have effect in accordance with section 236 of this Act.
2. The repeal in the Finance Act 1993 has effect in accordance with section 238 of this Act.

PART VII

STAMP DUTY

(1) EXCHANGE, PARTITION, ETC.

Chapter	Short title	Extent of repeal
1891 c. 39.	The Stamp Act 1891.	In section 73, the words from first "upon" to "heritable property, or" and the words "exchange or". In Schedule 1, the heading "Exchange of Excambion".
1991 c. 31.	The Finance Act 1991.	In section 110, subsection (3)(e) and, in subsection (4), the words following "exempt property".

These repeals have effect in accordance with section 241(6) of this Act.

(2) PRODUCTION OF INSTRUMENTS IN NORTHERN IRELAND

Chapter	Short title	Extent of repeal
1936 c. 33 (N.I.).	The Finance Act (Northern Ireland) 1936.	Section 9.

This repeal has effect in accordance with section 245(8) of this Act.

PART VIII

MISCELLANEOUS

(1) COMPANIES TREATED AS NON-RESIDENT

Chapter	Short title	Extent of repeal
1988 c. 1.	The Income and Corporation Taxes Act 1988.	In section 468F, in subsection (1)(c) the words "and not a dual resident" and in subsection (8) the definition of "dual resident".

Chapter	Short title	Extent of repeal
		In section 742(8) the words ", or regarded for the purposes of any double taxation arrangements having effect by virtue of section 788 as resident in a territory outside the United Kingdom,".
		In section 745(4) the words ", or regarded for the purposes of any double taxation arrangements having effect by virtue of section 788 as resident in a territory outside the United Kingdom,".
		Section 749(4A).
		Section 751(2)(bb).
1990 c. 29.	The Finance Act 1990.	Section 66.
		In section 67, subsections (1) and (2).
1992 c. 12.	The Taxation of Chargeable Gains Act 1992.	Section 139(3).
		Section 160.
		In section 166(2) the words "or a company" and the words "or company".
		In section 171(2), paragraph (e) and the word "or" immediately preceding it.
		Section 172(3)(a).
		In section 175(2) the words from "or a company which" to the end of paragraph (b).
		Section 186.
		In section 187, in subsection (1)(a) the words "or 186" and in subsection (6) the words "or, as the case may be, section 186(2)," and the words "or, as the case may be, section 186(1)".
		Section 188.
		In section 211(3) the words "(and would not be a gain on which, under any double taxation relief arrangements, it woud not be liable to tax)".
1993 c. 34.	The Finance Act 1993.	Section 61(3).

These repeals have effect in accordance with section 251 of this Act.

(2) RAILWAY TAXATION PROVISIONS

Chapter	Short title	Extent of repeal
1992 c. 12.	The Taxation of Chargeable Gains Act 1992.	In section 35(3)(d), the word "and" immediately preceding sub-paragraph (viii).

This repeal shall be deemed to have come into force on 11th January 1994.

(3) ASSIGNED MATTERS: MINOR CORRECTIONS

Chapter	Short title	Extent of repeal
1979 c. 2.	The Customs and Excise Management Act 1979.	In section 188A, subsection (7).
1983 c. 55.	The Value Added Tax Act 1983.	In Schedule 7, in paragraph 7, sub-paragraph (6).

INDEX

References are to sections and Schedules

RACE RELATIONS (REMEDIES) ACT 1994

(1994 c. 10)

An Act to remove the limit imposed by subsection (2) of section 56 of the Race Relations Act 1976 on the amount of compensation which may be awarded under that section and to make provision for interest in connection with sums so awarded; and for connected purposes. [3rd May 1994]

PARLIAMENTARY DEBATES
Hansard, H.C. Vol. 237, col. 1232; H.L. Vol. 553, cols. 182, 983, 1388.

INTRODUCTION
This Act provides for the removal of the limit imposed by s.56(2) of the Race Relations Act 1976 on the amount of compensation which may be awarded by industrial tribunals under that section. The Secretary of State is empowered to make Regulations with regard to interest in relation to compensation awards made by tribunals in race discrimination cases.

Removal of limit on amount of awards

1.—(1) In section 56 of the Race Relations Act 1976 (remedies on complaint to industrial tribunal in respect of acts of racial discrimination), subsection (2) (limit on the amount of compensation) shall cease to have effect.

(2) In consequence of subsection (1) above, section 76(2) of the Employment Protection (Consolidation) Act 1978 (limit on aggregate amount of compensation which may be awarded in respect of an act which constitutes both racial discrimination and unfair dismissal) shall cease to have effect.

Power to make provision as to interest in relation to awards

2.—(1) In section 56 of the Race Relations Act 1976, at the end there shall be inserted—

"(5) The Secretary of State may by regulations make provision—
(a) for enabling a tribunal, where an amount of compensation falls to be awarded under subsection (1)(b), to include in the award interest on that amount; and
(b) specifying, for cases where a tribunal decides that an award is to include an amount in respect of interest, the manner in which and the periods and rate by reference to which the interest is to be determined;
and the regulations may contain such incidental and supplementary provisions as the Secretary of State considers appropriate.

(6) The Secretary of State may by regulations modify the operation of any order made under paragraph 6A of Schedule 9 to the Employment Protection (Consolidation) Act 1978 (power to make provision as to interest on sums payable in pursuance of industrial tribunal decisions) to the extent that it relates to an award of compensation under subsection (1)(b)."

(2) In section 74(2) of that Act (parliamentary procedure in relation to certain orders and regulations), after the words "under section" there shall be inserted "56(5), (6) or".

Short title, repeals, commencement, and extent

3.—(1) This Act may be cited as the Race Relations (Remedies) Act 1994.

(2) The enactments mentioned in the Schedule to this Act are hereby repealed to the extent specified in the third column of the Schedule.

(3) This Act shall come into force at the end of the period of two months beginning with the date on which it is passed.

(4) This Act does not extend to Northern Ireland.

SCHEDULE

Chapter	Short Title	Extent of repeal
1976 c.74.	The Race Relations Act 1976.	In section 56, subsection (2) and, in subsection (4), the words "(subject to the limit in subsection (2))".
1978 c.44.	The Employment Protection (Consolidation) Act 1978.	Section 76(2). In Schedule 16, paragraph 25(2).

INDEX

References are to sections

ROAD TRAFFIC REGULATION (SPECIAL EVENTS) ACT 1994*

(1994 c. 11)

An Act to make provision, in connection with sporting or social events held on roads or entertainments so held, for the restriction or regulation of traffic on roads; and for connected purposes. [3rd May 1994]

PARLIAMENTARY DEBATES
Hansard, H.C. Vol. 238, col. 1182; Vol. 239, cols. 504, 587; H.L. Vol. 553, cols. 1162, 1623; Vol. 554, col. 346.

INTRODUCTION AND GENERAL NOTE
This Act enables traffic authorities to make orders temporarily restricting or prohibiting traffic in connection with the holding of sporting or social events or entertainments on roads.

The Act, which began its parliamentary life as a Private Member's Bill sponsored by the M.P. for Hexham, Peter Atkinson, became known during its passage as the "Tour de France" Bill. This was a reflection of the Bill's origins, which lay in the visit of the Tour de France to south-east England on July 6 and 7, 1994, as part of the events held to mark the opening of the Channel Tunnel. This was one of the largest sporting occasions held in the U.K. in recent years, involving some 200 riders and 1,500 other vehicles, mostly belonging to the Tour's sponsors.

The affected local authorities, in considering the road closures and other traffic regulation measures that would be necessary to accommodate this cavalcade, found the available legislation to be archaic and flawed, to the extent that there was a real possibility of a successful legal challenge to any measures that might be taken. It became clear that these flaws could also affect other major sporting and social events held in the country, such as the London Marathon, the Notting Hill Carnival, the Great North Run and the Lewes bonfire party.

The relevant legislation confers a miscellany of powers with respect to road closure on the police, district councils and traffic authorities. In London, under s.52 of the Metropolitan Police Act 1839 (c. 47), the Commissioner of Police for the Metropolis has power to "make regulations for the route to be observed by all carts, carriages, horses, and persons, and for preventing obstruction of the streets and thoroughfares ... in all times of public processions, public rejoicings, or illuminations". Similar powers are conferred on the Commissioner of Police for the City of London by s.22 of the City of London Police Act 1839 (c. xciv), and on district councils outside London by s.21 of the Town Police Clauses Act 1847 (c. 89). But these powers appear to permit only limited road closures, and it is doubtful whether they allow for associated traffic management such as, for example, the closure of parking bays, the removal of left or right turns, the introduction of one-way systems, the direction of traffic through pedestrianized areas or the removal of speed limits.

In addition, s.31 of the RTA 1988 (c. 52) empowers chief constables to close roads to allow authorised cycle races to take place. Cycle races are authorised under the Cycle Racing on Highways Regulations 1960 (S.I. 1960 No. 250), which impose conditions as to the number of participants, the length of a race through a built-up area and the length of the route that must be covered before a race repasses a certain point. These powers may be adequate to deal with races such as the Tour de France itself, or the Milk Race, but they suffer from the same defects as the nineteenth-century legislation in relation to traffic management, and are also inadequate to deal with the procession of vehicles that accompany a major race, or indeed with the other sporting and social events mentioned above.

The most recent legislation is s.14 of the RTRA 1984 (c. 27), as substituted by the RT(TR)A 1991 (c. 26), which allows a traffic authority to make an order restricting or prohibiting the use of roads in certain circumstances. However, these powers were designed for use where works are executed on or near a road or where there is a likelihood of danger to the public or of serious damage to the road. They are not available to deal with traffic management problems in connection with major sporting or social events.

For these reasons, the view was taken that new primary legislation was needed to allow proper traffic regulation for such events. The object of this Act is to supply traffic authorities with the full range of powers necessary for that purpose, and to ensure that those powers are used only after proper consultation and with due regard to the interests of those affected. However, the Act does not repeal any of the earlier legislation, which remains available for use for smaller events which are unlikely to cause major traffic control problems.

---

* Annotations by Robert Ward, M.A., LL.B. (Cantab.), LL.M. (U.B.C.), Barrister.

Scheme of the Act
    Section 1 introduces the new ss.16A, 16B and 16C to the RTRA 1984, setting out the powers of traffic authorities to restrict or prohibit traffic.

COMMENCEMENT
    The Act received the Royal Assent and came into force on May 3, 1994.

ABBREVIATIONS
    RTA 1988 (c. 52)   : Road Traffic Act 1988.
    RTRA 1984 (c. 27)   : Road Traffic Regulation Act 1984.
    RT(TR)A 1991 (c. 26) : Road Traffic (Temporary Restrictions) Act 1991.

Prohibition or restriction on roads in connection with certain events

    1.—(1) After section 16 of the Road Traffic Regulation Act 1984 there shall be inserted—

"Prohibition or restriction on roads in connection with certain events
    16A.—(1) In this section "relevant event" means any sporting event, social event or entertainment which is held on a road.
    (2) If the traffic authority for a road are satisfied that traffic on the road should be restricted or prohibited for the purpose of—
    (a) facilitating the holding of a relevant event,
    (b) enabling members of the public to watch a relevant event, or
    (c) reducing the disruption to traffic likely to be caused by a relevant event,
the authority may by order restrict or prohibit temporarily the use of that road, or any part of it, by vehicles or vehicles of any class or by pedestrians, to such extent and subject to such conditions or exceptions as they may consider necessary or expedient.
    (3) Before making an order under this section the authority shall satisfy themselves that it is not reasonably practicable for the event to be held otherwise than on a road.
    (4) An order under this section—
    (a) may not be made in relation to any race or trial falling within subsection (1) of section 12 of the Road Traffic Act 1988 (motor racing on public ways);
    (b) may not be made in relation to any competition or trial falling within subsection (1) of section 13 of that Act (regulation of motoring events on public ways) unless the competition or trial is authorised by or under regulations under that section; and
    (c) may not be made in relation to any race or trial falling within subsection (1) of section 31 of that Act (regulation of cycle racing on public ways) unless the race or trial is authorised by or under regulations made under that section.
    (5) An order under this section may relate to the road on which the relevant event is to be held or to any other road.
    (6) In the case of a road for which the Secretary of State is the traffic authority, the power to make an order under this section is also exercisable, with his consent, by the local traffic authority or by any local traffic authority which is the traffic authority for any other road to which the order relates.
    (7) In the case of a road for which a local traffic authority is the traffic authority, the power to make an order under this section is also exercisable, with the consent of that local traffic authority, by a local traffic authority which is the traffic authority for any other road to which the order relates.

(8) When considering the making of an order under this section, an authority shall have regard to the safety and convenience of alternative routes suitable for the traffic which will be affected by the order.

(9) The provision that may be made by an order under this section is—

(a) any such provision as is mentioned in section 2(1), (2) or (3) or 4(1) of this Act;

(b) any provision restricting the speed of vehicles; or

(c) any provision restricting or prohibiting—

    (i) the riding of horses, or

    (ii) the leading or driving of horses, cattle, sheep or other animals,

but no such order shall be made with respect to any road which would have the effect of preventing at any time access for pedestrians to any premises situated on or adjacent to the road, or to any other premises accessible for pedestrians from, and only from, the road.

(10) An order under this section may—

(a) suspend any statutory provision to which this subsection applies; or

(b) for any of the purposes mentioned in subsection (2) above, suspend any such provision without imposing any such restriction or prohibition as is mentioned in that subsection.

(11) Subsection (10) above applies to—

(a) any statutory provision of a description which could have been contained in an order under this section;

(b) an order under section 32(1)(b), 35, 45, 46 or 49 of this Act or any such order as is mentioned in paragraph 11(1) of Schedule 10 to this Act; and

(c) an order under section 6 of this Act so far as it designates any parking places in Greater London.

Restrictions on orders under s.16A

16B.—(1) An order under section 16A of this Act shall not continue in force for a period of more than three days beginning with the day on which it comes into force unless—

(a) the order is made by the Secretary of State as the traffic authority for the road concerned; or

(b) before the order is made, he has agreed that it should continue in force for a longer period.

(2) Where an order under section 16A of this Act has not ceased to be in force and the relevant event to which it relates has not ended, the Secretary of State may, subject to subsections (4) and (5) below, from time to time direct that the order shall continue in force for a further period not exceeding three days beginning with the day on which it would otherwise cease to be in force.

(3) A direction under subsection (2) above may relate to all the roads to which the order under section 16A of this Act relates or only to specified roads.

(4) Where an order under section 16A of this Act relates only to roads for which the Secretary of State is not himself the traffic authority, he shall not give a direction under subsection (2) above except at the request of the traffic authority for any road to which the order relates.

(5) Where an order under section 16A of this Act relates to any road for which the Secretary of State is not himself the traffic authority, he shall not give a direction under subsection (2) above affecting that road except with the consent of the traffic authority for that road.

(6) Where an order has been made under section 16A of this Act in any calendar year, no further order may be made under that section in that year so as to affect any length of road affected by the previous order, unless the further order—

(a) is made by the Secretary of State as the traffic authority for the road concerned; or

(b) is made with his consent.

(7) For the purposes of subsection (6) above, a length of road is affected by an order under section 16A of this Act if the order contains provisions—

(a) prohibiting or restricting traffic on that length of road; or

(b) suspending any statutory provision applying to traffic on that length of road.

Supplementary provisions as to orders under s.16A

16C.—(1) A person who contravenes, or who uses or permits the use of a vehicle in contravention of, a restriction or prohibition imposed by an order under section 16A of this Act shall be guilty of an offence.

(2) The Secretary of State may make regulations with respect to the procedure to be followed in connection with the making of orders under section 16A of this Act including provision for notifying the public of the exercise or proposed exercise of the powers conferred by that section and of the effect of orders made in the exercise of those powers.

(3) Without prejudice to the generality of subsection (2) above, the Secretary of State may by regulations under that subsection make, in relation to such orders as he thinks appropriate, provision—

(a) for the making and consideration of representations relating to a proposed order; and

(b) for any of the matters mentioned in paragraph 22(1)(a), (c), (d) or (e) of Schedule 9 to this Act;

and paragraph 25 of that Schedule shall apply to regulations under that subsection as it applies to regulations under Part III of that Schedule."

(2) In Part I of Schedule 2 to the Road Traffic Offenders Act 1988 (prosecution and punishment of offences), after the entry relating to section 16(1) of the Road Traffic Regulation Act 1984 there shall be inserted—

"RTRA section 16C(1).	Contravention of prohibition or restriction relating to relevant event.	Summarily.	Level 3 on the standard scale.	—	—	—"

GENERAL NOTE

New s.16A of the RTRA 1984

Section 16A(1) and (2) enables a traffic authority to make orders restricting or prohibiting the use of a road or any part of a road by vehicles or vehicles of any class or by pedestrians to the extent that they consider it necessary or expedient. The power arises only wherJe the authority are satisfied that traffic should be restricted or prohibited for the purpose of either facilitating the holding of a "relevant event", enabling members of the public to watch such an event or reducing the disruption to traffic likely to be caused by an event. A "relevant event" is defined as any sporting event, social event or entertainment which is held on a road. Under s.142(1) of the RTRA 1984 (c. 27), a "road" in England and Wales is defined as "any length of highway or of any other road to which the public has access, and includes bridges over which a road passes". In Scotland, "road" has the same meaning as in s.151(1) of the Roads (Scotland) Act 1984 (c. 54), namely "any way (other than a waterway) over which there is a public right of passage (by whatever means and whether subject to a toll or not) and includes the road's verge, and any bridge (whether permanent or temporary) over which, or tunnel through which, the road passes".

Subsection (3) requires a traffic authority to satisfy themselves, before making an order, that it is not reasonably practicable for the event to be held otherwise than on a road.

Subsection (4) prevents the making of orders to allow motor races or speed trials on the highway, which are illegal under s.12 of the RTA 1988 (c. 52). It also requires other motoring events or cycle races to be authorised in accordance with s.13 or 31 of the RTA 1988 (c. 52) (as appropriate); if they are not so authorised, they also are illegal. The omission from the Bill of motor races generated some criticism in the Commons, but Mr Atkinson frankly acknowledged that the priority was to ensure the Bill's smooth passage, which could have been jeopardised by opposition from environmental groups and others if the inclusion of such events in the Bill had been sought (*Hansard,* H.C. Vol. 238, col. 1189).

Subsection (5) allows orders to be made both for the road on which the event is to take place and on any other road.

Subsections (6) and (7) are designed to simplify the making of orders that affect two or more traffic authorities, for example where an event crosses a county boundary. In such cases, one authority may make all the orders for the event, with the consent of the other affected authorities. A local authority may also make an order affecting a trunk road if the Secretary of State consents.

Subsection (8) requires traffic authorities, when considering the making of an order, to have regard to the safety and convenience of alternative routes for affected traffic. The aim is to ensure that traffic disruption is kept to a minimum.

Subsection (9) specifies the provisions that may be made by an order, namely any provision that may be made by a traffic regulation order under s.2(1), (2), (3) or 4(1) of the RTRA 1984 (c. 27), any provision restricting the speed of vehicles or any provision restricting or prohibiting the riding of horses or the leading or driving of animals. The subsection also prohibits the making of any order the effect of which is to prevent pedestrian access to premises situated on or adjacent to the road, or to premises which are accessible by pedestrians only from the road. For this purpose, access is "prevented" only if it is precluded and not if it is merely hindered, and premises are "adjacent to" a road only if their access leads directly onto it (*Corfe Transport* v. *Gwynedd County Council* [1984] RTR 79 (decided under s.3 of the RTRA 1984 (c. 27))).

Subsections (10) and (11) enable orders under s.16A to suspend existing statutory provisions or orders so that, for example, it will be possible to allow events to go the wrong way down a one-way street or through a pedestrianized area.

New s.16B of the RTRA 1984

Section 16B limits the duration of orders under s.16A and the frequency with which they may be made in relation to any given length of road. They may not last for more than three days and they may affect a stretch of road only once in any calendar year, unless the order is made by the Secretary of State as traffic authority for the road concerned, or the order is made with the Secretary of State's consent. The Secretary of State may also extend an order from time to time for a further period of up to three days at the request of the local traffic authority. This might be necessary if, for example, owing to unexpected circumstances such as freak weather conditions an event does not finish when originally planned.

New s.16C of the RTRA 1984

Section 16C contains supplementary provisions dealing with contraventions of orders made under s.16A and with the making of regulations. Subsection (1) makes it an offence to contravene an order. The maximum penalty is a fine at level 3 on the standard scale (currently £1,000). Subsection (2) empowers the Secretary of State to make regulations setting out the procedure for making orders. The Minister for Roads and Traffic, Mr Robert Key, stated in the Commons that the regulations will make detailed provision for notification of and consultation with those who may be adversely affected by an order (*Hansard,* H.C. Vol. 238, col. 1237).

Expenses

2. There shall be paid out of money provided by Parliament any increase attributable to this Act in the sums payable out of such money under any other Act.

Consequential amendments, short title and extent

3.—(1) The Schedule to this Act (which contains consequential amendments) shall have effect.

(2) This Act may be cited as the Road Traffic Regulation (Special Events) Act 1994.

(3) This Act does not extend to Northern Ireland.

SCHEDULE

CONSEQUENTIAL AMENDMENTS

Road Traffic Regulation Act 1984

1. In section 68 of the Road Traffic Regulation Act 1984 (placing of traffic signs in connection with exercise of other powers), in subsection (1)(a) after "14" there shall be inserted "16A".

2. In section 124 of that Act (provisions as to certain orders), in subsection (2) after "14" there shall be inserted "16A".

3. In section 130 of that Act (application of Act to Crown), in subsection (2)(a) (provisions applying to vehicles and persons in the public service of the Crown) for "to 16" there shall be substituted "to 16C".

4. In section 141A of that Act (application of provisions to tramcars and trolley vehicles), in subsection (2) after "14" there shall be inserted "16A to 16C".

5.—(1) Schedule 9 to that Act (special provisions as to certain orders) shall be amended as follows.

(2) In Part IV (variation or revocation of certain orders), in paragraph 27(1) after "14" there shall be inserted "16A".

(3) In Part VI (validity of certain orders), in paragraph 34(1)(a) after "9" there shall be inserted "16A".

Roads (Scotland) Act 1984

6. In section 62(1) of the Roads (Scotland) Act 1984 (temporary prohibition or restriction of traffic etc. on roads for reasons of public safety or convenience), for the words from "under" to "made" there shall be substituted "can be made under neither section 14 nor section 16A of the Road Traffic Regulation Act 1984 (temporary prohibition or restriction of traffic and foot passage on roads in certain circumstances and in connection with certain events)".

INDEX

**References in roman are to sections of this Act;
those in italic are to sections of the Road Traffic Regulation Act 1984 (as amended)**

INSOLVENCY (NO. 2) ACT 1994*

(1994 c. 12)

ARRANGEMENT OF SECTIONS

An Act to amend the law relating to company insolvency and winding up, and the insolvency and bankruptcy of individuals, so far as it concerns the adjustment of certain transactions; and for connected purposes.

[26th May 1994]

PARLIAMENTARY DEBATES
Hansard, H.C. Vol. 239, col. 1297; H.L. Vol. 554, cols. 346, 1642, Vol. 555, col. 355.

INTRODUCTION AND GENERAL NOTE
This Act was introduced to remedy perceived errors in the drafting of ss.241 and 342 of the Insolvency Act 1986. The problem arose from the way these sections sought to protect purchasers from the effect of a previous transaction at an undervalue.

The common understanding of these provisions was that a gift, or other transaction, at an undervalue in a deed less than the relevant number of years old created a material risk for a future purchaser which led to the title being unacceptable. To "paper over this crack" in the title many purchasers took out indemnity insurance and many building societies insisted on such a precaution.

The deficiencies of the existing provisions are discussed for example in [1992] *Gazette* 22 and [1994] *Gazette* 23. In commenting on this Act a full explanation of its operation is given in the note on s.2. Section 1 deals with setting aside transactions by companies in their insolvency and s.2 with transactions by individuals. In the operation of the 1986 Act it is transactions by individuals which have caused the greatest difficulty and since ss.1 and 2 are very similar in structure, fuller treatment has been given to s.2.

Effectively the Act restores the position that applied under the Bankruptcy Act 1914 as a result of judicial decision, so that a later purchaser was safeguarded from the risk of his transaction being set aside unless he had notice of actual or potential bankruptcy of the donor at completion of the later transaction. The corporate provisions which were new in 1985 (the 1986 Act being a consolidation) are brought into line with these for bankruptcy.

Adjustment of certain transactions in case of liquidation etc: England and Wales

1.—(1) In subsection (2) of section 241 of the Insolvency Act 1986 (which relates to orders under section 238 or 239 and, in paragraphs (a) and (b), protects certain interests and certain persons who received benefits) in each of paragraphs (a) and (b), for the words "in good faith, for value and without notice of the relevant circumstances" there shall be substituted "in good faith and for value".

(2) After that subsection there shall be inserted the following subsection—

"(2A) Where a person has acquired an interest in property from a person other than the company in question, or has received a benefit from the transaction or preference, and at the time of that acquisition or receipt—

(a) he had notice of the relevant surrounding circumstances and of the relevant proceedings, or

(b) he was connected with, or was an associate of, either the company in question or the person with whom that company entered into the transaction or to whom that company gave the preference,

---

* Annotations by Professor Phillip H. Kenny, LL.B., Dip. Crim., LL.M., Solicitor, Property Consultant, Messrs. Dickinson Dees, Newcastle upon Tyne.

then, unless the contrary is shown, it shall be presumed for the purposes of paragraph (a) or (as the case may be) paragraph (b) of subsection (2) that the interest was acquired or the benefit was received otherwise than in good faith."

(3) For subsection (3) of that section there shall be substituted the following subsections—

"(3) For the purposes of subsection (2A)(a), the relevant surrounding circumstances are (as the case may require)—

(a) the fact that the company in question entered into the transaction at an undervalue; or

(b) the circumstances which amounted to the giving of the preference by the company in question;

and subsections (3A) to (3C) have effect to determine whether, for those purposes, a person has notice of the relevant proceedings.

(3A) In a case where section 238 or 239 applies by reason of the making of an administration order, a person has notice of the relevant proceedings if he has notice—

(a) of the fact that the petition on which the administration order is made has been presented; or

(b) of the fact that the administration order has been made.

(3B) In a case where section 238 or 239 applies by reason of the company in question going into liquidation immediately upon the discharge of an administration order, a person has notice of the relevant proceedings if he has notice—

(a) of the fact that the petition on which the administration order is made has been presented;

(b) of the fact that the administration order has been made; or

(c) of the fact that the company has gone into liquidation.

(3C) In a case where section 238 or 239 applies by reason of the company in question going into liquidation at any other time, a person has notice of the relevant proceedings if he has notice—

(a) where the company goes into liquidation on the making of a winding-up order, of the fact that the petition on which the winding-up order is made has been presented or of the fact that the company has gone into liquidation;

(b) in any other case, of the fact that the company has gone into liquidation."

GENERAL NOTE

Section 241(2) of the 1986 Act

In order to make clear the effect of this change to the Insolvency Act 1986 the amended part of s.241 is set out:

"(2) *[Restriction on orders]* An order under section 238 or 239 may affect the property of, or impose any obligation on, any person whether or not he is the person with whom the company in question entered into the transaction or (as the case may be) the person to whom the preference was given; but such an order—

(a) shall not prejudice any interest in property which was acquired from a person other than the company and was acquired [*in good faith and for value*] or prejudice any interest deriving from such an interest, and

(b) shall not require a person who received a benefit from the transaction or preference in good faith, for value and without notice of the relevant circumstances to pay a sum to the office-holder, except where that person was a party to the transaction or the payment is to be in respect of a preference given to that person at a time when he was a creditor of the company".

The words in subs. (2) in italics "in good faith and for value" replaced the words "in good, for value and without notice of the relevant circumstances" which are repealed. New subss. (2A) and (3), (3A), (3B) and (3C) were inserted by s.1 of the 1994 Act (subss. (2) and (3)).

The new provisions work as follows. Suppose that Company A transferred land at an undervalue to Company B and Company B sold that land to C. Suppose Company A becomes insolvent and there is a possibility of the Company A to Company B transaction being set aside.

When can C be affected by this? The effect of s.241 of the 1986 Act as amended is that C will not be affected if he is a purchaser in good faith and for value. In certain circumstances C will be presumed not to be in good faith. This is if C had notice of the relevant surrounding circumstances and of the relevant proceedings. Important points to note are as follows:

(a) the relevant surrounding circumstances are defined in the new s.241(3) of the 1986 Act and are either:

    (i) the fact that the transaction was at an undervalue. In unregistered land this will often be transparent from examining the title. In registered land it will not be a fact discovered usually by a purchaser. However, where the pre-registration deeds are made available they may contain this information or the purchaser may have knowledge from elsewhere: or

    (ii) the circumstances which amount to the giving of a preference (these are set out in s.239 of the Insolvency Act 1986).

The relevant proceedings are defined in three new subsections and apply as follows:

New s.241(3A): if the transaction which leads to the challenge is an administration order under Pt. II of the Insolvency Act 1986.

New s.241(3B): where the company goes into liquidation immediately following an administration order. In this case notice of the relevant proceedings can be notice of any of the three things mentioned.

New s.241(3C): where the company is in liquidation then notice can be either of the winding-up order or the petition on which the liquidation of the company is based or that the company is in liquidation.

It is suggested in the note on s.2 that the drafting of the provision requires some attention to normal conveyancing practice. Query if that would be the case in relation to s.1?

The various facts in s.241(2A), (2B) or (2C) of the 1986 Act *may* be discovered in the course of conveyancing as follows?

(a) by enquiries to the company concerned or other factual enquiries.

(b) by a search (a company search) of the company's records at Companies House. This relates to the discovery of: the appointment of an administrator; or a winding-up order made by the court; or a company resolution leading to voluntary winding-up.

(c) by enquiry of the Supreme Court Office. This relates to the discovery of winding-up petitions or applications for an administration order.

A purchaser such as C in the example will have notice of anything which would be discovered by the enquiries which he ought reasonably to have made (see s.199(i)(ii)(a) of the Law of Property Act 1925); or which is registered in the Land Charges Registry. When s.711A of the Companies Act 1985 (as added by the Companies Act 1989) is brought into force a purchaser will clearly not have notice merely because of registration at Companies House (see s.711A(i) of the Companies Act 1985) but this provision does not affect the fact that he is deemed to have notice by failure to make such enquiries as ought reasonably to be made in s.711A(2). Until that provision is brought into force the long-standing doctrine of deemed notice of documents filed at Companies House (see, *e.g. Mahony* v. *East Holyford Mining Co.* (1875) LR 7HL 869, 893) may cause problems. The existence of this doctrine suggests that enquiries about Company A must be made at Companies House.

Accordingly a purchaser will consider the following practices advisable.

(1) If the land is unregistered land then a company search and enquiries at the court will be advisable in any case where the deeds reveal or the purchaser otherwise knows that an estate owner ("Company A") made a transaction at an undervalue during the relevant period.

(2) If the land is registered then the title will reveal that a previous estate owner made a transaction which is liable to be set aside. This, however, may be revealed from the pre-registration deeds or other information fortuitously available to a purchaser. In such a case the purchaser is vulnerable and is advised to make all the searches and enquiries mentioned above. Land registration principles would suggest that a purchaser would be safe from attack once it was established that the Land Registry was clear or the title was actually registered. However, this is not necessarily so. Vulnerability under the present Act depends on notice and notice may be held to be the constructive notice which would arise from the further enquiries and searches which a purchaser would make who had notice of the nature of the previous transaction.

The example has been used of the position of the first purchaser, "C" after a gift between Company A and Company B. The Act applies in exactly the same way to subsequent purchasers.

Adjustment of certain transactions in case of bankruptcy: England and Wales

2.—(1) In subsection (2) of section 342 of the Insolvency Act 1986 (which relates to orders under section 339 or 340 and, in paragraphs (a) and (b), protects certain interests and certain persons who received benefits) in each of paragraphs (a) and (b), for the words "in good faith, for value and without notice of the relevant circumstances" there shall be substituted "in good faith and for value".

(2) After that subsection there shall be inserted the following subsection—

"(2A) Where a person has acquired an interest in property from a person other than the individual in question, or has received a benefit from the transaction or preference, and at the time of that acquisition or receipt—

    (a) he had notice of the relevant surrounding circumstances and of the relevant proceedings, or

    (b) he was an associate of, or was connected with, either the individual in question or the person with whom that individual entered into the transaction or to whom that individual gave the preference,

then, unless the contrary is shown, it shall be presumed for the purposes of paragraph (a) or (as the case may be) paragraph (b) of subsection (2) that the interest was acquired or the benefit was received otherwise than in good faith."

(3) For subsection (4) of that section there shall be substituted the following subsections—

"(4) For the purposes of subsection (2A)(a), the relevant surrounding circumstances are (as the case may require)—

    (a) the fact that the individual in question entered into the transaction at an undervalue; or

    (b) the circumstances which amounted to the giving of the preference by the individual in question.

(5) For the purposes of subsection (2A)(a), a person has notice of the relevant proceedings if he has notice—

    (a) of the fact that the petition on which the individual in question is adjudged bankrupt has been presented; or

    (b) of the fact that the individual in question has been adjudged bankrupt.

(6) Section 249 in Part VII of this Act shall apply for the purposes of subsection (2A)(b) as it applies for the purposes of the first Group of Parts."

GENERAL NOTE

In order to understand the effect of this change the amended part of the Insolvency Act 1986 is set out:

"*[Effect of order]*   An order under section 339 or 340 may affect the property of, or impose any obligation on, any person whether or not he is the person with whom the individual in question entered into the transaction or, as the case may be the person to whom the preference was given; but such an order—

    (a) shall not prejudice any interest in property which was acquired from a person other than that individual and was acquired [*in good faith and for value*] or prejudice any interest deriving from such an interest, and

    (b) shall not require a person who received a benefit from the transaction or preference in good faith, for value and without notice of the relevant circumstances to pay a sum to the trustee of the bankrupt's estate, except where he was a party to the transaction or the payment is to be in respect of a preference given to that person at a time when he was a creditor of that individual".

The words in italics "in good faith and for value" were inserted by the 1994 Act and the former words "in good faith, for value and without notice of the relevant circumstances" removed. New subss. (4), (5) and (6) were substituted and inserted by s.2 of the 1994 Act (subs. (3)).

The operation of the amended provisions is best illustrated by an example: A gives a property to B; B subsequently sells to C. It transpires that A's financial position was precarious and A becomes insolvent. Can C's title be impeached by A's trustee in bankruptcy? The purpose of s.341(2) of the Insolvency Act 1986 is to provide protection for innocent purchasers. As amended it provides that C's purchase will not be prejudiced in the following circumstances:

(i) The first principle is that C is protected if he has acquired the property in good faith and for value (see s.342(2)(a) of the 1986 Act as amended).

(ii) The new s.342(2A) of the 1986 Act specifies circumstances where it is to be assumed that C has not acted in good faith. These are set out in s.342(2A)(a) and (b) and are as follows:

    (a) Where C had notice at the time of the transaction of the relevant surrounding circumstances and of the relevant proceedings. These two concepts are discussed in the note on new s.342(4) and (5) in which they are defined. Notice for these purposes will be given its normal meaning, to include actual knowledge, constructive notice and imputed notice.

    (b) Where C is an associate or a person connected with the bankruptcy. Connected person is defined in s.435 of the Insolvency Act 1986; if the person with whom that person entered into a transaction was a company then the definition of connected person in s.249 of the Insolvency Act 1986 is relevant.

(iii) The new s.342(4) of the 1986 Act defines "the relevant surrounding circumstances" as being *notice* that the transaction between A and B was at an undervalue and or that the circumstances were such that they amounted to a preference. A preference is defined in s.340(3) of the Insolvency Act 1986.

(iv) The new s.342(5) of the 1986 Act explains what is meant by notice of the relevant proceedings. This is notice either of (a) the bankruptcy petition against A or (b) the bankruptcy order against A. This is the "heart" of the change made by the new Act. If the Land given by A to B is unregistered land then B will not have to register the title. (Note however that a sale at an undervalue will trigger registration.) When C purchases, C will effect a Land Charges Search and if there is no entry revealed against A, C may safely proceed with the purchase. C will not be able to proceed in the wholly exceptional circumstance where C acquires notice other than from the Land Charges Search of a petition or a bankruptcy order, for example, where a creditor of A's informs C — "I have just filed a bankruptcy petition against A".

If the Land is registered land then the purchaser will not make a bankruptcy search against A so will not discover the entry on the register (by virtue of s.198 of the Law of Property Act 1925 C will still have notice of the entry). C will still usually not be deemed not to be in good faith because C will not acquire any knowledge from the register of title of the fact that the transaction between A and B was a preference or at an undervalue.

So far as conveyancing practice is concerned this analysis means that there are circumstances when C will have to vary traditional conveyancing practice. The relevant circumstances are noted below.

(1) If C has notice of a previous transaction in unregistered land (within the five-year period within which a transaction may be set aside) then a Land Charges Search must be effected against the donor not limited to the donor's period of ownership but until the date of C's purchase. For example, if A who purchased in 1980, gave the property to B in 1992 and C purchases in 1994. C must have a clear search against A covering the period from 1980 to 1994 not the period 1980 to 1992. This is because C knows of the gift and s.198 of the Law of Property Act 1925 gives C notice of any bankruptcy entry against A's name in the Land Charges Registry. A purchaser in C's position, thus, has to vary the usual practice in making his Land Charges Search by extending the period of the search.

(2) If the land in the above example is registered land then the requirement for a change in practice occurs in the *unlikely* event that C is aware that the A to B transaction is a gift or preference. In this case C has notice of the surrounding circumstances and if there is a bankruptcy petition or order registered against A, C will also have notice of that by virtue of the Law of Property Act 1925, s.198. Here there is a conflict between the principles of the Land Registration Act 1925 and the effect of the Insolvency Act 1986 which survives the new act. In such a case C will need to effect a Land Charges Search for A for the period until his purchase to avoid the possibility of being affected by A's bankruptcy. Once C has a clear Land Registry Search and can register or has registered pursuant to that search then land registration principles require that this title is unimpeachable.

(3) Where the gift involving registered land took place before this Act came into force there may, in some cases, be an entry on the register referring to the possibility of the gift being set aside under the Insolvency Act 1986. In this case a purchaser who can produce clear searches against the donor should achieve registration free of this entry. This is because as against that new proprietor the transaction will then no longer be vulnerable. The purchaser from the existing entry will have notice of the surrounding circumstances. If a bankruptcy proceeding is registered against the donor at the Land Charges Registry the purchaser will have notice of the relevant proceedings. However, a clear Land Charges Search will show that the purchaser is entitled to be registered

free of the existing entry—as he does not have notice of the relevant proceedings because there are none. The purchaser may not without further enquiries from the present proprietor be able to tell who the donor is for the purpose of making an effective Land Charges Search. The need to make a Land Charges Search or take the risk of being deemed not to be a purchaser in good faith under the present Act erodes the basic Land Registry principle and is a vital step for a purchaser in C's position to take. However, under the amended s.342 of the Insolvency Act 1986 there is a possibility of C's title being challenged where C both has notice of the gift and the bankruptcy proceedings. For this reason a bankruptcy search against A is required. This need will arise where C is told that the transaction between A and B was at an undervalue. It could arise where the transaction between A and B gave rise to first registration and, B in deducing title to C, has produced the pre-registration deeds which reveal fortuitously that the A to B transaction was at an undervalue.

The example has been used of the position of a first purchase (by C) after an avoidable transaction between A and B. The Act applies in the same way to subsequent purchases.

Adjustment of certain transactions in case of liquidation etc: Northern Ireland

3.—(1) In paragraph (2) of Article 205 of the Insolvency (Northern Ireland) Order 1989 (which relates to orders under Article 202 or 203 and, in sub-paragraphs (a) and (b), protects certain interests and certain persons who received benefits) in each of sub-paragraphs (a) and (b), for the words "in good faith, for value and without notice of the relevant circumstances" there shall be substituted "in good faith and for value".

(2) After that paragraph there shall be inserted the following paragraph—

"(2A) Where a person has acquired an interest in property from a person other than the company in question, or has received a benefit from the transaction or preference, and at the time of that acquisition or receipt—

(a) he had notice of the relevant surrounding circumstances and of the relevant proceedings, or

(b) he was connected with, or was an associate of, either the company in question or the person with whom that company entered into the transaction or to whom that company gave the preference,

then, unless the contrary is shown, it shall be presumed for the purposes of sub-paragraph (a) or (as the case may be) sub-paragraph (b) of paragraph (2) that the interest was acquired or the benefit was received otherwise than in good faith."

(3) For paragraph (3) of that Article there shall be substituted the following paragraphs—

"(3) For the purposes of paragraph (2A)(a), the relevant surrounding circumstances are (as the case may require)—

(a) the fact that the company in question entered into the transaction at an undervalue; or

(b) the circumstances which amounted to the giving of the preference by the company in question;

and paragraphs (3A) to (3C) have effect to determine whether, for those purposes, a person has notice of the relevant proceedings.

(3A) In a case where Article 202 or 203 applies by reason of the making of an administration order, a person has notice of the relevant proceedings if he has notice—

(a) of the fact that the petition on which the administration order is made has been presented; or

(b) of the fact that the administration order has been made.

(3B) In a case where Article 202 or 203 applies by reason of the company in question going into liquidation immediately upon the discharge of an administration order, a person has notice of the relevant proceedings if he has notice—

(a) of the fact that the petition on which the administration order is made has been presented;

(b) of the fact that the administration order has been made; or

(c) of the fact that the company has gone into liquidation.

(3C) In a case where Article 202 or 203 applies by reason of the company in question going into liquidation at any other time, a person has notice of the relevant proceedings if he has notice—

> (a) where the company goes into liquidation on the making of a winding-up order, of the fact that the petition on which the winding-up order is made has been presented or of the fact that the company has gone into liquidation;

> (b) in any other case, of the fact that the company has gone into liquidation."

Adjustment of certain transactions in case of bankruptcy: Northern Ireland

4.—(1) In paragraph (2) of Article 315 of the Insolvency (Northern Ireland) Order 1989 (which relates to orders under Article 312 or 313 and, in sub-paragraphs (a) and (b), protects certain interests and certain persons who received benefits) in each of sub-paragraphs (a) and (b), for the words "in good faith, for value and without notice of the relevant circumstances" there shall be substituted "in good faith and for value".

(2) After that paragraph there shall be inserted the following paragraph—

> "(2A) Where a person has acquired an interest in property from a person other than the individual in question, or has received a benefit from the transaction or preference, and at the time of that acquisition or receipt—

> (a) he had notice of the relevant surrounding circumstances and of the relevant proceedings, or

> (b) he was an associate of, or was connected with, either the individual in question or the person with whom that individual entered into the transaction or to whom that individual gave the preference,

> then, unless the contrary is shown, it shall be presumed for the purposes of sub-paragraph (a) or (as the case may be) sub-paragraph (b) of paragraph (2) that the interest was acquired or the benefit was received otherwise than in good faith."

(3) For paragraph (4) of that Article there shall be substituted the following paragraphs—

> "(4) For the purposes of paragraph (2A)(a), the relevant surrounding circumstances are (as the case may require)—

> (a) the fact that the individual in question entered into the transaction at an undervalue; or

> (b) the circumstances which amounted to the giving of the preference by the individual in question.

> (5) For the purposes of paragraph (2A)(a), a person has notice of the relevant proceedings if he has notice—

> (a) of the fact that the petition on which the individual in question is adjudged bankrupt has been presented; or

> (b) of the fact that the individual in question has been adjudged bankrupt.

> (6) Article 7 shall apply for the purposes of paragraph (2A)(b) as it applies for the purposes of Parts II to VII."

Application to the Crown

5.—(1) The amendments of the Insolvency Act 1986 made by this Act bind the Crown.

(2) The amendments of the Insolvency (Northern Ireland) Order 1989 made by this Act bind the Crown in accordance with Article 378 of that Order.

<small>GENERAL NOTE</small>

The importance of this Act applying to the Crown is that in whatever position the Crown appears in a title the above provisions and the explanations given are unaltered.

Short title, commencement and extent

6.—(1) This Act may be cited as the Insolvency (No. 2) Act 1994.

(2) This Act shall come into force at the end of the period of two months beginning with the day on which it is passed.

(3) This Act has effect in relation to interests acquired and benefits received after this Act comes into force.

(4) Sections 1, 2 and 5(1) above extend to England and Wales only.

(5) Sections 3, 4 and 5(2) above extend to Northern Ireland only.

(6) This section extends to England and Wales and Northern Ireland only.

<small>GENERAL NOTE</small>

This Act comes into force on July 26, 1994. The important issue to resolve is how it applies in respect of transactions at an undervalue before this date. Lord Coleraine when introducing the Bill in the House of Lords (*Hansard*, H.L. Vol. 554, col. 347): said:

"... the Bill will apply only to interests acquired and benefits received after the Bill has come into force. I am advised that that means that the Bill will cover all third party transactions taking place after the Bill comes into force".

The position is thus that whenever a transaction at an undervalue takes place a purchaser before the Act came into force is tested by reference to the 1986 Act and a purchase after the Act came into force is tested by reference to that Act as amended by the 1994 Act.

INDEX

References are to sections

INTELLIGENCE SERVICES ACT 1994*

(1994 c. 13)

ARRANGEMENT OF SECTIONS

An Act to make provision about the Secret Intelligence Service and the Government Communications Headquarters, including provision for the issue of warrants and authorisations enabling certain actions to be taken and for the issue of such warrants and authorisations to be kept under review; to make further provision about warrants issued on applications by the Security Service; to establish a procedure for the investigation of complaints about the Secret Intelligence Service and the Government Communications Headquarters; to make provision for the establishment of an Intelligence and Security Committee to scrutinise all three of those bodies; and for connected purposes. [26th May 1994]

PARLIAMENTARY DEBATES
    Hansard, H.L. Vol. 550, col. 1023; Vol. 551, cols. 72, 234, 251, 1380; Vol. 552, col. 10; Vol. 555, col. 538; H.C. Vol. 238, col. 153; Vol. 242, col. 251.
    The Bill was discussed in Standing Committee E between March 8–29, 1994.

INTRODUCTION AND GENERAL NOTE
    The Security Service Act 1989 (c.5) ("the 1989 Act"), placed on a statutory footing the activities of the Security Service (M.I.5); publicly describing its activities; providing for its direction by

---

* Annotations by Philip Kolvin and Timothy Straker, Barristers, 2–3 Gray's Inn Square, Gray's Inn, London WC1.

a government appointee; outlawing entry on or interference with property except by warrant; creating the post of Commissioner for the purposes of reviewing and reporting upon its activities; and establishing a tribunal for the investigation of complaints, with power to order remedies, including the destruction of records and the payment of compensation.

The Intelligence Services Act 1994 (c.13) ("the 1994 Act") performs similar functions in relation to the Secret Intelligence Service (M.I.6) and the Government Communications Headquarters (GCHQ). In addition, it establishes a committee of parliamentarians from both Houses to examine the expenditure, administration and policy of all three Services. The latter represents a considerable advance in the policy and attitude of the Government, which refused to establish such a committee upon the promulgation of the 1989 Act.

The foundation of both Acts was, according to the Lord Chancellor: "this Government's policy to be as open as possible about security and intelligence matters without prejudicing national security, the effectiveness of the security and intelligence services or the safety of their staff" (*Hansard*, H.L. Vol. 550, col. 1023).

In seeking to define the activities of M.I.6 and the GCHQ, the 1994 Act subjects them to the control of the Secretary of State, to the scrutiny of a tribunal and a Commissioner, and to the oversight, in non-operational areas, of a parliamentary committee. Critics of the Act might argue that it might have gone further without prejudicing national interests. For example:

(1) the functions of M.I.6 and the GCHQ are widely defined in ss.1(1) and 3(1), and then made subject only to nebulous limitations in ss.1(2) and 3(2);

(2) the Commissioner's reports are not delivered directly to Parliament, but are filtered through the Prime Minister who may censor their contents (see s.8(7));

(3) the Intelligence and Security Committee may not review operational matters and may not summon witnesses; and, like the Commissioner, may find its reports censored by the Prime Minister (s.10(5));

(4) the Tribunal has no power to compel the attendance of witnesses, its reasoning is not disclosable, even to the complainant (see Sched. 2, para. 4(2)) and its decisions are unchallengeable.

However, there is general recognition that while openness and accountability are desirable goals, they need to be tempered with caution, and the balance is one of delicate political judgment. In this instance, the Government responded to a number of relaxing measures mooted during the passage of the Bill, and has clearly taken a substantial step towards the attainment of those goals.

EXTENT

The Act extends to Northern Ireland (s.12(3)) and may be extended by Order in Council to the Isle of Man, the Channel Islands or to any colony (s.7(4)).

ABBREVIATIONS

the 1989 Act : Security Service Act 1989 (c. 5).
the 1994 Act : Intelligence Services Act 1994 (c. 13).

The Secret Intelligence Service

The Secret Intelligence Service

1.—(1) There shall continue to be a Secret Intelligence Service (in this Act referred to as "the Intelligence Service") under the authority of the Secretary of State; and, subject to subsection (2) below, its functions shall be—

(a) to obtain and provide information relating to the actions or intentions of persons outside the British Islands; and

(b) to perform other tasks relating to the actions or intentions of such persons.

(2) The functions of the Intelligence Service shall be exercisable only—

(a) in the interests of national security, with particular reference to the defence and foreign policies of Her Majesty's Government in the United Kingdom; or

(b) in the interests of the economic well-being of the United Kingdom; or

(c) in support of the prevention or detection of serious crime.

GENERAL NOTE

Section 1 provides for the continuation, regulated by the 1994 Act, of the Secret Intelligence Service, now termed the Intelligence Service, under the authority of the Secretary of State.

Subs. (1)

The Secretary of State is an indivisible office of all of the Secretaries of State (see the Interpretation Act 1978, s.5 and Sched. 1). It is conceivable that the Foreign, Home and Defence Secretaries as well as the President of the Board of Trade could exercise the functions of the Secretary of State under this Act.

"British Islands" are defined in the Interpretation Act 1978, s.5 and Sched. 1 as being the U.K., the Channel Islands and the Isle of Man.

This subsection states that the functions of the Intelligence Service shall be to obtain and provide information relating to the actions or intentions of persons outside the British Islands, and to perform other tasks relating to the actions or intentions of such persons. The functions are deliberately drawn in wide terms.

The use of the word "outside" in subpara. (a) refers presumably to the persons whose actions or intentions are being monitored. Thus, M.I.6 is confirmed to be a Service the operations of which are abroad. However, provided that the persons being monitored are outside the British Islands, there is nothing preventing the obtaining of information within the British Islands. Thus, at least some of the operations of M.I.6 may be local.

Subs. (2)

This subsection limits the activities of the Intelligence Service by reference to the purpose for which they may be carried out.

For the meaning attached by the Government to the term "national security" see the note to s.1(2) of the 1989 Act. The fact that the term is intended to refer to the nation as a whole and not its sectional or lesser interests, is supported by the particular reference to defence and foreign policies. However, the reference to such policies is not intended to be exhaustive with regard to the term "national security".

The term "economic well-being of the United Kingdom" is clearly susceptible to the widest construction. The expression is not limited, for example, by use of the word "substantial", which was urged unsuccessfully during the passage of the Bill (see *Hansard*, H.L. Vol. 551, col. 234), so even a slight economic effect would fall within the purview of M.I.6. The well-being of any company through, for instance, the obtaining of an order from abroad, may impinge on the economic well-being of the U.K. The Lord Chancellor prays in aid safeguards in the form of the Commissioner, the Committee and the Tribunal, as well as the ultimate control of the Secretary of State (*Hansard*, H.L. Vol. 551, cols. 236, 240) but these do not affect the lawfulness of the activities of M.I.6, which are here couched in wide terms. Note, however, that the economic interests to be protected are those of the U.K., and not the British Islands as a whole.

The term "serious crime" is defined nowhere. The definition in s.10(3) of the Interception of Communications Act 1985 (c.56) (*i.e.* that it "involves the use of violence, results in substantial financial gain or is conducted by a large number of persons in pursuit of a common purpose ... or [is a crime] for which a person ... who has attained the age of twenty-one and has no previous convictions could ... be expected to be sentenced to imprisonment for a term of three years or more ...") was expressly disavowed by the Lord Chancellor (*Hansard*, H.L. Vol. 551, cols. 240–241) who considered it right to use a general phrase without specific further definition. Nor is the "serious crime" limited to that perpetrated in the U.K., since crime has, increasingly, a multi-national dimension (*ibid.*).

The Chief of the Intelligence Service

2.—(1) The operations of the Intelligence Service shall continue to be under the control of a Chief of that Service appointed by the Secretary of State.

(2) The Chief of the Intelligence Service shall be responsible for the efficiency of that Service and it shall be his duty to ensure—
  (a) that there are arrangements for securing that no information is obtained by the Intelligence Service except so far as necessary for the proper discharge of its functions and that no information is disclosed by it except so far as necessary—
      (i) for that purpose;
      (ii) in the interests of national security;
      (iii) for the purpose of the prevention or detection of serious crime; or
      (iv) for the purpose of any criminal proceedings; and
  (b) that the Intelligence Service does not take any action to further the interests of any United Kingdom political party.

(3) Without prejudice to the generality of subsection (2)(a) above, the disclosure of information shall be regarded as necessary for the proper discharge of the functions of the Intelligence Service if it consists of—

    (a) the disclosure of records subject to and in accordance with the Public Records Act 1958; or

    (b) the disclosure, subject to and in accordance with arrangements approved by the Secretary of State, of information to the Comptroller and Auditor General for the purposes of his functions.

(4) The Chief of the Intelligence Service shall make an annual report on the work of the Intelligence Service to the Prime Minister and the Secretary of State and may at any time report to either of them on any matter relating to its work.

DEFINITIONS

"Secretary of State": see the General Note to s.1.

GENERAL NOTE

Subs. (1)

Subsection (1) provides for the appointment, by the Secretary of State, of a Chief of the Intelligence Service, who shall then control the operations of that Service.

Subs. (2)

This subsection adumbrates the statutory duty of the Chief of the Intelligence Service. There is no sanction for breach save, presumably, revocation of his appointment.

The Intelligence Service may only obtain information for the discharge of the functions set out in s.1. It may only disclose such information for that purpose, or in the interest of national security, for the prevention or detection of serious crime or for the purpose of any criminal proceedings. Thus, it seems, the Intelligence Service may not disclose information in the interests of the economic well-being of the U.K. The use of the words "for that purpose" does not import all of the purposes in s.1(2), otherwise s.2(2)(a)(ii) and (iii) would be otiose. The reason for the omission of "economic well-being" disclosures is unclear.

The Chief of the Intelligence Service must ensure that the Service takes no action to further the interests of any U.K. political party. There is, apparently, nothing to prevent its furthering the interests of a foreign political party, provided that such action furthers the purposes specified in s.1(2).

Subs. (3)

This specifically permits disclosure of records to the Public Record Office, and subject to the approval of the Secretary of State, to the Comptroller and Auditor General for the purposes of his functions. The Lord Chancellor stated that: "The purpose of the provision is solely to enable the services to place their records, if and when appropriate, in the Public Record Office" (*Hansard*, H.C. Vol. 130, col. 1075). It is not intended to affect the operation of the Public Record Office.

Subs. (4)

The Chief of the Intelligence Service is required to make an annual report on the work of the Intelligence Service to the Prime Minister and the Secretary of State and may, as he sees fit, report to either of them on any matter concerning the work of the Service. Neither the Prime Minister nor the Secretary of State is obliged to lay the report before Parliament. See, however, ss.8(6) and 10(6) for the Prime Minister's duty to lay before Parliament the reports of the Commissioner and the Intelligence and Security Committee respectively.

GCHQ

The Government Communications Headquarters

3.—(1) There shall continue to be a Government Communications Headquarters under the authority of the Secretary of State; and, subject to subsection (2) below, its functions shall be—

    (a) to monitor or interfere with electromagnetic, acoustic and other emissions and any equipment producing such emissions and to obtain and provide information derived from or related to such emissions or equipment and from encrypted material; and

    (b) to provide advice and assistance about—

(i) languages, including terminology used for technical matters, and
(ii) cryptography and other matters relating to the protection of information and other material,
to the armed forces of the Crown, to Her Majesty's Government in the United Kingdom or to a Northern Ireland Department or to any other organisation which is determined for the purposes of this section in such manner as may be specified by the Prime Minister.

(2) The functions referred to in subsection (1)(a) above shall be exercisable only—

(a) in the interests of national security, with particular reference to the defence and foreign policies of Her Majesty's Government in the United Kingdom; or

(b) in the interests of the economic well-being of the United Kingdom in relation to the actions or intentions of persons outside the British Islands; or

(c) in support of the prevention or detection of serious crime.

(3) In this Act the expression "GCHQ" refers to the Government Communications Headquarters and to any unit or part of a unit of the armed forces of the Crown which is for the time being required by the Secretary of State to assist the Government Communications Headquarters in carrying out its functions.

DEFINITIONS
"British Islands": s.1.
"Secretary of State": s.1.

GENERAL NOTE
This section provides for the continuation, regulated by the 1994 Act, of the Government Communications Headquarters ("GCHQ") under the authority of the Secretary of State. The GCHQ is engaged principally in the interception, decoding and analysis of communications signals in the national interest.

Subs. (1)
This sets out the functions of the GCHQ. It is empowered to monitor and interfere with communications signals and equipment, obtain or provide information derived from or related to such signals or equipment, and also from encrypted material. It may also provide advice and assistance about languages, cryptography and other matters relating to the protection of information and other material to the armed forces, the Government or any other body determined in a matter specified by the Prime Minister.

Subs. (2)
This subsection limits the purposes of the activities of the GCHQ, and replicates the purposes of the Intelligence Service in s.1(2). In relation to "economic well-being" the persons being monitored must be outside the British Islands, which mirrors s.1(1)(a).

Subs. (3)
This effectively permits the Secretary of State to second any unit of the armed forces to the GCHQ, whereupon the unit adopts the GCHQ's statutory role.

The Director of GCHQ

4.—(1) The operations of GCHQ shall continue to be under the control of a Director appointed by the Secretary of State.

(2) The Director shall be responsible for the efficiency of GCHQ and it shall be his duty to ensure—

(a) that there are arrangements for securing that no information is obtained by GCHQ except so far as necessary for the proper discharge of its functions and that no information is disclosed by it except so far as necessary for that purpose or for the purpose of any criminal proceedings; and

(b) that GCHQ does not take any action to further the interests of any United Kingdom political party.

(3) Without prejudice to the generality of subsection (2)(a) above, the disclosure of information shall be regarded as necessary for the proper discharge of the functions of GCHQ if it consists of—

(a) the disclosure of records subject to and in accordance with the Public Records Act 1958; or

(b) the disclosure, subject to and in accordance with arrangements approved by the Secretary of State, of information to the Comptroller and Auditor General for the purposes of his functions.

(4) The Director shall make an annual report on the work of GCHQ to the Prime Minister and the Secretary of State and may at any time report to either of them on any matter relating to its work.

DEFINITIONS
    "GCHQ": s.3(3).
    "Secretary of State": s.1.

GENERAL NOTE
    Subsection (1) provides for the appointment by the Secretary of State of a Director of the GCHQ, who shall then control the operations of that Service.
    In general, see the General Note to s.2.

Authorisation of certain actions

Warrants: general

    5.—(1) No entry on or interference with property or with wireless telegraphy shall be unlawful if it is authorised by a warrant issued by the Secretary of State under this section.

(2) The Secretary of State may, on an application made by the Security Service, the Intelligence Service or GCHQ, issue a warrant under this section authorising the taking, subject to subsection (3) below, of such action as is specified in the warrant in respect of any property so specified or in respect of wireless telegraphy so specified if the Secretary of State—

(a) thinks it necessary for the action to be taken on the ground that it is likely to be of substantial value in assisting, as the case may be,—
    (i) the Security Service in carrying out any of its functions under the 1989 Act; or
    (ii) the Intelligence Service in carrying out any of its functions under section 1 above; or
    (iii) GCHQ in carrying out any function which falls within section 3(1)(a) above; and

(b) is satisfied that what the action seeks to achieve cannot reasonably be achieved by other means; and

(c) is satisfied that satisfactory arrangements are in force under section 2(2)(a) of the 1989 Act (duties of the Director-General of the Security Service), section 2(2)(a) above or section 4(2)(a) above with respect to the disclosure of information obtained by virtue of this section and that any information obtained under the warrant will be subject to those arrangements.

(3) A warrant authorising the taking of action in support of the prevention or detection of serious crime may not relate to property in the British Islands.

(4) Subject to subsection (5) below, the Security Service may make an application under subsection (2) above for a warrant to be issued authorising that Service (or a person acting on its behalf) to take such action as is specified in the warrant on behalf of the Intelligence Service or GCHQ and, where such a warrant is issued, the functions of the Security Service shall include the carrying out of the action so specified, whether or not it would otherwise be within its functions.

(5) The Security Service may not make an application for a warrant by virtue of subsection (4) above except where the action proposed to be authorised by the warrant—

(a) is action in respect of which the Intelligence Service or, as the case may be, GCHQ could make such an application; and

(b) is to be taken otherwise than in support of the prevention or detection of serious crime.

DEFINITIONS

"British Islands": s.1.
"GCHQ": s.3(3).
"interfere": s.11(1)(e).
"Secretary of State": s.1.
"the 1989 Act": s.11(1)(a).
"the Intelligence Service": s.1(1).
"wireless telegraphy": s.11(1)(e).

GENERAL NOTE

This section provides for the issuing by the Secretary of State to any of the three Services, of warrants permitting the entry on, or interference with, property or with wireless telegraphy. A warrant renders lawful that which might otherwise be unlawful, namely, a trespass to land or to goods.

Subs. (1)

The grant of a warrant can not be retrospective, so as to give *ex post facto* justification to an unlawful act.

Subs. (2)

This both grants power to the Secretary of State and circumscribes that power, *i.e.* he must be satisfied that the warrant is likely to be of substantial value to one of the Services in the execution of their statutory functions, and that the purpose of the warrant cannot reasonably be achieved otherwise; and that the provisions in ss.2(2)(a) and 4(2)(a) as to limited disclosure of information are being observed.

Subs. (3)

A warrant which authorises the taking of action in support of the prevention or detection of serious crime may not be made in relation to property in the British Islands, presumably because that would encroach on the function of the police under the Police and Criminal Evidence Act 1984 (c.60).

Subs. (4)

Subject to subs. (5), the Security Service may apply for and execute a warrant on behalf of the Intelligence Service or the GCHQ.

Subs. (5)

The powers of the Security Service under subs. (4) may only be exercised where the action authorised by the warrant falls within the statutory functions of the Intelligence Service or the GCHQ and is for a purpose other than the prevention or detection of serious crime.

Warrants: procedure and duration, etc.

6.—(1) A warrant shall not be issued except—

(a) under the hand of the Secretary of State; or

(b) in an urgent case where the Secretary of State has expressly authorised its issue and a statement of the fact is endorsed on it, under the hand of a senior official of his department.

(2) A warrant shall, unless renewed under subsection (3) below, cease to have effect—

(a) if the warrant was under the hand of the Secretary of State, at the end of the period of six months beginning with the day on which it was issued; and

(b) in any other case, at the end of the period ending with the second working day following that day.

(3) If at any time before the day on which a warrant would cease to have effect the Secretary of State considers it necessary for the warrant to continue to have effect for the purpose for which it was issued, he may by an instrument under his hand renew it for a period of six months beginning with that day.

(4) The Secretary of State shall cancel a warrant if he is satisfied that the action authorised by it is no longer necessary.

(5) In the preceding provisions of this section "warrant" means a warrant under section 5 above.

(6) As regards the Security Service, this section and section 5 above have effect in place of section 3 (property warrants) of the 1989 Act, and accordingly—

(a) a warrant issued under that section of the 1989 Act and current when this section and section 5 above come into force shall be treated as a warrant under section 5 above, but without any change in the date on which the warrant was in fact issued or last renewed; and

(b) section 3 of the 1989 Act shall cease to have effect.

DEFINITIONS
"Secretary of State": s.1.
"senior official": s.11(1)(d).
"the 1989 Act": s.11(1)(a).
"working day": s.11(1)(f).

GENERAL NOTE
This section provides for warrants to be issued on behalf of the Secretary of State and with his authority in urgent cases. Such warrants endure for only two days, as opposed to six months for warrants issued under his hand.

Subs. (1)
Subsection (1) enjoins the Secretary of State to issue warrants personally, except in an urgent case where a senior official may issue the warrant, and then only under the authority of the Secretary of State.

Subs. (2)
A warrant endures for six months, or two working days after issue if issued on behalf of the Secretary of State in an urgent case.

Subs. (3)
The Secretary of State may extend a warrant for six months, and may do so more than once, but this cannot be effected retrospectively.

Subs. (4)
The Secretary of State must cancel a warrant if he is satisfied that the action authorised by it is no longer necessary. Presumably, therefore, the Secretary of State must monitor the execution of the warrant.

Subs. (6)
By repealing s.3 of the Security Services Act 1989 (c.5), and bringing warrants issued to the Security Service within the purview of this Act, provisions relating to the issue of warrants to all three Services are harmonised, and governed by a single legislative provision.

Authorisation of acts outside the British Islands

7.—(1) If, apart from this section, a person would be liable in the United Kingdom for any act done outside the British Islands, he shall not be so liable if the act is one which is authorised to be done by virtue of an authorisation given by the Secretary of State under this section.

(2) In subsection (1) above "liable in the United Kingdom" means liable under the criminal or civil law of any part of the United Kingdom.

(3) The Secretary of State shall not give an authorisation under this section unless he is satisfied—

(a) that any acts which may be done in reliance on the authorisation or, as the case may be, the operation in the course of which the acts may be done will be necessary for the proper discharge of a function of the Intelligence Service; and

(b) that there are satisfactory arrangements in force to secure—
    (i) that nothing will be done in reliance on the authorisation beyond what is necessary for the proper discharge of a function of the Intelligence Service; and
    (ii) that, in so far as any acts may be done in reliance on the authorisation, their nature and likely consequences will be reasonable, having regard to the purposes for which they are carried out; and

(c) that there are satisfactory arrangements in force under section 2(2)(a) above with respect to the disclosure of information obtained by virtue of this section and that any information obtained by virtue of anything done in reliance on the authorisation will be subject to those arrangements.

(4) Without prejudice to the generality of the power of the Secretary of State to give an authorisation under this section, such an authorisation—

(a) may relate to a particular act or acts, to acts of a description specified in the authorisation or to acts undertaken in the course of an operation so specified;

(b) may be limited to a particular person or persons of a description so specified; and

(c) may be subject to conditions so specified.

(5) An authorisation shall not be given under this section except—

(a) under the hand of the Secretary of State; or

(b) in an urgent case where the Secretary of State has expressly authorised it to be given and a statement of that fact is endorsed on it, under the hand of a senior official of his department.

(6) An authorisation shall, unless renewed under subsection (7) below, cease to have effect—

(a) if the authorisation was given under the hand of the Secretary of State, at the end of the period of six months beginning with the day on which it was given;

(b) in any other case, at the end of the period ending with the second working day following the day on which it was given.

(7) If at any time before the day on which an authorisation would cease to have effect the Secretary of State considers it necessary for the authorisation to continue to have effect for the purpose for which it was given, he may by an instrument under his hand renew it for a period of six months beginning with that day.

(8) The Secretary of State shall cancel an authorisation if he is satisfied that any act authorised by it is no longer necessary.

DEFINITIONS
"British Islands": s.1.
"Secretary of State": s.1.

GENERAL NOTE
This section provides for the conferring of authorisation by the Secretary of State upon the Intelligence Service in relation to acts abroad. The authorisation may be defined in relation to particular acts, classes of acts or operations, and exempts the person authorised from civil or criminal liability in the U.K. Whether the acts authorised fall foul of the law of the country in which they are perpetrated must depend on that country's domestic law.

Subss. (1) and (2)
These subsections exempt a person authorised under this section from any domestic civil or criminal liability for authorised acts committed abroad.

Subs. (3)

This subsection prevents the Secretary of State from granting an authorisation unless:
(1) the acts or operations authorised are for the proper discharge of the function of the Intelligence Service;
(2) there are satisfactory arrangements in force:
    (a) to secure that nothing will be done in purported reliance on the authorisation which goes beyond such purposes;
    (b) that the nature and likely consequences of the acts authorised will be reasonable, having regard to the purposes for which they are carried out;
    (c) to secure that the provisions of s.2(2)(a) as to limiting disclosure of information will be observed.

Subs. (4)

The authorisation may relate to particular acts, a specified description of acts or a specified operation. It may be limited to particular persons or a specified class of persons. It may also be subject to specified conditions. All of these matters fall within the absolute discretion of the Secretary of State.

Subss. (6), (7) and (8)

These provide for the duration of an authorisation under this section, and mirror the warrant provisions in s.6(2), (3) and (4).

The Commissioner, the Tribunal and the investigation of complaints

The Commissioner

8.—(1) The Prime Minister shall appoint as a Commissioner for the purposes of this Act a person who holds or has held high judicial office within the meaning of the Appellate Jurisdiction Act 1876.

(2) The Commissioner shall hold office in accordance with the terms of his appointment and there shall be paid to him by the Secretary of State such allowances as the Treasury may determine.

(3) In addition to his functions under the subsequent provisions of this Act the Commissioner shall keep under review the exercise by the Secretary of State of his powers under sections 5 to 7 above, except in so far as the powers under sections 5 and 6 above relate to the Security Service.

(4) It shall be the duty of—
(a) every member of the Intelligence Service,
(b) every member of GCHQ, and
(c) every official of the department of the Secretary of State,
to disclose or give to the Commissioner such documents or information as he may require for the purpose of enabling him to discharge his functions.

(5) The Commissioner shall make an annual report on the discharge of his functions to the Prime Minister and may at any time report to him on any matter relating to his discharge of those functions.

(6) The Prime Minister shall lay before each House of Parliament a copy of each annual report made by the Commissioner under subsection (5) above together with a statement as to whether any matter has been excluded from that copy in pursuance of subsection (7) below.

(7) If it appears to the Prime Minister, after consultation with the Commissioner, that the publication of any matter in a report would be prejudicial to the continued discharge of the functions of the Intelligence Service or, as the case may be, GCHQ, the Prime Minister may exclude that matter from the copy of the report as laid before each House of Parliament.

(8) The Secretary of State may, after consultation with the Commissioner and with the approval of the Treasury as to numbers, provide the Com-

missioner with such staff as the Secretary of State thinks necessary for the discharge of his functions.

    "GCHQ": s.3(3).
    "Secretary of State": s.1.
    "the Commissioner": s.11(1)(b).
    "the Intelligence Service": s.1(1).

GENERAL NOTE

Subss. (1) and (2)
    This establishes the office of Commissioner, appointed by the Prime Minister. The Commissioner must be a serving or ex-judge of at least High Court level.

Subss. (3)–(8)
    The Commissioner is provided with functions in relation to the investigation of complaints against the Intelligence Service or the GCHQ (see Sched. 1, paras. (2)(5) and (7)). He must keep under review the exercise of the power of the Secretary of State to issue warrants and authorisations.
    The Intelligence Service, the GCHQ and the Secretary of State (through their staff) are obliged to disclose documents to him, which he may require in order to perform his functions.
    The Commissioner must report annually to the Prime Minister on the discharge of his functions, and may do so more frequently, at his discretion. The Prime Minister must place the annual report before both Houses of Parliament, save that if the continued discharge of the functions of the Intelligence Service or the GCHQ would be prejudiced, he may, after consultation with the Commissioner, excise prejudicial matters. The Prime Minister must inform the Houses whether he has censored any part of the reports.
    The Secretary of State may provide the Commissioner with the requisite staff.

Investigation of complaints

9.—(1) There shall be a Tribunal for the purpose of investigating complaints about the Intelligence Service or GCHQ in the manner specified in Schedule 1 to this Act.

(2) The Commissioner shall have the functions conferred on him by Schedule 1 to this Act and give the Tribunal all such assistance in discharging their functions under that Schedule as they may require.

(3) Schedule 2 to this Act shall have effect with respect to the constitution, procedure and other matters relating to the Tribunal.

(4) The decisions of the Tribunal and the Commissioner under Schedule 1 to this Act (including decisions as to their jurisdictions) shall not be subject to appeal or liable to be questioned in any court.

DEFINITIONS
    "GCHQ": s.3(3).
    "the Commissioner": s.11(1)(b).
    "the Intelligence Service": s.1(1).
    "the Tribunal": Sched. 2.

GENERAL NOTE
    This is an important section which establishes a Tribunal, constituted as provided by Sched. 2, for the purpose of investigating complaints about the Intelligence Service or the GCHQ. Section 9(1) and (2) are plainly drawn from s.10(1), (2) and (3) of the Security Service Act 1989 (c.5) which established a Tribunal for the purpose of investigating complaints about the security service.

Subs. (1)
   See further the note to Sched. 1.

Subs. (3)
   See further the note to Sched. 2.

Subs. (4)
   This takes the same form as s.5(4) of the Security Service Act 1989 (c.5). The ability to question any such decision has not been tested in any court and can be expected to be severely, if not
entirely, constrained by this subsection. Ouster clauses have been propounded in a number of
different ways in a number of different statutes. In *Anisminic* v. *Foreign Compensation Commission* [1969] 2 A.C. 147, there was an apparent absolute prohibition on recourse to any court of
law. However, the House of Lords held that it did not prohibit calling in question whether what
purported to be a determination was truly a determination in law. Here the subsection expressly
includes within the scope of the privative clause decisions as to jurisdiction. This potentially
raises a very interesting point as, in administrative law, it has been the conventional view that
decisions as to jurisdiction are decisions for the court rather than for the Tribunal because, to
allow otherwise, may be to permit unfettered power on the part of the Tribunal to determine its
own jurisdiction. However, here the plain parliamentary intention is to provide a system of
complaints about underlying matters and exclude decisions as to jurisdiction from the ambit of
the court's jurisdiction. This is of significance in determining the true effect of the privative
clause and the courts recently have been more inclined to take the words of privative clauses as
meaning what they say (see, *e.g. R.* v. *Cornwall County Council,* ex p. *Huntington* [1994] 1 All
E.R. 694, C.A.).

The Intelligence and Security Committee

The Intelligence and Security Committee

   10.—(1) There shall be a Committee, to be known as the Intelligence and
Security Committee and in this section referred to as "the Committee", to
examine the expenditure, administration and policy of—
   (a) the Security Service;
   (b) the Intelligence Service; and
   (c) GCHQ.
   (2) The Committee shall consist of nine members—
   (a) who shall be drawn both from the members of the House of Commons
         and from the members of the House of Lords; and
   (b) none of whom shall be a Minister of the Crown.
   (3) The members of the Committee shall be appointed by the Prime Minister after consultation with the Leader of the Opposition, within the meaning
of the Ministerial and other Salaries Act 1975; and one of those members
shall be so appointed as Chairman of the Committee.
   (4) Schedule 3 to this Act shall have effect with respect to the tenure of
office of members of, the procedure of and other matters relating to, the
Committee; and in that Schedule "the Committee" has the same meaning as
in this section.
   (5) The Committee shall make an annual report on the discharge of their
functions to the Prime Minister and may at any time report to him on any
matter relating to the discharge of those functions.
   (6) The Prime Minister shall lay before each House of Parliament a copy of
each annual report made by the Committee under subsection (5) above
together with a statement as to whether any matter has been excluded from
that copy in pursuance of subsection (7) below.
   (7) If it appears to the Prime Minister, after consultation with the Committee, that the publication of any matter in a report would be prejudicial to
the continued discharge of the functions of either of the Services or, as the

case may be, GCHQ, the Prime Minister may exclude that matter from the copy of the report as laid before each House of Parliament.

DEFINITIONS
"GCHQ": s.3(3).
"Minister of the Crown": s.11(c).
"the Intelligence Service": s.1(1).

GENERAL NOTE

Subss. (1)–(4)
This important section establishes an Intelligence and Security Committee of nine persons, drawn from parliamentarians from both Houses, although none shall be a Minister. The Committee is appointed by the Prime Minister, in consultation with the Leader of the Opposition.
The Committee shall examine the expenditure, administration and policy (but, note, not the operation) of all three Services.
Substantive matters relating to the tenure of office of the Committee, its procedure and access to information are dealt with in Sched. 3.

Subss. (5)–(7)
These provisions concern the making of reports by the Committee to the Prime Minister, and mirror the reporting and censorship provisions relating to the Commissioner in s.8(5)–(7).

Supplementary

Interpretation and consequential amendments

11.—(1) In this Act—
(a) "the 1989 Act" means the Security Service Act 1989;
(b) "the Commissioner" means the Commissioner appointed under section 8 above;
(c) "Minister of the Crown" has the same meaning as in the Ministers of the Crown Act 1975;
(d) "senior official" in relation to a department is a reference to an office of or above Grade 3 or, as the case may require, Diplomatic Service Senior Grade;
(e) "wireless telegraphy" has the same meaning as in the Wireless Telegraphy Act 1949 and, in relation to wireless telegraphy, "interfere" has the same meaning as in that Act;
(f) "working day" means any day other than a Saturday, a Sunday, Christmas Day, Good Friday or a day which is a bank holiday under the Banking and Financial Dealings Act 1971 in any part of the United Kingdom.
(2) In consequence of the preceding provisions of this Act, the 1989 Act, the Official Secrets Act 1989 and the Official Secrets Act 1989 (Prescription) Order 1990 shall have effect subject to the amendments in Schedule 4 to this Act.

Short title, commencement and extent

12.—(1) This Act may be cited as the Intelligence Services Act 1994.
(2) This Act shall come into force on such day as the Secretary of State may by an order made by statutory instrument appoint, and different days may be so appointed for different provisions or different purposes.
(3) This Act extends to Northern Ireland.

(4) Her Majesty may by Order in Council direct that any of the provisions of this Act specified in the Order shall extend, with such exceptions, adaptations and modifications as appear to Her to be necessary or expedient, to the Isle of Man, any of the Channel Islands or any colony.

SCHEDULES

Section 9   SCHEDULE 1

INVESTIGATION OF COMPLAINTS

Preliminary

1. Any person may complain to the Tribunal if he is aggrieved by anything which he believes the Intelligence Service of GCHQ has done in relation to him or to any property of his; and, unless the Tribunal consider that the complaint is frivolous or vexatious, they shall deal with it in accordance with this Schedule.

References and investigations by the Tribunal

2. If and so far as the complaint alleges that anything has been done in relation to any property of the complainant, the Tribunal shall refer the complaint to the Commissioner.

3. Subject to paragraph 2 above and paragraph 4 below, the Tribunal shall investigate—
(a) whether the Intelligence Service or, as the case may be, GCHQ has obtained or provided information or performed any other tasks in relation to the actions or intentions of the complainant; and
(b) if so, whether, applying the principles applied by a court on an application for judicial review, the Intelligence Service of GCHQ has reasonable grounds for doing what it did.

4. If, in the course of the investigation of a complaint by the Tribunal, the Tribunal consider that it is necessary to establish whether an authorisation was given under section 7 of this Act to the doing of any act, they shall refer so much of the complaint as relates to the going of that act to the Commissioner.

Functions of the Commissioner in relation to complaints

5.—(1) Where a reference is made to the Commissioner under paragraph 2 or paragraph 4 above, the Commissioner shall investigate, as the case may require,—
(a) whether a warrant was issued under section 5 of this Act in relation to the property concerned; or
(b) whether an authorisation was given under section 7 of this Act to the doing of the act in question.

(2) If the commissioner finds that a warrant was issued or an authorisation was given, he shall, applying the principles applied by a court on an application for judicial review, determine whether the Secretary of State was acting properly in issuing or renewing the warrant or, as the case may be, in giving or renewing the authorisation.

(3) The Commissioner shall inform the Tribunal of his conclusion on any reference made to him under paragraph 2 or paragraph 4 above.

Report of conclusions

6.—(1) Where the Tribunal determine under paragraph 3 above that the Intelligence Service or, as the case may be, GCHQ did not have reasonable grounds for doing what it did, they shall—
(a) give notice to the complainant that they have made a determination in his favour; and
(b) make a report of their findings to the Secretary of State and to the Commissioner.

(2) The Tribunal shall also give notice to the complainant of any determination in his favour by the Commissioner under paragraph 5 above.

(3) Where in the case of any complaint no such determination as is mentioned in sub-paragraph (1) or sub-paragraph (2) above is made by the Tribunal or the Commissioner, the Tribunal shall give notice to the complainant that no determination in his favour has been made on his complaint.

Special references by Tribunal to Commissioner

7.—(1) If in any case investigated by the Tribunal—
(a) the Tribunal's conclusions on the matters which they are required to investigate are such that no determination is made by them in favour of the complainant; but

(b) it appears to the Tribunal from the allegations made by the complainant that it is appropriate for there to be an investigation into whether the Intelligence Service or GCHQ has in any other respect acted unreasonably in relation to the complainant or his property,

they shall refer that matter to the Commissioner.

(2) The Commissioner may report any matter referred to him under sub-paragraph (1) above to the Secretary of State.

Remedies

8.—(1) Where the Tribunal give a complainant notice of such a determination as is mentioned in paragraph 6(1) above, the Tribunal may do either or both of the following, namely,—

(a) direct that the obtaining and provision of information in relation to the complainant or, as the case may be, the conduct of other activities in relation to him or to any property of his shall cease and that any records relating to such information so obtained or provided or such other activities shall be destroyed;

(b) direct the Secretary of State to pay to the complainant such sum by way of compensation as may be specified by the Tribunal.

(2) Where the Tribunal give a complainant notice of such a determination as is mentioned in paragraph 6(2) above, the Tribunal may do either or both of the following, namely,—

(a) quash any warrant or authorisation which the Commissioner has found to have been improperly issued, renewed or given and which he considers should be quashed;

(b) direct the Secretary of State to pay to the complainant such sum by way of compensation as may be specified by the Commissioner.

(3) Where the Secretary of State receives a report under paragraph 7(2) above, he may take such action in the light of the report as he thinks fit, including any action which the Tribunal have power to take or direct under the preceding provisions of this paragraph.

Supplementary

9. The persons who may complain to the Tribunal under this Schedule include any organisation and any association or combination or persons.

10.—(1) No complaint shall be entertained under this Schedule if and so far as it relates to anything done before the date on which this Schedule comes into force.

(2) Where any activities in relation to any peron or his property were instituted before that date and no decision had been taken before that date to discontinue them, paragraphs 2 and 3 above shall have effect as if they had been instituted on that date.

11. Any reference in this Schedule to a complainant's property includes—

(a) a reference to any wireless telegraphy transmission originated or received or intended to be received by him; and

(b) a reference to any place where the complainant resides or works.

DEFINITIONS
"GCHQ": s.3(3).
"the Commissioner": s.8(1).
"the Intelligence Service": s.1(1).

GENERAL NOTE
This Schedule provides for complaints to the Tribunal established under s.9. There are two pre-conditions for a complaint to be dealt with in accordance with the Schedule. First the complainant must be aggrieved by anything which he believes the Intelligence Service or the GCHQ has done in relation to him or to any property of his. Secondly, the Tribunal must not consider the complaint to be frivolous or vexatious. It should be observed that the first pre-condition imposes a requirement that the complainant be affected personally. This serves to remove from the ambit of the Tribunal that which might be a source of complaint, namely concerned individuals who, or organisations which seek to complain about the treatment meted out to others.

Para. (2)
If a complaint includes an allegation relating to property of a complainant it is referred to the Commissioner.

Para. (3)
This is an important provision as it reveals the scope of the Tribunal's investigation. First, they have to investigate whether the Intelligence Service or the GCHQ have obtained or provided information or performed any other tasks in relation to the actions or intentions of the complainant. That might be described as a fact-finding exercise. Secondly, they have, by applying

judicial review grounds, to investigate whether the Intelligence Service or the GCHQ had reasonable grounds for doing what it did. It can then be noted that this Tribunal cannot be described as an appellate body or as a body significantly concerned with the merits of any action on the part of the Intelligence Service or the GCHQ. This is because the grounds for judicial review, classically set out by Lord Diplock in *Council of Civil Service Unions* v. *Minister for the Civil Service* [1985] A.C. 374, at 410 as illegality, impropriety and irrationality, do not encompass consideration of the merits of that which has been done but rather consideration of the way in which it has been done. Irrationality, to succeed, generally predicates a decision-maker having taken leave of his senses (Lord Scarman in *Nottinghamshire County Council* v. *Secretary of State for the Environment*; *Bradford Metropolitan City Council* v. *Same* [1986] A.C. 240, at 248) or behaving in a way which no reasonable decision maker could behave. It may be thought unlikely that irrationality in that sense will ever succeed as a ground for complaint. This is because as there is only one Intelligence Service it is difficult to maintain the proposition that no reasonable Intelligence Service could have acted as the Intelligence Service in fact did. In short there is little scope for any comparison.

Para. (5)

Reference may be made to the Commissioner under paras. (2) or (4). He considers whether a warrant was issued under s.5 or whether an authorisation was given under s.7, of this Act. In either such case he applies judicial review principles to determine whether the Secretary of State was acting properly in issuing the warrant or in giving or renewing the authorisation. As to judicial review see the note to the preceding paragraph.

Para. (8)

This provides for remedies. They depend upon the Tribunal having determined that the GCHQ or the Intelligence Service did not have reasonable grounds for doing what they did.

Para. (10)

As at the date of this note no Statutory Instrument bringing this Schedule into effect has been made.

Section 9   SCHEDULE 2

THE TRIBUNAL

Constitution of the Tribunal

1.—(1) The Tribunal shall consist of not less than three or more that five members each of whom shall be—
    (a) a person who has a 10 year general qualification within the meaning of section 71 of the Courts and Legal Services Act 1990;
    (b) an advocate or solicitor in Scotland of at least ten years' standing; or
    (c) a member of the Bar of Northern Ireland or solicitor of the Supreme Court of Northern Ireland of at least 10 years' standing.
  (2) The members of the Tribunal shall be appointed by Her Majesty by Royal Warrant.
  (3) A member of the Tribunal shall vacate office at the end of the period of five years beginning with the day of his appointment but shall be eligible for re-appointment.
  (4) A member of the Tribunal may be relieved of office by Her Majesty at his own request.
  (5) A member of the Tribunal may be removed from office by Her Majesty on an Address presented to Her by both Houses of Parliament.

President and Vice-President

2.—(1) Her Majesty may by Royal Warrant appoint as President or Vice-President of the Tribunal a person who is, or by virtue of that Warrant will be, a member of the Tribunal.
  (2) If at any time the President of the Tribunal is temporarily unable to carry out the functions of the President under this Schedule, the Vice-President shall carry out those functions.
  (3) A person shall cease to be President or Vice-President of the Tribunal if he ceases to be a member of the Tribunal.

Procedure

3. The functions of the Tribunal in relation to any complaint shall be capable of being carried out, in any place in the United Kingdom, by any two or more members of the Tribunal designated for the purpose by the President; and different members of the Tribunal may carry out functions in relation to different complaints at the same time.

4.—(1) It shall be the duty of every member of the Intelligence Service or, as the case may be, GCHQ to disclose or give to the Tribunal such documents or information as they may require for the purpose of enabling then to carry out their functions under this Act.

(2) Subject to paragraph 6(2) below, the Tribunal shall carry out their functions under this Act in such a way as to secure that no document or information disclosed or given to the Tribunal by any person is disclosed without his consent to any complainant, to any person (other than the Commissioner) holding office under the Crown or to any other person; and accordingly the Tribunal shall not, except in reports under paragraph 6(1)(b) of Schedule 1 to this Act, give any reasons for a determination notified by them to a complainant.

(3) Subject to sub-paragraph (2) above, the Tribunal may determine their own procedure.

Salaries and expenses

5.—(1) The Secretary of State shall pay to the members of the Tribunal such remuneration and allowances as he may with the approval of the Treasury determine.

(2) The Secretary of State shall defray such expenses of the Tribunal as he may with the approval of the Treasury determine.

Staff

6.—(1) The Secretary of State may, after consultation with the Tribunal and with the approval of the Treasury as to numbers, provide the Tribunal with such staff as he thinks necessary for the proper discharge of their functions.

(2) The Tribunal may authorise any member of their staff to obtain any documents or information on the Tribunal's behalf.

Parliamentary disqualification '

7.—(1) In Part II of Schedule 1 to the House of Commons Disqualification Act 1975 (bodies whose members are disqualified) there shall be inserted at the appropriate place—

"The Tribunal established under section 9 of the Intelligence Services Act 1994".

(2) The same amendment shall be made in Part II of Schedule 1 to the Northern Ireland Assembly Disqualification Act 1975.

DEFINITIONS
"GCHQ": s.3(3).
"the Commissioner": s.8(1).
"the Intelligence Service": s.1(1).

GENERAL NOTE
This Schedule provides for the constitution of the Tribunal and records (para. (3)) that its functions can be carried out in any place in the U.K. by any two or more members of the Tribunal.

Para. (4)
This deals with documents. The Intelligence Service and the GCHQ have to provide documents to the Tribunal but nothing is passed on by the Tribunal without the consent of the person giving the document to any person, which would include the complainant. The complainant is also bereft of reasons for any determination or complaint made. This would undoubtedly provide (quite apart from any other restraint) a great inhibition on the ability of a complainant to pursue a matter in the Courts and beyond the Tribunal.

Section 10(4)   SCHEDULE 3

THE INTELLIGENCE AND SECURITY COMMITTEE

Tenure of office

1.—(1) Subject to the provisions of this paragraph, a member of the Committee shall hold office for the duration of the Parliament in which he is appointed.

(2) A member of the Committee shall vacate office—

(a) if he ceases to be a member of the House of Commons;
(b) if he ceases to be a member of the House of Lords;
(c) if he becomes a Minister of the Crown; or
(d) if he is required to do so by the Prime Minister on the appointment, in accordance with section 10(3) of this Act, of another person as a member in his place.

(3) A member of the Committee may resign at any time by notice to the Prime Minister.

(4) Past service is no bar to appointment as a member of the Committee.

Procedure

2.—(1) Subject to the following provisions of this Schedule, the Committee may determine their own procedure.

(2) If on any matter there is an equality of voting among the members of the Committee, the Chairman shall have a second or casting vote.

(3) The Chairman may appoint one of the members of the Committee to act, in his absence, as chairman at any meeting of the Committee, but sub-paragraph (2) above shall not apply to a chairman appointed under this sub-paragraph.

(4) The quorum of the Committee shall be three.

Access to information

3.—(1) If the Director-General of the Security Service, the Chief of the Intelligence Service or the Director of GCHQ is asked by the Committee to disclose any information, then, as to the whole or any part of the information which is sought, he shall either—

(a) arrange for it to be made available to the Committee subject to and in accordance with arrangements approved by the Secretary of State; or

(b) inform the Committee that it cannot be disclosed either—

(i) because it is sensitive information (as defined in paragraph 4 below) which, in his opinion, should not be made available under paragraph (a) above; or

(ii) because the Secretary of State has determined that it should not be disclosed.

(2) The fact that any particular information is sensitive information shall not prevent its disclosure under sub-paragraph (1)(a) above if the Director-General, the Chief or the Director (as the case may require) considers it safe to disclose it.

(3) Information which has not been disclosed to the Committee on the ground specified in sub-paragraph (1)(b)(i) above shall be disclosed to them if the Secretary of State considers it desirable in the public interest.

(4) The Secretary of State shall not make a determination under sub-paragraph (1)(b)(ii) above with respect to any information on the grounds of national security alone and, subject to that, he shall not make such a determination unless the information appears to him to be of such a nature that, if he were requested to produce it before a Departmental Select Committee of the House of Commons, he would think it proper not to do so.

(5) The disclosure of information to the Committee in accordance with the preceding provisions of this paragraph shall be regarded for the purposes of the 1989 Act or, as the case may be, this Act as necessary for the proper discharge of the functions of the Security Service, the Intelligence Service or, as the case may require, GCHQ.

Sensitive information

4. The following information is sensitive information for the purposes of paragraph 3 above—

(a) information which might lead to the identification of, or provide details of, sources of information, other assistance or operational methods available to the Security Service, the Intelligence Service or GCHQ;

(b) information about particular operations which have been, are being or are proposed to be undertaken in pursuance of any of the functions of those bodies; and

(c) information provided by, or by an agency of, the Government of a territory outside the United Kingdom where that Government does not consent to the disclosure of the information.

DEFINITIONS

"Committee": s.10(1).

"GCHQ": s.3(3).

"Secretary of State": s.1.

"the Intelligence Service": s.1(1).

GENERAL NOTE

Para. (1)

A member of the Intelligence and Security Committee holds office for the duration of the Parliament in which he is appointed, unless he resigns, is replaced by the Prime Minister, ceases to be a member of the House of Commons or Lords, or becomes a Minister.

Para. (2)

The Committee may determine its own procedure, but cannot, apparently, compel attendance of witnesses to give evidence before it unlike, for example, a Select Committee.

Paras. (3) and (4)

The Committee may ask the heads of the Services to provide information. They may only refuse on two grounds:

(1) the information is sensitive within the meaning of para. (4), and the head of the relevant Service does not consider it safe to disclose it. In this case, the Secretary of State has an overriding discretion to disclose the information to the Committee in the public interest;

(2) the Secretary of State has determined that it should not be disclosed. He may only so determine if he would be justified in refusing its disclosure to a Departmental Select Committee of the House of Commons, and may not refuse on grounds of national security alone.

Section 11(2)   SCHEDULE 4

CONSEQUENTIAL AMENDMENTS

The Security Service Act 1989

1.—(1) In section 2 of the Security Service Act 1989 (duties of the Director-General of the Security Service) in subsection (2) after the words "serious crime" there shall be inserted "or for the purpose of any criminal proceedings".

(2) After subsection (3) of that section there shall be inserted the following subsection—

"(3A) Without prejudice to the generality of subsection (2)(a) above, the disclosure of information shall be regarded as necessary for the proper discharge of the functions of the Security Service if it consists of—

(a) the disclosure of records subject to and in accordance with the Public Records Act 1958; or

(b) the disclosure, subject to and in accordance with arrangements approved by the Secretary of State, of information to the Comptroller and Auditor General for the purposes of his functions."

2. In section 4(3) of that Act (Security Service Commissioner to review exercise of powers by Secretary of State), for the words "powers under section 3 above" there shall be substituted "powers, so far as they relate to applications made by the Service, under sections 5 and 6 of the Intelligence Services Act 1994".

3. In paragraph 4(1) of Schedule 1 to that Act (Security Service Commissioner to investigate whether the Secretary of State acted properly in issuing or renewing warrant), after the words "section 3 of this Act" there shall be inserted "or section 5 of the Intelligence Services Act 1994".

The Official Secrets Act 1989

4. In section 4 of the Official Secrets Act 1989 (disclosure of information which results in commission of an offence etc.) in subsection (3)(b) after the words "under section 3 of the Security Service Act 1989" there shall be inserted "or under section 5 of the Intelligence Services Act 1994 or by an authorisation given under section 7 of that Act".

The Official Secrets Act 1989 (Prescription) Order 1990

5. At the end of Schedule 3 to the Official Secrets Act 1989 (Prescription) Order 1990 (bodies giving official authorisations etc.) there shall be added the following entry—

"The Tribunal established   Section 7(5)".
under section 9 of the
Intelligence Services Act
1994.

INDEX

References are to sections and Schedules

PARLIAMENTARY COMMISSIONER ACT 1994

(1994 c. 14)

An Act to include among the matters subject to investigation by the Parliamentary Commissioner for Administration actions taken in the exercise of administrative functions by the administrative staff of certain tribunals.   [5th July 1994]

PARLIAMENTARY DEBATES
Hansard, H.C. Vol. 239, col. 588; Vol. 240, col. 525; Vol. 241, col. 601; H.L. Vol. 555, cols. 318, 1084, 1818.

INTRODUCTION
This Act extends the jurisdiction of the Parliamentary Commissioner for Administration to include actions taken in exercise of administrative functions by administrative staff of certain tribunals. The Parliamentary Commissioner Act 1967 is amended to provide for this extension of jurisdiction and the tribunals, the members of which are covered by this new statute, are listed in new Sched. 4 to the 1967 Act.

Extension of jurisdiction

1.—(1) After subsection (6) of section 5 of the Parliamentary Commissioner Act 1967 there shall be inserted the following subsections—

"(7) For the purposes of this section, administrative functions exercisable by any person appointed as a member of the administrative staff of a relevant tribunal—

(a) by a government department or authority to which this Act applies; or

(b) with the consent (whether as to remuneration and other terms and conditions of service or otherwise) of such a department or authority,

shall be taken to be administrative functions of that department or authority.

(8) In subsection (7) of this section, 'relevant tribunal' means a tribunal listed in Schedule 4 to this Act.

(9) Her Majesty may by Order in Council amend the said Schedule 4 by the alteration or removal of any entry or the insertion of any additional entry; and any statutory instrument made by virtue of this subsection shall be subject to annulment in pursuance of a resolution of either House of Parliament."

(2) After paragraph 6A of Schedule 3 to that Act (matters not subject to investigation) there shall be inserted the following paragraph—

"6B.—(1) Action taken by any member of the administrative staff of a relevant tribunal, so far as that action is taken at the direction, or on the authority (whether express or implied), of any person acting in his capacity as a member of the tribunal.

(2) In this paragraph, 'relevant tribunal' has the meaning given by section 5(8) of this Act."

(3) After Schedule 3 to that Act there shall be inserted the following Schedule—

"SCHEDULE 4

RELEVANT TRIBUNALS FOR PURPOSES OF SECTION 5(7)

Tribunals constituted in Great Britain under regulations made under section 4 of the Vaccine Damage Payments Act 1979.

Child support appeal tribunals constituted under section 21 of the Child Support Act 1991.

Social security appeal tribunals constituted under section 41 of the Social Security Administration Act 1992.

Disability appeal tribunals constituted under section 43 of that Act.

Medical appeal tribunals constituted under section 50 of that Act."

Financial provisions

2. There shall be paid out of money provided by Parliament any increase attributable to this Act in the sums payable out of money so provided under the Parliamentary Commissioner Act 1967.

Short title, commencement and extent

3.—(1) This Act may be cited as the Parliamentary Commissioner Act 1994.

(2) This Act shall come into force at the end of the period of two months beginning with the day on which it is passed.

(3) This Act extends to Northern Ireland.

INDEX

References are to sections

ANTARCTIC ACT 1994*

(1994 c. 15)

ARRANGEMENT OF SECTIONS

PART I

PRELIMINARY

* Annotations by Catherine Redgwell, Senior Lecturer in Law at the University of Nottingham.

26. Power to extend the application of sections 6 to 12.

An Act to make new provision in connection with the Antarctic Treaty signed at Washington on 1st December 1959; to make provision consequential on the Protocol on Environmental Protection to that Treaty done at Madrid on 4th October 1991; to make provision consequential on the Convention on the Conservation of Antarctic Marine Living Resources drawn up at Canberra on 20th May 1980; to provide for the taking of criminal proceedings against, and the punishment of, British citizens and others in respect of certain acts and omissions occurring in that part of Antarctica that lies between 150° West longitude and 90° West longitude; and for connected purposes.   [5th July 1994]

PARLIAMENTARY DEBATES
    Hansard, H.C. Vol. 238, cols. 557, 585; Vol. 241, col. 583; H.L. Vol. 555, cols. 832, 1292, 1877. The Bill was discussed in Standing Committee D between March 23–30, 1994.

INTRODUCTION AND GENERAL NOTE
    The Antarctic Act 1994 (c. 15) received its Royal Assent on July 5, 1994. The Act repeals all of the Antarctic Treaty Act 1967 (c. 65) and most of the Antarctic Minerals Act 1989 (c. 21) save for ss.14 and 20. It is designed to enable the U.K. to ratify the Protocol on Environmental Protection to the Antarctic Treaty made in Madrid on October 4, 1991 (Cm. 1960). The Protocol requires ratification by all 26 Antarctic Treaty Consultative Parties, including the U.K., to enter into force. At the time of the passage of the Act, six States had ratified: Argentina, Spain, France, Norway, Peru and Ecuador. The Government expects to ratify the Protocol by the end of 1994.
    The Protocol was negotiated in response to the strong opposition which was mounted to the Convention on the Regulation of Antarctic Mineral Resource Activities (CRAMRA). The main achievement of the Protocol is the commitment of the Parties "to the comprehensive protection of the Antarctic environment and dependent and associated ecosystems" and the designation of Antarctica as a "natural reserve, devoted to peace and science" (Art. 1, Protocol). All activities proposed to take place in Antarctica are subject to environmental impact assessment before taking place (Art. 8, Protocol). Mineral resources activities are prohibited indefinitely (Art. 7, Protocol) thus marking a return to consensus within the Antarctic Treaty System following opposition to CRAMRA.
    In addition to the main body of the Protocol, it presently contains five Annexes. An additional annex on tourism is under discussion, but unlikely to emerge in the near future since many Consultative Parties consider that the Protocol and its Annexes are sufficient to regulate all activities in Antarctica, including tourism. The five annexes address environmental impact assessment (Annex I), conservation of Antarctic fauna and flora (Annex II), waste disposal and waste management (Annex III), prevention of marine pollution (Annex IV) and area protection and management (Annex V). Annex V was not part of the Protocol signed at Madrid but was added subsequently at the XVIth Antarctic Treaty Consultative Meeting in Bonn later that same month. The Act does not address Annex III on waste disposal nor Annex IV on marine

pollution. The U.K. Government intends to fulfil its treaty obligations in respect of the former by means of conditions attached to permits granted under the Act (*Hansard*, H.L. Vol. 555, col. 834). The marine pollution provisions of Annex IV track closely MARPOL 73/78 to which U.K. merchant shipping legislation has already given effect. For this reason no further primary legislation was considered necessary to regulate U.K.-registered vessels in Antarctica (*Hansard*, H.L. Vol. 555, col. 834).

The Act is divided into three parts. Part I is preliminary and includes definitions of Antarctica and the principal treaties. Part II is the core of the Act which contains the permitting requirements for expeditions to Antarctica and for activities to be carried out there when an expedition is British or has departed from the U.K. Part III confers criminal jurisdiction over U.K. nationals in that segment of Antarctica not claimed by any State as its territory, and over U.K. nationals carrying out their tasks in Antarctica as inspectors under the 1967 Antarctic Treaty or the Convention on the Regulation of Antarctic Marine Living Resources.

The Act was the consequence of a Private Member's Bill presented by Mr Michael Jopling but enjoyed all-party support. Although few matters proved contentious, some concern was expressed in Committee regarding the lack of transparency in the permitting process, particularly in respect of refusal, suspension or revocation of permits, and in respect of the number of matters left to subsequent regulations to specify. A concession was won only in respect of an undertaking by the Government to include, in regulations to be made pursuant to s.14, the requirement that the fact of an application for a permit having been made under ss.3–6 of Pt. II would be published in the *London Gazette* (*Hansard*, H.L. Vol. 555, col. 1878).

The only substantive amendment of the Bill concerned cl. 20 in respect of penalties. The original Bill provided that upon conviction for an offence under the Act the penalty would be a fine, unlimited for conviction on indictment but restricted to the statutory maximum for summary conviction. This was challenged in Committee as being too modest in the light of the importance of the Antarctic environment and the impact which offences under the Act might have upon that environment. An amendment introducing a maximum of two years' imprisonment on conviction upon indictment was agreed on Report, thus presenting courts in such circumstances with the flexibility either to fine, imprison, or both, upon conviction on indictment. The penalty upon summary conviction was left untouched. In moving the amendment Mr Jopling stated: "following consultations with the Home Office, the Department of the Environment and the Scottish Office, I have been led to conclude that those penalties are appropriate given the special situation of Antarctica, in particular its distance from the U.K. and the consequent difficulties of policing it, and the paramount need to protect its pristine ecological state and its priceless flora and fauna" (*Hansard*, H.C. Vol. 238, col. 587).

COMMENCEMENT

The Act comes into force on such day as the Secretary of State may, by order, appoint and different days may be appointed for different provisions and different purposes. Indications were given that ss.6–11 may enter into force first (Standing Committee D, col. 58, March 30, 1994).

EXTENT

The Act extends to Northern Ireland, and may be extended, in whole or in part, by Order in Council to the Channel Islands, the Isle of Man, or any colony.

ABBREVIATIONS

The 1967 Act	:	The Antarctic Treaty Act 1967 (c. 65).
The 1989 Act	:	The Antarctic Minerals Act 1989 (c. 21).
Consultative Party	:	Antarctic Treaty Consultative Party.
CRAMRA	:	Convention on the Regulation of Antarctic Mineral Resources Activities.
The Protocol	:	The Protocol on Environmental Protection to the Antarctic Treaty done at Madrid on October 4, 1991.

PART I

PRELIMINARY

Meaning of "Antarctica"

1.—(1) In this Act "Antarctica" means—
(a) the continent of Antarctica (including all its ice-shelves),
(b) all islands south of 60° South latitude (including all their ice-shelves),
(c) all areas of continental shelf which are adjacent to that continent or those islands and which are south of 60° South latitude, and

(d) all sea and airspace south of 60° South latitude.

(2) For the purposes of subsection (1) "continental shelf" shall be construed in accordance with the rules of international law.

GENERAL NOTE

Subs. (1)

Antarctica. This comprises not only the land mass of Antarctica but also the superjacent islands, ice shelves, continental shelf and sea and air space south of 60 degrees latitude. A similar definition is found in s.1(4) of the 1989 Act. An issue which arose repeatedly in debates was the status of the seabed beyond the continental shelf but within the area of 60 degrees south latitude. The Act does not extend to the deep seabed. In the U.K., mineral resource activities on the deep seabed are regulated by the Deep Seabed Mining (Temporary Provisions) Act 1981 (c. 53). This Act prohibits U.K. nationals from mining the deep seabed or exploring for minerals there without a licence. Assurances were given on behalf of the Government that: "licences for exploration or exploitation of the deep seabed in Antarctica will not be granted under the Deep Seabed Mining (Temporary Provisions) Act 1981 (c. 53) except for the purposes of scientific research; in other words, only for purposes which would be permitted under the [Antarctic Act] with respect to the continental shelf of Antarctica" (*Hansard*, H.L. Vol. 555, col. 846).

Land. This is defined to include ice shelves (s.31(1)).

The Antarctic Treaty, the Protocol and the Convention

2.—(1) In this Act—

"the Antarctic Treaty" means the Antarctic Treaty signed at Washington on 1st December 1959,

"the Protocol" means the Protocol on Environmental Protection to the Antarctic Treaty done at Madrid on 4th October 1991, and

"the Convention" means the Convention on the Conservation of Antarctic Marine Living Resources drawn up at Canberra on 20th May 1980.

(2) In this Act "another Contracting Party" means any State other than the United Kingdom that is a party to the Protocol.

GENERAL NOTE

Subs. (1)

The Antarctic Treaty and the Convention are presently in force and binding upon the U.K. Domestic implementation of the Antarctic Treaty was effected by the Antarctic Treaty Act 1967 (c. 65) which is repealed by this Act. The Antarctic Minerals Act 1989 (c. 21) which implemented the 1988 Convention on the Regulation of Antarctic Mineral Resource Activities is repealed leaving only s.14 dealing with jurisdiction with respect to proceedings under the law of the British Antarctic Territory and s.20 retaining the title of the 1989 Act. One consequence of the negotiation of the Protocol is that it is unlikely that CRAMRA will ever enter into force.

Subs. (2)

Under international law a State becomes a "party" to a treaty when that State has consented to be bound by the treaty and the treaty has entered into force. All 26 States which are Consultative Parties must ratify the Protocol before it enters into force. At the time of passage of the Act six States, all Consultative Parties, had ratified the Protocol: Argentina, Spain, France, Norway, Peru and Ecuador.

PART II

ENVIRONMENTAL PROTECTION

Permits for entering and remaining in Antarctica

Permits required for British expeditions to Antarctica

3.—(1) No person who is on a British expedition may enter or remain in Antarctica except in accordance with a permit granted under this section.

(2) Subsection (1) does not apply—

(a) to a person travelling through, on or above the high seas to an immediate destination outside Antarctica, or

(b) to a person entering or remaining in Antarctica for the sole purpose of fishing for profit.

(3) Subject to subsection (4), for the purposes of this section an expedition is a British expedition if—

(a) it was organised in the United Kingdom, or

(b) the place of final departure for Antarctica of the persons on the expedition was in the United Kingdom.

(4) An expedition organised in and authorised in writing by another Contracting Party shall not be regarded as a British expedition.

(5) Any person who contravenes subsection (1) shall be guilty of an offence.

(6) If subsection (1) is contravened by a person who—

(a) is on an expedition in respect of which a permit has been granted under this section to another person, and

(b) is specified or of a description specified in that permit,

that other person shall be guilty of an offence.

(7) If a person whose place of final departure for Antarctica was in the United Kingdom enters Antarctica in contravention of subsection (1)—

(a) the operator of the vessel or aircraft on which he enters Antarctica, and

(b) the master of that vessel or the commander of that aircraft,

shall each be guilty of an offence.

(8) The Secretary of State may on the application of any person grant to him a permit authorising any person specified or of a description specified in the permit to enter and remain in Antarctica on a British expedition.

DEFINITIONS

"another Contracting Party": s.2(2).
"Antarctica": s.1(1).
"commander": s.31(1).
"contravenes": s.31(1).
"expedition": s.31(1).
"master": s.31(1).
"operator": s.31(1).
"person": Sched. 1 to the Interpretation Act 1978 (c. 30).
"Secretary of State": Sched. 1 to the Interpretation Act 1978 (c. 30).
"vessel": s.31(1).

GENERAL NOTE

This section prohibits British expeditions from entering and remaining in Antarctica except in accordance with a permit granted by the Secretary of State, in practice being the Foreign Secretary (*Hansard*, H.C. Vol. 238, col. 600). This power will not be delegated (Standing Committee D, col. 34, March 23, 1994). Virtually all activities in Antarctica will require permits because of the broad definition of "expedition" which encompasses activities ranging from individual walking or mountaineering expeditions to large tourist and scientific expeditions. Excluded from the permit requirement are persons travelling on or above the high seas in Antarctica to an immediate destination outside of Antarctica and persons entering or remaining in Antarctica for the sole purpose of fishing for profit (subs. (2)).

There is no statutory requirement for publication of applications for permits under this or any other section of the Act, which attracted some criticism in the Committee stage of the Bill. An undertaking was given by the Government that regulations to be made pursuant to s.14 of the Act will require publication in the *London Gazette* of the fact of applications for permits under ss.3–6 (*Hansard*, H.L. Vol. 555, col. 1878).

Subs. (1)

British expedition. This means an expedition organised in the U.K. or using the U.K. as a final point of departure (subs. (3)), unless the expedition is organised in, and authorised in writing by, another Contracting Party (subs. (4)).

Contravention of subs. (1) is an offence (see further subs. (5) and ss.17–20 and 27).

Subs. (2)

Although Antarctica is not a major thoroughfare for vessels and aircraft in the southern hemisphere, this subsection is intended to exempt from the permit requirement persons travelling on or above the high seas in Antarctica to an immediate destination outside Antarctica in the lawful exercise of a high seas freedom. Persons entering or remaining in Antarctica for the sole purpose of fishing for profit are exempt from the permitting requirements of the Act.

Subs. (5)

It is an offence to contravene subs. (1). Not only the permit-holder but other persons on the expedition and specified or described in the permit are guilty of an offence if subs. (1) is contravened (see subs. (6)). Where the final point of departure of an expedition is the U.K., the master and operator of the vessel or commander and operator of the aircraft on which a person enters Antarctica in contravention of subs. (1) shall each also be guilty of an offence (see subs. (7)).

Offences under Pt. II are addressed further in ss.17–20 and 27 of the Act.

Subs. (8)

The power of the Secretary of State to grant permits under this section will not be delegated (Standing Committee D, col. 34, March 23, 1994).

The Government intends to provide in regulations for the publication in the *London Gazette* of the fact that an application for a permit has been made under this section (*Hansard*, H.L. Vol. 555, col. 1878).

Section 13 empowers the Secretary of State to attach conditions to the permit. It is an offence to contravene a condition attached to the permit. For further limitations upon the Secretary of State's discretion, see s.15.

An expedition requiring permits under ss.3, 4 and 5 may be granted a single, overarching permit (*Hansard*, H.C. Vol. 241, col. 600).

Permits required for British stations in Antarctica

4.—(1) No person may remain on a British station in Antarctica except in accordance with a permit granted under this section.

(2) For the purposes of this section a station is a British station if it is maintained by or on behalf of a United Kingdom national.

(3) Any person who contravenes subsection (1) shall be guilty of an offence.

(4) If subsection (1) is contravened by a person who—

(a) is on a station in respect of which a permit has been granted under this section to another person, and

(b) is specified or of a description specified in that permit,

that other person shall be guilty of an offence.

(5) The Secretary of State may on the application of any person grant to him a permit authorising any person specified or of a description specified in the permit to remain on any British station in Antarctica specified in the permit or of a description specified in the permit.

DEFINITIONS

"Antarctica": s.1(1).
"contravenes": s.31(1).
"person": Sched. 1 to the Interpretation Act 1978 (c. 30).
"Secretary of State": Sched. 1 to the Interpretation Act 1978 (c. 30).
"station": s.31(1).
"United Kingdom national": s.31(1).

GENERAL NOTE

Subs. (1)

British station. This is defined in subs. (2) as meaning a station maintained by or on behalf of a U.K. national. See also s.6(4)(b).

Subs. (3)
On offences under Pt. II of the Act see further ss.17–20 and 27.

Subs. (5)
The power of the Secretary of State to grant permits under this section will not be delegated (Standing Committee D, col. 34, March 23, 1994).

The Government intends to provide in regulations for the publication in the *London Gazette* of the fact that an application for a permit has been made under this section (*Hansard*, H.L. Vol. 555, col. 1878).

Section 13 empowers the Secretary of State to attach conditions to the permit. It is an offence to contravene a condition attached to the permit. For further limitations upon the Secretary of State's discretion, see s.15.

An expedition requiring permits under ss.3, 4 and 5 may be granted a single, overarching permit (*Hansard*, H.C. Vol. 241, col. 600).

Permits required for British vessels and aircraft entering Antarctica

5.—(1) No British vessel or British aircraft may enter Antarctica except in accordance with a permit granted under this section or under the written authorisation of another Contracting Party.

(2) Subsection (1) does not apply—

(a) to a vessel or aircraft travelling to an immediate destination outside Antarctica, or

(b) to a vessel entering Antarctica for the sole purpose of fishing for profit.

(3) In this section—

"British vessel" means a United Kingdom ship within the meaning of section 21(1) of the Merchant Shipping Act 1979, and

"British aircraft" means a British-controlled aircraft within the meaning of section 92 of the Civil Aviation Act 1982.

(4) If subsection (1) is contravened—

(a) the operator of the vessel or aircraft, and

(b) the master of the vessel or the commander of the aircraft,

shall each be guilty of an offence.

(5) The Secretary of State may on the application of any person grant to him a permit authorising any British vessel or aircraft of which he is the operator and which is specified or of a description specified in the permit to enter Antarctica on occasions or in circumstances specified in the permit.

DEFINITIONS
"another Contracting Party": s.2(2).
"Antarctica": s.1(1).
"commander": s.31(1).
"contravenes": s.31(1).
"master": s.31(1).
"operator": s.31(1).
"person": Sched. 1 to the Interpretation Act 1978 (c. 30).
"Secretary of State": Sched. 1 to the Interpretation Act 1978 (c. 30).
"vessel": s.31(1).

GENERAL NOTE
This section mirrors the provisions of s.3 in respect of persons in connection with British vessels and British aircraft (both defined in subs. (3)). A potential loophole identified at Committee stage was the launching of an aircraft or helicopter from a vessel already present in Antarctica and otherwise complying with the permitting requirements of subs. (1) (Standing Committee D, cols. 8–9, March 23, 1994). An undertaking was given that further consultations would be carried out with the appropriate authorities, including the Department of Transport and the Civil Aviation Authority. Tourist flights to and across Antarctica have been suspended since the 1970s following the crash of a Boeing 747 on Mount Erebus.

Subs. (1)
British vessel and *British aircraft*. These terms are defined in subs. (3) in accordance with s.21(1) of the Merchant Shipping Act 1979 (c. 39) and s.92 of the Civil Aviation Act 1982 (c. 16), respectively.

Subs. (4)
On offences under Pt. II of the Act see further ss.17–20 and 27.

Subs. (5)
The power of the Secretary of State to grant permits under this section will not be delegated (Standing Committee D, col. 34, March 23, 1994).

The Government intends to provide in regulations for the publication in the *London Gazette* of the fact that an application for a permit has been made under this section (*Hansard*, H.L. Vol. 555, col. 1878).

Section 13 empowers the Secretary of State to attach conditions to the permit, including conditions to be complied with by both the master or commander and the crew of the vessel or aircraft to which the permit relates. It is an offence to contravene a condition attached to the permit. For further limitations upon the Secretary of State's discretion, see s.15.

An expedition requiring permits under ss.3, 4 and 5 may be granted a single, overarching permit (*Hansard*, H.C. Vol. 241, col. 600).

Mineral resources

Mineral resource activities

6.—(1) No United Kingdom national may in Antarctica—
(a) drill, dredge or excavate for mineral resources,
(b) collect any samples of mineral resources, or
(c) do anything for the purpose of identifying specific mineral resource occurrences or deposits, or areas where such occurrences or deposits may be found,
except in accordance with a permit granted under this section.

(2) Any person who contravenes subsection (1) shall be guilty of an offence.

(3) The Secretary of State may on the application of any person grant to him a permit authorising any United Kingdom national who is specified or of a description specified in the permit to do anything so specified or of a description so specified that would otherwise constitute a contravention of subsection (1).

(4) The Secretary of State shall not grant a permit under this section unless he is satisfied that the activities authorised by the permit will be carried on—
(a) only for the purposes of scientific research, or
(b) only for purposes connected with the construction, maintenance or repair in Antarctica of a British station within the meaning of section 4 or of any other structure, road, runway or jetty maintained by or on behalf of a United Kingdom national.

(5) In this section "mineral resource" means any natural resource that is neither living nor renewable.

DEFINITIONS
"Antarctica": s.1(1).
"contravenes": s.31(1).
"person": Sched. 1 to the Interpretation Act 1978 (c. 30).
"Secretary of State": Sched. 1 to the Interpretation Act 1978 (c. 30).
"station": s.31(1).
"United Kingdom national": s.31(1).

GENERAL NOTE
It was the characterisation of CRAMRA as a "miners' charter" which led to its rejection and the negotiation of the Protocol which prohibits mineral resource activities in Antarctica indefinitely.

This section prohibits mineral resource activities such as drilling, sample collecting or any other activity designed to assist in the identification of specific mineral deposits, except in accordance with a permit under this section. Such permits may only be granted by the Secretary of State where he is satisfied that such activities are for the purposes of scientific research or logistical support. Similar restrictions are not found in connection with the grant of permits under the preceding sections (ss.3–5).

The 1989 Act required a licence for the carrying out of "prospecting activities". These are defined in s.2(1) of the 1989 Act to exclude low-level drilling and dredging and excavating for the purpose of obtaining small-scale samples. In practice these activities which, under the 1989 Act, would previously have fallen outside the remit of the licence regime will now require a permit under subs. (3) so long as the Secretary of State is satisfied that the activity to be carried out is for one of the purposes set forth in subs. (4).

Subs. (1)
Mineral resource. This is defined in subs. (5), which adopts a similar definition to that contained in s.1(4) of the 1989 Act.
United Kingdom national. This is defined in s.31(1) to include Scottish partnerships and bodies incorporated under the law of any part of the U.K. This is to ensure that legal persons are caught by the prohibition on mineral resource activities except in accordance with a permit.

Subs. (2)
On offences under Pt. II of the Act see further ss.17–20 and 27.

Subs. (3)
The Act does not permit delegation of this power by the Secretary of State (s.16) and assurances in this connection were given in Committee (Standing Committee D, col. 34, March 23, 1994).
The Government intends to provide in regulations for the publication in the *London Gazette* of the fact that an application for a permit has been made under this section (*Hansard*, H.L. Vol. 555, col. 1878).
Section 13 empowers the Secretary of State to attach conditions to the permit. It is an offence to contravene a condition attached to the permit. In Committee an amendment that would have required public disclosure of such conditions was defeated (Standing Committee D, col. 16, March 23, 1994).

Subs. (4)
Any permits granted for scientific research require the U.K. in the fulfilment of its international obligations to circulate information about proposed scientific programmes to the other Antarctic Treaty Parties and to exchange information regarding research carried out (Art. III(1)(a) and (c) of the Antarctic Treaty).

Subs. (5)
This is a similar definition to that found in s.1(4) of the 1989 Act.

Fauna and flora

Conservation of Antarctic fauna and flora

7.—(1) No United Kingdom national may in Antarctica—
  (a) intentionally kill, injure, capture, handle or molest any native mammal or native bird,
  (b) while on foot intentionally disturb a breeding or moulting native bird, or a concentration of native mammals or native birds,
  (c) use a vehicle, vessel or aircraft in a manner that disturbs a concentration of native mammals or native birds,
  (d) use explosives or firearms in such a manner,
  (e) remove or damage such quantities of any native plant that its local distribution or abundance will be significantly affected,
  (f) significantly damage a concentration of native plants, or
  (g) do anything that is likely to cause significant damage to the habitat of any native mammal, bird, plant or invertebrate,
except in accordance with a permit granted under section 12 or under the written authorisation of another Contracting Party.

  (2) Any person who contravenes subsection (1) shall be guilty of an offence.

DEFINITIONS
  "another Contracting Party": s.2(2).
  "Antarctica": s.1(1).
  "contravenes": s.31(1).

"native bird": s.31(1).
"native invertebrate": s.31(1).
"native mammal": s.31(1).
"native plant": s.31(1).
"person": Sched. 1 to the Interpretation Act 1978 (c. 30).
"United Kingdom national": s.31(1).
"vessel": s.31(1).

GENERAL NOTE
    The 1967 Act, repealed by this Act, was intended, *inter alia*, to give effect to measures for the
conservation of Antarctic flora and fauna. The 1967 Act contained a prohibition upon the wilful
killing, injury, molestation or taking of any native mammal or native bird and prohibited gathering native plants within specially protected areas and driving vehicles through such areas (s.1(1)
of the 1967 Act). Similar prohibitions form the core of this section, with significant extension of
the protection afforded plants and invertebrates in particular.

Subs. (1)
    On the delegation of the power to grant, revoke or suspend permits, see s.16.
    The Government's commitment to providing for the publication of the fact of applications for
permits made under ss.3–6 does not extend to this section (*Hansard*, H.L. Vol. 555, col. 1878).

Subs. (2)
    On offences under Pt. II of the Act see further ss.17–20 and 27.

Permits required for introducing non-native animals and plants into Antarctica

8.—(1) No United Kingdom national may introduce into any part of Antarctica any animal of a species that is not indigenous to Antarctica, or any
plant that is not a native plant, except in accordance with a permit granted
under section 12 or under the written authorisation of another Contracting
Party.
    (2) The keeping of an animal or plant on board a vessel in Antarctica shall
not be regarded as a contravention of subsection (1).
    (3) Any person who contravenes subsection (1) shall be guilty of an
offence.

DEFINITIONS
    "another Contracting Party": s.2(2).
    "Antarctica": s.1(1).
    "contravenes": s.31(1).
    "native plant": s.31(1).
    "person": Sched. 1 to the Interpretation Act 1978 (c. 30).
    "United Kingdom national": s.31(1).
    "vessel": s.31(1).

Subs. (1)
    On the delegation of the power to grant, revoke or suspend permits, see s.16.
    The Government's commitment to providing for the publication of the fact of applications for
permits made under ss.3–6 does not extend to this section (*Hansard*, H.L. Vol. 555, col. 1878).

Subs. (3)
    On offences under Pt. II of the Act see further ss.17–20 and s.27.

Special areas

Areas restricted under the Protocol

9.—(1) No United Kingdom national may enter or remain in an area in
Antarctica designated by regulations as an area restricted under the Protocol
except in accordance with a permit granted under section 12 or under the
written authorisation of another Contracting Party.
    (2) Any person who contravenes subsection (1) shall be guilty of an
offence.

DEFINITIONS
"another Contracting Party": s.2(2).
"Antarctica": s.1(1).
"contravenes": s.31(1).
"person": Sched. 1 to the Interpretation Act 1978 (c. 30).
"United Kingdom national": s.31(1).

GENERAL NOTE
This section is designed to reinforce the system of special areas under Annex of the Protocol. Special areas have been a feature of the Antarctic Treaty System since the 1964 Agreed Measures. See, for example, the prohibition upon the gathering of any native plants or the driving of vehicles in specially protected areas found in s.1(1)(b) of the 1967 Act.

Subs. (1)
On the delegation of the power to grant, revoke or suspend permits, see s.16.
The Government's commitment to providing for the publication of the fact of applications for permits made under ss.3–6 does not extend to this section (*Hansard*, H.L. Vol. 555, col. 1878).

Subs. (2)
On offences under Pt. II of the Act see further ss.17–20 and 27.

Historic Sites and Monuments

10.––(1) No United Kingdom national may damage, destroy or remove any part of a site or monument designated by regulations as an Antarctic Historic Site or Monument.

(2) Any person who contravenes subsection (1) shall be guilty of an offence.

DEFINITIONS
"another Contracting Party": s.2(2).
"Antarctica": s.1(1).
"contravenes": s.31(1).
"person": Sched. 1 to the Interpretation Act 1978 (c. 30).
"United Kingdom national": s.31(1).

GENERAL NOTE

Subs. (2)
On offences under Pt. II of the Act see further ss.17–20 and 27.

Places protected under the Convention

11.—(1) No United Kingdom national may enter or remain in a place that is in the area south of the Antarctic Convergence and that has been designated by regulations as a place protected under the Convention (in this section referred to as a "protected place") except in accordance with a permit granted under this section.

(2) Any person who contravenes subsection (1) shall be guilty of an offence.

(3) The Secretary of State may on the application of any person grant to him a permit authorising any United Kingdom national specified or of a description specified in the permit to enter and remain in any protected place specified in the permit.

DEFINITIONS
"another Contracting Party": s.2(2).
"Antarctic Convergence": s.31(2).
"contravenes": s.31(1).
"person": Sched. 1 to the Interpretation Act 1978 (c. 30).
"Secretary of State": Sched. 1 to the Interpretation Act 1978 (c. 30).
"United Kingdom national": s.31(1).

GENERAL NOTE

Subs. (2)
On offences under Pt. II of the Act see further ss.17–20.

Subs. (3)
On the delegation of the power to grant, revoke or suspend permits, see s.16.
The Government's commitment to providing for the publication of the fact of applications for permits made under ss.3–6 does not extend to this section (*Hansard*, H.L. Vol. 555, col. 1878).

Permits under Part II: further provisions

Grant of permits for activities prohibited by sections 7, 8 and 9

12. The Secretary of State may on the application of any person grant to him a permit authorising any United Kingdom national who is specified or of a description specified in the permit to do anything specified or of a description specified in the permit that would otherwise constitute a contravention of section 7(1), 8(1) or 9(1).

DEFINITIONS
"contravenes": s.31(1).
"person": Sched. 1 to the Interpretation Act 1978 (c. 30).
"Secretary of State": Sched. 1 to the Interpretation Act 1978 (c. 30).
"United Kingdom national": s.31(1).

GENERAL NOTE
This section makes provision for the Secretary of State, or any person upon whom the power has been delegated under s.16, to grant, revoke or suspend a permit to carry out the activities prohibited under s.7(1) (interference with fauna and flora), s.8(1) (introduction of non-indigenous species) or s.9(1) (special areas). An amendment that would have required the compulsory publication of applications in the *London Gazette* was defeated in Committee (Standing Committee D, col. 29, March 23, 1994). One argument given against publication was the need for confidentiality in respect of the reasons given for the refusal of a permit (Standing Committee D, cols. 30–31, March 23, 1994).
The Government's assurances in respect of publication apply only to applications made under ss.3, 4 and 5 to which s.16 (delegation of powers) does not apply. In Committee this caused some concern, since the power to grant, revoke or suspend permits in connection with activities under ss.7–9 could be granted to the same body which seeks the permit, with no concomitant obligation to reveal either the conditions attached to the permit or even the fact of the application having been made.

Conditions attached to permits under Part II

13.—(1) The Secretary of State may on granting a permit under this Part attach to it such conditions as he thinks fit, including—
   (a) conditions to be complied with by persons doing anything authorised by the permit,
   (b) in the case of a permit granted under section 5, conditions to be complied with by the master and crew of any vessel to which the permit relates or by the commander and crew of any aircraft to which the permit relates, and
   (c) conditions requiring the person to whom the permit is granted to provide information to the Secretary of State.
   (2) If any person contravenes a condition attached to a permit under subsection (1)—

(a) he shall be guilty of an offence, and
(b) if the permit was granted to another person, that other person shall be guilty of an offence.

"contravenes": s.31(1).
"master": s.31(1).
"person": Sched. 1 to the Interpretation Act 1978 (c. 30).
"Secretary of State": Sched. 1 to the Interpretation Act 1978 (c. 30).
"vessel": s.31(1).

GENERAL NOTE
This section makes provision for the Secretary of State to attach conditions to permits issued under Pt. II of the Act. In certain cases he is required to have regard to the provisions of the Protocol in so doing: see further s.15, below. Compliance with the permit conditions is required of both the master or commander and crew of any vessel or aircraft, or any member of an expedition permitted under the Act.

Subs. (1)
Freedom of scientific research and the exchange of information are the hallmarks of the Antarctic Treaty System, enshrined in Art. III thereof. Paragraph (c) of this subsection is designed to ensure, *inter alia*, that the Government obtains information sufficient to comply with its Antarctic Treaty obligation to circulate information.

Subs. (2)
On offences under Pt. II of the Act see further ss.17–20 and 27.

Permits: applications, production, revocation and suspension

14.—(1) Regulations may make provision—
(a) as to the procedure for making applications for permits under this Part,
(b) as to the circumstances in which, the persons to whom, and the persons by whom, permits may be required to be produced,
(c) as to the circumstances in which permits are liable to be revoked or suspended by the Secretary of State,
(d) as to the notice to be given before permits are revoked or suspended, and as to the other procedure to be followed in relation to the revocation or suspension of permits, and
(e) for appeals against the revocation or suspension of permits, and as to the procedure to be followed in relation to such appeals (including provision in accordance with which such procedure is to be determined).

(2) Any person who without reasonable excuse fails to produce a permit in compliance with a requirement made in accordance with regulations under subsection (1)(b) shall be guilty of an offence.

DEFINITIONS
"person": Sched. 1 to the Interpretation Act 1978 (c. 30).
"Regulations": s.31(1).
"Secretary of State": Sched. 1 to the Interpretation Act 1978 (c. 30).

GENERAL NOTE
Details of the procedures for applying for permits and for their revocation and suspension are to be laid out in regulations under this section. Certain requirements of the Protocol will need incorporation within these procedures, most notably the requirement of publication of draft and final Comprehensive Environmental Evaluations (Standing Committee D, col. 26, March 23, 1994).
There is no statutory duty to consult other bodies in considering the grant, suspension or revocation of a permit. The Government gave an undertaking that: "when the Secretary of State is considering applications for permits, he will, in addition to complying with the requirements of [section] 15, take into account any representations which he may receive from any quarter, whether governmental or non-governmental. It will, of course, be for the Secretary of State to

determine, in the light of all the circumstances, what weight to give to such representations" (*Hansard*, H.L. Vol. 555, col. 1878).

One aspect of this section gave rise to particular discussion. Under subs. (1)(e) the right to appeal is limited to revocation or suspension of permits, with no appeal against the refusal to grant a permit. Concern was expressed that a legitimate expedition by Greenpeace or the World Wide Fund for Nature might have its application refused where, for example, its purpose was to protect or observe the Antarctic environment (Standing Committee D, cols. 29–30, March 23, 1994). To meet this concern an amendment was moved which would have required the Secretary of State to make public the reasons for refusal of a permit. This was resisted, though an assurance was given in the House of Lords "that the Secretary of State will provide in regulations that the applicant must be given the reasons for refusal of his application" (*Hansard*, H.L. Vol. 555, col. 1879). It is then up to the applicant whether to make those reasons more publicly available.

Duty to have regard to the Protocol and to measures implementing the Protocol

15. The Secretary of State shall have regard to the provisions of the Protocol and to any measures for the implementation of the Protocol that have become effective by virtue of paragraph 4 of Article IX of the Antarctic Treaty—

(a) in considering in any case whether to grant a permit under section 3, 4, 5 or 12,

(b) in any case where he grants a permit under section 3, 4, 5 or 12, in considering whether to attach any conditions to it under section 13(1), and

(c) in exercising his power to make regulations under section 14(1)(c) in relation to a permit granted under section 3, 4, 5 or 12.

DEFINITIONS
"Antarctic Treaty": s.2(1).
"Protocol": s.2(1).
"regulations": s.31(1).
"Secretary of State": Sched. 1 to the Interpretation Act 1978 (c. 30).

GENERAL NOTE
The power of the Secretary of State to grant permits under this section may be delegated (see s.16). The Government-funded British Antarctic Survey is one body to whom such powers might be delegated (s.16(1)(b)). The Survey is also likely to be an applicant for such permits, raising the potential for conflicts of interest. In Committee, Mr Jopling made the following clarification in respect of the delegation of powers: "The power of delegation of British Antarctic Survey officials is unlikely to be exercised so as to empower them to issue permits for activities that could cause the sorts of harm referred to in cll. 7(1)(f) and 7(1)(g). The activities that require permits are most likely to be the activities of the British Antarctic Survey. It would clearly be inappropriate for the developer to be seen to be acting as the regulatory agency. The delegation of permits is ultimately discretionary and the power will be tailored to each case" (Standing Committee D, cols. 36–37, March 23, 1994).

In deciding whether to attach conditions to permits under s.3 (expeditions), s.4 (British stations), s.5 (British vessels and aircraft) and s.12 (permits under ss.7(1), 8(1) and 9(1)) the Secretary of State is obliged to "have regard to" the provisions of the Protocol. Total disregard of the provisions of the Protocol would amount to a possible breach of the U.K.'s international obligations as well as providing possible grounds for judicial review of the Secretary of State's decision (Standing Committee D, col. 33, March 23, 1994).

"... and to any measures ... Antarctic Treaty". This wording was introduced to ensure that the Secretary of State will also have regard to measures subsequently adopted by the Consultative Parties and binding upon them in accordance with Art. IX of the Treaty. Article 10(1)(b) of the Protocol envisages such measures being adopted for the implementation of the Protocol. This is also the mechanism for approval of management plans for protected areas under Annex V (*Hansard*, H.C. Vol. 238, col. 585).

Delegation of powers under sections 11 and 12 etc.

16.—(1) Any of the Secretary of State's powers relating to the granting of permits under section 11 or 12, or the revocation or suspension of permits granted under section 11 or 12, may be delegated by him to any person—

(a) who holds office as Administrator of the British Antarctic Territory (or who holds an appointment, by whatever name called, having functions similar to those performed by the person holding that office on the date of the passing of this Act),

(b) who holds office as Director of the British Antarctic Survey (or who holds an appointment, by whatever name called, having functions similar to those performed by the person holding that office on the date of the passing of this Act), or

(c) who is for the time being running a station in Antarctica on behalf of a person such as is mentioned in paragraph (b).

(2) Where any powers have been delegated under subsection (1) to a person such as is mentioned in paragraph (a) or (b) of that subsection, they may be exercised by any person who—

(a) is for the time being exercising the functions of the person to whom the powers have been delegated, and

(b) is authorised (whether generally or specially) for the purposes of this section by that person or by the Secretary of State.

(3) References in sections 13 to 15 to the Secretary of State include references to any person exercising any powers by virtue of this section.

(4) Any person to whom powers have been delegated under subsection (1) shall, as soon as practicable after the end of—

(a) the period ending with the first 30th June after the delegation took effect, and

(b) every subsequent period of twelve months ending with 30th June during any part of which the delegation has effect,

give a report to the Secretary of State in respect of that period.

(5) A report given under subsection (4) in respect of a period shall contain such particulars as the Secretary of State may require of—

(a) any permits granted, revoked or suspended during that period by the person giving the report (or by any other person exercising the powers delegated to that person), and

(b) any information received during that period by the person giving the report (or by any other person exercising the powers delegated to that person) in accordance with conditions attached to permits.

(6) The Secretary of State may from time to time by notice in writing to a person to whom powers have been delegated substitute a different period for any period in respect of which that person is required to give a report under subsection (4).

DEFINITIONS
"Secretary of State": Sched. 1 to the Interpretation Act 1978 (c. 30).

GENERAL NOTE

Subs. (4)
A similar annual reporting requirement is found in s.3(6) of the 1967 Act and is designed to ensure that even where the power to grant, revoke or suspend permits has been delegated under subs. (1), the U.K. Government is nonetheless supplied with information sufficient to meet the reporting requirements of the Antarctic Treaty and the Protocol. For example, in respect of wildlife and protected areas the U.K. is under an obligation under Art. VI of Annex II and Art. X of Annex V of the Protocol to submit information regarding the number of permits issued and their purpose. This information must be supplied to all other Consultative Parties and to the Committee on Environmental Protection established under the Protocol (Standing Committee D, col. 34, March 23, 1994).

Offences under Part II

Proceedings for offences under Part II

17. Proceedings for an offence under this Part may be taken, and the offence may for incidental purposes be treated as having been committed, in any place in the United Kingdom.

GENERAL NOTE
This section finds numerous precedents in, for example, ss.5(1) and 8(1) of the 1989 Act; s.3 of the Continental Shelf Act 1964 (c. 29); and s.8 of the Mineral Workings (Offshore Installations) Act 1971 (c. 61). It provoked considerable debate in Committee, where the potential for conflicting laws applicable to actions in Antarctica was raised. If an offence under the Act is committed in Antarctica this section permits proceedings to be taken against an alleged offender anywhere in the U.K.

Section 14 of the 1989 Act, which is not repealed by this Act, confers on any court in England and Wales civil and criminal jurisdiction in respect of matters arising under the law of the British Antarctic Territory.

Defences

18.—(1) Where a person is charged with an offence under section 3(5), (6) or (7), 4(3) or (4), 5(4) or 13(2) it shall be a defence to prove that the contravention in question occurred by reason of matters outside his control and that he took all reasonable precautions to avoid such a contravention.

(2) Subject to subsection (3), where a person is charged with an offence under this Part it shall be a defence to prove that the contravention in question occurred in a case of emergency relating to—

(a) the safety of human life, vessels or aircraft,
(b) the safety of equipment and facilities of high value, or
(c) the protection of the environment.

(3) Subsection (2) does not apply where the contravention in question is a contravention of section 6(1) or of a condition attached to a permit granted under section 6(3).

(4) Where a person is charged with an offence under section 7(2) in respect of a contravention of section 7(1)(a), it shall be a defence to prove that the act in question was done for the relief of the suffering of the mammal or bird in question.

DEFINITIONS
"contravention": s.31(1).
"person": Sched. 1 to the Interpretation Act 1978 (c. 30).
"vessel": s.31(1).

GENERAL NOTE

Subs. (1)
The defences of *force majeure* and due diligence provided for in this subsection do not avail persons charged with offences under ss.6–9. An additional defence is available under subs. (3) for contraventions of s.7(2) where the act in question is to free the bird or mammal in question from suffering.

Subs. (2)
These defences mirror those found in the Protocol and are available to persons charged with offences under Pt. II save for contraventions of s.6 (mineral resource activities).

Offences committed by bodies corporate and Scottish partnerships

19.—(1) Where an offence under this Part has been committed by a body corporate and the contravention in question is proved to have occurred with the consent or connivance of, or to be attributable to any neglect on the part of—

(a) a director, manager, secretary or other similar officer of the body corporate, or
(b) any person who was purporting to act in any such capacity,
he as well as the body corporate shall be guilty of that offence and shall be liable to be proceeded against and punished accordingly.

(2) In subsection (1) "director", in relation to a body corporate whose affairs are managed by its members, means a member of the body corporate.

(3) Where an offence under this Part has been committed by a Scottish partnership and the contravention in question is proved to have occurred with the consent or connivance of, or to be attributable to any neglect on the part of, a partner, he as well as the partnership shall be guilty of that offence and shall be liable to be proceeded against and punished accordingly.

DEFINITIONS
"contravention": s.31(1).
"person": Sched. 1 to the Interpretation Act 1978 (c. 30).

GENERAL NOTE
This section provides for the responsibility of bodies corporate and Scottish partnerships for offences under Pt. II. Similar language is found in s.10(4) of the 1989 Act repealed by this Act.

Subs. (2)
Director. This definition is also found in s.10(4) of the 1989 Act repealed by this Act.

Penalties

20. Any person who is guilty of an offence under this Part shall be liable on conviction on indictment to imprisonment for a term not exceeding two years, to a fine or to both, and on summary conviction to a fine not exceeding the statutory maximum.

DEFINITIONS
"person": Sched. 1 to the Interpretation Act 1978 (c. 30).

GENERAL NOTE
A person convicted of an offence under Pt. II is liable on conviction on indictment to an unlimited fine, or imprisonment for up to two years, or both. The penalty upon summary conviction is a fine alone, limited to the statutory maximum.

The original wording of this section reflected the penalties contained in s.10(1) of the 1989 Act, which provided only for an (unlimited) fine for conviction on indictment or, on summary conviction, to a fine not exceeding the statutory maximum. This was considered in Committee not to reflect adequately the severity with which offences under Pt. II of the Act should be viewed. The penalty of imprisonment for a term not exceeding two years for conviction on indictment was added on Report to the existing provision for unlimited fine, with the flexibility to use either or both penalties (*Hansard*, H.C. Vol. 238, cols. 587–588).

PART III

APPLICATION OF CRIMINAL LAW TO UNITED KINGDOM NATIONALS

GENERAL NOTE
This Part is designed to ensure criminal jurisdiction over U.K. nationals in respect of acts committed outside British Antarctic Territory. In respect of acts committed within that Territory, s.14 of the 1989 Act, which is not repealed by this Act, confers on any court in England and Wales civil and criminal jurisdiction in respect of matters arising under the law of the British Antarctic Territory.

United Kingdom nationals in the unclaimed sector of Antarctica

21. Where a United Kingdom national does or omits to do anything on any land lying south of 60° South latitude and between 150° West longitude and

90° West longitude and that act or omission would have constituted an offence under the law of any part of the United Kingdom if it had occurred in that part, he shall be guilty of the like offence as if the act or omission had taken place in that part, and shall be liable to be proceeded against and punished accordingly.

DEFINITIONS
"United Kingdom national": s.31(1).

GENERAL NOTE
This section is designed to ensure criminal jurisdiction may be effectively exercised over U.K. nationals in the unclaimed sector of Antarctica. The unclaimed sector is defined by the coordinates south of 60 degrees South latitude and between 150 degrees West longitude and 90 degrees West longitude. A similar provision is found in the 1967 Act, repealed by this Act. Without such extension U.K. nationals in the unclaimed sector would be subject only to those limited criminal offences in respect of which the U.K. exercises extra-territorial jurisdiction.

United Kingdom nationals working under the Antarctic Treaty

22.—(1) Where a United Kingdom national who—
(a) is an Antarctic Treaty official, and
(b) is in any part of Antarctica, other than the area mentioned in section 21, for the purpose of exercising his functions as an Antarctic Treaty official,
does or omits to do anything, and that act or omission would have constituted an offence under the law of any part of the United Kingdom if it had taken place in that part, he shall be guilty of the like offence as if the act or omission had taken place in that part, and shall be liable to be proceeded against and punished accordingly.
(2) In subsection (1) "Antarctic Treaty official" means a person who—
(a) has been designated as an observer by or on behalf of Her Majesty's government in the United Kingdom in accordance with Article VII of the Antarctic Treaty,
(b) is a scientist who has been exchanged in accordance with Article III(1)(b) of the Antarctic Treaty, or
(c) is a member of the staff accompanying a person such as is mentioned in paragraph (a) or (b).

DEFINITIONS
"Antarctica": s.1(1).
"United Kingdom national": s.31(1).

GENERAL NOTE
This section extends jurisdiction over U.K. nationals acting as Antarctic Treaty officials (defined in subs. (2)) and exercising their functions in any part of Antarctica outside of the unclaimed sector (*cf.* s.21) or British Antarctic Territory (*cf.* s.14 of the 1989 Act).

United Kingdom nationals working under the Convention

23.—(1) Where a United Kingdom national—
(a) who is a Convention official, and
(b) who is on a vessel in any part of the area south of the Antarctic Convergence for the purpose of exercising his functions as a Convention official,
does or omits to do anything, and that act or omission would have constituted an offence under the law of any part of the United Kingdom if it had taken place in that part, he shall be guilty of the like offence as if the act or omission had taken place in that part, and shall be liable to be proceeded against and punished accordingly.
(2) In subsection (1) "Convention official" means any person designated as an inspector or observer by a Member of the Commission for the Conser-

vation of Antarctic Marine Living Resources under Article XXIV of the Convention.

DEFINITIONS
"Antarctic Convergence": s.31(2).
"the Convention": s.2(1).
"U.K. official": s.31(1).
"vessel": s.31(1).

GENERAL NOTE
This section extends jurisdiction over U.K. nationals acting as Convention officials and operating within the Antarctic Convergence.

Proceedings for offences under Part III

24. Where by virtue of section 21, 22 or 23 a person is liable to be proceeded against for an offence in any part of the United Kingdom, the proceedings may be taken, and the offence may for incidental purposes be treated as having been committed, in any place in that part.

DEFINITIONS
"person": Sched. 1 to the Interpretation Act 1978 (c. 30).

GENERAL NOTE
"... *any part of the United Kingdom*". See the comments under s.17 above.

PART IV

MISCELLANEOUS AND SUPPLEMENTARY

International rights, obligations and arrangements

Power to make further provision in connection with the Antarctic Treaty, the Protocol and the Convention

25.—(1) Regulations may make provision for the purpose of implementing any right or obligation of the United Kingdom created or arising by or under any of the Agreements.
(2) In subsection (1) "the Agreements" means—
(a) the Antarctic Treaty, the Protocol and the Convention (as they have effect on the date of the passing of this Act or subsequently), and
(b) any annex or protocol to the Antarctic Treaty, the Protocol or the Convention (as any such annex or protocol has effect on the date of the passing of this Act or, if later, the date on which it is made, or subsequently).
(3) Regulations may make provision for the purpose of giving effect to any recommendations made in accordance with Article IX(1) of the Antarctic Treaty (recommendations to the governments of the parties to the Antarctic Treaty of measures in furtherance of its principles and objectives).
(4) Regulations under subsection (1) or (3) may not create any new criminal offence punishable with a penalty greater than that provided for in section 20 in respect of offences under Part II.

Power to extend the application of sections 6 to 12

26. Where the Secretary of State thinks fit in the light of any arrangements made by Her Majesty's government in the United Kingdom with another State, regulations may provide for any of the provisions of sections 6 to 12 to apply in relation to persons having such connection with that other State as may be specified in the regulations as they apply in relation to United Kingdom nationals.

Offences under this Act: further provisions

Meaning of "offence under this Act"

27. In the following provisions of this Act "offence under this Act" includes any offence committed by virtue of section 21, 22 or 23 and any offence (wherever committed) of incitement to commit an offence under Part II, conspiracy to commit an offence under Part II or attempting to commit an offence under Part II.

GENERAL NOTE

This section defines "offences under this Act" to encompass conspiracy, incitement, and attempt, to commit an offence under Pt. II.

Institution of proceedings

28.—(1) Proceedings for an offence under this Act shall not be instituted in England and Wales except—
 (a) by the Secretary of State or a person authorised by him for the purposes of this section, or
 (b) by or with the consent of the Director of Public Prosecutions.
 (2) Proceedings for an offence under this Act shall not be instituted in Northern Ireland except—
 (a) by the Secretary of State or a person authorised by him for the purposes of this section, or
 (b) by or with the consent of the Director of Public Prosecutions for Northern Ireland.

GENERAL NOTE

It was not considered necessary to legislate for the position in Scotland where criminal proceedings may only be brought by, or on behalf of, the Lord-Advocate or the procurator fiscal (Standing Committee D, col. 53, March 30, 1994).

Power of arrest etc.

29.—(1) Regulations may make provision for the arrest—
 (a) in any part of the area south of the Antarctic Convergence of any person suspected of committing an offence under section 11(2), under section 13(2) in relation to a condition attached to a permit granted under section 11, or by virtue of section 23, and
 (b) in any part of Antarctica of any person suspected of committing any other offence under this Act.
 (2) Regulations may make provision for—
 (a) the conveyance in custody of any person arrested under regulations made by virtue of subsection (1) to any place where he can be tried for the offence in question,
 (b) the seizure and detention of any article which may be evidence of an offence under this Act and its conveyance to any place where a person charged with that offence can be tried, and
 (c) securing the attendance, before any court by which a person can be tried for an offence under this Act, of any person required to give evidence or produce documents in proceedings relating to that offence.

Evidence

30.—(1) For the purposes of any proceedings for an offence under this Act a certificate signed by or on behalf of the Secretary of State and stating that at the time specified in the certificate—
 (a) a State was or was not a party to the Protocol,
 (b) a person was or was not an Antarctic Treaty official as defined in section 22, or

(c) a person was or was not a Convention official as defined in section 23, shall be conclusive evidence of the facts stated in it.

(2) A document purporting to be a certificate such as is mentioned in sub-section (1) shall be deemed to be such a certificate unless the contrary is proved.

(3) A document purporting to be a written authorisation such as is mentioned in section 3(4), 5(1), 7(1), 8(1) or 9(1) shall be deemed to be such an authorisation unless the contrary is proved.

Interpretation

Interpretation

31.—(1) In this Act—
"commander", in relation to an aircraft, means the member of the flight crew designated as commander by the operator of the aircraft, or if there is no such person, the person who is for the time being the pilot in command of the aircraft;
"contravenes" includes fails to comply with (and "contravention" has a corresponding meaning);
"expedition" includes any tour or other journey, whatever its purpose, made by one or more persons;
"land" includes any ice-shelf;
"master", in relation to a vessel, includes any person for the time being in charge of the vessel (other than a pilot);
"native bird" means a bird of any species indigenous to Antarctica or occurring there seasonally through natural migrations (and includes an egg of such a bird);
"native invertebrate" means a terrestrial or freshwater invertebrate indigenous to Antarctica (at any stage of its life cycle);
"native mammal" means a mammal of any species indigenous to Antarctica or occurring there seasonally through natural migrations;
"native plant" means any terrestrial or freshwater vegetation, including bryophytes, lichens, fungi and algae, indigenous to Antarctica, and includes such vegetation at any stage of its life cycle (including seeds and other propagules of such vegetation);
"operator", in relation to a vessel or aircraft, means the person for the time being having the management of that vessel or aircraft;
"regulations" means regulations made by the Secretary of State;
"station" includes any building or group of buildings;
"United Kingdom national" means—
(a) a British citizen, a British Dependent Territories citizen, a British National (Overseas) or a British Overseas citizen;
(b) a British subject under the British Nationality Act 1981;
(c) a British protected person within the meaning of that Act;
(d) a Scottish partnership;
(e) a body incorporated under the law of any part of the United Kingdom;
"vessel" includes a hovercraft.

(2) For the purposes of this Act the Antarctic Convergence shall be taken to be a line running along parallels of latitude and meridians of longitude that joins the following points—
50° South latitude 0°;
50° South latitude 30° East longitude;
45° South latitude 30° East longitude;
45° South latitude 80° East longitude;
55° South latitude 80° East longitude;

55° South latitude 150° East longitude;
60° South latitude 150° East longitude;
60° South latitude 50° West longitude;
50° South latitude 50° West longitude; and
50° South latitude 0°.

Supplementary

Orders and regulations

32.—(1) Regulations under this Act may make—
(a) different provision for different cases or circumstances, and
(b) incidental and supplementary provision.
(2) Any power to make an order or regulations under this Act shall be exercisable by statutory instrument.
(3) A statutory instrument containing any regulations under this Act shall be subject to annulment in pursuance of a resolution of either House of Parliament.

Repeals

33. The enactments mentioned in the Schedule to this Act (which include enactments that have not come into force and enactments superseded by provisions of this Act) are repealed to the extent specified in the third column of that Schedule.

Extent

34.—(1) This Act extends to Northern Ireland.
(2) Her Majesty may by Order in Council direct that any provision of this Act shall extend to the Channel Islands, the Isle of Man or any colony.
(3) An Order in Council under subsection (2) may provide for such provisions as may be specified in the Order to have effect in any territory in respect of which it is made—
(a) with the substitution for any reference to a United Kingdom national of a reference to a different description of person;
(b) with the substitution for any reference to the United Kingdom (or to a place in, or part of, the United Kingdom) of a reference to that territory (or to a place in, or part of, that territory);
(c) with such other modifications (including additions or omissions) as may be specified in the Order.

Commencement

35.—(1) This Act shall come into force on such day as the Secretary of State may by order appoint.
(2) Different days may be appointed under this section for different provisions and different purposes.

Short title

36. This Act may be cited as the Antarctic Act 1994.

SCHEDULE

R<small>EPEALS</small>

Chapter	Short title	Extent of repeal
1967 c. 65.	The Antarctic Treaty Act 1967.	The whole Act.
1981 c. 61.	The British Nationality Act 1981.	In Schedule 7, the entry relating to the Antarctic Treaty Act 1967.
1989 c. 21.	The Antarctic Minerals Act 1989.	Sections 1 to 13 and 15 to 19 and the Schedule.
1990 c. 40.	The Law Reform (Miscellaneous Provisions) (Scotland) Act 1990.	In Schedule 8, paragraph 39.

INDEX

References are to sections

STATE HOSPITALS (SCOTLAND) ACT 1994*

(1994 c. 16)

An Act to amend the National Health Service (Scotland) Act 1978 and the Mental Health (Scotland) Act 1984 in relation to the provision, control and management of state hospitals in Scotland.   [5th July 1994]

INTRODUCTION AND GENERAL NOTE
  This Act re-enacts the existing powers in the National Health Service (Scotland) Act 1978 (c. 29) and the Mental Health (Scotland) Act 1984 (c. 36) dealing with the provision, control and management of state hospitals in Scotland. Its purpose is to bring all such powers within the 1978 Act so that they are covered by the power in s.2 of that Act, as amended by the National Health Service and Community Care Act 1990 (c. 19), s.28, to set up a Special Health Board to exercise such of the Secretary of State's functions under the 1978 Act as he may determine.

State hospitals

1. For section 102 of the National Health Service (Scotland) Act 1978 (state hospitals) there shall be substituted the following section—

"State hospitals

102.—(1) The Secretary of State shall provide such hospitals as appear to him to be necessary for persons subject to detention under the Mental Health (Scotland) Act 1984 who require treatment under conditions of special security on account of their dangerous, violent or criminal propensities.

(2) Hospitals provided by the Secretary of State under subsection (1) are referred to in this* Act as "state hospitals".

(3) Subject to subsection (4) and section 2, state hospitals shall be under the control and management of the Secretary of State.

(4) The Secretary of State may provide for the management of a state hospital to be undertaken on his behalf by—

   (a) a committee constituted under section 91 of the Mental Health (Scotland) Act 1984; or

   (b) a Health Board or the Agency to the extent that power to do so is delegated to the Board or Agency by the Secretary of State.

(5) A committee managing a state hospital by virtue of subsection (4)(a) shall do so subject to such directions as the Secretary of State may give.".

DEFINITIONS
  "the Agency"   : National Health Service (Scotland) Act 1978, s.10.
  "Health Board"   : National Health Service (Scotland) Act 1978, s.108(1) (as amended by the National Health Service and Community Care Act 1990, Sched. 9, para. 19(22)(a)).

GENERAL NOTE
  This section implements the purpose described in the General Note to the Act. The provisions of the new s.102 derive as follows: subs. (1): 1984 Act, s.90(1); subs. (2): 1984 Act, s.90(2); subs. (3): 1984 Act, s.91(1); subs. (4): 1978 Act, s.102(1); subs. (5): 1984 Act, s.91(2) (part).

Consequential amendments and repeals

2.—(1) In section 105(4)(b) of the National Health Service (Scotland) Act 1978 (procedure as respects orders), the words "and 102(2)" are hereby repealed.

---

*Annotations by Peter Nicholson, LL.B., Solicitor.

(2) In section 108(1) of that Act (interpretation), for the definition of "state hospital" there shall be substituted the following—

" "state hospital" has the meaning indicated in section 102(2);".

(3) Sections 90 and 91(1) of the Mental Health (Scotland) Act 1984 are hereby repealed.

(4) In section 91(2) of that Act (constitution of State Hospital Management Committee), for the words "on his behalf and subject to such directions as he may give" there shall be substituted the words "by virtue of section 102(4)(a) of the National Health Service (Scotland) Act 1978".

(5) In section 125(1) of that Act (interpretation), in the definition of "State hospital", for the words "Part VIII of this Act" there shall be substituted the words "section 102(2) of the National Health Service (Scotland) Act 1978".

GENERAL NOTE

Subs. (1)
The original s.102(2) of the 1978 Act (dissolution of committee set up under s.102(1)) was repealed by the Mental Health (Amendment) (Scotland) Act 1983 (c. 39), Sched. 3: see now the 1984 Act, s.91(3).

Subs. (2)
The administration provisions in s.91(2)–(6) of the 1984 Act remain, but the management of a state hospital by a committee is now "by virtue of s.102(4)(a) of the [1978 Act]".

Short title, commencement and extent

3.—(1) This Act may be cited as the State Hospitals (Scotland) Act 1994.

(2) This Act shall come into force on such date as the Secretary of State may appoint by order made by statutory instrument.

(3) An order under subsection (2) above may contain such transitional provisions and savings as the Secretary of State may consider appropriate.

(4) This Act extends to Scotland only.

INDEX

References are to sections

CHIROPRACTORS ACT 1994*

(1994 c. 17)

---

* Annotations by Jonathan Montgomery, B.A., LL.M., Senior Lecturer in Law, University of Southampton.

An Act to establish a body to be known as the General Chiropractic Council; to provide for the regulation of the chiropractic profession, including making provision as to the registration of chiropractors and as to their professional education and conduct; to make provision in connection with the development and promotion of the profession; to amend, and make provision in connection with, the Osteopaths Act 1993; and for connected purposes.
[5th July 1994]

PARLIAMENTARY DEBATES
Hansard, H.C. Vol. 237, col. 1168; Vol. 238, col. 1173; Vol. 242, col. 939; H.L. Vol. 555, cols. 892, 1324; Vol. 556, col. 177.
The Bill was discussed in Standing Committee B on March 23, 1994.

INTRODUCTION AND GENERAL NOTE
This Act establishes a General Chiropractic Council to regulate the chiropractic profession. Chiropractic is one of a number of popular therapeutic approaches that do not derive from the orthodox western medical tradition that have become known as complementary therapies. The Act contains no definition of chiropractic, but its philosophy was described by Lord Walton (see *Hansard,* H.L. Vol. 555, col. 893). It is based on the premise that the human spine carries and protects the body's central nervous system. If the mobility of the spine is altered, to become too stiff or too mobile, then the nervous system may be affected and pain may result. Chiropractic is a method of assessing the position of the spine and correcting problems through adjustment or manipulation. It is similar to osteopathy, but uses different manipulative techniques and has different approaches to the philosophy and practice of training. Around 900 chiropractors are currently working in the U.K., seeing approximately 75,000 patients each week. Sufficient students are in training to suggest that the size of the profession may well double by the year 2000.
Chiropractic was developed in the U.S.A. in the late nineteenth century. It came to the U.K. in the early twentieth century, and the British Chiropractic Association was founded in 1925. The first permanent British training institution for the profession was set up in 1965. In the 1970s, chiropractors unsuccessfully sought registration under the Professions Supplementary to Medicine Act 1960 (c. 66). The current Government position on complementary therapies is that they should move towards statutory regulation when they can show that they are based on a systematic body of knowledge and already have a system of voluntary registration with an appropriate code of conduct. So long as the transformation to a statutory regime is supported by the profession itself, and has the support and acceptance of the medical profession, then the Government believes it is appropriate to seek Parliamentary legislation. However, the Government does not see its role as sponsoring a bill, instead the private members' bill is thought to be the appropriate procedure (*Hansard,* H.C. Vol. 237, cols. 1204–1205).
Medical hostility to complementary therapies has now been replaced by an increasing willingness to work with them (see British Medical Association, *Complementary Medicine: New Approaches to Good Practice,* 1993). The Osteopaths Act 1993 (c. 21) established a statutory regulatory regime for that profession. In the same year, the King's Fund established a Working Party, chaired by the Master of the Rolls, to examine the case for a similar Act to govern

Chiropractors. The report supported such a scheme (Sir Thomas Bingham M.R. (Chair), *Report of a Working Party on Chiropractic*, 1993). In some ways the claim is even stronger than that of osteopaths because chiropractic has received additional support from research, part-funded by the Medical Research Council, showing that patients with back pain treated by chiropractors fared better than those who received NHS hospital treatment (Meade et al.: "Low back pain of mechanical origin: randomised comparison of chiropractic and hospital outpatient treatment" (1990) 300 *B.M.J.* 1431).

ARRANGEMENT OF THE ACT
   The General Chiropractic Council and its statutory committees are established by s.1. Provision is made for a scheme of registration, including transitional arrangements for those already in practice (see ss.2–10). The supervision of professional education is governed by ss.11–18. In future the right to register will depend on acquiring an approved qualification, to demonstrate that an appropriate standard of proficiency has been obtained. Chiropractors may also be required to undertake post-registration professional training. Under s.19 the General Council is to publish a Code of Practice. Powers to discipline practitioners and prevent those too sick to practise from doing so are provided by ss.20–26. There is provision for appeals in ss.29–31. The title "chiropractor" and related terms are reserved to those on the register by s.32.
   The Act also makes a number of amendments to the Osteopaths Act 1993 (c. 21) (s.42, Sched. 2).

EXTENT
   The Act extends to the whole of the U.K., with the exception of ss.38 and 40 which contain provisions that deal separately with Great Britain, Northern Ireland, Scotland, and England and Wales (s.44(8)).

COMMENCEMENT
   Section 42 of and Sched. 2 to the Act came into force on July 5, 1994, the day on which it received the Royal Assent (s.44(2)). The other provisions will be brought into force on days to be appointed by the Secretary of State (s.44(3)). It is anticipated that the General Council will be established within two years of the Royal Assent, and that the statutory register will be opened about two years after that (*Hansard*, H.C. Vol. 237, cols. 1175–1176).

The General Council and its committees

The General Chiropractic Council and its committees

   1.—(1) There shall be a body corporate to be known as the General Chiropractic Council (referred to in this Act as "the General Council").
   (2) It shall be the duty of the General Council to develop, promote and regulate the profession of chiropractic.
   (3) The General Council shall have such other functions as are conferred on it by this Act.
   (4) Part I of Schedule 1 shall have effect with respect to the constitution of the General Council.
   (5) There shall be four committees of the General Council, to be known as—
      (a) the Education Committee;
      (b) the Investigating Committee;
      (c) the Professional Conduct Committee; and
      (d) the Health Committee.
   (6) The four committees are referred to in this Act as "the statutory committees".
   (7) Each of the statutory committees shall have the functions conferred on it by or under this Act.
   (8) The General Council may establish such other committees as it considers appropriate in connection with the discharge of its functions.

(9) Part II of Schedule 1 shall have effect with respect to the statutory committees.

(10) At the request of the General Council, Her Majesty may by Order in Council make such provision with respect to the matters dealt with by Schedule 1 as Her Majesty considers appropriate in consultation with the General Council.

(11) Any such Order in Council shall be subject to annulment in pursuance of a resolution of either House of Parliament.

(12) Any provision under subsection (10) may be made either in substitution for, or as an addition to, that made by any provision of Schedule 1.

GENERAL NOTE

Subs. (3)

The other mandatory functions conferred by the Act are: to establish the four statutory committees (s.1(4)); to appoint the Registrar of Chiropractors (s.2); to maintain a list of registered chiropractors approved to supervise those with provisional registration (s.5(6)); to make the register available to the public for inspection (s.9(1)), and publish it at least annually (s.9(2)); to determine and publish standards of proficiency (s.13); to recognise qualifications (s.14) and withdraw recognition (s.16); to prepare, publish and keep under review, a Code of Practice (s.19); to make rules governing disciplinary and health procedures (ss.20(10), 26, 30(3)); to appoint and remunerate legal assessors (s.27); and to maintain and publish audited accounts (s.41).

The Council also has a number of powers: to establish committees (s.1(8)); to limit newly qualified practitioners to provisional registration when their work needs to be supervised (s.5); to require registered chiropractors to undertake further training (s.17(1)); to appoint and remunerate medical assessors (s.28); and to require registered chiropractors to be insured (s.37). Schedule 1, para. 15 contains the financial and procedural powers to enable the Council to function. The Council is also empowered to make rules under ss.3(6), 4(4), (9), 5(1), (3), 6(2), 8(8), 9(3), 10(4), 14(4), (9), 17(1), 20(4), (10), 26(1), 27(3), 28(3), 29(2), 30(3). The making of rules is subject to approval by the Privy Council (see ss.35, 36).

If the Council fails to perform any of its functions, the Privy Council may give such directions as it considers appropriate and if necessary exercise default powers (s.34).

Subs. (4)

Schedule 1 provides that the General Council shall consist of 20 members. Ten members will be elected by registered chiropractors (para. 9), although the initial membership in this category will be appointed by the Privy Council under the transitional provisions in para. 44. Six members will be appointed by the Privy Council, of whom one must be a registered medical practitioner and five must be lay people (para. 11). Three members of the Council are to be appointed by the Education Committee, to advise on matters relating to education and training in chiropractic (para. 12). The final member is to be appointed by the Secretary of State to advise the council on matters of professional education (para. 13).

The Schedule also makes provision in respect of quorum, the duration of terms of office, retirement, and the position of Chairman.

The Schedule may be amended by Order in Council at the request of the General Council (s.1(10)).

Subs. (5)

For the functions and constitution of the Education Committee, see ss.11, 12, 16(1), 18 and Sched. 1, paras. 25–29. For the functions and constitution of the Investigating Committee, see ss.20, 21 and Sched. 1, paras. 30–33. For the functions and constitution of the Professional Conduct Committee, see ss.22, 24, 25, 26 and Sched. 1, paras. 34–37. For the functions and constitution of the Health Committee, see ss.23, 24, 25, 26 and Sched. 1, paras. 38–41.

Registration of chiropractors

GENERAL NOTE

There are three types of registration envisaged by the Act: full registration (s.3), conditional registration (s.4) and provisional registration (s.5). Provisional registration provides for supervised practice for newly qualified chiropractors. Conditional registration is a transitional category to enable chiropractors who do not have the formal qualifications required for full registration to continue to practice as chiropractors while they undertake prescribed steps to convert their status into full registration. All three types of registration enable practitioners to describe themselves as chiropractors without penalty (ss.32, 43).

The fees payable in relation to registration will be prescribed by rules to be made under s.6.

The Registrar of Chiropractors

2.—(1) The General Council shall appoint a person to be the registrar for the purposes of this Act.

(2) The person appointed shall be known as the Registrar of Chiropractors (referred to in this Act as "the Registrar") and shall hold office for such period and on such terms as the General Council may determine.

(3) It shall be the duty of the Registrar to establish and maintain a register of chiropractors in accordance with the provisions of this Act.

(4) The Registrar shall have such other functions as the General Council may direct.

(5) Where the terms on which the Registrar holds office include provision for the payment to him of any allowances or expenses, the rate at which those allowances or expenses are paid shall be determined by the General Council.

(6) The terms on which the Registrar holds office may, in addition to providing for his remuneration, include provision for the payment of such pensions, allowances or gratuities to or in respect of him, or such contributions or payments towards provision for such pensions, allowances or gratuities, as may be determined by the General Council.

DEFINITIONS
"General Council": ss.1, 43.

GENERAL NOTE
The Registrar need not be a chiropractor. Attempts to require that he or she be legally qualified were rejected in Parliament. Under s.27 the General Council must appoint a legal assessor to give advice to, *inter alia*, the Registrar on questions of law. Under s.28 the General Council may appoint a medical assessor to play a similar role in relation to medical issues.

Full registration

3.—(1) Subject to the provisions of this Act, any person who satisfies the conditions mentioned in subsection (2) shall be entitled to be registered as a fully registered chiropractor.

(2) The conditions are that the application is made in the prescribed form and manner and that the applicant—
  (a) has paid the prescribed fee;
  (b) satisfies the Registrar that he is of good character;
  (c) satisfies the Registrar that he is in good health, both physically and mentally; and
  (d) has a recognised qualification.

(3) Where an application for registration is made during the transitional period by a person who was in practice as a chiropractor at any time before the opening of the register, he shall be treated as having a recognised qualification if he satisfies the Registrar that for a period of at least five years (which need not be continuous) he has spent a substantial part of his working time in the lawful, safe and competent practice of chiropractic.

(4) For the purposes of subsection (3), no account shall be taken of any work done by the applicant before the beginning of the period of seven years ending with the opening of the register.

(5) For the purposes of subsection (3), the question whether the applicant has spent any part of his working time in the lawful, safe and competent practice of chiropractic shall be determined in accordance with such rules (if any) as may be made by the General Council.

(6) The General Council may by rules provide for treating a person who—
  (a) has obtained a qualification in chiropractic outside the United Kingdom,
  (b) does not hold a recognised qualification, but

(c) satisfies the Registrar that he has reached the required standard of proficiency,

as holding a recognised qualification for the purposes of this Act.

(7) In this section "transitional period" means the period of two years beginning with the opening of the register.

<small>DEFINITIONS</small>
"General Council": ss.1, 43.
"opening of the register": s.43.
"recognised qualification": ss.14(1), 43.
"register": ss.2, 43.
"Registrar": s.2.
"required standard of proficiency": ss.13, 43.

<small>GENERAL NOTE</small>

Subs. (1)
Registration is as of right provided that the conditions set out in the section are met. Rights of appeal against refusal of registration are provided by s.29.

Subs. (2)
Requirements of good character also exist as a prerequisite for registration in s.4, and under the Nurses, Midwives and Health Visitors Act 1979 (c. 36), s.11(2), the Dentists Act 1984 (c. 24), s.15(4), the Opticians Act 1989 (c. 44), s.8(2), and the Osteopaths Act 1993 (c. 21), s.3(2). There have been no reported cases on the meaning of the term in those sections. Some guidance may be found in the case law concerning the meaning of unprofessional conduct. While in the past general immorality has been found to constitute professional misconduct (*e.g.* living in an adulterous union, see *Stock* v. *Central Midwives Board* [1915] 3 K.B. 756), it is now probable that only defects of character that are relevant to professional practice would be taken into account. As a result of s.40, chiropractors applying for registration may be asked to declare convictions that are spent under the Rehabilitation of Offenders Act 1974 (c. 53).

A requirement of good health is also imposed before registration in the Dentists Act 1984 (c. 24), s.15(4), and the Osteopaths Act 1993 (c. 21), s.3(2).

In the absence of precise definitions of good character and good health, the fact that the Registrar must be satisfied will import a highly subjective assessment that may be difficult to challenge. The General Council may make rules that will establish the manner in which the Registrar is to satisfy himself as to good health, character and competence. An appeal lies to the General Council against refusals to register, and the Council will presumably be able to substitute its own subjective definition of the terms, subject to any contrary provision in rules made under s.29(2). Appeal against the decision of the General Council lies only on a point of law (s.29(4)).

Subs. (3)
This provision permits those who have been practising chiropractic for at least five years to seek full registration even though they may not have a recognised qualification. They must have spent a substantial part of their working time over this period practising chiropractic lawfully, safely and competently. The terms "competent" and "safe" may be defined by any rules made under subs. (5) and, in the absence of such provision, by reference to the standard of proficiency that will be determined and published under s.13. Only practice during the period of seven years prior to the end of the transitional period will count towards the five years of practice (subs. (4)). The transitional period ends two years after the register is opened (subs. (7)).

Subs. (6)
These conditions would seem to be cumulative, so that the subsection empowers the Council to make rules dealing with those who have overseas qualifications that are not recognised, but which can be the basis of registration if accompanied by evidence of proficiency without the period of experience that subs. (3) requires and without limitation to the transitional period.

Conditional registration

4.—(1) Subject to the provisions of this Act, any person who satisfies the conditions mentioned in subsection (2) shall be entitled to be registered as a conditionally registered chiropractor.

(2) The conditions are that the application is made in the prescribed form and manner during the transitional period and that the applicant—

(a) has paid the prescribed fee;

(b) satisfies the Registrar that he is of good character;

(c) satisfies the Registrar that he is in good health, both physically and mentally;

(d) satisfies the Registrar that for a period of at least four years (which need not be continuous) he has spent a substantial part of his working time in the lawful, safe and competent practice of chiropractic;

(e) if required to do so by the Registrar in accordance with rules made by the General Council, passes—

(i) the prescribed test of competence; or

(ii) such part of that test as the Registrar may specify; and

(f) gives the required undertaking.

(3) In the application of subsection (2)(d), in relation to any person, no account shall be taken of any work done by him before the beginning of the period of six years ending with the opening of the register.

(4) The General Council may by rules provide for the conversion, in prescribed circumstances and subject to the chiropractor concerned complying with such conditions (if any) as may be prescribed, of conditional registration into full registration.

(5) Unless it is converted into full registration in accordance with the rules, any conditional registration shall cease to have effect—

(a) at the end of the period of five years beginning with the opening of the register; or

(b) where a shorter period has been specified by the Registrar in accordance with subsection (10) in relation to the chiropractor in question, at the end of that shorter period.

(6) In dealing with an application for registration made during the transitional period by a person who—

(a) cannot meet the requirement of subsection (2)(d), but

(b) has a qualification in chiropractic which, while not being a recognised qualification, has not been refused recognition by the General Council,

the Registrar shall refer the matter to the Education Committee.

(7) Where a reference is made to the Education Committee under subsection (6), it shall be the duty of the Committee to advise the General Council.

(8) If, after considering the advice of the Education Committee, the General Council is satisfied that it is appropriate to do so, it shall direct the Registrar to disregard subsection (2)(d) in relation to the application in question.

(9) For the purposes of subsection (2)(d), the question whether the applicant has spent any part of his working time in the lawful, safe and competent practice of chiropractic shall be determined in accordance with such rules (if any) as may be made by the General Council.

(10) In this section—

"required undertaking" means an undertaking that the person giving it will, before the end of the period of five years beginning with the opening of the register or such shorter period as the Registrar may specify in relation to the applicant—

(a) complete such additional training and acquire such experience as may be specified by the Registrar in accordance with rules made by the General Council; and

        (b) comply with such other conditions (if any) as may be imposed on him by the Registrar in accordance with such rules; and

    "transitional period" means the period of two years beginning with the opening of the register.

(11) Rules made by virtue of paragraph (b) in the definition of "required undertaking" in subsection (10) may, in particular, provide for the Registrar to be able to impose, as a condition, the passing of a test of competence specified by the Registrar.

DEFINITIONS
    "Education Committee": ss.1, 11.
    "full registration": s.3.
    "General Council": ss.1, 43.
    "opening of the register": s.43.
    "recognised qualification": ss.14(1), 43.
    "register": ss.2, 43.
    "Registrar": s.2.
    "required standard of proficiency": ss.13, 43.

GENERAL NOTE
    Conditional registration will be available for those who do not have the formal qualifications required for full registration, but are experienced chiropractors. It enables them to continue to practice as chiropractors while they undertake prescribed steps to convert their status into full registration. The precise content of those steps will only become clear when the rules are made under s.6. The Registrar will be able to tailor the conditions imposed on registration to reflect the circumstances and experience of the particular chiropractor (*e.g.* subss. (4)(e)(ii), (5)(b), (10)).
    Conditional registration is a transitional category and will only be available to those who apply during the first two years of the operation of the register (subs. (2)). Conditionally-registered chiropractors must have met the conditions within the first five years of the operation of the register, or their registration will lapse (subs. (5)).

Subs. (2)
    Requirements of good character also exist as a prerequisite for registration in s.3, and under the Nurses, Midwives and Health Visitors Act 1979 (c. 36), s.11(2), the Dentists Act 1984 (c. 24), s.15(4), the Opticians Act 1989 (c. 44), s.8(2), and the Osteopaths Act 1993 (c. 21), s.3(2). There have been no reported cases on the meaning of the term in those sections. Some guidance may be found in the case law concerning the meaning of unprofessional conduct. While in the past general immorality has been found to constitute professional misconduct (*e.g.* living in an adulterous union in *Stock* v. *Central Midwives Board* [1915] 3 K.B. 756), it is now probable that only defects of character that are relevant to professional practice would be taken into account. As a result of s.40, chiropractors applying for registration may be asked to declare convictions that are spent under the Rehabilitation of Offenders Act 1974 (c. 53).
    A requirement of good health is also imposed by s.3, and before registration in the Dentists Act 1984 (c. 24), s.15(4), and the Osteopaths Act 1993 (c. 21), s.3(2).
    In the absence of precise definitions of good character and good health, the fact that the Registrar must be satisfied will import a highly subjective assessment that may be difficult to challenge. The General Council may make rules that will establish the manner in which the Registrar is to satisfy himself as regards good health, character and competence. An appeal lies to the General Council against refusals to register, and the Council will presumably be able to substitute its own subjective definition of the terms, subject to any contrary provision in rules made under s.29(2). Appeal against the decision of the General Council lies only on a point of law (s.29(4)).
    The terms "competent" and "safe" may be defined by any rules made under subs. (9) and, in the absence of such provision, by reference to the standard of proficiency that will be determined and published under s.13.
    Where a chiropractor has a qualification that has not yet been considered by the Education Committee, then provision is made by subss. (6)–(8) for reference to be made to that Committee, and for the General Council to waive the requirement of four years' experience.

Provisional registration

    5.—(1) The General Council may make rules providing for all applicants for registration who are entitled to be registered with full registration, or all such applicants falling within a prescribed class, to be registered initially with provisional registration.

(2) Before making any rules under subsection (1), the General Council shall take such steps as are reasonably practicable to consult those who are registered chiropractors.

(3) The General Council may by rules provide for the conversion, in prescribed circumstances and subject to the chiropractor concerned complying with such conditions (if any) as may be prescribed, of provisional registration into full registration.

(4) Unless it is converted into full registration in accordance with the rules, any provisional registration shall cease to have effect at the end of the period of one year beginning with the date on which it is entered in the register.

(5) A provisionally registered chiropractor shall not practise chiropractic except under the supervision of a fully registered chiropractor who is approved by the General Council for the purposes of this subsection.

(6) The General Council shall maintain a list of those fully registered chiropractors who are for the time being approved by the Council for the purposes of subsection (5).

DEFINITIONS
"full registration": s.3.
"fully registered chiropractor": ss.3, 43.
"General Council": ss.1, 43.
"registered chiropractors": ss.3, 4, 5, 43.

GENERAL NOTE
This section allows the Council to make rules requiring that qualified chiropractors must initially practise under supervision. This is expected to be applied to newly-qualified chiropractors. The rules may also provide for conditions, such as in-service training, that must be met in order to convert provisional registration into full registration. Such conditions must be met within a year of the practitioner's provisional registration, which can last only one year (subs. (4)).

The Act does not itself oblige the Council to introduce a scheme of provisional registration. The necessary rules can only be made after such consultation as is reasonably practicable with registered chiropractors (subs. (2)).

Subs. (5)
No definition of "supervision" is provided by the Act, so the degree of control required remains unclear.

Registration: supplemental provision

6.—(1) The register shall show, in relation to each registered chiropractor—

(a) whether he is registered with full, conditional or provisional registration; and

(b) the address at which he has his practice or principal practice or, if he is not practising, such address as may be prescribed.

(2) The General Council may make rules in connection with registration and the register and as to the payment of fees.

(3) The rules may, in particular, make provision as to—

(a) the form and keeping of the register;

(b) the form and manner in which applications for registration are to be made;

(c) the documentary and other evidence which is to accompany applications for registration;

(d) the manner in which the Registrar is to satisfy himself as to the good character and competence of any person applying for registration and the procedure for so doing;

(e) the manner in which the Registrar is to satisfy himself as to the physical and mental health of any person applying for registration and the procedure for so doing;

    (f) the description of persons from whom references are to be provided for persons applying for registration;

    (g) in the case of an application for conditional registration, the conditions or kinds of condition which may be imposed on the chiropractor concerned;

    (h) the making, periodic renewal and removal of entries in the register;

    (i) the giving of reasons for any removal of, or refusal to renew, an entry in the register;

    (j) any failure on the part of a registered chiropractor to comply with any conditions subject to which his registration has effect, including provision for the Registrar to refuse to renew his registration or for the removal of his name from the register;

    (k) the issue and form of certificates;

    (l) the content, assessment and conduct of any test of competence imposed under section 4;

    (m) the meaning of "principal practice" for the purposes of subsection (1).

    (4) The rules may, in particular, also make provision—

    (a) prescribing the fee to be charged for making an entry in the register or restoring such an entry;

    (b) prescribing the fee to be charged in respect of the retention in the register of any entry in any year following the year in which the entry was first made;

    (c) providing for the entry in the register of qualifications (whether or not they are recognised qualifications) possessed by registered chiropractors and the removal of such an entry;

    (d) prescribing the fee to be charged in respect of the making or removal of any entry of a kind mentioned in paragraph (c);

    (e) authorising the Registrar—

        (i) to refuse to make an entry in the register, or restore such an entry, until the prescribed fee has been paid;

        (ii) to remove from the register any entry relating to a person who, after the prescribed notice has been given, fails to pay the fee prescribed in respect of the retention of the entry.

    (5) A person who has failed to renew his registration as a chiropractor shall be entitled to have his entry restored to the register on payment of the prescribed fee.

DEFINITIONS
    "conditional registration": s.4.
    "full registration": s.3.
    "General Council": ss.1, 43.
    "provisional registration": s.5.
    "register": ss.2, 43.
    "registered chiropractor": ss.3, 4, 5, 43.
    "Registrar": s.2.

GENERAL NOTE
    Subsection (1) sets out the information to be entered on the statutory register. Provision relating to the entry of suspensions is made by s.7. Under s.9 the public are entitled to access to this register, and a "published register" must be issued annually giving at least the names and addresses of registered chiropractors. Allegations of fraudulently-obtained registration are to be investigated under s.10.

    The detailed picture of the scheme for registration will appear from the rules made under this section.

Suspension of registration

    7.—(1) Where the Registrar suspends the registration of a chiropractor in accordance with any provision of this Act, the Registrar shall enter in the register a note of—

(a) the suspension;
(b) the period of the suspension; and
(c) the provision under which the suspension was made.
(2) Where the period of the suspension is extended, the Registrar shall note the extension in the register.
(3) Any chiropractor whose registration has been suspended shall, for the period of his suspension, cease to be a registered chiropractor for the purposes of section 32(1).

DEFINITIONS
  "register": ss.2, 43.
  "registered chiropractor": ss.3, 4, 5, 43.
  "Registrar": s.2.

GENERAL NOTE
  Powers to suspend registration are provided by ss.10(3), 21(2), 22(4)(9), 23(2)(5), 24(2), 30(12), 31(8).

Subs. (3)
  This subsection prevents the use of the title chiropractor and related terms by suspended practitioners.

Restoration to the register of chiropractors who have been struck off

8.—(1) Where a person who has had his entry as a fully registered chiropractor removed from the register as the result of an order under section 22(4)(d) wishes to have his entry restored to the register he shall make an application for registration to the Registrar.
(2) No such application may be made before the end of the period of ten months beginning with the date on which the order under section 22(4)(d) was made.
(3) Any application for registration in the circumstances mentioned in subsection (1) (an "application for restoration") shall be referred by the Registrar to the Professional Conduct Committee for determination by that Committee.
(4) For the purposes of determining an application for restoration—
(a) the Committee shall exercise the Registrar's functions under section 3; and
(b) subsection (2) of that section shall have effect as if paragraph (d) were omitted.
(5) The Committee shall not grant an application for restoration unless it is satisfied that the applicant not only satisfies the requirements of section 3 (as modified) but, having regard in particular to the circumstances which led to the making of the order under section 22(4)(d), is also a fit and proper person to practise the profession of chiropractic.
(6) On granting an application for restoration, the Committee—
(a) shall direct the Registrar to register the applicant as a fully registered chiropractor; and
(b) may make a conditions of practice order with respect to him.
(7) The provisions of section 22 shall have effect in relation to a conditions of practice order made by virtue of subsection (6) as they have effect in relation to one made by virtue of subsection (4)(b) of that section.
(8) The General Council may by rules make provision in relation to the restoration to the register of conditionally registered chiropractors or provisionally registered chiropractors, and any such rules may provide for restoration, in prescribed circumstances, as a fully registered chiropractor.

DEFINITIONS
  "conditionally registered chiropractor": ss.4, 43.
  "conditions of practice order": s.22(4)–(8)(10).

"fully registered chiropractor": ss.3, 43.
"General Council": ss.1, 43.
"Professional Conduct Committee": ss.1, 22.
"provisionally registered chiropractor": ss.5, 43.
"register": ss.2, 43.
"Registrar": s.2.

GENERAL NOTE

This section allows chiropractors who have been removed from the register as a result of disciplinary proceedings under s.22 to apply for restoration to the register after 10 months. The decision whether to restore the practitioner to the register will be taken by the Professional Conduct Committee not the Registrar. That Committee will be able to impose conditions on the chiropractor's practice. Such orders are governed by the supplementary provisions set out in s.22(5)–(8), (10), (11), (13).

Rules made under subs. (8) will make provision relating to the restoration of chiropractors who were previously conditionally or provisionally registered. They may include the possibility that restoration of such practitioners may be as fully registered.

Appeal lies to Her Majesty in Council against decisions of the Professional Conduct Committee under this section, see s.31.

Access to the register etc.

9.—(1) The General Council shall make the register available for inspection by members of the public at all reasonable times.

(2) The General Council shall—

(a) before the end of the period of twelve months which begins on the date on which the register is opened, and

(b) at least once in every subsequent period of twelve months which begins on the anniversary of that date,

publish a list (referred to in this section as the "published register"), giving the names and registered addresses of those who, at the date of publication, are registered chiropractors.

(3) The published register shall also contain, in respect of each registered chiropractor, such other information, derived from the register, as may, by rules made by the General Council, be determined to be appropriate for publication.

(4) Any chiropractor whose registration has been suspended shall, for the period of his suspension, cease to be a registered chiropractor for the purposes of subsections (2) and (3).

(5) Any person who asks the General Council for a copy of the most recently published register shall be entitled to have one on payment of such reasonable fee as the Council may determine.

(6) Subsection (5) shall not be taken as preventing the General Council from providing copies of the published register free of charge whenever it considers it appropriate.

(7) Any copy of, or extract from, the published register shall be evidence (and in Scotland sufficient evidence) of the matters mentioned in it.

(8) A certificate purporting to be signed by the Registrar, certifying that a person—

(a) is registered in a specified category,

(b) is not registered,

(c) was registered in a specified category at a specified date or during a specified period,

(d) was not registered in a specified category, or in any category, at a specified date or during a specified period, or

(e) has never been registered,

shall be evidence (and in Scotland sufficient evidence) of the matters certified.

DEFINITIONS
    "General Council": ss.1, 43.
    "opening of the register": s.43.
    "register": ss.2, 43.
    "registered chiropractor": ss.3, 4, 5, 43.

GENERAL NOTE
    This section provides for public access to the register and for the annual publication of a list of registered chiropractors. The latter list, to be called the "published register" will not include the names of those whose registration has been suspended (subs. (4)), even though they must be recorded on the full register (s.7). The published register is to be supplied on request, subject to payment of a reasonable fee fixed by the General Council (subs. (5)). However, it is open to the Council to supply free copies at its discretion (subs. (6)).
    The precise details to be included in the published register in addition to the names and addresses of practitioners will be determined by rules made under subs. (3).
    Provision is made in subs. (8) for certificates of registration.

Fraud or error in relation to registration

10.—(1) The Registrar shall investigate any allegation that an entry in the register has been fraudulently procured or incorrectly made and report on the result of his investigation to the General Council.
    (2) An entry which has been restored to the register under section 6(5) or section 8, or under rules made by virtue of section 8(8), may be treated for the purposes of this section as having been fraudulently procured or incorrectly made if any previous entry from which the restored entry is derived was fraudulently procured or incorrectly made.
    (3) The Registrar may, at any time during his investigation, suspend the registration in question if he is satisfied that it is necessary to do so in order to protect members of the public.
    (4) The General Council shall by rules make provision, in relation to any case where the Registrar proposes to suspend a chiropractor's registration under subsection (3)—
    (a) giving the chiropractor concerned an opportunity to appear before the Investigating Committee and argue his case against suspension;
    (b) allowing him to be legally represented; and
    (c) for the Registrar to be made a party to the proceedings.
    (5) If, having considered any report of the Registrar, the General Council is satisfied that the entry in question has been fraudulently procured or incorrectly made it may order the Registrar to remove the entry.
    (6) Where such an order is made, the Registrar shall without delay notify the person whose entry is to be removed—
    (a) of the order; and
    (b) of the right of appeal given by subsection (7).
    (7) Where such an order is made, the person whose entry is to be removed may appeal to Her Majesty in Council.
    (8) Any such appeal—
    (a) must be brought before the end of the period of 28 days beginning with the date on which the order is made; and
    (b) shall be dealt with in accordance with rules made by Her Majesty by Order in Council for the purposes of this section.
    (9) On an appeal under this section, the General Council shall be the respondent.
    (10) The Judicial Committee Act 1833 shall apply in relation to the General Council as it applies in relation to any court from which an appeal lies to Her Majesty in Council.
    (11) Without prejudice to the application of that Act, on an appeal under this section to Her Majesty in Council the Judicial Committee may, in their report, recommend to Her Majesty in Council—
    (a) that the appeal be dismissed; or

(b) that it be allowed and the order appealed against quashed.

(12) The General Council may by rules make such further provision as it considers appropriate with respect to suspensions under subsection (3), including in particular provision as to their duration.

DEFINITIONS
   "General Council": ss.1, 43.
   "Investigating Committee": ss.1, 20.
   "register": ss.2, 43.
   "Registrar": s.2.

GENERAL NOTE
   This section deals with allegations that registration has been obtained fraudulently. The Registrar is obliged to investigate all such allegations and make a report to the General Council (subs. (1)). The Registrar is empowered to suspend a registration that is under investigation in order to protect the public (subs. (3)), but the practitioner is entitled to a hearing before the Investigating Committee before such suspension (subs. (4)).
   It is for the General Council to decide whether to order the removal of a chiropractor's registration. It may do so if registration is found to have been fraudulently procured or incorrectly made (subs. (5)). An appeal against such a step lies to Her Majesty in Council (subs. (7)) provided that it is brought within 28 days (subs. (8)).

Professional education

The Education Committee

   11.—(1) The Education Committee shall have the general duty of promoting high standards of education and training in chiropractic and keeping the provision made for that education and training under review.
   (2) Where it considers it to be necessary in connection with the discharge of its general duty, the Education Committee may itself provide, or arrange for the provision of, education or training.
   (3) The General Council shall consult the Education Committee on matters relating to education, training, examinations or tests of competence.
   (4) It shall be the duty of the Education Committee to give advice to the General Council on the matters mentioned in subsection (3), either on being consulted by the Council or where it considers it appropriate to do so.

DEFINITIONS
   "Education Committee": s.1, Sched. 1, paras. 25–29.
   "General Council": ss.1, 43.

GENERAL NOTE
   The Education Committee is empowered by subs. (2) to provide education and training. However, the principal task of the Committee is to oversee and advise on the education of chiropractors. The General Council is obliged to consult the Education Committee on matters within its remit (subs. (3)).
   It should be noted that the key function of recognising qualifications as sufficient to entitle those who hold them to registration is reserved to the General Council and is not within the scope of the Education Committee's powers (s.14).

Visitors

   12.—(1) The Education Committee may appoint persons to visit any place at which or institution by which or under whose direction—
   (a) any relevant course of study is, or is proposed to be, given;

(b) any examination is, or is proposed to be, held in connection with any such course;

(c) any test of competence is, or is proposed to be, conducted in connection with any such course or for any other purpose connected with this Act.

(2) In subsection (1) "relevant course of study" means any course of study which forms, or is intended to form, part of—

(a) the complete course of study required in order to obtain a recognised qualification or a qualification for which recognition is being sought; or

(b) any training which a registered chiropractor may be required to undergo after registration.

(3) No person appointed as a visitor may exercise his functions under this section in relation to—

(a) any place at which he regularly gives instruction in any subject; or

(b) any institution with which he has a significant connection.

(4) A person shall not be prevented from being appointed as a visitor merely because he is a member of—

(a) the General Council; or

(b) any of its committees.

(5) Where a visitor visits any place or institution, in the exercise of his functions under this section, he shall report to the Education Committee—

(a) on the nature and quality of the instruction given, or to be given, and the facilities provided or to be provided, at that place or by that institution; and

(b) on such other matters (if any) as he was required to report on by the Committee.

(6) Requirements of the kind mentioned in subsection (5)(b) may be imposed by the Education Committee—

(a) generally in relation to all visits;

(b) generally in relation to all visits made to a specified kind of place or institution; or

(c) specifically in relation to a particular visit.

(7) Where a visitor reports to the Education Committee under subsection (5), the Committee shall on receipt of the report—

(a) send a copy of it to the institution concerned; and

(b) notify that institution of the period within which it may make observations on, or raise objections to, the report.

(8) The period specified by the Committee in a notice given under subsection (7)(b) shall not be less than one month beginning with the date on which a copy of the report is sent to the institution under subsection (7)(a).

(9) The Education Committee shall not take any steps in the light of any report made under subsection (5) before the end of the specified period.

(10) The General Council may—

(a) pay fees, allowances and expenses to persons appointed as visitors; or

(b) treat any such person, for the purposes of paragraph 15(2)(c) to (e) of Schedule 1, as a member of its staff.

(11) In the case of a visitor who is also such a member as is mentioned in subsection (4), any payment made to him in his capacity as a visitor shall be in addition to any to which he is entitled as such a member.

DEFINITIONS
"Education Committee": ss.1, 11.
"recognised qualification": ss.14(1), 43.
"registered chiropractor": ss.3, 4, 5, 43.

GENERAL NOTE
The Education Committee is empowered to appoint "visitors" to institutions that provide training leading to a recognised pre-registration qualification or post-registration training. Insti-

tutions must be given at least a month to comment on any report and no action can be taken before the period for comment expires (subss. (7)–(9)). If the Education Committee forms the opinion that a recognised qualification is inadequate, it must refer the matter to the General Council (s.16(1)). The Committee itself has no power to withdraw recognition.

The standard of proficiency

13.—(1) The General Council shall from time to time determine the standard of proficiency which, in its opinion, is required for the competent and safe practice of chiropractic.

(2) The Council shall publish a statement of the standard of proficiency determined by it under this section.

(3) If the Council at any time varies the standard so determined it shall publish a statement of the revised standard, accompanied by a statement of the differences between that standard and the standard as it was immediately before the revision.

(4) No variation of the standard shall have effect before the end of the period of one year beginning with the date on which the Council publishes the statements required by subsection (3) in connection with that variation.

DEFINITIONS
  "General Council": ss.1, 43.

GENERAL NOTE
  The standard of proficiency will play a pivotal role in decisions about the recognition of qualifications, which must be evidence that the standard has been attained (s.14(2)). Withdrawal of recognition may follow from a finding that a qualification can no longer be taken to be evidence that the prescribed standard has been reached (s.16). The standard of proficiency also plays an important part in applications by practitioners who seek to rely on experience rather than qualifications to obtain registration (s.3(6)). It probably assists in determining the meaning of safe and competent practice, which play a similar role in ss.3(3) and 4(4)(d).
  Although it is for the General Council to determine the standard of proficiency, it will be necessary to consult the Education Committee on educational issues and tests for competence relating to the standard (s.11(3)).

Recognition of qualifications

14.—(1) For the purposes of this Act, a qualification is a "recognised qualification" if it is recognised by the General Council under this section.

(2) Where the General Council is satisfied that—

  (a) a qualification granted by an institution in the United Kingdom is evidence of having reached the required standard of proficiency, or

  (b) a qualification which such an institution proposes to grant will be evidence of having reached that standard,

it may, with the approval of the Privy Council, recognise that qualification for the purposes of this Act.

(3) Where the General Council is satisfied that a qualification granted by an institution outside the United Kingdom is evidence of having reached the required standard of proficiency, or of reaching a comparable standard, it may, with the approval of the Privy Council, recognise that qualification for the purposes of this Act.

(4) The General Council may by rules—

  (a) impose additional conditions for registration, or

  (b) provide for any provision made by this Act in relation to conditions for registration to have effect subject to prescribed modifications,

in the case of any application for registration based on a person's holding a qualification which is recognised under subsection (3).

(5) The General Council shall maintain and publish a list of the qualifications which are for the time being recognised under this section.

(6) Before deciding whether or not to recognise a qualification under this section, the General Council shall consult the Education Committee.

(7) When requesting the approval of the Privy Council for the purposes of subsection (2) or (3), the General Council shall make available to the Privy Council—
   (a) the information provided to it by the Education Committee; or
   (b) where the Privy Council considers it appropriate, a summary of that information.

(8) The Privy Council shall have regard to the information made available to it under subsection (7) before deciding whether or not to give its approval.

(9) The General Council may by rules make provision requiring the Education Committee to publish a statement indicating—
   (a) matters on which the Committee will wish to be satisfied before advising the General Council to recognise a qualification under subsection (2); and
   (b) matters which may cause the Committee to advise the General Council not to recognise a qualification under subsection (2).

(10) Where, by virtue of Community law a person ("the chiropractor") is to be authorised to practise the profession of chiropractic on the same conditions as a person who holds a recognised qualification—
   (a) the chiropractor shall be treated for the purposes of this Act as having a recognised qualification; but
   (b) the General Council may, subject to Community law, require him to satisfy specified additional conditions before being registered.

(11) In subsection (10) "Community law" means any enforceable Community right or any enactment giving effect to a Community obligation.

DEFINITIONS
   "Education Committee": ss.1, 11.
   "General Council": ss.1, 43.
   "required standard of proficiency": ss.13, 43.

GENERAL NOTE
   The importance of recognised qualifications is that they entitle a chiropractor to registration. Once conditional registration ceases to be available, two years after the opening of the register, acquiring a recognised qualification will be the only way of securing registration. Although the Education Committee must be consulted about recognition, the decision is for the General Council, and is subject to approval by the Privy Council. Supplementary provisions in relation to recognition of qualification are made by s.15. Withdrawal of recognition may take place under s.16.

Subs. (10)
   The relevant E.C. Directives are *Council Directive of 21 December 1988 on a general system for the recognition of higher-education diplomas awarded on completion of professional education and training of at least three years duration* (89/48/EEC; O.J. 1989, L19/16) and *Council Directive of 18 June 1992 on a second general system for the recognition professional education and training to supplement Directive 89/48/EEC* (92/51/EEC; O.J. 1992, L209/25). The Directive to apply depends on the length of study for the qualification and whether it is taken in higher education. The Directives do not preclude the requirement of a period of adaptation or an aptitude test.

Recognition of qualifications: supplemental

   15.—(1) A qualification may be recognised by the General Council under section 14—
   (a) only in respect of awards of that qualification made after a specified date;
   (b) only in respect of awards made before a specified date; or
   (c) only in respect of awards made after a specified date but before a specified date.

(2) Any date specified under subsection (1) may be earlier than the date on which this Act is passed.

(3) Where the General Council recognises a qualification in one or other of the limited ways allowed for by subsection (1), the limitation shall be specified in the list issued by the Council under section 14(5).

(4) The General Council may, in recognising a qualification under section 14, direct that the qualification is to remain a recognised qualification only so long as such conditions as the General Council sees fit to impose are complied with in relation to the qualification.

(5) Any such condition may at any time be removed by the General Council.

(6) The General Council shall not exercise any of its functions under subsection (4) or (5) without the approval of the Privy Council.

(7) Any institution which is, or is likely to be, affected by a direction given by the General Council under subsection (4) shall be notified by the Council of the direction as soon as is reasonably practicable.

(8) Where an application is made by any institution for the recognition of a qualification under section 14, the General Council shall notify the institution of the result of its application as soon as is reasonably practicable after the Council determines the application.

(9) Where the General Council refuses such an application it shall, when notifying the institution concerned, give reasons for its refusal.

DEFINITIONS
   "General Council": ss.1, 43.
   "recognised qualification": ss.14(1), 43.

GENERAL NOTE
   This section provides for various supplementary provisions in respect of recognised qualifications under s.14. It ensures that decisions that are taken by the General Council imposing conditions on recognition can only take effect with the approval of the Privy Council. It also provides that reasons must be given for a refusal of recognition. There is no provision for appeal (as there is in the Opticians Act 1989 (c. 44), s.4 and the Professions Supplementary to Medicine Act 1960 (c. 66), s.4), but refusal of recognition would in principle be amenable to judicial review.

Withdrawal of recognition

16.—(1) Where, as a result of any visitor's report or other information acquired by the Education Committee, the Committee is of the opinion—
   (a) that a recognised qualification is no longer, or will no longer be, evidence of having reached the required standard of proficiency,
   (b) that a proposed qualification which has yet to be granted, but which was recognised by virtue of section 14(2)(b), will not be evidence of having reached that standard, or
   (c) that a condition for the continued recognition of a qualification (imposed under section 15(4)) has not been complied with,
it shall refer the matter to the General Council.

(2) If the General Council is satisfied that the circumstances of the case are as mentioned in subsection (1)(a), (b) or (c) it may, with the approval of the Privy Council, direct that the qualification is no longer to be a recognised qualification for the purposes of this Act.

(3) A direction under subsection (2) shall have effect from the date of the direction or from such later date as may be specified in the direction.

(4) In considering any matter referred to it under subsection (1), the General Council shall have regard to the information on which the Education Committee formed its opinion together with any other relevant information which the Council may have.

(5) When requesting the approval of the Privy Council for the purposes of subsection (2), the General Council shall make available to the Privy Council the information to which it had regard under subsection (4).

(6) The Privy Council shall have regard to the information made available to it under subsection (5) before deciding whether or not to give its approval.

(7) Where the recognition of any qualification is withdrawn under this section, the General Council shall use its best endeavours to secure that any person who is studying for that qualification at any place, at the time when recognition is withdrawn, is given the opportunity to study at that or any other place for a qualification which is recognised.

(8) The withdrawal under this section of recognition from any qualification shall not affect the entitlement of any person to be registered by reference to an award of that qualification made to him before the date on which the direction withdrawing recognition had effect.

DEFINITIONS
"Education Committee": ss.1, 11.
"General Council": ss.1, 43.
"recognised qualification": ss.14(1), 43.
"required standard of proficiency": ss.13, 43.

GENERAL NOTE
This section enables recognition to be withdrawn from a qualification by the General Council, with the approval of the Privy Council. The Education Committee is charged with the task of alerting the Council to the possible need to withdraw recognition (subs. (1)) and would need to be consulted by the Council if it became concerned without the Committee's involvement (s.11(3)). As the required standard of proficiency may change (s.13(3)) withdrawal of recognition may be proper even though there has been no change in the qualification in question. There is no provision for appeal against withdrawal of recognition, the safeguard being the involvement of the Privy Council, but judicial review would lie.

Post registration training

17.—(1) The General Council may make rules requiring registered chiropractors to undertake further courses of training.

(2) The rules may, in particular, make provision with respect to registered chiropractors who fail to comply with any requirements of the rules, including provision for their registration to cease to have effect.

(3) Before making, or varying, any rules under this section the General Council shall take such steps as are reasonably practicable to consult those who are registered chiropractors and such other persons as the Council considers appropriate.

DEFINITIONS
"General Council": ss.1, 43.
"registered chiropractor": ss.3, 4, 5, 43.

GENERAL NOTE
There is increasing interest amongst the health professions in improving the standards of practitioners. Registration ensures only that the necessary standard of proficiency has been reached at the time the practitioner was originally registered, it does not ensure that they have kept their skills up-to-date. This provision allows for rules to be made, after consultation with the profession, to require post-registration training. It should be seen, along with the power to discipline for "professional incompetence" (s.20(1)), as a commitment to a high standard of practice throughout professional life.

Information to be given by institutions

18.—(1) This section applies to any institution by which, or under whose direction—
    (a) any relevant course of study is, or is proposed to be, given;
    (b) any examination is, or is proposed to be, held in connection with any such course; or

(c) any test of competence is, or is proposed to be, conducted in connection with any such course or for any other purpose connected with this Act.

(2) In subsection (1) "relevant course of study" has the same meaning as in section 12.

(3) Whenever required to do so by the Education Committee, any such institution shall give to the Committee such information as the Committee may reasonably require in connection with the exercise of its functions under this Act.

(4) The matters with respect to which the Education Committee may require information under subsection (3) include—

(a) the requirements which must be met by any person pursuing the course of study, undergoing the course of training or taking the examination or test in question;

(b) the financial position of the institution;

(c) the efficiency of the institution's management.

(5) Where an institution refuses any reasonable request for information made by the Education Committee under this section, the Committee may recommend to the General Council that recognition of the qualification in question be either—

(a) refused, or

(b) withdrawn.

(6) Where a recommendation is made to the General Council under subsection (5), the Council may—

(a) in a case to which subsection (5)(a) applies, refuse to recognise the qualification under section 14; or

(b) in a case to which subsection (5)(b) applies, give a direction under section 16(2) (with the required approval of the Privy Council) in respect of the qualification.

DEFINITIONS
"Education Committee": ss.1, 11.
"General Council": ss.1, 43.

GENERAL NOTE
This section obliges institutions providing or proposing to provide professional training or qualifications to supply reasonably requested information to the Education Committee. A refusal to supply information may lead to a recommendation to the General Council to withdraw or refuse recognition (subs. (5)). Recognition can only be withdrawn by the Council, with the approval of the Privy Council (subs. (6)(b)).

Subs. (3)
For the functions of the Education Committee, see ss.11, 12, 16(1).

Professional conduct and fitness to practise

The Code of Practice

19.—(1) The General Council shall prepare and from time to time publish a Code of Practice—

(a) laying down standards of conduct and practice expected of registered chiropractors; and

(b) giving advice in relation to the practice of chiropractic.

(2) It shall be the duty of the General Council to keep the Code under review and to vary its provisions whenever the Council considers it appropriate to do so.

(3) Before issuing the Code or varying it, the General Council shall consult such representatives of practising chiropractors as it considers appropriate.

(4) Where any person is alleged to have failed to comply with any provision of the Code, that failure—

(a) shall not be taken, of itself, to constitute unacceptable professional conduct on his part; but

(b) shall be taken into account in any proceedings against him under this Act.

(5) Any person who asks the General Council for a copy of the Code shall be entitled to have one on payment of such reasonable fee as the Council may determine.

(6) Subsection (5) is not to be taken as preventing the General Council from providing copies of the Code free of charge whenever it considers it appropriate.

DEFINITIONS
"General Council": ss.1, 43.
"registered chiropractor": ss.3, 4, 5, 43.
"unacceptable professional conduct": s.20.

GENERAL NOTE
The giving of advice of professional standards and ethics is a long established role of professional bodies. The General Council is obliged to consult *representatives* of *practising* chiropractors on the contents of the Code of Practice, not the whole registered profession (subs. (3)). In principle, the power to issue the code is amenable to judicial review, but the prospects of success are limited, see *R.* v. *General Medical Council*, ex p. *Colman* [1990] 1 All E.R. 489 and *Pharmaceutical Society of Great Britain* v. *Dickson* [1970] A.C. 403.

The relevance of the Code of Practice to disciplinary proceedings under the Act is set out in subs. (4). It could also be of relevance in negligence actions, although it would only constitute evidence as to the proper standard of care expected of responsible practitioners under the test in *Bolam* v. *Friern Hospital Management Committee* [1957] 1 W.L.R. 582.

Professional conduct and fitness to practise

20.—(1) This section applies where any allegation is made against a registered chiropractor to the effect that—

(a) he has been guilty of conduct which falls short of the standard required of a registered chiropractor;

(b) he has been guilty of professional incompetence;

(c) he has been convicted (at any time) in the United Kingdom of a criminal offence; or

(d) his ability to practise as a chiropractor is seriously impaired because of his physical or mental condition.

(2) In this Act conduct which falls short of the standard required of a registered chiropractor is referred to as "unacceptable professional conduct".

(3) Where an allegation is made to the General Council, or to any of its committees (other than the Investigating Committee), it shall be the duty of the Council or committee to refer the allegation to the Investigating Committee.

(4) The General Council may make rules requiring any allegation which is made or referred to the Investigating Committee to be referred for preliminary consideration to a person appointed by the Council in accordance with the rules.

(5) Any rules made under subsection (4)—

(a) may allow for the appointment of persons who are members of the General Council; but

(b) may not allow for the appointment of the Registrar.

(6) Any person to whom an allegation is referred by the Investigating Committee in accordance with rules made under subsection (4) shall—

(a) consider the allegation with a view to establishing whether, in his opinion, power is given by this Act to deal with it if it proves to be well founded; and

(b) if he considers that such power is given, give the Investigating Committee a report of the result of his consideration.

(7) Where there are rules in force under subsection (4), the Investigating Committee shall investigate any allegation with respect to which it is given a report by a person appointed under the rules.

(8) Where there are no such rules in force, the Investigating Committee shall investigate any allegation which is made or referred to it.

(9) Where the Investigating Committee is required to investigate any allegation, it shall—

(a) notify the registered chiropractor concerned of the allegation and invite him to give it his observations before the end of the period of 28 days beginning with the day on which notice of the allegation is sent to him;

(b) take such steps as are reasonably practicable to obtain as much information as possible about the case; and

(c) consider, in the light of the information which it has been able to obtain and any observations duly made to it by the registered chiropractor concerned, whether in its opinion there is a case to answer.

(10) The General Council shall by rules make provision as to the procedure to be followed by the Investigating Committee in any investigation carried out by it under this section.

(11) In the case of an allegation of a kind mentioned in subsection (1)(c), the Investigating Committee may conclude that there is no case to answer if it considers that the criminal offence in question has no material relevance to the fitness of the chiropractor concerned to practise chiropractic.

(12) Where the Investigating Committee concludes that there is a case to answer, it shall—

(a) notify both the chiropractor concerned and the person making the allegation of its conclusion; and

(b) refer the allegation, as formulated by the Investigating Committee—

(i) to the Health Committee, in the case of an allegation of a kind mentioned in subsection (1)(d); or

(ii) to the Professional Conduct Committee, in the case of an allegation of any other kind.

(13) Where the Investigating Committee concludes that there is no case to answer, it shall notify both the chiropractor concerned and the person making the allegation.

(14) In this section "allegation" means an allegation of a kind mentioned in subsection (1).

DEFINITIONS
"General Council": ss.1, 43.
"Health Committee": ss.1, 23.
"Investigating Committee": s.1.
"Professional Conduct Committee": ss.1, 22.
"registered chiropractor": ss.3, 4, 5, 43.
"Registrar": s.2.

GENERAL NOTE
This section provides for the initial stages of professional disciplinary investigations against registered chiropractors. The first statutory stage in the process involves the Investigating Committee, but the Council is empowered to make rules to introduce a preliminary screening process even before that stage (subss. (4)–(6)). This is the procedure used by the General Medical Council.

The task of the Investigating Committee is to consider whether there is a case to answer (subs. (9)(c)). If there is such a case, then the matter is to be remitted to either the Health Committee or the Professional Conduct Committee. Subsection (9)(a) ensures that the chiropractor against whom allegations have been made is given an opportunity to comment on them. Other procedural issues will be governed by the rules to be made under subs. (10).

If the Investigating Committee finds that there is no case to answer, they must inform the complainant and the chiropractor (subs. (13)). There is no appeal available to the complainant against such a finding, although where there is a case to answer the chiropractor has a full opportunity to defend himself or herself in the subsequent proceedings. This is an aspect of the fact that professional disciplinary proceedings are not primarily concerned with resolving complaints by individuals, but with protecting the public (Sir Thomas Bingham M.R. (Chair), *Report of a Working Party on Chiropractic* 1993, para. 55).

The Investigating Committee has the power to suspend a chiropractor during investigations if necessary in the public interest (s.21). Under s.27 the General Council is obliged to appoint a legal assessor to advise the Investigating Committee on points of law and medical advice will be available from the medical assessor appointed under s.28.

Subs. (1)

Para. (a)
The disciplinary test introduced by this Act is different from the term "professional misconduct" used in most of the statutes governing the longer established health professions, although the same wording is used in the Osteopaths Act 1993 (c. 21). It is unclear how far case law on the older statutes will provide a guide for the new test of "unacceptable professional conduct". It is probable that behaviour that has been found to be "professional misconduct" would also constitute "unacceptable professional conduct" but that the new terminology would embrace a wider range of circumstances. It could be argued that "misconduct" implies culpability, while "conduct which falls short of the standard required of a registered chiropractor" imports something nearer strict liability.

A more precise understanding of what will constitute "unacceptable professional conduct" will appear when the Code of Practice is published under s.19. Failure to comply with that Code will not, of itself, be "unacceptable professional conduct" but it will be taken into account (s.19(4)).

Para. (b)
Conferring jurisdiction to discipline incompetent practitioners marks a new direction in professional regulation in the U.K. Similar provision was made in the Osteopaths Act 1993 (c. 21), s.20. However, some professional bodies have come close to defining "misconduct" in such a way as to enable them to deal with practitioners who make errors even when they are not culpable errors. This has probably been done most clearly under the Pharmacy Act 1954 (c. 61), and has been affirmed by the High Court, see *R.* v. *Pharmaceutical Society of Great Britain*, ex p. *Sokoh, The Times*, December 4, 1986. A summary of relevant decisions of the Statutory Committee of the Royal Pharmaceutical Society can be found in Dale and Appelbe, *Pharmacy Law and Ethics* (5th ed. 1993), chap. 21. Some decisions of the United Kingdom Central Council for Nursing, Midwifery and Health Visiting could also be seen as addressing incompetence, even though the statutory term is "professional misconduct" (Nurses, Midwives and Health Visitors Act 1979 (c. 36), s.12). Examples of decisions from the nursing professional body can be found in the UKCC pamphlet ... *With a view to removal from the register ... ?* and in R. Pyne, *Professional Discipline in Nursing, Midwifery and Health Visiting* (2nd ed. 1992).

Para. (c)
The types of criminal offence that are relevant are limited by subs. (11) to those that have a material relevance to the fitness of the chiropractor to practise chiropractic (see also s.22(3)). An offence committed outside the U.K. may be covered by para. (a).

A potential difficulty arises in relation to the drafting of ss.20(1)(c) and 22(4) that is avoided in relation to other regulatory statutes. It is usual for the professional bodies to have a discretion to administer no punishment, even if an allegation is established. Under the Dentists Act 1984 (c. 24), s.27(1), practitioners may be disciplined by the professional body "if they think fit". Under the Opticians Act 1989 (c. 44), s.17(1), and the Medical Act 1983 (c. 54), s.36(1), similar discretions are imported by the word "may". Under s.22(4) of this Act it appears that some punishment is mandatory (the word used is "shall") whenever an allegation (in this case that the chiropractor has been convicted of a material criminal offence) is substantiated. There must, therefore, be at least an admonition.

Interim suspension powers of the Investigating Committee

21.—(1) This section applies where, under section 20, the Investigating Committee is investigating an allegation against a registered chiropractor.

(2) If the Committee is satisfied that it is necessary to do so in order to protect members of the public, it may order the Registrar to suspend the chiropractor's registration.

(3) The order shall specify the period of the suspension, which shall not exceed two months beginning with the date on which the order is made.

(4) The Committee shall not—

(a) make an order in any case after it has referred the allegation in question to the Professional Conduct Committee or the Health Committee; or

(b) make more than one order in respect of the same allegation.

(5) Before making an order, the Investigating Committee shall give the chiropractor concerned an opportunity to appear before it and to argue his case against the making of the proposed order.

(6) At any such hearing the chiropractor shall be entitled to be legally represented.

DEFINITIONS

"Health Committee": ss.1, 23.

"Investigating Committee": ss.1, 20.

"Professional Conduct Committee": ss.1, 22.

"registered chiropractor": ss.3, 4, 5, 43.

"Registrar": s.2.

GENERAL NOTE

This section empowers the Investigating Committee to suspend the registration of a chiropractor for a two-month interim period while allegations are being investigated. Only one suspension is permitted in respect of an allegation (subs. (4)(b)). Suspension can only occur after the chiropractor has been given the opportunity to argue against it (subs. (5)) with legal representation if desired (subs. (6)). Legal advice will be available to the Investigating Committee from the legal assessor appointed under s.27.

Subs. (4)(a)

The Professional Conduct Committee and the Health Committee have their own powers to impose interim suspensions under s.24.

Consideration of allegations by the Professional Conduct Committee

22.—(1) Where an allegation has been referred to the Professional Conduct Committee under section 20 or by virtue of any rule made under section 26(2)(a), it shall be the duty of the Committee to consider the allegation.

(2) If, having considered it, the Committee is satisfied that the allegation is well founded it shall proceed as follows.

(3) If the allegation is of a kind mentioned in section 20(1)(c), the Committee may take no further action if it considers that the criminal offence in question has no material relevance to the fitness of the chiropractor concerned to practise chiropractic.

(4) Otherwise, the Committee shall take one of the following steps—

(a) admonish the chiropractor;

(b) make an order imposing conditions with which he must comply while practising as a chiropractor (a "conditions of practice order");

(c) order the Registrar to suspend the chiropractor's registration for such period as may be specified in the order (a "suspension order"); or

(d) order the Registrar to remove the chiropractor's name from the register.

(5) A conditions of practice order must specify one or both of the following—

(a) the period for which the order is to have effect;

(b) a test of competence which must be taken by the chiropractor.

(6) A conditions of practice order shall cease to have effect—

(a) if a period is specified in the order, when that period ends;

(b) if no such period is specified but a test of competence is so specified, when the chiropractor concerned passes the test; or

(c) if both a period and a test are so specified, when the period ends or when the chiropractor concerned passes the test, whichever is the later to occur.

(7) At any time while a conditions of practice order is in force under this section or by virtue of a recommendation under section 31(8)(c), the Committee may (whether or not of its own motion)—

(a) extend, or further extend, the period for which the order has effect;
(b) revoke or vary any of the conditions;
(c) require the chiropractor concerned to pass a test of competence specified by the Committee;
(d) reduce the period for which the order has effect; or
(e) revoke the order.

(8) Where the period for which a conditions of practice order has effect is extended or reduced under subsection (7), or a test of competence is specified under that subsection, subsection (6) shall have effect as if—

(a) the period specified in the conditions of practice order was the extended or reduced period; and
(b) the test of competence was specified in that order.

(9) At any time while a suspension order is in force with respect to a chiropractor under this section or by virtue of a recommendation under section 31(8)(c), the Committee may (whether or not of its own motion)—

(a) extend, or further extend, the period of suspension; and
(b) make a conditions of practice order with which the chiropractor must comply if he resumes the practice of chiropractic after the end of his period of suspension.

(10) The period specified in a conditions of practice order or in a suspension order under this section, and any extension of a specified period under subsection (7) or (9), shall not in each case exceed three years.

(11) Before exercising its powers under subsection (4), (7) or (9), the Committee shall give the chiropractor concerned an opportunity to appear before it and to argue his case.

(12) At any such hearing the chiropractor shall be entitled to be legally represented.

(13) In exercising its powers under subsection (7) or (9), the Committee shall ensure that the conditions imposed on the chiropractor concerned are, or the period of suspension imposed on him is, the minimum which it considers necessary for the protection of members of the public.

(14) The Committee shall, before the end of the period of twelve months beginning with the commencement of this section, and at least once in every succeeding period of twelve months, publish a report setting out—

(a) the names of those chiropractors in respect of whom it has investigated allegations under this section and found the allegations to be well founded;
(b) the nature of those allegations; and
(c) the steps (if any) taken by the Committee in respect of the chiropractors so named.

(15) Where the Committee has investigated any allegation against a chiropractor under this section and has not been satisfied that the allegation was well founded, it shall include in its report for the year in question a statement of that fact if the chiropractor so requests.

DEFINITIONS
    "Professional Conduct Committee": s.1.
    "Registrar": s.2.

GENERAL NOTE
    Under this section, the Professional Conduct Committee must consider allegations in two stages. First, it must consider whether an allegation is well founded. Second, if it is satisfied that the allegations are well founded, it must consider what disciplinary action should be taken.

There would appear to be no scope for finding that an allegation is substantiated, but that no disciplinary action is called for. This is unusual. Under the Dentists Act 1984 (c. 24), s.27(1), practitioners may be disciplined by the professional body "if they think fit". Under the Opticians Act 1989 (c. 44), s.17(1), and the Medical Act 1983 (c. 54), s.36(1), similar discretions are imported by the word "may". However, with chiropractors it appears that some punishment is mandatory (the word used is "shall") whenever an allegation is proved. The most lenient step available is therefore an admonition.

Procedure before the Professional Conduct Committee will be governed by rules to be made under s.26. Those rules will give the chiropractor (but not the person making the allegation) the right to elect a hearing at which he or she may be legally represented (s.26(2)). Legal advice will be available to the Committee from the legal assessor appointed under s.27 and medical advice from the medical assessor appointed under s.28. Reasons for the decision will have to be given both to the practitioner and to the person making the allegation (s.26(2)(f)(g)). The Committee will also be given powers to require witnesses to attend, give evidence and produce documents (provided that their disclosure could be required in civil proceedings) (s.26(2)(h), (3)). Failure to comply with requirements to give evidence constitutes an offence under s.32(2).

Cases on the other regulatory statutes for the health professions suggest that the standard of proof required to establish unacceptable professional conduct is high (*De Gregory* v. *General Medical Council* [1961] A.C. 957, *Lanford* v. *General Medical Council* [1990] 1 A.C. 13, *R.* v. *General Dental Council*, ex p. *Brown*, *The Daily Telegraph*, November 9, 1990).

Although the drafting of the statute is slightly obscure, it appears that the two stages of fact-finding and determination of the penalty need to be kept strictly apart. The right to a hearing to answer the allegation is guaranteed by s.26(2)(c). Section 22(11) explicitly requires that chiropractors be given an opportunity to argue their case before the punishment is determined.

A power to make an interim suspension order pending investigation is provided by s.24.

Provision is made for appeals against decisions under this section by s.31.

Subs. (4)

Para. (b)

The "conditions of practice order" is in some ways similar to the conditional registration that can be imposed under the Medical Act 1983 (c. 54), s.36. However, the explicit mention of competence tests is new. Although the same phrase also appears in the Osteopaths Act 1993 (c. 21), that Act is not yet in operation. Subsection (10) limits the initial period of such an order to three years, but it can be extended for up to three years on any number of occasions if it is the minimum period necessary to protect the public (subs. (13)). At any time while a conditions of practice order is in force, the Professional Conduct Committee may vary it (subs. (7)), but the only way in which a chiropractor may seek such variation is by making an appeal within 28 days (s.31(1)). There is no equivalent provision to that in s.23(6), which enables those subject to conditions imposed for health reasons to apply for the variation or discharge of such orders. The right to apply to the Registrar to be restored to the register (s.8) applies only to those who have been struck off.

In *Finegan* v. *General Medical Council* [1987] 1 W.L.R. 121 it was held that a condition could be imposed under the Medical Act 1983 (c. 54) that would effectively prevent the doctor practising. It is unlikely that a similar condition could be made under the 1994 Act as the conditions must be complied with while practising.

Para. (c)

Subsection (10) limits the initial period of suspension to three years, but it can be extended for up to three years on any number of occasions if it is the minimum period necessary to protect the public (subs. (13)). At any time while a suspension order is in force, the Professional Conduct Committee may vary it of its own motion (subs. (7)), but the only way in which a chiropractor may seek such variation is by making an appeal within 28 days (s.31(1)).

Para. (d)

Removal from the register is expected to be used only in the most extreme cases, but the courts have shown themselves reluctant to interfere with the decisions of professional bodies; *Carmichael* v. *General Dental Council* [1990] 1 Med. L.R. 338, *Finegan* v. *General Medical Council* [1987] 1 W.L.R. 121.

Consideration of allegations by the Health Committee

23.—(1) Where an allegation has been referred to the Health Committee under section 20 or by virtue of any rule made under section 26(2)(a), it shall be the duty of the Committee to consider the allegation.

(2) If, having considered it, the Committee is satisfied that the allegation is well founded, it shall—

   (a) make an order imposing conditions with which the chiropractor concerned must comply while practising as a chiropractor (a "conditions of practice order"); or

   (b) order the Registrar to suspend the chiropractor's registration for such period as may be specified in the order (a "suspension order").

(3) Any condition in a conditions of practice order under this section shall be imposed so as to have effect for a period specified in the order.

(4) At any time while a conditions of practice order is in force under this section or under section 30 or by virtue of a recommendation under section 31(8)(c), the Committee may (whether or not of its own motion)—

   (a) extend, or further extend, the period for which the order has effect; or

   (b) make a suspension order with respect to the chiropractor concerned.

(5) At any time while a suspension order is in force with respect to a chiropractor under this section or under section 30 or by virtue of a recommendation under section 31(8)(c), the Committee may (whether or not of its own motion)—

   (a) extend, or further extend, the period of suspension;

   (b) replace the order with a conditions of practice order having effect for the remainder of the period of suspension; or

   (c) make a conditions of practice order with which the chiropractor must comply if he resumes the practice of chiropractic after the end of his period of suspension.

(6) On the application of the chiropractor with respect to whom a conditions of practice order or a suspension order is in force under this section or under section 30 or by virtue of a recommendation under section 31(8)(c), the Committee may—

   (a) revoke the order;

   (b) vary the order by reducing the period for which it has effect; or

   (c) in the case of a conditions of practice order, vary the order by removing or altering any of the conditions.

(7) Where a chiropractor has made an application under subsection (6) which has been refused ("the previous application"), the Committee shall not entertain a further such application unless it is made after the end of the period of twelve months beginning with the date on which the previous application was received by the Committee.

(8) The period specified in a conditions of practice order or in a suspension order under this section, and any extension of a specified period under subsection (4) or (5), shall not in each case exceed three years.

(9) Before exercising its powers under subsection (2), (4), (5) or (6), the Committee shall give the chiropractor concerned an opportunity to appear before it and to argue his case.

(10) At any such hearing the chiropractor shall be entitled to be legally represented.

(11) In exercising any of its powers under this section, the Committee shall ensure that any conditions imposed on the chiropractor concerned are, or any period of suspension imposed on him is, the minimum which it considers necessary for the protection of members of the public.

DEFINITIONS

   "Registrar": s.2.

GENERAL NOTE

   Under this section, the Health Committee must consider allegations of unfitness to practise due to ill health in two stages. First, it must consider whether an allegation is well founded. Second, if it is satisfied that the allegations are well founded, it must consider what action should be taken. There would appear to be no scope for finding that an allegation is substantiated, but that no action is called for. The orders available to the committee are either to suspend the practitioner from practice, or to impose a conditions of practice order.

Procedure before the Committee will be governed by rules to be made under s.26. Those rules will give the chiropractor (but not the person making the allegation) the right to elect a hearing, at which he or she may be legally represented (s.26(2)). Legal advice will be available to the Committee from the legal assessor appointed under s.27 and medical advice from the medical assessor appointed under s.28. Reasons for the decision will have to be given to both the practitioner and to the person making the allegation (s.26(2)(f)(g)). The Committee will also be given powers to require witnesses to attend, give evidence and produce documents (provided that their disclosure could be required in civil proceedings) (s.26(2)(h), (3)). Failure to comply with requirements to give evidence constitutes an offence under s.32(2).

Although the drafting of the statute is slightly obscure, it appears that the two stages of fact-finding and determination of what order should be made need to be kept strictly apart. The right to a hearing to answer the allegation is guaranteed by s.26(2)(c). Section 23(9) explicitly requires that chiropractors be given an opportunity to argue their case before the orders are made.

A power to make an interim suspension order pending investigation is provided by s.24.

Subsection (8) limits the initial period of conditions of practice and suspension orders to three years, but they can be extended for up to three years on any number of occasions if it is the minimum period necessary to protect the public (subs. 11). At any time while a conditions of practice order is in force, the Professional Conduct Committee may vary it (subs. (5)). A chiropractor may seek such variation by making an appeal within 28 days (s.30(1)) or applying to the Health Committee under subs. (6). Once such an application is made it cannot be renewed within 12 months (subs. (7)).

Provision is made for appeals against decisions under this section by s.30.

Interim suspension powers of the Professional Conduct Committee and the Health Committee

24.—(1) This section applies where—

(a) an allegation against a registered chiropractor has been referred under section 20, or by virtue of any rule made under section 26(2)(a), to the Professional Conduct Committee or the Health Committee and the Committee has not reached a decision on the matter; or

(b) the Professional Conduct Committee or the Health Committee reaches a relevant decision on any such allegation.

(2) The Committee concerned may, if it is satisfied that it is necessary to do so in order to protect members of the public, order the Registrar to suspend the registration of the chiropractor concerned.

(3) An order under subsection (2) (an "interim suspension order") shall cease to have effect—

(a) in a case falling within subsection (1)(a), when the Committee reaches a decision in respect of the allegation in question; and

(b) in a case falling within subsection (1)(b)—

(i) if there is no appeal against the decision, when the period for appealing expires; or

(ii) if there is an appeal against the decision, when the appeal is withdrawn or otherwise disposed of.

(4) Before making an interim suspension order, the Committee shall give the chiropractor in question an opportunity to appear before it and to argue his case against the making of the proposed order.

(5) At any such hearing the chiropractor shall be entitled to be legally represented.

(6) Where an interim suspension order has been made, the chiropractor concerned may appeal against it to the appropriate court.

(7) Any such appeal must be brought before the end of the period of 28 days beginning with the date on which the order appealed against is made.

(8) On an appeal under subsection (6) the court may terminate the suspension.

(9) On such an appeal the decision of the court shall be final.

(10) In this section—

"the appropriate court" means—
> (a) in the case of a chiropractor whose registered address is in Scotland, the Court of Session;
> (b) in the case of a chiropractor whose registered address is in Northern Ireland, the High Court of Justice in Northern Ireland; and
> (c) in any other case, the High Court of Justice in England and Wales;

"relevant decision" means an order under section 22(4)(c) or (d), or an order under section 23(2)(b).

DEFINITIONS
"Health Committee": ss.1, 23.
"Professional Conduct Committee": ss.1, 22.
"Registrar": s.2.

GENERAL NOTE
The power of interim suspension may only be used where necessary to protect the public (subs. (2)), and after hearing the chiropractor's case against the making of it (subs. (4)). Legal representation must be permitted (subs. (5)), with appeal lying to a court (subs. (6)) within 28 days (subs. (7)).
Revocation of interim suspension orders by the relevant Committee is governed by s.25.

Revocation of interim suspension orders

25.—(1) On an application made by the chiropractor concerned, in a case falling within section 24(1)(a), an interim suspension order may be revoked by the Committee which made it on the ground that a change in the circumstances of the case has made the order unnecessary.

(2) Where a chiropractor has made an application under subsection (1) which has been refused, he may appeal to the appropriate court against the refusal.

(3) Where, in relation to an interim suspension order—
(a) an appeal has been made under section 24(6) against the making of the order, or
(b) a further application for the order to be revoked has been made after an unsuccessful appeal under this section against the refusal of an earlier application,
leave of the appropriate court shall be required for any appeal under subsection (2) in relation to that order.

(4) Except in a case falling within subsection (5), no application under subsection (1) shall be entertained by the Committee concerned if it is made before the end of the period of six months beginning—
(a) with the date on which the order was imposed; or
(b) where an unsuccessful appeal against the order has been made under section 24(6), the date on which the appeal was dismissed.

(5) Where a previous application has been made under subsection (1) in relation to an interim suspension order, no further such application shall be entertained by the Committee concerned if it is made before the end of the period of six months beginning with the date on which the previous application was finally disposed of.

(6) Any appeal under subsection (2) must be brought before the end of the period of 28 days beginning with the date on which notice of the refusal is sent to the chiropractor.

(7) On an appeal under subsection (2) the court may terminate the suspension.

(8) On such an appeal the decision of the court shall be final.

(9) In this section "the appropriate court" has the same meaning as in section 24.

<small>DEFINITIONS</small>
"interim suspension order": ss.24, 43.

<small>GENERAL NOTE</small>
Chiropractors may apply to the Health and Professional Conduct Committees for revocation of interim suspension orders if they are no longer necessary due to a change in circumstances. Applications can be made after six months and thereafter every six months (subss. (4) and (5)). Appeal lies to a court against refusal to lift suspensions (sub. (2)).

Investigation of allegations: procedural rules

26.—(1) The General Council shall make rules as to the procedure to be followed by the Professional Conduct Committee or the Health Committee in considering any allegation under section 22 or 23.

(2) The rules shall, in particular, include provision—

(a) empowering each Committee to refer to the other any allegation which it considers would be better dealt with by that other Committee;

(b) requiring the chiropractor to whom the allegation relates to be given notice of the allegation;

(c) giving the chiropractor an opportunity to put his case at a hearing if—
(i) before the end of the period of 28 days beginning with the date on which notice of the allegation is sent to him, he asks for a hearing; or
(ii) the Committee considers that a hearing is desirable;

(d) entitling the chiropractor to be legally represented at any hearing in respect of the allegation;

(e) securing that—
(i) any hearing before the Professional Conduct Committee is held in public unless the Committee decides that it is in the interests of the person making the allegation, or of any person giving evidence or of any patient, to hold the hearing or any part of it in private; and
(ii) any hearing before the Health Committee is held in private unless the Committee considers that it is appropriate to hold the hearing or any part of it in public;

(f) requiring the chiropractor to be notified by the Committee of its decision, its reasons for reaching that decision and of his right of appeal;

(g) requiring the person by whom the allegation was made to be notified by the Committee of its decision and of its reasons for reaching that decision;

(h) empowering the Committee to require persons to attend and give evidence or to produce documents;

(i) about the admissibility of evidence;

(j) enabling the Committee to administer oaths.

(3) No person shall be required by any rules made under this section to give any evidence or produce any document or other material at a hearing held by either Committee which he could not be compelled to give or produce in civil proceedings in any court in that part of the United Kingdom in which the hearing takes place.

<small>DEFINITIONS</small>
"General Council": ss.1, 43.

"Health Committee": ss.1, 23.
"Professional Conduct Committee": ss.1, 22.

Legal assessors

27.—(1) The General Council shall appoint persons to be legal assessors.
(2) They shall have the general function of giving advice to—
(a) any person appointed in accordance with rules made under section 20(4),
(b) the Investigating Committee,
(c) the Professional Conduct Committee,
(d) the Health Committee, or
(e) the Registrar,
on questions of law arising in connection with any matter which he or (as the case may be) the committee is considering.
(3) They shall also have such other functions as may be conferred on them by rules made by the General Council.
(4) To be qualified for appointment as a legal assessor under this section, a person must—
(a) have a 10 year general qualification (within the meaning of section 71 of the Courts and Legal Services Act 1990);
(b) be an advocate or solicitor in Scotland of at least 10 years' standing; or
(c) be a member of the Bar of Northern Ireland or solicitor of the Supreme Court of Northern Ireland of at least 10 years' standing.
(5) The General Council may pay such fees, allowances and expenses to persons appointed as legal assessors as it may determine.
(6) In the case of a legal assessor who is also a member of the General Council or of any of its committees, any such payment made to him in his capacity as a legal assessor shall be in addition to any to which he is entitled as such a member.

DEFINITIONS
"General Council": ss.1, 43.
"Health Committee": ss.1, 23.
"Investigating Committee": ss.1, 20.
"Professional Conduct Committee": ss.1, 22.
"Registrar": s.2.

Medical assessors

28.—(1) The General Council may appoint registered medical prac-titioners to be medical assessors.
(2) They shall have the general function of giving advice to—
(a) any person appointed in accordance with rules made under section 20(4),
(b) the Investigating Committee,
(c) the Professional Conduct Committee,
(d) the Health Committee, or
(e) the Registrar,
on matters within their professional competence arising in connection with any matter which he or (as the case may be) the committee is considering.
(3) They shall also have such other functions as may be conferred on them by rules made by the General Council.
(4) The General Council may pay such fees, allowances and expenses to persons appointed as medical assessors as it may determine.
(5) In the case of a medical assessor who is also a member of the General Council or of any of its committees, any such payment made to him in his

capacity as a medical assessor shall be in addition to any to which he is entitled as such a member.

Appeals

Appeals against decisions of the Registrar

29.—(1) Where the Registrar—
(a) refuses to register an applicant for registration under this Act,
(b) registers such an applicant with provisional or conditional registration,
(c) refuses to renew any registration,
(d) removes the name of a registered chiropractor from the register on the ground that he has breached one or more of the conditions subject to which his registration had effect (otherwise than under an order of the Professional Conduct Committee), or
(e) refuses to grant an application for the conversion of a conditional, or provisional, registration into full registration,
the person aggrieved may appeal to the General Council.

(2) Any such appeal shall be subject to such rules as the General Council may make for the purpose of regulating appeals under this section.

(3) An appeal to the General Council must be made before the end of the period of 28 days beginning with the date on which notice of the Registrar's decision is sent to the person concerned.

(4) Any person aggrieved by the decision of the General Council on an appeal under this section may appeal, on a point of law, to the appropriate court.

(5) Any right of appeal given by this section shall be in addition to any right which the person concerned may otherwise have to appeal to a county court or, in Scotland, to the sheriff; but only one such right of appeal may be exercised in relation to the same decision.

(6) In this section "the appropriate court" means—
(a) in the case of a person whose registered address is (or if he were registered would be) in Scotland, the Court of Session;
(b) in the case of a person whose registered address is (or if he were registered would be) in Northern Ireland, the High Court of Justice in Northern Ireland; and
(c) in any other case, the High Court of Justice in England and Wales.

GENERAL NOTE
This section provides for appeals against decisions of the Registrar. Such appeals are to be made to the General Council, with a subsequent appeal to the courts on points of law.

Subs. (1)(d)
The conditions in question must be distinguished from conditions of practice orders under s.22. Conditions imposed under s.4 are within this subsection, as are those imposed by the Health Committee under s.23 (also called a conditions of practice order).

Appeals against decisions of the Health Committee

30.—(1) Any person with respect to whom a decision of the Health Committee is made under section 23 may, before the end of the period of 28 days beginning with the date on which notification of the decision is sent to him, appeal against it in accordance with the provisions of this section.

(2) An appeal under subsection (1) shall lie to an appeal tribunal, consisting of a chairman and two other members, established for the purposes of the appeal in accordance with rules made by the General Council for the purposes of this section.

(3) The General Council shall make rules as to the procedure to be followed by an appeal tribunal hearing an appeal under this section.

(4) The rules may, in particular, make similar provision to that made by virtue of section 26(2)(d), (f), (g), (h), (i) or (j).

(5) No decision against which an appeal may be made under this section shall have effect before—

(a) the expiry of the period within which such an appeal may be made; or

(b) the appeal is withdrawn or otherwise disposed of.

(6) The chairman of an appeal tribunal—

(a) shall be selected in accordance with rules made by the General Council; and

(b) shall be qualified as mentioned in section 27(4).

(7) Each of the other two members of an appeal tribunal shall be selected in accordance with rules made by the General Council—

(a) one of them being a fully registered chiropractor, and

(b) the other being a registered medical practitioner.

(8) The rules may not provide for the selection of any member of an appeal tribunal to be by the General Council.

(9) The chairman of an appeal tribunal shall appoint a person approved by the members of the tribunal to act as clerk of the tribunal.

(10) Subject to any provision made by the rules, an appeal tribunal shall sit in public and shall sit—

(a) in Northern Ireland, in the case of a chiropractor whose registered address is in Northern Ireland;

(b) in Scotland, in the case of a chiropractor whose registered address is in Scotland; and

(c) in England and Wales, in any other case.

(11) On any appeal under this section—

(a) the appeal shall be by way of a rehearing of the case;

(b) the General Council shall be the respondent; and

(c) the tribunal hearing the appeal shall have power to make any decision which the Health Committee had power to make under section 23.

(12) An appeal tribunal shall have the same powers of interim suspension as the Health Committee has by virtue of section 24(1)(b) and that section shall have effect in relation to suspension orders made by appeal tribunals with the necessary modifications.

(13) No person shall be required by any rules made under this section to give any evidence or produce any document or other material at a hearing

held by an appeal tribunal which he could not be compelled to give or produce in civil proceedings in any court in that part of the United Kingdom in which the hearing takes place.

(14) An appeal tribunal shall have power to award costs.

(15) Any expenses reasonably incurred by a tribunal, including any incurred in connection with the appointment of a clerk, shall be met by the General Council.

DEFINITIONS
"fully registered chiropractor": ss.3, 43.
"General Council": ss.1, 43.
"Health Committee": ss.1, 23.
"registered medical practitioner": the Medical Act 1983.

GENERAL NOTE
This section provides for appeal from decisions of the Health Committee to an appeal tribunal. The tribunal will be chaired by a lawyer of 10 years' standing (subs. (6)) and will consist of two further members: a chiropractor and a doctor (subs. (7)). Independence from the General Council is ensured by subs. (8), which prevents the Council selecting the tribunal members.

The details of procedure before the tribunal will be governed by rules made under subs. (3), but it is clear that costs may be awarded (subs. (14)). The appeal will be by way of rehearing (subs. (11)(a)) and the tribunal will have the same powers to dispose of the case as the Health Committee (subs. (11)(c)) including interim suspension (subs. (12)).

Appeals against decisions of the Professional Conduct Committee and appeal tribunals

31.—(1) Any person with respect to whom—

(a) a decision of the Professional Conduct Committee is made under section 8 or 22, or

(b) a decision is made by an appeal tribunal hearing an appeal under section 30,

may, before the end of the period of 28 days beginning with the date on which notification of the decision is sent to him, appeal against it in accordance with the provisions of this section.

(2) No such decision shall have effect—

(a) before the expiry of the period within which an appeal against the decision may be made; or

(b) where an appeal against the decision has been duly made, before the appeal is withdrawn or otherwise disposed of.

(3) An appeal under this section shall lie to Her Majesty in Council.

(4) An appeal under subsection (1)(b) may only be on a point of law.

(5) Any such appeal shall be dealt with in accordance with rules made by Her Majesty by Order in Council for the purposes of this section.

(6) On an appeal under this section, the General Council shall be the respondent.

(7) The Judicial Committee Act 1833 shall apply in relation to the Professional Conduct Committee, an appeal tribunal and the General Council as it applies in relation to any court from which an appeal lies to Her Majesty in Council.

(8) Without prejudice to the application of that Act, on an appeal under this section to Her Majesty in Council, the Judicial Committee may in their report recommend to Her Majesty in Council—

(a) that the appeal be dismissed;

(b) that the appeal be allowed and the decision questioned by the appeal quashed;

(c) that such other decision as the Professional Conduct Committee or (as the case may be) Health Committee could have made be substituted for the decision questioned by the appeal; or

(d) that the case be remitted to the Committee or appeal tribunal concerned to be disposed of in accordance with the directions of the Judicial Committee.

DEFINITIONS
"appeal tribunal": s.30.
"General Council": ss.1, 43.
"Health Committee": ss.1, 23.
"Professional Conduct Committee": ss.1, 22.

GENERAL NOTE
Appeals against decisions on health matters made by appeal tribunals can only be made on a point of law (subs. (4)). Appeals against decisions of the Professional Conduct Committee are not so restricted, but in relation to the other health professions the courts have proved themselves reluctant to scrutinise the substance of decisions on appeal, see, *e.g. Libman (Julius)* v. *General Medical Council* [1972] A.C. 217, *Carmichael* v. *General Dental Council* [1990] 1 Med. L.R. 338, *Finegan* v. *General Medical Council* [1987] 1 W.L.R. 121.

Offences

Offences

32.—(1) A person who (whether expressly or by implication) describes himself as a chiropractor, chiropractic practitioner, chiropractitioner, chiropractic physician, or any other kind of chiropractor, is guilty of an offence unless he is a registered chiropractor.

(2) A person who, without reasonable excuse, fails to comply with any requirement imposed by—
(a) the Professional Conduct Committee,
(b) the Health Committee, or
(c) an appeal tribunal hearing an appeal under section 30,
under rules made by virtue of section 26(2)(h) or under any corresponding rules made by virtue of section 30(4) is guilty of an offence.

(3) A person guilty of an offence under this section shall be liable on summary conviction to a fine not exceeding level five on the standard scale.

DEFINITIONS
"appeal tribunal": s.30.
"Health Committee": ss.1, 23.
"Professional Conduct Committee": ss.1, 22.
"registered chiropractor": ss.3, 4, 5, 43.

GENERAL NOTE

Subs. (1)
All three types of registration enable practitioners to describe themselves as chiropractors without penalty.

Monopolies and competition

Competition and anti-competitive practices

33.—(1) In this section "regulatory provision" means—
(a) any rule made by the General Council;
(b) any provision of the Code of Practice issued by the Council under section 19; and
(c) any other advice or guidance given by the Council, any of its committees or any sub-committee of such a committee.

(2) Schedule 8 to the Fair Trading Act 1973 (powers exercisable when making certain orders) shall, for the purposes of a competition order, have effect in relation to a regulatory provision as it has effect in relation to an agreement, but with the necessary modifications.

(3) A competition order may be made so as to have effect in relation to a regulatory provision even though that provision was properly made in exercise of functions conferred by this Act.

(4) In this section "a competition order" means—

(a) an order under section 56 of the Act of 1973 (orders following reports on monopoly references); or

(b) an order under section 10 of the Competition Act 1980 (orders following reports on competition references).

(5) For the purposes of any order under section 56 of the Act of 1973 or section 10 of the Act of 1980, section 90(4) of the Act of 1973 (power to apply orders to existing agreements) shall have effect in relation to a regulatory provision as it has effect in relation to an agreement.

DEFINITIONS
"Code of Practice": s.19.
"General Council": ss.1, 43.

GENERAL NOTE
This section ensures that the General Council will be subject to competition law when making rules and issuing advice.

Miscellaneous

Default powers of Privy Council

34.—(1) If it appears to the Privy Council that the General Council has failed to perform any functions which, in the opinion of the Privy Council, should have been performed, the Privy Council may give the General Council such direction as the Privy Council considers appropriate.

(2) If the General Council fails to comply with any direction given under this section, the Privy Council may itself give effect to the direction.

(3) For the purpose of enabling it to give effect to a direction under subsection (1), the Privy Council may—

(a) exercise any power of the General Council or do any act or other thing authorised to be done by the General Council; and

(b) do, of its own motion, any act or other thing which it is otherwise authorised to do under this Act on the instigation of the General Council.

DEFINITIONS
"General Council": ss.1, 43.

GENERAL NOTE
The functions of the General Council are discussed in the General Note to s.1.

Rules

35.—(1) The approval of the Privy Council shall be required for any exercise by the General Council of a power to make rules under this Act.

(2) Any rules made by the General Council or by Order in Council under this Act may make different provision with respect to different cases or classes of case and, in particular, different provision with respect to different categories of chiropractor or registered chiropractor.

(3) Any Order in Council made under section 10(8)(b) or 31(5) shall be subject to annulment in pursuance of a resolution of either House of Parliament.

(4) Nothing in any rules made under this Act shall be taken to oblige or entitle any person to act in breach of the law relating to confidentiality.

DEFINITIONS
"General Council": ss.1, 43.
"registered chiropractor": ss.3, 4, 5, 43.

Exercise of powers of Privy Council

36.—(1) Where the approval of the Privy Council is required by this Act in respect of the making of any rules by the General Council, it shall be given by an order made by the Privy Council.

(2) Any power of the Privy Council under this Act to make an order shall be exercisable by statutory instrument.

(3) Any order approving rules made under section 5, 8(8), 17 or 30 shall be subject to annulment in pursuance of a resolution of either House of Parliament.

(4) For the purposes of exercising any powers conferred by this Act (other than the power of hearing appeals) the quorum of the Privy Council shall be two.

(5) Any act of the Privy Council under this Act shall be sufficiently signified by an instrument signed by the Clerk of the Council.

(6) Any document purporting to be—

(a) an instrument made by the Privy Council under this Act, and

(b) signed by the Clerk of the Privy Council,

shall be evidence (and in Scotland sufficient evidence) of the fact that the instrument was so made and of its terms.

DEFINITIONS
"General Council": ss.1, 43.

Professional indemnity insurance

37.—(1) The General Council may by rules make provision requiring—

(a) registered chiropractors who are practising as chiropractors, or

(b) prescribed categories of registered chiropractors who are practising as chiropractors,

to secure that they are properly insured against liability to, or in relation to, their patients.

(2) The rules may, in particular—

(a) prescribe risks, or descriptions of risk, with respect to which insurance is required;

(b) prescribe the amount of insurance that is required either generally or with respect to prescribed risks;

(c) make such provision as the General Council considers appropriate for the purpose of securing, so far as is reasonably practicable, that the requirements of the rules are complied with;

(d) make provision with respect to failure to comply with their requirements (including provision for treating any failure as constituting unacceptable professional conduct).

DEFINITIONS
"General Council": ss.1, 43.
"registered chiropractor": ss.3, 4, 5, 43.

GENERAL NOTE
This section permits the General Council to make rules requiring registered chiropractors to carry proper insurance. The possibility that patients injured by poor practice in complementary therapies would be unable to recover damages because practitioners might not carry insurance has been one of the concerns expressed about "alternative medicine". Most members of the established professions would carry professional liability insurance where they are not employed by the NHS (when indemnity arrangements apply), but this is not usually a formal requirement. The General Chiropractic Council can make it mandatory under this provision. In contrast to other rule-making powers conferred by the Act, there is no duty to consult the profession before making rules under this section.

Data protection and access to personal health information

38.—(1) In section 2(1) of the Access to Health Records Act 1990 (definition of health professionals), after paragraph (f) there shall be inserted—
"(fa) a registered chiropractor;".

(2) In Article 4(1) of the Access to Health Records (Northern Ireland) Order 1993 (meaning of "health professional"), after sub-paragraph (d) there shall be inserted—
"(da) a registered osteopath within the meaning of the Osteopaths Act 1993;
(db) a registered chiropractor within the meaning of the Chiropractors Act 1994;".

(3) The following instruments shall be amended as mentioned in subsection (4)—
(a) the Data Protection (Subject Access Modification) (Health) Order 1987;
(b) the Access to Personal Files (Social Services) Regulations 1989;
(c) the Access to Personal Files (Social Work) (Scotland) Regulations 1989;
(d) the Access to Personal Files (Housing) Regulations 1989; and
(e) the Access to Personal Files (Housing) (Scotland) Regulations 1992.

(4) In each case, at the end of the Table in the Schedule there shall be inserted—

"Registered chiropractor   Chiropractor Act 1994, section 43."

(5) The reference in section 2(1) of the Access to Medical Reports Act 1988 to the order mentioned in subsection (3)(a) shall be read as a reference to that order as amended by this section.

(6) The amendments made by this section shall not be taken to prejudice the power to make further orders or (as the case may be) regulations varying or revoking the amended provisions.

DEFINITIONS
"registered chiropractor": ss.3, 4, 5, 43.
"registered osteopath": ss.3, 4, 5, 41 of the Osteopaths Act 1993.

GENERAL NOTE
These amendments ensure that the patients of chiropractors will be entitled to access to their records in the same way as would apply to those held by other professions. It is important that the statutory rights are extended as there is no common law right to such access, *R.* v. *Mid-Glamorgan Family Health Services*, ex p. *Martin, The Times*, August 16, 1994. Subsection (2) contains an amendment relating to osteopaths that was overlooked in the equivalent section of the Osteopaths Act 1993 (c. 21).

Supply of video recordings for use in training to be exempted supply

39. In subsection (11) of section 3 of the Video Recordings Act 1984 (exempted supplies), for "or the Medical Act 1983" substitute "the Medical Act 1983, the Osteopaths Act 1993 or the Chiropractors Act 1994".

GENERAL NOTE
These amendments facilitate the making of videos for the purposes of training osteopaths and chiropractors.

Exemption from provisions about rehabilitation of offenders

40.—(1) In this section—
"the 1975 Order" means the Rehabilitation of Offenders Act 1974 (Exceptions) Order 1975 (professions etc. with respect to which provisions of the Act of 1974 are excluded); and

"the 1979 Order" means the Rehabilitation of Offenders (Exceptions) Order (Northern Ireland) 1979 (professions etc. with respect to which provisions of the Rehabilitation of Offenders (Northern Ireland) Order 1978 are excluded).

(2) In Part I of Schedule 1 to the 1975 Order, there shall be inserted at the end—

"12. Registered chiropractor."

(3) In Part I of Schedule 1 to the 1979 Order, there shall be inserted at the end—

"11. Registered chiropractor."

(4) In both the 1975 Order and the 1979 Order, in each case in Part IV of Schedule 1, there shall be inserted in the appropriate place—

" "registered chiropractor" has the meaning given by section 43 of the Chiropractors Act 1994."

(5) The amendment of the 1975 Order and the 1979 Order by this section shall not be taken to prejudice the power to make further orders varying or revoking the amended provisions.

DEFINITIONS
"registered chiropractor": ss.3, 4, 5, 43.

Financial provisions

41.—(1) The General Council shall keep proper accounts of all sums received or paid by it and proper records in relation to those accounts.

(2) The accounts for each financial year of the General Council shall be audited by persons appointed by the Council.

(3) No person may be appointed as an auditor under subsection (2) unless he is eligible for appointment as a company auditor under section 25 of the Companies Act 1989 or Article 28 of the Companies (Northern Ireland) Order 1990.

(4) As soon as is reasonably practicable after the accounts of the General Council have been audited, the Council shall—

(a) cause them to be published, together with any report on them made by the auditors; and

(b) send a copy of the accounts and of any such report to the Privy Council.

(5) The Privy Council shall lay any copy sent to it under subsection (4) before each House of Parliament.

DEFINITIONS
"General Council": ss.1, 43.

Osteopaths Act 1993

Amendments of the Osteopaths Act 1993

42. The amendments of the Osteopaths Act 1993 set out in Schedule 2 shall have effect.

GENERAL NOTE
Schedule 2 makes a number of amendments to the Osteopaths Act 1993 (c. 21). Some of these are only drafting amendments. Paragraph 1 ensures that the published register under that Act

will not include the names of those whose registration has been suspended. Paragraph 3 provides for the Education Committee carrying out functions that had been reserved for the General Osteopathic Council. Paragraph 5 specifies the content of a conditions of practice order under s.22.

Supplemental

Interpretation

43. In this Act—
"conditionally registered chiropractor" means a person who is registered with conditional registration;
"fully registered chiropractor" means a person who is registered with full registration;
"the General Council" means the General Chiropractic Council;
"interim suspension order" has the meaning given in section 24(3);
"opening of the register" means the date on which section 3 comes into force;
"prescribed" means prescribed by rules made by the General Council;
"provisionally registered chiropractor" means a person who is registered with provisional registration;
"recognised qualification" has the meaning given by section 14(1);
"the register" means the register of chiropractors maintained by the Registrar under section 2;
"registered" means registered in the register;
"registered address" means the address which is entered in the register, in relation to the chiropractor in question, in accordance with the requirements of section 6(1) and does not include any other address which may be entered in the register, in relation to him, by virtue of rules made under section 6(2);
"registered chiropractor" means a person who is registered as a fully registered chiropractor, as a conditionally registered chiropractor or as a provisionally registered chiropractor;
"the Registrar" has the meaning given in section 2(2);
"the required standard of proficiency" means the standard determined by the General Council under section 13;
"the statutory committees" has the meaning given by section 1(6);
"unacceptable professional conduct" has the meaning given by section 20(2);
"visitor" means a person appointed under section 12.

Short title, commencement, transitional provisions and extent

44.—(1) This Act may be cited as the Chiropractors Act 1994.

(2) Section 42 and Schedule 2 shall come into force on the passing of this Act.

(3) The other provisions of this Act shall come into force on such day as the Secretary of State may by order appoint.

(4) The power conferred by subsection (3) shall be exercisable by statutory instrument.

(5) Different days may be appointed by an order under subsection (3) for different purposes and different provisions.

(6) Any order under subsection (3) may make such transitional provision as the Secretary of State considers appropriate.

(7) The transitional provisions of Part III of Schedule 1 shall have effect.

(8) This Act extends to the United Kingdom except that—
(a) section 38(1) and section 40(2) extend only to Great Britain;
(b) section 38(2) and section 40(3) extend only to Northern Ireland;
(c) section 38(3)(b) and (d) extends only to England and Wales; and
(d) section 38(3)(c) and (e) extends only to Scotland.

GENERAL NOTE
It is anticipated that the General Council will be established within two years of Royal Assent, and that the statutory register will be opened about two years after that (*Hansard*, H.C. Vol. 237, cols. 1175–1176). It should also be noted that the application of a number of provisions of the Act depend on time restrictions dating from the "opening of the register" which is defined as the date on which s.3 comes into effect (s.43).

SCHEDULES

Sections 1 and 44   SCHEDULE 1

THE GENERAL COUNCIL AND COMMITTEES

PART I

THE GENERAL COUNCIL

Membership

1. The General Council shall consist of—
(a) 10 members elected by fully registered chiropractors;
(b) 6 members appointed by the Privy Council;
(c) 3 members appointed by the Education Committee; and
(d) 1 member appointed by the Secretary of State.
2. The quorum of the General Council shall be 10.
3. Subject to paragraphs 4 to 7, each member's term of office shall be for a period of 5 years.
4.—(1) This paragraph applies where a member fails to complete his full term of office.
(2) In such circumstances as may be prescribed, if the unexpired term is less than the prescribed period the vacancy need not be filled before the end of that term.
(3) If the member's successor is elected or (as the case may be) appointed during the unexpired term, the successor's term of office shall, subject to paragraphs 5 to 7, be for the residue of the unexpired term.
(4) Rules made by the General Council under sub-paragraph (2) shall not prescribe a period of more than twelve months.
(5) In this paragraph "the unexpired term" means the period beginning with the date on which the member ceased to be a member and ending with the date on which his full term of office would have expired.
5. Any member may at any time resign by notice in writing addressed to the Registrar.
6. Every member shall retire on reaching the age of 70.
7. The General Council shall by rules make provision as to the grounds (such as repeated absence from meetings or unacceptable professional conduct) on which any member may be removed from office and the procedure involved.
8. No person shall be prevented from being elected or from being appointed merely because he has previously been a member of the General Council.

Members elected by fully registered chiropractors

9.—(1) This paragraph and paragraph 10 apply in relation to the 10 members elected by fully registered chiropractors.
(2) Each member—
(a) shall be a fully registered chiropractor at the time of his election, and
(b) may be a registered medical practitioner.
(3) Of the 10 members—
(a) 7 shall be elected by fully registered chiropractors whose registered addresses are in England;

(b) 1 shall be elected by fully registered chiropractors whose registered addresses are in Wales;

(c) 1 shall be elected by fully registered chiropractors whose registered addresses are in Scotland; and

(d) 1 shall be elected by fully registered chiropractors whose registered addresses are in Northern Ireland.

10. The General Council shall make further provision by rules in relation to the election of the 10 members and as to by-elections.

Members appointed by the Privy Council

11.—(1) Of the 6 members appointed by the Privy Council—

(a) 1 shall be a registered medical practitioner at the time of his appointment and shall be appointed after consultation with the Conference of Medical Royal Colleges and their Faculties in the United Kingdom; and

(b) the other 5 shall be persons who are not registered chiropractors at the time of their appointment.

(2) If the body mentioned in sub-paragraph (1)(a) ceases to exist, the Privy Council shall appoint the member in question after consultation with such other representative body or bodies as it thinks fit.

(3) The member appointed in accordance with sub-paragraph (1)(a) shall not be a registered chiropractor.

(4) Any of the other members may be a registered medical practitioner.

Members appointed by the Education Committee

12.—(1) The 3 members appointed by the Education Committee shall be persons appearing to the Committee to be qualified to advise the General Council on matters relating to education and training in chiropractic.

(2) Before making any such appointment, the Committee shall consult—

(a) those institutions in the United Kingdom by which or under whose direction any relevant course of study is given; and

(b) such other bodies (if any) as the Education Committee considers appropriate.

(3) In this paragraph "relevant course of study" has the same meaning as in section 12(2).

The member appointed by the Secretary of State

13. The member appointed by the Secretary of State shall be a person appearing to him to be qualified to advise the General Council on matters relating to professional education.

The Chairman

14.—(1) The members of the General Council shall elect a Chairman from among themselves.

(2) The Chairman may resign the office of Chairman at any time by notice in writing addressed to the Registrar.

(3) The Chairman shall hold office until—

(a) he resigns as Chairman;

(b) he ceases to be a member of the General Council;

(c) he is removed by a majority vote of the other members of the Council; or

(d) a period of 7 years, beginning with his assuming office as Chairman, has elapsed and no other person has been elected (and served) as Chairman during that time.

(4) A person shall not be prevented from being elected as Chairman merely because he has previously been Chairman, but if he has ceased to hold office by virtue of sub-paragraph (3)(d) he may not be elected as Chairman until some other person has served as the elected Chairman.

(5) The General Council shall by rules—

(a) make further provision in relation to the election of a Chairman; and

(b) make provision for the appointment of an acting Chairman in the event of a vacancy in the office of Chairman or in such other circumstances as may be prescribed.

Powers of the General Council

15.—(1) Subject to any provision made by or under this Act, the General Council shall have power to do anything which is calculated to facilitate the discharge of its functions or which is incidental or conducive to the discharge of its functions.

(2) The General Council shall, in particular, have power—

(a) to borrow;

(b) to appoint such staff as it may determine;

(c) to pay its staff such salaries as it may determine;
(d) to pay its staff, and the members of its committees and any of their sub-committees, such allowances and expenses as it may determine;
(e) to make such provision for the payment of such pensions, allowances or gratuities, or such contributions or payments towards provision for such pensions, allowances or gratuities, to or in respect of its staff as it may determine;
(f) to pay its members such allowances and expenses as it may determine;
(g) to establish such sub-committees of any of its committees as it may determine;
(h) subject to any provision made by or under this Act, to regulate the procedure of any of its committees or their sub-committees;
(i) to abolish any of its committees, other than a statutory committee, or any sub-committee of any of its committees;
(j) to delegate to any of its committees any functions of the General Council other than any power to make rules.

(3) The powers of the General Council may be exercised even though there is a vacancy among its members.

(4) No proceedings of the General Council shall be invalidated by any defect in the election or appointment of a member.

(5) Subject to any provision made by or under this Act, the General Council may regulate its own procedure.

PART II

THE STATUTORY COMMITTEES

General

16.—(1) The members of the statutory committees, other than co-opted members, shall be appointed by the General Council from among the members of the Council.

(2) The General Council shall make provision by rules as to the procedure for such appointments.

17.—(1) The co-option of any person to any of the statutory committees shall be subject to the approval of the General Council.

(2) A co-opted member of any of the statutory committees may also be a member of the General Council.

(3) The term of office of a co-opted member shall not exceed the period of 3 years beginning with the date of his co-option.

(4) The General Council shall make further provision by rules in relation to co-option, including provision as to the procedure involved.

18. A person shall not be prevented from being a member of a statutory committee merely because he has previously been a member of that committee.

19. Any member of a statutory committee (other than a co-opted member) shall hold office until he ceases to be a member of the General Council or, where he is a member of the committee by virtue of being Chairman of the General Council, until he ceases to be Chairman of the General Council.

20. The General Council may by rules make provision with respect to any sub-committee of a statutory committee including, in particular, provision as to the functions and powers to be conferred on the sub-committee, its composition and its relationship with the statutory committee.

21.—(1) The General Council shall make rules regulating the procedure of the statutory committees and their sub-committees (if any) including, in particular, provision as to rules of evidence to be observed in proceedings before any such committee or sub-committee.

(2) Subject to any provision made by or under this Act, each statutory committee and any sub-committee of such a committee may regulate its own procedure.

22.—(1) If it appears to the General Council that any statutory committee is failing to perform its functions adequately, the General Council may give a direction as to the proper performance of those functions.

(2) Where the General Council, having given a direction under sub-paragraph (1), is satisfied that the committee has failed to comply with the direction, it may exercise any power of that committee or do any act or other thing authorised to be done by that committee.

23.—(1) The powers of any statutory committee may be exercised even though there is a vacancy among its members.

(2) No proceedings of a statutory committee shall be invalidated by any defect in the appointment of a member.

24.—(1) A person may be a member of more than one statutory committee.

(2) No member of the Professional Conduct Committee or the Health Committee shall take part in dealing with an allegation referred to either committee by another committee if he is also a member of the committee which referred the allegation.

The Education Committee

25.—(1) The Education Committee shall consist of—
(a) 4 of the members of the General Council elected by fully registered chiropractors;
(b) 2 of the members of the General Council appointed by the Privy Council;
(c) the 3 members of the General Council appointed by the Education Committee;
(d) the member of the General Council appointed by the Secretary of State.
(2) In appointing the members of the Committee, the General Council shall secure, so far as is compatible with the provisions of sub-paragraph (1), that its Chairman is a member of the Committee.
26. The Committee may co-opt up to 6 further members.
27.—(1) Subject to sub-paragraph (2), the members of the Committee shall elect a Chairman from among themselves.
(2) The Chairman shall not be the Chairman of the General Council or a co-opted member of the Committee.
(3) In the event of a tie in any voting, the Chairman of the Committee shall have an additional casting vote.
28. The quorum of the Committee shall be 5, of whom at least 3 shall be members of the General Council.
29.—(1) The 3 members appointed to the General Council by the Committee shall not be entitled to take part in the appointment of any of their successors.
(2) The member appointed to the General Council by the Secretary of State shall also not be entitled to take part in the appointment of any of the successors to the 3 members mentioned in sub-paragraph (1).
(3) Where the Chairman of the Committee is prevented by sub-paragraph (1) or (2) from taking part in an appointment the appointment shall be made in accordance with rules made by the General Council.

The Investigating Committee

30. The Investigating Committee shall consist of at least 6 members of the General Council, of whom at least 2 shall be members of the General Council appointed by the Privy Council.
31. The Committee may co-opt up to 6 further members.
32.—(1) Subject to sub-paragraph (2), the members of the Committee shall elect a Chairman from among themselves.
(2) The Chairman shall not be the Chairman of the General Council or a co-opted member of the Committee.
(3) In the event of a tie in any voting, the Chairman of the Committee shall have an additional casting vote.
(4) In the event of a tie in voting in respect of a decision under section 20(9)(c) or section 21(2), the Chairman shall cast his additional vote in favour of the chiropractor concerned.
33. The quorum of the Committee shall be 5, of whom at least 3 shall be members of the General Council.

The Professional Conduct Committee

34. The Professional Conduct Committee shall consist of at least 5 members of the General Council, of whom at least 2 shall be members of the General Council appointed by the Privy Council.
35. The Committee may co-opt up to 4 further members.
36.—(1) If the Chairman of the General Council is a member of the Committee he shall be Chairman of the Committee.
(2) If he is not a member of the Committee, the members shall elect a Chairman from among those members who are not co-opted members.
(3) In the event of a tie in any voting, the Chairman of the Committee shall have an additional casting vote.
(4) In the event of a tie in voting in respect of a decision under section 22 or section 24, the Chairman shall cast his additional vote in favour of the chiropractor concerned.

37. The quorum of the Committee shall be 4, of whom at least 3 shall be members of the General Council.

The Health Committee

38. The Health Committee shall consist of at least 6 members of the General Council, of whom—
(a) at least 2 shall be members of the General Council appointed by the Privy Council; and
(b) at least one shall be a registered medical practitioner at the time of his appointment.
39. The Committee may co-opt up to 4 further members.
40.—(1) If the Chairman of the General Council is a member of the Committee he shall be Chairman of the Committee.
(2) If he is not a member of the Committee, the members shall elect a Chairman from among those members who are not co-opted members.
(3) In the event of a tie in any voting, the Chairman of the Committee shall have an additional casting vote.
(4) In the event of a tie in voting in respect of a decision under section 23 or section 24, the Chairman shall cast his additional vote in favour of the chiropractor concerned.
41. The quorum of the Committee shall be 5, none of whom need be registered medical practitioners but at least 3 of whom shall be members of the General Council.

Part III

Transitional Provisions

The initial membership of the General Council

42. When first constituted, the membership of the General Council shall be determined in accordance with the provisions of this Schedule as modified by this Part.

The transitional periods

43. In this Part—
"the three year transitional period" means the period beginning with the passing of this Act and ending with the third anniversary of the opening of the register;
"the four year transitional period" means the period beginning with the passing of this Act and ending with the fourth anniversary of the opening of the register; and
"the five year transitional period" means the period beginning with the passing of this Act and ending with the fifth anniversary of the opening of the register.

The chiropractic members

44.—(1) During the three year transitional period, paragraph 1(a) shall have effect as if it provided for the appointment of 10 members by the Privy Council.
(2) Each of those members shall be appointed by the Privy Council after consultation with bodies in the United Kingdom appearing to the Privy Council to represent practising chiropractors.
(3) When appointing any such member the Privy Council shall designate him as a person appointed as one of the 10 members provided for by paragraph 1(a) (as modified by this paragraph).
(4) In this paragraph "chiropractic member" means a member designated under this paragraph.
(5) Each of the chiropractic members shall, at the time of his appointment, be a person appearing to the Privy Council to be a practising chiropractor.
(6) Paragraph 6 shall not apply to any of the chiropractic members.
(7) Subject to paragraphs 4, 5 and 7, the term of office of each of the chiropractic members shall end at the end of the three year transitional period.

The lay members

45.—(1) The members appointed by the Privy Council under paragraph 1(b) during the five year transitional period shall each be designated by the Privy Council as a person appointed under paragraph 1(b).
(2) In this Part "lay member" means a member designated under this paragraph.
(3) Paragraph 11 shall have effect during the five year transitional period as if "registered chiropractors" and "registered chiropractor" read, respectively, "persons appearing to the Privy

Council to be practising chiropractors" and "a person appearing to the Privy Council to be a practising chiropractor".

(4) Subject to paragraphs 4 to 7, the term of office of each of the lay members shall end at the end of the five year transitional period.

The education members

46.—(1) During the four year transitional period, paragraph 1(c) shall have effect as if it provided for the appointment of 3 members by the Privy Council.

(2) Each of those members shall be appointed by the Privy Council after consultation with the Secretary of State.

(3) When appointing any such member the Privy Council shall designate him as a person appointed as one of the 3 members provided for by paragraph 1(c) (as modified by this paragraph).

(4) The 3 education members shall be persons appearing to the Privy Council to be qualified to advise the General Council on matters relating to education and training in chiropractic.

(5) In this paragraph "education member" means a member designated under this paragraph.

(6) Paragraph 6 shall not apply to any of the education members.

(7) Subject to paragraphs 4 to 7, the term of office of each of the education members shall end at the end of the four year transitional period.

The Secretary of State's nominee

47. Subject to paragraphs 4, 5 and 7, the term of office of any person appointed by the Secretary of State under paragraph 1(d) during the four year transitional period shall come to an end at the end of that period.

Appointment of first Chairman

48.—(1) The first Chairman of the General Council shall be appointed by the Privy Council from among the lay members to serve as such until the end of the first meeting of the Council to be held after the first election of members under paragraph 1(a).

(2) If a person appointed as Chairman of the Council during the three year transitional period fails to serve his full term of office as Chairman, his successor as Chairman shall be appointed by the Privy Council from among the lay members for the residue of the unexpired term.

(3) Paragraph 14(3) shall have effect in relation to any Chairman appointed by the Privy Council under this paragraph as if for paragraph (c) there were substituted—

"(c) his removal by the Privy Council, where the Privy Council agrees to a request for his removal made by a majority of the other members of the General Council;".

(4) Paragraph 14(3)(d) shall not apply in relation to any person serving as the Chairman appointed by the Privy Council under this paragraph.

Section 42   SCHEDULE 2

AMENDMENTS OF THE OSTEOPATHS ACT 1993

1.—(1) In section 9 of the Osteopaths Act 1993 (access to the register etc.), in subsection (1), the words from "and" at the end of paragraph (a) to the end of paragraph (b) are hereby repealed.

(2) After subsection (1) of that section insert—

"(1A) The General Council shall—

(a) before the end of the period of twelve months which begins on the date on which the register is opened, and

(b) at least once in every subsequent period of twelve months which begins on the anniversary of that date,

publish a list (referred to in this section as the "published register"), giving the names and registered addresses of those who, at the date of publication, are registered osteopaths.

(1B) The published register shall also contain, in respect of each registered osteopath, such other information, derived from the register, as may, by rules made by the General Council, be determined to be appropriate for publication.

(1C) Any osteopath whose registration has been suspended shall, for the period of his suspension, cease to be a registered osteopath for the purposes of subsections (1A) and (1B)."

(3) In subsection (3) of that section, after "copies of the" insert "published".

2. In section 13 (the standard of proficiency)—

(a) in subsection (3), omit "—(a)", and for "standard; and (b)" at the end of paragraph (a) substitute "standard, accompanied by"; and

(b) in subsection (4), for "statement" substitute "statements".

3.—(1) In section 18 (information to be given by institutions)—

(a) in subsection (3) for "the Council" (in both places) substitute "the Committee"; and

(b) in subsections (3) and (4) for "General Council" substitute "Education Committee".

(2) For subsection (5) of that section substitute—

"(5) Where an institution refuses any reasonable request for information made by the Education Committee under this section, the Committee may recommend to the General Council that recognition of the qualification in question be either—

(a) refused, or

(b) withdrawn.

(6) Where a recommendation is made to the General Council under subsection (5), the Council may—

(a) in a case to which subsection (5)(a) applies, refuse to recognise the qualification under section 14; or

(b) in a case to which subsection (5)(b) applies, give a direction under section 16(2) (with the required approval of the Privy Council) in respect of the qualification."

4. In subsection (10) of section 20 (professional conduct and fitness to practise), for "may" substitute "shall".

5.—(1) After subsection (4) of section 22 (consideration of allegations by the Professional Conduct Committee) insert—

"(4A) A conditions of practice order must specify one or both of the following—

(a) the period for which the order is to have effect;

(b) a test of competence which must be taken by the osteopath."

(2) In subsection (5)(a) of that section the words "for the purposes of this subsection" are hereby repealed.

6. In sections 27 (legal assessors) and 28 (medical assessors), in subsection (2)—

(a) the word "or" at the end of paragraph (c) is hereby repealed; and

(b) at the end of paragraph (d) insert "or

(e) the Registrar,".

7. In section 30 (appeals against decisions of the Health Committee), in subsection (12) for "under" substitute "by virtue of".

8. In section 31 (appeals against decisions of the Professional Conduct Committee and appeal tribunals)—

(a) in subsection (1)(a) after "section" insert "8 or"; and

(b) in subsection (7) for "the Health Committee" substitute "an appeal tribunal".

9. In section 41 (interpretation), for the definition of "registered address" substitute—

" "registered address" means the address which is entered in the register, in relation to the osteopath in question, in accordance with the requirements of section 6(1) and does not include any other address which may be entered in the register, in relation to him, by virtue of rules made under section 6(2);".

10.—(1) The Schedule (the General Council and its committees) is amended as follows.

(2) In paragraph 15, after paragraph (e) insert—

"(ee) to pay its members such allowances and expenses as it may determine;".

(3) In paragraph 21(2), for the words from "rules made" to "paragraph 15(2)(g)" substitute "provision made by or under this Act".

(4) Paragraph 15 shall be deemed always to have had effect as amended by sub-paragraph (2).

INDEX

References are to sections and Schedules

SOCIAL SECURITY (INCAPACITY FOR WORK) ACT 1994*

(1994 c. 18)

ARRANGEMENT OF SECTIONS

Incapacity benefit

An Act to provide for incapacity benefit in place of sickness benefit and invalidity benefit; to make provision as to the test of incapacity for work for the purposes of that benefit and other social security purposes; to make provision as to the rate of statutory sick pay; to make other amendments as to certain allowances payable to a person who is or has been incapable of work; and for connected purposes. [5th July 1994]

PARLIAMENTARY DEBATES
Hansard, H.C. Vol. 236, col. 35; Vol. 239, col. 155; Vol. 245, col. 134; H.L. Vol. 552, col. 1456; Vol. 553, col. 501; Vol. 554, cols. 95, 287, 350, 1436, 1520; Vol. 555, cols. 355, 377; Vol. 556, col. 725.
The Bill was discussed in Standing Committee E between February 1 and March 1, 1994.

INTRODUCTION AND GENERAL NOTE
This is arguably the single most important piece of social security legislation since the Social Security Act 1986, which came into force in April 1988. The main purpose of this Act is to abolish sickness benefit and invalidity benefit and to replace them with a new and less generous benefit—incapacity benefit. Since the introduction of statutory sick pay (SSP) in 1983, sickness

* Annotations by Professor N.J. Wikeley, M.A. (Cantab.), Barrister, Faculty of Law, University of Southampton.

benefit has diminished in importance. Invalidity benefit, however, is still the principal long-term contributory benefit providing income maintenance for those incapable of work. Although modifications have been made over the years to the conditions of entitlement to the various long-term insurance benefits, this is the first time that such a benefit has been abolished.

Social security is the largest single component of public expenditure, and a major review of social security provision has been under way for some time. In 1993 the Government published *The Growth of Social Security* (DSS), which highlighted three benefit areas which were contributing most to future growth. These were invalidity benefit, housing benefit and lone parents on income support. The report noted that the number of invalidity benefit recipients had increased from 600,000 in 1978–79 to almost 1.5 million in 1992–93, at a time when the nation's health had improved. The cost of this benefit had doubled since 1982–83 (paras. 4.5–4.6).

The suggestion in some quarters that this increase is because it has become too easy to claim invalidity benefit is not supported by the empirical data. The Policy Studies Institute has estimated that the increase in claims can be accounted for as follows: 29 per cent. of the extra cases are people over pensionable age, drawing invalidity benefit rather than their state pension for tax reasons; 16 per cent. are due to the increased participation of women in the labour market; and 13 per cent. are due to a gradual increase in the number of disabled people in the relevant age groups. This leaves 42 per cent. of the extra cases arising from genuine growth in the rate of claiming (Berthoud, *Invalidity Benefit: Where will the savings come from?* (PSI 1993), p. 5). Further research suggests that demographic factors (especially age and health conditions) are the prime determinants of both the inflow into invalidity benefit and the duration of claims. Invalidity benefit may also be used as a form of early retirement or hidden unemployment, especially in areas with high levels of joblessness (Holmes, Lynch and Molho (1991) 20 Jnl Soc Pol 87 and Disney and Webb (1991) 101 Econ Jnl 252). The level of invalidity benefit itself does not seem to be a major factor in the increase in numbers (Erens and Ghate, *Invalidity benefit: a longitudinal survey of new recipients*, DSS (1993) Research Report No. 20). This last report also showed that the majority of claimants are aged over 50 and living on low incomes.

The Government nonetheless concluded that reform was essential as, in its view, invalidity benefit was poorly targeted and not means tested, taking no account of increased occupational pension provision. It also continues for five years beyond pension age and is the last pre-pension benefit to contain an earnings-related component. In addition, the Government expressed its concern at the current operation of the test for incapacity for work. It has argued that the case law in this area has developed in such a way that non-medical factors are taken into account, with the result that the rules have been progressively widened and made more complicated.

Thus, according to the Secretary of State for Social Security, this Act has three main objectives: "first, to ensure that the huge and rising sums devoted to sickness benefits are properly focused on those who are genuinely too unwell to work; secondly, to ensure that the cost is affordable; and thirdly, to provide a more rational structure of benefits" (Mr P. Lilley, *Hansard*, H.C. Vol. 236, col. 35).

The structure of incapacity benefit

Statutory sick pay, sickness benefit and invalidity benefit
The structure of incapacity benefit cannot be understood fully without reference to the existing benefit arrangements. At present most employees who are off work sick qualify for SSP for the first 28 weeks. Although currently paid at two flat rates, with no additions, this will be paid at one rate as from April 1995. Claimants who do not qualify for SSP, but satisfy the contributions conditions, may be entitled to sickness benefit for the same maximum period. After 28 weeks those claimants who meet the contributions conditions and remain incapable of work become entitled to invalidity benefit. Claimants with an inadequate insurance record but who are seriously disabled may qualify for the non-contributory severe disablement allowance.

Invalidity benefit is a long-term benefit payable until the person is able to work again or retires (it can be paid for up to five years after reaching pensionable age). The benefit actually consists of a basic invalidity pension and an invalidity allowance. The invalidity pension is paid at the same rate as the standard state retirement pension and may be supplemented by adult and child dependants' additions.

The invalidity allowance is paid in addition to invalidity pension at one of three rates for those who were aged under 60 (for men) or 55 (for women) on the first day in their period of incapacity for work. The highest rate is paid for claimants aged under 40 at the relevant time, the middle rate for those aged between 40–49 and the lowest rate for men aged between 50–59 and women aged between 50–54. The discrimination against women aged between 55–59 has been ruled unlawful under EC law (see CS/27/1991).

Some existing claimants may have a third component to their invalidity benefit, namely an earnings-related additional pension. The calculation of the additional pension is based on contributions paid in the tax years 1978–79 to 1990–91. Contributions paid since April 1991 do not give rise to any entitlement to an additional pension (see the Social Security Act 1990, s.4). Any entitlement to an additional pension is offset against invalidity allowance entitlement.

Incapacity benefit
Incapacity benefit is markedly less generous. There are two types of incapacity benefit, described as short-term and long-term, and three different levels of benefit. A person incapable of work will receive the lower rate of short-term incapacity benefit for the first 28 weeks (see the Social Security Contributions and Benefits Act 1992, s.30B(2), inserted by s.2(1) of the 1994 Act), assuming he does not qualify for SSP. This lower rate will be equivalent to the current rate of sickness benefit. Between 29 and 52 weeks the claimant will qualify for the higher rate of the short-term incapacity benefit (SSCBA 1992, ss.30A(4) and 30B(2), inserted by ss.1(1) and 2(1) of the 1994 Act), which will be the same as the current higher rate of SSP. It is only after 52 weeks that the long-term rate of incapacity benefit (equivalent to invalidity pension at present) will become payable (SSCBA 1992, s.30A(5), inserted by s.1(1) of the 1994 Act). Thus claimants will only receive their maximum entitlement to benefit after one year, although they will be required to satisfy the "all work" test after 28 weeks (see below).

Two special groups of claimants will qualify for the highest rate of benefit after 28 weeks rather than the normal 52 weeks. These are the terminally ill and claimants in receipt of the highest rate of the care component of disability living allowance. These concessions were forced on the Government following debates and votes in the House of Lords.

Dependants' additions. These will remain payable, although the criteria have been tightened. Additions for adult dependants will be available after 28 weeks, as at present, but will only be payable if the dependant is aged over 60 or caring for children (see the SSCBA 1992, s.86A, inserted by s.2(5) of the 1994 Act). Child dependency additions will remain payable after 28 weeks, contrary to the Government's original intentions (s.2(4)).

Age allowances. These will also still be payable, but only at two rates: a higher rate for those incapacitated before the age of 35 and a lower one for those incapacitated between the ages of 35 and 45. No age additions will be payable where the incapacity for work starts after the age of 45 (see the SSCBA 1992, s.30B(7), inserted by s.2(1) of the 1994 Act).

The earnings-related additional pension. This is abolished and existing recipients will have that component of their benefit frozen in cash terms. Thus it will not be up-rated in subsequent years, contrary to the undertakings given when the SSA 1990 was passing through Parliament.

Long-term incapacity benefit will cease when the claimant reaches pensionable age, although short-term incapacity benefit will continue to be paid so long as the incapacity arose before attaining that age (see the SSCBA 1992, s.30A(2), inserted by s.1(1) of the 1994 Act).

The new test for incapacity for work
Although entitled the Social Security (Incapacity for Work) Act 1994, there is no actual definition of incapacity for work on the face of the Act. However, s.5 introduces two tests for incapacity for work, the "own occupation" test and the "all work" test.

The "own occupation test". This will apply for the first 28 weeks of incapacity but only for those who have been engaged in remunerative work for more than eight weeks in the previous 21 weeks. The test is whether the claimant "is incapable by reason of some specific disease or bodily or mental disablement of doing work which he could reasonably be expected to do in the course of the occupation in which he was so engaged" (see the SSCBA 1992, s.171B(2), inserted by s.5 of the 1994 Act). This is essentially the same test which the Benefits Agency currently applies for the first six months of a claimant's incapacity.

The "all work test". This is more problematic. This will apply from the outset of the claim to claimants who have no "own occupation", and after 28 weeks for those whose incapacity for work is initially judged according to the requirements of their own occupation. Although introduced by the SSCBA 1992, s.171C (again, as inserted by s.5 of the 1994 Act), the details of the new test have been left to delegated legislation. The Government's goal is to establish some form of objective and universal measure of incapacity. An outline of the type of approach envisaged was published by the DSS in 1993 in *A consultation on the medical assessment for Incapacity Benefit.* Since then, the DSS has been developing a medical test which seeks to quantify functional abilities and to rate the relative severity of combinations of specific limitations of functions. A specialist panel of independent advisers was appointed to assist in this process. The report evaluating this new test is expected to be published in August 1994, and the key regulations embodying its proposals will be brought before Parliament in the Autumn. There remains serious doubts as to whether incapacity for work is susceptible to such a form of objective assessment (see in particular the reservations expressed by a Government backbencher, Mr A. Howarth, at *Hansard*, H.C. Vol. 239, col. 172 and Vol. 245, col. 138).

According to ministerial statements, the principle underlying the new test is that it "should be based on medical, objective criteria and on the way in which illness affects the capacity to perform a range of physical and mental tasks. It is how those effects are related to the illness that determines whether a person qualifies for benefit. It does not depend on whether work is available, but purely on how the illness affects a person's physical or mental capacity to perform those tasks" (Mr A. Burt, Standing Committee E, col. 331). The "all work" test will seek to identify "the point at which the ability to do any form of work is substantially reduced—not the point at which all work becomes impossible" (Mr A. Burt, *Hansard*, H.C. Vol. 239, col. 197). The new test will operate as follows: "It will involve completion of a questionnaire by the claimant, a statement of diagnosis from the claimant's G.P., a list of principal disabling conditions and, when required, referral to a departmental doctor for a report or examination" (Mr A. Burt, Standing Committee E, col. 282).

Not all claimants will be subject to the "all work" test. The Government has undertaken to exclude certain categories of claimant from the new provisions. It is estimated that 850,000 out of 1.5 million claimants of invalidity benefit will remain under old regime (Viscount Astor, *Hansard*, H.L. Vol. 553, col. 504). See further the annotations to s.4(5).

The financial effect on claimants

Existing recipients of invalidity benefit will be transferred to incapacity benefit (s.4) but will see no reduction in the amount of benefit they receive. In the future, however, they may be affected in either or both of two ways. First, they may be subject to review under the arrangements for the new medical tests. Secondly, as indicated above, any additional pension will be frozen as at the point of change.

Many new claimants of incapacity benefit will be substantially disadvantaged in financial terms. For example, persons claiming for the first time in May 1995 will, over a period of time, receive less than they would have done had they claimed invalidity benefit in May 1994. The reasons for this are discussed above under the heading "Incapacity Benefit".

It follows from the less generous nature of incapacity benefit that many claimants will turn to income support to top up their contributory benefit. At present only about 7 per cent. of invalidity benefit claimants receive income support (*Hansard*, H.L. Vol. 554, col. 1448). However, it has been estimated that 25 per cent. of people awarded incapacity benefit after April 1995 will also be entitled to income support between weeks 28 and 52 of incapacity (*Hansard*, H.C. Vol. 238, col. 367 Written Answers).

So far as the inter-relationship with the tax system is concerned, the Government has indicated that the lower rate of short-term incapacity benefit will be free of tax (*i.e.* for the first 28 weeks). Thereafter incapacity benefit will be taxable (Mr N. Scott, Standing Committee E, col. 188).

Benefit savings

The Government has estimated that the Act will produce gross savings of £550 million in 1995–96 and £1,450 million in 1996–97; these figures must be offset by extra expenditure on income support and unemployment benefit of £135 million in 1995–96 and £265 million in 1996–97. The Act is expected to cause administrative costs to increase by some £50 million in the first two years (see "the Explanatory and Financial Memorandum" to the Bill). The Government has stressed, however, that the purpose is not to cut the cost of income replacement benefits for those incapable of work, but "to constrain the growth in the case load and the cost" (Mr N. Scott, Standing Committee E, col. 51).

The effect on other benefits

The effects of this Act are not confined to the incapacity benefits; two further consequences are worthy of note. The first is that the tighter test for incapacity for work will mean that about 100,000 more people will claim unemployment benefit in 1995–96 and 200,000 more in 1996–97 (Standing Committee E, col. 26). These claimants may be affected by an even more fundamental shift away from insurance-based benefits when the proposed "Jobseeker's Allowance" comes into force in April 1996. The second is that the new incapacity tests will apply throughout the social security system, except for SSP and the industrial injuries scheme (see the SSCBA 1992, s.171G(1), inserted by s.6(1)). They will therefore affect assessment of entitlement to the disability premium for income support where it is claimed on grounds of incapacity for work. At present a person incapable of work may qualify for the disability premium as part of income support (or housing benefit or council tax benefit) after 28 weeks. In future, entitlement to this premium will not arise until one year after the period of incapacity begins.

The scheme of the Act

The Act operates principally by way of amendments to the SSCBA 1992 and the SSAA 1992. One major feature of the Act is the reliance on regulation-making powers; in all there are over 30 separate provisions of this nature. See further the report of the House of Lords Select Committee on the Scrutiny of Delegated Powers (*5th Report*, 1993–94, H.L. Paper 41).

Section 1 deals with entitlement to and duration of incapacity benefit.

Section 2 concerns the rates of benefit payable for incapacity benefit.

Section 3 defines a "day of incapacity" and a "period of incapacity" for the purposes of incapacity benefit. It also makes provision for the position of incapacity benefit claimants who receive a councillor's allowance.

Section 4 makes provision for the main body of regulations concerning the transition from sickness and invalidity benefit to incapacity benefit.

Section 5 introduces the new tests of incapacity for work, the "own occupation" test and the "all work" test.

Section 6 makes supplementary provisions for the new incapacity tests, including deeming rules, disqualification rules and provisions governing the position of councillors.

Section 7 covers the transition from the current test of incapacity to the new test of incapacity for all other benefits.

Section 8 abolishes the lower rate of statutory sick pay.

Section 9 amends the conditions for entitlement to severe disablement allowance.

Section 10 amends the conditions for entitlement to disability working allowance.

Section 11 introduces the amendments and repeals in Scheds. 1 and 2.

Section 12 provides a general power to make minor transitional and consequential amendments.

Section 13 makes savings in respect of existing legislation.

Section 14 makes provision for Northern Ireland.

Section 15 concerns expenses under the Act.

Section 16 deals with the short title, commencement and extent of the Act.

COMMENCEMENT

The enabling provisions in ss.14, 15 and 16 came into force on Royal Assent (July 5, 1994) (s.16(2)). The bulk of the Act will come into force as and when the Secretary of State so appoints (s.16(3)). It is understood that the new system of incapacity benefit will come into operation on April 13, 1995.

ABBREVIATIONS

Bonner	: *Non-Means Tested Benefits: The Legislation* commentary by D. Bonner, I. Hooker and R. White (1993)
DAT	: disability appeal tribunal
DWA	: disability working allowance
Ogus and Barendt	: *The Law of Social Security* (3rd edn., 1988)
SDA	: severe disablement allowance
SSA 1986	: The Social Security Act 1986 (c. 50)
SSA 1990	: The Social Security Act 1990 (c. 27)
SSAA 1992	: The Social Security Administration Act 1992 (c. 5)
SSAT	: social security appeal tribunal
SSCBA 1992	: The Social Security Contributions and Benefits Act 1992 (c. 4)
SSP	: statutory sick pay

Incapacity benefit

Incapacity benefit: entitlement

1.—(1) In Part II of the Social Security Contributions and Benefits Act 1992 (contributory benefits), after section 30 insert—

"Incapacity benefit

Incapacity benefit: entitlement
30A.—(1) Subject to the following provisions of this section, a person who satisfies either of the following conditions is entitled to short-term incapacity benefit in respect of any day of incapacity for work which forms part of a period of incapacity for work.
(2) The conditions are that—
(a) he is under pensionable age on the day in question and satisfies the contribution conditions specified for short-term incapacity benefit in Schedule 3, Part I, paragraph 2; or
(b) on that day he is over pensionable age but not more than 5 years over that age, the period of incapacity for work began before he attained pensionable age, and—
    (i) he would be entitled to a Category A retirement pension if his entitlement had not been deferred or if he had not made an election under section 54(1) below, or
    (ii) he would be entitled to a Category B retirement pension by virtue of the contributions of his deceased spouse, but for any such deferment or election.
(3) A person is not entitled to short-term incapacity benefit for the first 3 days of any period of incapacity for work.
(4) In any period of incapacity for work a person is not entitled to short-term incapacity benefit for more than 364 days.
(5) Where a person ceases by virtue of subsection (4) above to be entitled to short-term incapacity benefit, he is entitled to long-term incapacity benefit in respect of any subsequent day of incapacity for work in the same period of incapacity for work on which he is not over pensionable age.".
(2) In Schedule 3 to the Social Security Contributions and Benefits Act 1992 (contribution conditions for entitlement to benefit), in the heading before paragraph 2 and in sub-paragraph (1) of that paragraph for "sickness benefit" substitute "short-term incapacity benefit".

DEFINITIONS
"day of incapacity for work": s.3(1) (s.30C(1)(a) of the SSCBA 1992).
"pensionable age": s.122(1) of the SSCBA 1992.
"period of incapacity for work": s.3(1) (s.30C(1)(b) of the SSCBA 1992).

GENERAL NOTE
This section, which inserts a new s.30A into the SSCBA 1992, sets out the conditions of entitlement to incapacity benefit.

Subs. (1)

Section 30A(1) of the SSCBA 1992
This provides that a person is entitled to short-term incapacity benefit for each "day of incapacity for work" which forms part of a "period of incapacity for work". Both these latter terms are defined by s.30C(1) of the SSCBA 1992, introduced by s.3(1) of this Act. The notion of "incapacity for work" itself is subject to regulations to be made under Pt. XIIA of the SSCBA 1992, introduced by ss.5 and 6 of this Act. In addition, one of the supplementary conditions laid down in s.30A(2) must be satisfied.

Section 30A(2) of the SSCBA 1992
There are two alternative supplementary conditions for entitlement to short-term incapacity benefit. The first, and most commonly relied upon in practice, is that the claimant is under pensionable age and satisfies the contribution conditions laid down in Sched. 3, para. 2 to the SSCBA 1992 (*i.e.* the existing contributions conditions for sickness benefit). The second is that the claimant is over pensionable age (but not more than five years over that age), his period of incapacity for work began before he reached pensionable age and *either* he would be entitled to a Category A retirement pension (but for deferment or an election to "de-retire" under the

SSCBA 1992, s.54) *or* he would be entitled to a Category B retirement pension but for such deferment or election (again, this essentially mirrors the existing alternative basis of entitlement to sickness benefit).

Section 30A(3) of the SSCBA 1992
As with sickness benefit, there are three waiting days in any period of incapacity for work for which short-term incapacity benefit will not be paid.

Section 30A(4) of the SSCBA 1992
This limits entitlement to short-term incapacity benefit to 364 days in any period of incapacity for work, and so the long-term rate of benefit only becomes payable after one year, as against six months for invalidity benefit.

No clear justification for the choice of 52 weeks has been advanced by the Government. According to one minister, "We decided to replace [invalidity benefit] with a new benefit and it was up to us to make a judgment about both the scope and the levels payable. The figures for the introduction of the new benefit were arrived at using that element of judgment. I cannot say that there is any justification for it besides that simple assertion" (Mr N. Scott, Standing Committee E, col. 195). An amendment to restrict payment of the lower rate of benefit to 196 days was lost by two votes at the Report stage in the House of Lords (*Hansard*, H.L. Vol. 554, cols. 1436–1451).

Section 30A(5) of the SSCBA 1992
After the maximum 364 days on short-term incapacity benefit have been exhausted, the claimant moves on to the long-term rate of incapacity benefit *providing* he is not over pensionable age. This proviso is an important difference from the position with invalidity benefit.

Subs. (2)
This is essentially a consequential amendment which ensures that the contribution conditions set out in Sched. 3, Pt. I, para. 2 to the SSCBA 1992 refer to short-term incapacity benefit rather than sickness benefit. The contribution conditions themselves remain the same. However, the existing concession which deems industrial injury claimants to have satisfied these conditions is to be repealed (Sched. 1, para. 29 and Sched. 2). This provision was introduced in 1982 following the abolition of short-term industrial injury benefit. Its repeal now will affect about 1,500 people (Standing Committee E, col. 23) and is symptomatic of the continuing erosion of the industrial injuries scheme.

Incapacity benefit: rate

2.—(1) In Part II of the Social Security Contributions and Benefits Act 1992, after section 30A (inserted by section 1 above), insert—

"Incapacity benefit: rate
30B.—(1) The amount payable by way of incapacity benefit in respect of any day is 1/7th of the appropriate weekly rate.

(2) Subject to the following provisions of this section, the weekly rate of short-term incapacity benefit is the lower or higher rate specified in Schedule 4, Part I, paragraph 2.

The benefit is payable at the lower rate so specified for the first 196 days of entitlement in any period of incapacity for work and at the higher rate so specified thereafter.

(3) In the case of a person over pensionable age the weekly rate of short-term incapacity benefit is, subject to subsection (4) below, that at which the relevant retirement pension referred to in section 30A(2)(b) above would have been payable.

But in determining that rate any increase of the following descriptions shall be disregarded—
   (a) any increase (for married women) under section 53(2) below or (for deferred retirement) under Schedule 5 to this Act;
   (b) any increase (for dependants) under section 80, 83 or 85 below; and
   (c) any increase (for Category A or Category B pensioners) under section 150 of the Administration Act (annual up-rating) of the sums mentioned in subsection (1)(e) of that section.

(4) In the case of a person who has been entitled to short-term incapacity benefit for 196 days or more in any period of incapacity for work and—

(a) is terminally ill, or

(b) he is entitled to the highest rate of the care component of disability living allowance,

the weekly rate of short-term incapacity benefit payable, if greater than the rate otherwise payable to him under subsection (2) or (3) above, shall be equal to the rate at which long-term incapacity benefit under section 30A above would be payable to him if he were entitled to it.

For the purposes of this subsection a person is terminally ill if he suffers from a progressive disease and his death in consequence of that disease can reasonably be expected within 6 months.

(5) References to short-term incapacity benefit at the higher rate shall be construed as including short-term incapacity benefit payable to any person who has been entitled to that benefit for 196 days or more in a period of incapacity for work, notwithstanding that the rate of benefit is determined in accordance with subsection (3) or (4) above.

(6) Subject as follows, the weekly rate of long-term incapacity benefit under section 30A above is that specified in Schedule 4, Part I, paragraph 2A.

(7) Regulations may provide that if a person is, on the qualifying date in relation to a period of incapacity for work, under such age as may be prescribed, the rate of long-term incapacity benefit under section 30A above payable to him in respect of any day in that period shall be increased by such amount as may be prescribed.

For this purpose 'the qualifying date' means the first day of the period of incapacity for work or such earlier day as may be prescribed.".

(2) In Part I of Schedule 4 to the Social Security Contributions and Benefits Act 1992 (rates of benefit, &c.: contributory periodical benefits), for paragraph 2 (sickness benefit) substitute—

| "2. Short-term incapacity benefit. | (a) lower rate . . . £43.45 |
| | (b) higher rate . . . £52.50"; |

and after that paragraph insert—

| "2A. Long-term incapacity benefit. | £57.60". |

(3) In section 150 of the Social Security Administration Act 1992 (annual up-rating of benefits), in subsection (1) (sums to be reviewed) after paragraph (a) insert—

"(aa) specified in regulations under section 30B(7) of that Act;";

and in subsection (3) (sums subject to mandatory up-rating), after "(a)(ii) or (iii)," insert "(aa),".·

(4) In section 80 of the Social Security Contributions and Benefits Act 1992 (increases for beneficiary's dependent children), in subsection (2) (benefits to which the section applies) for paragraphs (b) and (c) substitute—

"(b) short-term incapacity benefit at the higher rate or where the beneficiary is over pensionable age;

(c) long-term incapacity benefit; and".

(5) After section 86 of the Social Security Contributions and Benefits Act 1992 insert—

"Incapacity benefit: increase for adult dependants

86A.—(1) The weekly rates of short-term and long-term incapacity benefit shall, in such circumstances as may be prescribed, be increased for adult dependants by the appropriate amount specified in relation to benefit of that description in Schedule 4, Part IV, column (3).

(2) Regulations may provide that where the person in respect of whom an increase of benefit is claimed has earnings in excess of such amount as may be prescribed there shall be no increase in benefit under this section.".

(6) In Part IV of Schedule 4 to the Social Security Contributions and Benefits Act 1992 (rates of benefit, &c.: increases for dependants), after paragraph 1 insert—

"1A. Short-term incapacity benefit—		
(a) where the beneficiary is under pensionable age	11.00	26.90
(b) where the beneficiary is over pensionable age	11.00	33.10"

and for paragraph 2 substitute—

"2. Long-term incapacity benefit	11.00	34.50".

(7) Any order under section 150 of the Social Security Administration Act 1992 (up-rating orders) made by the Secretary of State before the commencement of this section shall include provision—

(a) making such increase (if any) in the sum specified in the provision inserted by subsection (2) above as the amount of short-term incapacity benefit at the higher rate as is necessary to make that sum equal to the higher rate or, if there is only one such rate, to the rate of statutory sick pay payable after the order comes into force; and

(b) making such increases in the other sums specified in the provisions inserted by subsections (2) and (6) above in Schedule 4 to the Social Security Contributions and Benefits Act 1992 as would have been required if the provisions in question had been in force at all material times.

DEFINITIONS

"Administration Act": s.174 of the SSCBA 1992.
"earnings": s.89(1) of the SSCBA 1992.
"entitled": s.122(1) of the SSCBA 1992.
"pensionable age": s.122(1) of the SSCBA 1992.
"qualifying date": s.30B(7) of the SSCBA 1992.
"terminally ill": s.30B(4) of the SSCBA 1992.

GENERAL NOTE

This section, which inserts a new s.30B into the SSCBA 1992, deals with the different rates of incapacity benefit. It also makes other consequential amendments to the SSCBA 1992 and the SSAA 1992.

Subs. (1)

Section 30B(1) of the SSCBA 1992

Incapacity benefit, like income support and SSP, is a daily benefit based on a seven-day week. In this respect it differs from sickness benefit and invalidity benefit which are based on a six-day week (excluding Sundays). The move to a seven-day benefit is not thought to have any significant financial implications (Standing Committee E, col. 86).

Section 30B(2) of the SSCBA 1992

Short-term incapacity benefit for claimants *under* pensionable age (those over pensionable age are covered by s.30B(3)) is payable at one of two rates; a lower rate for the first 196 days (28 weeks) of any period of incapacity and the higher rate thereafter. The lower rate will be equivalent to the current rate of sickness benefit and the higher rate to the higher rate of SSP. After 364 days the long-term rate of incapacity benefit is payable, which is at a higher rate still (ss.30A(5) and 30B(6)). This will be equivalent to the invalidity pension.

Section 30B(3) of the SSCBA 1992

Short-term incapacity benefit for claimants *over* pensionable age is payable at the same rate as the retirement pension that would have been payable. As with sickness benefit and invalidity benefit (see the SSCBA 1992, ss.31(6), (7) and 33(4), (5)), the weekly rate for this group does not include increases for married women, deferred retirement, dependants or guaranteed minimum pension.

Section 30B(4) of the SSCBA 1992

This provides for two special groups of claimants to qualify for what is essentially the long-term rate of incapacity benefit after 196 days instead of the usual 364 days. The two groups in question are the terminally ill and those entitled to the highest rate of the care component of disability living allowance (see the SSCBA 1992, s.72). Both these concessions were forced on the Government following pressure from the House of Lords.

Terminally ill. This definition is identical to that in the provisions governing attendance allowance and disability living allowance (the SSCBA 1992, s.66; see the discussion in *Bonner*).

Section 30B(5) of the SSCBA 1992

This provision was added at the same time as s.30B(4). Its purpose is to ensure that all claimants, including those who are over pensionable age, or terminally ill, or entitled to the highest rate of the care component of disability living allowance, will be able to benefit from training and DWA long-linking rules.

Section 30B(6) of the SSCBA 1992

This provides merely that the long-term rate of incapacity benefit, payable after 364 days, is as specified in the SSCBA 1992, Sched. 4, Pt. I, para. 2A (see subs. (2) below). This basic rate can be supplemented by age additions payable under regulations made by virtue of s.30B(7).

Section 30B(7) of the SSCBA 1992

This enables regulations to provide for the long-term rate of incapacity benefit to be increased by age-related additions. The "qualifying date" for this purpose will be *either* the first day of the period of incapacity of work *or* such earlier date as may be prescribed, *e.g.* for those previously on SSP or serving as members of H.M. Forces.

The age bands for the current age-related additions to invalidity benefit are set out in primary legislation (see the SSCBA 1992, s.34(3)). The higher rate invalidity allowance is paid for those under 40 years old on the first day of incapacity, the middle rate for those aged 40–49 and the lower rate for those aged 50–59 (or 50–54 if female).

The failure to adopt the same approach for incapacity benefit makes it easier for any future government to minimise parliamentary scrutiny of any erosion of these rates, although the age additions will be subject to mandatory uprating in the annual uprating round. Indeed, as originally drafted, the Bill would have enabled such regulations to be made without referral to the Social Security Advisory Committee. Following doubts expressed by the House of Lords Select Committee on the Scrutiny of Delegated Powers (*5th Report*, 1993–94, H.L. Paper 41, para. 16), the Government accepted an amendment reinstating the SSAC's role in this respect (*Hansard*, H.L. Vol. 554, col. 169). According to the DSS *Notes on Clauses*, regulations under this provision will specify that a higher rate age addition is payable for claimants aged under 35 and a lower rate if they are between 35 and 44 on the qualifying date. This in itself represents a significant reduction in the scope of these allowances, given that the majority of invalidity benefit claimants are aged 50 or over.

Subs. (2)

This simply substitutes the various rates of incapacity benefit for the existing rates of sickness benefit and invalidity benefit currently found in Sched. 4 to the SSCBA 1992. These rates are subject to annual up-rating in accordance with s.150 of the SSAA 1992.

Subs. (3)

This amendment to the SSAA 1992, s.150, ensures that the Secretary of State is under a duty to review annually the level of the age-related additions for incapacity benefit and to increase them in line with price inflation. The principal rates of incapacity benefit itself are automatically subject to this procedure, as was the case with sickness benefit and invalidity benefit.

Subs. (4)

Under the present law, child dependant additions can be paid with sickness benefit (but only if the claimant is over pensionable age) and with invalidity benefit. The original draft of this sub-section provided for such additions to be payable with short-term incapacity benefit (for claim-ants over pensionable age) and long-term incapacity benefit. The effect of this would have been that most claimants of incapacity benefit would not be eligible for child dependant additions in their first year of sickness. However, the House of Lords approved an amendment, against the Government's wishes, which enables such additions to be payable either immediately (for claim-ants over pensionable age) or after 196 days, *i.e.* at the point of transfer from the lower to the higher rate of short-term incapacity benefit, and thereafter with long-term incapacity benefit (*Hansard*, H.L. Vol. 554, cols. 1452–63 and Vol. 555, col. 377). This therefore maintains the existing position with regard to child dependant additions to invalidity benefit.

Subs. (5)

This inserts a new s.86A into the SSCBA 1992. Section 86A(1) is an enabling power providing for regulations to increase the rates of short-term and long-term incapacity benefit where the claimant has an adult dependant. According to the DSS *Notes on Clauses*, the main conditions of entitlement to such an increase will be that:

(a) the claimant has a dependent spouse aged 60 or over; or

(b) the claimant has a dependent spouse or other partner and is also receiving an increase for a dependent child; or

(c) the claimant (i) is under pensionable age and receiving short-term incapacity benefit, and (ii) has a dependent spouse or other partner, and (iii) has a dependent child, for whom an increase would be payable if child dependency additions were available with the lower rate of short-term incapacity benefit.

This is obviously less generous than the existing provision for adult dependency additions.

Section 86A(2) allows regulations to be made to prevent the payment of adult dependency increases where the adult dependant in question has earnings over a prescribed level. "Earn-ings" in this context includes occupational or personal pensions (see the SSCBA 1992, s.89(1)).

Subs. (6)

This subsection simply substitutes the rates of dependency increases for incapacity benefit for those relating to sickness and invalidity benefit.

Subs. (7)

This provides for the higher rate of short-term incapacity benefit, specified in subs. (2) above, to be increased before the commencement of the Act, but only if the Secretary of State decides to increase the rate of SSP. It also enables the other sums specified in subss. (2) and (6) to be up-rated in line with the April 1995 benefits up-rating. The Government is committed to increasing all the basic rates, age-related additions and dependency increases in line with the general up-rating of benefits (*Hansard*, H.C. Vol. 239, col. 207).

Incapacity benefit: supplementary provisions

3.—(1) In Part II of the Social Security Contributions and Benefits Act 1992, after section 30B (inserted by section 2(1) above) insert—

"Incapacity benefit: days and periods of incapacity for work

30C.—(1) For the purposes of any provisions of this Act relating to incapacity benefit, subject to the following provisions and save as other-wise expressly provided—

(a) a day of incapacity for work means a day on which a person is incapable of work;

(b) a period of incapacity for work means a period of 4 or more con-secutive days, each of which is a day of incapacity for work; and

(c) any two such periods not separated by a period of more than 8 weeks shall be treated as one period of incapacity for work.

(2) Any day which falls within the maternity allowance period (as defined in section 35(2) below) shall be treated for the purposes of any provision of this Act relating to incapacity benefit as a day of incapacity for work unless the woman is disqualified for receiving a maternity allowance for that day by virtue of regulations under section 35(3)(a) below.

(3) Regulations may make provision (subject to the preceding provisions of this section) as to the days which are or are not to be treated as days of incapacity for work for the purposes of any provision of this Act relating to incapacity benefit.

(4) The Secretary of State may by regulations provide—

(a) that paragraph (b) of subsection (1) above shall have effect as if the reference there to 4 consecutive days were to such lesser number of days, whether consecutive or not, within such period of consecutive days as may be prescribed; and

(b) that paragraph (c) of that subsection shall have effect as if for the reference to 8 weeks there were substituted a reference to such larger number of weeks as may be prescribed.

(5) Where—

(a) a person who is engaged and normally engaged in remunerative work ceases to be so engaged, and

(b) he is entitled to a disability working allowance for the week in which there falls the last day on which he is so engaged, and

(c) he qualified for a disability working allowance for that week by virtue of the higher rate of short-term incapacity benefit, or long-term incapacity benefit under section 30A above, having been payable to him, and

(d) the first day after he ceases to be engaged as mentioned in paragraph (a) above is for him a day of incapacity for work and falls not later than the end of the period of two years beginning with the last day for which he was entitled to such benefit,

any day since that day which fell within a week for which he was entitled to a disability working allowance shall be treated for the purposes of any claim for such benefit for a period commencing after he ceases to be engaged as mentioned in paragraph (a) above as having been a day of incapacity for work.

(6) Where—

(a) a person becomes engaged in training for work, and

(b) he was entitled to the higher rate of short-term incapacity benefit, or to long-term incapacity benefit under section 30A above, for one or more of the 56 days immediately before he became so engaged, and

(c) the first day after he ceases to be so engaged is for him a day of incapacity for work and falls not later than the end of the period of two years beginning with the last day for which he was entitled to such benefit,

any day since that day in which he was engaged in training for work shall be treated for the purposes of any claim for such benefit for a period commencing after he ceases to be so engaged as having been a day of incapacity for work.

In this subsection "training for work" means training for work in pursuance of arrangements made under section 2(1) of the Employment and Training Act 1973 or section 2(3) of the Enterprise and New Towns (Scotland) Act 1990 or training of such other description as may be prescribed.

(7) For the purposes of this section "week" means any period of 7 days.

Incapacity benefit: construction of references to days of entitlement
30D.—(1) The following provisions have effect in calculating for the purposes of—
  (a) section 30A(4) above (length of entitlement to short-term incapacity benefit),
  (b) section 30B(2) above (period after which short-term incapacity benefit is payable at higher rate),
  (c) section 30B(4) above (period after which incapacity benefit is payable at long-term rate in case of terminal illness), and
  (d) section 30B(5) above (construction of references to short-term incapacity benefit at the higher rate),
the number of days for which a person has been entitled to short-term incapacity benefit.
  (2) There shall be included—
  (a) the first three days of the period of incapacity for work, and
  (b) in the case of a woman, any days for which she was entitled to maternity allowance.
  (3) There shall also be included such days as may be prescribed in respect of which a person was entitled to statutory sick pay, and on the first of which he satisfied the contribution conditions for short-term incapacity benefit.
  (4) There shall be excluded any days in respect of which a person was disqualified for receiving incapacity benefit.

Incapacity benefit: reduction for councillor's allowance
30E.—(1) Where the net amount of councillor's allowance to which a person is entitled in respect of any week exceeds such amount as may be prescribed, an amount equal to the excess shall be deducted from the amount of any incapacity benefit to which he is entitled in respect of that week, and only the balance remaining (if any) shall be payable.
  (2) In this section "councillor's allowance" means—
  (a) in England or Wales, an allowance under or by virtue of—
          (i) section 173 or 177 of the Local Government Act 1972, or
          (ii) a scheme made by virtue of section 18 of the Local Government and Housing Act 1989,
      other than such an allowance as is mentioned in section 173(4) of the Local Government Act 1972, or
  (b) in Scotland, an allowance under or by virtue of section 49 of the Local Government (Scotland) Act 1973 or a scheme made by virtue of section 18 of the Local Government and Housing Act 1989;
and where any such allowance is paid otherwise than weekly, an amount calculated or estimated in accordance with regulations shall be regarded as the weekly amount of the allowance.
  (3) In subsection (1) above "net amount", in relation to any councillor's allowance to which a person is entitled, means the aggregate amount of the councillor's allowance or allowances to which he is entitled for the week in question, reduced by the amount of any expenses incurred by him in that week in connection with his membership of the council or councils in question.".
  (2) In Schedule 3 to the Social Security Contributions and Benefits Act 1992 (contribution conditions for entitlement to benefit), at the end of paragraph 2 (conditions for entitlement to short-term incapacity benefit) add—
      "(7) Where a person makes a claim for incapacity benefit and does not satisfy the second contribution condition (specified in sub-paragraph (3) above) and, in a later benefit year in which he would satisfy that

condition had no such claim been made, he makes a further claim for incapacity benefit, the previous claim shall be disregarded.".

DEFINITIONS
"councillor's allowance": s.30E(2) of the SSCBA 1992.
"day of incapacity for work": s.30C(1)(a) of the SSCBA 1992.
"entitled": s.122(1) of the SSCBA 1992.
"net amount": s.30E(3) of the SSCBA 1992.
"period of incapacity for work": s.30C(1)(b) of the SSCBA 1992.
"training for work": s.30C(6) of the SSCBA 1992.
"week": s.30C(7) of the SSCBA 1992.

GENERAL NOTE
This section, which makes further amendments to the SSCBA 1992, sets out supplementary provisions for entitlement to incapacity benefit. Subsection (1) inserts new ss.30C–30E into the SSCBA 1992. Section 30C defines days and periods of incapacity for the purposes of incapacity benefit. Section 30D defines the days to be included when calculating the number of days of entitlement to short-term incapacity benefit. Section 30E concerns entitlement to incapacity benefit for persons in receipt of a councillor's allowance. Subsection (2) makes provision for claimants who do not satisfy the contribution conditions for incapacity benefit when they first make their claim.

Subs. (1)

Section 30C(1) of the SSCBA 1992
The definitions of "day of incapacity for work" and "period of incapacity for work" are broadly familiar in that they follow the model contained in the SSCBA 1992, s.57(1). Thus a period of incapacity for work is defined as four or more consecutive days of incapacity for work, and periods of such incapacity separated by a period of eight weeks or less will be treated as a single period of incapacity under the linking rule (*cf.* the SSCBA 1992, s.57(1)(d)). (These definitions are subject to amendment in special cases by regulations made under s.30C(4)).
There are two reasons for the linking rule. First, it allows claimants suffering from repeated bouts of incapacity to link up those periods in order to establish entitlement to the higher rates of incapacity benefit where appropriate. Secondly, it provides some incentive for claimants to try to return to work knowing that they will be able to receive their previous rate of benefit should that work last no more than eight weeks.
The one vital difference as compared with the existing provisions is that the concept of incapacity for work itself is not defined in primary legislation. For the purposes of sickness benefit and invalidity benefit, a day of incapacity for work is one on which the claimant "is, or is deemed in accordance with regulations to be, incapable of work by reason of some specific disease or bodily or mental disablement"; also "work" means "work which the person can reasonably be expected to do" (see the SSCBA 1992, s.57(1)(a)). Under the new provisions, incapacity for work is to be defined by regulations made under the SSCBA 1992, Pt. XIIA (see s.5 below, and the Introduction and General Note, above).

Section 30C(2) of the SSCBA 1992
This provides that any day within the maternity allowance period is to be treated as a day of incapacity for work for incapacity benefit purposes, unless a disqualification is in operation. This carries forward a provision already found in the SSCBA 1992, s.57(2).

Section 30C(3) of the SSCBA 1992
This regulation making power will be used to provide that days where, *e.g.* a person is in prison or outside Great Britain will not count as days of incapacity for work.

Section 30C(4) of the SSCBA 1992
This enables regulations to be made modifying the definitions in s.30C(1)(b) and (c). This power will be used to make special provision for people with short and intermittent spells of incapacity for work, *e.g.* for medical treatment, who would otherwise have difficulty in building up an unbroken period of incapacity for work (DSS *Notes on Clauses*).

Section 30C(5) of the SSCBA 1992
This is a special and more generous linking rule for claimants who have been in receipt of DWA and have to return to claiming incapacity benefit. The normal linking rule is that separate

periods of incapacity for work can only be aggregated if they are eight weeks or less apart (see s.30C(1)(c)). This subsection applies to claimants who have been working and receiving DWA, and who qualified for DWA on the basis of receiving either short-term incapacity benefit at the higher rate or the long-term rate of incapacity benefit. It allows such claimants to return to the relevant rate of incapacity benefit on leaving their job, without having to serve the appropriate qualifying period again, providing the two periods of incapacity for work are separated by no more than two years. It therefore carries forward the concession which currently applies in respect of DWA recipients who formerly claimed invalidity benefit (see the SSCBA 1992, s.33(7)).

Section 30C(6) of the SSCBA 1992
This provision is analogous to new s.30C(5) of the SSCBA 1992, but extends the two-year linking rule to claimants who have been engaged in training for work, rather than being in remunerative work and in receipt of DWA, between two periods of incapacity for work. Relevant training courses for these purposes are likely to include three official programmes, namely Employment Rehabilitation, Community Action and North Norfolk Action. Non-government training courses will be included providing they are full-time (*i.e.* 16 hours or more a week) and have the sole or main purpose of enabling trainees to acquire occupational or vocational skills (*Hansard*, H.L. Vol. 554, col. 1465).

Section 30D of the SSCBA 1992
This new section defines the days to be included when calculating the number of days of entitlement to the various rates of incapacity benefit (including the special cases covered by s.30B(4) and (5)). Days to be taken into account include the three waiting days (see subs. (2)(a) and s.30A(3) of the SSCBA 1992) and days of entitlement to maternity allowance (subs. (2)(b)). Regulations may also provide for days of entitlement to SSP to count for these purposes, so long as the contribution conditions for incapacity benefit were satisfied on the first such day (subs. (3)). Days for which the person is disqualified are excluded for these purposes (subs. (4)).

Section 30E of the SSCBA 1992
This new section deals with the inter-relationship between incapacity benefit and allowances received by councillors. Where the net amount of a councillor's allowance exceeds a prescribed sum, the excess will be deducted from the relevant weekly amount of incapacity benefit. The definitions of "councillor's allowance" and "net amount" (subss. (2) and (3)) are in identical terms to those used in the SSCBA 1992, s.58 in relation to invalidity benefit.

Subs. (2)
This amendment to the SSCBA 1992, Sched. 4, Pt. I, para. 2, concerns the contribution conditions for incapacity benefit. The effect is that where a person does not satisfy these conditions at the outset of his claim, the claim will be disregarded if a further claim is made from a later date on which the contribution conditions would be met.

Power to provide for the transition to incapacity benefit

4.—(1) The Secretary of State may by regulations make such provision as appears to him to be necessary or expedient for the purposes of, or in connection with, the transition to incapacity benefit from sickness benefit and invalidity benefit.

Nothing in the following provisions of this section shall be construed as restricting the generality of that power.

(2) In this section—
"commencement" means the commencement of sections 1 to 3 above and the consequent repeal of the provisions of the Social Security Contributions and Benefits Act 1992 relating to sickness benefit and invalidity benefit; and
"prescribed" means prescribed by regulations under this section.

(3) Regulations under this section may provide that where a person was entitled to sickness benefit or invalidity benefit immediately before commencement any award of sickness benefit or invalidity benefit shall have effect after commencement, in accordance with the regulations and subject to such modifications as may be prescribed, as an award of incapacity benefit.

In the following provisions of this section such awards are referred to as "transitional awards" of incapacity benefit.

(4) The reference in subsection (3) above to a person who was entitled to sickness benefit or invalidity benefit includes a person who would have been so entitled but for being disqualified by virtue of regulations under section 32 or 59 of the Social Security Contributions and Benefits Act 1992; and regulations under this section may provide that any such disqualification shall have such corresponding effect as may be prescribed in relation to the transitional award.

(5) Regulations under this section may provide that a person's entitlement under a transitional award of incapacity benefit shall, except as may be prescribed, be subject to satisfying the conditions of entitlement to incapacity benefit, and may in particular provide—

(a) for the determination in accordance with Part XIIA of the Social Security Contributions and Benefits Act 1992 of the question whether that person is incapable of work; and

(b) for the termination of his entitlement on his attaining pensionable age.

Excepted cases may be defined, in particular, by reference to the age of the person on commencement and whether he was receiving invalidity benefit on 1st December 1993 (the date of the announcement of the new scheme).

(6) Regulations under this section may provide—

(a) that days before commencement which were days of incapacity for work for the purposes of sickness benefit or invalidity benefit, and such other days as may be prescribed, shall be treated as having been days of incapacity for work for the purposes of incapacity benefit, and

(b) that days of entitlement to sickness benefit or invalidity benefit, and such other days as may be prescribed, shall be treated as having been days of entitlement to incapacity benefit.

Such provision may be made for the purposes of a transitional award of incapacity benefit or of enabling a claim for incapacity benefit to be made after commencement on the basis that a day of incapacity for work after commencement forms part of a period of incapacity for work beginning before commencement; and such cases are referred to in the following provisions of this section as "transitional cases".

(7) Regulations under this section may provide—

(a) for the rate of short-term incapacity benefit under a transitional award to be increased, in such cases as may be prescribed, as if that benefit were sickness benefit and the provisions of Part IV of the Social Security Contributions and Benefits Act 1992 (increases for dependants) continued to apply to that benefit; and

(b) for the payment in transitional cases, in such circumstances as may be prescribed, of long-term incapacity benefit to persons over pensionable age.

(8) Regulations under this section may provide that in transitional cases the rate of short-term incapacity benefit at the higher rate or of long-term incapacity benefit shall be calculated—

(a) by reference to the rate of invalidity benefit, and of any relevant related allowance, addition or increase, paid or payable immediately before commencement, with such up-rating (if any) as may be provided for in accordance with the regulations (whether by applying the provisions of section 150 of the Social Security Administration Act 1992 or otherwise), and

(b) without any increase or addition which would otherwise be payable with incapacity benefit.

(9) If regulations make provision of the kind mentioned in subsection (8) above they may also make with respect to any additional pension element of incapacity benefit provision corresponding to any of the provisions in force before commencement with respect to the additional pension element of invalidity pension.

(10) Regulations under this section may provide, in relation to transitional cases where the rate of incapacity benefit falls to be calculated by reference to the rate of dependency allowance paid or payable before commencement, that any old saving provisions shall have effect subject to the regulations or shall cease to have effect in accordance with the regulations.

For the purposes of this subsection—

"dependency allowance" means an allowance of the kind provided for in Part IV of the Social Security Contributions and Benefits Act 1992, and

"old saving provisions" means provisions of any description, including administrative provisions, in connection with a previous change affecting entitlement to or the amount of dependency allowances, preserving a person's position in any respect.

(11) Section 175(2) to (4) of the Social Security Contributions and Benefits Act 1992 (general provisions as to regulations and orders) apply in relation to the power conferred by subsection (1) above as they apply in relation to power conferred by that Act to make regulations.

(12) For the period of four years from Royal Assent a statutory instrument which contains (whether alone or with other provisions) any regulations under this section shall not be made unless a draft of the instrument has been laid before Parliament and approved by a resolution of each House.

(13) A statutory instrument—

(a) which contains (whether alone or with other provisions) any regulations made under this section, and

(b) which is not subject to any requirement that a draft of the instrument be laid before and approved by a resolution of each House of Parliament,

shall be subject to annulment in pursuance of a resolution of either House of Parliament.

DEFINITIONS
"commencement": subs. (2).
"dependency allowance": subs. (10).
"entitled": s.122(1) of the SSCBA 1992.
"old savings provisions": subs. (10).
"pensionable age": s.122(1) of the SSCBA 1992.
"prescribed": subs. (2).
"transitional awards": subs. (3).
"transitional cases": subs. (6).

GENERAL NOTE
This section enables regulations to be made in connection with the transition from sickness benefit and invalidity benefit to incapacity benefit. Statutory instruments under this section are to be subject to the affirmative resolution procedure for four years from the date of Royal Assent (subs. (12)), and the negative procedure thereafter.

Subs. (1)
This is a very broad enabling power, which is not to be regarded as fettered by any of the specific regulation making powers that follow.

Subs. (3)
This provides that sickness benefit and invalidity benefit awards, in existence immediately before the coming into force of ss.1–3 of this Act, will become awards of incapacity benefit and be known as "transitional awards". By virtue of subs. (4), this includes claimants subject to disqualification at the point of change-over, so that such disqualifications will continue to run.

Subs. (5)
This allows regulations to be made providing that entitlement under transitional awards (see subs. (3)) will be subject to satisfying the entitlement conditions for incapacity benefit. Thus entitlement will be dependent upon meeting the new test to be laid down in regulations under the SSCBA 1992, Pt. XIIA (see s.5) and will cease on reaching pensionable age.

It also provides for certain claimants to be exempt from meeting the new conditions of entitlement. It is anticipated that this group will constitute about half of all those entitled to invalidity benefit in April 1995. These will include: those aged 58 and over on the day that the new scheme is introduced and who have been continuously in receipt of invalidity benefit since December 1, 1993; people in receipt of the highest rate of the disability living allowance care component; people who are terminally ill; and those suffering from one of a number of severe incapacitating conditions to be prescribed in regulations.

Most claimants exempt from the new tests are likely to fall into the first of these categories, which is also the most controversial. The age limit for exemption has been set at 58 years old "as a balance between the competing concerns of the taxpayer and the existing recipients" (*per* Baroness Cumberlege, *Hansard*, H.L. Vol. 554, col. 164). However, on the basis of the DSS's own research evidence, there is at least a good argument for setting the age at 50 rather than 58. This is because claimants aged over 50 are more likely to have a combination of health problems and to show less attachment to the labour market (see Erens and Ghate, *Invalidity Benefit: a longitudinal survey of new recipients*, DSS Research Report No. 20 (1993)).

Subs. (6)

This introduces the concept of "transitional cases" (to be distinguished from "transitional awards" under subs. (3) above). The category of transitional cases consists of transitional awards and those cases where the claim is based on periods of incapacity both before and after the new provisions come into effect. Thus this subsection enables regulations to be made providing for days of incapacity for work both before and after ss.1–3 of the Act come into force to be treated as days of incapacity for work for incapacity benefit. Similarly, days of entitlement to sickness benefit or invalidity benefit are to be treated as days of entitlement to incapacity benefit.

Subs. (7)

This enables the rate of short-term incapacity benefit under a transitional award (see subs. (3)) to be increased by dependency additions in the same way as sickness benefit. It also allows long-term incapacity benefit to be paid in transitional cases (see subs. (6)) to persons who are over pensionable age. The long-term rate is not normally payable to such claimants (s.30A(5)).

Subs. (8)

This regulation-making power applies to transitional cases (see subs. (6)). It enables awards of short-term incapacity benefit at the higher rate and of long-term incapacity benefit to be based on the appropriate rate of invalidity benefit prior to the change-over. This will include any relevant additions or increases, subject to any up-rating. To avoid duplication, any analogous additions to incapacity benefit will not be payable in such cases. Note, however, subs. (9) below, in connection with the additional pension element.

Subs. (9)

Separate provision is required for transitional cases in respect of the additional pension element of invalidity benefit. The reason is that whereas the greater part of individual awards in transitional cases are to be subject to up-rating (see subs. (8)), the Government's intention is to freeze the rate of additional pension at the rate in payment immediately before the new provisions come into force.

Subs. (10)

This allows for regulations to be made enabling existing forms of transitional protection for dependency increases to be rationalised from April 1995. This will only affect a small number of claimants, none of whom will experience any losses at the point of change-over. The Government also intends to use this power to abolish the old earnings rule providing for the tapered withdrawal of adult dependency increases of invalidity benefit. Instead an absolute ceiling will be set on this form of protection, equating to the point at which protection currently ceases. When earnings exceed this limit for more than eight weeks, protection will be lost (*Hansard*, H.L. Vol. 554, cols. 1466–67).

Test of incapacity for work

Test of incapacity for work

5. In the Social Security Contributions and Benefits Act 1992 (general provisions), after section 171 insert—

"PART XIIA

INCAPACITY FOR WORK

Test of incapacity for work

171A.—(1) For the purposes of this Act, save as otherwise expressly provided, whether a person is capable or incapable of work shall be determined in accordance with the provisions of this Part of this Act.

(2) Regulations may make provision as to—

(a) the information or evidence required for the purpose of determining whether a person is capable or incapable of work, and

(b) the manner in which that information or evidence is to be provided, .

and may provide that if a person without good cause fails to provide that information or evidence, or to do so in the manner required, he shall be treated as capable of work.

(3) Regulations may provide that in any case where a question arises as to whether a person is capable of work—

(a) he may be called to attend for such medical examination as may be required in accordance with regulations, and

(b) if he fails without good cause to attend for or submit himself to such examination, he shall be treated as capable of work.

(4) Regulations may prescribe for the purposes of this section—

(a) matters which are or are not to be taken into account in determining whether a person does or does not have good cause for any act or omission, or

(b) circumstances in which a person is or is not to be regarded as having or not having good cause for any act or omission.

The own occupation test

171B.—(1) Where a person has been engaged in remunerative work for more than 8 weeks in the 21 weeks immediately preceding the day with respect to which it falls to be determined whether he is or was incapable of work, the test applicable is the own occupation test.

(2) The own occupation test is whether he is incapable by reason of some specific disease or bodily or mental disablement of doing work which he could reasonably be expected to do in the course of the occupation in which he was so engaged.

(3) Where for any purpose of this Act it is determined in relation to a person—

(a) that the test applicable with respect to any day is the own occupation test, and

(b) that he is on that test incapable of work,

that test remains applicable in his case until the end of the spell of incapacity beginning with that day or, as the case may be, in which that day falls, or until the 197th day of incapacity for work in that spell, whichever is the earlier.

For this purpose a "spell of incapacity" means a series of 4 or more consecutive days of incapacity for work; and any two such spells not separated by a period of more than 8 weeks shall be treated as one spell of incapacity.

(4) For the purposes of subsection (3) above a day of incapacity for work means a day—

(a) with respect to which it has been determined for any purpose of this Act that the person in question was incapable of work, or

(b) in respect of which he was entitled to statutory sick pay, or

(c) in the case of a woman, which falls within the maternity allowance period, or

(d) which in accordance with regulations is to be treated for those purposes as a day of incapacity for work.

(5) Any provision of this Act apart from subsection (4) above under or by virtue of which a day is or is not to be treated for any purpose as a day of incapacity for work shall be disregarded for the purposes of this section.

(6) Provision may be made by regulations defining for the purposes of this section what is meant by "remunerative work".

The regulations may, in particular, provide—

(a) for "remunerative work" to be defined by reference to the number of hours worked per week; and

(b) for training of any prescribed description to be treated as if it were remunerative work.

(7) Provision may be made by regulations as to the application of this section in cases where a person engages in more than one occupation or in different kinds of work.

(8) The Secretary of State may by regulations provide that subsection (3) above shall have effect as if—

(a) the reference there to 4 consecutive days were to such lesser number of days, whether consecutive or not, within such period of consecutive days as may be prescribed; and

(b) for the reference to 8 weeks there were substituted a reference to such larger number of weeks as may be prescribed.

The all work test

171C.—(1) Where in any case the own occupation test is not applicable, or has ceased to apply, the test applicable is the all work test.

(2) Provision shall be made by regulations—

(a) defining the all work test by reference to the extent of a person's incapacity by reason of some specific disease or bodily or mental disablement to perform such activities as may be prescribed, and

(b) as to the manner of assessing whether the all work test is satisfied.

(3) Regulations may provide that where the all work test applies the test shall, if the prescribed conditions are met, be treated as satisfied until the person has been assessed or he falls to be treated as capable of work in accordance with regulations under section 171A(2) or (3) above or section 171E below.

The prescribed conditions may include the condition that it has not previously been determined, within such period as may be prescribed, that the person in question is or is to be treated as capable of work.".

Definitions
"day of incapacity for work": s.171B(4) of the SSCBA 1992.
"maternity allowance period": s.35(2) of the SSCBA 1992.
"medical examination": s.121(1) of the SSCBA 1992.
"remunerative work": s.171B(6) of the SSCBA 1992.
"spell of incapacity": s.171B(3) of the SSCBA 1992.

General Note
In many ways this is the core of the Act. This section inserts three new sections into the SSCBA 1992 which lay down new tests for incapacity for work. These tests are not confined to incapacity benefit, but are of general application throughout the social security system (s.171A (1), but see s.171G(1), inserted by s.6 below). There are two tests involved. The first is the test of a person's ability to carry out his own occupation (the "own occupation" test), which applies for the first 196 days of incapacity where a person has worked for more than eight weeks in the previous 21 weeks (s.171B). The second is the "all work" test, which applies in all other cases (s.171C). In both cases, the full details of the new tests will not be known until regulations are made later in 1994.

Section 171A of the SSCBA 1992

Section 171A(1) provides that the question as to whether a person is incapable of work for the purposes of benefits under the SSCBA 1992 generally is to be determined in accordance with Pt. XIIA of that Act, as inserted by ss.5 and 6 of the 1994 Act. The tests laid down by Pt. XIIA will therefore apply to SDA and be relevant to entitlement to the disability premiums for income support, housing benefit and council tax benefit. The new tests do not apply to SSP or the industrial injuries scheme (s.171G(1), inserted by s.6 of the 1994 Act). The remainder of s.171A consists of self-explanatory regulation-making powers.

Section 171B of the SSCBA 1992

This section introduces the "own occupation" test; this test will normally apply for the first 28 weeks of any period of incapacity, subject to the qualifications below.

Subs. (1)

The "own occupation" test, which judges a person's incapacity for work by reference to his normal occupation, only applies if that individual has been engaged in remunerative work for more than eight weeks in the 21 weeks immediately before the incapacity begins.

As originally drafted, the Bill required a normal occupation to be established by eight weeks' work in the previous 12. The Government accepted that this period was too short, and brought forward an amendment at the Committee stage in the House of Lords to increase it to 21 weeks (*Hansard*, H.L. Vol. 554, cols. 311–314). There is some logic in the choice of 21 weeks as it represents the aggregate of eight weeks' work plus the maximum of 13 weeks during which a claimant of unemployment benefit is allowed to restrict his search for work to his own occupation.

Has been engaged in remunerative work. The use of the expression "has been engaged" is sufficient to cover people on paid leave from their employment. The term "remunerative work" is to be defined by regulations under s.171B(6) and (7).

Subs. (2)

This defines the "own occupation" test (in contrast the "all work" test, introduced by s.171C, is not defined on the face of the Act). This test is very similar to the existing test of incapacity for work which applies to the early part of a claim for benefit (an important distinction is that there is currently no statutory maximum for the period during which this test applies, although DSS practice is not to look beyond the claimant's occupation for the first six months). The "own occupation" test "will assess a person's capacity to do his normal job. It will take into account relevant factors, including a person's general state of physical and mental health, disabilities and capacity to cope with pain or stress. However, it will only take these factors into account in so far as they affect a person's capacity to do his usual job" (*per* Baroness Cumberlege, *Hansard*, H.L. Vol. 554, col. 300).

Some specific disease or bodily or mental disablement. This expression is identical to that currently used in the existing test of incapacity for work under s.57(1)(a)(ii) of the SSCBA 1992. It will therefore presumably be interpreted in the same way (see *Bonner*, pp. 193–194 and *Ogus and Barendt*, pp. 149–150).

Work which he can reasonably be expected to do. Again, this replicates the terminology used in the existing test for incapacity for work under s.57(1)(a) of the SSCBA 1992 (see *Bonner*, pp. 188–190 and *Ogus and Barendt*, pp. 150–152). There is, however, a subtle difference in context. In invalidity benefit appeals, the issue is often whether the job(s) suggested by the adjudication officer as appropriate employment for the appellant constitute "work which the person can reasonably be expected to do" within s.57(1). In such cases the appellant has usually been on invalidity benefit for some time and it is clear that incapacity should be judged against a wider range of jobs, and not just the previous employment (see, *e.g.* R(S) 3/81). In the definition of the new "own occupation" test, the question is whether the claimant is capable of work "which he could reasonably be expected to do" in the course of that occupation. This means that incapacity for work must be judged for the first 28 weeks according to the normal physical demands of the "own occupation".

Subs. (3)

This specifies the period of time during which the "own occupation" test applies. So long as the claimant has been found to be incapable of work according to the "own occupation" test, that standard applies for the first 28 weeks of incapacity, or until the end of the spell of incapacity, whichever is the shorter. It also provides a linking rule for periods of incapacity for work.

Day of incapacity for work. This is defined by s.171B(4) below.

Subs. (4)

Maternity allowance period. This is defined by s.35(2) of the SSCBA 1992 as the equivalent of the maternity pay period under s.165 of that Act, were the claimant entitled to statutory maternity pay.

Subs. (5)

The purpose of this opaquely drafted provision is to ensure that claimants who benefit from the DWA or training long-linking rules (s.30C(5) and (6), inserted by s.3 above) are not disadvantaged. Those rules treat days following certain periods in receipt of DWA or training as days of incapacity for work. The intention behind subs. (5) is to ensure that in such cases the "own occupation" and not the "all work" test will be applicable (*per* Viscount Astor, *Hansard*, H.L. Vol. 554, cols. 322–323).

Subs. (6)

Remunerative work. This is defined for the purposes of the income-related benefits as 16 hours' work a week, which is done for payment or in expectation of payment (see, *e.g.* Income Support (General) Regulations 1987 (S.I. 1987 No. 1967), reg. 5(1)). It remains to be seen whether the same definition will be adopted for the purposes of the "own occupation" test, but this would seem likely.

Subs. (7)

This enables regulations to make special provision for establishing the "own occupation" where a claimant has more than one job. The Government has given no indications as to how it intends to exercise this power.

Subs. (8)

This allows regulations to make exceptions to the definition of a spell of incapacity for work. This will enable persons who are incapable of work for short periods but on a regular basis to aggregate those periods of incapacity. This could apply to claimants undergoing kidney dialysis or chemotherapy.

Section 171C of the SSCBA 1992

Subs. (1)

Section 171C(1) provides for a general "all work" test. This applies where the "own occupation" test (s.171B) either is not applicable (because the claimant does not have an "own occupation" as defined by s.171B(1) and (2)) or has ceased to apply (because the 196 days period has expired).

Subs. (2)

If s.5 is the core of this Act, s.171C(2) is the heart of the core. However, this provision gives no hint as to the precise nature of the "all work" test. See further the Introduction and General Note above.

Some specific disease or bodily or mental disablement. See the annotations to subs. (2) above.

Subs. (3)

This enables regulations to be made which will treat the "all work" test as satisfied in certain circumstances. This will enable benefit to remain in payment after the first 28 weeks while information is gathered and any medical examinations carried out in order to reach a determination under the "all work" test. Obviously this deeming rule will not apply where the person has been treated as capable of work in accordance with s.171A(2) or (3) or s.171E of the SSCBA 1992, *i.e.* where the claimant has not shown good cause for failing to provide information, attend for a medical examination, etc.

The final paragraph in s.171C(3) is designed to ensure that a claimant who has previously been found to be capable of work, or treated as so capable, should not be deemed incapable if he makes a further claim for benefit when his circumstances have not changed. It is therefore intended to stop people "playing the system" (*per* Viscount Astor, *Hansard*, H.L. Vol. 554, col. 310).

Test of incapacity for work: supplementary provisions

6.—(1) In the Social Security Contributions and Benefits Act 1992, after the sections inserted by section 5 above, insert—

"Incapacity for work: persons to be treated as incapable or capable of work

171D.—(1) Regulations may provide that a person shall be treated as capable of work, or as incapable of work, in such cases or circumstances as may be prescribed.

(2) Regulations may, in particular, provide that a person shall be treated as capable of work if he does work of a prescribed description, or more than the prescribed amount of work of a prescribed description.

Accordingly regulations may provide that a person shall not be treated as capable of work by reason only of his doing such work as may be prescribed, or no more than the prescribed amount of work of a prescribed description.

Incapacity for work: disqualification, &c.

171E.—(1) Regulations may provide for disqualifying a person for receiving any benefit, allowance or other advantage under any provision for the purposes of which this Part of this Act applies, or, in such cases as may be prescribed, provide that a person shall be treated as capable of work, if—

(a) he has become incapable of work through his own misconduct;

(b) he fails without good cause to attend for or submit himself to such medical or other treatment as may be required in accordance with the regulations; or

(c) he fails without good cause to observe any prescribed rules of behaviour.

(2) Regulations shall provide that any such disqualification shall be, or as the case may be that the person shall be treated as capable of work, for such period not exceeding 6 weeks as may be determined in accordance with Part II of the Administration Act.

(3) Regulations may prescribe for the purposes of this section—

(a) matters which are or are not to be taken into account in determining whether a person does or does not have good cause for any act or omission, or

(b) circumstances in which a person is or is not to be regarded as having or not having good cause for any act or omission.

Incapacity for work: work as councillor to be disregarded

171F.—(1) In determining whether a person is capable or incapable of work, there shall be disregarded any work which that person has undertaken as a councillor.

(2) For this purpose "councillor" means—

(a) in relation to England and Wales, a member of a London borough council, a county council, a district council, a parish or community council, the Common Council of the City of London or the Council of the Isles of Scilly; and

(b) in relation to Scotland, a member of a regional, islands or district council.

(3) The reference in subsection (1) above to the work which a person undertakes as a councillor shall be taken to include any work which he undertakes as a member of any of the bodies referred to in section 177(1) of the Local Government Act 1972, or section 49(1) or (1A) of the Local Government (Scotland) Act 1973, of which he is a member by virtue of his being a councillor.

(4) In making any such determination as is mentioned in subsection (1) above a person shall be treated as having been incapable of work on any day which falls in the pre-commencement period and which—

(a) would have been treated as a day on which he was so incapable, were there disregarded any work which he undertook (or was capable of undertaking) as a councillor; but

(b) would not have been so treated apart from this subsection.

The "pre-commencement period" means the period beginning with 11th May 1987 and ending immediately before 9th October 1989 (the coming into force of paragraph 2 of Schedule 8 to the Social Security Act 1989 which made provision corresponding to the provision made by this section).

Incapacity for work: supplementary provisions

171G.—(1) The provisions of this Part of this Act do not apply—

(a) for the purposes of Part V of this Act (benefit for industrial injuries: see section 94(6) above);

(b) for the purposes of Part XI of this Act (statutory sick pay: see section 151(4) above); or

(c) for such other purposes as may be prescribed.

(2) In this Part of this Act—

"prescribed" means specified in or determined in accordance with regulations; and

"week" means any period of 7 days.".

(2) In Part II of the Social Security Administration Act 1992 (adjudication), after section 61 insert—

"Incapacity for work

Adjudication: incapacity for work

61A.—(1) The following provisions apply in relation to the determination, for any purpose for which the provisions of Part XIIA of the Contributions and Benefits Act apply, whether a person—

(a) is, or is to be treated as, capable or incapable of work, or

(b) falls to be disqualified for any period in accordance with regulations under section 171E of that Act,

and to the determination for any such purpose of such other related questions as may be prescribed.

(2) Provision may be made by regulations for a determination made for one such purpose to be treated as conclusive for another such purpose.

Regulations may in particular provide that a determination that a person is disqualified for any period in accordance with regulations under section 171E of the Contributions and Benefits Act shall have effect for such purposes as may be prescribed as a determination that he is to be treated as capable of work for that period, and *vice versa*.

(3) Provision may be made by regulations for questions of such descriptions as may be prescribed to be determined by an adjudication officer, notwithstanding that other questions fall to be determined by another authority.

(4) Provision may be made by regulations—

(a) requiring a social security appeal tribunal to sit with one or more medical assessors in such classes of case as may be prescribed, and

(b) as to the constitution of panels of medical practitioners to act as medical assessors in such cases;

and regulations under this subsection may confer on the President, or such other person as may be prescribed, such functions as may be prescribed.".

(3) For the period of four years from Royal Assent a statutory instrument which contains (whether alone or with other provisions) any regulations made under any of the following provisions shall not be made unless a draft

of the instrument has been laid before Parliament and approved by a resolution of each House—
- (a) in the Social Security Contributions and Benefits Act 1992—
  section 171A(2), (3), or (4),
  section 171B(4)(d), (6), (7) or (8),
  section 171C(2) or (3),
  section 171D,
  section 171E(1), (2) or (3), or
  section 171G(1)(c);
- (b) in the Social Security Administration Act 1992, section 61A(2), (3) or (4).

DEFINITIONS

"councillor": s.171F(2) of the SSCBA 1992.
"medical treatment": s.121(1) of the SSCBA 1992.
"pre-commencement period": s.171F(4) of the SSCBA 1992.
"prescribed": s.171G(2) of the SSCBA 1992.
"week": s.171G(2) of the SSCBA 1992.

GENERAL NOTE

Subsection (1) inserts four further new sections into the SSCBA 1992. Section 171D enables regulations to provide for persons to be treated as capable or incapable of work, and for persons doing certain work to be treated as capable or incapable of work. Section 171E enables regulations to provide for disqualifications from incapacity benefit. Section 171F provides for work as a councillor to be disregarded. Section 171G makes further supplementary provision for the whole of Pt. XIIA of the SSCBA 1992, as inserted by ss.5 and 6 of this Act.

Subsection (2) inserts a new s.61A into the SSAA 1992, which provides for regulations dealing with the adjudication aspects of the new provisions on incapacity for work. Subsection (3) sets out the circumstances in which regulations made under various of the provisions in ss.171A–171G of the SSCBA 1992 and s.61A of the SSAA 1992 are subject to the affirmative resolution procedure.

Subs. (1)

Section 171D(1) of the SSCBA 1992

This enables regulations to provide for persons to be treated as either capable or incapable of work, irrespective of the new tests of incapacity for work. It is designed for exceptional cases. Thus where a person's medical condition is such that he is clearly incapable, he will be deemed by the regulations to satisfy the new tests. A provisional list of the exempt categories was given by the Under-Secretary of State for Social Security during the debates in Standing Committee E:
> "The list includes terminal illness, tetraplegia, paraplegia, persistent vegetative state, registered blind, severe learning difficulties, severe and progressive neurological or muscle-wasting diseases, active and progressive forms of inflammatory polio arthritis, impairment of cardio-respiratory function which severely and persistently limits effort tolerance, dementia, dense paralysis of the upper limb, trunk and lower limb on one side of the body, multiple effects of impairment of the function of the brain and/or nervous system causing motor sensory and intellectual deficits" (Standing Committee E, col. 332).

Section 171D(2) of the SSCBA 1992

This allows the Secretary of State to make regulations deeming persons to be capable of work if they do work of a prescribed description, or more than the prescribed amount of such work. Conversely, persons will not be treated as capable of work if they do other work of a prescribed nature, or no more than the prescribed limit. This will enable claimants to undertake certain therapeutic and voluntary work without jeopardising their entitlement to incapacity benefit. See to similar effect the Social Security (Sickness and Invalidity Benefit and Severe Disablement Allowance) Miscellaneous Amendments Regulations 1994 (S.I. 1994 No. 1101). The Government intend to make regulations to ensure that the voluntary work provisions apply to any voluntary work undertaken by any claimant for any public body, committee or advisory group, and not just for those which are charities or deal solely with disability issues (*Hansard*, H.L. Vol. 554, col. 1529).

Section 171E of the SSCBA 1992

Section 171E(1) allows regulations to make provision for disqualifying claimants who have become incapable of work through their own misconduct. Disqualifications can also be imposed for failure, without good cause, to attend for medical or other treatment or to observe any pre-scribed rules. On the case law on the analogous provisions relating to sickness benefit and inval-idity benefit, see *Ogus and Barendt*, pp. 156–160. Any such disqualification is for a maximum period of six weeks (subs. (2)). Once the period of disqualification is over, entitlement is auto-matically reinstated without the need for a fresh claim. The concept of "good cause" will be defined by regulations (subs. (3)).

As these provisions appear in Pt. XIIA of the SSCBA 1992, they apply not just to incapacity benefit, but also to SDA and the disability premiums for income support, housing benefit and council tax benefit, where these are paid on account of incapacity for work (see s.61A(2) of the SSAA 1992, inserted by s.6(2) below).

Section 171F of the SSCBA 1992

This section allows work carried out by a claimant as a councillor to be disregarded in assess-ing capacity or incapacity for work. It is in the same terms as s.58 of the SSCBA 1992, which deals with sickness benefit and invalidity benefit.

See also s.30E of the SSCBA 1992, inserted by s.3(1) above, on the treatment of councillors' allowances.

Section 171G of the SSCBA 1992

The important provision in this section is subs. (1), which excludes the industrial injuries scheme and SSP from the new incapacity tests. Other exemptions may be made by regulations.

Subs. (2)

This inserts a new s.61A into the SSAA 1992. It appears at the end of the regulation-making powers in Pt. II of that Act, *i.e.* the adjudication provisions. The most important provision is s.61A(4), which will require SSATs to sit with a medical assessor when hearing incapacity ben-efit appeals.

Section 61A(1) of the SSAA 1992

The enabling provisions in s.61A(2)–(4) apply to all determinations made under Pt. XIIA of the SSCBA 1992.

Section 61A(2) of the SSAA 1992

Regulations made under this power will enable an adjudication decision on incapacity to be valid across the whole social security system, with the exception of those areas excluded by s.171G. It follows that a person found capable of work in respect of a claim for incapacity benefit will be regarded as capable of work for other purposes, such as in respect of entitlement to the disability premium in income support or when applying for national insurance credits.

Section 61A(3) of the SSAA 1992

This enables regulations to be made allowing an adjudication officer to determine whether or not a person is incapable of work for the purposes of housing benefit or council tax benefit. This is clearly important in order to achieve consistency of approach. Such provision will, of course, include a right of appeal to a social security appeal tribunal. This measure reinforces the broader argument that these tribunals should have jurisdiction generally in relation to housing benefit and council tax benefit, given the degree of harmonisation which exists between the various income-related benefits.

Section 61A(4) of the SSAA 1992

This is a remarkable provision. At present appeals concerning questions of incapacity for work in the context of invalidity benefit are heard by SSATs. Social Security Appeal Tribunals consist of a legally qualified chairman and two lay members appointed because they have "knowledge and experience of conditions in the area and [are] representative of people living or working in the area" (see the SSAA 1992, s.40(2)).

Social Security Appeal Tribunals will continue to be the appellate body for incapacity benefit. However, regulations made under this provision will require SSATs to sit with one or more medical assessors in prescribed cases. The intention is that these assessors will be drawn from a panel appointed by the President of the Independent Tribunal Service, and so be independent of the DSS.

Social Security Appeal Tribunals, like other social security adjudicating authorities, already enjoy the power to direct that they should sit with assessors (see the SSAA 1992, s.56). In prac-tice this power is very rarely exercised. The function of such an assessor was explained by the Commissioner in *R(I) 14/51* at para. 7:

> "It is true that the sole function of assessors is to give the Tribunal information and advice on the medical questions involved in the case including the effect and value of any medical

evidence submitted by the claimant or the Insurance Officer. The assessor must not be regarded as a witness, for he cannot be cross-examined by the claimant or the local Insurance Officer (see, *per* Viscount Simon, L.C. in *Richardson* v. *Redpath, Brown & Co.* 36 B.W.C.C. 259 at p. 265). He is not a member of the Tribunal and has no judicial powers or duties; the Tribunal alone must decide all the issues in the case and must not accept the advice of the medical assessor on any medical matter unless they are satisfied that having regard to all the evidence in the case the advice is correct".

Research has shown that appellants are often far from clear about the role of the participants in tribunal hearings. Appellants may therefore find it difficult to appreciate the position of the assessor and may perceive him as the effective decision-maker in their case. Thus there is a very real risk that the use of medical assessors will undermine the work that has been done over the years to establish the independence of SSATs. The Council on Tribunals has argued that if there is to be a medically qualified person involved in the adjudicatory process, it would be better if he were a member of the tribunal itself in order to avoid these problems (*per* Lord Archer of Sandwell, *Hansard*, H.L. Vol. 554, col. 343).

It would, of course, have been quite possible to provide for incapacity benefit appeals to be heard by a specialist tribunal without the need for assessors to sit with SSATs. Disability Appeal Tribunals have jurisdiction in relation to the medical and disability aspects of claims for disablement living allowance, attendance allowance and DWA. Disability Appeal Tribunals consist of a legally-qualified chairman, a medical member and a member who is either disabled or has experience of caring for or working with people with disabilities (see the SSAA 1992, s.42). The Government's stated reason for not giving DATs jurisdiction to deal with appeals under this Act is the desire to preserve the distinction between disability and incapacity. This is hardly very compelling, given that the critical issue in relation to both disability and incapacity is often the effect the condition has on the particular individual in their social environment.

Subs. (3)
This is in similar terms to ss.4(12) and 7(5), although the affirmative resolution procedure applies to all regulations made under the powers listed in this section.

Power to provide for the transition to the new test of incapacity for work

7.—(1) The Secretary of State may by regulations make such provision as appears to him to be necessary or expedient for the purposes of, or in connection with, the transition to the test of incapacity for work provided for by sections 5 and 6 above.

Nothing in the following provisions of this section shall be construed as restricting the generality of that power.

(2) In this section—

"commencement" means the commencement of those sections; and

"prescribed" means prescribed by regulations under this section.

(3) Regulations under this section may provide—

(a) that days of incapacity for work before commencement, and such other days as may be prescribed, shall be taken into account for the purposes of section 171B(3) of the Social Security Contributions and Benefits Act 1992 (period after which the all work test applies);

(b) that a person's continued enjoyment after commencement of any allowance or other advantage under any provision for the purposes of which Part XIIA of the Social Security Contributions and Benefits Act 1992 applies shall, except as may be prescribed, be subject to satisfying the test of incapacity for work under that Part; and

(c) for the determination in accordance with that Part of the question whether the person is incapable of work.

(4) Section 175(2) to (4) of the Social Security Contributions and Benefits Act 1992 (general provisions as to regulations and orders) apply in relation to the power conferred by subsection (1) above as they apply in relation to a power conferred by that Act to make regulations.

(5) For the period of four years from Royal Assent a statutory instrument which contains (whether alone or with other provisions) any regulations under this section shall not be made unless a draft of the instrument has been laid before Parliament and approved by a resolution of each House.

(6) A statutory instrument—

(a) which contains (whether alone or with other provisions) any regulations made under this section, and

(b) which is not subject to any requirement that a draft of the instrument be laid before and approved by a resolution of each House of Parliament,

shall be subject to annulment in pursuance of a resolution of either House of Parliament.

DEFINITIONS

"commencement": subs. (2).

"prescribed": subs. (2).

GENERAL NOTE

This section deals with the transition from the existing test of incapacity to the new test of incapacity for all benefits other than incapacity benefit itself. It gives the Secretary of State a very broad regulation-making power in order to provide for all possible contingencies, both foreseen and unforeseen. Thus subs. (3) sets out specific enabling powers, while the generality of subs. (1) mirrors the terms of s.4(1). Regulations under this section are subject to the affirmative resolutions procedure for four years after July 5, 1994 (Royal Assent); subs. (5).

Statutory sick pay

Rate of statutory sick pay

8.—(1) In section 157(1) of the Social Security Contributions and Benefits Act 1992 (statutory sick pay: rates of payment), for the words following "at the weekly rate of" substitute "£52.50".

(2) Any order under section 150 of the Social Security Administration Act 1992 (up-rating orders) made by the Secretary of State before the commencement of this section shall include provision making such increase (if any) in the sum specified in the amendment made by subsection (1) above as the amount of statutory sick pay as is necessary to make that sum equal to the higher rate of statutory sick pay payable after the order comes into force.

(3) In subsection (2) of section 157 of the Social Security Contributions and Benefits Act 1992 (power to make provision by order as to rates of payment, &c.), for paragraph (a) substitute—

"(a) amend subsection (1) above so as to substitute different provision as to the weekly rate or rates of statutory sick pay; and".

(4) In sections 155(4) and 158(2)(b) of that Act for "the appropriate weekly rate set out in" substitute "the weekly rate applicable in accordance with".

GENERAL NOTE

When statutory sick pay (SSP) was introduced in 1983 it was payable at three different rates, depending on the person's earnings. In April 1987 the rates were reduced to two, a higher and lower rate. This section creates a single rate of SSP, equal to the existing higher rate, by abolishing the lower rate. This should ease administration of SSP for employers and assist the lower paid, as well as integrating more neatly with the new incapacity benefit.

Two other important changes to SSP were made by the Statutory Sick Pay Act 1994, s.1. The first of these was the withdrawal of reimbursement for employers of the costs of SSP (except for "small employers", *i.e.* those with a national insurance liability of no more than £20,000 in 1994–95: see the Statutory Sick Pay (Small Employers' Relief) Amendment Regulations 1994 (S.I. 1994 No. 561)). The second was the extension of entitlement to SSP to working women aged between 60 and 65.

Other amendments

Severe disablement allowance

9.—(1) Section 68 of the Social Security Contributions and Benefits Act 1992 (severe disablement allowance) is amended as follows.

(2) After subsection (10) insert—
"(10A) Where—
(a) a person becomes engaged in training for work, and
(b) he was entitled to a severe disablement allowance for one or more of the 56 days immediately before he became so engaged, and
(c) the first day after he ceases to be so engaged is for him a day on which he is incapable of work and falls not later than the end of the period of two years beginning with the last day for which he was entitled to a severe disablement allowance,
any day since that day in which he was engaged in training for work shall be treated for the purposes of any claim for a severe disablement allowance as having been a day on which he was both incapable of work and disabled.

In this subsection "training for work" means training for work in pursuance of arrangements made under section 2(1) of the Employment and Training Act 1973 or section 2(3) of the Enterprise and New Towns (Scotland) Act 1990 or training of such other description as may be prescribed.".
(3) In subsection (11) (regulation-making powers), after paragraph (c) insert—
"(cc) may prescribe evidence which is to be treated as establishing that a person suffers from loss of physical or mental faculty such that the extent of the resulting disablement amounts to not less than 80 per cent.;".
(4) In section 150 of the Social Security Administration Act 1992 (annual up-rating of benefits), in subsection (3) (sums subject to mandatory up-rating), in paragraph (a) for "paragraph 1, 2, 4, 5 or 6 of Part III" substitute "paragraphs 1 to 6 of Part III".

DEFINITIONS
"training for work": s.68(10A) of the SSCBA 1992.

GENERAL NOTE
This section makes consequential amendments to s.68 of the SSCBA 1992 which deals with entitlement to severe disablement allowance (SDA). Severe disablement allowance is a non-contributory benefit paid to people who have been incapable of work and have satisfied an extra condition of severe disability for a continuous period of 196 days (28 weeks). It is paid at a lower rate than the contributory invalidity benefit (and incapacity benefit, the successor to that benefit under this Act) but may be supplemented by age-related additions. There are three consequential changes involved.

Subs. (2)
The first change concerns persons who undertake training for work after having been entitled to SDA within 56 days of starting that training. If they then have to claim SDA after the training ceases, they are to be treated as both incapable of work and disabled for the purposes of SDA entitlement, providing that the first day after the end of the training is within two years of the last entitlement to SDA.

Subs. (3)
The second amendment is a clarifying provision which enables the Secretary of State to prescribe by regulations the evidence needed to meet the SDA threshold of an assessment of at least 80 per cent. disablement. This is likely to be by way of a medical examination or by passporting evidence which deems the test to be satisfied.

Subs. (4)
The third reform is to add the age-related additions for SDA to the list of benefits which are subject to mandatory up-rating in line with price inflation under s.150 of the SSAA 1992. The ordinary rate of SDA is already included in this list.

Disability working allowance

10.—(1) Section 129 of the Social Security Contributions and Benefits Act 1992 (disability working allowance) is amended as follows.

(2) In subsection (1) (conditions of entitlement) for "qualifies under subsection (2) below" substitute "qualifies under subsection (2) or (2A) below".

(3) After subsection (2) insert—

"(2A) A person qualifies under this subsection if—

(a) on one or more of the 56 days immediately preceding the date when the claim for a disability working allowance is made or is treated as made he was engaged in training for work and

(b) a relevant benefit was payable to him for one or more of the 56 days immediately preceding—

(i) the first day of training for work falling within the 56 days mentioned in paragraph (a) above or

(ii) an earlier day of training for work which formed part of the same period of training for work as that day.

(2B) For the purposes of subsection (2A) above—

(a) the following are relevant benefits—

(i) the higher rate of short-term incapacity benefit

(ii) long-term incapacity benefit

(iii) a severe disablement allowance,

or a corresponding benefit under any enactment having effect in Northern Ireland;

(b) "training for work" means training for work in pursuance of arrangements made under section 2(1) of the Employment and Training Act 1973 or section 2(3) of the Enterprise and New Towns (Scotland) Act 1990 or training of such other description as may be prescribed; and

(c) a period of training for work means a series of consecutive days of training for work, there being disregarded for this purpose such days as may be prescribed.".

DEFINITIONS
"training for work": s.129(2B)(b) of the SSCBA 1992.

GENERAL NOTE
Disability working allowance (DWA) is a means-tested benefit for disabled people who are low earners, introduced in April 1992 by the Disability Living Allowance and Disability Working Allowance Act 1991. Disability Working Allowance is modelled closely on family credit. The conditions of entitlement are set out in s.129 of the SSCBA 1992 and the Disability Working Allowance (General) Regulations 1991 (S.I. 1991 No. 2887).

The principal requirements for DWA are laid down in s.129(1) of the SSCBA 1992. These are that the claimant (a) is in remunerative work, (b) has a physical or mental disability that puts him at a disadvantage in getting a job, (c) satisfies the means-test and (d) is not in receipt of family credit. In addition, a claimant must either be in receipt of a qualifying benefit (*e.g.* disability living allowance) at the time of the DWA claim, or have been entitled to payment of another specified benefit (*e.g.* invalidity benefit, now incapacity benefit) within 56 days preceding the date of that claim (SSCBA 1992, s.129(2)). This section provides an alternative means of access to the new benefit to that of the qualifying benefit test under s.129(2) by extending entitlement to persons undertaking training for work.

Under the new s.129(2A) inserted by this section, a person can qualify for DWA if, within 56 days of claiming, he was engaged in training for work which was in turn preceded by a period of entitlement to the higher rate of the short-term incapacity benefit, the long-term incapacity benefit, SDA or a corresponding benefit in Northern Ireland.

This reform may lead to a marginal increase in the take-up of DWA, which has been very disappointing to date. The Government originally predicted that there would be about 50,000 DWA claimants (*Hansard*, H.C. Vol. 182, col. 303), but by May 1993 there were just 3,184 current awards (*Hansard*, H.C. Vol. 242, col. 506, Written Answer). The Government is introducing a series of further reforms in an attempt to improve take-up. As from October 1994, there will be a child care costs exemption of £40 per week in cash terms, as with the other income-related benefits (except income support itself). Four other reforms are due to be implemented in April 1995; the automatic remission of NHS charges for DWA claimants with capital of less than £8,000; an increase in the allowance for lone parents and couples; an increase in the threshold for single people to 75 per cent. of the couple's threshold; and the introduction of a disabled child's premium (*Hansard*, H.L. Vol. 554, col. 1547).

General

Consequential amendments and repeals

11.—(1) The enactments mentioned in Schedule 1 have effect subject to the amendments specified there which are consequential on the provisions of this Act.

> Part I contains amendments of the Social Security Contributions and Benefits Act 1992; and

> Part II contains amendments of the Social Security Administration Act 1992 and certain other enactments.

(2) The enactments mentioned in Schedule 2 are repealed to the extent specified.

GENERAL NOTE

This section introduces Scheds. 1 and 2 which deal with consequential amendments and repeals to the SSCBA 1992 and SSAA 1992 respectively.

General power to make transitional and consequential provision

12.—(1) The Secretary of State may by regulations make such transitional provision, and such consequential provision or savings, as appear to him to be necessary or expedient in preparation for or in connection with the coming into force of any provision of this Act or the operation of any enactment repealed or amended by any such provision during any period when the repeal or amendment is not wholly in force.

(2) The power conferred by subsection (1) above is not exercisable in respect of any matter for which provision may be made under section 4 (power to provide for transition to incapacity benefit) or section 7 (power to provide for the transition to new test of incapacity for work).

(3) Section 175(2) to (4) of the Social Security Contributions and Benefits Act 1992 (general provisions as to regulations and orders) apply in relation to the power conferred by subsection (1) above as they apply in relation to a power conferred by that Act to make regulations.

(4) A statutory instrument—

(a) which contains (whether alone or with other provisions) any regulations made under this section, and

(b) which is not subject to any requirement that a draft of the instrument be laid before and approved by a resolution of each House of Parliament,

shall be subject to annulment in pursuance of a resolution of either House of Parliament.

GENERAL NOTE

This section enables the Secretary of State to deal with routine transitional and consequential arrangements connected with the introduction of incapacity benefit. Such provision is subject to the negative resolution procedure (subs. (4)). This power does not extend to regulations under ss.4 or 7, which must be laid before both Houses for approval if made within four years of Royal Assent (ss.4(12) and 7(5)).

Saving for existing enactments

13.—(1) The amendments of the Social Security Contributions and Benefits Act 1992 made by this Act shall be treated as repealing and re-enacting with modifications the provisions of that Act relating to incapacity for work, so that, subject to any amendment, repeal or revocation—

   (a) any reference in any enactment to any such provision shall be construed as a reference to the corresponding new provision or, as the case may be, to the provision as amended by this Act; and

   (b) subordinate legislation made under any such provision—

      (i) shall continue in force and have effect as if made under the corresponding new provision or, as the case may be, the provision as amended by this Act, and

      (ii) shall be construed as if originally so made.

(2) In any enactment, subject to any amendment—

   (a) any reference to sickness benefit shall be construed as a reference to short-term incapacity benefit at the lower rate, and

   (b) any reference to invalidity benefit or invalidity pension shall be construed as a reference to short-term incapacity benefit at the higher rate or long-term incapacity benefit.

(3) In this section "enactment" includes an enactment contained in subordinate legislation, and "subordinate legislation" has the meaning given by section 21(1) of the Interpretation Act 1978.

DEFINITIONS
  "enactment": subs. (3).
  "subordinate legislation": subs. (3).

GENERAL NOTE
  This section deals with savings provisions. In particular, references within existing legislation to legislation which has been replaced by the provisions of this Act are to be read as references to the new legislation. Furthermore, any regulations made under existing legislation are to be deemed as having been made under the corresponding provisions in this Act. References in existing legislation (which includes subordinate legislation) to sickness benefit, invalidity benefit or invalidity pension are to be taken as references to short-term incapacity benefit at the lower rate or higher rate, or to long-term incapacity benefit, as appropriate.

Corresponding provision for Northern Ireland

14. An Order in Council under paragraph 1(1)(b) of Schedule 1 to the Northern Ireland Act 1974 (legislation for Northern Ireland in the interim period) which states that it is made only for purposes corresponding to those of this Act—

   (a) shall not be subject to paragraph 1(4) and (5) of that Schedule (affirmative resolution of both Houses of Parliament), but

   (b) shall be subject to annulment in pursuance of a resolution of either House of Parliament.

GENERAL NOTE
  This Act itself is inapplicable in Northern Ireland, subject to the exceptions specified in s.16(4). As is customary with social security legislation, corresponding provisions will be made under the Northern Ireland Act 1974 (c. 28) by an Order in Council. As this will be identical in all material respects to the legislation on the mainland, this section provides for such an Order to be subject to the negative resolution procedure.

Expenses

15. There shall be paid out of money provided by Parliament—

   (a) any expenses incurred by a Minister of the Crown in consequence of this Act; and

   (b) any increase attributable to this Act in the sums payable out of money so provided under any other enactment.

Short title, commencement and extent

16.—(1) This Act may be cited as the Social Security (Incapacity for Work) Act 1994.

(2) The following provisions of this Act come into force on Royal Assent—
section 14 (corresponding provision for Northern Ireland),
section 15 (expenses), and
this section.

(3) The other provisions of this Act come into force on such day as the Secretary of State may appoint by order made by statutory instrument, and different days may be appointed for different provisions and for different purposes.

(4) Section 14 above, subsections (1) and (2) above and this subsection extend to Northern Ireland, but otherwise this Act does not extend there.

GENERAL NOTE

With the exception of s.14 and s.16(1), (2) and (4), this Act does not have effect in Northern Ireland. However, corresponding provisions will be made for Northern Ireland under the powers contained in the Northern Ireland Act 1974 (c. 28).

SCHEDULES

Section 11(1)   SCHEDULE 1

CONSEQUENTIAL AMENDMENTS

PART I

AMENDMENTS OF THE CONTRIBUTIONS AND BENEFITS ACT

1. In section 4 of the Social Security Contributions and Benefits Act 1992 (payments treated as remuneration and earnings), in subsection (3) (meaning of "sickness payment") omit the words "within the meaning of section 57 below".

2.—(1) Section 20 of the Social Security Contributions and Benefits Act 1992 (descriptions of contributory benefits) is amended as follows.

(2) In subsection (1) (list of benefits), for paragraphs (b) and (c) substitute—
"(b) incapacity benefit, comprising—
(i) short-term incapacity benefit, and
(ii) long-term incapacity benefit;".

(3) In subsection (2)—
(a) in the definition of "long-term benefit" for paragraph (a) substitute—
"(a) long-term incapacity benefit;";
(b) in the definition of "short-term benefit" for paragraph (b) substitute—
"(b) short-term incapacity benefit; and".

3.—(1) Section 21 of the Social Security Contributions and Benefits Act 1992 (contribution conditions) is amended as follows.

(2) In subsection (1) (benefits which are subject to contribution conditions being satisfied) for "other than invalidity benefit" substitute "other than long-term incapacity benefit under section 30A below or short-term or long-term incapacity benefit under section 40 or 41 below".

(3) In subsection (2), in the first part of the table (classes of contributions relevant in relation to benefits), for "Sickness benefit" substitute "Short-term incapacity benefit under section 30A below".

4. In section 25(6) of the Social Security Contributions and Benefits Act 1992 (unemployment benefit: increases to be disregarded in determining rate of relevant retirement pension)—
(a) in paragraph (a) for "invalidity" substitute "incapacity"; and
(b) in paragraph (d) after "under section 150 of the Administration Act (annual up-rating)" insert "of the sums mentioned in subsection (1)(e) of that section".

5. After section 25 of the Social Security Contributions and Benefits Act 1992 (unemployment benefit) insert—

"Determination of days for which unemployment benefit is payable
25A.—(1) For the purposes of any provisions of this Act relating to unemployment benefit—
(a) subject to the provisions of this Act, a day shall not be treated in relation to any person as a day of unemployment unless on that day—
(i) he is capable of work, and
(ii) he is, or is deemed in accordance with regulations to be, available to be employed in employed earner's employment,

and that day falls in a week in which he is, or is deemed in accordance with regulations to be, actively seeking such employment;

(b) where a person is an employed earner and his employment as such has not been terminated, then in any week a day on which in the normal course that person would not work in that employment or in any other employed earner's employment shall not be treated as a day of unemployment unless each other day in that week (other than the day referred to in paragraph (e) below) on which in the normal course he would so work is a day of interruption of employment;

(c) "day of interruption of employment" means a day which is a day of unemployment or of incapacity for work;

(d) the following periods, namely—

(i) any 2 days of unemployment, whether consecutive or not, within a period of 6 consecutive days,

(ii) any 4 or more consecutive days of incapacity for work,

shall be treated as a period of interruption of employment, and any 2 such periods not separated by a period of more than 8 weeks ("week" for this purpose meaning any period of 7 days) shall be treated as one period of interruption of employment;

(e) Sunday or such other day in each week as may be prescribed shall not be treated as a day of unemployment and shall be disregarded in computing any period of consecutive days.

(2) For the purposes of any provision of this Act relating to unemployment benefit, references to a day or period of incapacity for work have the same meaning as they have for the purposes of incapacity benefit.

(3) Regulations may—

(a) make provision (subject to subsections (1) and (2) above) as to the days which are or are not to be treated for the purposes of unemployment benefit as days of unemployment;

(b) make provision with respect to—

(i) steps which a person is required to take in any week if he is to be regarded as actively seeking employed earner's employment in that week;

(ii) the meaning of "week" in subsection (1)(a) above or in any other provision relating to a person's actively seeking employed earner's employment;

(c) prescribe respective circumstances in which, for the purposes of subsection (1)(b) above—

(i) employment which has not been terminated may be treated as if it had been terminated; or

(ii) a day which falls in a period when an employed earner's employment is suspended but does not fall to be so treated and which, apart from the regulations, would not fall to be treated as a day of interruption of employment may be treated as such a day.

(4) Where it has been determined that a person is to be deemed in accordance with regulations to be available for employment in employed earner's employment in respect of any day, the question of his actual availability for such employment in respect of that day may be subsequently determined on a review of the determination as to his deemed availability.

(5) Where it has been determined that a person is to be deemed in accordance with regulations to be actively seeking employed earner's employment in any week, the question of his actually doing so in that week may be subsequently determined on a review of the determination as to his deemed doing so.

(6) If regulations under paragraph (a) of subsection (3) above provide that for the purposes of unemployment benefit days falling in a post-employment period are not to be treated in relation to a person as days of unemployment, then, for the purpose of determining that period, the regulations may, in particular, make provision—

(a) for calculating or estimating the amount or value of any payment made, or goods or services provided, to or for that person by his employer,

(b) for calculating or estimating that person's level of earnings in the employment in question during any period or for treating him as having such a level of earnings as may be prescribed, and

(c) for calculating or estimating the amount or value of any other sum which falls to be taken into account under the regulations.

In this subsection "post-employment period" means a period following the termination of a person's employment and falling to be determined in accordance with the regulations by reference to the amount or value of payments made, or goods or services provided, to or for the person by his employer at the time of, or within a prescribed period before or after, the termination of the employment.

Power to amend provisions as to days of entitlement

25B.—(1) Subsections (1) and (3) of section 25A above shall, on and after such day as the Secretary of State may by order appoint, have effect—

(a) with the substitution for paragraph (b) of subsection (1) of the following paragraph—

"(b) where a person is an employed earner and his employment as such has not been terminated but has been suspended by the employer, a day shall not be treated in relation to that person as a day of unemployment unless it is the 7th or a later day in a continuous period of days on which that suspension has lasted, there being disregarded for the purposes of determining the first 6 days of the period (but for no other purpose)—

(i) Sunday or such other day in each week as may have been prescribed under paragraph (e) of this subsection,

(ii) any day of recognised or customary holiday in connection with the suspended employment,

(iii) such other day or days as may be prescribed;"; and

(b) with the substitution for paragraph (c) of subsection (3) of the following paragraph—

"(c) prescribe respective circumstances in which for the purposes of subsection (1)(b) above an employed earner's employment may be treated—

(i) as having been or, as the case may be, as not having been terminated, or

(ii) as having been or, as the case may be, as not having been suspended.".

(2) The Secretary of State may by regulations provide—

(a) that paragraph (d) of section 25A(1) above shall have effect as if for the reference to 8 weeks there were substituted a reference to a larger number of weeks specified in the regulations; and

(b) that sub-paragraph (ii) of that paragraph shall have effect as if the reference there to 4 consecutive days were to such lesser number of days, whether consecutive or not, within such period of consecutive days as may be specified.

(3) Regulations under subsection (2)(b) above may be made to have effect from such date, not earlier than 14th September 1980, as may be specified in the regulations.".

6. In section 30 of the Social Security Contributions and Benefits Act 1992 (abatement of unemployment benefit on account of payments of occupational or personal pension), in subsection (3)(e) for "section 26(1) above and section 57(1) below" substitute "sections 25A(1) and 26(1) above".

7. Omit sections 31 to 34 of the Social Security Contributions and Benefits Act 1992 (sickness benefit and invalidity benefit).

8. For section 40 of the Social Security Contributions and Benefits Act 1992 (invalidity pension for widows) substitute—

"Long-term incapacity benefit for widows

40.—(1) Subject to subsection (2) below, this section applies to a woman who—

(a) on her late husband's death is not entitled to a widowed mother's allowance or subsequently ceases to be entitled to such an allowance;

(b) is incapable of work at the time when he dies or when she subsequently ceases to be so entitled;

(c) either—

(i) would have been entitled to a widow's pension if she had been over the age of 45 when her husband died or when she ceased to be entitled to a widowed mother's allowance; or

(ii) is entitled to such a pension with a reduction under section 39(4) above; and

(d) is not entitled to incapacity benefit apart from this section.

(2) This section does not apply to a woman unless—

(a) her husband died after 5th April 1979; or

(b) she ceased to be entitled to a widowed mother's allowance after that date (whenever her husband died).

(3) A woman to whom this section applies is entitled to long-term incapacity benefit under this section for any day of incapacity for work which—

(a) falls in a period of incapacity for work that began before the time when her late husband died or she subsequently ceased to be entitled to a widowed mother's allowance; and

(b) is after that time and after the first 364 days of incapacity for work in that period.

(4) A woman to whom this section applies who is not entitled to long-term incapacity benefit under subsection (3) above, but who is terminally ill, is entitled to short-term incapacity benefit under this section for any day of incapacity for work which—

(a) falls in a period of incapacity for work that began before the time when her late husband died or she subsequently ceased to be entitled to a widowed mother's allowance, and

(b) is after that time and after the first 196 days of incapacity for work in that period.

For the purposes of this subsection a woman is terminally ill if she suffers from a progressive disease and her death in consequence of that disease can reasonably be expected within 6 months.

(5) The weekly rate of incapacity benefit payable under this section is—

(a) if the woman is not entitled to a widow's pension, that which would apply if she were entitled to long-term incapacity benefit under section 30A above; and

(b) if she is entitled to a widow's pension with a reduction under section 39(4) above, the difference between the weekly rate of that pension and the weekly rate referred to in paragraph (a) above.

(6) A woman is not entitled to incapacity benefit under this section if she is over pensionable age; but if she has attained pensionable age and the period of incapacity for work mentioned in subsection (3)(a) or (4)(a) above did not terminate before she attained that age—

(a) she shall, if not otherwise entitled to a Category A retirement pension, be entitled to such a pension, and

(b) the weekly rate of the Category A retirement pension to which she is entitled (whether by virtue of paragraph (a) above or otherwise) shall be determined in the prescribed manner.

(7) Where a woman entitled to short-term incapacity benefit under subsection (4) above attains pensionable age and defers her entitlement to a Category A pension or makes an election under section 54(1) below, the days of incapacity for work falling within the period of incapacity for work mentioned in that subsection shall, for the purpose of determining any subsequent entitlement to incapacity benefit under section 30A above or the rate of that benefit, be treated as if they had been days of entitlement to short-term incapacity benefit.

(8) References to short-term incapacity benefit at the higher rate shall be construed as including short-term incapacity benefit payable under subsection (4) above.".

9. For section 41 of the Social Security Contributions and Benefits Act 1992 (invalidity pension for widowers) substitute—

"Long-term incapacity benefit for widowers

41.—(1) This section applies to a man whose wife has died on or after 6th April 1979 and who either—

(a) was incapable of work at the time when she died, or

(b) becomes incapable of work within the prescribed period after that time,

and is not entitled to incapacity benefit apart from this section.

(2) A man to whom this section applies is entitled to long-term incapacity benefit under this section for any day of incapacity for work which—

(a) falls in a period of incapacity for work that began before the time when his wife died or within the prescribed period after that time, and

(b) is after that time and after the first 364 days of incapacity for work in that period.

(3) A man to whom this section applies who is not entitled to long-term incapacity benefit under subsection (2) above, but who is terminally ill, is entitled to short-term incapacity benefit under this section for any day of incapacity for work which—

(a) falls in a period of incapacity for work that began before the time when his wife died or within the prescribed period after that time, and

(b) is after that time and after the first 196 days of incapacity for work in that period.

For the purposes of this subsection a man is terminally ill if he suffers from a progressive disease and his death in consequence of that disease can reasonably be expected within 6 months.

(4) The weekly rate of incapacity benefit payable under this section is that which would apply if he were entitled to long-term incapacity benefit under section 30A above.

(5) A man is not entitled to incapacity benefit under this section if he is over pensionable age; but if he has attained pensionable age, and the period of incapacity for work mentioned in subsection (2)(a) or (3)(a) above did not terminate before he attained that age—

(a) he shall, if not otherwise entitled to a Category A retirement pension and also not entitled to a Category B retirement pension by virtue of section 51 below, be entitled to Category A retirement pension; and

(b) the weekly rate of the Category A retirement pension to which he is entitled (whether by virtue of paragraph (a) above or otherwise) shall be determined in the prescribed manner.

(6) Where a man entitled to short-term incapacity benefit under subsection (3) above attains pensionable age and defers his entitlement to a Category A pension or makes an election under section 54(1) below, the days of incapacity for work falling within the period of incapacity for work mentioned in that subsection shall, for the purpose of determining any subsequent entitlement to incapacity benefit under section 30A above or the rate of that benefit, be treated as if they had been days of entitlement to short-term incapacity benefit.

(7) References to short-term incapacity benefit at the higher rate shall be construed as including short-term incapacity benefit payable under subsection (3) above.".

10. For section 42 of the Social Security Contributions and Benefits Act 1992 (entitlement to invalidity pension on termination of employment after period of entitlement to disability working allowance) substitute—

"Entitlement under s.40 or 41 after period of employment or training for work

42.—(1) Where—
 (a) a person who is engaged and normally engaged in remunerative work ceases to be so engaged, and
 (b) he is entitled to a disability working allowance for the week in which there falls the last day on which he is so engaged, and
 (c) he qualified for a disability working allowance for that week by virtue of incapacity benefit under section 40 or 41 above having been payable to him, and
 (d) the first day after he ceases to be engaged as mentioned in paragraph (a) above is for him a day of incapacity for work and falls not later than the end of the period of two years beginning with the last day for which he was entitled to incapacity benefit under that section,

any day since that day which fell within a week for which he was entitled to a disability working allowance shall be treated for the purposes of any claim for incapacity benefit under that section for a period commencing after he ceases to be engaged as mentioned in paragraph (a) above as having been a day of incapacity for work.

(2) Where—
 (a) a person becomes engaged in training for work, and
 (b) he was entitled to incapacity benefit under section 40 or 41 above for one or more of the 56 days immediately before he became so engaged, and
 (c) the first day after he ceases to be so engaged is for him a day of incapacity for work and falls not later than the end of the period of two years beginning with the last day for which he was entitled to incapacity benefit under that section,

any day since that day in which he was engaged in training for work shall be treated for the purposes of any claim for incapacity benefit under that section for a period commencing after he ceases to be so engaged as having been a day of incapacity for work.

In this subsection "training for work" means training for work in pursuance of arrangements made under section 2(1) of the Employment and Training Act 1973 or section 2(3) of the Enterprise and New Towns (Scotland) Act 1990 or training of such other description as may be prescribed.

(3) For the purposes of this section "week" means any period of 7 days.".

11. In section 44(4) of the Social Security Contributions and Benefits Act 1992 (Category A retirement pension: basic rate), for "the rate of sickness benefit under section 31(6) above" substitute "the rate of short-term incapacity benefit under section 30B(3) above".

12. In section 46 of the Social Security Contributions and Benefits Act 1992 (modifications of section 45 for calculating additional pension in certain cases), omit—
 (a) subsection (1); and
 (b) in subsection (2), the words "or 41(4)".

13. In section 47 of the Social Security Contributions and Benefits Act 1992 (increase of Category A retirement pension for invalidity), in subsections (1) and (5) for "invalidity allowance" substitute "age addition to long-term incapacity benefit by virtue of regulations under section 30B(7) above".

14. Omit section 57 of the Social Security Contributions and Benefits Act 1992 (determination of days for which benefit is payable).

15. Omit section 58 of the Social Security Contributions and Benefits Act 1992 (incapacity for work: work as councillor to be disregarded).

16. Omit section 59 of the Social Security Contributions and Benefits Act 1992 (invalidity benefit: disqualifications, &c.).

17.—(1) Section 61 of the Social Security Contributions and Benefits Act 1992 (exclusion of increase of benefit in case of failure to satisfy contribution conditions) is amended as follows.

(2) In subsection (2) for paragraph (b) substitute—

"(b) to short-term incapacity benefit at a rate determined under section 30B(3) above.".

(3) In the same subsection omit—

(a) paragraph (c) and the word "or" preceding it; and

(b) the words "or invalidity pension" (twice).

18.—(1) Section 68 of the Social Security Contributions and Benefits Act 1992 (severe disablement allowance) is amended as follows.

(2) In subsection (8) (daily rate of allowance to be 1/6th of appropriate weekly rate) for "one sixth of the weekly rate referred to in subsection (7) above" substitute "1/7th of the weekly rate".

(3) In subsection (11) (regulation-making powers), for paragraph (c) substitute—

"(ca) may prescribe circumstances in which a person is or is not to be treated as incapable of work;

(cb) may prescribe the circumstances in which a person is or is not to be treated as receiving full-time education;".

(4) In the same subsection, for paragraph (d) (reduction in respect of councillor's allowance) substitute—

"; and

(d) may make in relation to severe disablement allowance any such provision as is made in relation to incapacity benefit by section 30E above.".

(5) In the same subsection, omit paragraph (e) and the word "and" preceding it.

(6) Omit subsection (12).

(7) For subsection (13) substitute—

"(13) In this section 'retiring age' means 70 in the case of a man and 65 in the case of a woman.".

19. In section 82 of the Social Security Contributions and Benefits Act 1992 (short-term benefit: increase for adult dependants)—

(a) in subsection (1) omit "or sickness benefit" and for "the benefit in question" substitute "that benefit"; and

(b) in subsection (2)(a) omit "or sickness benefit".

20. In section 83(1) of the Social Security Contributions and Benefits Act 1992 (pension increase for dependent wife: pensions to which section applies), omit paragraph (b).

21. In section 84 of the Social Security Contributions and Benefits Act 1992 (pension increase for dependent husband), in subsection (1) for paragraph (a) substitute—

"(a) which began immediately upon the termination of a period for which the pensioner was entitled—

(i) to an increase in unemployment benefit by virtue of section 82(3) above, or

(ii) to an increase in incapacity benefit by virtue of any provision of regulations under section 86A below prescribed for the purposes of this sub-paragraph, and".

22. In section 85(1) of the Social Security Contributions and Benefits Act 1992 (pension increase for non-spouse having care of dependent child: pensions to which section applies), omit paragraph (c).

23. Omit section 86 of the Social Security Contributions and Benefits Act 1992 (increase of wife's invalidity pension for dependent husband).

24.—(1) Section 87 of the Social Security Contributions and Benefits Act 1992 (rate of increase where associated retirement pension is attributable to reduced contributions) is amended as follows.

(2) In subsection (1)(a) (benefits in relation to which the section applies)—

(a) for sub-paragraph (ii) substitute—

"(ii) to short-term incapacity benefit under section 30A(2)(b);" and

(b) omit sub-paragraph (iii).

(3) In subsection (1)(b), in the words immediately following subsection (1)(b) and in subsection (2) omit "or invalidity pension".

(4) For the words in subsection (1) following paragraph (b) substitute—

"the amount of any increase of the benefit attributable to sections 82 to 86A above shall be determined in accordance with regulations under this section.".

25. For section 88 of the Social Security Contributions and Benefits Act 1992 (pension increases to be in respect of only one adult dependant) substitute—

"**Increases to be in respect of only one adult dependant**

88. A person shall not under or by virtue of sections 83 to 86A above be entitled for the same period to an increase of benefit in respect of more than one person.".

26. In section 89 of the Social Security Contributions and Benefits Act 1992 (references to earnings to include occupational and personal pensions) for "sections 82 to 86 above" substitute "sections 82 to 86A above, and in regulations under section 86A above,".

27. In section 91(1) of the Social Security Contributions and Benefits Act 1992 (effect of trade disputes on entitlement to increases: increases to which section applies), in paragraph (a) for "under sections 82 to 88 above" substitute "under or by virtue of sections 82 to 88 above".

28. In section 93 of the Social Security Contributions and Benefits Act 1992 (dependency increases on termination of employment after period of entitlement to disability working allowance)—

(a) for paragraph (a) substitute—
    "(a) a person becomes entitled—
        (i) to the higher rate of short-term incapacity benefit, or to long-term incapacity benefit, by virtue of section 30C(5) or (6) or section 42 above, or
        (ii) to severe disablement allowance by virtue of section 68(10) or (10A) above; and";

(b) in paragraph (b) and the closing words for "pension or" (four times) substitute "benefit or".

29. Omit section 102 of the Social Security Contributions and Benefits Act 1992 (sickness benefit in respect of industrial injury).

30. In section 122(1) of the Social Security Contributions and Benefits Act 1992 (interpretation of Parts I to VI), for the definition of "day of incapacity for work" and "day of interruption of employment" substitute—
    "'day of interruption of employment' has the meaning given by section 25A(1)(c) above;".

31. In section 126(1) of the Social Security Contributions and Benefits Act 1992 (income support: trade disputes), in the closing words, omit "by reason of disease or bodily or mental disablement".

32. In section 129 of the Social Security Contributions and Benefits Act 1992 (disability working allowance), in subsection (2)(a) for paragraph (i) substitute—
    "(i) the higher rate of short-term incapacity benefit or long-term incapacity benefit;".

33. In section 150(1) of the Social Security Contributions and Benefits Act 1992 (qualifying benefits for purposes of Christmas bonus for pensioners), for paragraph (b) substitute—
    "(b) long-term incapacity benefit;".

34. In section 151(4) of the Social Security Contributions and Benefits Act 1992 (employer's liability to pay statutory sick pay: days to be treated as days of incapacity for work), for the words from "a day shall not be treated as a day" to "unless on that day" substitute "a day of incapacity for work in relation to a contract of service means a day on which".

35. In section 163(1) of the Social Security Contributions and Benefits Act 1992 (interpretation of Part XI), in the definition of "period of interruption of employment"—

(a) omit ", sickness benefit and invalidity benefit";
(b) for "57(1)(d)" substitute "25A(1)(d)".

36. In section 175 of the Social Security Contributions and Benefits Act 1992 (regulations, schemes and orders), in subsection (5) (powers excepted from general provision as to exercise of discretion), for "57(9)(a)" substitute "25B(2)(a)".

37. In section 176(1) of the Social Security Contributions and Benefits Act 1992 (parliamentary control: instruments subject to affirmative procedure)—

(a) in paragraph (a) (regulations), omit "section 32(2)" and "section 59(2)";
(b) in paragraph (c) (orders), omit "section 57(8)" and at the appropriate place insert "section 25B(1)".

38.—(1) Schedule 3 to the Social Security Contributions and Benefits Act 1992 (contribution conditions for entitlement to benefit) is amended as follows.

(2) In paragraph 2(6)(b) (meaning of "relevant benefit year" for purposes of contribution conditions for short-term incapacity benefit), for "period of interruption of employment" substitute "period of incapacity for work".

(3) In paragraph 5(6) (widowed mother's allowance, widow's pension and Category A and B retirement pensions), for "an invalidity pension" substitute "long-term incapacity benefit".

(4) In paragraph 8 (persons deemed to satisfy contribution conditions by virtue of entitlement to another short-term benefit) for "sickness benefit" (twice) substitute "short-term incapacity benefit".

39. In Schedule 4 to the Social Security Contributions and Benefits Act 1992 (rates of benefit, &c.)—
    (a) in Part I (contributory periodical benefits), omit paragraph 3; and
    (b) in Part IV (increases for dependants), in paragraph 1 omit "or sickness" and sub-paragraphs (c) and (d).

40. In Schedule 5 to the Social Security Contributions and Benefits Act 1992 (increase of pension where entitlement is deferred), in paragraph 7(1)(a) for "under section 150(1)(e)" substitute "by virtue of section 150(1)(e)".

41.—(1) Schedule 7 to the Social Security Contributions and Benefits Act 1992 (industrial injuries benefits) is amended as follows.
    (2) In paragraph 3 (restriction on increase of unemployability supplement)—
    (a) in sub-paragraph (2) omit "or an invalidity pension"; and
    (b) in sub-paragraph (3) omit "or invalidity pension".
    (3) In paragraph 13(10) (retirement allowance: meaning of "day of interruption of employment") omit ", sickness benefit or invalidity benefit".

42. In Part I of Schedule 8 to the Social Security Contributions and Benefits Act 1992 (workmen's compensation and industrial diseases benefit in respect of employment before 5th July 1948: nature and amount of benefit under industrial diseases benefit schemes), in paragraph 6(4)(d)—
    (a) for "section 82" substitute "section 86A"; and
    (b) for "sickness benefit" substitute "short-term incapacity benefit".

43.—(1) Schedule 11 to the Social Security Contributions and Benefits Act 1992 (circumstances in which entitlement to statutory sick pay does not arise) is amended as follows.
    (2) In paragraph 2, for sub-paragraphs (d) and (e) substitute—
      "(d) in the period of 57 days ending immediately before the relevant date the employee had at least one day on which—
        (i) he was entitled to incapacity benefit (or would have been so entitled had he satisfied the contribution conditions mentioned in section 30A(2)(a) above), or
        (ii) she was entitled to a maternity allowance, or
        (iii) he was entitled to a severe disablement allowance;".
    (3) Omit paragraph 5.

44.—(1) Schedule 12 to the Social Security Contributions and Benefits Act 1992 (relationship of statutory sick pay with benefits and other payments, &c.) is amended as follows.
    (2) In paragraph 1 (day of entitlement to statutory sick pay not to count as day of incapacity for work for certain purposes), after "period of interruption of employment" insert "for the purposes of unemployment benefit or a period of incapacity for work for the purposes of incapacity benefit".
    (3) For paragraphs 3 and 4 (sickness benefit) substitute—

"Incapacity benefit

    3.—(1) This paragraph and paragraph 4 below have effect to exclude, where a period of entitlement as between an employee and an employer of his comes to an end, the provisions by virtue of which short-term incapacity benefit is not paid for the first three days.
    (2) If the first day immediately following the day on which the period of entitlement came to an end—
    (a) is a day of incapacity for work in relation to that employee, and
    (b) is not a day in relation to which paragraph 1 above applies by reason of any entitlement as between the employee and another employer,
that day shall, except in prescribed cases, be or form part of a period of incapacity for work notwithstanding section 30C(1)(b) above (by virtue of which a period of incapacity for work must be at least 4 days long).
    (3) Where each of the first two consecutive days, or the first three consecutive days, following the day on which the period of entitlement came to an end is a day to which paragraphs (a) and (b) of sub-paragraph (2) above apply, that sub-paragraph has effect in relation to the second day or, as the case may be, in relation to the second and third days, as it has effect in relation to the first.
    4.—(1) Where a period of entitlement as between an employee and an employer of his comes to an end, section 30A(3) above (exclusion of benefit for first 3 days of period) does not apply in relation to any day which—
    (a) is or forms part of a period of incapacity for work (whether by virtue of paragraph 3 above or otherwise), and
    (b) falls within the period of 57 days immediately following the day on which the period of entitlement came to an end.

(2) Where sub-paragraph (1) above applies in relation to a day, section 30A(3) above does not apply in relation to any later day in the same period of incapacity for work.".

(4) For paragraph 5 substitute—

"Incapacity benefit for widows and widowers

5. Paragraph 1 above does not apply for the purpose of determining whether the conditions specified in section 40(3) or (4) or section 41(2) or (3) above are satisfied.".

45.—(1) Schedule 13 to the Social Security Contributions and Benefits Act 1992 (relationship between statutory maternity pay and other benefits) is amended as follows.

(2) For paragraph 1 (the general principle) substitute—

"1. Except as may be prescribed, a day which falls within the maternity pay period shall not be treated for the purposes of this Act—

(a) as a day of unemployment for the purpose of determining whether it forms part of a period of interruption of work, or

(b) as a day of incapacity for work for the purpose of determining whether it forms part of a period of incapacity for work for the purposes of incapacity benefit.".

(3) For paragraph 2 (invalidity) substitute—

"Incapacity benefit

2.—(1) Regulations may provide that in prescribed circumstances a day which falls within the maternity pay period shall be treated as a day of incapacity for work for the purpose of determining entitlement to the higher rate of short-term incapacity benefit or to long-term incapacity benefit.

(2) Regulations may provide that an amount equal to a woman's statutory maternity pay for a period shall be deducted from any such benefit in respect of the same period and a woman shall be entitled to such benefit only if there is a balance after the deduction and, if there is such a balance, at a weekly rate equal to it.".

PART II

AMENDMENTS OF THE ADMINISTRATION ACT AND OTHER ENACTMENTS

Social Security Administration Act 1992 (c. 5)

46. In section 20(1) of the Social Security Administration Act 1992 (questions to be submitted to adjudication officer), for paragraph (c) (disqualification) substitute—

"(c) any question whether, if he otherwise had a right to it, a person would be disqualified under or by virtue of any provision of the Contributions and Benefits Act for receiving a benefit to which this section applies.".

47. In section 25(1)(e) of the Social Security Administration Act 1992 (review of decisions) for "57(4) or (5)" substitute "25A(4) or (5)".

48. In section 27(2) of the Social Security Administration Act 1992 (supplementary provisions as to review: payments not to be affected), in paragraph (a) for "invalidity pension" substitute "incapacity benefit".

49. In section 130 of the Social Security Administration Act 1992 (duties of employers: statutory sick pay and claims for other benefits), in subsection (1) (claims for purposes of which information may be required)—

(a) for paragraph (a) substitute—

"(a) short-term incapacity benefit;"; and

(b) for paragraph (c) substitute—

"(c) long-term incapacity benefit;".

50. In section 132 of the Social Security Administration Act 1992 (duties of employers: statutory maternity pay and claims for other benefits), in subsection (1) (claims for purposes of which information may be required)—

(a) in paragraph (b) for "sickness benefit" substitute "short-term incapacity benefit"; and

(b) in paragraph (c) for "invalidity pension under section 33" substitute "long-term incapacity benefit under section 30A".

51. In section 170 of the Social Security Administration Act 1992 (Social Security Advisory Committee) in the definition of "relevant enactments" in subsection (5), for "and this Act" substitute ", this Act and the Social Security (Incapacity for Work) Act 1994".

52. In section 191 of the Social Security Administration Act 1992 (interpretation: general), omit the definition of "invalidity benefit".

53. In Schedule 2 to the Social Security Administration Act 1992 (supplementary provisions with respect to tribunals, &c.), in paragraph 7(2) (persons to whom remuneration and travelling and other allowances may be paid), after paragraph (a) insert—

"(aa) a person appointed as medical assessor to a social security appeal tribunal under regulations under section 61A(4) above; and".

54. In paragraph 4(1)(b) of Schedule 3 to the Employment Protection (Consolidation) Act 1978 (rights of employee in period of notice: sickness or industrial injury benefit), for "sickness benefit" substitute "short-term incapacity benefit".

55. In section 24(4) of the Criminal Justice Act 1991 (recovery of fines, &c. by deduction from income support: interpretation), in the definition of "income support" for "sickness or invalidity" substitute "or incapacity".

56.—(1) Section 46 of the Pension Schemes Act 1993 (effect of entitlement to guaranteed minimum pensions on payment of social security benefits) is amended as follows.

(2) In subsection (1), for ", a widow's pension or a widower's invalidity pension" substitute "or a widow's pension".

(3) Omit subsection (2).

(4) For subsection (3) substitute—

"(3) Where for any period—

(a) a person is entitled to one or more guaranteed minimum pensions; and

(b) he is also entitled to long-term incapacity benefit under section 30A of the Social Security Contributions and Benefits Act 1992,

for that period an amount equal to the weekly rate or aggregate weekly rates of the guaranteed minimum pension or pensions shall be deducted from any increase payable under regulations under section 30B(7) of that Act and he shall be entitled to such an increase only if there is a balance after the deduction and, if there is such a balance, at a weekly rate equal to it.".

(5) In subsection (6), omit paragraph (b)(i).

(6) In subsection (8), omit paragraph (a) and the word "and" immediately following it.

(7) Omit subsection (9).

57. In section 47(1) of the Pension Schemes Act 1993 (further provisions concerning entitlement to guaranteed minimum pensions for the purposes of section 46), omit the words from "in any case" to "construed".

58. In section 48(2) of the Pension Schemes Act 1993 (reduced benefits where minimum payments or minimum contributions paid), for "sections 34(4) and" substitute "section".

Section 11(2)   SCHEDULE 2

REPEALS

Chapter	Short title	Extent of repeal
1992 c. 4.	Social Security Contributions and Benefits Act 1992.	In section 4(3), the words "within the meaning of section 57 below". Sections 31 to 34. In section 46— (a) subsection (1); (b) in subsection (2) the words "or 41(4)". Sections 57 to 59. In section 61(2)— (a) paragraph (c) and the word "or" preceding it; (b) the words "or invalidity pension" (twice). In section 68— (a) in subsection (11), paragraph (e) and the word "and" preceding it; (b) subsection (12). In section 82(1) and (2)(a), the words "or sickness benefit".

Chapter	Short title	Extent of repeal

1992 c. 4—*cont.*	Social Security Contributions and Benefits Act 1992—*cont.*	Section 83(1)(b).
		Section 85(1)(c).
		Section 86.
		In section 87—
		  (a) in subsection (1)(a), sub-paragraph (iii);
		  (b) in subsection (1)(b), the words immediately following subsection (1)(b) and subsection (2), the words "or invalidity pension".
		Section 102.
		In section 126(1), in the closing words, the words "by reason of disease or bodily or mental disablement".
		In section 163(1), in the definition of "period of interruption of employment", the words "sickness benefit and invalidity benefit".
		In section 176(1)—
		  (a) in paragraph (a), the words "section 32(2)" and "section 59(2)";
		  (b) in paragraph (c), the words "section 57(8)".
		In Schedule 4, in Part I, paragraph 3.
		In Schedule 4, in Part IV, in paragraph 1—
		  (a) the words "or sickness";
		  (b) sub-paragraphs (c) and (d).
		In Schedule 7—
		  (a) in paragraph 3(2), the words "or an invalidity pension";
		  (b) in paragraph 3(3), the words "or invalidity pension";
		  (c) in paragraph 13(10), the words ", sickness benefit or invalidity benefit".
		In Schedule 11, paragraph 5.

1992 c. 5.	Social Security Administration Act 1992.	In section 191, the definition of "invalidity benefit".

1993 c. 48.	Pension Schemes Act 1993.	In section 46—
		  (a) subsection (2);
		  (b) subsection 6(b)(i);
		  (c) subsection 8(a) and the word "and" immediately following it;
		  (d) subsection (9).
		In section 47(1), the words from "in any case" to "construed".

INDEX

References are to sections and Schedules

LOCAL GOVERNMENT (WALES) ACT 1994*

(1994 c. 19)

Arrangement of Sections

Part I

Local Government Areas in Wales

The new areas and their councils

Part II

Functions

General

Planning

Education

---

* Annotations by Paul Griffiths, assistant secretary, the Council of Welsh Districts; additional commentary by Colin Crawford, Senior Lecturer, Faculty of Law, University of Birmingham.

62. Sheriffs.
63. Regulations, orders and directions.
64. Interpretation.
65. Expenses.
66. Short title, commencement, extent etc.

SCHEDULES:

An Act to make provision with respect of local government in Wales.

[5th July 1994]

PARLIAMENTARY DEBATES
Hansard, H.L. Vol. 550, col. 1269; Vol. 551, cols. 123, 327, 388, 724, 782, 1379, 1698, 1719, 1757; Vol. 552, cols. 819, 1244; H.C. Vol. 239, cols. 754, 932; Vol. 244, cols. 636, 770.
    The Bill was considered in Standing Committee A from April 12 to May 24, 1994.

GENERAL NOTE AND INTRODUCTION
    The Local Government (Wales) Act 1994 (c. 19) is a milestone in the legislative history of Wales. It is the first Act to deal exclusively with matters of Welsh local government. The Acts of 1888 and 1894 which established county, borough and district councils throughout England and Wales made no specific reference to Wales, uniformly applying the same legislation to the two countries. The Local Government Act 1972 (c. 70) ("the 1972 Act") made a comprehensive reform of the structure of local government in both England and Wales but there was little separate recognition of Wales in so far as in some particulars it made special legislative provisions for Wales.
    It is a measure of the growing administrative devolution to Wales and the increasing significance of the Welsh Office, established in 1965, that on this occasion there was no suggestion that there should be anything other than a separate Bill to deal with a reform of local government in Wales. This is not to say that the politics and policy processes of the two countries are not inextricably linked, they are. It is not to suggest that the Welsh Office is not well tied into the ways and means of the Whitehall village, but the outlying hamlet has grown in scale, has developed much of its own infrastructure and increasingly has a self-confidence based on a perceptibly separate identity.
    When, in 1990, the Government adopted the proposal to merge counties and districts into unitary authorities, it appeared to be adopting a consensus view. The three main opposition

parties in Wales; Labour, Plaid Cymru and the Liberal Democrats, had used the luxury of opposition status to propose a radical re-shaping of Welsh government through the establishment of unitary local authorities and some form of Welsh Assembly. The two main local authority associations in Wales; the Assembly of Welsh Counties and the Council of Welsh Districts, had adopted the same proposals. Perhaps inevitably, when a government offers, at least in part, to convert aspiration into action, consensus descends to dissension as shared values hit the hard rock of conflicting interests.

After more than a decade of upheaval and change in local government, and precipitated by the poll tax debacle and change in Prime Minister, the rôle of local government was again under scrutiny and the Secretary of State, Michael Heseltine, in 1990, initiated a characteristically sweeping review of the finance structure and internal management of local government in England. Within a year a Bill was drafted to establish a Local Government Commission to review English local government in the shire areas with enabling powers for the government to create new structures by order.

In 1991, the Secretary of State for Wales initiated a different policy process. He consulted the local authority associations and was informed of the shared support for unitary authorities, albeit with the caveat of a Welsh Assembly. The decision was made not to create a Commission but for the Welsh Office itself to organise the conventional policy process of a green paper, white paper and primary legislation that encompassed the detail of the proposed policy.

In June 1991, the Welsh Office published a green paper on the structure of local government in Wales. It stated a clear Government preference for reform into unitary authorities arguing the advantages of clearer accountability, less friction, improved co-ordination and greater efficiency. It suggested options for reform based on 13, 20 or 24 unitary authorities.

The responses to the consultation paper illustrated the emerging divergence of views. The Assembly of Welsh Counties proposed eight unitary authorities whilst the Council of Welsh Districts proposed 27 such authorities. The counties stressed a need to have authorities that could develop strategies over significant geographical areas in land use, economic development, transportation, social services and education. The counties argued the need for the direct employment of a full range of service specialisms in order to guarantee a supply and ensure an effective client side. The districts argued that the future for local government lay in units which could command local loyalty and that these units were often relatively small. The districts argued that there would be incentives for regional strategies to be developed through collaboration and that specialist resources could be made available through a market between authorities and other organisations. Whatever the merits of the arguments, the greater flexibility of the districts may have given them the greater political influence.

The Welsh Office continued its consultation process by establishing joint working parties of civil servants and local government officers, known as the Structures Group, which reported to a Welsh Consultative Council on Local Government which included the Secretary of State and elected members nominated by the local government associations. These institutions operated as advocacy fora in which the districts and counties presented their various arguments. Nevertheless copious documentation was developed on the costings of reform and the service delivery mechanisms which might develop from the various options. Much of the detail of the legislation was anticipated by this "collaborative" policy process.

Ultimately a White Paper was published in March 1993 and a Bill was published in November 1993. Both documents proposed 21 unitary authorities. By this time the initial consensus had been utterly fragmented, at least in terms of public postures. In May 1994 the Wales Labour Party Conference had determined a position of total non-co-operation with the reform process with the organised support of the county councils, the public sector trade unions and the Wales TUC. Along with Plaid Cymru, the Wales Labour Party had adopted the position of no local government reform without the simultaneous establishment of a Welsh Assembly. The scene was set for the traditional legislative process in Parliament wherein the Government proposes and the Opposition opposes, although the opposition was never designed to delay unduly or frustrate a reform that would ultimately serve the purposes of the opposition parties.

In the minds of the opposition parties in Wales this Act is part of a two-stage process, the latter part of which introduces some form of Welsh Assembly. Should there be an alternative Government at some stage in the future, this Act may stand as unfinished business. The debate would move on to the complex and potentially contentious matter of the relationship between the principal councils created by this Act and some proposed Assembly.

Progress of the Act

The Local Government (Wales) Bill had its first reading in the House of Lords on November 30, 1993. After two days in the Committee of the Whole House and two days at Report stage, it received its Third Reading on March 7, 1994. The Minister who presented the Bill in the House of Lords was the Lord Advocate, Lord Rodger of Earlsferry.

The Bill had its Second Reading in the House of Commons on March 15, 1994. After 18 days in Committee and two days at Report stage, it received its Third Reading on June 16, 1994. The Welsh Office Ministers who took the Bill through Committee and Report stages were Sir Wyn Roberts and Gwilym Jones. The Bill was enacted on July 5, 1994.

Structure of the Act
Part I of the Act defines the new local government areas. The Bill as initially published provided for 21 unitary authorities. The only significant amendment made to the boundaries initially specified in the Bill was that proposed by the Government at Committee Stage in the Commons which separated the Heads of the Valleys authority into two parts: Blaenau Gwent and Merthyr Tydfil. By amendment, the community of Llanelli Hill originally in Blaenau Gwent was moved from Powys to Monmouthshire. Much time was spent in both Houses as other boundary amendments were proposed with many M.P.'s defending constituency interests by proposing separate authorities within his or her constituency. At various times further unitary authorities were proposed for Meirionnydd, Montgomeryshire, Radnorshire, Brecknock, Llanelli, Neath, Port Talbot, Rhondda, Cynon Valley and Taff Ely. The alteration to Bridgend's boundary was much contested. There was only one amendment proposed which would decrease the number of authorities and that was to extend the boundaries of Cardiff – that amendment was supported by neither the Government nor the Official Opposition.
Part II of the Act makes for a general transfer of functions to the new principal councils and thereupon in a number of sections and schedules specifically amends existing legislation to that effect.
Part III of the Act provides for a mechanism wherein the new principal authorities can establish area committees within themselves with responsibilities guaranteed by the Secretary of State. This provision was intended as a conciliation to those areas of Wales which had not gained the unitary authorities that they sought. If the intention was pacification, the effect was to create one of the most criticised aspects of the Act with arguments that such area committees would confuse accountability. Part III also provides the Secretary of State with a series of reserve powers to ensure various forms of joint working if he believes they are necessary in future.
Part IV amends legislation relating to the financing of Welsh local government largely to the effect that each of the new authorities becomes a billing authority.
Part V provides for the transfer of assets and staff. It establishes a Residuary Body to advise on the transfer of assets and to manage and dispose of assets not otherwise transferred to the new principal councils. It establishes a Staff Commission to advise on the transfer of staff. Part V provides a legal framework for the transfer of staff and compensation to staff who may become redundant as a consequence of the Act. The provisions of Pt. V are related to the Transfer of Undertakings (Protection of Employment) Regulations 1981 (S.I. 1981 No. 1794). That relationship was much considered during the legislative process and the Government's declared intentions may yet be modified.
Parts VI and VII make provisions which are transitional, miscellaneous and supplemental.
No notes have been provided to the schedules but, wherever necessary, reference is made to the schedules in the General Notes on the sections which introduce the schedules.

PART I

LOCAL GOVERNMENT AREAS IN WALES

The new areas and their councils

The local government areas

   1.—(1) For section 20 of the Local Government Act 1972 ("the 1972 Act") substitute—

   "New principal local government areas in Wales
      20.—(1) For the administration of local government on and after 1st April 1996, the local government areas in Wales shall be—
         (a) the new principal areas; and
         (b) the communities.
      (2) The new principal areas (determined by reference to areas which, immediately before the passing of the Local Government (Wales) Act

1994, are local government areas) are set out in Parts I and II of Schedule 4 to this Act.

(3) Each of the new principal areas shall have the name given to it in Schedule 4.

(4) The new principal areas set out in Part I of Schedule 4 shall be counties and those set out in Part II of that Schedule shall be county boroughs.

(5) In this Act "principal area", in relation to Wales, means a county or county borough.

(6) The counties which were created by this Act, as originally enacted, as counties in Wales, and the districts within them, shall cease to exist on 1st April 1996 except that the preserved counties shall continue in existence (with, in some cases, modified boundaries) for certain purposes.

(7) The councils of the counties and districts mentioned in subsection (6) above shall cease to exist on 1st April 1996.

(8) The areas of the preserved counties are set out in Part III of Schedule 4 and are determined by reference to local government areas in existence immediately before the passing of the Local Government (Wales) Act 1994.

(9) The Secretary of State may by order change the name by which any of the preserved counties is for the time being known.

(10) Any such order shall be subject to annulment in pursuance of a resolution of either House of Parliament.

(11) The Welsh name of each of the new principal areas is shown in Schedule 4 immediately after its English name."

(2) Schedule 1 substitutes new Parts I, II and III in Schedule 4 to the 1972 Act.

(3) Schedule 2 provides for the application of certain enactments in relation to the preserved counties.

(4) Section 270(1) of the 1972 Act (definitions) is amended as follows.

(5) In the definition of "local authority" for "or community council" substitute "council but, in relation to Wales, means a county council, county borough council or community council;".

(6) In the definition of "local government area", for paragraph (b), substitute—

"(b) in relation to Wales, a county, county borough or community;".

(7) After the definition of "prescribed" insert—

" "preserved county" means any county created by this Act as a county in Wales, as it stood immediately before the passing of the Local Government (Wales) Act 1994 but subject to any provision of the Act of 1994, or any provision made under this Act, redrawing its boundaries;".

(8) In the definition of "principal area" insert at the end "but, in relation to Wales, means a county or county borough."

DEFINITIONS

"community": s.20(4) of the 1972 Act.
"community council": s.28(1) of the 1972 Act, as substituted by s.9 of this Act.
"county": s.270 of the 1972 Act.
"district": s.270 of the 1972 Act.
"local authority": s.270 of the 1972 Act, as amended by ss.(5).
"local government area": s.270 of the 1972 Act, as amended by ss.(6).
"new": s.64(1).
"preserved county": ss.(7).
"principal area": ss.20(5) and 270 of the 1972 Act, as substituted and amended by s.1(1), (4) and (8) of this Act.
"the 1972 Act": s.64(1).
"Wales": s.64(4) of this Act, and s.269 of the 1972 Act.

GENERAL NOTE
Subsection (1) replaces s.20 of the 1972 Act. In so doing this subsection abolishes, on April 1, 1996, the eight County Councils and 37 District Councils established by that Act and replaces them with 22 new principal councils: 11 counties and 11 county boroughs identified in Pts. I and II of Sched. 1 to this Act. These 22 councils are "unitary authorities" and this Act transfers to them, subject to specified amendments, the powers, rights and responsibilities previously held by the two tiers of districts and counties.

The titles county and county borough are not intended to imply any difference in status or power. The titles merely refer to historical tradition or reflect the degree of rurality or urbanisation. The chairman of a county borough council is entitled to the style of mayor (maer).

The provisions for changing the name of a council requiring a two-thirds majority support of the council, as provided for in s.74 of the 1972 Act, are maintained subject to the consent of the Secretary of State being required before October 1, 1996 (see Sched. 15, para 20(5)).

The new s.20(8) creates eight preserved counties based on the boundaries of the previous eight county councils as listed in Pt. III of Sched. 1. Schedule 2 provides a specification of the purposes of the preserved counties. Their purposes do not directly affect the role of the new local governments; they relate, for instance, to parliamentary constituency boundaries, Lieutenancies and sheriffs.

The new s.20(11) states that each of the new principal areas has been accorded both an English and a Welsh name which have equal status.

Constitution of new principal councils in Wales

2. For section 21 of the 1972 Act substitute—

"Constitution of principal councils in Wales

21.—(1) For every principal area in Wales there shall be a council consisting of a chairman and councillors.

(2) Each such council shall be a body corporate and shall have the functions given to them by this Act or otherwise.

(3) Each council for a county in Wales shall have the name of the county with the addition—

    (a) in the case of their English name, of the words "County Council" or the word "Council" (as in "Cardiganshire County Council" or "Cardiganshire Council"); and

    (b) in the case of their Welsh name, of the word "Cyngor" (as in "Cyngor Sir Aberteifi").

(4) Each council for a county borough in Wales shall have the name of the county borough with the addition—

    (a) in the case of their English name, of the words "County Borough Council" or the word "Council" (as in "Caerphilly County Borough Council" or "Caerphilly Council"); and

    (b) in the case of their Welsh name, of the words "Cyngor Bwrdeistref Sirol" or the word "Cyngor" (as in "Cyngor Bwrdeistref Sirol Caerffili" or "Cyngor Caerffili").

(5) In the case of Abertawe, Caerdydd and Powys subsection (3)(b) above shall have effect as if it required the addition of the words "Cyngor Sir"."

DEFINITIONS
"county": s.270 of the 1972 Act.
"district": s.270 of the 1972 Act.
"principal area": ss.20(5) and 270 of the 1972 Act, as substituted and amended by s.1(1), (4) and (8) of this Act.
"the 1972 Act": s.64(1).
"Wales": s.64(4) of this Act, and s.269 of the 1972 Act.

GENERAL NOTE
This section substitutes a new s.21 in the 1972 Act and provides for each of the new principal areas in Wales to have a council and for each council to have both Welsh and English titles. Each new council will be a body corporate and will consist of a chairman and councillors. Eleven of the councils are designated counties and will use the title County Council (Cyngor Sir) or Council

(Cyngor). Eleven are county boroughs and will use the title County Borough Council (Cyngor Bwrdeistref Sirol) or Council (Cyngor).

Cardiff and Swansea are designated counties which appears to belie their urban traditions; however, it is anticipated that they will petition to be granted royal charters re-conferring city status which, if granted, would allow them to be called the City and County of ... (Dinas a Sir ...).

As bodies corporate, the authorities may sue and be sued in their own name, and see annotations in the *Encyclopedia* on s.2 of the 1972 Act. For the functions, see Part IX of the 1972 Act, and Part II of this Act. For election, term of office and allowances for chaiman, see ss.22 and 23 of the 1972 Act, and for those matters in relation to councillors see ss.25 and 26 of that Act, as amended by s.4 of this Act.

Establishment of new principal councils

3. Schedule 3 makes provision (by substituting a new Schedule for Schedule 5 to the 1972 Act) with respect to the establishment of the new principal councils, on a date in 1995 to be fixed by the Secretary of State, and the election of their members.

DEFINITIONS
"principal council": s.270 of the 1972 Act.
"the 1972 Act": s.64(1).

GENERAL NOTE
This section makes provision for the establishment of the new principal councils by the election of its members on a date in 1995 to be fixed by the Secretary of State. At the Third Reading of the Bill in the House of Commons the Secretary of State fixed the date of May 4, 1995 (*Hansard*, H.C. Vol. 244, col. 851). These authorities will be "shadow authorities" until the existing authorities are abolished on April 1, 1996, *i.e.* they can plan for their future responsibilities and set a budget but will not hold any responsibilities until that date.

This section provides for Sched. 3 to this Act to substitute a new Sched. 5 to the 1972 Act.

Paragraph 2 of Sched. 3 allows the Secretary of State to make an order specifying the electoral divisions for the first elections to the new authorities and the number of councillors to be elected within each division. Consultations by the Secretary of State reveal his intention to propose existing district wards or combinations thereof as the electoral divisions for the 1995 elections. The consultations suggest that the number of councillors in Wales will initially be reduced from 1,950 to about 1,300 with, on average, each councillor representing 1,700 electors.

Paragraph 3 makes provision for the appointment of returning officers for the first election by existing councils designated by order of the Secretary of State and makes provision for the sharing of the expenses of the first election by the existing district councils.

Paragraph 4 makes provision for the declaration of acceptance of office by councillors of the new authorities by the head of paid service of an existing authority designated by the appropriate transition committee.

Paragraphs 5 to 7 set out the procedures for convening and holding the first meeting of the new council.

Paragraph 8 ensures the application of s.79 of the 1972 Act with reference to the qualification for membership.

Paragraph 9 suspends elections to the existing councils after December 31, 1994.

Elections of councillors

4.—(1) For section 25(2) of the 1972 Act (electoral divisions) substitute—

"(2) For the purpose of the election of councillors, every principal area in Wales shall be divided into electoral divisions, each returning such number of councillors as may be provided by an order under paragraph 2 of Schedule 5 to this Act or under or by virtue of the provisions of Part IV of this Act.

(3) There shall be a separate election for each electoral division."

(2) For section 26 of the 1972 Act substitute—

"**Elections of councillors**

26.—(1) The ordinary elections of councillors of the new principal councils shall take place in 1995 and in every fourth year after 1995.

(2) The term of office of every such councillor shall be four years.

(3) On the fourth day after any such ordinary election—

(a) the persons who were councillors immediately before the election shall retire; and

(b) the newly elected councillors shall assume office."

DEFINITIONS
"new": s.64(1).
"principal area": ss.20(5) and 270 of the 1972 Act, as substituted and amended by s.1(1), (4) and (8) of this Act.
"principal council": s.270 of the 1972 Act.
"the 1972 Act": s.64(1).
"Wales" s.64(4) of this Act, and s.269 of the 1972 Act.

GENERAL NOTE
This section substitutes ss.25(2) and 26 of the 1972 Act. It provides for the elections to the new authorities in 1995 and, for the whole of the council, every four years thereafter. As such, this Act removes the option of a council in Wales choosing to have 'election by thirds'. This may be argued to increase public understanding of the electoral process and increase the prominence of local elections. Opposition spokesmen argued that the standardisation of electoral procedures should be towards annual elections in all councils which they claimed would make for more continuous public accountability.

Change of status from county to county borough

5. For section 245A of the 1972 Act substitute—

"Change of status of Welsh county to county borough
245A.—(1) Where a petition is presented to Her Majesty by the council of a county in Wales praying for the grant of a charter under this section, Her Majesty, on the advice of Her Privy Council, may by charter confer on that county the status of a county borough.
(2) No such petition shall be presented unless a resolution of the council has been passed by not less than two-thirds of the members voting at a meeting of the council specially convened for the purpose.
(3) No charter under this section shall take effect before 1st April 1996.
(4) A county borough which has acquired that status by a charter under this section—
(a) shall be a county borough; but
(b) shall not be treated as a borough for the purposes of any Act passed before 1st April 1974.
(5) This section shall have effect subject to any provision made by a grant under Her Majesty's prerogative and, in particular, to any provision granting the status of a royal borough or conferring any style on any person."

DEFINITIONS
"county": s.270 of the 1972 Act.
"the 1972 Act": s.64(1).
"Wales": s.64(4) of this Act, and s.269 of the 1972 Act.

GENERAL NOTE
This section inserts a new s.245A into the 1972 Act and allows for the status of a Welsh county to be changed to that of county borough by Royal Charter if Her Majesty is petitioned by a county council on the basis of a resolution passed by not less than two-thirds of the members voting at a meeting specially convened for the purpose.
The status of a county borough does not affect the powers, rights and responsibilities of a council; it does, however, allow the chairman to assume the style Mayor (Maer).
The status of county borough may not affect the title employed by the council. Given the provision of s.2(4), the council may refer to itself as the Council (Cyngor) even if it has gained the

status of county borough. Therefore if, for instance, Monmouthshire gained the status of county borough by Royal Charter, its chairman may gain the style Mayor (Maer) but the council may use the title Monmouthshire Council (Cyngor Sir Fynwy).

Electoral arrangements

Review of electoral arrangements for new principal areas

6. For section 64 of the 1972 Act (special community review and review of electoral arrangements) substitute—

"Review of electoral arrangements for Welsh principal areas
        64.—(1) As soon as practicable after the ordinary election of councillors for any of the Welsh principal areas held in 1995, the Welsh Commission shall—
        (a) review the electoral arrangements for that area with a view to considering future electoral arrangements; and
        (b) formulate proposals for those arrangements.
        (2) The provisions of Part IV of this Act shall apply to a review under subsection (1) above as they apply to a review under section 57 above.
        (3) In its application to a review under subsection (1) above, section 58 above shall have effect as if it required—
        (a) the Welsh Commission to submit a report for any principal area before such date as the Secretary of State may direct, and
        (b) the Secretary of State to make an order under section 58 above giving effect to the proposals of the Commission under subsection (1) above (whether as submitted to him or with modifications)."

Definitions
    "electoral arrangements": s.78 of the 1972 Act.
    "principal area": ss.20(5) and 270 of the 1972 Act, as substituted and amended by s.1(1), (4) and (8) of this Act.
    "the 1972 Act": s.64(1).
    "Welsh Commission": ss.270 and 53 of the 1972 Act.

General Note
    Although the 1995 elections will be conducted on the basis of existing district wards, or combinations thereof, this section makes provision for a general review of electoral areas after 1995 and substitutes s.64 of the 1972 Act for this purpose. The section retains the provisions of s.57 of the 1972 Act in requiring the initial review to be supplemented by further reviews at 10 to 15-year intervals after the initial review. Section 58 of the 1972 Act which concerns submission, consideration and implementation of the Local Government Boundary Commission's (LGBC) reports continues to apply.

Rules to be observed in considering electoral arrangements

7.—(1) Schedule 11 to the 1972 Act (rules to be observed in considering electoral arrangements) shall be amended as follows.
        (2) In paragraph 1 (rules for counties)—
        (a) in sub-paragraph (1), at the end add "but does not apply in relation to any county in Wales"; and
        (b) in sub-paragraph (2)(c) and (d), omit "or community", in each place.
        (3) After paragraph 1 insert—

"Welsh counties and county boroughs
        1A.—(1) This paragraph applies to the consideration by the Secretary of State or the Welsh Commission of the electoral arrangements for elections of councillors for principal areas in Wales.

(2) Subject to any direction under sub-paragraph (3) below, the Welsh Commission shall, when considering the arrangements for elections of councillors for any principal area in Wales, provide for there to be a single member for each electoral division.

(3) The Secretary of State may give a direction to the Welsh Commission requiring it to consider the desirability of providing for multi-member electoral divisions for the area to which the direction relates (which may be the whole or a specified part of a principal area in Wales).

(4) For the purposes of this paragraph, an electoral division is a multi-member division if the arrangements made for the elections of councillors provide for a specified number of councillors (greater than one) to be elected for that division.

(5) Having regard to any change in the number or distribution of the local government electors of the principal area likely to take place within the period of five years immediately following the consideration—

(a) subject to paragraph (b), the number of local government electors shall be, as nearly as may be, the same in every electoral division in the principal area;

(b) where there are one or more multi-member divisions, the ratio of the number of local government electors to the number of councillors to be elected shall be, as nearly as may be, the same in every electoral division in the principal area (including any that are not multi-member divisions);

(c) every ward of a community having a community council (whether separate or common) shall lie wholly within a single electoral division; and

(d) every community which is not divided into community wards shall lie wholly within a single electoral division.

(6) Subject to sub-paragraph (5) above, in considering the electoral arrangements referred to in sub-paragraph (1) above, regard shall be had to—

(a) the desirability of fixing boundaries which are and will remain easily identifiable; and

(b) any local ties which would be broken by the fixing of any particular boundary."

(4) In paragraph 4, after "Commissions" insert "by a Welsh principal council".

DEFINITIONS

"common community council": s.29(1)(a) of the 1972 Act, as substituted by s.10 of this Act.
"community": s.20(4) of the 1972 Act.
"community council": s.28(1) of the 1972 Act, as substituted by s.9 of this Act.
"county": s.270 of the 1972 Act.
"electoral arrangements": s.78 of the 1972 Act.
"local government elector": s.270 of the 1972 Act.
"principal area": ss.20(5) and 270 of the 1972 Act, as substituted and amended by s.1(1), (4) and (8) of this Act.
"principal council": s.270 of the 1972 Act.
"the 1972 Act": s.64(1).
"Wales": ss.64(4) and 269 of the 1972 Act.
"Welsh Commission": ss.270 and 53 of the 1972 Act.

GENERAL NOTE

This section establishes a number of new criteria for a s.6 review and amends Sched. 11 to the 1972 Act for this purpose. The section requires that there will be a single member for each electoral division unless the Secretary of State gives a direction to the Welsh Commission that it should consider the desirability of multi-member electoral divisions in specified areas. The section also states that the review should aim to achieve, as far as possible, a standard ratio of councillors to electors in each electoral division within a principal area.

Communities and their councils

Community meetings and continuation of community councils

8. For section 27 of the 1972 Act substitute—

"*Communities*

Community meetings and continuation of community councils

27.—(1) A meeting of the local government electors for a community ("a community meeting") may be convened for the purpose of discussing community affairs and exercising any functions conferred by any enactment on such meetings.

(2) The community councils in existence on 1st April 1996 shall, subject to any provision made under this Act, continue in existence after that date.

(3) Subsection (4) below applies where—

(a) the name of a community was given only in its English form or only in its Welsh form; but

(b) there is a generally accepted alternative form of that name, or alternative name, in Welsh or (as the case may be) in English.

(4) The principal council within whose area the community lies shall, before 1st October 1997, take such steps as may be prescribed with a view to securing that there is both an English and a Welsh name for the community."

DEFINITIONS

"community": s.20(4) of the 1972 Act.
"community council": s.28(1) of the 1972 Act, as substituted by s.9 of this Act.
"community meeting": s.27(1) of the 1972 Act as substituted by this section.
"local government elector": s.270 of the 1972 Act.
"principal council": s.270 of the 1972 Act.
"the 1972 Act": s.64(1).

GENERAL NOTE

Communities in Wales are the equivalent of parishes in England. As a result of s.64 of the 1972 Act the Local Government Boundary Commission has identified community boundaries throughout Wales, thereby designating 865 communities.

This section is a substitute for s.27 of the 1972 Act. Subsection 27(1) reaffirms the right of a community to convene a community meeting to discuss the affairs of the community and to exercise any functions conferred on such meetings, including consideration of the establishment or dissolution of a community.

Over 700 communities have established community councils since 1974 and subs. (2) maintains the continued existence of these councils. Subss. (3) and (4) require all community councils to secure, by October 1, 1997, both Welsh and English names where there are generally accepted forms.

Establishment, dissolution and grouping etc. of community councils

9. For section 28 of the 1972 Act substitute—

"Establishment or dissolution of community councils

28.—(1) A community meeting of a community which does not have a separate community council may apply to the principal council within whose area it lies for an order establishing a council for the community.

(2) A community meeting of a community which has a separate community council may apply to the principal council within whose area it lies for an order dissolving the community council.

(3) If, on any application under this section, the principal council are satisfied that the relevant requirements of section 29B below and Schedule 12 to this Act have been complied with, they shall make the order applied for.

(4) An order under this section establishing a separate community council for a community shall make such provision as appears to the

council making it to be necessary for the election of a community council in accordance with this Act and Part I of the Representation of the People Act 1983.

(5) An order under this section establishing a separate community council for a community grouped under a common community council shall not be made unless—

(a) the community is separated from the group, or

(b) the group is dissolved,

by the order, or by an order under section 29A below.

(6) Where, in a case to which subsection (5) above applies, the group is not dissolved, the order under this section shall make such provision as appears to the principal council making it to be necessary for the alteration of the group's community council.

(7) Subject to section 30 below, an application under subsection (1) or (2) above may be made at any time.

(8) This section is subject to section 29B below."

DEFINITIONS

"common community council" s.29(1)(a) of the 1972 Act, as substituted by s.10 of this Act.
"community": s.20(4) of the 1972 Act.
"community council": s.28(1) of the 1972 Act, as substituted by this section.
"community meeting": s.27(1) of the 1972 Act as substituted by s.8 of this Act.
"principal council": s.270 of the 1972 Act.
"the 1972 Act": s.64(1).

GENERAL NOTE

This section provides that a community may apply to the principal council for the establishment or dissolution of a community council. The procedures for such applications are provided in detail in s.12 of this Act.

Community councils for groups of communities

10. For section 29 of the 1972 Act substitute—

"Community councils for groups of communities

29.—(1) A community meeting of a community may apply to the principal council within whose area the community is situated—

(a) for an order grouping the community with some neighbouring community or communities which lie in the same principal area as the applicant, under a common community council, or

(b) for an order adding the community to a group of communities—

(i) which are all in the area of the same principal council as the community; and

(ii) for which there is a common community council.

(2) If, on any application under this section, the principal council are satisfied that—

(a) the relevant requirements of section 29B below and Schedule 12 to this Act have been complied with, and

(b) in the case of an application under subsection (1)(b) above, that a community meeting of each of the communities in the group has consented to the applicant becoming a member of the group,

they shall make the order applied for.

(3) Subject to section 30 below, an application under subsection (1) above may be made at any time.

(4) An order under this section shall provide for the name of the group in both an English and a Welsh form.

(5) An order under this section shall—

(a) make such provision as appears to the council making it to be necessary for the election, in accordance with this Act and Part I of the Representation of the People Act 1983, of separate representatives on the community council for each community or for the wards of any community or, in the case of an order which adds a community to a group, for that community or for the wards of that community; and

(b) provide for the dissolution of the separate community council of any community included in the group.

(6) An order under this section shall make such provision as appears to the council making it to be necessary for the application to the communities included in the group of all or any of the provisions of section 79 of the Charities Act 1993 (parochial charities) and of any of the provisions of this Act with respect to the custody of community documents, so as to preserve the separate rights of each community.

(7) An order under this section may provide for any necessary adaptations of this Act in relation to the group of communities.

(8) This section is subject to section 29B below."

DEFINITIONS
"common community council": s.29(1)(a) of the 1972 Act, as substituted by this section.
"community": s.20(4) of the 1972 Act.
"community council": s.28(1) of the 1972 Act, as substituted by s.9 of this Act.
"community meeting": s.27(1) of the 1972 Act as substituted by s.8 of this Act.
"principal area": ss.20(5) and 270 of the 1972 Act, as substituted and amended by s.1(1), (4) and (8) of this Act.
"principal council": s.270 of the 1972 Act.
"the 1972 Act": s.64(1).

GENERAL NOTE
Section 29 of the 1972 Act provided for communities to group themselves in the establishment of a common community council. A small number of communities in Wales have taken advantage of this provision. This section is a substitute for s.29 of the 1972 Act. It provides the same principle of grouped communities but makes the applications subject to the amendments to s.29 laid out in s.12 of this Act.

The application to create a common community council for a group of communities, or to add to the group, must be supported by community meetings in each of the communities concerned. The proposed group must lie entirely within a single principal area. In considering an application, the principal council must have ensured that the required procedures have been adhered to. Section 30 of the 1972 Act continues to apply and this requires applications to a group to be made during reviews of the area concerned by the LGBC or within two years of such reviews, although under s.30(4) this restriction may be set aside by the Secretary of State at the request of the relevant district council, community council or community meeting.

Community councils for groups of communities: dissolution

11. After section 29 of the 1972 Act, insert—

"Community councils for groups of communities: dissolution

29A.—(1) The council of a group of communities may apply to the principal council within whose area the communities lie for an order dissolving the group.

(2) A community meeting of a community included in a group of communities may apply to the principal council within whose area the community lies for an order separating the community from the group.

(3) If, on any application under this section, the principal council are satisfied that—

(a) the relevant requirements of section 29B below and Schedule 12 to this Act have been complied with, and

(b) in the case of an application under subsection (1) above, that a community meeting of each of the communities in the group has consented to the dissolution of the community council,

they shall make the order applied for.

(4) Where a community council are dissolved by an order under this section, the order shall make such provision as appears to the principal council to be necessary for the election of a community council for any of

the communities in the group in accordance with this Act and Part I of the Representation of the People Act 1983.

(5) Where a community is separated from a group by an order under this section, the order shall make such provision as appears to the principal council to be necessary for the election of a community council for the community in accordance with this Act and Part I of the Representation of the People Act 1983.

(6) Subject to section 30 below, an application under subsection (1) above may be made at any time.

(7) This section is subject to section 29B below."

DEFINITIONS

"common community council": s.29(1)(a) of the 1972 Act, as substituted by s.10 of this Act.
"community": s.20(4) of the 1972 Act.
"community council": s.28(1) of the 1972 Act, as substituted by s.9 of this Act.
"community meeting": s.27(1) of the 1972 Act as substituted by s.8 of this Act.
"group of communities": s.29 of the 1972 Act, as substituted by s.10 of this Act.
"principal council": s.270 of the 1972 Act.
"the 1972 Act": s.64(1).

GENERAL NOTE

This section inserts s.29A into the 1972 Act.

Subsection (1) allows the council of a group of communities to apply to the principal council for its own dissolution. Such an application must be supported by community meetings in each of the communities in the group.

Subsection (2) allows a community meeting of a community within a group to apply to the principal council for its separation from the group. All such applications are subject to s.30 of the 1972 Act with reference to their timing and to s.29B (inserted by s.12 of this Act) with reference to their procedures.

Community councils: supplemental provisions

12.—(1) After section 29A of the 1972 Act, insert—

"**Community councils: applications under section 28, 29 or 29A**

29B.—(1) An application under section 28, 29 or 29A above may be made only if—

(a) a poll of the local government electors in the community has been held;

(b) a majority of those voting in the poll supports the proposal; and

(c) in the case of an application under section 29(1)(a), the application is made jointly with the communities to be grouped under the common community council.

(2) In the case of an application under section 29A(1), paragraphs (a) and (b) of subsection (1) above apply in relation to each of the communities concerned.

(3) The consent required by section 29(2)(b) or 29A(3)(b) above may be given by a community meeting only if—

(a) a poll of the local government electors in the community has been held; and

(b) a majority of those voting in the poll supports the proposal.

(4) At any community meeting at which there is discussed a proposal—

(a) for the establishment, or for the dissolution, of a community council,

(b) for the grouping of the community with another community or communities (on an application under section 29(1)(a) or (b) above), under a common community council;

(c) for the separation of the community from the communities with which it is grouped under a common community council;

(d) for the dissolution of the common community council for the communities with which it is grouped;

(e) for the giving of the consent required by section 29(2)(b) or 29A (3)(b) above,

a decision to hold a poll on the question shall be effective only if not less than the required number of local government electors is present and voting.

(5) The required number of local government electors is such number as is equal to 30 per cent. of the local government electorate or, if that number exceeds 300, is 300.

(6) No poll shall be held for the purposes of this section before the end of the period of 42 days beginning with the day on which the decision to hold the poll was taken.

(7) Paragraph 34 of Schedule 12 to this Act (voting at community meetings) shall have effect subject to the provisions of this section.

(8) Where the result of any poll ("the previous poll") held for the purposes of this section is the rejection of the proposal with respect to which the poll was held, no further poll on that question shall be held before the end of the period of two years beginning with the date on which the previous poll was held."

(2) For sub-paragraphs (2) and (3) of paragraph 30 of Schedule 12 to the 1972 Act substitute—

"(2) Except in a case falling within sub-paragraph (3) below, public notice of any community meeting shall be given not less than 7 clear days before the meeting.

(3) Where any business proposed to be transacted at a community meeting relates to any of the matters mentioned in section 29B(4) of this Act, public notice of the meeting shall be given not less than 30 clear days before the meeting.

(3A) The notice required by sub-paragraph (2) or (3) above shall—

(a) specify the time and place of the intended meeting;

(b) specify the business to be transacted at the meeting; and

(c) be signed by the person or persons convening the meeting."

DEFINITIONS

"common community council": s.29(1)(a) of the 1972 Act, as substituted by s.10 of this Act.

"community": s.20(4) of the 1972 Act.

"community council": s.28(1) of the 1972 Act, as substituted by s.9 of this Act.

"community meeting": s.27(1) of the 1972 Act as substituted by s.8 of this Act.

"grouped": s.270 of the 1972 Act.

"local government elector": s.270 of the 1972 Act.

"the 1972 Act": s.64(1).

GENERAL NOTE

This section inserts s.29B into the 1972 Act. Section 29B alters the procedures for the establishment and dissolution of community councils. Under the 1972 Act a community meeting could apply to the principal council for the establishment or dissolution of a community council. There was a provision for the decision of the meeting to be verified by a poll if one-third of the meeting or 10 persons, whichever was the less, requested a poll.

These provisions have been regarded as too limited and an encouragement for a few citizens to seek to disband a council merely because they disagree with its decisions. This new section significantly increases the consent required for both the establishment and dissolution of community councils by requiring the following procedures:

(a) in the convening of a community meeting to discuss dissolution or establishment of a community council and other related matters, the period of notice to be given is increased from 14 to 30 days;

(b) a decision of a community meeting to establish or dissolve a community council must be supported by a majority of those voting in a poll conducted to question the proposal;

(c) a majority vote at the meeting in favour of a poll of local government electors to decide upon dissolution or establishment of a community council will be valid only if 300 local

government electors or 30 per cent. of the local government electorate (whichever is the lower) is present at the meeting and votes;
   (d) following a valid vote of a community meeting to hold a poll, there will be a minimum period of 42 days between the community meeting and the poll;
   (e) if the poll is a rejection of the proposal put before the electorate there should be no further poll for at least two years.

The above procedure is a requirement for: the establishment of a community council; the proposal to join a community council to a group of communities; the proposal to dissolve a community council; and the proposal to separate from a group of community councils.

Constitution and powers of community councils

13. For section 33 of the 1972 Act substitute—

"Constitution and powers of community councils
   33.—(1) A community council shall be a body corporate consisting of the chairman and community councillors and shall have the functions given to them by this Act or otherwise.
   (2) Each community council shall have the name of the community, with the addition—
     (a) in English, of the words "Community Council" (as in "Dale Community Council" or "Llandrillo Community Council"); and
     (b) in Welsh, of the words "Cyngor Cymuned" (as in "Cyngor Cymuned Dale" or "Cyngor Cymuned Llandrillo").
   (3) A community council need not have a common seal.
   (4) Where a community council do not have a seal, any act of theirs which is required to be signified by an instrument under seal may be signified by an instrument signed and sealed by two members of the council."

DEFINITIONS
   "community": s.20(4) of the 1972 Act.
   "community council": s.28(1) of the 1972 Act, as substituted by s.9 of this Act.
   "the 1972 Act": s.64(1).

GENERAL NOTE
   This section substitutes s.33 of the 1972 Act and is very largely a replication of it. It provides for a community council to be a corporate body which has a chairman and performs functions as defined in legislation. The only addition is for the provision of an official title in both Welsh and English.

Consultation with community councils

14. After section 33 of the 1972 Act insert—

"Consultation with community councils
   33A.—(1) The Secretary of State may by order designate any matter—
     (a) for the purposes of subsection (2) below; or
     (b) for the purposes of subsection (3) below.
   (2) Where a new principal council are to consider any proposal which relates to a matter which is designated for the purposes of this subsection, the council shall—
     (a) afford the relevant community councils an opportunity to make representations to them about the proposal;
     (b) before making any decision in relation to the proposal, take into account any representations made to them by any relevant community council with respect to the proposal; and
     (c) when they take a decision with respect to the proposal, notify without delay any relevant community council by whom any such representations have been made.

(3) If a community council have given written notice to the relevant principal council—

    (a) that they wish to be consulted about a specified proposal which is to be considered by the principal council, and which relates to a matter designated for the purposes of this subsection, or

    (b) that they wish to be consulted about any proposal which is to be considered by the principal council and which relates to such a matter,

the principal council shall take the steps mentioned in subsection (2) above in relation to that community council.

(4) An order under this section may—

    (a) prescribe circumstances (including, in particular, the need to act with urgency) in which subsections (2) and (3) above do not apply;

    (b) give the Secretary of State power, in such circumstances as may be prescribed by the order, to provide that in relation to any principal council specified by him, those subsections shall not apply or shall apply only to the extent specified by him.

(5) A contravention of the duty imposed by subsection (2) or (3) above shall not affect the validity of any decision of a principal council or of anything done in pursuance of any such decision.

(6) In this section—

    "relevant community council", in relation to a principal council, means the council of any community which is, or group of communities which are, within the area of the principal council; and

    "relevant principal council", in relation to any community council, means the principal council within whose area the community is, or group of communities are, situated.

(7) The power to make an order under this section shall include power—

    (a) to make such incidental, consequential, transitional or supplemental provision as the Secretary of State thinks necessary or expedient; and

    (b) to make different provision for different areas, including different provision for different localities and for different authorities."

DEFINITIONS

"community council": s.28(1) of the 1972 Act, as substituted by s.9 of this Act.
"prescribed": s.270 of the 1972 Act.
"principal council": s.270 of the 1972 Act.
"relevant community council": subs. (6).
"relevant principal council": subs. (6).
"the 1972 Act": s.64(1).

GENERAL NOTE

It is recognised that it is the representational role of community councils which is most clearly applicable to the very wide diversity of community councils that exist, *i.e.* their role in identifying community opinion and representing that opinion to other organisations, such as their principal councils. Given the diversity of community councils the extent to which they can practice their representational role may, in itself, vary.

This section inserts s.33A into the 1972 Act. Subsection 33A(2) empowers the Secretary of State to designate, by order, those matters upon which principal councils must consult the community councils in their area. Subsection (3) empowers the Secretary of State to designate, by order, those matters upon which individual community councils can require to be consulted by their principal council. It may be envisaged that this formula will allow a diversity of practice which can reflect the resources and aspirations of different community councils.

At the time of enactment the Government had provided no indication of the scope of consultation that it envisaged. Moreover, in its Notes on Clauses, the Government had suggested that in the first instance it would do no more than issue general guidance and would only use its powers to make orders if compliance with guidance was, in its view, inadequate. Again, no indication of the general guidance was available at the time of enactment although the intention to give guidance had been confined by the Minister (see *Hansard* H.C. Vol. 242 col. 218).

One has to conclude that this Act leaves the role of community councils as vaguely determined as it was by the 1972 Act. Community councils have no duties beyond that of appointing a chairman. They have a range of powers, but a limited financial base for the exercise of those powers. They can be consulted and they can act as the agents of the principal councils, if this is agreed by the two councils – hitherto, an uncommon event.

Elections of community councillors

15. In section 35 of the 1972 Act (community councillors), for subsection (2) substitute—

"(2) There shall be ordinary elections of community councillors in 1995 and in every fourth year thereafter.

(2A) The term of office of the community councillors shall be four years.

(2B) On the fourth day after any such ordinary election—

(a) the persons who were councillors immediately before the election shall retire; and

(b) the newly elected councillors shall assume office."

DEFINITIONS
"the 1972 Act": s.64(1).

GENERAL NOTE
This section substitutes s.35(2) of the 1972 Act. It updates that section to take account of other changes in this Act and to improve the drafting. The elections to community councils will take place on May 4, 1995 which was the due date notwithstanding this Act. The elections will be every four years thereafter and will be for the whole council.

Community having the status of a town

16. After section 245A of the 1972 Act insert—

"**Community having the status of a town**

245B.—(1) The council of a community which is not grouped with any other community may, subject to subsection (3) below, resolve that the community shall have the status of a town.

(2) Where a community has the status of a town—

(a) the town council shall have the name of the community with the addition—

(i) in English, of the words "Town Council"; and

(ii) in Welsh, of the words "Cyngor Tref";

(b) the chairman of the town council shall be entitled to the style of "town mayor" or "maer y dref"; and

(c) the vice-chairman of the town council shall be entitled to the style of "deputy town mayor" or "dirprwy faer y dref".

(3) Where the provisions of section 27(4) above apply in relation to a community, the council of that community shall not pass a resolution under subsection (1) above unless it is satisfied that those provisions have been complied with in relation to the community.

(4) Any such resolution shall cease to have effect if the community to which it relates ceases to exist.

(5) If a community council which has passed such a resolution is dissolved without the community ceasing to exist, the dissolution shall not affect the status of the community.

(6) A community council by whom a resolution has been passed under subsection (1) above or, if the council has been dissolved, a community meeting of the community may resolve that the resolution shall cease to have effect.

(7) On the passing of a resolution under subsection (6) above, the community shall cease to have the status of a town.

(8) This section shall have effect subject to any provision made by a grant under Her Majesty's prerogative and, in particular, to any provision conferring any style on any person."

DEFINITIONS
  "community": s.20(4) of the 1972 Act.
  "community council": s.28(1) of the 1972 Act, as substituted by s.9 of this Act.
  "community meeting": s.27(1) of the 1972 Act, as substituted by s.8 of this Act.
  "grouped": s.270 of the 1972 Act.
  "the 1972 Act": s.64(1).

GENERAL NOTE
  This section provides for the insertion of s.245B into the 1972 Act. It allows any community council which is not part of a group to resolve that its community should have the status of a town. The only requirement is that the title and, where appropriate, the name should be expressed in both Welsh and English.

PART II

FUNCTIONS

General

General provision for transfer of functions

17.—(1) This section has effect for the purpose of adapting relevant legislative provisions and in particular for the purpose of providing for the exercise of functions conferred by such provisions.

(2) A provision is a "relevant legislative provision" for the purposes of this section if it is a provision of—

  (a) any public general Act passed before, or during the same Session as, this Act; or
  (b) an instrument which—
        (i) was made before the passing of this Act, under a public general Act; and
        (ii) is of a legislative character but is not in the nature of a local enactment.

(3) This section has effect subject to any provision made by, or by any instrument under, this Act and is not to be taken as affecting any provision so made.

(4) In any relevant legislative provision—

  (a) any reference to an area which is the area of a county council or the area of a district council, and
  (b) any reference which is to be construed as a reference to such an area,

shall be construed, in relation to Wales, as a reference to a new principal area.

(5) In any relevant legislative provision—

  (a) any reference to the council of a county or district, and
  (b) any reference which is to be construed as such,

shall be construed, in relation to Wales, as a reference to the council of a new principal area.

(6) Where, in relation to any relevant legislative provision, any question arises as to which new principal area is the appropriate new principal area for the purposes of that provision, that question shall be determined by order made by the Secretary of State.

(7) Where any relevant legislative provision is by virtue of this section to be construed in accordance with subsection (4) or (5)—

  (a) it shall be so construed subject to any modifications necessary to give full effect to the provision; and

(b) the Secretary of State may by order make such amendments or other modifications of the provision as he considers necessary or expedient in consequence of any provision made by or under this Act.

DEFINITIONS
"county": s.270 of the 1972 Act.
"district": s.270 of the 1972 Act.
"principal area": ss.20(5) and 270 of the 1972 Act, as substituted and amended by s.1(1), (4) and (8) of this Act.
"relevant legislative provisions": subs. (2).
"Wales": s.64(4) of this Act, and s.269 of the 1972 Act.

GENERAL NOTE
This section provides for the general transfer of existing local authority functions to the new councils. Any "relevant legislative provision" which refers to an existing county or district council is adapted to the creation of the new unitary authorities. In itself, this section makes no change to the powers of local government although subs. (3) provides for this general transfer to be qualified by any other provision elsewhere in the Act.

When originally drafted, the Government may have anticipated that this relatively simple section would dispense with any need to specify the wide range of legislation relevant to local government. The section appears to have been drafted with this aim. However, from the onset of the Bill's consideration by Parliament, it became clear that the Government intended to amend the Bill with many new sections and schedules which directly referred to the relevant legislative provisions. Lord Rodger of Earlsferry explained on behalf of the Government the changing nature of this section when he first introduced an amendment specifying a particular relevant legislative provision: "The Bill could go through and rely upon the general power in section 17. The amendment improves the Bill for practitioners not because the Bill, as originally drafted, would not have the effect of transferring the functions, but because it would be difficult for practitioners to use. A schedule like this makes the Bill more user-friendly". (*Hansard*, H.L. Vol. 551, col. 416).

Notwithstanding the extensive reference to specific legislation which was introduced into the Bill, this section remains significant. Unless the Act makes specific reference to the contrary, this section allows the assumption that any existing power of local government is transferred to the new authorities.

Planning

New principal councils to be local planning authorities in Wales

18.—(1) In this Act references to the planning Act are references to the Town and Country Planning Act 1990.

(2) Section 1 of the planning Act (local planning authorities) is amended as follows.

(3) After subsection (1), insert—

"(1A) Subsection (1) does not apply in relation to Wales.

(1B) In Wales—

(a) the local planning authority for a county is the county council; and

(b) the local planning authority for a county borough is the county borough council."

(4) After subsection (4), insert—

"(4A) Subsection (4) does not apply in relation to Wales.

(4B) As to any site in Wales, the local planning authority is also the mineral planning authority."

(5) At the end of the section add—

"(6) The exercise, in relation to Wales, of functions conferred on local planning authorities is subject to section 4(3) and Schedule 1A."

(6) In subsection (3), omit the words "and in Wales" and in subsection (5)—

(a) in paragraph (a), for "subsections (1) to (4) have" substitute "this section has"; and

(b) in paragraph (b), for "(1) and (2)" substitute "(1) to (2)".

(7) Schedule 4 inserts a new Schedule 1A in the planning Act.

"county": s.270 of the 1972 Act.
"the Planning Act": subs. (1).
"Wales": s.64(4) of this Act, and s.269 of the 1972 Act.

GENERAL NOTE
This section provides for the new authorities to be the local planning authorities in Wales and simply amends the Town and Country Planning Act 1990 (c. 8) to make reference to the new county and county borough councils in Wales. Subsection (7) introduces Sched. 4 to this Act which adds Sched. 1A to the 1990 Act. Schedule 1 to the 1990 Act now only applies to England. Schedule 4 distributes the local authority planning function in Wales in a manner which is consistent with the establishment of unitary authorities whilst reproducing the nature of those functions. In particular, the Schedule reproduces the requirements to notify and consult with community councils in determining applications for planning permission.

Joint and special planning boards in Wales

19.—(1) In section 2 of the planning Act (joint planning boards), after subsection (1) insert—

"(1A) Subsection (1) does not apply in relation to Wales.

(1B) If it appears to the Secretary of State that it is expedient that a joint board should be established as the local planning authority for two or more areas, each of which is the whole or part of a Welsh county or county borough, he may by order—

    (a) constitute those areas or parts as a united district for the purposes of this Act; and

    (b) constitute a joint board as the local planning authority for that united district.

(1C) A joint board constituted under subsection (1) or (1B) shall be known as a "joint planning board"."

(2) In Schedule 17 to the 1972 Act (National Parks), after paragraph 3 insert—

"3A.—(1) Where a National Park is wholly comprised in one planning area in Wales, the Secretary of State may by order constitute a special planning board to discharge, as respects the area of the Park, the functions to which this Part of this Schedule applies.

(2) Any enactment relating to joint planning boards constituted by an order under section 2 of the Town and Country Planning Act 1990 shall apply in relation to a special planning board constituted under this paragraph as it applies in relation to a joint planning board constituted under subsection (1B) of that section, but as if—

    (a) the area of the National Park were a united district; and

    (b) any reference (however expressed) to the constituent councils of the joint board (or which is to be construed as such a reference) were a reference to the council of the principal area in question.

3B. A board reconstituted under paragraph 3 above or constituted under paragraph 3A above shall be known as "a special planning board"."

(3) Section 2(2) of the planning Act (local inquiry to be held in the absence of consent of councils concerned) shall not apply to the making of any order—

    (a) under section 2(1B) of that Act, where the united district constituted by the order comprises or includes the whole or any part of the area of a National Park; or

    (b) under paragraph 3A of Schedule 17 to the 1972 Act,

if the board constituted by the order is to come into existence before 31st March 1997.

(4) In section 2 of the planning Act—

    (a) in subsection (1), omit the words "(in this Act referred to as a "joint planning board")";

   (b) in subsection (2), for the words "such an order" substitute "an order under subsection (1) or (1B)";

   (c) in subsection (3), after "county" insert "or county borough" (in both places); and

   (d) in subsection (4), after "(1)" insert "or (1B)".

DEFINITIONS

   "county": s.270 of the 1972 Act.

   "district": s.270 of the 1972 Act.

   "the Planning Act": subs. (1).

   "united district": s.2 of the Town and Country Planning Act 1990, as amended by this section.

   "Wales": s.64(4) of this Act, and s.269 of the 1972 Act.

GENERAL NOTE

   This section continues, in relation to the new unitary authorities, the existing power of the Secretary of State to constitute the whole or part of the area of two or more authorities as a united area and to establish a joint board as the local planning authority for that area. The procedures for the establishment of a joint planning board are still governed by regulations made under the Town and Country Planning Act 1990 (c. 8) and any order is by statutory instrument and will require a local inquiry unless there is consent by the councils concerned.

   Subsection (2) empowers the Secretary of State to constitute a special planning board for a national park whose area is wholly within a planning area in Wales. Any such order is governed by the procedures set out in Sched. 17 to the 1972 Act and does not require parliamentary approval.

   Subsection (3) disapplies the requirement for a local inquiry into the establishment of a joint planning board where the united district includes part of a national park and where the board is constituted before March 31, 1997. This provision was explained by Viscount St. Davids in the House of Lords (*Hansard*, H.L. Vol. 551, col. 413) as being necessary to ensure that the three planning boards in Wales for national park areas were reconstituted speedily to ensure their continuing operation.

Unitary development plans and National Parks

   20.—(1) After section 10 of the planning Act (application of Chapter I), insert—

"Application of Chapter I in relation to Wales

   10A.—(1) This Chapter also applies to the area of any local planning authority in Wales.

   (2) Subsections (3) and (4) apply where the area of a local planning authority in Wales includes—

   (a) the whole or any part of an area prescribed under section 23B(2) in relation to a National Park, and

   (b) other land.

   (3) The provisions of this Chapter apply separately in relation to—

   (a) the Park area or, if there is more than one, each Park area, and

   (b) the remaining area.

   (4) Any reference in any of the following sections of this Chapter to the area of the local planning authority (including any reference which falls to be so construed) shall be construed—

   (a) in its application in relation to any Park area, as a reference to that Park area, and

   (b) in its application in relation to the remaining area, as a reference to that area.

   (5) In this section—

   "the Park area", in relation to a National Park, means the part of the local planning authority's area which is within the area prescribed under section 23B(2) in relation to that Park or, where there is more than one such part, those parts taken as a whole;

   "the remaining area" means the part of the local planning authority's area which is not within the area so prescribed in relation to any National Park."

(2) In Chapter I of Part II of the planning Act, insert after section 28—

"**Application of Chapter I in relation to Wales: transitional provisions**
28A.—(1) Until a unitary development plan becomes fully operative for the area of any local planning authority in Wales—
  (a) Part IA of Schedule 2, and
  (b) Part III of Schedule 5 to the Local Government (Wales) Act 1994 (transitional provisions in relation to structure and local plans),
shall apply in relation to that area.
    (2) For the purposes of this Chapter, a unitary development plan for the area of a local planning authority in Wales has become fully operative when—
  (a) it has become operative under this Chapter; or
  (b) where different parts have become operative at different times, when all parts of it have become so operative."
(3) Schedule 5 shall have effect—
(a) Part I making minor and consequential amendments to Part II of the planning Act,
(b) Part II inserting a new Part IA in Schedule 2 to the planning Act, and
(c) Part III making transitional provision, including provision with respect to the completion and adoption by new authorities of—
        (i) local plans, and
        (ii) proposals for alteration or replacement of structure plans and local plans,
prepared or in course of preparation on 1st April 1996.
(4) Schedule 6 shall have effect—
(a) Part I making minor and consequential amendments to the 1972 Act in relation to National Parks and countryside functions, and
(b) Part II making minor and consequential amendments to enactments concerned with planning.

DEFINITIONS
"the Planning Act": subs. (1).
"Wales": s.64(4) of this Act, and s.269 of the 1972 Act.

GENERAL NOTE
Subsection (1) of this section introduces s.10A to the Town and Country Planning Act 1990 (c. 8). The effect of this new section is to apply the provisions of Chap. 1 of Pt. II of that Act to Wales, provisions which had previously applied only to the unitary authorities of London and metropolitan England. The new unitary authorities in Wales will therefore adopt the planning system of the existing unitary authorities in England.
    Subsections (2)–(5) of s.10A apply the requirement for unitary development plans to the national park areas of Wales.
    Subsection (2) of s.20 inserts s.28A into the 1990 Act and subs. (3) provides authority for Sched. 5 of this Act to make other consequential amendments to the 1990 Act. Together these make transitional provisions for the planning system. Paragraph 8 of Sched. 5 introduces a new Pt. IA to Sched. 2 to the 1990 Act and states clearly: "Every existing plan which relates to any part of Wales shall continue in force on and after April 1, 1996". This refers to any existing structure or local and any existing structure, local or old development plan. Any existing plan which is for the time being in force and any interim plan shall cease to have effect only when a unitary development plan has become fully operative for the area of a local planning authority in Wales.
    Subsection (4) introduces Sched. 6 to the Act. Part I of Sched. 6 makes minor and consequential amendments to specified sections of the 1972 Act which deal with the national parks. Part II of Sched. 6 makes minor and consequential amendments to other enactments.

Education

Local education authorities and minor authorities in Wales

21.—(1) In section 114 of the Education Act 1944 (interpretation), in the definition of "local education authority" in subsection (1), after "the county," insert "in relation to a county borough, the council of the county borough,".

(2) In section 192 of the 1972 Act (education), in subsection (1), after "non-metropolitan county" insert "in England" and at the end add "but, for each principal area in Wales, the local education authority shall be the council of that principal area".

(3) In section 114(1) of the Act of 1944, in the definition of "minor authority", omit, in paragraph (b), "is a community having no community council or" and, in paragraph (c)(iii), "which is a community having no community council or".

DEFINITIONS
"community": s.20(4) of the 1972 Act.
"community council": s.28(1) of the 1972 Act, as substituted by s.9 of this Act.
"principal area": ss.20(5) and 270 of the 1972 Act, as substituted and amended by s.1(1), (4) and (8) of this Act.
"Wales": s.64(4) of this Act, and s.269 of the 1972 Act.

GENERAL NOTE
This section amends the Education Act 1944 (c. 31) and the 1972 Act so that the local education authority in Wales is defined as the council of both a county and county borough. The section therefore transfers the existing powers of a local education authority to the new unitary authorities in Wales.

Transfer of other specific functions

Transfer of other specific functions

22.—(1) Schedule 7 makes provision for the transfer to the new principal councils of functions in relation to highways, road traffic and transport.

(2) Schedule 8 makes provision for the transfer to the new principal councils of functions in relation to housing.

(3) Schedule 9 makes provision for the transfer to the new principal councils of functions in relation to public health and related matters.

(4) Schedule 10 makes provision for the transfer to the new principal councils of functions in relation to social services.

(5) Schedule 11 makes provision for the transfer to the new principal councils of functions in relation to water, land drainage and coast protection.

(6) Each of the Schedules referred to in this section includes minor and consequential amendments of other enactments.

DEFINITIONS
"principal council": s.270 of the 1972 Act.

GENERAL NOTE
This section introduces Scheds. 7–11 which make provision for the transfer of functions in relation to; highways, road traffic and transport, housing, public health, social services, water, land drainage and coast protection. Each of the Schedules make amendments which are described as minor and consequential.

Only one paragraph in these various Schedules was questioned during the parliamentary process and that related to para. 2(2) of Sched. 7 (see *Hansard*, H.L. Vol. 551, col. 427). The Highways Act 1980 (c. 66) allowed the Minister to delegate trunk road agency work to a council outside its own area only with the consent of the council in whose area the road lay. This is amended in para. 2(2) to allow such delegation "after consultation" with the relevant councils. This amendment reflects the Government's declared intention to appoint eight or less of the new councils as trunk road agents in Wales each of which will be expected to work on trunk roads outside their own areas.

Fire services

23.—(1) In section 4 of the Fire Services Act 1947 (fire authorities), after second "county" insert "or, in Wales, of every county or county borough".

(2) A combination scheme may be made under section 5 or 6 of the Act of 1947, before 1st April 1996, with respect to two or more areas each of which is a new principal area.

(3) Where any such combination scheme is made before 1st April 1996, it shall not come into force until that date, except so far as it relates to—

(a) the constitution of an authority as the fire authority for the combined area constituted by the scheme, and

(b) the performance by that authority of any functions necessary for bringing the scheme into full operation on that date.

(4) Where the Secretary of State proposes to make such a combination scheme—

(a) subsection (2) of section 6 of the Act of 1947 shall until 1st April 1996 be taken to require him to give notice to—

(i) any existing fire authority whose area lies wholly or partly within the proposed combined area; and

(ii) each of the new principal councils concerned; and

(b) the requirement in that subsection with respect to public local inquiries shall not apply if—

(i) the proposed scheme relates only to new principal areas; and

(ii) the notice is given before 1st April 1996.

(5) Any such notice shall specify a period for making representations with respect to the proposed scheme.

(6) Where the Secretary of State has given notice of a proposed scheme, in a case to which subsection (4) applies, he shall consider any representations which are made to him before the end of the specified period by any body to whom notice was given.

DEFINITIONS

"county": s.270 of the 1972 Act.

"principal area": ss.20(5) and 270 of the 1972 Act, as substituted and amended by s.1(1), (4) and (8) of this Act.

"Wales": s.64(4) of this Act, and s.269 of the 1972 Act.

GENERAL NOTE

Each of the eight existing county councils in Wales is a fire authority for its own separate fire service. However, the Government in a separate policy process from that relating to the restructuring of local government had decided to reduce the number of fire services to three. There is therefore a need to create combined fire authorities in Wales. The Fire Services Act 1947 (c. 41) requires a public local inquiry to be held to consider a combination proposal. The main effect of this section is to disapply the requirement for a local public inquiry if notice of the proposal for such a scheme is given before April 1, 1996. By way of an alternative, if more limited, procedure the Secretary of State is required to give notice to existing fire authorities and to the new principal authorities concerned and consider representations made in response to such notice. The Government sought to justify the suspension of the requirement for local public inquiries by arguing that combination schemes would need to be in place by April 1, 1996 (*Hansard*, H.C. Vol. 244, col. 296).

Police

24.—(1) In section 1(1) of the Police Act 1964 (police areas), omit the words "and Wales" from paragraph (a) and after that paragraph insert—

"(aa) for every county and county borough in Wales;".

(2) In section 2 of that Act (police authorities), at the end add—

"(8) In this section any reference to a non-metropolitan county is to be read, in relation to Wales, as including a reference to a county borough."

(3) An amalgamation scheme may be made under section 21(2) of the Act of 1964 (Secretary of State's amalgamation schemes), before 1st April 1996, with respect to two or more areas each of which is a new principal area.

(4) Where any such amalgamation scheme is made before 1st April 1996, it shall not come into force until that date, except so far as it relates to—

(a) the constitution of an authority as the police authority for the combined area constituted by the scheme, and

(b) the performance by that authority of any functions necessary for bringing the scheme into full operation on that date.

(5) Where the Secretary of State proposes to make such an amalgamation scheme—

(a) paragraphs 1 and 2 of Schedule 3 to the Act of 1964 shall until 1st April 1996 be taken to require him to give notice—

(i) to any existing police authority whose area lies wholly or partly within the area of the proposed combined police authority;

(ii) where that police authority is a combined authority, to the councils of each of the counties comprised in the combined area; and

(iii) to each of the new principal councils concerned; and

(b) the requirement in paragraph 3 of that Schedule with respect to public local inquiries shall not apply if—

(i) the proposed scheme relates only to new principal areas; and

(ii) the notice is given before 1st April 1996.

(6) Any such notice shall specify a period for making representations with respect to the proposed scheme.

(7) Where the Secretary of State has given notice of a proposed scheme, in a case to which subsection (5) applies, he shall, before the end of the specified period, consider any representations which are made to him by any body to whom notice was given.

DEFINITIONS
"county": s.270 of the 1972 Act.
"principal area": ss.20(5) and 270 of the 1972, as substituted and amended by s.1(1), (4) and (8) of this Act.
"Wales": s.64(4) of this Act, and s.269 of the 1972 Act.

GENERAL NOTE
There are four police authorities in Wales, three of which are amalgamated authorities. At the time of consideration of the Bill the Government Minister stated that there were no Government proposals to change the number of police authorities (*Hansard*, H.C. Vol. 244, col. 315). Nevertheless in the context of 22 new authorities it was the Government's view that the amalgamation schemes would need to be reconstituted making "minor and consequential changes" in response to the new boundaries and that these new schemes would need to be in place by April 1, 1996.

Services

Provision of services by one new principal council for another

25.—(1) Any new principal council ("the contracting council") may enter into an agreement with another such council ("the supplying council") for the provision by the supplying council of services which the contracting council require for the purpose of, or in connection with, the discharge of any of their functions.

(2) Any agreement under subsection (1) (a "service agency agreement") may be made on such terms as to payment or otherwise as the parties consider appropriate.

(3) Subsection (1) is subject to—

(a) the provisions made by or under this Act;

(b) any other enactment which provides for specific functions of a local authority to be discharged only by that authority;

(c) any other enactment which imposes requirements which must be satisfied before a local authority may enter into any agreement of the kind provided for by subsection (1) including, in particular, the provisions of—

        (i) Part III of the Local Government, Planning and Land Act 1980 (restrictions on use by local authorities of direct labour organisations); and

        (ii) Part I of the Local Government Act 1988 (local authorities to undertake certain activities only if they can do so competitively).

(4) The power conferred by subsection (1) shall be exercisable subject to such regulations (if any) as the Secretary of State sees fit to make for the purposes of this section.

(5) Any such regulations may, in particular, make provision—

(a) excluding prescribed matters from those which may be the subject of a service agency agreement;

(b) restricting (whether by reference to one or more areas or otherwise) the councils with which a principal council may make a service agency agreement;

(c) restricting the area or areas with respect to which the supplying council may provide services under a service agency agreement.

(6) As respects the exercise of any of their other statutory powers, anything which falls to be done by the supplying council under a service agency agreement shall be treated as one of their statutory functions.

(7) The provisions of the Local Authorities (Goods and Services) Act 1970 (supply of goods and services by local authorities) do not affect, and are not affected by, the powers conferred on new principal councils by this section.

(8) In section 1(4) of that Act (authorities to which Act applies), for "any county" substitute "any county, county borough".

(9) For the purposes of this section the Residuary Body shall be treated as a new principal council.

DEFINITIONS
"county": s.270 of the 1972 Act.
"contracting council": subs. (1).
"principal council": s.270 of the 1972 Act.
"service agency agreement": subs. (2).
"supplying council": subs. (1).
"the Residuary Body": s.64(1).

GENERAL NOTE
This section enables the new authorities to enter into agreements with each other for the purchase of services by one authority from another. The section also enables the Secretary of State to make regulations governing such agreements.

This is a new power for local authorities in Wales which is not at present available to authorities in England. It is in addition to the power to trade services made available under the Local Authorities (Goods and Services) Act 1970 (c. 39) which the Audit Commission has interpreted as being limited to the supply of services created by some temporary surplus capacity of resources employed only for the discharge of functions within the authorities' own boundaries. The power is in addition to the powers to create agency agreements under s.101 of the 1972 Act which require the delegation of a function.

This power appears more flexible than the previous powers. This may be in recognition of the likelihood that 22 unitary authorities will be less self-sufficient in the employment of specialist resources relating to county services than the existing eight county councils. This section offers the new authorities the opportunity to purchase services, most likely specialist services, from each other.

Subsection (3) affirms that this power is subject to the constraints of other enactments and refers specifically to the requirement to subject certain services to competitive tendering as provided for in the Local Government, Planning and Land Act 1980 (c. 65) and the Local Government Act 1988 (c. 9).

Subsections (4) and (5) enable the Secretary of State to regulate the agreements that may be made restricting both the services that may be traded and the geographical areas within which trade may take place. At the House of Lords Committee Stage (*Hansard*, H.L. Vol. 551, col. 435), Lord Rodger of Earlsferry indicated that the Government would use such powers of regulation extensively to prevent trading in any service which was subject to competitive tendering and to restrict trading to geographically adjacent authorities. However, by the Report Stage in the House of Commons (*Hansard*, H.C. Vol. 244, col. 827) the Government had moderated its position. The statements of Mr Gwilym Jones are worth noting in full:

"... we do not intend to impose any geographic restrictions unless there is clear evidence of authorities abusing their freedom to provide services to authorities throughout Wales.

In the case of services subject to competitive tendering, we see no case for cross-border tendering for work such as refuse collection, building maintenance and catering. We have considered carefully the professional services that will become subject to competitive tendering after reorganisation. We have concluded that personnel, legal and financial services that are already adequately dealt with by even the smallest district council, and where there are many potential private sector suppliers, should not be used for the purposes of clause 25. However, we are considering the possibility that authorities appointed as my Right Hon. Friend's agents for trunk road agents should be allowed to provide professional services to other authorities ... If genuine difficulties emerged, it would always be possible for my Right Hon. Friend to amend the regulations to provide a more relaxed regime".

In the light of the above statements it is possible to predict that the new authorities will be able to trade specialist services relating to, for instance, education, trading standards and social services across the whole of Wales – such services not being subject to compulsory competitive tendering. A small number of trunk road agent authorities will be able to supply professional highways services to other authorities. The Government appears to have no declared view at the present time on the regulation of trading in relation to professional services concerned with information technology and non-highways construction related services.

Service delivery plans

26.—(1) Every new principal council shall prepare and publish a plan ("a service delivery plan")—
  (a) describing the manner in which they propose to perform their functions during the period beginning on 1st April 1996 and ending with 31st March 1997; and
  (b) giving particulars of the arrangements for organisation and management which they propose to adopt.
(2) Each new principal council shall—
  (a) publish a draft of their proposed service delivery plan before 1st November 1995; and
  (b) complete and publish their service delivery plan before 1st February 1996.
(3) In preparing their service delivery plan, a council shall take into account any guidance given by the Secretary of State as to consultation or as to the contents of the plan.
(4) A council's service delivery plan shall be published in such manner as the council consider likely to bring it to the attention of persons (both inside and outside their area) who may be affected by the performance of their functions.
(5) Copies of their service delivery plan shall be made readily available by each new principal council for inspection by any person during office hours.
(6) Subsections (4) and (5) also apply to the draft service delivery plan required to be published by subsection (2)(a).

DEFINITIONS
  "new": s.64(1).
  "principal council": s.270 of the 1972 Act.
  "service delivery plan": subs. (1).

GENERAL NOTE
  This section requires each new principal council to prepare and publish for consultation a service delivery plan which describes the manner in which they propose to perform their services and gives particulars of their intended organisation and management for the year following April 1, 1996. The new principal councils will undertake this task in their shadow year, publishing a draft by November 1, 1995 and a completed plan by February 1, 1996.
  This is likely to be a unique provision for Wales as it is not proposed to include an equivalent provision exists in the legislation for the reform of local government in England and Scotland.

Subsection (3) requires the councils to take into account any guidance given by the Secretary of State as to consultation or as to the contents of the plans. That guidance was published in draft by the Welsh Office in July 1994.

Subsections (4) and (5) require that the plans should be readily available and brought to the attention of persons who may be affected by the performance of the council's functions. The guidance refers specifically to voluntary organisations and community councils.

The plans do not have to be submitted to the Secretary of State and do not require his approval. However, the Minister (*Hansard*, H.C. Vol. 243, col. 362) noted that the Secretary of State has reserve powers in s.32 to seek information from the new councils and powers in ss.33 and 34 to impose arrangements on those councils if satisfactory arrangements are in his view unlikely to be in effect by April 1, 1996. The Act does not overtly relate the service delivery plans to the reserve powers. However, there appeared to be a relationship in the mind of the Minister.

PART III

DECENTRALISATION AND JOINT WORKING

Decentralisation schemes

Decentralisation schemes: preparation

27.—(1) If the conditions mentioned in subsection (2) are satisfied, the Secretary of State may give a direction to a new principal council requiring them to prepare and submit to him a decentralisation scheme for such area falling within the area of the council as the Secretary of State sees fit to specify in the direction.

(2) The conditions are that—

(a) an application relating to the council has been made to the Secretary of State under this section by ten or more of their members;

(b) the application is expressed to be made in relation to a specified area falling within the area of the council; and

(c) at least ten of those persons making the application are members of the council who are connected with the area specified in the application.

(3) In this section—

"decentralisation scheme", in relation to a council, means a scheme which provides for the exercise of specified functions of the council to be discharged by a committee of the council established for the purposes of the scheme; and

"direction" means a direction under subsection (1).

(4) Any council to whom a direction has been given shall submit the required decentralisation scheme to the Secretary of State in accordance with the direction.

(5) A direction may require a decentralisation scheme to be submitted before a specified date.

(6) A committee established for the purposes of a decentralisation scheme is referred to in this Act as an area committee.

(7) No application under subsection (2) may be made after 1st January 1996 and no direction may be given after 1st July 1996.

(8) The Secretary of State shall not give a direction unless he is satisfied that a decentralisation scheme is likely to be appropriate for the area in question.

(9) In considering whether a decentralisation scheme is likely to be appropriate for any area ("the local area"), the Secretary of State shall have regard to—

(a) the desirability of providing for the efficient administration of local government functions both in relation to the area of the principal council as a whole and in relation to the local area; and

(b) the particular circumstances of the local area including its geographical, historical, cultural and demographic circumstances.

(10) A direction may specify any area to which it relates by reference to specific boundaries or by a general description.

(11) The Secretary of State may from time to time issue guidance with respect to the preparation and content of decentralisation schemes.

(12) Any such guidance may be—

(a) general, relating to all decentralisation schemes or all schemes of a specified description; or

(b) specific to a particular scheme.

(13) In specifying any area in a direction, the Secretary of State shall have regard to, but not be bound by, the terms of the application in response to which it is given.

(14) For the purposes of subsection (2), a member of a council is connected with a specified area if he is a member for an electoral division which, or any part of which, falls within that area.

DEFINITIONS

"area committee": subs. (6).
"decentralisation scheme": subs. (3) and s.64(1).
"direction": subs. (3).
"local area": subs. (9).
"principal council": s.270 of the 1972 Act.

GENERAL NOTE

This section introduces a feature into Welsh local government which it is not proposed to introduce in either England or Scotland. The Secretary of State is enabled to require, approve and direct a scheme of decentralisation which allocates responsibilities to area committees within principal councils in specified areas in a manner guaranteed by the Secretary of State for an indefinite period.

In developing proposals for the restructuring of Welsh local government, the Government perceived a dilemma. In its view an economical system of local government required an undeclared limit on the number of local authorities and some undeclared minimum population size for the authorities. On the other hand, in many parts of Wales there was a clear popular demand for more unitary authorities than the Government considered to be economic and of a size that the Government did not consider to be efficient. In the period between the publication of the White Paper in March 1993 and the publication of the Bill in December 1993 the Government introduced this concept of a "unitary authority" within which would exist area committees with responsibilities guaranteed by the Secretary of State. The concept originally derived from the proposal to unite the historic counties of Montgomeryshire, Radnorshire and Brecknock into the single unitary authority of Powys. In order, in part, to avoid drafting a hybrid bill, the concept was made of general application throughout Wales.

This proposal was one of the most contested parts of the Bill. Critics claimed that: (i) it would recreate a two-tier system which was more confused than, and equally ill co-ordinated as, the one it replaced; (ii) it created area committees with responsibilities but without the commensurate powers to employ staff, control finances, own assets and award contracts; and (iii) it made for unclear political, legal and administrative accountability.

This section does not affect the established means whereby local authorities may choose to decentralise their activities which remain an alternative to the provisions of this section: decentralising consumer access, service delivery arrangements and managerial responsibility, and political control to committees under s.101 of the 1972 Act.

Subsection (1) enables the Secretary of State to give a direction before July 1, 1996 (subs. (7)) to a principal council to submit a decentralisation scheme for some specified area which becomes subject to his approval or modification and thereupon implemented with his guarantee (s.28).

Subsection (2) provides conditions under which the Secretary of State may give a direction under subs. (1): there must have been an application for a decentralisation scheme from at least 10 elected members of the area which is to be the subject of the direction. Such applications must be made by January 1, 1996 (subs. (7)).

Subsection (3) defines a decentralisation scheme as a scheme which provides for the exercise of specified functions by an area committee. At the Commons Committee Stage the Minister gave a Government view on the range of functions that might be included in a decentralisation scheme, such as: environmental health, trading standards, leisure, management and allocation of council housing, maintenance of minor highways, planning applications, aspects of education and social services and libraries (*Hansard*, H.C. Vol. 243, col. 383). The schemes would not be able to devolve responsibilities for funding schools, housing revenue account, setting the council tax, archives, emergency planning, child protection, trunk road agencies, superannuation, internal audit, benefit and council tax administration, community care plans, or unitary development plans (*ibid.*, col. 389). The Government has stated that the schemes will specify the arrangements for the financing of the area committees and for establishing accountability. The area committees will not be corporate bodies and thus the scheme will acknowledge that the area committees cannot employ staff, own assets or enter into contracts.

Subsections (4) and (5) require councils to respond to a direction with a submitted decentralisation scheme by a specified date.

Subsections (8) and (9) indicate that the Secretary of State will only respond to an application for a scheme by giving a direction in certain circumstances – having regard to the efficient administration of functions and the geographical, historical, cultural and demographic circumstances. In a Welsh Office consultation paper issued in January 1994, the Secretary of State indicated that he was unlikely to issue a direction in areas where the unitary authority was largely based on a former district. Ministers have stated that they are most likely to issue directions resulting from applications from areas which have some previous history as a local government unit.

Subsections (11) and (12) enable the Secretary of State to give guidance with respect to the preparation and content of decentralisation schemes.

Decentralisation schemes: approval and implementation

28.—(1) Where a council have submitted a decentralisation scheme to the Secretary of State under section 27 he shall, before the end of the period of six months beginning with the date on which the scheme was submitted to him—

(a) approve the scheme as submitted;

(b) approve the scheme subject to such modifications as he considers appropriate; or

(c) reject the scheme.

(2) Where he proposes not to approve the scheme as submitted, the Secretary of State shall notify the council concerned, before the end of that six month period, of the modifications which he proposes to make to the scheme, or (as the case may be) that he proposes to reject the scheme.

(3) Before he approves a scheme subject to modifications, or rejects a scheme, the Secretary of State shall have regard to any representations which have been made to him by the council concerned.

(4) Where the Secretary of State approves a decentralisation scheme, it shall be the duty of the council concerned to implement and maintain the scheme.

(5) The Secretary of State's decision under subsection (1) shall be given in writing.

(6) Where the Secretary of State approves a decentralisation scheme, he may give a direction to the council concerned as to the date by which the scheme is to be implemented.

(7) Where the Secretary of State has rejected a decentralisation scheme, he may at any time before the end of the period of six months beginning with the date on which he rejected the scheme, direct the council concerned to prepare and submit to him a revised scheme under section 27.

(8) Nothing in section 27(7) shall be taken to prevent the giving of a direction under subsection (7).

(9) A direction under subsection (7) may require the revised scheme to be submitted to the Secretary of State before a specified date.

Definitions

"decentralisation scheme": ss.27(3) and 64(1).

General Note

This section specifies the procedures for the approval and implementation of decentralisation schemes which were required from principal councils by direction under s.27.

Subsection (1) allows the Secretary of State, within six months of receiving a scheme, to approve, modify or reject a scheme; having regard to any representations made by the council (subs. (3)).

If the Secretary of State approves a scheme, he may give a direction requiring it to be implemented by a specified date (subs. (6)) and it shall be a duty of the council to implement and maintain the scheme (subs. (4)).

If the Secretary intends to approve a scheme subject to his modifications he must notify the council of his modifications within the six months of his consideration of the scheme (subs. (2)), presumably allowing the council to make further representations under subs. (3).

Where the Secretary of State rejects a scheme which he can do within six months of its submission, he may direct a council to submit a revised scheme (subs. (7)) under s.27. There appear to be no time constraints on the procedures for submitting and approving a revised scheme as s.28(8) removes the restriction imposed by s.27(7) where a direction is given under s.28(7).

Area committees: safeguards

29.—(1) Where an area committee has been established by a council in accordance with an approved decentralisation scheme—

    (a) the council shall not, except with the agreement of the committee, abolish the committee or alter any arrangements in force with respect to the committee which were made in accordance with the scheme as originally approved or which have subsequently been agreed with the committee; and

    (b) nothing in section 101(4) of the 1972 Act (power of local authority to exercise functions otherwise discharged by committee) shall be taken to authorise the council to exercise any functions which are to be discharged by the committee, except as provided for by the scheme.

(2) Every decentralisation scheme shall include provision, to be given effect to by the standing orders of the council concerned, for the majority required in order for any suspending resolution to be passed to be such majority greater than a simple majority as may be specified by the scheme.

(3) In subsection (2) "suspending resolution", in relation to a decentralisation scheme, means a resolution to suspend any of the arrangements in force with respect to an area committee established in accordance with the scheme.

DEFINITIONS
    "area committee": s.27(6).
    "decentralisation scheme": ss.27(3) and 64(1).
    "suspending resolution": subs. (3).
    "the 1972 Act": s.64(1).

GENERAL NOTE
    Subsection (1) ensures that no principal council will be able to abolish an area committee approved under s.28 or alter the approved arrangements except with the consent of the area committee concerned. This is the effect of the guarantee provided by the Secretary of State. It makes a committee established under s.28 distinctly different to any committee established under s.101 of the 1972 Act and, in the view of critics, creates problems of rigidity and accountability. Section 101(4) of the 1972 Act which specifically allows a principal council to exercise functions otherwise discharged by committee is disapplied by this subsection.

    Subsections (2) and (3) attempt to introduce some flexibility in the implementation of the decentralisation scheme by allowing the scheme to specify a procedure in standing orders for the suspension of any of the arrangements of the decentralisation scheme. Subsection (2) provides that the majority required for a suspending resolution must be more than a simple majority. The January 1994 Welsh Office Consultation Paper on decentralisation suggested that the scheme would need to ensure that the majority required was not so low as to allow a majority on the principal council to out-vote all the members of the area committee, *i.e.* potentially at least one member of the area committee would need to vote for the suspending resolution for it to have effect.

Area committees: membership etc.

30.—(1) This section applies where an area committee has been established by a council in accordance with an approved decentralisation scheme.

(2) The provisions of the 1972 Act with respect to arrangements for the discharge of functions by committees of local authorities and sub-com-

mittees, and the appointment of such committees and sub-committees, shall be subject to this section and section 31.

(3) Every person who is a member of the council for an electoral division which falls within the area for which the committee is established shall be entitled to be appointed to the committee at his request.

(4) The committee may appoint additional persons, including members of the council who are not entitled to membership of the committee under subsection (3), as members of the committee.

(5) No other persons shall be eligible for appointment to the committee.

(6) In this section, in relation to an area committee, "co-opted member" means any member appointed by the committee under subsection (4).

(7) Where the Secretary of State has given a direction under section 297 of the Education Act 1993 (power to direct appointment of members of certain committees) which applies to the committee and can only be complied with by the appointment of one or more additional members to the committee, it shall be the duty of the committee to exercise its powers of appointment to secure compliance with the direction.

(8) A co-opted member of an area committee shall not be entitled to vote at any meeting of the committee on any question which falls to be decided at that meeting.

(9) Nothing in subsection (8) shall prevent the appointment of a person, in compliance with a direction under section 297 of the Act of 1993, as a voting member of an area committee.

(10) In the application of section 101 of the 1972 Act (arrangement for discharge of functions by local authorities) in relation to the committee—
- (a) subsection (1) shall have effect as if it gave power to the committee, if authorised to do so by the decentralisation scheme, to arrange for the discharge of any of its functions by a local authority other than the authority who made the scheme;
- (b) subsection (2) shall have effect with the omission of the words "unless the local authority otherwise direct" and (in the second place where they occur) the words "the local authority or".

(11) Sections 102(3) of the 1972 Act (power to include persons who are not members of the local authority concerned) and 15 of the Local Government and Housing Act 1989 (political balance on committees) shall not apply in relation to membership of the committee.

(12) The term of office of each of the co-opted members of an area committee shall be fixed by the committee.

(13) Section 102(2) of the 1972 Act (number of members of committee and terms of office) shall not apply in relation to the committee.

(14) In the case of an appointment made in order to comply with a direction under section 297 of the Act of 1993, the committee shall exercise its powers under subsection (12) subject to any provision of the direction relating to terms of office.

DEFINITIONS
"area committee": s.27(6).
"co-opted member": subs. (6).
"decentralisation scheme": ss.27(3) and 64(1).
"the 1972 Act": s.64(1).

GENERAL NOTE
Subsection (3) requires that every member elected for a electoral division within the area of the area committee approved under s.28 is entitled to be appointed to the area committee at his request. This entitlement overrides any provision of the 1972 Act (subs. (2)).

Subsection (4) allows the area committee to appoint additional members who are not elected from divisions within the area who thereby become co-opted members (subs. (6)) for a period fixed by the committee (subs. (11)) without voting rights (subs. (8)). The additional members may or may not be members of the principal council which itself cannot appoint additional members (subs. (5)).

Subsection (7) ensures that if an area committee has responsibilities with regard to education then the Secretary of State has power to direct appointments to the area committees as defined under s.297 of the Education Act 1993 (c. 35). Such appointees may be appointed as voting members of the committee.

Subsection (10) allows an area committee to arrange for the discharge of its functions by another local authority, and exempts from provisions of the 1972 Act which would require such an act by a committee to be agreed by the principal council. Government ministers have stated that they anticipate this power to be used with reference to community councils within the area of the committee.

Subsections (11) and (12) disapply the provisions of s.102(2) and (3) of the 1972 Act relating to the number of members on committees and the membership of non-council members on the committees. They also exempt from the requirements for political balance in s.15 of the Local Government and Housing Act 1989 (c. 42).

Sub-committees of area committees

31.—(1) In this section "sub-committee" means a sub-committee of an area committee.

(2) The members of a sub-committee shall be appointed by the area committee from among persons who are—

(a) members of the area committee appointed under subsection (3) of section 30; or

(b) entitled to be members of the area committee by virtue of that subsection.

(3) Subject to subsection (10), a sub-committee may appoint additional persons, including persons who are not members of the area committee concerned, as members of the sub-committee.

(4) No other persons shall be eligible for appointment to a sub-committee.

(5) In this section, in relation to a sub-committee, "co-opted member" means any member of the sub-committee appointed under subsection (3).

(6) Where the Secretary of State has given a direction under section 297 of the Education Act 1993 (power to direct appointment of members of certain committees) which applies to a sub-committee, it shall be the duty of the area committee concerned and the sub-committee to secure compliance with the direction.

(7) A co-opted member of a sub-committee shall not be entitled to vote at any meeting of the sub-committee on any question which falls to be decided at that meeting.

(8) Nothing in subsection (7) shall prevent the appointment of a person in compliance with a direction under section 297 of the Act of 1993 as a voting member of a sub-committee.

(9) Sections 102(3) of the 1972 Act (power to include persons who are not members of the local authority concerned) and 15 of the Local Government and Housing Act 1989 (political balance on committees) shall not apply in relation to membership of a sub-committee.

(10) The number of members of a sub-committee and their terms of office shall be fixed by the area committee concerned.

(11) Section 102(2) of the 1972 Act (number of members of committee and terms of office) shall not apply in relation to the sub-committee.

(12) In the case of an appointment made in order to comply with a direction under section 297 of the Act of 1993, the area committee shall exercise its powers under subsection (10) subject to any provision of the direction relating to terms of office.

DEFINITIONS
"area committee": s.27(6).
"co-opted member": subs. (5).
"sub-committee": subs. (1).
"the 1972 Act": s.64(1).

GENERAL NOTE
   This section enables area committees to appoint sub-committees from within the membership of the area committees (subs. (2)) and gives the sub-committees the power to co-opt additional members (subs. (3)) without voting rights (subs. (7)) although the total membership of the sub-committee may be fixed by the area committee (subs. (10)). Other parts of the section apply the provisions of s.297 of the Education Act 1993 (c. 35) to the sub-committees and exempt from s.102(2) and (3) of the 1972 Act and s.15 of the Local Government and Housing Act 1989 (c. 42) to sub-committees.

Joint working

Provision of information to Secretary of State

32.—(1) The Secretary of State may at any time before 31st March 1999 direct any new principal council to give to him—
   (a) details of the arrangements which they have made, or propose to make, for the performance of specified functions of theirs; and
   (b) information of a specified kind or description as to the performance of specified functions of theirs.
   (2) In subsection (1) "specified", in relation to a direction, means specified in the direction.
   (3) Nothing in this section is to be taken as affecting the operation of any other provision under which a local authority may be required to provide information of any kind to the Secretary of State or to any other person.

DEFINITIONS
   "principal council": s.270 of the 1972 Act.
   "specified": subs. (2).

GENERAL NOTE
   Section 32 should be considered alongside ss.33 and 34. Taken together they represent a set of reserve powers which the Act awards the Secretary of State during the transition period of the reform which the Government considers to extend to March 31, 1999. Until that date, the Secretary of State is enabled by this section to require any information from the principal councils. By s.33, he may impose a joint arrangement where a joint working agreement has been agreed but has not been, or in the opinion of the Secretary of State is not likely to be, implemented. By s.34, where the joint arrangement imposed by direction under s.33 subsequently appears to the Secretary of State to be impractical, or has not been implemented, or are unlikely to continue working satisfactorily, he may impose a joint authority. The Government justified these sections by referring to the difficult challenge of managing the transition to the new structures and arguing that the Government should have the responsibility to monitor service delivery arrangements and intervene where it perceives actual breakdown or a danger of breakdown.
   These sections may be compared with s.21 of the Local Government Act 1992 (c. 19) which gives the Secretary of State in England the more simple but inflexible power to impose a joint authority at any time.
   Subsection (1) of s.32 enables the Secretary of State at any time before March 31, 1999 to require the new principal councils to provide information on existing arrangements, performance and proposed arrangements.
   Subsection (3) specifies that this power stands alongside any existing powers of the Secretary of State to require information. It is difficult to see how this section adds anything to the still applicable s.230 of the 1972 Act which requires all local authorities to send to the Secretary of State any information that he may require.

Joint working arrangements

33.—(1) Where it appears to the Secretary of State—
   (a) that particular functions of a new principal council should be discharged in accordance with arrangements entered into by that council and one or more other such councils in relation to the exercise of those functions, but

(b) that satisfactory arrangements for the exercise of those functions will not be, or are unlikely to be, in force on or after 1st April 1996,

he may, at any time before 31st March 1999, give a direction to the councils concerned requiring them to make specified arrangements in relation to the exercise of specified functions.

(2) The arrangements specified may, in particular, be, or include, arrangements for the joint exercise of functions.

(3) In this section "specified", in relation to a direction, means specified in the direction.

(4) In considering whether to give a direction under subsection (1), the Secretary of State shall have regard, in particular, to the desirability of the functions in question being discharged effectively and in a financially efficient manner.

(5) A direction under subsection (1) shall remain in force—

(a) until it is withdrawn by a notice in writing given by the Secretary of State to the councils concerned; or

(b) where a period is specified in the direction during which the direction is to have effect, and the direction has not been withdrawn by the Secretary of State, until the end of that period.

(6) A direction under subsection (1) may at any time while it is in force be varied by the Secretary of State.

(7) Nothing in subsection (5) or (6) shall be taken to affect the power of the Secretary of State to give a further direction under subsection (1).

DEFINITIONS

"new": s.64(1).

"principal council": s.270 of the 1972 Act.

"specified": subs. (3).

GENERAL NOTE

This section enables the Secretary of State before March 31, 1999 to give a direction requiring the new principal councils to make specified arrangements in relation to the exercise of specified functions. This is the second of the "reserve powers" described in the note to s.32.

Subsection (1) enables the Secretary of State to give a direction requiring principal councils to make a specified arrangement in relation to the exercise of specified functions. He may do so where it appears to him that a particular function should be discharged, having regard to effectiveness and financial efficiency (subs. (4)), in accordance with arrangements entered into by that council and one or more other councils, *i.e.* where it appears to him that there should be a joint arrangement but there is not one nor is there likely to be one. Sir Wyn Roberts stated that the power would be used "when it appears that there is likely to be a failure of a service or when failure has occurred (*Hansard*, H.C. Vol. 243 col. 454). It may be significant that this view of the Secretary of State need not depend on any information gained from a direction under s.32. Lord Rodger of Earlsferry in the House of Lords (*Hansard*, H.L. Vol. 552, cols. 859, 861) stated that the Secretary of State would be constrained by the possibility of judicial review to act in a proper manner and would, before he exercised powers under this section, consult with the local authorities.

Subsection (2) states that the specified arrangements may include arrangements for the joint exercise of functions. Presumably, therefore, the specified arrangement may not be a joint arrangement, which is interesting given that the power of the Secretary of State is contingent upon his view that the function is suffering from the absence of a joint arrangement.

Subsection (5) makes clear that a direction under this section may be limited to a period specified in the section or may continue for an indefinite period until it is withdrawn by the Secretary of State. Although the power to give a direction expires on April 1, 1999 any direction given before that date may continue thereafter.

Joint authorities

34.—(1) Where a direction has been given by the Secretary of State under section 33 but it appears to him that—

(a) it has proved impracticable to implement the arrangements required by the direction,

(b) the required arrangements have been implemented but are not working satisfactorily, or

(c) the required arrangements are, or have been, working satisfactorily but are unlikely to continue to work satisfactorily,

he may by order establish a body to act for the areas of the councils to which the direction relates.

(2) A body established under subsection (1) shall be known as a joint authority and may be established as a body corporate.

(3) A joint authority shall consist of such number of members as may be determined by the order establishing it.

(4) Those members shall be appointed by the councils to which the order relates, from among their members, each council being entitled to appoint such number of members as may be specified in the order.

(5) Where at any time the number of members of a joint authority is less than the required number, the Secretary of State may, if he is satisfied that the councils concerned have had a reasonable opportunity to make the necessary appointment or appointments—

(a) give such direction to the councils concerned or to any of them as he considers appropriate; and

(b) appoint such members (from among such persons as he considers appropriate) as may be required to complete the membership of the authority.

(6) The joint authority shall discharge the functions to which the direction relates, from a date specified in the order establishing the authority until such alternative arrangements for the exercise of the functions as appear to the Secretary of State to be satisfactory are brought into force.

(7) The power conferred on the Secretary of State by subsection (1) may not be exercised after 31st March 1999 but an order under subsection (1) which is made before that date shall continue in force until revoked by the Secretary of State.

(8) An order under this section may—

(a) provide for the joint authority concerned to be treated, for all purposes or only for the purposes of such enactments as may be prescribed, as a new principal council;

(b) provide for such enactments relating to new principal councils as may be prescribed (either generally or by reference to specified enactments) to have effect in relation to the joint authority concerned subject to such modifications as may be prescribed;

(c) make provision enabling the Secretary of State to require the joint authority concerned to submit to him a scheme for winding itself up and for the transfer to any of the councils for whose areas the joint authority is established of any of the joint authority's property, rights and liabilities or of any functions which it carries out.

(9) The Secretary of State may by order provide—

(a) for excluding any functions, or any functions in any area, from those falling to be carried out by a joint authority; and

(b) for giving effect (with or without modifications) to any scheme submitted to him under a provision made by virtue of subsection (8) for the dissolution of a joint authority.

(10) The power to make an order under this section includes, in particular, power to make provision for the transfer of property, rights and liabilities.

DEFINITIONS
"joint authority": subs. (2).
"new": s.64(1).
"principal council": s.270 of the 1972 Act.

GENERAL NOTE
If the Secretary of State believes that an arrangement directed under s.33 is not working satis-factorily, or may not in the future, he may under s.34, by order, up to March 31, 1999 (subs. (7)) establish a body to act for the areas to which the s.33 direction relates (subs. (1)). This body shall be known as a joint authority and may be a body corporate (subs. (2)), to be treated as a new principal council (subs. (8)(a)) to which the order may transfer property, rights and liabilities (subs. (10)). As bodies corporate, the authorities may sue and be sued in their own name; see annotations in the *Encyclopedia of Local Government Law* (Sweet & Maxwell) on s.2 of the 1972 Act.

Subsection (4) states that the members of the joint authority shall be elected members nomi-nated by the principal councils to which the order relates, with the number to be nominated by each council to be specified by the order (subs. (3)). The Secretary of State can only nominate members if the principal councils do not make the nominations they are entitled to make (subs. (5)).

An order under this section may enable the Secretary of State to require the joint authority to submit to him a scheme for winding itself up (subs. (8)(c)) to which he may give effect by a further order (subs. (9)(b)).

PART IV

FINANCE

Council tax, rating and the community charge

35.—(1) The new principal councils shall be billing authorities in relation to the financial year beginning on 1st April 1996 and in relation to subsequent financial years.

(2) In this section "billing authority" means an authority which is a billing authority for the purposes of—

   (a) Part I of the Local Government Finance Act 1992 (council tax); and

   (b) Part III of the Local Government Finance Act 1988 (non-domestic rating).

(3) In the period before 1st April 1996, the old authorities concerned shall continue to exercise their functions as billing authorities in respect of matters arising in connection with financial years before the financial year beginning on that date.

(4) After 31st March 1996, the new principal councils shall have the same functions in relation to council tax, rating (including non-domestic rating) and the community charge as the old authorities would have had—

   (a) in connection with those matters, and

   (b) in relation to any financial year beginning before 1996,

if the old authorities had not been abolished.

(5) For section 1(2) of the Act of 1992 substitute—

   "(2) In this Part "billing authority" means—

   (a) in relation to England, a district council or London borough council, the Common Council or the Council of the Isles of Scilly, and

   (b) in relation to Wales, a county council or county borough council."

(6) In section 39(1) of the Act of 1992 (precepting authorities), in para-graph (a) at the end add "in England".

DEFINITIONS
"billing authority": subs. (2) and s.1(2) of the Local Government Finance Act 1992 as amended by this section.
"community charge": s.1 of the Local Government Finance Act 1988.
"council tax": s.1(1) of the Local Government Finance Act 1992.
"financial year": s.64(1).
"new": s.64(1).
"non-domestic rating": Part III of the Local Government Finance Act 1988.
"old authority": s.64(1).
"precepting authorities": ss.39 and 69 of the Local Government Finance Act 1992.
"principal council": s.270 of the 1972 Act.

GENERAL NOTE
The Act does nothing to change in substance the arrangements for the financing of local government in Wales. Whereas previously the district councils were the billing authorities upon whom the county councils precepted their local taxes, this section provides for all the new principal councils to be billing authorities.

This section provides for the new authorities to be billing authorities for the financial year 1996–97 and beyond with the power to set and collect council tax and to collect non-domestic rates, inheriting the old authorities' rights and liabilities as to local authority taxation.

Valuation lists for Welsh billing authorities

36. After section 22 of the Local Government Finance Act 1992, insert—

"Amalgamated valuation lists for Welsh billing authorities

22A.—(1) Every new listing officer shall, on 1st April 1996, compile a list ("the amalgamated list") for the new billing authority for which he is appointed, based on the information provided for him under this section.

(2) The amalgamated list shall contain the information which was included in the valuation lists compiled on 1st April 1993 for the old billing authorities ("the current lists") so far as that information is relevant.

(3) The amalgamated list shall also include the information which was included in any current list by way of an alteration, so far as that information is relevant.

(4) A new listing officer's amalgamated list shall be treated, for the purposes of this Act, as the valuation list for his new billing authority and shall be deemed to have come into force on 1st April 1993.

(5) Where an amalgamated list contains information which is derived from any alteration made to any valuation list or lists from which it is derived, the amalgamated list shall be treated as having been varied on the date on which the alteration was made.

(6) Subsections (2) to (8) of section 22 above shall not apply in relation to an amalgamated list.

(7) Every listing officer shall—

(a) on or before 15th November 1995, provide the appropriate new listing officer with the information recorded in his valuation list as at 31st October 1995 so far as it is relevant; and

(b) on 31st March 1996, provide the appropriate new listing officer with the information recorded in his valuation list as at that date, so far as it is relevant.

(8) A new listing officer receiving any information under subsection (7)(a) above shall send a copy of it to his new billing authority as soon as is reasonably practicable.

(9) As soon as is reasonably practicable after compiling the amalgamated list, a new listing officer shall send a copy of it to his new billing authority.

(10) A new billing authority receiving a copy of an amalgamated list under subsection (9) above shall, as soon as is reasonably practicable, deposit it at its principal office.

(11) In this section—

"old authority" has the same meaning as in the Local Government (Wales) Act 1994;

"old billing authority" means a billing authority which is an old authority;

"new billing authority" means a billing authority which is a new principal council;

"listing officer" means a listing officer for an old billing authority;

"new listing officer" means a listing officer for a new billing authority; and "new principal council" has the same meaning as in the Local Government (Wales) Act 1994.

(12) For the purposes of this section—

(a) references to a listing officer's valuation list are references to the valuation list maintained by him under this Act;

(b) a new listing officer's area is the area of the new billing authority for which he is appointed;

(c) the appropriate new listing officer, in relation to any information which relates to a dwelling is the new listing officer for the new billing authority in whose area the dwelling is situated; and

(d) information is relevant in relation to a new listing officer, or his area, if it relates to a dwelling which is in his area."

DEFINITIONS

"amalgamated list": s.22A(1) of the Local Government Finance Act 1992, as enacted by this section.

"billing authority": s.1(2) of the Local Government Finance Act 1992, as amended by s.35(5) of this Act.

"current lists": s.22A(2) of the Local Government Finance Act 1992, as enacted by this section.

"dwelling": ss.3 and 69 of the Local Government Finance Act 1992.

"listing officer": s.22A(11) of the Local Government Finance Act 1992, as enacted by this section and ss.20 and 69 of the Local Government Finance Act 1992.

"new": s.64(1).

"new billing authority": s.22A(11) of the Local Government Finance Act 1992, as enacted by this section.

"new listing officer": s.22A(11) of the Local Government Finance Act 1992, as enacted by this section and ss.20 and 69 of the Local Government Finance Act 1992.

"old authority": s.64(1).

"old billing authority": s.22A(11) of the Local Government Finance Act 1992, as enacted by this section.

"principal council": s.270 of the 1972 Act.

"valuation list": s.22 of the Local Government Finance Act 1992.

GENERAL NOTE

This section inserts s.22A into the Local Government Finance Act 1992 (c. 14) to provide for the compilation of an amalgamated council tax list for each new billing authority. The amalgamated list is to contain any relevant information which was included in the valuation lists compiled for the old billing authorities and will be deemed to have come into force on April 1, 1993. The effect will be to furnish the new authorities with valuation lists concerning details of the dwellings situated in the area of each new authority and indicating the valuation band applicable to each dwelling.

Local non-domestic rating lists for Welsh billing authorities

37. After section 41 of the Local Government Finance Act 1988, insert—

"Local non-domestic rating lists for Welsh billing authorities

41A.—(1) Every new valuation officer shall, on 1st April 1996, compile a list ("the amalgamated list") for the new billing authority for which he is appointed, based on the information provided for him under this section.

(2) The amalgamated list shall contain the information which was included in the local non-domestic rating lists compiled on 1st April 1995 for the old billing authorities ("the current lists") so far as that information is relevant.

(3) The amalgamated list shall also include the information which was included in any current list by way of an alteration, so far as that information is relevant.

(4) A new valuation officer's amalgamated list shall be treated, for the purposes of this Act, as the local non-domestic rating list for his new

billing authority and shall be deemed to have come into force on 1st April 1995.

(5) Where an amalgamated list contains information which is derived from any alteration made to any list or lists from which it is derived, the amalgamated list shall be treated as having been varied on the date on which the alteration was made.

(6) Subsections (2) to (6B) of section 41 above shall not apply in relation to an amalgamated list.

(7) Every valuation officer shall—

(a) on or before 15th October 1995, provide the appropriate new valuation officer with the information recorded in his local non-domestic rating list as at 30th September 1995, so far as it is relevant; and

(b) on 31st March 1996, provide the appropriate new valuation officer with the information recorded in his local non-domestic rating list as at that date, so far as it is relevant.

(8) A new valuation officer receiving any information under subsection (7)(a) above shall send a copy of it to his new billing authority as soon as is reasonably practicable.

(9) As soon as is reasonably practicable after compiling an amalgamated list, a new valuation officer shall send a copy of it to his new billing authority.

(10) A new billing authority receiving a copy of an amalgamated list under subsection (9) above shall, as soon as is reasonably practicable, deposit it at its principal office.

(11) In this section—

"old authority" has the same meaning as in the Local Government (Wales) Act 1994;

"old billing authority" means a billing authority which is an old authority;

"new billing authority" means a billing authority which is a new principal council;

"new principal council" has the same meaning as in the Local Government (Wales) Act 1994;

"valuation officer" means a valuation officer for an old billing authority; and

"new valuation officer" means a valuation officer for a new billing authority.

(12) For the purposes of this section—

(a) references to a valuation officer's local non-domestic rating list are references to the local non-domestic rating list maintained by him under this Act;

(b) a new valuation officer's area is the area of the new billing authority for which he is appointed;

(c) the appropriate new valuation officer, in relation to any information which relates to any hereditament is the new valuation officer for the new billing authority in whose area the hereditament is situated; and

(d) information is relevant in relation to a new valuation officer, or his area, if it relates to a hereditament which is in his area."

DEFINITIONS

"amalgamated list": s.41A of the Local Government Finance Act 1992, as enacted by this section.

"billing authority": s.1(2) of the Local Government Finance Act 1992, as amended by s.35(5) of this Act.

"current lists": s.41A(2) of the Local Government Finance Act 1992, as enacted by this section.

"hereditament": ss.64 and 67 of the Local Government Finance Act 1988.

"local non-domestic rating list": s.41(1) of the Local Government Finance Act 1988.
"new": s.64(1).
"new billing authority": s.41A(11) of the Local Government Finance Act 1992, as enacted by this section.
"new valuation officer": s.41A(11) of the Local Government Finance Act 1992, as enacted by this section and s.67(2) of the Local Government Finance Act 1988.
"old authority": s.64(1).
"old billing authority": s.41A(11) of the Local Government Finance Act 1992, as enacted by this section.
"principal council": s.270 of the 1972 Act.
"valuation list": s.22 of the Local Government Finance Act 1992.
"valuation officer": s.41A(11) of the Local Government Finance Act 1992, as enacted by this section and s.67(2) of the Local Government Finance Act 1988.

GENERAL NOTE

The rates poundage for non-domestic rates is fixed nationally for Wales and then tied to annual increases in the retail prices index. The poundage is reset when the non-domestic rateable values are reassessed every five years (in 1990, 1995, etc.). They are currently collected locally by district councils and paid into a national pool, administered by the Secretary of State for Wales, from which they are redistributed to the Welsh counties and districts.

This section inserts s.41A into the Local Government Finance Act 1988 (c. 41) to provide for the compilation of an amalgamated local non-domestic rating list for each new billing authority. The amalgamated list is to contain any relevant information which was included in the local non-domestic rating lists compiled for the old billing authorities and will be deemed to have come into force on April 1, 1995.

Council funds for new principal councils

38.—(1) Each new principal council shall establish, and then maintain, a fund to be known as their council fund.

(2) Any sums received by a new principal council shall be paid into their council fund.

(3) All payments by a new principal council shall be made out of their council fund.

(4) Subsections (2) and (3) do not apply in relation to any sums to be paid into, or payments to be made out of, a trust fund.

(5) Section 101(1)(b) of the 1972 Act (delegation) shall not apply as regards the functions of a new principal council in relation to their council fund.

(6) Each new principal council shall keep accounts of sums paid into, and of payments made out of, their council fund.

(7) Any account kept only in respect of the general expenses of a new principal council shall be known as their general account and any account kept only in respect of any class of their special expenses shall be known as a special account.

(8) The Secretary of State may make regulations—
   (a) requiring assets of a prescribed description which fall within a council fund to be held in a separate fund within the council fund;
   (b) requiring any fund (other than a trust fund) of a prescribed description which is established by a new principal council to be maintained as a separate fund within their council fund.

(9) The Secretary of State may by regulations make provision with respect to the liability of new principal councils to make payments from their council funds in respect of precepts issued under Chapter IV of Part I of the Local Government Finance Act 1992.

(10) The regulations may, in particular, include provision—
   (a) that anything falling to be paid must be paid—
        (i) within a prescribed period; and
        (ii) in instalments of such amounts, and at such times, as are determined by the billing authority in accordance with prescribed rules;

(b) that the billing authority must inform any precepting authorities when instalments will be paid and how they are to be calculated;

(c) that if an instalment is not paid to a precepting authority in accordance with the regulations, it is to be entitled to interest on the amount of the instalment;

(d) as to the circumstances in which the billing authority is to be treated as having discharged the liability mentioned in subsection (9);

(e) as to the recovery (by deduction or otherwise) of any excess amount paid by the billing authority to any precepting authority in purported discharge of the liability mentioned in subsection (9).

(11) Schedule 12 makes minor and consequential amendments with respect to funds.

DEFINITIONS

"billing authority": s.1(2) of the Local Government Finance Act 1992, as amended by s.35(5) of this Act.

"council fund": ss.(1).

"new": s.64(1).

"precepting authority": ss.39 and 69 of the Local Government Finance Act 1992.

"prescribed": s.64(1).

"principal council": s.270 of the 1972 Act.

GENERAL NOTE

This section provides for each new authority to establish and maintain a council fund. With the exception of transactions relating to a trust fund or other funds specifically regulated by the Secretary of State (subs. (8)), any sums received by a new authority are to be paid into its council fund and all payments by a new authority are to be made out of its council fund.

Subsection (9) empowers the Secretary of State, by regulations, to make provision concerning the liability of new principal councils to make payments from their council funds in respect of precepts issued under the Local Government Finance Act 1992 (c. 14). Any regulations are subject to annulment in pursuance of a resolution of either House of Parliament.

By virtue of Chap. IV of Pt. I of the Local Government Finance Act 1992, precepting authorities in Wales are required to issue precepts to the new principal council for each financial year in order to seek from the new authorities the amounts needed to finance their spending. The new councils will be issued with precepts by (a) community councils (local precepting authorities) and (b) police authorities (major precepting authorities).

PART V

RESIDUARY MATTERS AND STAFF

The Residuary Body for Wales or Corff Gweddilliol Cymru

39.—(1) On 31st March 1996 or on such earlier day as the Secretary of State may by order appoint, there shall be a body corporate to be known as the Residuary Body for Wales or Corff Gweddilliol Cymru (but in this Act referred to as the Residuary Body).

(2) Schedule 13 shall have effect with respect to the Residuary Body.

DEFINITIONS

"the Residuary Body": s.64(1).

GENERAL NOTE

This section enables the Secretary of State to appoint a Residuary Body as a body corporate at any time on or before March 31, 1996.

Schedule 13 provides the framework for the Residuary Body. The purpose of the Residuary Body is to inherit assets, rights and liabilities not otherwise dealt with by the remaining provisions of the Act (para. 11). The Residuary Body will have powers to manage and dispose of surplus property, paying any such sums to the new principal councils in such proportions as the Secretary of State may direct (para. 13).

A key role for the Residuary Body (para. 9) will be to advise the Secretary of State in the exercise of his powers under s.54(2)(c) which allows the Secretary of State to make orders for the transfer of property, rights and liabilities, and of related functions, from an abolished body, or the Residuary Body, to a new principal council, or other public body or to the Residuary Body, in a manner which is incidental, consequential, transitional or supplemental to the provisions of the Act (s.54(1)). Sir Wyn Roberts gave the Government's view on circumstances when assets could be transferred to the Residuary Body within the constraints of s.54 (*Hansard*, H.C. Vol. 243, col. 499):

"In general that [s.54(2)(c)] limits the Secretary of State's powers to transfer assets to the residuary body to cases where administrative buildings are no longer required by the new authorities to carry out their functions. There are two exceptions. The first is when the ownership of the assets is in dispute. Those assets and liabilities could be transferred to the residuary body until the issue of ownership had been resolved. The second exception is other assets which are no longer needed by authorities for the purposes of carrying out their functions."

This statement does, however, leave open the question of who decides whether assets are "no longer needed".

Paragraph 1(1)–(3) enables the Secretary of State to appoint the Chairman and four to seven members of the Residuary Body.

Paragraph 2 declares that the members and officers of the Residuary Body are not Crown servants. For many purposes the Residuary Body is given the powers of a local authority (paras. 19 to 32). Paragraph 10 requires that the Residuary Body publishes an annual report which is sent to the Secretary of State who is required to lay such reports before Parliament. Paragraph 15 requires that the Residuary Body prepares an annual statement of accounts which complies with directions given by the Secretary of State with the consent of the Treasury. Paragraph 16 requires that the Residuary Body is subject to audit as if it were a local authority. Paragraph 17 subjects the Residuary Body to the potential scrutiny of the Parliamentary Commissioner for Administration.

Paragraph 18 provides for the winding up of the Residuary Body after a period of five years from its establishment although para. 18(4) does allow for an extension of this period subject to an order laid before Parliament through the negative resolution procedure.

The Staff Commission for Wales or Comisiwn Staff Cymru

40.—(1) There shall be a body corporate to be known as the Staff Commission for Wales or Comisiwn Staff Cymru (but in this Act referred to as the Commission).

(2) The Commission shall—

(a) advise the Secretary of State on the steps necessary to safeguard the interests of staff employed by—
     (i) the old authorities;
     (ii) the new principal councils; or
     (iii) the Residuary Body;

(b) consider and keep under review—
     (i) arrangements for the recruitment of the staff of any of those bodies; and
     (ii) the organisation, management and remuneration of the staff of the new principal councils;

(c) consider and keep under review the arrangements for the transfer of staff from any of the old authorities in consequence of any provision made by or under this Act; and

(d) consider such staffing problems and other staffing matters as may be referred to it by the Secretary of State as arising out of any provision made by or under this Act.

(3) The Secretary of State may give directions to the Commission as to its procedure and to any of the new principal councils or old authorities, or the Residuary Body, with respect to—

(a) the supply of any information requested, and the implementation of any advice given, by the Commission; and

(b) the payment by such a council or authority, or by the Residuary Body, of any expenses incurred by the Commission in doing anything requested by that council or authority or by the Residuary Body.

(4) Schedule 14 makes provision with respect to the constitution of the Commission and related matters.

DEFINITIONS
 "new": s.64(1).
 "old authority": s.64(1).
 "principal council": s.270 of the 1972 Act.
 "the Commission": s.64(1).
 "the Residuary Body": s.64(1).

GENERAL NOTE
 This section provides for the establishment of the Staff Commission for Wales on enactment.
 The Commission has the tasks normally associated with Staff Commissions for local government reorganisations: to advise the Secretary of State on the steps necessary to safeguard the
interests of staff (subs. (2)(a)); and to consider arrangements for the transfer of staff (subs.
(2)(c)). It has a novel function in subs. (2)(b) in considering the organisation, management and
remuneration of staff of the new principal councils – issues which many consider to be central to
the local authority's own responsibilities.
 Whilst the Staff Commission is in itself only an advisory body, subs. (3)(a) enables the Secretary of State to direct the implementation of any advice given.
 Schedule 14 provides the constitutional and administrative arrangements for the Commission. It provides for the winding-up of the Staff Commission after three years of its existence,
i.e. on July 5, 1997; although this period may be extended by order.

Continuity of employment in certain cases of voluntary transfer

41.—(1) This section applies to a person ("the employee") who at any time
ceases to be employed by an old authority if—
 (a) the termination of his employment is attributable to any provision
     made by or under this Act;
 (b) he is subsequently employed by another person; and
 (c) by virtue of section 84 of the Employment Protection (Consolidation)
     Act 1978 (renewal or re-engagement) that subsequent employment
     precludes his receiving any redundancy payment under Part VI of that
     Act with respect to his terminated employment.
 (2) Schedule 13 to the Act of 1978 (computation of period of employment
for the purposes of that Act) shall have effect as if it provided—
 (a) for the period of the employee's employment by the old authority to
     count as a period of employment with his new employer; and
 (b) for the change of employer not to break the continuity of the period of
     his employment.
 (3) For the purposes of any provision of the employee's contract of
employment with his new employer which depends on his length of service
with that employer, the period of his employment with the old authority shall
count as a period of employment with his new employer.

DEFINITIONS
 "new": s.64(1).
 "old authority": s.64(1).
 "the employee": subs. (1).

GENERAL NOTE
 This section ensures that if an employee loses employment with one authority, as a result of
the reorganisation, but gains employment in another local authority body, then that employee is
not entitled to redundancy payments from the original authority. This effect is achieved by
ensuring that such a transfer of employment within British local government is considered as a
re-engagement within the terms of s.84 of the Employment Protection (Consolidation) Act 1978
(c. 44). Under that Act the re-engagement or transfer must take place within four weeks of the
loss of employment from the original employing authority.
 Subsections (2) and (3) provide for all service with the old employer to be deemed as service
with the new authority for the purposes of the Employment Protection (Consolidation) Act
1978 or for the purposes of any other provision of the employee's contract of employment.

Transfers of staff

42.—(1) This section applies to any person ("a designated employee")
who, immediately before 1st April 1996 was employed by an abolished body

under a contract of employment which would have continued but for the abolition of that body and who is designated, or falls within a class or description of person designated, for the purposes of this section by an order made, at any time, by the Secretary of State.

(2) The contract of employment between a designated employee and the abolished body concerned shall not be terminated by the abolition of the body but shall have effect from 1st April 1996 as if originally made between him and such new employer as may be specified by the relevant designation order under this section.

(3) Such an order may specify as the new employer a new principal council or the Residuary Body.

(4) Without prejudice to subsection (2)—

(a) all the rights, powers, duties and liabilities of the abolished body under, or in connection with, the contract shall by virtue of this section be transferred on 1st April 1996 to the new employer; and

(b) anything done before 1st April 1996 by or in relation to the abolished body in respect of the contract or the designated employee shall be deemed from that date to have been done by or in relation to the new employer.

(5) Nothing in this section affects any right of a designated employee to terminate his contract of employment if a substantial change is made in his working conditions, to his detriment, but no such right shall arise by reason only of the change of employer effected by this section.

(6) A class or description of person may be specified by an order under subsection (1) by reference to such list or other document or documents as may be identified in accordance with the order.

(7) In this section "abolished body" means an old authority or any joint board which ceases to exist as a result of section 59.

DEFINITIONS
"abolished body": subs. (7).
"designated employee": subs. (1).
"new": s.64(1).
"old authority": s.64(1).
"principal council": s.270 of the 1972 Act.
"the Residuary Body": s.64(1).

GENERAL NOTE
This section empowers the Secretary of State to transfer staff by order from the existing local authorities to the new authorities.
Sir Wyn Roberts gave the Government view on the transfer process with the following statement (*Hansard*, H.C. Vol. 244, col. 787):

"The transfer arrangements would be as follows. First there would be a competition for chief executive and chief officer posts. I would expect that process to be completed by the end of summer 1995. Staff whose jobs were not changing would be identified and listed in draft transfer orders, which would be published no later than the end of November 1995. Any other staff with the right of transfer, under TUPE [Transfer of Undertakings (Protection of Employment) Regulations 1981], would be included in supplementary transfer orders.

Volunteers for redundancy would be sought from the remaining staff … We hope that sufficient volunteers for redundancy would come forward so as to avoid the need for any compulsory redundancies on March 31, 1996. But if that were not the case, some redundancy notices may need to be served before reorganisation. If such notices had not expired by March 31, 1996, it would be possible to transfer the staff concerned to serve out their notice in a new authority.

Perhaps this is the point at which to emphasise that section 53(4) provides for new authorities to take over contractual responsibilities of the old authorities".

The issue which was contested during the legislative process was the efficacy of distinguishing staff with TUPE rights and those without. The above process requires that the existing authorities in the period up to March 31, 1996 identify those staff without posts in the new authorities and without TUPE rights and serve redundancy notices. It is likely that such a distinction would discriminate against staff whose authorities are not being transferred as a whole entity (seven county councils and two district councils). The above process may therefore not achieve the objective of the Government stated by Lord Rodger of Earlsferry, "that the transfer arrangements treat staff from counties and districts on the basis of equality" (*Hansard*, H.L. Vol. 551, col. 773).

It may be significant that whereas the Act allows for the discrimination between staff deemed to have TUPE rights and those not so deemed, the Act may not require such discrimination. On the advice of the Staff Commission it would be possible for the Government to alter its expectations such that no notices of compulsory redundancy are issued before April 1, 1996.

Subsection (1) refers to staff identified in staff transfer orders as "designated" and makes provision for their transfer by order.

Subsection (2) ensures that for the staff who are transferred, their contract of employment is uninterrupted and unchanged by the transfer process and this continuation of all aspects of the employment contract, including accrued and future pension rights, is confirmed in subs. (4).

Subsection (5) provides for a designated employee to retain any right to terminate his contract of employment if a substantial change is made in his working conditions to his detriment. However, no such right will arise solely because of the change of employer.

Compensation for loss of office or diminution of emoluments

43.—(1) Where any person—
  (a) is, at any time after the passing of this Act, in the service of an old authority, a new principal council or the Residuary Body, and
  (b) suffers loss of employment or diminution of emoluments which is attributable to any provision made by or under this Act,
compensation in respect of any such loss or diminution suffered by him shall be paid only in accordance with regulations made under section 24 of the Superannuation Act 1972.

(2) Accordingly, none of the bodies mentioned in subsection (1) shall pay any such compensation under any other statutory provision, by virtue of any provision in a contract or otherwise.

(3) Subsections (1) and (2) do not preclude the making of any payment to which a person is entitled by virtue of contractual rights acquired by him before 1st December 1993.

(4) No compensation shall be payable under regulations made under the Superannuation Act 1972, to or in respect of a person to whom subsection (1) applies, in respect of any loss or diminution attributable to the termination of a late contract on or before 1st April 1996.

(5) In subsection (4)—
  "late contract" means a contract which is made after 30th November 1993 and provides for the employment of the person concerned for a fixed term extending beyond 31st March 1996; and
  "loss or diminution" means loss or diminution of a kind mentioned in subsection (1).

(6) For the purpose of determining under section 82(5) or (6) or 84(3) of the Employment Protection (Consolidation) Act 1978—
  (a) whether the provisions of a new contract offered to a person employed by any such body as is mentioned in subsection (1) differ from the corresponding provisions of his previous contract, and
  (b) whether employment under the new contract is suitable in relation to that person,
there shall be treated as forming part of the remuneration payable under the new contract any compensation to which that person is or, if he accepted the offer, would be entitled in accordance with this section.

(7) Subject to subsection (6), nothing in this section shall be taken to affect any entitlement to a redundancy payment under Part VI of the Act of 1978 or to any payment by virtue of any provision of the Superannuation Act 1972 other than section 24 of that Act.

Definitions
"late contract": subs. (5).
"loss or diminution": subs. (5).
"new": s.64(1).
"old authority": s.64(1).
"principal council": s.270 of the 1972 Act.
"the Residuary Body": s.64(1).

General Note
This section specifies that the only compensation which may be paid to staff, who suffer loss of employment or diminution of emoluments because of the reorganisation, shall be in accordance with the regulations made under s.24 of the Superannuation Act 1972 (c. 11) (see subs. (1)). This does not preclude the making of any payment to which a person is entitled by virtue of contractual rights acquired before December 1, 1993 (see subs. (3)). Employees entering into an employment contract after December 1, 1993 for a fixed term shall not be eligible for compensation under regulations made under the Superannuation Act 1972 (see subs. (4)).

At the time of enactment the Government was still consulting on its proposals for new regulations to be made under s.24 of the Superannuation Act 1972. Those proposals were for a maximum compensation payment of 66 weeks salary with, in such cases of maximum compensation, payments above 44 weeks to be at the discretion of the council. This section is similar in form to s.53 of the Local Government Act 1985 (c. 51) but at that time the regulations required compensation payments of up to 82 weeks.

Redundancy payments

44.—(1) In determining the effect of any provision of—
(a) Part IV, V or VI of the Employment Protection (Consolidation) Act 1978, or
(b) Chapter II of Part IV of the Trade Union and Labour Relations (Consolidation) Act 1992,
in relation to a person whose contract of employment is terminated as a result of this Act, it shall be assumed that he was dismissed by the old authority concerned by reason of redundancy immediately before 1st April 1996 and that his dismissal was proposed by the authority.

(2) For the purposes of this section—
(a) a person's contract of employment is terminated as a result of this Act if—
(i) immediately before 1st April 1996 he was in the service of an old authority under a contract of employment which would have continued in force if that authority had not been abolished; and
(ii) his contract of employment is not transferred to a new principal council or to the Residuary Body; and
(b) a contract of employment is transferred—
(i) to a new principal council, if it is treated by any provision made by this Act, or by or under any other enactment, as continued in force with that council on 1st April 1996; or
(ii) to the Residuary Body, if it is so treated as continued in force with the Residuary Body on that date.

(3) The new principal council to whom an old authority's liability as respects any redundancy payment under Part VI of the Act of 1978 is transferred under this Act shall be treated as the employer of the person concerned for the purposes of sections 101, 102, 108 and 119 of the Act of 1978 (ancillary provisions about redundancy payments).

(4) As respects any such redundancy payment, references to the relevant date in sections 81(4), 82(1) and 101 of the Act of 1978, and in Schedule 4 to that Act, shall be construed as references to 31st March 1996.

Definitions
"new": s.64(1).
"old authority": s.64(1).
"principal council": s.270 of the 1972 Act.
"the Residuary Body": s.64(1).

This section provides that in relation to any person whose contract is terminated as a result of this Act, it shall be assumed that he was dismissed by reason of redundancy immediately before April 1, 1996 and that his dismissal was proposed by the authority. The effect of this assumption is to ensure that there can be no suggestion that employment contracts were terminated due to frustration given the abolition of the old employer. The result is that any dismissal will be governed by the requirements of the Employment Protection (Consolidation) Act 1978 (c. 44) and the Trade Union and Labour Relations (Consolidation) Act 1992 (c. 52) which, in particular, make provision for consultation with staff and trade unions about prospective redundancies and notice of redundancy.

This section was substantially amended during the legislative process. As originally drafted, the Bill contained the premise that all employment contracts were frustrated by the abolition of the employing authorities and that employees would only have such employment rights as were specified in the Bill.

Other compensation payments

45.—(1) This section applies where any contract of employment made before 1st December 1993 is terminated as a result of this Act.

(2) Subsection (2) of section 44 applies for the purposes of this section as it applies for the purposes of that section.

(3) If the contract—

(a) provided for the employee's employment for a fixed term extending beyond 31st March 1996, but

(b) did not provide for the earlier termination of the contract by the authority concerned,

the employee shall be treated as having been entitled, immediately before 1st April 1996, to receive from the old authority an amount equal to the damages which he would have been entitled to recover from that authority if they had not been abolished but had dismissed him immediately before that date.

(4) If the contract (whether or not for a fixed term) provided for its termination by the old authority on payment of compensation for loss of employment, the employee shall be treated as having been entitled, immediately before 1st April 1996, to receive from the old authority an amount equal to the compensation which he would have been entitled to receive from that authority if they had not been abolished but had terminated the contract immediately before that date.

(5) In subsection (4) "compensation for loss of employment" does not include any payment to be made under the contract in lieu of notice.

(6) Where the amount of compensation payable under a contract differs according to the reasons for termination of the contract, the amount payable by virtue of subsection (4) shall be determined on the assumption that the contract was terminated by reason of redundancy within the meaning of the Employment Protection (Consolidation) Act 1978.

(7) The Secretary of State may by regulations exclude the operation of this section in prescribed circumstances (and, in particular, in cases of engagement by new principal councils).

DEFINITIONS

"new": s.64(1).
"old authority": s.64(1).
"prescribed": s.64(1).
"principal council": s.270 of the 1972 Act.

This section makes provision for the compensation which should be paid to staff on fixed term contracts entered into before December 1, 1993. The provisions apply a similar principle to that established in s.43 for staff not on fixed term contracts, *i.e.* that the member of staff whose contract is terminated as a result of this Act shall on any occasion be treated as if he were an employee of an old authority immediately before April 1, 1966 and shall be entitled to such damages or compensation as would be required by that circumstance.

The Act places any employee who entered employment after December 1, 1993 in a particularly weak position. Such employees are not eligible for compensation under the Local Government Act 1972 nor is there any provision for compliance with the terms of their contracts. The Act appears to assert that contracts entered into after December 1, 1993 are frustrated, with no obligations on the new or old authority.

PART VI

TRANSITIONAL PROVISIONS

Committees of existing councils for consideration of certain matters

46.—(1) The councils of each of the old authorities whose areas will be wholly or partly included in the area of a new principal council shall, as soon as is practicable after the passing of this Act, establish a joint committee ("a transition committee") to consider and advise on transitional matters.

(2) Each transition committee shall consist of such number of representatives of the authorities by whom it is established as may be agreed between them or, in default of agreement, as may be determined by the Secretary of State.

(3) In making any determination under subsection (2), the Secretary of State shall secure that the number of persons who represent county councils is equal to the number who represent district councils.

(4) A transition committee may co-opt additional persons to serve as members of the committee.

(5) For the purposes of this section a matter is a transitional matter in relation to a new principal council if, in the opinion of the transition committee for that council, it is one which it is expedient for the committee to consider in order to ensure that the council will be able to function effectively as from 1st April 1996.

(6) The Secretary of State may give a direction requiring—

(a) a particular transition committee,

(b) every transition committee falling within a class specified in the direction, or

(c) every transition committee,

to consider any such matter as may be specified in the direction.

(7) Any expenses incurred by a committee established under this section shall be defrayed by the authorities by whom the committee was established in such proportions as may be agreed between them or, in default of agreement, as may be determined by the Secretary of State.

DEFINITIONS

"county": s.270 of the 1972 Act.
"district": s.270 of the 1972 Act.
"new": s.64(1).
"old authority": s.64(1).
"principal council": s.270 of the 1972 Act.
"transition committee": subs. (1).

GENERAL NOTE

This section requires the existing local authorities in the area of a new unitary authority to set up a joint transition committee to consider and advise on transitional matters. There is no provision for winding up these committees before the abolition of the existing authorities on April 1, 1996 but the role of the committees after the election of shadow authorities on May 4, 1995 is left as a matter for local determination and will presumably be limited. The Welsh Office published guidance for transition committees in July 1994.

Subsection (1) requires that these committees are established as soon as is practicable after enactment.

Subsection (2) allows the existing councils to determine the size and composition of the committees to be drawn from representatives of the authorities. The Welsh Office guidance note suggested between 10 and 20 members. Section 15 of the Local Government and Housing Act

1989 (c. 42) requiring political balance does not apply to these committees although the Welsh Office guidance reported that "the transition committee should be representative of the area of the new authority". If the councils cannot agree the size and composition of the transition committee, subs. (2) allows the Secretary of State to determine those matters and he will do so in a manner which secures equal numbers of county members as district members (subs. (3)). The transition committees may co-opt additional members (subs. (4)).

Subsection (5) defines transitional matters that may be considered by the transition committee as any matter which in the opinion of the committee is one which it is expedient for the committee to consider in order to ensure that the council will be able to function effectively as from April 1, 1996. The guidance suggests that there is a need to organise audits of existing arrangements relating to property, staff, information technology, rights and liabilities, contracts, agreements including agreements with Direct Service Organisations, grants, etc. The guidance also suggests that the transition committee should set out the main service delivery options which the shadow authorities may choose to consider.

Old and new principal areas with the same name

47.—(1) Where a local government area established by this Act ("the new area") has the same name as a local government area ("the old area") in existence at any time before the commencement of section 1(1), references in any enactment passed before this Act to the old area by name are not to be read as references to the new area.

(2) This section is subject to any provision to the contrary made by or under this Act.

GENERAL NOTE

References in previous legislation may be to areas with the same title as revised areas in this Act. This section ensures that references to areas in previous legislation cannot be read as references to areas specified in this Act, even if they are referred to by the same title, *e.g.* references to the area of Monmouthshire before 1974 cannot be taken to apply to the much contracted area of Monmouthshire created by this Act.

Groups of communities

48.—(1) Where, as a result of the creation of new principal areas by this Act, the communities within an existing group of communities will not all be within the same new principal area, the district council concerned shall, before 1st April 1996 make an order—
  (a) dissolving the group; or
  (b) separating one or more of the communities from the group in order to secure that the remaining members of the group will all be within the same new principal area.

(2) Any order under subsection (1) shall make such provision as appears to the district council necessary for the election, in accordance with the 1972 Act and Part I of the Representation of the People Act 1983, of a community council for any community which, as a result of the order, is no longer a member of the group.

(3) Section 31 of the 1972 Act (provisions supplementary to sections 27 to 29 of that Act), applies in relation to an order made under this section as it applies to one made under section 29 of that Act.

DEFINITIONS
  "community": s.20(4) of the 1972 Act.
  "community council": s.28(1) of the 1972 Act, as substituted by s.9 of this Act.
  "district": s.270 of the 1972 Act.
  "group": s.270 of the 1972 Act.
  "new": s.64(1).
  "principal area": ss.20(5) and 270 of the 1972 Act, as substituted and amended by s.1(1), (4) and (8) of this Act.

GENERAL NOTE
  Section 29 of the 1972 Act allows communities to form a group for the purpose of creating a single community council. This section prevents new groups being created which cross over the

boundaries of the new principal councils. It also requires existing district councils to make an order dissolving an existing group which crosses over the boundary of a new principal council.

Charities

49.—(1) Where, immediately before the commencement of this section, any property is held exclusively for charitable purposes by any of the old authorities, as sole trustee, that property shall vest on the same trusts in the appropriate council.

(2) Where, immediately before the commencement of this section, any power with respect to a charity was vested in the proper officer of an old authority or in the holder of any other office of an old authority that power shall vest in the corresponding officer of the appropriate council.

(3) Where, immediately before the commencement of this section, an old authority or any officer of an old authority is included among the charity trustees of a charity, those trustees shall include instead the appropriate council or (as the case may be) the corresponding officer of that council.

(4) Where subsection (1) applies and the property in question is held for the benefit of—

(a) a specified area,
(b) the inhabitants of a specified area, or
(c) any particular class or body of persons in a specified area,

the appropriate council is the new principal council whose area comprises the whole, or the greater part, of the specified area.

(5) In any other case falling within this section, the appropriate council is the new principal council whose area comprises the whole, or the greater part, of the area of the old authority in question.

(6) The Secretary of State may by order make provision with respect to any of the matters dealt with by this section, either in substitution for the provision made by this section or by way of supplementing or modifying that provision, and either generally or in relation to prescribed cases or classes of case.

(7) Nothing in this section—

(a) affects any power of Her Majesty, the court or any other person to alter the trusts of any charity; or
(b) applies in a case to which section 50 applies.

(8) In this section "charity", "charitable purposes", "charity trustees", "court" and "trusts" have the same meaning as in the Charities Act 1993.

DEFINITIONS
"appropriate council": subss. (4) and (5).
"charity": subs. (8).
"charitable purposes": subs. (8).
"charity trustees": subs. (8).
"court": subs. (8).
"new": s.64(1).
"old authority": s.64(1).
"principal council": s.270 of the 1972 Act.
"trusts": subs. (8).

GENERAL NOTE
This section provides for the transfer to the new authorities of charity property, charity trusteeship and the rights and powers relating to charities held by the former local authorities.

Welsh Church funds

50.—(1) The Secretary of State shall by order designate such new principal councils in relation to such areas in Wales as he considers appropriate for the purposes of this section.

(2) Any property which, immediately before the commencement of this section, is vested in an old authority and is required to be applied in accord-

ance with a scheme shall be vested in such designated new principal council as the Secretary of State may by order specify.

(3) Where, by virtue of this section, property is vested in a designated council whose designated area does not comprise the whole of the area of the old authority in question, the designated council shall transfer an apportioned part of the property to any other designated council whose designated area includes part of the area of the old authority.

(4) The terms of any apportionment made for the purposes of subsection (3)—

(a) shall be agreed between the designated councils concerned, or

(b) if they fail to agree, shall be determined by arbitration before a single arbitrator appointed—

    (i) by agreement between those councils, or

    (ii) if they fail to agree, by the Secretary of State.

(5) The vesting or transfer of any property by virtue of this section shall not affect—

(a) the application of the property in accordance with the scheme which is applicable to it immediately before the commencement of this section, or

(b) the amendment or revocation of any scheme by a further scheme.

(6) In this section—

"designated" means designated by order under subsection (1); and

"scheme" means a scheme under section 19 of the Welsh Church Act 1914 (application of Welsh Church funds for charitable or eleemosynary purposes).

DEFINITIONS

"designated": subs. (6).

"new": s.64(1).

"old authority": s.64(1).

"principal council": s.270 of the 1972 Act.

"scheme": subs. (6).

"Wales": s.64(4) of this Act, and s.269 of the 1972 Act.

GENERAL NOTE

This section provides the mechanism for the transfer of property held by existing county councils and required to be applied in accordance with a scheme under s.19 of the Welsh Church Act 1914 (c. 91). The 1914 Act transferred property from the previously established Church in Wales to the counties and county boroughs of the time requiring those local authorities under s.19 to apply the relevant property "to any charitable or eleemosynary purpose of local or general utility including the aiding of poor scholars" giving due regard "to the wants and circumstances of the parish in which the property is situate or from which it is or has been derived".

Existing s.19 schemes will continue to be applicable until new schemes are made. Responsibility for making s.19 schemes will lie with each of the new principal councils although they may choose to make joint schemes.

In order to avoid a division of the property currently held and managed by the eight county councils this section provides for the Secretary of State to designate eight 'lead' authorities to manage the funds. However, subs. (5) makes it clear that the application of the funds shall be in accordance with the existing s.19 schemes and any new schemes which the new principal councils will make.

Control of disposals and contracts

51.—(1) On and after the operative date no old authority may, without the appropriate consent—

(a) dispose of any land or building if the consideration for the disposal exceeds £100,000;

(b) enter into any contract, other than a capital contract, in respect of which the consideration exceeds £100,000 where—

  (i) the period of the contract extends beyond 31st March 1996; or

  (ii) under the terms of the contract, that period may be extended
beyond that date; or

 (c) enter into any capital contract in respect of which the consideration
exceeds £1,000,000.

(2) In this section—

"appropriate consent" means the written consent of the successor to the
old authority or, where there is more than one successor, the written consent of each successor;

"capital contract" means a contract in respect of which the consideration payable by the old authority concerned is expenditure for
capital purposes;

"expenditure for capital purposes" has the same meaning as it has for
the purposes of Part IV of the Local Government and Housing Act
1989 (revenue accounts and capital finance of local authorities), by
virtue of section 40 of that Act, and includes any expenditure which
the authority concerned may (by virtue of a direction given under
subsection (6) of that section) treat as expenditure for capital
purposes;

"operative date" means the date fixed by order of the Secretary of State
under paragraph 1 of Schedule 5 to the 1972 Act (as substituted by
this Act); and

"successor", in relation to an old authority, means any new authority
whose area includes the whole, or any part, of the area of the old
authority.

(3) Any disposal made in contravention of this section shall be void.

(4) No contract entered into in contravention of this section shall be
enforceable against a successor.

(5) Any consent for the purposes of this section may be given—

 (a) in respect of a particular disposal or contract, or in respect of disposals
or contracts of any class or description; and

 (b) unconditionally or subject to conditions.

(6) The provisions of section 123 of the 1972 Act (power to dispose of
land), and of any other enactment relating to the disposal of land by local
authorities, shall have effect subject to this section.

(7) The consent required by this section is in addition to any consent
required by any of those provisions.

(8) In this section references to disposing of land include references to—

 (a) granting or disposing of any interest in land;

 (b) entering into a contract to dispose of land or to grant or dispose of any
such interest; and

 (c) granting an option to acquire any land or any such interest.

(9) For the purpose of determining whether a limit specified in subsection
(1) is exceeded in any case, there shall be taken into account the
consideration—

 (a) with respect to any other disposal of land or any building effected by
the old authority after 30th November 1993, or

 (b) under any other contract entered into by the old authority after that
date,

so far as the disposal or contract relates to the same or a similar description of
matter as that to which the case under consideration relates.

(10) Where the consideration or any of the consideration under a contract
is not in money, the limits specified in subsection (1) shall apply to the value
of the consideration.

(11) Where a question arises under this section as to the value of any consideration and the authorities concerned fail to reach agreement, it shall be
determined by the Secretary of State.

"appropriate consent": subs. (2).
"capital contract": subs. (2).
"exependiture for capital purposes": subs. (2).
"old authority": s.64(1).
"operative date": subs. (2).
"successor": subs. (2).

GENERAL NOTE

This section prevents the existing authorities from disposing of assets, or entering into contracts, above specified values without the consent of the shadow authorities once elected. The objective is to minimise the extent to which the existing authorities undertake actions which constrain the future actions of the new councils. The section refers to the "operative date" which is defined in the 1972 Act, as the date of election to the shadow authorities, which in the case of this Act is May 4, 1995.

Applications of Part I of the Local Government Act 1988 during transitional period

52.—(1) Sections 9 to 16 of the Local Government Act 1988 (accounts, reports and other information in relation to defined activities) shall apply in relation to work—

(a) carried out by a Welsh authority in the transitional period (whether or not before the passing of this Act), and

(b) falling within an exempt activity,

even though (as a result of its falling within that activity) sections 4 to 8 of that Act (restrictions in relation to works contracts and functional work) do not apply.

(2) An activity is an exempt activity if—

(a) on 31st March 1994, it was a defined activity for the purposes of the Act of 1988 and not the subject of an order under section 2(9) of the Act of 1988; and

(b) it is treated, by an exempting order having effect in relation to a period beginning after that date, as not being a defined activity.

(3) In this section—

"exempting order" means an order under section 2(9) of the Act of 1988 which specifies, as the period during which an activity is to be treated as not being a defined activity, a period ending on a date earlier than 1st April 1997;

"transitional period", in relation to an exempt activity, means the period specified in the exempting order; and

"Welsh authority" means a county or district council, a new principal council or a combined fire authority for an area in Wales.

(4) The Secretary of State may by order (an "extension order") provide that, in relation to a particular order under section 2(9) of the Act of 1988, subsection (3) is to have effect as if the date mentioned in the definition of "exempting order" were such date later than 1st April 1997 as may be specified in the extension order.

(5) Where sections 9 to 16 of the Act of 1988 apply by virtue of this section they shall be read with the following omissions—

(a) in section 9 (keeping of accounts), subsection (4), and the references to subsection (4) in subsections (5) and (6);

(b) in section 11 (reporting for financial year), subsections (2)(c) and (e);

(c) in section 12 (providing information), subsections (1) and (2); and

(d) in section 13 (serving of notices for purpose of getting information), paragraphs (a), (b) and (ba) of subsection (1).

(6) In the application of section 9, 10 or 11 of the Act of 1988 by virtue of this section, any condition which is required to have been fulfilled for that section to apply shall be taken to have been fulfilled.

DEFINITIONS
   "county": s.270 of the 1972 Act.
   "district": s.270 of the 1972 Act.
   "exempting order": subs. (3).
   "extension order": subs. (4).
   "new": s.64(1).
   "principal council": s.270 of the 1972 Act.
   "transitional period": subs. (3).
   "Wales": s.64(4) of this Act, and s.269 of the 1972 Act.
   "Welsh authority": subs. (3).

GENERAL NOTE
   The requirements upon local authorities to subject activities to competitive tendering by the Local Government, Planning and Land Act 1980 (c. 65) and the Local Government Act 1988 (c. 9) have been suspended by order in Wales for a three-year period which began on April 1, 1994. This was considered necessary during the period of transition to the new councils. The timing of the exemption period was based on the Government's former intention to reform local government in Wales in 1995.
   The suspension of the requirement to tender under the 1988 Act has led, perhaps inadvertently, to a suspension of the associated accounting requirements. This section is designed to reinstate the accounting requirements of ss.9–16 of the 1988 Act, notwithstanding the suspension of the requirement to tender.

Continuity of exercise of functions

53.—(1) The abolition of the old authorities shall not affect the validity of anything done by any of those authorities before their abolition.

(2) Anything which at 1st April 1996 is in the process of being done by or in relation to an old authority in the exercise of, or in connection with, any relevant functions may be continued by or in relation to the authority ("the successor authority") by which those functions become exercisable or, as the case may be, become exercisable in respect of the area in question.

(3) Where immediately before 1st April 1996 any relevant functions exercisable by an old authority are exercisable concurrently by another such authority, or by other such authorities in respect of their respective areas, subsection (2) shall have effect as if those functions had by virtue of this Act become functions of that other authority or of those other authorities in respect of their respective areas.

(4) Anything done by or in relation to an old authority before 1st April 1996 in the exercise of or in connection with any relevant functions shall, so far as is required for continuing its effect on and after that date, have effect as if done by or in relation to the successor authority.

(5) Subsection (4) applies in particular to—
   (a) any decision, determination, declaration, designation, agreement or instrument made by an old authority;
   (b) any regulations or byelaws made by an old authority;
   (c) any licence, permission, consent, approval, authorisation, exemption, dispensation or relaxation granted by or to an old authority;
   (d) any notice, direction or certificate given by or to an old authority;
   (e) any application, request, proposal or objection made by or to an old authority;
   (f) any condition or requirement imposed by or on an old authority;
   (g) any fee paid by or to an old authority;
   (h) any appeal allowed by or in favour of or against an old authority;
   (i) any proceedings instituted by or against an old authority.

(6) Any reference in this section to anything done by or in relation to an old authority includes a reference to anything which by virtue of any enactment is treated as having been done by or in relation to that authority.

(7) Any reference (however framed) to an old authority in any document constituting, or relating to, anything to which the provisions of this section

apply shall, so far as is required for giving effect to those provisions, be construed as a reference to the successor authority.

(8) The provisions of this section are without prejudice to any provision made by or under this Act in relation to any particular functions and shall not be construed as continuing in force any contract of employment made by any of the old authorities.

(9) The Secretary of State may, in relation to any particular functions, by order exclude, modify or supplement any of the provisions of this section or make such other transitional provision as he thinks necessary or expedient.

(10) In this section "relevant functions" means statutory functions which by virtue of any provision made by or under this Act become functions of another authority, or of other authorities in respect of their respective areas.

DEFINITIONS
"old authority": s.64(1).
"relevant functions": subs. (10).
"successor authority": subs. (2).

GENERAL NOTE
This section ensures that decisions made by abolished authorities remain valid despite the abolition of those authorities and ensures that the new authorities inherit the implications of those decisions, such that anything done by an old authority shall be deemed to have been done by the new authority for its continuing effect. Subsection (5) provides a specific list of the general application of the subs. (4) principle.

Consequential and supplementary provision

54.—(1) The Secretary of State may by order make such incidental, consequential, transitional or supplemental provision as he thinks necessary or expedient—
  (a) for the general purposes, or any particular purpose, of this Act or in consequence of any of its provisions or for giving full effect to it; or
  (b) in consequence of such of the provisions of any other Act passed in the same Session as this Act as apply to any area or authority affected by this Act.

(2) An order under subsection (1) may, in particular, make provision—
  (a) for enabling any authority or body by whom any powers will become exercisable, on a date specified by or under this Act, by virtue of any provision made by or under this Act to take before that date any steps which are necessary as a preliminary to the exercise of those powers;
  (b) for the making before any date specified by or under this Act of arrangements for securing the satisfactory operation from that date of any provision made by or under this Act and for defraying the cost of any such arrangements;
  (c) for the transfer of property, rights or liabilities, and of related functions, from an abolished body or the Residuary Body to a new principal council or other public body or to the Residuary Body;
  (d) for the management or custody of transferred property (whether real or personal);
  (e) for applying (with or without modifications) or amending, repealing or revoking (with or without savings) any provision of an Act passed before this Act or in the same Session, or an instrument made under such an Act before 1st April 1996;
  (f) for making savings, or additional savings, from the effect of any repeal made by this Act;
  (g) with respect to the membership of any body, so far as that membership consists of persons elected by or appointed by or on the nomination of—
    (i) any authority affected by this Act; or
    (ii) any group of bodies which includes such an authority;

(h) dissolving any body corporate established by any Act passed, or any instrument made, before 1st April 1996;

(i) with respect to the functions or jurisdiction of any public body or of—

 (i) any coroner, lord-lieutenant, lieutenant or high sheriff; or

 (ii) any other officers (including police officers) within the area of any local authority affected by any provision of or made under this Act,

and the costs and expenses of such public bodies and persons.

(3) In subsection (2)(c) "abolished body" means an old authority or any joint board which ceases to exist as a result of section 59.

(4) Any transfer made in accordance with any provision made by virtue of subsection (2)(c)—

(a) may be made subject to terms, including financial terms; and

(b) may impose new rights or liabilities in respect of the property transferred.

(5) The amendments that may be made under this section shall be in addition, and without prejudice, to those made by or under any other provision of this Act.

(6) Any question arising under this Act as to which is the successor authority in respect of any particular functions may be determined by a direction given by the Secretary of State.

(7) No other provision of this Act shall be taken to restrict the powers conferred by this section.

DEFINITIONS

"abolished body": subs. (3).

"new": s.64(1).

"principal council": s.270 of the 1972 Act.

"the Residuary Body": s.64(1).

GENERAL NOTE

This section enables the Secretary of State to make, by order, such incidental, consequential, transitional or supplementary provision as he thinks necessary or expedient for the general or particular purposes of this Act or any other Act passed in the same Session. This follows similar formulations in s.254. It is based on the similar s.254 in the 1972 Act and s.84 of the London Government Act 1963 (c. 33).

Subsection (2) gives particular examples of the general power given in subs. (1). Subsection (2)(c) is of particular significance as it enables the Secretary of State to make orders relating to the transfer of property. This was considered in the general note relating to s.39 concerning the Residuary Body.

Magistrates' courts, justices of the peace etc.

55.—(1) The Lord Chancellor may by order make, with respect to any matters mentioned in subsection (2), such incidental, consequential, transitional or supplemental provision as he thinks necessary or expedient in consequence of any of the provisions of this Act.

(2) The matters are—

(a) the functions or areas of jurisdiction of any justice of the peace, stipendiary magistrate, magistrates' court or keeper of the rolls for a commission area (within the meaning of the Justices of the Peace Act 1979); and

(b) commission areas, petty sessions areas and areas to which magistrates' courts committees relate.

(3) The Lord Chancellor may by order alter, in such manner as appears to him expedient in connection with the alteration in any local government area made by this Act, any of—

(a) the commission areas in Wales specified in section 1 of the Act of 1979,

(b) the areas in Wales which constitute petty sessions areas under section 4 of that Act, or

(c) the areas in Wales to which magistrates' courts committees relate under section 19 of that Act.

(4) Any order under this section may, in particular—

(a) make provision with respect to the costs and expenses of any persons with respect to whom provision is made by the order;

(b) apply (with or without modifications) or amend or repeal or revoke (with or without savings) any provision of an Act passed before this Act or in the same Session, or an instrument made under such an Act before 1st April 1996.

(5) Subsections (5) and (7) of section 54 apply in relation to this section as they apply in relation to that section.

DEFINITIONS
"Wales": s.64(4) of this Act, and s.269 of the 1972 Act.

GENERAL NOTE
Whilst s.54 enables the Secretary of State to make incidental, consequential, transitional or supplemental provisions, this section enables the Lord Chancellor to make equivalent provisions with regard to his responsibilities.

Subsection (2) specifies the matters which may be altered as a consequential provision: the functions and areas of jurisdiction of any justice of the peace; stipendiary magistrate; magistrates' court or keeper of the rolls for a commission area; commission areas; petty sessions areas and areas to which magistrates' courts committees relate.

This section was introduced to the Bill at Report Stage in the House of Commons, at the very last stage of detailed consideration. This unsatisfactory procedure left a number of questions unanswered. The Minister was unable to give a single illustration of how the "function" of any part of the judicial system might require change in consequence of this Act. The Police and Magistrates' Courts Bill considered in the same Session provides for a structured consultation procedure for proposals to change geographical areas. It is not clear whether the same procedures would appear not to be required for changes under this Act.

Transitional agreements as to property and finance

56.—(1) Any public bodies affected by the alteration, abolition or constitution of any area by this Act may make agreements with respect to any property, income, rights, liabilities or expenses (so far as affected by the alteration, abolition or constitution) of, and any financial relations between, the parties to the agreement.

(2) In subsection (1) "public body" does not include an old authority but does include a new principal council.

(3) Any such agreement may provide—

(a) for the transfer or retention of any property, rights or liabilities, with or without conditions, and for the joint use of any property;

(b) for the making of payments by either party to the agreement in respect of property, rights or liabilities so transferred or retained, or of such joint use, and in respect of the remuneration or compensation payable to any person; and

(c) for the making of any such payment either by way of a capital sum or of a terminable annuity.

(4) In default of agreement as to any disputed matter, the matter shall be referred to the arbitration of a single arbitrator—

(a) agreed on by the parties; or

(b) in default of agreement, appointed by the Secretary of State.

(5) The award of the arbitrator may make any provision which may be included in an agreement under this section.

(6) In subsection (4) "disputed matter" means any matter—

(a) which might be dealt with in an agreement under this section;

(b) which is the subject of an unresolved dispute between two or more public bodies; and

(c) for the resolution of which no provision is otherwise made.

DEFINITIONS
"disputed matter": subs. (6).
"new": s.64(1).
"old authority": s.64(1).
"principal council": s.270 of the 1972 Act.
"public body": subs. (2).

GENERAL NOTE
 The purpose of this section is to make provision for agreements between public bodies affected by the changes in local government areas and to provide for arbitration in default of
agreement.

Local Acts and instruments

57.—(1) Any local statutory provision to which this section applies and
which is not continued in force by any other provision of this Act shall continue to apply on and after 1st April 1996 to the area, things or persons to
which or to whom it applies before that date, but subject to the modifications
made by subsections (3) to (5) and to any other necessary modifications.
   (2) The continuation by subsection (1) of an instrument made under any
enactment shall not be taken to affect any power to vary or revoke the instrument which is exercisable apart from that subsection.
   (3) Subsection (1) has effect subject to the provisions of—
   (a) this Act;
   (b) any Act passed after this Act but before 1st April 1996; and
   (c) any order made under section 54 or 55 or this section.
   (4) Any local statutory provision to which this section applies and which
relates to functions exercisable by an old authority of any description, by
virtue of any public general enactment, shall have effect as if for any reference to the authority by whom the functions are exercisable immediately
before 1st April 1996 or to their area there were substituted a reference to—
   (a) the authority by whom those functions are exercisable on and after
       that date; or
   (b) (as the case may be) to so much of the area of the latter authority as
       comprises the area of the former authority or any part of that area.
   (5) In any local statutory provision to which this section applies but which
does not fall within subsection (4), for any reference to the area of an old
authority or to an old authority there shall be substituted a reference to so
much of the new principal area as comprises the area of the old authority or
any part thereof or, as the case may be, the council of that new principal area.
   (6) Subsections (4) and (5) have effect subject to any provision to the contrary made by, or by any instrument made under, this Act.
   (7) The Secretary of State may by order provide for the exercise of functions conferred by any local statutory provision to which this section applies
and exclude the operation of any provision of this section where it would
otherwise conflict with any provision of the order.
   (8) This section applies to any local statutory provision which is in force in
Wales immediately before 1st April 1996 and is not expressly repealed or
revoked by this Act.
   (9) In this section "local statutory provision" means a provision of—
   (a) a local Act (including an Act confirming a provisional order);
   (b) a public general Act passed with respect only to the whole or part of a
       local government area in Wales as it existed immediately before the
       passing of this Act;
   (c) an instrument made under any such local or public general Act; or
   (d) an instrument in the nature of a local enactment made under any other
       Act.

"local statutory provision": subs. (9).
"new": s.64(1).
"old authority": s.64(1).
"principal area": ss.20(5) and 270 of the 1972 Act, as substituted and amended by s.1(1), (4) and (8) of this Act.
"Wales": s.64(4) of this Act, and s.269 of the 1972 Act.

GENERAL NOTE
This section provides for the continuation in force of any local statutory provision, not kept in force by any other provision of the Bill, subject to any necessary modifications to be made in accordance with subss. (3)–(5), at least until modification by order under s.58.

Modification etc. of local Acts and instruments

58.—(1) This section applies where any local statutory provision ("the relevant provision") is—
(a) continued in force in any area by section 57, or
(b) amended or modified in its application to any area by an order under section 54 or 55 (a "modifying order").
(2) The Secretary of State may by order or (as the case may be) the modifying order may—
(a) extend the relevant provision throughout the new principal area in which it is continued in force;
(b) provide that the relevant provision as so continued, amended, modified or extended shall have effect in that area to the exclusion of any enactment for corresponding purposes, including any enactment contained in or applied by this Act;
(c) make such modifications of any such enactment as will secure that the enactment and the relevant provision will operate harmoniously in that area;
(d) repeal or revoke any local statutory provision to which this section applies and which appears to the Minister to have become spent, obsolete or unnecessary or to have been substantially superseded by any enactment or instrument which applies or may be applied to the area, persons or things to which or to whom the relevant provision applies;
(e) transfer to any authority appearing to the Minister to be appropriate any functions of an old authority under any local statutory provision to which this section applies which are not to become functions of some other authority under any provision of this Act (except section 54, 55, 57 or this section) or under any other instrument made under this Act;
(f) without prejudice to paragraph (e), make such modifications of any local statutory provision to which this section applies in its application to any new local government area as appear to the Minister to be expedient.
(3) An order under this section which extends the area for which any local statutory provision is in force shall be provisional only.
(4) In this section "the Minister" means—
(a) in relation to an order made by the Secretary of State under subsection (2), the Secretary of State; and
(b) in relation to a modifying order containing provision made by virtue of subsection (2) of this section, the Minister making that order.

"local statutory provision": s.57(9).
"Minister": subs. (4).
"modifying order": subs. (10).
"new": s.64(1).

"old authority": s.64(1).
"principal area": ss.20(5) and 270 of the 1972 Act, as substituted and amended by s.1(1), (4) and (8) of this Act.
"relevant provision": subs. (1).

GENERAL NOTE
Section 58 enables the Secretary of State, by order, to modify any local statutory provision. Such orders may extend local legislation throughout any new local area, exclude corresponding enactments or modify them so that they fit in with the local legislation, and transfer to the new local authorities functions conferred under existing legislation.

Section 240 of the 1972 Act continues to have effect with respect to provisional orders, to allow for the holding of inquiries and other petitioning procedures. Any order is subject to annulment in pursuance of a resolution of either House of Parliament.

Existing joint boards and committees and port health districts

59.—(1) Where an existing joint board was constituted by or under any enactment for exercising functions for any area (including any united district), the board shall continue in existence on and after 1st April 1996 and to exercise for that area the same functions as before that date (to the exclusion of new principal councils).

(2) In subsection (1)—
"joint board" means a joint board every constituent member of which is a local authority in Wales; and
"area" does not include a port health district.

(3) Subsection (1) does not apply to a joint board constituted for an area which on 1st April 1996 will be wholly within the area of a single new principal council if the board was constituted for the purpose of exercising functions which on and after that date would (apart from the existence of the board) be exercisable by that council.

(4) Subsection (3) applies whether or not the board has additional functions which, apart from this section, would not be exercisable by the new principal council.

(5) In a case to which subsection (3) applies—
(a) the functions of the board shall on 1st April 1996 become functions of the new principal council; and
(b) the joint board shall cease to exist on that date.

(6) This subsection applies where—
(a) a port health district was constituted by an order under any enactment relating to public health; and
(b) a local authority or joint board, every constituent member of which is a local authority, is the port health authority for that district.

(7) Where subsection (6) applies, the district shall continue to exist as a port health district on and after 1st April 1996.

(8) Where, on 1st April 1996, a single new principal council will become the riparian authority in relation to a port health district continued in existence by subsection (7)—
(a) that authority shall, on that date, become the port health authority for that district; and
(b) any existing joint board constituted for that district shall cease to exist.

(9) Where, on 1st April 1996, two or more new principal councils will become riparian authorities in relation to a port health district continued in existence by subsection (7), the port health authority for the district shall be—
(a) the existing port health authority, if that authority is a joint board; and
(b) the new principal council whose area comprises or abuts on the greater part of the district, in any other case.

(10) Any question as to which new principal council's area comprises or abuts on the greater part of a port health district shall be determined by the Secretary of State.

(11) This subsection applies to any existing joint committee constituted under any enactment for the purpose of exercising functions for an area which on 1st April 1996 will lie within the areas of two or more new principal councils by whom those functions would apart from this subsection become exercisable on that date.

(12) A joint committee to which subsection (11) applies—

(a) shall continue to exist on and after 1st April 1996 as if duly appointed by or in connection with those new principal councils; and

(b) shall exercise those functions for the area for which the committee exercised them before that date.

(13) Nothing in subsection (12) is to be taken as preventing new principal councils from making different arrangements for the discharge of functions.

(14) The continuation in existence of any area or body by this section does not prejudice any power conferred by any enactment to amend or revoke the order constituting the area or body or the power to make provision with respect to the body conferred by section 54.

(15) Subsections (1) and (3) do not apply to a joint planning board for a National Park in Wales.

(16) The following provisions shall have effect for the construction of references to a local statutory provision to which section 57 applies—

(a) any reference to an existing joint board which ceases to exist by virtue of this section, or any reference which is to be construed as such a reference, shall be construed as a reference to the new principal council by whom the functions of that board will become exercisable by virtue of this section;

(b) any reference to a united district or other area the existing joint board for which ceases to exist by virtue of subsection (3), or any reference which is to be construed as such a reference, shall be construed as a reference to so much of the area of the new principal council by whom the functions formerly exercisable by the existing joint board become exercisable on 1st April 1996, as comprises the united district or other area for which the board acted; and

(c) any reference to an existing local authority whose functions as port health authority become exercisable on 1st April 1996 by virtue of this section by a new principal council, or any reference which is to be construed as such a reference, shall be construed as a reference to that council.

(17) In this section "existing" means existing immediately before 1st April 1996.

(18) This section has effect subject to any provision made by or under this Act.

DEFINITIONS

"area": subs. (2).
"district": s.270 of the 1972 Act.
"existing": subs. (17).
"joint board": subs. (2).
"new": s.64(1).
"principal council": s.270 of the 1972 Act.

GENERAL NOTE

This section makes provision with respect to existing joint boards, joint committees and port health authorities. Unless the new principal area covers the whole area of an existing joint institution, the section provides for the continued existence of that joint institution.

PART VII

MISCELLANEOUS AND SUPPLEMENTAL

Records

60.—(1) Each new principal council shall make and maintain a scheme setting out their arrangements for the proper care, preservation and management of their records.

(2) Each scheme shall include details of any relevant shared arrangements which the council concerned have made.

(3) The council by whom a scheme has been made shall keep the scheme under review and, where they consider that it should be modified, make such adjustments to it as they consider appropriate.

(4) Before making, or modifying, their scheme a new principal council shall consult the Secretary of State and have regard to any advice that he may give.

(5) Where the records of a new principal council relate to the area, or part of the area, of another such council, that other council shall have the right—

(a) to inspect those records at all reasonable times (without payment of any fee); and

(b) to take copies of any of them, in such manner as carries no risk of damage.

(6) The right conferred by subsection (5) is subject to any shared arrangements which affect the records concerned.

(7) In this section—

"documents" includes records, of whatever form and in whatever medium, which convey or are capable of conveying information;

"records", in relation to a council, means any documents which—

(a) belong to the council or of which they have custody; and

(b) have been retained for reference and research purposes or because of their likely historical interest; and

"shared arrangements", in relation to a council, means any arrangements which the council have made with any other authority under section 25 of this Act or section 101 of the 1972 Act (arrangements for the discharge of functions by other local authorities).

DEFINITIONS

"documents": subs. (7).

"new": s.64(1).

"principal council": s.270 of the 1972 Act.

"records": subs. (7).

"shared arrangements": subs. (7).

GENERAL NOTE

Each new principal council shall make and maintain a scheme setting out the arrangements for fulfilling its responsibilities in relation to records (subs. (1)) and that scheme shall include details of any intended joint arrangements (subs. (2)). In making a scheme the new principal councils shall consult the Secretary of State and have regard to the advice given (subs. (4)).

Lieutenancies

61.—(1) In section 130 of the Reserve Forces Act 1980 (lieutenancies in England and Wales), at the end add—

"(4) In this section and in sections 133 to 137 below "county" means, in relation to Wales, a preserved county (as defined by section 64 of the Local Government (Wales) Act 1994)."

(2) Her Majesty may by Order in Council make such amendments in section 130 of the Act of 1980, with respect to the area for which any lord-

lieutenant or lieutenant may be appointed, as Her Majesty considers appropriate in the light of the changes made by or under this Act with respect to the areas of local authorities in Wales.

(3) Any such Order may make such incidental, consequential, transitional or supplemental provision (including provision amending the Act of 1980 or any other enactment) as appears to Her Majesty to be necessary or expedient.

(4) In section 94 of the Act of 1980 (procedure for enlistment), at the end add—

"(4) In subsection (2) above "county" means, in relation to Wales, a preserved county (as defined by section 64 of the Local Government (Wales) Act 1994)."

(5) In section 133 of the Act of 1980 (deputy lieutenants), at the end add—

"(6) In relation to Wales, subsection (5) above shall have effect as if the words from "(at" to "rate)" were omitted."

(6) In Schedule 7 to the Act of 1980 (provision of schemes for the constitution of associations), in paragraph 8(5), after the definition of "air force member" insert—

" "county" means, in relation to Wales, a preserved county (as defined by section 64 of the Local Government (Wales) Act 1994);".

DEFINITIONS

"preserved county": ss.64(1), and 270 of the 1972 Act as amended by s.1(7) of this Act.
"Wales": s.64(4) of this Act, and s.269 of the 1972 Act.

GENERAL NOTE

Lieutenancies

Since 1974 the lieutenancies have been organised on the basis of the eight county areas. This section maintains the status quo. The lieutenancies will be organised on the basis of the preserved counties as defined in s.64 and listed in Pt. III of Sched. 1. Subsection (3) offers the possibility of the new principal areas gaining their own lieutenancies, by Order in Council.

Sheriffs

62.—(1) In section 3 of the Sheriffs Act 1887 (annual appointment of sheriff) at the end add—

"(4) In this Act "county", in relation to Wales, means a preserved county (as defined by section 64 of the Local Government (Wales) Act 1994)."

(2) Her Majesty may by Order in Council make such amendments in section 3 of the Act of 1887, with respect to the area for which any sheriff may be appointed, as Her Majesty considers appropriate in the light of the changes made by this Act with respect to the areas of local authorities in Wales.

(3) Any such Order may make such incidental, consequential, transitional or supplemental provision (including provision amending the Act of 1887 or any other enactment) as appears to Her Majesty to be necessary or expedient.

(4) In section 6 of the Act of 1887 (nomination and appointment of sheriffs), after subsection (3) insert—

"(3A) In relation to Wales—

(a) subsection (3) above shall apply as if it required the duplicate warrant to be transferred to, and enrolled and kept by, the proper officer of the appropriate county or county borough council; and

(b) section 3(4) above shall not apply.

(3B) Any question as to which is the appropriate county or county borough council in relation to a particular warrant shall be determined by the Secretary of State."

DEFINITIONS
"preserved county": ss.64(1), and 270 of the 1972 Act as amended by s.1(7) of this Act.
"Wales": s.64(4) of this Act, and s.269 of the 1972 Act.

GENERAL NOTE

Sheriffs
Since 1974 the sheriffs have been appointed on the basis of the geographical areas of the eight counties. This section maintains the status quo. The sheriffs will be appointed to the areas of the preserved counties as defined in s.64 and listed in Pt. III of Sched. 1. Subsection (2) offers the possibility of the new principal areas gaining their own sheriffs by Order in Council.

Regulations, orders and directions

63.—(1) Any power to make regulations or orders conferred on the Secretary of State or the Lord Chancellor by this Act shall be exercisable by statutory instrument.

(2) Any such instrument, other than one made under a provision mentioned in subsection (4), shall be subject to annulment in pursuance of a resolution of either House of Parliament.

(3) No order shall be made under section 34 unless a draft of the order has been laid before, and approved by a resolution of, each House of Parliament.

(4) The provisions mentioned in subsection (2) are—
(a) sections 17(6), 34, 39(1), 49(6), 53(9) and 66(3);
(b) paragraph 18 of Schedule 5;
(c) paragraph 1(3) of Schedule 13; and
(d) paragraphs 12 and 18 of Schedule 17.

(5) Any regulations or order made under this Act may—
(a) make such supplemental, incidental, consequential or transitional or saving provision as the Secretary of State or (as the case may be) the Lord Chancellor considers appropriate; and
(b) make different provision for different cases or classes of case or for different localities.

(6) Any power of the Secretary of State to give a direction under this Act shall—
(a) include power to make different provision for different cases, including different provision for different localities and for different bodies; and
(b) shall be exercised in writing.

Interpretation

64.—(1) In this Act—
"the 1972 Act" means the Local Government Act 1972;
"the Commission" means the Staff Commission for Wales or Comisiwn Staff Cymru;
"decentralisation scheme" has the meaning given in section 27;
"financial year" means the period of twelve months beginning with 1st April;
"new", in relation to any area or authority, means an area or authority established by or under this Act;
"old authority" means an authority which ceases to exist as a result of this Act;
"the planning Act" means the Town and Country Planning Act 1990;
"prescribed" means prescribed by an order or by regulations made by the Secretary of State;
"preserved county" means any county created by the 1972 Act as a county in Wales, as that county stood immediately before the passing of this Act but subject to any provision of this Act, or made under the 1972 Act, redrawing its boundaries;

"the Residuary Body" means the Residuary Body for Wales or Corff Gweddilliol Cymru.

(2) A county borough established by this Act shall not be treated as a borough for the purposes of any Act passed before 1st April 1974.

(3) Subject to the provisions of this section, this Act and the 1972 Act shall be construed as one.

(4) Subject to any provision to the contrary, in any amendment of an enactment made by or under this Act "Wales" has the same meaning as in section 269 of the 1972 Act.

Expenses

65.—(1) There shall be defrayed out of money provided by Parliament—
  (a) any expenses incurred by any Minister of the Crown under this Act; and
  (b) any increase attributable to the provisions of this Act in the sums payable out of money so provided under any other enactment.

(2) Any sums received by the Secretary of State under a provision of this Act shall be paid into the Consolidated Fund.

Short title, commencement, extent etc.

66.—(1) This Act may be cited as the Local Government (Wales) Act 1994.

(2) The following provisions of this Act—
  (a) sections 1(1), (2) and (7), 3, 6, 7, 39, 40, 43, 46, 47, 48, 54, 55, 63 and 64,
  (b) Schedules 1, 3, 13 and 14 and paragraphs 1, 4, 6 and 9 of Schedule 17, and
  (c) subsections (1) to (4) and (9) of this section,
shall come into force on the passing of this Act.

(3) The other provisions of this Act shall come into force on such day as the Secretary of State may by order appoint.

(4) Different days may be appointed by an order under subsection (3) for different purposes and different provisions.

(5) Schedule 15 makes minor and consequential amendments of the 1972 Act.

(6) Schedule 16 makes certain miscellaneous consequential amendments.

(7) Schedule 17 contains transitional provisions and savings.

(8) The repeals set out in Schedule 18, which include repeals of certain enactments which are spent, shall have effect.

(9) This Act does not extend to Scotland or Northern Ireland except that any amendment or repeal of another enactment by this Act has the same extent as the enactment amended or repealed.

SCHEDULES

Section 1(2)   SCHEDULE 1

THE NEW PRINCIPAL AREAS

Counties

1. For Part I of Schedule 4 to the 1972 Act substitute—

"PART I

COUNTIES

Name	Area
Anglesey Sir Fôn	The district of Ynys Môn —Isle of Anglesey.
Caernarfonshire and Merionethshire Sir Gaernarfon a Meirionnydd	The districts of Arfon, Dwyfor, and Meirionnydd.
Cardiff Caerdydd	The district of Cardiff, together with (from the district of Taff-Ely) the community of Pentyrch.
Cardiganshire Sir Aberteifi	The district of Ceredigion.
Carmarthenshire Sir Gaerfyrddin	The districts of Carmarthen, Llanelli and Dinefwr.
Denbighshire Sir Ddinbych	The district of Rhuddlan, together with (from the district of Glyndŵr) the communities of Aberwheeler, Cynwyd, Llandrillo, Henllan, Denbigh, Llandyrnog, Llangynhafal, Llanynys, Llanrhaeadr-yng-Nghinmeirch, Nantglyn, Cyffylliog, Ruthin, Llanbedr Dyffryn Clwyd, Llanferres, Clocaenog, Efenechtyd, Llandegla, Llanfair Dyffryn Clwyd, Llanarmon-yn-Iâl, Llanelidan, Derwen, Betws Gwerfil Goch, Gwyddelwern, Bryneglwys, Corwen, Llantysilio, Llangollen and Llangollen Rural with (from the district of Colwyn) the communities of Trefnant and Cefnmeiriadog.
Flintshire Sir y Fflint	The districts of Alyn and Deeside and Delyn.
Monmouthshire Sir Fynwy	The district of Monmouth together with (from the district of Blaenau Gwent) the community of Llanelly.
Pembrokeshire Sir Benfro	The districts of Preseli Pembrokeshire and South Pembrokeshire, together with Caldey Island and St Margaret's Island.
Powys Powys	The districts of Montgomeryshire, Radnorshire and Brecknock, together with (from the district of Glyndŵr) the communities of Llanrhaeadr-ym-Mochnant, Llansilin and Langedwyn.
Swansea Abertawe	The district of Swansea, together with (from the district of Lliw Valley) the communities of Gowerton, Llwchwr, Gorseinon, Grovesend, Pontardulais, Mawr, Pont-Lliw, Penllergaer, Llangyfelach and Clydach."

County boroughs

2. For Part II of Schedule 4 to the 1972 Act substitute—

"PART II

COUNTY BOROUGHS

Name	Area
Aberconwy and Colwyn Aberconwy a Cholwyn	The districts of Aberconwy and Colwyn, but excluding (from the district of Colwyn) the communities of Cefnmeiriadog and Trefnant.

Name	Area
Blaenau Gwent Blaenau Gwent	The district of Blaenau Gwent (excluding the community of Llanelly).
Bridgend Pen-y-bont ar Ogwr	The district of Ogwr, but excluding the communities of Wick, St Bride's Major and Ewenny.
Caerphilly Caerffili	The districts of Islwyn and Rhymney Valley.
Merthyr Tydfil Merthyr Tudful	The district of Merthyr Tydfil.
Neath and Port Talbot Castell-nedd a Phort Talbot	The districts of Neath and Port Talbot, together with (from the district of Lliw Valley) the communities of Pontar-dawe, Gwaun-Cae-Gurwen, Cwmllynfell, Ystalyfera and Cilybebyll.
Newport Casnewydd	The district of Newport.
Rhondda, Cynon, Taff Rhondda, Cynon, Taf	The districts of Rhondda, Cynon Valley, and Taff-Ely, but excluding (from the district of Taff-Ely) the community of Pentyrch.
Torfaen Tor-faen	The district of Torfaen.
The Vale of Glamorgan Bro Morgannwg	The district of Vale of Glamorgan, together with (from the district of Ogwr) the communities of Wick, St Bride's Major and Ewenny.
Wrexham Wrecsam	The district of Wrexham Maelor, together with (from the district of Glyndŵr) the communities of Chirk, Glyn-traian, Llansantffraid Glyn Ceiriog, and Ceiriog Ucha."

The preserved counties

3. For Part III of Schedule 4 to the 1972 Act substitute—

"PART III

THE PRESERVED COUNTIES AND THEIR AREAS

Name	Area
Clwyd	The county of Clywd, but excluding the communities of Llanrhaeadr-ym-Mochnant, Llansilin and Llangedwyn.
Dyfed	The county of Dyfed.
Gwent	The county of Gwent.
Gwynned	The county of Gwynedd.
Mid Glamorgan Morgannwg Ganol	The county of Mid Glamorgan, but excluding the communities of Wick, St Bride's Major, Ewenny and Pentyrch.
Powys	The county of Powys with the addition of the communities of Llanrhaeadr-ym-Mochnant, Llansilin and Llangedwyn from the county of Clwyd.
South Glamorgan De Morgannwg	The county of South Glamorgan with the addition of the communities of Wick, St Bride's Major, Ewenny and Pen-tyrch from the county of Mid Glamorgan.
West Glamorgan Gorllewin Morgannwg	The county of West Glamorgan."

SCHEDULE 2

PROVISIONS APPLYING TO PRESERVED COUNTIES

The Defence Act 1842 (c. 94)

1. The provisions of section 19 of the Defence Act 1842 (valuing of premises in default of agreement) shall be subsection (1) of that section and at the end add—
    "(2) In this section and in sections 23 and 24 "county" means, in relation to Wales, a preserved county (as defined by section 64 of the Local Government (Wales) Act 1994)."

The Licensing Act 1964 (c. 26)

2.—(1) In sections 85 (parties organised for gain) and 188 (closing of licensed premises in case of riot) of the Licensing Act 1964, in each case at the end add—
    "(4) In subsection (1) above "county", in relation to Wales, means a preserved county (as defined by section 64 of the Local Government (Wales) Act 1994)."
(2) In section 193 of that Act (disqualification of justices), at the end add—
    "(9) In subsections (1) and (2) above "county", in relation to Wales, means a preserved county (as defined by section 64 of the Local Government (Wales) Act 1994)."

The Sea Fisheries (Shellfish) Act 1967 (c. 83)

3. The provisions of section 10 of the Sea Fisheries (Shellfish) Act 1967 (jurisdiction in relation to fishery) shall be subsection (1) of that section and at the end add—
    "(2) In the application of this section in relation to Wales, the reference to a county in subsection (1) of this section includes a reference to a preserved county (as defined by section 64 of the Local Government (Wales) Act 1994)."

The Local Government Act 1972 (c. 70)

4. In section 54 of the 1972 Act (proposals for changes in local government areas in Wales), after subsection (1) insert—
    "(1A) The Welsh Commission may, in consequence of a review conducted by them under this Part of this Act make proposals to the Secretary of State for effecting changes in the area of a preserved county which appear to the Commission to be desirable having regard, in particular, to the purposes for which the preserved counties are retained."
5. For section 56(1) of the 1972 Act (power of Secretary of State to direct holding of reviews), substitute—
    "(1) The Secretary of State may direct the Welsh Commission to conduct a review of—
    (a) Wales as a whole,
    (b) any one or more local government areas or parts of such areas in Wales, or
    (c) any one or more preserved counties or parts of such counties,
    for the purpose of considering whether or not to make such proposals in relation to the area reviewed as are authorised by section 54 above and what proposals, if any, to make; and the Commission shall, if they think fit, formulate such proposals accordingly."
6. At the end of section 219 of the 1972 Act (sheriffs and under-sheriffs), after subsection (8) add—
    "(9) In subsections (1) and (5) above "county", in relation to Wales, means a preserved county."
7. At the end of section 224 of the 1972 Act (arrangements by principal councils for custody of documents) add—
    "(3) In subsection (1) above "county", in relation to Wales, means a preserved county."
8. For section 269 of the 1972 Act (meaning of "England" and "Wales") substitute—

"Meaning of "England" and "Wales"
    269. In this Act "Wales" means the combined area of the preserved counties and "England" does not include any area which is included in any of the preserved counties."

The Interpretation Act 1978 (c. 30)

9. In Schedule 1 to the Interpretation Act 1978 (words and expressions defined) for the definition of "Wales" substitute—

" "Wales" means the combined area of the counties which were created by section 20 of the Local Government Act 1972, as originally enacted, but subject to any alteration made under section 73 of that Act (consequential alteration of boundary following alteration of watercourse)."

The Justices of the Peace Act 1979 (c. 55)

10.—(1) In section 1 of the Justices of the Peace Act 1979 (commission areas), in paragraph (a), after "county" insert "in England" and after that paragraph insert—
"(aa) every preserved county in Wales;".
(2) In section 4 of that Act (petty sessions areas), after subsection (1) insert—
"(1A) In subsection (1) above, any reference to a non-metropolitan county is to be construed, in relation to Wales, as a reference to a preserved county."
(3) In section 19 of that Act (general provisions as to magistrates' courts committees), in subsection (2), in paragraph (a), after "county" insert "in England", and after paragraph (b) insert—
"(bb) every preserved county in Wales;".
(4) In section 70 of that Act (interpretation), after the definition of "prescribed" insert—
" "preserved county" has the meaning given by section 64 of the Local Government (Wales) Act 1994;".

The Magistrates' Courts Act 1980 (c. 43)

11.—(1) In section 1 of the Magistrates' Courts Act 1980 (issue of summons to accused or warrant for his arrest), in subsection (8) after "county" insert "in England, any preserved county in Wales".
(2) In section 2 of that Act (jurisdiction to deal with charges), in subsections (1) and (3) after first "county" insert "in England, a preserved county in Wales" and after second "county" insert ", the preserved county".
(3) In section 3 of that Act (offences committed on boundaries etc.), in subsection (4) after "county" insert "in England, any preserved county in Wales".
(4) In section 150(1) of that Act (interpretation), after the definition of "prescribed" insert—
" "preserved county" has the meaning given by section 64 of the Local Government (Wales) Act 1994;".

The Representation of the People Act 1983 (c. 2)

12.—(1) The provisions of section 177 of the Representation of the People Act 1983 (local election offence punishable summarily) shall be subsection (1) of that section and at the end add—
"(2) In subsection (1) above "county", in relation to Wales, means a preserved county (as defined by section 64 of the Local Government (Wales) Act 1994)."
(2) In Schedule 1 to that Act (parliamentary election rules), in the Appendix, in the entry relating to the form of the certificate to be endorsed on the writ, insert the following—
"Note: in relation to any constituency in Wales, "county" in this form refers to a preserved county (as defined by section 64 of the Local Government (Wales) Act 1994)."

The Parliamentary Constituencies Act 1986 (c. 56)

13. In paragraph 4 of Schedule 2 to the Parliamentary Constituencies Act 1986 (rules for redistributing seats), after sub-paragraph (1) insert—
"(1A) In sub-paragraph (1)(a) above "county" means, in relation to Wales, a preserved county (as defined by section 64 of the Local Government (Wales) Act 1994)."

Section 3   SCHEDULE 3

ESTABLISHMENT OF NEW PRINCIPAL COUNCILS

The following is substituted for Schedule 5 to the 1972 Act—

"SCHEDULE 5

ESTABLISHMENT OF NEW PRINCIPAL COUNCILS

Election of councillors

1. The elections of councillors of the new principal councils which are to be held in 1995 shall be held on a date fixed by the Secretary of State by order.

Electoral divisions

2.—(1) For the purpose of any election of such councillors, each principal area shall be divided into electoral divisions specified in an order made by the Secretary of State after carrying out (either before or after the passing of the Local Government (Wales) Act 1994) such consultations as he thinks appropriate.

(2) An order under this paragraph for any area shall specify the number of councillors to be returned for each electoral division.

(3) There shall be a separate election of councillors for each electoral division.

(4) An order under this paragraph may contain such incidental, consequential, transitional or supplemental provision as the Secretary of State considers appropriate.

First elections of new councils

3.—(1) At the first elections of councillors for each new principal area, the returning officer shall be an officer of the council appointed by such county council or district council as the Secretary of State may by order designate and not a person appointed under section 35 of the Representation of the People Act 1983.

(2) Section 36(4) of the Act of 1983 shall not apply to any such election.

(3) All expenditure properly incurred by a returning officer or other officer in relation to the holding of the first elections of councillors for a new principal area shall be paid in the first instance by the council by whom the returning officer was appointed and shall be defrayed by the district councils in the area—

(a) in such proportions as may be agreed between them; or

(b) in default of such agreement, as may be determined by the Secretary of State.

(4) In relation to the first elections of councillors for a new principal area, "the appropriate officer", in Parts II and III of the Representation of the People Act 1983, does not have the meaning given by section 67(7) of that Act but means the returning officer appointed under this paragraph.

Declarations of acceptance of office

4.—(1) For the purpose of taking and receiving delivery of declarations of acceptance of the office of councillor of any new principal council before the first meeting of that council, the head of paid service of an authority designated by the appropriate transition committee—

(a) shall be deemed to be and shall act as the proper officer of the new council; and

(b) shall transfer any such declaration which has been delivered to him to the custody of the proper officer of the new council on the appointment of the latter.

(2) In this Schedule "head of paid service", in relation to an authority, means the officer of that authority who is designated under section 4 of the Local Government and Housing Act 1989.

First meetings of new principal councils

5.—(1) The first meeting of each new principal council shall be held within 21 days immediately following the day of election and shall be treated as the annual meeting of the council for 1995.

(2) The meeting shall be convened by the head of paid service of an authority designated by the appropriate transition committee and shall be held at such place as he may appoint.

(3) The notice of the meeting required by paragraph 4(2) of Schedule 12 to this Act shall be published at the place where the meeting is to be held and the summons to attend the meeting shall be signed by the person convening it.

6.—(1) Until the completion of the election of a chairman at the first meeting of a new principal council, persons designated by the appropriate transition committee shall exercise any functions falling to be exercised by the chairman and vice-chairman of the council.

(2) Any person so designated shall not vote in the first instance at the election of the chairman unless he is a councillor for the new area.

(3) At the first meeting of a new principal council the head of paid service of an authority so designated shall exercise any functions falling to be exercised by the proper officer of the new council in relation to the meeting.

(4) The standing orders for the regulation of the proceedings and business of an authority so designated shall apply at the first meeting of a new principal council.

7. If he is requested to do so, the Secretary of State may himself exercise a committee's power of designation for the purposes of any provision of paragraph 4, 5 or 6 above on the ground that the committee is unlikely to exercise the power in time for that provision to operate.

Qualification for membership

8. For the purposes of section 79 above, in its application to a candidate for membership of a new principal council, the new principal areas shall be treated as having been established not less than 12 months before the day of his nomination as such a candidate or, in relation to an election not preceded by the nomination of candidates, before the day of election.

Suspension of elections

9.—(1) In this paragraph "council" means a county or district council which ceases to exist on 1st April 1996 by virtue of the Local Government (Wales) Act 1994.

(2) No election of councillors of a council shall be held after 31st December 1994, except—

(a) to fill a casual vacancy in the office of councillor of that council where before 31st December 1994—

(i) the office has been declared to be vacant; or

(ii) notice of the vacancy has been given under section 89(1) of this Act; or

(b) where the number of casual vacancies in the office of councillor of a council occurring after 31st December 1994 exceeds half of the total number of such offices.

(3) Any such councillor holding office immediately before 31st December 1994, or elected after that date to fill a casual vacancy, shall, unless he resigns his office or it otherwise becomes vacant, continue to hold office until 1st April 1996.

(4) It shall not be necessary—

(a) to fill any casual vacancy in the office of councillor of a council occurring after 31st December 1994; and accordingly section 89 of this Act shall have effect with the necessary modifications in relation to any such vacancy; or

(b) to fill any casual vacancy occurring during March 1996 in the office of chairman or vice-chairman of a council.

Appropriate transition committee

10. In this Schedule, "appropriate transition committee" means the committee established under section 46 of the Local Government (Wales) Act 1994 in relation to the new principal council in question."

Section 18(7)   SCHEDULE 4

EXERCISE OF PLANNING FUNCTIONS IN WALES

After Schedule 1 to the planning Act insert the following Schedule—

"SCHEDULE 1A

DISTRIBUTION OF LOCAL PLANNING AUTHORITY FUNCTIONS: WALES

1.—(1) Where a local planning authority are not the local highway authority, the Secretary of State may include in a development order such provisions as he thinks fit enabling the local highway authority to impose restrictions on the grant by the local planning authority of planning permission for the following descriptions of development relating to land in the area of the local highway authority—

(a) the formation, laying out or alteration of any means of access to—

(i) a road classified under section 12(3) of the Highways Act 1980 or section 27 of the Local Government Act 1966; or

(ii) a proposed road the route of which has been adopted by resolution of the local highway authority and notified as such to the local planning authority;

(b) any other operations or use of land which appear to the local highway authority to be likely to—

(i) result in a material increase in the volume of traffic entering or leaving such a classified or proposed road;

(ii) prejudice the improvement or construction of such a road; or

(iii) result in a material change in the character of traffic entering, leaving or using such a road.

(2) The reference to a local planning authority in sub-paragraph (1) shall not be construed as including a reference to an urban development corporation who are the local planning authority by virtue of an order under section 149 of the Local Government, Planning and Land Act 1980, and no provision of a development order which is included in it by virtue of that sub-paragraph is to be construed as applying to such a corporation.

(3) The Secretary of State may include in a development order provision enabling a local highway authority to impose restrictions on the grant by an urban development corporation who are the local planning authority of planning permission for such descriptions of development as may be specified in the order.

2.—(1) A local planning authority who have the function of determining applications for planning permission shall, if requested to do so by the council for any community or group of communities situated in their area, notify that council of—

  (a) any relevant planning application; and
  (b) any alteration to that application accepted by the authority.

(2) In sub-paragraph (1) "relevant planning application" means an application which—

  (a) relates to land in the community or (as the case may be) one of the communities concerned; and
  (b) is an application for—
        (i) planning permission; or
        (ii) approval of a matter reserved under an outline planning permission within the meaning of section 92.

(3) Any request made for the purposes of sub-paragraph (1) shall be in writing and shall state that the community council wishes to be notified of all relevant applications or all applications of a description specified in the request.

(4) An authority shall comply with the duty to notify a community council of an application by—

  (a) sending the council a copy of the application; or
  (b) indicating to the council the nature of the development which is the subject of the application and identifying the land to which it relates,

and any notification falling within paragraph (b) shall be in writing.

(5) An authority shall comply with their duty to notify a community council of an alteration by—

  (a) sending a copy of the alteration to the council; or
  (b) informing the council in writing of its general effect,

but they need not notify a community council of an alteration which in their opinion is trivial.

(6) A development order may require a local planning authority who are dealing with an application of which a community council is entitled to be notified—

  (a) to give to the council an opportunity to make representations to them as to the manner in which the application should be determined;
  (b) to take into account any such representations;
  (c) to notify the council of the terms of their decision or, where the application is referred to the Secretary of State, the date when it was so referred and, when notified to them, the terms of his decision.

3. Paragraphs 4 to 10 apply only in relation to any area for which, by virtue of any provision of or made under section 6, 7 or 8, there is more than one local planning authority.

4. In sections 178(1), 181(4)(b) and 190(2), (3) and (5) any reference to the local planning authority shall be construed as a reference to the authority who issued the notice or made the order in question or, in the case of a notice issued or an order made by the Secretary of State, the authority named in the notice or order.

5. The functions of a local planning authority under section 187B are exercisable by any body having the function of taking enforcement action in respect of the breach in question.

6. Where a local planning authority have made a tree preservation order under section 198 or the Secretary of State has made such an order by virtue of section 202, the powers of varying or revoking the order and the powers of dispensing with section 206 or serving, or appearing on an appeal relating to, a notice under section 207 shall be exercisable only by the authority who made the order or, in the case of an order made by the Secretary of State, the authority named in the order.

7.—(1) The copy of the notice required to be served by paragraph 4(5) of Schedule 8 on a local planning authority shall, in the case of a proposal that a government department should give a direction under section 90(1) or that development should be carried out by or on behalf of a government department, be served on the local planning authority who, in the opinion of the Secretary of State, would have been responsible for dealing with an application for planning permission for the development in question if such an application had fallen to be made.

(2) References in paragraphs 3(2) and 5(1) of that Schedule to the local planning authority shall be construed as references to the local planning authority on whom that copy is required to be served.

Compensation

8.—(1) Claims for payment of compensation under section 107 (including that section as applied by section 108) and sections 115(1) to (4) and 186 shall, subject to sub-paragraph (3), be made to and paid by the local planning authority who took the action by virtue of which the claim arose or, where that action was taken by the Secretary of State, the local planning authority from whom the appeal was made to him or who referred the matter to him or, in the case of an order made or notice served by him by virtue of section 100, 104 or 185, the appropriate authority, and references in those sections to a local planning authority shall be construed accordingly.

(2) In this paragraph "appropriate authority" means—

(a) in the case of a claim for compensation under section 107 or 108, the local planning authority who granted, or are to be treated for the purposes of section 107 as having granted, the planning permission the revocation or modification of which gave rise to the claim; and

(b) in the case of a claim for compensation under section 115(1) to (4) or 186, the local planning authority named in the relevant order or stop notice of the Secretary of State.

(3) The Secretary of State may, after consultation with all the authorities concerned, direct that where a local planning authority is liable to pay compensation under any of the provisions mentioned in sub-paragraph (1) in any particular case or class of case they shall be entitled to be reimbursed the whole of the compensation or such proportion of it as he may direct from one or more authorities specified in the direction.

9. Claims for payment of compensation under a tree preservation order by virtue of section 203, and claims for payment of compensation under section 204 by virtue of directions given in pursuance of such an order, shall be made to and paid by the local planning authority who made the order or, in the case of an order made by the Secretary of State, the authority named in the order; and the reference in section 204(2) to the authority exercising functions under the tree preservation order shall have effect subject to the provisions of this paragraph.

10. The local planning authority by whom compensation is to be paid under section 279(1)(a) to statutory undertakers shall be the authority who referred the application for planning permission to the Secretary of State and the appropriate Minister, or from whose decision the appeal was made to them or who served the enforcement notice appealed against, as the case may be.

Miscellaneous

11. In relation to land in the area of a joint planning board, a person entering into a planning obligation under section 106 or 299A may identify the council of the county or county borough in which the land is situated as the authority by whom the obligation is enforceable."

Section 20(3)   SCHEDULE 5

UNITARY DEVELOPMENT PLANS IN WALES

PART I

MINOR AND CONSEQUENTIAL AMENDMENTS

1. Part II of the planning Act is amended as provided in this Part of this Schedule.

2. In section 12 (preparation of unitary development plan), at the end add—

"(11) Any provision made by regulations under this section in its application by virtue of section 10 may differ from that made under this section in its application by virtue of section 10A."

3. In sections 15 and 18 (adoption of unitary development plan by local planning authority, and calling in of unitary development plan for approval by Secretary of State), in subsection (3) in each case, after "unitary development plan" insert "for an area in England".

4. After section 23 (joint unitary development plans), insert the following sections—

"Joint unitary development plans: Wales

23A.—(1) A joint unitary development plan or joint proposals for the alteration or replacement of such a plan may be prepared by two or more local planning authorities in Wales for their areas if—

(a) each of those areas adjoins each of the others; or

(b) the Secretary of State has given his approval.

(2) Subsection (1) does not apply in relation to a joint plan for any area which consists of or includes a National Park.

(3) The previous provisions of this Chapter shall, in relation to any joint plan or proposals of a kind mentioned in subsection (1), have effect subject to the following provisions of this section.

(4) Each of the local planning authorities by whom a joint unitary development plan is prepared shall have the duty imposed under section 13(2) of making copies of the plan available for inspection.

(5) Objections to such a plan may be made to any of those authorities and the statement required by section 13(3) to accompany copies of the plan shall state that objections may be so made.

(6) It shall be for each of the local planning authorities by whom a joint unitary development plan is prepared to adopt the plan under section 15(1) and, subject to the provisions of this Chapter, they may do so as respects the part of their area to which the plan relates, but any modifications subject to which the plan is adopted must have the agreement of all those authorities.

(7) Where a unitary development plan has been prepared jointly, the power of preparing proposals in respect of the plan under section 21 may be exercised as respects their respective areas by any of the authorities by whom it was prepared and the Secretary of State may under that section direct any of them to prepare proposals as respects their respective areas.

(8) The date of the coming into operation of a unitary development plan prepared jointly by two or more local planning authorities or for the alteration or replacement of such a plan in pursuance of proposals so prepared shall be a date jointly agreed by those authorities.

National Parks in Wales

Unitary development plans for National Parks in Wales

23B.—(1) A unitary development plan shall be prepared for each National Park in Wales.

(2) A Welsh National Park development plan shall relate to an area prescribed in relation to the National Park in question by order made by the Secretary of State.

(3) The prescribed area in relation to a National Park which falls wholly within, but does not comprise the whole of, the area of a single local planning authority shall be—

(a) where the local planning authority have so elected, the whole of the area of the local planning authority; and

(b) in any other case—

(i) the whole of the area of the National Park; or

(ii) a composite area.

(4) The prescribed area in relation to any other Welsh National Park shall be—

(a) the whole of the area of the National Park; or

(b) a composite area.

(5) For the purposes of this section and section 23C, "composite area", in relation to a National Park, means an area which consists of the whole of the Park together with any one or more other areas in Wales.

(6) The Secretary of State shall not under subsection (2) prescribe an area which is a composite area except with the consent of every local planning authority in whose area the prescribed area or any part of it would fall.

(7) Any order made by the Secretary of State under subsection (2) may make such saving or transitional provision as he considers appropriate.

(8) Where, by an order under subsection (2), the Secretary of State prescribes a composite area which comprises or includes part only of the area of a local planning authority, the provisions of this Chapter shall apply in relation to—

(a) the Welsh National Park development plan in question, or

(b) any proposals for its alteration or replacement,

subject to such modifications, if any, as may be prescribed by the order.

(9) Subsections (3) and (4) of section 10A do not apply for the purposes of—

(a) subsection (3) or (8) of this section, or

(b) section 23C(1), (2) or (4).

(10) For the purposes of this Act, "Welsh National Park development plan" means a unitary development plan prepared for a National Park in Wales.

Joint unitary development plans for National Parks in Wales

23C.—(1) A Welsh National Park development plan for a National Park which neither coincides with nor falls wholly within the area of a single local planning authority shall be a joint unitary development plan.

(2) A Welsh National Park development plan for any other National Park shall be a joint unitary development plan if it relates to a composite area unless the composite area coincides with or falls wholly within the area of a single local planning authority.

(3) Any Welsh National Park development plan which is required to be a joint plan shall be prepared by the authorities who will be the appropriate authorities in relation to the plan.

(4) For the purposes of this section, an authority are an appropriate authority in relation to a joint plan if—

(a) they are a local planning authority; and

(b) their area or any part of their area falls within the area to which the plan relates.

(5) Any proposals prepared under section 21 for the alteration or replacement of a joint plan of a kind mentioned in subsection (1) or (2) shall be joint proposals prepared by the appropriate authorities in relation to that plan, and any direction given by the Secretary of State under that section in relation to that plan shall be given jointly to those authorities.

(6) Subsections (3) to (6) and (8) of section 23A apply in relation to any joint plan or proposals of a kind mentioned in subsection (1), (2) or (5) as they apply in relation to any joint plan or proposals of a kind mentioned in section 23A(1)."

5. In section 26 (regulations and directions), after subsection (3) insert—

"(3A) Any provision made by regulations under this section in its application by virtue of section 10 may differ from that made under this section in its application by virtue of section 10A."

6. After section 27 insert the following section—

"Meaning of "development plan" in relation to Wales

27A. For the purposes of the enactments mentioned in section 27, the development plan for any area in Wales shall be taken as consisting of—

(a) the provisions of the unitary development plan for the time being in force for that area, together with a copy of the relevant local planning authority's resolution of adoption or of the Secretary of State's notice of approval or, where part of the plan has been adopted and the remainder approved, copies of the resolution and the notice; and

(b) any alteration to that plan, together with a copy of the relevant local planning authority's resolution of adoption, or the Secretary of State's notice of approval, of the alteration or, where part of the alteration has been adopted and the remainder approved, copies of the resolution and the notice."

7. For section 29 (application of Chapter II to non-metropolitan areas), substitute—

"Application of Chapter II to non-metropolitan areas in England

29.—(1) This Chapter applies only to—

(a) the area of any local planning authority in England outside Greater London and the metropolitan counties; and

(b) any part of a National Park in a metropolitan county in England.

(2) Subsection (1) is subject to the transitional provisions in—

(a) Schedule 2; and

(b) Part III of Schedule 5 to the Local Government (Wales) Act 1994."

PART II

COMMENCEMENT OF UNITARY DEVELOPMENT PLANS

8. In Schedule 2 to the planning Act (development plans: transitional provisions), after Part I insert—

"Part IA

Wales

Continuation of structure, local and old development plans

1.—(1) Every existing plan which relates to any part of Wales shall continue in force on and after 1st April 1996.

(2) When a unitary development plan has become fully operative for the area of a local planning authority in Wales—

(a) any existing plan which is for the time being in force; and

(b) any interim plan,

shall cease to have effect in respect of its plan area to the extent that it is comprised in the area of that local planning authority.

(3) Any existing plan or interim plan shall, while it continues in force in respect of the area, or part of the area, of any local planning authority in Wales, be treated for the purposes of—

(a) this Act,

(b) any other enactment relating to town and country planning,

(c) the Land Compensation Act 1961, and

(d) the Highways Act 1980,

as being, or as being comprised in, the development plan in respect of that area or, as the case may be, that part of that area.

(4) Sub-paragraphs (1) to (3) have effect subject to the provisions of this Part of this Schedule and the 1994 Act transitional provisions.

(5) In this paragraph—

"the 1994 Act transitional provisions" means the provisions of Part III of Schedule 5 to the Local Government (Wales) Act 1994;

"existing plan" means a—

(a) structure plan;

(b) local plan; or

(c) old development plan,

to the extent that it was in force in respect of any area in Wales immediately before 1st April 1996 (and includes any alteration made to, or replacement of, the plan after that date under the 1994 Act transitional provisions);

"interim plan" means any modified plan (within the meaning of the 1994 Act transitional provisions) which comes into force in respect of any area in Wales on or after 1st April 1996 under those provisions;

"old development plan" means any plan which was in force immediately before 1st April 1996 by virtue of Schedule 7 to the Town and Country Planning Act 1971 and Part III of this Schedule; and

"plan area", in relation to an existing plan or interim plan, means the area in respect of which it was in force immediately before 1st April 1996 or, as the case may be, comes into force on or after that date.

Revocation of structure plan

2.—(1) Where under Chapter I of Part II of this Act the Secretary of State approves all or any of Part I of a unitary development plan for the whole or part of the area of a local planning authority in Wales ("the relevant whole or part area"), he may by order—

(a) wholly or partly revoke an existing plan which is a structure plan in respect of the plan area, to the extent that it is comprised in the relevant whole or part area or any part of it; and

(b) make such consequential amendments to that existing plan as appear to him to be necessary or expedient.

(2) Before making an order under this paragraph, the Secretary of State shall consult the local planning authority for the area to which the unitary development plan relates.

Incorporation of current policy in unitary development plan

3.—(1) This paragraph applies where—

(a) a unitary development plan is being prepared for the area of a local planning authority in Wales;

(b) the local planning authority preparing that plan have published in the prescribed manner a statement in the prescribed form identifying a policy included in the plan as an existing policy;

(c) one or more local plans is or, as the case may be, are together in force throughout the policy area; and

(d) a local inquiry or other hearing is held for the purpose of considering any objection to the plan.

(2) The person holding the inquiry or other hearing need not allow an objector to appear if he is satisfied that—

(a) the objection is to a policy identified in the statement published under sub-paragraph (1)(b);

(b) the policy so identified is an existing policy; and

(c) there has been no significant change in circumstances affecting the existing policy since it first formed part of any plan mentioned in sub-paragraph (1)(c).

(3) In this paragraph—

"existing policy" means a policy the substance of which (however expressed) was contained in the local plan or local plans mentioned in sub-paragraph (1)(c);

"policy" includes a proposal; and

"policy area" means so much of the area of the local planning authority to which the policy concerned relates.

Meaning of "local plan"

4. In this Part of this Schedule, "local plan" includes—

(a) a minerals local plan;

(b) a waste local plan;

(c) a local plan adopted or approved before the commencement of Part I of Schedule 4 to the Planning and Compensation Act 1991 or under Part III of that Schedule."

PART III

TRANSITIONAL PROVISIONS

Introductory

9.—(1) The provisions of this Part of this Schedule apply in relation to the area of any local planning authority in Wales during the period—

(a) beginning on 1st April 1996, and

(b) ending when a unitary development plan has become fully operative for that area.

(2) For the purposes of sub-paragraph (1), a unitary development plan for the area of a local planning authority in Wales has become fully operative—

(a) when it has become operative under Chapter I of Part II of the planning Act; or

(b) where different parts of it have become operative at different times, when all parts of it have become so operative.

(3) Sub-paragraphs (4) and (5) apply where the area of a local planning authority in Wales includes—

(a) the whole or any part of an area prescribed under section 23B(2) of the planning Act in relation to a National Park, and

(b) other land.

(4) The provisions of this Part of this Schedule apply separately in relation to—

(a) the Park area or, if there is more than one, each Park area, and

(b) the remaining area.

(5) Any reference in this Part of this Schedule to the area of the local planning authority (including any reference which falls to be so construed) shall be construed—

(a) in its application in relation to any Park area, as a reference to that Park area, and

(b) in its application in relation to the remaining area, as a reference to that area.

(6) In this paragraph—

"the Park area", in relation to a National Park, means the part of the local planning authority's area which is within the area prescribed under section 23B(2) of the planning Act in relation to that Park or, where there is more than one such part, those parts taken as a whole;

"the remaining area" means the part of the local planning authority's area which is not within an area so prescribed in relation to any National Park.

Application in relation to National Parks

10. The functions of a local planning authority under this Part of this Schedule are functions to which Part I of Schedule 17 to the 1972 Act (discharge of planning and countryside functions in National Parks) applies.

Interpretation

11.—(1) In this Part of this Schedule—
"affected area", in relation to a new planning authority, means—
      (a) in the case of a required plan (or proposed required plan) or a structure plan, the plan area, and
      (b) in the case of alteration proposals or structure plan alteration proposals, the related area,
to the extent that, on 1st April 1996, it became comprised in the area of the new planning authority;
"alteration proposals" means proposals for the alteration or replacement of a required plan (or of a plan which is treated as such a plan by virtue of paragraph 44(2) of Schedule 4 to the Planning and Compensation Act 1991)—
      (a) previously permitted to be prepared under section 39(1) of the planning Act; or
      (b) previously required to be prepared by a direction of the Secretary of State under section 39(2) of that Act;
"modified plan", in relation to a required plan (or proposed required plan) and any area, means that plan to the extent that it relates or is to relate to the area;
"modified proposals", in relation to alteration proposals and any area, means those proposals to the extent that they relate or are to relate to the area;
"modified structure plan proposals", in relation to structure plan alteration proposals and any area, means those proposals to the extent that they relate or are to relate to the area;
"new planning authority" means a new principal council or a joint planning board who are the local planning authority for any area in Wales;
"old development plan" has the meaning given by paragraph 14(1)(b);
"plan area", in relation to a required plan (or proposed required plan) or structure plan, means the area to which the plan relates (or is to relate);
"previously" means immediately before 1st April 1996;
"related area", in relation to alteration proposals or structure plan alteration proposals, means, to the extent that the proposals relate or are to relate to it, the plan area of the relevant required plan or, as the case may be, structure plan;
"relevant authority" means a new planning authority in whose area any part of—
      (a) in the case of a proposed required plan, the plan area; or
      (b) in the case of alteration proposals or structure plan alteration proposals, the related area,
became comprised on 1st April 1996;
"required plan" means—
      (a) a local plan which previously had been prepared or was required to be prepared under section 36(1) of the planning Act;
      (b) a minerals local plan which previously had been prepared or was required to be prepared under section 37(1) or (3) of that Act; or
      (c) a waste local plan which previously had been prepared or was required to be prepared under section 38(2) or (4) of that Act;
and for this purpose a plan which was permitted to be prepared jointly is not to be treated on that ground alone as not being required to be prepared;
"saved local plan" has the meaning given by paragraph 14(1)(a);
"structure plan" means a structure plan previously in force under section 31 of the planning Act; and
"structure plan alteration proposals" means proposals for the alteration or replacement of a structure plan—
      (a) previously permitted to be prepared under section 32(1) of the planning Act; or
      (b) previously required to be prepared by a direction of the Secretary of State under section 32(2) of that Act.
(2) For the purposes of this Part of this Schedule—
(a) even if the part of a required plan that relates to a part of the plan area has been prepared, the plan is to be treated as being in course of preparation in relation to that part of the area if the plan as a whole is in course of preparation; and
(b) even if the part of alteration proposals or structure plan alteration proposals that relates to a part of their related area has been prepared, those proposals are to be treated as being in course of preparation in relation to that part of the area if the proposals as a whole are in course of preparation.

Preparation of modified schemes

12.—(1) Where any planning scheme was previously in course of preparation, any relevant authority may submit to the Secretary of State a request for approval to prepare a modified scheme for the affected area.

(2) The Secretary of State may approve any such request if he is satisfied that the planning scheme was previously in course of preparation in relation to the affected area, and that—

(a) it is expedient that preparation of the planning scheme be continued in the preparation of the modified scheme;

(b) continued preparation of the planning scheme in relation to the affected area is likely to be of assistance to the new planning authority in preparing the unitary development plan for their area; or

(c) the adoption or approval of a modified scheme is otherwise expedient or desirable.

(3) Any approval under sub-paragraph (2)—

(a) may be given subject to such conditions as the Secretary of State thinks fit, including conditions as to the period within which the modified scheme is to be prepared and a copy of it submitted to him;

(b) may be accompanied by a direction modifying in such manner, and for such period, as the Secretary of State thinks fit the duty of the new planning authority to prepare a unitary development plan under Chapter I of Part II of the planning Act.

(4) Where the Secretary of State gives a direction under sub-paragraph (3)(b), Chapter I of Part II of the planning Act shall have effect in relation to the new planning authority subject to that direction.

(5) Where a planning scheme for any area in Wales had previously been prepared but not adopted or approved under Chapter II of Part II of the planning Act, the Secretary of State may, on an application made to him by a relevant authority, give permission to prepare a modified scheme for the affected area.

(6) The Secretary of State shall, whenever he gives any approval under sub-paragraph (2) or permission under sub-paragraph (5), direct that such of—

(a) the provisions of Chapter II of Part II of the planning Act, and

(b) any regulations made under any provision of that Chapter,

as may be specified in the direction shall apply for the purpose of the preparation, adoption or approval of the modified scheme in relation to the affected area.

(7) The provisions applied by a direction under sub-paragraph (6)—

(a) may include any requirement with respect to a modified scheme (or its preparation) corresponding to one already satisfied with respect to the planning scheme;

(b) may be applied subject to such modifications as may be specified in the direction; and

(c) may be applied for such limited period (if any) as may be specified in the direction.

(8) For the purposes of this paragraph—

"planning scheme" means a required plan, alteration proposals or structure plan alteration proposals; and

"modified scheme", in relation to a planning scheme—

(a) which is a required plan, means a modified plan,

(b) which consists of alteration proposals, means modified proposals,

(c) which consists of structure plan alteration proposals, means modified structure plan proposals.

Default powers

13.—(1) This paragraph applies where—

(a) a new planning authority have been given approval or permission under paragraph 12(2) or (5);

(b) the Secretary of State has required that proposals for a modified plan or modified proposals or modified structure plan proposals be submitted to him; or

(c) a new planning authority have prepared, but have not adopted, a modified plan, modified proposals or modified structure plan proposals.

(2) Where this paragraph applies—

(a) if at any time the Secretary of State is satisfied, after holding a local inquiry or other hearing, that the new planning authority are not taking the steps necessary to enable them to submit or adopt the proposals for a modified plan or the modified proposals or modified structure plan proposals within a reasonable period, or

(b) in a case where a condition was imposed in the approval given under paragraph 12(2) for the submission of a copy of the plan or proposals within a specified period, if that copy has not been submitted within that period, the Secretary of State may take such steps, which may include the alteration of any plan, as he thinks fit.

(3) The provisions of Chapter II of Part II of the planning Act shall, so far as applicable, apply with any necessary modifications in relation to the doing of anything under this paragraph by the Secretary of State and the thing so done.

(4) The new planning authority shall on demand repay to the Secretary of State so much of any expenses incurred by him in connection with the doing of anything which should have been done by them as he certifies to have been incurred by him in the performance of their functions.

Effect of adoption or approval of modified plan

14.—(1) Upon the adoption or approval of a modified plan for which the related required plan was previously the only required plan or the last of the required plans for the affected area—
   (a) any local plan which was continued in operation in relation to that area by paragraph 44(1) of Schedule 4 to the Planning and Compensation Act 1991 (a "saved local plan"), and
   (b) any plan which was previously in force by virtue of Schedule 7 to the Town and Country Planning Act 1971 and Part III of Schedule 2 to the planning Act (an "old development plan"),
shall cease to have effect in relation to that area.

(2) If the Secretary of State so directs, any specified provisions of a saved local plan or of an old development plan shall continue in operation—
   (a) for such period as may be specified or determined in accordance with the direction;
   (b) in relation to the affected area or any specified part of the affected area to which the saved local plan or the old development plan relates.

(3) The Secretary of State may at any time revoke any direction given under sub-paragraph (2).

(4) Before giving or revoking any such direction the Secretary of State shall consult the new planning authority.

(5) Any provision of a saved local plan or old development plan in force for any area in Wales by virtue of a direction under this paragraph shall have effect subject to the provisions of any modified plan in force for that area.

(6) For the purposes of this paragraph, "specified" means specified in the direction given under sub-paragraph (2).

Other plans to prevail over old development plans and saved local plans

15.—(1) Where an old development plan is in force for any area in Wales, the provisions of—
   (a) any structure plan,
   (b) any part of the unitary development plan, or
   (c) any local plan,
in force in respect of that area shall, to the extent that they conflict with it, prevail over any provision of the old development plan for the purposes of Parts III, V, VI, VII, VIII and IX of the planning Act, the Planning (Listed Buildings and Conservation Areas) Act 1990 and the Planning (Hazardous Substances) Act 1990.

(2) Where a saved local plan is in force in respect of any area in Wales, the provisions of—
   (a) any local plan, minerals local plan, or waste local plan,
   (b) any part of a unitary development plan,
in force in that area shall, to the extent that they conflict with it, prevail for all purposes over any provision of the saved local plan.

Local plans to prevail over structure plans

16.—(1) The provisions of a local plan in force by virtue of paragraph 1 of Part IA of Schedule 2 to the planning Act (continuation of structure, local and old development plans) for any area in Wales prevail for all purposes over any conflicting provisions in the structure plan so in force for that area unless the local plan is one which—
   (a) before 1st April 1996 had been stated under section 35C of the planning Act not to be in general conformity with the structure plan; and
   (b) has been neither altered nor replaced after the statement was supplied.

(2) Where, in relation to a modified plan in force for any area in Wales, the required plan was a local plan, the provisions of that modified plan prevail for all purposes over any conflicting provisions in the structure plan in force for that area.

Development plans for compensation purposes

17.—(1) This paragraph applies where, in relation to any area in Wales, there is no local plan in force.

(2) For any of the purposes of the Land Compensation Act 1961, the development plan or current development plan shall as respect that area be taken as being—

(a) if any part of the unitary development plan is in force for that area, that part of that plan; or

(b) if no part of such a plan is in force for that area, whichever of the structure plan and the old development plan (if any) in force for that area gives rise to those assumptions as to the grant of planning permission which are more favourable to the owner of the land in question.

(3) For any of the purposes of the Act of 1961, land situated in an area defined in the current development plan as an area of comprehensive development ("the defined area") shall be taken to be situated in whichever of the following areas leads to such assumptions as are mentioned in sub-paragraph (2)(b)—

(a) any area which is wholly or partly within the defined area and is selected by the structure plan as an action area; and

(b) the area so defined in the old development plan.

Revocation of old development plan

18. The Secretary of State may, after consultation with a new planning authority, by order wholly or partly revoke an old development plan continued in force under paragraph 1 of Part IA of Schedule 2 to the planning Act in respect of the whole or any part of so much of the area to which it relates as is comprised in the area of the new planning authority.

Temporary duty in relation to existing structure plan

19. It is the duty of a local planning authority in Wales, when exercising their functions under section 70 of the planning Act (determination of applications for planning permission) in relation to an application for planning permission, to seek the achievement of the general objective of the structure plan (if any) for the time being in force in their area (or, where different structure plans apply in respect of different parts of their area, in that part of their area to which the application relates).

Unitary development plan to prevail over other plans

20. Where a unitary development plan is operative in part, but has not become fully operative, in the area of a new planning authority, to the extent that they conflict with any provision of any—

(a) structure plan,

(b) local plan,

(c) minerals local plan,

(d) waste local plan, or

(e) modified plan,

in force for that area or any part of it, the provisions of the unitary development plan shall prevail for the purposes of Parts III, V, VI, VII, VIII and IX of the planning Act and of the Planning (Listed Buildings and Conservation Areas) Act 1990 and the Planning (Hazardous Substances) Act 1990.

Planning blight: structure plans

21.—(1) Paragraph 1 of Schedule 13 to the planning Act (blighted land) shall apply with the omission of Notes (2), (5A) and (7) and as modified by sub-paragraphs (2) to (6).

(2) References to a structure plan in force for the district in which land is situated are to be read as if they were references to a structure plan in force where that land is situated by virtue of Part IA of Schedule 2 to the planning Act.

(3) Note (1) to that paragraph shall apply as if—

(a) in paragraph (a), after "inspection" there were inserted "before 1st April 1996" and at the end there were added "and not withdrawn before that date";

(b) after that paragraph there were inserted—

"(aa) modified structure plan proposals made available for inspection under that section as it is applied by virtue of Part III of Schedule 5 to the Local Government (Wales) Act 1994;";

(c) in paragraph (b), after "published" there were inserted "either before 1st April 1996" and at the end there were added "or after that date in accordance with regulations or a direction made by virtue of that Part of that Schedule".

(4) Note (3) to that paragraph shall apply as if, after paragraph (b), there were inserted—
"or
   (c) copies of the unitary development plan for the area in which the land is situated have been made available under section 13(2).".
(5) Note (4) to that paragraph shall apply as if at the end there were added "or paragraph 13 of Schedule 5 to the Local Government (Wales) Act 1994".
(6) In Note (5) to that paragraph—
(a) the reference to a local plan is to be read as if it were a reference to—
     (i) a local plan within the meaning of paragraph 4 of Part IA of Schedule 2 to the planning Act; or
     (ii) a modified plan in force where that land is situated; and
(b) any reference to a district for which a local plan is in operation is to be read as if it were a reference to the area in which the plan mentioned in paragraph (a)(i) or (ii) is in force by virtue of Part IA of Schedule 2 to the planning Act.

Planning blight: local plans and modified plans

22.—(1) Paragraph 2 of Schedule 13 to the planning Act (blighted land) shall apply as modified by sub-paragraphs (2) to (5).
(2) Paragraph (a) shall apply as if for "for the district" there were substituted "where the land is situated".
(3) Note (1) to that paragraph shall apply as if—
(a) for the words from "includes a reference" to "also" there were substituted "is a reference to a local plan within the meaning of paragraph 4 of Part IA of Schedule 2 or a modified plan within the meaning of Part III of Schedule 5 to the Local Government (Wales) Act 1994, and, until copies of the unitary development plan for the area in which the land is situated have been made available under section 13(2),";
(b) in paragraph (a), after "proposals have" there were inserted "before 1st April 1996", and after "1991" there were inserted "and not withdrawn before that date"; and
(c) in paragraph (b)—
     (i) after "published" there were inserted "either before 1st April 1996", and
     (ii) at the end of that paragraph there were added "or after that date in accordance with regulations or a direction made by virtue of Part III of Schedule 5 to the Local Government (Wales) Act 1994".
(4) Note (3) to that paragraph shall apply as if, in paragraph (b), the words "the local planning authority decide to abandon" were omitted.
(5) Note (4) to that paragraph shall apply as if, at the end, there were added "or paragraph 13 of Schedule 5 to the Local Government (Wales) Act 1994".

Regulations and directions

23.—(1) The Secretary of State may by regulations make provision corresponding to any provision which he could previously have made by regulations under any provision of Chapter II of Part II of the planning Act.
(2) The Secretary of State may by regulations provide for—
(a) any regulations made or directions given under any provision of that Chapter and previously in force to continue to apply for such period as may be prescribed; and
(b) any regulations made under sub-paragraph (1) or applied under paragraph (a) or by or under any other provision of this Schedule to apply in relation to—
     (i) modified plans, modified proposals or, as the case may be, modified structure plan proposals, or
     (ii) the preparation of any such plan or proposals,
    subject to such modifications (if any) as may be prescribed.
(3) The Secretary of State may by a direction given under this paragraph make provision corresponding to any provision which he could previously have made by a direction given under any provision of Chapter II of Part II of the planning Act.
(4) Any power exercisable by virtue of sub-paragraph (1) or (3) to make regulations or give a direction in relation to required plans, proposals for the alteration or replacement of a required plan or structure plan, or the preparation of any such plan or proposals, shall be exercisable, with the necessary modifications, in relation to—
(a) modified plans, modified proposals or, as the case may be, modified structure plan proposals, or
(b) the preparation of any such plan or proposals.

SCHEDULE 6

MINOR AND CONSEQUENTIAL AMENDMENTS: PLANNING

PART I

THE 1972 ACT: NATIONAL PARKS AND COUNTRYSIDE FUNCTIONS

1. In section 184 of the 1972 Act (National Park and countryside functions), for subsection (1) substitute—
    "(1) The functions conferred on a local planning authority by or under the National Parks and Access to the Countryside Act 1949 and the Countryside Act 1968 shall—
    (a) as respects England elsewhere than in the metropolitan counties, Greater London and the Isles of Scilly, be exercisable in accordance with the following provisions of this section; and
    (b) as respects Wales, be exercisable in accordance with subsections (6) to (8) below."
2. Schedule 17 to the 1972 Act is amended as provided in paragraphs 3 to 14.
3. In paragraph 2 (functions which may be conferred on joint board), after "National Park" insert "in England".
4. In paragraph 4 (functions which may be conferred on joint and special planning boards), for "1 or 3" substitute "1, 3 or 3A".
5. In paragraph 6 (functions not to be discharged by National Park Committees), in paragraph (a), at the beginning insert "in the case of a council or councils for a planning area or areas in England,".
6. In paragraph 9 (discharge of functions by district planning authority), after "A National Park Committee" insert "for a National Park in England".
7. In paragraph 12A(1) (district council members for National Park Committees), after "a National Park" insert "in England".
8. In paragraph 13 (modification of section 101), in paragraphs (b) and (c), after "county" insert ", county borough" (in both places).
9. In paragraph 14(b) (members of National Park Committees), after "county" insert ", county borough".
10. In paragraph 19, after "Countryside Commission and" insert ", in the case of a National Park in England,".
11. In paragraph 20 (functions to which Part I of that Schedule applies), after "county council" insert ", county borough council".
12. In paragraph 21A (planning areas), at the end add "but, in relation to Wales, means a county or county borough".
13. After paragraph 35 (application of section 61 of National Parks and Access to the Countryside Act 1949) insert—
    "35A. In relation to Wales, paragraph 35 above has effect as if—
    (a) for "1974" there were substituted "1996";
    (b) for "and the county council" there were substituted "and the principal council"."
14. In paragraph 37 (identification of local planning authority), after "in relation to land" insert "in England".

PART II

OTHER ENACTMENTS

The National Parks and Access to the Countryside Act 1949 (c. 97)

15.—(1) In section 57 of the National Parks and Access to the Countryside Act 1949 (penalty for displaying on footpaths notices deterring public use), in subsection (3), after "district" insert "or, where they are not the highway authority, the council of the Welsh county or county borough".
(2) The provisions of section 69 of that Act (suspension of public access to avoid exceptional risk of fire) shall be subsection (1) of that section and at the end of that section add—
    "(2) The reference in subsection (1) of this section to the county planning authority is to be read, in relation to Wales, as a reference to the local planning authority."
(3) In Schedule 1 to that Act (orders designating National Parks and other orders)—
    (a) in paragraph 1(3)(a), for "area of every county planning authority whose area" substitute "every county or county borough which";

(b) in paragraph 2(5), after "county planning authority" insert "or, in Wales, the local planning authority".

The Local Government, Planning and Land Act 1980 (c. 65)

16.—(1) In section 148 of the Local Government, Planning and Land Act 1980 (planning control), in subsection (4) for "References" substitute "Except in relation to land in Wales, references".

(2) In Schedule 28 to that Act (powers of urban development corporations), in paragraph 11(2)(i), after "district planning authority" insert "or, in Wales, the local planning authority".

The Acquisition of Land Act 1981 (c. 67)

17.—(1) In section 17 of the Acquisition of Land Act 1981 (special parliamentary procedure for purposes of acquisition of local authority and statutory undertakers' land)—
(a) in subsection (3), after "Planning Board," insert "a Welsh planning board,"; and
(b) in subsection (4), after the definition of "statutory undertakers" add—
" "a Welsh planning board" means a board constituted under—
(a) section 2(1B) of the Town and Country Planning Act 1990; or
(b) paragraph 3A of Schedule 17 to the Local Government Act 1972."
(2) In paragraph 4 of Schedule 3 to that Act (acquisition of new rights over special kinds of land)—
(a) in sub-paragraph (3), after "Planning Board," insert "a Welsh planning board,"; and
(b) in sub-paragraph (4), after the definition of "statutory undertakers" add—
" "a Welsh planning board" means a board constituted under—
(a) section 2(1B) of the Town and Country Planning Act 1990; or
(b) paragraph 3A of Schedule 17 to the Local Government Act 1972."

The Litter Act 1983 (c. 35)

18. In section 10 of the Litter Act 1983 (interpretation), in the definition of "Park board"—
(a) after "1972; " at the end of paragraph (a), insert—
"(aa) in the case of a National Park in Wales, a joint planning board constituted under section 2(1B) of the Town and Country Planning Act 1990 for an area which comprises or includes the whole or any part of the area of that Park; ";
(b) in paragraph (b), after "reconstituted" insert "or constituted", after "3" insert "or 3A" and for "that Schedule" substitute "Schedule 17 to the Act of 1972".

The Housing Act 1985 (c. 68)

19. In section 573 of the Housing Act 1985 (meaning of "public sector authority"), in subsection (1), after "the Lake District Special Planning Board" insert—
"a Welsh planning board,"
and, after that subsection, insert—
"(1A) For the purposes of subsection (1), "a Welsh planning board" means a board constituted under—
(a) section 2(1B) of the Town and Country Planning Act 1990; or
(b) paragraph 3A of Schedule 17 to the Local Government Act 1972."

The Local Government Act 1988 (c. 9)

20. In Schedule 2 to the Local Government Act 1988 (public authorities for the purposes of public supply or works contracts), after "The Peak Park Joint Planning Board" insert—
"A joint planning board constituted under section 2(1B) of the Town and Country Planning Act 1990.
A special planning board constituted under paragraph 3A of Schedule 17 to the Local Government Act 1972."

The Local Government Finance Act 1988 (c. 41)

21. In section 74 of the Local Government Finance Act 1988 (power of Secretary of State to make regulations authorising a levying body to issue a levy) at the end add—
"(7) For the purposes of this section—
(a) a Welsh joint planning board constituted under section 2(1B) of the Town and Country Planning Act 1990; and
(b) a special planning board constituted under paragraph 3A of Schedule 17 to the Local Government Act 1972,

shall be treated as a levying body with respect to which regulations may be made under subsection (2) above."

The Electricity Act 1989 (c. 29)

22. In Schedule 8 to the Electricity Act 1989 (consents for generating stations and overhead lines), in paragraph 2(6), in paragraph (a) omit "and Wales" and after that paragraph insert— "(aa) in relation to Wales, means a local planning authority; ".

The Local Government and Housing Act 1989 (c. 42)

23.—(1) In section 21(1) of the Local Government and Housing Act 1989 (interpretation of Part I), in paragraph (m), for "1 or paragraph 3" substitute "1, 3 or 3A" and at the end add "or under section 2(1B) of the Town and Country Planning Act 1990".

(2) In section 39(1) of that Act (application of Part IV), in paragraph (h), for "1 or paragraph 3" substitute "1, 3 or 3A" and at the end add "or under section 2(1B) of the Town and Country Planning Act 1990".

(3) In section 67(3) of that Act (local authorities for the purposes of Part V), in paragraph (o), for "1 or paragraph 3" substitute "1, 3 or 3A" and at the end add "or under section 2(1B) of the Town and Country Planning Act 1990".

(4) In section 152(2) of that Act (relevant authorities for the purposes of imposing certain charges), in paragraph (k), for "1 or paragraph 3" substitute "1, 3 or 3A" and after "1992" add "or under section 2(1B) of the Town and Country Planning Act 1990".

The Town and Country Planning Act 1990 (c. 8)

24.—(1) In section 4 of the planning Act (National Parks)—
(a) in subsections (1) and (2), after "National Park" insert "in England" (in each place); and
(b) in subsection (3)—
(i) after "section 2" insert ", a special planning board is constituted under paragraph 3A of Schedule 17 to the Local Government Act 1972"; and
(ii) for "Schedule 17 to the Local Government Act 1972" substitute "that Schedule".

(2) In section 110(2) of that Act (registration of compensation for depreciation), after "district" insert ", Welsh county, county borough".

(3) In section 137(2) of that Act (service of purchase notice), after "district" insert ", Welsh county, county borough".

(4) In section 140(2) of that Act (notice to be given by Secretary of State where purchase notice referred to him), in paragraph (c)—
(a) at the beginning, insert "in England", and
(b) after "to that board;" insert—
"(cc) in Wales, to the local planning authority, where it is a joint planning board;".

(5) In section 188(1) of that Act (register of enforcement and stop notices), after "planning authority" insert ", every local planning authority for an area in Wales".

(6) In section 226 of that Act (compulsory acquisition of land for development and other planning purposes), in subsection (6)—
(a) in paragraph (a), after first "county" insert "in England"; and
(b) in paragraph (b), after "the district;" insert—
"(bb) if the land is in Wales, consult with the council of the county or county borough;"; and, in subsection (8), after "counties," insert "county boroughs,".

(7) In section 227(1) of that Act (acquisition of land by agreement), after "county," insert "county borough,".

(8) In section 231(1) of that Act (power of Secretary of State to require acquisition or development of land), after "county," insert "county borough,".

(9) In section 247(3)(b) of that Act (highways affected by development: orders by Secretary of State), after "county council," insert "county borough council,".

(10) In section 252 of that Act (procedure for making of orders under Part X), in subsection (12), in the definition of "local authority"—
(a) after "county," insert "county borough,"; and
(b) after first "parish" insert ", community".

(11) In section 253(4) of that Act (procedure in relation to orders for stopping up or diversion of highways in anticipation of planning permission), after "county," insert "county borough,".

(12) In section 307(1) of that Act (assistance for acquisition of property where objection made to blight notice in certain cases), after "county," insert "county borough,".

(13) In section 336 of that Act (interpretation), in subsection (1)—
(a) in the definition of "authority possessing compulsory purchase powers", after "or county council" insert "or county borough council";

(b) in the definition of "development plan", for "27" substitute "27, 27A"; and

(c) in the definition of "mineral planning authority", for "1(4)" substitute "1".

(14) After section 336(1) of that Act insert—

"(1A) In this Act—

(a) any reference to a county (other than one to a county planning authority) shall be construed, in relation to Wales, as including a reference to a county borough;

(b) any reference to a county council shall be construed, in relation to Wales, as including a reference to a county borough council; and

(c) section 17(4) and (5) of the Local Government (Wales) Act 1994 (references to counties and districts to be construed generally in relation to Wales as references to counties and county boroughs) shall not apply."

(15) In paragraph 8 of Schedule 1 to that Act (local planning authorities: distribution of functions), in sub-paragraphs (1) and (2)(a), omit "or community".

(16) In paragraph 3 of Schedule 13 to that Act (blighted land), for "for the district in which it" substitute "where the land".

(17) In paragraph 1 of Schedule 14 to that Act (procedure for footpaths and bridleways orders)—

(a) in sub-paragraph (2)(b)(ii), after first "rural parish" insert "or community"; and

(b) in sub-paragraph (3), in the definition of "council", after "county council," insert "a county borough council,".

(18) In Part I of Schedule 16 to that Act (provisions referred to in sections 314 to 319 of that Act), for "Section 1(1), (2), (3) and (5)" substitute "Section 1(1) to (3), (5) and (6)".

(19) In paragraph 4 of Schedule 17 to that Act (enactments exempted from section 333(6)), after "a county council" insert ", county borough council".

The Planning (Listed Buildings and Conservation Areas) Act 1990 (c. 9)

25.—(1) In section 2 of the Planning (Listed Buildings and Conservation Areas) Act 1990 (publication of lists)—

(a) in subsection (1), after "any district" insert ", Welsh county, county borough,", omit "and" at the end of paragraph (a), and at the end of that subsection add "and

(c) in the case of a Welsh county or county borough—

(i) with the county council or (as the case may be) the county borough council; and

(ii) with the local planning authority, if different from that council.", and

(b) in subsection (3)(a), after "district" insert ", Welsh county, county borough,".

(2) In section 3 of that Act (temporary listing: building preservation notices), in subsection (1), for ", other than" substitute "in Wales, or to a local planning authority in England who are not".

(3) In section 32(1) of that Act (purchase notice on refusal or conditional grant of listed building consent), after "district" insert ", Welsh county, county borough,".

(4) In section 34(2) of that Act (procedure on reference of listed building purchase notice to Secretary of State), in paragraph (c)—

(a) at the beginning insert "in England"; and

(b) after "to that board;" insert—

"(cc) in Wales, to the local planning authority, where it is a joint planning board;".

(5) In section 46(5) of that Act (issue of listed building enforcement notice by the Secretary of State), after "an area" insert "in England".

(6) In section 47(7) of that Act (compulsory acquisition of listed building in need of repair), in paragraph (a) of the definition of "the appropriate authority", after "county" insert ", county borough".

(7) In section 52(1) of that Act (acquisition of land by agreement), after "county," insert "county borough,".

(8) In section 57(7) of that Act (local authorities who may contribute to preservation of listed buildings etc.), in paragraph (a), after "county," insert "county borough,".

(9) In section 79(3) of that Act (local authorities for purposes of town scheme agreements), after paragraph (a) insert—

"(aa) a county borough council;".

(10) In Schedule 4 to that Act (further provisions as to exercise of functions by different authorities), the provisions of paragraph 1 shall be sub-paragraph (1) of that paragraph, and at the end of that paragraph add—

"(2) This Schedule shall apply in relation to Wales as if—

(a) paragraphs 2 to 5 were omitted;

(b) in paragraph 7, each reference to a district planning authority (or which is to be construed as such a reference) were a reference to the local planning authority."

The Planning (Hazardous Substances) Act 1990 (c. 10)

26.—(1) In section 1 of the Planning (Hazardous Substances) Act 1990 (hazardous substances authorities: general), after "district" insert ", Welsh county, county borough".

(2) In section 3(1) of that Act (hazardous substances authorities: other special cases), after "non-metropolitan county" insert "in England".

The Planning (Consequential Provisions) Act 1990 (c. 11)

27. In Schedule 3 to the Planning (Consequential Provisions) Act 1990 (transitional provisions and savings), in paragraph 8(1), after "district planning authority" insert "or, in Wales, the local planning authority".

The Environmental Protection Act 1990 (c. 43)

28. In section 88 of the Environmental Protection Act 1990 (fixed penalty notices for leaving litter), in subsection (10), in the definition of "Park board", omit "or" immediately before paragraph (b) and at the end add—

"(c) a joint planning board constituted under section 2(1B) of the Town and Country Planning Act 1990; or

(d) a special planning board constituted under paragraph 3A of Schedule 17 to the Local Government Act 1972;".

The Local Government (Overseas Assistance) Act 1993 (c. 25)

29. In section 1(10) of the Local Government (Overseas Assistance) Act 1993 (certain bodies on which powers are conferred by the Act), in paragraph (g), for "1 or 3" substitute "1, 3 or 3A" and at the end add "or under section 2(1B) of the Town and Country Planning Act 1990".

Section 22(1)   SCHEDULE 7

Highways, Road Traffic and Transport

Part I

Highways

The Highways Act 1980 (c. 66)

1.—(1) Section 1 of the Highways Act 1980 (which makes general provision for determining the highway authority) is amended as follows.

(2) After subsection (3) insert—

"(3A) In Wales the council of a county or county borough are the highway authority for all highways in the county or, as the case may be, the county borough, whether or not maintainable at the public expense, which are not highways for which the Minister is the highway authority under subsection (1) above."

(3) After subsection (4) add—

"(5) Subsection (3A) above is subject to any provision of this Act, or of any order made under this or any other Act, by virtue of which a council other than the Welsh council for the area in which the highway is situated are the highway authority."

2.—(1) Section 6 of that Act (delegation etc. of functions with respect to trunk roads) is amended as follows.

(2) After subsection (1A) of that section insert—

"(1B) The Minister shall not delegate functions to a council under subsection (1) above with respect to a trunk road or land outside their area but in Wales except after consultation with the Welsh council in whose area it is situated; and subsection (1A) does not apply in relation to a trunk road or land in Wales.".

(3) In subsection (6) of that section—

(a) after "the county council" insert "(the "responsible council")";

(b) after first "district council" insert "or Welsh council (the "contracting council")"; and

(c) for "district" in the second place in which it occurs substitute "contracting".

(4) In subsection (6A) of that section, for "district council" substitute "contracting council" and after paragraph (b) insert—

"(c) with respect to a trunk road or land in Wales but outside the area—

(i) of the responsible council; and

(ii) of the contracting council.

except after consultation with the Welsh council in whose area the trunk road or land is situated."

3. In section 8(4) of that Act (restrictions on certain agreements between local highway authorities)—

(a) after first "county" insert "(other than one in Wales)";

(b) after "another county" insert "or county borough";

(c) for "the counties" substitute "their areas";

(d) after "or of a county" insert "or county borough"; and

(e) after "the other county" insert "or, as the case may be, county borough".

4. In section 36(7) of that Act (highways maintainable at public expense), after "the council of a county" insert "in England".

5. In section 47(3) of that Act (procedure for applications with regard to unnecessary highways), after "relating to any highway" insert "in England".

6. In section 67 of that Act (guard-rails in private streets), in subsection (5), at the end add "but, in relation to a street in Wales, means a Welsh council".

7. In section 69 of that Act (subways), in subsection (3) at the end add "or, in the case of a road in Wales, as if the Welsh council in whose area it is situated were the highway authority for it".

8. In section 79 of that Act (prevention of obstruction at corners), after subsection (3) insert—

"(3A) In relation to any land in Wales—

(a) subsection (3) above does not apply; but

(b) if the Minister is the highway authority, he shall not serve a notice restraining the erection of any building on the land except with the consent of the Welsh council in whose area the land is situated."

9. In section 100 of that Act (drainage of highways), after subsection (6) insert—

"(6A) In subsection (6) above, "the district council" shall be read, in relation to Wales, as "the Welsh council".

(6B) Where the highway authority are a Welsh council—

(a) subsection (6) above does not apply; but

(b) before exercising any powers under sections 158, 159, 163, 165 and 168 of the Water Industry Act 1991 by virtue of subsection (5) above, they shall give notice of their intention to do so—

(i) to the sewerage undertaker; and

(ii) where they propose to exercise those powers outside their county or county borough, to the Welsh council or, as the case may be, the district council within whose area the powers are proposed to be exercised."

10. In section 114 of that Act (provision of public conveniences), after subsection (2) insert—

"(2A) In subsection (2) above, the reference to the council of the district in which the conveniences will be situated shall be read in relation to Wales as a reference to the Welsh council in whose area the conveniences will be situated.

(2B) Where the highway authority referred to in subsection (1) above are or, as the case may be, will be a Welsh council—

(a) subsection (2) above does not apply; but

(b) before providing any conveniences under subsection (1) above outside their county or county borough they shall give notice of their intention to do so to the Welsh council or, as the case may be, the district council in whose area the conveniences will be situated."

11. In section 116(3) of that Act (notice of application to stop up or divert highway), after paragraph (a) insert—

"(aa) if the highway is in Wales, the Welsh council for the area in which it is situated if they are not the highway authority for it; and";

and after "by the district council" insert "or Welsh council".

12. In section 120 of that Act (exercise of powers under sections 118 to 119A), in subsection (2)(a), for "the" immediately before "other council" substitute "any".

13. In section 151 of that Act (prevention of soil etc. being washed on to street), after subsection (1) insert—

"(1A) In relation to a street in Wales, the competent authorities for the purposes of this section are the highway authority for the street and, if different, the Welsh council in whose area the street is situated."

14. In section 154 of that Act (overhanging and dangerous trees etc.), after subsection (1) insert—

"(1A) In subsection (1)(a) above, any reference to a district includes a reference to a Welsh county or county borough."

15. In section 166 of that Act (forecourt abutting on streets), in subsection (5), after "Middle Temple," insert "a Welsh council".

16. In section 185 of that Act (power to install refuse or storage bins in streets), in subsection (1)(a), for "also" substitute "if different".

17. In section 204(2) of that Act (advance payments code), at the end add—

"(3) The areas in which the advance payments code applies by virtue of subsection (2)(b) above shall be taken to include any area in Wales—

(a) which is, or is in, a county borough; and

(b) in which the code applied immediately before 1st April 1996 by virtue of that subsection."

18.—(1) Section 205 of that Act (street works in private streets), is amended as follows.

(2) After subsection (4) insert—

"(4A) In the case of a street in Wales—

(a) subsection (4) above does not apply; but

(b) if the street works referred to in the resolution under subsection (1) above—

(i) are to be carried out in a part of the street which is treated as being in the area of a street works authority other than the local Welsh council for it; and

(ii) include the sewering of the street,

the proper officer of the council which are the street works authority shall, when preparing the specification required by subsection (3) above, consult the local Welsh council for it."

(3) At the end of subsection (5) add—

"and, in the case of any part of a street in Wales which is treated as being in the area of a street works authority which are not the local Welsh council for it, at the offices of the local Welsh council.

(5A) For the purposes of this section, the local Welsh council for a street in Wales are the council of the county or county borough in which it is situated."

19. In section 210 of that Act (power to amend specification, apportionment, etc.), at the end of subsection (2) insert "and, in the case of any part of a street in Wales, the Welsh council for the county or county borough in which it is situated, if different from the street works authority in whose area it is treated as situated."

20. In section 219 of that Act, (exceptions to application of advance payments code), after subsection (4) insert—

"(4A) In subsection (4)(c) above, "district council" is to be read in relation to plans deposited on or after 1st April 1996 for a building to be erected in Wales as "Welsh council"."

21. In section 220 of that Act (determination of payments under advance payments code), in subsection (1), after first "subsection (2)" insert "or (2A)", after "district council" insert "or Welsh council" and for second "subsection (2)" substitute "subsections (2) and (2A)" and, after subsection (2), insert—

"(2A) Where any required plans which—

(a) are deposited with a Welsh council; and

(b) relate to the erection of a building in an area—

(i) in which the advance payments code is in force; but

(ii) which is treated as being within the area of a street works authority other than that Welsh council,

are passed, the Welsh council shall, in any case to which section 219 above may be applicable, within one week inform the street works authority of that event."

22. In section 223 of that Act (determination to cease to have effect when plans not proceeded with), at the end add—

"(7) In any case—

(a) to which this section may be applicable; and

(b) which relates to plans for the erection of a building in any part of a street in Wales which is treated as being in the area of a street works authority other than the Welsh council for the county or county borough in which it is situated,

the Welsh council shall within one week inform the street works authority of the happening of any event of a kind described in paragraphs (a) to (c) of subsection (6) above."

23. In section 232 of that Act (power to treat as a private street land designated by development plan), in subsection (9), for "27" substitute "27, 27A".

24. In section 264 of that Act (vesting of drains etc. of certain roads), at the end insert—

"(4) Subsection (3)(a) above does not apply in Wales."

25. After section 272(5) of that Act (advances for purposes of works under section 96) insert—

"(5A) In relation to any work done in exercise of their powers under section 96 by a Welsh council in a highway within their area for which they are not the highway authority, subsection (5) above applies as though the reference to a district council were a reference to the Welsh council."

26. In section 287 of that Act (power to erect barriers in streets in cases of emergency etc.), in subsection (6), at the end add "but, in relation to Wales, means a Welsh council".

27.—(1) Section 329 of that Act (further provision as to interpretation) is amended as follows.

(2) In subsection (1)—

(a) in the definition of "local authority", at the end add "but, in relation to Wales, means a Welsh council"; and

(b) at the end add—

" "Welsh council" means the council of a Welsh county or county borough."

(3) After subsection (2) insert—

"(2A) In this Act—

(a) any reference to a county shall be construed in relation to Wales as including a reference to a county borough;

(b) any reference to a county council shall be construed in relation to Wales as including a reference to a county borough council; and

(c) section 17(4) and (5) of the Local Government (Wales) Act 1994 (references to counties and districts to be construed generally in relation to Wales as references to counties and county boroughs) shall not apply."

(4) After subsection (3) of that section insert—

"(3A) In a case where two or more communities are grouped under a common community council, references in this Act to a community are to be construed as references to those communities."

28. In Schedule 9 to that Act (improvement lines and building lines), after paragraph 2 insert—

"2A. Paragraph 2 above does not apply in relation to a street or highway in Wales."

29. In Schedule 12 to that Act (provisions as to orders under section 116 of that Act), in paragraph 1(d) after "district council" insert "if the highway is a classified road in a Welsh county or county borough and the council of that county or county borough is not the highway authority, to the council of that county or county borough".

The Conwy Tunnel (Supplementary Powers) Act 1983 (c. 7)

30. In section 8(4)(b) of the Conwy Tunnel (Supplementary Powers) Act 1983 (provisions supplementary to section 7), for "the Aberconwy Borough Council" substitute "the Aberconwy and Colwyn County Borough Council".

The Level Crossings Act 1983 (c. 16)

31. In section 1(11) of the Level Crossings Act 1983 (interpretation), in the definition of "local authority"—

(a) omit "and Wales", and

(b) after "City of London" insert ", in relation to Wales, means any council of a county or county borough".

The New Roads and Street Works Act 1991 (c. 22)

32.—(1) In section 94 of the New Roads and Street Works Act 1991 (power of street authority or district council to undertake street works), after subsection (1) insert—

"(1A) In subsection (1), the reference to a district council, is to be read, in relation to Wales, as a reference to a county council or a county borough council."

(2) In paragraph 2 of Schedule 2 to that Act (procedure in connection with toll orders), in sub-paragraph (3), after "City of London" insert "but, in relation to Wales, means a county council or county borough council".

The Severn Bridges Act 1992 (c. 3)

33.—(1) In section 39(1) of the Severn Bridges Act 1992 (interpretation), in the definition of "local authority", at the end insert "but, in relation to Wales, means a county council or a county borough council".

(2) In paragraph 8 of Schedule 2 to that Act (correction of deposited plans), in sub-paragraph (3), for "Monmouth Borough Council" substitute "Monmouthshire County Council".

(3) In of Schedule 3 to that Act (other highway works)—

(a) in paragraph 6(4)(b), for "Gwent County Council" substitute "Monmouthshire County Council"; and

(b) in paragraph 8(3), omit "Gwent County Council".

The Transport and Works Act 1992 (c. 42)

34.—(1) In section 11 of the Transport and Works Act 1992 (inquiries and hearings), in subsection (4), after "the Council of the Isles of Scilly" insert ", a county borough council,".

(2) In section 14 of that Act (publicity for making or refusal of orders), in subsection (7), at the end insert "but are, in relation to Wales, county councils and county borough councils".

(3) In section 48 of that Act (footpaths and bridleways over railways), in subsection (8), in the definition of "local authority" after "City of London" insert ", a county borough council,".

PART II

ROAD TRAFFIC AND TRANSPORT

The Transport Act 1968 (c. 73)

35. In section 159 of the Transport Act 1968 (interpretation), at the end add—
"(3) In this Act—

(a) any reference to a county (other than one to a metropolitan county) shall be construed in relation to Wales as including a reference to a county borough;

(b) any reference to a county council shall be construed in relation to Wales as including a reference to a county borough council; and

(c) section 17(4) and (5) of the Local Government (Wales) Act 1994 (references to counties and districts to be construed generally in relation to Wales as references to counties and county boroughs) shall not apply."

The Public Passenger Vehicles Act 1981 (c. 14)

36. In section 82 of the Public Passenger Vehicles Act 1981 (general interpretation provisions), at the end add—
"(3) In this Act—

(a) any reference to a county shall be construed in relation to Wales as including a reference to a county borough;

(b) any reference to a county council shall be construed in relation to Wales as including a reference to a county borough council; and

(c) section 17(4) and (5) of the Local Government (Wales) Act 1994 (references to counties and districts to be construed generally in relation to Wales as references to counties and county boroughs) shall not apply."

The Transport Act 1981 (c. 56)

37. In section 35 of the Transport Act 1981 (charges for licensing of cabs and cab drivers), after subsection (3) insert—
"(3A) In subsection (3) above, references to a district council shall be read, in relation to Wales, as references to a county council or a county borough council."

The Road Traffic Regulation Act 1984 (c. 27)

38.—(1) In section 39 of the Road Traffic Regulation Act 1984 (supplementary provisions as to exercise of powers under sections 32 to 35 in England or Wales), in subsection (4), omit "a district council in Wales proposes to make an order under section 32 or 35 of this Act, or", and after subsection (7) insert—
"(7A) Subsection (7) above does not apply in Wales."

(2) In section 44 of that Act (control of off-street parking outside Greater London)—

(a) in subsection (1)(a), for "Welsh counties" substitute "Welsh counties or county boroughs, by the county council or (as the case may be) county borough council"; and

(b) in subsection (3)(b) omit "and counties in Wales".

(3) In section 45(7) of that Act (definition of "local authority" for purposes of sections making provision for parking on highways)—

(a) in paragraph (b), for the words "or of a district" substitute "or county borough"; and

(b) omit "in England and Scotland" and the words from "and in Wales" to the end.

(4) In section 49 of that Act (supplementary provisions as to designation orders and designated parking places), omit subsection (3).

(5) Omit section 54 of that Act (designation orders in Wales).

(6) In section 55 of that Act (financial provisions relating to designation orders)—

(a) in subsections (2) and (4)(a) after "general fund" insert "or, in Wales, council fund"; and
(b) omit subsection (6).

(7) In section 59 of that Act (consents for, and provisions as to use of, parking places under section 57(1)(b)), in subsection (2), in paragraph (b) omit "or community" and after that subsection insert—

"(2A) In subsection (2) above, paragraph (b) and the words which follow it do not apply in relation to Wales."

(8) In section 100 of that Act (interim disposal of vehicles removed under section 99), in subsection (5), in paragraph (b) of the definition of "local authority", for "or of a district" substitute "or county borough".

(9) In section 125(4) of that Act (boundary roads), omit the words from "or, in relation to" to the end.

(10) In section 142 of that Act (interpretation), after subsection (1) insert—

"(1A) In this Act—
    (a) any reference to a county shall be construed in relation to Wales as including a reference to a county borough;
    (b) any reference to a county council shall be construed in relation to Wales as including a reference to a county borough council; and
    (c) section 17(4) and (5) of the Local Government (Wales) Act 1994 (references to counties and districts to be construed generally in relation to Wales as references to counties and county boroughs) shall not apply."

(11) In Schedule 9 to that Act (special provisions as to certain orders)—
(a) omit paragraph 11;
(b) in paragraph 24, for "sections 39 and 54" substitute "section 39"; and
(c) in paragraph 27(2), omit "54(5)".

The Transport Act 1985 (c. 67)

39.—(1) In section 63(4) of the Transport Act 1985 (functions of local councils with respect to passenger transport outside passenger transport areas), omit "and Wales".

(2) In section 64(1) of that Act (consultation and publicity with respect to policies as to services), omit "and Wales".

(3) In section 66(1) of that Act (exclusions of powers of certain councils to run bus undertakings) for "and Wales" substitute "a county council or county borough council in Wales".

(4) Section 81 of that Act (provision, maintenance and operation of bus stations) is amended as provided in subsections (5) to (7).

(5) After subsection (2) insert—

"(2A) Where, immediately before 1st April 1996, a council (the "former council") had power, by virtue of subsection (2) above, to maintain, repair and operate a bus station and any associated facilities, that power is, on and after that date, exercisable—
    (a) where the bus station and any such associated facilities—
            (i) was or were, immediately before 1st April 1996, situated wholly within the area of the former council, and
            (ii) is or are, on and after that date, situated wholly within a single Welsh county or county borough,
        by the council of that county or county borough; and
    (b) in any other case, by such Welsh county council or county borough council as the Secretary of State may by order designate."

(6) After subsection (5) of that section insert—

"(5A) Any Welsh county council or county borough council by whom any power is exercisable in relation to a bus station and any associated facilities by virtue of subsection (2A) above shall have power—
    (a) to make reasonable charges for the use of accommodation for public service vehicles at that bus station; and
    (b) to make reasonable charges for the use of, or let on hire to any person, those facilities (if any)."

(7) In subsection (6) of that section, for "(3) or (5)" substitute "(3), (5) or (5A)".

(8) In section 87 of that Act (interpretation of Part IV), at the end add—
    "and
    (f) references to a district council shall be read, in relation to Wales, as references to a county council or county borough council, and references to a district shall be so read as references to a county or, as the case may be, county borough."

(9) In section 105 of that Act (travel concessions on services provided by local authorities), after subsection (2) insert—

"(2A) In subsection (2) above, the reference to the general fund shall be read, in relation to Wales, as a reference to the council fund."

(10) In section 137 of that Act (general interpretation), after subsection (2) insert—

"(2A) In this Act—

(a) any reference to a county shall be construed in relation to Wales as including a reference to a county borough;

(b) any reference to a county council shall be construed in relation to Wales as including a reference to a county borough council; and

(c) section 17(4) and (5) of the Local Government (Wales) Act 1994 (references to counties and districts to be construed generally in relation to Wales as references to counties and county boroughs) shall not apply."

The Road Traffic Act 1988 (c. 52)

40.—(1) In section 192 of the Road Traffic Act 1988 (general interpretation of Act), after subsection (1) insert—

"(1A) In this Act—

(a) any reference to a county shall be construed in relation to Wales as including a reference to a county borough; and

(b) section 17(4) and (5) of the Local Government (Wales) Act 1994 (references to counties and districts to be construed generally in relation to Wales as references to counties and county boroughs) shall not apply."

(2) In paragraph 1(b) of Schedule 2 to that Act (deferred tests of condition of vehicles)—

(a) omit "and Wales"; and

(b) after "Greater London" insert "in such county or county borough in Wales".

The Road Traffic Offenders Act 1988 (c. 53)

41.—(1) Section 4 of the Road Traffic Offenders Act 1988 (offences for which local authorities in England and Wales may institute proceedings) is amended as follows.

(2) In subsection (5)—

(a) for "or district" substitute "or county borough"; and

(b) omit the words from "except, in Wales," to the end.

(3) After subsection (7) add—

"(8) In relation to Wales, any reference in subsections (1) to (4) above to a county shall be read as including a reference to a county borough."

The Road Traffic Act 1991 (c. 40)

42. In section 47 of the Road Traffic Act 1991 (applications for licences to drive hackney carriages etc.), after subsection (2) add—

"(3) In subsection (2), the reference to a district council shall be read in relation to Wales as including a reference to a county council or county borough council."

43. In Schedule 3 to the Road Traffic Act 1991 (permitted and special parking areas outside London)—

(a) in paragraphs 1(1)(a) and 2(1)(a), omit "and Wales";

(b) after paragraphs 1(1)(a) and 2(1)(a) insert, in both places—

"(aa) with respect to the whole, or any part, of their area, by a county council or county borough council in Wales;"; and

(c) omit paragraphs 1(1)(e) (except the word "or" immediately before paragraph (f)) and (2) and 2(2).

Section 22(2)   SCHEDULE 8

HOUSING

The Leasehold Reform Act 1967 (c. 88)

1.—(1) In section 28 of the Leasehold Reform Act (retention or resumption of land required for public purposes), after subsection (6) insert—

"(6A) In subsections (5) and (6) above, any reference to a county council shall be read, in relation to Wales, as including a reference to a county borough council."

(2) In Schedule 4A to that Act (exclusion of certain shared ownership leases), in paragraph 2(2)(a), after "county," insert "county borough,".

The Rent (Agriculture) Act 1976 (c. 80)

2. In section 5 of the Rent (Agriculture) Act 1976 (no statutory tenancy where landlord's interest belongs to Crown or to local authority, etc.), in subsection (3)(a), after "county" insert ", county borough".

The Rent Act 1977 (c. 42)

3.—(1) In section 14 of the Rent Act 1977 (landlord's interest belonging to local authority, etc.), in paragraph (a), after "county" insert "or county borough".

(2) In section 62 of that Act (registration areas for registration of rents), in paragraph (a), after "counties" insert "and county boroughs".

(3) In section 83 of that Act (local authorities for Part V), in paragraph (a), after "question," insert—

"(aa) in a Welsh county or county borough, the council of the county or county borough in question,".

(4) In section 124(8) of that Act (which defines "local authority" for the purposes of that section), at the end add "or, in Wales, the council of a county or county borough".

(5) In section 149 of that Act (powers of local authorities for the purposes of giving information), in subsection (2), after paragraph (a) insert—

"(aa) councils of Welsh counties and county boroughs;".

The Protection from Eviction Act 1977 (c. 43)

4.—(1) In section 3A of the Protection from Eviction Act 1977 (excluded tenancies and licences), in subsection (8)(a), after "county," insert "county borough,".

(2) In section 6 of that Act (prosecution of offences), after paragraph (a) insert—

"(aa) councils of Welsh counties and county boroughs;".

The Housing Act 1985 (c. 68)

5.—(1) In section 1 of the Housing Act 1985 (local housing authorities), after "City of London" insert "a Welsh county council or county borough council".

(2) In section 2(1) of that Act (the district of a local housing authority), after "City of London" insert "the Welsh county or county borough,".

(3) In section 4 of that Act (other descriptions of authority), in paragraph (e), after "county," insert "county borough,".

(4) In section 14 of that Act (exercise of powers by authority outside district), in subsection (2), in paragraph (b), after "outside that county" insert "but in England" and after that subsection insert—

"(2A) Where a Welsh county council or county borough council propose to exercise the power in England they shall before doing so give notice of their intention to the council of the county in which they propose to exercise the power, but failure to give notice does not invalidate the exercise of the power.";

and, in subsection (3), after "county," insert "county borough,".

(5) In section 16(2) of that Act (exercise outside Greater London of powers of authorities in London), after "district" insert "or, in Wales, of the county or county borough".

(6) In section 28 of that Act (reserve powers to provide housing accommodation), in subsection (1), after "councils" insert "in England".

(7) In sections 105(6)(b) and 106(3)(b) of that Act (consultation on matters of housing management and information about housing allocation), after "district" insert ", Welsh county or county borough" in each place.

The Housing Associations Act 1985 (c. 69)

6.—(1) In section 34 of the Housing Associations Act 1985 (provision of land by county councils), in subsection (1), after "wishes to erect houses" insert "in England".

(2) In section 106(1) of that Act (minor definitions: general), in the definition of "local authority", after "county," insert "county borough,".

The Landlord and Tenant Act 1985 (c. 70)

7. In section 38 of the Landlord and Tenant Act 1985 (minor definitions), in the definition of "local authority" after "county" insert "county borough".

The Landlord and Tenant Act 1987 (c. 31)

8. In section 58 of the Landlord and Tenant Act 1987 (exempt landlords and resident land-lords), in subsection (1)(a) after "county" insert ", county borough".

The Housing Act 1988 (c. 50)

9.—(1) In section 66(4) of the Housing Act 1988 (planning control), in paragraph (a), immedi-ately before "Greater London" insert "Wales,".

(2) In Schedule 1 to that Act (tenancies which cannot be assured tenancies), in paragraph 12(2)(a) (local authority tenancies etc.), after "county," insert "county borough,".

The Local Government and Housing Act 1989 (c. 42)

10.—(1) In section 114 of the Local Government and Housing Act 1989 (approval of appli-cations to provide certain facilities for the disabled), in subsection (1), for "the local housing authority" substitute "a local housing authority in England".

(2) In section 127(3) of that Act (ineligibility for certain bodies as assisted participants in group repair scheme), in paragraph (a) after "county," insert "county borough,".

(3) In section 172 of that Act (transfer of new town housing stock)—
(a) in subsections (2)(a) and (7)(c), after "district council" insert "or Welsh county council or county borough council" in both places; and
(b) in subsection (2)(a), for second "district" substitute "area".

The Social Security Administration Act 1992 (c. 5)

11. In section 15A of the Social Security Administration Act 1992 (payment out of benefit of sums in respect of mortgage interest etc.), in subsection (3)(d), after "county council," insert "county borough council,".

Section 22(3)   SCHEDULE 9

PUBLIC HEALTH

The Celluloid and Cinematograph Film Act 1922 (c. 35)

1. In section 9 of the Celluloid and Cinematograph Film Act 1922 (definitions), in the defi-nition of "local authority", after "of a county" insert "or county borough".

The Petroleum (Consolidation) Act 1928 (c. 32)

2. In section 2(1)(c) of the Petroleum (Consolidation) Act 1928 (local authorities empowered to grant petroleum-spirit licences outside Greater London), after "county council" insert "or county borough council".

The Public Health Act 1936 (c. 49)

3.—(1) In section 1 of the Public Health Act 1936 (local authorities), in paragraph (a) of subsection (1), at the beginning insert "except in Wales," and omit "or community", and after that paragraph insert—
    "(aa) in Wales, the county council or county borough council as respects all matters, without prejudice, however, to the exercise by a community council of any powers conferred upon such a council;".

(2) In subsection (2) of section 1—
(a) in the definition of "district", at the end add "and, in relation to a local authority in Wales, means a county or (as the case may be) county borough"; and
(b) in the definition of "local authority", at the end add "but, in relation to Wales, means the council of a county or county borough".

(3) In section 6 of that Act (union of districts, etc.), at the end add—
    "(6) In relation to Wales, the proviso in subsection (2) of this section does not apply and subsection (4) of this section applies as if the words "and also the county council" and "or council" were omitted."

(4) In section 267 of that Act (application to ships and boats), after subsection (2) insert—
    "(2A) Subsection (2) of this section does not apply if the point on land which is nearest to the spot where the vessel is lying is in Wales."

(5) In section 309 of that Act (expenses of joint boards), at the end add—
    "(6) In subsection (5) of this section, the reference to a county council shall not include a reference to the council of a Welsh county or county borough."

The Rag Flock and Other Filling Materials Act 1951 (c. 63)

4. In section 35 of the Rag Flock and Other Filling Materials Act 1951 (interpretation), in the definition of "local authority", at the end add "but, in relation to Wales, means the council of a county or county borough;".

The Nurses Agencies Act 1957 (c. 16)

5. In section 2 of the Nurses Agencies Act 1957 (licensing of agencies), at the end of subsection (1) add "but, in relation to a county or county borough in Wales, means the council of that county or county borough."

The Scrap Metal Dealers Act 1964 (c. 69)

6. In section 9(2) of the Scrap Metal Dealers Act 1964 (interpretation), in the definition of "local authority", after "London borough" insert "but, in relation to Wales, means the council of a county or county borough."

The Riding Establishments Act 1964 (c. 70)

7. In section 6(4) of the Riding Establishments Act 1964 (interpretation), in the definition of "local authority", after "City of London;" insert "in Wales means the council of a county or county borough;".

The Fire Precautions Act 1971 (c. 40)

8. In section 43(1) of the Fire Precautions Act 1971 (interpretation), in the definition of "local authority", in paragraph (a) omit "and Wales" and after that paragraph insert—
    "(aa) as respects Wales, the council of a county or county borough;".

The Health and Safety at Work etc. Act 1974 (c. 37)

9. In section 53(1) of the Health and Safety at Work etc. Act 1974 (general interpretation of Part I), in the definition of "local authority", in paragraph (a) omit "and Wales" and after that paragraph insert—
    "(aa) in relation to Wales, a county council or a county borough council,".

The Control of Pollution Act 1974 (c. 40)

10.—(1) In section 22 of the Control of Pollution Act 1974 (street cleaning etc.), in subsection (4), in the definition of "local authority", after "City of London" insert "but, in relation to Wales, means the council of a county or county borough".
    (2) In section 30 of that Act (interpretation etc. of Part I), in subsection (1), after "following subsection" insert "and to subsection (6) below", and at the end add—
        "(6) In the application of this Part of this Act to Wales—
        "collection authority" means a county council or county borough council; and
        "disposal authority" means a county council or county borough council."
    (3) In section 73(1) of that Act (interpretation of Part III), in paragraph (a) of the definition of "local authority" omit "and Wales" and after "Middle Temple;" insert—
        "(aa) in Wales, the council of a county or a county borough;".
    (4) In section 98 of that Act (interpretation of Part V), in paragraph (a) of the definition of "relevant authority" omit "and Wales" and at the end of that paragraph insert—
        "(aa) in Wales, the Secretary of State, a county council or a county borough council and, for the purposes of sections 91 to 93 of this Act, a sewerage undertaker; and".
    (5) In section 105(1) of that Act (general interpretation), after " "county" " insert ", "county borough" ".

The Refuse Disposal (Amenity) Act 1978 (c. 3)

11. In section 11(1) of the Refuse Disposal (Amenity) Act 1978 (interpretation), in paragraph (c) of the definition of "local authority", for "district council" substitute "county council or county borough council".

The Litter Act 1983 (c. 35)

12. The provisions of section 10 of the Litter Act 1983 (interpretation) shall be subsection (1) of that section, and at the end of that section add—
    "(2) In the application of this Act in relation to Wales, any reference to a county shall be read as including a reference to a county borough and any reference to a county council shall be read as including a reference to a county borough council."

The Public Health (Control of Disease) Act 1984 (c. 22)

13.—(1) In section 1 of the Public Health (Control of Disease) Act 1984 (authorities administering the Act), in subsection (1), after paragraph (a) insert—

"(aa) in Wales, a county council or county borough council,";

and in subsection (4)(c), after "county councils" insert "or county borough councils".

(2) In section 13 of that Act (regulations for control of certain diseases), in subsection (4)(a), after "county councils," insert "county borough councils,".

(3) In section 53 of that Act (interpretation of Part IV), in the definition of "canal", after "county" insert "or county borough".

(4) In section 64 of that Act (restriction on right to prosecute), in subsection (2)(a), after "district council" insert "Welsh county council, county borough council".

(5) In section 74 of that Act (general interpretation), in the definition of "district", at the end add "and, in relation to a local authority in Wales, means a county or county borough".

The Food Act 1984 (c. 30)

14. In section 61 of the Food Act 1984 (interpretation for Part III), in the definition of "local authority", after "parish" insert "council but, in relation to Wales, means a county council, county borough council".

The Building Act 1984 (c. 55)

15.—(1) In section 18 of the Building Act 1984 (building over sewer etc.), after subsection (2) insert—

"(2A) In subsection (2) above, the reference to the council of the district or borough shall be read, in relation to Wales, as a reference to the council of the county or county borough."

(2) In section 87 of that Act (application of provisions to Crown property), after subsection (2) insert—

"(2A) Subsection (2) above shall apply in relation to property in Wales as if—

(a) in paragraph (a) the reference to a county included a reference to a county borough; and

(b) paragraph (b) were omitted."

(3) In section 126 of that Act (general interpretation), in the definition of "local authority", after "Isles of Scilly" insert "but, in relation to Wales, means the council of a county or county borough;".

The Food Safety Act 1990 (c. 16)

16.—(1) In section 5 of the Food Safety Act 1990 (definition of food authority), in subsection (1) omit "and Wales", and after that subsection insert—

"(1A) Subject to subsection (3)(a) and (b) below, the food authorities in Wales are, as respects each county or county borough, the council of that county or county borough."

(2) In section 27(5) of that Act (appointment of public analysts), after "district" insert "in England".

The Environmental Protection Act 1990 (c. 43)

17.—(1) In section 4(11) of the Environmental Protection Act 1990 (which defines "local authority" for the purposes of Part I), in paragraph (b), at the beginning insert "in England" and after "Isles of Scilly;" insert—

"(bb) in Wales, a county council or county borough council;".

(2) In section 30 of that Act (authorities for purposes of Part II), for each of subsections (1)(f) and (2)(f) substitute—

"(f) for any county or county borough in Wales, the council of the county or county borough;".

(3) In subsection (3) of section 30, in paragraph (a) omit "and Wales" and after paragraph (b) insert—

"(bb) for any county or county borough in Wales, the council of the county or county borough;".

(4) In section 50(5)(a) of that Act (consultation in relation to waste disposal plans), omit sub-paragraph (iii).

(5) In section 79(7) of that Act (miscellaneous definitions for purposes of Part III), in paragraph (b) of the definition of "local authority", at the beginning insert "in England" and after "council;" insert—

"(bb) in Wales, a county council or county borough council;".

(6) In section 86 of that Act (preliminary provisions relating to litter), in subsection (2), after paragraph (a) insert—

"(aa) a county borough council,".

(7) In subsection (9)(b) of section 86, at the beginning insert "in England" and after "district;" insert—

"(bb) in Wales, the council of the county or county borough;".

(8) In section 88 of that Act (fixed penalty notices for leaving litter), in subsection (9)—

(a) in paragraph (a), for "a county" substitute "an English county"; and

(b) in paragraph (b), immediately before "county council" insert "English".

(9) In that Act, in each of—

(a) section 90(3) (litter control areas),

(b) section 92(1) (summary proceedings by litter authorities), and

(c) section 95(1) (public registers),

for "a" immediately before "county council" substitute "an English", and immediately before each of "regional" and "joint" insert "a".

(10) In section 93(1) of that Act (street litter control notices), for "a" immediately before "county council" substitute "an English", and immediately before "regional" insert "a".

(11) In section 99(5) of that Act (provisions relating to abandoned trolleys), in paragraph (d), after "Isles of Scilly;" insert—

"(dd) in Wales, the council of a county or county borough;".

(12) In section 143 of that Act (public registers of land which may be contaminated), in subsection (6), in paragraph (b) of the definition of "local authority", omit "and Wales" and after "council;" insert—

"(bb) in Wales, a county council or county borough council;".

(13) In section 149 of that Act (seizure of stray dogs), in subsection (11), in the definition of "local authority" omit "and Wales" and after "Isles of Scilly" insert "in relation to Wales, means a county council or a county borough council".

The Clean Air Act 1993 (c. 11)

18. In section 64(1) of the Clean Air Act 1993 (general provisions as to interpretation) in the definition of "local authority", in paragraph (a) omit "and Wales" and after "Middle Temple" insert—

"(aa) in Wales, the council of a county or county borough;".

Section 22(4)   SCHEDULE 10

SOCIAL SERVICES

The Children and Young Persons Act 1933 (c. 12)

1.—(1) Section 96 of the Children and Young Persons Act 1933 (provisions as to local authorities) is amended as follows.

(2) In subsection (1A), at the end add "but, in relation to Wales, shall be the councils of counties and county boroughs".

(3) After subsection (4) insert—

"(4A) Subsection (4) above does not apply in relation to the council of any Welsh county or county borough."

The National Assistance Act 1948 (c. 29)

2.—(1) In section 47 of the National Assistance Act 1948 (removal to suitable premises of persons in need of care and attention), in subsection (12), after "City of London" insert ", in Wales the councils of counties and county boroughs".

(2) In section 64(1) of that Act (interpretation), in the definition of "local authority" at the end add "but in relation to Wales means the council of a county or county borough".

The Disabled Persons (Employment) Act 1958 (c. 33)

3. In section 3 of the Disabled Persons (Employment) Act 1958 (provision of sheltered employment by local authorities), in subsection (5), omit "or Wales" and at the end add "and in relation to Wales, the council of a county or county borough".

The Children and Young Persons Act 1963 (c. 37)

4.—(1) In section 56 of the Children and Young Persons Act 1963 (prosecution of certain offences), after subsection (1) insert—

"(1A) Subsection (1) above shall have effect in relation to Wales as if the reference to a county were a reference to a Welsh county or county borough."

(2) In section 63 of that Act (interpretation), in subsection (1A), after "metropolitan counties)," insert "of county boroughs,".

The Health Services and Public Health Act 1968 (c. 46)

5.—(1) In section 45 of the Health Services and Public Health Act 1968 (promotion, by local authorities, of the welfare of old people), in subsection (11), after "county, or of a" insert "county borough,".

(2) In section 64 of that Act (financial assistance to certain voluntary organisations), in subsection (3)(b), after "non-metropolitan county," insert "county borough,".

(3) In section 65 of that Act (which makes similar provision relating to financial assistance by local authorities), in subsection (3)(a), after "county, or of a" insert "county borough,".

The Children and Young Persons Act 1969 (c. 54)

6. In section 70(1) of the Children and Young Persons Act 1969 (interpretation), in the definition of "local authority", after "county or of a" insert "county borough,".

The Local Authority Social Services Act 1970 (c. 42)

7. In section 1 of the Local Authority Social Services Act 1970 (local authorities for the purposes of the Act), at the end add "but, in relation to Wales, shall be the councils of counties and county boroughs".

The Chronically Sick and Disabled Persons Act 1970 (c. 44)

8. In section 21 of the Chronically Sick and Disabled Persons Act 1970 (badges for display on motor vehicles used by disabled persons), in subsection (8), omit "or Wales" and after "London borough" insert ", the council of a Welsh county or county borough".

The Adoption Act 1976 (c. 36)

9. In section 72(1) of the Adoption Act 1976 (interpretation), in the definition of "local authority", after "City of London" insert "but, in relation to Wales, means the council of a county or county borough".

The Supplementary Benefits Act 1976 (c. 71)

10. In Schedule 5 to the Supplementary Benefits Act 1976 (re-establishment courses and resettlement units)—
   (a) in paragraph 2(2), after "counties" insert ", of county boroughs"; and
   (b) in paragraph 4(2), after "county," insert "a county borough,".

The National Health Service Act 1977 (c. 49)

11.—(1) In section 22 of the National Health Service Act 1977 (co-operation between health authorities and local authorities), in the Table, in column 2 of the entry relating to an Area or District Health Authority in Wales, after "county" insert "or county borough" and after first "district" insert "in England".

(2) In section 28A of that Act (power to make payments towards expenditure on community services), in subsection (2)(b), after "district council," insert "or to a Welsh county council or county borough council,".

(3) In section 128(1) of that Act (interpretation)—
   (a) in the definition of "local authority", after "county council," insert "a county borough council,"; and
   (b) in the definition of "local social services authority", after "county," insert "of a county borough".

(4) In Schedule 7 to that Act (Community Health Councils), in paragraph 7, in the definition of "local authority", for "of a county or district mentioned in section 20(3) of that Act (which relates to Wales)" substitute "the council of a Welsh county or county borough".

The Health and Social Services and Social Security Adjudications Act 1983 (c. 41)

12. In Part II of Schedule 9 to the Health and Social Services and Social Security Adjudications Act 1983 (meals and recreation for old people)—
   (a) in paragraphs 1 and 2, after "council" insert "or Welsh county council or county borough council" in each place; and

(b) in paragraph 3, after "district councils" insert "or Welsh county councils or county borough councils" in all places.

The Children Act 1989 (c. 41)

13. In section 105 of the Children Act 1989 (interpretation), in the definition of "local authority" in subsection (1), omit "and Wales" and after "City of London" insert ", in relation to Wales, the council of a county or a county borough".

The National Health Service and Community Care Act 1990 (c. 19)

14. In section 46 of the National Health Service and Community Care Act 1990 (local authority plans for community care services), in subsection (3), in the definition of "local authority", after "county," insert "a county borough,".

Section 22(5)   SCHEDULE 11

WATER, LAND DRAINAGE AND COAST PROTECTION

PART I

WATER

The Reservoirs Act 1975 (c. 23)

1. In section 2 of the Reservoirs Act 1975 (functions of local authorities), in subsection (1)—
(a) omit "and Wales"; and
(b) after "London boroughs" insert ", in Wales, the councils of counties and county boroughs".

The Water Industry Act 1991 (c. 56)

2.—(1) In section 191 of the Water Industry Act 1991 (duties to make recreational facilities available when building reservoirs in Wales), in subsection (2)(b), for "district" substitute "county or county borough".
(2) In section 219 of that Act (interpretation), in subsection (1), in the definition of "local authority", at the end add "but, in relation to Wales, means the council of a county or county borough".

The Water Resources Act 1991 (c. 57)

3.—(1) In section 10 of the Water Resources Act 1991 (composition of regional flood defence committees), in subsection (5), after "county," insert "county borough,".
(2) In section 13 of that Act (composition of local flood defence committees), in subsection (7), after "county," insert "county borough,".
(3) In section 140 of that Act (appeals relating to contributions from internal drainage boards), in subsection (1)(b), after "county" insert ", county borough".
(4) In section 167 of that Act (power to dispose of spoil in connection with flood defence works), in subsection (3), after "London borough" insert "or Welsh county or county borough".
(5) In section 184 of that Act (duties to make recreational facilities available when building reservoirs in Wales), in subsection (2)(b), for "district" substitute "county or county borough".
(6) In section 221 of that Act (general interpretation), in the definition of "local authority" in subsection (1), after "county," insert "county borough,".
(7) In Schedule 8 to that Act (proceedings on applications for drought orders), in the Table in paragraph 1(2), for "a county" in each place substitute "an English county".
(8) In Schedule 14 to that Act (orders transferring main river functions to the Authority), in paragraph 2(2)(a), after "county council" insert ", county borough council".
(9) In Schedule 15 to that Act (drainage charges), in paragraph 13(4), after "London borough" in each place insert "or Welsh county or county borough".

(10) In Schedule 16 to that Act (schemes imposing special drainage charges)—
(a) in paragraph 1(2)(a)(i), after "county," insert "county borough,"; and
(b) in paragraph 3(2)(a), after "county council" insert ", county borough council".
(11) In Schedule 19 to that Act (orders conferring compulsory works powers), in paragraph 1(3)(a), for "a county" substitute "an English county".

PART II

LAND DRAINAGE

The Land Drainage Act 1991 (c. 59)

4.—(1) In section 10 of the Land Drainage Act 1991 (exercise of default powers by local authorities), in subsection (1), after "county," insert "county borough,".
(2) In section 14 of that Act (general drainage powers of boards and local authorities), in subsection (4)(b), for "a county" substitute "an English county".
(3) In section 15 of that Act (disposal of spoil by boards and local authorities), in subsection (5), for "London borough," substitute "London borough or Welsh county or county borough,".
(4) In section 16 of that Act (exercise of local authority powers under sections 14 and 15), in subsection (1), for "subsection (3)" substitute "subsections (3) and (3A)", in subsection (2), after "borough council" insert "or Welsh county council or county borough council", and at the end add—
"(3A) Subsection (1) above does not apply in relation to powers conferred on a Welsh county council or county borough council."
(5) In section 18 of that Act (drainage of small areas), after subsection (1) insert—
"(1A) Subsection (1) above has effect in relation to land in Wales with the omission of the words "other than a district council"."
(6) In section 20 of that Act (arrangements with other persons for carrying out drainage works), at the end add—
"(5) Subsection (2) above has effect in relation to Wales with the omission of "other than the council of a non-metropolitan district"."
(7) In section 55 of that Act (powers to borrow), in subsection (2), after "county" insert ", county borough".
(8) In section 57 of that Act (contributions by the NRA to expenses of internal drainage boards), in subsection (4)(b), after "county" insert ", county borough".
(9) In section 58 of that Act (allocation of NRA revenue for its functions as an internal drainage board), in subsection (4), after "county" insert ", county borough".
(10) In section 62 of that Act (powers to acquire land), in subsection (2), after "London borough" insert "or Welsh county or county borough".
(11) In section 66 of that Act (powers to make byelaws), in subsections (1) and (2), for "a county" in each place substitute "an English county".
(12) In section 72 of that Act (interpretation), in the definition of "local authority" in subsection (1), after "county," insert "county borough,".
(13) In Schedule 2 to that Act (expenses and proceedings etc. of internal drainage boards), in paragraphs 4(1)(b) and 5(1)(b), after "county" in each place insert ", county borough".
(14) In Schedule 3 to that Act (procedure with respect to certain orders), in paragraph 2(2)(a), after "county council", insert ", county borough council".
(15) In Schedule 4 to that Act (schemes for small drainage works), in paragraph 3(2), after "county," insert "county borough,".

PART III

COAST PROTECTION

The Coast Protection Act 1949 (c. 74)

5.—(1) In section 2 of the Coast Protection Act 1949 (constitution of coast protection boards), in subsection (2)(a), after "county" insert "(other than one in Wales)".
(2) In section 20 of that Act (contributions towards expenses of coast protection)—
(a) in subsection (1), omit "or Wales";
(b) in subsection (4), omit "or Wales";
(c) in subsection (5), for "or Wales" substitute ", the council of a county or county borough in Wales".
(3) In section 21 of that Act (grants), in subsection (1)(b), after "county" insert "or county borough".

19–104

(4) In section 22 of that Act (incidental use of land acquired for coast protection), in subsection (2), for "or Wales" substitute ", the council of a county or county borough in Wales".

(5) In section 45 of that Act (service of notices and other documents), in subsection (1)(b), after "county," insert "county borough,".

(6) In section 49 of that Act (interpretation), in the definition of "maritime district", after second "district" insert "or Welsh county or county borough".

(7) In Schedule 1 to that Act (orders), in paragraph 1(a), after "county," insert "county borough,".

Section 38(11) SCHEDULE 12

Funds

The 1972 Act

1. In section 148 of the 1972 Act (principal councils' funds and accounts) at the end add—
   "(6) This section does not apply in relation to a Welsh county council or county borough council."

The Local Government Finance Act 1988 (c. 41)

2. After section 89 of the Local Government Finance Act 1988 insert—

"Principal councils in Wales
   89A. This Part does not apply to a Welsh county council or county borough council (for whom provision as to the establishment of a council fund is made by section 38 of the Local Government (Wales) Act 1994)."

3. In section 111(2) of that Act (relevant authorities for purposes of provisions relating to financial administration) after paragraph (a) insert—
   "(aa) a county borough council,".

The Local Government Finance Act 1992 (c. 14)

4.—(1) Section 32 of the Local Government Finance Act 1992 (calculation of budget requirement) is amended as follows.

(2) In subsection (3)(a), after "fund" insert "or (as the case may be) council fund".

(3) After subsection (3) insert—
   "(3A) In the case of any billing authority in Wales, subsection (3)(a) above does not require the estimation of sums payable into their council fund in respect of council tax or non-domestic rates."

(4) In subsection (7)(a)(i), after "general fund" insert "or (as the case may be) council fund".

(5) After subsection (8) insert—
   "(8A) Subsections (2)(e), (3)(b), (7)(a)(ii) and (8) above do not apply in relation to a Welsh county council or county borough council.

   (8B) Subsection (5) above shall have effect in relation to a Welsh county council or county borough council as if for paragraphs (a) and (b) there were substituted—
   "(a) payments which must be met from a trust fund;
   (b) payments to be made to the Secretary of State under paragraph 5 of Schedule 8 to the 1988 Act or regulations made under paragraph 5(15) of that Schedule;
   (c) payments to be made in respect of the amount of any precept issued by a major precepting authority under Part I of this Act (but not payments to be so made in respect of interest on such an amount); and
   (d) payments to be made to another person in repaying, under regulations under the 1988 Act or Part I of this Act, excess receipts by way of non-domestic rates or council tax." "

(6) In subsection (9)(b), for "(8)" substitute "(8B)".

5.—(1) Section 33 of that Act (calculation of basic amount of council tax) is amended as follows.

(2) In subsection (1), after "general fund" insert "or (as the case may be) council fund".

(3) At the end of subsection (3), insert—
   "This subsection does not apply in relation to a Welsh county council or county borough council."

6. In section 35 of that Act (definition of "special items"), at the end add—
   "(4) Subsection (2) above shall have effect in relation to a Welsh county council or county borough council as if for paragraphs (b) and (c) there were substituted—
   "(b) any expenses incurred by a billing authority and arising in connection with property which it holds in trust for a part of its area are its special expenses;

(c) any expenses incurred by a billing authority which relates to a part of its area and which are of the same kind as expenses which—

(i) relate to another part of its area; and

(ii) are to be met out of property held in trust for that part;

are its special expenses;".

(5) Expenses of a billing authority are not to be treated as its special expenses for the purposes of subsection (1) above if they are expenses of meeting a levy issued to it by, or anticipated by it from—

(a) a Welsh joint planning board constituted under section 2(1B) of the Town and Country Planning Act 1990 for a united district which comprises or includes the whole or part of the area of a National Park; or

(b) a special planning board constituted under paragraph 3A of Schedule 17 to the Local Government Act 1972."

7. In sections 37 and 60 of that Act (substitute calculations), in each case in subsection (5)(a), after "general fund" insert "or (as the case may be) council fund".

8. In section 62 of that Act (failure to make substitute calculations), at the end add—

"(5) Subsection (2) above does not apply in relation to a Welsh county council or county borough council."

Section 39   SCHEDULE 13

THE RESIDUARY BODY FOR WALES: CORFF GWEDDILLIOL CYMRU

Membership

1.—(1) The Residuary Body shall consist of not less than 4 nor more than 7 members appointed by the Secretary of State.

(2) The Secretary of State shall appoint one of the members to be chairman.

(3) The Secretary of State may by order alter either of the numbers in sub-paragraph (1).

Status

2. The Residuary Body and its members and staff are not Crown servants and are not to be regarded as acting on behalf of the Crown.

Tenure of office of members

3.—(1) Every member of the Residuary Body shall hold and vacate office in accordance with the terms of his appointment but subject to the following provisions of this paragraph.

(2) Any member may resign his office by notice in writing to the Secretary of State.

(3) The Secretary of State may remove a member from office if that member—

(a) has become bankrupt or made an arrangement with his creditors;

(b) is incapacitated by physical or mental illness;

(c) has been absent from meetings of the Residuary Body for a period of three months otherwise than for a reason approved by it; or

(d) is, in the opinion of the Secretary of State, otherwise unable or unfit to discharge the functions of a member.

(4) A person shall cease to be chairman of the Residuary Body if he—

(a) resigns as such by notice in writing to the Secretary of State; or

(b) ceases to be a member of the Residuary Body.

Remuneration etc. of members

4.—(1) The Residuary Body shall pay to each member such remuneration and allowances (if any) as the Secretary of State may determine.

(2) The Residuary Body shall pay, or make provision for the payment of, such sums by way of pension, allowances and gratuities, to or in respect of such members as the Secretary of State may determine.

(3) Where a person ceases to be a member otherwise than on the expiration of his term of office and it appears to the Secretary of State that there are special circumstances which make it right for him to receive compensation, the Residuary Body shall pay as compensation to that person such amount as the Secretary of State may determine.

(4) The consent of the Treasury is required for any determination of the Secretary of State under this paragraph.

House of Commons and Northern Ireland Assembly disqualification

5. In Part III of Schedule 1 to the House of Commons Disqualification Act 1975 and Part III of Schedule 1 to the Northern Ireland Assembly Disqualification Act 1975 (disqualifying offices) insert, at the appropriate place—
"Any member of the Residuary Body for Wales (Corff Gweddilliol Cymru) in receipt of remuneration."

Proceedings

6.—(1) Subject to the provisions of this paragraph and paragraph 12(1), the Residuary Body shall regulate its own proceedings.
(2) The validity of any proceedings of the Residuary Body shall not be affected by any vacancy among its members or by any defect in the appointment of any of its members.
(3) A member who is directly or indirectly interested in any matter brought up for consideration at a meeting of the Residuary Body shall disclose the nature of his interest to the meeting.
(4) Where such a disclosure is made, the member shall not take part in any deliberation or decision of the Residuary Body with respect to that matter.

Application of seal and proof of instruments

7.—(1) The application of the seal of the Residuary Body shall be authenticated by the signature of any member of the Residuary Body, or of its staff, who has been authorised by the Residuary Body, whether generally or specially, for the purposè.
(2) Any document purporting to be a document duly executed under the seal of the Residuary Body shall be received in evidence and shall, unless the contrary is proved, be deemed to have been so executed.

Access to documents

8.—(1) Any person authorised in that behalf by the Residuary Body shall be entitled on producing, if so required, evidence of his authority—
(a) at all reasonable times to inspect and make copies of any document belonging to or under the control of any authority or body whose staff, assets, rights or liabilities are affected by any provision made by or under this Act; and
(b) to require copies of any such documents to be delivered to him.
(2) In this paragraph "document" includes any record of information and, where the record is not in legible form, the rights conferred by sub-paragraph (1) include the right to require the information to be made available in legible form for inspection or copying and to require copies of it in that form to be delivered.
(3) References in this paragraph to copies of a document include references to copies of any part of it.

Giving of advice to Secretary of State

9. The Residuary Body—
(a) may from time to time give such advice to the Secretary of State with respect to the exercise by him of his powers under section 54(2)(c) as it considers appropriate; and
(b) shall give to the Secretary of State advice on such matters connected with the exercise of those powers as he may specify.

Reports and information

10.—(1) The Residuary Body shall—
(a) publish an annual report on the discharge of its functions;
(b) send a copy of every such report to the Secretary of State; and
(c) give the Secretary of State such information relating to the discharge of its functions as he may require.
(2) The Secretary of State shall lay before each House of Parliament a copy of any report sent to him under sub-paragraph (1).
(3) For the purposes of sub-paragraph (1)(c), the Residuary Body shall—
(a) permit any person authorised by the Secretary of State to inspect and make copies of—
(i) any part of the accounts of the Residuary Body; or
(ii) any document in the possession of the Residuary Body, or any part of such a document; and

(b) provide such explanation of the accounts or document as that person or the Secretary of State may require.

(4) In this paragraph "document" has the same meaning as in paragraph 8.

Acquisitions and disposals

11.—(1) On 1st April 1996 all property, rights and liabilities of the old authorities, in respect of which provision is not otherwise made by or under this Act as to vesting, shall, by virtue of this paragraph, vest in the Residuary Body.

(2) This paragraph shall not be construed—

(a) as continuing in force any contract of employment made by an old authority, or

(b) as imposing any liability on the Residuary Body in respect of the termination of any such contract by the abolition of an old authority,

but the rights and liabilities to which this paragraph applies shall include any rights and liabilities attributable to anything done or omitted under or in respect of such a contract before 1st April 1996 except any liability to make a payment which is prohibited by section 43(2).

(3) The Residuary Body may, with the consent of the Secretary of State, acquire by agreement any land or additional land required by it for carrying out its functions.

(4) The Residuary Body—

(a) may dispose of any land held by it in such manner as it considers appropriate, and

(b) shall dispose of any land which is not required by it for the carrying out of its functions,

subject to the same restrictions as those imposed by section 123(2) and (2A) of the 1972 Act (disposal of land of principal councils) in the case of disposals by a principal council under section 123(1) of that Act and any other restrictions imposed by or under this Act.

Power of Secretary of State to give directions

12.—(1) The Residuary Body shall exercise its functions subject to such directions as the Secretary of State may from time to time give to it.

(2) No transaction entered into by the Residuary Body in the exercise of its functions shall be invalid by reason only of a failure to comply with any direction given under this paragraph.

(3) The Secretary of State shall publish any directions given by him under this paragraph.

Application of receipts

13.—(1) Any sum received by the Residuary Body (together with any accrued interest) which would be treated as a capital receipt for the purposes of section 58 of the Local Government and Housing Act 1989 if received by a local authority shall be paid—

(a) to such new principal council, or

(b) to such new principal councils, in such proportions,

as the Secretary of State may direct.

(2) Any sum received by a principal council under sub-paragraph (1) shall be treated as a capital receipt for the purposes of section 58 of the Act of 1989.

(3) Any direction under this paragraph may be given so as to operate generally in relation to all cases or descriptions of case or in relation to a particular case.

Funding

14. For the purposes of section 74 of the Local Government Finance Act 1988 (power to make regulations authorising a levying body to issue a levy) the Residuary Body shall be treated as a levying body with respect to which regulations may be made under subsection (2) of that section.

Accounts

15.—(1) The Residuary Body shall—

(a) keep proper accounts;

(b) keep proper records in relation to the accounts; and

(c) prepare a statement of accounts in respect of each financial year.

(2) The statement shall comply with any directions given by the Secretary of State with the consent of the Treasury, as to—

(a) the information to be contained in the statement;

(b) the manner in which the information is to be presented;

(c) the methods and principles according to which the statement is to be prepared.

(3) Without prejudice to paragraph 12, the Secretary of State may give directions to the Residuary Body requiring it—

(a) to keep accounts in respect of such matters, and records relating to them, as may be specified in the directions, and

(b) to apply such methods and principles as may be so specified with respect to any accounts or records kept by the Residuary Body.

Audit

16.—(1) The accounts of the Residuary Body shall be included among those which are required to be audited in accordance with Part III of the Local Government Finance Act 1982 and, subject to sub-paragraph (2), that Part shall accordingly have effect in relation to the Residuary Body and its accounts.

(2) Sections 15(1)(a), 17, 19, 20, 22, 23 and 24 of that Act shall not apply in relation to the Residuary Body or its accounts.

(3) At each audit of the accounts of the Residuary Body under Part III of the Act of 1982, any local government elector for any area to which the accounts to be audited relate may inspect those accounts and all books, deeds, contracts, bills, vouchers and receipts relating to them and make copies of all or any part of the accounts and those other documents.

(4) At the request of any such local government elector, the auditor shall give the elector, or any representative of the elector, an opportunity to question him about those accounts or to draw his attention to any matter on which he could make a report under section 15(3) of the Act of 1982.

(5) As soon as the audit of the accounts of the Residuary Body has been concluded, a copy of—

(a) any statement prepared for the accounting year in question under paragraph 15(1), and

(b) any report made by the auditor on the statement or on the accounts,

shall be sent by the Residuary Body to the Secretary of State.

(6) The Secretary of State shall lay a copy of the statement and report before each House of Parliament.

(7) Any person, on applying to the Residuary Body, shall be entitled—

(a) to inspect and make copies of any statement prepared by it under paragraph 15(1) and any report made by an auditor on the statement or on its accounts; and

(b) to be supplied with copies of any such statement or report on payment of such reasonable sum as the Residuary Body may determine.

(8) Any document which a person is entitled to inspect under sub-paragraph (3) or (7) may be inspected by him at all reasonable times and without payment.

Parliamentary supervision

17. The Residuary Body shall be included among the authorities to which the Parliamentary Commissioner Act 1967 applies.

Winding up

18.—(1) Except as respects any of its functions for the discharge of which provision will be required, or is likely to be required, after the end of the transitional period, the Residuary Body shall use its best endeavours to secure that its work is completed as soon as practicable and in any event by the end of the transitional period.

(2) In this paragraph "the transitional period" means the period of five years beginning with the establishment of the Residuary Body.

(3) Subject to sub-paragraph (4), the Residuary Body shall be wound up at the end of the transitional period.

(4) The Secretary of State may by order provide for sub-paragraph (3) to have effect with the substitution for the transitional period of such longer period as may be specified in the order.

(5) The Residuary Body shall—

(a) not later than the end of the period of four years beginning with its establishment, or

(b) where it proposes to complete its work before the end of the transitional period, not later than one year before the proposed date of completion, or

(c) where under sub-paragraph (4) the transitional period is extended, not later than one year before the end of the extended period,

submit to the Secretary of State a scheme for winding it up and disposing of its remaining functions, property, rights and liabilities.

(6) The Residuary Body shall as respects—

(a) any of its functions for the discharge of which provision will be or is likely to be required after the end of the transitional period,

(b) any property held by it for the purposes of any such functions, and

(c) any of its rights or liabilities which will or are likely to subsist beyond its being wound up, make such arrangements as are practicable for their transfer to another body or bodies or submit proposals to the Secretary of State for effecting such transfers by orders made by him in that behalf.

(7) The Secretary of State may by order provide—

(a) for any such transfer or disposal as is mentioned in sub-paragraph (5) or (6), whether as proposed by the Residuary Body or as modified by the Secretary of State; and

(b) for giving effect (with or without modifications) to any scheme submitted to him under sub-paragraph (5).

(8) In making any supplemental or transitional provision in an order under sub-paragraph (7), the Secretary of State may include provision amending any enactment or any instrument made under any enactment.

Application of other enactments

19. The Residuary Body shall be treated as a local authority or (as the case may be) as a principal council for the purposes of the following provisions of the 1972 Act—

(a) section 111(1) and (3) (subsidiary powers);

(b) sections 112 to 115 and 117 to 119 (staff);

(c) section 128(2) (protection of purchasers);

(d) section 140, 140A and 140C (insurance of members etc.);

(e) section 146 (transfer of securities);

(f) section 223 (appearance in legal proceedings);

(g) sections 224, 225 and 229 to 233 (documents); and

(h) section 239, so far as it relates to opposing a local or personal Bill in Parliament but without the procedural requirements in subsection (2).

20. The Residuary Body shall be treated as a local authority for the purposes of—

(a) the Landlord and Tenant Act 1954 (c. 56);

(b) the Caravan Sites and Control of Development Act 1960 (c. 62);

(c) the Local Government (Records) Act 1962 (c. 56);

(d) section 13(7)(f) of the Employment Agencies Act 1973 (c. 35) (circumstances in which Act does not apply);

(e) section 28 of the Health and Safety at Work etc. Act 1974 (c. 37) (restrictions on disclosure of information);

(f) sections 30 (repayment of advances of remuneration), 38 (use of spare capacity) and 41 (resolutions, minutes, etc.) of the Local Government (Miscellaneous Provisions) Act 1976 (c. 57);

(g) section 71 of the Race Relations Act 1976 (c. 74) (general statutory duty of local authorities);

(h) section 64 of the Justices of the Peace Act 1979 (c. 55) (disqualification in certain cases of justices who are members of local authorities);

(i) section 41 of the Local Government (Miscellaneous Provisions) Act 1982 (c. 30) (lost property etc.);

(j) paragraph 7 of Schedule 1 to the Stock Transfer Act 1982 (c. 41) (specified securities);

(k) section 60 of the County Courts Act 1984 (c. 28) (rights of audience);

(l) sections 84(5)(b) (agreements to indemnify certain lenders) and 85(4) (meaning of "relevant advance") of the Housing Associations Act 1985 (c. 69);

(m) sections 7 (transfer of local authority mortgages) and 9 (interpretation etc.) of the Local Government Act 1986 (c. 10); and

(n) section 157 of the Local Government and Housing Act 1989 (c. 42) (periodic payment of grants).

21. The Residuary Body shall be treated as a local authority for the purposes of the following provisions of the Housing Act 1985—

(a) sections 43 and 44 (consent required for certain disposals of houses);

(b) sections 45 to 51 (restrictions on recovery of service charges after disposal of house);

(c) section 80 (secure tenancy: landlord condition);

(d) sections 442 (so far as relates to agreements within subsection (1)(b)) and 443 (local authority contributions to mortgage costs); and

(e) Part XVI (assistance for owners of defective premises disposed of by local authorities and others).

22. The Residuary Body shall be treated as a housing authority for the purposes of sections 444, 452 and 453 of the Housing Act 1985 (provision in connection with local authority mortgages).

23. The Residuary Body shall be treated as a local authority for the purposes of the following provisions of the Landlord and Tenant Act 1985—

(a) section 14(4) (exclusion of implied repairing obligation);

(b) sections 18 to 30 (service charges); and

(c) paragraph 9(1) of the Schedule (rights of tenants with respect to insurance: exceptions).

24. The Residuary Body shall be included among the authorities or bodies to which the following enactments apply—

(a) section 11 of the Trustee Investments Act 1961 (c. 62) (local authority investment schemes);

(b) section 28(5)(a) of the Leasehold Reform Act 1967 (c. 88) (retention or resumption of land required for public purposes);

(c) paragraph 2 of Schedule 4A to the Act of 1967 (exclusion of certain shared ownership leases);

(d) section 3(1) of the Employers' Liability (Compulsory Insurance) Act 1969 (c. 57) (employers exempted from insurance); and

(e) section 5(2) of the Rent (Agriculture) Act 1976 (c. 80) (statutory tenancies).

25. The Residuary Body shall be included among the bodies specified in—

(a) section 99(4) (directions to dispose of land) of and Schedule 16 (bodies to whom Part X applies) to the Local Government, Planning and Land Act 1980 (c. 65);

(b) section 58(1) of the Landlord and Tenant Act 1987 (c. 31) (exempt landlords and resident landlords);

(c) Schedule 2 to the Local Government Act 1988 (c. 9) (public authorities to which section 17 of the Act applies); and

(d) section 144(2)(a) of the Road Traffic Act 1988 (c. 52) (third party insurance or security: exceptions).

26. The Residuary Body shall be treated as a local authority for the purposes of the Local Authorities (Goods and Services) Act 1970.

27. Paragraph 64A of Schedule 2 to the Pensions (Increase) Act 1971 (official pensions) shall have effect as if the reference to a residuary body established by the Local Government Act 1985 included a reference to the Residuary Body.

28. After paragraph (h) of section 14 of the Rent Act 1977 (landlord's interest belonging to local authority etc.) insert—

"(i) The Residuary Body for Wales (Corff Gweddilliol Cymru);".

29. In section 33(9) of the Local Government (Miscellaneous Provisions) Act 1982 (enforceability of certain covenants relating to land)—

(a) in paragraph (a), after "the London Residuary Body" insert "the Residuary Body for Wales (Corff Gweddilliol Cymru)"; and

(b) in paragraph (b), after "Greater London," insert "in relation to the Residuary Body for Wales (Corff Gweddilliol Cymru) means Wales".

30. Paragraph 1 of Schedule 1 to the Access to Personal Files Act 1987 shall have effect as if the reference to a Housing Act local authority in the table included a reference to the Residuary Body.

31. In Part I of Schedule 1 to the Housing Act 1988 (tenancies which cannot be assured tenancies), after paragraph 12(1)(g) insert—

"(gg) The Residuary Body for Wales (Corff Gweddilliol Cymru);".

32. In subsection (12) of section 252 of the planning Act (procedure for the making of orders under Part X), in the definition of "local authority", after "Housing Act 1988" insert ", the Residuary Body for Wales (Corff Gweddilliol Cymru)".

33. In section 19(3) of the Local Government Finance Act 1992 (exclusion of Crown exemption in certain cases), at the end add—

"(g) The Residuary Body for Wales (Corff Gweddilliol Cymru)."

Section 40(4)   SCHEDULE 14

THE STAFF COMMISSION FOR WALES: COMISIWN STAFF CYMRU

Membership

1.—(1) The Commission shall consist of not less than 4 and not more than 7 members, at least one of whom shall be Welsh-speaking.

(2) The members shall be appointed by the Secretary of State.

(3) The Secretary of State shall appoint one of the members to be chairman.

(4) Subject to the provisions of this paragraph, each member shall hold and vacate office in accordance with the terms of his appointment.

(5) A person who ceases to be a member shall be eligible for re-appointment.

(6) A member may resign his office by notice in writing to the Secretary of State.

(7) The Secretary of State may remove a member from office if he is satisfied that the member—

(a) is unable or unfit to carry out the functions of a member; or

(b) has not complied with the terms of his appointment.

(8) A person shall cease to be chairman of the Commission—

(a) if he resigns by notice in writing to the Secretary of State; or

(b) if he ceases to be a member of the Commission.

Remuneration, pensions etc.

2.—(1) The Commission shall pay to its members such remuneration and allowances (if any) as the Secretary of State may determine.

(2) The Commission shall—

(a) pay such pensions, allowances or gratuities to or in respect of any persons who have been or are its members as the Secretary of State may determine;

(b) make such payments as the Secretary of State may determine towards provision for the payment of pensions, allowances or gratuities to or in respect of any such persons.

(3) If, when any member ceases to hold office, the Secretary of State determines that there are special circumstances which make it right that that member should receive compensation, the Commission shall pay to him by way of compensation such sum as the Secretary of State may determine.

(4) The consent of the Treasury is required for any determination of the Secretary of State under this paragraph.

Staff

3.—(1) The Commission shall appoint a person to act as its secretary and may appoint such other staff as it may determine.

(2) The consent of the Secretary of State is required for the appointment of any person as secretary to the Commission.

(3) The terms and conditions of appointment of any person under this paragraph shall be determined by the Commission with the consent of the Secretary of State.

(4) The Commission shall pay to its staff such remuneration, and such allowances, as the Secretary of State may determine.

(5) The Commission may—

(a) pay such pensions, allowances or gratuities to or in respect of any persons who have been or are members of its staff as the Secretary of State may determine;

(b) make such payments as the Secretary of State may determine towards provision for the payment of pensions, allowances or gratuities to or in respect of any such persons.

(6) Any reference in sub-paragraph (5) to pensions, allowances or gratuities to or in respect of any persons includes a reference to payments by way of compensation to or in respect of any members of the Commission's staff who suffer loss of office or employment or loss or diminution of emoluments.

(7) The consent of the Treasury is required for the giving of any consent under sub-paragraph (3) or for the making of any determination under sub-paragraph (4) or (5).

Incidental powers

4.—(1) Without prejudice to any powers exercisable apart from this paragraph, the Commission shall have power to do anything (whether or not involving the acquisition or disposal of any property or rights) which—

(a) is calculated to facilitate the carrying out of any of its functions; or

(b) is conducive or incidental to the carrying out of its functions.

(2) The Commission shall not by virtue of this paragraph have power to borrow money or to cause any local inquiry to be held.

(3) Where the Commission asks a public body to supply it with any information which it reasonably requires in connection with any of its functions, it shall be the duty of that body to supply the Commission with that information.

(4) The Secretary of State may give directions as to the exercise by the Commission of its powers under this paragraph.

Proceedings

5.—(1) Subject to the following provisions of this Schedule, the Commission may regulate its own proceedings.

(2) The validity of any proceedings of the Commission shall not be affected by a vacancy amongst its members or by a defect in the appointment of a member, or by a contravention of paragraph 7.

Delegation of powers

6. Anything authorised or required by or under this Act to be done by the Commission may be done by—
 (a) any member of the Commission, or of its staff, who has been authorised for the purpose, whether generally or specially, by the Commission; or
 (b) any committee or sub-committee of the Commission which has been so authorised.

Members' interests

7.—(1) A member who is directly or indirectly interested in any matter brought up for consideration at a meeting of the Commission shall disclose the nature of his interest to the meeting.

 (2) Where such a disclosure is made, the member shall not take part in any deliberation or decision of the Commission with respect to that matter.

Application of seal and proof of instruments

8.—(1) The application of the seal of the Commission shall be authenticated by the signature of any member of the Commission, or of its staff, who has been authorised by the Commission, whether generally or specially, for the purpose.

 (2) Any document purporting to be a document duly executed under the seal of the Commission shall be received in evidence and shall, unless the contrary is shown, be deemed to have been so executed.

Finances of the Commission

9.—(1) The Secretary of State shall, in respect of each accounting year, pay to the Commission such amount as he may, with the consent of the Treasury, determine to be the amount required by the Commission for the discharge of its functions during that year.

 (2) In this paragraph and paragraph 10 "accounting year" means the period beginning with the day on which the Commission is established and ending with the financial year current on that day, and each successive financial year.

Accounts

10.—(1) The Commission shall—
 (a) keep proper accounts and records in relation to the accounts; and
 (b) prepare in respect of each accounting year a statement of accounts in such form as the Secretary of State may, with the consent of the Treasury, direct.

 (2) The accounts shall be audited by persons appointed for the purpose for each accounting year by the Secretary of State.

 (3) A copy of any accounts audited under sub-paragraph (2) and of the report made on those accounts by the persons appointed to audit them shall be sent to the Secretary of State as soon as is reasonably practicable after the report is received by the Commission.

 (4) The Secretary of State shall lay before each House of Parliament a copy of any accounts or report sent to him under this paragraph.

The Parliamentary Commissioner

11. In the Parliamentary Commissioner Act 1967, in Schedule 2 (departments and authorities subject to investigation), insert at the appropriate place—
 "The Staff Commission for Wales (Comisiwn Staff Cymru)".

House of Commons and Northern Ireland Assembly disqualification

12. In Part II of Schedule 1 to the House of Commons Disqualification Act 1975 (bodies of which all members are disqualified for membership of the House of Commons) and in Part II of Schedule 1 to the Northern Ireland Assembly Disqualification Act 1975 (bodies of which all members are disqualified for membership of the Northern Ireland Assembly), insert at the appropriate place—
 "The Staff Commission for Wales (Comisiwn Staff Cymru)".

Winding up

13.—(1) The Commission shall use its best endeavours to secure that its work is completed as soon as practicable and in any event by the end of the transitional period.

(2) In this paragraph "the transitional period" means the period of three years beginning with the commencement of section 40.

(3) Subject to sub-paragraph (4), the Commission shall be wound up at the end of the transitional period.

(4) The Secretary of State may by order provide for sub-paragraph (3) to have effect with the substitution for the transitional period of such longer period as may be specified in the order.

Section 66(5)   SCHEDULE 15

MINOR AND CONSEQUENTIAL AMENDMENTS OF THE 1972 ACT

1. The 1972 Act is amended as follows.

2. For section 22(4) (which makes provision with respect to the chairmen of principal councils), substitute—

"(4) The chairman of a principal council shall have precedence in the area of that council, but not so as to affect Her Majesty's prerogative prejudicially."

3. After section 25, insert—

"Title of chairman or vice-chairman of county borough council
25A.—(1) The chairman of a county borough council is entitled to the style of "mayor" or "maer".

(2) The vice-chairman of a county borough council is entitled to the style of "deputy mayor" or "dirprwy faer"."

4. In section 30 (restriction on community applications during certain periods)—
(a) in subsection (1), omit paragraph (a) (including "or" at the end) and in paragraph (b), for "the county or district" substitute "any area";
(b) omit subsection (2);
(c) in subsection (3), for "district" substitute "principal";
(d) in subsection (4), for "subsections (1) and (2)" substitute "subsection (1)", for "district" substitute "area"; and
(e) in subsection (5), for "or 29" substitute ", 29 or 29A".

5. In section 31 (provisions supplementary to sections 27 to 29)—
(a) in subsection (1), for "27, 28 or 29" substitute "28, 29 or 29A"; and
(b) for "district" substitute (in both places) "principal".

6. For section 37 (establishment of new authorities in Wales), substitute—

"Establishment of principal councils in Wales
37. Schedule 5 to this Act shall have effect with respect to the establishment of principal councils in Wales and connected matters."

7.—(1) In section 54(1) (proposals for changes in local government areas in Wales), for "district" substitute "principal" and for paragraphs (b) and (c) substitute—
"(b) the constitution of a new local government area by—
(i) amalgamating two or more principal areas or two or more communities;
(ii) aggregating parts of principal areas or parts of communities; or
(iii) separating part of a principal area or part of a community;
(c) the abolition of a principal area and its distribution among other principal areas;
(cc) the abolition of a community and its distribution among other areas of the like description;".

(2) Before section 54(2) insert—
"(1B) Where the Welsh Commission make proposals for the constitution of a new principal area, those proposals shall specify whether the new area should be a county or a county borough."

8.—(1) In section 55(1) (review of local government areas in Wales), for "counties and districts" substitute "principal areas" and for "county or district" substitute "principal area".

(2) In section 55(2)—
(a) for the words from "Upon the completion" to "whole of their district" substitute "It shall be the duty of each Welsh principal council to keep the whole of their area";
(b) for "in their district" substitute "in their area"; and
(c) for "the district council" substitute (in both places) "the principal council".

(3) In section 55(3)—
(a) for "any district" substitute "any principal area";
(b) for "that district or" substitute "that principal area or";
(c) for "the district council" substitute "the principal council"; and
(d) for "that district for" substitute "that principal area for".

(4) In section 55(4)—
(a) for "one district" substitute "one principal area"; and

(b) for "districts" substitute (in both places) "principal areas".

(5) In section 55(5), for "district council" substitute "principal council", in paragraph (a) omit "(other than a community which is co-extensive with a district)" and after paragraph (e) insert—

"(f) the alteration of the boundaries of any preserved county;".

9.—(1) In section 56(2) (power of Secretary of State to direct holding of reviews)—

(a) for "the council of a district" substitute "a principal council"; and

(b) for "their district" substitute (in both places) "their area".

(2) In section 56(3)—

(a) for "any district" substitute "any principal area";

(b) for "that district" substitute (in both places) "that principal area"; and

(c) for "the district council" substitute "the principal council".

(3) In section 56(4), for "district" substitute (in both places) "principal".

(4) In section 56(5)—

(a) for "district" substitute "principal"; and

(b) for "local government areas" substitute "any areas".

10.—(1) In section 57(2) (substantive changes in electoral arrangements)—

(a) for "counties" substitute "principal areas"; and

(b) for "Schedule 10 below" substitute "section 64 of this Act (as substituted by the Local Government (Wales) Act 1994)".

(2) In section 57(4)—

(a) for "the council of each district" substitute "each principal council";

(b) for "their district" substitute "their area"; and

(c) for "district council" substitute (in both places) "principal council".

(3) In section 57(5) to (7), for "district" substitute (in each place) "principal".

11.—(1) In section 58(1) (Commission's reports and their implementation), for "district" substitute "principal".

(2) In section 58, for subsection (4) substitute—

"(4) Any statutory instrument containing an order under this section which—

(a) alters the area of a principal council,

(b) alters the area of a preserved county, or

(c) abolishes a principal area,

shall be subject to annulment in pursuance of a resolution of either House of Parliament."

12. In section 59 (directions about reviews)—

(a) in subsection (1), for "the council of a district" substitute "a principal council"; and

(b) in subsection (2), omit "all or any class of".

13.—(1) Section 60 (procedure for reviews) is amended as follows.

(2) For "district" substitute (in each place) "Welsh principal".

(3) In subsection (4)(b), for "any principal council" substitute "the principal council and of any other principal council in Wales".

(4) In subsection (5) omit "or a district council".

(5) After subsection (5) insert—

"(5A) Where a Welsh principal council make a report, proposals or recommendations under this Part of this Act they shall—

(a) make copies of the report, proposals or recommendations available for inspection at their offices for the period mentioned in subsection (5)(b) above;

(b) take the steps mentioned in subsection (5)(a); and

(c) comply with the requirements of subsection (5)(b) above in relation to any other principal council in Wales whose area may be affected by the report, proposals or recommendations."

(6) In subsection (6), for "(5)" substitute "(5A)".

14. In section 61 (local inquiries), for "district" substitute (in both places) "Welsh principal".

15. In section 67 (consequential and transitional provisions relating to Part IV), omit subsection (5)(f).

16. In section 69 (variation and revocation of orders made under Part IV)—

(a) in subsections (2) and (3) for "district" substitute "Welsh principal";

(b) in subsection (4), for first "district" substitute "Welsh principal" and omit second "district"; and

(c) in subsection (6), for "a county council" substitute "any predecessor of a Welsh principal council", for "new district" substitute "Welsh principal area" and for "the district" substitute "that area".

17.—(1) In section 71(1) (modification of seaward boundaries), for "county" substitute (in each place) "area".

(2) At the end of section 71 add—

"(6) In subsection (1) above, "area" (except in "area of the sea") means any local government area in Wales and any preserved county.

(7) No order may be made under this section extending any area into England."

18. In section 72(2) (accretions from the sea), omit "or community" (in both places) and after subsection (2) insert—

"(2A) Every accretion from the sea or part of the sea-shore which is annexed to and incorporated with a community under this section shall be annexed to and incorporated with the principal area and the preserved county in which that community is situated."

19. At the end of section 73 (alteration of local boundaries consequent on alteration of watercourse) add—

"(4) For the purposes of this section a preserved county is an area of local government."

20.—(1) In section 74 (change of name of local authority area), in subsection (1), after "county" insert (in both places) ", county borough".

(2) In section 74, after subsection (2) insert—

"(2A) Where a Welsh principal area which has, by charter or other grant or incorporation order, been granted the status of a county borough, city or royal borough subsequently changes the name of the council in pursuance of this section, the charter or other grant or incorporation order shall have effect as if the new name were substituted for the old."

(3) In section 74(3) and (4), omit "or by virtue of a resolution under section 21(5) above".

(4) In section 74(4), after "county" insert ", county borough".

(5) At the end of section 74 add—

"(6) The name of a Welsh principal area shall not be changed under this section before 1st October 1996 except with the consent of the Secretary of State.

(7) If the name of a Welsh principal area is changed under this section, and there are generally accepted alternative English and Welsh forms of that name, or alternative English and Welsh names, both forms of the new name or (as the case may be) both names shall be published."

21.—(1) In section 76 (change of name of community)—

(a) in subsection (1), for "district" substitute "principal area";

(b) in subsections (2) and (3), omit "or by virtue of a resolution under section 33(2B) above"; and

(c) in subsection (2), for "district" substitute (in both places) "principal".

(2) At the end of section 76 add—

"(4) If the name of any community is changed under this section, and there are generally alternative English and Welsh forms of that name, or alternative English and Welsh names, both forms of the new name or (as the case may be) both names shall be published."

22. In section 78(2) (electoral arrangements), after "every" insert "Welsh principal council and".

23. In section 83(1) (declaration of acceptance of office) after "county" insert ", county borough".

24. In section 91(1) (temporary appointment of members of community councils), after "district council" insert "or Welsh principal council".

25. In section 97 (removal or exclusion of disability, etc.)—

(a) in subsection (1), for first "or" substitute "council, the principal council, as respects a member of a" and omit "district" in the second and third places; and

(b) in subsections (2) and (3), omit "district".

26.—(1) Section 101 (arrangements for discharge of functions) is amended as follows.

(2) After subsection (7) insert—

"(7A) Subsection (7) above does not apply to arrangements as between principal councils in Wales."

(3) After subsection (10) insert—

"(10A) In determining what arrangements to make for the discharge of any functions, a principal council in Wales may act as if paragraph (f) were omitted from subsection (9) above."

27. In section 103 (expenses of joint committees), in paragraph (a), for "or communities or groups of parishes or communities" substitute "or groups of parishes" and after "council" insert—

"(aa) in any case in which those authorities are the councils of communities or groups of communities situated in the same principal area, by the council of that area;".

28. In section 125 (compulsory acquisition of land on behalf of community council) at the end add—

"(8) In relation to Wales—

(a) references in this section to a district council are to be read as references to a principal council; and

(b) references to a district are to be read as references to a principal area."

29. In section 134(2) (use of schoolrooms etc. in community), in paragraph (c), for "county council or district council" substitute "principal council".

30. In section 137 (power of local authorities to incur expenditure for certain purposes not otherwise authorised), after subsection (4B) insert—

"(4C) In relation to Wales, subsection (4AA) above shall have effect with the following substituted for paragraphs (a) and (b)—

"(a) the sum appropriate to a principal council is £3.80;".

31. In section 140B (insurance of voluntary assistants of probation committees), at the end add—

"(3) In relation to Wales—

(a) subsections (1) and (2)(a) above shall have effect as if they referred to a principal council; and

(b) subsection (2)(a) above shall have effect as if it referred to the area of the principal council."

32. In section 141 (research and collection of information), at the end add—

"(3) This section shall have effect in relation to Wales—

(a) as if any reference to a council were a reference to a principal council; and

(b) as if any reference to a county were a reference to a principal area."

33. In section 146 (transfer of securities on alteration of area etc.), after subsection (1) insert—

"(1A) In relation to Wales, subsection (1)(b) above shall have effect as if the reference to a county council were a reference to a principal council."

34. In section 150(3) (expenses of community meetings where there is no community council), for "district" substitute "principal area".

35. In section 180(1) (local authorities and sanitary authorities for certain enactments relating to public health), after paragraph (d) insert—

"(e) for a Welsh county or county borough, be the county council or county borough council;".

36. In section 181 (water and sewerage)—

(a) in subsection (1), add at the end "and for any principal area in Wales, be the principal council"; and

(b) in subsection (2), at the end add "except that for any area in Wales it shall be the principal council".

37. In section 187(3) (notices deterring public use of footpaths) after "district council" insert "or, where they are not the highway authority, a Welsh principal council".

38. In section 189(3) (town and village greens etc.)—

(a) in paragraph (c), after "district" insert "or Welsh principal area"; and

(b) in the words following that paragraph, after "district" insert "or (as the case may be) area".

39. In section 191 (ordnance survey)—

(a) in subsection (2), after "district council" insert "(or, in Wales, a principal council)";

(b) in subsection (4)(a), after "require" insert "(or, in Wales, the principal council)";

(c) in subsection (4)(b), after "require" insert "(or, in Wales, the principal council)"; and

(d) in subsection (5), after "any" insert "preserved county or".

40. In section 195 (social services)—

(a) in subsection (2) after first "county" insert "in England"; and

(b) in subsection (3) omit "as amended by subsection (1) above".

41.—(1) Section 204 (licensing) is amended as follows.

(2) In subsection (1)—

(a) for "districts" substitute "principal areas";

(b) for "district" substitute, in both places, "area";

(c) for "areas in which" substitute "localities in which"; and

(d) for "April 1, 1974" substitute "1st April 1996".

(3) In subsection (2), after "shall" insert "(except in relation to Wales)".

(4) In subsection (3), after "council" insert "or, in Wales, of the principal council".

42. Omit section 207 (public libraries and museums in Wales).

43. In section 213(1) (local licence duties), omit "and Wales" and at the end add "and, in Wales, be vested in the principal councils".

44. In section 214(1) (cemeteries and crematoria) after "councils of" insert "Welsh counties, county boroughs".

45.—(1) Section 215 (maintenance of closed churchyard) is amended as follows.

(2) In subsection (2)(c) for "district" substitute "county or county borough".

(3) In subsection (3)—

(a) for first "district" substitute "district, Welsh county or (as the case may be) county borough"; and

(b) for "council of the district" substitute "local authority to whom the notice is given".

46. In section 225 (deposit of documents with proper officer of authority), in subsection (2) for "district council" substitute "principal council".

47.—(1) Section 226 (custody of community documents) is amended as follows.

(2) In subsections (1) and (3)(c), for "district council" substitute "principal council".

(3) In subsection (4), after "if the area is in" insert "Wales or in".

(4) In subsection (5), omit "or community council" (in both places).

(5) At the end add—

"(6) Subsection (5) above shall also apply in relation to community councils but as if the functions conferred by it were functions of the principal council."

48. In section 227 (provision of depositories for community documents), in both subsections (1) and (2), omit third "or community" and after "is situated" insert "or the council of the principal area in which the community is situated".

49. In section 235 (power of councils to make byelaws for good rule and government and suppression of nuisances), in subsection (1) after first "district" insert "the council of a principal area in Wales" and after second "district" insert "principal area".

50. In section 236 (procedure etc. for byelaws), in subsection (9), after "district council" insert "or in Wales of a principal council" and after subsection (10) insert—

"(10A) Subsection (10) above does not apply to a principal council in Wales."

51. In section 245 (status of communities)—

(a) in subsections (6) to (9) omit "or community" (in each place);

(b) in subsection (6) omit "or a community meeting"; and

(c) in subsection (9) omit "or a community meeting in Wales".

52.—(1) Section 246 (powers, privileges and rights in relation to former cities and boroughs) is amended as follows.

(2) After subsection (2) insert—

"(2A) Any powers to appoint local officers of dignity exercisable immediately before 1st April 1996 in relation to any area by the council of a district in Wales by virtue of a charter granted under section 245 above shall, on and after that date, be exercisable in relation to that area by the council of the principal area in which, on that date, that area becomes comprised.

(2B) Where on 1st April 1996 that area becomes comprised partly in each of two or more principal areas, those powers shall be exercised on and after that date by such of the councils of those principal areas as may be agreed between them, or, in default of agreement, as the Secretary of State may designate."

(3) In subsection (6), after first "subject to" insert "subsection (2A) above,".

53. In section 247 (transfer of armorial bearings from old to new authorities), at the end add—

"(3) Subsections (1) and (2) above also apply in relation to new principal councils in Wales and authorities which ceased to exist as a result of the Local Government (Wales) Act 1994 but as if the reference to April 1, 1974 were a reference to 1st April 1996."

54. In section 248 (freemen and inhabitants of pre-1974 boroughs), at the end add—

"(6) This section shall have effect in relation to Wales as if—

(a) in subsections (2) and (3) the references to the relevant district council were references to the relevant principal council; and

(b) in subsection (2) the reference to the council of the district were a reference to the council of the principal area."

55. In section 249 (honorary aldermen and freemen), after subsection (6) insert—

"(7) A principal council in Wales may, by such a resolution as is required by subsection (5) above, admit to be honorary freemen of the county or county borough persons of distinction and persons who have, in the opinion of the council, rendered eminent services to the county or county borough.

(8) The admission of a person to be an honorary freeman under subsection (7) above shall not confer on him any such rights as are referred to in section 248(4) above.

(9) A principal council in Wales shall, in relation to any person on whom they have conferred the title of honorary alderman or whom they have admitted to be an honorary freeman, have the same powers as are conferred by subsection (6) above."

56. In section 255(1) (transfer of officers), for "27, 28 or 29" substitute "28, 29 or 29A".

57. In section 270(1) (interpretation), in the definition of "new", after "Act" add "including one established by virtue of any provision of the Local Government (Wales) Act 1994".

58. In Schedule 4 (local government areas in Wales), omit Part IV.

59. In Schedule 8 (constitution and proceedings of the Welsh Commission), in paragraph 8—

(a) at the end of paragraph (b) add ", and"; and

(b) omit paragraph (d) and the word "and" immediately before it.

60. Omit Schedule 10 (initial reviews in Wales).

61. In Schedule 11 (rules to be observed in considering electoral arrangements), in paragraph 3(2)(b) and (c), omit the words "or community" (in each place).

62. In paragraph 35(1) of Schedule 12 (minutes of proceedings of community meeting), for "district" substitute "principal area".

63. In paragraph 28 of Schedule 14 (consent of highway authority required in connection with functions relating to clocks, drinking fountains etc.) after "district council" insert "or, where they are not the highway authority, the council of a Welsh principal area".

64. In paragraph 55 of Schedule 16 (applications for certificates of appropriate alternative development)—

(a) in sub-paragraph (1), for "Elsewhere" substitute "In England, elsewhere"; and

(b) in sub-paragraph (2), after "National Park" insert "in England but".

65.—(1) Schedule 26 (cemeteries and crematoria) is amended as follows.

(2) In paragraph 4, in paragraph (a) omit "or communities" in both places, and after paragraph (a) insert—

"(aa) where those authorities are the councils of communities or groups of communities situated in the same principal area, by the council of that principal area;".

(3) In paragraph 7, after "district council" insert "or Welsh principal council" and after second "district" insert "or Welsh principal area".

(4) In paragraph 8, after "district council" insert "or Welsh principal council" and after second "district" insert "or (as the case may be) principal area".

(5) In paragraph 11, in sub-paragraph (1) omit "or community" and after that sub-paragraph insert—

"(1A) Subject to the provisions of any order made under section 214(3) above, a Welsh principal council may make byelaws with respect to the management of any cemetery provided by them and a community council may adopt for any cemetery provided by them any byelaws made under this paragraph by the principal council and duly confirmed."

66. In paragraph 20 of Schedule 29 (certificates under Schedule 3 to the Gas Act 1965), after sub-paragraph (2) insert—

"(3) Sub-paragraph (2) above does not apply in relation to Wales."

Section 66(6)   SCHEDULE 16

OTHER CONSEQUENTIAL AMENDMENTS

The Burial Act 1859 (c. 1)

1. In section 1 of the Burial Act 1859 (failure to comply with Order in Council) after "City of London" insert "or Welsh county council or county borough council".

The Game Licences Act 1860 (c. 90)

2. In section 14 of the Game Licences Act 1860 (obligations of persons licensed to deal in game) the words "from the justices of the peace" shall cease to have effect.

The Explosives Act 1875 (c. 17)

3. In subsection (3) of section 67 of the Explosives Act 1875 (definition of local authority), after "a county" insert "or county borough".

The Finance Act 1908 (c. 16)

4. In section 6 of the Finance Act 1908 (collection by local authorities of duties on game licences)—

(a) in subsection (1), omit "and Wales" and at the end add "and in Wales be vested in the councils of counties and county boroughs"; and

(b) in subsection (2), omit "district" and after "1st April 1974" add "or, in relation to Wales, to a council having power to levy those duties after 1st April 1996".

The Commons Act 1908 (c. 44)

5. In section 1 of the Commons Act 1908 (power of making regulations as to the turning out of entire animals on commons), in subsection (3), after "county" insert ", county borough".

The Welsh Church Act 1914 (c. 91)

6. In section 19 of the Welsh Church Act 1914 (application of residue of property)—
(a) in subsection (1)(a), for the words from "The property" to "council either" substitute "Property vested in a Welsh county council or county borough council by virtue of a designation made under section 50 of the Local Government (Wales) Act 1994 shall be applied, in accordance with one or more schemes made by a Welsh county council or county borough council either"; and
(b) in subsection (1)(b), after "county" insert "or county borough".

The Law of Property Act 1925 (c. 20)

7.—(1) In section 193 of the Law of Property Act 1925 (rights of the public over commons and waste lands), in subsection (1)(d)(ii), after "county" insert ", county borough".
(2) In section 194 of that Act (restrictions on inclosure of commons)—
(a) in subsection (2), after second "county" insert "or county borough"; and
(b) in subsection (3)(b), after "county" insert ", county borough".

The Education Act 1944 (c. 31)

8. In section 54 of the Education Act 1944 (power to ensure cleanliness), at the end add—
"(9) Subsection (4) above has effect in relation to Wales as if the words from "and where" to the end were omitted."

The Requisitioned Land and War Works Act 1945 (c. 43)

9. In section 59(1) of the Requisitioned Land and War Works Act 1945, in the definition of "local authority" at the end add "but in relation to Wales means a county or county borough".

The Fire Services Act 1947 (c. 41)

10.—(1) In section 8 of the Fire Services Act 1947 (constitution and powers of fire authorities constituted under combination schemes)—
(a) in subsection (3), after "counties" insert "or, in Wales, counties or county boroughs"; and
(b) in subsection (4), after "county" insert "or, in Wales, of a county or county borough".
(2) In section 9 of that Act (amendment and revocation of combination schemes)—
(a) in subsection (2)(a), after "counties" insert "or, in Wales, counties or county boroughs"; and
(b) in subsection (4), after "county" insert "or, in Wales, of any county or county borough".
(3) In section 11 of that Act (adaptation of local Acts relating to fire services), in subsection (1), after "county" insert "or, in Wales, the county or county borough".

The Shops Act 1950 (c. 28)

11. In section 73 of the Shops Act 1950 (local authorities), in subsection (1), after "the borough;" insert "as respects any county or county borough in Wales, the council of that area;".

The Registration Service Act 1953 (c. 37)

12. In section 21 of the Registration Service Act 1953 (interpretation), in subsection (2)(b), at the end add "and any reference to a non-metropolitan county includes a reference to a county borough".

The Trading Representations (Disabled Persons) Act 1958 (c. 49)

13. In section 1(5) of the Trading Representations (Disabled Persons) Act 1958 (definition of "local authority" for purposes of registration of sellers of certain goods), after "means" insert ", in relation to England," and after "City of London," insert "in relation to Wales, the council of a county or county borough,".

The Opencast Coal Act 1958 (c. 69)

14. In section 15A of the Opencast Coal Act 1958 (suspension of public rights of way), in subsection (5)(a), in sub-paragraph (i) omit "and Wales" and "or community", and after "meeting;" insert—

"(ia) in Wales, the county council or county borough council, and any community council".

The Weeds Act 1959 (c. 54)

15. In section 5 of the Weeds Act 1959 (exercise of powers by local authority), after "county" insert ", county borough" (in both places).

The Caravan Sites and Control of Development Act 1960 (c. 62)

16.—(1) In section 23 of the Caravan Sites and Control of Development Act 1960 (power to prohibit caravans on commons), at the end add—

"(9) This section and the Second Schedule to this Act shall apply in relation to land in Wales as if for every reference to a district council or to the district council (however expressed), or which falls to be construed as such a reference, there were substituted a reference to a Welsh county council or county borough council (as the case may be) the Welsh county council or county borough council."

(2) In section 24(8) of that Act (local authorities who have power to provide sites for caravans), after "county" insert "in England" and omit "constituted under section four of the Act of 1947".

(3) In section 29(1) of that Act (interpretation of Part I), in the definition of "local authority", at the end add "but, in relation to Wales, means the council of a Welsh county or county borough".

The Land Compensation Act 1961 (c. 33)

17. In section 39(1) of the Land Compensation Act 1961 (interpretation), in the definition of "authority possessing compulsory purchase powers" for "or county council" substitute ", county council or county borough council".

The Factories Act 1961 (c. 34)

18. In section 176 of the Factories Act 1961 (general interpretation), after subsection (8) insert—

"(8A) In the application of this Act in relation to Wales—
(a) any reference to a district council shall be construed as a reference to a county council or (as the case may be) county borough council; and
(b) any reference to the district of a district council shall be construed as a reference to a county or county borough."

The Trustee Investments Act 1961 (c. 62)

19.—(1) In section 11 of the Trustee Investments Act 1961 (local authority investment schemes), in subsection (4)(a), after "county," insert "a county borough,".

(2) In Part IV of Schedule 1 to that Act (manner of investment), in paragraph 4, in paragraph (a) of the definition of "local authority", after "county," insert "a county borough,".

The Local Government (Records) Act 1962 (c. 56)

20.—(1) In section 2 of the Local Government (Records) Act 1962 (acquisition and deposit of records), in subsection (6) after "county," insert "county borough,".

(2) In section 8(1) of that Act (interpretation), in the definition of "local authority", after "county," insert "county borough,".

The Pipe-lines Act 1962 (c. 58)

21. In section 35 of the Pipe-lines Act 1962 (deposit of maps of pipe-lines with local authorities), in subsection (6), omit "and Wales" and after "City of London," insert "for the purpose of the application of this section to Wales, that expression means the council of a county or county borough,".

The Licensing Act 1964 (c. 26)

22.—(1) In section 58(1)(a) of the Licensing Act 1964 (meaning of "local authority"), after "district," insert "or, in Wales, the council of the county or county borough,".

(2) In section 66 of that Act (Sunday closing in Wales)—
(a) in subsection (1), for "district" substitute "county or county borough";
(b) omit subsection (2);

(c) in subsection (3), for the first and third "district" substitute "county or county borough" (in each case), and for the second and fourth "district" substitute "county or, as the case may be, county borough" (in each case);

(d) in subsection (4)—

(i) for "district council" substitute "county council or, as the case may be, county borough council";

(ii) for "district", in every other case, substitute "county or county borough"; and

(iii) for "1975" substitute "1996";

(e) in subsection (5), for "districts" substitute "counties and county boroughs"; and

(f) in subsection (7), for "district council" substitute "county council or county borough council" and for second "district" substitute "county or county borough".

(3) In section 67 of that Act (Welsh Sunday polls)—

(a) in subsection (2)(a), for the first "district" substitute "county or county borough" and for "district councillors" substitute "councillors of the county or (as the case may be) county borough";

(b) in subsection (3), for the first "district" substitute "county or county borough", and for "district council" substitute (in both places) "county council or (as the case may be) county borough council";

(c) in subsection (4), for "district" substitute "county or county borough"; and

(d) in subsection (5), for "district councillors" substitute "councillors of the county or county borough".

(4) In section 98 of that Act (grounds for refusing applications for Part IV licences), in subsection (5)(a) after "district" insert "or, in Wales, the council of the county or county borough".

(5) In section 180 of that Act (consent to grant of occasional licence), in subsection (1)(a), for "a district or part thereof" substitute "any area".

(6) In Schedule 2 to that Act (applications for justices' licences), in paragraph 5, in paragraph (a), after "licensed are" insert "in England but" and, after paragraph (a) insert—

"(aa) if the premises to be licensed are in Wales, to the proper officer of the county council or county borough council; and".

(7) In Schedule 8 to that Act (Sunday polls in Wales), in paragraph 6—

(a) in sub-paragraph (1), omit the first "district", for the second "district" substitute "county or county borough" and for the third "district" substitute "county or (as the case may be) county borough";

(b) in sub-paragraph (2), for the first "district" substitute "county or county borough" and omit "district" in both other places;

(c) in sub-paragraph (3), omit the first "district" and for the second "district" substitute "county or county borough";

(d) in sub-paragraph (4), for the first "district" substitute "county or county borough", omit the second "district" and for "district council" substitute "county council or (as the case may be) county borough council".

(8) In paragraph 7 of Schedule 8 to that Act—

(a) in sub-paragraph (1), for the first "district" substitute "county or county borough", for the second "district" substitute "county or (as the case may be) county borough", omit the third "district" and for "councillor for the district" substitute "councillor of the county or (as the case may be) county borough"; and

(b) in sub-paragraphs (2), (3) and (4) omit "district".

(9) After paragraph 7 of Schedule 8 to that Act insert—

"(7A) In paragraphs 6 and 7 above "returning officer", in relation to a county or county borough, means the returning officer for elections of councillors of the county or county borough."

(10) In the Appendix to Schedule 8 to that Act—

(a) in form A, for "[district of]" substitute "[county/county borough of]";

(b) in form B, for "[district of]", substitute, in each place, "[county/county borough of]";

(c) in form D, for "[ward of the district of]" substitute, in each place, "[division of the county/county borough of]" and for "said district" substitute "said [county/county borough]"; and

(d) in form E, for "[district of]" substitute, in each place, "[county/county borough of]".

The Harbours Act 1964 (c. 40)

23. In Schedule 3 to the Harbours Act 1964 (procedure for making harbour orders), in paragraph 3(ba)—

(a) omit "and Wales" and "or community"; and

(b) after "parish council" insert ", in Wales, a county council, a county borough council and a community council".

The Public Libraries and Museums Act 1964 (c. 75)

24.—(1) Omit the following provisions from the Public Libraries and Museums Act 1964—
(a) in section 4 (library authorities and areas), from "—(a)" to "(b)", in subsection (2);
(b) in section 5 (joint boards), the proviso in subsection (3);
(c) section 6 (special provisions as to Welsh districts);
(d) in section 10 (default powers of Secretary of State), in subsection (2)—
    (i) paragraph (a);
    (ii) in paragraph (b), in sub-paragraph (i) the words "other than any council of a district in Wales" and sub-paragraph (ii);
(e) in section 11 (supplemental provisions as to transfers of officers, assets and liabilities), in subsection (2) the words from "or (b)" to "library authority";
(f) section 21 (expenses of county councils in Wales).
(2) In section 4 of that Act, at the end add—
    "(3) In Wales, county councils and county borough councils shall, subject to section 5 below, be library authorities for the purposes of this Act."
(3) In section 25 of that Act (interpretation), after the definition of "library officer" insert—
    " "local authority", in relation to Wales, means a county council or county borough council;".
(4) In Schedule 2 to that Act (management of funds for purchase of exhibits), in paragraphs 2 and 5 after "county fund" insert (in each place) "council fund".

The Gas Act 1965 (c. 36)

25. In section 28 of the Gas Act 1965 (interpretation of Part II), in the definition of "local authority" in subsection (1), omit "and Wales" and after "City of London," insert "in Wales, the council of a county or county borough,".

The Sea Fisheries Regulation Act 1966 (c. 38)

26.—(1) In section 1 of the Sea Fisheries Regulation Act 1966 (sea fisheries districts and local fisheries committees), in subsection (1), for "county" substitute "county, county borough" (in both places).
(2) In section 2 of that Act (constitution of local fisheries committee), in subsection (1), for "county" substitute "county, county borough" (in both places).
(3) In section 3 of that Act (application by inhabitants in case of refusal by council), for "county" substitute "county, county borough" (in both places).
(4) In section 19 of that Act (contributions to river authority's expenses), for "county" substitute "county, county borough".

The Local Government Act 1966 (c. 42)

27. In section 41(1) of the Local Government Act 1966 (interpretation), in the definition of "local authority", after "London borough" insert "or county borough".

The Plant Health Act 1967 (c. 8)

28. In section 5 of the Plant Health Act 1967 (execution of Act by local authorities), in subsection (3), at the end add "but, in relation to Wales, shall be the councils of counties and county boroughs".

The Private Places of Entertainment (Licensing) Act 1967 (c. 19)

29. In the table in Part I of the Schedule to the Private Places of Entertainment (Licensing) Act 1967 (adopting and licensing authorities) at the end add—

| "A Welsh county. | The county council. | The county council. |
| A county borough. | The county borough council. | The county borough council." |

The Agriculture Act 1967 (c. 22)

30. In section 75(2) of the Agriculture Act 1967 (interpretation), in the definition of "local authority", omit "and Wales" and, immediately before "and, in Scotland", insert "in Wales, the council of a county or county borough".

The Slaughter of Poultry Act 1967 (c. 24)

31. In section 8 of the Slaughter of Poultry Act 1967 (interpretation), in the definition of "local authority" in subsection (1), omit "and Wales" and, after "City of London" insert ", as respects Wales, the council of a county or county borough".

The Theatres Act 1968 (c. 54)

32. In section 18 of the Theatres Act 1968 (interpretation), in subsection (1), in paragraph (b) of the definition of "licensing authority" omit "and Wales" and at the end of that paragraph insert—

"(bb) as respects premises in a county or county borough in Wales, the council of that area;".

The Medicines Act 1968 (c. 67)

33. In section 108 of the Medicines Act 1968 (enforcement)—
(a) in subsection (8), after "county" insert "or county borough"; and
(b) in subsection (12)(a), after "district" insert ", county borough" (in both places).

The Mines and Quarries (Tips) Act 1969 (c. 10)

34. In section 11(3) of the Mines and Quarries (Tips) Act 1969 (local authorities having functions under Part II of that Act), in paragraph (a), omit "and Wales" and after "Isles of Scilly" insert—

(aa) in Wales, the council of a county or county borough,".

The Post Office Act 1969 (c. 48)

35. In section 86(1) of the Post Office Act 1969 (interpretation), in the definition of "local authority", in paragraph (a) omit "and Wales" and after that paragraph insert—
"(aa) in relation to Wales, means the council of a county or county borough;".

The Late Night Refreshment Houses Act 1969 (c. 53)

36. In section 2(2) of the Late Night Refreshment Houses Act 1969 (licensing authorities), after "are" insert ", Welsh county councils and county borough councils".

The Employers' Liability (Compulsory Insurance) Act 1969 (c. 57)

37. In section 3 of the Employers' Liability (Compulsory Insurance) Act 1969 (employers exempted from insurance), in subsection (2)(b), for "or Wales" substitute "the council of a county or county borough in Wales,".

The Agriculture Act 1970 (c. 40)

38.—(1) In section 38 of the Agriculture Act 1970 (smallholdings authorities), in paragraph (b) omit "and Wales" and after that paragraph insert—
"(bb) the council of every county or county borough in Wales;".
(2) In section 48 of that Act (acquisition of land for purpose of smallholdings), in subsection (1), after "county" insert "or county borough".
(3) In section 60 of that Act (cottage holdings), in subsection (1), after "county council" insert ", a county borough council".
(4) In section 62 of that Act (provisions as to Wales), in subsection (1)(a), after "county" insert "or county borough".
(5) In section 67 of that Act (enforcement authorities), in subsection (1) omit "and Wales" and after that subsection insert—
"(1A) In Wales it shall be the duty of each county council and each county borough council to enforce this Part of this Act within its area.".

The Poisons Act 1972 (c. 66)

39. In section 11 of the Poisons Act 1972 (interpretation), in subsection (2) in paragraph (a) of the definition of "local authority" omit "and Wales" and after "City of London," insert—
"(aa) in relation to Wales, the council of a county or county borough,".

The Land Compensation Act 1973 (c. 26)

40.—(1) In section 8 of the Land Compensation Act 1973 (restrictions on compensation), in subsection (4), after "London borough" insert "or Welsh county or county borough".
(2) In section 19 of that Act (interpretation of Part I), in the definition of "the appropriate highway authority" in subsection (1)—
(a) in paragraph (a), after "1985" insert "or the Local Government (Wales) Act 1994"; and
(b) in paragraph (b), after "that Act" insert "either of those Acts".

(3) In section 52 of that Act (right to advance payment of compensation), in subsection (8), after "London borough" insert "or Welsh county or county borough".

The Employment Agencies Act 1973 (c. 35)

41. In section 13 of the Employment Agencies Act 1973 (interpretation), in subsection (1), in the definition of "local authority", omit "and Wales" and after "London borough council" insert "and in relation to Wales, means a county council or a county borough council,".

The Breeding of Dogs Act 1973 (c. 60)

42. In section 5(2) of the Breeding of Dogs Act 1973 (interpretation), in the definition of "local authority", omit "and Wales", and after "City of London" insert "and in Wales the council of a county or county borough".

The Slaughterhouses Act 1974 (c. 3)

43.—(1) In section 27 of the Slaughterhouses Act 1974 (local authorities for purposes of licensing slaughterhouses), omit "and" immediately before paragraph (c) and, in that paragraph, after first "district" insert "in England" and after second "district" add—
> "and
> (d) as respects any county or county borough in Wales, the council of the county or county borough."

(2) In section 34 of that Act (interpretation of Part I), in the definition of "district", at the end add—
> "and, in relation to—
> (a) a local authority who are the council of a Welsh county or county borough, and
> (b) the officers of such an authority,
> means that county or county borough;".

(3) In section 45 of that Act (interpretation of Part II)—
(a) after the definition of "contravention" insert—
> " "district", in relation to a local authority who are the council of a Welsh county or county borough, means that county or county borough;"; and
(b) in the definition of "local authority", after first "council" insert "of a Welsh county or county borough or".

The Local Government Act 1974 (c. 7)

44. In section 34(1) of the Local Government Act 1974 (interpretation), in the definition of "local authority", after "Broads Authority" insert "a Welsh county council, a county borough council".

The Consumer Credit Act 1974 (c. 39)

45. In section 189(1) of the Consumer Credit Act 1974 (interpretation), in the definition of "local authority" omit "and Wales" and after "Scilly," insert "in relation to Wales means a county council or a county borough council,".

The Guard Dogs Act 1975 (c. 50)

46. In section 7 of the Guard Dogs Act 1975 (interpretation), in the definition of "local authority" omit "and Wales", and after "City of London," insert "in relation to Wales, a county council or county borough council,".

The Safety of Sports Grounds Act 1975 (c. 52)

47.—(1) In the following provisions of the Safety of Sports Grounds Act 1975, after "where the local authority is in" insert (in each place) "Wales,"—
(a) section 3(3) (applications for certificates);
(b) in section 4 (amendment etc. of certificates), subsections (7) and (8);
(c) section 5(5)(d) (interested parties for purposes of appeals);
(d) section 10(8)(b) (copies of prohibition notices);
(e) section 10A(7)(d) (appeals against orders relating to prohibition notices); and
(f) section 11(c) (powers of entry and inspection).
(2) In section 17(1) of that Act (interpretation)—
(a) in the definition of "building authority", in paragraph (a) omit "or in Wales,"; and

(b) in the definition of "local authority", in paragraph (c) omit "or in Wales," and, after that paragraph insert—
"(cc) in Wales, the county council or county borough council;".

The Welsh Development Agency Act 1975 (c. 70)

48. In section 16 of the Welsh Development Agency Act 1975 (derelict land), in paragraph (a) of the definition of "local authority" in subsection (9), for "district" substitute "county borough".

The Local Land Charges Act 1975 (c. 76)

49. In section 3(1) of the Local Land Charges Act 1975 (registering authorities), after paragraph (a) insert—
"(aa) a Welsh county council;
(ab) a county borough council;".

The Lotteries and Amusements Act 1976 (c. 32)

50.—(1) In section 23(1) of the Lotteries and Amusements Act 1976 (interpretation), in paragraph (b) of the definition of "local authority", for "district" substitute "county borough".
(2) In Schedule 1 to that Act (registration of societies), in paragraph 1(2)(b), for "district" substitute "county council or county borough".
(3) In paragraph 1(2) of Schedule 3 to that Act (permits for commercial provision of amusements with prizes: interpretation), in paragraph (b) of the definition of "local authority", for "district" substitute "county council or county borough".

The Dangerous Wild Animals Act 1976 (c. 38)

51. In section 7 of the Dangerous Wild Animals Act 1976 (interpretation), in subsection (4), in the definition of "local authority", omit "and Wales" and after "City of London," insert "in relation to Wales, a county council or county borough council,".

The Race Relations Act 1976 (c. 74)

52. In section 19A of the Race Relations Act 1976 (discrimination by planning authorities), in subsection (2)(a), after "county," insert "county borough,".

The Development of Rural Wales Act 1976 (c. 75)

53.—(1) In section 1 of the Development of Rural Wales Act 1976 (establishment and general function of Development Board for Rural Wales)—
(a) in subsection (2), for "the county of Powys and the districts of Ceredigion and Meirionnydd" substitute "the area for which it was so responsible immediately before 1st April 1996"; and
(b) in subsection (4), in paragraphs (a) and (b), for "and of each district" substitute "or county borough".
(2) In section 34 of that Act (interpretation), in the definition of "local authority" in subsection (1), for "of a district" substitute "or county borough".
(3) In paragraph 3(3)(a) of Schedule 1 to that Act (constitution etc. of the Development Board for Rural Wales), for "and of each district" substitute "or county borough".
(4) In Schedule 3 to that Act (the new towns code)—
(a) omit paragraph 1(6); and
(b) in paragraph 38(2)—
(i) in sub-paragraph (i), for "district planning authority in whose area the land is situated" substitute "local planning authority"; and
(ii) in sub-paragraph (ii), at the end add "if they are not the local planning authority".

The European Parliamentary Elections Act 1978 (c. 10)

54.—(1) In paragraph 4 of Schedule 1 to the European Parliamentary Elections Act 1978 (returning officers etc.), in sub-paragraph (5)(a) omit "and Wales" and at the end insert—

"(aa) in Wales, a county or county borough;".

(2) In paragraph 5A of Schedule 2 to that Act (local inquiries held by Boundary Commission), in sub-paragraph (4)(a) omit "and Wales" and after "district" insert—

"(aa) in Wales, the council of a county or county borough;".

The Inner Urban Areas Act 1978 (c. 50)

55.—(1) In section 1 of the Inner Urban Areas Act 1978 (designation of districts by Secretary of State)—

(a) in subsection (1), after "district" insert "or Welsh county or county borough"; and

(b) in subsection (2), at the end add "but, in relation to a designated district which is a Welsh county or county borough, means the council of that county or county borough".

(2) In section 2 of that Act (loans for acquisition of or works on land), in subsection (1)(a), after "within the designated district or" insert "(except where the land is in Wales)".

(3) In section 7 of that Act (power to enter into arrangements), in subsection (1), after "district" in the first and last places where it occurs insert "or Welsh county or county borough" (in each place), and, in paragraph (a), at the beginning insert "as respects any such district,", and after "both;" insert—

"(aa) as respects any such Welsh county or county borough, the council of that county or county borough;".

(4) After subsection (2) of that section, insert—

"(2A) For the purposes of subsection (2) above, references to districts include references to Welsh counties and county boroughs."

(5) In section 17 of that Act (interpretation), in the definition of "designated district" in sub-section (1), after "any district" insert "or Welsh county or county borough".

(6) In the Schedule to that Act (improvement areas), after paragraph 1(1), insert—

"(1A) In the application of sub-paragraph (1) above in relation to Wales, the words "after consulting the other designated district authority," shall not apply."

The Ancient Monuments and Archaeological Areas Act 1979 (c. 46)

56.—(1) In section 8(2A) of the Ancient Monuments and Archaeological Areas Act 1979 (recovery of compensation on subsequent grant of scheduled monument consent), in paragraph (c), for "district" substitute "county or county borough".

(2) In section 35(5) of that Act (notice required of operations in areas of archaeological importance), in paragraph (a) omit "and Wales" and after that paragraph insert—

"(aa) in the case of land in Wales, on the council of each county or county borough in which the site of the operations is wholly or partly situated;".

(3) In section 61(1) of that Act (interpretation), in the definition of "local authority", in paragraph (a) omit "and Wales" and after "City of London;" insert—

"(aa) in Wales, the council of a county or county borough;".

The Local Government, Planning and Land Act 1980 (c. 65)

57.—(1) In section 2 of the Local Government, Planning and Land Act 1980 (duty of author-ities to publish information), in subsection (1) after paragraph (a) insert—

"(aa) a county borough council;".

(2) In section 4 of that Act (bodies which may be directed to publish information)—

(a) in subsection (4)(g), after "councils" insert "or Welsh county councils or county borough councils"; and

(b) in subsection (7), omit "district".

(3) In section 20(1) of that Act (interpretation of Part III), in the definition of "local auth-ority", in paragraph (a) omit "and Wales" and after that paragraph insert—

"(aa) in relation to Wales, a county council or county borough council or a police auth-ority established under section 3 of the Police Act 1964;".

(4) In section 98 of that Act (disposal of land at direction of Secretary of State), in subsection (8A) after paragraph (a) insert—

"(aa) a county borough council;".

(5) In section 99 of that Act (provisions supplementing section 98), in subsection (4) after paragraph (a) insert—

"(aa) a county borough council;".

(6) In section 100 of that Act (interpretation of Part X), in subsection (1)(a) after "county council," insert "county borough council,".

58.—(1) Section 103 of that Act (functions of the Land Authority for Wales), is amended as follows.

(2) In subsection (2)(c), for "county and district councils in whose area the land is situated" substitute "—

(i) the council of any county or county borough in which the land, or any part of the land, is situated, and

(ii) the joint planning board (if any) for the area in which the land, or any part of the land, is situated,".

(3) For subsection (6) substitute—

"(6) The council of a county or county borough in Wales which makes an assessment of land in its area which is, in its opinion, available and suitable for development may be assisted by the Authority in making that assessment.

(6A) A joint planning board in Wales which makes an assessment of land in its district which is, in its opinion, available and suitable for development may be assisted by the Authority in making that assessment."

(4) In subsection (7), for "or (6)" substitute "(6) or (6A)".

(5) In subsection (8), for "or district council" substitute "council, county borough council or joint planning board" and after "the council" insert "or board".

59.—(1) In section 116 of that Act (assessment of development land), in subsection (4), in paragraph (a) omit "and Wales" and after that paragraph insert—

"(aa) (in the application of the section to Wales) the councils of counties and county boroughs;".

(2) In section 162 of that Act (inner urban areas)—

(a) in subsection (5)—

(i) in paragraph (a) after "district" insert "or Welsh county or county borough"; and

(ii) in paragraph (b) after "district" insert "or (as the case may be) Welsh county or county borough"; and

(b) in subsection (6)(b), after "(a)" insert "or (aa)".

(3) In section 165 of that Act (power to transfer undertaking), in subsection (9) in paragraph (a) omit "and Wales" and after that paragraph insert—

"(aa) (in the application of the sections to Wales) a county council or county borough council;".

(4) In section 185 of that Act (pleasure boat byelaws) in subsection (1) after "London" insert—

"(iv) the council of a Welsh county or county borough,".

(5) In Schedule 16 to that Act (bodies to whom Part X applies), after paragraph 1 insert—

"1A. A county borough council.".

(6) In Schedule 19 to that Act (public authorities who may seek advice from the Land Authority for Wales), in paragraph 1 after sub-paragraph (a) insert—

"(aa) a county borough council,

(ab) a joint planning board in Wales,".

(7) In Schedule 20 to that Act (Land Authority for Wales: acquisition of land), after paragraph 4 insert—

"4A. Where the compulsory purchase order was made by the Authority and the land is situated in the district of a joint planning board in Wales—

(a) a notice under section 12 shall also be served on the board,

(b) the board shall have a right to object in accordance with the notice,

(c) the references in section 13 to objections made by an owner, lessee or occupier shall also include references to an objection made by the board."

(8) In Schedule 21 to that Act (further functions of the Land Authority for Wales)—

(a) in paragraph 9(1), after "local authority" insert "and joint planning board"; and

(b) in paragraph 9(2) for "district council" substitute "local planning authority" and for "the council" substitute "the local planning authority".

(9) In Schedule 32 to that Act (enterprise zones)—

(a) in paragraph 1(1) insert, after paragraph (a)—

"(aa) the council of a Welsh county or county borough;"

(b) in sub-paragraph (3) after the first "district" insert "county, county borough"; and

(c) in paragraph 2(2)(a)(ii) omit "or Wales" and after "situated" insert—

"(iia) if the area for which the scheme is to be prepared is in Wales, adequate publicity is given to its provisions in the county or county borough in which the area is situated;".

The Disused Burial Grounds (Amendment) Act 1981 (c. 18)

60. In the Schedule to the Disused Burial Grounds (Amendment) Act 1981 (disposal of human remains and tombstones, monuments or other memorials), in paragraph 10(1)(a), after "district," insert "or Welsh county or county borough,".

The Animal Health Act 1981 (c. 22)

61. In section 50 of the Animal Health Act 1981 (local authorities), in subsection (2), after paragraph (b) insert—
"(bb) as respects a county borough, the county borough council,".

The Zoo Licensing Act 1981 (c. 37)

62.—(1) In section 1 of the Zoo Licensing Act 1981 (licensing of zoos by local authorities), in subsection (3), in paragraph (a) omit "and Wales" and after that paragraph insert—
"(aa) in Wales, the councils of counties and county boroughs;".
(2) In section 3(2) of that Act (persons whose representations are to be taken into account in consideration of applications for licences), in paragraph (e), after "the licence" insert "—(i)" and at the end of that paragraph insert—
"or
(ii) if the part is situated in Wales, the local planning authority for the area in which it is situated;".

The New Towns Act 1981 (c. 64)

63.—(1) In section 2 of the New Towns Act 1981 (reduction of designated areas), in subsection (1)(b), after "district council" insert "or, in the case of land in Wales, any county council or county borough council".
(2) In section 7 of that Act (planning control), in subsection (3), immediately before "in a metropolitan county" insert "in Wales or".
(3) In section 23 of that Act (extinguishment of public rights of way), in subsection (2)—
(a) in paragraph (i), after "authority" insert "or, in the case of land in Wales, the local planning authority"; and
(b) in paragraph (ii), at the beginning insert "if different".
(4) In section 33 of that Act (new town may be united district for Public Health Acts), for "districts" substitute "areas".
(5) In section 38 of that Act (local authorities and work for Commission), in subsection (1), after "a county" insert ", county borough".
(6) In section 39 of that Act (power of development corporation to transfer undertakings), after subsection (2) insert—
"(2A) Subsection (2) above shall have effect in relation to Wales as if for "and of every district" there were substituted "or county borough"."
(7) In section 41 of that Act (transfer of property to Commission and dissolution of corporation), after subsection (1) insert—
"(1A) Subsection (1) above shall have effect in relation to Wales as if for "and of every district" there were substituted "or county borough"."
(8) In section 77 of that Act (regulations and orders), in subsection (4)(a)(ii), after "county planning authority" insert "or, where the order is one designating an area in Wales, by the local planning authority".
(9) In Schedule 1 to that Act (procedure for designating area of new town), in paragraph 2(3), after "district" insert "or, in the case of land in Wales, every county or county borough".

The Acquisition of Land Act 1981 (c. 67)

64.—(1) In section 17 of the Acquisition of Land Act 1981 (local authorities for purposes of orders subject to special parliamentary procedure), in subsection (4), in paragraph (b) of the definition of "local authority", for "district" substitute "county borough".
(2) In paragraph 4 of Schedule 3 to that Act (acquisition of new rights over special kinds of land), in sub-paragraph (4), in paragraph (b) of the definition of "local authority", for "district" substitute "county borough".

The Wildlife and Countryside Act 1981 (c. 69)

65.—(1) In section 3 of the Wildlife and Countryside Act 1981 (areas of special protection), in subsection (4), for "district" substitute "locality".
(2) In section 27(1) of that Act (interpretation of Part I), in paragraph (a) of the definition of "local authority", omit "and Wales" and after that paragraph insert—

"(aa) in relation to Wales, a county council or county borough council;".

(3) In section 34 of that Act (limestone pavement orders), in paragraph (a) of the definition of "the relevant authority" in subsection (6), after "non-metropolitan county" insert "in England", and after that paragraph insert—

"(aa) in relation to any area in Wales, the local planning authority;".

(4) In section 36 of that Act (marine nature reserves), in paragraph (a) of the definition of "local authority" in subsection (7), after "county council," insert "a county borough council,".

(5) In section 39(5) of that Act (relevant authorities for purposes of management agreements with owners and occupiers of land), after "land" in paragraph (a), insert "in England".

(6) In section 52 of that Act (interpretation of Part II), in subsection (2) omit "and to Wales".

(7) In section 57 of that Act (supplementary provisions as to definitive maps and statements), after subsection (5) insert—

"(5A) Subsection (5) shall apply in relation to land in Wales as if "in each district comprised" were omitted."

(8) In section 66(1) of that Act (interpretation of Part III), in the definition of "surveying authority", after "county council," insert "county borough council,".

(9) In section 72(10) of that Act (functions to which Part I of Schedule 17 to the 1972 Act applies), after "county council" insert ", county borough council".

(10) In Schedule 12 to that Act (procedure in connection with marine nature reserve orders), in paragraph 9(1), in the definition of "area", at the end add "or Welsh county or county borough".

(11) In Schedule 14 to that Act (applications for certain orders under Part III), in paragraph 5(1), in the definition of "local authority", omit "or community" and at the end of that definition add "but, in relation to Wales, means a community council".

(12) In Schedule 15 to that Act (procedure in connection with certain orders under Part III), in paragraph 13(2), in the definition of "local authority" omit "or community" and at the end of that definition add "but, in relation to Wales, means a community council".

The Civil Aviation Act 1982 (c. 16)

66.—(1) In section 79 of the Civil Aviation Act 1982 (grants towards cost of sound-proofing buildings), in subsection (7), omit "and Wales".

(2) In section 105(1) of that Act (interpretation), in paragraph (a) of the definition of "local authority" omit "and Wales" and, after that paragraph, insert—

"(aa) in relation to Wales, means a county council or a county borough council;".

The Aviation Security Act 1982 (c. 36)

67. In section 30 of the Aviation Security Act 1982 (supplementary orders), in subsection (3)(c), after "a county" insert "in England".

The Representation of the People Act 1983 (c. 2)

68.—(1) In section 8 of the Representation of the People Act 1983 (registration officers), in subsection (2) omit "and Wales" and after subsection (2) insert—

"(2A) In Wales, the council of every county or county borough shall appoint an officer of the council to be registration officer for any constituency or part of a constituency coterminous with or situated in the area of the council."

(2) In section 18(2) of that Act (polling districts), omit "and Wales" and after "borough" insert ", and in Wales it is the duty of the council of each county or county borough,".

(3) In section 24(1) of that Act (returning officers), in paragraphs (a), (b) and (c) after "constituency" insert, in each case, "in England" and insert the following paragraphs in the appropriate places—

"(aa) in the case of a county constituency in Wales which is coterminous with or wholly contained in a preserved county as defined by section 64 of the Local Government (Wales) Act 1994, the sheriff of the county;";

"(bb) in the case of a borough constituency in Wales which is coterminous with or wholly contained in a county or county borough, the chairman of the county or county borough council;";

"(cc) in the case of any other constituency in Wales, such sheriff or chairman of a county or county borough council as may be designated in an order by the Secretary of State so made;".

(4) In section 28(1) of that Act (discharge of returning officer's functions), in paragraph (a) after "constituency" insert "in England" and after that paragraph insert—

"(aa) in the case of a constituency in Wales for which the chairman of a county or county borough council is returning officer by virtue of that section, by the registration officer appointed by that council;".

(5) In section 28(5) of that Act (power of acting returning officer to appoint deputies), after "and a" insert "Welsh county council or county borough council or a".

(6) In section 31 of that Act (polling districts and stations at local government elections), in subsection (1) after "county councillors" insert "in England" and after that subsection insert—

"(1A) For elections of county or county borough councillors in Wales, the county or county borough council may divide an electoral division into polling districts and may alter any polling district."

(7) In section 35 of that Act (returning officers for local elections), in subsection (1) omit "and Wales" and "or communities" and after that subsection insert—

"(1A) In Wales the council of every county or county borough shall appoint—

(a) an officer of the council to be the returning officer for elections of councillors of the county or county borough; and

(b) an officer of the council to be the returning officer for elections of councillors of communities within the county or county borough."

(8) In section 36 of that Act (local elections), in subsection (3) omit "or community" in both places in paragraph (b) and after that subsection insert—

"(3AB) Where the polls at—

(a) the ordinary election of councillors for any electoral division of a Welsh county or county borough or an election to fill a casual vacancy occurring in the office of such a councillor, and

(b) the ordinary election of community councillors for any community or an election to fill a casual vacancy occurring in the office of such a councillor,

are to be taken on the same day and the elections are for related electoral areas, the polls at those elections shall be taken together."

(9) In section 36(4) of that Act (payment of expenses), after "county" insert "a county borough".

(10) In section 36 of that Act, in subsection (5) omit "or community", in both places, and "or the community" and after that subsection insert—

"(5A) All the expenditure properly incurred by a returning officer in relation to the holding of an election of a community councillor shall, in so far as it does not, in cases where there is a scale fixed for the purposes of this section by the council of the county or county borough in which the community is situated ("the principal council"), exceed that scale, be paid by the principal council; and if the principal council so require, any expenditure so incurred shall be repaid to them by the community council."

(11) In section 39 of that Act (void local elections)—

(a) in subsections (4) and (6)(a), after "district council" insert, in each case, "or Welsh county or county borough council"; and

(b) in subsection (6)(b), omit "district".

(12) In section 52(4) of that Act (discharge of registration duties), in paragraph (a) omit "and Wales" and for second "and" substitute—

"(aa) in Wales, of a county or county borough council, and".

(13) In section 69(2) of that Act (location of offices of election agents and sub-agents), in paragraphs (a) and (b), in each case for "or in a London borough or district" substitute "or in a Welsh county or county borough, or London borough or district,".

(14) In section 82(4) of that Act (persons before whom declaration as to expenses may be made), in paragraph (a), after "county council" insert ", a county borough council".

(15) In section 159 of that Act (candidate reported guilty of corrupt or illegal practice), in the definition of "corporate office" in subsection (3) after "county" insert ", county borough".

(16) In section 203(1) of that Act (interpretation)—

(a) in the definition of "local authority", after "county council," insert "a county borough council,"; and

(b) in the definition of "local government area", after "county," insert "county borough,".

(17) In Schedule 1 to that Act (parliamentary election rules), in paragraph 10(2)(c) after "district" insert "or Welsh county or county borough".

(18) In Schedule 2 to that Act (provisions which may be contained in regulations as to registration etc.), in paragraph 1(1) after "district" insert ", Welsh county or county borough".

(19) In Schedule 3 to that Act (form of return and declaration), in the first passage in brackets in each form (which provides for an alternative in relation to a local government election), after "county of" insert "county borough of".

(20) In Schedule 5 to that Act (use of certain rooms for parliamentary election meetings), in paragraph 3(1) after "council" insert "and every Welsh county and county borough council".

The Licensing (Occasional Permissions) Act 1983 (c. 24)

69. In section 1(5) of the Licensing (Occasional Permissions) Act 1983 (restriction on occasional permissions), for "district in Wales or Monmouthshire" substitute "locality".

The Value Added Tax Act 1983 (c. 55)

70. In section 20 of the Value Added Tax Act 1983 (refunds of tax to local authorities and other bodies), in subsection (6) after "county," insert "county borough,".

The Pastoral Measure 1983 (No. 1)

71. In section 87 of the Pastoral Measure 1983 (general interpretation), in the definition of "local planning authority" in subsection (1), after "(a)" insert "in England".

The Telecommunications Act 1984 (c. 12)

72. In section 97 of the Telecommunications Act 1984 (contributions by local authorities towards provision of facilities), in subsection (3)—
(a) in paragraph (a) omit "and Wales", after "City of London" insert "or" and omit "or a community council"; and
(b) after that paragraph insert—
    "(aa) in relation to Wales, means a county council, a county borough council or a community council;".

The Cinemas Act 1985 (c. 13)

73. In section 21 of the Cinemas Act 1985 (interpretation), in subsection (1), in the definition of "local authority", in paragraph (a) omit "and Wales" and after that paragraph insert—
    "(aa) in Wales, a county council or a county borough council;".

The Representation of the People Act 1985 (c. 50)

74.—(1) In the Representation of the People Act 1985, in sections 6(2A)(c) (absent vote at elections for an indefinite period) and 9(5)(c) (voting as proxy) after "county" insert, in each case, "or county borough".
(2) In section 21 of that Act (insufficient nominations at ordinary elections of community councils), in subsection (2)(b)—
(a) after "district council" insert "or, in the case of a community council, the county council or county borough council"; and
(b) omit "of district council".

The Weights and Measures Act 1985 (c. 72)

75. In section 69 of the Weights and Measures Act 1985 (local weights and measures authorities), in subsection (2), at the end add "and for each county borough shall be the county borough council".

The Health Service Joint Consultative Committees (Access to Information) Act 1986 (c. 24)

76. In section 1 of the Health Service Joint Consultative Committees (Access to Information) Act 1986 (interpretation), in subsection (1), in the definition of "local authority", after "county council," insert "a county borough council,".

The Airports Act 1986 (c. 31)

77. In section 12 of the Airports Act 1986 (interpretation of Part II), in the definition of "principal council" in subsection (1), in paragraph (a) omit "and Wales", and after that paragraph insert—
    "(aa) in relation to Wales, means the council of a county or of a county borough;".

The Gas Act 1986 (c. 44)

78. In paragraph 5 of Schedule 7 to the Gas Act 1986 (modifications of the Pipe-lines Act 1962), in sub-paragraph (5), in the definition of "local authority", in paragraph (a) omit "and Wales" and after "City of London;" insert—
    "(aa) in Wales, the council of a county or county borough;".

The Building Societies Act 1986 (c. 53)

79. In Schedule 8 to the Building Societies Act 1986 (powers to provide services) in paragraph 8 of Part IV, in the definition of "local authority in Great Britain", in paragraph (a) omit "and Wales" and "or community" and after that paragraph insert—

"(aa) in Wales, a county council, a county borough council and a community council;".

The Parliamentary Constituencies Act 1986 (c. 56)

80. In section 6(4)(a) of the Parliamentary Constituencies Act 1986 (local inquiries), after "county" insert "county borough".

The Fire Safety and Safety of Places of Sport Act 1987 (c. 27)

81.—(1) In the following provisions of the Fire Safety and Safety of Places of Sport Act 1987, after "where the local authority is in" insert (in each place) "Wales,"—
   (a) section 28(10) (copies of applications for safety certificates);
   (b) in section 29 (amendment, cancellation etc. of certificates), subsections (7) and (8);
   (c) section 30(8)(d) (interested parties for purposes of appeals); and
   (d) section 35(c) (powers of entry and inspection).

(2) In section 41 of that Act (interpretation), in paragraph (a) of the definition of "building authority" and paragraph (c) of the definition of "local authority" omit "or in Wales," and after paragraph (c) of the definition of "local authority" insert—

"(cc) in Wales, the county council or county borough council;".

The Coroners Act 1988 (c. 13)

82.—(1) In section 1 of the Coroners Act 1988 (appointment of coroners)—
   (a) in subsection (1)—
      (i) for "county or Greater London" substitute "county, Greater London or Wales";
      (ii) after first "non-metropolitan county" insert "in England"; and
      (iii) in paragraph (c), after first "county" insert "in England"; and
   (b) in subsection (2), after second "(b)" insert "or (bb)".

(2) In section 1 of that Act, after subsection (1)(b) insert—

"(ba) in the case of a coroner's district consisting of or included in a Welsh principal area, the council of that area;

(bb) in the case of a coroner's district lying partly in each of two or more Welsh principal areas, such one of the councils of those areas as may be designated by an order made by the Secretary of State by statutory instrument;".

(3) In section 2 of that Act (qualifications for appointment as coroner), in subsection (3), after first "county" insert "in England", and after subsection (2) insert—

"(2A) A person shall, so long as he is a councillor of a Welsh principal area, and for six months after he ceases to be one, be disqualified for being a coroner for a coroner's district which, or any part of which, falls within that area."

(4) In section 4 of that Act (coroners' districts), in subsections (2) and (4), after first "county" in each case insert "in England", and in subsection (5)(a), after "administrative area" insert "in England".

(5) After section 4 of that Act insert—

"Coroners' districts: Wales

4A.—(1) The Secretary of State may by order divide, amalgamate or otherwise alter—
   (a) any coroner's district for the time being existing in Wales; or
   (b) any such coroners' districts.

(2) Before making any order under subsection (1) above, the Secretary of State shall consult the councils and coroners appearing to him to be affected by the order and such other persons as he thinks appropriate.

(3) The Secretary of State may, in relation to any area in Wales (the "review area"), direct the council or councils for each Welsh principal area which, or any part of which, falls within the review area to consider any of the following questions—
   (a) whether any alteration should be made in a boundary between coroners' districts which falls within the review area;
   (b) whether a new coroner's district should be created for the whole or any part of the review area;
   (c) whether a coroner's district which falls wholly within the review area should be abolished.

(4) The council or councils to whom such a direction is given shall submit their conclusions to the Secretary of State, together with a statement of their reasons for reaching those conclusions.

(5) In making an order under subsection (1) above in a case where he has given a direction under subsection (3) above, the Secretary of State shall have regard to any proposals made to him under subsection (4) above.

(6) Where the Secretary of State intends to give effect to any such proposals without modification, subsection (2) above shall not require him to consult the council or councils who made those proposals.

(7) An order made under subsection (1) above may make such incidental, consequential, transitional or supplemental provision as appears to the Secretary of State to be appropriate.

(8) Except as provided by this Act, a coroner appointed for any coroner's district in Wales—

   (a) shall for all purposes be regarded as a coroner for the whole of Wales; and
   (b) shall have the same jurisdiction, rights, powers and authorities throughout Wales as if he had been appointed as coroner for the whole of Wales.

(9) The power to make orders under this section shall be exercisable by statutory instrument.

(10) Any such statutory instrument shall be laid before each House of Parliament after being made."

(6) In section 22 of that Act (removal of body for post mortem examination), in the definition of "local authority" in subsection (6), for "district or London borough" substitute "district, London borough or Welsh principal area".

(7) In section 27 of that Act (coroner's accounts), in subsection (3)(b), after "county council" insert "in England" and after "fund;" insert—

   "(bb) in the case of the council of a Welsh principal area, out of the council fund;".

(8) In section 27(4) of that Act, for the words from "district consisting of" to "districts or boroughs" substitute—

   "district—

   (a) consisting of two or more metropolitan districts or London boroughs, or
   (b) which lies partly in each of two or more Welsh principal areas,

the expenses of the councils of those districts, boroughs or areas".

(9) In section 31 of that Act (provision of accommodation), for "district or London borough" substitute "district, London borough or Welsh principal area".

(10) In section 35(1) of that Act (interpretation), in the definition of "administrative area", after "means" insert "Wales," and after "county" insert "in England", and after the definition of "relevant council" insert—

   " "Welsh principal area" means Welsh county or county borough".

The Education Reform Act 1988 (c. 40)

83. In section 235 of the Education Reform Act 1988 (interpretation), in subsection (1), in the definition of "local authority", after "county council," insert "a county borough council,".

The Local Government Finance Act 1988 (c. 41)

84. In section 55 of the Local Government Finance Act 1988 (alteration of lists), in subsection (7A)(a) after "41(6B)" insert "or 41A(10)".

85. In section 88(2) of that Act (councils to whom transport grants may be paid), after paragraph (a) insert—

   "(aa) a county borough council,".

86. In Schedule 9 to that Act (non-domestic rating: administration), in paragraph 8(2)(a) after "41(6B)" insert "or 41A(10)".

The Football Spectators Act 1989 (c. 37)

87. In section 13 of the Football Spectators Act 1989 (licensing authority's powers in relation to safety at football grounds), in subsection (3) after "is in" insert "Wales,".

The Local Government and Housing Act 1989 (c. 42)

88. In section 39 of the Local Government and Housing Act 1989 (revenue accounts and capital finance of local authorities), in subsection (1), after paragraph (a) insert—

   "(bb) a county borough council;".

The Broadcasting Act 1990 (c. 42)

89. In Part I of Schedule 2 to the Broadcasting Act 1990 (restrictions on the holding of licences), in paragraph 1(1), in the definition of "local authority", in paragraph (a) omit "and Wales" and after "Scilly;" insert—

"(aa) in relation to Wales, means a county council or county borough council;".

The Caldey Island Act 1990 (c. 44)

90.—(1) In section 1(1) of the Caldey Island Act 1990—
(a) for "(in" substitute "are in"; and
(b) omit the closing bracket after " "Caldey" " and the rest of the subsection.
(2) The following provisions shall be omitted from that Act—
(a) section 1(2)(a);
(b) in section 1(3), the words "and district";
(c) section 1(4);
(d) section 2;
(e) section 4(1)(a); and
(f) section 4(2).

The Coal Mining Subsidence Act 1991 (c. 45)

91. In section 47 of the Coal Mining Subsidence Act 1991 (notices to local authorities), in subsection (6), in paragraph (a) omit "and Wales" and after "county;" insert—

"(aa) in relation to Wales, the council of a county or county borough;".

The Deer Act 1991 (c. 54)

92. In section 11 of the Deer Act 1991 (licensed game dealers to keep records), in the definition of "authorised officer" in subsection (9), after "council of a" insert "Welsh county or county borough,".

The Social Security Contributions and Benefits Act 1992 (c. 4)

93. In section 58 of the Social Security Contributions and Benefits Act 1992 (incapacity for work: work as councillor to be disregarded), in subsection (4)(a), after "county" insert "or county borough".

The Social Security Administration Act 1992 (c. 5)

94. In section 191 of the Social Security Administration Act 1992 (interpretation), in the definition of "local authority", in paragraph (a), omit "and Wales" and after "Scilly;" insert—

"(aa) in relation to Wales, the council of a county or county borough;".

The Further and Higher Education Act 1992 (c. 13)

95. In section 90 of the Further and Higher Education Act 1992 (interpretation), in subsection (1), in the definition of "local authority", after "county council," insert "a county borough council,".

The Local Government Finance Act 1992 (c. 14)

96. In section 24 of the Local Government Finance Act 1992 (alteration of lists), in subsection (9)(b) after "22(8)" insert "or 22A(10)".

97. In section 28 of that Act (information about lists), in subsection (2)(a) after "22(8)" insert "or 22A(10)".

98. In section 54 of that Act (power to designate authorities for purposes of limiting council tax and precepts), in subsection (2), after "subsection (3)" insert "or (3A)", in subsection (3), after "classes" insert ", in relation to England," and after subsection (3) insert—

"(3A) The classes, in relation to Wales, are—
(a) county councils and county borough councils; and
(b) police authorities established under section 3 of the Police Act 1964.".

The Charities Act 1992 (c. 41)

99. In section 65 of the Charities Act 1992 (interpretation of Part III), in the definition of "local authority" in subsection (4), after "council of a" insert "Welsh county or county borough, of a".

The Judicial Pensions and Retirement Act 1993 (c. 8)

100. In section 21 of the Judicial Pensions and Retirement Act 1993 (pensions payable to judicial officers etc. by local authorities), in subsection (4), in the definition of "local authority", after "county council," insert "county borough council,".

The Charities Act 1993 (c. 10)

101.—(1) In section 76 of the Charities Act 1993 (local authority's index of local charities), in subsection (1), after "county" insert "or county borough".

(2) In section 77 of that Act (reviews of local charities by local authority), in subsection (1), after "county" insert "or county borough", and after subsection (4) insert—

"(4A) Subsection (4) above does not apply in relation to Wales."

(3) In section 78(1) of that Act (co-operation between charities and local authorities), in the definition of "local council"—

(a) after "means" insert ", in relation to England,";

(b) for "parish or (in Wales) community" substitute "or parish"; and

(c) at the end add "and, in relation to Wales, the council of a county, county borough or community".

(4) In section 79 of that Act (parochial charities), in subsection (7), in paragraphs (b) and (c), for "district council" substitute "council of the county or (as the case may be) county borough" (in each place).

(5) In Schedule 3 to that Act (enlargement of areas of local charities), after paragraph 3, insert—

"3A. A Welsh county or county borough	Any area comprising that county or county borough."

(6) In paragraph 4 of Schedule 3 to that Act, in paragraph (iv) in column 2, at the end add "or in any adjacent Welsh county or county borough" and after that paragraph insert—

"4A. Any area in a Welsh county or county borough	(i) Any area in the county or county borough; (ii) the county or county borough; (iii) any area comprising the county or county borough; (iv) any area partly in the county or county borough and partly in any adjacent Welsh county or county borough or in any adjacent district."

The Radioactive Substances Act 1993 (c. 12)

102. In section 47(1) of the Radioactive Substances Act 1993 (general interpretation provisions), in the definition of "local authority"—

(a) in paragraph (a) omit "and Wales"; and

(b) after paragraph (a) insert—

"(aa) in Wales, the council of a county or county borough;".

The Local Government (Overseas Assistance) Act 1993 (c. 25)

103. In section 1(9) of the Local Government (Overseas Assistance) Act 1993 (definition of "local authority"), in paragraph (a), for "and" substitute ", the council of a county or county borough in".

The Leasehold Reform, Housing and Urban Development Act 1993 (c. 28)

104. In section 161 of the Leasehold Reform, Housing and Urban Development Act 1993 (vesting of land by order in Urban Regeneration Agency), in subsection (7), in the definition of "local authority", after "county council," insert "a county borough council,".

The Education Act 1993 (c. 35)

105.—(1) In section 166 of the Education Act 1993 (duty of District Health Authority or local authority to help local education authority), in subsection (5), after "county council," insert "a county borough council,".

(2) In section 305 of that Act (interpretation), in subsection (1), in the definition of "local authority", after "county council," insert "a county borough council,".

The Welsh Language Act 1993 (c. 38)

106.—(1) In section 6 of the Welsh Language Act 1993 (meaning of "public body"), in subsection (1)(a), after first "council" insert "county borough council,".

(2) In section 25 of that Act (powers to give Welsh names to statutory bodies), for subsection (3) substitute—

"(3) Subsection (1) above does not apply in relation to a name conferred on any area or local authority by the Local Government Act 1972."

The Railways Act 1993 (c. 43)

107. In section 151 of the Railways Act 1993 (general interpretation), in subsection (1), in the definition of "local authority", after "county council," insert "county borough council,".

The Health Service Commissioners Act 1993 (c. 46)

108. In section 19 of the Health Service Commissioners Act 1993 (interpretation), in paragraph (a) of the definition of "local authority" omit "and Wales" and after that paragraph insert—

"(aa) in relation to Wales, a county council or county borough council,".

The Probation Service Act 1993 (c. 47)

109.—(1) Section 29 of the Probation Service Act 1993 (responsible authorities) is amended as follows.

(2) In subsection (1)(a), after second "probation area" insert—

"(aa) for any probation area in Wales, any county or county borough in whose area is situated the whole, or any part of, the probation area;".

(3) In subsection (2) after "county" insert "the council of a county borough".

Section 66(7)   SCHEDULE 17

SAVINGS AND TRANSITIONAL PROVISIONS

PART I

SAVINGS

Administration of local government before 1st April 1996

1. The provisions of section 20 of the 1972 Act in force immediately before the passing of this Act shall continue to have effect in relation to the administration of local government in Wales before 1st April 1996.

Former cities and boroughs—privileges and rights of inhabitants

2. Any privileges or rights belonging immediately before 1st April 1996 to the inhabitants of any area in Wales by virtue of—
   (a) section 246(1) of the 1972 Act (saving for privileges and rights of citizens and burgesses); or
   (b) any provision made under subsection (2)(b) of that section by a charter granted under section 245 of the 1972 Act (grant of borough status);
shall belong on and after that date to the inhabitants of that area.

Honorary aldermen

3. Any person who, immediately before 1st April 1996, is an honorary alderman by reference to his past membership of an old authority—

(a) shall continue to have that status even though the old authority has ceased to exist as a result of this Act; but

(b) shall not, while serving as a councillor of any new principal council in Wales, be entitled to be addressed as alderman or to attend or take part in any civic ceremonies of that council as an alderman.

Agricultural wages committees

4. Subject to any provision made under section 54 which amends or modifies the Agricultural Wages Act 1948, "county" shall, in relation to Wales, have the same meaning for the purposes of that Act as it had for those purposes immediately before the passing of this Act.

Inner urban areas

5.—(1) The area of any district in Wales which, immediately before 1st April 1996, was a designated district for the purposes of the Inner Urban Areas Act 1978 by virtue of an order under section 1(1) of that Act shall, subject to any further provision made by or under that Act, continue to be a designated district for those purposes.

(2) The designated district authority in relation to any such designated district which comprises or falls wholly within a new principal area shall be the council of that area.

(3) Where any such designated district falls partly within the areas of two or more new principal councils, each of those councils shall be the designated district authority in relation to the part of the designated district that falls within their area.

Effect of amendments

6. Where this Act, or any provision made under this Act, amends (whether by substituting a new definition for an existing definition or otherwise) any reference to any kind of local government area or any kind of local authority (in an enactment which has effect in England), the amendment shall not be taken to affect the operation of any provision of, or made under, the Local Government Act 1992 in relation to the enactment so amended.

Part II

Transitional Provisions

Election of principal councillors in 1995

7.—(1) Section 26(3) of the 1972 Act (as substituted by section 4 of this Act) shall not apply in relation to the ordinary election of councillors of the new principal councils which takes place in 1995.

(2) The councillors elected at that election shall assume office immediately.

(3) The term of office of every such councillor shall extend until he retires in accordance with section 26(3)(a) of the 1972 Act.

Election of community councillors in 1995

8.—(1) Any ordinary election of community councillors otherwise due to take place in May 1995 shall take place on the same day as the ordinary election in that year of councillors for the new principal area in which the community is situated.

(2) Any such councillor who otherwise would ordinarily have retired on 8th May 1995 shall (unless he resigns his office or it otherwise becomes vacant) hold office until the fourth day after the day on which the election of community councillors in 1995 takes place.

(3) The term of office of every councillor elected at that election shall extend until he retires in accordance with section 35(2B)(a) of the 1972 Act.

Grouping of communities

9. During the period beginning with the passing of this Act and ending with 1st April 1996, an order under section 29(1) of the 1972 Act (before the commencement of section 10) may be made only if all the communities concerned—

(a) were, immediately before the passing of this Act, situated within the same district; and

(b) will, after that date, be situated within the area of a single principal council.

Disclosure of officers' interests

10. For the purposes of section 117 of the 1972 Act (disclosure by officers of interests in contracts), any contract which—

(a) was entered into by an old authority, and

(b) to which any of the new principal councils becomes a party by virtue of this Act, shall be treated as a contract entered into by the new principal council.

Local land charges registers

11.—(1) The obligation imposed on local authorities to keep local land charges registers by section 3 of the Local Land Charges Act 1975 shall apply in relation to the new principal councils as if it required them to keep such registers from 1st April 1996.

(2) The local land charges registers kept by the old authorities shall be reconstituted as registers kept by the new principal councils in accordance with such directions as the Secretary of State considers appropriate to give to any of the old authorities or new principal councils.

Closure of old authorities' accounts

12.—(1) For the purposes of this paragraph, the Secretary of State shall by order designate such of the new principal councils as he considers appropriate.

(2) Each designated council shall be designated with respect to one or more old authorities.

(3) Each designated council shall, in relation to the accounts for any period ending before 1st April 1996 of each old authority with respect to which they are designated, discharge—

(a) any functions under regulations in force under Part III of the Local Government Finance Act 1982 (accounts and audit) which would have fallen to be discharged on or after that date by that old authority or any of its officers; and

(b) any functions under those regulations which fell to be so discharged before that date but which have not been discharged.

(4) As respects anything falling to be done on or after 1st April 1996 in relation to those accounts, the provisions of Part III of the Act of 1982 shall have effect as if they were accounts of the designated council but—

(a) the documents to which an auditor has the right of access under section 16(1) of that Act shall include any documents relating to the old authority concerned which are in the possession of any of the new principal councils or of the Residuary Body; and

(b) the persons who may be required to give information or an explanation under section 16(2) or 28(1) of that Act shall include any person who was an officer or member of the authority concerned at any time during the period to which the accounts relate.

(5) Any requirement under section 29(1) of the Act of 1982 in respect of a claim, return or account of an old authority, and any consent under section 30(1)(a) of that Act in respect of information relating to such an authority, may, on or after 1st April 1996, be made or given by the appropriate designated council.

(6) Any designated council—

(a) shall have a right of access at all reasonable times to all such documents—

(i) as are in the possession, or under the control, of an old authority, or

(ii) as are mentioned in sub-paragraph (4)(a),

which appear to the council to be needed for the purpose of discharging functions under this paragraph; and

(b) may require—

(i) any such person as is mentioned in sub-paragraph (4)(b), or

(ii) any person who is or has been an officer or member of that or any other new principal council,

to give to the council any such information or explanation as they think necessary for that purpose.

(7) It shall be the duty of every new principal council to take such steps, after 1st April 1996, as may reasonably be required of them by a designated council to enable the accounts of an old authority to be closed.

(8) Any person who without reasonable excuse fails to comply with any requirement under sub-paragraph (6) shall be liable on summary conviction to a fine not exceeding level 3 on the standard scale.

(9) In sub-paragraph (4) "document" includes any record of information and, where the record is not in legible form, the rights conferred by that sub-paragraph and sub-paragraph (6) include the right to require the information to be made available in legible form for inspection or copying and to require copies of it in that form to be delivered.

(10) In this paragraph "designated council" means a council designated under sub-paragraph (1).

Planning

13.—(1) If section 19 is brought into force before 1st April 1996, it shall have effect before that date only so far as is necessary to enable the establishment of any joint planning board or special planning board in Wales.

(2) Where any such board is established before 1st April 1996, it may before that date exercise such of its functions as it considers necessary to enable it to be fully operational on and after that date.

14.—(1) This paragraph applies where an old authority have, by virtue of paragraph 5 of Schedule 17 to the 1972 Act, made arrangements which, immediately before 1st April 1996, are in force for the discharge of any of the functions through a National Park Committee.

(2) The abolition of the old authority shall not affect the validity of anything done by the National Park Committee before the abolition of the authority.

(3) Anything which, on 1st April 1996, is in the process of being done by or in relation to an old authority in the exercise of, or in connection with, any functions discharged through a National Park Committee may be continued by or in relation to the successor authority.

(4) For the purposes of this paragraph "successor authority" means—

(a) where a joint or special planning board is established for the area of the National Park in question, that board; and

(b) in any other case, the local planning authority by whom the functions become exercisable (acting through a National Park Committee).

15.—(1) This paragraph applies where, immediately before 1st April 1996—

(a) a planning obligation is in force, in relation to any land in Wales, under section 106 of the planning Act (planning obligations: general) or any provision in any earlier enactment from which that provision was derived; and

(b) the enforcing authority are the county planning authority or the district planning authority for the area in which the land is situated.

(2) On and after 1st April 1996 the enforcing authority shall be the new planning authority and—

(a) the provision in the instrument by which the planning obligation was entered into identifying the enforcing authority in accordance with section 106(9)(d) shall be read as if it instead so identified the new planning authority, and

(b) section 106 shall have effect accordingly.

(3) In this paragraph—

"enforcing authority" means the authority by whom the obligation is enforceable;

"new planning authority" means—

(a) the local planning authority who are a county council, county borough council, joint planning board or special planning board in whose area that land becomes situated on 1st April 1996; but

(b) where a part of the land becomes situated in the area of each of two or more such authorities, such of those authorities as they may agree between them, or, in default of agreement, as may be determined by the Secretary of State.

(4) This paragraph has effect in relation to planning obligations entered into under section 299A of the planning Act (Crown planning obligations) as it has effect in relation to planning obligations entered into under section 106 of that Act, but as if for references to section 106, and to subsection (9)(d) of that section, there were substituted references to section 299A of that Act, and to subsection (2)(d) of section 299A, respectively.

16.—(1) Except as provided by section 287 of the planning Act (proceedings for questioning validity of development plans) as applied by this paragraph, the validity of—

(a) a modified plan, or

(b) any alteration made to or replacement of a local plan, a minerals local plan, a waste local plan or a structure plan under Part III of Schedule 5,

whether before or after the plan, alteration or replacement has been approved or adopted, shall not be questioned in any legal proceedings.

(2) Section 287 of the planning Act applies in relation to any such plan, alteration or replacement as it applies in relation to—

(a) a local plan, minerals local plan, or waste local plan adopted or approved, or

(b) any alteration made to or replacement of any such plan or a structure plan,

before 1st April 1996, but with the omission of subsection (3) and as modified by sub-paragraphs (3) to (5).

(3) Subsection (1)(a) shall apply as if after "Part II" there were inserted "or by or under Part III of Schedule 5 to the Local Government (Wales) Act 1994".

(4) Subsections (1)(b) and (2)(b) shall apply as if any reference to Part II of the planning Act included a reference to Part III of Schedule 5.

(5) Subsection (5)(a) shall apply as if for "under section 26 or, as the case may be, section 53" there were substituted 'under Part III of Schedule 5 to the Local Government (Wales) Act 1994".

(6) Terms used in this paragraph have the same meanings as they have in Part III of Schedule 5.

17.—(1) In section 306 of the planning Act (contributions by local authorities and statutory undertakers), subsection (2)(a) applies—

(a) in relation to the preparation of a modified plan as it applies in relation to the preparation of a local plan; and

(b) as if the reference to Part II of the planning Act included a reference to Part III of Schedule 5.

(2) In section 324 of the planning Act (rights of entry), subsection (1)(a) applies—

(a) in relation to a modified plan as it applies in relation to a local plan; and

(b) as if any reference to Part II of the planning Act included a reference to Part III of Schedule 5.

(3) In this paragraph "modified plan" has the meaning given by paragraph 11 of Schedule 5.

Highways

18.—(1) This paragraph applies where a bridge in Wales carries a highway for which the Secretary of State is not the highway authority.

(2) If—

(a) part of the bridge is situated in one new principal area and part in another; and

(b) the highway authority for the bridge is not otherwise determined under or by virtue of any provision of this Act,

the highway authority for the highway carried by the bridge and the approaches to it is such one of the councils of those new principal areas as may be agreed between them before such a day as the Secretary of State may by order appoint or, in default of such agreement, as may be determined by him.

(3) Where the Secretary of State has made a determination under sub-paragraph (2) the determination—

(a) may be varied at the request of the council of either of the new principal areas concerned; and

(b) shall be varied to give effect to any request made jointly to the Secretary of State by those councils.

(4) Any such variation shall take effect on the 1st April falling not less than 3 months, and not more than 15 months, after the date on which the determination is varied.

(5) For the purposes of sub-paragraph (2), the approaches to a bridge consist of so much of the highway or highways on either side of the bridge as is situated within 100 yards of either end of the bridge.

19.—(1) An order under section 188 of the Highways Act 1980 (new street orders) or under any enactment from which that section was derived made in relation to a highway in Wales before the date on which section 81 of the Planning and Compensation Act 1991 came into force shall have effect from 1st April 1996 as if made by the new principal council in whose area, on that date, the highway becomes situated.

(2) The new principal council shall have all the powers of a local authority exercisable under Part X of the Act of 1980 in respect of such an order.

Transport

20.—(1) This paragraph applies where, immediately before 1st April 1996, the authority or one of the authorities concerned in establishing a scheme under section 93 of the Transport Act 1985 (travel concession schemes) were a district or county council in Wales.

(2) Section 93 of that Act shall have effect on and after 1st April 1996 as if any new principal council who are a relevant council had been concerned in establishing the scheme.

(3) For the purposes of sub-paragraph (2), a council are a relevant council in relation to a scheme if the area which is the principal area (for the purposes of section 93 of that Act) or any part of that area is situated in the area of that council.

(4) This paragraph is subject to the power of the Secretary of State under section 54 to make such alternative or supplementary provision as he thinks necessary in relation to a scheme under section 93 of the Act of 1985.

(5) For the purposes of sections 93 to 102 of the Act of 1985—

(a) the substitution of a new principal council as the authority or one of the authorities responsible for administering a scheme; and

(b) any alteration to the scheme made by the Secretary of State in exercise of his power under section 54,

shall not be treated as a variation of the scheme.

Limitation of council tax

21.—(1) The Secretary of State may, in a report made by him in relation to the financial year beginning in 1996 and any Welsh county council or county borough council, specify a notional amount for the purposes of this paragraph.

(2) Any such report—

(a) shall contain such explanation as the Secretary of State considers desirable of the calculation by him of the notional amount;

(b) shall be laid before the House of Commons;

(c) may relate to two or more authorities; and

(d) may be amended by a subsequent report under this paragraph.

(3) If any such report is approved by resolution of the House of Commons, the Secretary of State may designate any authority to whom the report relates if in his opinion, taking any excess in the amount calculated by the authority as their budget requirement for the financial year beginning in 1996 over the notional amount as representing an increase, that increase is excessive".

(4) The Secretary of State may by order make such provision as he considers appropriate for the purpose of supplementing this paragraph.

(5) Subject to any such order, the provisions of Chapter V of Part I of the Local Government Finance Act 1992 (limitation of council tax and precepts) shall have effect in relation to a designation under this paragraph as they have effect in relation to a designation under section 54(1)(b) of that Act.

Freemen and aldermen

22.—(1) Nothing in this Act shall be taken to affect any person's status as a freeman or honorary freeman, or the right of any person to be admitted as a freeman of any place.

(2) Services rendered to an old authority, the area of which becomes wholly or partly included in a new principal area, shall be treated for the purposes of section 249 of the 1972 Act (honorary aldermen and freemen) as services rendered to the council of the new principal area.

Coroners

23.—(1) Any person who, immediately before 1st April 1996, is a coroner assigned to a particular coroner's district in Wales ("an existing coroner") shall, on and after that date, be deemed to have been duly appointed for that district.

(2) Nothing in this Act affects the validity of anything done before 1st April 1996 by an existing coroner.

(3) Anything done before 1st April 1996 by or in relation to an existing coroner shall, on and after that date, be deemed to have been done by or in relation to the coroner appointed for the coroner's district in question.

(4) Any person who, immediately before 1st April 1996 is a deputy coroner or assistant deputy coroner in relation to a particular coroner's district shall, on that date, be deemed to have been duly appointed as the deputy or assistant deputy of the coroner for that district.

(5) No order may be made under section 4A of the Coroners Act 1988 so as to have effect before 1st April 1996.

(6) Any person who, on or after 1st October 1995, ceases to be a councillor for a county in Wales which ceases to exist on 1st April 1996 ("the old county") shall, for six months after he ceases to be such a councillor, be disqualified for being a coroner for any district which, or any part of which, falls within the area of the old county.

Section 66(8)   SCHEDULE 18

REPEALS

Chapter	Short Title	Extent of repeal
23 and 24 Vict. c. 90.	Game Licences Act 1860.	In section 14, the words "from the justices of the peace".
8 Edw. 7. c. 16.	Finance Act 1908.	In section 6, in subsection (1) the words "and Wales" and in subsection (2) the word "district".
1936 c. 49.	Public Health Act 1936.	In section 1(1)(a), the words "or community".
1944 c. 31.	Education Act 1944.	In section 114(1), in the definition of "minor

Chapter	Short Title	Extent of repeal
		authority", in paragraph (b), the words "is a community having no community council or" and, in paragraph (c)(iii), the words "which is a community having no community council or".
1949 c. 74.	Coast Protection Act 1949.	In section 20, in subsections (1) and (4), the words "or Wales".
1958 c. 33.	Disabled Persons (Employment) Act 1958.	In section 3(5), the words "or Wales".
1958 c. 69.	Opencast Coal Act 1958.	In section 15A(5)(a)(i), the words "and Wales" and "or community".
1960 c. 62.	Caravan Sites and Control of Development Act 1960.	In section 24(8), the words "constituted under section four of the Act of 1947".
1962 c. 58.	Pipe-lines Act 1962.	In section 35(6), the words "and Wales".
1964 c. 26.	Licensing Act 1964.	Section 66(2). In paragraphs 6 and 7 of Schedule 8, in the expression "district returning officer", the word "district" in each place.
1964 c. 40.	Harbours Act 1964.	In paragraph 3(ba) of Schedule 3, the words "and Wales" and "or community".
1964 c. 48.	Police Act 1964.	In section 1(1)(a), the words "and Wales".
1964 c. 75.	Public Libraries and Museums Act 1964.	In section 4(2), the words from "—(a)" to "(b)". In section 5(3), the proviso. Section 6. In section 10(2), paragraphs (a) and (b)(ii) and in paragraph (b)(i) the words "other than any council of a district in Wales". In section 11(2), the words from "or (b)" to "library authority". Section 21.
1965 c. 36.	Gas Act 1965.	In section 28(1), in the definition of "local authority", the words "and Wales".
1967 c. 22.	Agriculture Act 1967.	In section 75(2), in the definition of "local authority", the words "and Wales".
1967 c. 24.	Slaughter of Poultry Act 1967.	In section 8(1), in the definition of "local authority", the words "and Wales".
1968 c. 54.	Theatres Act 1968.	In section 18(1), in paragraph (b) of the definition of "licensing authority", the words "and Wales".
1969 c. 10.	Mines and Quarries (Tips) Act 1969.	In section 11(3)(a), the words "and Wales".
1969 c. 48.	Post Office Act 1969.	In section 86(1), in paragraph (a) of the definition of "local authority", the words "and Wales".
1970 c. 40.	Agriculture Act 1970.	In section 38(b), the words "and Wales". In section 67(1), the words "and Wales".
1970 c. 44.	Chronically Sick and Disabled Persons Act 1970.	In section 21(8), the words "or Wales".
1971 c. 40.	Fire Precautions Act 1971.	In section 43(1), in paragraph (a) of the definition of "local authority", the words "and Wales".
1972 c. 66.	Poisons Act 1972.	In section 11(2), in paragraph (a) of the definition of "local authority", the words "and Wales".
1972 c. 70.	Local Government Act 1972.	In section 30, in subsection (1), paragraph (a) (including the word "or" at the end) and subsection (2).

Chapter	Short Title	Extent of repeal
		In section 55(5)(a), the words "(other than a community which is co-extensive with a district)".
		In section 59(2), the words "all or any class of".
		In section 60(5), the words "or a district council".
		Section 67(5)(f).
		In section 69(4), the word "district" (in the second place).
		In section 72(2), the words "or community" (in both places).
		In section 74(3) and (4), the words "or by virtue of a resolution under section 21(5) above".
		In section 76(2) and (3), the words "or by virtue of a resolution under section 33(2B) above".
		In section 97, in subsection (1), the word "district" (in the second and third places), and in subsections (2) and (3), the word "district".
		In section 195(3), the words "as amended by subsection (1) above".
		Section 200.
		Section 207.
		In section 213(1), the words "and Wales".
		In section 226(5), the words "or community council" (in both places).
		In section 227(1) and (2), the words "or community" (in each case in the third place).
		In section 245, in subsections (6) to (9) the words "or community" (in each place), in subsection (6) the words "or a community meeting" and in subsection (9) the words "or a community meeting in Wales".
		In Schedule 4, Part IV.
		In Schedule 8, in paragraph 8, paragraph (d) and the word "and" immediately before it.
		Schedule 10.
		In Schedule 11, in paragraphs 1(2)(c) and (d) and 3(2)(b) and (c), the words "or community" (in each place).
		In Schedule 26, in paragraph 4(a), the words "or communities" in both places, and in paragraph 11(1), the words "or community".
1973 c. 35.	Employment Agencies Act 1973.	In section 13(1), in the definition of "local authority", the words "and Wales".
1973 c. 60.	Breeding of Dogs Act 1973.	In section 5(2), in the definition of "local authority", the words "and Wales".
1974 c. 3.	Slaughterhouses Act 1974.	In section 27, the word "and" immediately before paragraph (c).
1974 c. 37.	Health and Safety at Work etc. Act 1974.	In section 53(1), in paragraph (a) of the definition of "local authority", the words "and Wales".
1974 c. 39.	Consumer Credit Act 1974.	In section 189(1), in the definition of "local authority", the words "and Wales".
1974 c. 40.	Control of Pollution Act 1974.	In section 73(1), in paragraph (a) of the definition of "local authority", the words "and Wales".
		In section 98, in paragraph (a) of the definition of "relevant authority", the words "and Wales".

Chapter	Short Title	Extent of repeal
1975 c. 23.	Reservoirs Act 1975.	In section 2(1), the words "and Wales".
1975 c. 50.	Guard Dogs Act 1975.	In section 7, in the definition of "local authority", the words "and Wales".
1975 c. 52.	Safety of Sports Grounds Act 1975.	In section 17(1), in paragraph (a) of the definition of "building authority", and in paragraph (c) of the definition of "local authority", the words "or in Wales,".
1976 c. 38.	Dangerous Wild Animals Act 1976.	In section 7(4), in the definition of "local authority", the words "and Wales".
1976 c. 75.	Development of Rural Wales Act 1976.	In Schedule 3, paragraph 1(6).
1978 c. 10.	European Parliamentary Elections Act 1978.	In Schedule 1, in paragraph 4(5)(a) the words "and Wales". In Schedule 2, in paragraph 5A(4)(a) the words "and Wales".
1979 c. 46.	Ancient Monuments and Archaeological Areas Act 1979.	In section 35(5)(a), the words "and Wales". In section 61(1), in paragraph (a) of the definition of "local authority", the words "and Wales".
1980 c. 65.	Local Government, Planning and Land Act 1980.	In section 4(7), the word "district". In section 20(1), in paragraph (a) of the definition of "local authority", the words "and Wales". In section 116(4)(a), the words "and Wales". In section 165(9)(a), the words "and Wales". In Schedule 32, in paragraph 2(2)(a)(ii), the words "or Wales".
1981 c. 37.	Zoo Licensing Act 1981.	In section 1(3)(a), the words "and Wales".
1981 c. 69.	Wildlife and Countryside Act 1981.	In section 27(1), in paragraph (a) of the definition of "local authority", the words "and Wales". In section 52(2), the words "and to Wales". In Schedule 14, in paragraph 5(1), in the definition of "local authority", the words "or community". In Schedule 15, in paragraph 13(2), in the definition of "local authority", the words "or community".
1982 c. 16.	Civil Aviation Act 1982.	In section 79(7), the words "and Wales". In section 105(1), in paragraph (a) of the definition of "local authority", the words "and Wales".
1983 c. 2.	Representation of the People Act 1983.	In section 8(2), the words "and Wales". In section 18(2), the words "and Wales". In section 35(1), the words "and Wales" and "or communities". In section 36(3)(b), the words "or community" (in both places). In section 36(5), the words "or community" (in both places) and the words "or the community". In section 39(6)(b), the word "district". In section 52(4)(a), the words "and Wales".
1983 c. 16.	Level Crossings Act 1983.	In section 1(11), in the definition of "local authority", the words "and Wales".
1984 c. 12.	Telecommunications Act 1984.	In section 97(3)(a), the words "and Wales" and the words "or a community council".

Chapter	Short Title	Extent of repeal
1984 c. 27.	Road Traffic Regulation Act 1984.	In section 39(4), the words "a district council in Wales proposes to make an order under section 32 or 35 of this Act, or". In section 44(3)(b), the words "and counties in Wales". In section 45(7), the words "in England or Scotland" and the words from "and in Wales" to the end. Section 49(3). Section 54. Section 55(6). In section 59(2)(b), the words "or community". In section 125(4), the words from "or, in relation to" to the end. In Schedule 9, paragraph 11 and, in paragraph 27(2)(a), the words "54(5)".
1985 c. 13.	Cinemas Act 1985.	In section 21(1), in the definition of "local authority", in paragraph (a) the words "and Wales".
1985 c. 50.	Representation of the People Act 1985.	In section 21(2)(b), the words "of district council".
1985 c. 67.	Transport Act 1985.	In section 63(4), the words "and Wales". In section 64(1), the words "and Wales".
1986 c. 31.	Airports Act 1986.	In section 12(1), in the definition of "principal council" in paragraph (a) the words "and Wales".
1986 c. 44.	Gas Act 1986.	In paragraph 5(5) of Schedule 7, in paragraph (a) of the definition of "local authority", the words "and Wales".
1986 c. 53.	Building Societies Act 1986.	In paragraph 8 of Part IV of Schedule 8, in paragraph (a) of the definition of "local authority in Great Britain", the words "and Wales" and "or community".
1987 c. 27.	Fire Safety and Safety of Places of Sport Act 1987.	In section 41, in paragraph (a) of the definition of "building authority", and in paragraph (c) of the definition of "local authority", the words "or in Wales".
1988 c. 52.	Road Traffic Act 1988.	In Schedule 2, in paragraph 1(b), the words "and Wales".
1988 c. 53.	Road Traffic Offenders Act 1988.	In section 4(5), the words from "except, in Wales" to the end.
1989 c. 29.	Electricity Act 1989.	In Schedule 8, in paragraph 2(6)(a) the words "and Wales".
1989 c. 41.	Children Act 1989.	In section 105(1), in the definition of "local authority", the words "and Wales".
1990 c. 8.	Town and Country Planning Act 1990.	In section 1(3), the words "and in Wales". In section 2(1), the words "(in this Act referred to as a "joint planning board")". In Schedule 1, in paragraph 8, in sub-paragraphs (1) and (2)(a), the words "or community".
1990 c. 9.	Planning (Listed Buildings and Conservation Areas) Act 1990.	In section 2(1), the word "and" at the end of paragraph (a).
1990 c. 16.	Food Safety Act 1990.	In section 5(1), the words "and Wales".
1990 c. 42.	Broadcasting Act 1990.	In paragraph 1(1) of Part I of Schedule 2, in paragraph (a) of the definition of "local authority", the words "and Wales".

Chapter	Short Title	Extent of repeal
1990 c. 43.	Environmental Protection Act 1990.	In section 30(3)(a), the words "and Wales". Section 50(5)(a)(iii). In section 88(10), in the definition of "Park board", the word "or" immediately before paragraph (b). In section 143(6), in paragraph (b) of the definition of "local authority", the words "and Wales". In section 149(11), in the definition of "local authority", the words "and Wales".
1990 c. 44.	Caldey Island Act 1990.	In section 1, in subsection (1), the closing bracket after ""Caldey"" and the rest of the subsection, subsection (2)(a), in subsection (3), the words "and district" and subsections (4) and (5). Section 2. In section 4, subsections (1)(a) and (2).
1991 c. 40.	Road Traffic Act 1991.	In Schedule 3, in paragraphs 1(1)(a) and 2(1)(a) the words "and Wales", and paragraphs 1(1)(e) (except the word "or" immediately before paragraph (f)) and (2) and 2(2).
1991 c. 45.	Coal Mining Subsidence Act 1991.	In section 47(6)(a), the words "and Wales".
1992 c. 3.	Severn Bridges Act 1992.	In Schedule 3, in paragraph 8(3), the words "Gwent County Council".
1992 c. 5.	Social Security Administration Act 1992.	In section 191, in the definition of "local authority", the words "and Wales".
1993 c. 11.	Clean Air Act 1993.	In section 64, in paragraph (a) of the definition of "local authority", the words "and Wales".
1993 c. 12.	Radioactive Substances Act 1993.	In section 47(1), in paragraph (a) of the definition of "local authority", the words "and Wales".
1993 c. 46.	Health Service Commissioners Act 1993.	In section 19, in paragraph (a) of the definition of "local authority", the words "and Wales".

INDEX

**References in roman type are to sections and Schedules of this Act:
references in italic are to the Local Government Act 1972 (as amended)**

ACCOUNTS, 52
AMENDMENTS,
  consequential, 66(6), Sched. 16
  1972 Act, 66(5), Sched. 15
AREA COMMITTEES, *see* DECENTRALISATION
  SCHEMES
AREAS OF LOCAL GOVERNMENT, *see* PRINCIPAL
  AREAS

CHARITIES, 49
COAST PROTECTION, *see* SERVICES
COMMENCEMENT, 66(2)–(4)
COMMUNITIES,
  community councils,
    constitution and powers, 13, *33*
    consultation with, 14, *33A*
    continuation of, 8, *27*
    election of councillors, 15, *35*
    establishment or dissolution of, 9, *28*
    for groups of communities,
      dissolution of, 11, *29A*
      orders for, 10, *29*
    supplementary provisions, 12, *29B*
  community meeetings, 8, *27*
  town status, 16, *245B*
CONTRACTS, 51
CORFF GWEDDILLIOL CYMRU, 39, Sched. 13
COUNTIES,
  change of status to county borough, 5, *245A*
  new principal areas, 1(1), 1(2), Sched. 1,
    Part I, *20(4)*, *Sched. 4*
  1972 Act counties ceasing to exist, 1(1),
    20(6)–(7)
  preserved,
    areas of, 1(1), Sched. 1, Part III, *20(8)*,
      Sched. 4
    continuation of for certain purposes,
      1(1), *20(6)*
    described, 1(2), Sched. 1, Part III
    names of, 1(1), *20(9)–(10)*
    provisions applying to, 1(3), Sched. 2
  as principal areas, 1(1), *20(5)*
  see also PRINCIPAL AREAS
COUNTY BOROUGHS,
  change of status to, 5, *245A*
  described, 1(1), 1(2), Sched. 1, Part II,
    20(4), *Sched. 4*
  as principal areas, 1(1), *20(5)*

DECENTRALISATION SCHEMES,
  approval and implementation, 28

DECENTRALISATION SCHEMES—*cont.*
  area committees,
    membership, 30
    safeguards, 29
    sub-committees, 31
  preparation, 27
DEFINITIONS, 1(4)–(8), *270(1)*
DISPOSALS, 51

EDUCATION,
  local education authorities, 21(1)–(2)
  minor authorities, 21(3)
EXPENSES, 65
EXTENT, 66(9)

FINANCE,
  billing authorities, 35
  council funds, 38, Sched. 12
  non-domestic rating lists, 37
  transitional provisions, 56
  valuation lists, 36
FIRE SERVICES, *see* SERVICES
FUNCTIONS, *see* EDUCATION; PLANNING;
  SERVICES; TRANSFER OF FUNCTIONS

HIGHWAYS, *see* SERVICES
HOUSING, *see* SERVICES

INTERPRETATION, 64

JOINT WORKING,
  arrangements, 33
  information as to, 32
  joint authorities, 34
  transitional provisions, 59
JUSTICES OF THE PEACE, 55

LAND DRAINAGE, *see* SERVICES
LIEUTENANCIES, 61
LOCAL ACTS AND PROVISIONS,
  continuation of, 57
  modification of, 58

MAGISTRATES' COURTS, 55

NATIONAL PARKS, 20, Sched. 5